Torts

A Modern Approach

Alex B. Long
Williford Gragg Distinguished Professor of Law
University of Tennessee College of Law

Teri Dobbins Baxter
Williford Gragg Distinguished Professor of Law
University of Tennessee College of Law

CAROLINA ACADEMIC PRESS
Durham, North Carolina

ISBN 978-1-5310-1723-1
e-ISBN 978-1-5310-1724-8
LCCN 2019953043

Carolina Academic Press
700 Kent Street
Durham, North Carolina 27701
Telephone (919) 489-7486
Fax (919) 493-5668
www.cap-press.com

Printed in the United States of America

Contents

Table of Cases

Authors' Note

Torts is the most interesting course in the first-year law school curriculum. Admittedly, the authors of this book are biased when it comes to this issue. But, as you will see, Torts is a subject to which everyone can relate.

This casebook has been designed to make the subject matter as relatable as possible for first-year law students. The book tries to take a modern approach to the learning that takes place in the first year of law school. As part of this effort, the authors have incorporated the following tools throughout the book:

Organizational tools to encourage active learning

Each chapter or section within a chapter begins with an outline of key concepts to help guide student learning. These outlines are designed to help focus students' attention on some of the most relevant content. The outlines are included to: (1) help students read cases in a more active manner, (2) make the organization of each chapter clear, and (3) facilitate class note-taking and outlining. Note that these outlines are not meant to be comprehensive. Your professor may not cover all of the topics listed or may cover topics not included in the outline.

A mixture of classic and modern cases

The book utilizes a mix of classic Torts cases as well as more recent cases. There are certain cases that every lawyer who has been to law school in the past 50 years studied—and with good reason. These cases are part of the vernacular of the legal profession. But when possible, this casebook incorporates modern cases on the theory that they are more relatable and at least as illustrative of the relevant legal principles as older cases.

Shorter notes

Some casebooks require the reader to read voluminous notes following the primary cases. This sometimes causes the reader to lose focus on the most important issues. The notes in this casebook are somewhat limited in number and length in the hopes of keeping students engaged. Instructors can expand on the topics presented or to bring out additional concepts in class as they see fit.

The use of problems

Each chapter begins with a hypothetical set of facts that students can use to orient themselves throughout the chapter. There are short problems throughout each chapter that build on the hypothetical at the beginning and that require students to apply the law covered in the chapter. Regardless of whether your instructor covers these problems in detail in class, the problems should help you to learn the law by applying what you have learned to a specific set of facts.

Formative assessment

At the end of each chapter or section, there is a short essay question involving the material covered. The questions are structured like bar exam essay questions, *i.e.*, short, issue-spotting questions requiring rule application. Like bar exam essay questions, each question should take approximately 30 minutes to answer. Students can use these questions as a formative assessment tool to help assess their understanding of the primary material covered in the chapter.

Inclusion of professionalism and professional identity material

The book makes an effort to direct students to relevant issues of professional responsibility and professionalism issues raised by the cases, as well as encouraging students to consider what sort of lawyers they wish to be. Cases sometimes raise issues of professional ethics and professionalism. The book tries to take advantage of opportunities to encourage consideration of those issues.

As you read the material in the chapters, we encourage you to take advantage of these tools.

Torts

Chapter 1

Introduction

A. History
- The difference between tort law and criminal law
- How tort law evolved as a historical matter
- Other concepts developed in class or in readings assigned by the professor

B. Fault as the Standard Basis for Liability
- The difference between fault-based liability and strict liability
- The different types of fault for purposes of tort law
- Other concepts developed in class or in readings assigned by the professor

C. Policies Underlying Tort Law
- The main policy values underlying tort law
- Other concepts developed in class or in readings assigned by the professor

Chapter Problem. The vehicle Dana was driving crossed the center line on the highway and collided with the oncoming vehicle Paul was driving. Paul had no time to avoid the collision. Paul suffered serious injuries as a result of the collision. He has now filed a civil action against Dana, seeking to recover for his injuries.

Tort law is the vehicle by which a party who is injured by another seeks compensation or other relief. Tort law and criminal law both deal with wrongful acts on the part of a defendant. But whereas an individual who violates the criminal law faces potential jail time or other penalties imposed by the state, an individual who runs afoul of tort law faces potential civil liability in the form of a lawsuit. In other words, tort law deals with wrongful conduct for which there is a civil remedy, typically in the form of monetary compensation.

The phrase "tort law" often conjures images of car crashes, customers slipping and falling, injuries resulting from fights, and scalding hot coffee. And the average personal injury lawyer may see plenty of those kinds of cases. But even the run-of-the mill tort case may involve complicated issues of causation, calculation of damages, or immunity from suit. At law schools where Torts is a one-semester course, most of the focus will be on intentional torts (like battery or false imprisonment) or negligence (with perhaps some products liability cases or defamation cases as well). But tort law encompasses a variety of fact patterns and legal theories, including the making of false and defamatory statements, fraud, invasion of privacy, unfair business practices, defective products, and violations of an individual's constitutional rights. If Torts is a two-semester course at your school, you may address some or all of these issues.

A. History

Historically, tort law looked little like it does today until well until the nineteenth century. Early English law was based on the writ system, whereby a party seeking a remedy for an injury had to obtain a written order known as a writ in order to bring a defendant to court. The writ of trespass applied when the injury was "direct" in the sense that the injury was the uninterrupted result of force. The example that is almost always used to illustrate this concept is that of the defendant who throws a log that hits the plaintiff. The question of whether the defendant was blameworthy for the resulting injury did not enter into the analysis. If, instead, the injury was indirect or not the result of force, the writ of case applied. So, if the defendant threw a log in the road and sometime later the plaintiff tripped over it and suffered injury, the proper writ was case. In order to recover under this theory, an injured party needed to prove fault on the part of the defendant.

Eventually, the writ system gave way to the development of defined tort theories of recovery. One of the most important U.S. tort cases in this regard was *Brown v. Kendall*, 60 Mass. (6 Cush.) 292, (Mass. 1850). The defendant tried to stop two dogs from fighting by hitting them with a stick. When he raised the stick, he accidentally hit the plaintiff in the eye. Since the plaintiff's injury was direct and the result of force, the proper cause of action would seem to have been trespass, and the plaintiff would not need to establish fault on the part of the defendant. Instead, the Massachusetts Supreme Judicial Court altered the development of tort law and held that if "the conduct of the defendant was free from blame, he will not be liable."

This basic principle gradually became the norm. Perhaps the most common explanation for the shift toward fault-based liability is that it "was partly inspired by the desire to protect the growth of industry," *Magrine v. Spector*, 241 A.2d 637 (N.J. Super. Ct. 1968), at a time when industrialization was resulting in more personal injuries. *See* Charles O. Gregory, *Trespass to Negligence to Absolute Liability*, 37 VA. L. REV. 359, 368 (1951) ("While it is pure speculation, one of Chief Justice Shaw's motives underlying his opinion [in *Brown v. Kendall*] appears to have been a desire to make risk-creating enterprise less hazardous to investors and entrepreneurs than it had been previously at common law."). In time, courts also replaced the writ system with the kinds of specific legal theories (battery, false imprisonment, negligence, etc.) that are covered in this book.

B. Fault as the Standard Basis for Liability

Van Camp v. McAfoos

156 N.W.2d 878 (Iowa 1968)

BECKER, Justice.

This case comes to us on appeal from trial court's action in sustaining defendant's motion to dismiss. We are therefore limited to what can be gleaned from the pleadings.

In Division I of her petition plaintiff sues Mark McAfoos alleging in pertinent part, "That at said time and place defendant Mark McAfoos was operating a tricycle on said public sidewalk, and drove the tricycle into the rear of the plaintiff without warning, striking the right leg of the plaintiff thereby causing an injury to the Achilles' tendon of that leg.

"That as a direct and proximate cause of this defendant's action, plaintiff's tendon was injured and subsequently required surgery . . ."

Division I does not reveal Mark's age but Division II alleges he was three years one month old at the time of the incident. Defendant moved to dismiss the petition urging it fails to state a claim upon which relief can be granted [and because it] fails to allege negligence . . .

. . .

I. Plaintiff's sole assignment of error as to Division I is "The trial court erred in failing to recognize categories of tort liability other than negligence, in evaluating the pleading in plaintiff's first division."

Plaintiff states her petition contains the following ultimate facts (1) she was rightfully using the public sidewalk (and thus had a right to the reasonably free use thereof and to remain uninjured during such use), (2) defendant used his tricycle on the public sidewalk (and thus had a duty to use the same without injurious interference with others), (3) surprise intrusion of the tricycle into the right rear ankle of plaintiff (thus interfering with plaintiff's right and stating defendant activated the mechanism causing the injury) and (4) damage resulted from the intrusion. She stands firmly on the proposition that invasion of her person is in itself a wrong and she need plead no more. We do not agree.

. . .

In essence plaintiff urges a person has a right not to be injuriously touched or struck as she lawfully uses a public sidewalk. She was injuriously struck by Mark. Therefore Mark is liable. She argues that no more need be pleaded. It follows that no more need be proved in order to justify submission of the case. Plaintiff's posture satisfies us she would have us impose liability without fault. We are not prepared to extend this concept to childish acts (by children).

II. Plaintiff's reply brief states: "If the absence of a single word or conclusory label remains the *sine qua non* of pleading a valid cause of action, we have restored today's jurisprudence to the specious procedural formalism of the 18th Century common courts."

. . .

The trial court's ruling was not a return to legal formalism. Plaintiff makes it abundantly clear she insists on a right to recovery by proof of an accident caused by another, independent of fault or wrong doing. Where an essential element of the cause of action is missing, the question is not what may be shown under the pleading but whether a cause of action has been pled.

Here no ultimate facts giving rise to the concept of *wrongful* action are pled. Plaintiff insists they need not be set forth. In her reply she poses the question in stark terms. "Any social or public policy decision involves a collision of rights. Which right merits judicial recognition? The right of a pedestrian to walk uninjured upon a public sidewalk, or the right of a child to propel a tricycle upon that public sidewalk to the injury of that pedestrian? As a matter of public policy, which right is more valuable?"

Faced with this choice of social policy, we hold liability will not be imposed for use of a tricycle on a public sidewalk without a showing (and thus a pleading) of some fault. Unless and until we are ready to recognize liability without fault for otherwise innocent childish actions, fault must be discernible in the pleading and in proof. No statute or ordinance is cited prohibiting use of a tricycle on a public sidewalk. Intentionally wrongful or negligently wrongful use of the tricycle is neither pled nor can it be made out from the bare allegation defendant "operated a tricycle on said public sidewalk and drove the tricycle into the rear of the plaintiff without warning."

. . .

Affirmed.

Notes

Fault as the basis for liability. Why does the court say there was no showing of fault? What type of fault on the part of the defendant would the plaintiff be required to prove in order to establish liability?

A short note on the civil litigation process. In *Van Camp*, the plaintiff filed a *petition* (more commonly known as a *complaint*), alleging a right to recover for her injuries. The defendant then filed *a motion to dismiss for failure to state a claim upon which relief can be granted.* When a defendant makes a motion to dismiss for failure to state a claim upon which relief can be granted, the court considers whether the facts alleged, if true, would provide the plaintiff with a legal right to recover. Why did the court grant the defendant's motion in *Van Camp*? Assuming the plaintiff's complaint survives a motion to dismiss, the parties will engage in a process known as *discovery*, in which both sides seek to gather evidence relevant to the case. Each side is permitted to request relevant documents from the other side, take the depositions of relevant witnesses, and pose questions to the other side (called interrogatories) that the other side must respond to in writing. Sometimes at the conclusion of this process, one or both sides (but most often the defendant) will file *a motion for summary judgment*, in which the party asks the court to enter judgment in the party's favor on the grounds that there is no genuine dispute as to any material fact and that the moving party is entitled to judgment as a matter of law because no reasonable juror could find in the other side's favor. At any point in this process, the parties may also agree to *settle* the dispute. The vast majority of civil cases are settled or dismissed prior to trial. If a case is not dismissed or settled, the parties may try the case in front of a jury or a judge. Most of the decisions in law school casebooks will be appellate decisions, in which one side appeals an adverse pretrial ruling or an adverse trial outcome.

Problem 1.1. Going back to the Chapter Problem, assume that you represent Dana. As Dana's lawyer, you learn that the reason why Dana's vehicle crossed the center line and collided with Paul's vehicle is because Dana suffered a completely unforeseeable heart attack while driving and was unable to control her vehicle as a result. Will Paul be able to recover from Dana in his tort action? Is the case likely to proceed all the way to trial?

C. Policies Underlying Tort Law

Tort law sometimes generates significant disagreement among policymakers. For example, different states have different legal rules regarding the amount of compensation an injured party may recover in some types of actions, what sort of proof a plaintiff must offer in a given case, the extent to which a plaintiff's own fault may impact the plaintiff's ability to recover, and a host of other legal rules. Whether you think an individual rule is proper or whether you think the rule was applied correctly by a court may depend on your view of the proper role of tort law and the values that underlie it.

There are several policy values that virtually all courts recognize as being essential to the development of tort rules. There are others that may influence legislators, judges, lawyers, litigants, and jurors as well.

(1) *Compensation:* "The primary purpose of tort law is to provide just compensation to the tort victim." Anderson v. State ex rel. Cent. Bering Sea Fishermen's Ass'n, 78 P.3d 710, 717 (Alaska 2003). Chapter 19 addresses the issue of damages in a tort case in detail. But, for now, it's enough to note that, as its name suggests, *compensatory damages* are available in a tort action to compensate an injured party.

(2) *Deterrence*: While compensating injured parties is the most obvious policy goal of tort law, deterring wrongful conduct is perhaps an equally

strong value. *See* Fu v. Fu, 733 A.2d 1133, 1141 (N.J. 1999) (referring to deterrence and compensation as "the fundamental goals of tort law"). Tort rules "are designed to encourage socially beneficial conduct and deter wrongful conduct." Denver Publ'g Co. v. Bueno, 54 P.3d 893, 897–98 (Colo. 2002). Another way tort law seeks to deter wrongful conduct is by allowing for the recovery of *punitive damages* in cases of particularly egregious conduct. Again, a later chapter will address this issue in much greater detail.

There are a host of other policy values underlying tort rules. The importance one attaches to them is likely to vary from person to person. These values might include (among others) distributing the loss resulting from harm in the most efficient manner; establishing a process by which a victim may seek compensation in order to discourage parties from having to resort to self-help measures (such as violence); promoting individual responsibility; and establishing clear rules that courts can administer and parties can rely upon. To some extent, most tort rules involve a balancing between these types of policy concerns.

The following case involves a plaintiff seeking to hold a defendant liable absent any showing of fault on the part of the defendant. As you read, consider how the policy values underlying tort law are implicated by the court's decision.

Rhodes v. MacHugh

361 P.3d 260 (Wash. Ct. App. 2015)

SIDDOWAY, C.J.

In this case, Jay Rhodes asks us to hold the owner of a ram (a male sheep) strictly liable for harm caused by the ram on account of the ram's gender-based dangerousness, rather than any abnormal dangerousness of which the owner was aware. [Rhodes was injured when a young ram, owned by his friend and neighbor, MacHugh, attacked him. Rhodes did not claim that MacHugh was negligent in any way with respect to the ram, that the ram was abnormally dangerous for his breed, or that MacHugh "thought there was anything wrong" with the ram. Instead, he sought to hold MacHugh strictly liable, that is, liable without any showing of fault.]

Because Mr. Rhodes relied exclusively on a theory of strict liability that he asked the court to extend to the owners of all rams, not just those known to be abnormally dangerous, the parties presented the legal issue to the trial court on summary judgment. Mr. MacHugh's motion for summary judgment dismissing the claim was granted. Mr. Rhodes appeals.

[The rule in Washington was that if an individual domesticated animal (like livestock) was known to be abnormally dangerous, a defendant could be held liable without proof of fault on the defendant's part for injuries caused by the animal. But when the animal was not known to be abnormally dangerous for its class, a plaintiff must establish negligence on the part of the defendant.]

It is [partly] for policy reasons that owners of male domestic animals have not been held to a standard of strict liability, because often it is the very characteristics that cause the males to be dangerous that make them useful to society. The comments to § 518 of the Restatement (Second) [of Torts] observe that "[t]he high temper normal to stud animals is so inseparable from their usefulness for breeding purposes that they are not kept at the risk of the liability stated in § 509." Restatement (Second) § 518 cmt. f. The comments explaining the rationale for § 509's rule of strict liability similarly observe that

> the virility which makes [bulls, stallions, and rams] dangerous is necessary for their usefulness in performing their function in the socially essential breeding of livestock, justifies the risk involved in their keeping. Therefore, the law has not regarded bulls, stallions and rams as being abnormally dangerous animals to be kept under the strict liability stated in this Section.

Id. § 509 cmt. e; *see also id.* § 509 cmt. d ("[T]he slightly added risk due to their dangerous character is counterbalanced by the desirability of raising livestock.").

. . .

"Rules of law . . . should not be changed for light or transient causes; but, when time and events prove the need for a change, changed they must be." State ex rel. Wash. State Fin. Comm. v. Martin, 62 Wash.2d 645, 666, 384 P.2d 833 (1963). Here, the utility of domestic animals remains undiminished. Those who raise them and face the greatest exposure to relatively more dangerous genders or breeds will be familiar with their characteristics. Third parties continue to have recourse for an owner's negligence, and owners are required to take greater precautions to confine and control animals in light of their characteristics. Mr. Rhodes's unfortunate excursion with Mr. MacHugh's ram does not persuade us that the limited scope of strict liability that Washington has historically imposed on the owners of domestic animals should be enlarged.

Affirmed.

Notes

Strict liability. What does it mean to say that a defendant can be held strictly liable? Strict liability for engaging in abnormally dangerous activities is discussed in Chapter 12.

Resolving disputes. Every case in this book involves litigation. But maybe not every case needed to result in litigation. Imagine you were the lawyer representing Rhodes. Were there any alternatives to litigation that you might have recommended to your client?

Problem 1.2. Why must a plaintiff ordinarily establish fault on the part of a defendant in order to recover damages? Why, for example, should Paul be required to prove fault on Dana's part if it is clear that Dana caused Paul's injuries?

Part 1
Intentional Torts

Perhaps the easiest type of tort claim to conceptualize is the intentional tort. With an intentional tort claim, the allegation is typically that the defendant acted with the intent to bring about some type of harmful or offensive consequence. Chapter Two will explore intentional harms to persons, including the torts of battery, assault, false imprisonment, and intentional infliction of emotional distress. This chapter will also examine the related defenses or privileges that may be raised by a defendant in a tort action. Chapter Three focuses on intentional wrongs involving property, such as the tort of trespass.

Chapter 2

Intentional Harms to Persons

A. Battery
- The purpose of the tort
- The basic elements of a battery claim
- The following concepts
  - To "act"
  - To act with the necessary "intent"
  - Transferred intent
  - The difference between the single intent and dual intent approaches
  - For conduct to result in "contact"
  - For conduct to result in "harmful" or "offensive" contact
  - Liability in general
  - Extended liability
  - Other concepts developed in class or in readings assigned by the professor

B. Assault
- The purpose of the tort
- The difference with battery
- The basic elements of an assault claim
- The following concepts:
  - To "act" versus "words alone"
  - To act with the necessary intent
  - Apprehension
  - Imminent contact
  - Conditional threats
  - Transferred intent
  - Other concepts developed in class or in readings assigned by the professor

C. False Imprisonment
- The purpose of the tort
- The basic elements of a false imprisonment claim
- The following concepts:
  - Confinement within fixed boundaries
  - Forms of confinement
  - Other concepts developed in class or in readings assigned by the professor

D. Intentional Infliction of Emotional Distress
- The purpose of the tort
- The basic elements of an IIED claim

- The following concepts:
  - Recklessness
  - Extreme and outrageous conduct
    - Indicators of extreme and outrageous conduct
    - What does not amount to extreme and outrageous conduct
    - Special rules when third parties suffer distress
  - Severe emotional distress
  - Other concepts developed in class or in readings assigned by the professor

E. Defenses and Privileges

- Consent
  - The impact of the plaintiff's consent on the plaintiff's intentional tort claim
  - What qualifies as consent generally
  - The difference between actual consent and apparent consent
  - How courts treat cases of medical battery
  - The plaintiff's incapacity as it impacts consent
  - When consent is otherwise not effective
  - Other concepts developed in class or in readings assigned by the professor
- Self-Defense
  - The basic elements of a self-defense claim
  - The special rule regarding the use of deadly force
  - The special rules regarding retreat and the "castle doctrine"
  - Other concepts developed in class or in readings assigned by the professor
- Defense of Others
  - The basic elements of a claim of defense of others
  - The privilege of defense of others as it relates to the privilege of self-defense
  - Other concepts developed in class or in readings assigned by the professor
- Shopkeeper's Privilege
  - The basic elements of the modern shopkeeper's privilege
  - The concept of reasonableness as it relates to the privilege
  - Other concepts developed in class or in readings assigned by the professor

Chapter Problem. The town of Pleasant Hill experienced several instances involving possible civil rights violations on the part of local police officers. These incidents led to a group of protesters gathering downtown to protest what they believed to be police abuses. The protesters were met by a group of opposing protesters expressing their support for law enforcement. The two groups faced each other on opposite sides of a street, separated by police barricades. There were dozens of protesters on both sides, all of whom were packed closely together within one single block of the town. After lots of taunts and name-calling on both sides, several violent incidents occurred. These incidents led to police arrests and, in a few cases, civil lawsuits. These incidents form the basis for the problems below.

A. Battery

1. Act with Intent

Garratt v. Dailey

279 P.2d 1091 (Wash. 1955)

HILL, Justice.

The liability of an infant for an alleged battery is presented to this court for the first time. Brian Dailey (age five years, nine months) was visiting with Naomi Garratt, an adult and a sister of the plaintiff, Ruth Garratt, likewise an adult, in the back yard of the plaintiff's home, on July 16, 1951. It is plaintiff's contention that she came out into the back yard to talk with Naomi and that, as she started to sit down in a wood and canvas lawn chair, Brian deliberately pulled it out from under her. The only one of the three persons present so testifying was Naomi Garratt. (Ruth Garratt, the plaintiff, did not testify as to how or why she fell.) The trial court, unwilling to accept this testimony, adopted instead Brian Dailey's version of what happened, and made the following findings:

> 'III. . . . that while Naomi Garratt and Brian Dailey were in the back yard the plaintiff, Ruth Garratt, came out of her house into the back yard. Some time subsequent thereto defendant, Brian Dailey, picked up a lightly built wood and canvas lawn chair which was then and there located in the back yard of the above described premises, moved it sideways a few feet and seated himself therein, at which time he discovered the plaintiff, Ruth Garratt, about to sit down at the place where the lawn chair had formerly been, at which time he hurriedly got up from the chair and attempted to move it toward Ruth Garratt to aid her in sitting down in the chair; that due to the defendant's small size and lack of dexterity he was unable to get the lawn chair under the plaintiff in time to prevent her from falling to the ground. That plaintiff fell to the ground and sustained a fracture of her hip, and other injuries and damages as hereinafter set forth.
>
> 'IV. That the preponderance of the evidence in this case establishes that when the defendant, Brian Dailey, moved the chair in question *he did not have any wilful or unlawful purpose in doing so; that he did not have any intent to injure the plaintiff, or any intent to bring about any unauthorized or offensive contact with her person* or any objects appurtenant thereto; that the circumstances which immediately preceded the fall of the plaintiff established that the defendant, *Brian Dailey, did not have purpose, intent or design to perform a prank or to effect an assault and battery upon the person of the plaintiff.*'

It is conceded that Ruth Garratt's fall resulted in a fractured hip and other painful and serious injuries. To obviate the necessity of a retrial in the event this court determines that she was entitled to a judgment against Brian Dailey, the amount of her damage was found to be $11,000. Plaintiff appeals from a judgment dismissing the action and asks for the entry of a judgment in that amount or a new trial.

The authorities generally . . . state that when a minor has committed a tort with force he is liable to be proceeded against as any other person would be.

In our analysis of the applicable law, we start with the basic premise that Brian, whether five or fifty-five, must have committed some wrongful act before he could be liable for appellant's injuries.

It is urged that Brian's action in moving the chair constituted a battery. A definition (not all-inclusive but sufficient for our purpose) of a battery is the intentional infliction of a harmful bodily contact upon another. The rule that determines liability for battery is given in 1 *Restatement, Torts*, 29, § 13, as:

> 'An act which, directly or indirectly, is the legal cause of a harmful contact with another's person makes the actor liable to the other, if
>
> '(a) the act is done with the intention of bringing about a harmful or offensive contact or an apprehension thereof to the other or a third person, and
>
> . . .

. . . In the comment on clause (a), the *Restatement* says:

> '*Character of actor's intention.* In order that an act may be done with the intention of bringing about a harmful or offensive contact or an apprehension thereof to a particular person, either the other or a third person, the act must be done for the purpose of causing the contact or apprehension or with knowledge on the part of the actor that such contact or apprehension is substantially certain to be produced.' See, also, Prosser on Torts 41, § 8.

We have here the conceded volitional act of Brian, *i.e.*, the moving of a chair. Had the plaintiff proved to the satisfaction of the trial court that Brian moved the chair while she was in the act of sitting down, Brian's action would patently have been for the purpose or with the intent of causing the plaintiff's bodily contact with the ground, and she would be entitled to a judgment against him for the resulting damages.

The plaintiff based her case on that theory, and the trial court held that she failed in her proof and accepted Brian's version of the facts rather than that given by the eyewitness who testified for the plaintiff. After the trial court determined that the plaintiff had not established her theory of a battery (*i.e.*, that Brian had pulled the chair out from under the plaintiff while she was in the act of sitting down), it then became concerned with whether a battery was established under the facts as it found them to be.

In this connection, we quote another portion of the comment on the 'Character of actor's intention,' relating to clause (a) of the rule from the *Restatement* heretofore set forth:

> 'It is not enough that the act itself is intentionally done and this, even though the actor realizes or should realize that it contains a very grave risk

> of bringing about the contact or apprehension. Such realization may make the actor's conduct negligent or even reckless but unless he realizes that to a substantial certainty, the contact or apprehension will result, the actor has not that intention which is necessary to make him liable under the rule stated in this section.'

A battery would be established if, in addition to plaintiff's fall, it was proved that, when Brian moved the chair, he knew with substantial certainty that the plaintiff would attempt to sit down where the chair had been. If Brian had any of the intents which the trial court found, in the italicized portions of the findings of fact quoted above, that he did not have, he would of course have had the knowledge to which we have referred. The mere absence of any intent to injure the plaintiff or to play a prank on her or to embarrass her, or to commit an assault and battery on her would not absolve him from liability if in fact he had such knowledge. Without such knowledge, there would be nothing wrongful about Brian's act in moving the chair and, there being no wrongful act, there would be no liability.

While a finding that Brian had no such knowledge can be inferred from the findings made, we believe that before the plaintiff's action in such a case should be dismissed there should be no question but that the trial court had passed upon that issue; hence, the case should be remanded for clarification of the findings to specifically cover the question of Brian's knowledge, because intent could be inferred therefrom. If the court finds that he had such knowledge the necessary intent will be established and the plaintiff will be entitled to recover, even though there was no purpose to injure or embarrass the plaintiff. If Brian did not have such knowledge, there was no wrongful act by him and the basic premise of liability on the theory of a battery was not established.

Polmatier v. Russ

537 A.2d 468 (Conn. 1988)

GLASS, Associate Justice.

The principal issue on this appeal is whether an insane person is liable for an intentional tort. The plaintiff, Dorothy Polmatier, executrix of the estate of her deceased husband, Arthur R. Polmatier, brought this action against the defendant, Norman Russ, seeking to recover damages for wrongful death. The state trial referee, exercising the power of the Superior Court, rendered judgment for the plaintiff. The defendant has appealed from that judgment. We find no error.

The trial court's memorandum of decision and the record reveal the following undisputed facts. On the afternoon of November 20, 1976, the defendant and his two month old daughter visited the home of Arthur Polmatier, his father-in-law. Polmatier lived in East Windsor with his wife, Dorothy, the plaintiff, and their eleven year old son, Robert. During the early evening Robert noticed a disturbance in the living room where he saw the defendant astride Polmatier on a couch beating him on the head with a beer bottle. Robert heard Polmatier exclaim, "Norm, you're killing me!" and ran to get help. Thereafter, the defendant went into Polmatier's bedroom where he took a box of 30-30 caliber ammunition from the bottom drawer of a dresser and went to his brother-in-law's bedroom where he took a 30-30 caliber Winchester rifle from the closet. He then returned to the living room and shot Polmatier twice, causing his death.

The defendant was taken to a local hospital and was later transferred to Norwich Hospital. While in custody he was confined in Norwich Hospital or the Whiting Forensic Institute. The defendant was charged with the crime of murder pursuant to General Statutes § 53a-54a(a),1 but was found not guilty by reason of insanity pursuant to General Statutes § 53a-13.2 Dr. Walter Borden, a psychiatrist, testified at both the criminal and this civil proceeding regarding the defendant's sanity. In the present civil case Borden testified that, at the time of the homicide, the defendant was suffering from a severe case of paranoid schizophrenia that involved delusions of persecution, grandeur, influence and reference, and also involved auditory hallucinations. He concluded that the defendant was legally insane and could not form a rational choice but that he could make a schizophrenic or crazy choice. He was not in a fugue state. The trial court found that at the time of the homicide the defendant was insane.

I

Connecticut has never directly addressed the issue of whether an insane person is civilly liable for an intentional tort. The majority of jurisdictions that have considered this issue have held insane persons liable for their intentional torts....

Our adoption of the majority rule holding insane persons civilly liable, in appropriate circumstances, for their intentional torts finds support in other Connecticut case law. We have elsewhere recognized the vitality of the common law principle that "'where one of two innocent persons must suffer loss from an act done, it is just that it should fall on the one who caused the loss rather than upon the other who had no agency in producing it and could not by any means have avoided it.'" Verrilli v. Damilowski, 140 Conn. 358, 360, 100 A.2d 462 (1953), citing Granniss v. Weber, 107 Conn. 622, 625, 141 A. 877 (1928); Grissell v. Housatonic R. Co., 54 Conn. 447, 461, 9 A. 137 (1887).

II

... The defendant argues that for an act to be done with the requisite intent, the act must be an external manifestation of the actor's will. The defendant specifically relies on the *Restatement (Second) of Torts* § 14, comment b, for the definition of what constitutes an "act," where it is stated that "a muscular movement which is purely reflexive or the convulsive movements of an epileptic are not acts in the sense in which that word is used in the Restatement. So too, movements of the body during sleep or while the will is otherwise in abeyance are not acts. An external manifestation of the will is necessary to constitute an act, and an act is necessary to make one liable [for a battery]...." The defendant argues that if his "activities were the external manifestations of irrational and uncontrollable thought disorders these activities cannot be acts for purposes of establishing liability for assault and battery." We disagree.

We note that we have not been referred to any evidence indicating that the defendant's acts were reflexive, convulsive or epileptic. Furthermore, under the *Restatement (Second) of Torts* § 2, "act" is used "to denote an external manifestation of the actor's will and does not include any of its results, even the most direct, immediate, and intended." Comment b to this section provides in pertinent part: "A muscular reaction is always an act unless it is a purely reflexive reaction in which the mind and will have no share." Although the trial court found that the defendant could not form a rational choice, it did find that he could make a schizophrenic or crazy choice. Moreover, a rational choice is not required since "[a]n insane person may have an intent to invade the interests of another, even though his reasons and motives for forming that intention may be entirely irrational." Restatement (Second), Torts § 895J, comment c.

We recognize that the defendant made conflicting statements about the incident when discussing the homicide. At the hospital on the evening of the homicide the defendant told a police officer that his father-in-law was a heavy drinker and that he used the beer bottle for that reason. He stated he wanted to make his father-in-law suffer for his bad habits and so that he would realize the wrong that he had done. He also told the police officer that he was a supreme being and had the power to rule the destiny of the world and could make his bed fly out of the window. When interviewed by Dr. Borden, the defendant stated that he believed that his father-in-law was a spy for the red Chinese and that he believed his father-in-law was not only going to kill him, but going to harm his infant child so that he killed his father-in-law in self-defense. The explanations given by the defendant for committing the homicide are similar to the illustration of irrational reasons and motives given in comment c to § 895J of the *Restatement*, set out above.

Under these circumstances we are persuaded that the defendant's behavior at the time of the beating and shooting of Polmatier constituted an "act" within the meaning of comment b, § 2, of the *Restatement*. Following the majority rule in this case, we conclude that the trial court implicitly determined that the defendant committed an "act" in beating and shooting Polmatier. Accordingly, the trial court did not err as to the first prong of the defendant's claim.

III

The second prong of the defendant's claim is that the trial court erred in failing to determine whether the defendant intended the resulting injury to the decedent.

As discussed above, the defendant gave the police and Borden several reasons why he killed Polmatier. Under comment c to § 895J of the Restatement, it is not necessary for a defendant's reasons and motives for forming his intention to be rational in order for him to have the intent to invade the interests of another. Considering his statements to the police and to Borden that he intended to punish Polmatier and to kill him, we are persuaded that the defendant intended to beat and shoot him.

Notes

***Garratt v. Dailey* on remand.** After the case was remanded, the trial judge, applying the standard provided by the Washington Supreme Court, found that five-year-old Brian Dailey *did* act with the necessary intent. *See* Garratt v. Dailey, 304 P.2d 681 (Wash. 1956).

The "act" requirement in intentional tort cases. An act must be volitional to qualify as an "act" for purposes of an intentional tort claim. A purely reflexive action does not qualify. *See* Restatement (Second) of Torts § 2 cmt. a. What would be an example of a situation in which an individual did not "act" for purposes of an intentional tort claim under the rule described in *Polmatier*?

The "intent" requirement in intentional tort cases. The definition of "intent" used in the *Garratt* and *Polmatier* cases with respect to battery claims is the same definition used in other kinds of intentional tort cases.

Insane defendants and children. Think back to Chapter 1. What are some of the policy justifications for the majority rules regarding intentional tort liability for insane individuals and minors? What are the counterarguments?

Transferred intent. The intent requirement for battery is also satisfied "if the actor intends to cause the relevant tortious consequence to a third party, rather than to the plaintiff, but the actor's conduct causes that consequence to the plaintiff." Restatement (Third) of Torts § 110. As you will see in this chapter, this transferred intent rule also applies to other intentional torts.

Problem 2.1. Bobby is one of the opposing protesters in Pleasant Hill. He had been holding a placard over his head for an hour when he noticed that his shoulders were sore. So, Bobby put the placard down and began swinging his arm for the purpose of loosening his shoulder. To a neutral observer, it looked for sure like Bobby's fist would end up hitting Carly, who was walking up from behind Bobby with her head down as Bobby swung his arm, oblivious to her presence. All of a sudden, Alice walked in front of Carly. Bobby's fist ended up hitting Alice in the face and breaking her nose.

Bobby's actions obviously resulted in a harmful contact. Can Alice establish that Bobby acted with the intent to cause a contact if she brings a battery claim against Bobby?

Problem 2.2. Dennis is part of the original group of protesters. The two groups stand on opposite sides of the street, hurling insults at each other. Each side is packed close together, shoulder to shoulder. Dennis becomes so angered by taunts from the other side that, out of sheer frustration, he throws a glass bottle high into the air toward the opposing protesters. The bottle falls from above and hits Alice, an opposing protester.

Dennis' actions obviously resulted in a harmful contact. Did Dennis act with the intent to cause a contact with respect to Alice?

2. Intent to Cause Harmful or Offensive Contact

With any intentional tort, a defendant must do something more than bring about a result through an intentional act. The defendant must intend that the act produce consequences. In the case of battery, the defendant must intend to cause a harmful or offensive contact. Section 3 below will discuss the causation aspect of the battery tort as well as what it means to say that the contact was harmful or offensive. But this section first briefly focuses on what it means to say that the defendant acted with the intent to bring about this result.

White v. Muniz

999 P.2d 814 (Colo. 2000)
(en banc)

I.

In October of 1993, Barbara White placed her eighty-three year-old grandmother, Helen Everly, in an assisted living facility, the Beatrice Hover Personal Care Center. Within a few days of admission, Everly started exhibiting erratic behavior. She became agitated easily, and occasionally acted aggressively toward others.

On November 21, 1993, the caregiver in charge of Everly's wing asked Sherry Lynn Muniz, a shift supervisor at Hover, to change Everly's adult diaper. The caregiver informed Muniz that Everly was not cooperating in that effort. This did not surprise Muniz because she knew that Everly sometimes acted obstinately. Indeed, initially Everly refused to allow Muniz to change her diaper, but eventually Muniz thought that Everly relented. However, as Muniz reached toward the diaper, Everly struck Muniz on the jaw and ordered her out of the room.

The next day, Dr. Haven Howell, M.D. examined Everly at Longmont United Hospital. Dr. Howell deduced that "she [had] a progressive dementia with characteristic gradual loss of function, loss of higher cortical function including immediate and short term memory, impulse control and judgment." She diagnosed Everly with "[p]rimary degenerative dementia of the Alzheimer type, senile onset, with depression."

[Muniz sued for battery. As part of the instructions to the jury, the trial court stated the following:]

> The fact that a person may suffer from Dementia, Alzheimer type, does not prevent a finding that she acted intentionally. You may find that she acted intentionally if she intended to do what she did, even though her reasons and motives were entirely irrational. *However, she must have appreciated the offensiveness of her conduct.*

(Emphasis added.) In selecting the instruction on intent, the trial court determined that Everly's condition rendered her mental state comparable to that of a child.

Muniz's counsel objected to the last sentence of the instruction, claiming that it misstated the law.... The jury rendered verdicts in favor of Everly and White.

The court of appeals reversed the decision of the trial court and remanded the case for a new trial [reasoning that the jury instruction was flawed.]

II.

The question we here address is whether an intentional tort requires some proof that the tortfeasor not only intended to contact another person, but also intended that the contact be harmful or offensive to the other person.

A.

State courts and legal commentators generally agree that an intentional tort requires some proof that the tortfeasor intended harm or offense. *See* W. Page Keeton et al., *Prosser and Keeton on the Law of Torts* § 8 (5th ed.1984); Dan B. Dobbs, *The Law of Torts* § 30 (2000).

Historically, the intentional tort of battery required a subjective desire on the part of the tortfeasor to inflict a harmful or offensive contact on another. *See* Restatement, *supra*, § 8A; Keeton, *supra*, § 8; 6 Am.Jur.2d *Assault and Battery* § 8 (1999). Thus, it was not enough that a person intentionally contacted another resulting in a harmful or offensive contact. *See* Restatement, *supra*, § 18 cmt. e; Keeton § 8. Instead, the actor had to understand that his contact would be harmful or offensive.

B.

More recently, some courts around the nation have abandoned this dual intent requirement in an intentional tort setting, that being an intent to contact and an intent that the contact be harmful or offensive, and have required only that the tortfeasor intend a contact with another that results in a harmful or offensive touching. . . .

C.

In this case, we have the opportunity to examine intent in the context of an injury inflicted by a mentally deficient, Alzheimer's patient. White seeks an extension of Horton to the mentally ill and Muniz argues that a mere voluntary movement by Everly can constitute the requisite intent. We find that the law of Colorado requires the jury to conclude that the defendant both intended the contact and intended it to be harmful or offensive.

III.

Because Colorado law requires a dual intent, we apply here the *Restatement*'s definition of the term. As a result, we reject the arguments of Muniz and find that the trial court delivered an adequate instruction to the jury.

Operating in accordance with this instruction, the jury had to find that Everly appreciated the offensiveness of her conduct in order to be liable for the intentional tort of battery. It necessarily had to consider her mental capabilities in making such a finding, including her age, infirmity, education, skill, or any other characteristic as to which the jury had evidence. We presume that the jury "looked into the mind of Everly," and reasoned that Everly did not possess the necessary intent to commit an assault or a battery.

Accordingly, we reverse the decision of the court of appeals, and remand the case to that court for reinstatement of the jury verdict in favor of White and consideration of any remaining issues.

Notes

Majority rule? As *White* suggests, the prevailing rule as to the intent of the defendant in a battery case is not entirely clear, or at least is in a state of flux. One author who has surveyed the law on the issue finds the decisional law to be unclear and the *Restatement*'s language to be somewhat confusing. As a result, it is difficult to state with any certainty what the majority rule is. *See* Joseph H. King, *The Torts Restatement's Inchoate Definition of Intent for Battery, and Reflections on the Province of Restatements*, 38 Pepp. L. Rev. 623, 628–38 (2011).

The better rule? The two most commonly cited policy justifications underlying tort rules are compensation of injured parties and deterrence of socially undesirable conduct. Which approach—the single intent or dual intent approach—better furthers those goals? There are also process-based concerns that may drive a court's reasoning as it decides which rule to adopt. For example, the single intent rule would, on average, likely lead to a greater number of battery claims in the court system. How should a court balance these competing policy concerns?

3. Such Contact Results

a. Causation

In order to establish liability for a battery, the plaintiff must establish that the defendant's actions resulted in a harmful or offensive contact. Basic issues of causation are typically not an issue in intentional tort cases. (As you will see, this is very much not the case in some negligence cases.) In most intentional tort cases, the plaintiff must simply show that the harmful or offensive contact would not have occurred absent the defendant's conduct. Restatement (Third) of Torts § 27 Tentative Draft (2015). But there are some wrinkles to this rule that are explored in greater detail in this section.

b. Contact

Reynolds v. MacFarlane

322 P.3d 755 (Utah Ct. App. 2014)

BENCH, Senior Judge

On August 5, 2009, MacFarlane walked into the break room at his workplace where his coworker, Reynolds, was standing in front of the microwave oven. Reynolds was holding a ten dollar bill somewhat loosely in his hand. Reynolds was unaware of MacFarlane's presence. MacFarlane approached Reynolds from behind and, without touching Reynolds, quickly snatched the ten dollar bill. Reynolds immediately spun around and faced MacFarlane. MacFarlane then stated, "That was too easy," and returned the ten dollar bill to Reynolds. As MacFarlane began to walk away, Reynolds struck MacFarlane, splitting his lip. MacFarlane asked why he hit him. Reynolds replied, "You pissed me off." Shortly after this incident, the two interacted with a larger group of employees outside, and the employees joked around and completed their break. The two men were together at an offsite employee lunch some days later, and on multiple occasions after the incident Reynolds sought out and voluntarily spoke with MacFarlane in MacFarlane's work area.

Nevertheless, the incident was reported to the parties' supervisor. During the ensuing investigation, Reynolds reported to the supervisor that the incident was "nothing" and that any contact between the parties was accidental. Reynolds was ultimately punished with a one-day suspension without pay for striking another employee. Thereafter, Reynolds received medical treatment for anxiety, which Reynolds explained to his physician had resulted from difficulties at work.

Nearly one year later, Reynolds filed a complaint against MacFarlane, alleging assault and intentional infliction of emotional distress. At a bench trial, the parties stipulated to the dismissal of Reynolds's claim for intentional infliction of emotional distress, but Reynolds moved to amend his complaint to include a claim for battery. The court granted Reynolds's motion. After hearing the evidence, the trial court found MacFarlane "to be more credible in that [his] testimony was more consistent and was corroborated by multiple parties." Accordingly, the court based its findings of fact largely on MacFarlane's testimony. The trial court concluded that Reynolds had not met his burden of proof to show that MacFarlane had committed an assault or a battery against him and then dismissed the case with prejudice. Reynolds appeals.

. . .

Utah has adopted the Restatement (Second) of Torts to define the elements of the intentional tort of battery. Wagner v. State, 2005 UT 54, ¶ 16, 122 P.3d 599. Consequently, an actor is liable for battery if "'(a) he acts intending to cause a harmful or offensive contact with the person of the other . . . or an imminent apprehension of such a contact, and (b) a harmful contact with the person of the other directly or indirectly results.'" *Id.* (quoting Restatement (Second) of Torts § 13 (1965)).

In this case, the trial court found that MacFarlane did not touch Reynolds when he grabbed the ten dollar bill from Reynolds's hand. Because "MacFarlane never touched or came into contact with Reynolds," the trial court concluded that Reynolds did not meet his burden of proof to show that a harmful contact resulted from MacFarlane's action. Reynolds asserts that the trial court's conclusion is erroneous because MacFarlane's grabbing of an object—the ten dollar bill—from his hand was sufficient contact with his person to constitute a battery.

For the intentional tort of battery, harmful or offensive contact "includes all physical contacts that the individual either expressly communicates are unwanted, or those contacts to which no reasonable person would consent." *Id.* ¶ 51. But "it is not necessary that the plaintiff's actual body be disturbed." Restatement (Second) of Torts § 18 cmt. c (1965). Rather, "[p]rotection of the interest in freedom from intentional and unpermitted contacts with the plaintiff's person extends to any part of the body, or to anything which is attached to it and practically identified with it." W. Page Keeton et al., *Prosser and Keeton on the Law of Torts* § 9, at 39 (5th ed.1984) (footnote omitted). "Thus, if all other requisites of a battery against the plaintiff are satisfied, contact with the plaintiff's clothing, or with a cane, a paper, or any other object held in the plaintiff's hand, will be sufficient" to support a battery claim because the "interest in the integrity of [a] person includes all those things which are in contact or connected with the person." *Id.* § 9, at 39–40 (footnotes omitted); *see also Morgan v. Loyacomo*, 190 Miss. 656, 1 So.2d 510, 511 (1941) ("[T]o constitute assault and battery, it is not necessary to touch the plaintiff's body or even his clothing; knocking or snatching anything from [the] plaintiff's hand or touching anything connected with his person, when done in a rude or insolent manner, is sufficient."); *Picard v. Barry Pontiac-Buick, Inc.*, 654 A.2d 690, 694 (R.I.1995) ("[D]efendant's offensive contact with an object attached to or identified with plaintiff's body was sufficient to constitute a battery."); *Fisher v. Carrousel Motor Hotel, Inc.*, 424 S.W.2d 627, 629 (Tex.1967) ("The intentional snatching of an object from one's hand is as clearly an offensive invasion of his person as would be an actual contact with the body.").... We consider the above authorities as persuasive and not inconsistent with our supreme court's battery analysis.

In this case, MacFarlane's act of taking the ten dollar bill held loosely in Reynolds's hand was sufficient contact to constitute the contact element of battery, *see Wagner*, 2005 UT 54, ¶ 16, 122 P.3d 599 notwithstanding the fact that MacFarlane did not touch Reynolds's body. When held in his hand, the ten dollar bill was connected to Reynolds such that when MacFarlane snatched the bill from Reynolds, MacFarlane's act resulted in offensive contact with Reynolds's person....

The trial court determined that Reynolds suffered no damages as a result of the August 5, 2009 incident. The Utah Supreme Court has explained that "[a] harmful or offensive contact is simply one to which the recipient of the contact has not consented either directly or by implication." "[H]armful or offensive contact is *not limited to that which is medically injurious* or perpetrated with the intent to cause some form of psychological or physical injury." (emphasis added). Instead, harmful or offensive contact "includes all physical contacts that the individual either expressly communicates are unwanted, or those contacts to which no reasonable person would consent." *Id.* Moreover, "[c]ommon law battery does not require that the nonconsensual contact be injurious. Rather, proof of an unauthorized invasion of the plaintiff's person, even if harmless, *entitles him to at least nominal damages*." *Lounsbury v. Capel*, 836 P.2d 188, 192–93 (Utah Ct.App.1992) (emphasis added); *see also id.* at 196 ("[A plaintiff] need not prove injury to sustain his battery claim; if he proves no more than the 'offense' of the nonconsensual touching, he is entitled to nominal damages.").

Here, the trial court found that "no injury resulted to Reynolds as a direct and proximate cause of MacFarlane's actions." Thus, the trial court ruled that Reynolds's claimed damages—the one-day suspension and his medical issues following the break-room incident with MacFarlane—were not proximately caused by MacFarlane's act. Reynolds has not effectively challenged this ruling on appeal. However, because we have concluded that MacFarlane committed a battery, Reynolds is entitled to nominal damages. Accordingly, we remand to the trial court for an award of nominal damages to Reynolds for battery.

Notes

Other forms of contact. Most battery cases involve some obvious form of contact, like a punch or a kick. But a defendant may cause "contact with the person" of the plaintiff in other ways. For example, the defendant who administers a drug that the plaintiff ingests has caused a contact. *See* Mink v. Univ. of Chicago, 460 F. Supp. 713, 718 (N.D. Ill. 1978). The act of blowing smoke in another's face has been held to be an act resulting in contact. *See* Leichtman v. WLW Jacor Commc'ns, Inc., 634 N.E.2d 697, 699 (Ohio Ct. App. 1994). What about shining a laser pointer at someone? Subjecting them to extreme heat or cold? How should the line be drawn as to what qualifies as contact?

Nominal damages. Nominal damages are awarded to establish that an individual's rights were violated even if the individual suffered no substantial harm. An award of $1 is common.

Problem 2.3. Edward, one of the original protesters, slips past the police barricade and approaches the group of opposing protesters and begins yelling at Bobby. Bobby thrusts the placard he was holding about an inch from Edward's face so that Edward can see the message on the placard. Bobby's actions were so swift that the breeze from the sign's movement blew back Edward's hair a little bit.

In a battery action against Bobby, could Edward establish the contact requirement of a battery claim?

c. Harmful or Offensive Contact

The most likely issue to arise in this part of the battery case is whether the contact that resulted was harmful or offensive. A harmful contact is easy enough to conceptualize—the plaintiff suffered a physical injury. The issue of what qualifies as an "offensive" contact is sometimes more complicated.

Balas v. Huntington Ingalls Industries, Inc.

711 F.3d 401 (4th Cir. 2013)

[Plaintiff, Karen Balas, appeals the entry of summary judgment in favor of the defendant by the lower court. Balas' supervisor was Brad Price.] In January 2010,

Price hugged Balas. Balas alleges that Price "trapped [her] in her work space and willfully, wantonly and forcibly put his arms around [her,] hugging her against her will." It is undisputed, however, that this hug occurred after Balas had given Price a gift of Christmas cookies for his family, and that immediately prior to the hug, Price had thanked her for the cookies and told her, "You never cease to amaze me."

For contact to rise to the level of battery, it must be "offensive," Restatement (Second) of Torts § 18 . . . "A bodily contact is offensive if it offends a reasonable sense of personal dignity." Restatement (Second) of Torts § 19. As Balas concedes, the quality of the act's offensiveness is judged by an objective standard, not by whether the plaintiff found the act offensive.

Balas . . . does not dispute that she never told Price to stop or that the hug was unwelcome. To the contrary, rather than objecting to the hug itself, she testified that it was the manner of the hug that made her uncomfortable: "the way [Price] swooped [her] up at [her] waist, or the way he grabbed [her] was what felt offensive."

Even if the hug was not consented to, . . . a reasonable person could not find it objectively offensive. To constitute battery, the challenged contact must be "unwarranted by the social usages prevalent at the time and place at which it is inflicted." Restatement (Second) of Torts § 19 cmt. a. Balas had just given Price a gift of Christmas cookies. Immediately before hugging Balas, Price thanked her and told her that she never ceased to amaze him. Given the circumstances surrounding the hug, we determine that Balas raises no genuine question of material fact as to whether the hug was objectively offensive.

Fuerschbach v. Southwest Airlines Co.

439 F.3d 1197 (10th Cir. 2006)

Several supervisors at Southwest Airlines convinced two Albuquerque police officers to stage an arrest of Marcie Fuerschbach, a Southwest Airlines employee, as part of an elaborate prank that included actual handcuffing and apparent arrest. This was a "joke gone bad," and turned out to be anything but funny, as Fuerschbach allegedly suffered serious psychological injuries as a result of the prank. [In addition to various claims against the officers, Southwest, and the supervisors, Fuerschbach sued the officers for battery.]

Any bodily contact is offensive "if it offends a reasonable sense of personal dignity." Restatement (Second) of Torts § 19. Viewing the evidence in the light most favorable to Fuerschbach, a jury could conclude that the officers' actions offended a reasonable sense of personal dignity. *See Ortega*, 827 P.2d at 155 (citing with approval *Fisher v. Carrousel Motor Hotel, Inc.*, 424 S.W.2d 627, 629 (Tex. 1967) (intentionally grabbing a plaintiff's plate constitutes battery because "[t]he intentional snatching of an object from one's hand is clearly an offensive invasion of his person"). A jury could find that placing a person's hands in position to be handcuffed, handcuffing the individual, and then leading the individual to walk fifteen feet offends a reasonable sense of personal dignity.

Moreover, the officers' demeanor is not probative of their intent to cause an offensive contact. Nor is the officers' intent merely to pull a prank on Fuerschbach an excuse. The record reveals that the officers intended to touch Fuerschbach's arms, to place her arms in position to be handcuffed, and to then handcuff her tightly, thus intending to cause an offensive contact. *See Love*, 524 N.E.2d at 167 ("The contact involved is plainly intentional; one cannot accidentally handcuff or subdue another."). Viewing the evidence in the light most favorable to Fuerschbach, the officers intended to cause an offensive contact with Fuerschbach's person and did cause an offensive contact. Accordingly, we reverse the district court's grant of summary judgment to the officers on Fuerschbach's assault and battery claim.

Notes

Offensive contact. In *Balas* and *Fuerschbach* the plaintiffs took offense to the contacts that resulted, yet the courts reached different results. Do you agree with both decisions? Why should tort law recognize a claim for a mere offensive contact? Why not limit the tort to harmful contacts?

Dual intent or single intent? *Balas* does not really focus on the issue of intent, whereas *Fuerschbach* does. Did *Fuerschbach* employ a single intent approach or a dual intent approach? Would the outcome have been different if the court had employed the competing approach?

Liability in general. In the case of a harmful contact, the plaintiff is obviously entitled to compensation for the monetary costs associated with the battery, as well as compensation for the emotional distress that results. *See* Black v. Comer, 38 So. 3d 16 (Ala. 2009). When a defendant's conduct is especially egregious—such as where the defendant was motivated by ill will or engaged in extreme misconduct—a plaintiff may also be entitled to punitive damages (*i.e.*, damages designed to punish the defendant and not merely to compensate the plaintiff). Fuerschbach allegedly suffered serious psychological injuries as a result of the prank, so assuming she could prove the existence of those injuries, she should be entitled to monetary compensation.

Extended liability for unforeseen harms. "When an actor's tortious conduct causes harm to a person that, because of a preexisting physical or mental condition or other characteristics of the person, is of a greater magnitude or different type than might reasonably be expected, the actor is nevertheless subject to liability for all such harm to the person." Restatement (Third) of Torts § 31 (2010). The classic example is *Vosburg v. Putney*, 56 N.W. 480, 480 (Wis. 1893), in which a child reached across an aisle at school and lightly touched the plaintiff's leg with his own foot. Due to a preexisting medical condition, this resulted in the plaintiff permanently losing the use of his leg. Vosburg v. Putney, 47 N.W. 99 (Wis. 1890). On appeal, the Wisconsin Supreme Court held that the plaintiff could recover on a battery claim for the full extent of the harm suffered. Vosburg v. Putney, 56 N.W. 480, 480 (Wis. 1893).

Consent. The issue of the plaintiff's consent (or lack thereof) to the defendant's contact is sometimes at issue, such as where the plaintiff is injured while engaged in horseplay or where a doctor performs a medical procedure without the patient's advance consent. Some courts define the tort of battery in terms of harmful or offensive contact that was not consented to by the plaintiff. Others treat the plaintiff's consent as a defense that prevents liability; if the plaintiff consents to the contact, the battery claim fails. Consent is addressed in Part E below as part of the treatment of defenses to intentional tort claims.

Problem 2.4. Recall that in Problem 2.2 Dennis threw a glass bottle high into the air toward the opposing protesters. The bottle falls from above and hits Alan, one of the opposing protesters. The glass shatters and ends up cutting Alan. Alan has hemophilia, a condition that impairs blood clotting and results in excessive bleeding, causing him to bleed profusely. Dennis watched in horror as the other protesters attempted to help Alan. Alan nearly died as a result.

Dennis' actions obviously resulted in a harmful contact. Assume that Dennis acted with the intent to cause an offensive contact when he threw the bottle. Can Dennis be held liable on a battery theory even though he did not intend to cause the degree of harm that resulted?

Problem 2.5. After Dennis threw the bottle in the direction of the opposing protesters, Francis, who was on Dennis' side, tapped Dennis on the shoulder to get his attention. When Dennis turns around, Francis puts her hand on Dennis' shoulder and angrily lectures him regarding his actions. The two begin arguing heatedly before they are pulled apart.

Did Francis cause a harmful or offensive contact?

Problem 2.6. **(Review)** Recall that in Problem 2.3 Bobby suddenly thrust the placard he had been holding in Edward's face. When Bobby thrust the placard in Edward's face, Edward was annoyed and responded by swatting at and hitting the placard, causing Bobby to drop it. Bobby suffers no physical harm as a result.

Can Edward be held liable for battery?

B. Assault

As perhaps the leading treatise on torts states, "[a]ssault and battery go together like ham and eggs." W. Page Keeton et al., Prosser and Keeton on the Law of Torts § 10, at 46 (5th ed.1984). But they are separate torts. Whereas the hallmark of a battery is harmful or offensive contact, the hallmark of an assault is the *apprehension* of such contact. Thus, the tort of assault seeks to protect one's right to be free from the apprehension of a battery.

Problem 2.7. When Dennis threw the glass bottle in the air toward the counter protesters, he lofted it so high in the air that it fell in such a way that Alan never saw it until after he had been hit. When Alan looked down, he noticed the glass on the ground and that he was covered in blood from where the bottle had cut him.

Could Alan recover from Dennis on an assault theory?

1. Act with Intent to Cause an Imminent Apprehension of a Harmful or Offensive Contact

Cullison v. Medley

570 N.E.2d 27 (Ind. 1991)

KRAHULIK, Justice.

Dan R. Cullison (Appellant-Plaintiff below) petitions this Court to accept transfer of this cause in order to reverse the trial court's entry of summary judgment against him and in favor of the Appellees-Defendants below (collectively "the Medleys"). The Court of Appeals affirmed the entry of summary judgment.

According to Cullison's deposition testimony, on February 2, 1986, he encountered Sandy, the 16-year-old daughter of Ernest, in a Linton, Indiana, grocery store parking lot. They exchanged pleasantries and Cullison invited her to have a Coke with him and to come to his home to talk further. A few hours later, someone knocked on the door of his mobile home. Cullison got out of bed and answered the door. He testified that he saw a person standing in the darkness who said that she wanted to talk to him. Cullison answered that he would have to get dressed because he had been in bed. Cullison went back to his bedroom, dressed, and returned to the darkened living room of his trailer. When he entered the living room and turned the lights on, he was confronted by Sandy Medley, as well as by father Ernest, brother Ron, mother Doris, and brother-in-law Terry Simmons. Ernest was on crutches due to knee surgery and had a revolver in a holster strapped to his thigh. Cullison testified that Sandy called him a "pervert" and told him he was "sick," mother Doris berated him while keeping her hand in her pocket, convincing Cullison that she also was carrying a pistol. Ron and Terry said nothing to Cullison, but their presence in his trailer home further intimidated him. Primarily, however, Cullison's attention was riveted to the gun carried by Ernest. Cullison testified that, while Ernest never withdrew the gun from his holster, he "grabbed for the gun a few times and shook the gun" at plaintiff while threatening to "jump astraddle" of Cullison if he did not leave Sandy alone. Cullison testified that Ernest "kept grabbing at it with his hand, like he was going to take it out," and "took it to mean he was going to shoot me" when Ernest threatened to "jump astraddle" of Cullison. Although no one actually touched Cullison, his testimony was that he feared he was about to be shot throughout the episode because Ernest kept moving his hand toward the gun as if to draw the revolver from the holster while threatening Cullison to leave Sandy alone.

As the Medleys were leaving, Cullison suffered chest pains and feared that he was having a heart attack. [Cullison also alleged that he suffered other forms of emotional distress stemming from the incident.]

... The Court of Appeals decided that, because Ernest never removed his gun from the holster, his threat that he was going to "jump astraddle" of Cullison constituted conditional language which did not express any present intent to harm Cullison and, therefore, was not an assault. Further, the Court of Appeals decided that even if it were to find an assault, summary judgment was still appropriate because Cullison alleged only emotional distress and made no showing that the Medleys' actions were malicious, callous, or willful or that the alleged injuries he suffered were a foreseeable result of the Medleys' conduct. We disagree.

It is axiomatic that assault, unlike battery, is effectuated when one acts intending to cause a harmful or offensive contact with the person of the other or an imminent apprehension of such contact. Restatement (Second) of Torts § 21 (1965). It is the right to be free from the apprehension of a battery which is protected by the tort action which we call an assault. As this Court held approximately 90 years ago in *Kline v. Kline* (1901), 158 Ind. 602, 64 N.E. 9, an assault constitutes "a touching of the mind, if not of the body." Because it is a touching of the mind, as opposed to the body, the damages which are recoverable for an assault are damages for mental trauma and distress. "Any act of such a nature as to excite an apprehension of a battery may constitute an assault. It is an assault to shake a fist under another's nose, to aim or strike at him with a weapon, or to hold it in a threatening position, to rise or advance to strike another, to surround him with a display of force. ..." *W. Prosser & J. Keaton, Prosser and Keaton on Torts* § 10 (5th ed. 1984). Additionally, the apprehension must be one which would normally be aroused in the mind of a reasonable person. *Id.* Finally, the tort is complete with the invasion of the plaintiff's mental peace.

The facts alleged and testified to by Cullison could, if believed, entitle him to recover for an assault against the Medleys. A jury could reasonably conclude that the Medleys intended to frighten Cullison by surrounding him in his trailer and threatening him with bodily harm while one of them was armed with a revolver, even if that revolver was not removed from the its holster. Cullison testified that Ernest kept grabbing at the pistol as if he were going to take it out, and that Cullison thought Ernest was going to shoot him. It is for the jury to determine whether Cullison's apprehension of being shot or otherwise injured was one which would normally be aroused in the mind of a reasonable person. It was error for the trial court to enter summary judgment on the count two allegation of assault.

Brower v. Ackerly

943 P.2d 1141 (Wash. Ct. App. 1997)

BECKER, Judge.

Jordan Brower, who alleges that Christopher and Theodore Ackerley made anonymous threatening telephone calls to him, appeals from a summary judgment dismissal of his claims against them.

The plaintiff, Jordan Brower, is a Seattle resident active in civic affairs. Christopher and Theodore Ackerley, in their early twenties at the time of the alleged telephone calls, are two sons of the founder of Ackerley Communications, Inc., a company engaged in various activities in Seattle including billboard advertising. Brower perceived billboard advertising as a visual blight. [As a result of Brower's efforts, the city pursued legal action against Ackerley related to its installation of possibly illegal billboards and took other measures to limit billboard advertising.]

Within two days an anonymous male caller began what Brower describes as "a campaign of harassing telephone calls" to Brower's home that continued over a period of 20 months.

On July 19, 1993, . . . [a]t about 7:30 p.m. [a] caller called and said, "I'm going to find out where you live and I'm going to kick your ass." At 9:43 p.m. Brower received another call from a voice disguised to sound, in Brower's words, "eerie and sinister". The caller said "Ooooo, Jordan, oooo, you're finished; cut you in your sleep, you sack of shit." Brower recorded the last two calls on his telephone answering machine.

Brower made a complaint to the police, reporting that he was very frightened by these calls. Because Brower had activated a call trapping feature of his telephone service after the third telephone call, the police were able to learn that the call had originated in the residence of Christopher Ackerley. When contacted by the police, Christopher Ackerley denied making the calls. He said Brower's telephone number was in his apartment, and that his brother Ted Ackerley had been in the apartment at the time and perhaps had made the calls.

The City filed no criminal charges based on the police report. Brower then brought this civil suit against Christopher and Theodore Ackerley seeking compensation for the emotional distress he suffered as the result of the telephone calls. . . .

The elements of civil assault have not been frequently addressed in Washington cases. The gist of the cause of action is "the victim's apprehension of imminent physical violence caused by the perpetrator's action or threat." In the 1910 case of *Howell v. Winters*, the Supreme Court relied on a definition provided in *Cooley, Torts* (3d ed.):

> An assault is an attempt, with unlawful force, to inflict bodily injuries upon another, accompanied with the apparent present ability to give effect to the attempt if not prevented. Such would be the raising of the hand in anger, with an apparent purpose to strike, and sufficiently near to enable

> the purpose to be carried into effect; the pointing of a loaded pistol at one who is in its range; the pointing of a pistol not loaded at one who is not aware of that fact and making an apparent attempt to shoot; shaking a whip or the fist in a man's face in anger; riding or running after him in threatening and hostile manner with a club or other weapon; and the like. The right that is invaded here indicates the nature of the wrong. Every person has a right to complete and perfect immunity from hostile assaults that threaten danger to his person; 'A right to live in society without being put in fear of personal harm.'

The discussion in *Howell* accords with the *Restatement (Second) of Torts*, which defines assault, in relevant part, as follows:

> (1) An actor is subject to liability to another for assault if
>
> (a) he acts intending to cause a harmful or offensive contact with the person of the other or a third person, or an imminent apprehension of such a contact, and
>
> (b) the other is thereby put in such imminent apprehension.

According to section 31 of the *Restatement*, words alone are not enough to make an actor liable for assault "unless together with other acts or circumstances they put the other in reasonable apprehension of an imminent harmful or offensive contact with his person." The comments to section 31 indicate infliction of emotional distress is a better-suited cause of action when mere words cause injury, "even though the mental discomfort caused by a threat of serious future harm on the part of one who has the apparent intention and ability to carry out his threat may be far more emotionally disturbing than many of the attempts to inflict minor bodily contacts which are actionable as assaults."

The Ackerleys argue that dismissal of Brower's assault claim was appropriate because the threatening words were unaccompanied by any physical acts or movements. Brower acknowledges that words alone cannot constitute an assault, but he contends the spoken threats became assaultive in view of the surrounding circumstances including the fact that the calls were made to his home, at night, creating the impression that the caller was stalking him.

Whether the repeated use of a telephone to make anonymous threats constitutes acts or circumstances sufficient to render the threats assaultive is an issue we need not resolve because we find another issue dispositive: the physical harm threatened in the telephone calls to Brower was not imminent.

To constitute civil assault, the threat must be of imminent harm. As one commentator observes, it is "the immediate physical threat which is important, rather than the manner in which it is conveyed." The *Restatement*'s comment is to similar effect: "The apprehension created must be one of imminent contact, as distinguished from any contact in the future." The *Restatement* gives the following illustration: "A threatens to shoot B and leaves the room with the express purpose of getting his revolver. A is not liable to B."

The telephone calls received by Brower on July 19 contained two explicit threats: "I'm going to find out where you live and I'm going to kick your ass"; and later, "you're finished; cut you in your sleep". The words threatened action in the near future, but not the imminent future. The immediacy of the threats was not greater than in the *Restatement*'s illustration where A must leave the room to get his revolver. Because the threats, however frightening, were not accompanied by circumstances indicating that the caller was in a position to reach Brower and inflict physical violence "almost at once," we affirm the dismissal of the assault claim.

Note

The plaintiff's prima facie case. Note all of the possible issues involved in establishing that a defendant acted with the required intent. A plaintiff must establish by a preponderance of the evidence that the defendant: (1) acted (2) with the intent (3) to cause the apprehension (4) of a contact (5) that was imminent and (6) that would be harmful or offensive.

Problem 2.8. After Dennis threw the glass bottle toward the opposing protesters, several of the protesters on Dennis' side chided Dennis for his actions. One of them was Eloise. After Eloise turned her back on Dennis, Dennis angrily picked up a nearby empty can and threw it at the back of Eloise's head for the purpose of startling her. At the last second, Eloise turned around and saw the can headed toward her face. She managed to duck out of the way and avoid the can.

Could Eloise establish that Dennis acted with the necessary intent to support an assault claim?

Problem 2.9. When Francis placed her hand on Dennis' shoulder and started lecturing Dennis about his behavior, the argument between the two escalated quickly. They soon began exchanging angry insults and it looked like a physical fight might occur. As the two were being pulled away from each other, Francis angrily pointed at Dennis and said, "I know where your car is parked! I'll be waiting for you!"

Can Dennis establish that Francis acted with the intent to cause the imminent apprehension of a harmful or offensive contact for purposes of an assault claim?

Note

Conditional threats. One recurring fact pattern involves the defendant who threatens the plaintiff with bodily harm if the plaintiff does not do what the defendant wants. ("Get out of that seat, or I'll punch you.") The decisions often speak of an "imminent" contact in terms of there being no significant delay. In the case of a conditional threat, the defendant is arguably not threatening an imminent battery since the battery can be avoided. However, courts have concluded that the fact that an individual can avoid by a battery by complying with the defendant's threat does not prevent the threatened contact from being imminent. Looked at slightly differently, if the plaintiff does not comply with the defendant's demand, the battery may still be imminent.

2. Such Apprehension Results

In order to establish a prima facie case of assault, the plaintiff must show that the defendant's act actually resulted in the reasonable apprehension of an imminent harmful or offensive contact. Most assault cases involve a plaintiff who fears an imminent battery. Look up the definition of the word "apprehend" or "apprehension." Is fear a requirement for an assault claim?

Note that under the majority approach, the plaintiff's apprehension of the contact must be reasonable. Recall, for example, in *Cullison* that the court stated that "the apprehension must be one which would normally be aroused in the mind of a reasonable person." Was Cullison's apprehension of an imminent harmful contact reasonable under the circumstances?

Some of the special rules that apply to battery claims apply with equal force to assault claims. So, for example, the fact that the plaintiff experiences a greater fear or distress than the defendant intended does not prevent the defendant from being liable for the full extent of the distress caused. In *Brower*, the type of distress the plaintiff suffered from the apparent death threats was perhaps of the sort the defendant intended. The *Brower* plaintiff experienced:

> feelings of panic, terror, and insecurity as well as a rising pulse, light-headedness, sweaty palms, sleeplessness, and an inability to concentrate that lasted for some time afterward: 'Every day I come home, I worry that someone has burned our house down, or if my wife is late from work, whether she has been harmed.'

In *Cullison*, the plaintiff's distress was heightened when he later learned that Ernest Medley had previously shot a man. As a result, Cullison alleged that he:

> sought psychological counseling and therapy and continued to see a therapist for approximately 18 months. Additionally, Cullison sought psychiatric help and received prescription medication which prevented him from operating power tools or driving an automobile, thus injuring Cullison in his sole proprietorship construction business. Additionally, Cullison testified that he suffered from nervousness, depression, sleeplessness, inability to concentrate and impotency following his run-in with the Medleys.

This sort of long-lasting distress might well have been greater than the defendants intended. But under the extended liability principle discussed in connection with battery, that would not prevent Cullison from recovering for the full value of his distress (provided it could be proven to the jury's satisfaction).

Problem 2.10. Recall that at one point during the protest, Bobby thrust his placard in Edward's face. Edward saw the sign rapidly approaching his face, but things happened so quickly that Edward didn't really have time to be afraid that the placard would cause him harm (although he did see the placard coming toward him). Nonetheless, Edward now suffers recurring nightmares as a result of the incident.

Can Edward establish that Bobby's actions resulted in the apprehension of an imminent harmful or offensive contact?

Problem 2.11. **(Review)** Assume for purposes of this problem only that Bobby thrust the placard in Edward's face for the purpose of making him think he was about to be struck. But Bobby lost control of the placard and accidentally hit Edward in the face with it.

Under what intentional tort theories could Edward recover?

C. False Imprisonment

The tort of false imprisonment protects one's interest in being free to choose one's own location. Therefore, the question of whether a plaintiff has been confined to a location chosen by another is often central in false imprisonment cases. The following case lays out the basic structure of a false imprisonment claim.

Dupler v. Seubert

230 N.W.2d 626 (Wis. 1975)

This is a false imprisonment action. On April 23, 1971, plaintiff-appellant Ethel M. Dupler was fired from her job with the defendant-respondent Wisconsin Telephone Company. She was informed of her discharge during an hour-and-a-half session with her two superiors, defendants-respondents Keith Peterson and Helen Seubert, who Dupler claims, falsely imprisoned her during a portion of this time period.

Dupler had worked for the Telephone Company as a customer service representative since 1960. At approximately 4:30 on April 23rd, Seubert asked Dupler to come to Peterson's office. When all three were inside, sitting down, with the door closed, Seubert told Dupler the Telephone Company would no longer employ her and that she could choose either to resign or be fired. Dupler testified that she refused to resign and that in the conversation that followed, Peterson discussed several alternatives short of dismissal, all of which had been considered but rejected.

At approximately 5 o'clock, Dupler testified, she began to feel sick to her stomach and said 'You have already fired me. Why don't you just let me go.' She made a motion to get up but Peterson told her to sit down in 'a very loud harsh voice.'

Then, Dupler testified, she began to feel violently ill and stated "I got to go. I can't take this any more. I'm sick to my stomach. I know I'm going to throw up." She got up and started for the door but Seubert also arose and stood in front of the door. After Dupler repeated that she was sick, Seubert allowed her to exit, but followed her to the men's washroom, where Dupler did throw up. Following this, at approximately 5:25, Seubert asked Dupler to return to Peterson's office where she had left her purse to discuss the situation further. Dupler testified that she went back to the office and reached for her purse; Seubert again closed the door and Peterson said '(i)n a loud voice 'Sit down. I'm still your boss. I'm not through with you.' At approximately 5:40 Dupler told Peterson her husband was waiting for her outside in a car and Peterson told her to go outside and ask her husband to come inside. Dupler then went outside and explained the situation to her husband who said "You get back in there and get you coat and if you aren't right out I'll call the police." Dupler returned to Peterson's office and was again told in a loud tone of voice to sit down. She said Seubert and Peterson were trying to convince her to resign rather than be fired and again reviewed the alternatives that had been considered. Dupler then said: "What's the sense of all this. Why keep torturing me. Let me go. Let me go." She stated that Peterson replied, "No, we still aren't finished. We have a lot of things to discuss, your retirement pay, your vacation, other things." Finally, at approximately 6:00 Peterson told Dupler they could talk further on the phone or at her house, and Dupler left. When asked why she had stayed in Peterson's office for such a long time, Dupler replied:

> Well, for one thing, Helen, Mrs. Seubert, had blocked the door, and tempers had been raised with all the shouting and screaming, I was just plain scared to make an effort. There were two against one.

Peterson and Seubert did not dispute that Dupler had been fired on April 23rd, or that the conference lasted from 4:30 to 6 p.m., or that Dupler became very upset and sick to her stomach and had to leave to throw up. Peterson admitted that Dupler had asked to leave and that he requested that she stay and continue talking so she could indicate whether she wished to resign or be fired. Seubert said Dupler did not so indicate until 'within three minutes of her leaving.' Both denied that any loud or threatening language had been used, or that Dupler was detained against her will. Peterson said neither he nor Seubert even raised their voices. He said the session was so lengthy because Dupler continued to plead for another chance, and to request reasons for the dismissal.

The jury found that both Peterson and Seubert falsely imprisoned Dupler and fixed her damages at $7,500. . . .

The issue raised by a motion for review filed by defendants-respondents is: Is the jury's verdict, finding that Dupler was falsely imprisoned, supported by the evidence?

The essence of false imprisonment is the intentional, unlawful, and unconsented restraint by one person of the physical liberty of another. In *Maniaci v. Marquette*

University, the court adopted the definition of false imprisonment contained in sec. 35 of the *Restatement of Torts 2d*, which provides in part:

> False Imprisonment
>
> (1) An actor is subject to liability to another for false imprisonment if
>
> (a) he acts intending to confine the other or a third person within boundaries fixed by the actor, and
>
> (b) his act directly or indirectly results in such a confinement of the other, and
>
> (c) the other is conscious of the confinement or is harmed by it.

Secs. 39 and 40 provide that the confinement may be caused by physical force or the threat of physical force, and the comment to sec. 40 indicates the threat may either be express, or inferred from the person's conduct. As Prosser comments:

> *Character of Defendant's Act*
>
> The restraint may be by means of physical barriers, or by threats of force which intimidate the plaintiff into compliance with orders. It is sufficient that he submits to an apprehension of force reasonably to be understood from the conduct of the defendant, although no force is used or even expressly threatened. . . . This gives rise, in borderline cases, to questions of fact, turning upon the details of the testimony, as to what was reasonably to be understood and implied from the defendant's conduct, tone of voice and the like, which seldom can be reflected accurately in an appellate record, and normally are for the jury.

This is precisely such a case and we conclude that the record contains sufficient evidence from which the jury could have concluded that Mrs. Dupler was intentionally confined, against her will, by an implied threat of actual physical restraint. She testified that defendant Peterson ordered her in a loud voice to remain seated several times, after she expressed the desire to leave. She reported being 'berated, screamed and hollered at,' and said the reason she did not just walk out of the room was that 'Mrs. Seubert had blocked the door, and tempers had been raised with all the shouting and screaming, I was just plain scared to make an effort. There were two against one.' The jury obviously believed Mrs. Dupler's rather than the defendants' account of what transpired, as it had the right to do, and we conclude her testimony was sufficient to support the jury's verdict.

Defendants rely upon the 1926 case of *Weiler v. Herzfeld-Phillipson Co.*, where this court held that an employer, who had detained an employee in his office for several hours upon suspicion of theft and then discharged her, was not liable for false imprisonment. This case is distinguishable, however, principally upon the ground that in *Weiler* the court emphasized several times that during the entire session the plaintiff was still employed by defendant and 'was compensated for every minute of the time spent by her in the office.' In the instant case, Dupler was compensated only through 5 p.m., and according to her testimony, she was not ordered to remain in the office, after she requested to leave, until after 5 p.m.

We conclude that *Weiler* is not controlling here and that the jury could properly find that defendants falsely imprisoned Dupler by compelling her to remain in Peterson's office against her will after 5 p.m. We conclude the imprisonment ceased when Dupler left the building to visit her husband, but resumed when she reentered Peterson's office to get her coat in order to leave, but was commanded to stay.

Notes

Prima facie case. Note again all of the possible issues involved in establishing a prima facie case. The central inquiry in many cases will be whether the defendant's actions resulted in the confinement of the plaintiff.

Forms of confinement. While confinement is often the key issue in false imprisonment cases, courts have been remarkably imprecise as to what qualifies as "confinement." One idea that sometimes emerges in decisions is the notion that the defendant must take action that "overcomes the plaintiff's will." *See* Oramalu v. Washington Mutual Bank, 699 F. Supp. 2d 898, 911 (S.D. Tex. 2009) (applying Texas law); Kalbfell v. Marc Glassman, Inc., 2003 Ohio App. LEXIS 3183, *15 (Ohio Ct. App. June 26, 2003) (focusing on whether the plaintiff's will "was sufficiently overcome"). Confinement can occur in a variety of ways:

(1) *Actual or apparent physical barriers*: For example, locking the plaintiff in a room. If the plaintiff is aware of a means of escape and can escape with only "slight inconvenience," there has been no confinement on the part of the defendant. *See* Restatement (Second) of Torts § 36 cmt. a (1965).

(2) *Overpowering physical force, or by submission to physical force*: Note that the force need not necessarily be overpowering in the sense that it is enough to overcome a reasonable person. It is enough that the force restrains the plaintiff (who attempts to resist) or that the plaintiff submits to the force applied. *Id.* § 39 cmt. a.

(3) *Threats of physical force*: The threat can be explicit or implicit. What matters is that the plaintiff reasonably believes that the defendant will physically restrain the plaintiff if the plaintiff attempts to leave. *See* McCann v. Wal-Mart Stores, Inc., 210 F.3d 51 (1st Cir. 2000).

(4) *Other duress*: The duress employed by the defendant must be sufficient to render the plaintiff's consent to remain ineffective. Examples include threatening to injure a member of the plaintiff's family or to damage the plaintiff's property. Restatement (Second) of Torts § 40 (1965).

(5) *Asserted legal authority*: For example, a security guard tells a customer that the customer will be arrested if the customer attempts to leave. *See* Bartolo v. Boardwalk Regency Hotel Casino, Inc., 449 A.2d 1339 (N.J. Super. Ct. 1982).

Other employee cases. One fact scenario that has arisen repeatedly is the employee who is accused of misconduct, questioned by her employer, and is afraid to leave an enclosed space for fear of losing her job. *See* Johnson v. UPS, Inc., 722 F. Supp. 1282 (D. Md. 1989); Hanna v. Marshall Field & Co., 665 N.E.2d 343 (Ill. Ct. App. 1996); Moen v. Las Vegas Intl. Hotel, Inc., 521 P.2d 370 (Nev. 1974). The general rule that emerges is that absent some other form of confinement, the implied or express threat of loss of the employee's job is not the sort of duress that can support a false imprisonment claim.

Transferred intent. As was the case with the torts of battery and assault, the theory of transferred intent applies to false imprisonment claims. *See* Adams v. Nat'l Bank of Detroit, 508 N.W.2d 464, 468 (Mich. 1993).

Shoplifters and the shopkeeper's privilege. Another common fact pattern involves the store employee or security guard who detains a suspected shoplifter. In many instances, the plaintiff will be able to make out a prima facie case of false imprisonment, but the defendant may have a defense in the form of a recognized privilege. The so-called shopkeeper's privilege is covered in Part E below, which deals with defenses to intentional tort claims.

Problem 2.12. Once more violence erupted during the protest, Edward decided he had had enough and decided to leave. As he walked down Elm Street back to his car, he was confronted by two protesters who asked him, "Where do you think you are going?" Wanting no further trouble, Edward turned around to try a different path back to his car. But when he turned, he saw another protester walking purposefully toward him, pounding his fist and asking, "Where do you think you're going?" This new individual was substantially smaller than Edward, who had wrestled in college. The three protesters stood silently on opposite sides of Edward in the street, blocking Edward's path, as Edward tried to figure out what to do. At that point, a police cruiser passed by, which caused the protesters to begin walking away. Edward then jogged back to the parking lot where his car was. As he started to pull out of the parking lot, the protesters whom he had encountered on the street blocked his exit. Edward quickly threw his car into reverse and backed out of the exit on the other side of the parking lot.

Assuming they could be identified, could any of the protesters be held liable for false imprisonment?

D. Intentional Infliction of Emotional Distress

Compared to the torts of battery, assault, and false imprisonment, the tort of intentional infliction of emotional distress (IIED) is a relatively recent addition to the world of torts. IIED (known in some jurisdictions as the tort of "outrage") is often referred to as a gap-filler tort that is "designed to capture behavior that a court finds troublesome, but which slips through the cracks between the well-defined, traditional tort categories." Russell Fraker, *Reformulating Outrage: A Critical Analysis of the Problematic Tort of IIED*, 61 Vand. L. Rev. 983, 996 (2008). Indeed, some courts say that there can be no IIED claim where the defendant's conduct invades other legally protected interests of the plaintiff. *See* K.G. v. R.T.R., 918 S.W.2d 795, 799 (Mo.1996); Creditwatch, Inc. v. Jackson, 157 S.W.3d 814, 816 (Tex. 2005). As its name suggests, the hallmark of the tort is conduct resulting in emotional distress. But the focus in most cases is on the extreme and outrageous nature of the defendant's conduct.

Agis v. Howard Johnson Co.

355 N.E.2d 315 (Mass. 1976)

QUIRICO, Justice.

This case raises the issue, expressly [reserved] in *George v. Jordan Marsh Co.*, 359 Mass. 244, 255, 268 N.E.2d 915 (1971), whether a cause of action exists in this Commonwealth for the intentional or reckless infliction of severe emotional distress without resulting bodily injury....

Briefly, the allegations in the plaintiffs' complaint, which we accept as true for purposes of ruling on this motion, are the following. Debra Agis was employed by the Howard Johnson Company as a waitress in a restaurant known as the Ground Round. On or about May 23, 1975, the defendant Dionne notified all waitresses that a meeting would be held at 3 P.M. that day. At the meeting, he informed the waitresses that "there was some stealing going on," but that the identity of the person or persons responsible was not known, and that, until the person or persons responsible were discovered, he would begin firing all the present waitresses in alphabetical order, starting with the letter 'A.' Dionne then fired Debra Agis.

The complaint alleges that, as a result of this incident, Mrs. Agis became greatly upset, began to cry, sustained emotional distress, mental anguish, and loss of wages and earnings. It further alleges that the actions of the defendants were reckless, extreme, outrageous and intended to cause emotional distress and anguish....

The defendants moved to dismiss the complaint pursuant to Mass.R.Civ.P. 12(b)(6), 365 Mass. 755 (1974), on the ground that, even if true, the plaintiffs' allegations fail to state a claim upon which relief can be granted because damages for emotional distress are not compensable absent resulting physical injury. The judge allowed the motion, and the plaintiffs appealed.

Our discussion of whether a cause of action exists for the intentional or reckless infliction of severe emotional distress without resulting bodily injury starts with our decision in *George v. Jordan Marsh Co.*, 359 Mass. 244, 268 N.E.2d 915 (1971). While in that case we found it unnecessary to address the precise question raised here, we did summarize the history of actions for emotional distress and concluded that the law of the Commonwealth should be, and is, 'that one who, without a privilege to do so, by extreme and outrageous conduct intentionally causes severe emotional distress to another, *with bodily harm resulting* from such distress, is subject to liability..." (emphasis supplied). The question whether such liability should be extended to cases in which there is no resulting bodily injury was 'left until it arises," and that question has arisen here.

In the *George* case, we discussed in depth the policy considerations underlying the recognition of a cause of action for intentional infliction of severe emotional distress with resulting physical injury, and we concluded that the difficulties presented in allowing such an action were outweighed by the unfair and illogical consequences of the denial of recognition of such an independent tort. In so doing, we examined the persuasive authority then recognizing such a cause of action, and we placed considerable reliance on the Restatement (Second) of Torts § 46 (1965). Our examination of the policies underlying the extension of that cause of action to cases where there has been no bodily injury, and our review of the judicial precedent and the Restatement in this regard, lead us to conclude that such extension is both warranted and desirable.

The most often cited argument for refusing to extend the cause of action for intentional or reckless infliction of emotional distress to cases where there has been no physical injury is the difficulty of proof and the danger of fraudulent or frivolous claims. There has been a concern that "mental anguish, standing alone, is too subtle and speculative to be measured by any known legal standard," that "mental anguish and its consequences are so intangible and peculiar and vary so much with the individual that they cannot reasonably be anticipated," that a wide door might "be opened not only to fictitious claims but to litigation over trivialities and mere bad manners as well," and that there can be no objective measurement of the extent or the existence of emotional distress. There is a fear that "[i]t is easy to assert a claim of mental anguish and very hard to disprove it.'"

While we are not unconcerned with these problems, we believe that "the problems presented are not . . . insuperable' and that 'administrative difficulties do not justify the denial of relief for serious invasions of mental and emotional tranquility . . . ." *State Rubbish Collectors Ass'n v. Siliznoff*, 38 Cal.2d 330, 338—339, 240 P.2d 282, 286 (1952). "That some claims may be spurious should not compel those who administer justice to shut their eyes to serious wrongs and let them go without being brought to account. It is the function of courts and juries to determine whether claims are valid or false. This responsibility should not be shunned merely because the task may be difficult to perform." *Samms v. Eccles*, 11 Utah 2d 289, 293, 358 P.2d 344, 347 (1961).

Furthermore, the distinction between the difficulty which juries may encounter in determining liability and assessing damages where no physical injury occurs and their performance of that same task where there has been resulting physical harm may be greatly overstated. "The jury is ordinarily in a better position . . . to determine whether outrageous conduct results in mental distress than whether that distress in turn results in physical injury. From their own experience jurors are aware of the extent and character of the disagreeable emotions that may result from the defendant's conduct, but a difficult medical question is presented when it must be determined if emotional distress resulted in physical injury. . . . Greater proof that mental suffering occurred is found in the defendant's conduct designed to bring it about than in physical injury that may or may not have resulted therefrom." *State Rubbish Collectors Ass'n v. Siliznoff, supra*, 38 Cal.2d at 338, 240 P.2d at 286. We are thus unwilling to deny the existence of this cause of action merely because there may be difficulties of proof. Instead, we believe "the door to recovery should be opened but narrowly and with due caution."

In light of what we have said, we hold that one who, by extreme and outrageous conduct and without privilege, causes severe emotional distress to another is subject to liability for such emotional distress even though no bodily harm may result. However, in order for a plaintiff to prevail in a case for liability under this tort, four elements must be established. It must be shown (1) that the actor intended to inflict emotional distress or that he knew or should have known that emotional distress was the likely result of his conduct, Restatement (Second) of Torts § 46, comment i (1965; (2) that the conduct was "extreme and outrageous," was "beyond all possible bounds of decency" and was "utterly intolerable in a civilized community," Restatement (Second) of Torts § 46, comment d (1965); (3) that the actions of the defendant were the cause of the plaintiff's distress; and (4) that the emotional distress sustained by the plaintiff was "severe" and of a nature "that no reasonable man could be expected to endure it." Restatement (Second) of Torts § 46, comment j (1965). These requirements are "aimed at limiting frivolous suits and avoiding litigation in situations where only bad manners and mere hurt feelings are involved," and we believe they are a "realistic safeguard against false claims . . ."

Testing the plaintiff Debra Agis's complaint by the rules stated above, we hold that she makes out a cause of action and that her complaint is therefore legally sufficient. While many of her allegations are not particularly well stated, we believe that the '[p]laintiff has alleged facts and circumstances which reasonably could lead the trier of fact to conclude that defendant's conduct was extreme and outrageous, having a severe and traumatic effect upon plaintiff's emotional tranquility." Because reasonable men could differ on these issues, we believe that "it is for the jury, subject to the control of the court," to determine whether there should be liability in this case. While the judge was not in error in dismissing the complaint under the then state of the law, we believe that, in light of what we have said, the judgment must be reversed and the plaintiff Debra Agis must be given an opportunity to prove the allegations which she has made.

Notes

The extreme and outrageous conduct element has proven difficult to define. Courts often explain the concept in reference to what does not qualify as extreme and outrageous conduct:

> The liability clearly does not extend to mere insults, indignities, threats, annoyances, petty oppressions, or other trivialities. The rough edges of our society are still in need of a good deal of filing down, and in the meantime plaintiffs must necessarily be expected and required to be hardened to a

> certain amount of rough language, and to occasional acts that are definitely inconsiderate and unkind.

Restatement (Second) of Torts §46 comment d. (1965).

Numerous commentators have criticized the vague nature of the "extreme and outrageous conduct" element. *See* Daniel Givelber, *The Right to Minimum Social Decency and the Limits of Evenhandedness: Intentional Infliction of Emotional Distress by Outrageous Conduct*, 82 COLUM. L. REV. 42, 43 (1982) ("[T]his is a most atypical intentional tort since it fails to define the proscribed conduct beyond suggesting that it is very bad indeed."). The *Restatement* takes the position that the question of whether conduct qualifies as extreme and outrageous is ordinarily a question for the finder of fact. Restatement (Second) of Torts §46 cmt. h (1977). However, numerous courts take the position that it is a question of law for the court. *See, e.g.*, Gray v. State, 624 A.2d 479, 484 (Me. 1993) ("The determination of extreme and outrageous conduct from undisputed facts is an issue for the court.").

Given the lack of clear standards as to what qualifies as extreme and outrageous conduct, it is sometimes difficult to predict how the issue will be resolved. The *Agis* decision above is actually unusual for a case involving an allegation of intentional infliction of emotional distress in the workplace. For example, at least one court has held that "as a general rule, sexual harassment alone does not rise to the level of outrageousness necessary to make out a cause of action for the intentional infliction of emotional distress." Hoy v. Angelone, 720 A.2d 745, 754 (Pa. 1998). Courts often say that they take "an especially strict approach" to workplace IIED claims and are "particularly hesitant" to recognize such claims given the stressful nature of many workplaces and the need for employers to sometimes make unpleasant decisions. *See* Burkhart v. Am. Railcar Indust., Inc., 603 F.3d 472, 478 (8th Cir. 2010); Jackson v. Blue Dolphin Communications of N.C., L.L.C., 226 F. Supp. 2d 785, 794 (W.D.N.C. 2002).

Despite the uncertainty inherent in the requirement of extreme and outrageous conduct, there are some recognized indicators or markers of such conduct. The next two cases address that point.

Costello v. Mitchell Public School Dist. 79

266 F.3d 916 (8th Cir. 2001)

WOLLMAN, Chief Judge.

James and Jamie Costello (the Costellos), and their daughter Sadonya Costello (Sadonya) (collectively, the plaintiffs), appeal from the district court's grant of summary judgment in favor of Mitchell Public School District 79, the school board and superintendent of Mitchell Public Schools, the principal of Mitchell High School (Mitchell or the school), and a teacher at Mitchell (collectively, defendants). We affirm.

[Sadonya was a seventh-grade student, who was struggling in school and possibly in need of special education.] At the end of her first semester at Mitchell, Sadonya was having difficulty with her band teacher, Roger Kercher. She testified in her deposition that he daily called her "retarded," "stupid," and "dumb," in front of her classmates. In one instance, after belittling her in front of the class for a bad grade on an assignment in her notebook, he threw the notebook at her, hitting her in the face. During a basketball game in either late December or early January at which the band was playing, Sadonya came to her mother and explained that Kercher had just told her that she could no longer play in the band because she was too stupid and that he did not have to teach students like her and that he would not. Jamie Costello asked Kercher about it, who just laughed and said "yeah, something like that."

Jamie Costello subsequently met with Halley, Yauney, Kercher, and Sadonya's therapist about the problems with band, although Kercher became angry and left the meeting. During the meeting, Jamie Costello asked Sadonya's therapist what she thought about Sadonya remaining in band class, and "she said if Mr. Kercher feels that way, [Sadonya's] not going to gain anything by being in one of his classes." Sadonya was then removed from band and placed in a required music appreciation class, which was also taught by Kercher. Sadonya completed the music appreciation class despite Kercher's comments. Several other students and parents mentioned to Jamie Costello that Kercher had also been verbally, and occasionally physically, abusive toward other students in his classes.

[Eventually, Sadonya was home schooled. She suffered from depression and suicidal thoughts and received counseling and treatment. Her parents filed a number of claims on her behalf regarding the failure of the school to provide appropriate special education as well a claim of intentional infliction of emotional distress.]

With regard to the intentional infliction of emotional distress claim, the district court concluded that the Costellos and Sadonya had failed to present a genuine issue of material fact under Nebraska law on whether Kercher's actions were so outrageous in character and so extreme in degree as to go beyond all possible bounds of decency.

To constitute intentional infliction of emotional distress, a plaintiff must show

> (1) [t]hat there has been intentional or reckless conduct; (2) [t]hat the conduct was so outrageous in character and so extreme in degree as to go beyond all possible bounds of decency and is to be regarded as atrocious and utterly intolerable in a civilized community; and (3) [t]hat the conduct caused emotional distress so severe that no reasonable person should be expected to endure it.

Gall v. Great W. Sugar Co., 219 Neb. 354, 363 N.W.2d 373, 377 (1985). Assuming that the plaintiffs have raised a genuine issue of material fact on the first and third parts of the test, we agree with the district court that Kercher's words and conduct, however unprofessional, intemperate, and unworthy of one entrusted with the responsibility of educating students, did not rise to the level that would satisfy part two of the test set forth in *Gall*. Accordingly, the district court did not err in granting summary judgment in favor of all defendants on the merits of this claim.

The judgment in affirmed.

HAMILTON, Circuit Judge, concurring in part and dissenting in part.

I concur in all of the court's opinion but the part that affirms the district court's grant of summary judgment in favor of Roger Kercher (Kercher) with respect to Sadonya Costello's (Sadonya) claim alleging intentional infliction of emotional distress under Nebraska common law....

A reasonable jury could infer that Kercher intended to inflict emotional distress on Sadonya from the nature of his statements to her under all the facts and circumstances of this case. In determining whether a defendant's conduct meets the second element of an intentional infliction of emotional distress claim, the extreme and outrageous element, all of the facts and circumstances of the particular case must be considered. For example, the relationship between the parties is an important factor to be considered because the extreme and outrageous character of the defendant's conduct may arise from the defendant's abuse of a position of power or trust, or a relation with the plaintiff, which gives the defendant actual or apparent authority over the plaintiff, or power to affect the plaintiff's interests. Restatement (Second) of Torts (Restatement) § 46 cmt. e (1965). Another important factor to be considered in determining whether a defendant's conduct meets the extreme and outrageous element is whether the defendant knew the plaintiff was particularly susceptible or vulnerable to emotional distress. Restatement § 46 cmt. f. "[C]onduct which might otherwise be considered merely rude or abusive may be deemed outrageous when the defendant knows that the plaintiff is particularly susceptible to emotional distress." *Brandon*, 624 N.W.2d at 621. Generally, the extreme and outrageous element is met when recitation of the facts to an average member of the community would arouse his resentment against the defendant, and lead such member "to exclaim, "'Outrageous!'" Restatement § 46 cmt. d.

There is no doubt that recitation of the facts in the present case, as set forth above, to an average member of the Nebraska community would arouse resentment against Kercher and lead such member of the community to exclaim "Outrageous!" In his capacity as Sadonya's teacher, Kercher intentionally attempted to publicly humiliate Sadonya, a child, on the topic of the inadequacy of her intelligence, knowing that she would be particularly susceptible to resulting emotional distress given her young age, the fact that she was a new student at Mitchell High School, and that she was already doing poorly in his class. Additionally, as of January 22, 1997, Kercher knew that Sadonya required the services of a mental health counselor. Under these facts, I cannot say, as a matter of law, that Kercher's conduct was not so outrageous as to exceed the bounds of decent society. Sadonya has met the second element of her intentional infliction of emotional distress claim against Kercher....

In sum, I concur in the court's opinion except that I would allow Sadonya's intentional infliction of emotional distress claim against Kercher to go to a jury. If all of Sadonya's allegations about Kercher's conduct are true, society would immeasurably benefit from the imposition of civil liability upon such conduct.

McDaniel v. Gile

230 Cal. App. 3d 363 (Cal. Ct. App. 1991)

[Defendant and cross-complainant Patricia Gile was represented in her marital dissolution action by plaintiff and cross-defendant attorney James H. McDaniel. McDaniel sued Gile for unpaid legal fees, and Gile cross-claimed for, *inter alia*, intentional infliction of emotional distress. The lower court entered in a summary disposition in favor of McDaniel on Gile's IIED claim.]

The facts are taken from defendant's answers to plaintiff's interrogatories, which were submitted by plaintiff in support of his motion for summary adjudication. In January of 1985, plaintiff met with defendant and "fill[ed] out a lengthy and intimate self-characterization document, seeking intimate details of [her] personal and sexual life." At their next meeting plaintiff "continually referred to [sic] back to the more intimate parts of [her] personal life, particularly remarking about the sexual problems [she] had in [her] marriage."

Several weeks later, when plaintiff and defendant were at the courthouse, plaintiff took defendant into a small room and when she attempted to leave he grabbed her and "pinned [her] against the wall and kissed [her] on the mouth." . . .

On numerous occasions during the following weeks, plaintiff called defendant both at home and at her work place and made "sexually suggestive remarks." When defendant asked plaintiff if he always talked to his clients like that, he answered, "that he only did so with 'the sexy ones.'" Plaintiff would also call defendant at home in the late evening and ask her to come to his office.

After defendant refused to have sexual relations with plaintiff, plaintiff abandoned her and failed to "[r]epresent [her] interests, appear in court to represent [her] interests, negotiate a complete and fair property settlement . . . , properly advise [her] of [her] rights," return her phone calls, or take any action at all except after numerous requests. In January of 1986, defendant needed a restraining order because she was having a problem with her ex-husband involving the police. She called plaintiff at his office for days. When she finally spoke to him, he told her that "if [she] had played the game 'the right way' [she] would have the right phone number to reach him immediately. [She] understood this to mean that if [she] gave him sexual favors he would have been available for [her] as an attorney and not otherwise."

When defendant brought a friend to meetings to protect herself from plaintiff, he made sexually suggestive remarks about her and other women. One time he told defendant's friend that "when a woman client came to him, she was extremely vulnerable, so if she went to bed to get better service from him, 'so be it.'" Defendant had heard that plaintiff had done the same things to other women in her position and that his reputation for this was "well known around the Ontario courthouse."

Ultimately, [defendant] was forced to settle her case alone to her disadvantage.

Defendant contends that there are triable issues of fact as to her cause of action for intentional infliction of emotional distress. She further contends that the trial court erred in granting summary adjudication of issues based on plaintiff's assertion[] that his conduct was not "outrageous" as a matter of law. We agree.

. . . Behavior may be considered outrageous if a defendant (1) abuses a relation or position which gives him power to damage the plaintiff's interest; (2) knows the plaintiff is susceptible to injuries through mental distress; or (3) acts intentionally or unreasonably with the recognition that the acts are likely to result in illness through mental distress.'"

. . . The withholding by a retained attorney of legal services when sexual favors are not granted by a client and engaging in sexual harassment of the client constitutes acts of outrageous conduct under these circumstances.

Nevertheless, plaintiff predicts "a floodgate of litigation" which will require courts to determine standards as to what statements can be made by an individual to a member of the opposite sex. Plaintiff's sweeping prediction belies the facts of this case and ignores his fiduciary relationship and coercive conduct toward a vulnerable woman. Indeed, the facts of this case are no different than those alleging sexual harassment in the workplace. Furthermore, our Supreme Court has held that fear of unfounded or fraudulent claims is not a valid reason for disallowing a tort action predicated upon a meritorious claim.

We conclude that the summary adjudication of defendant's claim for intentional infliction of emotional distress was improper.

Notes

Extreme and outrageous conduct in the legal context. Not surprisingly, IIED claims often arise over conduct occurring in connection with a legal proceeding. Often, the defendants are lawyers. *See* East River Savings Bank v. Steele, 311 S.E.2d 189 (Ga. Ct. App. 1983) (involving lawyer who engaged in such "severe cross-examination" of a witness that the witness had a heart attack); Wong v. Panis, 772 P.2d 695, 700 (Haw. Ct. App. 1986) (involving attorney's acts of submitting allegedly abusive interrogatories on behalf of clients). Most of the claims fail on the question of whether the conduct was extreme and outrageous. Sometimes, however, plaintiffs are at least able to raise a jury question on this issue. *See* Carney v. Rotkin, Schmerin & McIntyre, 206 Cal. App. 3d 1513, 1518–19 (Ct. App. 1988) (concluding plaintiff had stated a claim when a law firm, in an attempt to collect a debt on behalf of client, falsely told a 74-year-old woman that there was a bench warrant out for her arrest and that the firm would not recall the warrant until the debt was paid in full); Perk v. Worden, 475 F. Supp. 2d 565 (E.D. Va. 2007) (concluding plaintiff had stated a claim where lawyer, seeking to collect a debt on behalf of a client, "blatantly lied" to the plaintiff so that she would not appear for a court hearing and he could obtain a default judgment against her, knowingly filed state actions against her in an incorrect venue, and was verbally abusive to her on the telephone). It's worth noting that the actions in *Carney* and *Perk* would probably also subject the lawyers in question to professional discipline. *See* ABA Model Rules of Professional Conduct Rule 4.4(a) ("In representing a client, a lawyer shall not use means that have no substantial purpose other than to embarrass, delay, or burden a third person . . ."); *id.* Rule 8.4(c) (prohibiting deceit).

The extreme and outrageous conduct element is not the only issue that poses definitional problems for courts. A plaintiff must also suffer "severe emotional distress." The following case explores the meaning of this phrase.

Kazatsky v. King David Memorial Park

527 A.2d 988 (Pa. 1987)

The Kazatskys had purchased two plots of land in King David's cemetery for the burial of an infant son and daughter, prematurely born twins who had died shortly after birth. [After the funeral, a dispute arose between the parties regarding the location of the graves and the failure of King David to install grave-site markers. The Kazatskys planned to hold a subsequent unveiling at the grave-sites. Harvey Kazatsky told King David that he would bring payment for the grave-site markers to the unveiling, but was told that the markers would not be installed unless payment was made first. Eventually, King David relented and installed the markers, but told the Kazatskys that there would be no care or maintenance of the grave-sites unless the bill was paid.]

The unveiling took place during a "torrential downpour" with only the Kazatskys, their two surviving sons and their rabbi attending. The party left after a brief service but when they were half-way up the road out of the cemetery, a car drove up towards them. Mrs. Reinick emerged from that vehicle and expressed her condolences, and reminded the Kazatskys that there would be no care or maintenance unless the One Hundred Forty-three Dollars ($143.00) fee was paid. The Kazatskys found this "infuriating and extremely upsetting." As a result of this incident, the Kazatskys decided not to pay the disputed bill.

During the summer of 1982 the Kazatskys observed deteriorating conditions at the grave-sites, including crabgrass and weeds, during their visits. By December of 1982 the marker had begun to tip and sink for lack of a foundation and surrounding sod.

Harvey Kazatsky conceded on cross-examination that throughout their dispute with King David the Kazatskys did not seek medical or psychiatric counseling. On redirect he explained that they were very supportive of each other and did not feel they needed professional help.

The Kazatskys' claim for damages for emotional distress is based on King David's alleged use of threats to coerce them into purchasing a perpetual care contract for their deceased children's grave sites. Specifically they complain of King David's communication of its refusal to (1) permit the installation of the grave marker; (2)

allow the unveiling ceremony; and (3) provide care and maintenance for the grave sites. The Kazatskys' attempt to bring these contacts with King David within the parameters of a cause of action under section 46 of the Restatement (Second) of Torts for outrageous conduct causing severe emotional distress.

. . .

We are not required here to determine whether King David's conduct reached the level of "outrageousness" that would support recovery of money damages . . . , because of a glaring failure in the chain of proof required to establish this claim. The Kazatskys presented no expert testimony, indeed no evidence at all except their own unsubstantiated averments, concerning their alleged injuries. To permit recovery on the basis of such a questionable showing would necessitate a radical departure from settled principles of Pennsylvania tort doctrine.

. . .

It is basic to tort law that an injury is an element to be proven. Given the advanced state of medical science, it is unwise and unnecessary to permit recovery to be predicated on an inference based on the defendant's "outrageousness" without expert medical confirmation that the plaintiff actually suffered the claimed distress. Moreover, the requirement of some objective proof of severe emotional distress will not present an unsurmountable obstacle to recovery. Those truly damaged should have little difficulty in procuring reliable testimony as to the nature and extent of their injuries. We therefore conclude that if section 46 of the Restatement is to be accepted in this Commonwealth, at the very least, existence of the alleged emotional distress must be supported by competent medical evidence. In this case no such evidence was presented and the record further reflects that neither Mr. nor Mrs. Kazatsky sought medical assistance.

Accordingly, for the foregoing reasons, the order of the Superior Court sustaining the ruling of the trial court is affirmed.

Notes

Severe emotional distress. The *Restatement* explains that extreme and outrageous conduct is actionable "only where the distress inflicted is so severe that no reasonable man could be expected to endure it." Restatement (Second) of Torts § 46 cmt. j. (1965). This definition is perhaps as vague as the *Restatement*'s definition of extreme and outrageous conduct. The comments go on to note that severe emotional distress is normally accompanied or followed "by shock, illness, or other bodily harm, which in itself affords evidence that the distress is genuine and severe." But bodily harm is not always required in order to establish that the distress was severe. *Id.* § 46 cmt. j. *But see* Clift v. Narragansett Television L.P., 688 A.2d 805 (R.I. 1996) (requiring "resulting physical symptomology"). As *Kazatsky* illustrates, some courts have tried to bring clarity to this part of the prima facie case or have at least sought to impose evidentiary requirements.

Why is "severe" distress required, and why do some courts impose heightened evidentiary requirements regarding this element? Possible explanations include concerns that plaintiffs can more easily fake emotional distress than physical injury and the potential for expanded liability. *See* Martha Chamallas, *The Architecture of Bias: Deep Structures in Torts Law*, 146 U. Pa. L. Rev. 463, 494 (1998).

Intent versus recklessness. The torts of battery, assault, and false imprisonment all require that the defendant act with the intent to bring about particular consequences. But with intentional infliction of emotional distress, recklessness will do. Recklessness is a lower standard than intent. Recklessness on the part of a defendant requires "not only some appreciation of the unreasonable risk involved, but also a deliberate disregard of that risk and the high probability of harm involved." City of Jackson v. Lewis, 153 So. 3d 689, 694 (Miss. 2014).

Third-party distress. Defendant kills Husband. Wife learns about the murder from the police the next day and suffers severe emotional distress as a result. Should Wife have an IIED claim? As the law has developed, Wife would not have a claim since she was not present at the time of the murder or did not otherwise contemporaneously perceive the murder (for example, watching it occur online). If a friend witnessed the murder as it occurred, the friend would also not likely have an IIED claim since, as the rule has developed, only close relatives can recover in such instances. *See* Restatement (Third) of Torts § 46 cmt. m (2012). Why would courts adopt such a rule? What if, instead, Defendant intends to inflict emotional distress upon A—say, by falsely telling A that a family member has died—but, unbeknownst to Defendant, B also happens to be present and suffers severe emotional distress upon hearing the same news. Should B have a claim under such circumstances even though Defendant never intended to cause harm to B? *See* Restatement (Third) of Torts § 46 cmt. i.

Special rules for suicide. With battery and assault, the fact that the defendant did not intend to cause the full extent of harm that ultimately occurred to the plaintiff does not matter; the defendant remains liable for the extended consequences of his or her actions. There are numerous IIED cases in which the defendant's intentional conduct allegedly results in the plaintiff's suicide. The families of the decedents have sometimes sought recovery under a state's wrongful death statute, which typically allows for recovery by close relatives. In wrongful death actions involving suicide allegedly brought about by a defendant's extreme and outrageous conduct, courts have frequently adopted special rules that limit the scope of a defendant's liability. Some have imposed a higher standard of causation than that used in most intentional tort cases. *See* Tate v. Canonica, 180 Cal. App. 2d 898, 909 (Cal. Ct. App. 1960) (holding that a plaintiff must establish that the defendant's conduct was a substantial factor in causing the suicide); Watson v. Adams, 2015 U.S. Dist. LEXIS 41172, *24 (D.S.C. March 31, 2015) (stating as a general rule that that there cannot be recovery for suicide unless the defendant's conduct created an irresistible impulse to commit suicide). At least one court has held that a plaintiff may only recover "where the plaintiff can show that suicide was a likely result of the defendant's conduct." Turcios v. DeBruler Co., 32 N.E.3d 1117, 1127 (Ill. 2015).

Problem 2.13. Following the violence at the protests, police reviewed video of the incidents in an attempt to determine the identity of those who engaged in violence. Police ultimately came to the reasonable, but incorrect, conclusion that Francis was one of those who had engaged in violence. In fact, Francis had been out of town on the day of the protests. Nonetheless, police obtained a warrant for Francis' arrest and knocked on her front door to arrest her. When the police entered the house, Francis became hysterical. Sobbing, she told the police that she hadn't been at the protests and that she couldn't go to jail because she had to take care her of one-year-old daughter and her aged father, both of whom were present at the time. One of the officers called the Pleasant Hill District Attorney and asked how he should proceed. The officer put the District Attorney on speakerphone so she could hear for herself what was happening. After a few minutes, the District Attorney—still on speakerphone—said to the officer, "I don't care. She's a troublemaker. Lock the bitch up." After a few hours, police realized that they had misidentified Francis and all charges against her were dropped.

Francis suffered severe emotional distress following the incident. Could she establish a prima facie case of intentional infliction of emotional distress in a suit against the District Attorney?

E. Defenses and Privileges

A plaintiff bringing an intentional tort claim bears the burden of establishing a prima facie case. At that point, the defendant must either successfully assert a defense or privilege (sometimes called a justification) or face liability. And just as a plaintiff alleging an intentional tort bears the burden of proof with respect to the prima facie case, the defendant asserting an affirmative defense or privilege bears the burden of establishing that the elements of the defense or privilege are satisfied.

1. Consent

Volenti non fit injuria: to the willing, no injury is done. The fact that an individual is willing for conduct to occur prevents the individual from recovering in tort from the individual who engaged in the conduct. As mentioned in Part A of this chapter, there is sometimes something of an overlap between the defense of consent and the prima facie case for an intentional tort. If, for example, the plaintiff's words or actions would lead a reasonable person to believe that contact is welcome, the plaintiff has consented to the contact *and*, at the same time, the defendant probably did not intend to cause an offensive contact. For consent to be effective, however, the plaintiff must consent to the conduct that actually occurs or to substantially the same conduct. Historically, there was sometimes a dispute as to whether consent to an illegal act (for example, consent to engage in a fistfight) is effective to bar liability. Today, consent to a criminal act is often deemed to be effective for purposes of a tort action, despite the illegal nature of the act in question.

Consent can be actual or apparent in nature. Either form of consent is effective to bar recovery. Whether consent is actual or apparent is largely just a matter of classification.

a. Actual Consent

Actual consent (or "consent in fact") occurs where the plaintiff is actually willing to permit the conduct that occurs. This most obviously occurs when the plaintiff's words *expressly* indicate the plaintiff's assent to the defendant's conduct. ("Go ahead and hit me.") This is sometimes referred to as express consent. Sometimes, however, the plaintiff's actual consent is *implied* by his actions. If, for example, you play a game of basketball at the gym or on the playground, you probably actually consent to at least some measure of physical contact simply by agreeing to play, even if you never formally announce your willingness to the other players.

For each example below, consider whether the plaintiff actually consented to the defendant's conduct and, if so, what effect that consent would have on the plaintiff's right to recover in a tort suit:

(i) David asks Paul if he wants to fight. Paul nods his head. David hits Paul, shattering several bones Paul's face. Paul sues for battery.

(ii) Paul has played football since he was a child. As part of practice, his high school coach assigned a drill where one player would hold a blocking pad and another player, operating at less than full speed, would push the player holding the blocking pad back 10 yards. When it was Paul's turn to hold the blocking pad for David, David proceeded at full speed, pushed Paul back 15 yards, and gave him a violent shove at the end, causing Paul to fall backward and break his arm. Paul sues for battery. *See* Dorley v. South Fayette Township Sch. Dist., 129 F. Supp. 3d 220 (W.D. Pa. 2015).

b. Apparent Consent

O'Brien v. Cunard S.S. Co.

28 N.E. 66 (Mass. 1981)

[The plaintiff, a 17-year-old Irish woman traveling abroad for the first time, was a passenger onboard the defendant's ship. The ship was sailing to Boston where there were strict quarantine regulations regarding small pox. The ship's doctor administered a small-pox vaccination allegedly against the plaintiff's will, and the plaintiff sued.]

By the plaintiff's testimony, which, in this particular, is undisputed, it appears that about 200 women passengers were assembled below, and she understood from conversation with them that they were to be vaccinated; that she stood about 15 feet from the surgeon, and saw them form in a line, and pass in turn before him; that he "examined their arms, and, passing some of them by, proceeded to vaccinate those that had no mark;" that she did not hear him say anything to any of them; that upon being passed by they each received a card, and went on deck; that when her turn came she showed him her arm; he looked at it, and said there was no mark, and that she should be vaccinated; that she told him she had been vaccinated before, and it left no mark; "that he then said nothing; that he should vaccinate her again;" that she held up her arm to be vaccinated; that no one touched her; that she did not tell him she did not want to be vaccinated; and that she took the ticket which he gave her, certifying that he had vaccinated her, and used it at quarantine. She was one of a large number of women who were vaccinated on that occasion, without, so far as appears, a word of objection from any of them. They all indicated by their conduct that they desired to avail themselves of the provisions made for their benefit. There was nothing in the conduct of the plaintiff to indicate to the surgeon that she did not wish to obtain a card which would save her from detention at quarantine, and to be vaccinated, if necessary, for that purpose. Viewing his conduct in the light of the surrounding circumstances, it was lawful; and there was no evidence tending to show that it was not.

Note

As *O'Brien* illustrates, even if an individual does not actually consent to the defendant's conduct, the fact that a reasonable person would understand that the individual—through her words or actions—does consent to the defendant's conduct, the effect is the same: the apparent consent bars any subsequent recovery. It is noteworthy that the defendant in such a case may actually be mistaken about whether the plaintiff consents to the conduct. But, like the other defenses that are covered later in this chapter, the fact that the defendant's mistake was reasonable relieves the defendant of liability.

c. The Special Case of Medical Battery

As the law has developed, a doctor who fails to exercise reasonable care during a procedure is subject to liability on a medical malpractice theory. This theory will be addressed in Chapter 4. Sometimes, however, what the patient is complaining about is the fact that the patient consented to allow the doctor to perform a certain type of procedure and the doctor essentially performed a different procedure. For example, in *Mohr v. Williams*, 104 N.W. 12 (Minn. 1905), the patient underwent surgery on her right ear. While the patient was under anesthesia, the doctor performing the surgery concluded that the right ear was in better shape than he had thought but that a portion of the left ear was diseased. The doctor then successfully performed surgery on the left ear instead of the right. The plaintiff successfully sued for battery. The Minnesota Supreme Court stated that if an emergency situation arose or was discovered during surgery, a patient's consent to the doctor's treatment of the situation would be implied. But absent such an emergency, the doctor's surgery on the left ear amounted to an unconsented-to harmful or offensive contact. *Id.* at 15.

Other courts take a more doctor-friendly approach. In *Kennedy v. Parrott*, 90 S.E.2d 754 (N.C. 1956), the patient underwent an appendectomy. During the operation, the doctor discovered some large cysts on the patient's ovaries. The doctor punctured the cysts while the patient was still under anesthesia. Rejecting what it referred to as the "fetish of consent," the court adopted a rule providing doctors with greater latitude to address unanticipated issues during surgery:

> In major internal operations, both the patient and the surgeon know that the exact condition of the patient cannot be finally and definitely diagnosed until after the patient is completely anesthetized and the incision has been made. In such case the consent—in the absence of proof to the contrary—will be construed as general in nature and the surgeon may extend the operation to remedy any abnormal or diseased condition in the area of the original incision whenever he, in the exercise of his sound professional judgment, determines that correct surgical procedure dictates and requires such an extension of the operation originally contemplated. This rule applies when the patient is at the time incapable of giving consent, and no one with authority to consent for him is immediately available.
>
> In short, where an internal operation is indicated, a surgeon may lawfully perform, and it is his duty to perform, such operation as good surgery demands, even when it means an extension of the operation further than was originally contemplated, and for so doing he is not to be held in damages as for an unauthorized operation.

Id. at 759.

In other cases, the procedure that is performed is the same to which the plaintiff consented, but it occurs under different circumstances. In *Perna v. Pirozzi*, 457 A.2d 431 (N.J. 1983), the patient decided to undergo a surgical procedure and requested that Dr. Pirozzi perform the procedure. On the day of the surgery, the patient executed a consent form that named Dr. Pirozzi as the operating surgeon and authorized him to perform the surgery. Instead, the surgery was performed by another member of Dr. Pirozzi's medical group, Dr. Del Gaizo. The court determined that a battery claim may lie against the surgeon performing the surgery. *Id.* at 465. In *Ashcraft v. King*, 278 Cal. Rptr. 900 (Cal. Ct. App. 1991), the plaintiff consented to a surgical procedure, but allegedly on the condition that only family-donated blood would be used in the transfusions. Instead, non-family blood was used, and the patient was given blood contaminated with the Human Immuno-deficiency Virus (HIV). The court concluded the plaintiff had properly alleged a claim of battery. *Id.* at 905.

d. Capacity

In order for consent to be effective, the plaintiff must have the capacity to consent. The individual who supposedly consents to the defendant's conduct must be capable of appreciating the nature and likely consequences of the conduct. Therefore, the question may arise as to whether an individual with a mental impairment or a minor has the capacity to consent. Consider the two examples below and assess whether the plaintiff had the capacity to consent to the defendants' conduct.

(i) Plaintiff is 17 years old. She received treatment from a licensed osteopath for her back pain. The osteopath performed spinal manipulation upon Plaintiff, which allegedly results in injury to Plaintiff. The osteopath did not obtain consent from Plaintiff's parents prior to performing the manipulation. Plaintiff has now sued the osteopath for battery, among other claims. *See* Cardwell v. Bechtol, 724 S.W.2d 739 (Tenn. 1987).

(ii) Plaintiff is 15 years old. Defendant is 40. The two parties engage in "consensual" sexual intercourse. A criminal statute prohibits an individual from having sex with anyone who is at least 15 years of age but less than 17 years of age where the actor is at least 10 years older than the victim and is not the spouse of the victim. Plaintiff has now sued Defendant for battery. Did the plaintiff have the capacity to consent? What if the defendant had only been 18? *See* Lindeman v. Corporation of the President of the Church of Jesus Christ of Latter-Day Saints, 43 F. Supp. 3d 1197 (D. Colo. 2014).

e. Mistake, Misrepresentation, or Duress

Neal v. Neal

873 P.2d 881 (Idaho Ct. App. 1994)

[Thomas Neal was married to Mary Neal. Thomas had an affair with another woman. During that time, he had sexual relations with both women. When Mary discovered the affair, she filed for divorce and sued for battery.]

Where a person's consent to physical contact is given based upon a substantial mistake, known to or induced by the actor, concerning the nature of the contact itself or the extent of the harm to be expected therefrom, the consent is deemed to be ineffective, and the actor may be held liable as if no consent had been given. *See* Restatement (Second) of Torts § 57 (1965); Restatement (Second) of Torts § 892B(2) (1979). For this rule to apply, however, the mistake must extend to the essential character of the act itself, rather than to some collateral matter which merely operates as an inducement. *See* Prosser & Keeton, *supra*, § 18, at 120. "This is true, in general, whenever the other has given his consent with full understanding of the conduct, the invasion of his interests and the harm expected to follow, but has done so because of a mistake concerning some other reason for consenting." *Restatement, supra* § 892B(2) comment g.

In this case, we conclude that Thomas' failure to disclose his relationship with Jill LaGasse did not invalidate Mary's consent to engage in sexual intercourse with him. Although Thomas deceived Mary as to the exclusivity of their relationship—a factor arguably bearing upon her consent to sexual intercourse with him—it did not directly or substantially relate to the essential nature of the physical contact she consented to. Thus, Mary's misapprehension concerning Thomas' sexual fidelity did not operate to invalidate her consent to engage in sexual intercourse with him. Accordingly, we hold that Mary's allegations are insufficient to establish lack of consent. Her claim for battery, therefore, was properly dismissed.

Notes

Nature of the contact. Assume that in *Neal*, Thomas had contracted a sexually transmitted disease but failed to inform Mary about this fact during the time he was still sleeping with her. Would Mary's battery claim survive?

Duress. The fact that the plaintiff consents under duress to the defendant's conduct also vitiates consent. Whether the defendant's conduct amounts to the type of duress sufficient to render consent ineffective might depend on a host of factors, including the nature of the pressure applied, the relationship of the parties, and the type of conduct to which the plaintiff consents. *See* Reavis v. Slominski, 551 N.W.2d 528 (Neb. 1996) (involving disagreement among majority, concurring, and dissenting opinions as to whether the threat of losing one's job invalidates an employee's consent to an intentional tort); Grager v. Schudar, 770 N.W.2d 692 (N.D. 2009) (involving issue of whether prisoner's consent to jailer's alleged sexual abuse was effective).

Problem 2.14. As the protesters in Pleasant Hill started to head back to their cars, two individuals from the opposing sides, Harold and Isaiah, began arguing with each other. Both men clearly and expressly challenged the other to a fistfight. Eventually, Harold took Isaiah up on his challenge. But unbeknownst to Isaiah, Harold slipped on a pair of brass knuckles before he punched Isaiah, breaking Isaiah's nose. Isaiah now sues for battery. Harold argues that Isaiah consented to the contact as evidenced by the fact that the injury that resulted was no greater than might have occurred had he not put on the brass knuckles.

Is Harold's defense likely to succeed?

2. Self-Defense

"An actor is privileged to use reasonable force, not intended or likely to cause death or serious bodily harm, to defend himself against unprivileged harmful or offensive contact or other bodily harm which he reasonably believes that another is about to inflict intentionally upon him." Tatman v. Cordingly, 672 P.2d 1286, 1289 (Wyo. 1983) (quoting Restatement (Second) of Torts §63(1)). This rule uses the word "reasonable" several times, thus creating several possible issues when applied to a set of facts. The following case considers some of those issues but does so in the context of the use of *deadly force* allegedly used in self-defense.

Hagopian v. Fuchs

169 A.2d 172 (N.J. Super. Ct. 1961)

FOLEY, J.A.D.

Plaintiff appeals from a jury verdict of no cause of action in a suit for damages arising out of an alleged assault and battery.

The incident from which this action arose occurred on February 28, 1957 in a gasoline service station in Buttzville, New Jersey. Plaintiff, a dairy farmer, was a member of the Tri-State Master Dairy Farmers Grand Guild. Defendant, also a dairy farmer, was not a member of this guild. The guild members had been on a 'strike' for three or four days prior to the date of the occurrence. The strike, which consisted in withholding the milk supply from the creameries in the area in order to obtain a higher price therefor, had been terminated by an injunctive order issued on February 28 prior to the time of the happening.

In the early morning of that day defendant received a telephone call from a creamery in Pine Brook, N.J. was advised that the strike had ended, and invited to deliver milk to the creamery. He then loaded his own supply of milk on a truck, picked up milk from five other farmers in the area, and accompanied by another farmer, started for Pine Brook at about 8:30 a.m. Prior to doing so he notified the State Police of his intended route in order that it might be patrolled, and arranged with Harry Yohe, the other farmer, to drive behind him in his car "just in case something should happen due to the ... activities during the week." These "activities" included an incident in which defendant had been involved in Hackettstown three days previously when, while attempting to deliver milk, he had been intercepted and attacked by a group of striking guild members.

While proceeding westerly on route 46 from Hackettstown toward Buttzville, defendant's truck was passed by a passenger vehicle which plaintiff was driving in an easterly direction. Defendant, apprehensive of trouble, noticed that after the car had gone by, the driver turned it around and began to follow him. Defendant testified that because of the attack made on him in Hackettstown on February 25, he became fearful of his safety and accelerated the speed of his truck. Plaintiff said that he recognized defendant's vehicle as a milk truck and that he wanted to talk to the driver in the hope of persuading him to join the guild. Neither party knew the other.

While there are some deviations in detail, the facts concerning what happened thereafter were not in substantial dispute. After driving the truck at a high speed for about a mile in an effort to avoid being overtaken, defendant drove into a gasoline service station. Plaintiff's car arrived there at about the same time. The occupants of both vehicles got out. Defendant had in his hand a steel wedge weighing four pounds. Plaintiff approached defendant; he said his purpose was to talk to him. Neither he nor his companions were armed with weapons of any kind. Defendant, as he backed toward the rear of the truck, called for the police and for help, and warned the men not to come any closer. Plaintiff continued to advance. Defendant had noticed that two of plaintiff's companions had gone around on the other side of the truck. In the words of the defendant:

> . . . I saw two go that way; and I didn't see them until they appeared on the right side of the truck, at the tail. I was six feet beyond the tail slightly behind the truck.
>
> 'With that, Hagopian, not heeding any warning at all, continued and made a turn, and made a reach. And I struck because of the fact of the other two coming around; and the fear, I was going to get touched and I knowed they were going to do property damage.

Defendant further testified that he thought plaintiff had turned to reach for a rope to pull himself up on defendant's truck.

> . . . I swung and threw the wedge. That wedge struck him on the head as he started to rise up. And why or how, I don't know to this day yet, but I can see that wedge strike. The wedge glanced off and it came right back into my hand. I caught it, and I charged the fellows on the right side and they dispersed.

Cross-examination of defendant revealed that plaintiff was about four to six feet away when defendant threw the wedge at him; that at the moment the wedge was thrown, plaintiff's back was turned to defendant, and that defendant actually aimed the wedge at plaintiff's head. Defendant pleaded self-defense.

One of the points advanced by plaintiff on this appeal is that the trial court erred in refusing to charge plaintiff's written request that:

> In this case, defendant pleaded self-defense to justify his admitted assault and battery upon the plaintiff. This is what is known in law as an affirmative defense, and before you may seriously consider it, you must first find that defendant has proved by a preponderance of the credible evidence that the conduct of plaintiff was such as to cause a reasonably prudent person in defendant's position to be put in fear of his own safety. Unless the evidence so indicates, the defense of self-protection is not sustained and you must disregard it.

It is beyond dispute that the self-defense plea is an affirmative one and, therefore, that the burden of proof is carried by him who asserts it. . . .

We have examined the charge carefully and find the objection to be well founded. The court properly charged that the burden was on the plaintiff to establish 'his charges and damages by a preponderance of the credible evidence.' The court went on to say that if the jury found the testimony to be "evenly balanced, then the party, upon whom the burden rests to prove the same by a preponderance of the credible evidence, must be deemed to have failed in that regard." This was followed by a brief and accurate statement of the central issue in the case namely:

> . . . the plaintiff says, that he was the victim of an unprovoked assault and battery by the defendant. The defendant says, that his act in striking the plaintiff was justified, in order to protect himself from bodily harm.

The judge then discussed at considerable length the elements of self-defense and the circumstances under which it could be invoked. He did not, however, adequately distinguish between the degree of force permitted one who is in reasonable apprehension that he is in peril of death or serious bodily harm, and the force which he is privileged to use in circumstances, where the means used by his assailant are not intended or likely to cause death or serious bodily harm. We will discuss this distinction hereinafter, but whatever the degree of force the jury may have found that defendant was entitled to employ in the circumstances, it is plain that the jury was not told that the burden of proving the facts giving rise to the privilege was at all times upon the defendant.

The very nature of the case, as revealed by the uncontradicted facts, underscores the dangers implicit in the failure to charge defendant's burden. As the matter was presented to the jury, it was required to determine only whether the evidence offered by the defendant so weakened the effect of plaintiff's proof of an unlawful assault as to permit the jury to conclude that plaintiff had failed to sustain his burden of proof. However, the fact is that plaintiff proved, and defendant admitted, an assault with a deadly weapon. Consequently, the only question for the jury to determine was whether the defendant was privileged to commit the same. Obviously, the failure to advise the jury that defendant was burdened with proving this to be a fact, by a preponderance of the evidence, relieved him of an onerous task, properly cast upon him by the law in the interest of human life and safety. This was prejudicial error requiring reversal.

Since the case must be retried a consideration by the trial judge of applicable principles will be in order. At the outset, it can scarcely be denied that the steel wedge which defendant intentionally aimed at plaintiff's head while his back was turned was a deadly weapon. The use of a means of self-defense intended or likely to cause death or serious bodily harm is not privileged for the purpose of preventing the infliction of a lesser harm upon the actor. If the actor adopts such a means to protect himself against the lesser bodily harm, he is liable, although the harm which he actually inflicts is one which he would have been privileged to inflict by a less dangerous means. Restatement, Torts, § 63, p. 123 (1934).

The phrase "serious bodily harm" is used to describe a bodily harm, the consequence of which is so grave or serious that it is regarded as differing in kind, and not merely in degree, from other bodily harm. A harm which creates a substantial risk of fatal consequences is a "serious bodily harm" as is a harm, the infliction of which constitutes the crime of mayhem.[1] The permanent or protracted loss of the function

---

1. Editor's note: The crime of "mayhem" typically involves the infliction of serious physical injury that amounts to maiming of the person. *See* Nevada Rev. Stat. § 200.280 (defining the crime

of any important member or organ is also a "serious bodily harm." Restatement, Torts, § 63, comment (b), p. 121 (1934).

The intentional infliction upon another of a harmful contact by means intended or likely to cause death or serious bodily harm is privileged only if the actor reasonably believes that he is thereby put in peril of death or serious bodily harm which can be safely prevented only by the immediate use of such self-defensive means. Restatement, Torts, § 65, p. 135 (1934). Even then the intentional use of a deadly weapon is not privileged if the actor reasonably believes that he can with complete safety avoid the necessity of so defending himself by retreat, in any place other than his dwelling place.

In evaluating the conduct of this defendant in light of these principles the primary inquiry should be: were the circumstances which were known to him, or should have been known to him, such as would lead a reasonable man, one of ordinary firmness and courage, to entertain an apprehension that he was in danger of death or serious bodily harm?

We are not unmindful that although the threat which creates the privilege must be that of an immediate invasion of the actor's interests, previous threats or attacks may be important in connection with other circumstances to produce a situation which does create the privilege, although that alone would not justify the invasion. 1 Harper & James, The Law of Torts, s 311, p. 241 (1956). Hence, the prior attack on defendant and the circumstances surrounding the milk strike would be relevant to the reasonableness of defendant's belief that he was in peril of death or serious bodily harm. Yet, this factor should be considered in the context of the circumstances existing at the time he threw the lethal wedge at plaintiff's head. As noted, the uncontroverted evidence is that at that moment plaintiff had turned his back to defendant. He was unarmed and had made no threats nor manifested malice. It is at least doubtful that defendant as a reasonable man had the right to conclude that he was in peril of death or serious bodily harm, and it may be that if the trial court had been requested to do so he would have declared, as a matter of law, that in throwing the wedge, plaintiff exceeded the privilege which is granted to him. However, as we observed, this issue was litigated as a factual matter rather than one of law and we do not suggest that the trial court was under any obligation to take it from the jury, absent a motion to that effect by plaintiff. Nevertheless, we think it should be considered by the trial court on the retrial in the light of the evidence adduced therein, and if on such evidence the court concludes that a factual issue appears, care should be taken to inform the jury of the precise boundaries of defendant's privilege.

Reversed and remanded for a new trial.

---

of mayhem as "unlawfully depriving a human being of a member of his or her body, or disfiguring or rendering it useless.").

Notes

Reasonableness. Consider the following jury instruction: "When it is apparent to a person that he is threatened with a battery, he has the right to determine from appearances and the circumstances then existing the necessity of resorting to force to repel any such apparent, threatened battery, and he has the right to do what seems reasonably necessary to protect himself against any such apparent, threatened attack, whether it is real or not, provided he believes it to be real." Assume you represent the party who is resisting the argument that the other side acted in self-defense. What objection, if any, might you have to this jury instruction?

Duty to retreat. One issue that sometimes arises is whether a defendant has a duty to seek to avoid a harmful contact by retreating where it is reasonable to do so. The *Restatement* takes the position that a defendant need not retreat when he reasonably believes he is threatened with a harmful or offensive contact, even if he could do so safely. Restatement (Second) of Torts § 63 cmt. m (1965). Not all jurisdictions agree. *See, e.g.*, Conn. General Statutes, § 53a-19 (providing that "a person is not justified in using deadly physical force upon another person if he or she knows that he or she can avoid the necessity of using such force with complete safety . . . by retreating"). Even in states that impose a duty to retreat where feasible, there is no duty to retreat when one is threatened inside one's own home. Based on the idea that one's home is one's castle, this common law "castle doctrine" generally permits a person to use up to deadly force inside the person's home when the person reasonably believes he is threatened with like force inside his own home.

Stand your ground laws. A number of states have codified or modified the traditional common law rules regarding self-defense in one's home or other location where one has a right to be. For example, under Tennessee's Stand Your Ground statute, a "person who is not engaged in unlawful activity and is in a place where the person has a right to be has no duty to retreat before threatening or using force intended or likely to cause death or serious bodily injury" if the person has a reasonable belief that there is an imminent danger of death or serious bodily injury. The statute further provides:

> Any person using force intended or likely to cause death or serious bodily injury within a residence, dwelling or vehicle *is presumed to have held a reasonable belief* of imminent death or serious bodily injury to self, family, a member of the household or a person visiting as an invited guest when that force is used against another person, who unlawfully and forcibly enters or has unlawfully and forcibly entered the residence, dwelling or vehicle . . .

T. C. A. § 39-11-611 (emphasis added).

Problem 2.15. At one point during the demonstrations, a group of protesters pushed through the police barricade and charged toward the opposing protesters. Jack was part of that group. By this point, the demonstrations had devolved into chaos. Rocks and bottles were flying as both sides exchanged insults, threats, and punches. Jack punched one of opposing protesters, Kyle, causing Kyle to fall to the ground. Jack then knelt over Kyle and punched Kyle in the head three more times. Kyle is licensed to carry a firearm. After the third punch, Kyle pulls his gun and fires, hitting Jack in the chest. Jack dies from the gunshot, and his family brings a wrongful death action against Kyle.

Kyle defends on the ground that he was acting in self-defense. Is his affirmative defense likely to succeed?

3. Defense of Others

A defendant is also privileged to act in defense of others. Historically, some courts required that the defendant actually be correct in his or her belief that the person being threatened was actually being threatened. The more modern view is that this privilege tracks the self-defense privilege. Specifically, the defendant simply needs to have a reasonable belief that the plaintiff is about to inflict physical harm upon the third person. The same rules regarding the use of deadly force in self-defense also apply to this privilege. *See* Restatement (Second) of Torts § 76 (1965).

4. Shopkeeper's Privilege

A privilege at common law has long existed for individuals who make a citizen's arrest. The scope of this privilege is limited, however. To claim the privilege, the person being detained must have actually committed a felony or committed a breach of the peace in the presence of the defendant. *See* Restatement (Second) of Torts § 119 (1965). This privilege provided retail merchants and shopkeepers with only limited protection from potential liability if they sought to detain a suspected shoplifter, since most shoplifters do not commit felonies or engage in breaches of the peace. Therefore, shopkeepers enjoyed a special privilege that allowed them to detain shoplifters for the purpose of recapturing property. But the privilege was still limited in that the person detained must have actually had the property in his possession for the privilege to apply. The following case examines the more modern version of the shopkeeper's (or merchant's) privilege.

Barkley v. McKeever Enterprises, Inc.

456 S.W.3d 829 (Mo. 2015)
(en banc)

Paul C. Wilson, Judge

On May 24, 2009, Barkley went to Price Chopper in Independence. While shopping, she took various items (*e.g.*, notebooks, a book light, toothpaste, and batteries) from the shelves and placed them in a reusable shopping bag she carried next to her purse. In her other hand, Barkley carried other empty reusable shopping bags. Barkley's husband, who also went shopping with her, placed various items in a grocery cart. When they met to check out, Barkley's husband unloaded the cart onto the conveyor belt while Barkley walked past the register and handed the empty reusable bags to an employee for use in bagging their purchases. Barkley continued to carry the bag concealing her other items next to her purse. She made no effort to pay for the items in that bag, and they had not been scanned along with her husband's purchases. When the other items were paid for, Barkley headed for the exit.

Two loss prevention employees had been watching Barkley on Price Chopper's surveillance system. When they saw Barkley head for the exit without paying for the items in the bag next to her purse, they stopped her. They confiscated the bag containing the unpurchased items, escorted her to the store's security office, and told her she was being detained on suspicion of shoplifting. Barkley's husband waited for her in the nearby customer service area.

Inside the security office, Barkley and the two male loss prevention employees were joined by a female employee in accordance with Price Chopper's policy for female shoplifting suspects. Barkley was told to sit on a bench in the office while the employees searched her purse, itemized and photographed the merchandise Barkley had concealed in the reusable shopping bag, and began preparing their report. Approximately four minutes after Barkley was first detained, the employees summoned the police when they determined that the price of the items in Barkley's bag exceeded the store's threshold for prosecution.

As the employees were processing the items and preparing their report, Barkley stood and approached two of the employees from behind. The third employee, who could see her approaching, told Barkley to stay seated on the bench. Barkley refused and continued to approach the other employees. When they turned and saw her, one of them moved to handcuff her. Barkley resisted and, during the scuffle, she was pushed up against a file cabinet. When the employee cuffed one of her hands and started to handcuff the other hand behind her back, Barkley complained that this would be too painful. The employee acquiesced and handcuffed Barkley's hands in the front instead. He told Barkley to return to the bench, but she refused again.

At this point, one of the employees reached out to guide Barkley back to the bench. She evaded this employee and ran for the door. Barkley was able to open the door because her hands were cuffed in front of her. But, before she could get the door open enough to escape, the employees caught up to her. While one of them pushed the door shut and tried to pull Barkley's hands from the door handle, the other employee knocked Barkley's legs out from under her. With Barkley on the floor, the employees were able to move her handcuffs to the back so she would not be able to use her hands again. Then, they attempted to help Barkley up and over to the bench. She refused their assistance, however, and remained sitting on the floor until the employees completed their report.

When the report was finished, the employees moved Barkley's handcuffs back to the front and, again, tried to help her off the floor. Barkley did not resist this time, and the employees assisted her to the bench. Approximately eight minutes later, or about 46 minutes after Barkley was first detained near the store's exit, the police arrived to arrest Barkley and escort her from the store. She was charged with shoplifting in Independence Municipal Court but later was acquitted of this charge.

Barkley sued Price Chopper for actual and punitive damages arising out of her detention in the store. She alleged that . . . Price Chopper's employees . . . committed assault, battery, and false imprisonment. Price Chopper pleaded that the merchant's privilege and section 537.1251 protected it from all liability to Barkley for the acts alleged.

In October 2012, the case was tried to a jury. At the close of the evidence, Barkley abandoned all of her claims except false imprisonment and battery. These were submitted to the jury, together with Price Chopper's affirmative defense to each count. The jury found for Price Chopper on both counts. Barkley sought a new trial on the grounds that the trial court erred in submitting an affirmative defense to the charge of battery and that the trial court erred in admitting and excluding certain evidence. Her motion was overruled. Barkley appeals, and this Court has jurisdiction.

. . .

Analysis

The privilege of a merchant to detain a suspected shoplifter has long been recognized in Missouri. At first, the privilege applied only if the suspect in fact was guilty of the crime. *See Pandjiris v. Hartman*, 196 Mo. 539, 94 S.W. 270, 272 (1906) (the "only plea of justification or excuse is that plaintiff was guilty of the crime for which he was arrested"). As a result, no matter how reasonable the merchant's suspicion may have been, only a subsequent conviction would protect the merchant from civil liability to the person detained.

In 1941, however, this Court abandoned this restriction. Expressly overruling *Pandjiris*, this Court held:

> In an effort to harmonize the individual right to liberty with a reasonable protection to the person or property of the defendant, it should be said in such a charge of false imprisonment, where a defendant had probable cause to believe that the plaintiff was about to injure defendant in his person or property, even though such injury would constitute but a misdemeanor, that probable cause is a defense, provided, of course, that the detention was reasonable.

Teel v. May Dep't Stores Co., 348 Mo. 696, 155 S.W.2d 74, 78 (1941) (quoting *Collyer v. S.H. Kress & Co.*, 5 Cal.2d 175, 54 P.2d 20, 23 (1936)) (quotation marks omitted).

Based on the evidence in that case, *Teel* holds as a matter of law that there was no "unreasonable or unlawful detention of plaintiff . . . up to the time of obtaining the return of the goods." But, rather than let the plaintiff go when they recovered the stolen merchandise, the store employees detained her until she signed a confession admitting to the attempted theft. The Court held that this was actionable.

If the employees did not believe plaintiff's explanation, the Court noted that the employees "might have been within their rights if they had called the authorities to take [Plaintiff] into custody and preferred charges against [Plaintiff]. . . ." But *Teel* holds it is "well settled that unreasonable delay in releasing a person, who is entitled to be released, or such delay in calling, taking him before or turning him over to proper authorities . . . would thereafter amount to false imprisonment." As a result, the Court remanded the case for a new trial because "neither the privilege to restrain plaintiff for the purpose of obtaining return of the goods or in order to turn her over to the proper authorities . . . would give [a merchant] any authority to hold plaintiff to compel her to give a confession in violation of her civil rights under the Constitution of this State."

The General Assembly codified *Teel* in 1961 in what is now section 537.125 (later amended in 1985). Subsection 2 of this statute provides:

> 2. Any merchant, his agent or employee, who has reasonable grounds or probable cause to believe that a person has committed or is committing a wrongful taking of merchandise or money from a mercantile establishment, **may detain such person in a reasonable manner and for a reasonable length of time for the purpose of investigating whether there has been a wrongful taking of such merchandise or money.** Any such reasonable detention shall not constitute an unlawful arrest or detention, nor shall it render the merchant, his agent or employee, criminally or civilly liable to the person so detained.

§ 537.125.2 (emphasis added).

The remaining two subsections of section 537.125 expound on the privilege set forth in subsection 2. Subsection 3 explains when that privilege is triggered, *i.e.*, what constitutes "reasonable grounds or probable cause to believe that a person has committed or is committing a wrongful taking." It states:

> 3. Any person **willfully concealing unpurchased merchandise** of any mercantile establishment, either on the premises or outside the premises of such establishment, **shall be presumed** to have so concealed such merchandise with the intention of committing a wrongful taking of such merchandise within the meaning of subsection 1, and the finding of such unpurchased merchandise concealed upon the person or among the belongings of such

> person **shall be evidence of reasonable grounds and probable cause for the detention** in a **reasonable manner** and for a reasonable length of time, of such person by a merchant, his agent or employee, in order that recovery of such merchandise may be effected, and any such **reasonable detention shall not be deemed to be unlawful, nor render such merchant, his agent or employee criminally or civilly liable.**

§ 537.125.3 (emphasis added). Subsection 4 then describes the breadth of the privilege and the liabilities from which the merchant is protected:

> 4. Any merchant, his agent or employee, who has reasonable grounds or probable cause to believe that a person has committed a wrongful taking of property, as defined in this section, and who has detained such person and investigated such wrongful taking, **may contact law enforcement** officers and **instigate criminal proceedings** against such person. Any such contact of law enforcement authorities or instigation of a judicial proceeding shall not constitute malicious prosecution, **nor shall it render the merchant, his agent or employee criminally or civilly liable to the person so detained** or against whom proceedings are instigated.

§ 537.125.4 (emphasis added).

Accordingly, under the principles first adopted in *Teel* and later codified in section 537.125, a merchant is privileged to detain—in a reasonable manner and for a reasonable time—any person the merchant has a reasonable suspicion or probable cause to believe is committing (or has committed) a wrongful taking of the merchant's property. The merchant may detain such a person for the purpose of recovering the merchandise and also for the purpose of investigating whether a wrongful taking actually occurred (or was occurring) and, if so, for the purpose of contacting law enforcement and instigating criminal proceedings. Provided this detention is conducted in a reasonable manner and for a reasonable time, the merchant is protected from all liability (civil and criminal) to the person detained.

...

[Barkley argues] that Price Chopper was not privileged to use any force—even reasonable force—to prevent her from fleeing once the store employees had recovered the merchandise hidden in her bag. In other words, she contends that the protection of the merchant's privilege does not extend to claims of battery and, even if it does, Barkley contends that the privilege ends as soon as the merchant recovers its merchandise. Both contentions are incorrect.

First, even though *Teel* dealt with a claim of false imprisonment, the merchant's privilege is not limited to such claims. The privilege to detain necessarily includes the privilege to use reasonable force (*i.e.*, a battery), or to threaten the use of such force (*i.e.*, an assault), to accomplish this detention. As the Supreme Judicial Court of Massachusetts noted, the merchant's privilege would be "meaningless if reasonable force cannot be used. It makes no sense to assume that shoplifters caught in the act will simply comply with a request to wait for the police to arrive." *Commonwealth v. Rogers*, 459 Mass. 249, 945 N.E.2d 295, 306 (2011).

In addition, Barkley's argument that the merchant's privilege does not protect merchants from claims of battery contradicts the language of section 537.125. The statute explicitly permits the merchant to do several things, including detaining the suspect in a reasonable manner and for a reasonable time, investigating whether the suspect committed a wrongful taking, and contacting law enforcement to initiate criminal proceedings. But the protection for merchants provided by section 537.125 is not limited to the claims most closely associated with those actions, *i.e.*, false imprisonment, slander, or malicious prosecution. Instead, section 537.125 protects the merchant from all liability (civil and criminal) to the person detained.

Barkley's second contention also fails. She argues that the only purpose of the merchant's privilege is to recover stolen property and, therefore, the privilege ends as soon as that purpose is achieved. The only basis for her argument is section 537.125.3, which states that the merchant is permitted to detain the suspect "in a reasonable manner and for a reasonable length of time . . . in order that recovery of such merchandise may be effected." But Barkley's argument ignores the remainder of the statutory language and the common law breadth of this privilege.

Teel recognizes that a merchant is allowed to restrain a suspected shoplifter in a reasonable manner and for a reasonable time for three purposes, *i.e.*, "for the purpose of investigation," as well as "for the purpose of obtaining return of the goods or in order to turn her over to the proper authorities[.]" Section 537.125, too, permits reasonable detentions not only for the purpose of recovering the property, as noted in subsection 3, but also for the purpose of "investigating whether there has been a wrongful taking of such merchandise or money." § 537.125.2. The statute expressly authorizes that, once a merchant "has detained such person and investigated such wrongful taking, [it] may contact law enforcement officers and instigate criminal proceedings against such person[.]" § 537.125.4. As a result, not only does section 537.125 not reject the principle from *Teel* that a merchant may detain a suspect in a reasonable manner and for a reasonable time in order to turn her over to the police, it expressly incorporates and reinforces that principle.

Accordingly, the Court holds that the merchant's privilege is not extinguished the instant the merchandise is recovered. Instead, the merchant is privileged to detain the person to determine whether the person actually was committing (or had committed) a wrongful taking and—if so—to detain that person for the purpose of summoning the police and initiating criminal proceedings. As long as the detention is carried out in a reasonable manner and for a reasonable time, the merchant cannot be liable to the person detained under any theory, civil or criminal, including a claim that the merchant used or threatened to use reasonable force to accomplish the detention. Accordingly, Barkley's claim that there is no affirmative defense to her claim of battery is rejected.

Laura Denvir Stith, Judge

I concur in the principal opinion's holding that section 537.125, RSMo 2000 permits a merchant to detain a suspected shoplifter "in a reasonable manner and for a reasonable length of time for the purpose of investigating whether there has been a wrongful taking of such merchandise or money," § 537.125.2, and "in order that recovery of such merchandise may be effected," § 537.125.3. Such reasonable detention will not subject the merchant to the risk of suit for unlawful arrest or detention. Id. But this does not answer the key questions in this appeal—what is "a reasonable manner" and "a reasonable length of time" for a merchant to detain a person?

I differ from the principal opinion as to what constitutes a "reasonable manner" of detention, however. In particular, the statute, as just quoted, only authorizes use of "reasonable means" of detention for the purpose of investigating the allegedly wrongful taking and while awaiting law enforcement authorities. The principal opinion, by contrast, affirms a verdict based on an instruction that permitted the use of physical force when Ms. Barkley failed to follow the store employees' instructions and when she attempted to flee the store's security office. That instruction did not require the jury to find that such physical force was necessary to recover the merchandise or to detain her at the store while waiting for authorities to arrive. In light of Ms. Barkley's testimony that she simply wanted to go tell her husband where she was and what was going on, and in light of the irrelevance of obedience of employee instructions to any of these statutory issues, this distinction could have been dispositive.

More specifically, as the principal opinion correctly notes, Ms. Barkley was detained by two security employees at Price Chopper after they saw her fail to pay for some items she had placed in one of the reusable cloth bags she carried with her as she shopped. Although the principal opinion uses the term "concealed" in the cloth bag, thereby suggesting that she put the items in the bag to steal them, the jury acquitted her of shoplifting. In light of that verdict, a more appropriate term would be that the items were "placed" in the cloth bag.

After Ms. Barkley was acquitted of shoplifting, she sued Price Chopper on multiple theories including the theories of false imprisonment and battery. In support of these claims, she testified at the trial that she was diabetic, disabled, and on pain medication, and carried her medications with her when she went with her husband and granddaughters to buy groceries at Price Chopper. She says she went with one granddaughter to look for diabetes test strips while her husband took the cart and other granddaughters and collected groceries. As she shopped separately with the grandchild, she said, she picked up a few items and put them in the red cloth bag (her husband having the cart) and just forgot about them at checkout.

As shown on a videotape of the 46-minute detention, once Ms. Barkley was brought into the security office, the employees emptied everything out of her purse to examine it (presumably for stolen property) and took her driver's license for identification. For reasons not explained in the record, they looked at her prescription containers and then left them on the counter when they replaced her other items and moved her purse and shopping bags over to the top of a cabinet near where she was sitting. The security employees determined that the value of the items found in the shopping bag was sufficiently high that they called law enforcement. While everyone waited for the police, the employees filled out paperwork, Ms. Barkley took her cell phone out of her pocket to call her husband to let him know where she was and what was going on. One of the employees grabbed her phone from her and put it on the counter, where she could not use or reach it. She testified that she twice asked the employees to contact her husband. They refused and asked her questions for the paperwork. At this point, Ms. Barkley's identity was not in question—the employees had her purse, her cell phone, her prescription medicines, her driver's license, and had mostly filled out the paperwork with information about the incident. After waiting about two minutes, Ms. Barkley got up from the bench and walked over to where the employees were standing by the counter. She says she did so because of concern about her medications still being on the counter rather than back in her purse and to ask again about contacting her husband, but the employees said they did not hear what she said and just saw she had come up to stand next to them. They immediately grabbed her and handcuffed her, she claims while one stated, "I didn't tell you to get up off the f—ing bench" and called her a "druggie" and repeatedly used profanity. She says the employees refused her request that they contact her husband who was sitting outside with the grandchildren.

At this point, as noted by the principal opinion, Ms. Barkley tried to reach the door to the office—she says to let her husband know what was going on—the employees say so she could flee—and she was grabbed, her legs knocked out from under her, and her handcuffs were moved so that her arms were handcuffed behind her rather than in front of her. She was left sitting on her legs on the floor for a long period, before the employees finally helped her up and to walk back to the bench, where she sat down and the employees removed the handcuffs. She remained on the bench until a policewoman arrived....

[S]ection 537.125's defenses only apply for the purpose of reacquiring the merchandise and investigating and holding the person for law enforcement. Those means may not be used merely to make a person follow employee instructions or not leave the security office. And as the employees already knew who Ms. Barkley was and had her purse, ID, and medications, she was not fleeing to avoid identification. Had the jury been properly instructed that force was reasonable only if used to investigate or to hold her for law enforcement, it might well have found that the force was not used in a reasonable manner when it was used because she failed to follow instructions and tried to leave the office to talk with her husband....

For these reasons, I would remand for a new trial at which both parties should more carefully follow the statute in preparing the jury instructions.

Review Question

Each week, the Pleasant Hill Flag Football Association hosts flag football games for teams consisting of adults. Teams of firefighters, insurance salespeople, lawyers, etc. all gather weekly to play football and socialize afterward. Since flag football involves "tackling" players by pulling off flags attached by Velcro® instead of actual tackling, the games are not especially violent. Players do, however, sometimes get knocked down or pushed during play, and arguments do happen from time to time. There is also a lot of joking and horseplay that occurs. During a game between a local paper company and a group of software programmers, Alice dove in an attempt to grab one of Bob's flags as Bob ran for a touchdown. Alice missed and landed on the ground. Alice and Bob were friends, so Bob decided to have a bit of fun. Instead of spiking the ball in the end zone, he decided to spike it right next to Alice's head as she was still on the ground and scare her. "Take that," Bob yelled at Alice as he spiked the ball. Unfortunately, Alice happened to move at that instant, resulting in the ball hitting Alice squarely on the nose. Alice cried out in pain as her nose bled profusely. Bob was mortified and knelt down to help Alice. Chris, one of Alice's teammates, saw what had happened and saw Bob kneeling over Alice. Concerned that Bob was about to further injure Alice, Chris tackled Bob and began pummeling Bob before he was pulled away.

Assess the potential liability of Bob and Chris under any applicable intentional tort theories.

Chapter 3

Intentional Harms to Property

A. Conversion and Trespass to Chattels
- Conversion
  - Generally defined
  - The intent requirement
  - Conversion of tangible things versus intangibles
  - Other concepts developed in class or in readings assigned by the professor
- Trespass to chattels
  - Generally defined
  - The difference with conversion
  - Other concepts developed in class or in readings assigned by the professor

B. Trespass to Land
- Generally defined
- The intent requirement
- Special issues
- Other concepts developed in class or in readings assigned by the professor

C. Defenses and Privileges
- Defense of property
  - The basic elements of the defense
  - The use of deadly force
- Necessity
  - Public necessity
    - Generally defined
    - The difference with private necessity
  - Private necessity
    - Generally defined
    - The effect of satisfying the defense
  - Other concepts developed in class or in readings assigned by the professor

Chapter Problem. Al is the owner of Al's Auto Shop & Auto Sales. In addition to fixing cars, Al's also sells used cars. After a long night, sometimes Al will sleep on a cot in the office. One late night after Al's had long been closed, three individuals—Brad, Carter, and Donna—were walking home after a night of drinking when they passed by the shop. The three individuals decided to check out Al's inventory of cars. The three climbed over the front fence and entered Al's car lot.

A. Conversion and Trespass to Chattels

A chattel is an item of personal property, as opposed to real property (land). Therefore, the torts of conversion and trespass to chattels deal with wrongs to one's personal property. The two torts, although separate, are so closely related that it is difficult to understand one without understanding the other.

1. Conversion

Pearson v. Dodd

410 F.2d 701 (D.C. Cir. 1969)

J. SKELLY WRIGHT, Circuit Judge:

This case arises out of the exposure of the alleged misdeeds of Senator Thomas Dodd of Connecticut by newspaper columnists Drew Pearson and Jack Anderson. The District Court has granted partial summary judgment to Senator Dodd, appellee here, finding liability on a theory of conversion....

The undisputed facts in the case were stated by the District Court as follows:

> ... On several occasions in June and July, 1965, two former employees of the plaintiff, at times with the assistance of two members of the plaintiff's staff, entered the plaintiff's office without authority and unbeknownst to him, removed numerous documents from his files, made copies of them, replaced the originals, and turned over the copies to the defendant Anderson, who was aware of the manner in which the copies had been obtained. The defendants Pearson and Anderson thereafter published articles containing information gleaned from these documents....[1]

...

The District Court ruled that appellants' receipt and subsequent use of photocopies of documents which appellants knew had been removed from appellee's files without authorization established appellants' liability for conversion. We conclude that appellants are not guilty of conversion on the facts shown.

Dean Prosser has remarked that "conversion is the forgotten tort." That it is not entirely forgotten is attested by the case before us. History has largely defined its

---

1. Editor's note: There were over 4,000 documents copied. The documents purportedly showed, among other things, that Dodd misappropriated over $100,000 in campaign donations for personal use.

contours, contours which we should now follow except where they derive from clearly obsolete practices or abandoned theories.

Conversion is the substantive tort theory which underlay the ancient common law form of action for trover. A plaintiff in trover alleged that he had lost a chattel which he rightfully possessed,[23] and that the defendant had found it and converted it to his own use. With time, the allegations of losing and finding became fictional, leaving the question of whether the defendant had 'converted' the property the only operative one.

The most distinctive feature of conversion is its measure of damages, which is the value of the goods converted. The theory is that the 'converting' defendant has in some way treated the goods as if they were his own, so that the plaintiff can properly ask the court to decree a forced sale of the property from the rightful possessor to the converter.

The Second Restatement of Torts has [defined] conversion as:

> . . . An intentional exercise of dominion or control over a chattel which so seriously interferes with the right of another to control it that the actor may justly be required to pay the other the full value of the chattel.

It is clear that on the agreed facts appellants committed no conversion of the physical documents taken from appellee's files. Those documents were removed from the files a night, photocopied, and returned to the files undamaged before office operations resumed in the morning. Insofar as the documents' value to appellee resided in their usefulness as records of the business of his office, appellee was clearly not substantially deprived of his use of them.

This of course is not an end of the matter. It has long been recognized that documents often have value above and beyond that springing from their physical possession. They may embody information or ideas whose economic value depends in part or in whole upon being kept secret. The question then arises whether the information taken by means of copying appellee's office files is of the type which the law of conversion protects. The general rule has been that ideas or information are not subject to legal protection, but the law has developed exceptions to this rule. Where information is gathered and arranged at some cost and sold as a commodity on the market, it is properly protected as property. Where ideas are formulated with labor and inventive genius, as in the case of literary works or scientific researches, they are protected. Where they constitute instruments of fair and effective commercial

23. A threshold question, not briefed by either party and hence not decided by us, is the nature of the property right held by appellee in the contents of the files in his Senate office. Those files, themselves paid for by the United States, are maintained in an office owned by the United States, by employees of the United States. They are meant to contribute to the work of appellee as an officer of the United States. The question thus is not entirely free from doubt whether appellee has title to the contents of the files or has a right of exclusive possession of those contents, or is a bailee, or even a mere custodian of those contents.

competition, those who develop them may gather their fruits under the protection of the law.

The question here is not whether appellee had a right to keep his files from prying eyes, but whether the information taken from those files falls under the protection of the law of property, enforceable by a suit for conversion. In our view, it does not. The information included the contents of letters to appellee from supplicants, and office records of other kinds, the nature of which is not fully revealed by the record. Insofar as we can tell, none of it amounts to literary property, to scientific invention, or to secret plans formulated by appellee for the conduct of commerce. Nor does it appear to be information held in any way for sale by appellee, analogous to the fresh news copy produced by a wire service.

Appellee complains, not of the misappropriation of property bought or created by him, but of the exposure of information either (1) injurious to his reputation or (2) revelatory of matters which he believes he has a right to keep to himself. Injuries of this type are redressed at law by suit for libel and invasion of privacy respectively, where defendants' liability for those torts can be established under the limitations created by common law and by the Constitution.

Because no conversion of the physical contents of appellee's files took place, and because the information copied from the documents in those files has not been shown to be property subject to protection by suit for conversion, the District Court's ruling that appellants are guilty of conversion must be reversed.

So ordered.

Notes

Conversion of electronic data and other intangibles. Originally, the tort of conversion was fairly limited. The tort only provided a remedy for conversion of tangible things. Thus, there could be no recovery for conversion of trade secrets or electronic data. Eventually, courts began to expand the tort to recognize claims where a defendant took tangible property (*e.g.*, stock certificates) that served as the embodiment or representation of a plaintiff's property right (the stock itself). The legal fiction courts developed was that the tangible property and the thing it represented had merged. From there, it was only a matter of time before courts began to recognize conversion claims based on the taking of trade secrets, electronic data, and other intangible property. *See* Thyroff v. Nationwide Mut. Ins. Co., 864 N.E.2d 1272 (N.Y. 2007) (electronic records and data). At the same time, there are now dozens of federal and state statutes addressing a defendant's interference with a plaintiff's property rights in such material. DAN B. DOBBS ET AL., THE LAW OF TORTS § 712 (2d ed.). As such, it is possible that a common law conversion claim might be preempted by another body of law. *See* Coyne's & Co., Inc. v. Enesco, LLC, 565 F. Supp. 2d 1027 (D. Minn. 2008) (copyright); Mortgage Specialists, Inc. v. Davey, 904 A.2d 652 (N.H. 2006) (trade secrets).

Conversion of DNA. Several state statutes declare genetic information to be personal property. For example, the Alaska Genetic Privacy Act prohibits anyone from obtaining a DNA sample or disclosing the results of a DNA analysis without consent of the individual from whom the DNA was taken and expressly provides that "a DNA sample and the results of a DNA analysis performed on the sample are the exclusive property of the person sampled or analyzed." AK Stat. § 18.13.010(a)(1). The statute goes on to provide that a person may bring a civil action against a person who collects a DNA sample from the person, and, in addition to the actual damages suffered by the person, may collect "$5,000 or, if the violation resulted in profit or monetary gain to the violator, $100,000." *Id.* § 18.13.020.

Intent. Conversion is an intentional tort. But the intent element simply requires the intent to exercise dominion or control over the item, not necessarily the specific intent to prevent the owner from using the property. *See* Magley v. M & W Inc., 2018 Mich. App. LEXIS 2809 (Mich. Ct. App. 2018) ("Good faith, mistake, and ignorance are not defenses to a claim of conversion.").

Spoliation of evidence. There might also be legal consequences for destroying one's *own* property, albeit separate from the tort of conversion. Lawyers need to be particularly mindful of these potential consequences. Rule 37(e) of the Federal Rules of Civil Procedure addresses the failure to preserve electronic information subject to discovery as part of the litigation process. When a party acts with the intent to deprive the opposing party of discoverable information, the party is subject to potentially significant judicial sanctions. Some jurisdictions have recognized the tort of intentional spoliation of evidence where a party destroys evidence that is potentially relevant to litigation. *See* Hazen v. Municipality of Anchorage, 718 P.2d 456 (Alaska 1986); Coleman v. Eddy Potash, Inc., 120 905 P.2d 185 (N.M. 1995). Lawyers are also subject to professional discipline for obstructing another party' s access to evidence or unlawfully altering, destroying, or concealing a document or other material having potential evidentiary value. ABA Model Rules of Professional Conduct R. 3.4(a); Paula Schaefer, *Attorneys, Document Discovery, and Discipline*, 30 Geo. J. Legal Ethics 1 (2017).

2. Trespass to Chattels

Perhaps the easiest way to conceptualize the tort of trespass to chattels is as an interference with one's property rights that is less serious than conversion. As *Pearson* explained, "Where the intermeddling falls short of the complete or very substantial deprivation of possessory rights in the property, the tort committed is not conversion, but the lesser wrong of trespass to chattels." *Pearson*, 410 F.2d at 707. Obvious factors to consider in making this determination would include the duration of the defendant's control over the item and the extent of any harm done.

As the *Pearson* court explained, "The difference is more than a semantic one. The measure of damages in trespass is not the whole value of the property interfered with, but rather the actual diminution in its value caused by the interference." *Pearson*, 410 F.2d at 707. A trespass to chattels may occur where the defendant dispossesses the plaintiff of the item, uses the item in such a way as to impair its value, or deprives the owner of the use of the item for a substantial period. Restatement (Second) of Torts § 218.

Problem 3.1. While on Al's premises, Brad climbs into one of the used cars on the lot and pretends to drive. Eventually, he gets bored and begins walking down the line of used cars, scratching his own car key against the sides of the cars. Carter, who is highly intoxicated, picks up a nearby cinder block and tosses it onto the windshield of another car, completely shattering the windshield. Brad and Carter are laughing about what Carter has done when they notice that Donna, who was sitting in the front seat of a used car that she has apparently hotwired, was driving off the premises. Police eventually arrest Donna while she is still in possession of the car one year later. The car is in pristine condition.

- Is Brad subject to liability for conversion? Trespass to chattels? Neither?
- Is Carter subject to liability for conversion? Trespass to chattels? Neither?
- Is Donna subject to liability for conversion? Trespass to chattels? Neither?

B. Trespass to Land

The tort of trespass to land protects one's right of exclusive possession of one's land. Note that the term "land" should be construed to mean anything affixed to the defendant's property (like a house). One area in which trespass claims are often relevant is the environmental field.

Schwartzman, Inc. v. Atchison, Topeka & Santa Fe Railway Co.

857 F. Supp. 838 (D.N.M. 1994)

BURCIAGA, Chief Judge.

THIS MATTER came on for a hearing on June 28, 1994, on Defendant's February 15, 1994 motion for summary judgment . . .

Plaintiff owns land in the South Valley area of Bernalillo County. Defendant Atchison, Topeka and Santa Fe Railway Co. ("ATSF") owns a wood treatment and preservation facility adjacent to Plaintiff's property. From 1908 to 1972, Defendant used this facility to treat and preserve wooden railroad ties. On February 15, 1993, Plaintiff filed a complaint, subsequently removed to federal court, alleging Defendant improperly stored and disposed chemical waste which contaminated the groundwater and rendered Plaintiff's adjacent property unmarketable. [Plaintiff alleged multiple causes of action, including trespass.]

Count II of Plaintiff's complaint alleges trespass. Trespass is defined as a direct infringement of another's right of possession. Pacheco v. Martinez, 97 N.M. 37, 41, 636 P.2d 308 (Ct.App.1981). *See also* Restatement (Second) of Torts § 158 ("One is subject to liability to another for trespass, irrespective of whether he thereby causes harm . . . , if he intentionally (a) enters land [of another or] causes a thing or third person to do so. . . ."). A trespass may be committed on or beneath the surface of the earth. Restatement (Second) of Torts § 159 (1977). Count III avers maintenance of a private nuisance. A private nuisance is defined as "a nontrespassory invasion of another's interest in the private use and enjoyment of land." Restatement (Second) of Torts § 821D (1977). Defendant asserts that these claims should be dismissed because no genuine issue of material fact exists to support Plaintiff's contention that contamination has migrated on Plaintiff's property.

The theoretical differences between trespass and nuisance are important in this case. A claim of trespass contemplates actual physical entry or invasion, whereas nuisance liability arises merely by virtue of activity which falls short of tangible, concrete invasion, so as not to interfere with possession, but nevertheless interferes with the use and enjoyment of the land. . . .

Plaintiffs allege that all of its tracts have been trespassed upon by Defendant's alleged horizontal migration of contaminants in the groundwater . . . . This alleged contamination includes tracts 14 north, 14 south, 10 north, 10 south, 9 north, 9 south, and tract 15 of Plaintiff's property. As to tract 14 north, ATSF conducted limited soil and groundwater testing and found some evidence of creosote contamination. Aside from tract 14 north, however, the only evidence of physical contamination of the other tracts is based on the opinions of Plaintiff's experts. Plaintiff has not done any soil or groundwater testing of the other tracts, and incredibly, does not intend to conduct such testing[.]

. . . Apparently, Plaintiff labors under the quite mistaken notion that it is Defendant who bears the burden of proof in this case. To survive summary judgment, Plaintiff must identify specific facts, which show physical invasion of contaminants. *See also* Celotex Corp. v. Catrett, 477 U.S. 317, 322, 106 S.Ct. 2548, 2552, 91 L.Ed.2d 265 (1986) (party in opposition to summary judgment must show "sufficient support" for essential elements of its case).

Due to Plaintiff's dearth of evidence demonstrating contamination of the groundwater directly underneath Plaintiff's property, Defendant contends Plaintiff's trespass [claim] must fail. . . . Defendant does not dispute that tract 14 north's groundwater is contaminated.

. . . It appears, however, that Plaintiff's expert testimony provides the evidentiary support necessary to withstand summary judgment as to the trespass cause of action. In lieu of testing or sampling results, Plaintiff relies on the opinions of three experts in the applicable field, testifying by affidavit. One such expert, Philip B.

Bedient, opined, "It is highly likely that the contamination from ATSF's Albuquerque site has travelled a significant distance, given the extremely long period of time the treatment facility operated . . . and the relatively high velocities of groundwater in the area." Bedient believes that the contaminant plume is "moving east to northeast," based on a missing layer of clay which acts as a "very permeable conduit for the migration of groundwater contamination." Finally, Bedient stated that, based on his experience at other sites, it is also "highly likely" that contamination has reached tract 10 and it is "more likely than not" that it has reached tracts 8 and 9. [The other two experts provided similar opinions.]

Plaintiff's experts' testimony, however, does reveal a major deficiency of Plaintiff's case. Bedient noted that the extent of this supposed horizontal migration is impossible to determine "due to ATSF's limited and inadequate investigation." And McGinnis stated, "Additional sampling needs to be conducted both on and off the ATSF site to determine the extent of horizontal migration. . . ." Newcomer also disparaged ATSF's investigation and lamented the uncertainty. All of these experts, therefore, have admitted that more exploration of the area needs to be conducted in order to determine more precisely the extent of horizontal migration. As Plaintiff bears the burden of proof in this case, Plaintiff is the party responsible for conducting this exploration; yet, Plaintiff apparently does not intend to do so.

Nevertheless, summary judgment should not be granted, despite this deficiency. The experts' affidavits raise issues of credibility, and the rule is well-settled that the Court should not make credibility determinations on a motion for summary judgment. . . . Plaintiff has shown genuine issues of material fact by virtue of the experts' testimony, coupled with the undisputed facts that (1) the contamination is not limited to the ATSF site; (2) the groundwater underneath tract 14 north is contaminated; (3) the site had been actively discharging waste for nearly 65 years; and (4) the groundwater moves relatively quickly in this area and has changed direction over the years. Defendant failed to contradict or impeach the experts' testimony and did not attack their qualifications or their analysis. Consequently, Defendant's motion for summary judgment as to counts II and III is denied.

Notes

Intent. As is the case with conversion, the only intent required for a trespass claim is the intent to cause the entry onto the land of another. The fact that the defendant did not know that the property belonged to the defendant is irrelevant. *See* Restatement (Second) of Torts § 164 cmt. a.

Damages in trespass actions. With the tort of battery, the defendant's actions need not result in a harmful contact; it is enough that an offensive contact results. What if in *Schwartzman* the defendant's chemical waste reached the plaintiff's groundwater but caused no damage? Could the plaintiff still prevail on a trespass claim?

Trespasses above the surface of the earth. The Federal Aviation Administration (FAA) has the authority to regulate navigable airspace, which is generally defined as 500 feet above the surface of the earth in uncongested areas and at least 1,000 feet in more congested areas. 14 C.F.R. § 91.3(b). There can be no liability for trespass (for example, by an airplane) at these levels or above. Under FAA safety guidelines, drones may fly no higher than 400 feet above ground. How low should a drone have to fly over a defendant's land before there should be liability for trespass? *Cf.* U.S. v. Causby, 328 U.S. 256 (1946) (involving successful takings claim by farmer where military aircraft passed as low as 83 feet over farmer's land, thereby substantially interfering with farmer's use and enjoyment of land).

Other means of trespass. A trespass may also occur if the defendant remains on the land, or fails to remove from the land a thing that the defendant is under a duty to remove. *See* Restatement (Second) of Torts § 158 (1965).

C. Defenses and Privileges

1. Defense of Property

The previous chapter addressed the privilege of self-defense. The rule in the case of defense of property is similar: an individual is privileged to use the force he reasonably believes necessary to defend his property. As is the case with self-defense, there are some nuances involved with this privilege.

Katko v. Briney

183 N.W.2d 657 (Iowa 1971)

MOORE, Chief Justice.

The primary issue presented here is whether an owner may protect personal property in an unoccupied boarded-up farm house against trespassers and thieves by a spring gun capable of inflicting death or serious injury.

We are not here concerned with a man's right to protect his home and members of his family. Defendants' home was several miles from the scene of the incident to which we refer *infra*.

Plaintiff's action is for damages resulting from serious injury caused by a shot from a 20-gauge spring shotgun set by defendants in a bedroom of an old farm house which had been uninhabited for several years. Plaintiff and his companion, Marvin McDonough, had broken and entered the house to find and steal old bottles and dated fruit jars which they considered antiques.

At defendants' request plaintiff's action was tried to a jury consisting of residents of the community where defendants' property was located. The jury returned a verdict for plaintiff and against defendants for $20,000 actual and $10,000 punitive damages.

After careful consideration of defendants' motions for judgment notwithstanding the verdict and for new trial, the experienced and capable trial judge overruled them and entered judgment on the verdict. Thus we have this appeal by defendants. . . .

II. Most of the facts are not disputed. In 1957 defendant Bertha L. Briney inherited her parents' farm land in Mahaska and Monroe Counties. Included was an 80-acre tract in southwest Mahaska County where her grandparents and parents had lived. No one occupied the house thereafter. Her husband, Edward, attempted to care for the land. He kept no farm machinery thereon. The outbuildings became dilapidated.

For about 10 years, 1957 to 1967, there occurred a series of trespassing and housebreaking events with loss of some household items, the breaking of windows and 'messing up of the property in general'. The latest occurred June 8, 1967, prior to the event on July 16, 1967 herein involved.

Defendants, through the years, boarded up the windows and doors in an attempt to stop the intrusions. They had posted 'no trespass' signs on the land several years before 1967. The nearest one was 35 feet from the house. On June 11, 1967 defendants set 'a shotgun trap' in the north bedroom. After Mr. Briney cleaned and oiled his 20-gauge shotgun, the power of which he was well aware, defendants took it to the old house where they secured it to an iron bed with the barrel pointed at the bedroom door. It was rigged with wire from the doorknob to the gun's trigger so it would fire when the door was opened. Briney first pointed the gun so an intruder would be hit in the stomach but at Mrs. Briney's suggestion it was lowered to hit the legs. He admitted he did so 'because I was mad and tired of being tormented' but 'he did not intend to injure anyone'. He gave no explanation of why he used a loaded shell and set it to hit a person already in the house. Tin was nailed over the bedroom window. The spring gun could not be seen from the outside. No warning of its presence was posted.

Plaintiff lived with his wife and worked regularly as a gasoline station attendant in Eddyville, seven miles from the old house. He had observed it for several years while hunting in the area and considered it as being abandoned. He knew it had long been uninhabited. In 1967 the area around the house was covered with high weeds. Prior to July 16, 1967 plaintiff and McDonough had been to the premises and found several old bottles and fruit jars which they took and added to their collection of antiques. On the latter date about 9:30 p.m. they made a second trip to the Briney property. They entered the old house by removing a board from a porch window which was without glass. While McDonough was looking around the kitchen area plaintiff went to another part of the house. As he started to open the north bedroom door the shotgun went off striking him in the right leg above the ankle bone. Much of his leg, including part of the tibia, was blown away. Only by McDonough's assistance was plaintiff able to get out of the house and after crawling some distance was put in his vehicle and rushed to a doctor and then to a hospital. He remained in the hospital 40 days. . . .

III. Plaintiff testified he knew he had no right to break and enter the house with intent to steal bottles and fruit jars therefrom. He further testified he had entered a plea of guilty to larceny in the nighttime of property of less than $20 value from a private building. He stated he had been fined $50 and costs and paroled during good behavior from a 60-day jail sentence. Other than minor traffic charges this was plaintiff's first brush with the law. On this civil case appeal it is not our prerogative to review the disposition made of the criminal charge against him.

IV. The main thrust of defendants' defense in the trial court and on this appeal is that 'the law permits use of a spring gun in a dwelling or warehouse for the purpose of preventing the unlawful entry of a burglar or thief'. They repeated this contention in their exceptions to the trial court's instructions 2, 5 and 6. They took no exception to the trial court's statement of the issues or to other instructions....

Instruction 5 stated: 'You are hereby instructed that one may use reasonable force in the protection of his property, but such right is subject to the qualification that one may not use such means of force as will take human life or inflict great bodily injury. Such is the rule even though the injured party is a trespasser and is in violation of the law himself.'

Instruction 6 stated: 'An owner of premises is prohibited from willfully or intentionally injuring a trespasser by means of force that either takes life or inflicts great bodily injury; and therefore a person owning a premise is prohibited from setting out 'spring guns' and like dangerous devices which will likely take life or inflict great bodily injury, for the purpose of harming trespassers. The fact that the trespasser may be acting in violation of the law does not change the rule. The only time when such conduct of setting a 'spring gun' or a like dangerous device is justified would be when the trespasser was committing a felony of violence or a felony punishable by death, or where the trespasser was endangering human life by his act.' ...

The overwhelming weight of authority, both textbook and case law, supports the trial court's statement of the applicable principles of law.

Prosser on Torts, Third Edition, pages 116—118, states:

> ... the law has always placed a higher value upon human safety than upon mere rights in property, it is the accepted rule that there is no privilege to use any force calculated to cause death or serious bodily injury to repel the threat to land or chattels, unless there is also such a threat to the defendant's personal safety as to justify a self-defense ... Spring guns and other mankilling devices are not justifiable against a mere trespasser, or even a petty thief. They are privileged only against those upon whom the landowner, if he were present in person would be free to inflict injury of the same kind.

The legal principles stated by the trial court in instructions 2, 5 and 6 are well established and supported by the authorities cited and quoted supra. There is no merit in defendants' objections and exceptions thereto. Defendants' various motions based on the same reasons stated in exceptions to instructions were properly overruled.

Affirmed.

Notes

Reasonable force. In *Vancherie v. Siperly*, 221 A.2d 356 (Md. 1966), there was evidence that the plaintiff, a customer at a restaurant who had spent the afternoon drinking at another location, refused to leave the defendant's restaurant and was thus a trespasser. The plaintiff "was a six-foot tall, young and healthy sailor." The defendant "was sixty-five years old and partially disabled." In an effort to expel the plaintiff from his restaurant, the defendant struck the plaintiff in the head with a nightstick. Was the defendant privileged to use this force in defense of his property?

Use of mechanical devices in defending property. *Katko* involved the use of a spring gun. Other mechanical devices that are potentially implicated by the *Katko* rule include barbed wire, razor wire, and mantraps. *See* Restatement (Second) of Torts §§ 84–85.

When the use of mechanical devices might be permitted. The *Restatement* takes the position that the use of deadly force by means of mechanical devices is privileged to the same extent as the use of deadly force would otherwise be privileged. *See* Restatement (Second) of Torts § 85 cmt. a. Think back to the defenses discussed in the last chapter. When would that be the case?

The use of spring guns is illegal under the criminal law in some states. *See* S.C. Code § 16-23-450. Presumably, the criminal law might impact the tort rules in such states.

Threats of physical force. One is privileged to threaten a harmful or offensive contact in order to prevent a trespass to the same extent one is privileged to actually use such force. *See* State v. Buckley, 149 A.3d 928 (Vt. 2016) (defendant not privileged to point a shotgun at and threaten to shoot two men who were repossessing a vehicle).

Application to trespass to chattels and conversion. The privilege to use reasonable force in defense of one's property also applies where the wrongdoer is engaging in a conversion or trespass to chattels. *See* Restatement (Second) of Torts § 77.

Problem 3.2. Several trespassers had entered Al's lot in recent months. The part of the property that was the most vulnerable to trespass was the western boundary of the lot, so Al decided to attach electric wires to a fence along the western boundary in an attempt to protect the property from trespassing. The wires were connected to a 110-volt outlet. Voltage at this level is potentially lethal. Al put up warning signs at three different spots along the fence stating, "WARNING: Electrified fence."

If a trespasser were to be injured after coming into contact with the fence, would Al be able to successfully claim the privilege of defense of property?

2. Necessity

With the other defenses covered so far in this chapter and in the previous chapter, it is the plaintiff's initial conduct that allegedly triggers the need for the defendant to commit the actions about which the plaintiff complains. The defense of necessity is different in that, in the case of necessity, the defendant's supposed need to take action typically arises from some external force—such as a fire—rather than the actions of the plaintiff. Over time, a distinction has developed between a matter of public necessity and one of private necessity.

a. Public Necessity

In order to claim the defense of public necessity, the defendant must be acting to protect the public at large from a threatened danger, as opposed to merely herself or a small number of people. The classic case is *Surocco v. Geary*, 3 Cal. 69 (1853), in which a fire was spreading through a section of San Francisco. The defendant, a public official, acting on the advice of others, ordered the destruction of one building so as to save others in the path of the fire.

> The right to destroy property, to prevent the spread of a conflagration, has been traced to the highest law of necessity, and the natural rights of man, independent of society or civil government. . . . It rests upon the maxim, *Necessitas inducit privilegium quod jura privata.*

Id. at 73. To avoid liability, the defendant must show that he was acting out of "apparent or actual necessity."

In many public necessity cases, the actor causing the damage to the property is a public official. State constitutions frequently contain "takings" clauses, which prohibit a state actor from taking private property for public use without just compensation. Thus, the defense of public necessity may be in tension with the state constitutional provision providing for compensation in the event of a taking. In *Wegner v. Milwaukee Mutual Insurance Co.*, 479 N.W.2d 38 (Minn. 1991), the police did extensive damage to the plaintiff's property as part of an attempt to apprehend a suspect. The Minnesota Supreme Court held that there had been a taking for public use and that the defense of public necessity could not deprive the plaintiff of the right to just compensation. In contrast, the Texas Supreme Court held under similar facts that the police could defend against such a claim upon a showing of "great public necessity." *See* Steele v. City of Houston, 603 S.W.2d 786 (Tex. 1980).

Consider how those formulations of the defense of public necessity square with the defense of private necessity addressed in the next section.

b. Private Necessity

Ploof v. Putnam

71 A. 188 (Vt. 1908)

MUNSON, J.

It is alleged as the ground on recovery that on the 13th day of November 1904, the defendant was the owner of a certain island in Lake Champlain, and of a certain dock attached thereto, which island and dock were then in charge of the defendant's servant; that the plaintiff was then possessed of and sailing upon said lake a certain loaded sloop, on which were the plaintiff and his wife and two minor children; that there then arose a sudden and violent tempest, whereby the sloop and the property and persons therein were placed in great danger of destruction; that, to save these from destruction or injury, the plaintiff was compelled to, and did, moor the sloop to defendant's dock; that the defendant, by his servant, unmoored the sloop, whereupon it was driven upon the shore by the tempest, without the plaintiff's fault; and that the sloop and its contents were thereby destroyed, and the plaintiff and his wife and children cast into the lake and upon the shore, receiving injuries. [Plaintiff proceeded on a trespass theory, to which Defendant demurred.]

There are many cases in the books which hold that necessity, and an inability to control movements inaugurated in the proper exercise of a strict right, will justify entries upon land and interferences with personal property that would otherwise have been trespasses....

This doctrine of necessity applies with special force to the preservation of human life. One assaulted and in peril of his life may run through the close of another to escape from his assailant. One may sacrifice the personal property of another to save his life or the lives of his fellows....

It is clear that an entry upon the land of another may be justified by necessity, and that the declaration before us discloses a necessity for mooring the sloop. But the defendant questions the sufficiency of the counts because they do not negative the existence of natural objects to which the plaintiff could have moored with equal safety. The allegations are, in substance, that the stress of a sudden and violent tempest compelled the plaintiff to moor to defendant's dock to save his sloop and the people in it. The averment of necessity is complete, for it covers not only the necessity of mooring to the dock; and the details of the situation which created this necessity, whatever the legal requirements regarding them, are matters of proof, and need not be alleged. It is certain that the rule suggested cannot be held applicable irrespective of circumstance, and the question must be left for adjudication upon proceedings had with reference to the evidence or the charge....

Judgment affirmed and cause remanded.

Vincent v. Lake Erie Transp. Co.

124 N.W. 221 (Minn. 1910)

O'BRIEN, J.

The steamship Reynolds, owned by the defendant, was for the purpose of discharging her cargo on November 27, 1905, moored to plaintiff's dock in Duluth. While the unloading of the boat was taking place a storm from the northeast developed, which at about 10 o'clock p. m., when the unloading was completed, had so grown in violence that the wind was then moving at 50 miles per hour and continued to increase during the night. There is some evidence that one, and perhaps two, boats were able to enter the harbor that night, but it is plain that navigation was practically suspended from the hour mentioned until the morning of the 29th, when the storm abated, and during that time no master would have been justified in attempting to navigate his vessel, if he could avoid doing so. After the discharge of the cargo the Reynolds signaled for a tug to tow her from the dock, but none could be obtained because of the severity of the storm. If the lines holding the ship to the dock had been cast off, she would doubtless have drifted away; but, instead, the lines were kept fast, and as soon as one parted or chafed it was replaced, sometimes with a larger one. The vessel lay upon the outside of the dock, her bow to the east, the wind and waves striking her starboard quarter with such force that she was constantly being lifted and thrown against the dock, resulting in its damage, as found by the jury, to the amount of $500.

We are satisfied that the character of the storm was such that it would have been highly imprudent for the master of the Reynolds to have attempted to leave the dock or to have permitted his vessel to drift away from it.... Nothing more was demanded of them than ordinary prudence and care, and the record in this case fully sustains the contention of the appellant that, in holding the vessel fast to the dock, those in charge of her exercised good judgment and prudent seamanship....

The appellant contends by ample assignments of error that, because its conduct during the storm was rendered necessary by prudence and good seamanship under conditions over which it had no control, it cannot be held liable for any injury resulting to the property of others, and claims that the jury should have been so instructed. An analysis of the charge given by the trial court is not necessary, as in our opinion the only question for the jury was the amount of damages which the plaintiffs were entitled to recover, and no complaint is made upon that score.

The situation was one in which the ordinary rules regulating properly rights were suspended by forces beyond human control, and if, without the direct intervention of some act by the one sought to be held liable, the property of another was injured, such injury must be attributed to the act of God, and not to the wrongful act of the person sought to be charged. If during the storm the Reynolds had entered the harbor, and while there had become disabled and been thrown against the plaintiffs' dock, the plaintiffs could not have recovered. Again, if which attempting to hold fast to the dock the lines had parted, without any negligence, and the vessel carried against some other boat or dock in the harbor, there would be no liability upon her owner. But here those in charge of the vessel deliberately and by their direct efforts held her in such a position that the damage to the dock resulted, and, having thus preserved the ship at the expense of the dock, it seems to us that her owners are responsible to the dock owners to the extent of the injury inflicted....

Theologians hold that a starving man may, without moral guilt, take what is necessary to sustain life; but it could hardly be said that the obligation would not be upon such person to pay the value of the property so taken when he became able to do so. And so public necessity, in times of war or peace, may require the taking of private property for public purposes; but under our system of jurisprudence compensation must be made....

Order affirmed.

Notes

The limits of the necessity defense. Was the defendant in *Vincent* privileged to keep the boat moored to the plaintiff's dock? If so, why was the defendant still held liable?

Defining the defense. One is only privileged to commit what would otherwise be a trespass where the need to do so appears to be reasonably necessary. Moreover, the means used must also be reasonable. In *Lange v. Fisher Real Estate Dev. Corp.*, 832 N.E.2d 274 (Ill. Ct. App. 2005), a cab driver chased a non-paying customer onto the plaintiff's property without the plaintiff's permission in order to recover his fare. Ordinarily, this would make him a trespasser. Should the cab driver be able to claim the privilege of necessity? In *Benamon v. Soo Line R.R. Co.*, 689 N.E.2d 366 (Ill. Ct. App. 1997), a teenager was chased by a group of boys. The teenager found a hiding place and hid until the boys left. Afraid that the boys might return and see where he lived, the teenager attempted to go home a different way and entered onto the property of a railroad. Was the teenager's entry onto the property justified by private necessity?

Problem 3.3. While Brad and Carter were still on Al's car lot, it began to rain heavily. Brad and Carter decided to leave the premises, but as the intoxicated Carter attempted to scale the fence at the front of the lot, he slipped and fell. Carter was rendered unconscious and was bleeding profusely from his head. Brad had his cell phone with him, but decided to get Carter out of the pouring rain before he called for an ambulance. Brad picked up his friend and carried him over to the building where Al's office was located. Brad tried to open the locked door, but eventually kicked the door open and went inside to call for an ambulance.

If Al were to sue Brad for trespass for the damage to the door, would Carter be able to successfully assert the privilege of private necessity?

Problem 3.4 **(review)**. Al, the owner, happened to be sleeping on the cot in the office that night and heard Brad kick open the door. Al, fearing a burglary, came out of the office with a shotgun. He first fired a warning shot into the air, but when Brad, panicked by the gunshot, did not immediately flee, Al fired directly at Brad, thereby seriously injuring him.

Was Al's use of the shotgun privileged?

Review Question

Cameron and Phoebe were returning home after an afternoon of hiking at a state park. As they pulled out of the parking lot, Phoebe noticed a field full of wildflowers down the road near an old barn. Phoebe pulled the car over and she and Cameron entered the field to go pick some flowers. The couple picked a lovely bouquet, which they planned to bring home. While in the field, the couple noticed a cute dog with no collar or tags who kept following the couple around. Believing the dog to be a stray, Cameron and Phoebe decided to take the dog home and care for her. Cameron picked up the dog and put her in the back of their car. As it turned out, the field and the dog (named Cookie Monster) belonged to John, a nearby homeowner. When John saw Cameron and Phoebe on his property, he ran out of his house, shoved Phoebe down, and punched Cameron. As he did so, he shouted, "Get off my property! Give me my dog back!" Phoebe was uninjured, but Cameron suffered a broken nose.

(a) Discuss any claims John might bring against Cameron and Phoebe and the likely outcome of such claims.

(b) Assume that Cameron and Phoebe bring battery claims against John. Discuss any defense(s) John might assert and his likelihood of success.

Part 2
Negligence

The cases in Part 1 involved allegations that the defendants acted with the intent to bring about some type of harmful or offensive consequence. In contrast, a plaintiff bringing a negligence action alleges that the defendant failed to act reasonably and that this failure caused the plaintiff's injuries. An intent to bring about the injuries is not an element of the claim. Thus, the negligent defendant typically lacks the culpability of the intentional tortfeasor. Mark Geistfeld, *Negligence, Compensation, and the Coherence of Torts Law,* 91 GEO. L.J. 585, 626 (2003).

There is some disagreement among judges and scholars as to the origins of the negligence cause of action. As discussed in Chapter 1, historically, a defendant could be held liable even absent fault. Legal historian Lawrence Friedman has attributed the switch to a fault-based system to the industrial revolution and its reliance machines and their "marvelous capacity to cripple and maim" workers. LAWRENCE FRIEDMAN, A HISTORY OF AMERICAN LAW 300 (2d ed. 1985). Industrialization also resulted in products with a greater capacity to injure consumers. If industrialists could be forced to pay damages to individuals injured by their machines without any showing of fault, the budding American industrial economy would have never developed. Thus, the theory is that courts adopted a requirement that injured parties at least demonstrate the lack of reasonable or ordinary care on the part of a defendant in order to recover damages.

In order to establish a claim of negligence, a plaintiff must establish five elements: (1) the defendant had a duty to conform his conduct to a specific standard of care; (2) conduct by the defendant falling below the standard of care amounting to a breach of that duty; (3) harm; (4) the defendant's substandard conduct was a cause in fact of the plaintiff's harm; and (5) the defendant's substandard conduct was a proximate or legal cause of the plaintiff's harm.[1] Milbert v. Answering Bureau, Inc., 120 So. 3d 678, 688 (La. 2013); Coln v. City of Savannah, 966 S.W.2d 34, 39 (Tenn. 1998). This part of the book explores each of these elements, as well as the defenses that may apply, the special rules for government actors, and the related tort of negligent infliction of emotional distress.

1. Some courts list only four elements, with the fourth element of causation having two distinct components: causation in fact and proximate cause. Regardless of whether one speaks of four or five elements, the analysis remains the same.

Chapter 4

Duty and Breach

A. Duty (The Standard of Care)
- The duty owed in the typical case
- Exceptions to the general rule
- Other concepts developed in class or in readings assigned by the professor

B. Breach of Duty
- Determining breach
- The Hand formula
- Open and obvious risks
- Other concepts developed in class or in readings assigned by the professor

C. Special Issues Involving Breach of Duty
- Sudden emergencies
  - Jury instruction
  - The need for a special jury instruction?
- Negligence per se
  - Requirements
  - Excuse
  - Effect of defendant's negligence per se
- Industry Custom
- Minors
- Other special characteristics of the actor
- Circumstantial evidence and *res ipsa loquitur*
  - The basis for the theory
  - Limits on the theory
  - Black-letter requirements
    - The accident is one that ordinarily does not occur in the absence of someone's negligence
    - The agency or instrumentality is within the exclusive control of the defendant
    - Procedural effect
- Professional negligence
  - Establishing the standard of care
    - The role of experts
    - Specialties
    - Local or national standards

- The role of custom in establishing the standards of care
  - In general
  - Two schools of thought/respectable minority rule
  - Error in judgment rule
- Res ipsa loquitur in medical malpractice cases
- Informed consent
- Other concepts developed in class or in readings assigned by the professor

Chapter Problem. Adrian rented a second-floor apartment from Darren. Under the terms of the lease, Darren was responsible for maintenance of the stairs outside of the apartment. As Adrian was leaving her apartment one day, she slipped and fell down all 13 stairs. She ended up suffering a broken leg. She has now sued Darren on a negligence theory. In a separate incident, another tenant, Bill, was injured when he fell from the balcony in his apartment.

A. Duty (The Standard of Care)

In order to establish a claim of negligence, a plaintiff must first establish that the defendant had a duty to conform his conduct to a specific standard of care. The duty element of the prima case involves two distinct issues: (1) did the defendant owe a duty of care with respect to the plaintiff? and (2) if so, what was the standard of care? These are questions of law for the judge to decide. In many cases, the first issue is really a non-issue. In the next chapter, we will circle back to those situations in which there might be some question as to whether the defendant owed the plaintiff a duty of care. But for now, this chapter focuses on the duty element in terms of how one defines the standard of care in a typical negligence case.

Stewart v. Motts

654 A.2d 535 (Pa. 1995)

MONTEMURO, Justice.

The sole issue presented before us is whether there exists a higher standard of "extraordinary care" for the use of dangerous instrumentalities over and above the standard of "reasonable care" such that the trial court erred for failing to give an instruction to the jury that the Appellee should have used a "high degree of care" in handling gasoline. Because we believe that there is but one standard of care, the standard of "reasonable care," we affirm.

The pertinent facts of this case are simple and were ably stated by the trial court:

> On July 15, 1987, Plaintiff, Jonathon Stewart, stopped at Defendant, Martin Motts' auto repair shop and offered assistance to the Defendant in repairing an automobile fuel tank. In an effort to start and move the car with

> the gasoline tank unattached, the Plaintiff suggested and then proceeded to pour gasoline into the carburetor. The Defendant was to turn the ignition key at a given moment. While the exact sequence of events was contested, the tragic result was that the car backfired, caused an explosion and resulted in Plaintiff suffering severe burns to his upper body. On October 8, 1992, following a two day trial, a jury returned a verdict for the defendant thus denying the Plaintiff's claim for damages.

[The trial court refused to provide the jury instruction requested by the plaintiff. Specifically, the plaintiff wanted the jury instructed that due to the flammability of gasoline, the defendant was legally obligated to exercise "a high degree of care."]

We begin our discussion by reaffirming the principle that there is but one standard of care to be applied to negligence actions involving dangerous instrumentalities in this Commonwealth. This standard of care is "reasonable care" as well stated in the Restatement (Second) of Torts:

> The care required is always reasonable care. The standard never varies, but the care which it is reasonable to require of the actor varies with the danger involved in his act and is proportionate to it. The greater the danger, the greater the care which must be exercised....

Restatement (Second) of Torts § 298 comment b (1965)....

Properly read, our cases involving dangerous agencies reaffirm these well accepted principles found in the *Restatement*....

In summation, this Commonwealth recognizes only one standard of care in negligence actions involving dangerous instrumentalities—the standard of reasonable care under the circumstances. It is well established by our case law that the reasonable man must exercise care in proportion to the danger involved in his act.

With these principles in mind we must next examine the jury instructions in this case....

Reviewing the charge as a whole, we cannot conclude that it was inadequate. The trial judge explained to the jury that negligence is "the absence of ordinary care which a reasonably prudent person would exercise in the circumstances here presented." The trial judge further explained:

> It is for you to determine how a reasonably prudent person would act in those circumstances. Ordinary care is the care a reasonably prudent person would use under the circumstances presented in this case. It is the duty of every person to use ordinary care not only for his own safety and the protection of his property, but also to avoid serious injury to others. What constitutes ordinary care varies according to the particular circumstances and conditions existing then and there. The amount of care required by law must be in keeping with the degree of danger involved.

We find that this charge, when read as a whole, adequately instructed the jury.

Grotheer v. Escape Adventures, Inc.

14 Cal. App. 5th 1283 (2017)

SLOUGH, J.

Plaintiff and appellant Erika Grotheer is a non-English speaking German citizen who took a hot air balloon ride in the Temecula wine country and suffered a fractured leg when the basket carrying her and seven or eight others crash landed into a fence. Grotheer sued three defendants for her injuries: the balloon tour company, Escape Adventures, Inc. (Escape), the pilot and Escape's agent, Peter Gallagher (Gallagher), and Wilson Creek Vineyards, Inc. (Wilson Creek) (collectively, defendants or respondents). Grotheer alleged Escape and Gallagher negligently or recklessly operated the balloon by (1) failing to properly slow its descent during landing and (2) failing to give the passengers safe landing instructions before the launch. Grotheer alleged the hot air balloon company is a common carrier, and as such, owed its passengers a heightened duty of care. . . .

Grotheer claims Escape is a common carrier and therefore owed its passengers a heightened duty of care to ensure their safe carriage during the balloon tour. We conclude a hot air balloon operator like Escape is not a common carrier as a matter of law.

In general, every person owes a duty to exercise "reasonable care for the safety of others," however, California law imposes a heightened duty of care on operators of transportation who qualify as "common carriers" to be as diligent as possible to protect the safety of their passengers. (Civ. Code, §§ 1714, subd. (a), 2100, 2168.) "A carrier of persons for reward must use the utmost care and diligence for their safe carriage, must provide everything necessary for that purpose, and must exercise to that end a reasonable degree of skill." (Civ. Code, § 2100.)

Whether a hot air balloon operator is a common carrier is an issue of first impression in California. It is also a question of law, as the material facts regarding Escape's operations are not in dispute.

A common carrier of persons is anyone "who offers to the public to carry persons." (Civ. Code, § 2168.) The Civil Code treats common carriers differently depending on whether they act gratuitously or for reward. "A carrier of persons without reward must use ordinary care and diligence for their safe carriage." (Civ. Code, § 2096.) But "[c]arriers of persons for reward have long been subject to a heightened duty of care." (*Gomez*, at p. 1128, 29 Cal.Rptr.3d 352, 113 P.3d 41.) Such carriers "must use the utmost care and diligence for [passengers'] safe carriage, must provide everything necessary for that purpose, and must exercise to that end a reasonable degree of skill." (Civ. Code, § 2100). While common carriers are not insurers of their passengers' safety, they are required "to do all that human care, vigilance, and foresight reasonably can do under the circumstances." This duty originated in English common law and is "based on a recognition that the privilege of serving the public as a common carrier necessarily entails great responsibility, requiring common carriers to exercise a high duty of care towards their customers."

Common carrier status emerged in California in the mid-nineteenth century as a narrow concept involving stagecoaches hired purely for transportation. [The court noted that over time the concept had been applied to recreational transport, like scenic airplane and railway tours.]

It is in this critical regard we find a hot air balloon differs from those recreational vehicles held to a common carrier's heightened duty of care. [B]alloon pilots do not maintain direct and precise control over the speed and direction of the balloon. A pilot directly controls only the balloon's altitude, by monitoring the amount of heat added to the balloon's envelope. A pilot has no direct control over the balloon's latitude, which is determined by the wind's speed and direction. A balloon's lack of power and steering poses risks of mid-air collisions and crash landings, making ballooning a risky activity. This precedent teaches that the key inquiry in the common carrier analysis is whether passengers expect the transportation to be safe because the operator is reasonably capable of controlling the risk of injury. . . .

Because no amount of pilot skill can completely counterbalance a hot air balloon's limited steerability, ratcheting up the degree of care a tour company must exercise to keep its passengers safe would require significant changes to the aircraft and have a severe negative impact on the ballooning industry. For that reason, we conclude Escape is not a common carrier as a matter of law.

Notes

Reasonable care. The standard of care in the overwhelming majority of negligence cases is that of reasonable care. There are lots of different phrases used by courts to describe this idea: "reasonable care," "ordinary care," the care of a "reasonable person," the care of the "reasonable man," the care of a "reasonably prudent person," etc. They all mean the same thing. It is the care that a reasonable person would exercise under the same or similar circumstances. Nearly all of the rest of this chapter is devoted to trying to flesh out what that actually means.

Other situations. There are few situations in which a defendant owes the heightened duty discussed in *Grotheer.* In addition to common carriers, one situation that some courts have been willing to recognize as justifying a heightened duty is the duty owed by an innkeeper to a guest. *See* Taboada v. Dally Seven, Inc., 626 S.E.2d 428 (Va. 2007) (likening the innkeeper-guest relationship to the common carrier-passenger relationship and recognizing a duty of "utmost care and diligence"). What justifies this heightened standard? Other variations on and departures from the reasonable person standard are discussed in Chapter 5.

The historical rule and the modern trend. As *Grotheer* suggests, common carriers have long been subject to this heightened duty of care. But the modern trend has been to hold common carriers to the same standard of care as any potential tortfeasor, *i.e.*, reasonable care under the circumstances. *See* Bethel v. New York City Transp. Auth., 703 N.E.2d 1214 (N.Y. 1998) (rejecting older approach and adopting a reasonable care standard).

Highly specific standards of care. Justice Oliver Wendell Holmes believed that with time and experience confronting similar fact patterns, judges could devise more specific standards of care than the traditional standard of reasonable care. For example, in *Baltimore & O.R. Co. v. Goodman*, 275 U.S. 66 (1927), Holmes articulated a standard of care that required the driver of an automobile at a railroad crossing to get out of his vehicle, approach the tracks, and look both ways before returning to the car and proceeding. Citing the inherent problems with such a rule (such as the fact that the driver might place himself at greater risk by approaching the tracks), the Court effectively overruled *Goodman* a few years later and reverted to a standard of reasonable care. *See* Pokora v. Wabash Ry. Co., 292 U.S. 98 (1934). Vestiges of the Holmes approach still survive in some limited areas. For example, Pennsylvania courts have adopted the "hills and ridges" doctrine in slip-and-fall cases involving snow. Under this doctrine, a property owner has a duty to remove snow only when snow or ice has accumulated "in ridges or elevations" and the defendant fails to remove the snow within a reasonable time. *See* Biernacki v. Presque Isle Condos. Unit Owners Ass'n, 828 A.2d 1114, 1117 (Pa. Super. 2003).

B. Breach of Duty

If the defendant fails to live up to the applicable standard of care, there has been a breach of duty. Stated differently, the failure to meet the standard of care is negligence (although all of the remaining elements of a negligence claim must be satisfied before the defendant can be held liable). While it is for the judge to determine what the standard of care is in a given case (and, again, the standard is usually that of reasonable care under the circumstances), it is ordinarily for the jury to determine whether the defendant has met that standard. The focus is on what a reasonable person would do under the same or similar circumstances. The "reasonable person" isn't necessarily hyper-cautious. "[T]he reasonable person exercises care only about the kinds of harm that are foreseeable to reasonable people and risks that are sufficiently great to require precaution." Dan B. Dobbs, The Law of Torts § 117 (2000). Where risks are foreseeable, the reasonable person will do something within reason to avoid the risks. In other words, a reasonable person seeks to avoid conduct that results in unreasonable risks of harm. Restatement (Second) of Torts § 282 (1965).

The first case in this section, *United States v. Carroll Towing Co.*, is one of the most famous tort cases and introduces a framework for analysis on the issue of breach. The other cases in this section illustrate how courts analyze the issue and some of the special issues that factor into the analysis.

United States v. Carroll Towing Co.

159 F.2d 169 (2d Cir. 1947)

L. HAND, Circuit Judge.

The facts, as the judge found them, were as follows. On June 20, 1943, the Conners Company chartered the barge, 'Anna C.' to the Pennsylvania Railroad Company at a stated hire per diem, by a charter of the kind usual in the Harbor, which included the services of a bargee, apparently limited to the hours 8 A.M. to 4 P.M. On January 2, 1944, the barge, which had lifted the cargo of flour, was made fast off the end of Pier 58 on the Manhattan side of the North River, whence she was later shifted to Pier 52. At some time not disclosed, five other barges were moored outside her, extending into the river; her lines to the pier were not then strengthened. At the end of the next pier north (called the Public Pier), lay four barges; and a line had been made fast from the outermost of these to the fourth barge of the tier hanging to Pier 52. The purpose of this line is not entirely apparent, and in any event it obstructed entrance into the slip between the two piers of barges. The Grace Line, which had chartered the tug, 'Carroll,' sent her down to the locus in quo to 'drill' out one of the barges which lay at the end of the Public Pier; and in order to do so it was necessary to throw off the line between the two tiers. . . .

[The "Carroll" backed away] preparatory to 'drilling' out the barge she was after in the tier off the Public Pier. She had only got about seventy-five feet away when the tier off Pier 52 broke adrift because the fasts from the 'Anna C,' either rendered, or carried away. The tide and wind carried down the six barges, still holding together, until the 'Anna C' fetched up against a tanker, lying on the north side of the pier below—Pier 51—whose propeller broke a hole in her at or near her bottom. Shortly thereafter: *i.e.*, at about 2:15 P.M., she careened, dumped her cargo of flour and sank. The tug, 'Grace,' owned by the Grace Line, and the 'Carroll,' came to the help of the flotilla after it broke loose; and, as both had syphon pumps on board, they could have kept the 'Anna C' afloat, had they learned of her condition; but the bargee had left her on the evening before, and nobody was on board to observe that she was leaking. [The court below held, among other things, that the Carroll Company was liable to the United States for the loss of the barge's cargo of flour.] The Grace Line . . . and the Carroll Company . . . wish to charge the 'Anna C' with a share of all her damages, or at least with so much as resulted from her sinking. . . .

. . .

[T]here is no general rule to determine when the absence of a bargee or other attendant will make the owner of the barge liable for injuries to other vessels if she breaks away from her moorings. However, in any cases where he would be so liable for injuries to others obviously he must reduce his damages proportionately, if the injury is to his own barge. It becomes apparent why there can be no such general rule, when we consider the grounds for such a liability. Since there are occasions when every vessel will break from her moorings, and since, if she does, she becomes a menace to those about her; the owner's duty, as in other similar situations, to provide against resulting injuries is a function of three variables: (1) The probability that she will break away; (2) the gravity of the resulting injury, if she does; (3) the burden of adequate precautions. Possibly it serves to bring this notion into relief to state it in algebraic terms: if the probability be called P; the injury, L; and the burden, B; liability depends upon whether B is less than L multiplied by P: *i.e.*, whether B is less than PL. Applied to the situation at bar, the likelihood that a barge will break from her fasts and the damage she will do, vary with the place and time; for example, if a storm threatens, the danger is greater; so it is, if she is in a crowded harbor where moored barges are constantly being shifted about. On the other hand, the barge must not be the bargee's prison, even though he lives aboard; he must go ashore at times. We need not say whether, even in such crowded waters as New York Harbor, a bargee must be aboard at night at all; . . . but we hold that it is not in all cases a sufficient answer to a bargee's absence without excuse, during working hours, that he has properly made fast his barge to a pier, when he leaves her. In the case at bar the bargee left at five o'clock in the afternoon of January 3rd, and the flotilla broke away at about two o'clock in the afternoon of the following day, twenty-one hours afterwards. The bargee had been away all the time, and we hold that his fabricated story was affirmative evidence that he had no excuse for his absence. At the locus in quo—especially during the short January days and in the full tide of war activity—barges were being constantly 'drilled' in and out. Certainly it was not beyond reasonable expectation that, with the inevitable haste and bustle, the work might not be done with adequate care. In such circumstances we hold—and it is all that we do hold—that it was a fair requirement that the Conners Company should have a bargee aboard (unless he had some excuse for his absence), during the working hours of daylight.

. . .

Decrees reversed and cause remanded for further proceedings in accordance with the foregoing.

Indiana Consolidated Insurance Co. v. Mathew

402 N.E.2d 1000 (Ind. Ct. App. 1980)

HOFFMAN, Judge.

Appellant Indiana Consolidated Insurance Company seeks review of the finding that Robert D. Mathew (Mathew) did not act in a negligent manner so as to be liable for damages done to his brother's garage when a Toro riding lawnmower that Mathew was starting caught fire. Appellant insured the garage and premises under a homeowner's insurance policy and is pursuing this claim against Mathew by virtue of its subrogation rights.

. . .

[T]he facts favorable to Mathew disclose that on May 1, 1976 Mathew's brother was out of town for the weekend. The two brothers lived across the street from each other and took turns mowing both lawns. In the late afternoon Mathew decided to mow both lawns and went to his brother's garage where a twelve horsepower Toro riding lawnmower was stored. The mower was approximately eight years old, was kept in good mechanical condition, and had required only minor tune-ups and belt replacements for the rotary mower assembly. Mathew pulled the mower away from the side wall of the garage and after checking the gas gauge filled the lawnmower approximately three-fourths full with gasoline using a funnel. He then went back across the street to his home for approximately twenty minutes. Upon returning to the garage Mathew started the lawnmower. However, he noticed a flame in the engine area under the hood and immediately shut the engine off. He opened the hood and saw a flame four to five inches tall under the gas tank. Using some clean towels Mathew tried to snuff out the flame but was unsuccessful. He could find no other means to extinguish the fire. The flames continued to grow and the machine began spewing gasoline, so he ran to his home to call the fire department. He returned to find the garage totally engulfed in flames.

At trial Mathew testified that he was afraid to try to push the flaming machine outside the garage for fear that the tank would explode in his face.

...

On appeal appellant contends that the judgment is contrary to law because Mathew was negligent in filling the gas tank, in starting the mower in an enclosed area, and in failing to push the flaming mower out of the garage. The standard by which Mathew's conduct is to be measured is whether he exercised the duty to use due care in operating the mower that an ordinary prudent man would exercise under the same or similar circumstances.

The record amply supports the finding that Mathew did not act in a negligent manner in filling the gas tank. He testified that he did so carefully, with the use of a funnel. He did not fill the tank full, and he was adamant in his belief that he did not spill any gasoline. He hypothesized that even had any gas been spilled it would have evaporated in the cool air during the twenty-minute period before he started the mower. Appellant is merely asking this Court to reweigh the evidence in regard to any gasoline spillage due to Mathew's admission on cross-examination that he could have spilled some fuel. The trier of fact resolved this issue in favor of Mathew, finding that he exercised due care in fueling the mower, and it must remain undisturbed upon appeal. Appellant is again reminded that any conflicts in testimony when appeal from a negative judgment is taken must be resolved in favor of the appellee.

Appellant's contention that Mathew should be held liable for the act of negligently starting the mower inside the garage is also without merit. It cannot seriously be contended that the evidence shows that Mathew acted other than a reasonably prudent man in pulling the mower out into an open area of the garage and starting it. The mower was a riding type that was of considerable weight and size. Garages are designed to permit the starting of motorized vehicles such as automobiles and are commonly used for such purpose. That this particular mower would catch fire at this particular time was not reasonably foreseeable. As one is not required to anticipate that which is unlikely to happen, the trial court did not err in determining that Mathew was not negligent in starting the mower inside the garage.

Appellant's further allegation that Mathew negligently failed to push the flaming mower out of the garage area is refuted by the evidence that the machine was spewing gasoline and that he was afraid for his safety should the tank explode. Mathew therefore chose to leave and summon help from the local fire department.... The law values human life above property. Greater risk of one's person is justified to save life than is reasonable in protecting property. If Mathew had tried to push the riding mower ten feet into an open area the machine might have exploded and caused much graver damage to his person than was suffered by the destruction of the garage. Contrary to appellant's position several jurisdictions have ruled that one may be deemed negligent in voluntarily risking life or serious injury for the purpose of saving mere property.

...

The judgment is not contrary to law and is therefore affirmed.

Notes

The concept of foreseeability in negligence cases. In attempting to instruct jurors as to what qualifies as reasonable care or the care of an ordinary, prudent person, courts sometimes reference the concept of foreseeability of harm. For example, a standard jury instruction in New York explains that "[t]here is negligence if a reasonably prudent person could foresee injury as a result of his or her conduct and acted unreasonably in the light of what could be foreseen." Pelletier v. Lahm, 936 N.Y.S.2d 60 (N.Y. Sup. Ct. 2011) (quoting jury instructions).

The Hand Formula. Most courts do not formally instruct jurors to engage in the cost-benefit analysis in which Judge Hand engaged in *Carroll Towing. See* Patrick J. Kelley & Laurel A. Wendt, *What Judges Tell Juries About Negligence: A Review of Pattern Jury Instructions*, 77 Chi. Kent L. Rev. 587, 619 (2002). Nonetheless, the Hand Formula (as the *Carroll Towing* approach is often referred to) remains a useful tool in analyzing whether the individual's alleged act of negligence amounted to the failure to exercise care. *See* UDR Texas Properties, Inc. v. Petrie, 517 S.W.3d 98, 107 (Tex. 2017) (Willett, J., dissenting) (stating that the Hand Formula is "the subject of 28.1 million Google hits [and] is widely taught in law schools as a recognized definition of negligence").

Subsequent remedial measures. Assume that following the accident described in *Carroll Towing* that the defendant adopted a strict policy of requiring bargees to be onboard at least 18 hours out of every day. Should the plaintiff in that case be permitted to introduce this subsequent change in practice in order to establish that the burden on the defendant to keep a bargee onboard was not unreasonable? Rule 407 of the Federal Rules of Evidence prohibits a party from introducing evidence of such subsequent remedial measures as part of an effort to establish negligence on the part of the defendant.

Levi v. Southwest Louisiana Elec. Membership Co-op. (Slemco)

542 So. 2d 1081 (La. 1989)

DENNIS, Justice.

Facts

The plaintiff, Giovanni Levi, an oil field roustabout-pumper for Amoco Oil Company, sustained near fatal permanently disabling injuries when the erected mast of a paraffin removal truck rig upon which he was working came in contact or close proximity with an uninsulated 14,400 volt electric distribution line being operated by Southwest Louisiana Electric Membership Cooperative (Slemco). The accident occurred on February 16, 1982 at the E.C. Stuart # 2 Well in the Section 28 Dome Field, in St. Martin Parish, an oil field owned by Amoco Oil Company. In the 1960's Slemco had constructed an uninsulated electrical distribution line to serve most of the 22 wells producing in the field. The power company routed the line so as to avoid crossing a well driveway or coming in close proximity to the well by placing the line either across the main road from the well or behind the well, with the exception of the E.C. Stuart # 2 Well where the line crossed the access road leading to the well 40.5 feet from the well head and 25.7 feet overhead. Slemco failed to avoid a driveway traversal or a close encounter between its line and the E.C. Stuart # 2 Well because that well was omitted from the power company's original construction plan due to oversight or to the fact that no electricity was supplied to this well or both.

To remove paraffin from its wells the oil company used a rig mounted on a truck. A mast was attached to the rear of the truck with hinges. In the collapsed position, the other end was carried in a "headache rack" over the front of the truck. . . .

On the day of the accident Levi and another Amoco employee, while servicing wells in the field, found it necessary to dismantle the lubricator to make a repair. . . . It was necessary for the workers to raise the mast off the truck and lower the lubricator to the ground to make the repairs. Using control levers on the side of the truck, Levi raised the mast tip up, over the truck and back toward the power line. Levi had noticed the distribution line at this location on previous occasions but failed to pay attention to it on the day of the accident. Levi recalled only that he last saw the mast when it was at a 45° angle in front of the truck. Shortly thereafter, the mast either touched the power line or came close enough for electrical arcing to occur. 14,400 volts of electricity escaped from the power line and coursed through the mast, the truck and Levi's body.

As a result of the accident, Levi suffered the amputation of both legs just below the knees and severe burns over 25% of his body. At the time of the trial, he had been hospitalized 10 times for 11 different surgical procedures.

Levi filed suit against Slemco and its insurer. The case was tried before a jury. In response to written interrogatories, the jury found that Slemco's conduct did not fall below the . . . standard of care. The trial court denied plaintiff's motions for a judgment notwithstanding the verdict and for a new trial. Levi appealed, and the court of appeal affirmed. . . .

Statement and Application of Legal Precepts

The crucial questions are (a) whether the power company was required to recognize that its conduct involved a risk of causing physical injury or loss to another in the manner of that sustained by the plaintiff, and, if so, (b) whether the possibility of such injury or loss constituted an unreasonable risk of harm. These issues are decisive under either a duty-risk or a traditional negligence approach. [W]hen the power company realizes or should realize that the transmission of electricity through its line presents an unreasonable risk of causing physical harm to another, it is under a duty to exercise reasonable care to prevent the risk from taking effect.

(a) Whether the power company was required to recognize the hazard

A power company is required to recognize that its conduct involves a risk of causing harm to another if a reasonable person would do so while exercising such attention, perception of the circumstances, memory, knowledge of other pertinent matters, intelligence and judgment as a reasonable person would have.

[A] power company has an obligation to make reasonable inspections of wires and other instrumentalities in order to discover and remedy hazards and defects. Consequently, a company will be considered to have constructive knowledge of an electrical hazard which has existed for a period of time which would reasonably permit discovery had the company adequately performed its duties.

In the present case there is no dispute as to the fact that the power company had actual knowledge of the oil company's regular use of trucks with erectable high masts around its wells. Because this activity had continued on a regular basis over a long period of time the power company should have been aware of the physical characteristics of this equipment and any electrical hazard it might create. An Amoco employee testified that although the E.C. Stuart # 2 Well was not a "problem paraffin well", the paraffin was removed from it every two to three weeks. . . . Since the power company knew that its uninsulated 14,400 volt electric line passed near the oil wells at a level of only 25 to 26 feet above ground, the company should have known that electrical hazards would be created if masts were raised near the line.

The evidence clearly indicates that the power company was aware of these potential dangers and took significant precautions against them in choosing the route of its line. The 22 oil wells in the oil field had been completed when the power company constructed its transmission line. The company purposefully routed the line, in most instances, so as to give wide berth to each well and to avoid crossing over well access roads. Except for the E.C. Stuart # 2 Well, according to the exhibits, the power line was kept at distances of 76.5 to 212 feet from the wells. . . . Thus, the design of the power line route, except at the Stuart Well, afforded workers with high-masted equipment ample working area free of electrical hazards, and, at all wells except Stuart and one other, completely safe access, as margins of error against their negligence or inattentiveness.

We do not think reasonable minds can disagree with the conclusion that the power company, particularly with its superior knowledge, skill and experience in electrical safety, should have recognized that its conduct under these circumstances involved a risk of harm to oil field workers. Aside from the obvious serious possibility that an inattentive worker might raise the mast while parked on the access road too near the power line, there were similar chances that a falling mast could pass dangerously close to the line or that a careless roustabout might attempt to drive under the line on his way to another well without fully lowering his mast. The power company complains that it should not be charged with recognition of any risk that takes effect through a victim's negligence. But the ordinary reasonable person, and even more so the power company, is required to realize that there will be a certain amount of negligence in the world. When the risk becomes serious, either because the threatened harm is great, or because there is an especial likelihood that it will occur, reasonable care may demand precautions against "that occasional negligence which is one of the ordinary incidents of human life and therefore to be anticipated." Murphy v. Great Northern R. Co., 2 Ir.Rep. 301 (1897); *See* Prosser and Keeton on Torts, supra, § 33 at p. 198; Restatement (Second) Torts, supra, § 302A. . . .

(b) Whether the hazard was an unreasonable risk of harm

The test for determining whether a risk apparent to one in the position of the actor is unreasonable is supplied by the following formula: The amount of precautions "demanded of a person by an occasion is the resultant of three factors: the likelihood that his conduct will injure others, taken with the seriousness of the injury if it happens, and balanced against the interest which he must sacrifice to avoid the risk." L. Hand, J., in Conway v. O'Brien, 111 F.2d 611, 612 (2d Cir.1940). . . .

The facts of the present controversy and other similar power line cases invite a sharp focus upon the essential balancing process that lies at the heart of negligence. In such a case, a paraphrase of the Hand formula helps to bring the elements of the process into relief: Since there are occasions when high voltage electricity will escape from an uninsulated transmission line, and since, if it does, it becomes a menace to those about the point of its escape, the power company's duty, as in other similar situations, to provide against resulting injuries is a function of three variables: (1) the possibility that the electricity will escape; (2) the gravity of the resulting injury, if it does; (3) the burden of taking adequate precautions that would avert the mishap. When the product of the possibility of escape multiplied times the gravity of the harm, if it happens, exceeds the burden of precautions, the failure to take those precautions is negligence.

The cost of prevention is what Hand meant by the burden of taking precautions against the accident. It may be the cost of installing safety equipment or otherwise making the activity safer, or the benefit foregone by curtailing or eliminating the activity. No one, including Judge Hand thought reasonable care can be measured with mathematical precision, however. His formula in *Carroll Towing* merely suggests the kind of evidence that is relevant on the issue of reasonable care and how it should be weighed.

Applied to the situation in the present case, the likelihood that a roustabout's inattentiveness or that a malfunction of a rig would allow a mast to come close enough to the uninsulated power line to cause the electricity to escape varied between locations in the oil field. This danger was greatest on the E.C. Stuart # 2 well site at which the accident happened. This was the only location at which the power company suspended its uninsulated line completely across a road used by masted truck operators for access to a well. It was the one site where the uninsulated line was located only about two truck lengths from the well, leaving very little room for a high masted truck to maneuver safely. The fact that the power company systematically avoided these hazards elsewhere within the oil field possibly tended to make workers less wary of them at the accident site and thereby increased the likelihood of an accident. Under these circumstances, there was a significant chance that the power company's conduct would cause harm or death to one or more of the class of workers handling masted equipment at the well site.

The social value which the law attaches to each person's interest in life and freedom from physical harm is of the highest order. Fatal or disastrous harm is likely to be caused to these interests by a high voltage electrical accident. Moreover, electrical hazards located in oil fields or other industrial settings typically threaten harm to many workers when the risk takes effect. Consequently, the gravity of the harm, if the risk takes effect, is extreme.

Plaintiff's experts testified that several different kinds of precautions could and should have been taken to eliminate or reduce the hazard caused by the operation of the bare high voltage line at the E.C. Stuart # 2 Well: [Among other precautions, the utility could have replaced the line at the well with factory installed insulation or could have insulated the line temporarily with rubber hose type insulation, or the company simply could have raised the line to a safer level at the site of the accident.]

The defendants' expert only quibbled at the precaution of insulation. His objection to insulation was that it would deteriorate and might give workers a false sense of security. His criticism must be discounted as being directed evidently at rubber hose type temporary insulation, rather than factory installed permanent insulation. The record discloses no reason why permanent insulation could not have been used at the accident site. Even if only temporary insulation were available, we are convinced from the evidence that this lesser precaution would reduce the risk substantially and be worth the burden it cost. As for the company's evidence that insulation of the line would have to be replaced from time to time, it is clear that this small additional cost would not cause the burden of precautions to outweigh the gravity of the harm threatened when multiplied by the likelihood that it would happen.

The expert witness for the defendants apparently could find no fault with the suggested precautions of elevation of the line to a height safely above the reach of masted equipment or the precaution of underground installations. He was not asked about either safeguard and he did not volunteer any information on them.

When the components of the evidence are brought into relief and weighed in the light of their interrelationships, reasonable minds must agree that the minimal burden of adequate precautions was clearly outweighed by the product of the chance and the gravity of the harm. Accordingly, the power company was guilty of negligence that was a legal cause of plaintiff's injuries, or, in other words, the company breached its duty to take precautions against the risk that took effect as those injuries, and the lower courts committed manifest error in not reaching this conclusion.

For the reasons assigned, the judgment of the court of appeal is reversed, the judgment of the trial court is set aside, and the case is remanded to the court of appeal for it to review the balance of the merits of the controversy and to render a judgment consistently with this court's opinion.

Styles v. Eblen

436 S.W.2d 504 (Ky. 1969)

OSBORNE, Judge.

On December 24 or 25, 1965, 114 hogs belonging to Marvin D. Eblen and Wallace C. Eblen, appellees, were electrocuted when an electrical line constructed and maintained by W. E. Styles, appellant, was knocked down by a partially dead tree which fell during a period of high winds. Styles held an oil lease on the property where the incident occurred and was conducting a secondary oil recovery operation in the area under various leases and a unitization agreement.... The secondary recovery operation involved pumping water into certain wells to force the remaining oil to pool. Styles had erected electrical lines to operate the necessary pumps. The pumps attached to the lines which electrocuted the hogs had not been utilized in the recovery operation for a period of approximately two years and sometime during that period of time the pumps had been partially dismantled and the electrical lines disconnected at the pumps. However, although the power supplied by these lines was no longer being used, the lines had been left connected and were still energized at the time the hogs were electrocuted.

The energized lines were knocked down by one side of a double sycamore. According to the Eblens this part of the tree had been dead for some time. The tree fell during a period of high winds, with gusts of up to fifty miles an hour. The jury returned a verdict for the Eblens in the amount of $6000 for the loss of the hogs.

Appellant's primary contention is that the trial court should have granted a peremptory instruction because there was insufficient evidence of negligence in the construction, maintenance and operation of the lines to raise a jury question....

The lines in question extend from a tree near the property line for an undisclosed distance to the pumps in question. They had not been in use for a period of two years. Evidence shows that it would have taken only five minutes to disconnect them at the tree. The lines carried 480 volts of electrical current, which is sufficient when brought into contact with man or beast to cause serious injury or death. It is common knowledge that such lines are susceptible to wind and storm.

It is horn book law that the reasonableness of any conduct must be judged by the circumstances of the case. Where the necessity and utility of maintaining such lines are important, where the lines serve a useful function and are carefully constructed, the inherent danger is weighed against the social utility of their maintenance and there is no negligence. But when the utility of the instrumentality is extremely low and when the risk involved is so much greater, as is the case here, then further maintenance of the instrumentality constitutes negligent conduct.... The principle is aptly summarized by asking the question, 'Is the game worth the candle?' We have many times recognized that this is the basic question to be determined in deciding whether a particular act involves an unreasonable risk. It is our opinion that maintenance of highly-energized, uninsulated, electrical wires for a substantial period after their utility has ceased when there was no plan to place them in immediate reuse, and when the time and effort necessary to disconnect them would be insignificant compared to the risk involved to the general public constituted negligence....

Judgment affirmed.

Notes

Assessing the burden of adequate precaution. Obviously, the cost to the defendant in taking a precaution is a relevant consideration in assessing the breach question. Based on your reading of *Levi* and *Styles*, what other sorts of things should the finder of fact or reviewing court consider when assessing the burden of adequate precautions to avoid the accident? *See* Restatement (Second) of Torts § 291 (1965).

Judge versus jury. Ordinarily, it is for the judge to decide what the applicable standard of care is and for the jury to decide whether the defendant's conduct met that standard. Was it appropriate for the Louisiana Supreme Court to set aside the jury's conclusion in *Levi* with respect to negligence on the part of the defendant?

Frasca v. Prudential-Grace Lines, Inc.

394 F. Supp. 1092 (D. Md. 1975)

BLAIR, District Judge.

This is a maritime 'slip'n fall' case ... The plaintiff, a longshoreman, was injured when he slipped and fell off a ladder leading into the No. 4 hatch on the defendant's ship, the S.S. SANTA CLARA. [The jury found that the plaintiff, the plaintiff's stevedoring employer, and the shipowner were each negligent. The court entered judgment in favor of the plaintiff in the amount of $8,400.] The shipowner timely moved for a judgment notwithstanding the verdict under Fed.R.Civ.P. 50(b), having made a motion for a directed verdict at the close of all the evidence....

The accident occurred on May 29, 1973, a cloudy, overcast day, with an on-and-off drizzle. The longshoremen crew of which plaintiff was a member reported to work at 8:00 a.m. to finish unloading No. 4 hatch on the S.S. SANTA CLARA, which they had begun unloading the day before. They had quit work at noon the previous day due to inclement weather. . . .

To descend into the hatch using this ladder, a person had to swing one foot over the coaming[1] and feel for the top rung, while holding on to the deck lashing with one hand and the hatch coaming with the other. The other foot would then be swung over the coaming and placed on the ladder. Thus, the lashing wires provided the only firm hand hold.

When the members of plaintiff's gang descended into the lower hold on the morning of May 29, they noticed that the lashing wires, the coaming, and the ladder were all covered with a fine film of oil or grease. . . .

The general greasy condition of the lashing wires, hatch coaming, and ladder was not directly called to the attention of the ship's personnel by any of the longshoremen. However, a member of the ship's crew did descend into the hold by way of the port hatch ladder to open the lower hatch when the longshoremen first descended in the morning. A ship's crew member also descended into the hatch to close the upper 'tween deck lid at about 1:00 p.m. Neither the ship's crew nor the stevedoring company or its employees made any attempts to correct the oily and greasy conditions on the lashing wires, hatch coaming, and ladder.

The factual cause of the greasy conditions in the area was not certain. The condition could have been caused by ship's crew or longshoremen previously tracking the oil from the upper 'tween deck onto the ladder, coaming, and lashing wires, and/or from the presence of grease in the grooves of the hatch cover rollers on the top of the coaming. The greasy conditions were present when the longshoremen reported for work that morning. The condition became worse throughout the day due to the tracking of oil by the longshoremen as they went up and down the ladder.

From 8:00 a.m. until the time of plaintiff's fall shortly after 3:00 p.m., eight longshoremen used the ladder at least three times each. The plaintiff himself used the ladder four times. He admitted that he noticed the greasy and oily conditions when he first descended in the morning and remained aware of the condition until the time of his injury. Another ladder, known as the 'escape hatch' ladder, was available for use in the after end of No. 4 hatch. After 1:00 p.m. on May 29, however, this ladder became more difficult to use because the longshoremen would have had to climb over two large air conditioners that had been stowed in the after end of the upper 'tween deck in No. 4 hatch. None of the longshoremen used the escape hatch ladder, as their usual practice was to use the ladder leading directly into the hatch. The plaintiff was not instructed to use the escape hatch ladder rather than the port hatch ladder.

Shortly after 3:00 p.m. on May 29, the plaintiff ascended the ladder to get some coffee and use the restroom. He returned to No. 4 hatch, and, while attempting to

1. Editor's note: a "coaming" is a raised surface on a ship that is designed to keep out water.

swing his right foot over the coaming and descend the ladder, his left foot slipped off the top rung of the ladder, causing his hands to slip from the lashing wire and coaming. The plaintiff fell approximately 15 feet to the upper 'tween deck and suffered severe injuries. The question presented is whether these facts constitute sufficient evidence from which a reasonable jury could find that the defendant shipowner breached any duty that it owed to the plaintiff longshoreman....

... The court ... found no reasonable minds could differ as to the obviousness of the condition and the plaintiff's actual knowledge thereof. Further, there is no evidence that the ship's crew made any effort to alleviate the greasy and oily conditions in and surrounding No. 4 hatch. Thus, the narrow question is whether a reasonable jury could find that the owner should have expected that the stevedore would not correct and the longshoremen would not protect themselves against the known danger or that the owner should have otherwise anticipated the harm despite such knowledge. Otherwise stated, was it reasonably foreseeable to a reasonably prudent man in the shoes of the shipowner that, once the longshoremen discovered the danger, neither the plaintiff, his fellow employees, nor the stevedoring company, which also had a duty to remedy dangerous conditions, would have taken any steps to remedy the situation over the seven-hour work period prior to the injury, and if so, was it reasonably foreseeable that the longshoremen would nevertheless continue to work in the area without using the alternate route available or insisting that the ship take remedial measures to make the condition safe? If it was so foreseeable, then a reasonable jury could find that, by taking no corrective measures, the shipowner breached his duty of reasonable care to guard against the foreseeable risks. Such questions of foreseeability are, of course, generally for the jury to decide, unless reasonable minds could not differ.

Clearly, if the accident had occurred in the early morning upon the first descent down the hatch, a jury could find the shipowner liable. It is entirely foreseeable that the stevedoring company would not have had sufficient time or even would have neglected to perform its duty at that point, even once the condition was discovered....

This court concludes that reasonable minds could not differ concerning the unforeseeability that, even though the condition became worse during the day, the longshoremen would nevertheless continue to go in and out of the hold on at least 25-30 separate occasions without even protecting themselves by merely wiping the oil from the rungs of the ladder or by the use of the safer, alternate route, and that for at least seven hours, the stevedoring company would totally fail to ... remedy the unsafe conditions in the work area. The only reasonable conclusion to be drawn from the evidence is that, if any negligence was the cause of the plaintiff's injury, it was solely that of the stevedoring company and the plaintiff himself. In short, based on the evidence presented, and giving the plaintiff the benefit of every reasonable inference to be drawn therefrom, the shipowner had no reason to expect that the stevedore and longshoremen would fail to protect the plaintiff against a danger which they knew existed, which is frequently encountered in the type of work, and which could be so easily avoided. Stated otherwise, the shipowner had no reason to anticipate harm despite the longshoremen's actual knowledge of the condition. . . . Thus, the court concludes as a matter of law that the shipowner breached no duty that it owed to the plaintiff. Hence, the defendant's motion for a judgment n.o.v. will be granted.

Notes

Contributory negligence. Chapter 8 will address a defendant's affirmative defenses to a negligence action, including the defense of contributory negligence. Under this defense, if a plaintiff's own negligence is (in most jurisdictions) at least equal to or perhaps greater than the defendant's negligence, the plaintiff cannot recover. Note that this is not what happened in *Frasca*.

Open and obvious risks. Some courts take the position that where risks are "so obvious that the [plaintiff] might reasonably be expected to discover them," the defendant owes no duty to protect against the risks. Riddle v. McLouth Steel Products Corp., 485 N.W.2d 676 (Mich. 1992). An alternative approach would be to say that a defendant owes a duty of reasonable care even with respect to open and obvious risks, but that the defendant ordinarily does not breach this duty if he fails to take action to prevent harm. Which approach would you generally prefer if you represented defendants? Plaintiffs?

Problem 4.1. Adrian had taken two steps when she slipped and fell down the rest of the stairs in Darren's apartment building. The stairs were covered with linoleum. There was a metal strip at the edge of each stair. The linoleum was approximately 12 years old and was worn in the middle where people had stepped over the years. There was no handrail along the wall.

Imagine that you represent Adrian. As a matter of law, Darren owed his tenants, including Adrian, a duty of reasonable care. Be prepared to explain how you plan to argue that Darren, the landlord, breached his duty to exercise reasonable care with respect to the stairs.

C. Special Issues Involving Breach of Duty

Ordinarily, the standard of care in a negligence action is one of reasonable care under the circumstances. As the cases above suggest, determining breach is often an imprecise endeavor. But sometimes courts apply special rules with respect to either the reasonable person standard or the means by which we determine breach. The decisions in this section address some of those special situations.

1. Sudden Emergencies

Jackson v. Brown

801 S.E.2d 194 (W. Va. 2017)

Justice Ketchum:

On the morning of June 7, 2014, Defendant Jackson drove a 1999 Ford F-350 flatbed truck to a restaurant in Ritchie County, West Virginia, where he ate breakfast. Following breakfast, Defendant Jackson went to an Ace Hardware Store in Ritchie County where he purchased "six or seven joints of plastic pipe" that he was planning to install "in the ground as a French drain to get water away (from the residence that he lived in)." After loading the plastic pipes into his truck, Defendant Jackson drove a short distance before coming to a stop at the intersection of Ritchie Industrial Park Road and U.S. Route 50.

U.S. Route 50 is a four-lane divided highway. Defendant Jackson's truck was perpendicular to Route 50 as he was stopped at the intersection. His plan was to drive straight across the two eastbound lanes and make a left turn to merge into the westbound lanes of Route 50. Defendant Jackson testified that before attempting to drive his truck across the eastbound lanes of Route 50, he looked to his left and noticed a semi-truck coming toward him. Believing that he had enough time to clear the two eastbound lanes in front of the semi-truck, Defendant Jackson proceeded into the eastbound lanes of the highway. However, Defendant Jackson did not see a motorcycle that was also traveling eastbound on Route 50 that was being driven by the decedent, Harry Myer, Jr. ("Decedent Myer").

Decedent Myer was traveling in the right or slow eastbound lane of Route 50 when Defendant Jackson's truck entered the highway. Though Decedent Myer applied his brakes, as evidenced by skid marks in the slow lane of Route 50, he crashed his motorcycle into the left rear quarter panel of Defendant Jackson's truck. The collision occurred in the right or slow eastbound lane. Decedent Myer was injured and later died at the scene of the accident as a result of the injuries he suffered in the crash.

[Meyer's estate brought a wrongful death action against Jackson. Jackson defended by alleging that Meyer was himself negligent in terms of his reaction to the presence of Jackson's vehicle.] In support of this argument, Defendant Jackson argued that the motorcycle's skid marks started in the middle of the right lane and proceeded toward the "lane-dividing lines." However, the skid marks remained in the motorcycle's lane of travel. Essentially, Defendant Jackson argued that because the skid marks demonstrated that Decedent Myer's motorcycle traveled from the middle of the right lane toward the left edge of the right lane, the jury should decide "whether [Decedent] Myer acted as a reasonably prudent person . . . by swerving left instead of right and possibly avoiding the collision."

. . .

Importantly, there was no evidence indicating that the plaintiff was negligent in any manner. The only expert who testified in this matter stated that Defendant Jackson caused the accident by pulling onto Route 50 and failing to yield to Decedent Myer. This expert, Daniel Aerni, testified on behalf of the plaintiff and stated that Decedent Myer was traveling between 55 to 64 mph, which was below the posted speed limit, "at the start of the 89-foot skid [.]" Regarding the amount of time it took Decedent Myer to react to Defendant Jackson pulling onto Route 50, the expert testified:

> I calculated that the truck driven by Mr. Jackson accelerated over a distance of about 52 feet and that it took him about 4.2 seconds to do so.... Furthermore, I calculated that the skid by Mr. Myer took about 1.34 seconds, as I recall, the difference being about 2.8 seconds. That is the amount of time that I obtain between the very start of the acceleration by Mr. Jackson and the application of the brakes by Mr. Myer.
>
> ...

After review, we find that the material facts are undisputed and that "reasonable minds can draw but one inference from them." The undisputed material facts demonstrate that Decedent Myer was traveling below the speed limit in the right lane of Route 50 when Defendant Jackson failed to yield to oncoming traffic in violation of W.Va. Code § 17C-9-1. Confronted with the sudden emergency created by Defendant Jackson, Decedent Myer applied his brakes within 2.8 seconds of Defendant Jackson entering the highway. In Syllabus Point 3 of Poe v. Pittman, 150 W.Va. 179, 144 S.E.2d 671 (1965), this Court held:

> A person in a sudden emergency, not created in whole or in part by his own negligence, who acts according to his best judgment or who, because of insufficient time for reflection, fails to act in the most judicious manner, is not guilty of negligence if he exercises the degree of care which would be exercised by a reasonably prudent person in like circumstances.

We reiterate that Decedent Myer applied his brakes within 2.8 seconds of Defendant Jackson creating the sudden emergency by failing to yield to oncoming traffic and pulling onto Route 50. After applying his brakes, the skid mark evidence reveals that Decedent Myer's motorcycle skidded for approximately 89 feet, starting in the center of the right lane and colliding with Defendant Jackson's truck near the left edge of the right lane. There is no evidence that Decedent Myer left the right lane at any time during the course of this accident. Under these facts, we find that Decedent Myer acted as a reasonably prudent person by applying his brakes within 2.8 seconds and by staying in the right lane throughout the sudden emergency caused by Defendant Jackson....

Based on all of the foregoing, we find no error with the circuit court's ruling granting summary judgment to the plaintiff on the issue of Defendant Jackson's liability.

Note

Rejection of the special sudden emergency rule. A number of jurisdictions have held that juries should not be given any sort of special "sudden emergency" instruction when deciding the case. *See, e.g.*, Bjorndal v. Weitman, 184 P.3d 1115 (Or. 2008). Is such an instruction necessary? If you represented the party alleging negligence on the part of another, would you want such an instruction given to the jury? If not, what sort of instruction would be appropriate?

2. Negligence Per Se

Ordinarily, the standard of care is not defined with any specificity beyond reasonable care under the circumstances. Sometimes, however, criminal or administrative statutes or other forms of positive law may establish the standard of care in a given case, and the violation of that statute or other enactment amounts to a breach of duty for purposes of a negligence claim. As the *Restatement* explains it, "The unexcused violation of a legislative enactment . . . which is adopted by the court as defining the standard of conduct of a reasonable man, is negligence in itself." Restatement (Second) of Torts § 288(B)(1) (1965).

Winger v. C.M. Holdings, L.L.C.

881 N.E.2d 433 (Iowa 2016)

WATERMAN, Justice.

This wrongful-death action arises from a fatal fall from an apartment balcony and presents several issues on the applicability of the doctrine of negligence per se to an alleged municipal housing code violation. The thirty-two-inch high balcony railing complied with the local housing code when the apartment complex was constructed in 1968, but unless exempted under a grandfather provision, it is ten inches shorter than the current housing code allows. Before the accident, a local housing inspector cited the landlord for that code violation. The inspector reasoned that an attached plastic lattice modified the railings to eliminate grandfather status. The landlord did not appeal that finding but rather ordered the higher railings and asked for an extension of time to install them. The City of Des Moines Housing Appeal Board (HAB), without a contested hearing, found the property was in violation but granted a three-month extension to install compliant railings and suspended the $1090 fine. The plaintiffs' daughter fell over the original railing to her death three days later.

The plaintiffs filed a premises liability action alleging the thirty-two-inch railing violated the local housing code. Their expert testified the forty-two-inch railing would have prevented the accident. The district court ruled the landlord was bound by the HAB's determination that forty-two-inch railings were required and rejected the landlord's arguments that the property was grandfathered out of the current code or that the HAB's extension of time to install higher railings excused tort liability. The court instructed the jury that the landlord's violation of the housing code constituted negligence per se and limited the jury to deciding causation, comparative fault, and damages.... In posttrial rulings, the district court concluded the doctrine of negligence per se did not apply to a local housing code and ordered a new trial. Both sides appealed, and we transferred the case to the court of appeals, which affirmed with one judge dissenting and another specially concurring. We granted the applications for further review by both sides.

I. Background Facts and Proceedings.

Mark Critelli was the sole owner of the Grand Stratford Apartments until February 15, just over five months before Shannon's fatal fall. This apartment complex consists of a duplex and three larger buildings constructed in 1968. The apartments were built to comply with the 1968 housing code, which required guardrails between thirty- and thirty-four inches high.... In 2005, the guardrail ordinance stated, "Multiple family dwellings with porches, balconies or raised floor surfaces located more than 30 inches above the floor or below grade shall have guards not less than 42 inches in height." Des Moines, Iowa, Municipal Code §60-127(c) (2005). The grandfather provision was revised to state, "Any structure that was in compliance on the day previous to the adoption of this code will be allowed to remain." *Id.* §60-5. The ordinance was admitted into evidence without objection.

[The HAB had previously found that Critelli was a "habitual violator" of the code. Therefore, all properties under his ownership were put on an accelerated inspection schedule. A city inspector, Eddie Leedom, inspected the Grand Stratford Apartments on February 10 and found 106 code violations, including the guardrail height, broken window screens, and a broken garbage disposal. Critelli and his company, C.M. Holdings, began repairs. On an inspection on July 5, Leedom noted only six remaining violations. He imposed a $1090 fine for the guardrail-height violations. By July 13, the only remaining infraction was the height of the guardrails, and CM Holdings had ordered new forty-two-inch guardrails.]

...

III. Analysis.

The central fighting issue on appeal is whether CM Holdings was negligent *as a matter of law* by failing to replace the thirty-two-inch high balcony guardrails with forty-two-inch high guardrails....

A. Can a Violation of a City Ordinance Constitute Negligence Per Se? The court of appeals construed *Griglione* to hold that only the breach of a statewide standard can constitute negligence per se and affirmed the order granting a new trial on that basis. The court of appeals understandably relied on this language from *Griglione*:

> We believe rules of conduct that establish absolute standards of care, the violation of which is negligence per se, must be ordained by a state legislative body or an administrative agency regulating on a statewide basis under authority of the legislature. That is the position espoused in Restatement

> (Second) of Torts §286 (1965) and followed by this court in *Jorgensen* [*v. Horton*, 206 N.W.2d 100, 102 (Iowa 1973)]. We are persuaded that, for purposes of civil damages actions based on allegedly negligent actions by municipal employees, this principle is sound.

525 N.W.2d at 812. The plaintiffs argued that language is dicta, but the court of appeals concluded that language is controlling. We note that language was unnecessary to the decision and is not supported by the cited authorities. We resolve the issue by overruling *Griglione.*

Our court has long recognized the violation of a municipal safety ordinance can be negligence per se. However, the district court and court of appeals questioned the viability of this line of cases based on what we recently said in *Griglione*, a case that did not involve a municipal ordinance or code with the force of law.

The fighting issue in *Griglione* was whether the violation of a local police department's internal operating procedures constituted negligence per se.... The preamble to the operating procedures stated,

> The following Police Department Standard Operating Procedures are guidelines that are suggested for occurrences as specified as follows. They will never replace good, sound judgment or common sense, but when confronted with an unfamiliar situation should serve as an aid to the Officer.

Id. The provisions regarding deadly force included the following statement:

> The Deadly Force Policy is written to guide officers before the fact in approaching a potentially critical situation and not merely to assist in assessing the possible liability after the fact. The use of deadly force in effecting an arrest shall be based on the concept of protection of the officer or other person from the use, or threat of use of deadly force.

Id.

We concluded that violations of the department's internal operating procedures were not negligence per se for two reasons. First, we held that the operating procedures "do not involve the delineation of that type of precise standard required to invoke the negligence per se doctrine." Second, we stated that only the violation of a rule applying "statewide" could constitute negligence per se and cited *Jorgensen* and the Restatement (Second) of Torts section 286, in support of that proposition. That statement was broader than necessary to decide the narrow issue of whether an officer's violation of his department's internal procedures is negligent per se. We could have answered "no" without addressing local ordinances that have the force of law. Moreover, the cited authorities contradict the proposition that only violations of statewide standards constitute negligence per se. In *Jorgensen*, we considered whether the defendant's failure to follow a standard in a private construction safety code was negligence per se. We said,

> Statutes *and ordinances* such as these under discussion are a legislative prescription of a suitable precaution, or a fixing by law of the standard of care

> which is required under the circumstances, and it must follow that a failure to observe the standard of care thus fixed by law is negligence.

Id. (emphasis added. We ultimately held breach of the private safety code did not establish negligence per se, but we noted four times in that opinion that an ordinance may serve as the basis for negligence per se. Similarly, the Restatement (Second) of Torts expressly includes ordinances as a basis for a standard of care, the violation of which is negligent per se. The Restatement (Third) of Torts continues to recognize that the violation of a local ordinance is negligence per se. *See* Restatement (Third) of Torts: Liab. for Physical & Emotional Harm § 14 cmt. a, at 154–55 (Am. Law Inst.2010) ("This Section most frequently applies to statutes adopted by state legislatures, but equally applies to regulations adopted by state administrative bodies, ordinances adopted by local councils, and federal statutes as well as regulations promulgated by federal agencies.").

In *Wiersgalla v. Garrett*, we reiterated the governing standard as follows:

> [I]f a statute or regulation ... provides a rule of conduct specifically designed for the safety and protection of a certain class of persons, and a person within that class receives injuries as a proximate result of a violation of the statute or regulation, the injuries "would be actionable, as ... negligence per se." To be actionable as such, however, "the harm for which the action is brought must be of the kind which the statute was intended to prevent; and the person injured, in order to recover, must be within the class which [the statute] was intended to protect."

486 N.W.2d 290, 292 (Iowa 1992) (citations omitted) (quoting Koll, 253 N.W.2d at 270). We hold this standard applies equally to municipal ordinances.

The ordinance at issue here requires forty-two-inch high guardrails on second-floor or higher balconies. The obvious purpose for requiring a forty-two-inch high guardrail on balconies above ground level is to protect persons from getting killed or injured falling off the balcony. Shannon clearly was within the scope of persons intended to be protected from injury by the municipal ordinance. The requirement is sufficiently specific to prescribe a standard of care the violation of which constitutes negligence per se.

...

We see no good reason to limit application of the negligence per se doctrine to laws of statewide application. The negligence per se doctrine also applies to local ordinances. We next address whether the district court correctly instructed the jury that CM Holdings violated the ordinance as a matter of a law.

B. Does the Jury Instruction on Negligence Per Se Require a New Trial? CM Holdings argues it was entitled to a directed verdict because the grandfather provision in the ordinance applies as a matter of law to permit the thirty-two-inch guardrails, or alternatively, the HAB's extension of time to install forty-two-inch guardrails excused tort liability. ...

2. Was CM Holdings legally excused based on the HAB's extension? CM Holdings moved for a directed verdict and JNOV on grounds the HAB's extension of time to allow installation of forty-two-inch guardrails excused tort liability. The district court correctly concluded the extension merely suspended enforcement of the administrative penalty and did not excuse tort liability.

"The legal excuse doctrine allows a person to avoid the consequences of a particular act or type of conduct by showing justification for acts that otherwise would be considered negligent." Rowling v. Sims, 732 N.W.2d 882, 885 (Iowa 2007). We have identified four categories of legal excuse:

> (1) anything that would make it impossible to comply with the statute or ordinance;
>
> (2) anything over which the [person] has no control which places [him or her] in a position contrary to the provisions of the statute or ordinance;
>
> (3) where the [person] is confronted by an emergency not of [his or her] own making, and by reason of such an emergency, [he or she] fails to obey the statute; and
>
> (4) where a statute specifically provides an excuse or exception.

Hagenow v. Schmidt, 842 N.W.2d 661, 673 (Iowa 2014), *overruled on other grounds by Alcala*, 880 N.W.2d at 708 & n. 3. A jury may only be instructed on the category of legal excuse that is supported by the evidence.

CM Holdings relies on section 60-101(3): "The housing appeals board shall ... [r]ule on requests for additional time, provided that the granting of such additional time does not endanger the life, health or safety of the occupants or the integrity of the structure." Des Moines, Iowa, Municipal Code § 60-101(3). An extension for time under this section does not specifically excuse the violation. A request for time is made when the HAB has determined there has been a violation of the housing code. The notice granting an extension of time explicitly states the Grand Stratford Apartments are in violation of the housing code. The suspension of a fine and extra time to complete repairs does not mean the property complies with the code during the time allowed. To the contrary, the notice states, "The property was not brought into compliance" with the code.

CM Holdings cites no case holding that an agency's extension of time to remedy code violations provides the property owner a legal excuse in a third party's tort action arising from the violation. We affirm the district court's ruling rejecting CM Holdings' legal excuse.

3. Did the district court correctly rule the grandfather provision did not apply as a matter of law? CM Holdings argues the forty-two-inch guardrail requirement in the current municipal code did not apply to the Grand Stratford Apartments based on the grandfather provision in the housing code. [The court held that on remand, the parties may litigate the grandfather issue.]

IV. Conclusion.

For those reasons, we vacate the decision of the court of appeals and reverse the district court's post-trial rulings on the doctrine of negligence per se. We affirm the district court's ruling rejecting the legal-excuse doctrine. We remand this case for a new trial consistent with this opinion. Costs shall be assessed equally to the plaintiffs and the defendant.

Notes

Why negligence per se? "[A] court applying the doctrine of negligence per se substitutes the standard of conduct contained in the statute for the general standard of ordinary care, streamlining the fact-finder's breach determination." Barry L. Johnson, *Why Negligence Per Se Should Be Abandoned*, 20 N.Y.U. J. Legis. & Pub. Pol'y 247, 260 (2017). Why should this be the case? One argument is that "a reasonably prudent person should, by definition, follow the standards of conduct embodied in legislative commands." *Id.* at 259. But is that always right? In a minority of jurisdictions, violation of a statute is merely *some* evidence of breach, rather than conclusive evidence of breach. A jury is free to conclude that the defendant's conduct was nonetheless reasonable despite the violation of the statute. *Id.* at 261.

Divining legislative purpose. The principle of negligence per se forces a court to inquire into the purpose of the legislature or other rulemaking body. The obvious starting point is the statutory language itself. But there may be other potential clues as to the purpose underlying a statute, ordinance, or regulation. Imagine that Alice was driving her car at a lawful speed in the Iowa countryside when a boar—an uncastrated male pig—ran out in front of her car. Alice had no time to avoid a collision. Alice suffered injuries as a result of the collision and sued the owner of the boar. An 1898 Iowa criminal statute titled "Male animals running at large" provides, "The owner of any stallion, jack, bull, boar, or buck shall restrain the same, and any person may take possession of any such animal running at large." The owner of the boar that collided with Alice's car was in violation of the statute. Applying the test from *Winger*, does this violation amount to negligence per se?

Excuse. Section 288A(2) lists a series of related, but slightly different set of excuses to a violation of a statute than those listed in *Winger*:

(a) the violation is reasonable because of the actor's incapacity;

(b) he neither knows nor should know of the occasion for compliance;

(c) he is unable after reasonable diligence or care to comply;

(d) he is confronted by an emergency not due to his own misconduct.

(e) compliance would involve a greater risk of harm to the actor or to others.

Causation. Note that a finding of negligence per se is not a finding of liability per se. A plaintiff still must prove that the defendant's negligence was a cause in fact and proximate cause of the plaintiff's damages. For example, in one case, the court assumed that the defendant's illegal sale of ammunition to a person under the age of 21 was negligence per se, but not the proximate cause of the individual's use of the ammunition to commit suicide. Rains v. Bend of the River, 124 S.W.3d 580 (Tenn. 2003); *see also* Groover v. Johnston, 625 S.E.2d 406 (Ga. Ct. App. 2006) (concluding that even though negligence per was established in a medical malpractice action, summary judgment in favor of the plaintiff was not appropriate because a plaintiff still must prove proximate cause).

Problem 4.2. In addition to her common law negligence claim, Adrian has alleged negligence per se against Darren. Adrian points to a local ordinance that references stairways. Specifically, one section of the ordinance provides that a landlord "must maintain all exit stairways in sound condition and in a reasonably good state of maintenance and repair." Another section provides that "all exit stairways of four or more risers shall have at least one handrail and all stairways which are five feet or more in width, or which are open on both sides, shall have a handrail on each side." The stairway in question has eight risers and is two feet wide. Other sections in the ordinance address "unobstructed egress and ingress" in apartment complexes. The ordinance was enacted after a tragic fire in an apartment complex some years ago, which resulted in the deaths of several people. The victims were overcome by smoke in an apartment building while attempting to flee a fire when they came down the stairs and the door to the street opened inward rather than outward.

Can Adrian successfully assert negligence per se against Darren in order to establish the breach requirement?

3. Industry Custom

Cruz v. New York City Transit Authority

136 A.D.2d 196 (N.Y. Sup. Ct. App. Div. 1988)

BRACKEN, J.

In this personal injury action, the trial court determined, at the close of the plaintiffs' case, that the defendant was entitled to a judgment against the plaintiff as a matter of law. We reverse, and grant a new trial.

I

The pertinent trial evidence may be briefly summarized. While waiting for a friend to join him on the landing of an exterior stairway leading to the token booth and turnstile area of the Elderts Lane elevated station of the Jamaica Avenue subway line, the plaintiff Robert Cruz lifted himself up and sat on the landing's 43-inch-high railing. As Cruz sat, a number of young people began to climb the stairway. One of these youths "brushed" against Cruz, who fell to the sidewalk below. His resultant injuries have rendered him quadriplegic.

In addition, the plaintiffs adduced expert testimony from an engineer who was of the opinion that the stairway and railing in question had not been designed in accordance with good and accepted engineering principles. According to the witness, the platform was approximately seven feet above the sidewalk and the railing was an additional 43 inches in height. Thus, the railing should have been designed to preclude persons from sitting upon it, by increasing its height to four feet, or by dimpling it or placing spikes along its length to make it difficult to sit upon or by placing a wire mesh screen above the railing extending to the roof over the stairway. However, the trial court would not permit the witness to testify regarding whether such design features had been implemented either at the elevated subway station in question or at other elevated subway stations within the city, including those within close proximity to the station in question. . . .

[T]he trial court erred in precluding the plaintiffs from adducing testimony from their expert pertaining to the design and construction of exterior stairways at other elevated subway stations in the city, including those in close proximity to the scene of the accident. Proof of a generally accepted practice, custom or usage within a particular trade or industry is admissible as tending to establish a standard of care, and proof of a departure from that general custom or usage may constitute evidence of negligence. Of course, it need not be shown that the particular custom or usage is universally observed, so long as it is fairly well defined within the particular field. There must exist, however, an identity of conditions, so that the particular custom or usage is applicable to the circumstances of the case at hand. Thus, the plaintiffs in this case should have been afforded the opportunity to establish that there existed an accepted practice with respect to the railing design both at the elevated station in question and on similar exterior stairways at other elevated subway stations in the city, and the trial court was unduly restrictive in precluding such testimony.

The T.J. Hooper

60 F.3d 737 (2d Cir. 1932)

L. HAND, Circuit Judge.

The barges No. 17 and No. 30, belonging to the Northern Barge Company, had lifted cargoes of coal at Norfolk, Virginia, for New York in March, 1928. They were towed by two tugs of the petitioner, the "Montrose" and the "Hooper," and were lost off the Jersey Coast on March tenth, in an easterly gale. The cargo owners sued the barges under the contracts of carriage; the owner of the barges sued the tugs . . . All the suits were joined and heard together, and the judge found that all the vessels were unseaworthy; the tugs, because they did not carry radio receiving sets by which they could have seasonably got warnings of a change in the weather which should have caused them to seek shelter in the Delaware Breakwater en route. . . .

The weather bureau at Arlington broadcasts two predictions daily, at ten in the morning and ten in the evening. Apparently there are other reports floating about, which come at uncertain hours but which can also be picked up. The Arlington report of the morning read as follows: "Moderate north, shifting to east and southeast winds, increasing Friday, fair weather to-night." The substance of this, apparently from another source, reached a tow bound north to New York about noon, and, coupled with a falling glass, decided the master to put in to the Delaware Breakwater in the afternoon.

[T]he 'Montrose' and the "Hooper" would have had the benefit of the evening report from Arlington had they had proper receiving sets. This predicted worse weather . . . The master of the "Montrose" himself, when asked what he would have done had he received a substantially similar report, said that he would certainly have put in. The master of the "Hooper" was also asked for his opinion, and said that he would have turned back also . . .

. . . It is not fair to say that there was a general custom among coastwise carriers so to equip their tugs. One line alone did it; as for the rest, they relied upon their crews, so far as they can be said to have relied at all. An adequate receiving set suitable for a coastwise tug can now be got at small cost and is reasonably reliable if kept up; obviously it is a source of great protection to their tows. Twice every day they can receive these predictions, based upon the widest possible information, available to every vessel within two or three hundred miles and more. Such a set is the ears of the tug to catch the spoken word, just as the master's binoculars are her eyes to see a storm signal ashore.

Is it then a final answer that the business had not yet generally adopted receiving sets? There are, no doubt, cases where courts seem to make the general practice of the calling the standard of proper diligence; we have indeed given some currency to the notion ourselves. Indeed in most cases reasonable prudence is in fact common prudence; but strictly it is never its measure; a whole calling may have unduly lagged in the adoption of new and available devices. It never may set its own tests, however persuasive be its usages. Courts must in the end say what is required; there are precautions so imperative that even their universal disregard will not excuse their omission. But here there was no custom at all as to receiving sets; some had them, some did not; the most that can be urged is that they had not yet become general. Certainly in such a case we need not pause; when some have thought a device necessary, at least we may say that they were right, and the others too slack.

Notes

The role of custom. "Custom is relevant in determining the standard of care because it illustrates what is feasible [and] it suggests a body of knowledge of which the defendant should be aware . . . ." Darling v. Charleston Community Memorial Hospital, 211 N.E.2d 253, 257 (Ill. 1965). Part C7 below examines the role that custom plays in cases involving alleged negligence on the part of professionals, such as doctors.

Expert testimony. In order to establish that a custom exists within an industry or field, the plaintiff may need to introduce the testimony of an expert in that field. Under Rule 702 of the Federal Rules of Evidence, if "specialized knowledge will assist the trier of fact to understand the evidence or to determine a fact in issue, a witness qualified as an expert by knowledge, skill, experience, training, or education, may testify thereto in the form of an opinion or otherwise." This testimony may even include an opinion as to "an ultimate issue to be decided by the trier of fact." (*E.g.*, "In my opinion, the defendant did not exercise reasonable care.")

Wal-Mart Stores, Inc. v. Wright

774 N.E.2d 891 (Ind. 2002)

BOEHM, Justice.

Factual and Procedural Background

Ruth Ann Wright sued for injuries she sustained when she slipped on a puddle of water at the "Outdoor Lawn and Garden Corral" of the Carmel Wal-Mart. Wright alleged Wal-Mart was negligent in the maintenance, care and inspection of the premises, and Wal-Mart asserted contributory negligence. By stipulation of the parties, a number of Wal-Mart's employee documents assembled as a "Store Manual" were admitted into evidence at the jury trial that followed....

At the end of the trial, Wright tendered the following instruction:

> There was in effect at the time of the Plaintiff's injury a store manual and safety handbook prepared by the Defendant, Wal-Mart Stores, Inc., and issued to Wal-Mart Store, Inc. employees. You may consider the violation of any rules, policies, practices and procedures contained in these manuals and safety handbook along with all of the other evidence and the Court's instructions in deciding whether Wal-Mart was negligent.
>
> The violation of its rules, policies, practices and procedures are a proper item of evidence tending to show the degree of care recognized by Wal-Mart as ordinary care under the conditions specified in its rules, policies, practices and procedures.

Wal-Mart objected on the ground that "you can set standards for yourself that exceed ordinary care and the fact that you've done that shouldn't be used, as this second paragraph says, as evidence tending to show the degree that you believe is ordinary. The jury decides what ordinary care is." The court overruled the objection and the tendered instruction became Final Instruction 17....

The jury found Wal-Mart liable and assessed Wright's total damages at $600,000, reduced to $420,000 by 30% comparative fault attributed to Wright. Wal-Mart appealed, contending that the second paragraph of Final Instruction 17 was an improper statement of law that incorrectly altered the standard of care from an objective one to a subjective one. The Court of Appeals affirmed ...

... When an instruction is challenged as an incorrect statement of the law, ... appellate review of the ruling is de novo. Here, Wal-Mart argues that the second paragraph of Final Instruction 17 incorrectly stated the law because it invited jurors to apply Wal-Mart's subjective view of the standard of care as evidenced by the Manual, rather than an objective standard of ordinary care. Wright responds that the paragraph simply allows jurors to consider Wal-Mart's subjective view of ordinary care as some evidence of what was in fact ordinary care, and does not convert the objective standard to a subjective one. The Court of Appeals agreed with Wright, holding that the paragraph was proper because it "did not require the jury to find that ordinary care, as recognized by Wal-Mart, was the standard to which Wal-Mart should be held," and because the trial court had not "instructed the jury that reasonable or ordinary care was anything other than that of a reasonably, careful and ordinarily prudent person."

I. Work Rules as Standards of Ordinary Care

Initially, we note that implicit in each of these positions, and explicit in the second paragraph of the instruction, is the assumption that the Manual in fact "tend[s] to show the degree of care recognized by Wal-Mart as ordinary care under the conditions specified in [the Manual]." Wal-Mart also objected to this assumption, contending "you can set standards for yourself that exceed ordinary care and the fact that you've done that shouldn't be used, as this second paragraph says, as evidence tending to show the degree that you believe is ordinary." We agree. The second paragraph of the instruction told the jurors that because Wal-Mart has established certain rules and policies, those rules and policies are evidence of the degree of care recognized by Wal-Mart as ordinary care. But Wal-Mart is correct that its rules and policies may exceed its view of what is required by ordinary care in a given situation. Rules and policies in the Manual may have been established for any number of reasons having nothing to do with safety and ordinary care, including a desire to appear more clean and neat to attract customers, or a concern that spills may contaminate merchandise.

The law has long recognized that failure to follow a party's precautionary steps or procedures is not necessarily failure to exercise ordinary care. 57A Am.Jur.2d Negligence § 187 at 239 (1998) (failure to follow company rule does not constitute negligence per se; jury may consider rule, but rule does not set standard of conduct establishing what law requires of a reasonable person under the circumstances); 1 Dan B. Dobbs, The Law of Torts § 165 (2000) (defendant's rules or practices are evidence bearing on the reasonable care issue, but do not ordinarily count as the standard of care; limiting instruction may be required, advising jury that rules cannot set a higher duty than is required by law) ... We think this rule is salutary because it encourages following the best practices without necessarily establishing them as a legal norm.

II. Ordinary Care as an Objective Standard

There is a second problem with the instruction. Even if the Manual reflected Wal-Mart's subjective view of ordinary care, the second paragraph of the instruction incorrectly states the law because it invites jurors to apply Wal-Mart's subjective view—as evidenced by the Manual—rather than an objective standard of ordinary care. It is axiomatic that in a negligence action "[t]he standard of conduct which the community demands must be an external and objective one, rather than the individual judgment, good or bad, of the particular actor." W. Page Keeton et al., *Prosser & Keeton on the Law of Torts* § 32, at 173–74 & n. 3 (5th ed.1984) . . . An individual "actor's belief that he is using reasonable care is immaterial." Keeton, *supra*, § 32, at 174 n. 3. This door swings both ways. A defendant's belief that it is acting reasonably is no defense if its conduct falls below reasonable care. Similarly, a defendant's belief that it should perform at a higher standard than objective reasonable care is equally irrelevant. As one court succinctly put it, "a party's own rules of conduct are relevant and can be received into evidence with an express caution that they are merely evidentiary and not to serve as a legal standard." Mayo v. Publix Super Mkts., Inc., 686 So.2d 801, 802 (Fla.Dist.Ct.App.1997).

. . . We conclude that the second paragraph of Final Instruction 17 was an improper invitation to deviate from the accepted objective standard of ordinary care and therefore incorrectly stated the law.

. . .

The judgment of the trial court is reversed. This action is remanded for a new trial.

Problem 4.3. Recall from Problem 4.1 that the linoleum outside of Adrian's apartment was 12 years old. There are numerous trade publications and landlord discussion groups on the Internet that landlords like Darren can turn to for advice. Nearly all of these sources suggest that the lifespan of linoleum flooring is five years and that flooring should be replaced at this time. Can Adrian use this fact to establish Darren's breach of duty in her negligence case?

4. Minors

Schomp v. Wilkens by Leen

501 A.2d 1036 (N.J. Super. Ct. 1985)

LONG, J.A.D.

Here plaintiffs, Gregory Schomp and his father, John, challenge a trial court judgment entered upon a jury verdict of no cause for action in connection with the complaint they instituted against David Wilkens.[2] The complaint alleged that Greg-

2. David Wilkens, a minor, was represented in this action by his guardian ad litem, Philip Leen. His parents, Frederick and Virginia Wilkens were named as co-defendants in the complaint but

ory was injured in a bicycle collision as a result of the negligence of David Wilkens who was riding the other bicycle involved in the accident. Answers were filed and the case proceeded to trial where the following facts were established.

On June 16, 1981 Gregory Schomp, who was then 17 ½ years old, was riding his bicycle near his home in Watchung. Proceeding down Washington Drive, he made a right turn onto Scott Drive which is in a recently developed residential area. There were no cars travelling on the street or parked between the corner of Washington Drive and the scene of the accident. Gregory was riding about two feet from the curb and looking straight ahead. He estimated his speed to be approximately 10 m.p.h. As he rode down a slight decline, gently applying his brakes to maintain a constant speed, he was struck by the bicycle ridden by David Wilkens who was exiting his driveway on Scott Drive. As a result of the collision Gregory was injured. The Wilkens' driveway declines sharply to the street. There is sufficient foliage surrounding the Wilkens' driveway to prevent a clear view of it on approach from Washington Drive. Gregory testified that he neither saw David approach nor heard any kind of warning. David presented no evidence at trial. The trial judge instructed the jury, over the Schomps' objection, that the standard of care for a minor is that exercised by a person of similar age, judgment and experience. He declined to charge the jury, as requested by the Schomps on the effects of violation of the motor vehicle statutes relevant to the situation. The jury returned a verdict of no cause for action and this appeal ensued in which the Schomps claim that a reversal is warranted because the trial judge erroneously instructed the jury as to the applicable standard of care, improperly declined to charge violations of the motor vehicle statutes as evidence of negligence and because the verdict was against the weight of the evidence.

We begin with the Schomps' claim that the trial judge erred when he described the standard of care applicable to this case: "... the law tells us that the degree of care required of a child is such as is usually exercised by a person of similar age, judgment and experience." We view this instruction as entirely proper. In this respect, we conceive the Schomps' reliance on *Goss v. Allen*, 70 N.J. 442, 360 A.2d 388 (1976) to be misplaced. In *Goss*, the plaintiff was injured in a skiing accident with a 17 year old skier. Faced with the question of the standard of care applicable to the minor skier, the Appellate Division ruled that because skiing is an adult activity, an adult standard of care is appropriate. The Supreme Court reversed holding that while "certain activities engaged in by minors [for example, hunting, driving, operating a boat] are so potentially hazardous as to require that the minor be held to an adult standard of care ..." [70 N.J. at 447, 360 A.2d 388] skiing, as a recreational activity engaged in by persons of all ages, is governed in each individual case by the standard applicable to the age of the person so engaged. The Schomps here contend that

---

were dismissed by the trial judge at the end of plaintiffs' proofs. That dismissal is not the subject of this appeal.

bicycle riding is a "hazardous" activity as described in *Goss* and urge that because of the hazard the standard which ordinarily would have applied to David as a minor should have been replaced by an adult standard. We reject this argument. Bicycling is an ordinary recreational activity engaged in by persons at every stage of life from babyhood to old age. As is true with other relatively innocuous activities it is, of course, possible to ride a bicycle in a dangerous manner. Generally, however, bicycling is viewed as a safe method of exercise and recreation. To accept the Schomps' view of bicycling as hazardous within the intendment of *Goss* would require us to conclude that it is more dangerous than skiing, a quantum leap we are not prepared to venture. In our view it is not such a hazardous activity to warrant application of an adult standard.

Nor are we persuaded to the contrary by the Schomps' argument that in analyzing this issue it is critical to consider the provisions of N.J.S.A. 39:4-14.1 which require bicyclists to obey the motor vehicle statutes. . . .

Although no New Jersey court has ever addressed this precise issue, the courts in several other jurisdictions have been faced with the question of the interplay of a statute applying the rules of the road to bicycling and the question of the appropriate standard of care for a child bicyclist. In *Williams v. Gilbert*, 239 Ark. 935, 395 S.W.2d 333 (Sup.Ct.1965) a seven year old plaintiff was injured when his bicycle was struck by defendant's pick-up truck in Arkansas which has a statute virtually identical to N.J.S.A. 39:4-14.1. The Supreme Court of Arkansas ruled that nothing in the statute required the same treatment of an offender whether he be an adult or a child. Although a minor driving the motor vehicle would be held to an adult standard of care, the court noted that automobiles pose an inherent risk to others, while a bicycle "poses no threat of serious injury to anyone except the child himself." *Id.* Similarly, in *Ransom v. Melegi*, 18 Mich App. 476, 171 N.W.2d 482 (Ct.App.1969), the issue was the standard of care governing the behavior of a 12 year old bicyclist who was struck by defendant's car. A state statute similar to N.J.S.A. 39:4-14.1 was also implicated. The defendant argued, as do the Schomps, that this was a legislative expression of the dangerousness of bicycling which required that the child be tested by an adult standard of care. The Court of Appeals of Michigan disagreed: "The statute does not purport to change the standard by which a child's care is to be measured. It merely imposes upon a bicyclist the so-called 'rules of the road' which govern a driver's rights and duties." In each of these cases the appropriate standard of care was held to be that of a child of similar age, experience and judgment under similar circumstances. It should be noted that both Williams and Ransom were cited with approval in *Goss* and there is no contrary authority in any jurisdiction. Rather the great weight of authority supports the application of the child's standard of care to a minor bicyclist. . . .

In sum, we are satisfied that the trial judge properly charged the jury that David Wilkens' conduct was to be evaluated by the standard applicable to a person of "similar age, judgment and experience."

Notes

The adult standard of care. The *Restatement* frames the issue in *Schomp* as whether "the child is engaging in a dangerous activity that is characteristically undertaken by adults." Restatement (Third) of Torts § 10(a) (2005). In which of the following situations would a 12-year-old be held to the adult standard of care?

- The minor uses a pistol for target practice.
- The minor goes hunting with his parents with a rifle.
- The minor plays golf.
- The minor rides a motorized dirt bike in an open field.
- The minor rides a motorized dirt bike on the highway.

Justification for the rule? Why is a minor who engages in a dangerous activity that is characteristically undertaken by adults held to the standard of a reasonable adult?

Minors incapable of negligence. A number of jurisdictions have adopted "the rule of sevens" with respect to a minor's negligence. Children under the age of 7 are legally deemed to be incapable of negligence. There is a rebuttable presumption that children between the ages of 7 and 14 are incapable of negligence, and a rebuttable presumption that children over the age of 14 *are* capable of negligence.

5. Other Special Characteristics of the Actor

In deciding whether an individual exercised the care of a reasonable person under the circumstances, there may be special characteristics of the individual that must be considered. There are other characteristics that are generally not taken into account in deciding whether the individual acted reasonably.

a. Characteristics That Are Taken into Account

i. Special skills or knowledge. If an individual has special skills or knowledge beyond that possessed by most people, those skills or knowledge should be taken into account when assessing whether the individual exercised reasonable care under the circumstances. Restatement (Third) of Torts § 12 (2010). This rule most obviously applies in cases where the individual engages in a profession or trade requiring special skill. But it may apply in other situations as well. *See* Cerny v. Cedar Bluffs Junior/Senior Public School, 628 N.W.2d 697 (Neb. 2001) (holding that standard of care regarding diagnosis of injury owed by members of coaching staff was that of a reasonably prudent person holding a state teaching certificate with a coaching endorsement).

ii. Superior mental or physical abilities. The reasonable person standard assumes that the reasonable person comes equipped with some basic level of attention, perception, memory, knowledge, intelligence, and judgment when it comes to perceiving and responding to risks. But "[i]f the actor has in fact more than the minimum of these qualities, he is required to exercise the superior qualities that he has in a manner reasonable under the circumstances." Restatement (Second) of Torts § 289 cmt. m (1965). Under what circumstances might this rule come into play? Likewise, an actor is expected to utilize whatever superior physical qualities the actor may have where reasonable under the circumstances. *Id.* § 289 cmt. c.

iii. Involuntary intoxication. The reasonable person is sober. "In a rare case, a person might be the victim of involuntary intoxication." Restatement (Third) of Torts § 12 cmt. c (2010). In such cases, the individual's intoxication is taken into account, and the individual is not held to the standard of a reasonable sober person under the circumstances.

iv. Physical impairments. The fact that an individual has a physical impairment is taken into account when determining whether the individual exercised reasonable care. Thus, a person with a physical impairment must live up to the standard of care of a person with the same impairment. *See* Poyner v. Loftus, 694 A.2d 69 (D.C. 1997) (holding as a matter of law that legally blind pedestrian, injured after falling from an elevated walkway, failed to exercise reasonable care by not walking with a service animal or using a cane).

b. Characteristics That Are Not Taken into Account

i. Voluntary intoxication. In *Davies v. Butler*, 602 P.2d 605 (Nev. 1979), the decedent was undergoing the final initiation ritual of a "social drinking club." The initiation rule required new members to consume massive quantities of alcohol. Davies died from alcohol poisoning during the ritual. In defending against the parents' wrongful death action, the members of the club argued that Davies was himself comparatively negligent in voluntarily consuming the alcohol. And citing the well-established rule that an individual's voluntary intoxication is not taken into account when assessing whether the individual acted reasonably, the defendants argued Davies had acted negligently. However, the Nevada Supreme Court held that, under the circumstances, the trial court erred in instructing the jury under the circumstances that "(i)ntoxication is no excuse for failure to act as a reasonably prudent person would act. A person who is intoxicated or under the influence of intoxicating liquor is held to the same standard of care as a sober person." *Id.* at 612. Do you agree with the court's decision?

ii. Mental and emotional impairments. In contrast to its treatment of physical impairments, tort law typically does not take into account the fact that an individual has some type of mental or emotional impairment. Restatement (Third) of Torts § 12(c). For example, the fact that an individual has advanced Alzheimer's disease is not taken into account when determining whether the individual acted reasonably under the circumstances. *See, e.g.*, Colman v. Notre Dame Convalescent Home, Inc., 968 F. Supp. 809 (D. Conn. 1997). Why are the rules different for physical impairments versus mental ones? One older justification that is still sometimes asserted is that "if mental defectives are to live in the world they should pay for the damage they do, and that it is better that their wealth, if any, should be used to compensate innocent victims than that it should remain in their hands." Restatement (Second) of Torts § 283B cmt. b (1964). Other, somewhat less offensive, justifications have also been offered. There are concerns over fakery and proof as to the existence of an impairment, for example. There is also the concern that there is no practical way to draw a satisfactory line "between mental deficiency and those variations of temperament, intellect, and emotional balance which cannot, as a practical matter, be taken into account in imposing liability for damage done." *Id.* This might explain tort law's decision to ignore less severe forms of mental or emotional issues, but does it sufficiently explain the refusal to consider serious, diagnosable conditions with clearly physiological root causes in determining breach of duty? *See generally* Kristin Harlow, *Applying the Reasonable Person Standard to Psychosis: How Tort Law Unfairly Burdens Adults with Mental Illness*, 68 Ohio St. L.J. 1733 (2007).

Note that this rule has also been applied in the case of sudden, unexpected mental disorders. *See* Bashi v. Wodarz, 53 Cal. Rptr. 2d 635 (Ct. App. 1996) (involving car accident where driver experienced an "unanticipated onset of mental illness" just prior to the collision). In contrast, if an individual had a sudden, unanticipated heart attack, the fact that the individual was suffering from a heart attack would be taken into account in assessing whether the individual acted reasonably.

iii. Gender, race, and similar characteristics. Reviewing studies in the field, one author notes that there is "mounting evidence that gender, race, and other cultural factors shape our perceptions of risk." Martha Chamallas, *Gaining Some Perspective in Tort Law: A New Take on Third-Party Criminal Attack Cases*, 14 Lewis & Clark L. Rev. 1351, 1367 (2010). In the case of sexual harassment claims brought under employment discrimination statutes, for example, courts have been receptive to the idea of considering whether a "reasonable woman" would have perceived the conduct in question as harassing. In contrast, tort law has generally not been willing to depart from the traditional generic "reasonable *person*" standard. Should it? For example, would it be surprising for a woman to perceive a risk of physical harm in a situation in which the average male would not? For a woman to perceive a risk of physical harm in a situation in which the average male would not? If not, should that difference be taken into account when assessing the reasonableness of the response to that perceived threat?

6. Establishing Breach: Circumstantial Evidence and *Res Ipsa Loquitur*

With all of the cases thus far in this chapter, the plaintiffs have had enough evidence from which they could easily construct a theory as to why the defendants should be found to have breached a duty. The jury might believe the defendant's version of the facts over the plaintiff's or find that the defendant's actions were not negligent, but there was at least enough evidence that a jury was not asked to engage in rank speculation as to what had transpired. Sometimes, however, the plaintiff lacks clear evidence as to what happened, let alone whether the defendant was negligent.

a. Circumstantial Evidence

Byrne v. Wal-Mart Stores, Inc.

877 So. 2d 462 (Miss. Ct. App. 2004)

MYERS, J., for the Court.

The undisputed facts in this case are that Byrne was shopping in Wal-Mart on April 8, 1998. While walking through the ladies' apparel department on her way to the front of the store, Byrne stepped on an unidentified substance, thought to be a cookie, causing her to injure her back and knee. Byrne filed suit against Wal-Mart and two employees, Andrew Lightsey, Wal-Mart's manager, and Jane Doe on November 7, 2000. On June 17, 2002, a motion for summary judgment was made by the defendants. The trial court considered arguments from both sides and subsequently granted the defendants' motion for summary judgment. Finding no genuine issue of material fact and that the defendants are entitled to a judgment as a matter of law, we affirm.

This cause of action is one of negligence, particularly premises liability. The standard of proof for this type of action was outlined in the case of *Downs v. Choo*, 656 So.2d 84, 86 (Miss.1995). According to *Downs*, in order to succeed in a premises liability action, the plaintiff must prove one of three things: (1) a negligent act by the defendant caused the plaintiff's injury; or, (2) that defendant had actual knowledge of a dangerous condition, but failed to warn the plaintiff of the danger; or, (3) the dangerous condition remained long enough to impute constructive knowledge to the defendant.

[There was no evidence to support the first two theories.] Constructive knowledge is imputed to the store by a showing of the length of time the dangerous condition existed prior to the plaintiff's injury. Based on the length of time the condition was present, the store owner exercising reasonable care should have known of its existence. There was no proof offered by Byrne on this matter either. She stated in her deposition that she did not know how long the cookie had been on the floor and that she did not take a good look to see what type of object caused her injury. Byrne failed to show that the object was on the floor long enough for the defendants to have notice and remedy the situation.

... Byrne asserts that the trial court committed error by failing to apply the "mode of operation" theory to the present case. Byrne relies on the case of *Merritt v. Wal-Mart Stores, Inc.*, 911 F.Supp. 242 (S.D. Miss. 1995) for her argument that she did not need to prove actual or constructive notice. In her appellate brief, Byrne asserts that Mississippi has adopted a rule that when an owner of a self-service establishment has actual notice that his mode of operation creates certain risks of harm to customers, and those risks are foreseeable, it is not necessary for the plaintiff to prove notice of the hazard that caused the injury. Byrne asserts that by allowing customers to walk around its store with food, Wal-Mart is involved in a mode of operation that creates unreasonable risks for its business invitees.

Byrne's reliance on *Merritt* is misplaced because that case was decided on completely different facts. *Merritt* was a slip and fall case where the plaintiff slipped due to liquid spilled from a self-service drink area in the absence of slip-resistant mats. The court held that a jury question existed as to whether the store created an unreasonably safe condition by failing to provide non-skid mats near the drink dispenser. Byrne wants this court to extend *Merritt*'s limited holding to the entire area of the defendant's store. By accepting Byrne's argument, we would be subjecting store owners who allow customers to walk around the store with food, toys or other potentially "dangerous objects" to a strict liability standard. Even the *Merritt* case recognized a store owner's duty to business invitees as a duty of ordinary care to keep the premises in a reasonably safe condition, a negligence standard. Reasonably safe does not mean completely risk free. The evidence in this case demonstrates that Wal-Mart employees conduct safety sweeps and clean-ups to ensure that areas of the store are free from debris.

Evans v. Aydha

189 So. 3d 1225 (Miss. Ct. App. 2016)

FAIR, J., for the Court:

This is a premises-liability case. While pumping gas at JB's Convenience Store in Pontotoc, Janet Evans slipped and fell, hitting her head on the pavement. Evans sued the owner and manager, Mosleh Aydha, claiming he had failed to properly maintain the service station in a reasonably safe condition based on the presence of an oily spot on the concrete where she fell. The trial court granted JB's summary judgment after finding that there was "no evidence of what [the] spot was, how it got there, how long it had been there, or whether or not the Defendant knew or should have known about [it]." But after our own de novo review of the record, we conclude that, giving Evans the benefit of reasonable inferences, she produced sufficient circumstantial evidence to survive summary judgment. We reverse and remand.

Evans must prove either (1) that JB's negligence injured her, (2) that JB's had knowledge of the dangerous condition and failed to warn her, or (3) that the condition existed for a sufficient amount of time so that JB's should have had knowledge or notice of the condition (constructive knowledge). Evans takes the third path, alleging that she slipped and fell on a black, oily spot on the pavement, knowledge of which could be imputed to JB's based on its weathered, dirty condition.

JB's devotes much of its brief to arguing that Evans failed to show she was injured by a dangerous condition of its property in the first place. In the alternative, it contends she failed to prove the oily spot had been there long enough to constructively impart knowledge of its existence to JB's.

Evans offered the affidavit of her daughter, who said that she was notified after the accident. She went to the scene and found her mother's car still parked at the pump. She noticed a spot of "black oily residue or sludge" near the pump, where her mother had fallen. The spot was "mostly black, dirty, and it was obvious to me that the oily residue had been on the pavement for an extended period of time, at least several days." The spot "looked slippery."

. . . JB's presents a rather cursory argument that the spot described by the daughter was not necessarily the same spot upon which Evans slipped. The argument is based on the questionable assertion that the daughter's description of the spot "does not in any way match the description of the spot as testified to by Evans." Obviously, they are both black and in the same place. It is true that the daughter's description is more specific, describing it as slippery, dirty, and oily. But Evans had just fallen so hard that, it was observed, her head literally bounced off the ground and hit the pavement twice. It is certainly within the realm of reasonable inferences that the daughter was describing the same spot, and her description is more detailed because she was in a better position to make detailed observations.

As to whether the black spot observed by the daughter could have been created after the fall, it is true that the daughter did not state exactly how long it had been since her mother fell, other than it apparently occurring on the same day. But she described the spot as old, and she testified that her mother's car was still parked next to the pump when she arrived. The spot was in a rather confined space between Evans's vehicle and the pump—a place it would be unlikely for a third person to come along in the meantime and create another black spot, so long as Evans's vehicle remained parked at the pump. Evans must be given the benefit of reasonable inferences, and the inference that the two spots were one and the same is reasonable.

We are also quite convinced that the length of time the spot had existed can be reasonably inferred from the daughter's testimony describing it as "sludge," "dirty," and, in her judgment, at least a few days old. Circumstantial evidence may be used to prove the length of time a dangerous condition has existed, so long as it "creates a legitimate inference that places it beyond conjecture." In *Ducksworth v. Wal-Mart Stores Inc.*, 832 So.2d 1260, 1262 (¶ 4) (Miss.Ct.App.2002), this Court found that a directed verdict was erroneously entered for the defendant in a case where spilled liquid "was dirty, with shoe prints and cart tracks in it." Similarly, in *Moore v. Winn-Dixie Stores Inc.*, 252 Miss. 693, 697, 173 So.2d 603, 604 (1965), our supreme court reversed a directed verdict in a case where a banana peel was found after the fall to be "black in color," "soiled up," and "must have been there a little while." We are satisfied that from the daughter's description of the spot, a reasonable inference can be made that it existed long enough to place JB's on constructive notice of its existence.

Note

Direct evidence versus circumstantial evidence. Courts often draw a distinction between direct evidence and circumstantial evidence. Roughly stated, direct evidence is "[e]vidence that is based on personal knowledge or observation and that, if true, proves a fact without inference or presumption." In contrast, circumstantial evidence is "[e]vidence based on inference and not on personal knowledge or observation." State v. Silvernail, 831 N.W.2d 594, 604 (Minn. 2013) (Stras, J., concurring in part).

b. Res Ipsa Loquitur: *The Theoretical Basis for the Theory*

Byrne v. Boadle

Court of the Exchequer 1863
159 Eng. Rep. 299

At the trial before the learned Assessor of the Court of Passage at Liverpool, the evidence adduced on the part of the plaintiff was as follows: A witness named Critchley said: "On the 18th July, I was in Scotland Road, on the right side going north, defendant's shop is on that side. When I was opposite to his shop, a barrel of flour fell from a window above in defendant's house and shop, and knocked the plaintiff down. He was carried into an adjoining shop. A horse and cart came opposite the defendant's door. Barrels of flour were in the cart. I do not think the barrel was being lowered by a rope. I cannot say: I did not see the barrel until it struck the plaintiff. It was not swinging when it struck the plaintiff. It struck him on the shoulder and knocked him towards the shop. No one called out until after the accident." The plaintiff said: "On approaching Scotland Place and defendant's shop, I lost all recollection. I felt no blow. I saw nothing to warn me of danger. I was taken home in a cab. I was helpless for a fortnight." (He then described his sufferings.) "I saw the path clear. I did not see any cart opposite defendant's shop." Another witness said: "I saw a barrel falling. I don't know how, but from defendant's." The only other witness was a surgeon, who described the injury which the plaintiff had received. It was admitted that the defendant was a dealer in flour.

It was submitted, on the part of the defendant, that there was no evidence of negligence for the jury. The learned Assessor was of that opinion, and nonsuited the plaintiff, reserving leave to him to move the Court of Exchequer to enter the verdict for him with £50 damages, the amount assessed by the jury.

Littler, in the present term, obtained a rule *nisi* to enter the verdict for the plaintiff, on the ground of misdirection of the learned Assessor in ruling that there was no evidence of negligence on the part of the defendant; against which Charles Russell now shewed cause. First, there was no evidence to connect the defendant or his servants with the occurrence. . . .

Secondly, assuming the facts to be brought home to the defendant or his servants, these facts do not disclose any evidence for the jury of negligence. The plaintiff was bound to give affirmative proof of negligence. But there was not a scintilla of evidence, unless the occurrence is of itself evidence of negligence. There was not even evidence that the barrel was being lowered by a jigger-hoist as alleged in the declaration.

[Pollock, C. B. There are certain cases of which it may be said *res ipsa loquitur*, and this seems one of them. In some cases the Courts have held that the mere fact of the accident having occurred is evidence of negligence, as, for instance, in the case of railway collisions.] On examination of the authorities, that doctrine would seem to be confined to the case of a collision between two trains upon the same line, and both being the property and under the management of the same Company. [Bramwell, B. No doubt, the presumption of negligence is not raised in every case of injury from accident, but in some it is. We must judge of the facts in a reasonable way; and regarding them in that light we know that these accidents do not take place without a cause, and in general that cause is negligence.] The law will not presume that a man is guilty of a wrong. . . . There are many accidents from which no presumption of negligence can arise. [Bramwell, B. Looking at the matter in a reasonable way it comes to this—an injury is done to the plaintiff, who has no means of knowing whether it was the result of negligence; the defendant, who knows how it was caused, does not think fit to tell the jury.] Unless a plaintiff gives some evidence which ought to be submitted to the jury, the defendant is not bound to offer any defence. The plaintiff cannot, by a defective proof of his case, compel the defendant to give evidence in explanation. [Pollock, C. B. I have frequently observed that a defendant has a right to remain silent unless a prima facie case is established against him. But here the question is whether the plaintiff has not shewn such a case.] In a case of this nature, in which the sympathies of a jury are with the plaintiff, it would be dangerous to allow presumption to be substituted for affirmative proof of negligence.

Littler appeared to support the rule, but was not called upon to argue.

POLLOCK, C. B. We are all of opinion that the rule must be absolute to enter the verdict for the plaintiff. The learned counsel was quite right in saying that there are many accidents from which no presumption of negligence can arise, but I think it would be wrong to lay down as a rule that in no case can presumption of negligence arise from the fact of an accident. Suppose in this case the barrel had rolled out of the warehouse and fallen on the plaintiff, how could he possibly ascertain from what cause it occurred? It is the duty of persons who keep barrels in a warehouse to take care that they do not roll out, and I think that such a case would, beyond all doubt, afford prima facie evidence of negligence. A barrel could not roll out of a warehouse without some negligence, and to say that a plaintiff who is injured by it must call witnesses from the warehouse to prove negligence seems to me preposterous. So in the building or repairing a house, or putting pots on the chimneys, if a person passing along the road is injured by something falling upon him, I think the accident alone would be prima facie evidence of negligence. Or if an article calculated to cause damage is put in a wrong place and does mischief, I think that those whose duty it was to put it in the right place are prima facie responsible, and if there is any state of facts to rebut the presumption of negligence, they must prove them. The present case upon the evidence comes to this, a man is passing in front of the premises of a dealer in flour, and there falls down upon him a barrel of flour. I think it apparent that the barrel was in the custody of the defendant who occupied the premises, and who is responsible for the acts of his servants who had the controul of it; and in my opinion the fact of its falling is prima facie evidence of negligence, and the plaintiff who was injured by it is not bound to shew that it could not fall without negligence, but if there are any facts inconsistent with negligence it is for the defendant to prove them.

Bramwell, B. I am of the same opinion.

Notes

Distinguishing *res ipsa* cases from other circumstantial evidence cases. How does the plaintiff's evidence in *Byrne v. Boadle* (the *res ipsa* case) differ from that of the plaintiff in *Evans* (the oil case)?

Effect of *res ipsa*. In some jurisdictions, the fact that the requirements of *res ipsa* are met results in a presumption—which the defendant can attempt to rebut—that the defendant breached the duty of care. *See* Watson v. Ford Motor Co., 699 S.E.2d 169, 179 n. 7 (S.C. 2010). In others, *res ipsa* does not shift the burden of proof or create a rebuttable presumption. Instead, the court instructs the jury that it is permitted, but not required, to infer negligence on the part of the defendant. *See* Dover Elevator Co. v. Swann, 638 A.2d 762, 765 (Md. Ct. App. 1994).

Limits on the theory. Parts c and d below will explore the black-letter requirements that must be met before a court will instruct a jury with regard to the theory of *res ipsa loquitur.* But as should already be clear, the theory is potentially a powerful one for a plaintiff insofar as it may relieve the plaintiff of the burden of introducing specific evidence of negligence. Not surprisingly, courts often consider various factors in addition to the standard black-letter requirements in order to determine whether it is appropriate for *res ipsa* to apply. The following decision and the notes that follow provide examples of courts engaging in this sort of analysis before moving on to consideration of how the black-letter requirements of *res ipsa loquitur* apply in a case.

Deciutiis v. Six Flags America, LP

2017 Md. App. LEXIS 392 (Md. Ct. Spec. App. April 17, 2017)

Arthur, J.

Appellant Roxanne Deciutiis and her minor child were injured on a ride at a Six Flags amusement park. On the day on which their case was set for trial, Six Flags orally moved for judgment, arguing that Ms. Deciutiis needed an expert to explain the cause of her and her child's injuries, but did not have one. Ms. Deciutiis contended that an expert was unnecessary, because she would prove Six Flags' negligence under the doctrine of *res ipsa loquitur.*

The Circuit Court for Prince George's County granted judgment in favor of Six Flags on the ground that Ms. Deciutiis had not satisfied the conditions for invoking *res ipsa loquitur.* She appealed. We affirm.

Factual and Procedural History

A. The Penguin's Blizzard River Ride

On July 11, 2011, Ms. Deciutiis and her daughter visited the Six Flags amusement park in Mitchellville, Maryland. They decided to go on the Penguin's Blizzard River ride.

The ride is comprised of an elevated chute with rushing water and three loops. An inflated raft, carrying multiple persons, is "carried by the conveyer belt to the top of the chute[.]" From there, the raft is released into the chute. After it is released, the raft "twist[s], spin[s], [and] splash[es]" through the loops at a high rate of speed. Ultimately, the raft is deposited into a long, flat channel that leads to a "boathouse."

Multiple employees operate the ride. One employee "makes sure that [the occupants] are strapped in" with lap belts. At the top of the conveyor belt, another employee releases the raft into the rushing water in the chute, spacing the rafts "about 100 yards apart" from one another. Once the raft reaches the end of the chute and flows through the long, flat channel, a third employee guides it from the channel to the boathouse.

As the Deciutiises' raft was making its descent, the raft in front of them became stuck for some unknown reason. The rafts collided. Ms. Deciutiis sustained injuries to her neck and back, and her daughter hit her head.

B. Action for Negligence

On June 11, 2014, two years and 11 months after the incident, Ms. Deciutiis, individually and as the parent of her child, filed a complaint against Six Flags America Property Corporation in the Circuit Court for Prince George's County. The complaint alleged that Ms. Deciutiis and her daughter had suffered personal injuries because of the defendant's negligence. . . .

Discussion

I. *Res ipsa loquitur*

Res ipsa loquitur "afford[s] a plaintiff the opportunity to present a prima facie case when direct evidence of the cause of an accident is not available or is available solely to the defendant" and the circumstantial evidence permits the factfinder to infer that the defendant's negligence was the cause. Courts apply *res ipsa* only "'where the facts and circumstances and the demand of justice make its application essential[.]'"

. . .

C. Failure to Pursue Reasonably Accessible Evidence of Direct Negligence

Ms. Deciutiis made no effort to gather direct evidence of Six Flags' negligence even though that evidence was reasonably accessible. Her failure to do so precludes her from relying on *res ipsa loquitur.*

Although it would have been easy enough to require Six Flags to identify the employees who were operating the ride on the day of the accident, Ms. Deciutiis did not depose them to elicit their knowledge about how the accident occurred, let alone list them as potential witnesses. Similarly, although it would not have been exceedingly difficult to identify the patrons on the first raft or any other patrons on the Deciutiis's raft,[4] Ms. Deciutiis did not depose them to elicit their knowledge about

4. No one could reasonably expect Ms. Deciutiis to begin identifying and interviewing witnesses immediately after she and her daughter had been injured in an accident. Nonetheless,

how the accident occurred or indicate any intention to call them as witnesses. Consequently, Ms. Deciutiis adduced none of the readily accessible information about whether the first raft got stuck because it was underinflated as a result of something that Six Flags had done or failed to do; or whether a patron on the first raft had done something to stop the raft, slow its descent, or cause it to become deflated; or whether a Six Flags employee had released the Deciutiis's raft before he should have released it; or whether an employee had released the Deciutiis's raft even though he knew or should have known that the first raft had gotten stuck.

Furthermore, Ms. Deciutiis made no effort to obtain readily available information about the maintenance records for this particular ride or about Six Flags' knowledge of similar accidents on the Penguin's Blizzard River ride, whether in Mitchellville or at another Six Flags amusement park. Consequently, Ms. Deciutiis adduced none of the readily available information about whether Six Flags had notice about maintenance defects with this ride in particular or design defects with the Penguin's Blizzard River ride in general. In fact, Ms. Deciutiis offered no explanation at all about why her raft had collided with the other one....

... Ms. Deciutiis failed to pursue reasonably available information that might have assisted her in developing direct, rather than circumstantial, evidence of Six Flags' negligence. [T]herefore, the circuit court correctly concluded that Ms. Deciutiis could not proceed under a theory of *res ipsa loquitur.*

Notes

Evidentiary issues. "[R]es ipsa loquitur is a rule founded on the absence of specific proof of omissions or facts which constitute negligence." Barger v. Chelpon, 60 243 N.W. 97, 100 (S.D. 1932). "Thus, res ipsa loquitur is a rule of necessity and 'should be invoked sparingly and only when the facts and demands of justice make the application essential.'" Malloy v. Commonwealth Highland Theatres, Inc., 375 N.W.2d 631, 636 (S.D. 1985). In the typical *res ipsa* case, the court allows the plaintiff to rely upon a *res ipsa* theory to help overcome the plaintiff's lack of evidence regarding the defendant's alleged negligence. Logically, the converse should also be true: if the plaintiff has strong evidence regarding the defendant's alleged negligence, the theory of *res ipsa* is not needed and should not be available to the plaintiff. *See* Crawford v. Rogers, 406 P.2d 189, 193 (Alaska 1965) ("[I]f the evidence discloses the circumstances of the accident to the extent that there is nothing left to infer, then the doctrine of *res ipsa loquitur*, which is founded upon inference, is no longer needed."). This is most likely to be the case where the plaintiff has direct, rather than circumstantial, evidence regarding the alleged act of negligence. *See* Widmyer v. Southeast Skyways, Inc., 584 P.2d 1 (Alaska 1978).

---

entities like Six Flags frequently compile incident reports that identify witnesses and sometimes disclose what they observed. When prepared in the ordinary course of business, such reports are available in discovery.

Black-letter requirements. The excerpt from *Deciutiis* and the note above involve some of the preliminary considerations a court may undertake before moving on to consideration of the black-letter requirements of *res ipsa loquitur.* The following description of those requirements is fairly typical:

> (1) that the occurrence is one that ordinarily would not happen in the absence of negligence; and
>
> (2) that the defendant had exclusive control of the instrumentality that caused the event.

Dyback v. Weber, 500 N.E.2d 8, 12 (Ill. 1986). The rest of this section will focus on those requirements.

Problem 4.4. Assume that Adrian from the Chapter Problem attempts to rely upon *res ipsa* to establish negligence against Darren. Should the court permit her to do so?

c. Res Ipsa*: The Accident Is One That Does Not Ordinarily Occur Absent Negligence*

Eversole v. Woods Acquisition, Inc.

135 S.W.3d 425 (Mo. Ct. App. 2004)

LISA WHITE HARDWICK, Judge.

Factual and Procedural History

In July 2000, Eversole noticed antifreeze was leaking from his 1997 Ford Thunderbird. He was the original owner of the vehicle and had not previously experienced any mechanical problems with it. Eversole took the vehicle to Woods, where he learned the manufacturer had issued a recall on the engine's intake manifold from which the antifreeze was leaking. Woods replaced the intake manifold and conducted a ten-mile test drive to confirm the vehicle worked properly.

Eversole picked up the vehicle on July 5, 2000, when the repair work was completed. He drove it to work on July 6 and 7, and then used it to run a few errands on July 8. On July 9, Eversole was returning from a visit to his parents' home when he noticed flames coming from under the hood of the vehicle. He got out and called the fire department, but the fire destroyed the vehicle.

Eversole filed a lawsuit against Woods alleging alternative theories of breach of implied warranty and *res ipsa loquitur* negligence in the loss of his Thunderbird. He testified at the bench trial that he did not know what caused the vehicle to erupt in fire. Eversole had driven the vehicle 137 miles in the four days after picking it up from Woods and had no indication of a further mechanical problem until the fire broke out. . . .

After the close of evidence, the trial judge found "the issues in favor of the Plaintiff and against the Defendant." Woods was ordered to pay damages to Eversole in the amount of $12,000 for the loss of the Thunderbird. Woods appeals.

Sufficiency of Evidence on Negligence Theory

Eversole's negligence claim against Woods was based on a *res ipsa loquitur* theory. *Res ipsa* is a rule of evidence allowing a factfinder to infer from circumstantial evidence that a loss or injury arose from some negligent act of the defendant, without requiring the plaintiff to prove specific acts of negligence. To make a submissible case, plaintiff must establish that: (1) the incident causing the loss is of the kind that does not ordinarily occur in the absence of negligence; (2) the instrumentality causing the loss is under the control of the defendant; and (3) the defendant has superior knowledge about the cause of the loss. Plaintiff has the burden of proof and must establish by the greater weight of evidence that the loss resulted from defendant's negligence.

Woods contends Eversole failed to meet his burden of proof on the negligence claim because there was no substantial evidence to establish the three essential elements of a *res ipsa* theory. First, Woods argues Eversole did not produce any evidence to show that a car fire would not normally occur in the absence of negligence. This initial element requires proof that the loss occurred as a result of an "unusual" event, accident, or occurrence. Whether a given event is an unusual occurrence ordinarily resulting from negligence "is a judicial decision which is arrived at by judges applying their common experience in life to the event . . . and deciding whether the criteria for res ipsa loquitur are satisfied." City of Kennett v. Akers, 564 S.W.2d 41, 45 (Mo. banc 1978).

Woods suggests the fire incident was not unusual because "hundreds, if not thousands, of cars that catch fire each day" without negligence. Eversole's Thunderbird featured an internal combustion engine, made operational by sparks, electrical components, and highly explosive gasoline. The vehicle had been driven nearly 52,000 miles over a three-year period. Woods contends it was Eversole's burden to show that "a car with almost 60,000 miles" would not ordinarily erupt in fire in the absence of negligence.

In making this argument, Woods ignores the fact that the intake manifold repair work was an intervening factor in the circumstances leading to the fire. Eversole's burden was to show that a fuel fire would not ordinarily have occurred, given the vehicle's performance and repair history, without negligence. A party seeking to apply the doctrine of *res ipsa* need not submit facts surrounding the occurrence that exclude all reasonable hypotheses except defendant's negligence. Eversole was required to submit enough facts from which the court could conclude that, more often than not, a fire such as this one resulted from a failure to exercise reasonable care on the part of the person in charge of the automobile. If Eversole's evidence tended to show the cause of the fire, even if it left some doubt, he could not be deprived of the benefit of the *res ipsa* doctrine.

The evidence at trial was undisputed that Eversole's Thunderbird was destroyed by a fuel fire which erupted in the engine area. Just four days prior to the fire, Woods disconnected and reconnected fuel lines to the engine in the process of replacing the intake manifold. . . . Eversole had not had any trouble with the fuel lines before the repair work was performed. In light of this history, the fuel fire was an unusual event. Common life experience also suggests it would be extraordinary for fuel lines to leak and cause a major fire in a three-year old vehicle, even with 52,000 miles of use, without an intervening act of manipulation. The evidence established a reasonable inference that the fuel lines would not have ruptured in the absence of some negligence by Woods in performing the repair work.

Deciutiis v. Six Flags America, LP

2017 Md. App. LEXIS 392 (Md. Ct. Spec. App. April 17, 2017)

[See the facts and procedural history above regarding the accident on the Penguin's Blizzard River Ride. Before the court ruled that Ms. Deciutiis' failure to pursue reasonably available information precluded her ability to rely on a theory of *res ipsa loquitur*, the court considered whether the black-letter requirements of the theory were met.]

After the court granted the motion *in limine*, Six Flags made an oral motion for judgment, arguing that Ms. Deciutiis needed an expert to explain the cause of her and her daughter's injuries. Ms. Deciutiis contended that an expert was unnecessary, because she would prove Six Flags' negligence under the doctrine of *res ipsa loquitur.*

[Six Flags argued that "*res ipsa* does not apply 'in cases concerning the malfunction of complex machinery,' such as elevators, escalators, and (Six Flags argued) amusement park rides with rafts that ascend on conveyor belts and descend over running water, through a downward-sloping chute with multiple turns. In such cases, "an expert is required to testify that the malfunction is of a sort that would not occur absent some negligence."]

I. *Res ipsa loquitur*

Under the doctrine of *res ipsa loquitur*, the factfinder may draw an inference of negligence if the plaintiff proves three elements: (1) the plaintiff suffered an injury that does not ordinarily occur absent negligence; and (2) the injury was caused by an instrumentality exclusively in the defendant's control.

Res ipsa applies only when "'the circumstances attendant upon an accident are themselves of such a character as to justify a jury in inferring negligence as the cause of that accident.'" Holzhauer v. Saks & Co., 346 Md. at 338, quoting Benedick v. Potts, 88 Md. 52, 55, 40 A. 1067 (1898). "This is the case when 'the common knowledge of jurors [is] sufficient to support an inference or finding of negligence on the part of' a defendant." For example, courts have held that jurors may draw an inference of negligence when a barrel of flour falls out of a warehouse window (*id.* at

339, citing Byrne v. Boadle, 2 Hurl. & Colt. 722, 159 Eng. Rep. 299 (1863)) or where stairs collapse below a person's feet (*id.*, citing Blankenship v. Wagner, 261 Md. at 45), because it is a matter of common knowledge that such events ordinarily do not occur in the absence of someone's negligence....

B. Complex Mechanical Devices

Res ipsa loquitur applies only when jurors possess the background knowledge necessary to decide whether an event ordinarily occurs in the absence of someone's negligence. Consequently, a plaintiff may not employ *res ipsa loquitur* in cases involving injury caused by complex mechanical devices, such as elevators and escalators. As the Court of Appeals has explained:

> [W]hether an escalator is likely to stop abruptly in the absence of someone's negligence is a question that lay[persons] cannot answer based on common knowledge. The answer requires knowledge of "complicated matters" such as mechanics, electricity, circuits, engineering, and metallurgy.

Holzhauer v. Saks & Co., 346 Md. at 341.

In such cases, "'expert testimony is required to establish negligence and causation.'" Holzhauer v. Saks & Co., 346 Md. at 339, quoting Meda v. Brown, 318 Md. at 428.

In the circuit court, Six Flags likened the Penguin's Blizzard River ride to a complex mechanical device like an elevator or escalator. The circuit court agreed. So do we.

The successful design and operation of this particular ride depends on a number of scientific principles that are beyond the ken of anyone who lacks training in physics or engineering. To facilitate the descent of the rafts, the chute must be angled toward the ground, but the angle cannot be so steep as to allow the rafts to generate enough speed to overshoot the turns and fly out of the chute. Similarly, the radius of the turns cannot be so tight as to force the rafts to ride up, and possibly over, the walls. On the turns, the walls must be high enough to contain the rafts, but they cannot be banked at such a steep angle that they cause the rafts to flip over. Water must flow through the chute at a sufficient volume and rate as to keep the rafts moving, but not at such a volume or rate as to cause undue speed and acceleration. The rafts must be inflated with enough pressure to keep them afloat, but not enough to cause them to explode. The weight of the passengers cannot be so great as to cause a raft to run aground—and so on.

In view of the complex physical and mechanical principles that are involved in the design and successful operation of the Penguin's Blizzard River ride, Ms. Deciutiis could not rely on *res ipsa loquitur* to prove her prima facie case. Instead, she would have to adduce expert testimony as to negligence and causation. Because Ms. Deciutiis had no such testimony, the circuit court correctly entered judgment in Six Flags' favor.

Cox v. May Department Store Co.

903 P.2d 1119 (Ariz. Ct. App. 1995)

Factual and Procedural Background

On December 29, 1990, Janelle Cox ("Cox") was ascending the escalator at Robinson's Department Store ("Robinson's"), owned by May, when the jacket she was wearing became lodged between the escalator's moving handrail and stationary guide. This caused her to be thrown down and dragged to the top of the escalator, resulting in physical injury. Prior to the accident, Cox had noticed nothing unusual about the escalator's operation. Her jacket was not unusual and she was riding the escalator in a normal manner. Cox did not see how her jacket became caught under the handrail. [The trial court granted summary judgment in favor of the defendants.]

Discussion

...

B. *Res ipsa loquitur*

"*Res ipsa loquitur* is 'a theory of circumstantial evidence under which the jury may reasonably find negligence and causation from the fact of the accident and the defendant's relation to the accident." Ward v. Mount Calvary Lutheran Church, 178 Ariz. 350, 354, 873 P.2d 688, 692 (App.1994). A plaintiff who establishes the elements of *res ipsa loquitur* can withstand a motion for summary judgment and reach the jury without direct proof of negligence.

...

1. Likelihood of Negligence

The trial court concluded, and we agree, that this type of accident would not likely have occurred without negligence on someone's part. This first element merely requires a weighing of the probabilities of the cause of the accident. To survive summary judgment on this element, the evidence presented must be sufficient to allow the jury to infer that negligence was more likely than not the cause of the accident: "The facts must justify the conclusion that negligence is the most likely explanation for the occurrence." This issue, "in borderline cases, is properly left to the jury." Ruiz v. Otis Elevator, 146 Ariz. 98, 101, 703 P.2d 1247, 1250 (App.1985).

The jury, in turn, may find negligence based upon either its common knowledge, which generally is "past experience that is common to the community," or, where such common knowledge is lacking, through expert testimony that such an accident does not usually occur absent negligence.

We conclude that it is permissible for a trier of fact to find that the accident in the instant case would not likely have occurred without negligence. Cox was ascending the escalator in a normal fashion and wearing a normal jacket when her jacket became caught under the handrail. Its common experience with escalators would allow the jury to infer that such an accident would not occur absent the negligent design, construction, maintenance, inspection, or repair of the escalator. . . .

Note

Common sense and complexity. *Deciutiis* and *Cox* obviously disagree regarding the extent to which jurors are permitted to make their own decisions regarding the likelihood that an injury would not have occurred in the absence of negligence when it comes to "complex mechanical devices." Which court has the better view? The *Restatement* takes the position that in complex cases, an expert may be permitted to testify in order to help the jury determine whether an event usually does not occur absent negligence. Restatement (Second) of Torts § 328 cmt. d.

d. Res Ipsa*: Control of the Instrumentality*

Deciutiis v. Six Flags America, LP

2017 Md. App. LEXIS 392 (Md. Ct. Spec. App. April 17, 2017)

[See the facts and procedural history above regarding the accident on the Penguin's Blizzard River Ride. Before the court ruled that Ms. Deciutiis' failure to pursue reasonably available information precluded her ability to rely on a theory of *res ipsa loquitur*, the court considered whether the requirements of the theory were met. Six Flags contended that *res ipsa* should not apply because the theory only applies if an injury "was caused by an instrumentality exclusively in the defendant's control." According to Six Flags, it did not have exclusive control over all aspects of the ride, such as the operation of individual rafts.]

Ms. Deciutiis challenged Six Flags' contention. She asserted that Six Flags exercised exclusive control over the ride, because "they installed the ride in the park. They operated the ride. They have maintained the ride. They have people stationed [on the ride.]" . . .

I. *Res ipsa loquitur*

A. Exclusive Control

The circuit court rejected Ms. Deciutiis's reliance on *res ipsa loquitur* in part because she could not show that Six Flags had "exclusive control" over the raft with which her raft collided. Ms. Deciutiis responds that "[t]he force and speed of the water is determined by the amount of water pumped into the top of the chute, how steep the incline [is], and the number of directions it is required to follow," all of which, she says, were under Six Flags' complete control.

Ms. Deciutiis's argument fails to recognize that the occupants of the other raft also had some ability to stop the raft or to slow its descent. For example, Ms. Deciutiis does not rule out the prospect that the occupants of the other raft might have done something to deflate it. Nor does she rule out the prospect that the occupants of the other raft might have grabbed or touched the walls, particularly the walls in the long, flat channel through which the raft passes after it has descended through the chute. Simply put, Six Flags had control over some, but by no means every, aspect of the ride, because someone besides Six Flags had the ability to influence the movement of the other raft.

. . . The circuit court, therefore, did not err in entering judgment in Six Flags' favor.

Niman v. Plaza House, Inc.

471 S.W.2d 207 (Mo. 1971) (en banc)

MORGAN, Judge.

This is an action, brought under the res ipsa loquitur doctrine, for damages for personal injuries, loss of services, medical expenses and property damage. Plaintiffs received a verdict in a total amount of $25,800. Defendant have appealed. We affirm.

Factually, it appears that plaintiffs were tenants of a fifth floor apartment in an eleven-story apartment building owned by defendant Plaza House and managed by defendant Haas. On the night of December 16, 1964, plaintiffs retired. The next morning, Louis Niman awoke, got out of bed, and was shaving in the bathroom with the door closed. When Esther Niman awoke, she felt an intense heat and found the bedroom full of steam. She attempted to get out of bed, and when her feet touched the floor, it was so filled with hot water and slime that she fell on her buttocks. She suffered immediate pain and severe injuries, and the furnishings in the apartment were generally ruined.

It is agreed that the Plaza House had a hot-water heating system; that boilers in the basement heated the water; that it circulated through pipes into and out of the various apartments with the assistance of pumps, which pulled the water through the system and discharged it back into the boiler for reheating; that the radiator in plaintiffs' bedroom ran along the west side of the room under the windows; that the water circulated lengthwise through a pipe in the radiator to the southwest corner of the room, looped through a shut-off valve and two 90 ell fittings, and then ran lengthwise through a second pipe back across the west wall to the return line; that the hot water in the apartment had escaped through a ruptured portion of one of the fittings.

. . .

Did defendants have such control of the radiator as to make a res ipsa submission proper? It is agreed by all that the defendants were to provide heat for the apartment; and that they owned and maintained all portions of the heating mechanism, including the radiator in question. When defendant Haas was asked who had charge of the operation of the heating system, his answer was 'I did.' It was also conceded that tenants were to regulate the temperature in each of their particular apartments by turning the control knob and that no instructions or warnings were given that the radiator valve should not be completely closed. That a showing of the plaintiffs' possession of the apartment does not necessarily establish that they had 'control' of all appliances therein is well established. As said in *Gladden v. Walker & Dunlop, Inc.*, 83 U.S.App.D.C. 224, 168 F.2d 321, 322: "It is familiar law that a landlord who keeps control over parts of an apartment house must use reasonable care for safety. We have applied this principle to the lighting of a common entrance stairway. With regard to plumbing and heating systems, the principle extends to operative fixtures in the apartments leased to tenants and operation through them. We think the principle is equally broad with regard to the electrical system. Plumbing, heating, and electrical fixtures are not isolated either in use or maintenance. They must be maintained and used, if at all, in conjunction with the systems of which they are parts. Accordingly the tenant who uses them is usually not expected to maintain them, but only to notify the landlord when they appear to be out of order.... We think it immaterial whether the injury to appellant appears to have been caused by defects in operative fixtures or in other parts of the electric system. The law should follow custom and convenience in classifying such fixtures among the things that the landlord controls."

Basically, the same situation exists in the present case reference management and control of the heating pipe lines and radiators. The defendants owned, managed, controlled and operated the boiler system which heated the water that was circulated through the pipe lines and radiators of the apartment house. It is readily apparent that plaintiffs would have no control or even interest in such aspects of the heating system. There is no evidence, nor do defendants even suggest, that the plaintiffs had the right to alter or repair any part of the heating system, including the ruptured fitting, that was in their apartment.

Admittedly, plaintiffs had available a 'knob' to regulate the temperature in the apartment. Necessarily, when they made a temperature selection, by turning the knob, it was an accepted fact that the volume of hot water flowing through the radiator was to be affected. The knob was owned by defendants and provided for plaintiffs to allow them to use a part of the total heating system.... There is no contention that plaintiffs improperly operated the knob, nor that by turning the knob they affected the heating system in some way that was not intended. In short, all the evidence reflects that plaintiffs did precisely what the defendants expected them to do....

At trial, defendants established that the night in question was extremely cold, and that 'perhaps' plaintiffs had opened a window which caused the water to freeze and burst the ell fitting. Such evidence was not pertinent to the issue of "control" of the heating system, but only as to whether or not plaintiffs were contributorily negligent in their 'use' of it. Defendants pleaded contributory negligence, but did not submit that issue to the jury nor carry it forward in their briefs on appeal. For that reason we need not consider the effect, if any, of such evidence.

We have concluded that within the legal connotation of the word "control," as it is used in the res ipsa loquitur doctrine, the defendants had sole and exclusive control of the entire heating system and particularly that portion which ruptured and caused the damage suffered. Consistent therewith, we find that plaintiffs' cause of action was properly submitted under the res ipsa loquitur theory.

Notes

The purpose of the control requirement. What function does the requirement that the defendant have exclusive control over the instrumentality causing the harm serve? Why is it part of the test? The *Restatement (Second) of Torts* utilizes a slightly different test:

> (1) It may be inferred that harm suffered by the plaintiff is caused by negligence of the defendant when
>
> (a) the event is of a kind which ordinarily does not occur in the absence of negligence; [and]
>
> (b) other responsible causes, including the conduct of the plaintiff and third persons, are sufficiently eliminated by the evidence. . .

Restatement (Second) of Torts § 328D (1965). How are the two tests related? Would the results in *Deciutiis* and *Niman* have been the same under the *Restatement* test?

Control versus right of control. In some cases, the focus is less about whether the defendant actually had exclusive control over the instrumentality and more about whether the defendant had the *right* of control. *See, e.g.,* Weaks v. Rupp, 966 S.W.2d 387, 394–95 (Mo. App. W.D. 1998). For example, in *Hogland v. Klein*, 298 P.2d 1099 (Wash. 1956), the owner of a building hired a house mover to physically move the house. The mover supplied all of the equipment necessary to move the house, including the supporting timber. The owner and his employees were responsible for preparing the building for the move, but did so under the supervision of the mover's foreman. The mover's employees then hooked up the building to the mover's truck and began the move. Shortly thereafter, one of the supporting timbers broke, resulting in damage to the house. The mover asserted that *res ipsa loquitur* should not apply because the mover was not in physical control of the timber when the house was loaded. But according to the Washington Supreme Court, "the requirement, that the offending instrumentality be under the management and control of the defendant or his servants, does not mean actual physical control but refers rather to the right of control at the time of the accident." *Id.* at 1101.

Problem 4.5. Bill was the other tenant injured at the apartment complex owned by Darren. Bill was leaning against the metal railing on the balcony when the railing gave way, sending Bill falling 30 feet to the ground. The railing had just been replaced that same day. Darren had one of his employees replace the railings on several balconies. That employee has since moved and cannot be located. The railing has since been lost or discarded, and Darren installed a new railing a few days after Bill's fall. Bill's lawyer has been unable to gather enough evidence to determine the cause of the collapse. Bill has sued

Darren for negligence and seeks to rely on the *res ipsa loquitur* doctrine to establish the breach element. Can Bill rely upon a theory of *res ipsa loquitur* in order to satisfy the breach element?

7. Professional Negligence

Claims of professional negligence raise special issues. A claim of professional negligence (as opposed to simple or ordinary negligence) arises when there is an allegation against a professional and the professional's alleged negligence involved "the exercise of professional judgment and skill." MCG Health v. Casey, 603 S.E.2d 438, 441 (Ga. Ct. App. 2004). This section focuses primarily on the most recognizable type of professional negligence clam: medical malpractice. But many of the legal issues related to the standard of care that apply in claims against medical professionals also arise in claims against other professionals, including engineers, architects, and lawyers.

a. Establishing the Standard of Care and Breach

Custom has long played an important role in establishing the standard of care in professional negligence cases. The traditional view has been that "professional prudence is defined by actual or accepted practice within a profession, rather than theories about what 'should' have been done." Osborn v. Irwin Memorial Blood Bank, 7 Cal. Rptr. 2d 101 (Ct. App. 1992). In the medical field, this would mean that a malpractice claim would fail unless a plaintiff could establish departure from a custom within the field. *See* Philip G. Peters Jr., *The Quiet Demise of Deference to Custom: Malpractice at the Millennium*, 57 Wash. & Lee L. Rev. 163, 166, n. 15 (2000). But as this section illustrates, this statement of the law: (a) oversimplifies matters and (b) is less accurate in terms of the state of the law than it once was.

1. Local or National Standards

Gambill v. Stroud

531 S.W.2d 945 (Ark. 1976)

FOGLEMAN, Justice.

The appellants, the husband and the guardian of Yvonne Gambill, brought this action for damages assertedly resulting from medical malpractice. After an extended trial there was a verdict for the defendant, Dr. Stroud. The principal question on appeal is whether we should modify our prevailing 'same or similar locality' rule in malpractice cases, by which a physician, surgeon, or dentist is held only to the standard of competence that obtains in his own locality or in a similar locality. The rule is fully stated in [Arkansas Model Jury Instructions] AMI 1501, which the trial judge gave over the plaintiffs' objections.

. . .

The thrust of appellants' argument is that the rule set out in AMI 1501 is no longer applicable to modern medicine, because doctors practicing in small communities now have the same opportunities and resources as physicians in large cities to keep abreast of advances in the medical profession, due to availability of the Journal of the American Medical Association and other journals, drug company representatives and literature, closed circuit television, special radio networks, tape recorded digests of medical literature, medical seminars and opportunities for exchange of views between doctors from small towns and those from large cities where there are complexes of medical centers and modern facilities.

However desirable the attainment of this ideal may be, it remains an ideal. It was not shown in this case, and we are not convinced, that we have reached the time when the same postgraduate medical education, research and experience is equally available to all physicians, regardless of the community in which they practice. The opportunities for doctors in small towns, of which we have many, to leave a demanding practice to attend seminars and regional medical meetings cannot be the same as those for doctors practicing in clinics in larger centers. It goes without saying that the physicians in these small towns do not and cannot have the clinical and hospital facilities available in the larger cities where there are large, modern hospitals, and medical centers or the same advantage of observing others who have been trained, or have developed expertise, in the use of new skills, facilities and procedures, or consulting and exchanging views with specialists, other practitioners and drug experts, of utilizing closed circuit television, special radio networks or of studying in extensive medical libraries found in larger centers.

The rule we have established is not a strict locality rule. It incorporates the similar community into the picture. The standard is not limited to that of a particular locality. Rather, it is that of persons engaged in a similar practice in similar localities, giving consideration to geographical location, size and character of the community. Restatement of the Law, Torts, 2d, 75 Comment g, s 299A. . . .

Sheeley v. Memorial Hospital

710 A.2d 161 (R.I. 1998)

GOLDBERG, Justice.

This case is before the court on the appeal of Joanne Sheeley (Sheeley) from the directed verdict entered against her in the underlying medical malpractice action. Specifically Sheeley asserts that the trial justice erred in excluding the testimony of her expert witness, which exclusion resulted in the entry of the directed verdict. . . .

On May 19, 1987, Sheeley delivered a healthy child at Memorial Hospital (hospital) in Pawtucket, Rhode Island. At the time of the birth Sheeley was under the care of Mary Ryder, M.D. (Dr. Ryder), then a second-year family practice resident....

In conjunction with the delivery process Dr. Ryder performed an episiotomy on Sheeley. This procedure entails a cut into the perineum of the mother, the purpose being to prevent tearing during the delivery. After the baby had been delivered, Dr. Ryder performed a repair of the episiotomy, stitching the incision previously made into the perineum. [Plaintiff developed complications following the procedure and sued Dr. Ryder and the hospital.]

At the trial on the malpractice action, Sheeley sought to introduce the expert medical testimony of Stanley D. Leslie, M.D. (Dr. Leslie), a board certified obstetrician/gynecologist (OB/GYN). Doctor Leslie planned to testify about Dr. Ryder's alleged malpractice and the applicable standard of care as it relates to the performance of an episiotomy. The defendants objected and filed a motion in limine to exclude the testimony, arguing that Dr. Leslie, as an OB/GYN, was not qualified under G.L.1956 § 9-19-41[3] to testify against a family practice resident who was performing obstetric and gynecological care. A hearing on the motion was conducted, at which time it was disclosed that Dr. Leslie had been board certified in obstetrics and gynecology since 1961 and recertified in 1979. Doctor Leslie testified that board certification represents a level of achievement of skill and knowledge as established by a national standard in which the standard of care is uniform throughout the medical specialty. Doctor Leslie is currently a clinical professor of obstetrics and gynecology at the Hill-Science Center, State University, College of Medicine in Syracuse. He is a member of the New York Statewide Professional Standards Review Council, which reviews disputes between doctors and hospitals regarding diagnosis and management, and the Credentials and Certification Committee at the Crouse-Irving Hospital, where his responsibilities include drafting standards for family practice physicians. It was further revealed that Dr. Leslie has in the course of his career delivered approximately 4,000 babies and that even though he has been retired from the practice of obstetrics since 1975, he has maintained his familiarity with the standards and practices in the field of obstetrics through weekly conferences, active obstetric work, professorial responsibilities, and continuing education.

Nevertheless, relying on *Soares v. Vestal*, 632 A.2d 647 (R.I. 1993), defendants maintained that § 9-19-41 requires a testifying expert to be in the same medical field as the defendant physician. In *Soares* this court upheld the trial justice's decision to

---

3. General Laws 1956 § 9-19-41 states:

"In any legal action based upon a cause of action arising on or after January 1, 1987, for personal injury or wrongful death filed against a licensed physician, hospital, clinic, health maintenance organization, professional service corporation providing health care services, dentists or dental hygienist based on professional negligence, only those persons who by knowledge, skill, experience, training or education qualify as experts in the field of the alleged malpractice shall be permitted to give expert testimony as to the alleged malpractice."

exclude the testimony of the plaintiff's expert witness in a situation in which the expert was board certified in neurology and internal medicine, and the underlying malpractice action involved a family practitioner performing emergency medicine. Agreeing that *Soares* was determinative, the trial justice here granted defendants' motion, stating: "I fail to see where this case is distinguishable from *Soares*. I don't quarrel with the doctor's background and qualifications. I think he's the inappropriate expert to testify in this case." Sheeley did not have any other experts prepared to testify, nor was she able to procure one within the two-day period allowed by the trial justice. Consequently defendants' motion for a directed verdict was granted. This appeal ensued.

On appeal Sheeley argues that the trial justice's ruling constitutes an abuse of discretion and is clearly wrong because Dr. Leslie was amply qualified to testify concerning the alleged malpractice. The defendants . . . assert that Sheeley's expert is not competent to offer expert testimony on the appropriate standard of care because he has more specialized training than Dr. Ryder and because he lacks any recent experience in providing obstetric care.

. . . In a medical malpractice case expert testimony is an essential requirement in proving the standard of care applicable to the defendant, "unless the lack of care is so obvious as to be within the layman's common knowledge." Richardson v. Fuchs, 523 A.2d 445, 448 (R.I.1987). Accordingly we are of the opinion that in this instance, the nature of the evidence offered clearly evinces its relevance and competence such that an offer of proof was not necessary. That said, we turn to the specific issue on appeal.

"The determination of the competency of an expert witness to testify is within the discretion of the trial justice." This court will not disturb that decision in the absence of clear error or abuse. In fairness to the trial justice, we note that in making her determination with respect to the admissibility of the expert's testimony, she was without the benefit of our decisions in *Marshall v. Medical Associates of Rhode Island, Inc.*, 677 A.2d 425 (R.I.1996), and more importantly *Buja v. Morningstar*, 688 A.2d 817 (R.I. 1997), which have distinguished *Soares* and limited its holding to situations in which the physician-expert lacks knowledge, skill, experience, or education in the same medical field as the alleged malpractice. Nevertheless, after a review of these cases, we find it clear that the trial justice did in fact abuse her discretion and commit reversible error in excluding the testimony of Dr. Leslie.

In *Buja* the plaintiffs brought a medical malpractice action against their family practitioners when their child suffered severe medical complications, including cerebral palsy and mental retardation, after having been deprived of oxygen just prior to birth. At trial, the plaintiffs sought to introduce testimony of a board certified obstetrician. The trial justice, however, excluded the testimony and stated that testimony concerning the standard of care required of a family practitioner practicing obstetrics had to be introduced by an expert in family medicine, not an expert in OB/GYN. Relying on our previous holding in *Marshall*, this court reversed the trial justice and stated that even though the proposed expert did not practice in the same specialty as the defendants, he clearly had the prerequisite "knowledge, skill, experience, training or education . . . in the field of the alleged malpractice." The *Buja* court held that nothing in the language of § 9-19-41 requires the expert to practice in the same specialty as the defendant. "Such an additional requirement is unnecessary and is in contravention to the General Assembly's clear intentions, as expressed in § 9-19-41." In view of this holding and the striking factual similarities of the instant matter to *Buja*, there can be little doubt that we must reverse the decision of the trial justice and remand the case for a new trial.

Yet in spite of our holdings in *Buja* and *Marshall*, defendants continue to insist that Dr. Leslie is not qualified to testify. In essence defendants argue that Dr. Leslie is overqualified, stating that a board certified OB/GYN does not possess the same knowledge, skill, experience, training, or education as a second-year family practice resident performing obstetrics in Rhode Island. Furthermore defendants argue that because Dr. Leslie has not actually practiced obstetrics since 1975, his experience in providing obstetrical care is "clearly outdated" and he is therefore not competent to testify concerning the appropriate standard of care as it applied to the performance of an episiotomy and the repair of the same—even while they acknowledge that the standard of care relative to the procedures involved in the alleged malpractice have changed little over the last thirty years. Finally defendants assert that pursuant to the limitations of the "similar locality" rule, Dr. Leslie must be disqualified because he lacks any direct knowledge about the applicable standard of care for a family practice resident providing obstetric care in Rhode Island. The defendants suggest that Dr. Leslie, although he has attended national conferences and studied medical journals and treatises in addition to his national certification, is not qualified to testify about the applicable local standard of care. In light of these arguments and with a view toward preventing any further confusion regarding the necessary qualifications of an expert testifying about the proper standard of care in medical malpractice actions, we take this opportunity to revisit our position on the appropriate standard of care.

For over three-quarters of a century this court has subscribed to the principle "that when a physician undertakes to treat or diagnose a patient, he or she is under a duty to exercise 'the same degree of diligence and skill which is commonly possessed by other members of the profession who are engaged in the same type of practice in similar localities having due regard for the state of scientific knowledge at the time of treatment.'" DiFranco v. Klein, 657 A.2d 145, 148 (R.I.1995). This "same or similar locality" rule is a somewhat expanded version of the "strict locality" rule, which requires that the expert testifying be from the same community as the defendant. *See* Shilkret v. Annapolis Emergency Hospital Association, 276 Md. 187, 349 A.2d 245, 248 (1975) The rationale underlying the development of the "strict locality" rule was a recognition that opportunities, experience, and conditions may differ between densely and sparsely populated communities.

This restrictive rule, however, soon came under attack in that it legitimized a low standard of care in certain smaller communities and that it also failed to address or to compensate for the potential so-called conspiracy of silence in a plaintiff's locality that would preclude any possibility of obtaining expert testimony. Furthermore, as this court noted in *Wilkinson*, the locality rule is somewhat of an anachronism in view of "[m]odern systems of transportation and communication." Thus many jurisdictions, including our own, adopted the "same or similar locality" rule, which allows for experts from similarly situated communities to testify concerning the appropriate standard of care. Nevertheless, even with this somewhat expanded view, the medical malpractice bar has continually urged a narrow application of the rule, arguing the need for similar, if not identical, education, training, and experience. The obvious result of such an application, however, is to reduce the pool of qualified experts to its lowest common denominator. This is a consequence that we have never intended.

The appropriate standard of care to be utilized in any given procedure should not be compartmentalized by a physician's area of professional specialization or certification. On the contrary, we believe the focus in any medical malpractice case should be the procedure performed and the question of whether it was executed in conformity with the recognized standard of care, the primary concern being whether the treatment was administered in a reasonable manner. Any doctor with knowledge of or familiarity with the procedure, acquired through experience, observation, association, or education, is competent to testify concerning the requisite standard of care and whether the care in any given case deviated from that standard. The resources available to a physician, his or her specific area of practice, or the length of time he or she has been practicing are all issues that should be considered by the trial justice in making his or her decision regarding the qualification of an expert. No one issue, however, should be determinative. Furthermore, except in extreme cases, a witness who has obtained board certification in a particular specialty related to the procedure in question, especially when that board certification reflects a national standard of training and qualification, should be presumptively qualified to render an opinion.

This court is of the opinion that whatever geographical impediments may previously have justified the need for a "similar locality" analysis are no longer applicable in view of the present-day realities of the medical profession. As the *Shilkret* court observed:

> The modern physician bears little resemblance to his predecessors. As we have indicated at length, the medical schools of yesterday could not possibly compare with the accredited institutions of today, many of which are associated with teaching hospitals. But the contrast merely begins at that point in the medical career: vastly superior postgraduate training, the dynamic impact of modern communications and transportation, the proliferation of medical literature, frequent seminars and conferences on a

> variety of professional subjects, and the growing availability of modern clinical facilities are but some of the developments in the medical profession which combine to produce contemporary standards that are not only much higher than they were just a few short years ago, but are also national in scope.
>
> In sum, the traditional locality rules no longer fit the present-day medical malpractice case.

We agree. Furthermore, we note that in enacting § 9-19-41, the Legislature failed to employ any reference to the "similar locality" rule. We conclude that this omission was deliberate and constitutes a recognition of the national approach to the delivery of medical services, especially in the urban centers of this country, of which Rhode Island is certainly one.

Accordingly we join the growing number of jurisdictions that have repudiated the "same or similar" communities test in favor of a national standard and hold that a physician is under a duty to use the degree of care and skill that is expected of a reasonably competent practitioner in the same class to which he or she belongs, acting in the same or similar circumstances. In this case the alleged malpractice occurred in the field of obstetrics and involved a procedure and attendant standard of care that has remained constant for over thirty years. Doctor Leslie, as a board certified OB/GYN with over thirty years of experience, a clinical professor of obstetrics and gynecology at a major New York hospital, and a member of the New York Statewide Professional Standards Review Council, is undoubtedly qualified to testify regarding the appropriate standard of care.

For the foregoing reasons the plaintiff's appeal is sustained, and the judgment appealed from is reversed. The papers in the case are remanded to the Superior Court with our decision endorsed thereon for a new trial in accordance with this opinion.

Notes

The national standard. The national standard is now the majority approach. *See* Barry R. Furrow et al., Health Law § 6-2, at 360 (1995). Are there nonetheless valid reasons for retaining the same or similar locality approach?

Determining the relevant locality. What should it take for a locality to qualify as "similar" enough to be used to help determine the standard of care in a jurisdiction that retains the similar locality approach?

Expert testimony. "Unless the medical professional's negligence is so grossly apparent or the treatment at issue is so common that it is considered to be within the common knowledge of a layperson, expert medical testimony is required to establish the applicable standard of care and the medical professional's deviation therefrom." Gulino v. Zurawski, 43 N.E.3d 1102, 1123 (Ill. Ct. App. 2015). Particularly in jurisdictions that retain the same or similar locality approach, the need for expert testimony sometimes results in disputes as to whether an expert has sufficient familiarity with the locality to testify.

Specialties. Those who specialize within a particular field or who otherwise hold themselves out as specialists are typically held to the standard of care within that specialty. This is often treated as a national standard. *See* Bahr v. Harper-Grace Hosps, 528 N.W.2d 170, 172 (Mich. 1995).

Other professions. Many of the same issues regarding the relevant standard of care also come up in other types of professional negligence cases. *See* Cox ex rel. Cox v. Board of Hosp. Managers for City of Flint, 651 N.W.2d 356 (Mich. 2002) (holding that the standard of care for nurses is the degree of skill and care ordinarily possessed and exercised by practitioners of the profession in the same or similar localities); Hamilton v. Sommers, 855 N.W.2d 855 (S.D. 2014) (rejecting a locality approach in legal malpractice cases and opining that where locality is relevant to determining the standard of care, a statewide focus is usually appropriate).

Apology statutes. Assume that a medical professional apologizes or expresses regret to a patient over a bad outcome following treatment. Could the apology be relevant to the question of whether the professional failed to meet the standard of care? In an effort to shield medical providers from liability, close to 30 states have enacted statutes prohibiting "statements, writings or benevolent gestures expressing sympathy or a general sense of benevolence relating to the pain, suffering or death of a person involved in an accident" from being introduced as evidence of negligence in claims against health care providers. Fla. Stat. § 90.426.

Problem 4.6. When Bill fell from the balcony, he was taken to the emergency room in an ambulance for what appeared to be several broken bones. He also complained of chest pain upon arriving at the hospital. Dr. Douglas was the treating physician in the emergency room. Dr. Douglas had finished medical school, completed an internship at the hospital, was fully licensed, and was now completing a year-long residency at the hospital in order to become a board certified specialist in cardiology. Consistent with recognized practice, Dr. Douglas ordered an EKG, chest x-ray, and CT scan for Bill. When Dr. Douglas reviewed the tests, he saw nothing unusual in terms of any chest issues aside from general soreness and some bruised ribs. In fact, Bill was suffering from a pulmonary embolism brought on by the fall. Bill was released from the hospital that evening but died several hours later. His family has now brought a wrongful death claim based on Dr. Douglas' misdiagnosis. The plaintiff's expert is prepared to state that Dr. Douglas exercised the care that a cardiology resident would have exercised under the circumstances and that it is not uncommon for pulmonary emboli to be misdiagnosed. But he is also prepared to testify that a more experienced cardiologist would probably have correctly diagnosed the condition after reviewing the results of the test.

To what standard of care should Dr. Douglas be held?

2. The Role of Custom in Establishing the Standard of Care and Breach

Chiero v. Chicago Osteopathic Hospital

392 N.E.2d 203 (Ill. Ct. App. 1979)

[Plaintiff alleged various forms of negligence in connection with his prostate surgery, but his own expert testified in a deposition that the surgeon "met the prevailing standard of care in the medical community." The trial court granted the defendant's summary judgment motion.]

Plaintiff next contends that we should abrogate the requirement, in medical malpractice cases, that the standard of care be established through expert medical testimony. We note initially that this requirement "is broadly recognized throughout the country. Nevertheless, plaintiff argues that the expert testimony requirement elevates custom and practice to conclusive evidence of due care, and, thereby, permits the medical profession to set its own standards. We disagree.

Proper standards of practice in any profession, including the medical profession, are not conclusively fixed by local usage or general custom. While in most instances, reasonable prudence is in fact common prudence, strictly it is never its measure. *Texas v. Pacific Ry. Co. v. Behymer* (1903), 189 U.S. 468, 23 S.Ct. 622, 47 L.Ed. 905; *The T. J. Hooper* (2d Cir. 1932), 60 F.2d 737.

In a professional malpractice case, such as here, where expert testimony is required to establish the requisite standard of care, evidence that a defendant's conduct conformed with local usage or general custom is indicative of due care; it is not, however, conclusive. It may be overcome by contrary expert testimony (or its equivalent) that the prevailing custom or usage itself constitutes negligence.

Plaintiff's own medical expert, Dr. Streeter, stated in his deposition that the TUR was performed by the defendants in accordance with the prevailing standard of care in the medical community. While we agree that Dr. Streeter's testimony is only evidence of due care, and not Necessarily conclusive, plaintiff has not presented any expert testimony or any evidence whatsoever, in the seven years this suit has been on file, to support the proposition that the prevailing standard of care itself constitutes negligence. Consequently, in our view, the trial court properly entered summary judgment for the defendants.

Hood v. Phillips

554 S.W.2d 160 (Tex. 1977)

[The alleged act of negligence involved the physician's choice to perform carotid surgery in his treatment of the patient's emphysema. Three physicians testifying for the patient characterized carotid surgery as an unaccepted mode of treatment for emphysema, as a treatment not supported by medical evidence, and as a surgical procedure which had been tried by a number of physicians, found ineffectual, and abandoned. One issue on appeal was whether the jury should have been instructed as follows: "A physician is not guilty of malpractice where the method of treatment used is supported by a respectable minority of physicians, as long as the physician has adhered to the acceptable procedures of administering the treatment as espoused by the minority."]

It should be noted at the outset that Hood does not assert that the surgical removal of the carotid body was unskillfully or negligently performed. Nor does Hood contend that Dr. Phillips' diagnosis of emphysema was incorrect. Instead, the patient-plaintiff maintains that it was negligence to utilize this particular surgical procedure as a method of treating emphysema.

Both Hood and Dr. Phillips assert the court of civil appeals erred in adopting the "respectable minority" negligence standard. . . .

Some courts have held any variance from the accepted mode of treatment renders the physician liable. In *Jackson v. Burnham*, 20 Colo. 532, 39 P. 577, 580 (1895), it was stated that "when a particular mode of treatment is upheld by a consensus of opinion among the members of the profession, it should be followed by the ordinary practitioner; and if a physician sees fit to experiment with some other mode, he should do so at his peril."

The following standard has been applied in Texas in other medical malpractice suits ". . . what a reasonable and prudent doctor would have done under the same or similar circumstances." Snow v. Bond, 438 S.W.2d 549, 550 (Tex.1969).

This review of the various standards reveals most courts have not attempted to articulate a distinction among "experimental," "outmoded," "rejected," and "accepted" surgical procedures. Instead, the majority of courts have attempted to draw a line between the reasonable and prudent physician who, as a last resort, turns to an "experimental" or a "rejected" treatment in the hope of assisting the patient and the individual practitioner who attempts to beguile his patient with false or distorted promises. These courts have recognized, as we do, that physicians should be allowed to exercise their professional judgment in selecting a mode or form of treatment. Further, physicians should be allowed to experiment in order that medical science can provide greater benefits for humankind. Consequently, we reject the "any variance" standard.

The "respectable minority" standard adopted by the court of civil appeals and "considerable number" test could convey to a jury the incorrect notion that the standard for malpractice is to be determined by a poll of the medical profession. Accordingly, these standards are rejected.

We are of the opinion that the statement of the law most serviceable to this jurisdiction is as follows: A physician who undertakes a mode or form of treatment which a reasonable and prudent member of the medical profession would undertake under the same or similar circumstances shall not be subject to liability for harm caused thereby to the patient. The question which conveys to the jury the standard which should be applicable is as follows: Did the physician undertake a mode or form of treatment which a reasonable and prudent member of the medical profession would not undertake under the same or similar circumstances?

Notes

The respectable minority standard. Even in jurisdictions that follow the "respectable minority" or "two schools of thought" approach, the rule does not apply where the alleged negligence involves something other than the physician's choice as to which procedure to follow. *See* Choma v. Iyer, 871 A.2d 238 (Pa. Super. Ct. 2005) ("Where as here, the dispute is not to the course of treatment, but rather to a question of fact regarding plaintiff's condition, the 'two schools of thought' doctrine is inapplicable.").

Error in judgment. Somewhat related to the "two schools of thought"/"respectable minority" doctrine is the "error in judgment" rule (or the "honest error in judgment" rule). In some jurisdictions, jurors may be instructed that a physician "is not a guarantor of a cure or a good result from his treatment and he is not responsible for an honest error in judgment in choosing between accepted methods of treatment." Ouellette by Ouellette v. Subak, 391 N.W.2d 810, 814 (Minn. 1986).

Problem 4.7. Assume that Bill's malpractice case is tried in a jurisdiction that allows juries to be instructed on the error in judgment rule and two schools of thought/respectable minority doctrine.

(a) Should those instructions be given with respect to Dr. Douglas' treatment?

(b) Putting aside whether the instructions should be given in Bill's case, what objections might you have as a plaintiff's attorney to these sorts of instructions more generally?

Note

A brief note on medical malpractice reform. Later chapters will address tort reform measures, such as products liability and caps on punitive damages awards. The medical malpractice field is another area in which tort reform proponents have successfully pushed for legislative change. One of the chief concerns of proponents is that the threat of malpractice liability leads doctors to engage in defensive medicine. According to this argument, this sort of practice shifts the focus from the patient to the provider and results in potentially unhelpful and unnecessary treatment. This, in turn, leads to increased health care costs and perhaps physicians choosing to practice in states with more doctor-friendly rules.

One approach has been to require a plaintiff to obtain pre-certification of malpractice claims or certificates of good faith in malpractice cases. These types of measures require the plaintiff's lawyer to consult with medical experts prior to or shortly after filing a claim and to obtain a written statement from the experts that they believe there is a good faith basis for bringing the claim. *See* Tennessee Code § 29-26-122(a). Another approach places limits on who may serve as an expert witness in a malpractice action. *See* Tennessee Code § 29-26-115(b) (requiring an expert to have been licensed in the state or a border state during the year preceding the date of the injury). Damage caps are also common features of medical malpractice statutes.

3. *Res Ipsa Loquitur* in Medical Malpractice Cases

Ybarra v. Spangard

154 P.2d 687 (Cal. 1944)

GIBSON, Chief Justice.

This is an action for damages for personal injuries alleged to have been inflicted on plaintiff by defendants during the course of a surgical operation. The trial court entered judgments of nonsuit as to all defendants and plaintiff appealed.

On October 28, 1939, plaintiff consulted defendant Dr. Tilley, who diagnosed his ailment as appendicitis, and made arrangements for an appendectomy to be performed by defendant Dr. Spangard at a hospital owned and managed by defendant Dr. Swift. Plaintiff entered the hospital, was given a hypodermic injection, slept, and later was awakened by Drs. Tilley and Spangard and wheeled into the operating room by a nurse whom he believed to be defendant Gisler, an employee of Dr. Swift. Defendant Dr. Reser, the anesthetist, also an employee of Dr. Swift, adjusted plaintiff for the operation, pulling his body to the head of the operating table and, according to plaintiff's testimony, laying him back against two hard objects at the top of his shoulders, about an inch below his neck. Dr. Reser then administered the anesthetic and plaintiff lost consciousness. When he awoke early the following morning he was in his hospital room attended by defendant Thompson, the special nurse, and another nurse who was not made a defendant.

Plaintiff testified that prior to the operation he had never had any pain in, or injury to, his right arm or shoulder, but that when he awakened he felt a sharp pain about half way between the neck and the point of the right shoulder. He complained to the nurse, and then to Dr. Tilley, who gave him diathermy treatments while he remained in the hospital. The pain did not cease but spread down to the lower part of his arm, and after his release from the hospital the condition grew worse. He was unable to rotate or lift his arm, and developed paralysis and atrophy of the muscles around the shoulder. He received further treatments from Dr. Tilley until March, 1940, and then returned to work, wearing his arm in a splint on the advice of Dr. Spangard. [It was the opinion of two subsequent treating physicians that Plaintiff's condition was the result of trauma or injury by pressure or strain.]

Plaintiff's theory is that the foregoing evidence presents a proper case for the application of the doctrine of *res ipsa loquitur*, and that the inference of negligence arising therefrom makes the granting of a nonsuit improper. Defendants take the position that, assuming that plaintiff's condition was in fact the result of an injury, there is no showing that the act of any particular defendant, nor any particular instrumentality, was the cause thereof. They attack plaintiff's action as an attempt to fix liability 'en masse' on various defendants, some of whom were not responsible for the acts of others; and they further point to the failure to show which defendants had control of the instrumentalities that may have been involved. Their main defense may be briefly stated in two propositions: (1) that where there are several defendants, and there is a division of responsibility in the use of an instrumentality causing the injury, and the injury might have resulted from the separate act of either one of two or more persons, the rule of *res ipsa loquitur* cannot be invoked against any one of them; and (2) that where there are several instrumentalities, and no showing is made as to which caused the injury or as to the particular defendant in control of it, the doctrine cannot apply. We are satisfied, however, that these objections are not well taken in the circumstances of this case.

The doctrine of *res ipsa loquitur* has three conditions: "(1) the accident must be of a kind which ordinarily does not occur in the absence of someone's negligence; (2) it must be caused by an agency or instrumentality within the exclusive control of the defendant; (3) it must not have been due to any voluntary action or contribution on the part of the plaintiff."

There is, however, some uncertainty as to the extent to which *res ipsa loquitur* may be invoked in cases of injury from medical treatment. This is in part due to the tendency, in some decisions, to lay undue emphasis on the limitations of the doctrine, and to give too little attention to its basic underlying purpose. The result has been that a simple, understandable rule of circumstantial evidence, with a sound background of common sense and human experience, has occasionally been transformed into a rigid legal formula, which arbitrarily precludes its application in many cases where it is most important that it should be applied. If the doctrine is to continue to serve a useful purpose, we should not forget that "the particular force and justice of the rule, regarded as a presumption throwing upon the party charged the duty of producing evidence, consists in the circumstance that the chief evidence of the true cause, whether culpable or innocent, is practically accessible to him but inaccessible to the injured person." 9 Wigmore, Evidence, 3d Ed., s 2509, p. 382.

The present case is of a type which comes within the reason and spirit of the doctrine more fully perhaps than any other. The passenger sitting awake in a railroad car at the time of a collision, the pedestrian walking along the street and struck by a falling object or the debris of an explosion, are surely not more entitled to an explanation than the unconscious patient on the operating table. Viewed from this aspect, it is difficult to see how the doctrine can, with any justification, be so restricted in its statement as to become inapplicable to a patient who submits himself to the care and custody of doctors and nurses, is rendered unconscious, and receives some injury from instrumentalities used in his treatment. Without the aid of the doctrine a patient who received permanent injuries of a serious character, obviously the result of some one's negligence, would be entirely unable to recover unless the doctors and nurses in attendance voluntarily chose to disclose the identity of the negligent person and the facts establishing liability. If this were the state of the law of negligence, the courts, to avoid gross injustice, would be forced to invoke the principles of absolute liability, irrespective of negligence, in actions by persons suffering injuries during the course of treatment under anesthesia. But we think this juncture has not yet been reached, and that the doctrine of *res ipsa loquitur* is properly applicable to the case before us.

The condition that the injury must not have been due to the plaintiff's voluntary action is of course fully satisfied under the evidence produced herein; and the same is true of the condition that the accident must be one which ordinarily does not occur unless some one was negligent. We have here no problem of negligence in treatment, but of distinct injury to a healthy part of the body not the subject of treatment, nor within the area covered by the operation. The decisions in this state make it clear that such circumstances raise the inference of negligence and call upon the defendant to explain the unusual result.

The argument of defendants is simply that plaintiff has not shown an injury caused by an instrumentality under a defendant's control, because he has not shown which of the several instrumentalities that he came in contact with while in the hospital caused the injury; and he has not shown that any one defendant or his servants had exclusive control over any particular instrumentality. Defendants assert that some of them were not the employees of other defendants, that some did not stand in any permanent relationship from which liability in tort would follow, and that in view of the nature of the injury, the number of defendants and the different functions performed by each, they could not all be liable for the wrong, if any.

We have no doubt that in a modern hospital a patient is quite likely to come under the care of a number of persons in different types of contractual and other relationships with each other. For example, in the present case it appears that Drs. Smith, Spangard and Tilley were physicians or surgeons commonly placed in the legal category of independent contractors; and Dr. Reser, the anesthetist, and defendant Thompson, the special nurse, were employees of Dr. Swift and not of the other doctors. But we do not believe that either the number or relationship of the defendants alone determines whether the doctrine of res ipsa loquitur applies. Every defendant in whose custody the plaintiff was placed for any period was bound to exercise ordinary care to see that no unnecessary harm came to him and each would be liable for failure in this regard. Any defendant who negligently injured him, and any defendant charged with his care who so neglected him as to allow injury to occur, would be liable. The defendant employers would be liable for the neglect of their employees; and the doctor in charge of the operation would be liable for the negligence of those who became his temporary servants for the purpose of assisting in the operation.

In this connection, it should be noted that while the assisting physicians and nurses may be employed by the hospital, or engaged by the patient, they normally become the temporary servants or agents of the surgeon in charge while the operation is in progress, and liability may be imposed upon him for their negligent acts under the doctrine of *respondeat superior.* Thus, a surgeon has been held liable for the negligence of an assisting nurse who leaves a sponge or other object inside a patient, and the fact that the duty of seeing that such mistakes do not occur is delegated to others does not absolve the doctor from responsibility for their negligence.

It may appear at the trial that, consistent with the principles outlined above, one or more defendants will be found liable and others absolved, but this should not preclude the application of the rule of *res ipsa loquitur.* The control at one time or another, of one or more of the various agencies or instrumentalities which might have harmed the plaintiff was in the hands of every defendant or of his employees or temporary servants. This, we think, places upon them the burden of initial explanation. Plaintiff was rendered unconscious for the purpose of undergoing surgical treatment by the defendants; it is manifestly unreasonable for them to insist that he identify any one of them as the person who did the alleged negligent act.

The other aspect of the case which defendants so strongly emphasize is that plaintiff has not identified the instrumentality any more than he has the particular guilty defendant. Here, again, there is a misconception which, if carried to the extreme for which defendants contend, would unreasonably limit the application of the *res ipsa loquitur* rule. It should be enough that the plaintiff can show an injury resulting from an external force applied while he lay unconscious in the hospital; this is as clear a case of identification of the instrumentality as the plaintiff may ever be able to make.

An examination of the recent cases, particularly in this state, discloses that the test of actual exclusive control of an instrumentality has not been strictly followed, but exceptions have been recognized where the purpose of the doctrine of *res ipsa loquitur* would otherwise be defeated. Thus, the test has become one of right of control rather than actual control. . . .

[T]here can be no justification for the rejection of the doctrine in the instant case. As pointed out above, if we accept the contention of defendants herein, there will rarely be any compensation for patients injured while unconscious. A hospital today conducts a highly integrated system of activities, with many persons contributing their efforts. There may be, *e.g.*, preparation for surgery by nurses and interns who are employees of the hospital; administering of an anesthetic by a doctor who may be an employee of the hospital, an employee of the operating surgeon, or an independent contractor; performance of an operation by a surgeon and assistants who may be his employees, employees of the hospital, or independent contractors; and post surgical care by the surgeon, a hospital physician, and nurses. The number of those in whose care the patient is placed is not a good reason for denying him all reasonable opportunity to recover for negligent harm. It is rather a good reason for re-examination of the statement of legal theories which supposedly compel such a shocking result.

We do not at this time undertake to state the extent to which the reasoning of this case may be applied to other situations in which the doctrine of *res ipsa loquitur* is invoked. We merely hold that where a plaintiff receives unusual injuries while unconscious and in the course of medical treatment, all those defendants who had any control over his body or the instrumentalities which might have caused the injuries may properly be called upon to meet the inference of negligence by giving an explanation of their conduct.

The judgment is reversed.

Notes

The uncertain value of *Ybarra*. A number of courts have declined to follow *Ybarra*, often citing concerns over unfairness and imposing strict liability. *See* Hoven v. Rice Memorial Hosp., 396 N.W.2d 569 (Minn. 1986); Talbot v. Dr. W.H. Groves' Latter-Day Saints Hosp., Inc., 440 P.2d 872 (Utah 1968). Other courts have followed *Ybarra*'s logic. *See* Van Zee v. Sioux Valley Hosp., 315 N.W.2d 489, 494 (S.D. 1982). *Ybarra*-type cases are (thankfully) relatively uncommon in the medical field. *See* Saul Levmore, *Gamorrah to Ybarra and More: Overextraction and the Puzzle of Immoderate Group Liability*, 81 Va. L. Rev. 1561, 1565 n.12 (1995).

Expert testimony. While *res ipsa* is often referred to as a theory that relies upon common sense and common understanding, before a plaintiff may rely on the theory in a malpractice action, expert testimony must usually be introduced to establish that the injury was unlikely to occur absent negligence. *See* Van Zee v. Sioux Valley Hosp., 315 N.W.2d 489, 492 (S.D. 1982).

b. Informed Consent

Chapter 2 touched on battery claims in the medical context. These are cases in which the patient consented to allow the doctor to perform a certain type of procedure and the doctor performed what the patient claims was a fundamentally different procedure. *See* Mohr v. Williams, 104 N.W. 12 (Minn. 1905) (recognizing potential battery claim where plaintiff consented to surgery on right ear but doctor decided to perform surgery on left ear); Perna v. Pirozzi, 457 A.2d 431 (N.J. 1983) (recognizing potential battery claim where plaintiff consented to surgical procedure to be performed by one doctor but a different doctor performed the procedure). As the case below illustrates, informed consent cases differ from medical battery cases.

Matthies v. Mastromonaco

733 A.2d 456 (N.J. 1999)

POLLOCK, J.

This appeal presents the question whether the doctrine of informed consent requires a physician to obtain the patient's consent before implementing a nonsurgical course of treatment. It questions also whether a physician, in addition to discussing with the patient treatment alternatives that the physician recommends, should discuss medically reasonable alternative courses of treatment that the physician does not recommend. We hold that to obtain a patient's informed consent to one of several alternative courses of treatment, the physician should explain medically reasonable invasive and noninvasive alternatives, including the risks and likely outcomes of those alternatives, even when the chosen course is noninvasive.

. . .

In 1990, Matthies was eighty-one years old and living alone in the Bella Vista Apartments, a twenty-three-story senior citizen residence in Union City. On August 26, 1990, she fell in her apartment and fractured her right hip. For two days, she remained undiscovered. When found, she was suffering the consequences of a lack of prompt medical attention, including dehydration, distended bowels, and confusion. An emergency service transported her to Christ Hospital in Jersey City. She was treated in the emergency room and admitted to the intensive care unit.

One day after Matthies's admission, her initial treating physician called Dr. Mastromonaco, an osteopath and board-certified orthopedic surgeon, as a consultant. Dr. Mastromonaco reviewed Matthies's medical history, condition, and x-rays. He decided against pinning her hip, a procedure that would have involved the insertion of four steel screws, each approximately one-quarter inch thick and four inches long.

Dr. Mastromonaco reached that decision for several reasons. First, Matthies was elderly, frail, and in a weakened condition. Surgery involving the installation of screws would be risky. Second, Matthies suffered from osteoporosis, which led Dr. Mastromonaco to conclude that her bones were too porous to hold the screws. He anticipated that the screws probably would loosen, causing severe pain and necessitating a partial or total hip replacement. Third, forty years earlier, Matthies had suffered a stroke from a mismatched blood transfusion during surgery. The stroke had left her partially paralyzed on her right side. Consequently she had worn a brace and essentially used her right leg as a post while propelling herself forward with her left leg. After considering these factors, Dr. Mastromonaco decided that with bed rest, a course of treatment that he recognized as "controversial," Matthies's fracture could heal sufficiently to restore her right leg to its limited function. He prescribed a "bed-rest treatment," which consisted of complete restriction to bed for several days, followed by increasingly extended periods spent sitting in a chair and walking about the room.

Before her fall, Matthies had maintained an independent lifestyle. She had done her own grocery shopping, cooking, housework, and laundry. Her dentist of many years, Dr. Arthur Massarsky, testified that he often had observed Matthies climbing unassisted the two flights of stairs to his office. Matthies is now confined to a nursing home.

. . . Shortly after Matthies began her bed-rest treatment, the head of her right femur displaced. Her right leg shortened, and she has never regained the ability to walk. . . .

Dr. Mastromonaco's goal in conservatively treating Matthies was to help her "get through this with the least complication as possible and to maintain a lifestyle conducive to her disability." He believed that rather than continue living on her own, Matthies should live in a long-term care facility. He explained, "I'm not going to give her that leg she wanted. She wanted to live alone, but she couldn't live alone.... I wanted her to be at peace with herself in the confines of professional care, somebody to care for her. She could not live alone."

Matthies asserts that she would not have consented to bed rest if Dr. Mastromonaco had told her of the probable effect of the treatment on the quality of her life. She claims that Dr. Mastromonaco knew that without surgery, she never would walk again. He did not provide her, however, with the opportunity to choose between bed rest and the riskier, but potentially more successful, alternative of surgery....

A jury question existed whether Dr. Mastromonaco consulted either with plaintiff or her family about the possibility of surgery....

Matthies remained at Christ Hospital until October 1990. She was then discharged to the Andover Intermediate Care Center, a residential nursing home in which she received physical therapy. While at Andover, Matthies was attended by several physicians, including orthopedic surgeons. Those doctors continued the conservative treatment begun by Dr. Mastromonaco. Matthies also saw psychiatrists and was treated at Andover for depression because she grew increasingly despondent over her continued inability to walk.

In January 1993, Matthies was transferred to the Castle Hill Health Care Center, another residential care facility. Except for hospital stays, she has remained at Castle Hill....

Choosing among medically reasonable treatment alternatives is a shared responsibility of physicians and patients. To discharge their responsibilities, patients should provide their physicians with the information necessary for them to make diagnoses and determine courses of treatment. Physicians, in turn, have a duty to evaluate the relevant information and disclose all courses of treatment that are medically reasonable under the circumstances. Generally, a physician will recommend a course of treatment. As a practical matter, a patient often decides to adopt the physician's recommendation. Still, the ultimate decision is for the patient.

We reject defendant's contention that informed consent applies only to invasive procedures. Historically, the failure to obtain a patient's informed consent to an invasive procedure, such as surgery, was treated as a battery. The physician's need to obtain the consent of the patient to surgery derived from the patient's right to reject a nonconsensual touching. Eventually, courts recognized that the need for the patient's consent is better understood as deriving from the right of self-determination. A shrinking minority of jurisdictions persist in limiting informed consent actions to invasive procedures. In those jurisdictions, battery survives as the appropriate cause of action. Most jurisdictions view the failure to obtain a patient's informed consent as an act of negligence or malpractice, not battery.

The rationale for basing an informed consent action on negligence rather than battery principles is that the physician's failure is better viewed as a breach of professional responsibility than as a nonconsensual touching. As we have stated, "Informed consent is a negligence concept predicated on the duty of a physician to disclose to a patient information that will enable him to 'evaluate knowledgeably the options available and the risks attendant upon each' before subjecting that patient to a course of treatment." Analysis based on the principle of battery is generally restricted to cases in which a physician has not obtained any consent or has exceeded the scope of consent. The essential difference in analyzing informed consent claims under negligence, rather than battery principles, is that the analysis focuses not on an unauthorized touching or invasion of the patient's body, but on the physician's deviation from a standard of care.

In informed consent analysis, the decisive factor is not whether a treatment alternative is invasive or noninvasive, but whether the physician adequately presents the material facts so that the patient can make an informed decision. That conclusion does not imply that a physician must explain in detail all treatment options in every case. For example, a physician need not recite all the risks and benefits of each potential appropriate antibiotic when writing a prescription for treatment of an upper respiratory infection. Conversely, a physician could be obligated, depending on the circumstances, to discuss a variety of treatment alternatives, such as chemotherapy, radiation, or surgery, with a patient diagnosed with cancer. Distinguishing the two situations are the limitations of the reasonable patient standard, which need not unduly burden the physician-patient relationship. The standard obligates the physician to disclose only that information material to a reasonable patient's informed decision. Physicians thus remain obligated to inform patients of medically reasonable treatment alternatives and their attendant probable risks and outcomes. Otherwise, the patient, in selecting one alternative rather than another, cannot make a decision that is informed.

. . .

To assure that the patient's consent is informed, the physician should describe, among other things, the material risks inherent in a procedure or course of treatment. The test for measuring the materiality of a risk is whether a reasonable patient in the patient's position would have considered the risk material. Although the test of materiality is objective, a "patient obviously has no complaint if he would have submitted to the therapy notwithstanding awareness that the risk was one of its perils." Canterbury v. Spence, 464 F.2d 772, 790 (D.C.Cir.), cert. denied, 409 U.S. 1064, 93 S.Ct. 560, 34 L.Ed.2d 518 (1972) (citation omitted). As the court stated in *Canterbury*:

> We think a technique which ties the factual conclusion on causation simply to the assessment of the patient's credibility is unsatisfactory. . . . [W]hen causality is explored at a postinjury trial with a professedly uninformed patient, the question whether he actually would have turned the treatment down if he had known the risks is purely hypothetical. . . . And the answer

> which the patient supplies hardly represents more than a guess, perhaps tinged by the circumstance that the uncommunicated hazard has in fact materialized. In our view, this method of dealing with the issue on causation comes in second-best.... Better it is, we believe, to resolve the causality issue on an objective basis: in terms of what a prudent person in the patient's position would have decided if suitably informed of all perils bearing significance. If adequate disclosure could reasonably be expected to have caused that person to decline the treatment because of the revelation of the kind of risk or danger that resulted in harm, causation is shown, but otherwise not. The patient's testimony is relevant on that score of course but it would not threaten to dominate the findings. And since that testimony would probably be appraised congruently with the factfinder's belief in its reasonableness, the case for a wholly objective standard for passing on causation is strengthened.

For consent to be informed, the patient must know not only of alternatives that the physician recommends, but of medically reasonable alternatives that the physician does not recommend. Otherwise, the physician, by not discussing these alternatives, effectively makes the choice for the patient. Accordingly, the physician should discuss the medically reasonable courses of treatment, including nontreatment.

...

Because the patient has a right to be fully informed about medically reasonable courses of treatment, we are unpersuaded that a cause of action predicated on the physician's breach of a standard of care adequately protects the patient's right to be informed of treatment alternatives.... The physician's selection of one of several medically reasonable alternatives may not violate a standard of care, but it may represent a choice that the patient would not make. Physicians may neither impose their values on their patients nor substitute their level of risk aversion for that of their patients. One patient may prefer to undergo a potentially risky procedure, such as surgery, to enjoy a better quality of life. Another patient may choose a more conservative course of treatment to secure reduced risk at the cost of a diminished lifestyle. The choice is not for the physician, but the patient in consultation with the physician. By not telling the patient of all medically reasonable alternatives, the physician breaches the patient's right to make an informed choice.

...

The judgment of the Appellate Division is affirmed.

Notes

Material risks. Note that *Matthies* adopts an objective standard in terms of the information that must be disclosed to a patient and explains that "the physician should describe, among other things, the material risks inherent in a procedure or course of treatment." What types of information must be disclosed under this standard? The physician's success rate with a procedure? *See* Duttry v. Patterson,

771 A.2d 1255 (Pa. 2001); Johnson v. Kokemoor, 199 Wis. 2d 615, 639, 545 N.W.2d 495 (1996). The physician's experience (or lack thereof) with respect to a specific procedure? *See* Whiteside v. Lukson, 947 P.2d 1263 (Wash. Ct. App. 1997). The fact that a child died during a childbirth procedure the doctor had been involved with (as opposed to disclosing merely that there had been a "bad outcome" from the procedure)? Duffy v. Flagg, 905 A.2d 15 (Conn. 2006). The fact that a surgeon has relapsed in alcohol addiction during the period of treatment? *See* Williams v. Booker, 712 S.E.2d 617 (Ga. Ct. App. 2011); Hidding v. Williams, 578 So. 2d 1192, 1194 (La. Ct. App. 1991).

Causation. Should a patient have an informed consent claim where a physician fails to adequately inform the patient regarding a risk but the risk never actually materializes? *See* Canterbury v. Spence, 464 F.2d 772, 790 (D.C. Cir. 1972) ("An unrevealed risk that should have been made known must materialize, for otherwise the omission, however unpardonable, is legally without consequence. Occurrence of the risk must be harmful to the patient, for negligence unrelated to injury is nonactionable.").

Review Question

One fall evening, Maria decided to clean up all of the leaves that had fallen into her yard. After raking leaves for an hour, Maria decided around 6:00 p.m. to instead use an electric leaf blower she had just bought. Maria had never used a leaf blower but had seen other people around the neighborhood do so. Maria connected the extension cord to the leaf blower to turn it on. Unfortunately, when she did so, the leaf blower was pointing downward and toward Bill, Maria's next-door neighbor, who happened to be raking his own leaves just a few feet away. Maria's leaf blower blew dirt and rocks upward into Bill's eyes, causing damage. Bill has now sued Maria for negligence. A local ordinance permits the operation of electric leaf blowers between the hours of 9:00 a.m. and 5:00 p.m. weekdays and 10:00 a.m. to 4:00 p.m. weekends in residential areas. Did Maria breach any duty toward Bill?

Chapter 5

The Duty Element Revisited

A. Special Relationships
  - Landowners and occupiers
    - Traditional categories: trespasser, licensee, invitee
    - Abolishing traditional categories
      - Duty of reasonable care for licensees and invitees
      - Retention of limited duty to trespassers
      - Minors and attractive nuisances
    - Open and obvious dangers
  - Innkeepers and common carriers
    - Duty to protect against third-party criminal acts
  - Businesses
    - Duty to ill or injured patrons
  - Social hosts
  - Duty of colleges and universities to protect students
  - Duty to warn
  - Other concepts developed in class or in readings assigned by the professor

B. Duty When Actor Has Created Risk of Physical Harm
  - Duty to act when prior conduct is dangerous
  - Negligent entrustment
  - Other concepts developed in class or in readings assigned by the professor

C. Voluntarily Assumed Duties
  - Duty to exercise reasonable care when voluntarily rendering aid
  - Other concepts developed in class or in readings assigned by the professor

Chapter Problem. Fit 4 Life is a fitness and recreation facility. Members pay a fee and have access to fitness classes, personal trainers, exercise equipment, and spa and locker room facilities. Recently, Fit 4 Life has been sued by members alleging negligence by Fit 4 Life or its employees that resulted in injuries or death.

The general rule, as reflected in Restatement of Torts (Third) § 7, is that "[a]n actor ordinarily has a duty to exercise reasonable care when the actor's conduct creates a risk of physical harm" to persons or property. Therefore, in most instances the questions of whether a duty existed toward the plaintiff and what the applicable standard of care is are not at issue. However, in some circumstances, the courts have determined that public policy or notions of justice warrant denying or limiting liability, or modifying the duty of reasonable care.

Likewise, public policy concerns have prompted courts to impose duties to act in special circumstances. Although people generally have no duty to act for the benefit of another or to render aid to another unless that person's actions have created an unreasonable risk of harm, tort law has developed special rules that impose duties to act based upon the nature of the relationship between the parties or where the defendant voluntarily renders aid to another.

This chapter explores these special issues involving the duty element in a negligence case.

A. Special Relationships

Courts have traditionally recognized duties owed between the following: landowners and occupiers and those who are legally on their property; innkeepers and their guests; and common carriers and their passengers. More recently, courts have established limited duties owed by social hosts to their minor guests, business owners to their ill or injured customers, and even colleges and universities to their students.

1. Landowner and Occupier

Traditional Classifications: Historically, the law assigned duties to the landowner or occupier based upon the status of the person entering the land. Those who qualified as "invitees" were owed the highest duty of care, while a lesser duty was owed to "licensees." "Trespassers" were owed no duty and entered at their own risk. Because a duty is a prerequisite to recovery for damages (no duty, no breach of a duty, no damages), plaintiffs are highly motivated to prove that they are invitees (or at least licensees) while defendants seek to prove that they had no (or only a limited) duty of care.

Stitt v. Holland Abundant Life Fellowship

614 N.W. 2d 88 (Mich. 2000)

YOUNG, J.

. . .

On the evening of November 22, 1989, Violet Moeller accompanied her friend Pat Drake to defendant's church to attend bible study. Ms. Moeller was not a member of the church. Ms. Drake parked her car in the church parking lot. As she exited Ms. Drake's car, plaintiff tripped and fell over a tire stop, fracturing her left arm. Plaintiff subsequently sued the defendant church, asserting that defendant negligently placed the concrete tire stops and failed to provide adequate lighting in the parking lot.

Before trial, the church twice filed motions for summary disposition. The trial court denied both motions, but determined that Ms. Moeller was a licensee and not an invitee at the time of the accident. The case proceeded to trial, at which time the judge instructed the jury on the duties owed to licensees.[1] At the close of trial, the jury returned a verdict in favor of the defendant.

Plaintiff appealed, contending that the trial court erred in determining that she was a licensee at the time of her accident. The Court of Appeals held that the plaintiff was a "public invitee" . . . , reversed the trial court judgment and remanded the case for a new trial. We granted defendant's application for leave to appeal. 461 Mich. 861, 602 N.W.2d 577 (1999).

Analysis

A. The Common-Law Classifications

Historically, Michigan has recognized three common-law categories for persons who enter upon the land or premises of another: (1) trespasser, (2) licensee, or (3) invitee. *Wymer v. Holmes,* 429 Mich. 66, 71, n. 1, 412 N.W.2d 213 (1987). Michigan has not abandoned these common-law classifications. *Reetz v. Tipit, Inc.,* 151 Mich. App. 150, 153, 390 N.W.2d 653 (1986). Each of these categories corresponds to a different standard of care that is owed to those injured on the owner's premises. Thus, a landowner's duty to a visitor depends on that visitor's status. *Wymer, supra* at 71, n. 1, 412 N.W.2d 213.

A "trespasser" is a person who enters upon another's land, without the landowner's consent. The landowner owes no duty to the trespasser except to refrain from injuring him by "wilful and wanton" misconduct. *Id.*

A "licensee" is a person who is privileged to enter the land of another by virtue of the possessor's consent. *Id.* A landowner owes a licensee a duty only to warn the licensee of any hidden dangers the owner knows or has reason to know of, if the licensee does not know or have reason to know of the dangers involved. The landowner owes no duty of inspection or affirmative care to make the premises safe for the licensee's visit. *Id.* Typically, social guests are licensees who assume the ordinary risks associated with their visit. *Preston, supra* at 451, 175 N.W.2d 759.

The final category is invitees. An "invitee" is "a person who enters upon the land of another upon an invitation which carries with it an implied representation, assurance, or understanding that reasonable care has been used to prepare the premises, and make [it] safe for [the invitee's] reception." *Wymer, supra* at 71, n. 1, 412 N.W.2d

1. The trial court gave the following instructions:

The possessor of land or premises is liable for physical harm caused to the licensee by a condition on the premises if, but only if, (A) the possessor knew or should've known of the condition, and should have realized that it involved an unreasonable risk of harm to the licensee, and should have expected that she would not discover or realize the danger and (B) the possessor failed to exercise reasonable care to make the conditions safe or to warn the licensee of the condition and the risk involved, and (C) the licensee did not know or have reason to know of the condition and risk involved.

213. The landowner has a duty of care, not only to warn the invitee of any known dangers, but the additional obligation to also make the premises safe, which requires the landowner to inspect the premises and, depending upon the circumstances, make any necessary repairs or warn of any discovered hazards. *Id.* Thus, an invitee is entitled to the highest level of protection under premises liability law. *Quinlivan v. Great Atlantic & Pacific Tea Co., Inc.,* 395 Mich. 244, 256, 235 N.W.2d 732 (1975).

A possessor of land is subject to liability for physical harm caused to his invitees by a condition on the land if the owner: (a) knows of, or by the exercise of reasonable care would discover, the condition and should realize that the condition involves an unreasonable risk of harm to such invitees; (b) should expect that invitees will not discover or realize the danger, or will fail to protect themselves against it; and (c) fails to exercise reasonable care to protect invitees against the danger. *Id.* at 258, 235 N.W.2d 732, citing Restatement, § 343.

The Court of Appeals correctly recognized that invitee status is commonly afforded to persons entering upon the property of another for business purposes. See, *e.g., Nezworski, supra; Pelton v. Schmidt,* 104 Mich. 345, 62 N.W. 552 (1895). In this case, we are called upon to determine whether invitee status should extend to individuals entering upon church property for *non* commercial purposes. Because invitee status necessarily turns on the existence of an "invitation," we must examine our common law in order to ascertain the meaning of that term.

B. The Meaning of Invitation in Michigan's Common Law

Unfortunately, our prior decisions have proven to be less than clear in defining the precise circumstances under which a sufficient invitation has been extended to a visitor to confer "invitee" status. On the one hand, several of our decisions appear to support the requirement that the landowner's premises be held open for a commercial business purpose. Indeed, several panels of our Court of Appeals have interpreted our decisions as supporting the requirement of a business purpose. The "commercial purpose" distinction is sufficiently recognized in Michigan case law that there are even secondary authorities that include Michigan among those jurisdictions conferring invitee status only on business visitors. See, *e.g.,* 95 A.L.R.2d 992, § 4, p. 1014.

In contrast with the line of cases supporting a commercial purpose requirement, some of our earlier decisions are replete with broad language suggestive of the Restatement's "public invitee" definition, although the precise contours of the definition are difficult to discern.

. . .

Despite the divergence of our cases concerning the elements necessary to confer invitee status, one thing *has* been consistent: to our knowledge, this Court has never squarely addressed the question whether a mere "public invitee" such as a churchgoer is entitled to invitee status. . . .

C. The Restatement

We begin by noting that a large number of jurisdictions have adopted § 332 of the Restatement:

(1) An invitee is either a public invitee or a business visitor.

(2) A public invitee is a person who is invited to enter or remain on land as a member of the public for a purpose for which the land is held open to the public.

(3) A business visitor is a person who is invited to enter or remain on land for a purpose directly or indirectly connected with business dealings with the possessor of the land.

Subsection (2) of § 332 of the Restatement creates an invitee status that does not depend on a commercial purpose. In this case, the Court of Appeals interpreted *Preston, supra,* as having implicitly adopted the Restatement definition of "public invitee." We certainly agree that *Preston* relied on § 332 of the Restatement. However, the issue whether to adopt the Restatement definition of "public invitee" was not before this Court in *Preston.*

In *Preston,* the plaintiffs were social guests who had been invited to the defendant's cottage for the weekend. In order to access the cottage, the plaintiffs entered a lift. The lift consisted of a car that was controlled by cable and an electric winch. After the plaintiffs entered the lift, a shaft broke and the car crashed, injuring the plaintiffs. *Id.* at 445, 175 N.W.2d 759. The plaintiffs filed suit against the defendants. The jury returned a verdict in favor of the defendants. The Court of Appeals erroneously determined that the plaintiffs were invitees merely because they had been "invited" onto the premises. That Court reversed and remanded the case for a new trial. *Id.* This Court held that the Court of Appeals committed error requiring reversal because the trial judge properly instructed the jury on the duty owed by a host to his social guests, licensees. *Id.* at 454, 175 N.W.2d 759. As stated by the trial judge, a host has no duty to reconstruct his premises or make his home more convenient or more safe for those accepting his hospitality. The guest assumes the ordinary risks that come with the premises. *Id.* at 446, 175 N.W.2d 759.

There was no contention in *Preston* that the plaintiffs were "public invitees," because that case involved only the duty owed to social guests. Thus, the issue whether to adopt the Restatement definition of "public invitee" was not before this Court in *Preston* and there is room for doubt regarding whether *Preston* can properly be regarded as binding precedent on this point. However, to the extent *Preston* purported to adopt the Restatement definition, and this could be properly considered a binding holding, we overrule *Preston.* Moreover, as explained below, we decline to adopt § 332 of the Restatement here.

D. Business Purpose As A Precondition of Invitee Status

Given the divergence of our cases on what circumstances create invitee status, we must provide some form of reconciliation in this case. In harmonizing our cases, we conclude that the imposition of additional expense and effort by the landowner, requiring the landowner to inspect the premises and make them safe for visitors, must be directly tied to the owner's commercial business interests. It is the owner's desire to foster a commercial advantage by inviting persons to visit the premises that justifies imposition of a higher duty. In short, we conclude that the prospect of pecuniary gain is a sort of quid pro quo for the higher duty of care owed to invitees. Thus, we hold that the owner's reason for inviting persons onto the premises is the primary consideration when determining the visitor's status: In order to establish invitee status, a plaintiff must show that the premises were held open for a *commercial* purpose.

With regard to church visitors, we agree with the court in *McNulty v. Hurley*, 97 So.2d 185 (Fla., 1957), that such persons are licensees.[2] In *McNulty*, a churchgoer was injured when, as she was leaving the church, she was pushed to the ground by a crowd of people. The lower court granted the defendant church's motion to dismiss on grounds that the plaintiff failed to state a cause of action. The defendant contended that one entering church premises for the purpose of attending religious services is a mere licensee. Thus, the only duty of the church was to refrain from wanton negligence or wilful misconduct and to refrain from intentionally exposing her to danger. *Id.* at 187. The plaintiff, on the other hand, argued that she was on the church premises by invitation and that most religions urge members and others to enter their churches and hold their doors open as a standing invitation. *Id.* The Florida Supreme Court disagreed, stating:

> [A]n invitation to enter and worship, whether it be either express or implied, does not constitute one who accepts the invitation an invitee in the legal sense. In order for such relationship to arise the person entering onto the premises, *i.e.*, the invitee, must have done so for purposes which would have benefited the owner or occupant of the premises, *i.e.*, the invitor, or have been of mutual benefit to the invitee and the invitor. And as we view it this benefit must be of a material or commercial rather than of a spiritual, religious, or social nature. [*Id.* at 188.]

Thus, as we do, the *McNulty* court considered a business purpose or a business or commercial benefit to the landowner as a necessary requirement in order for a visitor to be deemed an invitee. The *McNulty* court rejected the argument that church members confer a benefit to the church by supporting the church, stating:

> It cannot be successfully or logically argued that a person enters a place of worship, call it by any name, and participates in worship and prayer to the God or Supreme Being of his choice for the benefit of the body or organization which owns the church, the religious or lay readers who conduct the services, or the God or Supreme Being whom he worships and asks for guidance, help or forgiveness. One of the concepts of all religious beliefs known to us is that participation in religious activities is for the benefit of the mortals who participate therein. [*Id.*]

2. The Florida Supreme Court has since moved away from *McNulty* and has adopted § 332 of the Restatement. See *Post v. Lunney*, 261 So.2d 146 (Fla., 1972). However, we continue to find *McNulty's* reasoning persuasive.

The *McNulty* court also addressed the issue whether financial contributions at a religious service provided a sufficient basis for invitee status. We find this analysis instructive because the plaintiff in the case at bar similarly alleges that on prior visits to the church she made financial contributions to the church to such an extent that she should be considered an invitee. The *McNulty* court stated:

> [N]or would it matter if the plaintiff had alleged that she made a contribution when the collection plate was passed, for this would not have changed her status.... It seems clear to us ... that one who attends a religious edifice for the purpose of attending a religious service, as did the plaintiff in this case, does so "for his own convenience, pleasure or benefit" and is at best a licensee. [*Id.* at 188–189.]

We agree that whether the plaintiff in the instant case previously gave an offering to the church has no bearing on whether she was a licensee or an invitee. Absent a showing that the church's invitation to attend its services was for an essential commercial purpose, Ms. Moeller should be considered a licensee and not an invitee. A person who attends church as a guest enjoys the "unrecompensed hospitality" provided by the church in the same way that a person entering the home of a friend would. *Hambright v. First Baptist Church,* 638 So.2d 865, 868 (Ala., 1994). We conclude that church visitors who are attending church for religious worship are more like social guests (licensees) than business visitors (invitees).[3]

Conclusion

We recognize that a majority of jurisdictions considering the issue have adopted the public invitee definition set forth in § 332 of the Restatement. However, in exercising our common-law authority, our role is not simply to "count heads" but to determine which common-law rules best serve the interests of Michigan citizens. We believe that Michigan is better served by recognizing that invitee status must be founded on a commercial purpose for visiting the owner's premises.

For the above stated reasons, we hold that persons on church premises for other than commercial purposes are licensees and not invitees. Accordingly, we reverse the decision of the Court of Appeals and reinstate the trial court's decision.

Problem 5.1. Robert is a member of Fit 4 Life. He pays monthly dues in exchange for the right to use the Fit 4 Life exercise and spa facilities.

What duties, if any, did Fit 4 Life owe to Robert?

---

3. The solicitation of entirely voluntary donations by a nonprofit organization is plainly not a commercial activity. Accordingly, a church providing an opportunity for voluntary donations during a religious service that are in no way required to attend the service, *i.e.*, passing a collection plate, does not transform one who attends the church service and elects to make a donation from a licensee into an invitee. Indeed, we imagine that many religious individuals would find it offensive to have their voluntary donations to a church regarded as part of a business or commercial transaction, rather than as a gift intended to aid in various religious good works.

Note

Abandoning Traditional Classifications. Some jurisdictions have moved away from the traditional classifications and instead have adopted a reasonable care standard for both licensees and invitees. *See, e.g., Dos Santos v. Coleta*, *infra*. The rationale for abandoning those classifications included the difficulty of determining the proper classification of plaintiffs, which led to confusion and costly litigation. *See, e.g., Koenig v. Koenig*, 766 N.W.2d 635, 643–44 (Iowa 2009). "The difficulty in distinguishing between invitees and licensees underscores another disadvantage of the classification—people do not alter their behavior based on an entrant's status as an invitee or licensee." *Id.* at 644.

However, as the next case illustrates, most jurisdictions have maintained the general rule that a landowner owes a very limited duty to trespassers.

Alexander v. Medical Assoc. Clinic

646 N.W.2d 74 (Iowa 2002)

TERNUS, Justice

The defendant/appellee, Medical Associates Clinic, P.C., owns land upon which its office building is located. The defendant's property includes an undeveloped, open field that abuts a residential area. Unknown to the defendant, the plaintiff/appellant, Monty Alexander, entered the field late one evening to retrieve his sister's dog. Walking in darkness, he fell in a ditch and injured his knee.

The plaintiff filed this suit to recover damages for his injury, asserting the defendant was negligent in its maintenance of the property. After discovery, the defendant filed a motion for summary judgment alleging the undisputed facts established that the plaintiff was a trespasser and there were no facts to support a finding that the defendant breached its limited duty of care to a trespasser. The plaintiff resisted. The district court granted summary judgment, ruling (1) as a matter of law, the plaintiff was a trespasser, (2) the applicable standard of care was the avoidance of willful and wanton injury, not negligence, and (3) there were no facts showing the defendant breached this duty of care. This appeal followed.

...

The issues raised on appeal are rather narrow. The plaintiff challenges only the second part of the district court's decision, namely, that the defendant must be judged by the common law duty to avoid willful and wanton injury to a trespasser. The plaintiff argues on appeal that the defendant should be held to a duty of reasonable care and that there is a factual issue as to whether that duty of care was breached. The plaintiff does not contest the district court's ruling that, as a matter of law, he was a trespasser and that the defendant did not breach its common law duty of care to the plaintiff. Thus, the determinative issue on appeal is whether Iowa should abandon its common law rule of trespasser liability and replace it with a duty of reasonable care under the circumstances.

Iowa has long adhered to the common law rule that "a possessor of land owes no duty to a trespasser other than not to injure him willfully or wantonly, and to use reasonable care after his presence becomes known to avoid injuring him." *Champlin v. Walker,* 249 N.W.2d 839, 842 (Iowa 1977); *accord Mann v. Des Moines Ry.,* 232 Iowa 1049, 1057, 7 N.W.2d 45, 51 (1942); *Gwynn v. Duffield,* 66 Iowa 708, 713, 24 N.W. 523, 525 (1885). Thus, a landowner's duty with respect to a trespasser is twofold: (1) the landowner may not use his land in such a way that he deliberately or maliciously causes injury to a trespasser, and (2) once the landowner is aware of the presence of a trespasser, the landowner must use reasonable care to avoid injuring the trespasser. *See generally Webster's Third New International Dictionary* 2575 (defining "wanton"), 2617 (defining "willful"). A "trespasser" is one who has no legal right to be upon another's land and enters the land without the express or implied consent of the owner. *Reasoner v. Chicago, Rock Island & Pac. R.R.,* 251 Iowa 506, 510, 101 N.W.2d 739, 741 (1960); *Mann,* 232 Iowa at 1056, 7 N.W.2d at 50.

The trespasser rule arose "out of the special privileges accorded the occupation of land" in feudal England. *Rosenau v. City of Estherville,* 199 N.W.2d 125, 135 (Iowa 1972); *accord Kermarec v. Compagnie Generale Transatlantique,* 358 U.S. 625, 630, 79 S.Ct. 406, 410, 3 L.Ed.2d 550, 554 (1959); 62 Am.Jur.2d *Premises Liability* § 79, at 431–32 (1990). The rule has continued to exist based on a belief that a property owner should not be obligated to make his or her property safe "or to keep it in any particular condition" for the benefit of intruders. *Mann,* 232 Iowa at 1062, 7 N.W.2d at 53. A well-known treatise on torts perhaps best articulates the rationale behind our trespasser rules:

> The possessor of land has a legally protected interest in the exclusiveness of his possession. In general, no one has any right to enter without his consent, and he is free to fix the terms on which that consent will be given. Intruders who come without his permission have no right to demand that he provide them with a safe place to trespass, or that he protect them in their wrongful use of his property.

W. Page Keeton et al., *Prosser and Keeton on the Law of Torts* § 58, at 393 (5th ed.1984) [hereinafter *Prosser on Torts*].

The plaintiff points out that several jurisdictions have abolished the traditional analysis that determines the duty owed by a landowner based on the status of the injured party—invitee, licensee or trespasser. *See Sheets v. Ritt, Ritt & Ritt, Inc.,* 581 N.W.2d 602, 604–05 (Iowa 1998) (citing cases that have rejected common law distinctions). In fact, in *Sheets,* four members of this court favored taking a first step down that path by abolishing the distinction between invitee and licensee. That position, however, did not gain the support of a majority of the court, and premises liability in Iowa remains dependent on the status of the plaintiff.

The present case presents a different question than that presented in *Sheets.* In this case, we are asked to impose upon landowners a duty of reasonable care with respect to *trespassers*—persons who enter the landowner's property without the express or implied consent of the landowner. Although, as already noted, a few courts have abandoned all classifications with respect to landowner liability, the majority of courts have retained the special duties of a property owner to a trespasser. We will briefly review the position of other courts on this issue, not because the law is a popularity contest where the side with the most votes wins, but because the judgment of other jurisdictions reflects, we think, a prevailing belief that the interests of trespassers do not warrant a further reduction in the right of property owners to use their land as they see fit.

The landmark case in which a court first abandoned the common law classifications historically used in premises liability law was *Rowland v. Christian,* 69 Cal.2d 108, 70 Cal.Rptr. 97, 443 P.2d 561 (1968), *abrogated in part by statute as stated in Calvillo-Silva v. Home Grocery,* 19 Cal.4th 714, 80 Cal.Rptr.2d 506, 968 P.2d 65, 72 (1998). By the end of the 1970s, seven states [Alaska, Colorado, Hawaii, Louisiana, New Hampshire, New York, and Rhode Island] had followed California's lead and five states [Alabama, Delaware, Idaho, Ohio, and Utah] had not, the latter group choosing instead to retain the traditional rules based on the entrant's status. During that same period six states [Florida, Maine, Massachusetts, Minnesota, North Dakota, and Wisconsin] chose to abolish or modify the distinction made between invitees and licensees, but did not take the same step with respect to trespassers. Thus, in the twelve years after *Rowland,* a total of eleven states rejected California's rule that the liability of property owners to trespassers should be judged by the same standard as their liability to persons legally on their land.

Since 1980, the rejection of California's one-rule-fits-all approach has been even more overwhelming. In Rhode Island, the Rhode Island Supreme Court partially overruled its earlier decision that had followed *Rowland* and held that the traditional rules governing liability to trespassers should be retained. *Tantimonico v. Allendale Mut. Ins. Co.,* 637 A.2d 1056, 1057 (R.I.1994), *overruling in part Mariorenzi v. DiPonte, Inc.,* 114 R.I. 294, 333 A.2d 127, 131–32 (1975). In addition, the state legislatures in California and Colorado abrogated or partially abrogated court decisions adopting a negligence standard for all premises liability actions. In Colorado, the legislature passed a statute that reinstated a classification-based system of liability for landowners. *See* Colo.Rev.Stat. § 13-21-115 (1997). In California, in response to cases in which trespassing criminals had recovered for injuries incurred during their unlawful intrusions, the state legislature enacted a law that limited landowners' liability to trespassers who were on the property to commit a crime, essentially reinstating the common law duty in such cases. *See* 1985 Cal. Stat. ch. 1541, § 1 (codified at Cal. Civil Code § 847 (West 2002)).

In addition to those jurisdictions retreating from a prior, wholesale adoption of negligence principles, eight states [District of Columbia, Kansas, Nebraska, New Mexico, North Carolina, Tennessee, West Virginia, and Wyoming] refused to change their conventional principles of trespasser liability, even though they judicially abolished or modified the distinction between an invitee and a licensee. Additionally, two states, Maryland and Oklahoma, decided to retain their common law rules governing liability to trespassers, but left open the question whether they would discard the invitee and licensee classifications. *Murphy v. Baltimore Gas & Elec. Co.,* 290 Md. 186, 428 A.2d 459, 463 (1981), *overruled in part on other grounds by Baltimore Gas & Elec. Co. v. Flippo,* 348 Md. 680, 705 A.2d 1144, 1151 (1998); *Lohrenz v. Lane,* 787 P.2d 1274, 1276–77 (Okla.1990); *see Abbott v. Wells,* 11 P.3d 1247, 1248 (Okla.2000) (applying status analysis to invitee in premises liability case). Finally, seven more states [Arkansas, Connecticut, Kentucky, Mississippi, Missouri, New Jersey, and Washington] chose to maintain the common law rules making the duty owed by a landowner dependent on the status of the injured party.

In stark contrast to this widespread rejection of negligence principles in trespasser cases, only one state since the 1970s has joined the minority position, abandoning all classifications.[4] *Moody v. Manny's Auto Repair,* 110 Nev. 320, 871 P.2d 935, 942 (1994).

In summary, presently six states use a negligence standard to govern trespasser liability; twenty-nine states have declined the opportunity to change their rule in such cases; and two state legislatures have reinstated the common law trespasser rule after it had been abolished by court decision. Given the fact that only one court in the last twenty-seven years has abandoned the common law trespasser rule, the so-called "trend" to adopt a universal standard of care for premises liability has clearly lost momentum. . . . Keeton, in his treatise on torts, suggests that courts are acquiring "a more healthy skepticism toward invitations to jettison years of developed jurisprudence in favor of beguiling legal panacea." *Prosser on Torts* § 62, at 434.

We think the California approach has failed to gain favor, at least with respect to trespasser liability, because the common law rule retains validity in modern day life. *See id.* (stating "courts are gaining a renewed appreciation for the considerations behind the traditional duty limitations toward trespassing adults"). Land ownership is not limited to the privileged few in modern American society; many, many persons own real property. The private ownership of land continues to be a treasured opportunity, and the interests of landowners are still deserving of consideration. We agree with one treatise writer that in a society such as ours, "it is considered a socially desirable policy to allow a person to use his own land in his own way, without the burden of watching for and protecting those who come there without permission or right." *Id.* § 58, at 395. As one court has stated, "It is unreasonable to subject an owner to a 'reasonable care' test against someone who isn't supposed to be there and about whom he does not know." *Wood v. Camp,* 284 So.2d 691, 693 (Fla.1973).

The common law rule is also better suited to achieve a reasonable balance between individual property rights and the interests of a trespasser. Under the common law rule, a landowner knows in advance what his duty is; he must refrain from

4. The state of Montana has on occasion been included in lists of states abolishing classifications as the basis for premises liability. While it is true the court has abandoned status-based liability rules, the Montana Supreme Court's decision to do so was based on a state statute that "prevented [the court] from distinguishing" between classes of injured parties. *See Limberhand v. Big Ditch Co.,* 218 Mont. 132, 706 P.2d 491, 496 (1985).

maliciously or deliberately injuring a trespasser. A duty of reasonable care, in contrast, despite its common usage, is based on a much more amorphous standard, providing little guidance to the landowner. *See id.* at 694 ("Such vague terminology applied in every circumstance affords no guidelines or distinctions . . . ; just to say that the rule is 'reasonable care under the circumstances' in all instances ignores the responsibility of the law to provide guidance."); *Carter v. Kinney,* 896 S.W.2d 926, 930 (Mo.1995) (refusing to abolish common law classifications, stating "[t]o abandon the careful work of generations for an amorphous 'reasonable care under the circumstances' standard seems—to put it kindly—improvident"); *Tantimonico,* 637 A.2d at 1059 (quoting another jurist's contrast of the common law rule, described as "'well-settled and reasonable,'" with the negligence standard, "'a single vague duty of reasonable care, under which the property owner acts at his peril with no standard by which he can judge his obligations in advance'" (citation omitted)). Moreover it is no solace to the landowner, who has spent emotional and monetary resources to defend a meritless suit, that a judge or jury eventually finds no liability. *See Wood,* 284 So.2d at 694 (noting the assurance that a jury might well find a landowner has not violated a duty of reasonable care "is a dangerous generality (and expense) to which to subject an owner"). Balanced against the need for a predictable standard by which landowners may govern their conduct is the absence of any right of a trespasser to claim more generous protection since the trespasser comes on the land without the express or implied consent or invitation of the property owner. *See Poulin v. Colby College,* 402 A.2d 846, 851 n. 5 (Me.1979) ("Whereas both invitees and licensees enter another's lands under color of right, a trespasser has no basis for claiming extended protection.").

In summary, we remain unconvinced that the rights of property owners have so little value in today's society that those rights should be diminished in favor of persons trespassing on another's land. The common law standard is just as viable today as it was a century ago: a landowner has a duty not to injure a trespasser maliciously or deliberately, and to use reasonable care after the trespasser's presence becomes known to avoid injuring the trespasser. *See Champlin,* 249 N.W.2d at 842. This duty strikes an appropriate balance between the interests of the landowner and the trespasser and therefore we decline the plaintiff's invitation to abandon it. We express no opinion on whether the differentiation made between invitees and licensees remains viable.

. . .

We conclude the district court applied the correct legal principles in determining that the defendant was entitled to judgment as a matter of law. Because the plaintiff claims no other error in the court's ruling, we affirm.

Note

Minors and attractive nuisance. Although the majority of jurisdictions have not adopted a duty of reasonable care to trespassers, special rules have been adopted to protect minors. In addition to the duty to refrain from maliciously or deliberately injuring minors who are trespassers, nearly every state has adopted some version of *Restatement (Second) of Torts* § 339 (1965). When specific conditions are met, that section imposes liability on landowners or occupiers for injuries to children due to artificial conditions on land.

Bennett v. Stanley

92 Ohio St. 3d 35 (2001)

PFEIFER, J.

In this case we are called upon to determine what level of duty a property owner owes to a child trespasser. We resolve the question by adopting the attractive nuisance doctrine set forth in Restatement of the Law 2d, Torts (1965), Section 339. We also hold that an adult who attempts to rescue a child from an attractive nuisance assumes the status of the child, and is owed a duty of ordinary care by the property owner.

Factual and Procedural Background

When Rickey G. Bennett, plaintiff-appellant, arrived home in the late afternoon of March 20, 1997, he found his two young daughters crying. The three-year-old, Kyleigh, told him that "Mommy" and Chance, her five-year-old half-brother, were "drowning in the water." Bennett ran next door to his neighbors' house to find mother and son unconscious in the swimming pool. Both died.

The Bennetts had moved next door to defendants-appellees, Jeffrey and Stacey Stanley, in the fall of 1996. The Stanleys had purchased their home the previous June. At the time of their purchase, the Stanleys' property included a swimming pool that had gone unused for three years. At that time, the pool was enclosed with fencing and a brick wall. After moving in, the Stanleys drained the pool once but thereafter they allowed rainwater to accumulate in the pool to a depth of over six feet. They removed a tarp that had been on the pool and also removed the fencing that had been around two sides of the pool. The pool became pond-like: it contained tadpoles and frogs, and Mr. Stanley had seen a snake swimming on the surface. The pool contained no ladders, and its sides were slimy with algae.

Rickey and Cher Bennett were married in 1995. They had two daughters, born in 1993 and 1995. Cher brought her son, Chance Lattea, into the marriage. The Bennetts rented the house next to the Stanleys. The houses were about one hundred feet apart. There was some fencing with an eight-foot gap between the two properties.

The Stanleys were aware that the Bennetts had moved next door and that they had young children. They had seen the children outside unsupervised. Stacey Stanley had once called Chance onto her property to retrieve a dog. The Stanleys testified, however, that they never had any concern about the children getting into the pool. They did not post any warning or "no trespassing" signs on their property.

Rickey Bennett testified that he had told his children to stay away from the pool on the Stanleys' property. He also stated that he had never seen the children playing near the pool.

Kyleigh told her father that she and Chance had been playing at the pool on the afternoon of the tragedy. The sheriff's department concluded that Chance had gone to the pool to look at the frogs and somehow fell into the pool. His mother apparently drowned trying to save him.

Bennett, in his capacity as Administrator of the Estate of Cher D. Bennett, as Administrator of the Estate of Chance C. Lattea, and as custodial parent of Kyleigh D. Bennett, filed a wrongful death and personal injury suit against the Stanleys. The complaint alleged that appellees had negligently maintained an abandoned swimming pool on their property and that appellees' negligence proximately caused the March 20, 1997 drowning of Chance and Cher. Appellant averred that appellees had created a dangerous condition by negligently maintaining the pool and that appellees reasonably should have known that the pool posed an unreasonable risk of serious harm to others. Appellant specifically alleged that appellees' pool created an unreasonable risk of harm to children who, because of their youth, would not realize the potential danger.

...

[The trial court granted Appellees's motion for summary judgment, finding "that Chance and Cher were trespassers on appellees' property and that appellees therefore only owed them a duty to refrain from wanton and willful misconconduct." The appellate court affirmed.]

The cause is now before this court upon the allowance of a discretionary appeal.

Law and Analysis

Ohio has long recognized a range of duties for property owners vis-à-vis persons entering their property.... Currently, to an invitee the landowner owes a duty "to exercise ordinary care and to protect the invitee by maintaining the premises in a safe condition." *Light v. Ohio Univ.* (1986), 28 Ohio St.3d 66, 68, 28 OBR 165, 167, 502 N.E.2d 611, 613. To licensees and trespassers, on the other hand, "a landowner owes no duty * * * except to refrain from willful, wanton or reckless conduct which is likely to injure [the licensee or trespasser]." *Gladon [v. Greater Cleveland Regional Transit Auth.*, 662 N.E.2d 287, 293 (Ohio 1996)]. Today, we face the issue of whether child trespassers should become another class of users who are owed a different duty of care.

This court has consistently held that children have a special status in tort law and that duties of care owed to children are different from duties owed to adults:

"[T]he amount of care required to discharge a duty owed to a child of tender years is necessarily greater than that required to discharge a duty owed to an adult under the same circumstances. This is the approach long followed by this court and we see no reason to abandon it. 'Children of tender years, and youthful persons generally, are entitled to a degree of care proportioned to their inability to foresee and avoid the perils that they may encounter. * * * The same discernment and foresight in discovering defects and dangers cannot be reasonably expected of them, that older and experienced persons habitually employ; and therefore the greater precaution should be taken, where children are exposed to them.'" *Di Gildo v. Caponi* (1969), 18 Ohio St.2d 125, 127, 47 O.O.2d 282, 283, 247 N.E.2d 732, 734, quoting Ohio Jurisprudence 2d 512 (1959), Negligence, Section 21.

Recognizing the special status of children in the law, this court has even accorded special protection to child trespassers by adopting the "dangerous instrumentality" doctrine:

"The dangerous instrumentality exception [to nonliability to trespassers] imposes upon the owner or occupier of a premises a higher duty of care to a child trespasser when such owner or occupier actively and negligently operates hazardous machinery or other apparatus, the dangerousness of which is not readily apparent to children." *McKinney v. Hartz & Restle Realtors, Inc.* (1987), 31 Ohio St.3d 244, 247, 31 OBR 449, 452, 510 N.E.2d 386, 390.

. . .

Despite the fact that in premises liability cases a landowner's duty is defined by the status of the plaintiff, and that children, even child trespassers, are accorded special protection in Ohio tort law, this court has never adopted the attractive nuisance doctrine. The doctrine as adopted by numerous states is set forth in Restatement of the Law 2d, Torts (1965), Section 339:

"A possessor of land is subject to liability for physical harm to children trespassing thereon caused by an artificial condition upon land if:

"(a) the place where the condition exists is one upon which the possessor knows or has reason to know that children are likely to trespass, and

"(b) the condition is one of which the possessor knows or has reason to know and which he realizes or should realize will involve an unreasonable risk of death or serious bodily harm to such children, and

"(c) the children because of their youth do not discover the condition or realize the risk involved in intermeddling with it or in coming within the area made dangerous by it, and

"(d) the utility to the possessor of maintaining the condition and the burden of eliminating the danger are slight as compared with the risk to children involved, and

"(e) the possessor fails to exercise reasonable care to eliminate the danger or otherwise to protect the children."

. . . .

Ohio is one of only three states that have not either created a special duty for trespassing children or done away with distinctions of duty based upon a person's status as an invitee, licensee, or trespasser. *Kessler v. Mortenson* (Utah 2000), 16 P.3d 1225, 1228; Comment, *supra*, 46 Ohio St.L.J. at 147; Drumheller, Maryland's Rejection of Attractive Nuisance Doctrine (1996), 55 Md.L.Rev. 807, 810, and fn. 32.

...

Adopting the attractive nuisance doctrine would be merely an incremental change in Ohio law, not out of line with the law that has developed over time. It is an appropriate evolution of the common law. While the present case is by no means a guaranteed winner for the plaintiff, it does present a factual scenario that would allow a jury to consider whether the elements of the cause of action have been fulfilled.

We therefore use this case to adopt the attractive nuisance doctrine contained in Restatement of the Law 2d, Torts (1965), Section 339. In doing so, we do not abandon the differences in duty a landowner owes to the different classes of users. In this case we simply further recognize that children are entitled to a greater level of protection than adults are. We remove the "distinctions without differences" between the dangerous instrumentality doctrine and the attractive nuisance doctrine. See *Wills,* 26 Ohio St.3d at 192, 26 OBR at 165, 497 N.E.2d at 1123, A.W. Sweeney, J., concurring. Whether an apparatus or a condition of property is involved, the key element should be whether there is a foreseeable, "unreasonable risk of death or serious bodily harm to * * * children." Restatement, Section 339(b).

The Restatement's version of the attractive nuisance doctrine balances society's interest in protecting children with the rights of landowners to enjoy their property. Even when a landowner is found to have an attractive nuisance on his or her land, the landowner is left merely with the burden of acting with ordinary care. A landowner does not automatically become liable for any injury a child trespasser may suffer on that land.

The requirement of foreseeability is built into the doctrine. The landowner must know or have reason to know that children are likely to trespass upon the part of the property that contains the dangerous condition. See Section 339(a). Moreover, the landowner's duty "does not extend to those conditions the existence of which is obvious even to children and the risk of which should be fully realized by them." *Id.* at Comment *i.* Also, if the condition of the property that poses the risk is essential to the landowner, the doctrine would not apply:

"The public interest in the possessor's free use of his land for his own purposes is of great significance. A particular condition is, therefore, regarded as not involving unreasonable risk to trespassing children unless it involves a grave risk to them which could be obviated without any serious interference with the possessor's legitimate use of his land." *Id.* at Comment *n.*

We are satisfied that the Restatement view effectively harmonizes the competing societal interests of protecting children and preserving property rights. In adopting the attractive nuisance doctrine, we acknowledge that the way we live now is different from the way we lived in 1907. . . . We are not a rural society any longer, our neighbors live closer, and our use of our own property affects others more than it once did.

Despite our societal changes, children are still children. They still learn through their curiosity. They still have developing senses of judgment. They still do not always appreciate danger. They still need protection by adults. Protecting children in a changing world requires the common law to adapt. Today, we make that change.

. . .

On remand, the evidence may establish that Cher's status was that of a rescuer. This court has held pertaining to rescuers that "if the rescuer does not rashly and unnecessarily expose himself to danger, and is injured, the injury should be attributed to the party that negligently, or wrongfully, exposed to danger, the person who required assistance." *Pennsylvania Co. v. Langendorf* (1891), 48 Ohio St. 316, 28 N.E. 172, paragraph three of the syllabus. See, also, *Pittsburg[h], Cincinnati, Chicago & St. Louis Ry. Co. v. Lynch* (1903), 69 Ohio St. 123, 68 N.E. 703. While the attractive nuisance doctrine is not ordinarily applicable to adults, it "may be successfully invoked by an adult seeking damages for his or her own injury if the injury was suffered in an attempt to rescue a child from a danger created by the defendant's negligence." 62 American Jurisprudence 2d (1990), Premises Liability, Section 288. Therefore, we hold that if Cher Bennett entered the Stanleys' property to rescue her son from an attractive nuisance, the Stanleys owed her a duty of ordinary care.

Accordingly, we reverse the judgment of the court of appeals and remand the cause to the trial court.

Note

Open and obvious dangers. Although landowners owe a duty of care to those who are lawfully on the premises, when the existence of a dangerous condition should be obvious to a reasonable person, courts have found that the landowner generally has no duty to warn of the danger. However, in some circumstances, courts have found that even if the dangerous condition is open and obvious, the landowner may still have a duty to remedy or protect against the harm.

Dos Santos v. Coleta

987 N.E.2d 1187 (Mass. 2013)

CORDY, J.

The plaintiff Cleber Coleta Dos Santos was injured when he unsuccessfully attempted to flip into an inflatable pool from a trampoline that had been set up directly adjacent to it in the backyard of a property he was renting from the defendants, Maria A. and Jose T. Coleta.[5] He brought an action in the Superior Court against the defendants, claiming that they were negligent in setting up and maintaining the trampoline next to the pool and in failing to warn him of the danger of jumping from the trampoline into the pool. The jury returned a verdict for the defendants. The plaintiff appealed.... The Appeals Court affirmed and we granted

5. Jose T. Coleta is the plaintiff's half-brother, and Maria A. Coleta is Jose's wife and the plaintiff's sister-in-law. Because they share a surname, we refer to the Coletas individually by their first names.

the plaintiff's application for further appellate review. Because we conclude that a landowner has a duty to remedy an open and obvious danger, where he has created and maintained that danger with the knowledge that lawful entrants would (and did) choose to encounter it despite the obvious risk of doing so, we now reverse.

. . . In the summer of 2005, the plaintiff lived with his wife and son in one unit of a two-family home in Framingham that he rented from the defendants. The defendants and their children lived in the other unit before moving to South Carolina on July 31, 2005. On or about June 18, 2005, the defendants' son received a trampoline as a birthday gift. Jose set up the trampoline immediately adjacent to an inflatable vinyl swimming pool that he had set up in the backyard earlier that spring. Although the backyard was large enough to allow the trampoline and pool to be placed apart from each other, Jose set up the trampoline directly beside the pool because he had seen it done before at other houses and wanted to enable persons to jump from the trampoline into the pool. The pool was approximately two feet deep, and the trampoline was three feet high. The trampoline was accessible by two ladders, one of which was placed directly in the pool. Jose disregarded warnings printed on the side of the pool cautioning against jumping or diving into the pool. He knew that setting up the trampoline next to the pool might be dangerous but thought it would be "fun."

Although the defendants moved to South Carolina on July 31, they maintained ownership of the home and continued to rent the other unit to the plaintiff and his family. The defendants left the pool and trampoline in the backyard and understood that both items would continue to be used by their friends and family.

On the evening of August 2, 2005, the plaintiff, who had never before used the trampoline, came home from work and decided to play with his son on the trampoline while his wife recorded a video of them to send to their extended family in Brazil. The plaintiff decided to entertain his son by flipping into the pool. The plaintiff testified that he was trying to "flip over and sit on [his] butt in the water." The video recording, a portion of which was shown to the jury at trial, shows the plaintiff attempting to perform a front flip into the pool. The plaintiff severely underrotated the flip, entered the water headfirst, and struck his head on the bottom of the pool. As a result of the impact, the plaintiff sustained a burst fracture of his C-5 vertebrae, and is permanently paralyzed from the upper chest down.

Officer Val Krishtal of the Framingham police department responded to the scene of the accident. He testified that immediately following the accident, while awaiting the arrival of emergency medical services, the plaintiff stated that he "dove into the pool from the trampoline and landed on his head." Police officers at the scene took photographs of the trampoline and pool, which showed the pool manufacturer's warning label printed on the side cautioning against jumping and diving. The warning appeared in six languages, including Portuguese, the plaintiff's and defendants' native language. The label also included pictographs conveying the same warning.

The plaintiff was hospitalized for an extended period of time following the accident, and in the years since, he has been hospitalized at various facilities for medical conditions related to his quadriplegia. His medical bills and related expenses exceeded $700,000 at the time of trial.

Although he instructed the jury on the "open and obvious danger" doctrine, the trial judge declined to give the plaintiff's requested instruction based on the Restatement (Second) of Torts, *supra* at § 343A(1) & comment f, which contemplates that a landowner may in certain circumstances be liable for injuries resulting from open and obvious dangers. Rather, after instructing the jury on a landowner's duty of care, he provided them with the following instructions on the open and obvious danger doctrine:

> "[A] landowner's duty to protect lawful visitors against dangerous conditions on his property ordinarily does not extend to dangers that would be obvious to persons of average intelligence. This is often referred to as the open and obvious danger rule. If the particular dangers inherent in a particular condition would be open and obvious to a person of average intelligence, then the landowner does not have a duty to warn the visitor to avoid encountering the danger. The standard is an objective one, that is, would a reasonable person of average intelligence be aware of the open and obvious danger of the condition?"

The jury were further instructed:

> "In the present case, it is undisputed that defendants had a trampoline and inflatable pool in their backyard. At the time of the accident, August 2nd, 2005, the pool and the trampoline were next to one another. In deciding whether the defendants, Maria and Jose, owed a duty to [the plaintiff], you must decide whether the dangerous condition that he encountered and which caused his injury was open and obvious to a person of average intelligence, having in mind the particular activity in which [the plaintiff] was engaged at the time of the accident. Whether other people may have engaged in this activity may be considered by you, but the question that you must decide is whether the danger of injury from engaging in this activity with the trampoline and the pool was open and obvious to a person of average intelligence. Apply this analysis in answering the first question on the verdict form. *If your answer is yes, your work is done.* Date and sign the form. If your answer is no, then you go to the next question which involves negligence." (Emphasis added.)

The judge then instructed the jury on negligence, including instructions on foreseeability. The first question on the verdict slip, special question no. 1, asked: "Was the dangerousness of the condition that [the plaintiff] encountered on the defendant's property and that caused his injury open and obvious to a person of average intelligence, having in mind the particular activity in which he was engaged at the time of the accident?" The jury answered, "Yes," in response to special question no. 1, and the court entered judgment for the defendants.

"We review objections to jury instructions to determine if there was any error, and, if so, whether the error affected the substantial rights of the objecting party." *Hopkins v. Medeiros*, 48 Mass.App.Ct. 600, 611, 724 N.E.2d 336 (2000). See Mass. R. Civ. P. 61, 365 Mass. 829 (1074).

"Before liability for negligence can be imposed, there must first be a legal duty owed by the defendant to the plaintiff, and a breach of that duty proximately resulting in the injury." *Davis v. Westwood Group,* 420 Mass. 739, 742–743, 652 N.E.2d 567 (1995). An owner or possessor of land owes a common-law duty of reasonable care to all persons lawfully on the premises. *Id.* at 743, 652 N.E.2d 567. This duty includes an obligation to maintain the "property in a reasonably safe condition in view of all the circumstances, including the likelihood of injury to others, the seriousness of the injury, and the burden of avoiding the risk." *Mounsey v. Ellard,* 363 Mass. 693, 708, 297 N.E.2d 43 (1973). It also includes an obligation "to warn visitors of any unreasonable dangers of which the landowner is aware or reasonably should be aware." *Davis v. Westwood Group, supra,* and cases cited. However, "[l]andowners are relieved of the duty to warn of open and obvious dangers on their premises because it is not reasonably foreseeable that a visitor exercising (as the law presumes) reasonable care for his own safety would suffer injury from such blatant hazards." *O'Sullivan v. Shaw,* 431 Mass. 201, 204, 211, 726 N.E.2d 951 (2000) (*O'Sullivan*) (holding landowner had no duty to warn visitor of open and obvious risk of diving into shallow end of in-ground pool). The landowner has no duty to warn of such hazards "because the warning would be superfluous for an ordinarily intelligent plaintiff." *Papadopoulos v. Target Corp.,* 457 Mass. 368, 379, 930 N.E.2d 142 (2010) (*Papadopoulos*), citing *O'Sullivan, supra* at 206, 726 N.E.2d 951. A landowner, though, "is not relieved from remedying an open and obvious danger where [the landowner] 'can and should anticipate that the dangerous condition will cause physical harm to the [lawful visitor] notwithstanding its known or obvious danger.'" *Papadopoulos, supra,* quoting *Soederberg v. Concord Greene Condominium Ass'n,* 76 Mass.App.Ct. 333, 338, 921 N.E.2d 1020 (2010) (*Soederberg*), quoting Restatement (Second) of Torts, *supra* at § 343A comment f.

Today, we consider the scope of a landowner's duty to remedy an open and obvious danger as contemplated in § 343A and most recently discussed by this court in *Papadopoulos, supra.* As an initial matter, it is clear that at least in some circumstances "[s]hould the jury ultimately conclude that the danger was, in fact, open and obvious, the question . . . remain[s] whether the plaintiff nevertheless may recover on a duty to remedy theory." *Quinn v. Morganelli,* 73 Mass.App.Ct. 50, 54, 895 N.E.2d 507 (2008) (*Quinn*). . . .

Having established that the existence of an open and obvious danger will not necessarily relieve a landowner of *all* duties to lawful entrants with regard to that danger, we set out to answer the following principal question: where the duty to warn has been negated, in what circumstances will the duty to remedy nevertheless exist—or, in other words, in what circumstances "can and should [a landowner] anticipate that the dangerous condition will cause physical harm to the [lawful entrant] notwithstanding its known or obvious danger"? *Papadopoulos, supra,* quoting *Soederberg, supra.* Section 343A states in relevant part:

> "Such reason to expect harm to the [lawful entrant] from known or obvious dangers may arise, *for example,* where the [landowner] has reason to expect that the [lawful entrant's] attention may be distracted, so that he will not discover what is obvious, or will forget what he has discovered, or fail to protect himself against it. Such reason may also arise where the [landowner] has reason to expect that the [lawful entrant] will proceed to encounter the known or obvious danger because to a reasonable man in his position the advantages of doing so would outweigh the apparent risk." (Emphasis added.)

Restatement (Second) of Torts, *supra* at § 343A comment f. As the defendants assert, reported cases in the Commonwealth applying § 343A have generally rested their conclusion that a landowner can and should anticipate a particular harm on a finding that "a reasonable man in [the plaintiff's] position [would conclude] the advantages of [encountering the danger] would outweigh the apparent risk." *Papadopoulos, supra* at 379–380, 930 N.E.2d 142 (duty to remedy exists where experience dictates that visitors will often choose to cross snow or ice-covered walkways despite risk); *Docos v. John Moriarty & Assocs., Inc.,* 78 Mass.App.Ct. 638, 642, 940 N.E.2d 501 (2011) (*Docos*) (fact finder could conclude "advantages of continuing to work in a setting more dangerous than the typical active construction site due to excessive debris would outweigh the apparent risk"); *Soederberg, supra* at 339, 921 N.E.2d 1020 (noting "examples [from the case law] demonstrate that it is entirely foreseeable that people will engage snow or ice hazards lying in well-traveled pathways, even if those hazards are open and obvious"). Based on its reading of these cases, the Appeals Court concluded that "[§ 343A] . . . involves[s] a cost-benefit determination in which the action taken in the face of the open and obvious unsafe condition is theoretically overcome by the benefit accrued, *e.g.,* walking on ice and snow to get to a parked car. Here, no similar cost-benefit analysis existed." *Dos Santos, supra* at 6, 957 N.E.2d 1125.

Critically, however, by its own language, application of § 343A is not limited to situations where the plaintiff encounters the danger only after concluding the benefit of doing so outweighs the risk. See *Quinn, supra* at 50–52, 54–55 & n. 7, 895 N.E.2d 507. The illustrations accompanying § 343A comment f are clearly meant to be illustrative, not exhaustive. See Restatement (Second) of Torts, *supra* at § 343A comment f & illustrations 2–5. The main text of § 343A merely states that a landowner is not liable for injuries caused by open and obvious dangers "unless the [landowner] should anticipate the harm despite such knowledge or obviousness." Restatement (Second) of Torts, *supra* at § 343A(1). As the illustrations accompanying § 343A comment f indicate, § 343A contemplates that a lawful entrant's encounter with an open or obvious hazard may in some instances be a result of the entrant's own negligence. See Restatement (Second) of Torts, *supra* at § 343A illustrations 2–4 (explaining landowner has a duty to remedy open and obvious dangers that he can reasonably anticipate lawful entrants will nonetheless encounter due to their being distracted, failing to look, or initially observing the condition but subsequently forgetting to avoid it). Indeed, this makes sense, as an open and obvious danger is by definition a danger that a reasonable person needs no warning to avoid. *O'Sullivan, supra* at 204, 726 N.E.2d 951. . . .

Section 343A thus instructs that although a duty to warn of an open and obvious danger would be superfluous because an open and obvious danger provides its own warning, a landowner is not relieved from remedying that danger where he knows or has reason to know that lawful entrants may not heed the warning for a variety of reasons, including their own failure to exercise reasonable care. In cases where the only viable theory of negligence is a negligent failure to warn, the open and obvious nature of the danger causing the injury will therefore relieve the landowner of any duty vis-à-vis that danger.[6] In cases where a negligent failure to warn is not the only viable theory of negligence, such as where the plaintiff alleges negligent design, or negligent failure to comply with a company safety policy, the landowner may still owe a duty to the lawful entrant to remedy an open and obvious danger.

In affirming judgment for the defendants, the Appeals Court essentially concluded that the *O'Sullivan* case controlled because it effectively established a per se rule of nonliability in "shallow diving" cases. Additionally, in addressing the effect, if any, of the *Papadopoulos* and *Soederberg* line of cases on *O'Sullivan*, the Appeals Court further reasoned that those cases are distinguishable from "shallow diving" cases, including the present case, on the grounds that a "property owner would have no reason to anticipate that a reasonable person of average intelligence would conclude that the advantage of performing the maneuver [*i.e.*, a flip or dive] outweighed the risk of serious injury." *Dos Santos, supra.* The Appeals Court thus relied heavily on the plaintiff's "'foolhardy' decision to attempt a risky maneuver in a shallow pool" in concluding that the defendants could not and should not have anticipated that the plaintiff would suffer injury as a result of the open and obvious danger posed by the trampoline-pool combination. We take a somewhat different view.

First, as previously discussed, application of § 343A is not limited to situations where the plaintiff chooses to encounter the danger only after conducting a favorable "cost-benefit" analysis. A plaintiff's own negligence in encountering the danger

6. We acknowledge that the text of § 343A comment f states that where a landowner can and should anticipate that a lawful entrant will encounter an open and obvious danger, he owes a duty to that entrant, and that "[t]his duty *may require him to warn* the [entrant], or to take other reasonable steps to protect him, against the known or obvious condition or activity . . ." (emphasis added). Restatement (Second) of Torts, *supra* at § 343A comment f. To the extent that § 343A thus contemplates that the residual duty owed by a landowner in regard to open and obvious dangers may include a duty to warn (as opposed to a duty to remedy), it is contrary to our holding in this case and the established law of the Commonwealth.

does not relieve the landowner of a duty to remedy that danger where the plaintiff's negligent act can and should be anticipated by the landowner. Second, as the defendants' own testimony made quite clear, Jose set up the trampoline next to the pool with the specific intent to enable the type of use that resulted in the plaintiff's injury, and both defendants knew that the trampoline and pool were in fact being used in this manner and that this use was dangerous. Therefore, it is simply incorrect to say the defendants did not anticipate the risk of injury.

Because the trial judge relied so heavily on the *O'Sullivan* case—stating that the present case is "very much, if not on all fours with *O'Sullivan*"—in declining to give the plaintiff's requested instruction and instead instructing the jury to cease deliberations if they concluded the danger was open and obvious, we turn now to that case. In *O'Sullivan, supra* at 201–202, 726 N.E.2d 951, this court affirmed a grant of summary judgment for the defendant homeowners on claims that they "were negligent in allowing visitors to dive into the shallow end of [an in-ground] pool and in failing to warn of the danger associated with this activity." In addition to the obvious fact that both cases involve injuries sustained by jumping or diving into shallow pools, the trial judge relied on *O'Sullivan* presumably for its statement that "the open and obvious danger rule . . . operates to negate the existence of a duty of care," and its citation to a long line of cases from across the country holding landowners not liable for injuries caused by shallow diving on the grounds that the danger posed by such activity is open and obvious. *Id.* at 206, 207–208, 726 N.E.2d 951. From this, the judge apparently concluded that *O'Sullivan* stands for the proposition that the existence of an open and obvious danger negates *any* duty of a landowner to protect lawful entrants from harm caused by that danger, at least insofar as the plaintiff made the unwise decision to encounter the danger. In light of our recognition of § 343A, that conclusion was incorrect. Nevertheless, some confusion is understandable, as it has been noted that (at least prior to *Papadopoulos*) "[o]ur case law [had] not squarely addressed" whether a landowner may have a duty to remedy an open and obvious danger in certain circumstances. *Quinn, supra* at 54, 895 N.E.2d 507.

A close reading of *O'Sullivan* suggests that while the court may have used the terms "duty to warn" and "duty of care" interchangeably, it is relatively clear that the only question presented to the court in that case was whether the defendants could be held liable for failing to warn the plaintiff not to dive into the shallow end of an in-ground swimming pool. There was no suggestion in *O'Sullivan* that there was anything unusual or unsafe about the design, installation, or maintenance of the pool. Nor could the plaintiff apparently have made such a claim; the pool was by all accounts a typical pool, with a shallow end, a deep end, and a diving board installed in the deep end. Put another way, there was nothing about the design of the pool in *O'Sullivan* that expressly facilitated and invited dangerous misuse. Because the only possible theory of liability was a negligent failure to warn, the negation of the duty to warn by operation of the open and obvious danger rule therefore negated any duty of care in that particular case. Accordingly, we find *O'Sullivan* to be distinguishable from the present case.

"While the open and obvious doctrine may relieve the defendant of its duty to warn, the doctrine does not mean that the defendant can maintain its property 'in an unreasonably unsafe condition as long as the unsafe condition is open and obvious.'" *Godsoe v. Maple Park Props., Inc., supra*, quoting *Martins v. Healy, supra*. Here, Jose set up a trampoline immediately adjacent to a two-foot-deep pool, with a ladder leading directly from the pool to the trampoline, for the very purpose of enabling people to jump from the trampoline into the pool. He knew that the pool warned against jumping of any kind, and he [and Maria] knew that the setup was dangerous but proceeded with the setup because he thought it would be "fun." In many ways, Jose's actions were equivalent to installing a diving board in the shallow end of an in-ground pool. The danger from using a diving board in the shallow end of an in-ground pool would be open and obvious, but a defendant who installs or maintains the diving board in this manner would surely have reason to anticipate that persons would use the board to propel themselves into the water despite the danger. Far from failing to warn users not to jump or dive into the shallow pool—which, standing alone, would not give rise to liability—Jose actively facilitated this improper and highly dangerous use. And while the defendants make much of the fact that the plaintiff attempted a front flip (or, as they variously suggest, a dive) into the pool, whereas Jose only intended for people to "jump" from the trampoline to the pool, this assertion misses the point. Even assuming the jury interpreted the defendants' testimony that the setup was intended to facilitate "jumping" to mean that the defendants did not anticipate anyone would attempt to flip or dive into the pool, "[t]o be held liable the defendant need not have foreseen the precise manner in which the injuries occurred." *Luz v. Stop & Shop, Inc., of Peabody*, 348 Mass. 198, 204, 202 N.E.2d 771 (1964). See *Moose v. Massachusetts Inst. of Tech.*, 43 Mass.App. Ct. 420, 425, 683 N.E.2d 706 (1997), quoting Restatement (Second) of Torts, *supra* at § 435(1). Given the shallow depth of the water, there was no reliably safe way to propel oneself from the trampoline into the pool.[7] The defendants knew that it was

7. It has been suggested that there is no fundamental difference between jumping off the trampoline and landing feetfirst on the ground, and jumping off the trampoline and landing feetfirst in two feet of water. We disagree. As an initial matter, there was no evidence adduced at trial regarding whether the trampoline manufacturer warned against jumping (or, more accurately, bouncing) directly from the trampoline onto the ground, and the jury were not asked to consider the reasonableness of doing so. However, Jose did testify that he disregarded the advice of the person who gifted the trampoline to his son, who told Jose that he should purchase a safety net designed to surround the trampoline. Such a safety net presumably would have prevented anyone from jumping off the trampoline, whether it be into the pool or onto the ground. In any event, regardless of the propriety or advisability of jumping from the trampoline with the intention of landing feetfirst on the ground, there is a discernible difference between that activity and the act of jumping feetfirst into a vinyl pool filled with two feet of water that specifically warned its users against jumping of any kind.

unsafe to do so and, therefore, could or should have anticipated injuries resulting from this activity.

On these facts, a jury were entitled to conclude that the defendants owed a duty of care—specifically a duty to remedy—despite the open and obvious nature of the danger. Accordingly, the judge erred in instructing the jury to cease deliberations if they concluded that the danger was open and obvious, and should have further instructed the jury that a landowner is not "relieved from remedying open and obvious dangers where he [or she] 'can or should anticipate that the dangerous condition will cause physical harm to the [lawful entrant] notwithstanding its known or obvious danger.'" *Soederberg, supra* at 338, 921 N.E.2d 1020, quoting Restatement (Second) of Torts, *supra* at § 343A comment f.

... Having established that the jury's determination that the danger created by the trampoline and pool was open and obvious was not dispositive of the defendants' duty of care, and that the judge should have further instructed the jury regarding the duty to remedy, the judge should have posed a special question to the jury directing them to determine whether, as a matter of fact, the defendants reasonably could and should have anticipated that someone would be injured as a result of jumping from the trampoline into the pool. Therefore, while there was nothing wrong with special question no. 1 as posed by the judge in that it asked the jury to determine whether the danger was open and obvious, the judge should have posed some form of the plaintiff's requested special question, see *supra* at note 9, as special question no. 2, allowing the jury next to determine whether the defendants reasonably could and should have anticipated that lawful entrants would jump from the trampoline to the pool causing injury despite the open and obvious danger of doing so.

... Based on the foregoing analysis, we conclude that the trial judge's failure to give the plaintiff's requested instruction affected his substantial rights. Accordingly, we set aside the verdict and remand the case to the Superior Court for a new trial with directions to the trial judge to instruct the jury in a manner consistent with this opinion.[8]

So ordered.

Problem 5.2. Andrew, another Fit 4 Life member, tripped over a power cord as he tried to walk to the locker room. The cord was usually plugged into an outlet on the floor a few inches in front of the treadmill, but there was a short in the wiring to that outlet, so the cord had been run from the back end of the treadmill to a wall outlet approximately four feet away. The cord crossed a

8. The liability analysis does not end here. Even if, on remand, the defendants are found to have owed and committed a breach of a duty of care, the plaintiff's damages would be reduced by his comparative negligence and his recovery would be barred altogether if he were found to be more than fifty per cent at fault. G.L. c. 231, § 85.

walkway behind a row of treadmills. Fit 4 Life members and guests frequently used the walkway and had to walk over the cord to get to and from the locker rooms to the fitness areas. While there were other paths to the locker room, the walkway behind the treadmills was the most direct route for those in the area with treadmills and elliptical machines. Members and guests using those machines would have to walk out of their way to walk around the machines to access another path to the locker rooms. The cord was taped down with fluorescent yellow tape and the carpet was a dark blue pattern, but nothing else highlighted or called attention to the presence of the cord.

Imagine that you represent Andrew. Did Fit 4 Life breach any duty or duties that it owed to Andrew?

2. Innkeeper and Guest

Gress v. Lakahani Hospitality, Inc.

110 N.E.3d 251 (Ill. App. 1 Dist. 2018)

LAVIN, J. delivered the judgment of the court, with opinion.

On the evening of October 2, 2013, Karla Gress was a guest at the Holiday Inn Chicago-Skokie (Skokie Holiday Inn), which was owned and/or managed by defendants Lakhani Hospitality, Inc. (LHI), and Mansoor Lakhani (Lakhani). After eating dinner and consuming an alcoholic beverage in the hotel restaurant, Karla went to her room where she was subsequently raped while unconscious, allegedly by the hotel security guard who also did some maintenance work at the hotel.

Karla and her husband ... brought a premises liability action against LHI.... As to the alleged offender, Alhagie Singhateh, plaintiffs claimed that he committed assault and battery, as well as intentional infliction of emotional distress and gender violence.... The trial court dismissed, with prejudice, the premises liability counts ....

For the reasons to follow, we reverse and remand the dismissal of the premises liability counts in plaintiffs' fourth-amended complaint that were directed at LHI, Lakhani, and Gilani. We agree with plaintiffs, finding that they adequately pleaded the existence of a special relationship duty of care between LHI and its employees as the innkeeper and Karla as the guest, and contrary to the trial court's finding, we find that plaintiffs adequately alleged that Singhateh's sexual assault was reasonably foreseeable under both the duty and causation elements of negligence....

Karla alleged that she was a guest at the Skokie Holiday Inn and that she had a drink at the hotel's Bar Louie restaurant/lounge. During that time, she alleged that, unbeknownst to her, Singhateh placed a narcotic substance in her drink. Singhateh, as a hotel security guard, had a key to Karla's room. On the evening in question, Singhateh was directed by another LHI employee to enter Karla's room alone, allegedly in order to repair a faulty air conditioner unit, even though LHI had been advised that Karla was intoxicated. The limited key card records show that "a duplicate key" was used to access Karla's room at 9:40 p.m. Once there, Singhateh raped Karla while she was unconscious. When Karla awoke, she realized that she had been sexually assaulted. A rape kit was taken the next morning at a nearby hospital, and police matched fluid to Singhateh's DNA at a subsequent date. Meanwhile, for reasons that are not disclosed in plaintiffs' complaint or the parties' briefs, Singhateh continued to work for LHI for several years after this occurrence.

Plaintiffs' complaint made numerous allegations about unseemly conduct by Singhateh and others at the Skokie Holiday Inn. Plaintiffs alleged that Singhateh had previously been arrested for solicitation of prostitution after offering an undercover police officer $10 for sexual relations. There was no indication that LHI was aware of that arrest, although the hotel was allegedly aware of another named employee's embezzlement of LHI funds, which was reported to police. In spite of this, LHI also continued to employ this employee. According to plaintiffs, prior to the incident in this case, several named LHI guests filed police reports of stolen property from their rooms, with the key card history of one guest showing that only LHI employees had accessed his room. Plaintiffs also alleged that employees often brought women into the hotel and gave them alcoholic beverages and fraternized with them in a hotel room. Prostitutes were alleged to have frequented the hotel and were served alcohol at the bar. These hotel employees also disabled surveillance cameras, presumably for improper purposes. In April 2011, an unnamed guest called the police department reporting a sexual assault (this allegation lacked further details). In December 2013, just two months after Karla's rape, another unnamed LHI guest allegedly had several drinks at the bar, then was approached by two males, only to later awake in her hotel room naked, and although she did not remember certain portions of the evening, she recalled one male on top of her having intercourse. She reported this rape to the Skokie police.

Additionally, Singhateh was allegedly known by management to have harassed managers and was seen searching their bags without consent. Some six years before this occurrence, plaintiffs alleged that Singhateh was working at the O'Hare Holiday Inn during which time a female guest complained about creepy behavior by the security guard, which included him contacting her at her hotel room via the hotel telephone, even though she had not given this security guard her name or room number. She also said that the same person offered to bring a Caesar salad to her room, even though she had not ordered any food. Finally, she became concerned when she saw a shadow outside her room, leading her to latch and barricade the door. She complained to management that she was concerned for her physical safety and that of other hotel guests based on the interaction. Although Singhateh was not identified by name, the resulting report was placed in his LHI file, implying that management knew that the guest was talking about Singhateh.

In response to these allegations, the trial court ruled that the hotel and its management employees could not have reasonably foreseen that their security guard (who doubled as a handyman) might sexually assault an intoxicated female guest if granted access to her room. Finding that plaintiffs' allegations "continue to lack relevant facts to support the foreseeability of [the] attack," primarily because none of the "additional incidents" alleged by plaintiffs included "a sexual assault by Singhateh or another employee of a hotel guest in her room," the court thereby relieved defendants of any duty to protect Karla from the security guard's criminal activities. The court likewise found that neither Karla's intoxication nor Singhateh's arrest provided a basis for foreseeability. Thus, in dismissing the premises liability counts, the trial court accepted defendants' argument that they had no duty to foresee that Singhateh might rape Karla since they had not known him to have done that previously and that plaintiffs failed to sufficiently plead causation. As stated, the court determined that the counts related to negligent hiring and retention, and also to negligent supervision and training against Intercontinental and Hostmark, should be dismissed because there was no nexus between Singhateh's alleged unfitness due to his arrest and the sexual assault of Karla. Plaintiffs appealed.

Analysis

Plaintiffs now challenge the trial court's judgment. The question presented by a motion to dismiss a complaint under section 2-615 of the [Illinois Code of Civil Procedure] is whether the complaint alleges sufficient facts that, if proved, would entitle the plaintiff to relief....

In an action like the present, where the plaintiff seeks recovery based on the defendant's alleged negligence, the plaintiff must plead and prove the existence of a duty owed by the defendant, a breach of that duty, and injury proximately resulting from that breach. *Bogenberger*, 2018 IL 120951, ¶ 21,——Ill.Dec.——,—— N.E.3d——. We begin our analysis with a discussion of duty. The touchstone of the duty analysis is to ask whether the plaintiff and the defendant stood in such a relationship to one another that the law imposes on the defendant an obligation of reasonable conduct for the benefit of the plaintiff. *Krywin v. Chicago Transit Authority*, 238 Ill. 2d 215, 226, 345 Ill.Dec. 1, 938 N.E.2d 440 (2010). Whether a duty exists is a question of law for the court to decide subject to our *de novo* review, and thus to determine whether dismissal was proper, we must examine whether the plaintiff alleged sufficient facts, which if proven, establish a duty of care owed to them by defendants. *Id.*; *Doe-3 v. McLean County Unit District No. 5 Board of Directors*, 2012 IL 112479, ¶ 20, 362 Ill.Dec. 484, 973 N.E.2d 880. On the other hand, questions of a breach of the duty and proximate cause of the injury are factual matters for the jury to decide, provided there is a genuine issue of material fact regarding those issues. *Krywin*, 238 Ill. 2d at 226, 345 Ill.Dec. 1, 938 N.E.2d 440; *Marshall*, 222 Ill. 2d at 430, 305 Ill.Dec. 897, 856 N.E.2d 1048.

...

Plaintiffs contend that they adequately pleaded the existence of a special relationship between the hotel and Karla, such that the hotel had a duty to protect her against the criminal actions of a third party, including the hotel's own employee. While generally speaking, the owner or possessor of property does not owe a duty to protect invitees from the criminal acts of third parties, however, a notable exception to this is if a special relationship exists between the parties, such as, in this case, an innkeeper and its guests, a common carrier and its passengers, a voluntary custodian and ward, or a business invitor and invitee. *Iseberg v. Gross*, 227 Ill. 2d 78, 88, 316 Ill.Dec. 211, 879 N.E.2d 278 (2007); see also Restatement (Second) of Torts § 314A (1965). As section 314A of the Restatement (Second) of Torts puts it,

> "A[n] [innkeeper] is under a duty to its [guests] to take reasonable action
>
> (a) to protect them against unreasonable risk of physical harm, and
>
> (b) to give them first aid after it knows or has reason to know that they are ill or injured, and to care for them until they can be cared for by others." Restatement (Second) of Torts § 314A, at 118 (1965).

The duty to protect against unreasonable risk of harm extends to risks arising from acts of third persons, whether innocent, negligent, intentional, or even criminal. Restatement (Second) of Torts § 314A cmt. d, at 119 (1965). Likewise, before duty can attach, a defendant must know or should know of the unreasonable risk of injury. Restatement (Second) of Torts § 314A cm t. f, at 120 (1965). This is another way of saying that the defendant must know of the chance of injury or the possibility of harm. See Black's Law Dictionary (10th ed. 2014) (defining "risk"). Pertinent to this case, the Restatement (Second) of Torts § 319 (1965) also states that when one actor (like the hotel) takes charge of a third person (like a hotel employee) "whom he knows or should know" would likely cause bodily harm to another (like Karla) if not controlled, that actor "is under a duty to exercise reasonable care to control the third person [like the employee] to prevent him from doing such harm."

Courts have historically held that a hotel or common carrier, for example, must exercise the "highest degree of care," which we interpret simply as another way of expressing the existence of a special relationship. See *Krywin*, 238 Ill. 2d at 226, 345 Ill.Dec. 1, 938 N.E.2d 440; *Danile v. Oak Park Arms Hotel, Inc.*, 55 Ill. App. 2d 2, 3, 9, 203 N.E.2d 706 (1964) ("a reasonable degree of care is a high degree of care"); *Fortney v. Hotel Rancroft, Inc.*, 5 Ill. App. 2d 327, 335, 125 N.E.2d 544 (1955). These special relationships give rise to an *affirmative duty* to *aid or protect* another against an "unreasonable risk of physical harm." *Simpkins*, 2012 IL 110662, ¶ 20, 358 Ill. Dec. 613, 965 N.E.2d 1092. Such duties are premised on a relationship between the parties that is independent of the specific situation which gave rise to the harm. Restatement (Second) of Torts § 314A cmt. b, at 119 (1965) (the "special relations between the parties * * * create a special responsibility, and take the case out of the general rule"); see also *Bogenberger*, 2018 IL 120951, ¶ 33,——Ill.Dec.——,—— N.E.3d——. The key to imposing a duty based on a special relationship is that the defendant's relationship with either the tortfeasor or the plaintiff "'places the defendant in the best position to protect against the risk of harm.'" *Bogenberger*, 2018

IL 120951, ¶ 39, —— Ill.Dec. ——, —— N.E.3d —— (quoting *Grand Aerie Fraternal Order of Eagles v. Carneyhan*, 169 S.W.3d 840, 850 (Ky. 2005)). With respect to the innkeeper-guest relationship, it has been said that "since the ability of one of the parties to provide for his own protection has been limited in some way by his submission to the control of the other, a duty should be imposed upon the one possessing control (and thus the power to act) to take reasonable precautions to protect the other one from assaults by third parties which, at least, could reasonably have been anticipated." (Internal quotation marks omitted.) *Hills v. Bridgeview Little League Ass'n*, 195 Ill. 2d 210, 244, 253 Ill.Dec. 632, 745 N.E.2d 1166 (2000).

Whether the rape in this case could have been reasonably anticipated by LHI and its employees, and was thus foreseeable, forms the crux of the parties' contentions on appeal. See *Bruns v. City of Centralia*, 2014 IL 116998, ¶ 33, 386 Ill. Dec. 765, 21 N.E.3d 684 ("something is foreseeable only if it is objectively reasonable to expect" (internal quotation marks omitted)). Plaintiffs assert that defendants created a "dangerous condition" by allowing Singhateh unfettered access to Karla's room while she was intoxicated and, in fact, directing him to the room, especially given Singhateh's background and the hotel's licentious atmosphere. They thus argue that a subsequent crime was generally foreseeable. The defendants argue contrarily that prior instances of criminal conduct must be similar in nature for foreseeability purposes. They specifically argue that there were no reported sexual assaults by Singhateh or other LHI employees, thus militating against a finding of foreseeability under the duty element.

To understand foreseeability as it relates to a special relationship duty of care at the pleading stage, we turn to Illinois Supreme Court law. In the seminal special duty case of *Marshall*, a Burger King customer was eating in the restaurant when Pamela Fritz lost control of her car in the parking lot, rendering it airborne, before it crashed into the building and killed the customer. The trial court dismissed the case . . . after finding no duty because the type of accident was unlikely and the burden to protect against the accident was onerous. The supreme court disagreed and affirmed the appellate court's reversal and remand of the case.

The supreme court held that due to the business invitor-invitee special relationship, the defendants, as owners and operators of the restaurant, owed an affirmative duty to the deceased customer to protect against the third-party negligent driving of Fritz. They specifically reasoned that the duty to protect arose out of the special relationship of the parties, noting that this special relationship and duty of care encompassed "the type of risk—*i.e.*, the negligent act of a third person—" that led to the customer's injury. *Marshall*, 222 Ill. 2d at 440, 305 Ill.Dec. 897, 856 N.E.2d 1048. While noting that the existence of duty turns in large part on public policy considerations, the court reasoned that "the policy justifying the business invitor's duty of reasonable care is related to the affirmative action the invitor takes in opening his business to the public and to the potential for harm that a business open to the general public poses." *Id.* at 441, 305 Ill.Dec. 897, 856 N.E.2d 1048.

Marshall then analyzed whether the defendants had shown that they were entitled to an exemption from the duty of protection. In doing so, the court examined the traditional four policy factors associated with "duty," including the reasonable foreseeability of the injury, the injury's likelihood, the burden of guarding against the injury, and the consequences of placing the burden on the defendant, before concluding that the defendants had not rebutted the existence of a duty to protect.[9] The court declined to fully address whether the business invitor's lack of knowledge of prior, similar incidents of negligent conduct, should limit his duty of care, finding the defendants' argument in that regard underdeveloped. Most pertinent to our analysis here is that the court also specifically found it *unpersuasive* that a defendant must have some *notice* of a prior incident or prior conduct before the law imposes a duty to protect a plaintiff from the conduct of a third party, or that the prior incident must be sufficiently similar to put a defendant on notice that there is a reasonable probability that the acts of the third party are likely to cause physical harm to others. *Id.* at 444–45, 305 Ill.Dec. 897, 856 N.E.2d 1048 (citing Restatement (Second) of Torts § 344 cmt. f (1965)). *Marshall* thus held that a special relationship, standing alone, was sufficient to establish an affirmative duty to protect against third-party negligence.

Other supreme court cases (both before and after *Marshall*), appear to require foreseeability as an inherent requirement in proving a special relationship duty to protect. In *Iseberg*, 227 Ill. 2d 78, 316 Ill.Dec. 211, 879 N.E.2d 278, a section 2-615 case decided in 2007, a year after *Marshall* and where no special relationship was found, the court stated that when one of the four special relationships "exists between the parties and an unreasonable risk of physical harm arises within the scope of that relationship, an obligation may be imposed on the one to exercise reasonable care to protect the other from such risk, *if the risk is reasonably foreseeable*, or to render first aid when it is known that such aid is needed." (Emphasis added.) *Id.* at 88, 316 Ill.Dec. 211, 879 N.E.2d 278. This echoed an earlier statement in *Hills* (decided in 2000) that, "[t]he existence of a special relationship does not, by itself, impose a duty upon the possessor of land to protect lawful entrants from the criminal acts of third parties. Before a duty to protect will be imposed it must also be shown that the criminal attack was reasonably foreseeable." *Hills*, 195 Ill. 2d at 243, 253 Ill.

9. In *Simpkins*, 2012 IL 110662, ¶ 21, 358 Ill.Dec. 613, 965 N.E.2d 1092, the supreme court identified a similar manner of proceeding with the duty analysis. The court wrote that the first question to be analyzed in a negligence case is whether the defendant, by his act or omission, contributed to the risk of harm to the particular plaintiff. If the answer is "yes," the *Simpkins* court stated one must weigh the traditional four factors to determine duty. *Id.* If the answer is "no," then one should address whether there were any recognized special relationships "that establish a duty running from the defendant to the plaintiff." *Id.* This suggests that "duty" along with foreseeability factors and "duty" along with a special relationship are distinct ways courts and practitioners may analyze duty in negligence cases at least at the pleading stage. As our analysis in this case reveals, we arguably have both a risk of harm created by the defendant, plus the satisfied four factors, and also a special relationship.

Dec. 632, 745 N.E.2d 1166. Likewise, the supreme court had long held in the common carrier-passenger case of *Letsos v. Chicago Transit Authority*, 47 Ill. 2d 437, 441, 265 N.E.2d 650 (1970), that the carrier's high degree of care it owed to passengers included, "the responsibility to prevent injuries which could have been reasonably foreseen and avoided by the carrier." We find *Marshall* particularly apt in this case, since as in *Marshall*, this case involves a special relationship complaint dismissed at the section 2-615 stage. We thus proceed in our analysis pursuant to *Marshall*. It merits mention, however, that whether foreseeability is a rebuttable contention on defendants' part or a requirement under a special relationship duty element, plaintiffs have adequately set forth a cause of action, which requires reversal of the trial court's judgment.

Here, as in *Marshall*, due to the hotel-guest special relationship pleaded in this case, defendants owed an affirmative duty to Karla to protect against third-party criminal attacks. Restatement (Second) of Torts § 314A cmt. d, at 119 (1965). This type of relationship encompassed the type of risk, a sexual assault by a hotel employee. Plaintiffs' complaint specifically alleged that while Karla was a paying guest at a hotel owned, operated, and managed by defendants, she was rendered intoxicated by defendants' employee and then sexually assaulted by him in her room. LHI's hotel management essentially facilitated the assault by sending this male security guard/repairman into that room, knowing that he had a key, despite being forewarned that the female guest was intoxicated. We observe that to "safely" commit his crime, Singhateh needed to be in Karla's room, alone with her, behind the locked door. Rather than affirmatively protecting her privacy and safety in her locked room, the hotel management vitiated it. See Restatement (Second) of Torts § 314A cmt. d, at 119 (1965). ("[t]he duty to protect the other against unreasonable risk of harm extends to risks arising out of the actor's own conduct"). In other words, the allegations establish that LHI and its management should have known that Singhateh could have entered Karla's room without her consent and then taken advantage of her.

> "A guest, who is either asleep in [her] room or about to enter [her] room, should not be subjected to the risk of an assault * * *. A guest has a right to rely upon the innkeeper doing all within his power to avoid or prevent such an assault, and to that end should be required to exercise a high degree of care." *Fortney*, 5 Ill. App. 2d at 335, 125 N.E.2d 544.

. . .

Conclusion

We therefore reverse the trial court's dismissal of the counts of plaintiffs' fourth-amended complaint directed against LHI . . . .

Affirmed in part and reversed in part; cause remanded.

3. Business Owner's Duty to Ill or Injured Patron

Drew v. Lejay's Sportsmen's Café, Inc.

806 P.2d 301 (Wyo. 1991)

Facts

Eddie Drew and Ted Gonzales drove from Rock Springs to Jackson on July 3, 1986, to "party" over the Independence Day weekend. After frequenting the bars for several hours on the 4th of July and continuing into the early hours of the 5th, they arrived at LeJay's restaurant about 1:30 a.m., July 5, where they continued to drink while waiting for a table and after they were seated. Drew started choking after only a few bites of his meal.

Gonzales' testimony about his reaction to Drew's choking demonstrates that he was slow to realize the seriousness of the situation. When Drew could no longer talk and did not move, Gonzales finally sought help. Gonzales' testimony is confusing about the sequence of those he spoke to for help and what kind of help he asked for. Initially, he simply asked three or four times for a cloth to wipe Drew's mouth, but he testified that he also said several times, "This man is dying over here." After several efforts to get the attention of restaurant employees regarding Drew's choking, a threat was made to Gonzales that the police would be called and Gonzales said to call them. From the testimony Gonzales talked to waitresses, the cashier, and the cook. It is not clear how many times Gonzales asked these employees for help, or in what order, but he did ask more than once.

Some time during all of this activity, Gonzales had asked customers near Drew for help, and they placed Drew on the floor and gave him mouth-to-mouth resuscitation. When the police arrived, they continued giving mouth-to-mouth resuscitation to Drew. Although Gonzales told the police Drew was dying and to call an ambulance, this was not done right away. It is not clear from the record how long the wait was for an ambulance to be called or who made the call.

By 2:38 a.m. the ambulance was en route to the restaurant; it began its return trip to the hospital by 2:52 a.m., arriving at 2:55 a.m. Efforts during the ambulance ride and at the hospital failed to revive Drew. At the hospital a two-inch by two-inch chunk of meat was removed from Drew's trachea. That chunk had caused Drew to have cardiorespiratory arrest. Despite a flight for life to a Denver hospital and further medical attention there, Drew was pronounced dead at 5:51 p.m.

Discussion

At the jury trial, Mrs. Drew's counsel offered two jury instructions . . . purporting to correctly state the law as found in Restatement (Second) of Torts, § 314A (1965). The Restatement section provides:

> § 314A. Special Relations Giving Rise to Duty to Aid or Protect
>
> (1) A common carrier is under a duty to its passengers to take reasonable action

(a) to protect them against unreasonable risk of physical harm, and

(b) to give them first aid after it knows or has reason to know that they are ill or injured, and to care for them until they can be cared for by others.

(2) An innkeeper is under a similar duty to his guests.

(3) A possessor of land who holds it open to the public is under a similar duty to members of the public who enter in response to his invitation.

(4) One who is required by law to take or who voluntarily takes the custody of another under circumstances such as to deprive the other of his normal opportunities for protection is under a similar duty to the other.

The trial court rejected Mrs. Drew's proposed jury instructions....

The trial court instructed the jury about the restaurant's duty of care to Drew in this language:

> A restaurant whose employees are reasonably on notice that a customer is in distress and in need of emergency medical attention has a legal duty to come to the assistance of that customer. However, a restaurant does not have a duty to provide medical training to its food service personnel, or medical rescue services to its customers who become ill or injured through no act of omission of the restaurant or its employees. A restaurant in these circumstances meets its legal duty to a customer in distress when it summons medical assistance within a reasonable time.

In her appeal Mrs. Drew argues that the Restatement (Second) of Torts § 314A is the appropriate rule of law. She claims that a customer who becomes ill or injured inside a business establishment is virtually in the custodial care of those persons operating the business. She asserts that the business invitor-invitee relationship is a special relationship that gives rise to a duty on the invitor's part to render first aid to the invitee.

...

[T]he restaurant owner's position that its duty of care to its customer is fulfilled if, after having notice of the customer's illness or injury, the business proprietor summons medical assistance within a reasonable time. One case offered by LeJay's, *Breaux v. Gino's, Inc.*, 153 Cal.App.3d 379, 200 Cal.Rptr. 260 (1984), is particularly instructive. There, the California court focused on the nature and extent of restaurants' duty to come to the assistance of their customers who become ill or need medical attention. The California court observed that loss compensability is an "essentially political" question which the courts may decide if neither the constitution nor the legislature has spoken on the subject. The court recognized a duty existed, and held that the legislature had already decided the question of the extent of duty in that by statute restaurants meet their legal duty to a customer in distress when they summon medical assistance within a reasonable time. *Id.*, 200 Cal.Rptr. at 262.

We agree with the analysis offered by the California court. Neither the Wyoming Constitution nor our statutes speak to this duty, nor have we been directed to any applicable regulations. Consequently, this issue is appropriately decided in Wyoming by court decision. We find no basis in this jurisdiction for disagreeing with the extent of the duty as declared by the able trial judge, the summoning of medical assistance within a reasonable time. We are concerned that a specific requirement of first aid, rather than aid in the form of a timely call for professional medical assistance, would place undue burdens on food servers and other business-invitors.

In the first instance, the likelihood of an invitee requiring first aid in this sort of circumstance is remote. LeJay's argues persuasively that approximately 270 billion meals are consumed annually in the United States, while only 3,000 choking deaths occur each year. These deaths are not further subdivided into categories such as eating or objects placed in the mouth, but it is apparent in any case that the likelihood of a food server being faced with this circumstance is very remote. Beyond the basic numbers involved, the chance of first aid succeeding in this circumstance is even more remote. Eddie Drew's condition was caused by a 2-inch by 2-inch chunk of meat lodged in his trachea. It is open whether any maneuver short of a surgical procedure would have made a difference.

Offset against the slim chance of this sort of event occurring on its premises are the burdens placed on the food server such as LeJay's by being required to provide first aid. Courses in first aid techniques require both time and money. Annual recertification classes are required in CPR and the Heimlich maneuver. Because employee turnover in the food service industry is high, continual training efforts might be required to provide a staff capable of providing first aid. This duty would apply to every food server, regardless of size, across the state. The same duty that rests on large scale restaurants would apply to the 24-hour convenience store, grocery stores, movie theaters, and corner newsstand. It would apply as well to all business-invitors, whatever products or services they offer to the public.

We note one further practical limitation. Ms. Zuber, of the Wyoming Heart Association, testified that lay persons receiving CPR training are advised that they may exercise their own discretion in choosing to administer CPR in any given situation. Clearly a business-invitor's employees remain lay persons and cannot be compelled to perform first aid against their better judgment. It would not be appropriate to either remove the employee's discretion or hold the employer liable if it is exercised. The only persons expected to perform rescue techniques regardless of circumstances are the professional medical responders called for just that purpose. Whether that call is made within a reasonable time is the appropriate factual issue for jury consideration.

Our prior decisions have held the duty to an invitee is that of reasonable care under all the circumstances. *Ruhs v. Pacific Power & Light*, 671 F.2d 1268, 1272 (10th Cir.1982). Nothing has been said previously in Wyoming about the extent of that duty in these circumstances. While we agree with Restatement (Second) of Torts § 314A to the extent that we acknowledge reasonable care must be exercised in this circumstance, we are satisfied that duty is met when medical assistance is summoned within a reasonable time, and decline to adopt § 314A.

Affirmed.

Problem 5.3. Robert collapsed after participating in a cycling class at Fit 4 Life. The cycling class instructor and others present at the fitness facility put a rolled-up towel under Robert's head and offered him cool water to drink. The Fit 4 Life employees waited almost 20 minutes before calling 911 because they believed he was simply overheated and needed a few minutes to cool off and hydrate. In reality, Robert was having a heart attack and in need of immediate medical care. An ambulance arrived five minutes after receiving the call and transported Robert to the hospital, but he later died. Sally, Robert's widow, sues Fit 4 Life, alleging negligence.

Imagine that you represent Robert. Did Fit 4 Life breach any duty or duties that it owed to Robert?

4. Social Hosts

Under the traditional classifications of premises liability, social guests are generally considered to be licensees. Consequently, hosts have a duty to warn their guests of any hidden dangers the host knows or has reason to know of, if the guest does not know or have reason to know of the dangers involved. *See Stitt, supra*. However, in recent years courts have been faced with the question of whether social hosts owe a duty to third persons injured by an intoxicated person who has obtained intoxicating liquor at his or her home. *Faulk v. Suzuki Motor Co., Ltd.*, below, reflects the majority view that no such duty should be imposed by the courts.

Faulk v. Suzuki Motor, Co. Ltd.

851 P.2d 332 (Haw. App. 1993)

BURNS, Chief Judge.

Plaintiff Ellen Faulk (Faulk) appeals the circuit court's October 18, 1991 judgment ... that, as a social host server of alcoholic beverages, defendant and third-party plaintiff Albert Cabral (Cabral) was not liable for injuries his intoxicated guest, third-party defendant Jaime M. Bumanglag (Bumanglag), negligently caused to Faulk in an automobile accident. We affirm.

I.

On May 11, 1988, Cabral had a party at his house in Wailuku. Later on that same day, approximately 0.9 miles north of Olowalu, there was a collision between the

Suzuki Samurai vehicle Faulk was driving and the automobile Bumanglag was driving. Faulk was seriously injured. Bumanglag's blood alcohol level was 0.0015 or 0.15 percent and beyond the 0.10 percent maximum tolerance specified in Hawaii Revised Statutes (HRS) § 291-4(a)(2) (Supp.1992).

On May 10, 1990, Faulk filed a complaint against Cabral and the other defendants.... On May 23, 1991, Cabral moved for a summary judgment with respect to Faulk's claims against him. In her July 25, 1991 memorandum in opposition, Faulk requested that Cabral's May 23, 1991 motion not be decided for six months to allow her time to conduct formal discovery.

At the July 30, 1991 hearing on Cabral's motion, the parties stipulated to the following facts:

> 1. [Cabral] owned and occupied the subject premises.
>
> 2. CABRAL was the host for a party at the subject premises, and invited [Bumanglag] to the subject premises for the purpose of attending the party.
>
> 3. CABRAL purchased the alcohol for the party, and controlled the supply, service and consumption of the alcohol at the subject premises.
>
> 4. CABRAL observed BUMANGLAG, knew BUMANGLAG had become intoxicated, and continued to serve alcohol to BUMANGLAG with that knowledge.
>
> 5. CABRAL knew of BUMANGLAG'S intention to drive after leaving the subject premises.
>
> 6. CABRAL knew that the consumption of the alcohol by BUMANGLAG would impair the driving ability of BUMANGLAG.
>
> 7. The injuries sustained by [Faulk] were a foreseeable consequence of supplying and serving alcohol to BUMANGLAG at the subject premises.

At the conclusion of the hearing, the court orally granted Cabral's motion. The October 18, 1991 judgment followed.

II.

HRS § 281-78(b)(1)(B) (Supp.1992) provides that "[a]t no time under any circumstances shall any [liquor] licensee or its employee... [s]ell or furnish any liquor to... [a]ny person at the time under the influence of liquor[.]"

On the basis of this statute and in the absence of dram shop legislation, the Hawaii Supreme Court permitted a person who was injured by an intoxicated driver of an automobile to recover tort damages from a liquor licensee tavern that furnished liquor to the intoxicated driver prior to her operating the vehicle. *Ono v. Applegate,* 62 Haw. 131, 612 P.2d 533 (1980). In Faulk's case, however, Cabral was not, on May 11, 1988, a liquor licensee under HRS Chapter 281 or an employee of a liquor licensee. Hawaii does not have a statute that imposes upon a non-liquor licensee social host a tort law duty emanating from the fact that the social host furnished liquor to a sober or intoxicated social guest for voluntary consumption.

Thus, the issue is whether, in Hawaii, a non-liquor licensee social host has a non-statutory tort law duty to protect third persons from risks of personal injury and/or property damage caused when the following three events occur in the following sequence: (1) at the social host's party at the social host's residence, the social host's invited adult guest becomes intoxicated and more intoxicated from consuming alcoholic beverage provided by the social host; (2) while intoxicated, the adult guest leaves the social host's residence and operates an automobile other than the social host's automobile; and (3) the intoxicated adult guest's negligent operation of the automobile causes injury to a third person and/or damage to a third person's property. This is a question of law. Based on *Johnston v. KFC Nat'l Management Co.*, 71 Haw. 229, 788 P.2d 159 (1990), the answer is no.

In *Johnston*, Kentucky Fried Chicken (KFC) employees held an authorized Christmas party for themselves at KFC's Aiea branch after it closed for operations on that day. KFC supplied some of the food and paper goods. The participants supplied the liquor. Travis, the KFC Aiea branch manager, invited Parks, a KFC employee at another branch. Cui, then age 19, was an employee at the KFC Aiea branch. Cui invited some of the participants to continue the Christmas party at Cui's parents' residence in Wahiawa. Parks was visibly intoxicated when she left the KFC Aiea branch party. Parks drove to Cui's parents' residence and consumed beer supplied by Cui. The party was on the residential premises but not in the house. Cui's parents were asleep in their bedroom. Parks then drove to her home on Ward Avenue, showered, changed clothes, and while driving her friend Wai home, drove into oncoming traffic on Kapiolani Boulevard and severely and permanently injured Johnston, who was operating a moped. The circuit court entered summary judgment in favor of KFC, Cui, and Cui's parents. The Hawaii Supreme Court affirmed, holding that "as a matter of law, [Cui and Cui's parents], and KFC, as an alleged social host or as an employer, owed no duty to Johnston under the facts of this case." *Id.* at 238, 788 P.2d at 164.

Faulk's attempt to distinguish the facts in her case from the facts in *Johnston* fails. There is no relevant difference.

Likewise, Faulk's suggestion that *Johnston* anticipated its own demise is wrong. In *Johnston*, the Hawaii Supreme Court saw "no clear judicial trend toward modifying the traditional common law, nor any statutory enactment or policy which leads [it] to conclude that a change in the common law [which imposes no duty upon social hosts] is appropriate at this time." *Id.* at 233–34, 788 P.2d at 162. Faulk has not demonstrated that the judicial trend or policy is relevantly different since *Johnston* was decided in 1990 or that it should be.

III.

Faulk also contends that the circuit court abused its discretion when it denied her request for a delay of six months to permit her to conduct formal discovery. We conclude that the circuit court did not abuse its discretion.

According to Faulk's Opening Brief, she wanted time to discover "facts as to the actual conduct of CABRAL and BUMANGLAG . . . which may have shown an exacerbated situation imposing a greater duty [than was imposed by the stipulated facts] or a duty based on other facts." Other than an intentional tort, we cannot imagine a situation more exacerbating than the situation described in the stipulated facts, and nothing in the record reasonably suggests the possible existence of any facts more exacerbating than the stipulated facts.

IV.

Accordingly, we affirm the circuit court's October 18, 1991 judgment entered in accordance with its October 18, 1991 Order Granting Defendant and Third-Party Plaintiff Albert Cabral's Motion for Summary Judgment.

Note

Social host liability when serving alcohol to minor guests. Other courts considering whether to impose social host liability have declined to do so because they believed that the decision whether to impose a duty is better left to the legislature. However, some courts have been willing to find a duty when social hosts furnish intoxicating beverages to underage guests.

Martin v. Marciano

871 A.2d 911 (R.I. 2005)

WILLIAMS, Chief Justice.

The plaintiff, Brian Martin (plaintiff), was attacked with a baseball bat while attending a high school graduation party that the defendant-parent, Lee Martin[10] (defendant), hosted in honor of her daughter, Jen Martin (Jen). The plaintiff brought suit against the assailant, Chijoke Okere (Okere), party guest Matthew J. Marciano (Marciano), and the defendant. A Superior Court motion justice granted the defendant's motion for summary judgment, concluding that the defendant owed no duty to the plaintiff to protect him from Okere's attack. The plaintiff timely appealed.

Based on the evidence before this Court, we are of the opinion that summary judgment was inappropriate. If defendant provided alcoholic beverages to underage partygoers as plaintiff alleges, or had actual knowledge of the presence and consumption of alcohol by underage drinkers on her property, then defendant was duty-bound to exercise reasonable care to protect plaintiff from physical assault by persons expected to be in attendance or those acting at their behest. Whether plaintiff's injuries are causally related to defendant's conduct, or Okere's actions

10. Although they share the same last name, plaintiff and defendant are not related.

constitute a supervening act, thus breaking the causal link, are unresolved questions of fact to be determined by the fact-finder. Accordingly, we vacate the judgment of the Superior Court.

I

Facts

...

The record establishes that defendant hosted a high school graduation party for Jen at her home in the City of Warwick on July 9, 2000. A large tent and port-a-john had been rented for the occasion; in the absence of a formal guest list, people were invited through word-of-mouth. The plaintiff arrived at the party with a group of friends at approximately 8 p.m. When he arrived, there were between forty and fifty guests already there, but the number grew to approximately seventy. According to plaintiff, despite the fact that most of the guests were between the ages of seventeen and twenty, two kegs of beer were available when he arrived and many guests supplemented that supply with their own alcohol. The plaintiff said in his deposition testimony that he consumed approximately six beers from the kegs.

Marciano was also among the guests. The plaintiff testified at his deposition that he knew Marciano and, approximately one year before the party, Marciano had punched him in the face "for no reason." At some point during the evening, a fight erupted between Marciano and some of plaintiff's friends. As the fight spilled onto the street, plaintiff's friends threatened to punch Marciano. The plaintiff told Marciano to leave so the situation would defuse and the party could continue. The record discloses that Marciano left the premises but called his friend Okere, intending to return with reinforcements. Significantly, Marciano supplied Okere with a baseball bat.

Approximately half an hour to an hour later, Marciano returned to the party with Okere, who was wielding a baseball bat and asking "Who f——ed with Matt Marciano?" Within minutes of Okere's arrival, plaintiff was struck on the head with the bat that Okere had been holding. Before being hit, plaintiff did not see Okere but he heard that there likely was going to be a fight and saw people "scrambling." According to one witness, after plaintiff was hit, defendant went inside her house and locked the door, excluding people who were looking for paper towels to tend to plaintiff's head injuries. According to his brief, plaintiff suffered considerable brain damage as a result of the injury.

The plaintiff brought the instant action against defendant, as well as Okere and Marciano. The defendant moved for summary judgment, arguing that she owed plaintiff no duty to protect him from an unforeseeable attack on her property or, alternatively, that Okere's actions constituted an intervening act that broke the chain of causation between plaintiff's injuries and any negligence on her part. The motion justice granted summary judgment on the ground that defendant did not have a duty to protect plaintiff because such an attack was unforeseeable.

II
Analysis

. . .

A legal duty is a question of law that the court alone is authorized to determine. *Volpe v. Gallagher,* 821 A.2d 699, 705 (R.I. 2003). As there is "[n]o clear cut formula" for determining the existence of a duty, the court will make the determination on a case-by-case basis. *Id.* In so doing, this court "'will consider all relevant factors, including the relationship between the parties, the scope and burden of the obligation to be imposed upon the defendant, public policy considerations,'" *id.,* and the "foreseeability of harm to the plaintiff." *Banks v. Bowen's Landing Corp.,* 522 A.2d 1222, 1225 (R.I. 1987).

As a general rule, a landowner has no duty to protect another from harm caused by the dangerous or illegal acts of a third party. *Luoni v. Berube,* 431 Mass. 729, 729 N.E.2d 1108, 1111 (2000). An exception to this rule exists, however, when a plaintiff and a defendant bear a special relationship to each other. *Id.* "A special relationship, when derived from common law, is predicated on a plaintiff's reasonable expectations and reliance that a defendant will anticipate harmful acts of third persons and take appropriate measures to protect the plaintiff from harm." *Id.* One such relationship exists between those who provide intoxicants and those whom they serve. 2 Stuart M. Speiser et al., *The American Law of Torts,* § 9:20 at 1125 (1985); *see also Grisham v. John Q. Long V.F.W. Post, No. 4057 Inc.,* 519 So.2d 413, 416 (Miss.1988) ("the keeper of a bar or tavern, though not an insurer of his guests' safety, has a duty to exercise reasonable care to protect them from reasonably foreseeable injury at the hands of other patrons").

As a party host who is alleged to have made alcohol illegally[11] available to underage guests, defendant owed plaintiff "the duty of exercising reasonable care to protect [him] from harm and criminal attack at the hands of fellow [guests] or other third persons." 2 Speiser, § 9:20 at 1125. Although this duty most often has been extended to tavern and barroom operators, *see, e.g., Grisham,* 519 So.2d at 416; *Fisher v. Robbins,* 78 Wyo. 50, 319 P.2d 116, 126 (1957), there is no valid justification for absolving an adult parent of this higher standard of care when she knowingly provides alcohol, or is aware that it is available, to underage individuals, for consumption on her property. Indeed, if a barroom patron may "rely on the belief that he is in an orderly house and that its operator, personally or by his delegated representative, is exercising reasonable care to the end that the doings in the house shall be orderly * * *," so too could plaintiff. *Fisher,* 319 P.2d at 126 (quoting 30 Am. Jur. *Intoxicating Liquors* § 609 at 575 (1940)).

This Court's holding in *Ferreira v. Strack,* 652 A.2d 965 (R.I.1995), does not preclude our recognition of defendant's duty to provide protection to her guests in this

---

11. *See* G.L.1956 § 3-8-11.1 (prohibiting adults from providing alcohol to individuals under the age of twenty-one).

case. In *Ferreira*, we held that a social host owed no duty of care to "an innocent third party who suffers injuries as a result of the negligent operation of a motor vehicle by an adult guest if the negligence is caused by the guest's intoxication." *Id.* at 967. Despite our recognition of the clear public policy against drunk driving, we noted that "[t]he imposition of liability upon social hosts for the torts of guests has such serious implications that any action taken should be taken by the Legislature after careful investigation, scrutiny, and debate." *Id.* at 968.

The "serious implications" that counseled in favor of judicial restraint in *Ferreira* are noticeably absent here. Here, defendant is alleged, at most, to have willingly provided alcohol to a group of underage partygoers and, at least, supervised a party at which the underage guests were drinking openly and freely from two kegs of beer. *Cf. Ferreira*, 652 A.2d at 969–70 (questioning whether the drunk driver even could properly be termed a social guest because the hosts did not invite him to the party, did not know of his presence in their home, and had no opportunity to observe his level of intoxication). Moreover, we reject the notion that imposing a duty on defendant and other similarly irresponsible parents and hosts to protect their guests from harm causally related to the consumption of alcohol by underage drinkers creates an unreasonable burden. To avoid assuming a duty of protection, the adult property owner must simply comply with existing law and refuse to provide alcohol or condone underage drinking on his or her property. Therefore, the consequences of imposing such a duty in cases such as this are not "economically and socially staggering;" in fact, they are negligible. *Keckonen v. Robles*, 146 Ariz. 268, 705 P.2d 945, 949 (Ct.App.1985) (declining to "extend to the social host the liability imposed upon the tavern keeper").

We conclude that burdening parent-hosts who provide alcohol to underage guests with a duty to take reasonable steps to protect their guests from injury is in accord with the clear public policy of this state. The General Assembly has devoted considerable attention to the issue of underage drinking and has prohibited individuals under the age of twenty-one from purchasing, G.L.1956 § 3-8-6(a)(1); consuming, § 3-8-6(a)(2); possessing, § 3-8-10; and transporting alcohol, § 3-8-9. Individuals under the age of eighteen are prohibited from acting as bartenders. Section 3-8-2. Adults are prohibited from purchasing or procuring alcohol for people under the age of twenty-one. Section 3-8-11.1. These statutes demonstrate an overriding policy against not only underage drinking, but also an adult's provision of alcohol to minors, who, by virtue of their tender age and inexperience, are presumed less capable of handling the deleterious effects of alcohol consumption. The imposition of a higher standard of care in this case may provide a valuable disincentive for adults who might otherwise be willing to provide alcohol to minors, or to turn a blind eye to its consumption on their premises.

. . .

Conclusion

In the context of this case, we hold that the defendant had a duty to protect her guests from unreasonable harm by other guests and third persons. Factual questions remain about whether the defendant breached her duty of care and whether Okere's conduct was a foreseeable supervening cause that severed the causal relationship between the defendant's conduct and the plaintiff's injuries. Therefore, we vacate the judgment of the Superior Court. The record shall be remanded to the Superior Court.

5. Duty of Colleges and Universities to Students

Until recently, courts were reluctant to find that colleges and universities had a duty to protect their adult students from the violent acts of third parties. That attitude has shifted in recent years, particularly in light of several high-profile mass murders on college campuses.

Regents of University of California v. Superior Court

4 Cal. 5th 607 (2018)

CORRIGAN, J.

After he enrolled in the University of California at Los Angeles (UCLA), Damon Thompson experienced auditory hallucinations. He believed other students in the classroom and dormitory were criticizing him. School administrators eventually learned of Thompson's delusions and attempted to provide mental health treatment. However, one morning Thompson stabbed fellow student Katherine Rosen during a chemistry lab. Rosen sued the university and several of its employees for negligence, arguing they failed to protect her from Thompson's foreseeable violent conduct.

This case involves whether, and under what circumstances, a college or university[12] owes a duty of care to protect students like Rosen from harm. Considering the unique features of the collegiate environment, we hold that universities have a special relationship with their students and a duty to protect them from foreseeable violence during curricular activities. Because the Court of Appeal reached a different conclusion, we reverse its decision and remand for further proceedings.

I. Background

A. Thompson's Behavior Preceding the Assault

Damon Thompson transferred to UCLA in the fall of 2008. He soon began experiencing problems with other students in both classroom and residence hall settings.

At the end of fall quarter, Thompson emailed his history professor that he was "angered" by "offensive" remarks from other students during the final examination and "outrage[d]" because their comments had affected his performance. Thompson also complained he had heard the professor calling him "'troubled' and 'crazy'

12. We use the terms "college" and "university" interchangeably to refer to all schools that provide postsecondary education to enrolled students.

among other things." When the professor forwarded Thompson's messages to his department chair, he was advised to calm Thompson and encourage him to visit the school's counseling services if he appeared "genuinely paranoid or a potential threat."

Thompson next complained about mistreatment by fellow dormitory residents. In a three-page letter to the Dean of Students, Thompson alleged a female resident had repeatedly made "unwelcomed verbal sexual advances" toward him, and others had spread rumors and "accusations of a sexual nature about [him] . . . throughout the entire student body." He claimed the residents frequently disrupted his sleep, called him "'stupid,'" and eavesdropped on his phone calls. Not only had he been "made the 'target'" of the residents' "teasing," but he also "receive[d] an immense amount of unwanted attention" around campus. Thompson warned that if the university failed to discipline the responsible parties, the matter would likely "escalate into a more serious situation," and he would "end up acting in a manner that will incur undesirable consequences." A week later, the school moved Thompson to a new dormitory.

In late January 2009, Thompson complained to three professors and teaching assistant Jenny Hernandez that students had been trying to distract him with offensive comments. Hernandez told her supervising professor she had never observed this behavior but Thompson himself acted oddly, frequently talking to himself. She believed he was displaying signs of schizophrenia and should be referred to the university's Counseling and Psychological Services (CAPS). Hernandez and the professor met with Thompson and urged him to use these services, but Thompson denied "'hearing things'" or "'making this up.'" Another professor forwarded Thompson's complaints to Assistant Dean of Students Cary Porter, who contacted the university's "Consultation and Response Team" (Response Team). The Response Team advises campus members who have concerns about the well-being of particular students. Dean Porter also met with Thompson and encouraged him to seek medical help at CAPS.

Thompson's dormitory problems escalated in February. He told resident director Janelle Rahyns there were "voices coming through the walls calling him an idiot." He heard a clicking noise above his room that sounded like a gun, and he believed the other residents were planning to shoot him. Thompson told Rahyns he had telephoned his father and was advised to "hurt the other residents." While admitting he had "thought about it," Thompson said he decided not to hurt anyone. Campus police arrived and searched the premises but found no weapon. They concluded Thompson needed a psychiatric evaluation and escorted him to the emergency room for that purpose. During the examination, Thompson reported a history of depression and complained of auditory hallucinations and paranoid thinking. For several months, he had heard people talking about him and insulting him, even when "'there's no one there.'" He denied suicidal or homicidal thinking. The examiner diagnosed Thompson with possible schizophrenia and major depressive disorder. Thompson agreed to take a low-dose antipsychotic medication and begin outpatient treatment at CAPS. Dean Porter and the Response Team were informed about the incident and Thompson's mental evaluation. The Response Team began discussing Thompson at its weekly meetings.

In March 2009, Thompson began sessions with CAPS psychologist Nicole Green. Although he denied wanting to hurt himself or others, he continued to report auditory hallucinations and paranoid thoughts. He had thrown away the prescribed antipsychotic medication. Green diagnosed schizophrenia and urged Thompson to see a CAPS psychiatrist. Thompson refused to consider medication until he could determine whether the voices were real. He expressed frustration that nobody believed him and said he would try to record the voices. Around this time, Rahyns notified CAPS that Thompson was "still having trouble" in the dormitory. The Response Team decided to move him to a single room and explore possibilities for transitioning him into different housing.

Later in March, Thompson told Green he was still hearing voices and being harassed by other students. He was now amenable to psychiatric evaluation. Later that day, at a session with CAPS psychiatrist Charles McDaniel, Thompson admitted thinking about harming others, although he had no identified victim or plan. He heard numerous distinct voices in his dormitory and classrooms. He wanted to harm the people insulting him but could not attribute the voices to specific individuals. McDaniel strongly urged Thompson to submit to voluntary hospitalization. He refused but agreed to take medication. While CAPS staff agreed Thompson did not meet the criteria for an involuntary hold, McDaniel recommended involuntary hospitalization if his thoughts of harming others worsened. Thompson attended additional CAPS sessions in April and continued to report auditory hallucinations. Although angered by this perceived harassment, Thompson said he did not intend to harm his tormentors. He withdrew from treatment in late April.

On June 3, 2009, campus police responded to an incident at Thompson's dormitory. A resident reported that Thompson had knocked on his door, accused him of making too much noise, and pushed him. When the resident denied making noise, Thompson pushed him again, saying this was his "'last warning.'" As a result of the incident, Thompson was expelled from university housing and ordered to return to CAPS at the beginning of fall quarter. After he moved to an apartment, Thompson twice called the police to complain neighbors were yelling at him through the floor.

Meanwhile, Thompson continued to experience auditory hallucinations in the classroom. During the summer, he complained to two faculty members about insults and harassment in his chemistry laboratory. After fall quarter started, Thompson emailed professor Alfred Bacher that the disruptive behavior of other students was interfering with his experiments. The next day, September 30, Thompson told CAPS psychologist Tanya Brown he still "occasionally" heard "voices of other students having 'malice' toward him and making critical and racist comments." Nevertheless, he denied an intent to harm anyone, including those criticizing him. Brown noted that Thompson displayed a guarded attitude, slowed speech, delusional thought processes, and impaired insight. CAPS psychiatrist Charles

McDaniel met with Thompson the same day and made similar observations. Due to Thompson's behavior, McDaniel was unsure whether he was reporting his symptoms accurately. Thompson agreed to start treatment at the university's behavioral health clinic.

B. The Assault

On October 6th, teaching assistant Adam Goetz emailed Professor Bacher describing "another incident" with Thompson in that day's chemistry lab. Shortly after the professor left the room, Thompson accused another student of calling him stupid. He insisted on learning the student's name. After Goetz gave him the name, Thompson "calmed down" and "seemed fine." But Goetz remained worried that Thompson's behavior was becoming a weekly "routine." Goetz later testified that Thompson frequently identified Katherine Rosen, who worked "right next to" Thompson in the lab, as one of the students calling him stupid.

The following day, another teaching assistant told Professor Bacher that Thompson had come into his chemistry lab from a different section and accused students of verbally harassing him. Although Thompson did not know the students' names, he did identify a specific student, other than Rosen, as one of his tormentors. The teaching assistant saw no harassment and was skeptical of Thompson's claims.

Bacher forwarded Goetz's email to Dean Porter on the morning of October 7th, seeking advice on how to handle the situation. Porter contacted Karen Minero of the Response Team, who expressed concern that Thompson had identified a specific student. Minero forwarded Porter's email to other Response Team members and CAPS personnel. The CAPS director contacted Green, suggesting Thompson "may need urgent outreach," and members of the Response Team tried to schedule a meeting to discuss Thompson. Thompson did not appear for a scheduled session with Green that afternoon. The next morning, Porter and Minero discussed Thompson and decided to investigate whether he was having similar difficulties in other classes.

Around noon on October 8th, Thompson was doing classwork in Professor Bacher's chemistry laboratory. Suddenly, without warning or provocation, he stabbed fellow student Katherine Rosen in the chest and neck with a kitchen knife. Rosen had been kneeling down, placing items in her lab drawer, when Thompson attacked her from behind. She was taken to the hospital with life-threatening injuries but ultimately survived. When campus police arrived, Thompson admitted he had stabbed someone and explained that the other students had been teasing him. Thompson ultimately pleaded not guilty by reason of insanity to a charge of attempted murder. (Pen. Code, §§ 187, subd. (a), 664, 1026.) He was admitted to Patton State Hospital and diagnosed with paranoid schizophrenia.

C. Procedural History

Rosen sued Thompson, the Regents of the University of California, and several UCLA employees, including Alfred Bacher, Cary Porter, Robert Naples, and CAPS psychologist Nicole Green. The complaint alleged a single cause of action against the UCLA defendants[13] for negligence. Rosen alleged UCLA had a special relationship with her as an enrolled student, which entailed a duty "to take reasonable protective measures to ensure her safety against violent attacks and otherwise protect her from reasonable foreseeable criminal conduct, to warn her as to such reasonable foreseeable criminal conduct on its campus and in its buildings, and/or to control the reasonably foreseeable wrongful acts of third parties/other students." She alleged UCLA breached this duty because, although aware of Thompson's "dangerous propensities," it failed to warn or protect her or to control Thompson's foreseeably violent conduct.

UCLA moved for summary judgment on three alternative grounds: (1) colleges have no duty to protect their adult students from criminal acts; (2) if a duty does exist, UCLA did not breach it in this case; and (3) UCLA and Green were immune from liability under certain Government Code provisions. In opposing the motion, Rosen argued UCLA owed her a duty of care because colleges have a special relationship with students in the classroom, based on their supervisory duties and the students' status as business invitees. Rosen also claimed UCLA assumed a duty of care by undertaking to provide campus-wide security.

The trial court denied the motion. The court concluded a duty could exist under each of the grounds Rosen identified, triable issues of fact remained as to breach of duty, and the immunity statutes did not apply.

UCLA challenged this order in a petition for writ of mandate. A divided panel of the Court of Appeal granted the petition. . . . We granted review.

II. Discussion

A. Standard of Review

. . .

The Court of Appeal determined summary judgment should have been granted because Rosen could not establish duty. "Duty, being a question of law, is particularly amenable to resolution by summary judgment." (*Parsons*, *supra*, 15 Cal.4th at p. 465, 63 Cal.Rptr.2d 291, 936 P.2d 70.) Contrary to the Court of Appeal, however, we conclude universities *do* have a legal duty, under certain circumstances, to protect or warn[14] their students from foreseeable violence in the classroom or during curricular activities. The trial court properly denied summary judgment on this ground.

---

13. We refer to these defendants collectively, and the school itself, by the acronym UCLA.

14. We speak here of a university's duty "to protect" its students from foreseeable harm. However, in an appropriate case, this duty may be fully discharged if adequate *warnings* are conveyed to the students at risk. (Cf. *Tarasoff v. Regents of University of California* (1976) 17 Cal.3d 425, 439–440, 131 Cal.Rptr. 14, 551 P.2d 334 (*Tarasoff*) [discussing therapist's duty to protect discharged through warnings].)

B. A College's Duty to Protect Students from Foreseeable Harm

...

In general, each person has a duty to act with reasonable care under the circumstances. (*Cabral v. Ralphs Grocery Co.* (2011) 51 Cal.4th 764, 771, 122 Cal.Rptr.3d 313, 248 P.3d 1170 (*Cabral*); see Civ. Code, § 1714, subd. (a).) However, "one owes no duty to control the conduct of another, nor to warn those endangered by such conduct." (*Davidson v. City of Westminster* (1982) 32 Cal.3d 197, 203, 185 Cal.Rptr. 252, 649 P.2d 894 (*Davidson*).) "A person who has not created a peril is not liable in tort merely for failure to take affirmative action to assist or protect another unless there is some relationship between them which gives rise to a duty to act." (*Williams v. State of California* (1983) 34 Cal.3d 18, 23, 192 Cal.Rptr. 233, 664 P.2d 137; see *Cabral*, at p. 771, 122 Cal.Rptr.3d 313, 248 P.3d 1170.)

...

Rosen's complaint alleges UCLA had separate duties to protect her *and* to "control the reasonably foreseeable wrongful acts of third parties/other students." Here, we have focused on the university's duty to protect students from foreseeable violence. Having concluded UCLA had a duty to protect Rosen under the circumstances alleged, we need not decide whether the school had a separate duty to control Thompson's behavior to prevent the harm.

1. College-Student Special Relationship Supports a Limited Duty

Whether UCLA was negligent in failing to prevent Thompson's attack depends first on whether a university has a special relationship with its students that supports a duty to warn or protect them from foreseeable harm. The determination whether a particular relationship supports a duty of care rests on policy and is a question of law. (Rest.3d Torts, Liability for Physical and Emotional Harm, § 40, coms. e & h, pp. 41–42.)

a. Features of a Special Relationship

The Restatement [Third of Torts] does not exclude colleges from the school-student special relationship. However, the drafters observe that reasonable care varies in different school environments, with substantially different supervision being appropriate in elementary schools as opposed to colleges. (*Id.*, § 40, com. l, p. 45.) State courts have reached different conclusions about whether colleges owe a special relationship-based duty to their students. (*Id.*, § 40, com. l, reporter's notes, p. 57.) We have not previously addressed the question.

Relationships that have been recognized as "special" share a few common features. Generally, the relationship has an aspect of dependency in which one party relies to some degree on the other for protection.... The Restatement authors observed over 50 years ago that the law has been "working slowly toward a recognition of the duty to aid or protect in any relation of dependence or of mutual dependence." (Rest.2d Torts, § 314A, com. b, p. 119.)

The corollary of dependence in a special relationship is control. Whereas one party is dependent, the other has superior control over the means of protection. "[A] typical setting for the recognition of a special relationship is where 'the plaintiff is particularly vulnerable and dependent upon the defendant who, correspondingly, has some control over the plaintiff's welfare.' [Citations.]" (Giraldo v. Department of Corrections & Rehabilitation (2008) 168 Cal.App.4th 231, 245–246, 85 Cal. Rptr.3d 371.) One court observed that "the epitome" of such a special relationship exists between a jailer and prisoner. (*Id.* at pp. 250–251, 85 Cal.Rptr.3d 371.) Common carriers and their passengers present another quintessential example. . . .

Special relationships also have defined boundaries. They create a duty of care owed to a limited community, not the public at large. We have held that police officers are not in a special relationship with the citizens in their jurisdiction (*see Williams v. State of California*, *supra*, 34 Cal.3d at pp. 27–28, 192 Cal.Rptr. 233, 664 P.2d 137), even when officers are aware of risks to a specific potential victim (see Davidson, supra, 32 Cal.3d at pp. 208–209, 185 Cal.Rptr. 252, 649 P.2d 894). Nor is a government entity in a special relationship with all citizens who use its facilities. (*Zelig v. County of Los Angeles*, *supra*, 27 Cal.4th at p. 1130, 119 Cal.Rptr.2d 709, 45 P.3d 1171.) In declining to find a duty of care owed to courthouse visitors, we observed that a "county, 'as with all public entities,' has the responsibility to 'exercise reasonable care to protect all of its citizens' [citation], but does not thereby become liable to each individual for all foreseeable harm." (*Id.* at p. 1131, 119 Cal.Rptr.2d 709, 45 P.3d 1171.) Because a special relationship is limited to specific individuals, the defendant's duty is less burdensome and more justifiable than a broad-ranging duty would be. (See Rest.3d Torts, Liability for Physical and Emotional Harm, § 40, com. h, p. 43.)

Finally, although relationships often have advantages for both participants, many special relationships especially benefit the party charged with a duty of care. (Rest.3d Torts, Liability for Physical and Emotional Harm, § 40, com. h, p. 43.) Retail stores or hotels could not successfully operate, for example, without visits from their customers and guests.

b. The College Environment

The legal significance of the college-student relationship has changed with shifting cultural attitudes. Before the 1960s, colleges stood in loco parentis to students, who were viewed as being under their custody and institutional control. (Sokolow et al., *College and University Liability for Violent Campus Attacks* (2008) 34 J.C. & U.L. 319, 321 (hereafter Sokolow).) Although the role of parental stand-in may have given colleges some obligation to protect students (see *Bradshaw v. Rawlings* (3d Cir. 1979) 612 F.2d 135, 139 (*Bradshaw*)), the era also recognized parental immunity. Parents were largely immune from suit by their children, and colleges often enjoyed the same immunity, at least with respect to disciplining or regulating student conduct. (Lake, *The Rise of Duty and the Fall of In Loco Parentis and Other Protective Tort Doctrines in Higher Education Law* (1999) 64 Mo. L.Rev. 1, 5 (hereafter Lake).)

When rigid immunity defenses gave way to more flexible doctrines during the 1970s and 1980s, the view that colleges stood in loco parentis shifted to what Professor Peter Lake calls the "bystander" era in university liability. (See Lake, *supra*, 64 Mo. L.Rev. at pp. 11, 16.) Dramatic social changes of that time expanded the privacy and autonomy rights of adult students and, correspondingly, reduced the authority of college administrators to control student behavior. (*Bradshaw*, *supra*, 612 F.2d at p. 140.) Courts generally reacted to these changes by treating colleges like businesses. (Lake, at p. 12.) While the university might owe a duty as a landowner to maintain a safe premises, courts typically resisted finding a broader duty based on a special relationship with students. (See, *e.g.*, *Nero v. Kansas State University* (1993) 253 Kan. 567, 580, 583–584 [861 P.2d 768, 778–780].) This was particularly so when injuries resulted from alcohol consumption or fraternity activity. (See Lake, at p. 12.)[15]

. . .

Considering the unique features of the college environment, we conclude postsecondary schools *do* have a special relationship with students while they are engaged in activities that are part of the school's curriculum or closely related to its delivery of educational services.

Although comparisons can be made, the college environment is unlike any other. Colleges provide academic courses in exchange for a fee, but a college is far more to its students than a business. Residential colleges provide living spaces, but they are more than mere landlords. Along with educational services, colleges provide students social, athletic, and cultural opportunities. Regardless of the campus layout, colleges provide a discrete *community* for their students. For many students, college is the first time they have lived away from home. Although college students may no longer be minors under the law, they may still be learning how to navigate the world as adults. They are dependent on their college communities to provide structure, guidance, and a safe learning environment. "In the closed environment of a school campus where students pay tuition and other fees in exchange for using the facilities, where they spend a significant portion of their time and may in fact live, they can reasonably expect that the premises will be free from physical defects and that school authorities will also exercise reasonable care to keep the campus free from conditions which increase the risk of crime." (*Peterson*, *supra*, 36 Cal.3d at p. 813, 205 Cal.Rptr. 842, 685 P.2d 1193.)

Colleges, in turn, have superior control over the environment and the ability to protect students. Colleges impose a variety of rules and restrictions, both in the classroom and across campus, to maintain a safe and orderly environment. They often employ resident advisers, mental health counselors, and campus police. They can monitor and discipline students when necessary. "While its primary function

---

15. "These cases have become known as the 'bystander' cases because in each of them the university was cast in the role of a legal bystander to 'uncontrollable' student actions and drinking." (Lake, *supra*, 64 Mo. L.Rev. at p. 16.)

is to foster intellectual development through an academic curriculum, the institution is involved in all aspects of student life. Through its providing of food, housing, security, and a range of extracurricular activities the modern university provides a setting in which every aspect of student life is, to some degree, university guided." (*Furek v. University of Delaware* (Del. 1991) 594 A.2d 506, 516.) Finally, in a broader sense, college administrators and educators "have the power to influence [students'] values, their consciousness, their relationships, and their behaviors." (de Haven, *The Elephant in the Ivory Tower: Rampages in Higher Education and the Case for Institutional Liability* (2009) 35 J.C. & U.L. 503, 611 (hereafter de Haven).)

The college-student relationship thus fits within the paradigm of a special relationship. Students are comparatively vulnerable and dependent on their colleges for a safe environment. Colleges have a superior ability to provide that safety with respect to activities they sponsor or facilities they control. Moreover, this relationship is bounded by the student's enrollment status. Colleges do not have a special relationship with the world at large, but only with their enrolled students. The population is limited, as is the relationship's duration.

Of course, many aspects of a modern college student's life are, quite properly, beyond the institution's control. Colleges generally have little say in how students behave off campus, or in their social activities unrelated to school. It would be unrealistic for students to rely on their college for protection in these settings, and the college would often be unable to provide it. This is another appropriate boundary of the college-student relationship: Colleges are in a special relationship with their enrolled students only in the context of school-sponsored activities over which the college has some measure of control. (Cf. *Avila*, *supra*, 38 Cal.4th at p. 163, 41 Cal. Rptr.3d 299, 131 P.3d 383 ["school-supervised" athletic events]; *Patterson v. Sacramento City Unified School Dist.* (2007) 155 Cal.App.4th 821, 830, 66 Cal.Rptr.3d 337 ["'school-sponsored'" community service project].) As commentators have observed, while there is an "emerging trend" of courts recognizing a special relationship between colleges and their students (Sokolow, *supra*, 34 J.C. & U.L. at p. 323), this relationship supports a duty of care only with respect to "risks that arise within the scope of the school-student relationship." (*Id.* at pp. 323–324; see Peters, *Protecting the Millennial College Student* (2007) 16 S. Cal. Rev. L. & Soc. Just. 431, 459–460; Dall, *Determining Duty in Collegiate Tort Litigation: Shifting the Paradigms of the College-Student Relationship* (2003) 29 J.C. & U.L. 485, 485–487.)

. . .

The special relationship we now recognize is . . . limited. It extends to activities that are tied to the school's curriculum but not to student behavior over which the university has no significant degree of control. The incident here occurred in a chemistry laboratory while class was in session. Education is at the core of a college's mission, and the classroom is the quintessential setting for curricular activities. Perhaps more than any other place on campus, colleges can be expected to retain a measure of control over the classroom environment. Although collegiate class attendance may not be as strictly monitored as in secondary school, this distinction is not especially significant. All college students who hope to obtain a degree must attend classes and required laboratory sessions. It is reasonable for them to expect that their schools will provide some measure of safety in the classroom.

2. Policy Considerations Support Recognizing a Limited Duty

As discussed, there is generally no duty to protect others from the conduct of third parties. The "special relationship" doctrine is an exception to this general rule. (*Delgado v. Trax Bar & Grill* (2005) 36 Cal.4th 224, 235, 30 Cal.Rptr.3d 145, 113 P.3d 1159; *Tarasoff, supra*, 17 Cal.3d at pp. 435–436, 131 Cal.Rptr. 14, 551 P.2d 334; Rest.3d Torts, Liability for Physical and Emotional Harm, § 40.) Accordingly, as a consequence of the special relationship recognized here, colleges generally owe a duty to use reasonable care to protect their students from foreseeable acts of violence in the classroom or during curricular activities.

...

The court may depart from the general rule of duty, however, if other policy considerations clearly require an exception. (*Kesner v. Superior Court* (2016) 1 Cal.5th 1132, 1143, 210 Cal.Rptr.3d 283, 384 P.3d 283 (*Kesner*); *Cabral, supra*, 51 Cal.4th at p. 771, 122 Cal.Rptr.3d 313, 248 P.3d 1170; see also *Verdugo v. Target Corp.* (2014) 59 Cal.4th 312, 344, 173 Cal.Rptr.3d 662, 327 P.3d 774 (conc. opn. of Werdegar, J.).) We have identified several factors that may, on balance, justify excusing or limiting a defendant's duty of care. These include: "the foreseeability of harm to the plaintiff, the degree of certainty that the plaintiff suffered injury, the closeness of the connection between the defendant's conduct and the injury suffered, the moral blame attached to the defendant's conduct, the policy of preventing future harm, the extent of the burden to the defendant and consequences to the community of imposing a duty to exercise care with resulting liability for breach, and the availability, cost, and prevalence of insurance for the risk involved." (*Rowland v. Christian* (1968) 69 Cal.2d 108, 113, 70 Cal.Rptr. 97, 443 P.2d 561 (*Rowland*).) These factors must be "evaluated at a relatively broad level of factual generality." (*Cabral*, at p. 772, 122 Cal.Rptr.3d 313, 248 P.3d 1170.) In considering them, we determine "not whether they support an exception to the general duty of reasonable care on the facts of the particular case before us, but whether carving out an entire category of cases from that general duty rule is justified by clear considerations of policy." (*Ibid.*) In other words, the duty analysis is categorical, not case-specific. (See *Kesner*, at p. 1144, 210 Cal.Rptr.3d 283, 384 P.3d 283.).

...

We conclude that violence against students in the classroom or during curricular activities, while rare, is a foreseeable occurrence, and considerations of public policy do not justify categorically barring an injured student's claim against the university.

a. Foreseeability Factors

(1) "The most important factor to consider in determining whether to create an exception to the general duty to exercise ordinary care ... is whether the injury

in question was *foreseeable*." (*Kesner*, *supra*, 1 Cal.5th at p. 1145, 210 Cal.Rptr.3d 283, 384 P.3d 283, italics added; see *Tarasoff*, *supra*, 17 Cal.3d at p. 434, 131 Cal. Rptr. 14, 551 P.2d 334.) In examining foreseeability, "the court's task . . . 'is not to decide whether a *particular* plaintiff's injury was reasonably foreseeable in light of a *particular* defendant's conduct, but rather to evaluate more generally whether the category of negligent conduct at issue is sufficiently likely to result in the kind of harm experienced that liability may appropriately be imposed . . . .'" (*Cabral*, *supra*, 51 Cal.4th at p. 772, 122 Cal.Rptr.3d 313, 248 P.3d 1170; accord *Parsons*, *supra*, 15 Cal.4th at p. 476, 63 Cal.Rptr.2d 291, 936 P.2d 70.)

Phrased at the appropriate level of generality, then, the question here is not whether UCLA could predict that Damon Thompson would stab Katherine Rosen in the chemistry lab. It is whether a reasonable university could foresee that its negligent failure to control a potentially violent student, or to warn students who were foreseeable targets of his ire, could result in harm to one of those students. Violent unprovoked attacks by and against college students, while still relatively uncommon, are happening more frequently. (See de Haven, *supra*, 35 J.C. & U.L. at p. 510.) One example occurred on April 16, 2007 at Virginia Polytechnic Institute and State University (Virginia Tech), when an emotionally disturbed underclassman barred the doors to a classroom building, then walked the halls shooting people, killing five professors and 24 students. (See *id.* at pp. 554–566.) He left over a dozen more wounded before taking his own life. (*Id.* at p. 566.) Although mass shootings on college campuses had occurred before, the record demonstrates that the Virginia Tech tragedy prompted schools to reexamine their campus security policies. A January 2008 report of the University of California Campus Security Task Force recommended several improvements in student mental health services, emergency communications, preparedness, and hazard mitigation across all campuses. In April 2008, almost exactly one year after the Virginia Tech shootings, a special review task force of the International Association of Campus Law Enforcement Administrators published a "Blueprint for Safer Campuses," with several recommendations for assessing and responding to potential threats. Colleges across the country, including the public universities of California, created threat assessment protocols and multidisciplinary teams to identify and prevent campus violence. Thus, particularly after the Virginia Tech shootings focused national attention on the issue, colleges have been alert to the possibility that students, particularly those with mental health issues, may lash out violently against those around them. Even a comparatively rare classroom attack is a foreseeable occurrence that colleges have been equipping themselves to address for at least the past decade.

Whether a university was, or should have been, on notice that a *particular* student posed a foreseeable risk of violence is a case-specific question, to be examined in light of all the surrounding circumstances. Any prior threats or acts of violence by the student would be relevant, particularly if targeted at an identifiable victim. (See *Mullins v. Pine Manor College*, *supra*, 449 N.E.2d at p. 337.) Other relevant facts could include the opinions of examining mental health professionals, or observations of students, faculty, family members, and others in the university community. Such case-specific foreseeability questions are relevant in determining the applicable standard of care or breach in a particular case. They do not, however, inform our threshold determination that a duty exists.

(2) The second factor, "the degree of *certainty* that the plaintiff suffered injury" (*Rowland, supra*, 69 Cal.2d at p. 113, 70 Cal.Rptr. 97, 443 P.2d 561, italics added), may come into play when the plaintiff's claim involves intangible harm, such as emotional distress. (*Kesner, supra*, 1 Cal.5th at p. 1148, 210 Cal.Rptr.3d 283, 384 P.3d 283.) Here, however, we are addressing claims for physical injuries that are capable of identification. (See *ibid.*)

(3) The third factor is "the *closeness of the connection* between the defendant's conduct and the injury suffered." (*Rowland, supra*, 69 Cal.2d at p. 113, 70 Cal.Rptr. 97, 443 P.2d 561, italics added.) "Generally speaking, where the injury suffered is connected only distantly and indirectly to the defendant's negligent act, the risk of that type of injury from the category of negligent conduct at issue is likely to be deemed unforeseeable. Conversely, a closely connected type of injury is likely to be deemed foreseeable." (*Cabral, supra*, 51 Cal.4th at p. 779, 122 Cal.Rptr.3d 313, 248 P.3d 1170.) The negligence alleged here is the failure to prevent a classroom assault, either by controlling the perpetrator or warning the potential victim. Although the immediate cause of injury in such cases will be the perpetrator's violent outburst, we have explained that the existence of an intervening act does not necessarily attenuate a defendant's negligence. Rather, "the touchstone of the analysis is the foreseeability of that intervening conduct." (*Kesner, supra*, 1 Cal.5th at p. 1148, 210 Cal.Rptr.3d 283, 384 P.3d 283.) When circumstances put a school on notice that a student is at risk to commit violence against other students, the school's failure to take appropriate steps to warn or protect foreseeable victims can be causally connected to injuries the victims suffer as a result of that violence. Although a criminal act is always shocking to some degree, it is not completely unpredictable if a defendant is aware of the risk. (See, *e.g.*, *Randi W. v. Muroc Joint Unified School Dist.* (1997) 14 Cal.4th 1066, 1077–1078, 60 Cal.Rptr.2d 263, 929 P.2d 582; cf. *Thompson v. County of Alameda* (1980) 27 Cal.3d 741, 758, 167 Cal.Rptr. 70, 614 P.2d 728 [crime committed after release of a potentially dangerous offender "is statistically foreseeable"].)

b. Policy Factors

Although *Rowland*'s foreseeability factors weigh in favor of recognizing a duty of care, we must also consider whether public policy requires a different result. (See *Kesner, supra*, 1 Cal.5th at pp. 1149–1150, 210 Cal.Rptr.3d 283, 384 P.3d 283; *Cabral, supra*, 51 Cal.4th at p. 781, 122 Cal.Rptr.3d 313, 248 P.3d 1170.) "A duty of care will not be held to exist even as to foreseeable injuries . . . where the social utility of the activity concerned is so great, and avoidance of the injuries so burdensome to society, as to outweigh the compensatory and cost-internalization values of negligence liability." (*Merrill v. Navegar, Inc., supra*, 26 Cal.4th at p. 502, 110 Cal.Rptr.2d 370, 28 P.3d 116; see *Parsons, supra*, 15 Cal.4th at p. 476, 63 Cal.Rptr.2d 291, 936 P.2d 70.)

(1) Some measure of *moral blame* does attach to a university's negligent failure to prevent violence against its students. "We have previously assigned moral blame, and we have relied in part on that blame in finding a duty, in instances where the plaintiffs are particularly powerless or unsophisticated compared to the defendants or where the defendants exercised greater control over the risks at issue." (*Kesner, supra*, 1 Cal.5th at p. 1151, 210 Cal.Rptr.3d 283, 384 P.3d 283.) With the decline of colleges' in loco parentis role, adult students can no longer be considered particularly powerless or unsophisticated. "While the college will take a lead role in campus security and safety issues, 'babysitting' would defeat the proper role of most colleges in most instances. Most often the proper student/college relationship is one of *shared* responsibility." (Lake, *supra*, 64 Mo. L.Rev. at p. 26.) Nevertheless, compared to students, colleges will typically have access to more information about potential threats and a superior ability to control the environment and prevent harm. This disparity in knowledge and control tips the balance slightly in favor of duty.

(2) "The overall *policy of preventing future harm* is ordinarily served, in tort law, by imposing the costs of negligent conduct upon those responsible. The policy question is whether that consideration is outweighed, for a category of negligent conduct, by laws or mores indicating approval of the conduct or by the undesirable consequences of allowing potential liability." (*Cabral, supra*, 51 Cal.4th at pp. 781–782, 122 Cal.Rptr.3d 313, 248 P.3d 1170, italics added.) UCLA argues imposing a duty of care would discourage colleges from offering comprehensive mental health and crisis management services. Rather than become engaged in the treatment of their mentally ill students, colleges would have an incentive to expel anyone who might pose a remote threat to others. We understand that the recognition of a duty of care will force schools to balance competing goals and make sometimes difficult decisions. The existence of a duty may give some schools a marginal incentive to suspend or expel students who display a potential for violence. It might make schools reluctant to admit certain students, or to offer mental health treatment. But colleges' decisions in this area are restricted to some extent by laws such as the Americans with Disabilities Act (42 U.S.C. § 12101 et seq.). In addition, the market forces that drove colleges across the country to adopt sophisticated violence prevention protocols in the wake of the Virginia Tech incident would likely weigh against the dismantling of these protections. Colleges and universities also may have options short of expelling or denying admission to deal with potentially violent students. What constitutes reasonable care will vary with the circumstances of each case. On the whole, however, if such steps can avert violent episodes like the one that occurred here, recognizing a duty serves the policy of preventing future harm.

UCLA also predicts that legal recognition of a duty might deter students from seeking mental health treatment, or being candid with treatment providers, for fear that their confidences would be disclosed. To a large extent, however, the conditions that might influence student perceptions about confidentiality already exist. Psychotherapists' duty to warn about patient threats is well established in California. Indeed, despite fears that this duty would deter people from seeking treatment and irreparably damage the psychotherapist-patient relationship (see, *e.g.*, *Tarasoff, supra*, 17 Cal.3d at pp. 458–460, 131 Cal.Rptr. 14, 551 P.2d 334 (dis. opn. of Clark, J.)), empirical studies have produced "no evidence thus far that patients have been discouraged from coming to therapy, or discouraged from speaking freely once there, for fear that their confidentiality will be breached" (Buckner & Firestone, *"Where the Public Peril Begins" 25 Years After Tarasoff*, 21 J. Legal Med. 187, 221). Moreover, as the record in this case demonstrates, threat assessment and violence prevention protocols are already prevalent on university campuses. Recognizing that the university owes its students a duty of care under certain circumstances is unlikely to appreciably change this landscape.

(3) Which leads to the next policy factor: the *burden* that recognizing a tort duty would impose on the defendant and the community. (See *Rowland, supra*, 69 Cal.2d at p. 113, 70 Cal.Rptr. 97, 443 P.2d 561.) UCLA and some amici curiae place considerable weight on this factor, arguing it would be prohibitively expensive and impractical to make university professors and administrators the "insurers" of student safety. But the record shows that UCLA, like other colleges across the country, has *already* developed sophisticated strategies for identifying and defusing potential threats to student safety. The school created multidisciplinary teams of trained staff members and professionals for this very purpose. Indeed, one of these teams was closely monitoring Thompson's behavior. UCLA also expressly marketed itself to prospective students, and their parents, as "one of the safest campuses in the country." These enhanced safety measures came at a price, but students paid the bill. In 2007, schools in the University of California system raised mandatory registration fees 3 percent to improve student mental health services, and they planned further increases to implement all of the violence prevention measures recommended by the Campus Security Task Force. Because the record reflects that colleges have already focused considerable attention on identifying and responding to potential threats, and have funding sources available for these efforts, it does not appear that recognizing a legal duty to protect students from foreseeable threats would pose an unmanageable burden.

The duty we recognize here is owed not to the public at large but is limited to enrolled students who are at foreseeable risk of being harmed in a violent attack while participating in curricular activities at the school. Moreover, universities are not charged with a broad duty to prevent violence against their students. Such a duty could be impossible to discharge in many circumstances. Rather, the school's duty is to take *reasonable* steps to protect students when it becomes aware of a *foreseeable* threat to their safety. The reasonableness of a school's actions in response to a potential threat is a question of breach.

(4) The final policy factor in a duty analysis is the *availability of insurance* for the risk involved. (*Rowland, supra*, 69 Cal.2d at p. 113, 70 Cal.Rptr. 97, 443 P.2d 561.) While not addressing this issue specifically, UCLA has offered no reason to doubt colleges' ability to obtain coverage for the negligence liability under consideration.

Accordingly, an examination of the *Rowland* factors does not persuade us to depart from our decision to recognize a tort duty arising from the special relationship between colleges and their enrolled students. Specifically, we hold that colleges have a duty to use reasonable care to protect their students from foreseeable violence during curricular activities.

We emphasize that a duty of care is not the equivalent of liability. Nor should our holding be read to create an impossible requirement that colleges prevent violence on their campuses. Colleges are not the ultimate insurers of all student safety. We simply hold that they have a duty to act with reasonable care when aware of a foreseeable threat of violence in a curricular setting. Reasonable care will vary under the circumstances of each case. Moreover, some assaults may be unavoidable despite a college's best efforts to prevent them. Courts and juries should be cautioned to avoid judging liability based on hindsight.

Our conclusion that universities owe a duty to protect students from foreseeable violence during curricular activities does not end the matter, however.[16] UCLA's petition for writ of mandate argued summary judgment should have been granted for three reasons. First, UCLA claimed it owed Rosen no duty of care; second, it did not negligently breach any duty to Rosen; and third, various immunity statutes shielded the school and individual defendants from liability.[17] The Court of Appeal majority agreed that UCLA owed no duty of care and did not reach the other arguments. Thus, while we conclude UCLA did owe a duty to protect Rosen, we will remand for the Court of Appeal to decide whether triable issues of material fact remain on the questions of breach and immunity. In regard to breach, we note that the appropriate *standard of care* for judging the reasonableness of the university's actions remains an open question, which the parties are free to litigate on remand. UCLA's argument that there was little more it reasonably could have done to prevent the assault may be relevant to this determination.

Finally, apart from their diverging views on duty, the majority and dissenting justices below agreed that Rosen had failed to plead or support a claim against UCLA psychologist Nicole Green under Civil Code section 43.92. That statute provides that a psychotherapist is not liable for failing to protect against a patient's violent behavior unless the patient has told the therapist about a serious threat of physical violence against a reasonably identifiable victim. (Civ. Code, § 43.92, subd. (a).) Because Rosen's petition for review was limited to the issue of duty and did not challenge the Court of Appeal's conclusion regarding section 43.92, we decline her invitation to revisit the ruling now.

---

16. Because we decide the university had a duty arising out of its special relationship with Rosen, we do not address Rosen's alternate theories of duty based on an implied-in-fact contract or the negligent undertaking doctrine.

17. Specifically, the school relied on Government Code section 856, which immunizes public entities' decisions about involuntary confinement, and section 820.2, which immunizes public employees' discretionary acts.

III. Disposition

The decision of the Court of Appeal is reversed. The case is remanded for further proceedings consistent with this opinion.

CHIN, J. concurring

I agree with the majority that universities have a duty to warn or protect their students from foreseeable acts of violence "in the classroom." (Maj. opn., *ante*, at 230 Cal.Rptr.3d at p. 424, 413 P.3d at p. 663.) However, for several reasons, I do not join the majority opinion insofar as it would extend this duty beyond the classroom, to encompass more broadly "curricular activities" (*ibid.*) and activities "closely related to [the] delivery of educational services" (*id.* at 230 Cal.Rptr.3d at 429, 413 P.3d at p. 667).

First, we need not decide whether the duty extends beyond the classroom, because the attack in this case occurred in a classroom and, as the majority states, "[t]he negligence alleged here is the failure to prevent a *classroom* assault." (Maj. opn., *ante.*, at 230 Cal.Rptr.3d at p. 434, 413 P.3d at p. 672, italics added.) Notably, the majority rightly declines to decide several other issues that we need not resolve in order to dispose of this case, *i.e.*, whether universities have a duty to control the behavior of students (*id.* at 230 Cal.Rptr.3d at p. 425, 413 P.3d at pp. 664–665.) and alternate theories of duty based on an implied-in-fact contract or the negligent undertaking doctrine (*id.* at 230 Cal.Rptr.3d at p. 437 fn. 8, 413 P.3d at p. 674 fn. 8). In my view, we should exercise similar restraint in addressing a university's duty to protect or warn, and should confine our consideration of the issue to what is necessary to decide this case.

Second, in terms of the various factors courts apply to determine whether to impose a duty as a matter of public policy, activities outside the classroom differ in potentially significant ways from activities inside the classroom. As the majority explains, among the relevant factors is the extent of the defendant's control in the particular setting over the environment and third party behavior. (Maj. opn., *ante*, at 230 Cal.Rptr.3d at pp. 429–431, 434–435,413 P.3d at pp. 668–669, 672.) As the majority also explains, "[p]erhaps more than any other place on campus, colleges can be expected to retain a measure of control over the classroom environment." (*Id.* at 230 Cal.Rptr.3d at p. 431, 413 P.3d at p. 669.) Implicit in this statement is recognition that the extent of a university's control over the environment and student behavior is likely to be considerably less outside of the classroom. Indeed, the extent of a university's control in a nonclassroom setting varies considerably depending on the particular activity and the particular setting. It may be that, as to any given nonclassroom activity, a university's control is sufficient, from a public policy perspective, to impose a duty to protect or warn. But I would leave that question for a case that presents the issue on concrete facts, rather than broadly conclude, in a case involving *classroom* activity, that a university's control in nonclassroom settings is sufficient to impose a duty to protect or to warn.

Finally, the majority's conclusion seems likely to create confusion, because the majority offers no guidance as to which nonclassroom activities qualify as either "curricular" (maj. opn., *ante*, at 230 Cal.Rptr.3d at pp. 423–424, 413 P.3d at p. 663.) or "closely related to [the] delivery of educational services" (*id.* at 230 Cal.Rptr.3d at p. 429, 413 P.3d at p. 667.), or what factors are relevant to this determination. This omission no doubt results from the circumstance, as already noted, that this case involves classroom activity, and that the majority is thus deciding the duty question as to nonclassroom activities in the abstract, without any concrete facts to guide its analysis. For this reason, and the others mentioned above, although I concur in the judgment, I do not join the majority's conclusion that a university's duty to warn or protect extends beyond the classroom, to encompass more broadly "curricular activities" (*id.* at 230 Cal.Rptr.3d at p. 424, 413 P.3d at p. 663) and activities "closely related to [the] delivery of educational services" (*id.* at 230 Cal.Rptr.3d at p. 429, 413 P.3d at p. 667).

6. Duty to Warn

Even if the law does not impose a duty to aid or protect, it may impose a duty to warn others of a known danger.

Tarasoff v. Regents of the University of California

551 P.2d 334 (Cal. 1976)

TOBRINER, Justice.

...

1. Plaintiffs' complaints.

The issue before us on this appeal is whether [Plaintiffs'] complaints now state, or can be amended to state, causes of action against defendants. We therefore begin by setting forth the pertinent allegations of the complaints.

Plaintiffs' first cause of action, entitled 'Failure to Detain a Dangerous Patient,' alleges that on August 20, 1969, Poddar was a voluntary outpatient receiving therapy at Cowell Memorial Hospital. Poddar informed Moore, his therapist, that he was going to kill an unnamed girl, readily identifiable as Tatiana, when she returned home from spending the summer in Brazil. Moore, with the concurrence of Dr. Gold, who had initially examined Poddar, and Dr. Yandell, Assistant to the director of the department of psychiatry, decided that Poddar should be committed for observation in a mental hospital. Moore orally notified Officers Atkinson and Teel of the campus police that he would request commitment. He then sent a letter to Police Chief William Beall requesting the assistance of the police department in securing Poddar's confinement.

Officers Atkinson, Brownrigg, and Halleran took Poddar into custody, but, satisfied that Poddar was rational, released him on his promise to stay away from

Tatiana. Powelson, director of the department of psychiatry at Cowell Memorial Hospital, then asked the police to return Moore's letter, directed that all copies of the letter and notes that Moore had taken as therapist be destroyed, and 'ordered no action to place Prosenjit Poddar in 72-hour treatment and evaluation facility.'

Plaintiffs' second cause of action, entitled 'Failure to Warn On a Dangerous Patient,' incorporates the allegations of the first cause of action, but adds the assertion that defendants negligently permitted Poddar to be released from police custody without 'notifying the parents of Tatiana Tarasoff that their daughter was in grave danger from Posenjit Poddar.' Poddar persuaded Tatiana's brother to share an apartment with him near Tatiana's residence; shortly after her return from Brazil, Poddar went to her residence and killed her.

. . .

2. Plaintiffs can state a cause of action against defendant therapists for negligent failure to protect Tatiana.

The second cause of action can be amended to allege that Tatiana's death proximately resulted from defendants' negligent failure to warn Tatiana or others likely to apprise her of her danger. Plaintiffs contend that as amended, such allegations of negligence and proximate causation, with resulting damages, establish a cause of action. Defendants, however, contend that in the circumstances of the present case they owed no duty of care to Tatiana or her parents and that, in the absence of such duty, they were free to act in careless disregard of Tatiana's life and safety.

In analyzing this issue, we bear in mind that legal duties are not discoverable facts of nature, but merely conclusory expressions that, in cases of a particular type, liability should be imposed for damage done. As stated in *Dillon v. Legg* (1968) 68 Cal.2d 728, 734, 69 Cal.Rptr. 72, 76, 441 P.2d 912, 916: 'The assertion that liability must . . . be denied because defendant bears no 'duty' to plaintiff 'begs the essential question—whether the plaintiff's interests are entitled to legal protection against the defendant's conduct . . . (Duty) is not sacrosanct in itself, but only an expression of the sum total of those considerations of policy which lead the law to say that the particular plaintiff is entitled to protection.' (Prosser, Law of Torts (3d ed. 1964) at pp. 332–333.)'

. . .

Although, as we have stated above, under the common law, as a general rule, one person owed no duty to control the conduct of another[18] (*Richards v. Stanley* (1954)

18. This rule derives from the common law's distinction between misfeasance and nonfeasance, and its reluctance to impose liability for the latter. (See Harper & Kime, *The Duty to Control the Conduct of Another* (1934) 43 Yale L.J. 886, 887.) Morally questionable, the rule owes its survival to 'the difficulties of setting any standards of unselfish service to fellow men, and of making any workable rule to cover possible situations where fifty people might fail to rescue . . .' (Prosser, Torts (4th ed. 1971) §56, p. 341.) Because of these practical difficulties, the courts have increased the number of instances in which affirmative duties are imposed not by direct rejection of the common

43 Cal.2d 60, 65, 271 P.2d 23; *Wright v. Arcade School Dist.* (1964) 230 Cal.App.2d 272, 277, 40 Cal.Rptr. 812; Rest.2d Torts (1965) s 315), nor to warn those endangered by such conduct (Rest.2d Torts, *supra*, § 314, com. c Prosser, Law of Torts (4th ed. 1971) § 56, p. 341), the courts have carved out an exception to this rule in cases in which the defendant stands in some special relationship to either the person whose conduct needs to be controlled or in a relationship to the foreseeable victim of that conduct (see Rest.2d Torts, *supra*, §§ 315—320). Applying this exception to the present case, we note that a relationship of defendant therapists to either Tatiana or Poddar will suffice to establish a duty of care; as explained in section 315 of the Restatement Second of Torts, a duty of care may arise from either '(a) a special relation . . . between the actor and the third person which imposes a duty upon the actor to control the third person's conduct, or (b) a special relation . . . between the actor and the other which gives to the other a right of protection.'

Although plaintiffs' pleadings assert no special relation between Tatiana and defendant therapists, they establish as between Poddar and defendant therapists the special relation that arises between a patient and his doctor or psychotherapist. Such a relationship may support affirmative duties for the benefit of third persons. Thus, for example, a hospital must exercise reasonable care to control the behavior of a patient which may endanger other persons.[19] A doctor must also warn a patient if the patient's condition or medication renders certain conduct, such as driving a car, dangerous to others.

Although the California decisions that recognize this duty have involved cases in which the defendant stood in a special relationship *both* to the victim and to the person whose conduct created the danger,[20] we do not think that the duty should logically be constricted to such situations. Decisions of other jurisdictions hold that the single relationship of a doctor to his patient is sufficient to support the duty to exercise reasonable care to protect others against dangers emanating from the

---

law rule, but by expanding the list of special relationships which will justify departure from that rule. (See Prosser, *supra*, § 56, at pp. 348—350.)

19. When a 'hospital has notice or knowledge of facts from which it might reasonably be concluded that a patient would be likely to harm himself *or others* unless preclusive measures were taken, then the hospital must use reasonable care in the circumstances to prevent such harm.' (*Vistica v. Presbyterian Hospital* (1967) 67 Cal.2d 465, 469, 62 Cal.Rptr. 577, 580, 432 P.2d 193, 196.) (Emphasis added.) A mental hospital may be liable if it negligently permits the escape or release of a dangerous patient (*Semler v. Psychiatric Institute of Washington, D.C.* (4th Cir. 1976) 44 U.S.L.Week 2439; *Underwood v. United States* (5th Cir. 1966) 356 F.2d 92; Fair v. United States (5th Cir. 1956) 234 F.2d 288). *Greenberg v. Barbour* (E.D.Pa. 1971) 322 F.Supp. 745, upheld a cause of action against a hospital staff doctor whose negligent failure to admit a mental patient resulted in that patient assaulting the plaintiff.

20. *Ellis v. D'Angelo* (1953) 116 Cal.App.2d 310, 253 P.2d 675, upheld a cause of action against parents who failed to warn a babysitter of the violent proclivities of their child; *Johnson v. State of California* (1968) 69 Cal.2d 782, 73 Cal.Rptr. 240, 447 P.2d 352, upheld a suit against the state for failure to warn foster parents of the dangerous tendencies of their ward; *Morgan v. City of Yuba* (1964) 230 Cal.App.2d 938, 41 Cal.Rptr. 508, sustained a cause of action against a sheriff who had promised to warn decedent before releasing a dangerous prisoner, but failed to do so.

patient's illness. The courts hold that a doctor is liable to persons infected by his patient if he negligently fails to diagnose a contagious disease (*Hofmann v. Blackmon* (Fla.App.1970) 241 So.2d 752), or, having diagnosed the illness, fails to warn members of the patient's family (*Wojcik v. Aluminum Co. of America* (1959) 18 Misc.2d 740, 183 N.Y.S.2d 351, 357–358; *Davis v. Rodman* (1921) 147 Ark. 385, 227 S.W. 612; *Skillings v. Allen* (1919) 143 Minn. 323, 173 N.W. 663; see also *Jones v. Stanko* (1928) 118 Ohio St. 147, 160 N.E. 456).

. . .

Defendants contend, however, that imposition of a duty to exercise reasonable care to protect third persons is unworkable because therapists cannot accurately predict whether or not a patient will resort to violence. In support of this argument amicus representing the American Psychiatric Association and other professional societies cites numerous articles which indicate that therapists, in the present state of the art, are unable reliably to predict violent acts; their forecasts, amicus claims, tend consistently to overpredict violence, and indeed are more often wrong than right. Since predictions of violence are often erroneous, amicus concludes, the courts should not render rulings that predicate the liability of therapists upon the validity of such predictions.

The role of the psychiatrist, who is indeed a practitioner of medicine, and that of the psychologist who performs an allied function, are like that of the physician who must conform to the standards of the profession and who must often make diagnoses and predictions based upon such evaluations. Thus the judgment of the therapist in diagnosing emotional disorders and in predicting whether a patient presents a serious danger of violence is comparable to the judgment which doctors and professionals must regularly render under accepted rules of responsibility.

We recognize the difficulty that a therapist encounters in attempting to forecast whether a patient presents a serious danger of violence. Obviously we do not require that the therapist, in making that determination, render a perfect performance; the therapist need only exercise 'that reasonable degree of skill, knowledge, and care ordinarily possessed and exercised by members of (that professional specialty) under similar circumstances.' (*Bardessono v. Michels* (1970) 3 Cal.3d 780, 788, 91 Cal.Rptr. 760, 764, 478 P.2d 480, 484; *Quintal v. Laurel Grove Hospital* (1964) 62 Cal.2d 154, 159–160, 41 Cal.Rptr. 577, 397 P.2d 161; see 4 Witkin, Summary of Cal. Law (8th ed. 1974) Torts, § 514 and cases cited.) Within the broad range of reasonable practice and treatment in which professional opinion and judgment may differ, the therapist is free to exercise his or her own best judgment without liability; proof, aided by hindsight, that he or she judged wrongly is insufficient to establish negligence.

In the instant case, however, the pleadings do not raise any question as to failure of defendant therapists to predict that Poddar presented a serious danger of violence. On the contrary, the present complaints allege that defendant therapists did in fact predict that Poddar would kill, but were negligent in failing to warn.

Amicus contends, however, that even when a therapist does in fact predict that a patient poses a serious danger of violence to others, the therapist should be absolved of any responsibility for failing to act to protect the potential victim. In our view, however, once a therapist does in fact determine, or under applicable professional standards reasonably should have determined, that a patient poses a serious danger of violence to others, he bears a duty to exercise reasonable care to protect the foreseeable victim of that danger. While the discharge of this duty of due care will necessarily vary with the facts of each case,[21] in each instance the adequacy of the therapist's conduct must be measured against the traditional negligence standard of the rendition of reasonable care under the circumstances. (Accord *Cobbs v. Grant* (1972) 8 Cal.3d 229, 243, 104 Cal.Rptr. 505, 502 p.2d 1.) As explained in Fleming and Maximov, *The Patient or His Victim: The Therapist's Dilemma* (1974) 62 Cal.L.Rev. 1025, 1067: '. . . the ultimate question of resolving the tension between the conflicting interests of patient and potential victim is one of social policy, not professional expertise. . . . In sum, the therapist owes a legal duty not only to his patient, but also to his patient's would-be victim and is subject in both respects to scrutiny by judge and jury.'

Contrary to the assertion of amicus, this conclusion is not inconsistent with our recent decision in *People v. Burnick, supra*, 14 Cal.3d 306, 121 Cal.Rptr. 488, 535 P.2d 352. Taking note of the uncertain character of therapeutic prediction, we held in *Burnick* that a person cannot be committed as a mentally disordered sex offender unless found to be such by proof beyond a reasonable doubt. (14 Cal.3d at p. 328, 121 Cal.Rptr. 488, 535 P.2d 352.) The issue in the present context, however, is not whether the patient should be incarcerated, but whether the therapist should take any steps at all to protect the threatened victim; some of the alternatives open to the therapist, such as warning the victim, will not result in the drastic consequences of depriving the patient of his liberty. Weighing the uncertain and conjectural character of the alleged damage done the patient by such a warning against the peril to the victim's life, we conclude that professional inaccuracy in predicting violence cannot negate the therapist's duty to protect the threatened victim.

The risk that unnecessary warnings may be given is a reasonable price to pay for the lives of possible victims that may be saved. We would hesitate to hold that the therapist who is aware that his patient expects to attempt to assassinate the President of the United States would not be obligated to warn the authorities because the therapist cannot predict with accuracy that his patient will commit the crime.

21. Defendant therapists and amicus also argue that warnings must be given only in those cases in which the therapist knows the identity of the victim. We recognize that in some cases it would be unreasonable to require the therapist to interrogate his patient to discover the victim's identity, or to conduct an independent investigation. But there may also be cases in which a moment's reflection will reveal the victim's identity. The matter thus is one which depends upon the circumstances of each case, and should not be governed by any hard and fast rule.

Defendants further argue that free and open communication is essential to psychotherapy (see *In re Lifschutz* (1970) 2 Cal.3d 415, 431–434, 85 Cal.Rptr. 829, 467 P.2d 557); that 'Unless a patient ... is assured that ... information (revealed by him) can and will be held in utmost confidence, he will be reluctant to make the full disclosure upon which diagnosis and treatment ... depends.' (Sen.Com. on Judiciary, comment on Evid.Code, § 1014.) The giving of a warning, defendants contend, constitutes a breach of trust which entails the revelation of confidential communications.[22]

We recognize the public interest in supporting effective treatment of mental illness and in protecting the rights of patients to privacy (see *In re Liftschutz, supra*, 2 Cal.3d at p. 432, 85 Cal.Rptr. 829, 467 P.2d 557), and the consequent public importance of safeguarding the confidential character of psychotherapeutic communication. Against this interest, however, we must weigh the public interest in safety from violent assault. The Legislature has undertaken the difficult task of balancing the countervailing concerns. In evidence Code section 1014, it established a broad rule of privilege to protect confidential Communications between patient and psychotherapist. In Evidence Code section 1024, the Legislature created a specific and limited exception to the psychotherapist-patient privilege: 'There is no privilege ... if the psychotherapist has reasonable cause to believe that the patient is in such mental or emotional condition as to be dangerous to himself or to the person or property of another and that disclosure of the communication is necessary to prevent the threatened danger.'[23]

---

22. Counsel for defendant Regents and amicus American Psychiatric Association predict that a decision of this court holding that a therapist may bear a duty to warn a potential victim will deter violence-prone persons from seeking therapy, and hamper the treatment of other patients. This contention was examined in Fleming and Maximov, The Patient or His Victim: The Therapist's Dilemma (1974) 62 Cal.L.Rev. 1025, 1038—1044; they conclude that such predictions are entirely speculative. In *In re Lifschutz, supra*, 2 Cal.3d 415, 85 Cal.Rptr. 829, 467 P.2d 557, counsel for the psychiatrist argued that if the state could compel disclosure of some psychotherapeutic communications, psychotherapy could no longer be practiced successfully. (2 Cal.3d at p. 426, 85 Cal. Rptr. 829, 467 P.2d 557.) We rejected that argument, and it does not appear that our decision in fact adversely affected the practice of psychotherapy in California. Counsel's forecast of harm in the present case strikes us as equally dubious.

We note, moreover, that Evidence Code section 1024, enacted in 1965, established that psychotherapeutic communication is not privileged when disclosure is necessary to prevent threatened danger. We cannot accept without question counsels' implicit assumption that effective therapy for potentially violent patients depends upon either the patient's lack of awareness that a therapist can disclose confidential communications to avert impending danger, or upon the therapist's advance promise never to reveal nonprivileged threats of violence.

23. Fleming and Maximov note that 'While [section 1024] supports the therapist's less controversial *right* to make a disclosure, it admittedly does not impose in him a *duty* to do so. But the argument does not have to be pressed that far. For if it is once conceded ... that a duty in favor of the patient's foreseeable victims would accord with general principles of tort liability, we need no longer look to the statute for a source of duty. It is sufficient if the statute can be relied upon ... for the purposes of countering the claim that the needs of confidentiality are paramount and must therefore defeat any such hypothetical duty. In this more modest perspective, the Evidence Code's

We realize that the open and confidential character of psychotherapeutic dialogue encourages patients to express threats of violence, few of which are ever executed. Certainly a therapist should not be encouraged routinely to reveal such threats; such disclosures could seriously disrupt the patient's relationship with his therapist and with the persons threatened. To the contrary, the therapist's obligations to his patient require that he not disclose a confidence unless such disclosure is necessary to avert danger to others, and even then that he do so discreetly, and in a fashion that would preserve the privacy of his patient to the fullest extent compatible with the prevention of the threatened danger. (See Fleming & Maximov, *The Patient or His Victim: The Therapist's Dilemma* (1974) 62 Cal.L.Rev. 1025, 1065–1066.)[24]

The revelation of a communication under the above circumstances is not a breach of trust or a violation of professional ethics; as stated in the Principles of Medical Ethics of the American Medical Association (1957), section 9: 'A physician may not reveal the confidence entrusted to him in the course of medical attendance . . . *unless he is required to do so by law or unless it becomes necessary in order to protect the welfare of the individual or of the community.*'[25] (Emphasis added.) We conclude that the public policy favoring protection of the confidential character of patient-psychotherapist communications must yield to the extent to which disclosure is essential to avert danger to others. The protective privilege ends where the public peril begins.

Our current crowded and computerized society compels the interdependence of its members. In this risk-infested society we can hardly tolerate the further exposure to danger that would result from a concealed knowledge of the therapist that his patient was lethal. If the exercise of reasonable care to protect the threatened victim requires the therapist to warn the endangered party or those who can reasonably be expected to notify him, we see no sufficient societal interest that would protect and justify concealment. The containment of such risks lies in the public interest. For the foregoing reasons, we find that plaintiffs' complaints can be amended to state a cause of action against defendants Moore, Powelson, Gold, and Yandell and against the Regents as their employer, for breach of a duty to exercise reasonable care to protect Tatiana.[]

. . .

'dangerous patient' exception may be invoked with some confidence as a clear expression of legislative policy concerning the balance between the confidentiality values of the patient and the safety values of his foreseeable victims.' (Emphasis in original.) Fleming & Maximov, *The Patient or His Victim: The Therapist's Dilemma* (1974) 62 Cal.L.Rev. 1025, 1063.

24. Amicus suggests that a therapist who concludes that his patient is dangerous should not warn the potential victim, but institute proceedings for involuntary detention of the patient. The giving of a warning, however, would in many cases represent a far lesser inroad upon the patient's privacy than would involuntary commitment.

25. See also Summary Report of the Task Force on Confidentiality of the Council on Professions and Associations of the American Psychiatric Association (1975).

Turning now to the police defendants, we conclude that they do not have any such special relationship to either Tatiana or to Poddar sufficient to impose upon such defendants a duty to warn respecting Poddar's violent intentions. (See *Hartzler v. City of San Jose* (1975) 46 Cal.App.3d 6, 9–10, 120 Cal.Rptr. 5; *Antique Arts Corp. v. City of Torrance* (1974) 39 Cal.App.3d 588, 593, 114 Cal.Rptr. 332.) Plaintiffs suggest no theory, and plead no facts that give rise to any duty to warn on the part of the police defendants absent such a special relationship. They have thus failed to demonstrate that the trial court erred in denying leave to amend as to the police defendants. (See *Cooper v. Leslie Salt Co.* (1969) 70 Cal.2d 627, 636, 75 Cal. Rptr. 766, 451 P.2d 406; *Filice v. Boccardo* (1962) 210 Cal.App.2d 843, 847, 26 Cal. Rptr. 789.)

...

Conclusion

For the reasons stated, we conclude that plaintiffs can amend their complaints to state a cause of action against defendant therapists by asserting that the therapists in fact determined that Poddar presented a serious danger of violence to Tatiana, or pursuant to the standards of their profession should have so determined, but nevertheless failed to exercise reasonable care to protect her from that danger....

Note

Legislative response. The California legislature enacted Civil Code § 43.92[26] in response to the court's decision in *Tarasoff.* The reasoning behind the legislation was explained in *Regents of Univ. of California v. Superior Court*, 240 Cal. Rptr. 3d 675, 686 (Ct. App. 2018), reh'g denied (Dec. 21, 2018), review denied (Mar. 13, 2019):

> The legislative history clarifies that section 43.92 "was not intended to overrule Tarasoff or Hedlund," but rather to "abolish" those decisions' "expansive rulings... that a therapist can be held liable for the mere failure to predict and warn of potential violence by his patient.'" (Ewing, supra, 120 Cal.App.4th at p. 816, 15 Cal.Rptr.3d 864.) The statute represents "a

26. That statute reads:

(a) There shall be no monetary liability on the part of, and no cause of action shall arise against, any person who is a psychotherapist as defined in Section 1010 of the Evidence Code in failing to protect from a patient's threatened violent behavior or failing to predict and protect from a patient's violent behavior except if the patient has communicated to the psychotherapist a serious threat of physical violence against a reasonably identifiable victim or victims.

(b) There shall be no monetary liability on the part of, and no cause of action shall arise against, a psychotherapist who, under the limited circumstances specified in subdivision (a), discharges his or her duty to protect by making reasonable efforts to communicate the threat to the victim or victims and to a law enforcement agency....

legislative effort to strike an appropriate balance between conflicting policy interests. On the one hand, the need to preserve a patient confidence recognizes that effective diagnosis and treatment of a mental illness or an emotional problem is severely undermined when a patient cannot be assured that a statement made in the privacy of his therapist's office will not be revealed. On the other hand is the recognition that, under limited circumstances, preserving a confidence is less important than protecting the safety of someone whom the patient intends to harm." (*Ibid.*)

B. Duty When Actor Has Created Risk of Physical Harm

1. Duty to Act When Prior Conduct Is Dangerous

Robertson v. LeMaster

171 W. Va. 607 (1983)

McGRAW, Chief Justice:

This is an appeal by Curtis and Karen Lee Robertson from an order entered by the Circuit Court of Wayne County granting the motion of Norfolk & Western Railway Company for a directed verdict, and dismissing the appellants' action on the merits....

The evidence adduced by the appellants at trial showed that on October 11, 1978, Tony K. LeMaster, then nineteen years old, was employed by the appellee as a section laborer. LeMaster reported for work at 7:00 a.m. at the appellee's Nolan section office, approximately 50 miles from his home in Fort Gay. After working three hours in the Nolan area, LeMaster's section was called in to work at a derailment that had occurred near Kermit, approximately half-way between the appellee's section office in Nolan and LeMaster's home in Fort Gay. LeMaster and his fellow workers were transported to the derailment site in a truck owned by the appellee.

Upon arriving at the derailment site, the section foreman, Ruben VanHoose, instructed his men to eat lunch. When they finished eating, the section crew began the work of removing debris and repairing the track that was damaged by the derailment. The derailment had completely blocked the appellee's single railway track between Fort Gay and Nolan, and thus was deemed an emergency under the railroad's contract with its union employees. Much of the work of removing the derailed train and the damaged track was performed by heavy equipment furnished by the appellee. However, the work performed by LeMaster and his co-workers was heavy manual labor which included lifting railroad ties and shoveling coal. The work was continuous, except for intermittent periods when the workers were required to step back out of the way of the heavy equipment. The work continued long past LeMaster's normal 3:30 p.m. quitting time.

At approximately 10:00 p.m. that night, LeMaster told his foreman, VanHoose, that he was tired and wanted to go home. VanHoose told LeMaster that he could not go home, but told him to speak with Bill Rowe, the road master in charge. LeMaster did not speak with Rowe at this time, but continued working.

At approximately 1:00 a.m. on the morning of October 12, 1978, LeMaster was given his first chance to eat since lunch the previous day. LeMaster ate in a dining car provided by the appellee. When he was finished eating, LeMaster left the dining car and sat down outside to rest. LeMaster testified that this was his first opportunity to rest since beginning work on the derailment. After sitting down, LeMaster was approached by Rowe and told to return to work.

LeMaster resumed working. Several times during the night he told his foreman that he was tired and wanted to go home. Each time the foreman told LeMaster that he should ask Rowe. LeMaster testified that he did not speak with Rowe for fear of being fired. Apparently, LeMaster and Rowe were involved in a work related dispute several months before, which resulted in LeMaster being laid off for a week. At 5:00 a.m. LeMaster ate breakfast in the dining car. After breakfast he again resumed work.

At 9:00 a.m. or 9:30 a.m. LeMaster talked with Les Conn, the assistant foreman, about going home. Shortly thereafter, LeMaster told VanHoose that he was too tired to work, and VanHoose then told him to talk with Rowe. LeMaster finally spoke with Rowe, telling him that he was too tired to continue working. Rowe told LeMaster that if he wouldn't work, he should get his bucket and go home. LeMaster asked for a ride to his car in Nolan.

An employee of the appellee drove LeMaster to his car. During the drive from the derailment site to Nolan, LeMaster fell asleep with a lighted cigarette in his hand. Upon arriving at Nolan, LeMaster got into his car and began the 50 mile trip to his house in Fort Gay. He decided to stop en route at the derailment site at Kermit to speak with Rowe and determine if he had been fired. When he arrived at the derailment site, LeMaster threw his hard hat at Rowe, told him to find some other person to work, and then asked if he was fired. Rowe told LeMaster that he was not fired and to "just go on home." They then shook hands, and LeMaster left in his car.

On the way home LeMaster claims that he fell asleep at the wheel and the accident with the Robertsons resulted. LeMaster has no memory of the details of the accident. Benjamin Jude, a witness to the accident, testified that he was travelling from Kermit to Louisa at approximately 10:45 a.m. when LeMaster passed his car. Jude was travelling 65 to 70 miles per hour at the time. He estimated that LeMaster was travelling about 75 miles per hour. Jude testified that LeMaster turned his head and looked at him when he passed, and that LeMaster appeared normal and his eyes were open.

After passing Jude's vehicle, LeMaster came upon the appellants' vehicle travelling in the same direction as LeMaster, but at a much slower speed. Jude testified that it appeared that LeMaster was attempting to pass the appellants' vehicle when the right front end of LeMaster's car struck the left rear end of the appellants' car, causing the accident. After the accident, Jude approached LeMaster's car to see if he was injured. Jude testified that it took approximately a minute for LeMaster to regain consciousness. LeMaster told Jude that he was "all right except I must have fallen asleep."

The section crew of which LeMaster was a member had worked throughout the night without rest breaks. Some of the men did slip away and go to sleep. One member of the section crew blacked out, fell over an embankment and slept for approximately an hour. LeMaster worked approximately 27 hours before Rowe gave him permission to quit work. The section crew, other than LeMaster, worked for 37 hours on the derailment. The appellee railroad company offered to drive all members of the crew, other than LeMaster, to their homes, rather than taking them back to Nolan to their vehicles.

The appellants' cause of action sounds in tort. They allege in their complaint that the appellee, Norfolk & Western Railway Company, "illegally, willfully, wantonly, negligently, and with a conscious disregard for the rights and safety of others, ordered, forced and required . . . LeMaster, its employee, to work for . . . 32 hours straight without rest, and then to leave the . . . place of employment without providing either rest or transportation home when it knew or should have known that its employee constituted a menace to the health and safety of the public." The appellants further allege that these acts of the appellee were the proximate cause of the automobile accident in which they were injured.

At the close of the plaintiff's case, the appellee moved for a directed verdict on the issue of liability. As grounds for the motion the appellee asserted that the appellants had made no factual showing to demonstrate that a duty of care existed on the part of the appellee towards the appellants, or to demonstrate that the conduct of the appellee was the proximate cause of the accident. The trial court agreed that the elements of duty and proximate cause had not been established, and granted the appellee's motion. We reverse.

I.

"In order to establish a *prima facie* case of negligence in West Virginia, it must be shown that the defendant has been guilty of some act or omission in violation of a duty owed to the plaintiff. No action for negligence will lie without a duty broken." Syllabus Point 1, *Parsley v. General Motors Acceptance Corporation,* 167 W.Va. 866, 280 S.E.2d 703 (1981). *See Hinkle v. Martin,* 163 W.Va. 482, 256 S.E.2d 768 (1979); *Morrison v. Roush,* 110 W.Va. 398, 158 S.E. 514 (1931); *Uthermohlen v. Bogg's Run Min. & Mfg. Co.,* 50 W.Va. 457, 40 S.E. 410 (1901). The appellee contends that it owed no duty of care to the appellants, and therefore the trial court correctly directed a verdict against the appellants. We disagree.

...

It is well established that one who engages in affirmative conduct, and thereafter realizes or should realize that such conduct has created an unreasonable risk of harm to another, is under a duty to exercise reasonable care to prevent the threatened harm. *See Restatement (Second) Torts* § 321 (1965). As Professor Prosser succinctly states: "'[Duty]' is a question of whether the defendant is under any obligation for the benefit of the particular plaintiff; and in negligence cases, the duty is always the same, to conform to the legal standard of reasonable conduct in light of the apparent risk." W. Prosser, *supra* § 53. The issue raised by the appellants is whether the appellee's conduct in requiring LeMaster to work over 27 hours and then setting him loose upon the highway without providing alternate transportation or rest facilities to its exhausted employee created an unreasonable risk of harm to others that was foreseeable....

In determining the scope of the duty which an actor owes to another, the court in *Dillon v. Legg, supra,* focused on the foreseeability of injury. A significant number of courts have since followed this approach. [Citations omitted] In these jurisdictions foreseeability that harm might result has become a primary factor in determining whether a duty exists.[27] As Harper and James state:

> [T]he obligation to refrain from particular conduct is owed only to those who are foreseeably endangered by the conduct and only with respect to those risks or hazards whose likelihood made the conduct unreasonably dangerous. Duty, in other words, is measured by the scope of the risk which negligent conduct foreseeably entails.

2 F. Harper & F. James, *The Law of Torts* § 18.2 (1956) (footnote omitted).

Beyond the question of foreseeability, the existence of duty also involves policy considerations underlying the core issue of the scope of the legal system's protection. Such considerations include the likelihood of injury, the magnitude of the burden of guarding against it, and the consequences of placing that burden on the defendant. Other broader policy considerations also enter the equation, but they are not so readily articulated.

Although we have never explicitly addressed the question of the existence of duty as a product of foreseeability of injury, we have held in the past that "[a]ctionable negligence necessarily includes the element of reasonable anticipation that some injury might result from the act of which complaint is made." *Matthews v. Cumberland & Allegheny Gas Co.,* 138 W.Va. 639, 653, 77 S.E.2d 180, 188 (1953). In a similar vein, we have held that "[d]ue care is a relative term and depends on time, place, and

27. The genesis of this approach can be found in Justice Cardozo's classic opinion in *Palsgraf v. Long Island R.R. Co., supra,* note 1, where he states: "The risk reasonably to be perceived defines the duty to be obeyed." 248 N.Y. at 344, 162 N.E. at 100.

other circumstances. It should be in proportion to the danger apparent and within reasonable anticipation." Syllabus Point 2, *Johnson v. United Fuel Gas Co.*, 112 W.Va. 578, 166 S.E. 118 (1932); *see also State ex rel. Cox v. Sims,* 138 W.Va. 482, 77 S.E.2d 151 (1953). And in syllabus point one of *Dicken v. Liverpool Salt & Coal Co.*, 41 W. Va. 511, 23 S.E. 582 (1895), we held that "[n]egligence is the violation of the duty of taking care under the given circumstances. It is not absolute, but is always relative to some circumstances of time, place, manner, or person." These past decisions implicitly support the proposition that the foreseeability of risk is a primary consideration in establishing the element of duty in tort cases.

"Upon a motion for a directed verdict, all reasonable doubts and inferences should be resolved in favor of the party against whom the verdict is asked to be directed." Syllabus Point 5, *Wager v. Sine,* 157 W.Va. 391, 201 S.E.2d 260 (1973); *see also Jividen v. Legg,* 161 W.Va. 769, 245 S.E.2d 835 (1978); *Lambert v. Goodman,* 147 W.Va. 513, 129 S.E.2d 138 (1963). In this case the appellee required its employee LeMaster to work for over 27 hours at hard labor without rest, despite repeated requests that he be permitted to go home. When the appellee finally permitted LeMaster to cease work, it did not provide him sleeping quarters to rest before driving. Neither did the appellee offer to provide LeMaster transportation home, as it later did all its other employees who worked on the derailment. Rather, the appellee provided LeMaster transportation to his car at Nolan, approximately twenty-five miles farther from his home than the derailment site. On the way to Nolan, the obviously exhausted LeMaster fell asleep with a lighted cigarette in his hand in the presence of another of the appellee's employees.

Viewing these facts in the light most favorable to the appellants, we believe that the appellee could have reasonably foreseen that its exhausted employee, who had been required to work over 27 hours without rest, would pose a risk of harm to other motorists while driving the 50 miles from the appellee's office to his home. Indeed, it could be said that the appellee's negligent conduct under these facts was not merely a failure to exercise appropriate precautionary measures, but includes an element of affirmative conduct in requiring LeMaster to work unreasonably long hours and then driving him to his vehicle and sending him out on the highway in such an exhausted condition as to pose a danger to himself or others. When such affirmative action is present, liability may be imposed regardless of the existence of a relationship between the defendant and the party injured by the incapacitated individual. *See Restatement (Second) of Torts* § 321, Comment a (1965); *Leppke v. Segura,* 632 P.2d 1057 (Colo.App.1981). *See also Clark v. Otis Engineering Corp.*, 633 S.W.2d 538 (Ct. of App.Tex.1982).

The appellee's reliance on *Pilgrim v. Fortune Drilling Co., Inc.*, 653 F.2d 982 (5th Cir.1981), is misplaced. In *Pilgrim,* where the plaintiff's claim was based on the employer's negligence in failing to prevent an employee from driving 117 miles to his home after completing a 12 hour shift, there was no evidence that the employee was incapacitated, or that the conduct of the employer involved an affirmative act which increased the risk of harm. Indeed, it appears that the issue raised by the appellants in this proceeding was specifically not addressed in *Pilgrim*.[28]

Accordingly, we conclude that the trial court erred in ruling that the appellee owed no duty to the appellants. We are unable to say as a matter of law that the appellee's conduct in requiring its employee to work such long hours and then setting him loose upon the highway in an obviously exhausted condition did not create a foreseeable risk of harm to others which the appellee had a duty to guard against.

. . .

For the foregoing reasons, the order of the Circuit Court of Wayne County which grants the motion of Norfolk & Western Railway Company for a directed verdict is reversed, and the case is remanded for proceedings consistent with this opinion.

Reversed and remanded.

Problem 5.4. Fit 4 Life offers a weekly water aerobics class for senior citizens. Some of the class members are healthy, but many of the members have physical ailments typical of older adults (such as joint problems, reduced muscle strength, and cardiovascular disease). Joyce is the class instructor, and while she has no formal medical training—a fact that is made clear to each student at the beginning of each class—she is aware that some of the students have physical ailments and limitations.

On one scheduled class day, the indoor pool that they usually use is closed for emergency maintenance. Rather than cancel, Joyce decides to hold the

---

28. The court in *Pilgrim* framed the issue in this manner:

> In their brief plaintiffs argue that "[i]t is negligent to allow a fatigued employee to drive on the public highways." They then suggested that "[t]he duty is to furnish transportation to exhausted employees, furnish sleeping quarters near the work site, reduce working hours, or otherwise supply alternatives to exhausted employees driving on public roads." We are not concerned here whether it is negligent for an employer to fail to furnish transportation to exhausted employees, to fail to provide sleeping quarters near the work site so exhausted employees can rest before driving, to fail to reduce working hours, or to otherwise fail to supply alternatives to exhausted employees driving on public roads. We are only concerned with whether it was negligent for this employer to *permit* its employee to drive home in an exhausted condition. That is the legal theory involved in the special issue submitted to the jury. We express no opinion on whether an employer could be negligent by failing to provide transportation to exhausted employees, to furnish sleeping quarters to them, etc. since we do not have the question before us.

653 F.2d at 982, fn. 8 (emphasis in original).

The appellants' complaint, on the other hand, alleges that the appellee was negligent in requiring LeMaster "to work for . . . approximately thirty-two (32) hours straight without rest, and then to leave the . . . place of employment without providing either rest or transportation home when it knew or should have known that its employee constituted a menace to the health and safety of the public." Thus, the issue raised by the appellants is precisely that unaddressed by the Fifth Circuit in *Pilgrim v. Fortune Drilling Co., Inc., supra*.

class outside. Although it is 95°F outside, the temperature in the pool is a comfortable 82°F. At the end of each class, Joyce has all of the students lie on their towels near the side of the pool to do some stretching exercises. Joyce chose an area in direct sunlight, because there was not enough room for all of the students in any of the shaded areas. Joyce, who is 30 years old, is hot but not uncomfortable, but she knows that adults over the age of 65 are more sensitive to high temperatures and more prone to heat stroke, although they may not be aware of any symptoms until it is too late.

Only after the class ended (after 20 minutes of stretching) did Joyce remember to offer the students water. By that time, several of the students had already headed to the locker room. Beatrice, an elderly woman from Joyce's class, passed out in the locker room suffering from heat stroke. When she passed out, she fell on Verna, causing Verna to injure her hip.

Beatrice recovers, but she sues Fit 4 Life to recover the $50,000 she incurred in medical costs. Assuming Fit 4 Life is liable for any action or omission of Joyce on these facts, did Fit 4 Life violate any duty to Beatrice? Did Fit 4 Life violate any duty to Verna?

2. Negligent Entrustment

Hays v. Royer

384 S.W.3d 330 (Mo. App. 2012)

MITCHELL, J.

This is a negligent entrustment case. The issue is whether an entrustee may have a viable claim against the entrustor when no third party was injured and when the entrustee's claim is dependent upon his own negligence (and not some independent negligent act of the entrustor). The Restatement view is that, in a state in which contributory negligence does not bar the plaintiff's claim, an entrustee may state a cause of action against the entrustor, and previous cases from this court have implicitly so recognized. Accordingly, we hold that such a claim does exist, and the circuit court therefore erred in dismissing the petition on the ground that it failed to state a claim.

Facts and Procedural Background

While intoxicated, Scott Hays drove and wrecked a company van. Hays died in the accident, but no other person and no other vehicle were involved. The van Hays was driving was owned and/or controlled by Respondents, Francis "Pete" Royer, Barbara Royer, Royer's Incorporated, and Royer Hays Funeral Services, LLC (collectively, "Royer"). Hays worked for Royer and was part owner of Royer Hays Funeral Services.

Appellant Brody Hays is Scott Hays's minor son, and Appellant Heather Hays was Scott Hays's wife. Brody Hays and Heather Hays filed a petition, asserting a wrongful death claim against Royer and alleging that Royer had negligently entrusted the van to Scott Hays. The petition alleged that Royer knew or should have known that Hays was an unsafe driver in that he was habitually intoxicated. Pete Royer had "meetings, discussions, and conferences" regarding Hays's drinking problem. In the past, Royer's employees had had to wake Hays after he had passed out from intoxication. Royer knew that Hays had received inpatient treatment for alcoholism but that the treatment had not cured him. Royer knew that Hays had drunk beer at work and had driven the company van after drinking. In short, Royer knew that Scott Hays "would habitually keep and consume alcohol while operating" the company van.

On the day of the accident, Hays drove the company van to a bar, where he became intoxicated. The accident occurred on his way home from the bar.

Royer filed a motion to dismiss the petition, arguing that it failed to state a claim upon which relief could be granted. Specifically, Royer argued that, under Missouri law, there is no duty to protect an adult from his own voluntary consumption of alcohol. The circuit court granted the motion to dismiss and entered a judgment accordingly. Brody Hays and Heather Hays appeal.

...

Analysis

In their sole point on appeal, the Hayses argue that the circuit court erred in dismissing the petition in that it states a claim for negligent entrustment because a person who negligently entrusts a motor vehicle to another may be held liable for the entrustee's injuries, even when no third party was injured, when the entrustor should have known that the entrustee would drive while intoxicated. We agree.

...

I. A cause of action for negligent entrustment may be maintained by the entrustee.

Negligent entrustment is a variant of the common law tort of negligence.

> To make a prima facie case on a negligence theory, a plaintiff must plead and prove: (1) a legal duty on the part of the defendant to use ordinary care to protect the plaintiff against unreasonable risk of harm; (2) a breach of that duty; (3) a proximate cause between the breach and the resulting injury; and (4) actual damages to the plaintiff's person or property.

O.L. v. R.L., 62 S.W.3d 469, 474 (Mo.App. W.D.2001).

The requisite elements of a claim for negligent entrustment are:

> (1) the entrustee was incompetent by reason of age, inexperience, habitual recklessness or otherwise; (2) the entrustor knew or had reason to know of the entrustee's incompetence; (3) there was entrustment of the chattel; and (4) the negligence of the entrustor concurred with the conduct of the entrustee to cause the plaintiff's injuries.

Hallquist v. Smith, 189 S.W.3d 173, 175–76 (Mo. App. E.D.2006).

a. An entrustor of chattel has a common law duty to the entrustee.

"As with all negligence claims, the threshold question is whether the defendant owed the injured party a duty of care." *O.L.*, 62 S.W.3d at 474.

. . .

Royer . . . argues that a duty to protect another from his own self-imposed injuries arises only in custodial situations regarding children, mental patients and prisoners. Royer cites several cases that found a duty in such situations. But the fact that the courts have found a duty to use ordinary care to protect a person of limited capacity who is entrusted to the care of the alleged tortfeasor, does not preclude the existence of a duty in other situations. Factors considered by the courts in determining whether a duty exists include, but are not limited to, the foreseeability and likelihood of injury.[29] [Citations omitted] Factors considered by courts in determining whether a duty exists in a negligent entrustment context include "the risk involved [and] the foreseeability and likelihood of injury as weighed against the social utility of the actor's conduct." *Casebolt,* 829 P.2d at 356 (quoting *Smith v. City and Cnty. of Denver,* 726 P.2d 1125, 1127 (Colo.1986)).[30]

Apart from the issue of whether public policy mandates that we not recognize such a duty (which we discuss below), we think the petition alleged sufficient facts to proceed with the claim that Royer owed a duty of care to Hays. We know that Royer had a "duty" not to entrust a vehicle to someone who it knew or should have known would drive it while intoxicated. *See Hallquist,* S.W.3d at 176–77. That is, there is no question that, if a third party had been injured by Hays's conduct, all four elements of negligence (including duty) would have applied, at least for the purposes of a motion to dismiss. *Id.* The fortuity that no third party was injured does not change that conclusion.

As noted above, foreseeability is a factor that must be considered in determining whether a duty exists. It is true that a negligent act (even assuming that it ultimately caused the plaintiff damages) does not impose liability upon the defendant when it was not foreseeable that the specific plaintiff would have been injured by the negligent act. *See Palsgraf v. Long Island R.R. Co.,* 248 N.Y. 339, 162 N.E. 99, 99–100 (1928); *see also Smith v. Brown & Williamson Tobacco Corp.,* 275 S.W.3d 748, 801 (Mo.App. W.D. 2008) ("[T]he duty owed in negligence cases is based on the foreseeable or reasonable anticipation that harm or injury is a likely result of acts or omissions.") (internal quotation marks omitted). But this is not such a case. We say that

---

29. Even in the case of an incapacitated individual in the care of an alleged tortfeasor, foreseeability is a concept that underlies the existence of a duty of care. But in such cases, foreseeability may be presumed. *See O.L. v. R.L.,* 62 S.W.3d 469, 474 (Mo.App. W.D.2001) (the court rejected grandmother's claim that she could not be subjected to a duty in this negligent supervision case unless she knew or should have known that grandfather posed a risk to granddaughter because "public policy expressed in the law has already determined that it is foreseeable that a child may be injured by himself or another if not adequately supervised.").

30. While factors other than foreseeability may be considered in determining whether the entrustor owed a duty to the entrustee, here, the issue is only whether the petition made sufficient allegations to survive a motion to dismiss for failure to state a claim upon which relief may be granted.

it is negligent to entrust a vehicle to an intoxicated person *precisely because* such an entrustment is likely to lead to a car accident, which is what *actually occurred* here. Assuming that the defendant's conduct constitutes a breach of the standard of care, the foreseeability of the plaintiff (and his injury) ties the defendant's act to the harm done, thereby establishing a legal duty. *Palsgraf,* 162 N.E. at 99–100. Here, the act of entrustment breached the standard of care, *Hallquist,* 189 S.W.3d at 176–77, and the foreseeability of the harm to Hays gave rise to the common law duty owed by Royer. *See Smith,* 275 S.W.3d at 801.

b. Missouri case law implicitly acknowledges a first party cause of action for negligent entrustment.

While negligent entrustment cases are *generally* brought by third parties who were injured by the entrustee's negligence, at least two Missouri cases have implicitly recognized a cause of action lying with the entrustee himself. *See Steenrod v. Klipsch Hauling Co., Inc.,* 789 S.W.2d 158, 164 (Mo.App. E.D.1990); *Thomasson v. Winsett,* 310 S.W.2d 33, 36 (Mo.App.1958). Neither case held that an entrustor owes no duty to an entrustee. Rather, in both cases, the plaintiff failed to prove the second element noted above—that the entrustor *knew or had reason to know* that the entrustee was incompetent to operate the entrusted chattel. *Steenrod,* 789 S.W.2d at 171; *Thomasson,* 310 S.W.2d at 38–39. Here, the petition alleges that Royer *did* know that Hays was incompetent to drive the company van. It may be that, like the plaintiffs in *Steenrod* and *Thomasson,* the Hayses will not succeed in proving that Royer had knowledge of Hays's incompetence. That, however, is a question of the sufficiency of the plaintiffs' *proof,* not of the sufficiency of their *allegations.* At this stage, we must assume that the proof will support the plaintiffs' factual allegations, and thus the defect that was fatal to the entrustees' claims in *Steenrod* and *Thomasson* does not exist here.

c. The Restatement supports the existence of a first party cause of action for negligent entrustment.

The Restatement illustrates as follows:

> A . . . rents his boat to B and C, who are obviously so intoxicated as to make it likely that they will mismanage the boat so as to capsize it or to collide with other boats. B and C by their drunken mismanagement collide with the boat of D, upsetting both boats. B, C, and D are drowned. *A is subject to liability to the estates of B, C, and D* under the death statute, although the estates of B and C may also be liable for the death of D.

RESTATEMENT (SECOND) TORTS § 390 cmt. c, illustration 7 (1965) (emphasis added). Under this illustration, B and C are the entrustees, and the Restatement states plainly that they have a cause of action against A, the entrustor.[31]

---

31. While the illustration states that B and C were "visibly" intoxicated, and the petition here alleges that Hays "habitually" drove the company van while intoxicated, this distinction does not

. . .

Conclusion

A cause of action for negligent entrustment may be stated by the entrustee himself. The petition here alleges facts that, if true, would entitle the plaintiffs to recover for negligent entrustment. Accordingly, we reverse and remand for further proceedings consistent with this opinion.

C. Voluntarily Assumed Duties

We return to the general rule that a person ordinarily has no duty to render aid to another. However, if a person having no duty to act voluntarily begins to render aid, the law may impose a duty to do so in a reasonable manner.

O'Malley v. Hospitality Staffing Solutions

20 Cal. App. 5th 21 (2018)

Ordinarily, a person has no legal duty to come to the aid of another. But if a person does come to the aid of another, and does so without exercising reasonable care, that person may be responsible for any damages caused under a "negligent undertaking" theory of liability. (*Paz v. State of California* (2000) 22 Cal.4th 550, 558–559, 93 Cal.Rptr.2d 703, 994 P.2d 975 (*Paz*).)

On March 29, 2014, at about 4:00 p.m., Priscilla O'Malley arrived at a Capistrano Beach hotel. Priscilla and her husband Michael lived about an hour away and owned timeshare privileges at the hotel. The front desk clerk, Kora Mann, who was employed by the hotel, checked Priscilla into a room. At about 5:30 p.m., Priscilla's husband Michael spoke to Priscilla by phone. At about 6:00 p.m., Priscilla spoke to her sister and told her that she was going to stay in for the evening.

Starting at about 7:00 p.m., Michael repeatedly called Priscilla's cell phone, but she did not answer. The couple ordinarily phoned each other on a regular basis. At 9:00 p.m., Michael became concerned and called the front desk to find out which

change our analysis. As set out above, the elements of a claim of negligent entrustment include that the entrustee was "incompetent by reason of . . . habitual recklessness or otherwise." *Hallquist,* 189 S.W.3d at 175. Thus, an entrustee may be otherwise incompetent by reason of intoxication at the time of entrustment or incompetent by reason of habitual recklessness. Here, the petition states more than just that Hays was a known alcoholic. Rather, it alleges that Hays *habitually* drove the company van while intoxicated. While we are dubious that merely lending one's car to a known alcoholic would be sufficient to establish the "knowledge of incompetency" element in that not all alcoholics drive while intoxicated at all, much less is it known that they do so habitually, *see Peters v. Henshaw,* 640 S.W.2d 197, 199 (Mo.App. W.D.1982) ("[B]efore liability can be imposed in . . . a [negligent entrustment] case[,] it must be shown that the reckless conduct of the borrower was so constantly committed as to constitute a habit of negligence.") (quoting *Lix v. Gastian,* 261 S.W.2d 497, 500 (Mo.App.1953)), here the petition alleges more.

room Priscilla had checked into. Over the next hour and a half, Michael made three more calls into Priscilla's room and another call to her cell phone, all of which went unanswered.

At about 10:30 p.m., Michael spoke to Mann at the front desk and asked for her help. Michael explained that his wife was not answering his calls and that he was worried that something might be wrong: specifically, that she might have injured herself and could not get to the phone. Michael wanted to see if Mann could send someone to the room in order to see if his wife was there, and if so, if she was okay. While Michael was on the phone, Mann called into the room and got no answer.

Mann told Michael that a maintenance worker (Saul Ramos) was standing right next to her at the front desk. Ramos was employed by Hospitality Staffing Solutions LLC (HSS), an agency that supplied maintenance staff to the hotel. Mann told Michael that she would have Ramos check the room. Mann instructed Ramos to go to the room and see if Priscilla was there. Ramos understood that Michael was trying to find out whether his wife was in the room, and if she was there, why she was not answering the phone. Ramos had been working at the hotel for a year, but he had never before been asked to do a welfare check of a guest in a room.

Ramos said that he went to the room, knocked several times on the door, and announced, "Maintenance." Ramos said that he opened the door, took one step into the room, and called out asking if anyone was there. He said that all the lights were off. Ramos said that when he stared into the dark room he could only see the shapes of the furniture.

Ramos returned to the front desk and told Mann that no one was in the room. Mann called Michael and related what Ramos had told her. Between 10:30 p.m. and 4:00 a.m., the next morning, Michael called Priscilla a dozen more times. At about 4:00 a.m., Michael decided to drive to the hotel to look for clues as to where Priscilla might be. Michael entered the room at about 5:00 a.m., and noticed that the bedroom and bathroom lights were on. Michael heard labored breathing; he saw Priscilla lying on the living room floor. Priscilla was taken to the hospital. It was later determined that she had suffered a brain aneurism. Priscilla continues to have memory disturbance, difficulty with balance, and other deficits. A doctor averred that Priscilla's injuries would have been less severe had she received treatment earlier in the evening.

On February 10, 2015, Michael and Priscilla filed a complaint alleging negligence and loss of consortium. The O'Malleys later amended the complaint to add HSS (the employer of maintenance worker Ramos) as a Doe defendant.[32] The trial court granted summary judgment in favor of HSS. The O'Malleys appeal.

32. Again, HSS is the only defendant involved in this appeal.

Discussion

Summary judgment "provide[s] courts with a mechanism to cut through the parties' pleadings in order to determine whether, despite their allegations, trial is in fact necessary to resolve their dispute." (*Aguilar v. Atlantic Richfield Co.* (2001) 25 Cal.4th 826, 844, 107 Cal.Rptr.2d 841, 24 P.3d 493.) The trial court properly grants the motion if all the papers submitted establish there is no triable issue of material fact and the moving party is entitled to judgment as a matter of law. (*Id.* at p. 843, 107 Cal.Rptr.2d 841, 24 P.3d 493; Code Civ. Proc., § 437c, subd. (c).)

Here, Ramos's employer, HSS, argues that it owed Priscilla and Michael O'Malley no duty of care. The O'Malleys argue there are disputed facts raising a reasonable inference that Ramos may have created a duty of care under the "negligent undertaking" theory of liability. We agree with the O'Malleys.

The Negligent Undertaking Theory of Liability

"The general rule is that a person who has not created a peril is not liable in tort for failing to take affirmative action to protect another unless they have some relationship that gives rise to a duty to act. [Citation] However, one who undertakes to aid another is under a duty to exercise due care in acting and is liable if the failure to do so increases the risk of harm or if the harm is suffered because the other relied on the undertaking." (*Paz*, *supra*, 22 Cal.4th at pp. 558–559, 93 Cal.Rptr.2d 703, 994 P.2d 975.)

"Thus, . . . a negligent undertaking claim of liability to third parties requires evidence that: (1) the actor undertook, gratuitously or for consideration, to render services to another; (2) the services rendered were of a kind the actor should have recognized as necessary for the protection of third persons; (3) the actor failed to exercise reasonable care in the performance of the undertaking; (4) the actor's failure to exercise reasonable care resulted in physical harm to the third persons; and (5) *either* (a) the actor's carelessness increased the risk of such harm, or (b) the actor undertook to perform a duty that the other owed to the third persons, or (c) the harm was suffered because either the other or the third persons relied on the actor's undertaking." (*Paz*, *supra*, 22 Cal.4th at p. 559, 93 Cal.Rptr.2d 703, 994 P.2d 975.)

The elements of a negligence claim are: a legal duty of care, a breach of that duty, and an injury proximately caused by the breach. Ordinarily, the existence of a duty and the scope of that duty are legal issues determined by courts.

However, under a negligent undertaking theory of liability, the scope of a defendant's duty presents a jury issue when there is a factual dispute as to the nature of the undertaking. (*Artiglio v. Corning Inc.* (1998) 18 Cal.4th 604, 615–616, 76 Cal.Rptr.2d 479, 957 P.2d 1313.) The issue of "whether [a defendant's] alleged actions, if proven, would constitute an 'undertaking' sufficient . . . to give rise to an actionable duty of care is a legal question for the court." *Id.* at p. 615. However, "there may be fact questions 'about precisely what it was that the defendant undertook to do.' That is, while '[t]he "precise nature and extent" of [an alleged negligent undertaking] duty "is a question of law . . . 'it depends on the nature and extent of the act undertaken, a question of fact.'" "Thus, if the record can support competing inferences, or if the facts are not yet sufficiently developed, 'an ultimate finding on the existence of a duty cannot be made prior to a hearing on the merits', and summary judgment is precluded." *Id.* (internal citations omitted).

Application and Analysis

In this case, we find that there are disputed material facts and inferences regarding precisely what the maintenance worker, Ramos, may have undertaken to do. The clerk at the front desk, Mann, said that she told Ramos "to knock on [Priscilla O'Malley's] room . . . and if she did not answer the door, to open the door and look in and see if she was in there." Ramos described what Mann had told him somewhat differently. Ramos said that, "I was told to go check on her, to go to [her] room and see if she's there."

Ramos was present at the front desk during the phone conversation when Michael told Mann his concerns about his wife's possible injuries. Although Ramos apparently heard only one side of the conversation, it is a reasonable inference that Ramos may have been alerted to the apparent urgency of Michael's request. This was the first time Ramos had ever been asked to go to a room to check on a hotel guest. Further, Ramos understood that Michael was trying to find out whether his wife was in the room, and if she was there, why she was not answering the phone. The risk that Priscilla may have been lying incapacitated somewhere in the hotel room (beyond the threshold of the front door) may have been reasonably foreseeable. Therefore, the scope of Ramos' duty may have been more than simply opening the door and peering inside what Ramos claimed was a dark room.

The case of *Bloomberg v. Interinsurance Exchange* (1984) 162 Cal.App.3d 571, 207 Cal.Rptr. 853 (*Bloomberg*), is instructive. In *Bloomberg*, a car broke down on the freeway and the two people in the car made arrangements to have the Automobile Club (AAA) send a tow truck for assistance. Unfortunately, the AAA driver was unable to locate the car, and an intoxicated driver struck the passenger of the stranded vehicle, killing him. The trial court ruled that as a matter of law AAA could not be held liable; the Court of Appeal reversed. (*Id.* at pp. 574–575, 207 Cal. Rptr. 853.) "Generally if the risk of injury might have been reasonably foreseen, a defendant is liable." (*Id.* at p. 576, 207 Cal.Rptr. 853.)

"A defendant who enters upon an affirmative course of conduct affecting the interests of another is regarded as assuming a duty to act, and will be liable for negligent acts or omissions." (*Bloomberg, supra*, 162 Cal.App.3d at p. 575, 207 Cal. Rptr. 853.) The appellate court held that once AAA had agreed to render aid, it had assumed a duty to do so in a nonnegligent manner. (*Id.* at p. 575, 207 Cal.Rptr. 853.) "To the extent that [the two people in the car] relied on respondent to come to their assistance and in so relying made no other arrangements for their rescue, to that extent respondent contributed to the risk of harm." (*Id.* at p. 576, 207 Cal.Rptr. 853.) The court found that foreseeability of the risk—that a drunk driver would run into a stranded car—was a question of fact for the jury. (*Id.* at p. 577, 207 Cal. Rptr. 853.)

Here, we find that a reasonable trier of fact might infer that Ramos assumed a duty to check on whether Priscilla was in her hotel room, and if she was there, why she was not answering the phone. If Ramos had such a duty, the scope of his duty would depend on the nature of the harm that was foreseeable. The risk that Priscilla was incapacitated and needed assistance may have been reasonably foreseeable, but this is a jury question, similar to the situation in *Bloomberg.* Further, it appears that Michael may have relied on Ramos's representation that Priscilla was not in the room, and that he delayed coming to the hotel, thereby possibly exacerbating Priscilla's injuries. In sum, a trier of fact may ultimately decide that some portion of the O'Malleys' injuries were the result of a lack of reasonable care exercised by Ramos (and ultimately his employer) under a negligent undertaking theory of liability. (See *Juarez v. Boy Scouts of America, Inc.* (2000) 81 Cal.App.4th 377, 393, 97 Cal.Rptr.2d 12 [respondeat superior liability when an "employee engages in tortious conduct while acting within the course and scope of employment"].)

HSS argues that: "A third party cannot just barge in on a spouse in the privacy of a residential space because another spouse directed him to do so." But this argument really goes to the issue of breach: whether any duty Ramos may have undertaken was arguably excused (as HSS argues) or breached (as the O'Malleys argue). It is settled law that in a negligence claim, any questions concerning breach (or causation) must be resolved by the trier of fact. (*Vasquez v. Residential Investments, Inc.* (2004) 118 Cal.App.4th 269, 278, 12 Cal.Rptr.3d 846.)

Indeed, the O'Malleys contend that Ramos may not have actually opened the door and peered inside the hotel room (as he claims he did), based on a factual dispute as to whether the lights were off (as Ramos contends) or on (as Michael contends). Further, according to the O'Malleys, had Ramos actually opened the door he might have been able to hear Priscilla's labored breathing. But these are all issues concerning the element of breach; they cannot be resolved in a summary judgment motion.

The judgment is reversed. The trial court's order granting defendant's motion for summary judgment is vacated. The court is directed to enter a new order denying defendant's motion for summary judgment. The plaintiffs are awarded their costs on appeal.

Jagneaux v. Louisiana Farm Bureau Cas. Ins. Co.

771 So. 2d 109 (La. Ct. App. 2000)

SULLIVAN, J.

This case arises out of an accident between a tractor and a van in rural Jefferson Davis Parish. The occupants of the van, Lawrence and Arlene Jagneaux, appeal the dismissal on summary judgment of a passenger in the tractor, who allegedly improperly signaled to the tractor driver that it was safe to proceed through an intersection.

Facts

On April 4, 1997, fifteen-year-old Jeremy Byrne was operating a single-seat, enclosed-cab tractor (with plow in tow) while his friend, Chris Edwards, fourteen, sat on the lefthand armrest. As the tractor traveled along a wet, unpaved road, its tires began spewing mud and dirt, eventually obstructing the views from both side windows. When the teenagers reached the stop sign at an intersection with a state highway, Jeremy asked Chris to check for traffic. Chris opened the door and stepped out of the cab onto the tractor's diesel tank to get a better view of the road. He signaled to Jeremy, but what that signal meant and Jeremy's understanding of it are in dispute. The result is that Jeremy entered the intersection before it was safe to do so and collided with the Jagneauxs' van.

The Jagneauxs sued Jeremy's and Chris's fathers, their insurers, and the manufacturer of the tractor. Jeremy's representatives settled with the Jagneauxs, but the trial court dismissed Chris's on summary judgment, after concluding that Chris did not breach any duties owed by a guest passenger. On appeal, the Jagneauxs argue the trial court erred in improperly weighing Jeremy's and Chris's conflicting testimony and in failing to recognize that Chris undertook a duty beyond that of a guest passenger.

Discussion

Appellate courts review summary judgments *de novo,* applying the same criteria as the trial court in deciding whether or not summary judgment should be granted. *Schroeder v. Board of Supervisors,* 591 So.2d 342 (La.1991). Although summary judgments are now favored, the mover must still show the absence of a genuine issue of material fact and that he is entitled to judgment as a matter of law. La.Code Civ.P. art. 966.

In support of their motion for summary judgment, Chris's father, Barry Edwards, and his insurer, State Farm Fire and Casualty Company, introduced the depositions of the two boys and an excerpt from Mr. Jagneaux's deposition.

Chris testified that he opened the cab door, looked to the left and said, "It's clear on this side," but before he could climb higher to see over the cab to the right, he felt the tractor move forward. He then got back in the cab and asked Jeremy, "What are you doing?" Jeremy said, "You said it's clear," and Chris replied, "No, I said it was clear on this side." Chris then instinctively turned around to look out of the back window and the accident happened. According to Chris, Jeremy later said, "I must have misunderstood you." Chris also testified: "He might have misunderstood me and heard that it was clear, plus I was talking away from him."

Jeremy testified that he did not remember Chris's exact words, but that he went forward because he understood, "You can go." He remembered Chris standing up on the diesel tank and then coming back in the cab. Although Chris was not sitting all the way down when he started moving forward, he did wait until Chris shut the cab door before he advanced. He thought Chris had come back into the cab to sit down, and he did not believe that Chris was still looking for traffic: "As far as I was concerned, he was finished." According to Jeremy, Chris never tried to stop him from going forward. Jeremy testified that he relied on Chris to check for traffic in both directions and that he did not remember Chris saying, "What are you doing?" or himself replying, "You told me it was okay to go." Although Jeremy said that he could not "contradict" Chris if Chris testified otherwise, Jeremy also testified that he would have remembered if Chris said these things and that Chris never blamed him for the accident.

In his deposition, Mr. Jagneaux testified that a policeman at the scene told him that the passenger left the tractor, looked to the north then signaled to the driver, who understood it to be an "all-clear" sign.

As the driver stopped at a stop sign, Jeremy had the duty to "yield the right of way to all vehicles which have entered the intersection from another highway or which are approaching so closely on said highway as to constitute an immediate hazard." La.R.S. 32:123(B). If the Jagneauxs contend that Chris negligently signaled for Jeremy to enter the intersection, they must prove the following as set out in *Lennard v. State Farm Mutual Automobile Insurance Co.*, 26,396, p. 4 (La.App. 2 Cir. 1/25/95); 649 So.2d 1114, 1118 (emphasis added):

> *Any person who waves or signals to indicate the way is clear for a motorist to turn has a duty to exercise reasonable care in doing so. See Martin v. New Orleans Public Service,* 553 So.2d 994, 995–96 (La.App. 4th Cir. 1989). However, before any person can be assessed with fault for failing to exercise reasonable care in waving or signaling, the party alleging the waver's negligence must prove the following: (1) the "waver" did indeed make a signal for the motorist to cross, (2) the "waver" intended to convey that he had checked for traffic, (3) the "waver" intended to indicate that it was entirely safe to cross the street, (4) the motorist reasonably relied on the signal in decid[ing] to cross, and (5) these circumstances, taken as a whole, caused the accident. *Id.*

In *Lennard*, the "waving" driver was a "phantom"; thus the driver relying on the "waver" was not in a position to know if the "phantom" had looked for traffic or intended to signal that it was clear. The court considered these factors in reversing a jury's assessment of fault to the "phantom waver":

> At trial, Peterson admitted he did not know the phantom driver. Peterson also admitted he did not know whether the phantom driver had looked to see if any oncoming traffic was approaching. Moreover, Peterson never testified that the phantom driver intended to convey he had checked for traffic or to indicate it was entirely safe to cross the highway. . . .
>
> . . . .
>
> We find, in regard to the phantom's fault in waving to Peterson, the jury's finding is clearly wrong. *There is no evidence in the record describing the phantom's conduct or communications with Peterson other than the evidence of the phantom driver's simple left-handed waving motion. There is no evidence in the record indicating the phantom had actually checked for traffic or intended to communicate to Peterson that it was safe to cross the highway.*

> Without any such evidence in the record, we conclude that the jury's finding regarding the phantom driver's fault is clearly wrong.

Id. at 1118–19 (emphasis added).

In the present case, Chris was not a "phantom waver." He was known to Jeremy, and the record contains testimony regarding his actions and what he intended to communicate. Movers for summary judgment argue that the boys' versions of the accident are not in conflict because Jeremy said he could not "contradict" Chris's testimony about what was said and because Jeremy admitted he may have "misunderstood" Chris. However, we find the teenagers' accounts differ on one key point. Chris testified that he got back into the cab because he felt the tractor move forward, but Jeremy testified that he waited until Chris shut the cab door before he began to advance. Whether Jeremy proceeded forward before or after Chris began entering the cab is relevant to at least three of the factors in *Lennard:* whether Chris, in fact, signaled for Jeremy to proceed; whether Chris intended to convey that he had checked for traffic; and whether Chris intended to communicate that it was safe to cross the street.

In granting summary judgment, the trial court expressed concern that every guest passenger in an accident would face liability if this case were allowed to proceed. However, we agree with the Jagneauxs that Chris was acting beyond the role of a guest passenger when he assumed the duty of checking for traffic. We further find the evidence does conflict as to whether Chris exercised reasonable care in assuming that duty. As stated in *Citizens Bank & Trust Co. v. Mitchell,* 31,435, pp. 4–5 (La. App. 2 Cir. 1/20/99); 727 So.2d 661, 664: "Even under the more liberalized summary judgment law, however, summary judgment may not be granted when the supporting and opposing documents reveal conflicting versions of the facts which may only be resolved by weighing contradictory testimony and assessing witness credibility."

For the above reasons, the judgment of the trial court is reversed, and the case is remanded for proceedings consistent with this opinion. Costs of this appeal are assessed to Appellees, Barry Edwards and State Farm Fire and Casualty Company.

REVERSED AND REMANDED

Problem 5.5. Aimee is a Fit 4 Life cycling class instructor. When Robert collapsed, Aimee was only a few feet away. She immediately went to his side and directed others to back away from him. Based on Robert's physical condition Aimee erroneously believed that Robert was having a seizure, not a coronary event. A bystander got the AED and brought it to where Aimee was kneeling next to Robert. The bystander asked if Aimee knew how to use the AED and she said that she was certified in operating AEDs (which was true), but she did not think it was necessary or appropriate to use it at that time. Instead, she placed a towel under his neck for support and waited for the ambulance.

Did Aimee violate any duty or duties to Robert?

Review Question

Family Central is a community center run by a nonprofit organization. The center has a gymnasium with a basketball court, and several rooms of varying sizes that are used for classes, meetings, and play areas for kids. The main goal of the center is to provide people in the community, especially youth, a safe place to play and gather and engage in healthy activities such as sports and exercise. The center charges a small fee to enter. The fee is only enough to cover part of the cost to maintain the center and pay employees and the fee is waived for those who cannot afford to pay. The rest of the cost of running the center is covered by donations from individuals and local businesses.

A local contractor volunteered to build an indoor obstacle course for adults and kids. The various obstacles test the strength, balance, and dexterity of those who attempt to complete the course. For example, one obstacle requires a person to travel 20 feet across a three-inch beam suspended three feet above the floor. There is also a rock wall and a rope suspended over a pit of foam cubes that is used to swing from one platform to another. The rope is four feet in front of the first platform and a person must jump from the platform to the rope, hang on while it swings over the pit, then leap off onto the second platform. If the person misses the rope or jumps too soon, she will fall into the foam pit and have to make her way to the side of the pit to climb out.

One afternoon, Erica went with her friend Gavin (both in their twenties) to Family Central to attempt the obstacle course. Erica paid $2.00 to enter the center. Gavin's entry fee was waived based on his income.

The two friends entered the room with the obstacle course and looked around, since it was their first time seeing the course. The only sign in the room prohibited food and drinks in the room. A staff member advised them that they could start at any point in the obstacle course, so the two of them split up.

Erica started at the balance beam. Although her socks did not have grips on the bottom and she could see that the wooden beam was polished and potentially slippery, the room was very cold so she decided to keep her socks on. About halfway across the beam, her right foot slipped and she fell backwards and hit her head on the wooden beam, giving her a concussion. There were no mats or other cushioning on the floor under or around the beam, and Erica fractured her wrist when she hit the floor. Zoe, another visitor to the community center who was standing near Erica when she fell, rushed to help Erica. In her haste to help Erica stand, Zoe yanked on Erica's injured wrist and caused further injury.

Meanwhile, Gavin went to the swinging rope. He leaped from the first platform and reached for the rope, but it slipped from his grip and he fell into the pit with the foam cubes. As he was climbing out of the pit, he cut his foot on a broken bottle that was in the pit. An investigation concluded that the bottle had been dropped into the pit the day before. Although the staff scan the area for potential hazards each morning, the staff member responsible for checking the pit missed it when she did her visual inspection because the bottle was made of glass the same color as the foam cubes. The staff admitted that they knew people were bringing glass bottles into the obstacle course room but said there were not enough staff members to effectively enforce the food and drink ban.

(a) Did Family Central or any of its staff violate any duty or duties owed to Erica?

(b) Did Zoe violate any duty owed to Erica?

(c) Did Family Central or any of its staff violate any duty or duties owed to Gavin?

Chapter 6

Harm and Cause in Fact

A. Harm
- The injury requirement
- Other concepts developed in class or in readings assigned by the professor

B. Cause in fact
- The but-for test
- Joint and several liability
  - In general
  - Contribution
  - Several liability
  - Modified joint and several liability
  - Other concepts developed in class or in readings assigned by the professor
- Alternate tests
  - Increased risk
  - Multiple sufficient cause
  - Alternative liability
  - Market share
  - Loss of opportunity (loss of chance)
  - Other concepts developed in class or in readings assigned by the professor

Chapter Problem. You represent plaintiffs in personal injury actions. Polly, Pedro, and Patty—a minor whose parents are acting on her behalf—have each come to you with different injuries and are seeking your help.

The elements of harm and cause in fact (or "factual cause" or "actual cause") are separate elements of a negligence claim, but they are closely connected. Some of the cases grouped under the cause-in-fact heading in this chapter are as much about harm or damages as they are the cause of those damages. Courts also sometimes talk about "causation" as one element in a negligence action but then break that element down into two parts: cause-in-fact and proximate cause. Despite the fact that both terms contain the word "cause," they serve quite different functions. Therefore, the concept of proximate cause is covered separately in Chapter 7. For now, this chapter focuses first on what qualifies as actionable harm for purposes of a negligence claim before turning to the concept of cause in fact.

A. Harm

Owens-Illinois v. Armstrong

591 A.2d 544 (Md. Ct. Special App. 1991)

BISHOP, Judge.

Issue Presented

Whether the court committed reversible error when it instructed the jury that damages could not be awarded solely for the medical condition of pleural plaques or pleural thickening.

Facts

Frederick Stormer worked as a stockman for the Wallace and Gale Company for six months in 1942. As part of his job, Stormer sorted and stacked asbestos-containing pipe coverings. He then became a warehouseman for Lever Brothers where he worked near pipes covered with asbestos-containing insulation for twenty-eight years. Dominic Celozzi was employed as a coppersmith at the Bethlehem Sparrows Point shipyard from 1937 to 1975. As part of his job, Celozzi worked with and near asbestos-containing insulation products in the engine and boiler rooms of ships.

Stormer and Celozzi presented evidence that they developed pleural plaques and pleural thickening from exposure to asbestos. They also presented evidence that they suffered from asbestosis.... [A]sbestosis is a scarring of the lungs caused by asbestos fibers which results in shortness of breath and difficulty in breathing. Pleural plaques and pleural thickening result from the scarring of the pleura, the thin membrane that keeps the lungs contained and configured to the chest wall and diaphragm. When asbestos fibers are inhaled into the lungs, they may pierce through the smallest airways into the pleura. The fibers that reach the pleura cause a localized reaction which results in a deposit of scar tissue. When the scarring of the pleura is localized, it is known simply as a pleural plaque. When the scarring is widespread, it is referred to as pleural thickening.

All of the medical experts agreed that pleural plaques and pleural thickening are an alteration of an otherwise healthy pleura. They also agreed that pleural scarring does not constitute any loss or detriment. Appellants' two medical experts often used the word "injury" to describe pleural scarring, yet they testified that pleural plaques and pleural thickening do not affect the human body, do not shorten life expectancy, do not cause complications or problems, do not cause pain and cannot be felt. Appellees' three medical experts testified that pleural plaques and pleural thickening have no health significance and do not cause any pain, dysfunction, symptoms or problems.

Based upon this evidence, the court instructed the jury as follows:

> You have heard testimony that one or more of these plaintiffs may have developed pleural plaques or pleural thickening as a result of exposure to

> asbestos. You are instructed that there is no evidence that pleural plaques or pleural thickening cause any impairment or disability. If you find that a plaintiff has only pleural plaques and/or pleural thickening and not asbestosis, then your answer to question one [on the verdict sheet] should be no as to that plaintiff. No damages may be awarded solely because of the pleural plaques or pleural thickening.

Question one on the verdict sheet instructed the jury that if they found that either Stormer or Celozzi did not have asbestosis they should not proceed any further in their deliberation of that case. The jury determined that neither Stormer nor Celozzi suffered from asbestosis and judgment was entered in favor of the defendants.

Discussion

... In the case *sub judice*, the evidence produced by Stormer and Celozzi demonstrated that pleural plaques and pleural thickening alter the pleura, but do not cause any loss or detriment. Consequently, the court's instruction on pleural plaques and pleural thickening was error only if mere alteration of the pleura is a legally compensable injury. We hold that it is not.

Sections 388 and 402A of The Restatement (Second) of Torts (1965) identify "harm" as one of the necessary elements of a cause of action in both negligence and strict liability. The Restatement, in Section 7(2), defines "[t]he word 'harm' [as] used throughout the Restatement ... to denote the existence of loss or detriment in fact of any kind to a person resulting from a cause." Comment b to section 7 further explains that "'[h]arm' implies a loss or detriment to a person, and not a mere change or alteration in some physical person, object or thing.... In so far as physical changes have a detrimental effect on a person, that person suffers harm." These definitions, as used in the Restatement (Second) of Torts, have been cited with approval in Maryland.

Stormer and Celozzi contend that their pleural scarrings are nonconsented alterations of their bodies and as such are grounds for compensation. In support of their contention, they cite the Restatement (Second) of Torts § 15, comment a (1965) which discusses the topic of "battery" and provides, "There is an impairment of the physical condition of another's body if the structure or function of any part of the other's body is altered to any extent even though the alteration causes no other harm." This is, however, only a partial quote from comment a which continues, "A contact which causes no bodily harm may be actionable as a violation of the right to freedom from the *intentional* infliction of offensive bodily contact." (Emphasis added). Section 15 is inapposite, therefore, because it broadly defines bodily harm only in the context of an action based on the intentional tort of battery. A similar argument was rejected in Wright v. Eagle-Picher, 80 Md.App. 606, 615, 565 A.2d 377 (1989). *See also* In re Hawaii Federal Asbestos Cases, 734 F.Supp. 1563, 1567 (D. Haw. 1990) ("Plaintiffs must show a compensable harm by adducing objective testimony of a functional impairment due to asbestos exposure.... In other words, the mere presence of asbestos fibers, pleural thickening or pleural plaques in the lung unaccompanied by an objectively verifiable *functionable impairment* is not enough." (Emphasis in original) (footnote omitted)).

In Maryland, compensatory damages are not to be awarded in negligence or strict liability actions absent evidence that the plaintiff suffered a loss or detriment. In the case sub judice, the medical evidence was clear and uncontradicted that pleural scarring does not cause a functional impairment or harm as defined in the Restatement § 7, supra. Consequently, the court did not err when it instructed the jury that damages were not to be awarded merely for pleural plaques or pleural thickening.

Notes

Similar decisions. Most other courts have reached the same conclusion on the specific issue in *Owens-Illinois. See* Ackison v. Anchor Packing, 897 N.E.2d 1118 (Ohio 2008); In re Haw. Fed. Asbestos Cases, 734 F. Supp. 1563 (D. Haw. 1990); Giffear v. Johns-Manville Corp., 632 A.2d 880 (Pa. Super. 1993). Where pleural thickening is accompanied by physical symptoms, such as shortness of breath, courts have been willing to find that a plaintiff has suffered a compensable injury. *See* Summers v. Certainteed Corp., 997 A.2d 1152 (Pa. 2010).

Emotional distress. Exposure to asbestos increases one's risk of developing cancer. Has an individual who has been exposed to asbestos and who has only pleural thickening but who fears being at increased risk of cancer suffered a compensable harm in the form of emotional distress? *See* Simmons v. Pacor, 674 A.2d 232 (Pa. 1996). Courts often say that physical harm is a necessary element of a negligence claim. *See* Alcala v. Marriott Intern., Inc., 880 N.W.2d 699 (Iowa 2016). Chapter 10 will cover the special situation of negligent infliction of emotional distress.

Risk of future injury. Under the standard "single recovery rule" in tort law, "all damages, future as well as past, must be presented and considered at the time of trial." *Dillon v. Evanston Hospital*, 771 N.E.2d 357, 369 (Ill. 2002). Has a plaintiff suffered a compensable injury when, due to the defendant's negligence, the plaintiff is at an increased risk of developing a disease or impairment in the future? In other words, is being put at an increased risk of future injury a present injury? In *Dillon v. Evanston Hospital*, a doctor negligently failed to completely remove a catheter from the plaintiff's vein. As a result, a fragment of the catheter was embedded in the plaintiff's heart. This failure put the plaintiff at an increased risk of developing future injuries. However, the risk of any of these injuries actually occurring was less than 50%. While traditional rules of causation would ordinarily bar recovery in such a case, the Illinois Supreme Court permitted the plaintiff to obtain "compensation for a future injury that is not reasonably certain to occur, but the compensation would reflect the low probability of occurrence." *Id.* at 370. The final case in this chapter involves a similar issue.

Would the individual who has no present physical injury but is at an increased risk of developing a future condition have a claim for damages based just on the increased future medical expenses involved in monitoring the condition? The majority of courts do not permit a claim for medical monitoring costs absent physical injury. *See, e.g.*, Wood v. Wyeth-Ayerst Laboratories, 82 S.W.3d 849, 853–54 (Ky. 2002); Henry v. Dow Chem. Co., 701 N.W.2d 684, 689 (Mich. 2005) ("Michigan law requires an actual injury to person or property as a precondition to recovery under a negligence theory."). *But see* Bower v. Westinghouse Elec. Corp., 522 S.E.2d 424 (W. Va. 1999) (holding that "a plaintiff asserting a claim for medical monitoring costs is not required to prove present physical harm resulting from tortious exposure to toxic substances [n]or is the plaintiff required to demonstrate the probable likelihood that a serious disease will result from the exposure.").

B. Cause in Fact

As the term suggests, causation in fact is all about whether the defendant's negligence did, in fact, cause the plaintiff's injury. In the average slip and fall or car crash case, this element does not pose much of a problem. But causation-in-fact issues sometimes prove to be complicated. Section 1 focuses on the test used in most cases. The sections that follow focus on the rules that may apply in more complicated factual scenarios.

1. The Standard Test: The But-for Test

Jordan v. Jordan

257 S.E.2d 761 (Va. 1979)

PER CURIAM

Defendant, called as an adverse witness, testified that she left [her] friend's home by the front door approximately forty-five to fifty minutes after she had told her husband that she was not ready to leave. When she left the house, she looked for her husband but did not see him. She assumed that he had become angry and walked home through the woods, since such a walk took only five minutes. After she unlocked the door on the passenger's side of the car, she entered the automobile, closed the door, and slid across the seat to the driver's side. She started the motor and backed up in order to avoid a hole in the driveway and a truck that had been parked nearby. The car struck her husband after she had backed up one and one-half to two feet. She testified that she did not look behind her or use the rearview mirror before backing her car, and that she could not have seen her husband if she had looked immediately before backing because of his "squatting position" behind the car.

The plaintiff testified that he squatted down approximately three to four feet behind the left back side of the car about twenty to thirty minutes before his wife came out of the house and entered her automobile.... The plaintiff said that he did not hear his wife leave the home and bid her friend good-bye, nor did he pay attention to the sound of the car door closing. The plaintiff attempted to move only after hearing the car engine start. When he stood up, the car knocked him down and ran over him. He sustained a broken leg, a fractured hip, and minor injuries.

...

The failure of the defendant to look in the rearview mirror at the very moment she started the engine and moved her car backward does not constitute actionable negligence under the evidence here. There is no evidence that the defendant could have seen the plaintiff if she had looked in the rearview mirror. Indeed, the uncontradicted testimony of the plaintiff indicates that her looking in the rearview mirror would not have detected his presence. Since there is no evidence to suggest that the plaintiff could have seen the defendant, we conclude that the defendant's failure to look in the rearview mirror did not cause the plaintiff's injuries and, therefore, does not constitute actionable negligence.

Salinetro v. Nystrom

341 So. 2d 1059 (Fla. Ct. App. 1977)

PER CURIAM.

Anna Salinetro appeals an adverse final judgment entered pursuant to a directed verdict in this action for alleged medical malpractice.

Anna Salinetro sustained back injuries in an automobile accident and applied for personal injury benefits from her insurer, State Farm Mutual Automobile Insurance Company. State Farm required Anna to submit to a medical examination and on December 10 x-rays were taken by Dr. Nystrom of her lower back and abdominal area. Although unknown to her, Anna was approximately four-six weeks pregnant at the time; however, neither Dr. Nystrom nor his receptionist or his x-ray technician inquired whether or not she was pregnant or the date of her last menstrual period. Thereafter, upon suspecting she was pregnant, on December 12 Anna visited her gynecologist, Dr. Emilio Aldereguia, who, after running some tests, confirmed her pregnancy. In January Dr. Aldereguia learned that Dr. Nystrom had taken x-rays of Anna's pelvis and advised her to terminate her pregnancy because of possible damage to the fetus by the x-rays. Anna underwent a therapeutic abortion and the pathology report stated that the fetus was dead at the time of the abortion. Thereafter, Anna filed the instant lawsuit against Dr. Nystrom for medical malpractice.... After the presentation of all the evidence on Anna's behalf, Dr. Nystrom moved for a directed verdict on the ground she failed to make a prima facie case of medical malpractice. The trial judge granted the motion and entered judgment for Dr. Nystrom.

Anna first contends that the record contains sufficient evidence to present to the jury a prima facie case of malpractice.

Liability for negligence depends on a showing that the injury suffered by plaintiff was caused by the alleged wrongful act or omission to act by the defendant. Merely to show a connection between the negligence and the injury is not sufficient to establish liability.

Assuming arguendo that Dr. Nystrom's conduct fell below the standard of care in failing to inquire of Anna whether she was pregnant or not on the date of her last menstrual period, this omission was not the cause of her injury. Anna herself testified that even if asked about being pregnant, she would have answered in the negative. Anna further testified to the effect that being a few days late with her menstrual period was not unusual and did not indicate to her that she may have been pregnant at the time she went to Dr. Nystrom; that six days prior thereto she had visited Dr. Aldereguia, and he had found no evidence that she was pregnant. We further note that simply because Anna was late with her menstrual period would not in and of itself mean that she was pregnant because further tests were required to ascertain whether she was pregnant. Thus, this point is without merit.

Notes

But-for causation. In the run-of-the-mill case, a court will instruct the jury to consider whether the plaintiff's injury would have occurred but for the defendant's negligence. As *Jordan* and *Salinetro* illustrate, this requires a juror to consider a hypothetical set of facts in which the defendant did what the plaintiff argues the defendant should have done in order to exercise reasonable care.

Preponderance of the evidence. As is the case with the other elements of a negligence claim, a plaintiff must prove it is more likely than not that, but for the defendant's negligent conduct, the plaintiff would not have been harmed.

Multiple necessary causes. The but-for test also works when multiple forces combine to produce a result, but none of them standing alone would have been sufficient to produce the result.

Problem 6.1. Dante drives his car in a negligent fashion. Denise drives her car in a slightly more negligent fashion. The two cars collide, spin out of control, and crash into Polly, a nearby pedestrian. Had they not collided, both cars would have passed Polly without incident. Polly suffers $100,000 in damages. Was Dante's negligence a cause in fact of Polly's injury? Was Denise's?

Dillon v. Twin State Gas & Electric Co.

163 A. 111 (N.H. 1932)

[The decedent, age 14, and other boys would climb on girders attached to a bridge that ran over a river. The defendant maintained wires to carry electric current over the bridge. The wires were insulated for weather protection but not against contact. The wires ran about a foot above the horizontal girder, which was 19 feet above the floor of the bridge. While the decedent was sitting on the horizontal girder, he "leaned over, lost his balance, instinctively threw out his arm, and took hold of one of the wires with his right hand to save himself from falling. The wires happened to be charged with a high voltage current at the time and he was electrocuted."

The administrator of the boy's estate brought an action against the power company. The defendant's motion for a directed verdict was denied. After concluding that the defendant owed a duty to the decedent, the court turned to the issue of causation.]

The circumstances of the decedent's death give rise to an unusual issue of its cause. In leaning over from the girder and losing his balance he was entitled to no protection from the defendant to keep from falling. Its only liability was in exposing him to the danger of charged wires. If but for the current in the wires he would have fallen down on the floor of the bridge or into the river, he would without doubt have been either killed or seriously injured. Although he died from electrocution, yet, if by reason of his preceding loss of balance he was bound to fall except for the intervention of the current, he either did not have long to live or was to be maimed. In such an outcome of his loss of balance, the defendant deprived him, not of a life of normal expectancy, but of one too short to be given pecuniary allowance, in one alternative, and not of normal, but of limited, earning capacity, in the other.

If it were found that he would have thus fallen with death probably resulting, the defendant would not be liable, unless for conscious suffering found to have been sustained from the shock. In that situation his life or earning capacity had no value. To constitute actionable negligence there must be damage, and damage is limited to those elements the statute prescribes.

If it should be found that but for the current he would have fallen with serious injury, then the loss of life or earning capacity resulting from the electrocution would be measured by its value in such injured condition. Evidence that he would be crippled would be taken into account in the same manner as though he had already been crippled.

His probable future but for the current thus bears on liability as well as damages. Whether the shock from the current threw him back on the girder or whether he would have recovered his balance, with or without the aid of the wire he took hold of, if it had not been charged, are issues of fact, as to which the evidence as it stands may lead to different conclusions.

2. Joint and Several Liability

a. Introduction to Joint and Several Liability

The principle of joint and several liability is well established:

> If two or more persons owe to another the same duty, and by their common neglect of that duty, he is injured, . . . the tort is joint, and upon well-settled principles each, any, or all of the tort[ ]feasors may be held. But when each of two or more persons owe to another a separate duty, which each wrongfully neglects to perform, then, although the duties were diverse and disconnected, and the neglect of each was without concert, if such several neglects occurred and united together in causing injury, the tort is equally joint, and the tort[ ]feasors are subject to a like liability.

Matthews v. Seaboard Air Line Railway, 46 S.E. 335 (S.C. 1903) (citations omitted).

Stated more simply, where the negligence of two or more defendants causes one indivisible injury, both may be held liable. As the excerpt above from *Matthews* suggests, joint and several liability might result where multiple defendants act in concert. *See* Restatement (Second) of Torts § 876(a) (1977). But it may also result where two completely unrelated defendants engage in completely separate actions that result in harm.

An important component of joint and several liability is the fact that a plaintiff has the right to seek to collect from any of multiple tortfeasors. The trial judge may instruct the jury to apportion responsibility among multiple defendants. But each defendant is individually responsible for the full amount of a plaintiff's damages. However, a paying defendant also has a right of *contribution* from the other defendants for their portion of the loss.

Landers v. East Texas Salt Water Disposal Co.

248 S.W.2d 731 (Tex. 1952)

CALVERT, Justice.

Suit by C. H. Landers, plaintiff, against East Texas Salt Water Disposal Company and Sun Oil Company, defendants, seeking a joint and several judgment of damages and injunctive relief was dismissed as to the damages feature by the trial court . . .

In his petition plaintiff alleged that he was the owner of a small lake which he had drained, cleaned and stocked with fish at considerable expense; defendant East Texas Salt Water Disposal Company was the owner of a pipe line which traversed land adjoining plaintiff's land on the west and into which the defendant pumped approximately 1500 barrels of salt water daily; that on or about April 1, 1949, such pipe line broke and the defendant Disposal Company negligently permitted . . . salt water to escape from the line and to flow over plaintiff's land and into his lake, killing his fish and otherwise injuring and damaging him. Plaintiff further alleged that the defendant Sun Oil Company was the owner of an oil well, located a short distance from plaintiff's property line, from which the defendant pumped small quantities of oil and large quantities of salt water each day, the oil and salt water being carried off through a pipe line which for some distance ran parallel to a spring branch; that the branch crossed plaintiff's property and emptied into his lake; that on or about April 1, 1949, the pipe line broke and the defendant Sun Oil Company negligently permitted large quantities of oil and salt water to escape and run into the branch and thence into plaintiff's lake, killing his fish and otherwise injuring and damaging him.

. . .

Did the plaintiff in his pleading allege facts which, if established by evidence, made the defendants jointly and severally liable for plaintiff's damages? From the face of the petition it appears that there was no concert of action nor unity of design between the defendants in the commission of their alleged tortious acts, an absence said by the court in the case of *Sun Oil Co. v. Robicheaux*, Tex.Com.App., 23 S.W.2d 713, 715, to be determinative of the nonexistence of joint liability. In that case the rule was thus stated:

> 'The rule is well established in this state, and supported by almost universal authority, that an action at law for damages for torts cannot be maintained against several defendants jointly, when each acted independently of the others and there was no concert or unity of design between them. In such a case the tort of each defendant is several when committed, and it does not become joint because afterwards its consequences, united with the consequences of several other torts committed by other persons in producing damages. Under such circumstances, each tort-feasor is liable only for the part of the injury or damages caused by his own wrong; that is, where a person contributes to an injury along with others, he must respond in damages, but if he acts independently, and not in concert of action which other persons in causing such injury, he is liable only for the damages which directly and proximately result from his own act, and the fact that it may be difficult to define the damages caused by the wrongful act of each person who independently contributed to the final result does not affect the rule. Sun Co. v. Wyatt, 48 Tex.Civ.App., 349, 107 S.W. 934; 38 Cyc. 484; 26 R.C.L. 766.'

It may be noted that the opinion of the Commission of Appeals in the *Robicheaux* case was not adopted by the Supreme Court. Nevertheless, it has been generally recognized as having correctly stated the law of this state, and it was specifically cited and followed by the Court of Civil Appeals in deciding this case.

. . .

The rule of the *Robicheaux* case, strictly followed, has made it impossible for a plaintiff, though gravely injured, to secure relief in the nature of damages through a joint and several judgment by joining in one suit as defendants all wrongdoers whose independent tortious acts have joined in producing an injury to the plaintiff, which, although theoretically divisible, as a practical matter and realistically considered is in fact but a single indivisible injury. As interpreted by the Courts of Civil Appeals the rule also denies to a plaintiff the right to proceed to judgment and satisfaction against the wrongdoers separately because in such a suit he cannot discharge the burden of proving with sufficient certainty, under pertinent rules of damages, the portion of the injury attributable to each defendant. Thus at the time he filed his suit the plaintiff in this case was confronted with a declared status of the law in this state which effectively relieved the two defendants of the consequences of their wrongs and required the innocent plaintiff to suffer his injuries without recompense. Whether he insisted on standing on his joint and several suit against the defendants or bowed to the ruling of the trial court and proceeded against the defendants separately, he could not prevail. In other words, our courts seem to have embraced the philosophy, inherent in this class of decisions, that it is better that the injured party lose all of his damages than that any of several wrongdoers should pay more of the damages than he individually and separately caused. If such has been the law, from the standpoint of justice it should not have been; if it is the law now, it will not be hereafter. The case of *Sun Oil Co. v. Robicheaux* is overruled. Where the tortious acts of two or more wrongdoers join to produce an indivisible injury, that is, an injury which from its nature cannot be apportioned with reasonable certainty to the individual wrongdoers, all of the wrongdoers will be held jointly and severally liable for the entire damages and the injured party may proceed to judgment against any one separately or against all in one suit. If fewer than the whole number of wrongdoers are joined as defendants to plaintiff's suit, those joined may by proper cross action under the governing rules bring in those omitted. To permit the joinder as defendants of such wrongdoers without at the same time imposing joint liability upon them would not relieve the inequities of the situation nor cure the ills of the plaintiff. Simple procedural joinder of the defendants would put the plaintiff in no better position to produce the required proof of the portion of the injury attributable to each of the defendants. In most such cases, under the decisions heretofore cited, he would still be the victim of an instructed verdict. It would be of no comfort or advantage to the plaintiff that the instructed verdict relieved all of the defendants of liability in one suit and at one time rather than in separate suits and one at a time.

. . .

The judgments of the Court of Civil Appeals and of the trial court are reversed and the cause is remanded to the trial court for further proceedings not inconsistent with this opinion.

Note

Apportioning responsibility. Chapter 8 will address the issue of apportioning responsibility among the parties. But for now, the *Restatement* lists two factors to consider in making this determination in the case of multiple parties whose negligence contributes to an indivisible injury:

> (a) the nature of the person's risk-creating conduct, including any awareness or indifference with respect to the risks created by the conduct and any intent with respect to the harm created by the conduct; and
>
> (b) the strength of the causal connection between the person's risk-creating conduct and the harm.

Restatement (Third) of Torts § 8 (2000).

Problem 6.2. Refer back to Problem 6.1. Polly suffers $100,000 in damages and sues Dante and Denise in the same action in a jurisdiction that employs a system of joint and several liability. The jury awards the full amount of requested damages and assigns 60% of responsibility to Denise and 40% to Dante. Polly seeks to collect $100,000 from Dante.

(a) Can she do that? What is likely to happen if she does?

(b) Assume for purposes of this question that Dante is insolvent and unable to pay. How much of the $100,000 judgment is Denise responsible for?

Problem 6.3. Don was not paying attention as he stood up from his table at Dominique's Restaurant. As a result, he ended up colliding with another customer, Pedro, and accidentally knocking out one of Pedro's teeth. As Pedro was walking out of the restaurant, he slipped on some water that had been left standing on the restaurant floor due to negligence on the part of an employee. He ended up breaking his ankle from the fall. Pedro's damages from the lost tooth were $4,000. His damages from the broken ankle were $6,000. In a jurisdiction that employs a system of joint and several liability, how much could Pedro recover from Don? How much could he recover from Dominique's?

b. The Move Away from Joint and Several Liability

Toward the latter half of the twentieth century, states began to move away from a system of pure joint and several liability. Some states moved toward a system of pure *several liability*, under which a defendant can only be held responsible for his or her portion of the fault for the injury. Even in a pure several liability jurisdiction, joint and several liability applies if the defendants were acting in concert or where an agency relationship exists between the defendants. *See* Ariz. Rev. Stat. § 12-2506; Resolution Trust Corp. v. Block, 924 S.W.2d 354 (Tenn.1996). The majority of jurisdictions now employ some type of modified joint and several liability.

South Carolina Code of Laws § 15-38-15

Liability of defendant responsible for less than fifty per cent of total fault . . . .

(A) In an action to recover damages resulting from personal injury, wrongful death, or damage to property . . . if indivisible damages are determined to be proximately caused by more than one defendant, joint and several liability does not apply to any defendant whose conduct is determined to be less than fifty percent of the total fault for the indivisible damages as compared with the total of: (i) the fault of all the defendants; and (ii) the fault (comparative negligence), if any, of plaintiff. A defendant whose conduct is determined to be less than fifty percent of the total fault shall only be liable for that percentage of the indivisible damages determined by the jury or trier of fact.

Arkansas Code § 16-55-201

Modification of joint and several liability

(a) In any action for personal injury, medical injury, property damage, or wrongful death, the liability of each defendant for compensatory or punitive damages shall be several only and shall not be joint.

(b) (1) Each defendant shall be liable only for the amount of damages allocated to that defendant in direct proportion to that defendant's percentage of fault.

Arkansas Code § 16-55-203

Increase in percentage of several share.

(a) (1) Notwithstanding the provisions of 16-55-201 . . . , in the event a several judgment has been entered against multiple-party defendants, a plaintiff may move the court no later than ten (10) days after the entry of judgment to determine whether all or part of the amount of the several share for which a defendant is liable will not be reasonably collectible.

(2) If the court determines, based upon a preponderance of the evidence, that any defendant's several share or multiple defendants' several shares will not be reasonably collectible, the court shall increase the percentage points of the several shares of each of the remaining defendants, subject to the limitations in subdivisions (a)(3) and (4) of this section.

(3) (A) If a defendant's percentage of fault is determined by the finder of fact to be ten percent (10%) or less, then the percentage points of that defendant's several share shall not be increased.

(B) If a defendant's percentage of fault is determined by the finder of fact to be greater than ten percent (10%) but less than fifty percent (50%), then the percentage points of that defendant's several share shall be increased by no more than ten (10) percentage points.

(C) If a defendant's percentage of fault is determined by the finder of fact to be fifty percent (50%) or greater, then the percentage points of that defendant's several share shall be increased by no more than twenty (20) percentage points.

Problem 6.4. Refer back to Problem 6.1 involving Polly, Dante, and Denise. The jury awards $100,000 in damages and assigns 60% of responsibility to Denise and 40% to Dante.

(a) How much could Polly recover from Denise in a pure several liability jurisdiction if Dante is solvent? How much could she recover from Denise if Dante is insolvent?

(b) How much could Polly recover from Denise in South Carolina if Dante is solvent? How much could she recover from Denise if Dante is insolvent?

(c) How much could Polly recover from Denise in Arkansas if Dante is solvent? How much could she recover from Denise if Dante is insolvent in a pure several liability jurisdiction?

3. Alternate Tests

As *Landers* illustrates, sometimes application of the standard but-for causation test would lead to unfair or illogical results. Sometimes plaintiffs face other obstacles establishing causation through no fault of their own. Thus, courts have been forced to devise alternative approaches to causation issues in some cases. The cases in this section illustrate how courts have sought to further the goal of compensation where standard causation rules prove problematic.

a. Increased Risk

Zuchowicz v. United States

140 F.3d 381 (2d Cir. 1998)

[The defendant was charged with negligence in prescribing the drug Danocrine in overdose amounts. The plaintiff eventually developed primary pulmonary hypertension (PPH) and died. Her medical expert, Dr. Richard Matthay, testified that he was confident to a reasonable medical certainty that the Danocrine caused Mrs. Zuchowicz's PPH. He added that he believed the overdose of Danocrine to have been responsible for the disease. Danocrine was approved by the Food and Drug Administration ("FDA") for use in dosages not to exceed 800 mg/day. Mrs. Zuchowicz was accidentally given a prescription instructing her to take twice this amount—1600 mg/day. According to one expert, no formal studies of the effects of Danocrine at such high doses have been performed, and very, very few women have received doses this high in any setting.]

4. Was Danocrine a But For Cause of Mrs. Zuchowicz's Illness and Death?

We hold that, on the basis of Dr. Matthay's testimony alone, the finder of fact could have concluded—under Connecticut law—that Mrs. Zuchowicz's PPH was, more likely than not, caused by Danocrine. While it was not possible to eliminate all other possible causes of pulmonary hypertension, the evidence presented showed that the experts had not only excluded all causes of secondary pulmonary hypertension, but had also ruled out all the previously known drug-related causes of PPH....

5. Was the Overdose a But For Cause of Mrs. Zuchowicz's Illness and Death?

To say that Danocrine caused Mrs. Zuchowicz's injuries is only half the story, however. In order for the causation requirement to be met, a trier of fact must be able to determine, by a preponderance of the evidence, that the defendant's negligence was responsible for the injury. In this case, defendant's negligence consisted in prescribing an overdose of Danocrine to Mrs. Zuchowicz. For liability to exist, therefore, it is necessary that the fact finder be able to conclude, more probably than not, that the overdose was the cause of Mrs. Zuchowicz's illness and ultimate death. The mere fact that the exposure to Danocrine was likely responsible for the disease does not suffice.

The problem of linking defendant's negligence to the harm that occurred is one that many courts have addressed in the past. A car is speeding and an accident occurs. That the car was involved and was a cause of the crash is readily shown. The accident, moreover, is of the sort that rules prohibiting speeding are designed to prevent. But is this enough to support a finding of fact, in the individual case, that speeding was, in fact, more probably than not, the cause of the accident? The same question can be asked when a car that was driving in violation of a minimum speed requirement on a super-highway is rear-ended. Again, it is clear that the car and its driver were causes of the accident. And the accident is of the sort that minimum speeding rules are designed to prevent. But can a fact finder conclude, without more, that the driver's negligence in driving too slowly led to the crash? To put it more precisely—the defendant's negligence was strongly causally linked to the accident, and the defendant was undoubtedly a but for cause of the harm, but does this suffice to allow a fact finder to say that the defendant's negligence was a but for cause?

At one time, courts were reluctant to say in such circumstances that the wrong could be deemed to be the cause. They emphasized the logical fallacy of *post hoc, ergo propter hoc*, and demanded some direct evidence connecting the defendant's wrongdoing to the harm.

All that has changed, however. And, as is so frequently the case in tort law, Chief Judge Cardozo in New York and Chief Justice Traynor in California led the way. In various opinions, they stated that: if (a) a negligent act was deemed wrongful because that act increased the chances that a particular type of accident would occur, and (b) a mishap of that very sort did happen, this was enough to support a finding by the trier of fact that the negligent behavior caused the harm. Where such a strong causal link exists, it is up to the negligent party to bring in evidence denying but for cause and suggesting that in the actual case the wrongful conduct had not been a substantial factor.

. . .

The case before us is a good example of the above-mentioned principles in their classic form. The reason the FDA does not approve the prescription of new drugs at above the dosages as to which extensive tests have been performed is because all drugs involve risks of untoward side effects in those who take them. Moreover, it is often true that the higher the dosage the greater is the likelihood of such negative effects. At the approved dosages, the benefits of the particular drug have presumably been deemed worth the risks it entails. At greater than approved dosages, not only do the risks of tragic side effects (known and unknown) increase, but there is no basis on the testing that has been performed for supposing that the drug's benefits outweigh these increased risks. It follows that when a negative side effect is demonstrated to be the result of a drug, and the drug was wrongly prescribed in an unapproved and excessive dosage (*i.e.* a strong causal link has been shown), the plaintiff who is injured has generally shown enough to permit the finder of fact to conclude that the excessive dosage was a substantial factor in producing the harm.

In fact, plaintiff's showing in the case before us, while relying on the above stated principles, is stronger. For plaintiff introduced some direct evidence of causation as well. On the basis of his long experience with drug-induced pulmonary diseases, one of plaintiff's experts, Dr. Matthay, testified that the timing of Mrs. Zuchowicz's illness led him to conclude that the overdose (and not merely Danocrine) was responsible for her catastrophic reaction.

Under the circumstances, we hold that defendant's attack on the district court's finding of causation is meritless.

b. Multiple Sufficient Causes

Anderson v. Minneapolis, St. Paul & Sault Ry.

179 N.W. 45 (Minn. 1920)

Plaintiff's case in chief was directed to proving that in August, 1918, one of defendant's engines started a fire in a bog near the west side of plaintiff's land; that it smoldered there until October 12, 1918, when it flared up and burned his property, shortly before it was reached by one of the great fires which swept through Northeastern Minnesota at the close of that day. Defendant introduced evidence to show that on and prior to October 12th fires were burning west and northwest of, and were swept by the wind towards, plaintiff's premises. It did not show how such fires originated, neither did it clearly and certainly trace the destruction of plaintiff's property to them. By cross-examination of defendant's witnesses and by his rebuttal evidence plaintiff made a showing which would have justified the jury in finding that the fires proved by defendant were started by its locomotive on or near its right of way in the vicinity of Kettle River.

[The Minnesota Supreme Court approved of the following jury instruction given at trial:]

> 'If you find that other fires not set by one of defendant's engines mingled with one that was set by one of defendant's engines, there may be difficulty in determining whether you should find that the fire set by the engine was a material or substantial element in causing plaintiff's damage. If it was, the defendant is liable; otherwise, it is not. * * *
>
> 'If you find that bog fire was set by defendant's engine, and that some greater fire swept over it before it reached plaintiff's land, then it will be for you to determine whether the bog fire * * * was a material or substantial factor in causing plaintiff's damage. If it was, defendant was liable. If it was not, defendant was not liable. If the bog fire was set by one of defendant's engines, and if one of defendant's engines also set a fire or fires west of Kettle River, and those fires combined and burned over plaintiff's property, then the defendant is liable.'

Ford Motor Co. v. Boomer

736 S.E.2d 724 (Va. 2013)

Opinion by Justice LEROY F. MILLETTE, JR.

Lokey served as a Virginia State Trooper for 30 years. Beginning in 1965 or 1966, for approximately seven and a half to eight years, his duties required that he observe vehicle inspections wherein mechanics used compressed air to blow out brake debris (dust) to allow for a visual inspection of the brakes. Lokey testified that, during these years, he observed vehicle inspections in approximately 70 garages a month, for five to six hours a day, ten days each month. Lokey testified to standing within ten feet of the inspectors who were blowing out brake linings with compressed air, and that these blow outs were a fairly common practice in inspections at the time. He also recalled breathing in visible dust in the garages, which to his knowledge had no specialized ventilation systems. He testified that he was not provided protective clothing or masks or warned that breathing brake dust was harmful to his health.

[Lokey was likely exposed to dust from brake linings in Ford and Oldsmobile cars during this timeframe. These linings contained asbestos materials. The Oldsmobile brake linings were made by Bendix. Lokey was diagnosed with mesothelioma, a malignant cancer of the pleura of the lungs, in 2005. He passed away in 2007 due to complications related to his disease. His estate brought a wrongful death action. Lokey's expert testified that the type of asbestos found in brakes can cause mesothelioma. They opined that the exposure to dust from Bendix brakes and brakes in new Ford cars were both substantial contributing factors to Lokey's mesothelioma. The jury found in favor of the estate as to negligence and awarded damages in the amount of $282,685.69. The trial court denied Bendix' and Ford's motions to strike the expert testimony and their motions to set aside the verdict or for a new trial and entered final judgment for the estate. Bendix and Ford appealed.]

We explained [in *Wells v. Whitaker*, 207 Va. 616, 622, 151 S.E.2d 422, 428 (1966)] that "[t]o impose liability upon one person for damages incurred by another, it must be shown that the negligent conduct was a necessary physical antecedent of the damages."

The requirement of but-for causation came with a caveat, however: "The 'but for' test is a useful rule of exclusion in all but one situation: where two causes concur to bring about an event and either alone *would have been sufficient* to bring about an identical result." *Id.* at 622 n. 1, 151 S.E.2d at 428 n. 1 (emphasis added).

Causation in a mesothelioma case, however, presents a challenge for the courts beyond even our standard concurring negligence instruction. Mesothelioma is a signature disease: it was uncontroverted at trial that the cause of mesothelioma is exposure to asbestos at some point during an individual's lifetime. The long latency period of the disease, however, makes it exceedingly difficult to pinpoint when the harmful asbestos exposure occurred and, in the presence of multiple exposures, equally difficult to distinguish the causative exposure(s).

Further complicating the issue, although numerous individuals were exposed to varying levels of asbestos during its widespread industrial use before safety measures became standard, not all persons exposed developed mesothelioma. It is not currently known why some are more susceptible than others to developing mesothelioma, or why even low levels of exposure may cause mesothelioma in some individuals while others exposed to higher dosages never develop the disease. Thus, in the context of a lifetime of potential asbestos exposures, designating particular exposures as causative presents courts with a unique challenge.

Despite this lack of certainty, we task juries with determining liability in multiple exposure mesothelioma cases. Virginia statutory and case law makes clear that the Commonwealth permits recovery for parties injured by asbestos exposure, including those with mesothelioma, even when a jury must draw inferences from indirect facts to determine whether an exposure was causal. The question before us is whether the Commonwealth's approach . . . should be modified to allow such recovery in multiple-causation cases and, if so, how. Certainly, if the traditional but-for [approach] was invoked, the injured party would virtually never be able to recover for damages arising from mesothelioma in the context of multiple exposures, because injured parties would face the difficult if not impossible task of proving that any one single source of exposure, in light of other exposures, was the sole but-for cause of the disease.

The circuit court, in an admirable attempt to offer guidance to the jury as to this point, invoked a supplemental term in its jury instructions: "substantial contributing factor." For example, in Instruction 16, the court stated:

> Before the plaintiff is entitled to recover from either defendant on the negligence theory, he must prove by a preponderance of the evidence . . . exposure to asbestos-containing products manufactured and/or sold by defendant was a *substantial contributing factor* in causing plaintiff's injury; . . .

(emphasis added)

In the last several decades, with the rise of asbestos-based lawsuits, the "substantial contributing factor" instruction has become prominent in some other jurisdictions. . . .

Considering it now for the first time, we find several problems with the substantial contributing factor instruction. . . . The term substantial contributing factor could be construed to mean any cause that is more than a merely *de minimis* factor. Conversely, the invocation of the term "substantial" could be interpreted to raise the standard for proof of causation beyond a mere preponderance of the evidence to some more elevated standard. In sum, some jurors might construe the term to lower the threshold of proof required for causation while others might interpret it to mean the opposite. We do not believe that substantial contributing factor has a single, common-sense meaning, and we conclude that a reasonable juror could be confused as to the quantum of evidence required to prove causation . . . .

Moreover, we agree with the explicit rejection of substantial contributing factor language in the recent Restatement (Third) of Torts: Liability for Physical and Emotional Harm (2010). The Restatement (Second) of Torts used substantial factor language, stating that, absent an independent but-for cause, "[i]f two forces are actively operating . . . and each of itself is sufficient to bring about harm to another, [one] actor's negligence may be found to be a substantial factor in bringing it about." Restatement (Second) of Torts § 432 (1965).

The latest revision of the Restatement, however, deliberately abandoned this language, explaining:

> [T]he substantial-factor rubric tends to obscure, rather than to assist, explanation and clarification of the basis of [causation] decisions. The element that must be established, by whatever standard of proof, is the but-for or necessary-condition standard of this Section. Section 27 provides a rule for finding each of two acts that are elements of sufficient competing causal sets to be factual causes without employing the substantial-factor language of the prior Torts Restatements. There is no question of degree for either of these concepts.

Restatement (Third) of Torts § 26, cmt. j. The comment also specifically references the tendency of courts to at times interpret the language as either raising or lowering the factual causation standard, leading to inconsistent and inaccurate statements of law. *Id.* If courts cannot be relied upon to consistently construe the language, we cannot expect lay jurors to accomplish the same task.

The Restatement (Third) of Torts relies instead on the combination of sections 26 and 27:

> § 26 Factual Cause
>
> Tortious conduct must be a factual cause of harm for liability to be imposed. Conduct is a factual cause of harm when the harm would not have occurred absent the conduct. Tortious conduct may also be a factual cause of harm under § 27.
>
> § 27 Multiple Sufficient Causes
>
> If multiple acts occur, each of which under § 26 alone would have been a factual cause of the physical harm at the same time in the absence of the other act(s), each is regarded as a factual cause of the harm.

This model, as explicated in the comments, is quite consistent with our statements in *Wells* regarding concurring causation. The rationale articulated in comment c of § 27 echoes the logic behind our long history of recognizing concurring causes:

> A defendant whose tortious act was fully capable of causing the plaintiff's harm should not escape liability merely because of the fortuity of another sufficient cause. . . . When two tortious multiple sufficient causes exist, to deny liability would make the plaintiff worse off due to multiple

> tortfeasors than would have been the case if only one of the tortfeasors had existed. Perhaps most significant is the recognition that, while *the but-for standard provided in § 26 is a helpful method for identifying causes, it is not the exclusive means for determining a factual cause. Multiple sufficient causes are also factual causes* because we recognize them as such in our common understanding of causation, even if the but-for standard does not. Thus, the standard for causation in this Section comports with deep-seated intuitions about causation and fairness in attributing responsibility.

Restatement (Third) of Torts § 27, cmt. c. (emphasis added). The multiple sufficient cause analysis allows multiple tortfeasors to be found jointly and severally liable.

. . .

While it might be clearly seen in a car accident or converging fires that both acts contributed in some degree to the harm, the nature of mesothelioma leaves greater uncertainty as to which exposure or exposures in fact constituted the triggering event. This is, however, a distinction without a difference: if the jurors, after hearing the testimony and evidence, believe that a negligent exposure was more likely than not sufficient to have triggered the harm, then the defendant can be found liable in the same way that a jury can conclude that a driver in a multiple-car collision or the negligent party in one of two converging fires is liable.

. . . The acts themselves do not have to be concurrent, so long as they are "operating and sufficient to cause the harm contemporaneously." Restatement (Third) of Torts § 27, cmt. e. . . .

While we reject defendants' strict interpretation of sole but-for cause argued to the circuit court at trial, we nonetheless conclude that the trial court erred in failing to sustain the defendants' objections to the substantial contributing factor jury instructions. We remand for further proceedings consistent with the multiple sufficient cause analysis.

Notes

Multiple necessary causes distinguished. The multiple sufficient cause scenario at issue in *Anderson* and *Boomer* should be distinguished from the multiple necessary cause scenario. In the latter scenario, multiple causes work in conjunction to bring about a result, and each is necessary to produce the result.

Substantial factor test. Despite the *Restatement*'s shift in language, some courts continue to use the substantial factor language. *See* Vasquez v. Davis, 228 F. Supp. 3d 1189, 1206 (D. Colo. 2016).

Problem 6.5. Patty is six years old. She has lived at her current residence her entire life. This house was built in 1970. Patty has been hospitalized for lead poisoning on three separate occasions. There is no doubt that exposure to lead pigment from paint from Patty's home caused her illnesses. Her parents wish to bring an action against the manufacturers of lead pigment in the lead paint in her home. You have done research and identified most, but not all, of the dozens of manufacturers who were producing lead pigment in 1970. (The production of lead pigment ceased in 1977 due to health concerns.) You have not been able to identify which manufacturer produced the pigments used in Patty's house. Each manufacturer used a different chemical process in producing their pigments. It is undisputed that each manufacturer was negligent in 1970 in continuing to produce pigment when the excessive dangers of such production were clear. Finally, it is undisputed that only one type of lead pigment was used in Patty's house.

If you were to sue each manufacturer in one action, could you rely upon the multiple sufficient cause concept from *Boomer* to help establish the cause-in-fact requirement with respect to each defendant?

c. Alternative Liability

Summers v. Tice

199 P.2d 1 (Cal. 1948) (en banc)

CARTER, Justice.

Plaintiff's action was against both defendants for an injury to his right eye and face as the result of being struck by bird shot discharged from a shotgun. The case was tried by the court without a jury and the court found that on November 20, 1945, plaintiff and the two defendants were hunting quail on the open range. Each of the defendants was armed with a 12 gauge shotgun loaded with shells containing 7 1/2 size shot.... Defendant Tice flushed a quail which rose in flight to a ten foot elevation and flew between plaintiff and defendants. Both defendants shot at the quail, shooting in plaintiff's direction. At that time defendants were 75 yards from plaintiff. One shot struck plaintiff in his eye and another in his upper lip. Finally it was found by the court that as the direct result of the shooting by defendants the shots struck plaintiff as above mentioned and that defendants were negligent in so shooting and plaintiff was not contributorily negligent.

The problem presented in this case is whether the judgment against both defendants may stand. It is argued by defendants that they are not joint tort feasors, and thus jointly and severally liable, as they were not acting in concert, and that there is not sufficient evidence to show which defendant was guilty of the negligence which caused the injuries the shooting by Tice or that by Simonson..... Further..., the court failed to find on plaintiff's allegation in his complaint that he did not know which one was at fault did not find which defendant was guilty of the negligence which caused the injuries to plaintiff.

...

. . . [W]e believe it is clear that the court sufficiently found on the issue that defendants were jointly liable and that thus the negligence of both was the cause of the injury or to that legal effect. It found that both defendants were negligent and 'That as a direct and proximate result of the shots fired by defendants, and each of them, a birdshot pellet was caused to and did lodge in plaintiff's right eye and that another birdshot pellet was caused to and did lodge in plaintiff's upper lip.' . . . It thus determined that the negligence of both defendants was the legal cause of the injury or that both were responsible. Implicit in such finding is the assumption that the court was unable to ascertain whether the shots were from the gun of one defendant or the other or one shot from each of them. The one shot that entered plaintiff's eye was the major factor in assessing damages and that shot could not have come from the gun of both defendants. It was from one or the other only.

. . .

When we consider the relative position of the parties and the results that would flow if plaintiff was required to pin the injury on one of the defendants only, a requirement that the burden of proof on that subject be shifted to defendants becomes manifest. They are both wrongdoers both negligent toward plaintiff. They brought about a situation where the negligence of one of them injured the plaintiff, hence it should rest with them each to absolve himself if he can. The injured party has been placed by defendants in the unfair position of pointing to which defendant caused the harm. If one can escape the other may also and plaintiff is remediless. Ordinarily defendants are in a far better position to offer evidence to determine which one caused the injury. This reasoning has recently found favor in this Court. In a quite analogous situation this Court held that a patient injured while unconscious on an operating table in a hospital could hold all or any of the persons who had any connection with the operation even though he could not select the particular acts by the particular person which led to his disability. Ybarra v. Spangard, 25 Cal.2d 486, 154 P.2d 687, 162 A.L.R. 1258. There the Court was considering whether the patient could avail himself of res ipsa loquitur, rather than where the burden of proof lay, yet the effect of the decision is that plaintiff has made out a case when he has produced evidence which gives rise to an inference of negligence which was the proximate cause of the injury. It is up to defendants to explain the cause of the injury. It was there said: "If the doctrine is to continue to serve a useful purpose, we should not forget that 'the particular force and justice of the rule, regarded as a presumption throwing upon the party charged the duty of producing evidence, consists in the circumstance that the chief evidence of the true cause, whether culpable or innocent, is practically accessible to him but inaccessible to the injured person." Similarly in the instant case plaintiff is not able to establish which of defendants caused his injury.

. . .

Cases are cited for the proposition that where two or more tort feasors acting independently of each other cause an injury to plaintiff, they are not joint tort feasors and plaintiff must establish the portion of the damage caused by each, even though it is impossible to prove the portion of the injury caused by each. In view of the foregoing discussion it is apparent that defendants in cases like the present one may be treated as liable on the same basis as joint tort feasors, and hence the last cited cases are distinguishable inasmuch as they involve independent tort feasors.

In addition to that, however, it should be pointed out that the same reasons of policy and justice shift the burden to each of defendants to absolve himself if he can relieving the wronged person of the duty of apportioning the injury to a particular defendant, apply here where we are concerned with whether plaintiff is required to supply evidence for the apportionment of damages. If defendants are independent tort feasors and thus each liable for the damage caused by him alone, and, at least, where the matter of apportionment is incapable of proof, the innocent wronged party should not be deprived of his right to redress. The wrongdoers should be left to work out between themselves any apportionment. Some of the cited cases refer to the difficulty of apportioning the burden of damages between the independent tort feasors, and say that where factually a correct division cannot be made, the trier of fact may make it the best it can, which would be more or less a guess, stressing the factor that the wrongdoers are not a position to complain of uncertainty.

The judgment is affirmed.

Note

Apportionment of damages. At the bench trial in *Summers*, each defendant was found liable for $10,000. So the trial judge apparently decided to apportion the damages equally between the two defendants.

Problem 6.6. Refer back to Problem 6.5. If you were to sue each manufacturer in one action, could you rely upon the alternative liability concept from *Summers v. Tice* to help establish the cause-in-fact requirement with respect to each defendant?

d. Market Share

Martin v. Abbott Laboratories

689 P.2d 368 (Wash. 1984)

DORE, Justice.

This case concerns whether plaintiffs, allegedly injured by the drug diethylstilbestrol (DES), have a cause of action against numerous DES manufacturers when they cannot identify the specific manufacturer of the DES ingested. The trial court held that plaintiffs had stated a cause of action when it denied summary judgment as to two drug manufacturers, finding material issues of fact under a theory of alternate liability.

Trial Court Proceedings

Rita Rene Martin was born on October 4, 1962. Her mother, Shirley Ann Martin, obtained a prescription for and ingested DES from May 1962 until the date Rita Martin was born. On January 4, 1980, Rita was diagnosed [with cancer.] On February 21, 1980, as a result of the cancer, Rita underwent a radical hysterectomy, pelvic node dissection, and partial vaginectomy.

Like many other women who have pursued judicial remedies for injuries they allege were caused by DES, Shirley Martin cannot remember which drug company manufactured the DES she ingested. Moreover, because of the passage of time and because DES was marketed generically, neither Shirley's physician nor her pharmacist, William Ludwig, Jr., f/d/b/a/ Lakewood Pharmacy, Inc., can remember which company manufactured or marketed the drug Shirley ingested. The only thing Shirley Martin can substantiate is that she took the drug in 100 mg doses.

Shirley and Rita Martin sued numerous drug companies on the [theory of negligence] for personal injuries, pain, suffering, and destruction of the parent-child relationship. The Martins alleged that all of the pharmaceutical companies were liable for their injuries because of the companies' concerted or joint action to gain FDA approval and to market DES. The Martins allege this concerted action is established by (1) the manufacturers' collaboration in testing and marketing DES, (2) the marketing of DES on a mutually agreed-upon formula, and (3) the marketing of DES as a fungible item which led to the selling of DES without reference to the brand prescribed.

[The trial judge granted summary judgment to over 15 defendants on the general grounds that they did not market DES in the dosage or form ingested by Shirley Martin, they did not market the product in Washington, and related grounds. The only remaining defendants were Stanley Drug Products, Inc. and Kirkman Laboratories, Inc.]

As to the two remaining defendants, the trial judge held that, under the theory of "alternate liability", there were material issues of fact as to the liability of Stanley Drug Products, Inc., and Kirkman Laboratories, Inc.

Although the trial judge found that there were arguable questions of fact concerning liability for concerted action, the trial judge rejected this theory because it would result in joint and several liability for a number of defendants who could prove that they did not manufacture the DES that caused plaintiffs' harm, and because he believed the theory of "alternate liability" more fairly accommodated the facts of this case.

The Martins endorse the trial court's ruling, but continue to argue that they have raised issues of fact which would justify even broader liability under concerted action, enterprise, or market-share theories of liability. They urge this court to reverse the trial court's order as to those respondents dismissed on summary judgment. The respondents argue that the trial court correctly dismissed the majority of the pharmaceutical companies joined in this action. Respondents contend, among other things, that adoption of any theory that would impose industrywide liability would hamper the development of new drugs, would impose enormous potential costs on pharmaceutical companies, and would not serve as an incentive to use greater care in producing drugs. Finally, respondents urge the Martins to seek broader liability through legislative enactment.

Stanley Drug Products, Inc. and Kirkman Laboratories, Inc. contend that the trial judge erred in not granting summary judgment in their favor. Their basic contentions are that neither was identified as the actual defendant that manufactured or distributed the DES ingested by Shirley Martin, and the probability that either was such party is very small, in that they are but two manufacturers from a large potential number of defendants.

Development and Marketing of DES

Crucial to an understanding of this litigation and resolution of the issues is the history of the development and marketing of DES. Much of the history is developed in the record here, and detailed in numerous reported cases and law journals.

...

In late 1940, the [Food & Drug Administration] (FDA) indicated that it was considering requesting the drug companies to pool their clinical data on DES. On December 20, 1940, the FDA convened a meeting with the drug companies, at which it formally requested that the companies submit their clinical data jointly in a "master file". The FDA believed that the individual [New Drug Applications (NDA)] did not contain sufficient clinical data to properly evaluate the safety and efficacy of DES. Pooling of the data, in the FDA's view, would eliminate this problem as well as expedite its evaluation of DES.

...

The FDA began approving the supplemental NDAs in July 1947. Soon thereafter, DES was marketed as a miscarriage preventative. Some companies marketed the drug under a trade name; others marketed it generically. Several companies supplied DES to competitors. Because the DES compounds produced by the drug companies were chemically identical, pharmacists often filled prescriptions for DES with whatever company's drug was in stock, a practice that the firms were aware of. None of the companies warned physicians about the possibility of carcinogenic or other risks to the offspring of women who took DES.

The number of firms marketing DES has fluctuated considerably over the years. Estimates are that up to 200 or 300 companies manufactured and marketed DES between 1947 and 1971.

...

In 1971, Dr. Arthur Herbst and several other physicians published a study linking the outbreak in young women of clear cell adenocarcinoma, a form of cancer, with the ingestion of DES by their mothers during pregnancy. In November of that same year, the FDA required the drug companies to include a statement on all labels that "DES is contraindicated for use in the prevention of miscarriages." Today, the FDA continues to permit the use of DES in treatments unrelated to problems of pregnancy.

Identification of Culpable Defendant

. . . "An essential element of the plaintiff's cause of action for negligence, or for that matter for any other tort, is that there be some reasonable connection between the act or omission of the defendant and the damage which the plaintiff has suffered." W. Prosser, Torts § 41 (4th ed. 1971), at 236.

The majority of the courts in DES litigation have followed the traditional approach, finding no cause of action when the plaintiff cannot identify the particular manufacturer of the pills which caused her injury.

Notwithstanding this general rule, four theories have been proposed, and in some cases adopted, to give DES plaintiffs a cause of action. These theories are (1) alternate liability, (2) concerted action, (3) enterprise liability, and (4) market-share liability.

Alternate Liability

Alternate liability arose as a cure for plaintiff causation problems. The theory was introduced in *Summers v. Tice*, 33 Cal.2d 80, 199 P.2d 1 (1948) and incorporated in Restatement (Second) of Torts § 433B(3) (1965), at 441–42:

> Where the conduct of two or more actors is tortious, and it is proved that harm has been caused to the plaintiff by only one of them, but there is uncertainty as to which one has caused it, the burden is upon each such actor to prove that he has not caused the harm.

. . .

Several DES cases have discussed alternate liability as a means of providing DES plaintiffs with a cause of action.

. . .

The Wisconsin Supreme Court in *Collins v. Eli Lilly Co.*, 116 Wis.2d 166, 342 N.W.2d 37 (1984) rejected the traditional alternate liability theory because it contemplated that all possible defendants be before the court. The court did, however, adopt a "risk contribution" theory which may be considered a modification of alternate liability. The court held that the plaintiff need commence suit against only one defendant and allege the following elements:

> [1] that the plaintiff's mother took DES; [2] that DES caused the plaintiff's subsequent injuries; [3] that the defendant produced or marketed the type of DES taken by the plaintiff's mother; [4] and that the defendant's conduct in producing or marketing the DES constituted a breach of a legally recognized duty to the plaintiff. In the situation where the plaintiff cannot allege and prove what type of DES the mother took, as to the third element the plaintiff need only allege and prove that the defendant drug company

> produced or marketed the drug DES for use in preventing miscarriages during pregnancy.

Collins, 342 N.W.2d at 50. The court fashioned this remedy on the grounds that as between an innocent plaintiff and the defendants, who may have provided the product and all who contributed to the risk of injury to the public, the interests of justice and fundamental fairness demand that the latter should bear the cost of injury. The court further held that the defendants may implead third party defendants, and defendants have the burden of proving that they did not produce or market the subject DES, either during the time period the plaintiff was exposed to DES or in the relevant geographic market area. The plaintiff is entitled to recover all damages from the one defendant, or in the situation where there are multiple defendants, plaintiff should recover from each their proportionate share of liability under principles of comparative negligence.

In sum, the short history of DES litigation shows that the alternate liability theory is not accepted in those jurisdictions which follow the traditional rules of products liability. Those courts demand that a defendant, that is, the manufacturer or distributor of the drug, be identified as the causal agent for plaintiff's injury. Although some courts have found this theory applicable, they have done so under only two conditions: (1) where the plaintiff can show all of the defendants were before the court, or (2) where not all of the defendants were joined but strong policy reasons and the "single indivisible injury" or "risk contribution" rules could be applied.

We find persuasive the commentators and courts that have concluded that strict application of alternate liability theory does not present a viable theory for DES cases. The alternate liability theory formulation contemplates that all tortious defendants will be joined in the suit. Thus, the court can be sure that at least one of the defendants was directly responsible for the plaintiff's harm. The alternate liability formula does not, in its pure form, provide a fair way to apportion damages among the defendants. Under the alternate liability theory, defendants that produced or marketed small amounts of DES and those that produced or marketed large amounts would be equally liable.

Concerted Action

The theory of concerted action derives from vicarious liability. The plaintiff must show a tacit agreement among defendants to perform a tortious act. . . .

The concerted action typically alleged by DES plaintiffs (and the Martins in this case) consists of the pharmaceutical manufacturers using one another's marketing techniques, manufacturing DES according to an agreed-upon formula, promoting its marketability as a generic drug, relying upon one another's testing, and encouraging one another not to perform adequate tests and not to provide adequate warnings.

[Most courts] have rejected, as a matter of law, DES plaintiffs' claims that the pharmaceutical manufacturers engaged in concerted action. These courts have generally rejected this theory because the plaintiff cannot show an agreement among the manufacturers to market the drug in 1947 for accidents of pregnancy. . . .

We agree with those jurisdictions which have rejected the concerted action theory as a basis of liability in DES cases. . . .

Enterprise Liability

. . . Enterprise liability holds the defendants liable for sharing in industrywide misconduct. *See e.g.*, Hall v. E.I. Du Pont De Nemours & Co., 345 F.Supp. 353 (E.D.N.Y.1972). In *Hall*, the plaintiffs, children who were injured by blasting caps, could not identify the manufacturers of the caps that injured them. The court held plaintiffs' claims contained issues of fact regarding whether the blasting cap manufacturers were jointly aware of the risks at issue and had a joint capacity to reduce those risks. At present, the theory of enterprise liability has not been accepted by any court involved in DES litigation. The courts have generally rejected this theory on the grounds that enterprise liability as described in *Hall*, is predicated upon industrywide cooperation of a much greater degree than occurred among DES manufacturers.

. . .

The underlying rationale in all of the decisions rejecting enterprise liability is that the law of torts does not include a theory of liability which would allow an entire industry to be held strictly liable for an injury caused by a defective product. Enterprise liability as described in *Hall* is predicated upon industrywide cooperation of a much greater degree than that alleged by the plaintiff. We agree.

Market-Share Liability

In *Sindell v. Abbott Laboratories*, 26 Cal.3d 588, 607 P.2d 924, 163 Cal.Rptr. 132, cert. denied, 449 U.S. 912, 101 S.Ct. 285, 66 L.Ed.2d 140 (1980), the Supreme Court of California modified the traditional alternate liability theory and adapted it to DES cases. Under the *Sindell* court's market-share theory, a plaintiff need only join a sufficient number of manufacturers to represent a "substantial share" of the market. Once the plaintiff has met this threshold requirement, the burden of proof shifts to each defendant to exculpate itself by showing that it could not have supplied the offending drug. Those defendants that are unable to prove their innocence are liable for the plaintiff's damages. The court in *Sindell*, however, recognized that holding each of the defendants jointly and severally liable for all of plaintiff's harm would have been unfair. In view of the large number of manufacturers, the court reasoned that there "may be a substantial likelihood" that none of them supplied the drug which caused plaintiff's harm. To overcome this difficulty, the court held that each defendant would be liable only for "the proportion of the judgment represented by its share of that market . . ." Underlying the court's reasoning is the notion that, although market share liability might not effect a correct matching of plaintiffs and defendants in each case, each defendant ultimately will be held liable only for the amount of harm that it statistically is likely to have caused. The *Sindell* court reasoned that the use of DES to prevent miscarriage causes harm in a certain percentage of cases. Therefore, according to the court, a defendant who produced 10 percent of the DES that was placed on the market to prevent miscarriage statistically would be likely to have caused 10 percent of the harm. Thus, if the court apportioned damages according to each defendant's market share, then theoretically each defendant would be held liable only for approximately as much harm as it caused.

. . .

Although the *Sindell* market-share theory is conceptually attractive, we find it also an inappropriate theory due to its inherent distortion of liability. Although the court in *Sindell* was unclear on this point, the decision arguably requires that defendants pay 100 percent of the plaintiff's damages even though these defendants may represent less than 100 percent of the market. The inherent distortion of defendants' actual liability under the market-share liability theory is best illustrated by a hypothetical. Assume that plaintiff's damages are $100,000, and she joins enough DES manufacturers to represent 60 percent of the relevant market. Defendant X occupies 20 percent of the relevant market and one-third of the market that all joined defendants represent. If defendant X is liable only for its share of the relevant market, it would be liable for 20 percent of the damages, or $20,000. If defendants are required to pay 100 percent of the judgment, however, then defendant X must pay one-third of the judgment, or $33,333, which is equivalent to one-third of the market that all the joined defendants represent. In other words, defendant X would have to pay 67 percent ($13,333) more than its share of the relevant market. It is evident that the definition of "substantial market share" directly affects the degree to which the defendant's liability is distorted. The lower the percentage of the market that is required to be joined, the higher will be the resulting distortion.

We reject the *Sindell* market-share theory of liability. Not only does the *Sindell* court fail to define "substantial" share of the relevant market, the theory distorts market liability by providing that the "substantial" market share bears joint responsibility for 100 percent of plaintiff's injuries.

Market-Share Alternate Liability

Having rejected the application of the four theories which to this date have been proposed in the DES context, this court is faced with a choice of either fashioning a method of recovery for the DES case which will deviate from traditional notions of tort law, or permitting possibly tortious defendants to escape liability to an innocent, injured plaintiff.

As noted earlier, the crux of the problem facing this DES plaintiff is that she cannot identify the drug company that she alleges caused her injury. Numerous commentators and courts have identified several reasons for this plight. First, DES was, for the most part, produced in a "generic" form which did not contain any clearly identifiable shape, color, or markings. DES was a fungible drug produced with a chemically identical formula, and often pharmacists would fill DES prescriptions from whatever stock they had on hand, whether or not a particular brand was specified in the prescription. Second, it has been estimated that possibly as many as 300 drug companies produced or marketed DES during the 24 years DES was on the market, with companies entering and leaving the market throughout this period. Third, it appears that many drug companies may not have kept, or may not be able to locate, pertinent records as to when, where, and what type of DES they produced or marketed. These problems result from the passage of many years between the plaintiff's in utero exposure and the manifestation of cancer. During the intervening years, memories may have faded, medical and pharmaceutical records may have been lost or destroyed, and witnesses may have died.

We are presented with a conflict between the familiar principle that a tortfeasor may be held liable only for damage that it has caused, and the sense of justice which urges that the victims of this tragedy should not be denied compensation because of the impossibility of identifying the individual manufacturer of these generic tablets if their manufacture and distribution were otherwise culpable.

We believe that a modification of the alternate liability theory somewhat along the lines of the *Sindell* market-share approach is warranted.

Because certain manufacturers and distributors produced or marketed an allegedly defective drug for accidents of pregnancy, those manufacturers and distributors all contributed to the risk of injury, even though they may not have contributed to the actual injury of a given plaintiff. Although the defendants in this case have not acted in concert under the concert of action theory, all participated in either gaining approval of DES for use in pregnancy or in producing or marketing DES in subsequent years. Each defendant contributed to the risk of injury to the public and, consequently, the risk of injury to individual plaintiffs. Thus, each defendant shares in some measure, a degree of culpability in producing or marketing DES. Moreover, as between the injured plaintiff and the possibly responsible drug company, the drug company is in a better position to absorb the cost of the injury. The drug company can either insure itself against liability, absorb the damage award, or pass the cost along to the consuming public as a cost of doing business. We conclude that it is better to have drug companies or consumers share the cost of the injury than to place the burden solely on the innocent plaintiff.

We hold that plaintiff need commence suit against only one defendant and allege the following elements: that the plaintiff's mother took DES; that DES caused the plaintiff's subsequent injuries; that the defendant produced or marketed the type of DES taken by the plaintiff's mother; and that the defendant's conduct in producing or marketing the DES constituted a breach of a legally recognized duty to the plaintiff. At the trial, the plaintiff will have to prove each of these elements to the satisfaction of the trier of fact. We emphasize, however, that the plaintiff need not prove that a defendant produced or marketed the precise DES taken by the plaintiff's mother. Rather, the plaintiff need only establish by a preponderance of the evidence that a defendant produced or marketed the type (*e.g.*, dosage, color, shape, markings, size, or other identifiable characteristics) of DES taken by the plaintiff's mother; the plaintiff need not allege or prove any facts related to the time or geographic distribution of the subject DES. While the type of DES ingested by the mother should be within the domain of her knowledge, facts relating to time and distribution should be particularly within the domain of knowledge of the DES manufacturers and distributors.

We reject the *Sindell* requirement of joinder of a "substantial share" of the market because it does not alter the probability under our market-share alternate liability theory that a particular defendant caused the injury. As will be demonstrated, a particular defendant's potential liability is proportional to the probability that it caused plaintiff's injury.

Individual defendants are entitled to exculpate themselves from liability by establishing, by a preponderance of the evidence, that they did not produce or market the particular type DES taken by the plaintiff's mother; that they did not market the DES in the geographic market area of plaintiff mother's obtaining the drug; or that it did not distribute DES in the time period of plaintiff mother's ingestion of the drug.

The defendants that are unable to exculpate themselves from potential liability are designated members of the plaintiffs' DES market; defined by the specificity of the evidence as to geographic market area, time of ingestion, and type of DES. These defendants are initially presumed to have equal shares of the market and are liable for only the percentage of plaintiff's judgment that represents their presumptive share of the market. These defendants are entitled to rebut this presumption and thereby reduce their potential liability by establishing their respective market share of DES in the plaintiff's particular geographic market. Upon proof of a market share by a preponderance of the evidence, that particular defendant is only liable for its share of the market as it relates to the total judgment. To the extent that other defendants fail to establish their actual market share, their presumed market share is adjusted so that 100 percent of the market is accounted for.

The defendants may implead third party defendants in order to reduce their presumptive share of the market or in order to establish an actual reduced market share.

This ability of a defendant to reduce its liability reduces the disproportion between potential liability that a particular defendant caused the injury by imposing liability according to respective market shares. In the case where each party carries its burden of proof, no defendant will be held liable for more harm than it statistically could have caused in the respective market.

We recognize that the elimination of individual causal responsibility as an element of plaintiff's case is liability enhancing. However, it is also liability limiting insofar as it permits the defendants to apportion liability according to respective market share and further provides that the plaintiff may not be able to recover her entire damages. Under this market share alternate liability theory, the dilution of causal blame that is attributable to a given defendant may be counterbalanced by the corresponding dilution of liability.

. . .

Conclusion

Having found that the Martins stated a cause of action as heretofore enunciated, we affirm the denial of summary judgment to Stanley Drug Products, Inc., and Kirkman Laboratories, Inc. We reverse the grant of summary judgment in favor of Raway Pharmaceutical Company and Stanlabs Pharmaceutical Company. All remaining grants of summary judgment are affirmed.

Note

The limits of market-share liability. To the extent courts have been willing to recognize market-share liability, they have done so primarily in cases like *Martin,* where the plaintiff has been injured by a fungible product. *See* Note, *The Price Tag on Designer Babies: Market Share Liability*, 59 B.C. L. Rev. 319, 336 (2018); Paul D. Rheingold, *Mass Torts—Maturation of Law and Practice*, 37 Pace L. Rev. 617, 625 (2017).

Problem 6.7. Refer back to Problem 6.5. If you were to sue each manufacturer in one action, could you rely upon one of the market-share approaches described in *Martin* to help establish the cause-in-fact requirement with respect to each defendant?

e. Loss of Opportunity (Loss of Chance)

Lord v. Lovett

770 A.2d 1103 (N.H. 2001)

NADEAU, J.

The plaintiff, Belinda Joyce Lord, appeals the Superior Court's (Perkins, J.) dismissal of her "loss of opportunity" action against the defendants, James Lovett, M.D., and Samuel Aldridge, M.D. We reverse and remand.

The plaintiff suffered a broken neck in an automobile accident on July 22, 1996, and was treated at the Lakes Region General Hospital by the defendants. She contends that because the defendants negligently misdiagnosed her spinal cord injury, they failed both to immobilize her properly and to administer steroid therapy, causing her to lose the opportunity for a substantially better recovery. She alleges that she continues to suffer significant residual paralysis, weakness and sensitivity.

Upon learning that the defendants intended to move to dismiss at the close of the plaintiff's case, the trial court permitted the plaintiff to make a pre-trial offer of proof. She proffered that her expert would testify that the defendants' negligence deprived her of the opportunity for a substantially better recovery. She conceded, however, that her expert could not quantify the degree to which she was deprived of a better recovery by their negligence.

Following the plaintiff's offer of proof, the defendants moved to dismiss on two grounds: (1) New Hampshire law does not recognize the loss of opportunity theory of recovery; and (2) the plaintiff failed to set forth sufficient evidence of causation. The trial court dismissed the plaintiff's action on the basis that her case is "clearly predicated on loss of . . . opportunity" and that "there's no such theory permitted in this State." This appeal followed.

. . .

The loss of opportunity doctrine, in its many forms, is a medical malpractice form of recovery which allows a plaintiff, whose preexisting injury or illness is aggravated by the alleged negligence of a physician or health care worker, to recover for her lost opportunity to obtain a better degree of recovery. *See Delaney v. Cade*, 255 Kan. 199, 873 P.2d 175, 178 (1994); King, *"Reduction of Likelihood" Reformulation and Other Retrofitting of the Loss-of-a-Chance Doctrine*, 28 U. Mem. L.Rev. 491, 492–93 (1998).

Generally, courts have taken three approaches to loss of opportunity claims.

The first approach, the traditional tort approach, is followed by a minority of courts. According to this approach, a plaintiff must prove that as a result of the defendant's negligence, the plaintiff was deprived of at least a fifty-one percent chance of a more favorable outcome than she actually received. Once the plaintiff meets this burden, she may recover damages for the entire preexisting illness or condition. *See King, "Reduction of Likelihood" Reformulation, supra.*

Under this approach, a patient whose injury is negligently misdiagnosed, but who would have had only a fifty percent chance of full recovery from her condition with proper diagnosis, could not recover damages because she would be unable to prove that, absent the physician's negligence, her chance of a better recovery was at least fifty-one percent. If, however, the patient could establish the necessary causal link by establishing that absent the negligence she would have had at least a fifty-one percent chance of a better outcome, not only would the patient be entitled to recover, but she would be awarded damages for her entire injury. This approach has been criticized as yielding an "all or nothing" result. *See* King, *"Reduction of Likelihood" Reformulation, supra*; *Delaney*, 873 P.2d at 183.

The second approach, a variation of the traditional approach, relaxes the standard of proof of causation. The causation requirement is relaxed by permitting plaintiffs to submit their cases to the jury upon demonstrating that a defendant's negligence more likely than not "increased the harm" to the plaintiff or "destroyed a substantial possibility" of achieving a more favorable outcome. *See* King, *"Reduction of Likelihood" Reformulation, supra* at 507.

Under this approach, the patient would not be precluded from recovering simply because her chance of a better recovery was less than fifty-one percent, so long as she could prove that the defendant's negligence increased her harm to some degree. The precise degree required varies by jurisdiction. Some courts require that the defendant's negligence increase the plaintiff's harm by any degree, while other courts require that the increase be substantial. As in the traditional approach, once the plaintiff meets her burden, she recovers damages for the entire underlying preexisting condition or illness rather than simply the loss of opportunity. This approach "represents the worst of both worlds [because it] continues the arbitrariness of the all-or-nothing rule, but by relaxing the proof requirements, it increases the likelihood that a plaintiff will be able to convince a jury to award full damages." King, *"Reduction of Likelihood" Reformulation, supra* at 508.

Under the third approach, the lost opportunity for a better outcome is, itself, the injury for which the negligently injured person may recover. As with the second approach, a plaintiff may prevail even if her chances of a better recovery are less than fifty-one percent.

In other words, if the plaintiff can establish the causal link between the defendant's negligence and the lost opportunity, the plaintiff may recover that portion of damages actually attributable to the defendant's negligence.

Under this approach, "[b]y defining the injury as the loss of chance . . . , the traditional rule of preponderance is fully satisfied." *Perez v. Las Vegas Medical Center,* 107 Nev. 1, 805 P.2d 589, 592 (1991).

We agree with the majority of courts rejecting the traditional "all-or-nothing" approach to loss of opportunity cases, and find the third approach most sound. The third approach permits plaintiffs to recover for the loss of an opportunity for a better outcome, an interest that we agree should be compensable, while providing for the proper valuation of such an interest.

> [T]he loss of a chance of achieving a favorable outcome or of avoiding an adverse consequence should be compensable and should be valued appropriately, rather than treated as an all-or-nothing proposition. Preexisting conditions must, of course, be taken into account in valuing the interest destroyed. When those preexisting conditions have not absolutely preordained an adverse outcome, however, the chance of avoiding it should be appropriately compensated even if that chance is not better than even.

King, Causation, *Valuation, and Chance in Personal Injury Torts Involving Preexisting Conditions and Future Consequences*, 90 Yale L.J. 1353, 1354 (1981).

Accordingly, we hold that a plaintiff may recover for a loss of opportunity injury in medical malpractice cases when the defendant's alleged negligence aggravates the plaintiff's preexisting injury such that it deprives the plaintiff of a substantially better outcome.

. . .

[D]efendant Lovett argues that we should not recognize the plaintiff's loss of opportunity injury because it is intangible and, thus, is not amenable to damages calculation. We disagree.

First, we fail to see the logic in denying an injured plaintiff recovery against a physician for the lost opportunity of a better outcome on the basis that the alleged injury is too difficult to calculate, when the physician's own conduct has caused the difficulty. Second, "[w]e have long held that difficulty in calculating damages is not a sufficient reason to deny recovery to an injured party." *Smith v. Cote*, 128 N.H. 231, 242, 513 A.2d 341(1986). Third, loss of opportunity is not inherently unquantifiable. A loss of opportunity plaintiff must provide the jury with a basis upon which to distinguish that portion of her injury caused by the defendant's negligence from the portion resulting from the underlying injury. *See Valliere v. Filfalt*, 110 N.H. 331, 332–33, 266 A.2d 843 (1970); King, *Causation, Valuation, and Chance, supra* at 1360. This can be done through expert testimony just as it is in aggravation of preexisting injury cases.

We decline to address the defendants' arguments disputing the sufficiency of the plaintiff's evidence because the trial court has not yet considered the issue. The trial court limited its ruling to the legal question of whether New Hampshire recognizes the loss of opportunity doctrine. We likewise limit our holding to that question.

Reversed and remanded.

Notes

Loss of chance in other jurisdictions. The majority of states to have considered the loss of chance theory in the medical malpractice context have adopted it. *See* Lauren Guest et al., *The "Loss of Chance" Rule as a Special Category of Damages in Medical Malpractice: A State-by-State Analysis*, 21 J. LEGAL ECON. 53, 58–60 (2015). Some require that a plaintiff establish that she lost a "substantial chance" of a better medical outcome due to the defendant's medical negligence. *See* Smith v. Providence Health & Services, 393 P.3d 1106 (Or. 2017) (declining to adopt a specific rule, but holding that plaintiff had alleged the loss of a substantial chance of a better outcome by alleging a 33 percent chance of total or close to total recovery from his stroke). In *Cohan v. Medical Imaging Consultants, P.C.*, 900 N.W.2d 732 (Neb. 2017), the Nebraska Supreme Court refused to recognize a loss of chance theory of recovery where a physician's negligence in diagnosing the plaintiff's breast cancer reduced the plaintiff's chances of non-recurrence of cancer. The court reasoned that recognizing the theory would require a jury to engage in mere speculation as to possible harm in the future that may never occur.

Loss of chance outside of the medical malpractice context. Recognition of the loss of chance theory has largely been limited to the medical malpractice context. For example, while the Oregon Supreme Court has adopted the rule in medical malpractice cases, it has refused to do so in legal malpractice actions. *See* Drollinger v. Mallon, 260 P.3d 482 (Or. 2011) ("Whatever the merits in the medical malpractice context, where the proof burden facing some plaintiffs otherwise would be insurmountable and where statistical evidence that can fill the void is readily available, the argument for its application in the legal malpractice context is less compelling . . .").

Review Question

Tommy was an employee of MCL Corp., a hazardous waste disposal plant. Tommy was injured when two safety devices failed. The first device, called a baghouse, is located adjacent to the plant, and is designed to collect and store the volatile aluminum dust that comes from inside the plant via a series of overhead ducts. The second, the back blast damper, is designed to keep the contents of the baghouse from returning to the plant via the ductwork. Tommy was injured when an excess of aluminum dust accumulated in the baghouse, which produced a fireball that traveled through the ductwork of the plant into the plant itself, where it injured Tommy. The baghouse was negligently maintained by DustCo. The back blast damper, which failed to prevent the contents of the baghouse from returning to the plant as it was designed to do, was negligently maintained by Davis Corp. Tommy has sued DustCo. and Davis Corp. on negligence theories.

(a) Was Davis Corp.'s negligence a cause in fact of Tommy's injuries?

(b) Was DustCo.'s negligence a cause in fact of Tommy's injuries?

(c) Assume for purposes of this question that Tommy could establish each element of a prima facie case against Davis Corp. and DustCo. Could Tommy recover the full amount of his damages from Davis Corp. in a joint and several liability jurisdiction?

Chapter 7

Proximate Cause

A. The Scope of Risk Test
- Generally defined
- Role of foreseeability
- Kind of harm foreseeably risked
  - Foreseeable kind of harm versus unforeseeable manner of occurrence
  - Extent of harm
- Class of person put at foreseeable risk

B. Superseding Cause
- Generally defined
- Intervening force/cause versus superseding cause
- Relation to scope of risk/proximate cause
- Intentional/criminal acts versus negligent acts
- Other types of intervening or superseding causes
- Extraordinary events or attenuated causes

C. Special Policy-Based Proximate Cause Rules
- The role of policy in proximate cause determinations
- Suicide
- The eggshell plaintiff rule
- Rescuers, emergency responders, and medical providers
- Fires

Chapter Problem. Austin drove his car in a negligent manner while intoxicated. But for Austin's negligence, Phil, Betty, Cliff, Elizabeth, and Francisco would not have been injured. Each has sued Austin for negligence. There is no dispute that Austin was negligent and that his negligence was a cause in fact of each plaintiff's injuries.

Establishing that a defendant's negligence was an actual cause or cause in fact of the plaintiff's injuries is only half of the causation battle. A plaintiff must also establish that the negligence was a proximate (or legal) cause of the injuries. Despite the inclusion of the word "cause" in the term, the proximate cause concept is only partly about causation. Courts and commentators have struggled to define this concept.

Some courts have suggested that term "defies precise definition." Cruz-Mendez v. ISU/Insurance Services of San Francisco, 722 A.2d 515, 525 (N.J. 1999). There is certainly an element of truth to this. Questions of basic fairness and policy sometimes play a large role in proximate cause determinations. Indeed, it is often noted that saying that the defendant's negligence was a "proximate cause" of the plaintiff's injuries is simply a way of saying that it is fair to hold the defendant liable under the circumstances. *See, e.g.*, Ashley County, Arkansas, v. Pfizer, Inc., 552 F.3d 659, 671 (8th Cir. 2009) ("Proximate cause is bottomed on public policy as a limitation on how far society is willing to extend liability for a defendant's actions."); Wankel v. A & B Contractors, Inc., 732 A.2d 333, 349 (Md. Ct. Spec. App. 1999) (stating that proximate cause "asks whether the defendant, in light of 'considerations of fairness and social policy,' should be held liable for the injury, even when cause in fact has been established").

Courts may also frame the rules regarding proximate cause in different ways. That said, the law has developed in such a way as to allow for at least some predictability when it comes to the proximate cause element. As the material below illustrates, there are legal rules that, while perhaps not perfectly explaining the result in every case, provide helpful guidance in the run of cases.

A. The Scope of the Risk Test

1. The Test in General

Thompson v. Kaczinski

774 N.W.2d 829 (Iowa 2009)

HECHT, Justice

I. Factual and Procedural Background.

James Kaczinski and Michelle Lockwood resided in rural Madison County, near Earlham, on property abutting a gravel road. During the late summer of 2006, they disassembled a trampoline and placed its component parts on their yard approximately thirty-eight feet from the road. Intending to dispose of them at a later time, Kaczinski and Lockwood did not secure the parts in place. A few weeks later, on the night of September 16 and morning of September 17, 2006, a severe thunderstorm moved through the Earlham area. Wind gusts from the storm displaced the top of the trampoline from the yard to the surface of the road.

Later that morning, while driving from one church to another where he served as a pastor, Charles Thompson approached the defendants' property. When he swerved to avoid the obstruction on the road, Thompson lost control of his vehicle. His car entered the ditch and rolled several times. Kaczinski and Lockwood were awakened by Thompson's screams at about 9:40 a.m., shortly after the accident. When they went outside to investigate, they discovered the top of their trampoline lying on the roadway. Lockwood dragged the object back into the yard while Kaczinski assisted Thompson.

Thompson and his wife filed suit, alleging Kaczinski and Lockwood breached statutory and common law duties by negligently allowing the trampoline to obstruct the roadway. Kaczinski and Lockwood moved for summary judgment, contending they owed no duty under the circumstances because the risk of the trampoline's displacement from their yard to the surface of the road was not foreseeable. The district court granted the motion, concluding Kaczinski and Lockwood breached no duty and the damages claimed by the plaintiffs were not proximately caused by the defendants' negligence. The Thompsons appealed. We transferred the case to the court of appeals, which affirmed the district court's ruling. We granted the Thompsons' application for further review.

. . .

III. Discussion.

[The court concluded that the lower court erred in granting summary judgment to the defendants on the issue of breach of duty.]

C. Causation. [T]he district court concluded the plaintiffs' claims must fail for the further reason that they did not establish a causal connection between their claimed injuries and damages and the acts and omissions of Kaczinski and Lockwood. Again relying on its determination that the risk of the trampoline's displacement from the yard to the roadway was not foreseeable, the court resolved the causation issue against the Thompsons as a matter of law.

We have held causation has two components: cause in fact and legal cause. The decisions of this court have established it is the plaintiff's burden to prove both cause in fact and legal (proximate) cause. The latter component requires a policy determination of whether "the policy of the law must require the defendant to be legally responsible for the injury." Gerst v. Marshall, 549 N.W.2d 810, 815 (Iowa 1996). Causation is a question for the jury, "'*save in very exceptional cases* where the facts are so clear and undisputed, and the relation of cause and effect so apparent to every candid mind, that but one conclusion may be fairly drawn therefrom.'" Lindquist v. Des Moines Union Ry., 239 Iowa 356, 362, 30 N.W.2d 120, 123 (1947) (quoting Fitter v. Iowa Tel. Co., 143 Iowa 689, 693–94, 121 N.W. 48, 50 (1909)).

We have previously applied the test articulated in the Restatement (Second) of Torts when determining if a defendant's conduct is a legal or proximate cause of the plaintiff's damages. This test holds "[t]he actor's negligent conduct is a legal cause of harm to another if (a) his conduct is a substantial factor in bringing about the harm, and (b) there is no rule of law relieving the actor from liability." Restatement (Second) of Torts § 431, at 428 (1965); *accord* Kelly v. Sinclair Oil Corp., 476 N.W.2d 341, 349 (Iowa 1991). . . .

The formulation of legal or proximate cause outlined above has been the source of significant uncertainty and confusion. This court's adherence to the formulation has been less than consistent. Even had it been applied consistently, the concept of legal or proximate cause itself has been criticized for confusing factual determinations (substantial factor in bringing about harm) with policy judgments (no rule of law precluding liability). Although we have previously noted our uneven approach to proximate cause questions and acknowledged the criticism of the doctrine, we have not yet had the opportunity to clarify this area of law. We do now.

"Tort law does not impose liability on an actor for all harm factually caused by the actor's tortious conduct." Restatement (Third) ch. 6 Special Note on Proximate Cause, at 574. This concept has traditionally been designated "proximate cause." While this term is used extensively and appropriately by courts, practitioners, and scholars, it causes considerable confusion for juries because it does not clearly express the idea it is meant to represent. *See id.* § 29 cmt. b, at 576–77. The confusion arises when jurors understand "proximate cause" as implying "there is but one cause—the cause nearest in time or geography to the plaintiff's harm—and that factual causation bears on the issue of scope of liability." *Id.* § 29 cmt. b, at 577. Thus, in an attempt to eliminate unnecessary confusion caused by the traditional vernacular, the drafters of the third Restatement refer to the concept of proximate cause as "scope of liability."

The drafters of the Restatement (Third) explain that the "legal cause" test articulated in the second Restatement included both the "substantial factor" prong and the "rule of law" prong because it was intended to address both factual and proximate cause. *Id.* ch. 6 Special Note on Proximate Cause, at 574. Although the "substantial factor" requirement has frequently been understood to apply to proximate cause determinations, *see Gerst*, 549 N.W.2d at 815–16, the drafters contend it was never intended to do so. Restatement (Third) § 29 cmt. a, at 576.[3] Accordingly, to eliminate the resulting confusion of factual and policy determinations resulting from the Restatement (Second) formulation of legal cause, the drafters have opted to address factual cause and scope of liability (proximate cause) separately. Restatement (Third) ch. 6 Special Note on Proximate Cause, at 575. The assessment of scope of liability under the Restatement (Third) no longer includes a determination of whether the actor's conduct was a substantial factor in causing the harm at issue, a question properly addressed under the factual cause rubric.

Most importantly, the drafters of the Restatement (Third) have clarified the essential role of policy considerations in the determination of the scope of liability. "An actor's liability is limited to those physical harms that result from the risks that made the actor's conduct tortious." *Id.* § 29, at 575. This principle, referred to as the "risk standard," is intended to prevent the unjustified imposition of liability by "confining liability's scope to the reasons for holding the actor liable in the first place." *Id.* § 29 cmt. d, at 579–80. As an example of the standard's application, the drafters provide an illustration of a hunter returning from the field and handing his loaded shotgun to a child as he enters the house. *Id.* cmt. d, illus. 3, at 581. The child drops the gun (an object assumed for the purposes of the illustration to be neither too heavy nor unwieldy for a child of that age and size to handle) which lands on her foot and breaks her toe. *Id.* Applying the risk standard described above, the hunter would not be liable for the broken toe because the risk that made his action negligent was the risk that the child would shoot someone, not that she would drop the gun and sustain an injury to her foot. *Id.*

The scope-of-liability issue is fact-intensive as it requires consideration of the risks that made the actor's conduct tortious and a determination of whether the harm at issue is a result of any of those risks. When, as in this case, the court considers in advance of trial whether

> the plaintiff's harm is beyond the scope of liability as a matter of law, courts must initially consider all of the range of harms risked by the defendant's conduct that the jury could find as the basis for determining [the defendant's] conduct tortious. Then, the court can compare the plaintiff's harm with the range of harms risked by the defendant to determine whether a reasonable jury might find the former among the latter.

Id. at 580.

. . .

The drafters of the Restatement (Third) explain that foreseeability is still relevant in scope-of-liability determinations. "In a negligence action, prior incidents or other facts evidencing risks may make certain risks foreseeable that otherwise were not, thereby changing the scope-of-liability analysis." Restatement (Third) § 29 cmt. d, at 584–85. In fact, they acknowledge the similarity between the risk standard they articulate and the foreseeability tests applied by most jurisdictions in making causation determinations in negligence cases.

> Properly understood, both the risk standard and a foreseeability test exclude liability for harms that were sufficiently unforeseeable at the time of the actor's tortious conduct that they were not among the risks—potential harms—that made the actor negligent. . . . [W]hen scope of liability arises in a negligence case, the risks that make an actor negligent are limited to foreseeable ones, and the factfinder must determine whether the type of harm that occurred is among those reasonably foreseeable potential harms that made the actor's conduct negligent.

Id. § 29 cmt. j, at 594. Although the risk standard and the foreseeability test are comparable in negligence actions, the drafters favor the risk standard because it "provides greater clarity, facilitates clearer analysis in a given case, and better reveals the reason for its existence." . . .

We find the drafters' clarification of scope of liability sound and are persuaded by their explanation of the advantages of applying the risk standard as articulated in the Restatement (Third), and, accordingly, adopt it.

Our next task, then, is to consider whether the district court erred in concluding the harm suffered by the Thompsons was, a matter of law, outside the scope of the risk of Kaczinski and Lockwood's conduct. We conclude the question of whether a serious injury to a motorist was within the range of harms risked by disassembling the trampoline and leaving it untethered for a few weeks on the yard less than forty feet from the road is not so clear in this case as to justify the district court's resolution of the issue as a matter of law at the summary judgment stage. A reasonable fact finder could determine Kaczinski and Lockwood should have known high winds occasionally occur in Iowa in September and a strong gust of wind could displace the unsecured trampoline parts the short distance from the yard to the roadway and endanger motorists. Although they were in their home for several hours after the storm passed and approximately two-and-a-half hours after daybreak, Kaczinski and Lockwood did not discover their property on the nearby roadway, remove it, or warn approaching motorists of it. On this record, viewed in the light most favorable to the Thompsons, we conclude a reasonable fact finder could find the harm suffered by the Thompsons resulted from the risks that made the defendants' conduct negligent. Accordingly, the district court erred in deciding the scope-of-liability question as a matter of law in this case.

Notes

Scope of the risk. The *Restatement (Third) of Torts* refers to the test described in *Thompson* as a "scope of the risk" test. *See id.* § 29 cmt. a. Perhaps the clearest formulation comes from Professor Dan Dobbs: "[A] negligent defendant is liable for all the general kinds of harms he foreseeably risked by his negligent conduct and the class of persons he put at risk by that conduct." DAN B. DOBBS, THE LAW OF TORTS § 181 (2000).

The Wagon Mound. One of the leading international cases in the field is *Overseas Tankship (U.K.) Ltd. v. Mort's Dock & Engineering Co., Ltd.* (The Wagon Mound) [1961] A.C. 388. A ship, called the Wagon Mound, negligently spilled furnace oil into the bay in Sydney Harbour, Australia. Some of the oil spread to the plaintiff's nearby wharf and was ignited while the plaintiff was welding. According to experts, it was not foreseeable to the defendant that the oil could be set afire when spread on water. Prior decisions had focused less on how foreseeable the harm was and more on whether the harm was the direct consequence of the defendant's negligence. In fact, it was for this reason that the trial court found in favor of the plaintiffs. But on appeal, the Privy Council rejected the older approach and focused instead on foreseeability. "The liability of negligence . . . is no doubt based upon a general public sentiment of moral wrongdoing for which the offender must pay." Foreseeability of harm, in the Privy Council's view, was a better indicator of blameworthiness than mere directness between negligence and resulting injury. As the defendant did not foreseeably risk the kind of harm that occurred, the plaintiff's action was dismissed.

Foreseeability in general. As *Thompson* notes, even in jurisdictions that have not formally adopted the *Restatement* approach to proximate cause, foreseeability of harm is typically the touchstone. In theory at least, the scope of risk test provides an additional level of specificity to the foreseeability analysis.

Other approaches. While foreseeability is the primary focus in most jurisdictions, some courts express the concept of proximate cause primarily in terms of the strength of the causal link between the defendant's wrongful act and the injury. *See, e.g.*, Yearty v. Scott Holder Enterprises, Inc., 824 S.E.2d 817, 821 (Ga. 2019) ("Proximate cause is defined as that which, in the natural and continuous sequence, unbroken by other causes, produces an event, and without which the event would not have occurred.").

Problem 7.1. As Austin was driving while intoxicated, he swerved and hit Betty, the driver of another nearby vehicle. Austin was traveling about 30 m.p.h. at the time. Betty suffered physical harm as a result of the collision. Using the language of the scope-of-risk approach to proximate cause, be prepared to explain why Austin's negligence was a proximate cause of Betty's injuries.

2. Scope of the Risk: Kinds of Harms Foreseeably Risked

Hughes (A.P.) v. Lord Advocate

[1963] A.C. 837 (H.L.)

[The facts of the case, as described by Lord Guest, were as follows:] In November 1958, some Post Office employees had opened a manhole in Russell Road, Edinburgh, for the purpose of obtaining access to a telephone cable. The manhole from which the cover had been removed was near the edge of the roadway. A shelter tent had been erected over the open manhole. The manhole was some nine feet deep, and a ladder had been placed inside the manhole to give access to the cable. Around the area of the site had been placed Four red warning paraffin lamps. The lamps were lit at 3:30 p.m. About 5 p.m. or 5:30 p.m. the Post Office employees left the site for a tea break, for which purpose they went to an adjoining Post Office building. Before leaving (they removed the ladder from the manhole and placed it on the ground beside the shelter and pulled a tarpaulin cover over the entrance to the shelter, leaving a space of two feet to two feet, six inches between the lower edge of the tarpaulin and the ground. The lamps were left burning.

After they left, the Appellant, aged eight, and his uncle, aged ten, came along Russell Road and decided to explore the shelter. According to the findings of the Lord Ordinary, the boys picked up one of the red lamps, raised up the tarpaulin sheet and entered the shelter. They brought the ladder into the shelter with a view to descending into the manhole. They also brought a piece of rope which was not the Post Office equipment, tied the rope to the lamp and, with the lamp, lowered themselves into the manhole. They both came out carrying the lamp. Thereafter, according to the evidence, the Appellant tripped over the lamp, which fell into the hole. There followed an explosion from the hole with flames reaching a height of thirty feet. With the explosion the Appellant fell into the hole and sustained very severe burning injuries....

[T]he cause of the explosion was as a result of the lamp which the Appellant knocked into the hole being so disturbed that paraffin escaped from the tank, formed vapour and was ignited by the flame.... This explanation of the accident was rated by the experts as a low order of probability. But as there was no other feasible explanation, [it] was accepted by the Lord Ordinary, and this House must take it as the established cause.

LORD REID:

It was argued that the Appellant cannot recover because the damage which he suffered was of a kind which was not foreseeable.... No doubt it was not to be expected that the injuries would be as serious as those which the Appellant in fact sustained. But a defender is liable, although the damage may be a good deal greater in extent than was foreseeable. He can only escape liability if the damage can be regarded as differing in kind from what was foreseeable.

So we have (first) a duty owed by the workmen, (secondly) the fact that if they had done as they ought to have done there would have been no accident, and (thirdly) the fact that the injuries suffered by the Appellant, though perhaps different in degree, did not differ in kind from injuries which might have resulted from an accident of a foreseeable nature. The ground on which this case has been decided against the Appellant is that the accident was of an unforeseeable type. Of course, the pursuer has to prove that the defender's fault caused the accident, and there could be a case where the intrusion of a new and unexpected factor could be regarded as the cause of the accident rather than the fault of the defender. But that is not this case. The cause of this accident was a known source of danger, the lamp, but it behaved in an unpredictable way.

The explanation of the accident which has been accepted, and which I would not seek to question, is that, when the lamp fell down the manhole and was broken, some paraffin escaped, and enough was vaporised to create in explosive mixture which was detonated by the naked light of the lamp the experts agree that no one would have expected that to happen: it was so unlikely as to be unforeseeable....

...

This accident was caused by a known source of danger, but caused in a way which could not have been foreseen, and in my judgment that affords no defence. I would therefore allow the appeal.

LORD JENKINS:

It is true that the duty of care expected in cases of this sort is confined to reasonably foreseeable dangers, but it does not necessarily follow that liability is escaped because the danger actually materialising is not identical with the danger reasonably foreseen and guarded against. Each case must depend on its own particular facts. For example (as pointed out in the Opinions), in the present case the paraffin did the mischief by exploding, not burning, and it is said that while a paraffin fire (caused, for example, by the upsetting of the lighted lamp or otherwise allowing its contents to leak out) was a reasonably foreseeable risk so soon as the pursuer got access to the lamp, an explosion was not.

To my mind the distinction drawn between burning and explosion is too fine to warrant acceptance. Supposing the pursuer had on the day in question gone to the site and taken one of the lamps, and upset it over himself, thus setting his clothes alight, the person to be considered responsible for protecting children from the dangers to be found there would presumably have been liable. On the other hand, if the lamp, when the boy upset it, exploded in his face, he would have had no remedy because the explosion was an event which could not reasonably be foreseen. This does not seem to me to be right. . . .

I would allow this appeal.

LORD PEARCE:

. . . When an accident is of a different type and kind from anything that a defender could have foreseen he is not liable for it (*see The Wagon Mound* [1961] A.C.388). But to demand too great precision in the test of foreseeability would be unfair to the pursuer since the facets of misadventure are innumerable. The obvious risks were burning and conflagration and a fall. All these in fact occurred, but unexpectedly the mishandled lamp instead of causing an ordinary conflagration produced a violent explosion. Did the explosion create an accident and damage of a different type from the misadventure and damage that could be foreseen? In my judgment it did not. The accident was but a variant of the foreseeable. It was, to quote the words of Denning, L.J. in *Roe v. Minister of Health and Another* {1954} 2 Q.B.66 at p. 85, "within the risk created by the negligence." No unforeseeable extraneous, initial occurrence fired the train. The children's entry into the tent with the ladder, the descent into the hole, the mishandling of the lamp, were all foreseeable. The greater part of the path to injury had thus been trodden, and the mishandled lamp was quite likely at that stage to spill and cause a conflagration. Instead, by some curious chance of combustion, it exploded and no conflagration occurred, it would seem, until after the explosion. There was thus an unexpected manifestation of the apprehended physical dangers. But it would be, I think, too narrow a view to hold that those who created the risk of fire are excused from the liability for the damage by fire because it came by way of explosive combustion. The resulting damage, though severe, was not greater than or different in kind from that which might have been produced had the lamp spilled and produced a more normal conflagration in the hole.

I would therefore allow the appeal.

Williams v. Stewart

703 P.2d 546 (Ariz. Ct. App. 1985)

LIVERMORE, Judge.

Plaintiff, Charles Lynn Williams, was employed by Don Stewart Evangelistic Association (Stewart) to assist in maintenance of association property. He was asked to clean a swimming pool. In order to do so he had to unclog the drain. He jumped into the pool. This may have caused a pre-existing sinus infection to spread to the brain, substantially damaging him.

[Williams argued that the association had been negligent in allowing the pool to become "murky, green, and leaf strewn" and that negligence created an unreasonable risk of harm to one charged with cleaning it.]

Even assuming that the pool was dirty because of a failure over a period of time to clean it and that such failure created an unreasonable risk of some kinds of harm, Williams' injury was well outside the scope of foreseeable risk, was unrelated to what made the conduct negligent, and no liability resulted. This is not a case "where the duty breached was one imposed to prevent the type of harm which plaintiff ultimately sustained." Thompson v. Sun City Community Hospital, Inc., 141 Ariz. 597, 608, 688 P.2d 605, 616 (1984).

Notes

Kind of harm foreseeably risked. What kind of harms did the association in *Williams* foreseeably risk by negligently allowing the pool to become murky, green, and leaf-strewn?

Unforeseeable manner of occurrence. The accident in *Hughes* occurred in a manner no one could have reasonably foreseen. Why did this fact not shield the defendant from liability?

Proximate cause and lawyering. As *Hughes* illustrates, how one classifies the kinds of harms foreseeably risked by the defendant's conduct is likely to go a long way toward the question of whether a plaintiff prevails. Thus, a good lawyer will give some thought as to how to classify the kind of harm at issue in a case. If the same basic set of facts of *Hughes* were to arise again today, how would you, as the defendants' lawyer, characterize the kind of harm foreseeably risked by the defendants' negligence?

Extent of harm. Assume that the defendant was negligently running through a crowd, bumping into people along the way. The defendant might foreseeably risk some sort of physical injury from such negligent behavior—perhaps a bruised shoulder or a sprained ankle. What if, instead, the defendant's negligence causes the victim to fall to the ground and hit his head, causing his death? Was the harm still within the foreseeable scope of risk even though no reasonable person would have expected anyone to die from running through a crowd? The general rule is that "[i]f the type of harm that occurs is within the scope of the risk, the defendant is liable for all such harm caused, regardless of its extent." Restatement (Third) of Torts § 29 cmt. p (2010). Isn't a bruised shoulder or a sprained ankle a different type of harm than death?

Problem 7.2. When Austin's car collided with Betty's car, Austin lost control of his car, went off the bridge, and crashed into the lake below. Austin was able to get out of the car, but his passenger, Phil, drowned. Phil's family has now brought a wrongful death action against Austin based on his negligence. Austin's lawyer argues that Phil's drowning was not the kind of harm foreseeably risked by Austin's negligence and that Austin's negligence was therefore not the proximate cause of Phil's injuries. You represent Phil's family. What argument will you make in response?

3. Scope of the Risk: Class of Persons Put at Foreseeable Risk

Ordinarily, there will be little question that an injured party was within the class of persons put at foreseeable risk of harm by the defendant's conduct. But sometimes in assessing whether the harm suffered by the plaintiff resulted from the risks that made the actor's conduct tortious, it may be helpful to consider whether the plaintiff was within the class of persons foreseeably put at risk by the conduct.

Palsgraf v. Long Island R. Co.

162 N.E. 99 (N.Y. 1928)

CARDOZO, C. J.

Plaintiff was standing on a platform of defendant's railroad after buying a ticket to go to Rockaway Beach. A train stopped at the station, bound for another place. Two men ran forward to catch it. One of the men reached the platform of the car without mishap, though the train was already moving. The other man, carrying a package, jumped aboard the car, but seemed unsteady as if about to fall. A guard on the car, who had held the door open, reached forward to help him in, and another guard on the platform pushed him from behind. In this act, the package was dislodged, and fell upon the rails. It was a package of small size, about fifteen inches long, and was covered by a newspaper. In fact, it contained fireworks, but there was nothing in its appearance to give notice of its contents. The fireworks when they fell exploded. The shock of the explosion threw down some scales at the other end of the platform many feet away. The scales struck the plaintiff, causing injuries for which she sues.

The conduct of the defendant's guard, if a wrong in its relation to the holder of the package, was not a wrong in its relation to the plaintiff, standing far away. Relatively to her it was not negligence at all. Nothing in the situation gave notice that the falling package had in it the potency of peril to persons thus removed. Negligence is not actionable unless it involves the invasion of a legally protected interest, the violation of a right. 'Proof of negligence in the air, so to speak, will not do.' Pollock, Torts (11th Ed.) p. 455. 'Negligence is the absence of care, according to the circumstances.' The plaintiff, as she stood upon the platform of the station, might claim to be protected against intentional invasion of her bodily security. Such invasion is not charged. She might claim to be protected against unintentional invasion by conduct involving, in the thought of reasonable men, an unreasonable hazard that such invasion would ensue. These, from the point of view of the law, were the bounds of her immunity, with perhaps some rare exceptions, survivals for the most part of ancient forms of liability, where conduct is held to be at the peril of the actor. If no hazard was apparent to the eye of ordinary vigilance, an act innocent and harmless, at least to outward seeming, with reference to her, did not take to itself the quality of a tort because it happened to be a wrong, though apparently not one involving the risk of bodily insecurity, with reference to someone else. 'In every instance, before negligence can be predicated of a given act, back of the act must be sought and found a duty to the individual complaining, the observance of which would have averted or avoided the injury.' 'The ideas of negligence and duty are strictly correlative.' The plaintiff sues in her own right for a wrong personal to her, and not as the vicarious beneficiary of a breach of duty to another.

A different conclusion will involve us, and swiftly too, in a maze of contradictions.... One who jostles one's neighbor in a crowd does not invade the rights of others standing at the outer fringe when the unintended contact casts a bomb upon the ground. The wrongdoer as to them is the man who carries the bomb, not the one who explodes it without suspicion of the danger. Life will have to be made over, and human nature transformed, before prevision so extravagant can be accepted as the norm of conduct, the customary standard to which behavior must conform.

The argument for the plaintiff is built upon the shifting meanings of such words as 'wrong' and 'wrongful,' and shares their instability. What the plaintiff must show is 'a wrong' to herself; *i.e.*, a violation of her own right, and not merely a wrong to some one someone else, nor conduct 'wrongful' because unsocial, but not 'a wrong' to any one anyone. We are told that one who drives at reckless speed through a crowded city street is guilty of a negligent act and therefore of a wrongful one, irrespective of the consequences. Negligent the act is, and wrongful in the sense that it is unsocial, but wrongful and unsocial in relation to other travelers, only because the eye of vigilance perceives the risk of damage. If the same act were to be committed on a speedway or a race course, it would lose its wrongful quality. The risk reasonably to be perceived defines the duty to be obeyed, and risk imports relation; it is risk to another or to others within the range of apprehension. This does not mean, of course, that one who launches a destructive force is always relieved of liability, if the force, though known to be destructive, pursues an unexpected path. 'It was not necessary that the defendant should have had notice of the particular method in which an accident would occur, if the possibility of an accident was clear to the ordinarily prudent eye.' Some acts, such as shooting are so imminently dangerous to any one anyone who may come within reach of the missile however unexpectedly, as to impose a duty of prevision not far from that of an insurer. Even today, and much oftener in earlier stages of the law, one acts sometimes at one's peril. Under this head, it may be, fall certain cases of what is known as transferred intent, an act willfully dangerous to A resulting by misadventure in injury to B. These cases aside, wrong is defined in terms of the natural or probable, at least when unintentional. The range of reasonable apprehension is at times a question for the court, and at times, if varying inferences are possible, a question for the jury. Here, by concession, there was nothing in the situation to suggest to the most cautious mind that the parcel wrapped in newspaper would spread wreckage through the station. If the guard had thrown it down knowingly and willfully, he would not have threatened the plaintiff's safety, so far as appearances could warn him. His conduct would not have involved, even then, an unreasonable probability of invasion of her bodily security. Liability can be no greater where the act is inadvertent.

Negligence, like risk, is thus a term of relation. Negligence in the abstract, apart from things related, is surely not a tort, if indeed it is understandable at all. Negligence is not a tort unless it results in the commission of a wrong, and the commission of a wrong imports the violation of a right, in this case, we are told, the right to be protected against interference with one's bodily security. But bodily security is protected, not against all forms of interference or aggression, but only against some. One who seeks redress at law does not make out a cause of action by showing without more that there has been damage to his person. If the harm was not willful, he must show that the act as to him had possibilities of danger so many and apparent as to entitle him to be protected against the doing of it though the harm was unintended. Affront to personality is still the keynote of the wrong. . . . The victim does not sue derivatively, or by right of subrogation, to vindicate an interest invaded in the person of another. Thus to view his cause of action is to ignore the fundamental difference between tort and crime. He sues for breach of a duty owing to himself.

The law of causation, remote or proximate, is thus foreign to the case before us. The question of liability is always anterior to the question of the measure of the consequences that go with liability. If there is no tort to be redressed, there is no occasion to consider what damage might be recovered if there were a finding of a tort. We may assume, without deciding, that negligence, not at large or in the abstract, but in relation to the plaintiff, would entail liability for any and all consequences, however novel or extraordinary. There is room for argument that a distinction is to be drawn according to the diversity of interests invaded by the act, as where conduct negligent in that it threatens an insignificant invasion of an interest in property results in an unforeseeable invasion of an interest of another order, as, e. g., one of bodily security. Perhaps other distinctions may be necessary. We do not go into the question now. The consequences to be followed must first be rooted in a wrong.

The judgment of the Appellate Division and that of the Trial Term should be reversed, and the complaint dismissed, with costs in all courts.

ANDREWS, J. (dissenting).

Assisting a passenger to board a train, the defendant's servant negligently knocked a package from his arms. It fell between the platform and the cars. Of its contents the servant knew and could know nothing. A violent explosion followed. The concussion broke some scales standing a considerable distance away. In falling, they injured the plaintiff, an intending passenger.

Upon these facts, may she recover the damages she has suffered in an action brought against the master? The result we shall reach depends upon our theory as to the nature of negligence. Is it a relative concept—the breach of some duty owing to a particular person or to particular persons? Or, where there is an act which unreasonably threatens the safety of others, is the doer liable for all its proximate consequences, even where they result in injury to one who would generally be thought to be outside the radius of danger? This is not a mere dispute as to words. We might not believe that to the average mind the dropping of the bundle would seem to involve the probability of harm to the plaintiff standing many feet away whatever might be the case as to the owner or to one so near as to be likely to be struck by its fall. If, however, we adopt the second hypothesis, we have to inquire only as to the relation between cause and effect. We deal in terms of proximate cause, not of negligence.

...

But we are told that 'there is no negligence unless there is in the particular case a legal duty to take care, and this duty must be one which is owed to the plaintiff himself and not merely to others.' This I think too narrow a conception. Where there is the unreasonable act, and some right that may be affected there is negligence whether damage does or does not result. That is immaterial. Should we drive down Broadway at a reckless speed, we are negligent whether we strike an approaching car or miss it by an inch. The act itself is wrongful. It is a wrong not only to those who happen to be within the radius of danger, but to all who might have been there—a wrong to the public at large.

...

The proposition is this: Every one owes to the world at large the duty of refraining from those acts that may unreasonably threaten the safety of others. Such an act occurs. Not only is he wronged to whom harm, might reasonably be expected to result, but he also who is in fact injured, even if he be outside what would generally be thought the danger zone. There needs be duty due the one complaining, but this is not a duty to a particular individual because as to him harm might be expected. Harm to some one being the natural result of the act, not only that one alone, but all those in fact injured may complain.... Unreasonable risk being taken, its consequences are not confined to those who might probably be hurt.

...

The right to recover damages rests on additional considerations. The plaintiff's rights must be injured, and this injury must be caused by the negligence. We build a dam, but are negligent as to its foundations. Breaking, it injures property down stream. We are not liable if all this happened because of some reason other than the insecure foundation. But, when injuries do result from out unlawful act, we are liable for the consequences. It does not matter that they are unusual, unexpected, unforeseen, and unforeseeable. But there is one limitation. The damages must be so connected with the negligence that the latter may be said to be the proximate cause of the former.

These two words have never been given an inclusive definition. What is a cause in a legal sense, still more what is a proximate cause, depend in each case upon many considerations, as does the existence of negligence itself. Any philosophical doctrine of causation does not help us.

. . .

A cause, but not the proximate cause. What we do mean by the word 'proximate' is that, because of convenience, of public policy, of a rough sense of justice, the law arbitrarily declines to trace a series of events beyond a certain point. This is not logic. It is practical politics. . . .

There are some hints that may help us. The proximate cause, involved as it may be with many other causes, must be, at the least, something without which the event would not happen. The court must ask itself whether there was a natural and continuous sequence between cause and effect. Was the one a substantial factor in producing the other? Was there a direct connection between them, without too many intervening causes? Is the effect of cause on result not too attenuated? Is the cause likely, in the usual judgment of mankind, to produce the result? Or, by the exercise of prudent foresight, could the result be foreseen? Is the result too remote from the cause, and here we consider remoteness in time and space. Bird v. St. Paul & M. Ins. Co., 224 N. Y. 47, 120 N. E. 86, 13 A. L. R. 875, where we passed upon the construction of a contract—but something was also said on this subject. Clearly we must so consider, for the greater the distance either in time or space, the more surely do other causes intervene to affect the result. When a lantern is overturned, the firing of a shed is a fairly direct consequence. Many things contribute to the spread of the conflagration—the force of the wind, the direction and width of streets, the character of intervening structures, other factors. We draw an uncertain and wavering line, but draw it we must as best we can.

Once again, it is all a question of fair judgment, always keeping in mind the fact that we endeavor to make a rule in each case that will be practical and in keeping with the general understanding of mankind.

. . .

Notes

The impact of *Palsgraf*. *Palsgraf* is unquestionably the most famous U.S. decision related to proximate cause. The decision has been cited nearly 2,000 times by state and federal courts.

Duty and proximate cause. The majority and dissenting opinions represent the tension that exists with respect to defining the concept of proximate cause. Notice that Justice Cardozo talks about the issue in terms of whether a *duty* was owed to Palsgraf based on the foreseeability of harm to her. Many courts similarly explain that "general negligence law imposes a general *duty* of reasonable care when the defendant's own conduct creates a foreseeable risk of injury to a *foreseeable plaintiff*." Domagala v. Rolland, 805 N.W.2d 14, 23 (Minn. 2011) (emphasis added). In contrast, the *Restatement (Third) of Torts* treats cases like *Palsgraf* as involving questions regarding the scope of risk created by the defendant's negligence (or proximate cause). *See id.* § 29 cmt. n; Thompson v. Kaczinski, 774 N.W.2d 829, 834–39 (Iowa 2009).

Problem 7.3. When Austin collided with Betty, Betty was rendered unconscious. Her right foot pressed down on the accelerator and her car lurched forward. The car went forward on the road for approximately 100 feet before it began to veer toward the pedestrian walkway on the side of the road. Cliff, a pedestrian, had just exited an ice cream store and was walking on the sidewalk when Betty's car ran over his foot, breaking it in several places.

Was Austin's negligence a proximate cause of Cliff's injuries?

B. Superseding Causes

"A 'superseding cause' is an intervening force or act that is deemed sufficient to prevent liability for an actor whose tortious conduct was a factual cause of harm." Restatement (Third) of Torts § 34 (2010). As you read the cases below, consider when an intervening force or act should be treated as a superseding cause sufficient to break the chain of causation. Consider also how the superseding cause analysis relates to the scope of risk analysis covered above.

Watson v. Kentucky & Indiana Bridge & R. Co.

126 S.W. 146 (Ky. 1910)

SETTLE, J.

This action was instituted by the appellant, John Watson, in the court below against the appellees, Kentucky & Indiana Bridge & Railroad Company, hereinafter called the Bridge & Railroad Company, the Southern Railway Company, the Southern Railway Company in Kentucky, and the Union Tank Line Company, to recover $20,000 damages for injuries sustained to his person on the night of June 14, 1907, from an explosion of gas caused, as alleged, by the negligence of the appellees. It was, in substance, alleged in the petition, as amended, that while a tank car, owned by the appellee Union Tank Line Company, and filled with a highly explosive substance known as gasoline, was being transported through a populous section of the city of Louisville over the roadbed of the appellee Bridge & Railroad Company, it was derailed and its valve broken, thereby causing all the gasoline to escape and flow in large quantities on the street and into the gutters; that from the gasoline thus flowing and standing in pools upon the street and gutters there arose and spread over the neighborhood of the place of derailment and into the houses of the residents thereof, great quantities of highly explosive and combustible gas which, three hours after the derailment of the tank car, exploded with force from contact with a lighted match thrown on the street by one Chas. Duerr, who claimed to have used it in igniting a cigar; that the explosion threw appellant from his bed and almost demolished his house, from the ruins of which he was taken unconscious and bleeding with a fractured jaw and one cheek nearly torn from his face.

. . .

The lighting of the match by Duerr having resulted in the explosion, the question is, was that act merely a contributing cause, or the efficient and, therefore, proximate cause of appellant's injuries?

. . .

. . . No better statement of the law of proximate cause can be given than is found in 21 Am. & Eng. Ency. of Law (2d Ed.) 490, quoted with approval in *Louisville Home Telephone Company v. Gasper*, 123 Ky. 128, 93 S. W. 1057, 29 Ky. Law Rep. 578, 9 L. R. A. (N. S.) 548: "It is well settled that the mere fact that there have been intervening causes between the defendant's negligence and the plaintiff's injuries is not sufficient in law to relieve the former from liability; that is to say, the plaintiff's injuries may yet be natural and proximate in law, although between the defendant's negligence and the injuries other causes or conditions, or agencies, may have operated, and, when this is the case, the defendant is liable. So the defendant is clearly responsible where the intervening causes, acts, or conditions were set in motion by his earlier negligence, or naturally induced by such wrongful act or omission, or even, it is generally held, if the intervening acts or conditions were of a nature the happening of which was reasonably to have been anticipated, though they may have been acts of the plaintiff himself. . . ."

If the presence, on Madison street in the city of Louisville, of the great volume of loose gas that arose from the escaping gasoline was caused by the negligence of the appellee Bridge & Railroad Company, it seems to us that the probable consequences of its coming in contact with fire and causing an explosion was too plain a proposition to admit of doubt. Indeed, it was most probable that someone would strike a match to light a cigar or for other purposes in the midst of the gas. In our opinion, therefore, the act of one lighting and throwing a match under such circumstances cannot be said to be the efficient cause of the explosion. . . . This conclusion, however, rests upon the theory that Duerr inadvertently or negligently lighted and threw the match in the gas.

If, however, the act of Duerr in lighting the match and throwing it into the vapor or gas arising from the gasoline was malicious, and done for the purpose of causing the explosion, we do not think appellees would be responsible, for while the appellee Bridge & Railroad Company's negligence may have been the efficient cause of the presence of the gas in the street, and it should have understood enough of the consequences thereof to have foreseen that an explosion was likely to result from the inadvertent or negligent lighting of a match by some person who was ignorant of the presence of the gas or of the effect of lighting or throwing a match in it, it could not have foreseen or deemed it probable that one would maliciously or wantonly do such an act for the evil purpose of producing the explosion. Therefore, if the act of Duerr was malicious, we quite agree with the trial court that it was one which the appellees could not reasonably have anticipated or guarded against, and in such case the act of Duerr, and not the primary negligence of the appellee Bridge & Railroad Company, in any of the particulars charged, was the efficient or proximate cause of appellant's injuries. The mere fact that the concurrent cause or intervening act was unforeseen will not relieve the defendant guilty of the primary negligence from liability, but if the intervening agency is something so unexpected or extraordinary as that he could not or ought not to have anticipated it, he will not be liable, and certainly he is not bound to anticipate the criminal acts of others by which damage is inflicted and hence is not liable therefor.

Britton v. Wooten

817 S.W.2d 443 (Ky. 1991)

LEIBSON, Justice.

On May 8, 1983, Wooten's Pic Pac Grocery in Louisa, Kentucky, was destroyed by fire. A portion of the grocery store premises consisted of a building owned by the movant, Genoa Britton (the lessor), and leased to L. Wayne Wooten d/b/a Wooten's Pic Pac and Wooten's Grocery Company, Inc. (collectively, the lessee). The movant filed suit against her lessee alleging negligence in the operation of the grocery store. Allegedly, the store employees stacked trash that was flammable, combustible material next to the building all the way up to the eaves, in violation of the fire marshal's regulations and the fire code of the State of Kentucky. Consequently, a fire originating in the trash progressed up the exterior wall to the combustible roof, causing the building to burn to the ground.

The only evidence of record specifically identifying how the fire started was the testimony of Andrew Reed, an arson investigator from the Kentucky State Police, who had investigated the cause of the fire at length. He stated that in his opinion "someone set fire to the paper boxes in or near the Dempsey dumpsters."

... The primary reason stated for granting the Summary Judgment was that the lease, as a matter of law, contracted away the lessor's right to sue the lessee for the destruction of the premises by fire. [The Kentucky Supreme Court held that summary judgment was erroneously granted in this respect.]

In seeking Summary Judgment, the lessee had also relied upon "several general principles of law pertaining to proximate causation" and, more specifically, "that the act of the arsonist in setting the fire was a superseding cause as a matter of law, thereby breaking the chain of causation." ...

To begin with, at this point the evidence that this fire constituted the crime of arson is far short of overwhelming. . . . We need not decide this subissue because we reject any all-inclusive general rule that, as respondent contends, "criminal acts of third parties . . . relieve the original negligent party from liability."

This archaic doctrine has been rejected everywhere. The only Kentucky case movant cites in support of it [is] *Watson v. Kentucky & Indiana Bridge and R. Co.*, 137 Ky. 619, 126 S.W. 146 (1910), a case over 80 years old. In it the court draws a distinction in the railroad company's liability for a fire ignited following a train derailment and gas spillage on the basis of a fact question presented as to whether the man who ignited the gasoline did so maliciously or inadvertently. That case indeed holds that the railroad company is "not bound to anticipate the criminal act of others by which damage is inflicted and hence is not liable therefor." *Id.* at 151, 126 S.W. 146. The question is whether that case is still viable.

Restatement (Second) of Torts, § 449 . . . postulates:

> If the likelihood that a third person may act in a particular manner is the hazard or one of the hazards which makes the actor [the defendant] negligent, such an act [by another person] whether innocent, negligent, intentionally tortious, or criminal, does not prevent the actor [the defendant] from being liable for harm caused thereby.

. . .

Seelbach v. Cadick, Ky., 405 S.W.2d 745, 749 (1966) states:

> . . . an intervening cause or agency which insulates from liability is [restricted to] 'an independent force, not naturally arising out of or related to the negligently created condition.' . . . it is not necessary that the party negligently creating the condition foresee the specific subsequent act in the chain of causation.

This reasoning applies with the same logic to the intentional acts of third persons as to those merely reckless or negligent. . . .

In the present case whether the spark ignited in the trash accumulated next to the building was ignited negligently, intentionally, or even criminally, or if it was truly accidental, is not the critical issue. . . .

The Summary Judgment in the trial court is vacated, and the decision in the Court of Appeals affirming it is reversed. The within case is remanded to the trial court for further proceedings consistent with this Opinion.

Fast Eddie's v. Hall

688 N.E.2d 1270 (Ill. Ct. App. 1997)

BAKER, Judge.

Appellant-defendant Fast Eddie's d/b/a Hyway Tavern, Inc., (Fast Eddie's) appeals the trial court's denial of its motions for summary judgment on a complaint filed by the plaintiff-appellee Judy Hall, as executor of the estate of Teresa Hall (Estate). Teresa Hall died after one of Fast Eddie's patrons shot and killed her. . . .

Facts

The facts most favorable to Hall, the non-movant, reveal that on the evening of June 4, 1993, Teresa Hall, Michael Lamb and John Schooley were patrons at Fast Eddie's. Schooley and Lamb arrived together around 7:00 p.m. and began to consume alcoholic beverages. Sometime later in the evening, Hall arrived at the tavern and began to drink and socialize with Schooley. At one point in the evening, after Schooley stepped outside the bar for moment, Lamb began to make advances toward Hall. At about the same time, the on-duty manager, Rita Stephens, noticed that Hall had become heavily intoxicated and was having difficulty sitting up on her bar stool. As a result, Stephens asked Lamb to take Hall out of the tavern. Lamb did as Stephens requested and escorted Hall to Schooley's car and returned to the bar. Schooley then drove Hall to his trailer in Terre Haute. After they arrived, Hall passed out in the passenger's seat of Schooley's car. Schooley then went inside his trailer and passed out on the couch.

Shortly thereafter, Lamb purchased a six-pack of beer from the tavern and drove to his home. After discovering that his wife was not there, he drove to Schooley's trailer. As he approached the trailer, he noticed Hall passed out in the passenger's seat of Schooley's car. Lamb removed Hall's body and placed her in his car. He then drove to the Riley Conservation Club where he shot Hall in the abdomen and head, killing her. When Hall's body was found, her blood alcohol was .23%, her skirt was twisted over her hips and her breasts were partially exposed. Lamb later confessed to killing Hall and pled guilty to her murder.

On September 30, 1994, Judy Hall, as administrator of the Estate of Teresa Hall, filed a complaint against Fast Eddie's alleging that it was negligent per se for violating IND.CODE § 7.1-5-10-15, Indiana's Dram Shop Act, by serving Lamb and Hall alcoholic beverages when they were visibly intoxicated. [Fast Eddie's filed a motion for summary judgment, arguing that any negligence on its part was not a proximate cause of Hall's death. The motion was denied.]

III. Proximate Cause Of Hall's Assault and Murder

Finally, Fast Eddie's argues that the trial court erroneously denied its motion for summary judgment because its alleged violation of the Dram Shop Act was not the proximate cause of Hall's sexual assault and death. According to the Dram Shop Act, a provider of alcoholic beverages is not liable in a civil action unless:

> (1) the person furnishing the alcoholic beverage had actual knowledge that the person to whom the alcoholic beverage was furnished was visibly intoxicated at the time the alcoholic beverage was furnished; and,
>
> (2) the intoxication of the person to whom the alcoholic beverage was furnished was a proximate cause of the death, injury, or damage alleged in the complaint.

I.C. § 7.1-5-10-15.5(b) (emphasis added). Thus, even though a proprietor may have a statutory duty to refrain from providing alcoholic beverages to intoxicated persons, it will not be liable unless the alleged violation is the proximate cause of a patron's death or injury.

Proximate cause is the limitation which courts have placed on the actor's responsibility for the consequences of his act or failure to act. A party's act is the proximate cause of an injury if it is the natural and probable consequence of the act and should have been reasonably foreseen and anticipated in light of the circumstances. However, a willful, malicious criminal act of a third party is an intervening act which breaks the causal chain between the alleged negligence and the resulting harm. Although proximate cause is generally a question of fact, it becomes a question of law where only a single conclusion can be drawn from the facts.

Here, even assuming Fast Eddie's breached its statutory duty under the Dram Shop Act, its breach was not the proximate cause of Hall's sexual assault and death. First, the chain of causation in the instant case is extremely tenuous. Although Lamb initially escorted Hall out of the tavern, he returned to the bar after Schooley drove Hall to his trailer. It was later in the evening, however, when Lamb left the tavern, returned home to discover his wife's absence, decided to proceed to Schooley's home, found Hall passed out in Schooley's car and killed her. The tavern could not have reasonably foreseen this series of events which culminated in Hall's unfortunate death. Additionally, even if the chain of causation were stronger, Lamb's intentional criminal acts were the intervening cause of Hall's death which broke the causal chain between Fast Eddie's negligence and Hall's sexual assault and death. Therefore, Fast Eddie's alleged violation of the statute was not the proximate cause of Hall's sexual assault and death.

Finally, we reject the Estate's contention that Lamb's intoxication was the proximate cause of Hall's death. In support of its contention, the Estate submitted Lamb's deposition testimony that his intoxication caused him to shoot Hall. The Estate concludes that this evidence creates a genuine issue of material fact regarding the proximate cause of Hall's death. We disagree.

Unlike automobile accidents which occur as the result of alcoholic beverage consumption, assault and murder are intentional acts of volition which are the result of an assailant's deliberate design. Here, Hall died because Lamb deliberately decided to kill her. This criminal intent would have been present whether or not Lamb was intoxicated. Thus, despite Lamb's contention, we find as a matter of law that Hall's death was the result of Lamb's deliberate design and volitional act and not his intoxication. The trial court, therefore, improperly denied Fast Eddie's motion for summary judgment on the issue of proximate cause. As a result, we reverse the trial court's order denying Fast Eddie's motions for summary judgment and instruct the trial court to enter summary judgment in its favor.

The trial court's denial of summary judgment is reversed.

Notes

Other types of superseding causes. The cases above all involve possibly intentional or criminal acts on the part of third persons. But there are other intervening forces that can amount to superseding causes. Forces of nature or "acts of God" may be treated as intervening and superseding causes that break the chain of causation. Smith v. Bd. of County Rd. Comm'rs, 146 N.W.2d 702, 703 (Mich. Ct. App. 1966) (torrential rain); Tel Oil Co. v. City of Schenectady, 303 A.D.2d 868, 873 (N.Y. Sup. Ct. A.D. 2003) (mudslide caused by convergence of warm temperatures, rapid snowmelt, heavy rain, and strong winds on same day).

Extraordinary events or attenuated causes. In describing what qualifies as a superseding cause, courts often reference the idea of an extraordinary event or one that is highly attenuated from the defendant's negligence. Losito v. Manlyn Dev. Group, Inc., 925 N.Y.S.2d 643 (N.Y. Sup. Ct. A.D. 2011).

Superseding causes and scope of risk analysis. Could the courts in *Britton* and *Fast Eddie's* have reached the same results without ever engaging in an analysis of whether the intervening forces in question were superseding causes? In other words, would the scope of risk analysis introduced in the previous section have been sufficient to enable the courts to reach the same result? Is tort law served by recognition of the concept of a "superseding cause"?

Problem 7.4. The reason why Austin originally swerved and crashed into Betty is because he was trying to avoid a cat that had run out into the road. Austin reacted badly when confronted with the cat's presence due to his intoxication. When Betty was rendered unconscious and her car began moving forward, Donna saw Betty's car headed directly toward her own car. Donna was stopped at a red light at the time, but when she saw Betty's car coming she quickly pulled her car toward the curb. When she did, she negligently hit a nearby light pole, causing it to fall and land on Elizabeth, another pedestrian.[1]

(a) Was the presence of the cat a superseding cause of Betty's injuries? (Stated differently, was Austin's negligence still a proximate cause of Betty's injuries despite the presence of the cat?)

(b) Were the actions of Donna a superseding cause of Elizabeth's injuries? (Stated differently, was Austin's negligence still a proximate cause of Elizabeth's injuries despite Donna's actions?)

(c) If it turns out that the pole was negligently installed or maintained by the local power company and was therefore likely to fall over upon impact, would Donna's negligence amount to a superseding cause of

1. Lest any readers believe that this fact pattern is unrealistic, see *Bernier v. Boston Edison Co.*, 403 N.E.2d 391 (Mass. 1980), on which it is based.

Elizabeth's injuries sufficient to relieve the power company of liability? (Stated differently, would the negligence of the power company still be a proximate cause of Elizabeth's injuries despite Donna's actions?)

C. Special Policy-Based Proximate Cause Rules

If the concept of proximate cause is truly "bottomed on public policy as a limitation on how far society is willing to extend liability for a defendant's actions," *Ashley County, Arkansas, v. Pfizer, Inc.*, 552 F.3d 659, 671 (8th Cir. 2009), there may be times when the legal rules that develop end up being based on policy considerations at least as much as straight application of scope of risk principles. The following section examines some of these situations.

1. Legislative Rules

Worley v. Weigels, Inc.

919 S.W.2d 589 (Tenn. 1996)

REID, Justice.

This case presents for review the liability of a seller of alcoholic beverages to a person under 21 years of age. The trial court granted summary judgment of no liability to the seller. The Court of Appeals reversed on the finding that the case presents issues for the jury. This Court finds that, pursuant to public policy expressly declared by the legislature regarding liability for the sale of intoxicating liquors, the seller in this case is not liable for the injuries alleged, as a matter of law.

I

For purposes of summary judgment, the facts are not in dispute. At about 2:50 a.m. on September 8, 1991, the plaintiffs' child, Phillip Worley, sustained serious and permanent personal injuries when the vehicle in which he was riding as a guest passenger and which was being operated by Anthony Kaiser, crashed into a utility pole while traveling at a high rate of speed.

On the prior evening, Worley, Kaiser, Scott Goosie, and several of their friends, all of whom were under 21 years of age, gathered at the residence of one of the group whose parents were away from home. During the evening, Goosie and Worley were dispatched to a store owned by the defendant, Weigel's, Inc., to purchase beer. Goosie, who was 20 years of age at the time, purchased a substantial quantity of beer. He purchased the beer without showing or being asked by the clerk to show any evidence of his age. Goosie did not drink any beer during the evening. However, Kaiser became intoxicated from drinking beer purchased by Goosie. While en route from the party, with Worley as a passenger, Kaiser, because of his intoxication, lost control of his vehicle and the collision resulted.

Worley's parents, individually and as his conservators, sued the defendant and alleged as a cause of action the violation of the provisions of Tenn. Code Ann. §§ 57-4-203(b)(1) and 57-5-301(c) (Supp.1995).[2]

. . .

III

The first issue is whether a seller may be held liable for injuries caused by an intoxicated minor who consumed alcoholic beverages furnished by another minor who purchased the beverages from the seller. The defendant contends that the statutes prohibit recovery unless the buyer consumes the beverage and, as a direct result of that consumption, causes injury. The plaintiffs contend that liability extends to injuries caused by other minors where it was reasonably foreseeable that the other minors would consume the alcoholic drink. Their position is that, even though Tenn. Code Ann. § 57-10-101 limits proximate causation generally, Tenn. Code Ann. § 57-10-102 preserves its usual application in the two particular situations set forth in the statute, sales to minors and sales to intoxicated persons.

In *Brookins v. The Round Table, Inc.*, 624 S.W.2d 547 (Tenn.1981), the Court summarized the development of the law at that time:

> At common law, an individual who sold or furnished alcohol to another generally was held not to be liable for damages resulting from the other's intoxication, even if those damages were foreseeable, in part because the other's acceptance and use of the intoxicants was considered an independent intervening cause, cutting off any liability. Today, even in the absence of statutes prohibiting the sale of intoxicating beverages to a minor or to an intoxicated person, courts generally recognize that the furnishing of intoxicants may be the proximate cause of an injury resulting from intoxication, the negligence consisting of the creation of a situation or condition which involves unreasonable risk because of the foreseeable action of another.

Id. at 549 (citations omitted). Reversing the lower court's grant of summary judgment, the *Brookins* court stated, "[W]hether the sale of intoxicants is the proximate cause of subsequent injuries is essentially a question of foreseeability. . . ." *Id. Brookins* noted the purpose of the legislation prohibiting the sale of alcohol to minors:

> These broad prohibitions are intended not only to protect minors from the folly of their own actions, but are for the protection of members of the general public as well. They are directed to minors as a class in recognition of their susceptibilities and the intensification of dangers inherent in the

---

2. "Any licensee or other person who sells, furnishes, disposes of, gives, or causes to be sold, furnished, disposed of, or given, any alcoholic beverage to any person under twenty-one (21) years of age is guilty of a Class A misdemeanor." Tenn.Code Ann. § 57-4-03(b)(1) (Supp.1995).

> consumption of alcoholic beverages, when consumed by a person lacking in maturity and responsibility.

Id. at 550. Under the *Brookins* decision, the plaintiffs' cause of action in the present case would survive summary judgment, and the issue for the jury to decide would be whether the injury sustained by Worley was reasonably foreseeable.

However, Title 57, Chapter 10, of the Tennessee Code, entitled "Alcohol-Related Injuries", replaced the rule stated in *Brookins.* Section 57-10-101 (1989) provides:

> The general assembly hereby finds and declares that the consumption of any alcoholic beverage or beer rather than the furnishing of any alcoholic beverage or beer is the proximate cause of injuries inflicted upon another by an intoxicated person.

Section 57-10-102 provides:

> Notwithstanding the provisions of § 57-10-101, no judge or jury may pronounce a judgment awarding damages to or on behalf of any party who has suffered personal injury or death against any person who has sold any alcoholic beverage or beer, unless such jury of twelve (12) persons has first ascertained beyond a reasonable doubt that the sale by such person of the alcoholic beverage or beer was the proximate cause of the personal injury or death sustained and that such person:
>
> (1) Sold the alcoholic beverage or beer to a person known to be under the age of twenty-one (21) years and such person caused the personal injury or death as the direct result of the consumption of the alcoholic beverage or beer so sold; or
>
> (2) Sold the alcoholic beverage or beer to an obviously intoxicated person and such person caused the personal injury or death as the direct result of the consumption of the alcoholic beverage or beer so sold.

With the enactment of these statutes, the legislature made a definite distinction between the basis for civil liability and the basis for criminal liability incident to the sale of alcoholic beverages. These statutes, rather than the duties imposed by criminal statutes, determine the civil liability of the seller. These statutes declare that the "consumption" rather than the "furnishing of" intoxicating beverages is deemed the "proximate cause of injuries inflicted" by the intoxicated person, except that a sale may be deemed to be the proximate cause when the sale is to a person known to be a minor and whose consumption causes the injury or to a person who is "obviously intoxicated" and whose consumption caused the injury. Since the purchaser in this case did not consume the beverage purchased, the accident was not caused by the purchaser's consumption of the beverage. Therefore, there is no liability on the seller.

Note

Multiple proximate causes. It is important to keep in mind that ordinarily there can be more than one proximate cause of an event. *See* Williams v. Joynes, 677 S.E.2d 261, 264 (Va. 2009). What would the result in *Worley* have been if the court had simply applied the scope of risk analysis discussed in this chapter? Chapter 8 will deal with the issue of how jurors should apportion fault among multiple negligent parties.

2. Suicide

One situation in which traditional notions of foreseeability and scope of risk may give way to broader policy is in the situation where a defendant's negligence allegedly results in the suicide of another.

One of the earliest statements of the law regarding suicide and proximate cause appears in the 1881 Supreme Court case of *Scheffer v. Washington City, V.M. & G.S.R. Co.*, 105 U.S. 249 (1881). Scheffer eventually killed himself after suffering severe physical and mental injuries as a result of a train collision, allegedly caused by the defendant's negligence. According to the Court, the proximate cause of Scheffer's death "was his own act of self-destruction." Suicide "was not the natural and probable consequence" of the defendant's negligence and, therefore, could not have been foreseen, according to the Court. *Id.* at 251. The overwhelming majority rule now is that an individual's act of suicide is "a supervening cause of the victim's loss of his life, breaking the chain of responsibility that would otherwise link the loss to the negligent act." Jutzi-Johnson v. United States, 263 F.3d 753, 755 (7th Cir. 2001). This rule has been applied even where common sense would suggest that suicide was one of the foreseeable risks of the defendant's negligence. *See* R.D. v. W.H., 875 P.2d 26 (Wyo. 1994) (stating the general rule where defendant helped plaintiff obtain prescription medication used to commit suicide just five days after an earlier suicide attempt and after a previous attempt involving the same medication).

The most common exception to the general rule that a decedent's suicide amounts to a superseding cause that breaks the chain of causation is where the defendant's negligence brings about "delirium or insanity" that causes the victim to commit suicide. *See, e.g.,* R.D. v. W.H., 875 P.2d 26 (Wyo. 1994) (applying this exception); Rimbert v. Eli Lilly and Co., 577 F. Supp. 2d 1174 (D.N.M. 2008) (declining to grant defendant's motion for summary judgment where genuine issue of material fact existed as to whether pharmaceutical company's failure to warn patient about possible Prozac-induced suicide induced a mental illness that led to patient's suicide). The other common exception is where the defendant enters into a custodial relationship with the decedent, knowing of the decedent's risk of suicide, and is negligent in caring for the individual. *See, e.g.,* Murdock v. City of Keene, 623 A.2d 755, 757 (N.H. 1993).

3. The "Eggshell Plaintiff" Rule

Benn v. Thomas, K-G, Ltd.

512 N.W.2d 537 (Iowa 1994)

McGIVERIN, Chief Justice.

The main question here is whether the trial court erred in refusing to instruct the jury on the "eggshell plaintiff" rule in view of the fact that plaintiff's decedent, who had a history of coronary disease, died of a heart attack six days after suffering a bruised chest and fractured ankle in a motor vehicle accident caused by defendant's negligence....

I. Background facts and proceedings. On February 15, 1989, on an icy road in Missouri, a semi-tractor and trailer rear-ended a van in which Loras J. Benn was a passenger. In the accident, Loras suffered a bruised chest and a fractured ankle. Six days later he died of a heart attack.

Subsequently, Carol A. Benn, as executor of Loras's estate, filed suit against defendants Leland R. Thomas, the driver of the semi-tractor, K-G Ltd., the owner of the semi-tractor and trailer, and Heartland Express, the permanent lessee of the semi-tractor and trailer. The plaintiff estate sought damages for Loras's injuries and death. For the purposes of simplicity, we will refer to all defendants in the singular.

At trial, the estate's medical expert, Dr. James E. Davia, testified that Loras had a history of coronary disease and insulin-dependent diabetes. Loras had a heart attack in 1985 and was at risk of having another. Dr. Davia testified that he viewed "the accident that [Loras] was in and the attendant problems that it cause[d] in the body as the straw that broke the camel's back" and the cause of Loras's death. Other medical evidence indicated the accident did not cause his death.

Based on Dr. Davia's testimony, the estate requested an instruction to the jury based on the "eggshell plaintiff" rule, which requires the defendant to take his plaintiff as he finds him, even if that means that the defendant must compensate the plaintiff for harm an ordinary person would not have suffered. The district court denied this request.

The jury returned a verdict for the estate in the amount of $17,000 for Loras's injuries but nothing for his death. In the special verdict, the jury determined the defendant's negligence in connection with the accident did not proximately cause Loras's death.

The estate filed a motion for new trial claiming the court erred in refusing to instruct the jury on the "eggshell plaintiff" rule. The court denied the motion, concluding that the instructions given to the jury appropriately informed them of the applicable law.

The plaintiff estate appealed. The court of appeals reversed the trial court, concluding that the plaintiff's evidence required a specific instruction on the eggshell plaintiff rule.

...

A tortfeasor whose act, superimposed upon a prior latent condition, results in an injury may be liable in damages for the full disability. This rule deems the injury, and not the dormant condition, the proximate cause of the plaintiff's harm. This precept is often referred to as the "eggshell plaintiff" rule, which has its roots in cases such as *Dulieu v. White & Sons*, [1901] 2 K.B. 669, 679, where the court observed:

> If a man is negligently run over or otherwise negligently injured in his body, it is no answer to the sufferer's claim for damages that he would have suffered less injury, or no injury at all, if he had not had an unusually thin skull or an unusually weak heart.

The proposed instruction here stated:

> If Loras Benn had a prior heart condition making him more susceptible to injury than a person in normal health, then the Defendant is responsible for all injuries and damages which are experienced by Loras Benn, proximately caused by the Defendant's actions, even though the injuries claimed produced a greater injury than those which might have been experienced by a normal person under the same circumstances.

See Iowa Uniform Jury Instruction 200.34 (1993) (citing *Becker*).

Defendant contends that plaintiff's proposed instruction was inappropriate because it concerned damages, not proximate cause. Although the eggshell plaintiff rule has been incorporated into the Damages section of the Iowa Uniform Civil Jury Instructions, we believe it is equally a rule of proximate cause.

We agree that the jury might have found the defendant liable for Loras's death as well as his injuries under the instructions as given. But the proximate cause instruction failed to adequately convey the existing law that the jury should have applied to this case. The eggshell plaintiff rule rejects the limit of foreseeability that courts ordinarily require in the determination of proximate cause. *Prosser & Keeton* § 43, at 291 ("The defendant is held liable for unusual results of personal injuries which are regarded as unforeseeable. . . ."). Once the plaintiff establishes that the defendant caused some injury to the plaintiff, the rule imposes liability for the full extent of those injuries, not merely those that were foreseeable to the defendant. Restatement (Second) of Torts § 461 (1965) ("The negligent actor is subject to liability for harm to another although a physical condition of the other . . . makes the injury greater than that which the actor as a reasonable man should have foreseen as a probable result of his conduct.").

The instruction given by the court was appropriate as to the question of whether defendant caused Loras's initial personal injuries, namely, the fractured ankle and the bruised chest. This instruction alone, however, failed to adequately convey to the jury the eggshell plaintiff rule, which the jury reasonably could have applied to the cause of Loras's death.

Defendant maintains "[t]he fact there was extensive heart disease and that Loras Benn was at risk any time is not sufficient" for an instruction on the eggshell plaintiff rule. Yet the plaintiff introduced substantial medical testimony that the stresses of the accident and subsequent treatment were responsible for his heart attack and death. Although the evidence was conflicting, we believe that it was sufficient for the jury to determine whether Loras's heart attack and death were the direct result of the injury fairly chargeable to defendant Thomas's negligence.

Defendant nevertheless maintains that an eggshell plaintiff instruction would draw undue emphasis and attention to Loras's prior infirm condition. We have, however, explicitly approved such an instruction in two prior cases. *See* Woode v. Kabela, 256 Iowa 622, 632, 128 N.W.2d 241, 247 (1964) ("It was proper for the court to instruct with reference to the condition because if the negligent actions of defendant were such that [plaintiff's] former poor physical condition was revived or was enhanced he was entitled to damages because of such condition."); Hackley v. Robinson, 219 N.W. 398, 398–99 (Iowa 1928) (approving instruction allowing plaintiff to recover upon a showing "that the injury directly caused the dormant or inactive tuberculosis to become revivified").

. . .

To deprive the plaintiff estate of the requested instruction under this record would fail to convey to the jury a central principle of tort liability.

Note

Policy-driven rule? *Benn* refers to the eggshell plaintiff rule as an exception to traditional foreseeability principles. If it is an exception, what policy justifies the exception? Or is the rule instead merely an extension of the rule discussed earlier regarding scope of risk and the extent of harm caused by the defendant's negligence?

4. Rescuers, Emergency Responders, and Medical Providers

One proximate cause scenario that sometimes arises is the situation in which a third party attempts to aid the party injured by the defendant's negligence. Sometimes the party providing assistance is injured in the process. How far does the causal chain extend in such cases? As observed by Justice Cardozo in the seminal case of *Wagner v. Int'l Ry. Co.*, 232 N.Y. 176 (N.Y.1921), "[d]anger invites rescue.... The wrong that imperils life is a wrong to the imperiled victim; it is a wrong also to the rescuer . . ." *Id.* at 180 (emphasis added).

McCarter v. Davis

2014 U.S. Dist. LEXIS 102399 (E.D. Mo. 2014)

[Davis lost control of his vehicle, causing the vehicle to turn over onto its passenger side and come to rest in the median between the east and westbound lanes on the interstate. McCarter, who was behind Davis, pulled her car over to the left shoulder of the interstate to see if Davis was okay. Other vehicles began pulling over behind McCarter's car and on the other side of the road. One of the cars on the other side of the road was driven Daniel Rozum. Daniel's wife, Tara, got out of the car to approach another vehicle to find out if 911 had been called. At this time, another driver instructed McCarter to move her car to the other side of the road. As

McCarter was moving her car across the interstate, she was hit by another vehicle. This caused McCarter's car to collide with Tara, resulting in serious injuries. As you might imagine, at this point, the procedural history becomes quite complicated. But the issue facing the court on Davis' motion for summary judgment was whether Davis' negligence was a proximate cause of Tara's injuries.]

The Rescue Doctrine. . . . Davis contends that the rescue doctrine does not apply because (a) the Rozums did not attempt to rescue him and (b) his negligence was not the proximate cause of the Rozums' injuries because there was an efficient intervening cause.

Davis' two arguments address the "two important benefits" of the rescue doctrine described by the Missouri Supreme Court in *Lowrey v. Horvath*, 689 S.W.2d 625 (Mo.1985) (en banc).

> First, under the rescue doctrine it is not negligence to knowingly and voluntarily place one's self in a position where the likelihood of receiving serious physical injury is great when the exposure to such danger is conducted in a reasonable manner and for the purpose of saving human life. Second, the plaintiff may invoke the rescue doctrine to establish that the defendant's negligence in creating the peril which induced the injured person to attempt to rescue another who was imperiled was the proximate cause of the injury for which recovery is sought. . . .

The undisputed facts are that Davis' accident was in the median of the Interstate, *i.e.*, between the westbound and eastbound lanes, and the Rozums pulled over on the shoulder of the right lane. They had not seen the accident occur. Neither Daniel nor Tara intended to cross the highway to get to Davis. Tara intended only to determine if "911" had been called. She did this by approaching the tractor trailer driver, also on the shoulder of the right lane, to ask if it had been called and, if it had not been, she planned to return to her car and make the call. When approaching the driver on foot, she walked as far away from the traffic lane as possible while avoiding the ravine. Thus, Tara purposefully avoided putting herself in a position where she might be injured. Moreover, the maximum assistance she, and Daniel, intended to render was to make a phone call if necessary to obtain assistance for Davis from someone else.

In *Allison v. Sverdrup & Parcel and Assocs.*, 738 S.W.2d 440, 454 (Mo.Ct.App.1987), cited by Plaintiff, the court applied the "forceful reasoning" of cases from other jurisdictions and held that "a person who sees another in imminent peril created by the negligence of defendant will not be charged with negligence in *risking his or her own life or serious injury in an attempt to rescue*, provided he or she does not act recklessly or rashly." (Emphasis added.) Citing cases from five other jurisdictions, the Massachusetts Court of Appeals noted that "[a] common thread runs through the cases which recognize the rescue doctrine, and that is some act of intervention, *e.g.*, moving a vehicle . . . administering first aid. . . ." Barnes v. Geiger, 446 N.E.2d 78, 82 (Mass.Ct.App.1983) (emphasis added). "To achieve the status of a rescuer, a claimant's purpose must be more than investigatory. There must be asserted some specific mission of assistance by which the plight of the imperiled could reasonably be ameliorated." *Id.*

McCarter argues that the Rozums did intervene "by attempting to assist [Davis] and obtain emergency aid for him" and, at a minimum, she has established that the question is one for the jury. In support of her argument, however, she has omitted several undisputed facts. She states that after exiting the Rozums' vehicle, Tara "began walking back to the scene of the accident." She did not. She and Daniel specifically testified that they had no intention of crossing the highway, which they would have to do to reach the scene of the accident. Instead, Tara walked toward the driver of the tractor trailer to ask if "911" had been called. In doing so, she purposefully placed herself as far out of danger of injury as possible.

If she had determined that "911" needed to be called, she would have made the call from her car, again removing herself from danger. Neither she nor Daniel had seen the accident and neither testified that the inquiry about whether "911" had been called was for the benefit of Davis and not to respond to a motor vehicle accident involving only property damage. *See* Welch v. Hesston Corp., 540 S.W.2d 127, 129 (Mo.Ct.App.1976) (Missouri rescue doctrine does not apply to rescuers of property).

The Court finds that, for the purposes of Missouri's rescue doctrine, Tara Rozum was not a rescuer by virtue of her activities of walking on the right shoulder of the highway for the sole purpose of determining from a bystander on that same shoulder whether "911" needed to be called to respond to an accident—not witnessed by either Rozum—in the median on the other side of the highway.

Notes

Logic or policy? Does the rescue doctrine flow naturally from the concept of foreseeability, or is it more a function of courts attempting to draw lines of convenience?

Proximate cause and lawyering. A lawyer has a professional obligation to diligently represent her client as well as a duty of candor toward the tribunal. *See* ABA Model Rules of Professional Conduct R. 1.3 & R. 3.1. Why did Tara's lawyer argue that Tara was walking back to the scene of the accident if she really wasn't?

Problem 7.5. Recall from Problem 7.4 that Donna's negligence resulted in a pole falling onto Elizabeth. When Elizabeth was injured by the falling pole, a bystander who knew Elizabeth ran two blocks to the business office park where Elizabeth's husband, Francisco, worked. The bystander told Francisco that Elizabeth had been injured, so Francisco leapt from his desk and ran toward the scene of the accident. On his way, Francisco slipped and fell on a patch of ice. He now seeks to recover from Donna for her negligence.

Does Francisco qualify as a rescuer, thus making Donna's negligence a proximate cause of his injuries?

Sometimes the party providing assistance does so in a negligent manner and compounds the existing injury or causes a new one. One issue that might come up is whether the new act of negligence breaks the chain of causation for purposes of proximate cause analysis. In *Banks v. Elks Club Pride of Tennessee*, 301 S.W.3d 214 (Tenn. 2010), the plaintiff was injured when the chair she was sitting in collapsed, causing injury to her back. Roughly two months later, the plaintiff's doctor performed surgery but operated on the wrong part of her back, thereby aggravating the original injury. Citing the traditional rule in such cases, the Tennessee Supreme Court held that the alleged act of original negligence on the part of the Elks Club could still be a proximate cause of the subsequent injuries, despite the intervening negligence on the part of the surgeon. *Id.* at 227. "[I]f one is injured by the negligence of another, and these injuries are aggravated by medical treatment (either prudent or negligent), the negligence of the wrongdoer causing the original injury is regarded as [a] proximate cause of the damage subsequently flowing from the medical treatment." *Id.* at 217 n.3 (quoting *Transports, Inc. v. Perry*, 414 S.W.2d 1, 4–5 (1967)). The surgeon's actions could likewise be a proximate cause.

Problem 7.6. Elizabeth was rushed to the hospital after the light pole fell on her. After a week in the hospital, it was decided that Elizabeth needed spinal surgery. The surgeon who performed the surgery, Dr. Franklin, was an expert in the field but was negligent in performing the surgery. As a result, Elizabeth was paralyzed from the waist down and suffered continuous and extreme pain. While convalescing at a different facility, Elizabeth developed a staph infection due to the negligence of the facility.

Assuming Donna was negligent, was her negligence a proximate cause of Elizabeth's paralysis? Was the negligence a proximate cause of her staph infection?

Problem 7.7. Elizabeth was eventually released from the hospital. Her pain following the surgery was so severe that something as simple as having a sheet touch her legs resulted in extreme pain. Attempts to alleviate the pain were unsuccessful and Elizabeth was told that she would likely experience this sort of pain for the rest of her life. Eventually, she decided the pain was unbearable and took her own life. Research suggests that people with spinal cord injuries resulting in paralysis have a significantly higher suicide rate than the general population, a fact that Dr. Franklin, as a surgeon, was aware of.

In a wrongful death action brought by Elizabeth's family against Dr. Franklin, should Dr. Franklin's negligence be treated as a proximate cause of Elizabeth's death?

5. Fires

Cases involving negligence leading to fire that spreads to adjoining property potentially present a challenge for courts. In the nineteenth-century case of *Kellogg v. Chicago & Northwestern R. Co.*, 26 Wis. 223 (1870), for example, sparks from a wood-burning locomotive landed on fields near the railroad tracks, resulting in fire that spread to other areas, damaging barns and other property along the way. If foreseeability is the touchstone, the issue of proximate cause with respect to damage to the barns and other property would seem to be an easy one. As one judge in the case wrote, "It was apparent in this case . . . that, if set at the time and under the circumstances, [the fire] would prove destructive of the property of the plaintiff or of others . . . It required no prophetic vision to see this. It was a matter within the common experience of mankind." *Id.* at 236. Yet the majority rule that emerged from these cases was that the sparks were too remote a cause to be considered the proximate cause of resulting fire damage. Joseph A. Ranney, *Shaping Debate, Shaping Society: Three Wisconsin Chief Justices and Their Counterparts*, 81 MARQ. L. REV. 923, 936 n.59 (1998); Ryan v. N.Y. Central R. Co., 35 N.Y. 210 (1866). Legal historians have explained the outcomes in these cases "as a leading example of 19th century courts' desire to foster enterprise and economic growth even at the expense of uncompensated individual loss." Ranney, *supra*, at 936 n.59 (citing LAWRENCE M. FRIEDMAN, A HISTORY OF AMERICAN LAW 410–12 (1973); Robert Heidt, *The Avid Sportsman and the Scope for Self-Protection: When Exculpatory Clauses Should Be Enforced*, 38 U. RICH. L. REV. 381, 433 (2004) ("The courts appreciated . . . that the liability risks being insufficiently independent, liability insurers for the defendant could not diversify against this potentially huge liability risk at a reasonable cost.").

A more modern counter-example is *Oberg v. Dept. of Natural Resources*, 787 P.2d 918 (Wash. 1999) (en banc), which involved a lightning strike on the defendant's property. The lightning triggered what became known as the "Barker Mountain fire," which burned 25,000 acres. The defendant was allegedly negligent in permitting the fire to escape the defendant's property, and the fire ended up damaging the plaintiff's nearby properties (amounting to 5,000 acres). The jury found that the defendant's negligence was a proximate cause of the plaintiff's damages. The Washington Supreme Court affirmed the verdict on appeal. The dissenting judge in the case, citing a series of older decisions, argued that there was an intervening force that amounted to a superseding cause: 30 m.p.h. winds. *Id.* at 929–30 (Dore, CJ, dissenting); *see also* Jacobsen v. State, 769 P.2d 694 (Mont. 1989) (finding that it was not error to instruct the jury about superseding causes when an "unusually strong wind" caused a fire to spread to plaintiff's property).

Review Question

Doug's job required him to pay a visit to Blaze Manufacturing to repair a piece of equipment in the heat-treatment department of the factory. On the floor of the department were two cauldrons, approximately four feet high each. Sodium cyanide powder was placed in each cauldron and then two chains would be lowered into the cauldron, passing an electric current through the powder. The powder would then become a molten liquid and reach a heat of 800° centigrade. At that point, metal parts would be dipped into the cauldron to be treated. The covers for the cauldron were made of a compressed compound of asbestos and cement known as Sindanyo. Sindanyo had been used for this purpose for more than 20 years in the industry without incident. Workers in the facility typically stored the covers on a metal rack near the cauldrons. While Doug was in the factory, another worker named Edward carelessly knocked one of the covers loose so that it fell into the cauldron. The cover did not cause a splash, and no one was alarmed at the time. But approximately two minutes later, molten liquid erupted from the cauldron, burning Doug as he passed by. It was later learned through experiments that when Sindanyo is immersed in the molten liquid and subjected to a temperature of more than 500°C, it creates such an eruption. Doug sued Blaze Manufacturing on a negligence theory, alleging that Blaze was negligent in the manner in which it stored the covers. You can assume there is sufficient evidence for Doug to reach the jury on the issues of breach of duty and causation in fact. Was Blaze's negligence a proximate cause of Doug's injuries?

Chapter 8

Defenses

A. Contributory Negligence
- In general
- The status of the rule
- Other concepts developed in class or in readings assigned by the professor

B. Comparative Fault
- In general
- Apportioning fault
- Different forms of comparative fault
  - Pure
  - Modified
    - 51%/not greater than
    - 50%/equal to
- Comparative fault involving multiple tortfeasors
- Other concepts developed in class or in readings assigned by the professor

C. Assumption of Risk
- In general
- Express assumption of risk
  - In general
  - Public policy concerns/determining the validity of an agreement
- Implied primary assumption of risk (no duty/no breach)
  - In general
  - Inherent risks of an activity
  - Status of defense in comparative fault jurisdictions
  - Intentional misconduct in an activity
  - Firefighter's rule
- Implied secondary assumption of risk (comparative fault)
  - In general
  - Status of defense in comparative fault jurisdictions
- Other concepts developed in class or in readings assigned by the professor

Chapter Problem. Phyllis, Pat, and Pauline were all injured in separate accidents. Each seeks to recover based on the negligence of others.

If a plaintiff establishes a prima facie case of negligence, the burden at that point shifts to the defendant to establish an affirmative defense. If the defendant is unable to do so, the defendant is liable for the full range of the plaintiff's damages. This chapter examines the traditional defense of contributory negligence, how it gave way to a system of comparative fault, and where the concept of assumption of risk fits into the analysis.

A. Contributory Negligence

Butterfield v. Forrester

11 East 60
(King's Bench 1809)

This was an action on the case for obstructing a highway, by means of which obstruction the plaintiff, who was riding along the road, was thrown down with his horse, and injured, etc. At the trial before Bayley, J., at Derby, it appeared that the defendant, for the purpose of making some repairs to his house, which was close by the roadside at one end of the town, had put up a pole across part of the road, a free passage being left by another branch or street in the same direction. That the plaintiff left a public house not far distant from the place in question at 8 o'clock in the evening in August, when they were just beginning to light candles, but while there was light enough left to discern the obstruction at one hundred yards distance; and the witness who proved this, said that if the plaintiff had not been riding very hard he might have observed and avoided it; the plaintiff, however, who was riding violently, did not observe it, but rode against it, and fell with his horse and was much hurt in consequence of the accident; and there was no evidence of his being intoxicated at the time. On this evidence, Bayley, J., directed the jury, that if a person riding with reasonable and ordinary care could have seen and avoided the obstruction; and if they were satisfied that the plaintiff was riding along the street extremely hard, and without ordinary care, they should find a verdict for the defendant, which they accordingly did.

. . .

BAYLEY, J. The plaintiff was proved to be riding as fast as his horse could go, and this was through the streets of Derby. If he had used ordinary care he must have seen the obstruction; so that the accident appeared to happen entirely from his own fault.

LORD ELLENBOROUGH, C.J. A party is not to cast himself upon an obstruction which had been made by the fault of another, and avail himself of it, if he does not himself use common and ordinary caution to be in the right. In cases of persons riding upon what is considered to be the wrong side of the road, that would not authorize another purposely to ride up against them. One person being in fault will not dispense with another's using ordinary care for himself. Two things must concur to support this action: an obstruction in the road by the fault of the defendant, and no want of ordinary care to avoid it on the part of the plaintiff . . .

[New trial denied.]

Notes

Contributory negligence. The Supreme Judicial Court of Massachusetts considered an almost identical set of facts 15 years later and applied the rule from *Butterfield. See* Smith v. Smith, 19 Mass. 621, 624 (1824) (holding that the plaintiff could not recover "unless the plaintiff can show that he used ordinary care"). This rule of contributory fault, whereby the plaintiff's own fault effectively barred recovery, gradually became the norm in the United States.

Rationales for the defense. The justifications for the rule include the idea that "the plaintiff should be penalized for his misconduct; the plaintiff should be deterred from injuring himself; and the plaintiff's negligence supersedes the defendant's so as to render defendant's negligence no longer proximate." McIntyre v. Balentine, 833 S.W.2d 52 (Tenn. 1992).

Last clear chance. Under the last clear chance exception to the contributory fault rule, a plaintiff who is contributorily negligent is not barred from recovery if the defendant could still have avoided the accident through the exercise of reasonable care, *i.e.*, if the defendant had the last clear chance to avoid the accident. *See* Restatement (Second) of Torts § 479.

The status of the rule. As the *McIntyre* decision in the next section illustrates, only a handful of jurisdictions (Alabama, the District of Columbia, Maryland, North Carolina, and Virginia) retain the all-or-nothing defense of contributory fault found in *Butterfield* and *Smith.*

Problem 8.1. The City of Pleasant Hill installed a water meter in Phyllis' front yard a few years ago. One year ago, Phyllis notified the city that the metal cover on the meter was broken. The city replaced the cover, but Phyllis notified the city that the new cover did not fit and that if one were to step on the cover, the cover would give way and the person's leg would slip into the hole. The city failed to respond to Phyllis' repeated requests to fix the cover. A few months later, Phyllis was carrying a bag of leaves to the curb when she stepped on the cover. Her foot slid into the hole, causing her to suffer injuries. Phyllis sued the city. At her deposition, Phyllis explained that the lid was visible at the time and that she had simply forgotten about the defective cover when she was walking to the curb. The city has now asserted Phyllis' own negligence as a defense. What effect, if any, should Phyllis' actions have on her right to recover in a jurisdiction that still employs a system of contributory negligence?

B. Comparative Fault

1. In General

McIntyre v. Balentine

833 S.W.2d 52 (Tenn. 1992)

DROWOTA, Justice.

In this personal injury action, we granted Plaintiff's application for permission to appeal in order to decide whether to adopt a system of comparative fault in Tennessee. . . .

In the early morning darkness of November 2, 1986, Plaintiff Harry Douglas McIntyre and Defendant Clifford Balentine were involved in a motor vehicle accident resulting in severe injuries to Plaintiff. The accident occurred in the vicinity of Smith's Truck Stop in Savannah, Tennessee. As Defendant Balentine was traveling south on Highway 69, Plaintiff entered the highway (also traveling south) from the truck stop parking lot. Shortly after Plaintiff entered the highway, his pickup truck was struck by Defendant's Peterbilt tractor. At trial, the parties disputed the exact chronology of events immediately preceding the accident.

Both men had consumed alcohol the evening of the accident. After the accident, Plaintiff's blood alcohol level was measured at .17 percent by weight. Testimony suggested that Defendant was traveling in excess of the posted speed limit.

Plaintiff brought a negligence action against Defendant Balentine and Defendant East-West Motor Freight, Inc. Defendants answered that Plaintiff was contributorily negligent, in part due to operating his vehicle while intoxicated. After trial, the jury returned a verdict stating: "We, the jury, find the plaintiff and the defendant equally at fault in this accident; therefore, we rule in favor of the defendant." . . .

I.

The common law contributory negligence doctrine has traditionally been traced to Lord Ellenborough's opinion in *Butterfield v. Forrester*, 11 East 60, 103 Eng.Rep. 926 (1809). There, plaintiff, "riding as fast as his horse would go," was injured after running into an obstruction defendant had placed in the road. Stating as the rule that "[o]ne person being in fault will not dispense with another's using ordinary care," plaintiff was denied recovery on the basis that he did not use ordinary care to avoid the obstruction.

. . .

In Tennessee, the rule as initially stated was that "if a party, by his own gross negligence, brings an injury upon himself, or contributes to such injury, he cannot recover;" for, in such cases, the party "must be regarded as the author of his own misfortune." Whirley v. Whiteman, 38 Tenn. 610, 619 (1858). In subsequent decisions, we have continued to follow the general rule that a plaintiff's contributory negligence completely bars recovery.

Equally entrenched in Tennessee jurisprudence are exceptions to the general all-or-nothing rule: contributory negligence does not absolutely bar recovery where defendant's conduct was intentional; where defendant's conduct was "grossly" negligent; where defendant had the "last clear chance" with which, through the exercise of ordinary care, to avoid plaintiff's injury; or where plaintiff's negligence may be classified as "remote."

In contrast, comparative fault has long been the federal rule in cases involving injured employees of interstate railroad carriers, *see* Federal Employers' Liability Act, ch. 149, § 3, 35 Stat. 66 (1908) (codified at 45 U.S.C. § 53 (1988)), and injured seamen. *See* Death On The High Seas Act, ch. 111, § 6, 41 Stat. 537 (1920) (codified at 46 U.S.C. § 766 (1988)); Jones Act, ch. 250, § 33, 41 Stat. 1007 (1920) (codified as amended at 46 U.S.C. § 688 (1988)).

Similarly, by the early 1900s, many states, including Tennessee, had statutes providing for the apportionment of damages in railroad injury cases. While Tennessee's railroad statute did not expressly sanction damage apportionment, it was soon given that judicial construction. In 1856, the statute was passed in an effort to prevent railroad accidents; it imposed certain obligations and liabilities on railroads "for all damages accruing or resulting from a failure to perform said dut[ies]." . . . The statute was then judicially construed to permit the jury to consider "[n]egligence of the person injured, which caused, or contributed to cause the accident . . . in determining the amount of damages proper to be given for the injury." *Louisville & N.R.R. v. Burke*, 46 Tenn. 45, 51–52 (1868). . . .

Between 1920 and 1969, a few states began utilizing the principles of comparative fault in all tort litigation. Then, between 1969 and 1984, comparative fault replaced contributory negligence in 37 additional states. In 1991, South Carolina became the 45th state to adopt comparative fault, leaving Alabama, Maryland, North Carolina, Virginia, and Tennessee as the only remaining common law contributory negligence jurisdictions.

Eleven states have judicially adopted comparative fault. Thirty-four states have legislatively adopted comparative fault.

II.

Over 15 years ago, we stated, when asked to adopt a system of comparative fault:

> We do not deem it appropriate to consider making such a change unless and until a case reaches us wherein the pleadings and proof present an issue of contributory negligence accompanied by advocacy that the ends of justice will be served by adopting the rule of comparative negligence.

Street v. Calvert, 541 S.W.2d at 586. Such a case is now before us. After exhaustive deliberation that was facilitated by extensive briefing and argument by the parties, amicus curiae, and Tennessee's scholastic community, we conclude that it is time to abandon the outmoded and unjust common law doctrine of contributory negligence and adopt in its place a system of comparative fault. Justice simply will not permit our continued adherence to a rule that, in the face of a judicial determination that others bear primary responsibility, nevertheless completely denies injured litigants recompense for their damages.

We recognize that this action could be taken by our General Assembly. However, legislative inaction has never prevented judicial abolition of obsolete common law doctrines, especially those, such as contributory negligence, conceived in the judicial womb. Indeed, our abstinence would sanction "a mutual state of inaction in which the court awaits action by the legislature and the legislature awaits guidance from the court," thereby prejudicing the equitable resolution of legal conflicts.

Nor do we today abandon our commitment to *stare decisis.* While "[c]onfidence in our courts is to a great extent dependent on the uniformity and consistency engendered by allegiance to *stare decisis*, . . . mindless obedience to this precept can confound the truth and foster an attitude of contempt." *Hanover*, 809 S.W.2d at 898.

[The case was remanded for a new trial.]

Notes

Impact of the switch to comparative fault. One obvious impact of the switch to comparative fault is that it renders any of the associated exceptions to the contributory negligence rule (such as the last clear chance exception mentioned in *McIntyre*) obsolete. *See* McIntyre v. Balentine, 833 S.W.2d 52, 57 (Tenn. 1992). The switch also created other issues to resolve, including whether a plaintiff should be permitted to recover if the plaintiff was deemed more responsible than the defendant, and the impact on joint and several liability. These issues are discussed in Sections B2 and B3 below.

Apportioning Fault. As the following section discusses, jurors are instructed to assign responsibility between the parties in a comparative fault system. The *Restatement* lists two factors to consider in making this determination:

> (a) the nature of the person's risk-creating conduct, including any awareness or indifference with respect to the risks created by the conduct and any intent with respect to the harm created by the conduct; and
>
> (b) the strength of the causal connection between the person's risk-creating conduct and the harm.

Restatement (Third) of Torts § 8 (2000). Courts instruct juries on this issue in various ways. A decision from Louisiana lists the following factors as relevant in the apportioning of fault:

> (1) whether the conduct resulted from inadvertence or involved an awareness of the danger, (2) how great a risk was created by the conduct, (3) the significance of what was sought by the conduct, (4) the capacities of the actor, whether superior or inferior, and (5) any extenuating circumstances which might require the actor to proceed in haste, without proper thought.

Rideau v. State Farm Mut. Auto. Ins. Co., 970 So. 2d 564, 574 (La. Ct. App. 2007).

Some jurisdictions say that the comparison should be "upon the extent to which their respective negligent conduct contributed to the occurrence of the harmful event." In other words, the comparison involves a question of causation, not fault. *See* Moffitt v. Carroll, 640 A.2d 169 (Del. 1994). A Maine statute provides that where a plaintiff was also at fault, the plaintiff's damages "must be reduced to such extent as the jury thinks *just and equitable* having regard to the claimant's share in the responsibility for the damage." Maine Rev. Stat. Ann. § 156 (emphasis added).

The rescue doctrine. Chapter 7, which dealt with proximate cause, covered the rescue doctrine, under which the negligence of a defendant that places another in a position of peril is treated as a proximate cause of a rescuer's injuries. Another feature of the rescue doctrine relates to contributory fault. "A rescuer who voluntarily attempts to save the life or secure the safety of another person in peril is protected by the rescue doctrine from a claim of contributory negligence *unless the rescuer has acted rashly or recklessly.*" Reed v. Ault, 969 N.E.2d 515, 527 (Ill. Ct. App. 2012) (emphasis added).

2. Different Forms of Comparative Fault

There are two basic forms of comparative fault: pure or modified. The majority of jurisdictions have adopted a form of modified comparative fault. Within the modified form, there are two basic types. The statutes below provide examples of each form.

a. Pure (or Complete) Comparative Fault

Alaska Statutes § 09.17.060.
Effect of Contributory Fault

In an action based on fault seeking to recover damages for injury or death to a person or harm to property, contributory fault chargeable to the claimant diminishes proportionately the amount awarded as compensatory damages for the injury attributable to the claimant's contributory fault, but does not bar recovery.

b. Modified (or Incomplete) Comparative Fault

Hawaii Revised Statutes Annotated § 666-31
Contributory negligence no bar; comparative negligence; findings of fact and special verdicts

(a) Contributory negligence shall not bar recovery in any action by any person or the person's legal representative to recover damages for negligence resulting in death or in injury to person or property, if such negligence was not greater than the negligence of the person or in the case of more than one person, the aggregate negligence of such persons against whom recovery is sought, but any damages allowed shall be diminished in proportion to the amount of negligence attributable to the person for whose injury, damage or death recovery is made.

Colo. Rev. Stat. § 13-21-111

Negligence cases—comparative negligence as measure of damages

(1) Contributory negligence shall not bar recovery in any action by any person or his legal representative to recover damages for negligence resulting in death or in injury to person or property, if such negligence was not as great as the negligence of the person against whom recovery is sought, but any damages allowed shall be diminished in proportion to the amount of negligence attributable to the person for whose injury, damage, or death recovery is made.

Note

Approximately 21 jurisdictions utilize the 51%/"not greater than" modified approach used in Hawaii. Approximately 12 jurisdictions utilize the 50%/"not as great as" modified approach used in Colorado.

Problem 8.2. Refer back to the facts of Problem 8.1. Assume that Phyllis suffered $10,000 in damages.

(a) Assume you are on the jury in Phyllis' case. How would you apportion fault between Phyllis and the city?

(b) Assume the jury determines Phyllis to be 60% at fault. How much, if any, could Phyllis recover if the accident occurred in Pleasant Hill, Alaska?

(c) Assume the jury determines Phyllis to be 50% at fault. How much, if any, could Phyllis recover if the accident occurred in Pleasant Hill, Hawaii?

(d) Assume the jury determines Phyllis to be 50% at fault. How much, if any, could Phyllis recover if the accident occurred in Pleasant Hill, Colorado?

3. Other Issues Involved in the Comparative Fault Evaluation

In the simple case, there is one plaintiff and one defendant, and that defendant has adequate financial resources to cover a damages award. But tort cases are often more complicated than that. Sometimes there are multiple defendants, insolvent parties, cross claims, settlements between parties, and non-parties who nonetheless contributed to the plaintiff's injuries. States have adopted a variety of approaches to deal with the complexity. The proposed uniform law below from the National

Conference of Commissioners on Uniform State Laws (NCCUSL) is included as one example of how a state might deal with these sorts of issues. The problem that follows the Act involves the application of the rules from the Act.

Uniform Comparative Fault Act

§ 1. [Effect of Contributory Fault]

(a) In an action based on fault seeking to recover damages for injury or death to person or harm to property, any contributory fault chargeable to the claimant diminishes proportionately the amount awarded as compensatory damages for an injury attributable to the claimant's contributory fault, but does not bar recovery. . . .

§ 2. [Apportionment of Damages]

(a) In all actions involving fault of more than one party to the action, including third-party defendants and persons who have been released under Section 6, the court, unless otherwise agreed by all parties, shall instruct the jury to answer special interrogatories or, if there is no jury, shall make findings, indicating:

(1) the amount of damages each claimant would be entitled to recover if contributory fault is disregarded; and

(2) the percentage of the total fault of all of the parties to each claim that is allocated to each claimant, defendant, third-party defendant, and person who has been released from liability under Section 6. For this purpose the court may determine that two or more persons are to be treated as a single party.

(b) In determining the percentages of fault, the trier of fact shall consider both the nature of the conduct of each party at fault and the extent of the causal relation between the conduct and the damages claimed.

(c) The court shall determine the award of damages to each claimant in accordance with the findings, subject to any reduction under Section 6, and enter judgment against each party liable on the basis of rules of joint-and-several liability. For purposes of contribution under Sections 4 and 5, the court also shall determine and state in the judgment each party's equitable share of the obligation to each claimant in accordance with the respective percentages of fault.

(d) Upon motion made not later than [one year] after judgment is entered, the court shall determine whether all or part of a party's equitable share of the obligation is uncollectible from that party, and shall reallocate any uncollectible amount among the other parties, including a claimant at fault, according to their respective percentages of fault. The party whose liability is reallocated is nonetheless subject to contribution and to any continuing liability to the claimant on the judgment.

§ 3. [Set-off]

A claim and counterclaim shall not be set off against each other, except by agreement of both parties. On motion, however, the court, if it finds that the obligation of either party is likely to be uncollectible, may order that both parties make payment into court for distribution. The court shall distribute the funds received and declare obligations discharged as if the payment into court by either party had been a payment to the other party and any distribution of those funds back to the party making payment had been a payment to him by the other party.

§4. [Right of Contribution]

(a) A right of contribution exists between or among two or more persons who are jointly and severally liable upon the same indivisible claim for the same injury, death, or harm, whether or not judgment has been recovered against all or any of them. It may be enforced either in the original action or by a separate action brought for that purpose. The basis for contribution is each person's equitable share of the obligation, including the equitable share of a claimant at fault, as determined in accordance with the provisions of Section 2.

(b) Contribution is available to a person who enters into a settlement with a claimant only (1) if the liability of the person against whom contribution is sought has been extinguished and (2) to the extent that the amount paid in settlement was reasonable.

§5. [Enforcement of Contribution]

(a) If the proportionate fault of the parties to a claim for contribution has been established previously by the court, as provided by Section 2, a party paying more than his equitable share of the obligation, upon motion, may recover judgment for contribution.

(b) If the proportionate fault of the parties to the claim for contribution has not been established by the court, contribution may be enforced in a separate action, whether or not a judgment has been rendered against either the person seeking contribution or the person from whom contribution is being sought.

(c) If a judgment has been rendered, the action for contribution must be commenced within [one year] after the judgment becomes final. If no judgment has been rendered, the person bringing the action for contribution either must have (1) discharged by payment the common liability within the period of the statute of limitations applicable to the claimant's right of action against him and commenced the action for contribution within [one year] after payment, or (2) agreed while action was pending to discharge the common liability and, within [one year] after the agreement, have paid the liability and commenced an action for contribution.

§6. [Effect of Release].

A release, covenant not to sue, or similar agreement entered into by a claimant and a person liable discharges that person from all liability for contribution, but it does not discharge any other persons liable upon the same claim unless it so provides. However, the claim of the releasing person against other persons is reduced by the amount of the released person's equitable share of the obligation, determined in accordance with the provisions of Section 2.

Note

Fault of a non-party. What if one of the tortfeasors was unable to be located or is otherwise not made a party to the action? Is that individual's fault taken into account when the jury apportions fault? *McIntyre, supra*, held that "where a non-party caused or contributed to the injury or damage for which recovery is sought, . . . the trial court shall instruct the jury to assign this nonparty the percentage of the total negligence for which he is responsible." McIntyre v. Balentine, 833 S.W.2d 52, 58 (Tenn. 1992). In contrast, the Uniform Comparative Fault Act excludes the fault of nonparties in the jury's apportionment. Uniform Comparative Fault Act § 2 cmt.

Problem 8.3. Pat went out drinking with his friend Dale. The two men split a fifth of Vodka and a few beers. Dale then decided to drive over to a friend's house. Pat knew Dale was heavily intoxicated but chose to get in the car with him anyway. As they were driving, another car, driven by Dwight, came around a turn and veered into their lane. Dwight was traveling well in excess of the speed limit on this winding road. Had Dale not been so intoxicated, he probably could have avoided Dwight while keeping his car on the road. Unfortunately, he did not and Pat was injured in the ensuing collision. Pat suffered $100,000 in damages and has sued Dale and Dwight. Assume that the jury assigns 40% of the fault for Pat's injuries to Dale, 40% to Dwight, and 20% to Pat himself for having chosen to get into the car with Dale. Assume further that the relevant jurisdiction has adopted the Uniform Comparative Fault Act.

(a) Assume that all parties are solvent. How much could Pat collect in damages? How much could he collect from Dale?

(b) Assume for purposes of this question only that Dwight is insolvent. How much can Pat recover from Dale?

(c) Assume for purposes of this question only that Pat settles with Dwight before trial for $10,000. How much can Pat recover from Dale?

(d) Assume for purposes of this question only that Dwight and Dale were also injured when Dale's car collided with Dwight's. Dale suffered $50,000 in damages and Dwight suffered $100,000. Each has sued the other for negligence. The jury found Dale to be 60% at fault and Dwight to be 40% at fault. How does all of this affect each person's right to recover?

C. Assumption of Risk

The assumption of the risk doctrine was a relative late-comer in the law of negligence. The basic principle of this defense is easily stated: if a person

> voluntarily consents to accept the danger of a known and appreciated risk, that person may not sue another for failing to protect him from it. In practice, however, this principle proved easier to state than to apply.

Coomer v. Kansas City Royals Baseball Corp., 437 S.W.3d 184, 191 (Mo. 2014) (en banc).

Before most courts dispensed with the all-or-nothing defense of contributory negligence, assumption of the risk played an important role in negligence law. Like contributory negligence, the defense of assumption of risk served as a complete bar to recovery. The concept still plays a role, but the switch to comparative fault principles has altered the way in which most courts consider the concept. There are three types of assumption of risk cases: where the plaintiff (1) expressly consented to assume a known and understood risk ("express assumption of the risk"); (2) implicitly consented to assume a known and understood risk that was not created by the defendant's own negligence ("implied primary assumption of the risk"); and (3) implicitly consented to assume a known and understood risk that resulted from the defendant's own negligence, provided that the plaintiff acted unreasonably in doing so ("implied secondary assumption of the risk"). *Id.* at 192. The following part considers what is left of the defense now that most jurisdictions have switched to a form of a comparative fault.

1. Express Assumption of Risk

The leading case on the issue of express (or contractual) assumption of risk is *Tunkl v. Regents of Univ. of Cal.*, 383 P.2d 441 (Cal. 1963). In *Tunkl*, the plaintiff had signed a release absolving a hospital of all liability as a condition of admission to the hospital. The California Supreme Court listed several factors that might result in a waiver being held invalid:

> It concerns a business of a type generally thought suitable for public regulation. The party seeking exculpation is engaged in performing a service of great importance to the public, which is often a matter of practical necessity for some members of the public. The party holds himself out as willing to perform this service for any member of the public who seeks it, or at least for any member coming within certain established standards. As a result of the essential nature of the service, in the economic setting of the transaction, the party invoking exculpation possesses a decisive advantage of bargaining strength against any member of the public who seeks his services. In exercising a superior bargaining power the party confronts the public with a standardized adhesion contract of exculpation, and makes no provision whereby a purchaser may pay additional reasonable fees and obtain protection against negligence. Finally, as a result of the transaction, the person or property of the purchaser is placed under the control of the seller, subject to the risk of carelessness by the seller or his agents.

Id. at 444–45. The following case involves a court applying a similar approach in the case of a waiver.

Thompson v. Hi Tech Motorsports, Inc.

945 A.2d 368 (Vt. 2008)

REIBER, C.J.

The following facts are undisputed for purposes of summary judgment. In May 2003, plaintiff went to defendant's motorcycle dealership to test drive a motorcycle. Plaintiff spoke with a salesperson and indicated that although she was a relatively new rider, she had a valid motorcycle driver's license and had experience riding a motorcycle with a 200cc engine. After further discussion with the salesperson, plaintiff signed a single-page release.[1] Then, as part of a group, plaintiff took a promotional test ride on a 750cc motorcycle. During the test ride, as plaintiff was turning, she downshifted, but was unable to control the bike, and she hit a guardrail, injuring herself.

Plaintiff filed a suit for damages in superior court, claiming that defendant's agents were negligent in encouraging her to ride a bike that they knew or should have known was too big for plaintiff and that she could not operate safely. Defendant filed a motion for summary judgment, claiming that the release plaintiff signed discharged it as a matter of law from any liability for her injuries. Plaintiff filed a cross-motion for partial summary judgment, arguing that the release was contrary to public policy. The trial court resolved both motions on the same day in single-line orders. First, the court denied defendant's motion, concluding that there were "factual disputes concerning the representations made by the defendant's salesman." Second, the court granted plaintiff's motion for partial summary judgment, concluding simply that "defendant's release was void for being contrary to public policy." The trial court granted defendant permission to appeal, and this Court accepted review of the question of whether the release is void as contrary to public policy.

...

I.

First, we consider whether the release is void as contrary to public policy. As we have explained in the past, evaluating whether a release from liability contravenes public policy does not follow a strict formula because "no single formula will reach the relevant public policy issues in every factual context." *Dalury v. S-K-I,*

1. The undersigned hereby acknowledges that he/she has had prior experience with the operation of a motorcycle . . . , has a valid motor vehicle operator's license with a motorcycle endorsement . . . , and that he/she has examined the vehicle to be test driven, and is familiar with its operation. He/she understands that the operation of this vehicle is inherently dangerous. He/she understands that the operation of this vehicle may result in serious injury or even death and accepts these risks in test driving a Land-Air vehicle. . . .

The undersigned waives any claim that he/she may have now or in the future against Land-Air, its employees, agents, officers, directors and shareholders for injury to him/her self as a result of his/her operation or the operation by some other person of a motorized vehicle owned by or under the control of Land-Air.

Ltd., 164 Vt. 329, 333, 670 A.2d 795, 798 (1995). Rather, we consider the totality of the circumstances and societal expectations to determine whether sufficient public interest exists to void a release. Although the public interest cannot be determined through a formulaic approach, some relevant characteristics of a public interest are the nature of the parties' relationship, including whether the party granting exculpation is in a position of dependency, and the type of service provided by the party seeking exculpation, including whether the service is laden with public interest. *See* Restatement (Third) of Torts: Apportionment of Liab. §2 cmt. e (2000); *see also Tunkl v. Regents of Univ. of Cal.*, 60 Cal.2d 92, 32 Cal.Rptr. 33, 383 P.2d 441, 445–46 (1963) (listing characteristics of contracts that affect a public interest).

Although we recognize the great public need for motorcycle safety, we conclude that the waiver of liability in this case for injuries occurring on test drives does not contravene public policy. We are so persuaded given the nature of the service that defendant provides, the lack of control defendant exercises over those test-driving its vehicles, and the absence of legislative policy to regulate or control dealerships.

We agree with defendant that this case is distinguishable from *Dalury v. S-K-I, Ltd.*, wherein we concluded that a ski resort could not exculpate itself from negligence liability through a release. In *Dalury*, a skier sued a ski area where he fell and was injured, claiming that the premises was negligently designed. We concluded that the release was void because it contravened a strong tradition of public policy that placed the responsibility for proper maintenance of grounds on those who own and control the property. We reasoned that "if defendants were permitted to obtain broad waivers of their liability, an important incentive for ski areas to manage risk would be removed, with the public bearing the cost of the resulting injuries." We concluded that "[i]t is illogical, in these circumstances, to undermine the public policy underlying business invitee law and allow skiers to bear risks they have no ability or right to control."

The same concerns, which prompted our decision in *Dalury*, are not present here because whereas public policy places the burden of maintaining safe premises on a landowner, public policy concerning motorcycle safety places the burden of safe driving on the operator of the motorcycle. In *Dalury*, we emphasized that the defendant ski area had the unique opportunity and means "to foresee and control hazards" on its premises, thus it was logical for the ski area to bear the risk of a negligently designed or maintained ski area. In contrast, dealerships, like defendant, do not have the opportunity or means to control a prospective customer's driving capability. Persons, who choose to take defendant's motorcycles out for a test ride, have the ability to undertake precautions to avoid hazards associated with operation, unlike skiers who "are not in a position to discover and correct risks of harm" on a ski hill.

...

Furthermore, we conclude that in undertaking to retail motorcycles by providing test drives, defendant is neither "performing a service of great importance to the public, which is often matter of practical necessity for some members of the public," nor holding itself "out as willing to perform this service for any member of the public who seeks it." *Tunkl*, 32 Cal.Rptr. 33, 383 P.2d at 445. Motorcycle dealerships do not provide a public service, which is a necessity for some members of the public. *See Jones v. Dressel*, 623 P.2d 370, 377 (Colo.1981) (concluding that flight service for parachute jumping was not a matter of public interest); *Mann v. Wetter*, 100 Or.App. 184, 785 P.2d 1064, 1066–67 (1990) (holding that diving school did not provide an essential public service); *Blide v. Rainier Mountaineering, Inc.*, 30 Wash.App. 571, 636 P.2d 492, 493 (1981) (holding that mountaineering does not implicate the public interest). In addition, unlike the ski area in *Dalury* that advertised to and invited all members of the general public, even those with no experience, defendant made no representation that it was making its motorcycles available to all members of the public or that it was providing training in the proper use of motorcycles. Defendant allowed only those persons who attested in a signed release that they were properly licensed with a motorcycle endorsement and had sufficient relevant experience and training to take defendant's bikes for a test ride.

In reply, plaintiff argues that if the release is upheld, this will (1) provide a disincentive for dealers to conduct test rides safely; and (2) contravene legislative intent to promote motorcycle safety. We are not persuaded. First, rather than encouraging all persons to drive their vehicles, including those with no experience, defendant requires prospective drivers to attest, in the release, that they have "prior experience with operation" of the relevant vehicle, have a valid license with the relevant endorsement, have examined the vehicle and are familiar with the vehicle's operation. Furthermore, as explained above, during the test drive the prospective buyer, not the dealer, has control of the motorcycle. It is logical to place the incentive for safe driving on the party who has actual control of the vehicle.

Second, there is no existing public policy, as evidenced through legislative enactment, which strives to promote motorcycle safety through regulation either of motorcycle dealerships in general or their test-drive practices in particular. Although motorcycle safety is an important public concern and motorcycle use is highly regulated, the motorcycle-safety statutes focus on the driver's responsibilities to be properly trained, to follow correct driving techniques and to wear appropriate equipment. Given this focus, we conclude that public policy, in general and as expressed through statute, does not prevent a motorcycle dealership from limiting its liability for injuries sustained during a test ride.

...

II.

Having concluded that the release is not void on its face for public policy reasons, we consider the scope of the release to determine if it covers actions for defendant's ordinary negligence. Plaintiff concedes that she read and signed defendant's release, which states, in relevant part:

> The undersigned waives *any* claim that he/she may have now or in the future against Land-Air, its employees, agents, officers, directors and shareholders for injury to him/her self as a result of his/her operation or the operation by some other person of a motorized vehicle owned by or under the control of Land-Air.

(Emphasis added.) Although the release does not include the word negligence, defendant contends that the release unambiguously includes "any claim," and consequently applies to negligence claims as a matter of law. We disagree.

As with other contract provisions, we interpret those limiting tort liability based on the language of the writing, and where that language is clear, we must implement the intent and understanding of the parties. At the same time, we have cautioned that contractual exclusions of negligence liability are traditionally disfavored, and thus their interpretation requires more exacting judicial scrutiny. In applying this heightened judicial scrutiny, we strictly construe an exculpatory agreement against the party relying on it. We have explained that "[t]he most effective way for parties to express an intention to release one party from liability flowing from that party's own negligence is to provide explicitly that claims based in negligence are included in the release." Although this language is not essential, in its absence there must be words that convey a similar intent.

In *Colgan v. Agway, Inc.*, we concluded that a waiver in the parties' construction contract did not cover claims for the builder's negligence. 150 Vt. at 375, 553 A.2d at 145. Our decision was grounded on the wording and organization of the parties' contract. The exculpatory language the defendant relied on was embedded in a paragraph entitled "One Year Limited Warranty," and focused solely on liability for workmanship and materials. In addition, although the contract used particular language in other areas to describe the parties' respective obligations, the contract did not employ the word negligence. We concluded that "[g]iven the manner in which the remainder of the contract is drafted, it defies both logic and common sense that the parties would intend to release the seller from all liability arising out of defective design of the structure by tacking broad exculpatory language to the end of a limited warranty clause."

Just as the organization of the parties' contract in *Colgan* persuaded us that it did not cover negligence claims, we conclude that this release does not exculpate defendant from liability arising out of its own negligence. Defendant correctly notes that the release contains broad language purporting to release any claim. The question is whether this general clause is specific enough to release defendant from liability, given that when a party wishes to exculpate itself from negligence liability "a greater degree of clarity is necessary to make the exculpatory clause effective than would be required for other types of contract provisions." *Id.* at 375, 553 A.2d at 145. The opening paragraph of the release recites that operating a motorcycle is inherently dangerous and that operation may result in injury. The release then waives "any claim" resulting from the operation. Based on this language, we conclude that the release waived claims for injuries resulting from dangers inherent to riding a motorcycle, not for those resulting from defendant's negligence. Although plaintiff waived claims for injuries resulting from dangers inherent in riding a motorcycle, the release did not cover claims for injury resulting from defendant's alleged negligent representations to plaintiff. *See* Sirek v. Fairfield Snowbowl, Inc., 166 Ariz. 183, 800 P.2d 1291, 1295 (1990) (concluding that language in a release for ski rental alerted renter to "the dangers inherent in skiing," but did not alert renter that she was also releasing ski area for "its own negligence in selecting appropriate skis or properly setting the bindings"); *Turnbough v. Ladner*, 754 So.2d 467, 469 (Miss.1999) (holding that release that participant in scuba diving class signed waived claims associated with risks inherent in sport, but did not waive right to recover for instructor's failure to follow accepted safety standards).

This interpretation is supported by the Alaska Supreme Court's decision in *Moore v. Hartley Motors Inc.*, 36 P.3d at 633, which involved a similarly worded release. In *Moore*, the plaintiff signed a release before beginning an ATV instruction class. After noting that the release did not contain the word negligence, the court observed that the release's "opening sentences refer only to unavoidable and inherent risks of ATV riding, and nothing in its ensuing language suggests an intent to release [the defendants] from liability for acts of negligence unrelated to those inherent risks." The court concluded that the plaintiff released the defendants "only from liability arising from the inherent risks of ATV riding and ordinary negligence associated with those inherent risks."

Similarly, we conclude that plaintiff released defendant from liability associated with the inherent dangers of riding a motorcycle but did not release defendant from injuries caused by its own negligence.

Remanded for further proceedings consistent with this opinion.

Notes

Conspicuousness of the release. In considering whether there was truly a meeting of the minds and the plaintiff truly assumed the relevant risk, courts often look to whether the language releasing the defendant from liability was conspicuous in nature, including how the release appears in the agreement. *See* Bagley v. Mt. Bachelor, Inc., 340 P.3d 27, 38 (Ore. 2014); Donahue v. Ledgends, Inc., 331 P.3d 342, 350 (Alaska 2014).

Recreational activities. *Thompson* references several other decisions involving defendants who offer recreational activities as opposed to more essential services like the medical care at issue in *Tunkl*. One common scenario involves skiing or snowboarding. Courts have sometimes reached different conclusions as to whether waivers releasing ski resort operators from liability for their own negligence are enforceable. *See* Bagley v. Mt. Bachelor, Inc., 340 P.3d 27, 38 (Or. 2014) (refusing to enforce agreement releasing ski area operator from negligence claims involving snowboarding); Chepkevich v. Hidden Valley Resort, L.P., 2 A.3d 1174 (Pa. 2010) (concluding agreement barring negligence claims was enforceable in case involving skier injured attempting to board ski lift).

Exculpatory clauses and minors. Many courts are unwilling to enforce releases signed by parents on behalf of their children who participate in sporting or recreational activities. *See* Childress v. Madison County, 777 S.W.2d 1, 6–7 (Tenn. Ct. App. 1989) (listing decisions). *But see* Colo. Rev. Stat. 13-22-107(3) (overruling judicial decision and allowing parents to "release or waive the child's prospective claim for negligence" on the grounds "that parents have a fundamental right to make decisions on behalf of their children, including deciding whether the children should participate in risky activities"). One common justification for refusing to enforce such agreements is that a parent or guardian cannot contract away the minor's rights and minors lack the capacity to enter into such agreements. *See* Woodman ex rel. Woodman v. Kera LLC, 785 N.W.2d 1, 5 (Mich. 2010).

Gross negligence and recklessness. The "overwhelming majority" of states hold that releases for reckless or grossly negligent conduct are unenforceable on public policy grounds. Tayar v. Camelback Ski Corp., Inc., 47 A.3d 1190, 1202 (Pa. 2012); Forman v. Brown, 944 P.2d 559, 564 (Colo. App. 1996).

Problem 8.4. When Pauline joined the Workout Now! Fitness Club, she signed a membership contract. Paragraph 7 of the contract consisted of the following exculpatory clause:

> By the use of the facilities of Seller and/or by the attendance at any of the gymnasiums owned by Seller, the Member expressly agrees that Seller shall not be liable for any damages arising from personal injuries sustained by the Member or his guest in, on or about the premises of the said gymnasiums or as a result of their using the facilities and the equipment therein. By the execution of this agreement Member assumes full responsibility of any such injuries or damages which may occur to the Member or guest in, on or about the said gymnasiums. Member assumes full responsibility for any injuries, damages or losses which may occur to Member or guest in, on or about the premises of said gymnasiums and does hereby fully and forever release and discharge Seller and all associated gymnasiums, their owners, employees and agents from any and all claims, demands, damages, rights of action, or causes of action, present or future, whether the same be known or unknown, anticipated, or unanticipated, resulting from or arising out of the Member's or his guests' use or intended use of the said gymnasium or the facilities and equipment thereof.

Pauline suffered injuries to her mouth and jaw while using an upright row machine at Fitness Now! The handle on the equipment detached from a weight cable and smashed into her face. The handle was connected to the weight cable by means of a pigtail hook. The clevis, a part which attached to the pigtail hook and ensured that the handle would not disengage from the cable, was missing. As a result of the accident, Pauline required extensive dental treatment, which ultimately required surgery. She has now sued Workout Now! for alleged negligence in failing to inspect and maintain its equipment.

(a) Will the exculpatory clause bar her recovery?

(b) If you represented Workout Now!, how would you advise the company to rewrite Paragraph 7?

2. Implied Primary Assumption of Risk (No Duty/No Breach of Duty)

Murphy v. Steeplechase Co., Inc.

166 N.E. 173 (N.Y. 1929)

CARDOZO, C. J.

The defendant, Steeplechase Amusement Company maintains, an amusement park at Coney Island, N.Y. One of the supposed attractions is known as 'the Flopper.' It is a moving belt, running upward on an inclined plane, on which passengers sit or stand. Many of them are unable to keep their feet because of the movement of the belt, and are thrown backward or aside. The belt runs in a groove, with padded walls on either side to a height of four feet, and with padded flooring beyond the walls at the same angle as the belt. An electric motor, driven by current furnished by the Brooklyn Edison Company, supplies the needed power.

Plaintiff, a vigorous young man, visited the park with friends. One of them, a young woman, now his wife, stepped upon the moving belt. Plaintiff followed and stepped behind her. As he did so, he felt what he describes as a sudden jerk, and was thrown to the floor. His wife in front and also friends behind him were thrown at the same time. Something more was here, as every one understood, than the slowly moving escalator that is common is shops and public places. A fall was foreseen as one of the risks of the adventure. There would have been no point to the whole thing, no adventure about it, if the risk had not been there. The very name, above the gate, 'the Flopper,' was warning to the timid. If the name was not enough, there was warning more distinct in the experience of others. We are told by the plaintiff's wife that the members of her party stood looking at the sport before joining in it themselves. Some aboard the belt were able, as she viewed them, to sit down with decorum or even to stand and keep their footing; others jumped or fell. The tumbling bodies and the screams and laughter supplied the merriment and fun. 'I took a chance,' she said when asked whether she thought that a fall might be expected.

Plaintiff took the chance with her, but, less lucky than his companions, suffered a fracture of a knee cap. . . .

. . .

Volenti non fit injuria. One who takes part in such a sport accepts the dangers that inhere in it so far as they are obvious and necessary, just as a fencer accepts the risk of a thrust by his antagonist or a spectator at a ball game the chance of contact with the ball. The antics of the clown are not the paces of the cloistered cleric. The rough and boisterous joke, the horseplay of the crowd, evokes its own guffaws, but they are not the pleasures of tranquility. The plaintiff was not seeking a retreat for meditation. Visitors were tumbling about the belt to the merriment of onlookers when he made his choice to join them. He took the chance of a like fate, with whatever damage to his body might ensue from such a fall. The timorous may stay at home.

Coomer v. Kansas City Royals Baseball Corp.

437 S.W.3d 184 (Mo. 2014) (en banc)

PAUL C. WILSON, Judge.

Background

Coomer is a longtime baseball fan and frequent spectator at Royals games in Kauffman Stadium. On September 8, 2009, he brought his father along to watch the Royals host the Detroit Tigers. Only about 12,000 people were on hand to watch the game because it had rained most of the day. With such a small crowd, Coomer and his father left their assigned seats early in the game and moved to empty seats six rows behind the visitor's dugout.

Shortly after Coomer changed seats, Sluggerrr [the Kansas City Royals mascot] mounted the visitor's dugout to begin the "Hotdog Launch," a feature of every Royals home game since 2000. The launch occurs between innings, when Sluggerrr uses an air gun to shoot hotdogs from the roof of the visitor's dugout to fans seated beyond hand-tossing range. When his assistants are reloading the air gun, Sluggerrr tosses hotdogs by hand to the fans seated nearby. Sluggerrr generally tossed the hotdogs underhand while facing the fans but sometimes throws overhand, behind his back, and side-armed.

Coomer estimates that he attended 175 Royals games before this game in September 2009. He admits that he frequently watched Sluggerrr toss hotdogs from the roof of the visitor's dugout and, on September 8, he saw Sluggerrr mount the dugout to begin the Hotdog Launch. Coomer and his father were seated approximately 15 to 20 feet from Sluggerrr, directly in his view. After employing his hotdog-shaped airgun to send hotdogs to distant fans, Sluggerrr began to toss hotdogs by hand to fans seated near Coomer. Coomer testified that he saw Sluggerrr turn away from the crowd as if to prepare for a behind-the-back throw, but, because Coomer chose that moment to turn and look at the scoreboard, he admits he never saw Sluggerrr throw the hotdog that he claims injured him. Coomer testified only that a "split second later . . . something hit me in the face," and he described the blow as "pretty forceful."

Coomer did not report this incident to the Royals when it happened because he did not realize he had been injured. Instead, he stayed for most of the rest of Tuesday's game (a thrilling 7–5 effort that snapped the first-place Tigers' six-game winning streak) and even returned to Kauffmann Stadium the following night to witness the Royals' further 5–1 drubbing of the Tigers. Thursday morning, however, Coomer felt he was "seeing differently" and something "wasn't right" with his left eye. The problem progressed until, approximately eight days after the incident, Coomer saw a doctor and was diagnosed with a detached retina. Coomer underwent surgeries to repair the retina and to remove a "traumatic cataract" in the same eye.

Coomer reported his injury to the Royals in September 2009, eight days after it occurred. In February 2010, Coomer filed this lawsuit alleging one count of negligence and one count of battery. Regarding the negligence count, Coomer asserted that the Royals (through its employee, Sluggerrr) failed to exercise ordinary care in throwing hotdogs into the stands, that the team failed to adequately train Sluggerrr on how to throw hotdogs into the stand safely, and that the team failed to adequately supervise Sluggerrr's hotdog toss. In its answer, the Royals admitted responsibility for Sluggerrr's acts but denied he had been negligent. The Royals also asserted affirmative defenses of assumption of the risk and comparative fault.

. . .

At the close of the evidence, Coomer moved for a directed verdict on the issues of comparative fault and assumption of the risk. He argued that implied primary assumption of the risk "only applies to risks that are inherent in the nature of the activity" and, in this case, "the harm of getting hit with a hotdog has absolutely no relationship to going to a baseball game." Regarding comparative fault, Coomer argued that, as a matter of law, he cannot have been negligent merely for not fleeing his seat during the Hotdog Launch. The trial court overruled Coomer's motion, holding that both (a) whether the risk of being injured by Sluggerrr's hotdog toss is one of the risks inherent in watching a Royals game and (b) the reasonableness of Coomer's actions were proper questions for the jury.

. . .

The jury returned a verdict in favor of the Royals. The verdict form states that the jury assessed zero percent of fault to the Royals and 100 percent of fault to Coomer, but it does not disclose the basis for this decision. Coomer moved for judgment notwithstanding the verdict and for a new trial based on the arguments asserted in his directed verdict motion and in his objections to the jury instructions. The trial court overruled Coomer's motions and entered judgment for the Royals. Coomer appeals and, after granting transfer, this Court has jurisdiction.

Analysis

This case presents the question of whether the century-old affirmative defense commonly referred to as "assumption of the risk" survived this Court's adoption of comparative fault in *Gustafson v. Benda*, 661 S.W.2d 11 (Mo. Banc 1983). To the extent it survives, Coomer claims that the application of this doctrine is to be decided by the court and not the jury. The Court agrees. Because the trial court erred in submitting the question of assumption of the risk to the jury, the judgment in this case must be vacated and the matter remanded.

I. Assumption of the Risk in a post-*Gustafson* World

The simplest application of [the assumption of risk] doctrine recognizes that, when a plaintiff makes an express statement that he is voluntarily accepting a specified risk, the plaintiff is barred from recovering damages for an injury resulting from that risk. This application (*i.e.*, "express assumption of the risk") most often involves a written waiver or release by the would-be plaintiff, but it can be based on any form of any explicit acquiescence.

In most cases, however, the plaintiff's consent cannot be proved so easily. There, the defendant contends that the plaintiff's voluntary acceptance of a known and appreciated risk should be inferred from the plaintiff's conduct and the surrounding circumstances....

When the risk arises from the circumstances (*e.g.*, from ... the inherent nature of the defendant's activity), "implied primary assumption of the risk" completely bars recovery by a plaintiff who knowingly and voluntarily encounters that risk.

The version of comparative fault adopted by this Court in *Gustafson* fundamentally altered [the] landscape [of contributory fault]. Section 1(a) of the Uniform Comparative Fault Act (the "UCFA") provides that "any contributory fault chargeable to the claimant diminishes proportionately the amount awarded as compensatory damages for an injury attributable to the claimant's contributory fault, but does not bar recovery." *Gustafson*, 661 S.W.2d at 18 (quoting from the UCFA, which is set forth in full in an appendix to that opinion). Section 1(b) of the UCFA defines "fault" for purposes of section 1(a) to include "unreasonable assumption of risk not constituting an enforceable express consent." *Id.*

... *Gustafson* does not reject or abandon "express assumption of the risk." Though this application of the assumption of the risk doctrine always has been subject to certain limitations as a matter of public policy, *Gustafson* and the adoption of comparative fault have no effect on this application or its limitations. This is because, in an "express assumption of the risk" case, the plaintiff's consent relieves the defendant of any duty to protect the plaintiff from injury. As a result, the defendant cannot be negligent and there is no "fault" to which the jury can compare the plaintiff's fault.

By the same token, *Gustafson* has no effect on the continued viability of "implied primary assumption of the risk." This is because, under the law of Missouri and most other jurisdictions, implied primary assumption of the risk "is ***not really an*** *affirmative defense*; rather, it indicates that the defendant ***did not even owe the plaintiff any duty of care.*** *Krause*, 787 S.W.2d at 711–12 (emphasis added). With no duty to protect the plaintiff, the defendant cannot be negligent and there is no "fault" for the jury to compare under comparative fault principles.

Missouri's characterization of the implied primary assumption of the risk doctrine in terms of "duty" is decidedly mainstream:

> Like express assumption of the risk, "'primary' implied assumption of the risk. . . . is really a principle of no duty, or no negligence, and so denies the existence of any cause of action."

W. Page Keeton, *PROSSER AND KEETON ON TORTS*, at 496–97 (5th ed.1984).

Accordingly, . . . because the "express" and "implied primary" applications of assumption of the risk result in determinations that the defendant has no duty to protect the plaintiff, the form of comparative fault adopted in *Gustafson* does not preclude these applications as a complete—not merely a partial—bar to the plaintiff's recovery.

II. Implied Primary Assumption of the Risk and the "Baseball Rule"

One of the most interesting—and certainly the most relevant—applications of implied primary assumption of the risk involves certain risks assumed by spectators at sporting events. Long before the Kansas City Athletics moved to Oakland and the fledging Royals joined the Junior Circuit, an overwhelming majority of courts recognized that spectators at sporting events are exposed to certain risks that are inherent merely in watching the contest. Accordingly, under what is described above as implied primary assumption of the risk, these courts held that the home team was not liable to a spectator injured as a result of such risks. *See* Augustine, *Who Is Responsible When Spectators Are Injured While Attending Professional Sporting Events?*, 2008 Den. U. Sports & Ent. L.J. 39, 42–46 (2008) ("When Spectators Are Injured ").

The archetypal example of this application of implied primary assumption of the risk is when a baseball park owner fails to protect each and every spectator from the risk of being injured by a ball or bat flying into the stands. Just as Missouri teams have led (and continue to lead) professional baseball on the field, Missouri courts helped lead the nation in defining this area of the law off the field. More than 50 years ago, this Court was one of the first to articulate the so-called "Baseball Rule:"

> [W]here a baseball game is being conducted under the customary and usual conditions prevailing in baseball parks, it is not negligence to fail to protect all seats in the park by wire netting, and that the special circumstances and specific negligence pleaded did not aid plaintiff or impose upon the defendant a duty to warn him against hazards which are necessarily incident to baseball and are perfectly obvious to a person in possession of his faculties.

Anderson v. Kansas City Baseball Club, 231 S.W.2d 170, 172 (Mo.1950) (emphasis added).

Anderson was based on this Court's earlier decision in *Hudson v. Kansas City Baseball Club*, 349 Mo. 1215, 164 S.W.2d 318, 320 (1942), which used the "no duty" language of implied primary assumption of the risk to explain its holding:

> The basis of the proprietor's liability is his superior knowledge and if his invitee knows of the condition or hazard there is no duty on the part of the proprietor to warn him and there is no liability for resulting injury because the invitee has as much knowledge as the proprietor does and then by voluntarily acting, in view of his knowledge, assumes the risks and dangers incident to the known condition.

Hudson, 164 S.W.2d at 323 (emphasis added) (applying Restatement (Second) of Torts, § 343).

. . .

Anderson and *Hudson* are just two of the many dozens of cases around the country holding that, as long as some seats directly behind home plate are protected, the team owes "no duty" to spectators outside that area who are injured by a ball or bat while watching a baseball game. Despite being decided by such different courts across so many decades, all of these cases reflect certain shared principles. First, it is not possible for baseball players to play the game without occasionally sending balls or bats (or parts of bats) into the stands, sometimes at unsafe speeds. Second, it is not possible for the home team to protect each and every spectator from such risks without fundamentally altering the game or the spectators' experience of watching it through such means as: (a) substituting foam rubber balls and bats that will not injure anyone (or be very fun to watch); (b) erecting a screen or other barrier around the entire field protecting all spectators while obstructing their view and making them feel more removed from the action; or (c) moving all spectators at least 600 feet away from home plate in all directions. Third, ordinary negligence principles do not produce reliably acceptable results in these circumstances because the risk of injury (and the extent of the harm) to spectators is substantial, yet the justification for not protecting spectators from that risk can be expressed only in terms of the amusement or entertainment value of watching the sport that brought the spectators to the stadium in the first place.

. . .

[E]ven though the "no duty" rationale of the Baseball Rule applies to risks inherent in watching a baseball game, the home team still owes a duty of reasonable care not to ***alter or increase*** such inherent risks. One example, useful both for its facts and its analysis, is *Lowe v. California League of Prof. Baseball*, 56 Cal.App.4th 112, 65 Cal.Rptr.2d 105 (1997). . . .

In *Lowe*, . . . even though the plaintiff was struck by a foul ball, he claimed that his injuries were not caused by that inherent risk. Instead, the plaintiff claimed he was prevented from watching for foul balls because he was repeatedly jostled and distracted by the team's dinosaur mascot. The court agreed that the Baseball Rule did not bar such a claim:

> ***[T]he key inquiry here is whether the risk which led to plaintiff's injury involved some feature or aspect of the game which is inevitable or unavoidable in the actual playing of the game.*** . . . Can [this] be said about the antics of the mascot? ***We think not.*** Actually, the . . . person who dressed up as Tremor, recounted that there were occasional games played when he was not there. In view of this testimony, as a matter of law, we hold that the antics of the mascot are not an essential or integral part of the playing of a baseball game. In short, the game can be played in the absence of such antics.

Id. (emphasis added).

. . .

Accordingly, the proper application of implied primary assumption of the risk in this case—unaffected by *Gustafson*—is this: if Coomer was injured by a risk that is an inherent part of watching the Royals play baseball, the team had no duty to protect him and cannot be liable for his injuries. But, if Coomer's injury resulted from a risk that is not an inherent part of watching baseball in person—or if the negligence of the Royals altered or increased one of these inherent risks and caused Coomer's injury—the jury is entitled to hold the Royals liable for such negligence and, to the extent the reasonableness of Coomer's actions are in dispute, the jury must apportion fault between the parties using comparative fault principles. This approach has been used in Missouri and around the country.

> Therefore, in the sports context, under comparative fault, if the plaintiff's ***injury is the result of a risk inherent in the sport in which he was participating, the defendant is relieved from liability*** on the grounds that by participating in the sport, the plaintiff assumed the risk and the defendant never owed the plaintiff a duty to protect him from that risk. ***If on the other hand, the plaintiff's injury is the result of negligence on the part of the defendant***, the issue regarding the plaintiff's assumption of that risk and whether it was a reasonable assumption of risk, is ***an element of fault to be compared to the defendant's negligence*** by the jury.

Sheppard, 904 S.W.2d at 263–64 (emphasis added).

III. Implied Primary Assumption of the Risk is a Question of Law

. . . As explained above, the doctrine of implied primary assumption of the risk negates any duty the defendant otherwise may have owed the plaintiff. The question of whether and to what extent the defendant owes a duty to the plaintiff is always a question for the court, not the jury.

IV. Being Injured by Sluggerrr's Hotdog Toss is Not a Risk Inherent in Watching Royals Baseball

. . .

Some fans may find Sluggerrr's hotdog toss fun to watch between innings, and some fans may even have come to expect it, but this does not make the risk of injury from Sluggerrr's hotdog toss an "inherent risk" of watching a Royals game. As noted above, "inherent" means "***structural*** or involved in the ***constitution or essential character*** of something: belonging ***by nature or settled habit,***" *Webster's Third New International Dictionary* (1966), at 1163 (emphasis added). There is nothing about the risk of injury from Sluggerrr's hotdog toss that is "structural" or involves the "constitution or essential character" of watching a Royals game at Kauffman Stadium.

. . .

Accordingly, the Court holds as a matter of law that the risk of injury from Sluggerrr's hotdog toss is not one of the risks inherent in watching the Royals play baseball that Coomer assumed merely by attending a game at Kauffman Stadium. This risk can be increased, decreased or eliminated altogether with no impact on the game or the spectators' enjoyment of it. As a result, Sluggerrr (and, therefore, the Royals) owe the fans a duty to use reasonable care in conducting the Hotdog Launch and can be held liable for damages caused by a breach of that duty. Sluggerrr's tosses may—or may not—be negligent; that is a question of fact for the jury to decide. But the Royals owe the same duty of reasonable care when distributing hotdogs or other promotional materials that it owes to their 1.7 million fans in all other circumstances, excepting only those risks of injury that are an inherent part of watching a baseball game in person.

V. The Jury Instructions Were Prejudicial

As held above, the trial court erred in submitting to the jury the question of whether the risk of injury from Sluggerrr's hotdog toss was an inherent risk of watching a baseball game at Kauffman Stadium. . . . Accordingly, the judgment is vacated, and the case is remanded. [The court also held the evidence was sufficient to justify submitting Coomer's comparative fault to the jury, so that issue could be considered by the jury on remand.]

Notes

No duty/No breach of duty. Some courts talk about primary assumption of risk in terms of there being no breach of duty as opposed to no duty existing. *See* Eischen v. Crystal Valley Co-op., 835 N.W.2d 629, 637 (Minn. 2013).

Inherent risks. Skiing is another situation in which the concepts of inherent risks and implied primary assumption of risk come up. Numerous jurisdictions have adopted statutes shielding ski resorts from liability for injuries arising out of the inherent dangers and risks of skiing. These statutes often define what is and is not an inherent risk of skiing. *See* Alaska Ski Safety Act of 1994," Alaska Stat. § 05.45.200 (listing "changing weather conditions" as one of the inherent risks of skiing but excluding the negligence of a ski area operator).

Intentional rulebreaking. One issue that sometimes comes up in the sports context is the extent to which a participant consents to intentional misconduct on the part of an opposing player. *See* Avila v. Citrus Cmty. Coll. Dist., 131 P.3d 383,

393, 394 (Cal. 2006) (concluding that the plaintiff assumed the risk of being hit by a pitch intentionally thrown at him by the pitcher because such conduct was not "totally outside the range of ordinary activity involved in the sport" and was an accepted custom of the game); Turcotte v. Fell, 502 N.E.2d 964, 969–70, 971 (N.Y. 1986) (discussing assumption of the risk and contrasting inherent dangers assumed with "flagrant infractions unrelated to the normal method of playing the game and done without any competitive purpose").

The Firefighter's Rule. The Firefighter's Rule generally prohibits recovery by a professional rescuer (like a firefighter) against the party whose negligence necessitated the rescuer's presence and ultimate injury. The rule bars public employees whose jobs require them to go to a location in order to confront specific risks to recover for injuries resulting from that risk. *See* Norfolk Southern Railway Company v. Johnson, 554 S.W.3d 315, 317 (Ky. 2018). Some decisions justify the rule, at least in part, on primary assumption of risk grounds. *See* Armstrong v. Mailand, 284 N.W.2d 343, 350 (Minn.1979) ("Firemen assume, in a primary sense, all risks reasonably apparent to them that are part of firefighting."). Also like implied primary assumption of risk, the rule is perhaps better phrased in terms of the absence of a breach of a duty. *See* Worley v. Winston, 550 So. 2d 694 (La. App. 2d Cir. 1989).

Problem 8.5. Refer back to the facts in Problem 8.4. Assume that the court holds that the exculpatory clause does not bar Pauline's claim. What impact, if any, would implied primary assumption of risk principles have on Pauline's claim?

3. Implied Secondary Assumption of Risk (Comparative Fault)

The first case in this section, *Morgan State University v. Walker*, is from Maryland, one of the few states that still recognizes implied assumption of the risk as an affirmative defense. The second is an excerpt from *Coomer*, which, as you recall, discussed the shift to comparative fault principles in Missouri.

Morgan State University v. Walker

919 A.2d 21 (Md. Ct. Special App. 2007)

GREENE, Judge.

Factual and Procedural Background

The pertinent facts of this case are not in dispute. It snowed approximately 22 inches in Baltimore, Maryland between February 16–18, 2003. MSU was closed through February 19, 2003 because of the snowfall. At that time, Respondent's daughter was a residential student at MSU. Carnegie Express, a company that MSU had hired to remove the snow, performed snow removal services on February 16 and 17. On February 18, MSU informed Carnegie Express that MSU would complete the snow removal process and that Carnegie Express did not have to do so.

At or around 8:00 a.m. on February 24, 2003, Respondent [Pamela Walker] drove approximately one hour from her home in Upper Marlboro to visit her daughter at MSU. Respondent stated that she needed to bring her daughter money because her daughter did not have an ATM card and needed money for gas and other things. Respondent arrived at MSU's campus with the intention of parking in parking lot T, the lot in front of her daughter's dormitory. The parking lot is an elevated lot. Respondent explained that she, therefore, did not notice the ice and snow until she was already on top of it. She testified that once she pulled into the parking lot she noticed that she was driving "on crunchy ice and snow." Respondent found a parking spot near the entrance to the dormitory and parked without looking for a spot in another portion of the lot. She explained that the only spots closer to the entrance were handicapped spaces. Respondent testified that she "didn't think of danger," she just thought "doggone, they didn't clean this parking lot." She also testified that she "had no other choice," aside from that parking lot, as to where to park her car.

Respondent parked and exited her car. She noticed snow and ice on the ground between her car and the entrance to the dormitory. She therefore held onto the cars next to her as she walked to reach her daughter's building. Respondent's daughter testified that, like the parking lot, the driveway and steps in front of her dormitory had not been cleared. Respondent testified that she held onto the railing when walking on the steps and walked very slowly. She also noted that she had on Timberland boots and stated "I mean I don't have any problems with walking or anything like that. Actually I'm a dare devil to be honest with you." She reached her daughter's dormitory without incident.

Respondent visited with her daughter for approximately one hour. On her way back to her car, she walked slowly and tapped each car, while looking down at the ground "to make sure that [she] didn't slip and fall." She saw snow and ice on the ground as she was walking and testified that she was "trying to be safe." When Respondent reached her vehicle, she lost her footing, fell to the ground and fractured her leg, an injury that she claims has cost her approximately $50,000 in medical bills and lost earnings.

Respondent instituted a personal injury action against MSU in the Circuit Court for Baltimore City, alleging negligent failure to clear the parking lot of snow and ice, and negligent hiring, training and supervision, on the basis that MSU's employees failed to clear adequately the snow and ice in the parking lot. The Circuit Court granted summary judgment for MSU based on the theory that, as a matter of law, Respondent voluntarily assumed the risk of her injuries by walking on the snow and ice. Respondent appealed to the Court of Special Appeals. In an unreported opinion, the intermediate appellate court reversed the Circuit Court, holding that, under the circumstances, the jury should decide whether Respondent's decision to park in the lot and walk on the snow and ice was voluntary. MSU filed a petition for writ of certiorari in this Court, which we granted.

Discussion

Respondent's Assumption of the Risk

We agree with MSU and the Circuit Court that the question of voluntariness, in the context of an assumption of the risk analysis, is measured by an objective standard. Therefore, when the uncontroverted evidence demonstrated that Respondent knowingly and voluntarily walked across a snow and ice covered parking lot and injured herself, she assumed the risk of her injuries as a matter of law. The Circuit Court was therefore correct to grant MSU's motion for summary judgment and not send the question to the jury.

Assumption of the risk is an affirmative defense in a negligence action. The two leading cases on this issue are *ADM P'ship v. Martin*, 348 Md. 84, 702 A.2d 730 (1997), and *Schroyer v. McNeal*, 323 Md. 275, 592 A.2d 1119 (1991). In *ADM P'ship*, we set forth the principles of an assumption of the risk analysis:

> In Maryland, it is well settled that in order to establish the defense of assumption of risk, the defendant must show that the plaintiff: (1) had knowledge of the risk of the danger; (2) appreciated that risk; and (3) voluntarily confronted the risk of danger.
>
> * * *
>
> 'The doctrine of assumption of risk rests upon an intentional and voluntary exposure to a known danger and, therefore, consent on the part of the plaintiff to relieve the defendant of an obligation of conduct toward [her] and to take [her] chances from harm from a particular risk.'
>
> * * *
>
> Assumption of risk means 'voluntary incurring that of an accident which may not occur, and which the person assuming the risk may be careful to avoid after starting.' Thus, if established, it functions as a complete bar to recovery because 'it is a previous abandonment of the right to complain if an accident occurs.'
>
> * * *
>
> 'In determining whether a plaintiff had knowledge and appreciation of the risk, an objective standard must be applied and a plaintiff will not be heard to say that he did not comprehend a risk which must have been obvious to him.' Thus, 'when it is clear that a person of normal intelligence in the position of the plaintiff must have understood the danger, the issue is for the court.'

...

In accordance with the test most clearly articulated in *ADM P'ship*, and our reasoning and holding in *Schroyer*, it is clear that Respondent had knowledge of the risk of danger of walking across the snowy and icy parking lot and appreciated that risk. The issue, therefore, is whether she voluntarily confronted the risk of that danger. In addition, as explained *supra*, these three factors are analyzed by an objective standard.

Respondent's own testimony made clear that she was aware of the snow and ice in the parking lot. She testified that as soon as she drove into the parking lot, she noticed that she was driving "on crunchy ice and snow." She stated further that she thought, "doggone, they didn't clean this parking lot." Respondent's behavior demonstrates that she was also aware of the risk, and appreciated the risk, of danger of walking on snow and ice. She explained that she walked very slowly, held onto the cars as she walked, and held onto the railing as she walked slowly up the steps. In addition, Respondent explained that she looked down at the ground "to make sure that [she] didn't slip and fall." Moreover, as we stated in both *ADM P'ship* and *Schroyer*, "[t]he danger of slipping on ice . . . [is] one of the 'risks which any one of adult age must be taken to appreciate.'"

Nothing in the record suggests that Respondent was forced against her will to confront the risk of danger of walking on the snow and ice, such that her behavior could be classified as involuntarily. After hearing the crunch of ice and snow under her tires and acknowledging that MSU had not removed the ice and snow from the parking lot, she proceeded to get out of her car and visit with her daughter. Respondent's motivation stemmed from the fact that she believed that her daughter needed money. In accordance with our prior holdings, Respondent's actions would be considered involuntary only if she lacked the free will to avoid the situation. *See ADM P'ship*, 348 Md. at 94–95, 702 A.2d at 736 (holding that Martin proceeded voluntarily in the face of danger despite the fact that she thought she would lose her job if she did not deliver the blueprints); . . . Therefore, the fact that Respondent wanted to bring her daughter money for gas does not render her actions involuntary.

Relevancy of MSU's Negligence

Respondent argues that several questions need to be answered to assess correctly whether Respondent voluntarily walked across the icy parking lot, and that, the jury should then determine whether she assumed the risk of her injuries based on the answers to those questions. We disagree. Many of the questions posed by Respondent examine whether MSU was negligent in its failure to clear the parking lot of snow and ice. In an assumption of the risk analysis, however, the defendant's or a third party's negligence is irrelevant.

We can assume, for the sake of argument, that Respondent is correct and that MSU was negligent in failing to clear the parking lot and walkways of snow and ice. This assumption does not change our analysis or our conclusion. As this Court has previously explained "the assumption of the risk defense exists independently of the conduct of another person, whether the defendant or a third party." . . .

JUDGMENT OF THE COURT OF SPECIAL APPEALS REVERSED AND CASE REMANDED TO THAT COURT WITH INSTRUCTIONS TO AFFIRM THE JUDGMENT OF THE CIRCUIT COURT FOR BALTIMORE CITY. . . .

Coomer v. Kansas City Royals Baseball Corp.

437 S.W.3d 184 (Mo. 2014)
(en banc)

[The facts and the Missouri Supreme Court's discussion of whether the affirmative defenses of express assumption of risk and implied primary assumption of risk survived Missouri's switch to comparative fault in the *Gustafson* decision appear in Part B2 *supra*.]

Gustafson rejects any further application of "implied secondary assumption of the risk." When a plaintiff acts unreasonably in deciding to assume a risk created by a defendant's negligence, such "fault" may reduce—but not bar—the plaintiff's recovery under *Gustafson*. By the same token, when the plaintiff's decision was reasonable, it cannot be used to reduce his recovery because reasonable behavior does not constitute "fault" under the UCFA. [Simons, *Reflections on Assumption of Risk*, 50 UCLA L. Rev. 481, 489 (2002) 489] (noting that the "predominant modern position" of most courts and the Restatement (Third) of Torts is that secondary implied assumption of the risk has be assimilated into comparative fault).

. . .

Accordingly, when the plaintiff is injured by the defendant's negligence, this Court holds that the adoption of comparative fault in *Gustafson* precludes any consideration of the plaintiff's conduct in assuming that risk (*i.e.*, implied secondary assumption of the risk) except as a partial defense under a proper comparative fault instruction. . . .

[T]he Court holds that the evidence was sufficient to justify submitting Coomer's comparative fault to the jury. Coomer contends that, because he was "just sitting there," this cannot constitute negligence. The jury might reach that conclusion and, as a result, not attribute any percentage of the fault to Coomer. But that is not the only conclusion supported by this evidence. The evidence also was sufficient for the jury to find that Coomer acted unreasonably by: (a) watching Sluggerrr go into his leonine wind-up in preparation for a behind-the-back hotdog toss and then (b) choosing the precise moment that Sluggerrr was releasing the hotdog to let his gaze—and attention—wander elsewhere. The jury may find that this failure to keep a careful lookout, among other reasons, was sufficient to assess some percentage of fault to Coomer.

Note

Secondary assumption of the risk in comparative negligence jurisdictions. *Coomer* states the general rule regarding secondary assumption of the risk in jurisdictions that have moved to a system of comparative fault.

Problem 8.6. When Pauline used the rowing machine, she noticed that the handle felt looser than normal, but did not think much of it. Assume that she brings her claim in a Maryland state court. What impact, if any, would implied secondary assumption of risk principles have on her claim?

Problem 8.7. Assume that Pamela Walker from *Morgan State University v. Walker* had slipped and fallen in Missouri instead of Maryland. Would her negligence claim have survived summary judgment? What impact would her assumption of the risk of slipping have had on her claim if the facts had occurred in a modified comparative fault jurisdiction?

Review Question

Sheryl has skied for about 15 years. She's not an expert, but she goes skiing a few times a year. She was recently injured while skiing at the Brushy Mountain Ski Resort. Before Sheryl could purchase her lift ticket, she was required to sign a release in which she agreed "not to sue Brushy Mountain Ski Resort or its employees if injured while using the facilities even if such injuries result from the inherent risks associated with skiing." Sheryl was skiing on the black diamond (expert level) Widowmaker Trail with her friend Holly. Sheryl rarely skied black diamond trails but did so this time in order to accompany Holly. Sheryl was having difficulty staying upright on the steep trail when she was suddenly slammed into from behind by Zander, a college student. Zander had been drinking with some of his friends all day and was heavily intoxicated. Due to his intoxication, Zander lost control and ended up plowing into Sheryl. Sheryl suffered a broken leg as a result and sued Zander and the Brushy Mountain Ski Resort for failing to prevent (what she claims was) the obviously intoxicated Zander from getting on the ski lift.

(a) To what extent, if any, will Sheryl's recovery be limited by the waiver she signed?

(b) [Alternatively] To what extent, if any, will Sheryl's own actions limit her recovery in a jurisdiction that follows the majority rules with respect to comparative fault and assumption of risk?

Chapter 9

Immunities and Tort Actions Involving Government Actors

A. Charitable and Intrafamily Immunity
- Charitable immunity
- Intrafamily immunity
  - In general
  - Exceptions
  - Justifications
- Other concepts developed in class or in readings assigned by the professor

B. Governmental Immunity
- Sovereign immunity
- Governmental immunity statutes
- Discretionary function immunity
- Other concepts developed in class or in readings assigned by the professor

C. Public Duty Doctrine
- In general
- Special relationship exception
- Other concepts developed in class or in readings assigned by the professor

D. Other Tort Claims Involving Government Actors
- Federal Tort Claims Act
  - In general
  - The *Feres* doctrine
- Constitutional tort actions
- Other concepts developed in class or in readings assigned by the professor

Chapter Problem. Jordan and Leah Allen have brought separate negligence claims against the Pleasant Hill Police Department, a local 911 operator, and Leah's father Grant, stemming from violent acts committed by Grant.

The previous chapter focused on defenses stemming from the behavior of the injured party; the plaintiff was comparatively negligent or assumed the risk of injury. This chapter focuses on immunities and other theories limiting liability that are not based on the behavior of the injured party but are instead based on policy concerns.

A. Charitable and Intrafamily Immunity

1. Charitable Immunity

Charities in the United States enjoyed broad immunity from tort liability until well until the twentieth century. Among the justifications offered were the concerns that liability would drain the charitable coffers or discourage the formation of charities, both of which would have the effect of deterring charitable good works. Eventually, the *Restatement* took the position that charities do not enjoy any special immunity. *See* Restatement (Second) of Torts § 895E (1979). Most states have eliminated or abrogated the special immunity for charities. Some states have created exceptions to charitable immunity, for example, by permitting liability where the charity carries insurance that would cover the damages in question. *See* James v. Prince George's County, 288 Md. 315, 418 A.2d 1173 (1980). Others have placed caps on the amount of damages. *See, e.g.*, S.C. Code § 33-56-180 (imposing a $250,000 cap involving an action against a charity based on the acts of an employee).

2. Intrafamily Immunity

Historically, there were two common types of intrafamily immunity. The first applied to bar suits between married couples. Under common law, a husband and wife were treated as a single entity (with the wife's rights subsumed into those of her husband) and thus were not able to sue one another. As society evolved, this form of immunity has been abolished (or at least substantially limited) in nearly every jurisdiction. *See, e.g.*, Freehe v. Freehe, 81 Wash.2d 183, 500 P.2d 771 (1972), *overruled in part on other grounds by* Brown v. Brown, 100 Wash.2d 729, 675 P.2d 1207 (1984). The second form of intrafamily immunity barred tort claims by children against their parents. The decision below deals with this form of immunity.

Zelmer v. Zelmer

188 P.3d 497 (Wash. 2008)
(en banc)

MADSEN, J.

Three-year-old Ashley McLellan drowned in a backyard swimming pool while under the supervision of her stepfather, Joel Zellmer. The trial court ruled the parental immunity doctrine shields Zellmer from liability for negligence in connection with her death. Petitioners Stacey Ferguson and Bruce McLellan, Ashley's biological parents, challenge that ruling. They contend the parental immunity doctrine should be abolished in favor of a reasonable parent standard. Alternatively, they argue the doctrine does not apply under the facts of this case.

. . .

... Like other jurisdictions, this court has substantially limited the scope of parental immunity in accordance with changing views of public policy on the family relation. A parent is not immune when acting outside his or her parental capacity. *See Merrick*, 93 Wash.2d 411, 610 P.2d 891 (operating a motor vehicle); *Borst*, 41 Wash.2d 642, 251 P.2d 149 (driving a business truck). For example, when operating a business or driving a car, a parent owes a child the same duty of reasonable care applicable to the world at large, and may be held liable notwithstanding the parent/child relationship. Even when acting in a parental capacity, a parent who abdicates his or her parental responsibilities by engaging in willful or wanton misconduct is not immune from suit. *See* Hoffman v. Tracy, 67 Wash.2d 31, 406 P.2d 323 (1965) (driving while intoxicated); Livingston v. City of Everett, 50 Wash.App. 655, 660, 751 P.2d 1199 (1988) (parent left four-year-old child unattended in a small room with two Doberman pinschers).

But this court has consistently held a parent is not liable for ordinary negligence in the performance of parental responsibilities. *Jenkins*, 105 Wash.2d 99, 713 P.2d 79 (disallowing contribution claim where parents allowed child to wander free in neighborhood; child electrocuted at utility power station); Talarico v. Foremost Ins. Co., 105 Wash.2d 114, 712 P.2d 294 (1986) (disallowing negligent supervision claim where parent started backyard fire then left three-year-old son unattended, resulting in severe burns); Baughn v. Honda Motor Co., 105 Wash.2d 118, 119, 712 P.2d 293 (1986) (disallowing contribution claim where parents allowed sight-impaired child to ride motorbike, resulting in fatal crash); Stevens v. Murphy, 69 Wash.2d 939, 421 P.2d 668 (1966) (disallowing suit against divorced parent who negligently injured children while transporting them home from a scheduled visitation), overruled in part by *Merrick*, 93 Wash.2d at 413, 610 P.2d 891; DeLay v. DeLay, 54 Wash.2d 63, 337 P.2d 1057 (1959) (disallowing negligence action against parent who instructed son to siphon gas, resulting in burn injuries); Cox v. Hugo, 52 Wash.2d 815, 329 P.2d 467 (1958) (disallowing contribution claim against parent who failed to prevent child from wandering into neighbor's yard where she was burned by trash fire).

...

There now appears to be nearly universal consensus that children may sue their parents for personal injuries caused by intentionally wrongful conduct. However, the overwhelming majority of jurisdictions hold parents are not liable for negligent supervision of their child, whether stated in terms of a limited parental immunity (among jurisdictions that have partially abrogated the parental immunity doctrine), parental privilege (among those that either abolished the immunity doctrine outright or declined to adopt it in the first instance), or lack of an actionable parental duty to supervise.

A minority of states have followed the lead of the California Supreme Court, allowing children to sue parents for negligent supervision under a "reasonable parent" standard. Gibson v. Gibson, 3 Cal.3d 914, 479 P.2d 648, 92 Cal.Rptr. 288 (1971) (remanding for trial where son was struck by car after entering highway at father's direction); Broadbent v. Broadbent, 184 Ariz. 74, 907 P.2d 43 (1995) (remanding for trial where child fell into swimming pool and nearly drowned while mother left to answer telephone).

In a trio of cases decided in 1986, we "reaffirmed the vitality of the doctrine of parental immunity with respect to assertions of negligent supervision." *Baughn*, 105 Wash.2d at 119, 712 P.2d 293; *Jenkins*, 105 Wash.2d at 103, 713 P.2d 79; *Talarico*, 105 Wash.2d 114, 712 P.2d 294. We expressly rejected the "reasonable parent" standard and concluded the better approach was to continue to recognize a limited form of parental immunity in cases of ordinary negligence when a parent is acting in a parental capacity. In explaining our decision, we stated:

> "Parents should be free to determine how the physical, moral, emotional, and intellectual growth of their children can best be promoted." *Foldi* [*v. Jeffries*], 93 N.J. [533,] 545, 461 A.2d [1145,] 1152 [(1983).] Parents should not routinely have to defend their child-rearing practices where their behavior does not rise to the level of wanton misconduct. There is no correct formula for how much supervision a child should receive at a given age.

Jenkins, 105 Wash.2d at 105, 713 P.2d 79.

The petitioners offer no persuasive arguments for overruling *Jenkins*, *Baughn*, and *Talarico*. Instead, they direct much of their criticism at long-discarded rationales underlying the original form of the parental immunity doctrine. Following *Jenkins*, the primary objective of the modern parental immunity doctrine is to avoid undue judicial interference with the exercise of parental discipline and parental discretion. This rationale remains as vital today as it was in 1986. Parents have a right to raise their children without undue state interference.

. . .

Next, petitioners argue it would be inappropriate to extend the parental immunity doctrine to stepparents in view of the modern trend to limit or abolish it.

Notwithstanding the limitations courts have placed on the scope of conduct shielded by the parental immunity doctrine, a majority of states addressing the issue hold it applies to stepparents who stand in loco parentis to the same extent as to legal parents.

Authority to the contrary exists only in jurisdictions where stepparents either have no legal obligation to support a child, or where parental immunity otherwise bars suit in the case of motor vehicle torts. In recognition of the waning support for a broad rule of parental immunity, these jurisdictions have restricted its application to biological or adoptive parents, thus limiting the scope of persons to whom it applies rather than the range of conduct it protects.

This court has, more appropriately, limited the scope of conduct protected by the parental immunity doctrine to conform to changing societal views about the appropriate boundaries of parental discretion. State interference in the parent/child relationship is deemed justified under a broader range of circumstances than formerly recognized. Our legislature has narrowed the range of unfettered parental discretion through the enactment of statutes designed to protect children from abuse and exploitation. Because this court already has placed appropriate limitations on the scope of the parental immunity doctrine to accord with its modern rationale, restricting the scope of parental immunity to biological and adoptive parents is unwarranted.

No court has allowed a stepparent to claim parental immunity solely by virtue of his or her marriage to the injured child's biological parent. This is consistent with the common law rule that a stepparent gains no parental rights and assumes no obligations merely by reason of the relationship. On the other hand, a stepparent standing in loco parentis has a common law duty to support and educate a child to the same extent as does a natural parent.

The term "in loco parentis" means, "[i]n the place of a parent; instead of a parent; charged, factitiously, with a parent's rights, duties, and responsibilities." BLACKS LAW DICTIONARY 787 (6th ed.1990). It refers to a person who has put himself or herself in the situation of a lawful parent by assuming all obligations incident to the parental relation without going through the formalities of legal adoption and embodies the two ideas of assuming the status and discharging the duties of parenthood.

We agree with those courts that find no principled distinction between a legal parent and a stepparent who assumes all the obligations and exercises all the responsibilities of parenthood, as the public policy reasons supporting immunity for a biological or adoptive parent apply equally to one standing in loco parentis. As the Court of Appeals stated, stepparents need the same "wide sphere of discretion as legal parents" when they have assumed the responsibility to discipline and educate a child.

A stepparent may or may not act as a parent with respect to a given child. Whether a stepparent stands in loco parentis is primarily a question of intent to be determined in view of the facts of each case. The intention required to create an in loco parentis relationship "should not lightly or hastily be inferred." The relevant focus is the stepparent's overall relationship with the child, rather than with the particular conduct upon which the child's complaint is based.

...

The loco parentis relationship should be found to exist only if the facts and circumstances show the stepparent intends to assume the responsibilities of a legal parent not only in providing financial support but also with respect to educating, instructing, and caring for the child's general welfare. This is generally a question of fact that should not be resolved as a matter of law when the issue is in conflict and different inferences may reasonably be drawn from the evidence.

We agree with the petitioners that a genuine issue of fact exists as to whether Zellmer stood in loco parentis to Ashley. It is undisputed Zellmer had been married to Ashley's primary residential parent for 88 days, he provided Ashley with housing for a majority of that time, and Ashley's mother at least occasionally entrusted her to his care.

. . .

In opposition to summary judgment, the plaintiffs presented evidence Zellmer did not provide financial and emotional support to Ashley, did not treat her as his own daughter, and did not otherwise demonstrate a genuine concern for her welfare characteristic of a parent/child relationship. Moreover, Zellmer was not generally authorized to discipline Ashley or exercise parental discretion on her behalf.

. . .

Taking into account the short duration of the relationship, and viewing the facts in the light most favorable to the nonmoving party, a genuine issue of material fact exists as to whether Zellmer stood in loco parentis to Ashley. Thus, summary judgment was improper.

Notes

Intentional wrongs. As originally developed, parental immunity extended to intentional wrongs, including sexual abuse. *See* Roller v. Roller, Roller, 79 P. 788, 788–89 (Wash. 1905) (holding minor child could not sue father for rape); *see also* Broadbent v. Broadbent, 907 P.2d 43 (Ariz. 1995) (describing history of parental immunity). As *Zelmer* notes, today parental immunity does not apply to a "willful, malicious, or intentional wrong" committed by a parent against a child. *See* McCullough v. Godwin, 214 S.W.3d 793, 801 (Tex. Ct. App.-Tyler 2007).

Justifications for intrafamily immunity. As described by the Arizona Supreme Court, the traditional justifications for parental immunity included the following:

(1) Suing one's parents would disturb domestic tranquility;

(2) Suing one's parents would create a danger of fraud and collusion;

(3) Awarding damages to the child would deplete family resources;

(4) Awarding damages to the child could benefit the parent if the child predeceases the parent and the parent inherits the child's damages; and

(5) Suing one's parents would interfere with parental care, discipline, and control.

Broadbent v. Broadbent, 907 P.2d 43, 48 (Ariz. 1995). *Zelmer* refers to these justifications as "long-discarded." Why might a court conclude that some of these justifications do not withstand scrutiny?

Problem 9.1. Grant and Jordan Allen divorced six months ago. They retain joint custody over their daughter Leah. Leah was staying at Grant's house overnight per the couple's custody agreement when Grant punished Leah for spilling grape juice on the floor. The punishment consisted of locking Leah inside the cupboard under the sink in Grant's kitchen. By the time Jordan picked Leah up later that afternoon, Leah was experiencing dehydration and hyperthermia due to the extreme heat in the cupboard. Jordan rushed Leah to the hospital where she remained for several days. Jordan now seeks to bring a negligence action against Grant on Leah's behalf. You represent Leah. What is your advice about the likely success of such a claim?

B. Governmental Immunity

1. Sovereign Immunity

Under the old English common law concept of sovereign immunity, the King could do no wrong. This meant that "the Crown is immune from any suit to which it has not consented." Feres v. United States, 340 U.S. 135, 139 (1950). The concept was imported into U.S. law. In some states, sovereign immunity was enshrined within the state constitution. In others, it was adopted as a common law principle. *See* Coleman v. East Joliet Fire Protection Dist., 46 N.E.3d 741, 748 (Ill. 2016) (describing the history of the rule in Illinois). The criticisms of sovereign immunity are obvious. Immunity serves as a complete bar to suit, regardless of the fault of the sovereign. Thus, an innocent victim of the state's failure to exercise reasonable care may be left without a remedy.

2. Governmental Immunity Statutes

Sovereign immunity gradually gave way to more limited forms of government immunity. At the federal level, Congress passed the Federal Torts Claims Act (FTCA) in 1946. *See* 28 U.S.C. § 2671 et seq. The Act waived the federal government's immunity from suit where the government, if a private person, would be liable under like circumstances. However, the Act also created a number of exceptions where immunity remains. The FTCA is addressed in more detail in Part D below.

Following the enactment of the FTCA, states gradually began to abolish sovereign immunity and instead enacted statutes spelling out when state actors can and cannot be sued. Some states took the approach of generally retaining immunity but carving out certain areas where suits against governmental entities would be permitted. Other states take the opposite approach and waive sovereign immunity except in certain cases.

South Carolina Code § 15-78-20

Legislative findings; declaration of public policy; extent of, and construction of, waiver of immunity.

(a) The General Assembly finds that while a private entrepreneur may be readily held liable for negligence of his employees within the chosen ambit of his activity, the area within which government has the power to act for the public good has been without limit and, therefore, government did not have the duty to do everything which might have been done. The General Assembly further finds that each governmental entity has financial limitations within which it must exercise authorized power and discretion in determining the extent and nature of its activities. Thus, while total immunity from liability on the part of the government is not desirable, . . . neither should the government be subject to unlimited nor unqualified liability for its actions. . . .

South Carolina Code § 15-78-40

Tort liability of State, agency, political subdivision, or governmental entity, generally.

The State, an agency, a political subdivision, and a governmental entity are liable for their torts in the same manner and to the same extent as a private individual under like circumstances, subject to the limitations upon liability and damages, and exemptions from liability and damages, contained herein.

South Carolina Code § 15-78-60

Exceptions to waiver of immunity

The governmental entity is not liable for a loss resulting from:

(1) legislative, judicial, or quasi-judicial action or inaction;

(2) administrative action or inaction of a legislative, judicial, or quasi-judicial nature;

(3) execution, enforcement, or implementation of the orders of any court or execution, enforcement, or lawful implementation of any process;

. . .

(8) snow or ice conditions or temporary or natural conditions on any public way or other public place due to weather conditions unless the snow or ice thereon is affirmatively caused by a negligent act of the employee;

(9) entry upon any property where the entry is expressly or impliedly authorized by law;

(10) natural conditions of unimproved property of the governmental entity, unless the defect or condition causing a loss is not corrected by the particular governmental entity responsible for the property within a reasonable time after actual or constructive notice of the defect or condition;

. . .

(16) maintenance, security, or supervision of any public property, intended or permitted to be used as a park, playground, or open area for recreational

> purposes, unless the defect or condition causing a loss is not corrected by the particular governmental entity responsible for maintenance, security, or supervision within a reasonable time after actual notice of the defect or condition; . . .
>
> [This section lists a total of 40 exceptions.]

State statutes also may immunize public entities and public employees from liability for the negligent performance of certain designated activities, but permit liability in the case of willful or wanton behavior. *See* 745 ILCS 10/3-108(a) (extending immunity to a local public entity or a public employee who undertakes to supervise an activity on or the use of any public property "unless the public entity or public employee is guilty of willful and wanton conduct in its supervision proximately causing such injury").

3. Discretionary Function Immunity

Individual state government officials typically retain immunity from liability stemming from their performance of discretionary functions. This form of immunity exists to prevent judicial "'second guessing of' . . . administrative decisions grounded in social, economic, and political policy through tort litigation, thereby protecting [states] from liability that would seriously handicap efficient government operations." Ette ex rel. Ette v. Linn-Mar Cmty. Sch. Dist., 656 N.W.2d 62, 67 (Iowa 2002).

Anderson v. State

692 N.W.2d 360 (Iowa 2005)

WIGGINS, Justice.

Kecia Anderson brought a tort claim against Marilyn Mercado and the State of Iowa for injuries she sustained in a fall on the campus of the University of Northern Iowa. Anderson alleged Mercado and the State were negligent in failing to close the library early due to the weather conditions. . . .

On February 8, 2001, Anderson arrived at the library on the campus of the University of Northern Iowa in the early evening to study for an exam. The library closed at 12 a.m. Andersen left the library at approximately 11:55 p.m. By that time, a winter storm had caused icy conditions on the campus's streets and sidewalks. As soon as Anderson walked beyond the overhang of the library, she slipped and fell on the ice injuring herself.

[Mercado, the interim dean of the library, was in charge of the library until she left the building sometime after 5 p.m. Another librarian, Barb Weeg, reported to Linda McLaury, a library assistant, the sidewalks were starting to get a little slick and that McLaury should contact Mercado about the icy conditions and to inquire whether the library should remain open under these weather conditions. Mercado had the authority to close the library early under severe weather conditions. Mercado attempted to ascertain how dangerous the weather conditions were and how many employees were present.]

Mercado also asked McLaury how many people were in the building, because the number of persons using the library bears on Mercado's decision whether to shut down the library. McLaury responded about thirty to thirty-five people were in the building. Mercado then made the decision to keep the library open until closing. She told McLaury to call her back if anything else came up that evening.

At trial, Mercado testified two other factors not discussed in her phone conversation with McLaury influenced her decision to keep the library open. First, was the library's written weather/working policy. Although the university intended the weather/working policy to clarify the policy for library personnel, it contained the following statement from an article in the December 9, 1996 Campus News Network, which provided:

> It is the policy of the University to continue normal hours of operation and maintain a regular work schedule for staff members during periods of severe weather and/or adverse working conditions. It is a basic premise of this policy that University faculty, staff, and students shall have the opportunity to make their own decision about reporting to work or class with due consideration for travel safety conditions.

The second factor to influence Mercado's decision to keep the library open was Weeg's tendency to exaggerate and to be over-concerned about things.

[Anderson's] case proceeded to trial. At the close of Anderson's evidence, defendants moved for a directed verdict on several grounds, including the discretionary function immunity. The district court granted the motion and entered a directed verdict in favor of Mercado and the State on the basis the decision not to close the library was subject to discretionary function immunity. . . . Anderson appealed.

The court of appeals held Mercado's decision to keep the library open was not subject to discretionary function immunity. It stated "the simple determination that weather conditions did not warrant the early closing of the library is not . . . a policy driven analysis. It is not a decision supported by social, political, or economic policies." The court of appeals affirmed on the premises liability claim. This court granted further review.

. . .

The district court granted Mercado and the State's directed verdict by concluding the decision to keep the library open was a discretionary function under Iowa Code section 669.14(1) (2001). The question we must decide is whether the district court correctly interpreted section 669.14(1) and applied it to the evidence.

The State does not waive its sovereign immunity for actions "based upon the exercise or performance or the failure to exercise or perform a discretionary function or duty on the part of a state agency or an employee of the state, whether or not the discretion be abused." Iowa Code § 669.14(1). For purposes of determining whether an action is a discretionary function under Iowa Code chapter 669, the Iowa Tort Claims Act, our analysis is effectively identical to a discretionary function analysis under Iowa Code chapter 670 governing the tort liability of governmental subdivisions. Schmitz v. City of Dubuque, 682 N.W.2d 70, 73 (Iowa 2004). Immunity is the exception, and liability is the rule under the tort claims acts. The discretionary function immunity is an affirmative defense raised by the defendant, and the party asserting immunity has the burden to prove the immunity.

We utilize a two-step test for determining whether a challenged action falls within the discretionary function exception, and thus is entitled to statutory immunity from tort liability. The test requires the court to consider whether the action is a matter of choice for the acting employee and when the challenged conduct involves an element of judgment, to determine whether that judgment is of the kind the discretionary function exception was designed to shield. Iowa Code § 670.4(3); Bellman v. City of Cedar Falls, 617 N.W.2d 11, 19 (Iowa 2000).

Anderson concedes Mercado and the State met the first prong of the test. Therefore, we must decide whether the second prong is satisfied. This court has adopted the Supreme Court's holding that the discretionary function exception "protects only governmental actions and decisions based on considerations of public policy." Berkovitz v. United States, 486 U.S. 531, 536–37, 108 S.Ct. 1954, 1959, 100 L.Ed.2d 531, 541 (1988); Goodman v. City of Le Claire, 587 N.W.2d 232, 237–38 (Iowa 1998)....

The common thread running through [our] decisions defeating the discretionary function immunity was the record in each of these cases did not show the governmental entity based its actions on the required policy considerations, as distinguished from an action arising out of the day-to-day activities of the business of government. Unless a governmental entity can demonstrate that when it exercised its judgment, it genuinely could have considered and balanced factors supported by social, economic, or political policies, we will not recognize the discretionary function immunity.

Applying this standard to the present case, we think the district court was correct in concluding Mercado and the State were entitled to immunity under the discretionary function exception. Our review of the record reveals the university had a policy to continue the normal hours of operation for the library during periods of severe weather. The purpose of keeping the library open was to afford the maximum opportunity for students and staff to utilize the library facilities. Keeping the library open furthered the public policy of providing the best college education to its students at a reasonable cost. Persons who desired to use the library for studying or research needed to count on the fact the library would be available to them during its normal hours of operation, except when it would be impossible to keep it open those hours.

Mercado's decision not to close the library was consistent with the university's policy to keep the library open during periods of severe weather. Although she did have the authority to close the library if the conditions made it impossible to keep it open, she considered and balanced the same factors used by the university when it formulated its policy. Before Mercado made the decision to keep the library open, she queried the staff on how many persons were using the library facilities. She also ascertained whether there would be sufficient personnel to staff the library if it remained open. She then weighed the number of persons using the library, the adequacy of the staff, and the knowledge that if the weather conditions deteriorated further she could have closed the library against the weather conditions as reported to her by her staff. Balancing all these considerations, she made the decision to keep the library open during its normal hours of operation in spite of the weather and allow the faculty, staff, and students to make their own decision as to whether they wanted to remain in the library that evening. People who were not in the library at the time of Mercado's decision were free to come to the library to study or find an alternate place of study if they felt the weather prohibited them from making the trip to the library. People in the library were free to leave the library upon learning of the weather condition from other students, weather reports available to the users on the internet, or by looking outside and observing the weather conditions first hand. The evidence confirms people entered and exited the library, without incident, after Mercado made the decision to keep the library open.

Thus, Mercado not only could have considered and balanced the factors supported by public policy, but did engage in the required public policy analysis before deciding to continue the normal hours of operation for the library during periods of severe weather. Under these circumstances, Mercado and the State are entitled to immunity for keeping the library open that evening under the discretionary function exception.

Notes

Garden-variety discretion. As *Anderson* hints, the exercise of what one court has referred to as "garden-variety discretion" is not protected by discretionary immunity. Cope v. Scott, 45 F.3d 445, 448 (D.C. Cir. 1991). To use an extreme example, if a government official "drove an automobile on a mission connected with his official duties and negligently collided with another car, the exception would not apply. Although driving requires the constant exercise of discretion, the official's decisions in exercising that discretion" are not the type intended to be covered by the immunity. U.S. v. Gaubert, 499 U.S. 315, 325 n.7 (1991).

Planning versus operation. Some courts state the analysis in terms of a planning/operation test. Even if a public employee has some discretion as to how to act and is not simply following a well-defined policy, discretionary immunity is only likely to apply where the actor is making policy-type decisions (planning decisions) as opposed to decisions regarding more routine or operational matters (operational decisions). *See* Mullin v. Municipal City of South Bend, 639 N.E.2d 278 (Ind. 1994).

Problem 9.2. Jordan and Grant wound up getting into a heated argument about Grant's punishment of Leah. The argument grew so heated that Jordan eventually became fearful and called 911 for assistance, reporting that Grant had threatened her with physical violence. After speaking with Jordan and Grant, the police officer who responded to the call decided not to arrest Grant. Later that night, Grant returned to Jordan's apartment and physically assaulted her. Jordan now seeks to bring a negligence action against the police officer. Would discretionary immunity bar recovery in this instance?

C. The Public Duty Doctrine

The public duty doctrine is separate from the concept of immunity, although it may sometimes produce the same result. The public duty doctrine "is not based upon immunity from existing liability. Instead, it is based on absence of duty in the first instance." Holsten v. Massey, 490 S.E.2d 864, 871 (W. Va. 1997).

Riss v. City of New York

240 N.E.2d 860 (N.Y. 1968)

BREITEL, Judge.

[Linda Riss broke off a relationship with Burton Pugach. Pugach then harassed Riss for over six months. He repeatedly threatened to have Riss killed or maimed if she did not take him back and at one point told Riss, "If I can't have you, no one else will have you, and when I get through with you, no one else will want you." Riss sought help from the police, who apparently did not put a stop to Pugach's behavior. On June 14, 1959 Riss became engaged to another man. At a party held to celebrate the event, she received a phone call warning her that it was her "last chance." Riss called the police for help, but the police refused to help. The next day, an individual hired by Pugach threw lye in Riss' face. She was blinded in one eye, lost a good portion of her vision in the other, and her face was permanently scarred.]

This appeal presents, in a very sympathetic framework, the issue of the liability of a municipality for failure to provide special protection to a member of the public who was repeatedly threatened with personal harm and eventually suffered dire personal injuries for lack of such protection.... The issue arises upon the affirmance by a divided Appellate Division of a dismissal of the complaint, after both sides had rested but before submission to the jury.

It is necessary immediately to distinguish those liabilities attendant upon governmental activities which have displaced or supplemented traditionally private enterprises, such as are involved in the operation of rapid transit systems, hospitals, and places of public assembly. Once sovereign immunity was abolished by statute the extension of liability on ordinary principles of tort law logically followed. To be equally distinguished are certain activities of government which provide services and facilities for the use of the public, such as highways, public buildings and the like, in the performance of which the municipality or the State may be liable under ordinary principles of tort law. The ground for liability is the provision of the services or facilities for the direct use by members of the public.

In contrast, this case involves the provision of a governmental service to protect the public generally from external hazards and particularly to control the activities of criminal wrongdoers. The amount of protection that may be provided is limited by the resources of the community and by a considered legislative-executive decision as to how those resources may be deployed. For the courts to proclaim a new and general duty of protection in the law of tort, even to those who may be the particular seekers of protection based on specific hazards, could and would inevitably determine how the limited police resources of the community should be allocated and without predictable limits. This is quite different from the predictable allocation of resources and liabilities when public hospitals, rapid transit systems, or even highways are provided.

Before such extension of responsibilities should be dictated by the indirect imposition of tort liabilities, there should be a legislative determination that that should be the scope of public responsibility.

...

When one considers the greatly increased amount of crime committed throughout the cities, but especially in certain portions of them, with a repetitive and predictable pattern, it is easy to see the consequences of fixing municipal liability upon a showing of probable need for and request for protection. To be sure these are grave problems at the present time, exciting high priority activity on the part of the national, State and local governments, to which the answers are neither simple, known, or presently within reasonable controls. To foist a presumed cure for these problems by judicial innovation of a new kind of liability in tort would be foolhardy indeed and an assumption of judicial wisdom and power not possessed by the courts.

...

For all of these reasons, there is no warrant in judicial tradition or in the proper allocation of the powers of government for the courts, in the absence of legislation, to carve out an area of tort liability for police protection to members of the public. Quite distinguishable, of course, is the situation where the police authorities undertake responsibilities to particular members of the public and expose them, without adequate protection, to the risks which then materialize into actual losses (Schuster v. City of New York, 5 N.Y.2d 75, 180 N.Y.S.2d 265, 154 N.E.2d 534).

Accordingly, the order of the Appellate Division affirming the judgment of dismissal should be affirmed.

KEATING, Judge (dissenting).

Linda has turned to the courts of this State for redress, asking that the city be held liable in damages for its negligent failure to protect her from harm. With compelling logic, she can point out that, if a stranger, who had absolutely no obligation to aid her, had offered her assistance, and thereafter Burton Pugach was able to injure her as a result of the negligence of the volunteer, the courts would certainly require him to pay damages. Why then should the city, whose duties are imposed by law and include the prevention of crime (New York City Charter, § 435) and, consequently, extend far beyond that of the Good Samaritan, not be responsible? If a private detective acts carelessly, no one would deny that a jury could find such conduct unacceptable. Why then is the city not required to live up to at least the same minimal standards of professional competence which would be demanded of a private detective?

. . .

It is not a distortion to summarize the essence of the city's case here in the following language: "Because we owe a duty to everybody, we owe it to nobody." Were it not for the fact that this position has been hallowed by much ancient and revered precedent, we would surely dismiss it as preposterous. To say that there is no duty is, of course, to start with the conclusion. The question is whether or not there should be liability for the negligent failure to provide adequate police protection.

The foremost justification repeatedly urged for the existing rule is the claim that the State and the municipalities will be exposed to limitless liability. The city invokes the specter of a "crushing burden" if we should depart from the existing rule and enunciate even the limited proposition that the State and its municipalities can be held liable for the negligent acts of their police employees in executing whatever police services they do in fact provide.

The fear of financial disaster is a myth. The same argument was made a generation ago in opposition to proposals that the State waive its defense of 'sovereign immunity'. The prophecy proved false then, and it would now. The supposed astronomical financial burden does not and would not exist. No municipality has gone bankrupt because it has had to respond in damages when a policeman causes injury through carelessly driving a police car or in the thousands of other situations where, by judicial fiat or legislative enactment, the State and its subdivisions have been held liable for the tortious conduct of their employees. . . .

Cuffy v. City of New York

505 N.E.2d 937 (N.Y. 1987)

TITONE, Judge.

The violence that led to plaintiffs' injuries originated in a landlord-tenant dispute between Joseph and Eleanor Cuffy, who occupied the upper apartment of their two-family house in The Bronx, and Joel and Barbara Aitkins, who had leased the ground-floor apartment from the Cuffys for approximately a year. Even before the incidents that are directly involved in this action, there had been episodes between the two couples which the police had been called to mediate. Eleanor Cuffy had previously filed a formal criminal complaint against the Aitkinses, and a prior effort at supervised informal dispute resolution had terminated in an arbitrator's order directing Ms. Cuffy and the Aitkinses to avoid further contact. This history of repeated confrontation and police intervention forms the backdrop for the events at issue in the trial of the Cuffys' claims against the City.

Viewed in the light most favorable to plaintiffs, the evidence at the trial showed that on July 27, 1981, the night immediately preceding the incident, Joel Aitkins physically attacked Eleanor Cuffy, tearing her blouse and bruising her eye. Officer Pennington, who had responded to reports of skirmishes between the Aitkinses and the Cuffys on two or three prior occasions, came to the house once again to investigate, but declined to take any specific action because, in his judgment, the offense was merely a matter of "harassment" between landlord and tenant and an arrest was not warranted.

In frustration, Joseph Cuffy, who had been to see the police four or five times before, went to the local precinct with a neighbor at about 11:00 that night to ask for protection for his family. Cuffy spoke with Lieutenant Moretti, the desk officer, and told him that the Aitkinses had threatened his family's safety. According to both Cuffy and his neighbor, Cuffy specifically told Moretti that he intended to move his family out of its upper floor apartment immediately if an arrest was not made. In response, Moretti told Cuffy that he should not worry and that an arrest would be made or something else would be done about the situation "first thing in the morning." Cuffy then went back to his family and instructed his wife to unpack the family's valises, thereby signifying his intention to remain in the house. Despite Lieutenant Moretti's assurances, the police did not, in fact, undertake any further action in response to Cuffy's complaint.

At approximately 7:00 P.M. on the following evening, the Cuffys' son Ralston, who did not live with his parents, came to their house for a visit. Immediately after Ralston alit from his car, Joel Aitkins accosted him and the two men had an altercation, which culminated in Ralston's being struck with a baseball bat. Eleanor Cuffy, who observed the fight from her upstairs window, and another son, Cyril, rushed to Ralston's rescue. Barbara Aitkins then joined in the attack, slashing at both Eleanor and Cyril with a knife. Joseph Cuffy, who had come home from work at about 6:30 and then gone to his neighbor's house, arrived at the scene while the fight was in progress, but was not in time to avert the harm. By the time the fight was over, all three Cuffys had sustained severe injuries.

Eleanor, Cyril and Ralston Cuffy thereafter commenced this action against the City, alleging that the police had a "special duty" to protect them because of the promise that Lieutenant Moretti had made on the night preceding the incident The ensuing trial ended in a verdict awarding each of the plaintiffs substantial damages. The City appealed to the Appellate Division, which unanimously affirmed the judgment, without opinion. We conclude, however, that the judgment should have been reversed.

As a general rule, a municipality may not be held liable for injuries resulting from a simple failure to provide police protection. This rule is derived from the principle that a municipality's duty to provide police protection is ordinarily one owed to the public at large and not to any particular individual or class of individuals. Additionally, a municipality's provision of police protection to its citizenry has long been regarded as a resource-allocating function that is better left to the discretion of the policy makers. Consequently, we have generally declined to hold municipalities subject to tort liability for their failure to furnish police protection to individual citizens.

There exists, however, a narrow class of cases in which we have recognized an exception to this general rule and have upheld tort claims based upon a "special relationship" between the municipality and the claimant The elements of this "special relationship" are: (1) an assumption by the municipality, through promises or actions, of an affirmative duty to act on behalf of the party who was injured; (2) knowledge on the part of the municipality's agents that inaction could lead to harm; (3) some form of direct contact between the municipality's agents and the injured party; and (4) that party's justifiable reliance on the municipality's affirmative.

As was made clear in *Yearwood v. Town of Brighton*, 101 A.D.2d 498, 475 N.Y.S.2d 958, affd. 64 N.Y.2d 667, 485 N.Y.S.2d 252, 474 N.E.2d 612, the injured party's reliance is as critical in establishing the existence of a "special relationship" as is the municipality's voluntary affirmative undertaking of a duty to act. That element provides the essential causative link between the "special duty" assumed by the municipality and the alleged injury. Indeed, at the heart of most of these "special duty" cases is the unfairness that the courts have perceived in precluding recovery when a municipality's voluntary undertaking has lulled the injured party into a false sense of security and has thereby induced him either to relax his own vigilance or to forego other available avenues of protection. On the other hand, when the reliance element is either not present at all or, if present, is not causally related to the ultimate harm, this underlying concern is inapplicable, and the invocation of the "special duty" exception is then no longer justified.

Another element of the "special duty" exception is the requirement that there be "some direct contact between the agents of the municipality and the injured party." This element, which is conceptually related to the reliance element, exists first as a natural corollary of the need to show a "special relationship" between the claimant and the municipality, beyond the relationship with government that all citizens share in common. In addition, the "direct contact" requirement serves as a basis for rationally limiting the class of citizens to whom the municipality's "special duty" extends.

As a rule based partially on policy considerations, the direct contact requirement has not been applied in an overly rigid manner. Thus, in *Sorichetti v. City of New*

York, a case involving a preexisting judicial order of protection, we allowed recovery for an infant's injuries, although it was the infant's distraught mother, and not the injured infant, who had the direct contact with the law enforcement officials. Our deviation from the "direct contact" requirement in that case, however, may be explained by the close relationship between the interests of the mother and those of the child, as well as by the fact that the mother's contact with the police had been initiated solely for the purpose of obtaining protection for the child, who was herself helpless. Moreover, the presence of a judicial order of protection contributed to our conclusion in *Sorichetti* that an actionable relationship existed. In any event, what *Sorichetti* and similar "special duty" cases teach is that the proper application of the "direct contact" requirement depends on the peculiar circumstances of each case, all of which must be considered in light of the policies underlying the narrow "special duty" doctrine.

In this case, the requirement that there be some direct contact with an agent of the municipality is fatal to the cause of action asserted by plaintiff Ralston Cuffy, the older son who was not a member of Joseph and Eleanor Cuffy's household and did not himself have any direct contact with the police. The absence of direct contact is dispositive of Ralston's claim for two reasons. First, unlike in *Sorichetti*, none of the factors militating in favor of relaxing the "direct contact" requirement are present in his case. Since Ralston did not live in the Cuffy's home, his interests were not tied to those of the rest of his family, and it cannot be said that the assurances of protection his father had received directly from Lieutenant Moretti were obtained on his behalf. Accordingly, Ralston's connection to the official promises that form the basis of this action is simply too remote to support recovery.

Second, and perhaps more importantly, there was no indication Ralston even knew of the promise of protection that his father had received. His presence at the house on the day of the incident was thus merely an unfortunate coincidence and, in any event, was certainly not the result of his own reliance on any promise of protection that the police might have made. In the absence of such reliance, his claim is insufficient as a matter of law.

The claims asserted against the City by Eleanor and Cyril Cuffy present a more complex problem. Although neither of those parties had "direct contact" with the public servant who had promised to provide the family with protection, the "special duty" undertaken by the City through its agent must be deemed to have run to them. It was their safety that prompted Joseph Cuffy to solicit the aid of the police, and it was their safety that all concerned had in mind when Lieutenant Moretti promised police assistance. It would thus be wholly unrealistic to suggest that Eleanor and Cyril Cuffy were in no different position from any other citizen or that the City owed them no "special duty" simply because Joseph Cuffy, rather than they, had been the party who had "direct contact" with Lieutenant Moretti.

Nonetheless, Eleanor and Cyril Cuffy's recovery is precluded for the entirely separate reason that, as a matter of law, their injuries cannot be deemed to have been the result of their justifiable reliance on the assurances of police protection that

Joseph Cuffy had received. It is true that the evidence supported an inference that both of these plaintiffs remained in the house during the night of July 27, 1981 and throughout the following morning primarily because of their reliance on Lieutenant Moretti's promise to Joseph that Joel Aitkins would be arrested or something else would be done "first thing in the morning." However, Ms. Cuffy also testified that she had periodically looked out her front window throughout the day of the incident and had not seen any police cars pull up in front of her house and that she continued to be nervous about the situation. Thus, plaintiffs' own evidence established that by midday on July 28th Ms. Cuffy was aware that the police had not arrested or otherwise restrained Mr. Aitkins as had been promised.

This evidence was sufficient, as a matter of law to defeat any colorable claim that Eleanor and Cyril Cuffy's injuries were the result of any justifiable reliance on the lieutenant's assurances. Although both of them knew or should have known by midday that the promised police action would not be forthcoming, they remained in the house hours after any further reliance on those assurances could reasonably be deemed justified. It was this continued presence in the house and the consequent continued exposure to danger that ultimately led to their participation in the melee, which was prompted, in the immediate sense, by Ralston's arrival and his unfortunate confrontation with Aitkins.

In this regard, it is noteworthy that, according to the uncontradicted evidence, Ms. Cuffy had entertained relatives that day, her husband had been in and out of the house twice that very evening and the couple had plans to go out to dinner later that night. Thus, it certainly cannot be said that, having remained in the house overnight in reliance on the officer's promise, the family was thereafter trapped and unable to take steps to protect itself when its members knew or should have known that police assistance would not be forthcoming.

It may well be that the police were negligent in misjudging the seriousness of the threat to the Cuffys that the Aitkinses' continued presence posed and in not taking any serious steps to assure their safety. It may also be that the police had a "special duty" to Eleanor and Cyril Cuffy because of the promise that Lieutenant Moretti had made and those plaintiffs' overnight, justifiable reliance on that promise. It is clear, however, that those plaintiffs' justifiable reliance, which had dissipated by midday, was not causally related to their involvement in the imbroglio with the Aitkinses on the evening of July 28th. Thus, they too failed to meet the requirements of the doctrine allowing recovery for a municipality's failure to satisfy a "special duty," and their claims, like those of Ralston Cuffy, should have been dismissed.

For all of the foregoing reasons, the order of the Appellate Division should be reversed, with costs, and the complaint dismissed.

Notes

Types of actions subject to the doctrine. The majority of public duty doctrine cases involve the failure to provide police protection, fire protection, or other emergency services (like paramedics). *See* Woods v. District of Columbia, 63 A.3d 551, 559 (D.C. 2013). Indeed, many decisions define the concept in those terms. But some courts have applied the doctrine to more generalized duties to the public. *See* Estate of McFarlin v. State, 881 N.W.2d 51 (Iowa 2016) (applying the doctrine in action against state for failure to mark a pipe in a public waterway); Ravenscroft v. Washington Water Power Co., 969 P.2d 75, 85–86 (Iowa 1998) (en banc) (applying the doctrine to action against county for failure to warn of submerged tree stumps in a public waterway); State ex rel. Barthelette v. Sanders, 756 S.W.2d 536, 537–38 (Mo. 1988) (en banc) (applying the doctrine in a claim against state park superintendent for failing to close a dangerous river to public access); Cox v. Department of Natural Resources, 699 S.W.2d 443, 449 (Mo. Ct. App.1985) (applying the doctrine in a claim based on the failure of the county to provide a safe public swimming area).

911 calls. The alleged negligence of 911 dispatchers has resulted in numerous lawsuits. *See, e.g.*, Upchurch v. McDowell County 911, 750 S.E.2d 644 (W. Va. 2013). In addition to recognizing the application of the public duty doctrine in such cases, *see id.*, some states have extended statutory immunity to 911 operators. *See* W. Va. Code § 24-6-8 (providing immunity to public agencies, telephone companies, and employees of such entities except in the case of willful or wanton misconduct); N.J.S.A. 52:17C-10(e) (similar).

Abrogation of the doctrine. The public duty doctrine is recognized in the overwhelming majority of jurisdictions. A few courts abolished the doctrine, only to have the state legislature revive the rule via legislation. *See* Coleman v. East Joliet Fire Protection Dist., 46 N.E.3d 741, 754 (Ill. 2016) (describing the history of the rule). In 2016, the Illinois Supreme Court abolished the rule, relying primarily on three grounds:

> (1) the jurisprudence has been muddled and inconsistent in the recognition and application of the public duty rule and its special duty exception; (2) application of the public duty rule is incompatible with the legislature's grant of limited immunity in cases of willful and wanton misconduct; and (3) determination of public policy is primarily a legislative function and the legislature's enactment of statutory immunities has rendered the public duty rule obsolete.

Id. at 756. Some states recognize an exception to the public duty doctrine where the behavior of the governmental entity is "egregious" or "reckless." *See* Estate of Graves v. Circleville, 922 N.E.2d 201 (Ohio 2010); Schultz v. Foster-Glocester Regional School Dist., 755 A.2d 153 (R.I. 2000); Ezell v. Cockrell, 902 S.W.2d 394 (Tenn. 1995).

Problem 9.3. Refer back to Problem 9.2. Regardless of the application of discretionary immunity, how would the public duty doctrine apply to Jordan's claim against the responding police officer?

Problem 9.4. Refer back to Problem 9.2. When Grant returned to Jordan's apartment the second time, he pounded on the door and demanded to be let in. Jordan refused and called 911. The operator told Jordan to stay on the line and that she would dispatch an officer to the apartment. A few seconds later, Grant announced that he was leaving. The operator told Jordan that she would cancel the response by the police officer. Jordan asked, "What if he comes back?" The operator replied that Jordan could call again and she would dispatch a police officer immediately. A few minutes after Jordan hung up, Grant returned, kicked the door down, and physically assaulted Jordan. Jordan has now sued the 911 operator on a negligence theory for failing to dispatch an officer. How would the public duty doctrine apply to Jordan's claim against the operator?

D. Other Tort Claims Involving Government Actors

1. Federal Tort Claims Act

a. In general

As mentioned, with the Federal Torts Claims Act, Congress consented to suit in federal court subject to a number of exceptions. Under the Act, the federal government may be liable if a private person, under like circumstances, would be liable in accordance with the law of the place where the act or omission occurred. The federal government maintains immunity for claims arising out of several intentional torts, such as battery, false imprisonment, and defamation. *See* 28 U.S.C. § 2680(h). The *U.S. v. Shearer* case in subsection b below touches on this part of the statute.

The government may face liability stemming from negligence. But the discretionary immunity discussed previously may apply to such claims. For example, alleged negligence in failing to enact a particular statute or regulation is not actionable. *See* Dalehite v. United States, 346 U.S. 15, 43 (1953). The *Fang v. U.S.* excerpt below provides an illustration of the discretionary immunity concept within the context of the FTCA.

Fang v. United States

140 F.3d 1238 (9th Cir. 1998)

On September 3, 1994, Freda Fang ("Fang") was a passenger in a 1988 Toyota Camry travelling through Sequoia National Park. While travelling down a hill in one of the least visited sections of the park, the car's brakes failed. The vehicle left the roadway, proceeded over an embankment, and plunged approximately 210 feet down the side of a mountain with a 45-degree slope. Both rear-seat passengers, including Fang, were ejected from the car during the accident.

. . .

After the arrival of additional medical support and equipment, Fang was placed in a cervical collar and strapped to a backboard. Then, using climbing ropes, the EMTs transported her up the mountain. This process took approximately fifty-five minutes, during which CPR was continuously administered. Unfortunately, Fang was pronounced dead upon her arrival at the top of the hill. The cause of death was listed as "cervical fracture."

Fang's mother, Pearl Bei Fei Fang ("plaintiff"), subsequently brought this wrongful death action. The suit . . . alleged the negligent failure of National Park Service ("NPS") employees to (1) properly stabilize Fang's spine prior to treatment; (2) administer to Fang proper CPR; (3) carry all of the equipment necessary to Fang's treatment with them to the accident site.

. . .

1. Stabilization of Fang's Spine.

Plaintiff claims that in the course of their rescue efforts the EMTs failed to properly stabilize Fang's spine before treating her. . . .

No social, economic, or political policy is implicated in the decision whether to stabilize the spine of a person who may have suffered a head, neck, or back injury prior to treatment. This is simply an ordinary judgment made by EMTs in applying their training and expertise to an emergency situation. Therefore, we conclude that the district court erred in determining that plaintiff's claim that the EMTs failed to properly stabilize Fang's spine was barred by the discretionary function exception.

2. The CPR.

Plaintiff additionally claims that the EMTs failed "to render proper CPR to the decedent after she had gone into cardiac arrest." . . .

[L]ike the spinal immobilization claim, the CPR claim is not the type of governmental discretion which Congress wanted to immunize from liability through the discretionary function exception. Competing policy rationales do not dictate or influence this conduct. . . .

3. The Equipment.

Finally, plaintiff claims that the EMTs negligently failed to take a cervical collar and backboard to the accident site. . . . To the extent that plaintiff is claiming that additional equipment should have been kept at the site, her claim is barred by the discretionary function exception.

b. The Feres *Doctrine*

The Federal Tort Claims Act did not waive immunity for claims "arising out of the combatant activities of the military or naval forces, or the Coast Guard, during time of war." 28 U.S.C. § 2680(j). In *Feres v. United States*, 340 U.S. 135 (1950), the Supreme Court took this notion a step further. *Feres* involved the claims of three soldiers, one of whom was killed by fire in his barracks while stationed in New York and two of whom alleged medical malpractice on the part of military physicians. The Court held "that the Government is not liable under the Federal Tort Claims Act for injuries to servicemen where the injuries arise out of or are in the course of activity *incident to service*." *Id.* at 146 (emphasis added).

United States v. Shearer

473 U.S. 52 (1985)

Chief Justice BURGER delivered the opinion of the Court, except as to Part II-A.

We granted certiorari to decide whether the survivor of a serviceman, who was murdered by another serviceman, may recover from the Government under the Federal Tort Claims Act for negligently failing to prevent the murder.

I

Respondent is the mother and administratrix of Army Private Vernon Shearer. While Private Shearer was off duty at Fort Bliss and away from the base, he was kidnaped and murdered by another serviceman, Private Andrew Heard. A New Mexico court convicted Private Heard of Shearer's murder and sentenced him to a term of 15 to 55 years' imprisonment.

Respondent brought this action under the Federal Tort Claims Act, 28 U.S.C. §§ 1346(b) and 2671 et seq., claiming that the Army's negligence caused Private Shearer's death. Respondent alleged that Private Heard, while assigned to an Army base in Germany in 1977, was convicted by a German court of manslaughter and sentenced to a 4-year prison term. Upon his discharge from that confinement in Germany, the Army transferred Private Heard to Fort Bliss. Respondent alleged that, although the Army knew that Private Heard was dangerous, it "negligently and carelessly failed to exert a reasonably sufficient control over" him and "failed to warn other persons that he was at large."

The United States District Court for the Eastern District of Pennsylvania granted summary judgment in favor of the Government. The Court of Appeals reversed. 723 F.2d 1102 (CA3 1983). The court held that *Feres v. United States*, 340 U.S. 135, 71 S.Ct. 153, 95 L.Ed. 152 (1950), did not bar respondent's suit because "[g]enerally an off-duty serviceman not on the military base and not engaged in military activity at the time of injury, can recover under FTCA." ...

We granted certiorari. 469 U.S. 929, 105 S.Ct. 321, 83 L.Ed.2d 259 (1984). We reverse.

II

B.

Our holding in *Feres v. United States*, 340 U.S. 135, 71 S.Ct. 153, 95 L.Ed. 152 (1950), was that a soldier may not recover under the Federal Tort Claims Act for injuries which "arise out of or are in the course of activity incident to service." Although the Court in *Feres* based its decision on several grounds,

> "[i]n the last analysis, *Feres* seems best explained by the 'peculiar and special relationship of the soldier to his superiors, the effects of the maintenance of such suits on discipline, and the extreme results that might obtain if suits under the Tort Claims Act were allowed for negligent orders given or negligent acts committed in the course of military duty.'" *United States v. Muniz*, 374 U.S. 150, 162 [83 S.Ct. 1850, 1858, 10 L.Ed.2d 805] (1963), quoting *United States v. Brown*, 348 U.S. 110, 112 [75 S.Ct. 141, 143, 99 L.Ed. 139] (1954).

The *Feres* doctrine cannot be reduced to a few bright-line rules; each case must be examined in light of the statute as it has been construed in *Feres* and subsequent cases. Here, the Court of Appeals placed great weight on the fact that Private Shearer was off duty and away from the base when he was murdered. But the situs of the murder is not nearly as important as whether the suit requires the civilian court to second-guess military decisions, and whether the suit might impair essential military discipline.

Respondent's complaint strikes at the core of these concerns. In particular, respondent alleges that Private Shearer's superiors in the Army "negligently and carelessly failed to exert a reasonably sufficient control over Andrew Heard, ... failed to warn other persons that he was at large, [and] negligently and carelessly failed to ... remove Andrew Heard from active military duty." This allegation goes directly to the "management" of the military; it calls into question basic choices about the discipline, supervision, and control of a serviceman.

... To permit this type of suit would mean that commanding officers would have to stand prepared to convince a civilian court of the wisdom of a wide range of military and disciplinary decisions; for example, whether to overlook a particular incident or episode, whether to discharge a serviceman, and whether and how to place restraints on a soldier's off-base conduct. But as we noted in *Chappell v. Wallace*, such "'complex, subtle, and professional decisions as to the composition, training, ... and control of a military force are essentially professional military judgments.'" 462 U.S., at 302, 103 S.Ct., at 2366, quoting *Gilligan v. Morgan*, 413 U.S. 1, 10, 93 S.Ct. 2440, 2446, 37 L.Ed.2d 407 (1973).

Finally, respondent does not escape the *Feres* net by focusing only on this case with a claim of negligence, and by characterizing her claim as a challenge to a "straightforward personnel decision." By whatever name it is called, it is a decision of command. The plaintiffs in *Feres* and *Stencel Aero Engineering* did not contest the wisdom of broad military policy; nevertheless, the Court held that their claims did not fall within the Tort Claims Act because they were the type of claims that, if generally permitted, would involve the judiciary in sensitive military affairs at the expense of military discipline and effectiveness. Similarly, respondent's attempt to hale Army officials into court to account for their supervision and discipline of Private Heard must fail.

Notes

Incident to service. Would the *Feres* doctrine bar a claim by a soldier who was injured as a result of sexual harassment by a drill sergeant on base? *See* Stubbs v. United States, 744 F.2d 58 (8th Cir. 1984). When an off-duty solider is injured while riding a horse he rented from a military stable operated by a civilian? *See* Hass for Use & Benefit of U.S. v. United States, 518 F.2d 1138, 1141 (4th Cir.1975)?

Criticism. *Feres* and its progeny have been the subject of repeated criticism, both as a matter of statutory interpretation and policy. *See* United States v. Johnson, 481 U.S. 681, 693–94 (1987) (Scalia, J., dissenting) (criticizing the *Feres* decision on statutory interpretation grounds); Costo v. U.S., 248 F.3d 863, 867 (9th Cir. 2001) (noting the criticism of the justifications for the doctrine).

Family members. The claim of a family who seeks to recover for the wrongful death of a service member is also barred by the *Feres* doctrine. *See* Ritchie v. U.S., 733 F.3d 871 (9th Cir. 2013). However, family members may recover for their own injuries, such as where a military hospital's negligence causes injury to the child of a solder. *See* Williams v. United States, 435 F.2d 804, 805 (1st Cir. 1970).

2. Constitutional Tort Actions

Another area where governmental immunity may apply is in the case of a tort action based on the violation of a constitutional right. Under 42 U.S.C. § 1983, one who acts under color of law (*i.e.*, ordinarily a government employee) and "subjects, or causes to be subjected, any citizen of the United States or other person within the jurisdiction thereof to the deprivation of any rights, privileges, or immunities secured by the Constitution and laws, shall be liable to the party injured." Examples of § 1983 claims include prisoners' claims under the Eighth Amendment or deprivations of life, liberty, or property under the Fourteenth Amendment. While state law immunities do not bar claims for damages against individual state or local employees, employees may be able to claim immunity under § 1983 provided "their conduct does not violate clearly established statutory or constitutional rights of which a reasonable person would have known." Harlow v. Fitzgerald, 457 U.S. 800, 818 (1982).

In one famous § 1983 case, the Supreme Court held that the failure of a county's Department of Social Services (DSS) to prevent suspected abuse of a four-year-old child by the child's parent did not violate the child's liberty interest under the Fourteenth Amendment. DeShaney v. Winnebago County Dept. of Social Services, 489 U.S. 189 (1989). In *DeShaney*, a representative from the DSS noted multiple suspected instances of child abuse over the course of six months, but did nothing to remove the child from the father's custody. Eventually, the father beat the child so badly that the child entered into a coma, whereupon it was discovered that the child had suffered a series of traumatic events to the head over an extended period. The child's resulting brain damage was so severe that he was expected to be confined to an institution for the rest of his life. In a decision reminiscent of *Riss* and *Cuffy*, the Supreme Court held that the county had no constitutional duty to protect the child from abuse, so the failure to protect the child could not form the basis of a § 1983 claim. *Id.* at 200; *see also* Castle Rock v. Gonzales, 545 U.S. 748 (2005) (affirming dismissal of § 1983 claim based on police failure to enforce a restraining order against husband, who eventually murdered the couple's children).

Review Question

Angela was a prospective firefighter. In order to complete her training, she was required to pass a physical ability test. Given the intensity of the test, paramedics employed by the city were onsite in case a candidate experienced physical difficulties. After the test was over, Angela complained of nausea and chest pain. She soon passed out. Bill, another candidate, ran to the room where the paramedics were located and asked for their assistance. Carol, a paramedic, checked Angela's vital signs and administered oxygen. Carol told Angela that she was calling for a life support unit to transport Angela. Carol called a dispatcher and requested that a life support unit be dispatched to the scene. She informed the dispatcher that the patient was stable and that classified the situation as a "Priority 3" or the lowest emergency priority. A life support unit arrived 15 minutes later and transported Angela to a nearby hospital. Unfortunately, Angela died shortly after arrival. Her family has now brought a wrongful death action against Carol (among others). The theory is that Carol's failure to properly diagnose and classify Angela's life-threatening condition as one of the utmost urgency led to delay in her treatment. Carol has responded that her actions were subject to discretionary function immunity or, alternatively, that the public duty doctrine applies and prohibits liability. Assess the validity of Carol's argument.

Chapter 10

Negligent Infliction of Emotional Distress and Loss of Consortium

A. Historical Treatment of Negligent Infliction of Emotional Distress
- Other concepts developed in class or in readings assigned by the professor

B. Direct Victim Cases
- The impact rule
  - Generally
  - Justifications
  - Status of the Rule
- The physical manifestation rule
  - Generally
  - Justifications
  - Evidence of physical manifestation of distress
- The Zone of Danger Rule
  - Generally
  - Justifications
- Rules Based on Guaranties of Genuineness and Foreseeability
  - Activities, undertakings, or relationships in which negligent conduct is especially likely to cause serious emotional harm.
  - General negligence principles
- Other concepts developed in class or in readings assigned by the professor

C. Harm to Third Persons Cases
- Generally
- *Dillon v. Legg* approach
- *Thing v. La Chusa* approach
- Justifications
- Other concepts developed in class or in readings assigned by the professor

D. Loss of Consortium
- Other concepts developed in class or in readings assigned by the professor

Chapter Problem. The Pleasant Hill Hospital was recently sued by several individuals, all of whom allege that the Hospital's negligence caused them to suffer severe emotional distress. In one case, the plaintiff seeks damages resulting from the fright caused by the negligence of a Hospital employee. In the others, the plaintiffs seek compensation for the emotional distress suffered as a result of watching a loved one suffer due to the negligence of the Hospital.

When a defendant's negligence causes physical injury, a plaintiff can recover for any resulting emotional distress. So, the defendant who negligently collides with a plaintiff and causes the plaintiff to suffer a broken leg is liable for the emotional distress that accompanies the broken leg. The cases discussed in this chapter are different, however. This chapter explores cases in which the defendant's negligence causes emotional distress without necessarily causing a direct physical injury.

Claims of negligent infliction of emotional distress (NIED) occupy an uncertain place in tort law. On the one hand, they are close aligned with other negligence claims. However, physical injury has historically been a requirement in a negligence action. With NIED claims, the alleged injury is emotional, not necessarily physical, in nature. This focus on emotional distress also creates a close connection between claims of intentional infliction of emotional distress (IIED)—covered in Chapter 2—and claims of negligent infliction of emotional distress. Thus, there is some question as to whether NIED claims are best viewed as a subspecies of negligence claims or whether they are better viewed as a freestanding tort that focuses on emotional distress. Gregory C. Keating, *Is Negligent Infliction of Emotional Distress a Freestanding Tort?*, 44 Wake Forest L. Rev. 1131 (2009).

As has been the case with the courts' treatment of IIED claims, courts have taken a cautious approach to NIED claims:

> Over time, the rationales for limiting claims of mental distress have shifted somewhat. Early cases tended to doubt the genuineness of mental distress claims. There were fears that plaintiffs could easily fake injuries and that it would be impossible to trace the invisible causal chain from the accident to the plaintiff's injury. The courts also often faulted the plaintiff for not being "tougher," suggesting that mental distress was more a function of the idiosyncrasies of the victim than of the dangerous quality of the defendant's actions. These concerns about proof still sometimes surface today, despite the wealth of medical knowledge describing and documenting various types of mental disturbances and widespread acknowledgment that there is no bright line between physical and mental injury.
>
> In more recent decisions, however, the hesitation to award damages for mental distress is more often couched in terms of concerns about disproportionate liability for defendants and the lack of a clear stopping point for liability.

See Martha Chamallas, *The Architecture of Bias: Deep Structures in Torts Law*, 146 U. Pa. L. Rev. 463, 494 (1998).

These types of concerns largely explain the limitations courts have placed on claims of negligent infliction of emotional distress and the variety of tests courts employ. NIED claims tend to involve one of the following factual scenarios: (1) the plaintiff is the direct victim of the defendant's negligence and suffers emotional distress as a result or (2) the plaintiff suffers emotional distress after the defendant's negligence causes harm to a third person. Different rules may apply in these scenarios, and, indeed, some courts may not permit recovery at all in the latter category. *See* Straub v. Fisher & Paykel Health Care, 990 P.2d 384, 388 (Utah 1999) ("A plaintiff cannot recover for negligent infliction of emotional distress unless the plaintiff is a direct victim of the defendant's negligence. This rule applies regardless of whether the plaintiff's emotional distress resulted from fear for her own safety or from witnessing harm to another.").

A. Historical Treatment of NIED Claims

The two decisions in this part of the chapter—separated by more than 100 years—illustrate the courts' historical reluctance when it comes to NIED claims. To varying degrees, these concerns persist today.

Mitchell v. Rochester Ry. Co.

45 N.E. 354 (N.Y. 1896)

MARTIN, J.

The facts in this case are few, and may be briefly stated. On the 1st day of April, 1891, the plaintiff was standing upon a crosswalk on Main street, in the city of Rochester, awaiting an opportunity to board one of the defendant's cars which had stopped upon the street at that place. While standing there, and just as she was about to step upon the car, a horse car of the defendant came down the street. As the team attached to the car drew near, it turned to the right, and came close to the plaintiff, so that she stood between the horses' heads when they were stopped. She testified that from fright and excitement caused by the approach and proximity of the team she became unconscious, and also that the result was a miscarriage, and consequent illness. Medical testimony was given to the effect that the mental shock which she then received was sufficient to produce that result. Assuming that the evidence tended to show that the defendant's servant was negligent in the management of the car and horses, and that the plaintiff was free from contributory negligence, the single question presented is whether the plaintiff is entitled to recover for the defendant's negligence which occasioned her fright and alarm, and resulted in the injuries already mentioned. While the authorities are not harmonious upon this question, we think the most reliable and better-considered cases, as well as public policy, fully justify us in holding that the plaintiff cannot recover for injuries occasioned by fright, as there was no immediate personal injury.

... The difficulty which often exists in cases of alleged physical injury, in determining whether they exist, and, if so, whether they were caused by the negligent act of the defendant, would not only be greatly increased, but a wide field would be opened for fictitious or speculative claims. To establish such a doctrine would be contrary to principles of public policy. Moreover, it cannot be properly said that the plaintiff's miscarriage was the proximate result of the defendant's negligence. Proximate damages are such as are the ordinary and natural results of the negligence charged, and those that are usual, and may, therefore, be expected. It is quite obvious that the plaintiff's injuries do not fall within the rule as to proximate damages. The injuries to the plaintiff were plainly the result of an accidental or unusual combination of circumstances, which could not have been reasonably anticipated, and over which the defendant had no control, and hence her damages were too remote to justify a recovery in this action. These considerations lead to the conclusion that no recovery can be had for injuries sustained by fright occasioned by the negligence of another, where there is no immediate personal injury.

Dowty v. Riggs

385 S.W.3d 117 (Ark. 2010)

JIM HANNAH, Chief Justice.

Appellants Karen Dowty and Karen Dowty and Alvis Eugene Dowty, Sr. ("Gene"), as next friends of Riggs Dowty, a minor, appeal from an order of summary judgment entered against them in their suit against appellee Evelyn Riggs to recover damages for negligence and for negligent infliction of emotional distress....

The claims in this case arose from an incident that occurred on October 29, 2004, at the home of Evelyn, who is Karen's mother. That day, Karen, Gene, and Riggs traveled to Evelyn's residence to help her with some yard work. When they arrived, Evelyn's adult son, Perry Riggs, approached the vehicle and displayed a .25-caliber pistol. When Gene got out of the vehicle, Perry shot him in the arm. Karen exited the vehicle, and Perry continued to fire the gun. Thereafter, Karen removed Riggs from the vehicle and left the scene. Neither Karen nor Riggs was physically injured....

Arkansas does not recognize the tort of negligent infliction of emotional distress. This court has long held that "there can be no recovery for fright or mental pain and anguish caused by negligence, where there is no physical injury." *Erwin v. Milligan*, 188 Ark. 658, 663, 67 S.W.2d 592, 594 (1934). "The reason that mental suffering unaccompanied by physical injury is not considered as an element of recoverable damages is that it is deemed to be too remote, uncertain, and difficult of ascertainment; and the reason that such suffering is allowed as an element of damages, when accompanied by physical injury, is that the two are so intimately connected that both must be considered because of the difficulty in separating them." *Chi., Rock Island & Pac. Ry. Co. v. Caple*, 207 Ark. 52, 58–59, 179 S.W.2d 151, 154 (1944) (quoting St. Louis Iron Mountain & S. Ry. Co. v. Taylor, 84 Ark. 42, 47, 104 S.W. 551, 552 (1907)).

The appellants contend that, even though they did not suffer any physical injury, they should be allowed to recover for the mental anguish and emotional distress caused by Evelyn's negligence. In support of their argument, they cite cases from jurisdictions that allow recovery for negligent infliction of emotional distress. While the appellants offer rules for recovery used by other jurisdictions, they do not advocate that this court adopt a particular set of rules. In essence, we are asked to adopt a test that will most likely allow the appellants to recover damages in this case. They contend that a negligent-infliction-of-emotional-distress claim provides the only relief for them because "[t]he attacker, Perry Riggs, cannot be held responsible due to considerable, debilitating mental defects." But this court cannot simply overrule precedent and recognize a new tort due to the appellants' inability to recover damages from the person they have identified as their "attacker."

. . .

We do not overrule our common law cavalierly or without giving considerable thought to the change. In this case, the appellants have failed to demonstrate that great injury or injustice would result were we to continue to uphold the prior decisions of this court. We are mindful that the majority of jurisdictions in this country allow recovery for negligent infliction of emotional distress. *See* John J. Kircher, *The Four Faces of Tort Law: Liability for Emotional Harm*, 90 MARQ. L. REV. 789, 809 (2007). And we acknowledge that advances in the understanding of the effects of emotional trauma may belie our rejection of claims that we have previously "deemed to be too remote, uncertain, and difficult of ascertainment." Accordingly, we may revisit the issue in the future. Here, however, the facts in the present case do not warrant the creation of a new tort.

Note

Mitchell stated the original rule in these cases. By the time *Dowty* was decided in 2010, the vast majority of states had moved away from *Mitchell* and permitted recovery in at least some circumstances. But as *Dowty* illustrates, courts also have serious concerns about permitting recovery for emotional distress absent physical injury. Originally, some courts began to recognize narrow exceptions to the rule articulated in *Mitchell.* For example, in the so-called "dead body cases," some courts began to recognize the claims of loved ones in the case of negligent mishandling or embalming of a corpse. These cases were not specifically classified as negligent infliction of emotional distress cases but were instead treated as a freestanding tort. *See* Muchow v. Lindblad, 435 N.W.2d 918, 922 (N.D. 1989). In some instances, such as the case of negligent delivery of a death notice to a loved one, the claims were sometimes grounded on breach of contract principles. *See* Gardner v. Cumberland Tel. Co., 268 S.W. 1108, 1109 (Ky. 1925). Over time, however, claims of negligent infliction of emotional distress began to develop more concrete form and the law began to expand.

B. NIED: Direct Victim Cases

The most commonly recognized NIED claim is the case where the plaintiff is the direct victim of the defendant's negligence and suffers emotional distress as a result. Courts have applied a variety of rules to these sorts of cases.

1. The Impact Rule

Gilliam v. Stewart

291 So. 2d 593 (Fla. 1974)

DREW, Justice, Retired:

This cause is here by virtue of a certificate of the District Court of Appeal, Fourth District, that the decision below passes upon a question of great public interest, viz:

> Where a person suffers a definite and objective physical injury, *i.e.*, heart attack, as a result of emotional stress, *i.e.*, fright, induced by a defendant's alleged negligent conduct may such person maintain an action against the defendant even though no physical impact from an external force was imposed upon the injured person?

[The District Court of Appeal below described the facts as follows: Plaintiffs Jane R. Stewart and J. Parks Stewart, her husband, originally initiated their complaint against the defendants, Gilliam and Bradley, seeking compensatory damages and alleging, inter alia, that on January 20, 1970, defendants negligently and carelessly operated their motor vehicles so as to collide with each other and ultimately to collide with the residence of the plaintiffs. The complaint further alleged that "as a direct and proximate result of the negligence of the Defendants, Freddie LaVerne Gilliam and Robert Leo Bradley, the Plaintiff, Jane R. Stewart, Suffered serious and grievous personal injuries, including a shock to her nervous system which resulted in a coronary insufficiency and myocardial infarction and a left lateral cerebellar lesion." Defendants' vehicles were involved in an intersectional collision, both being propelled over the curb, the Gilliam vehicle coming to rest at an oak tree on the Stewarts' property and the Bradley vehicle directly striking the masonry residence of the plaintiffs causing minor damage to the dwelling. The accident occurred shortly before nine in the morning; Mrs. Stewart was still in bed but not asleep. Mrs. Stewart heard the crash at the intersection and then heard the crash of the cars striking the tree and the house. When Mrs. Stewart heard the car hit the house she got out of bed, went to the front porch, looked through the window and saw Bradley's car against her house with steam coming out of the radiator; she was also able to observe the Gilliam vehicle resting against the oak tree. She was unable to get out the back door of her house through the kitchen because of the Bradley vehicle so she ran back through the den and out another back door to ascertain if anyone was hurt. She then went back into her house to use the telephone also permitting various people to come into her house to use the phone.

Within 15 minutes after returning to the house, Mrs. Stewart went back to bed because of chest pains and approximately two hours later she was in the intensive care unit of the Orange Memorial Hospital. At the time the car struck Mrs. Stewart's house she said she felt no physical impact. Following the accident on January 20, Dr. Morton Levy, who had been Mrs. Stewart's family physician for a 20-year period, examined her and diagnosed her condition as being myocardial infarction.] [Dr. Levy attributed the myocardial infarction to the fright associated with the incident.]

Judge Mager's opinion for the majority below ably presents the case for receding from the impact doctrine. No useful purpose will be served by repeating here what he has so ably set forth there. We do not agree that, especially under the facts in this case, there is any valid justification to recede from the long standing decisions of this Court in this area. There may be circumstances under which one may recover for emotional or mental injuries, as when there has been a physical impact or when they are produced as a result of a deliberate and calculated act performed with the intention of producing such an injury by one knowing that such act would probably—and most likely—produce such an injury, but those are not the facts in this case.

The decision below is quashed with directions to reinstate the trial court's summary judgment.

It is so ordered.

Notes

Injury and impact. Note that under some formulations of the impact rule, a plaintiff could recover if the defendant's negligence resulted in *either* physical impact or physical injury. The amount of impact or injury could be "slight, trifling, or trivial" and still satisfy the requirement. *See* Deutsch v. Shein, 597 S.W.2d 141, 146 (Ky. 1980).

Justifications for the impact rule. Recall some of the justifications listed at the beginning of the chapter and in *Mitchell* for limiting the ability of plaintiffs to recover for emotional distress absent physical injury. How, if at all, does the impact rule address the concerns identified by courts concerning such claims?

Status of the rule today. Most courts have done away with the impact rule, *see, e.g., Osborne v. Keeney*, 399 S.W.3d 1 (Ky. 2012), although a few still follow it. *See* Indiana. Atl. Coast Airlines v. Cook, 857 N.E.2d 989 (Ind. 2006). As we will see in Part B4 below, however, even in states that still follow the rule, some exceptions often exist.

Problem 10.1. Bob sometimes drives his elderly mother, Patricia, to the store. As he was driving his mother one day, Bob noticed a Pleasant Hill Hospital ambulance running straight through a stop sign and entering the intersection at a high rate of speed. Patricia saw the ambulance too and began screaming as she feared the two vehicles would collide. Chris was driving the ambulance and he too became afraid as he entered the intersection. The Hospital had failed to maintain the brakes on the ambulance and Chris was unable to stop at the intersection as a result. Fortunately, the two vehicles swerved and missed each other. However, Patricia was deeply shaken by the near miss and sobbed uncontrollably following the incident. She remained agitated and nervous for several days afterward and would sometimes begin crying out of nowhere as she replayed the incident in her mind. Bob was able to move past the incident fairly quickly. If Patricia were to sue the Hospital on a theory of negligent infliction of emotional distress, could she recover in a jurisdiction that applies the impact rule?

2. The Physical Manifestation Rule

Daley v. LaCroix

179 N.W.2d 390 (Mich. 1970)

T. M. KAVANAGH, Judge.

This appeal presents as a threshold question . . . whether the "impact" rule in emotional distress has any continued vitality in the Michigan civil jurisprudence.

On July 16, 1963, about 10:00 p.m., defendant was traveling west on 15 Mile Road near plaintiffs' farm in Macomb County. Defendant's vehicle left the highway, traveled 63 feet in the air and 209 feet beyond the edge of the road and, in the process, sheared off a utility pole. A number of high voltage lines snapped, striking the electrical lines leading into plaintiffs' house and caused a great electrical explosion resulting in considerable property damage.

Plaintiffs claimed, in addition to property damage, that Estelle Daley suffered traumatic neurosis, emotional disturbance and nervous upset, and that Timothy Daley suffered emotional disturbance and nervousness as a result of the explosion and the attendant circumstances.

[The Court of Appeals affirmed the trial court's grant of a directed verdict upon the ground that Michigan law denies recovery for negligently caused emotional disturbance absent a showing of physical impact.]

The life of the law . . . has not been logic but experience. Bowing to the onslaught of exceptions and the growing irreconcilability between legal fact and decretal fiction, a rapidly increasing majority of courts have repudiated the "requirement of impact" and have regarded the physical consequences themselves or the circumstances of the accident as sufficient guarantee.

. . .

Based upon close scrutiny of our precedential cases and the authority upon which they rested and cognizant of the changed circumstances relating to the factual and scientific information available, we conclude that the "impact" requirement of the common law should not have a continuing effect in Michigan and we therefore overrule the principle to the contrary contained in our previous cases.

We hold that where a definite and objective physical injury is produced as a result of emotional distress proximately caused by defendant's negligent conduct, the plaintiff in a properly pleaded and proved action may recover in damages for such physical consequences to himself notwithstanding the absence of any physical impact upon plaintiff at the time of the mental shock.

The rule we adopt today is, of course, subject to familiar limitations.

Generally, defendant's standard of conduct is measured by reactions to be expected of normal persons. Absent specific knowledge of plaintiff's unusual sensitivity, there should be no recovery for hypersensitive mental disturbance where a normal individual would not be affected under the circumstances. As stated in comment c, Restatement, Torts (Second), § 313, at p. 114:

> On the other hand, one who unintentionally but negligently subjects another to such an emotional distress does not take the risk of any exceptional physical sensitiveness to emotion which the other may have unless the circumstances known to the actor should apprise him of it. Thus, one who negligently drives an automobile through a city street in a manner likely merely to startle a pedestrian on a sidewalk, is not required to take into account the possibility that the latter may be so constituted that the slight mental disturbance will bring about an illness.

. . .

In view of the above holding it becomes necessary to discuss another issue raised by plaintiffs—whether, considering the evidence in the light most favorable to plaintiffs, sufficient evidence was presented to create a jury question. . . .

From an examination of the evidence presented on behalf of Timothy Daley, we believe that, even though the question is a close one, on favorable view, he presented facts from which under our new rule, as announced in this case, a jury could reasonably find or infer a causal relation between defendant's alleged negligence and the injuries alleged. We conclude that Timothy Daley should be given an opportunity to prove his alleged cause of action, if he can do so, at a new trial.

Plaintiff Estelle Daley's claim that she suffered physical consequences naturally arising from the fright proximately caused by defendant's conduct is amply supported by the record. Her sudden loss of weight, her inability to perform ordinary household duties, her extreme nervousness and irritability, repeatedly testified to by plaintiffs, are facts from which a jury could find or infer a compensable physical injury.

The plaintiffs' testimony is also supported by the medical expert witness, who diagnosed plaintiff Estelle Daley as "a chronic psychoneurotic . . . in partial remission," and who attributed this state or condition to the explosion directly caused by defendant's acts.

. . .

The order of the trial court granting directed verdicts against plaintiffs Estelle Daley and Timothy Daley and the Court of Appeals' affirmance thereof are reversed and the causes remanded for new trials.

Notes

Justifications for the physical manifestation rule. Recall some of the justifications listed at the beginning of the chapter and in *Mitchell* for limiting the ability of plaintiffs to recover for emotional distress absent physical injury. How, if at all, does the physical manifestation rule address the concerns identified by courts concerning such claims?

Evidence of physical manifestation of distress. One federal court has said that Michigan courts "are very lenient" in terms of finding evidence of the definite and objective physical injury caused by emotional distress that *Daley* requires. Stites v. Sundstrand Heat Transfer, Inc., 660 F. Supp. 1516, 1527 (W.D. Mich. 1987). In the case of Timothy Daley, for example, there was no expert testimony offered regarding his emotional distress. Some courts that retain the rule require stronger evidence of physical injury. *See* Leaon v. Washington County, 397 N.W.2d 867, 875 (Minn. 1986) (concluding plaintiff did not satisfy the physical manifestation test when he "lost weight (later regained), became depressed, and exhibited feelings of anger, fear, and bitterness"). Some require that the distress result in "physical harm manifested by objective symptomology," *Sullivan v. Boston Gas Co.*, 414 Mass. 129, 132 (1993), which requires "objective corroboration of the emotional distress alleged." Payton v. Abbott Labs, 386 Mass. 540, 547 (1982).

Problem 10.2. Refer back to the facts from Problem 10.1. Could Patricia recover from the Hospital on her NIED claim in a jurisdiction that employs the physical manifestation test?

3. The Zone of Danger of Rule

Sometimes "a near miss may be as frightening as a direct hit." *Williams v. Baker*, 572 A.2d 1062, 1067 (D.C. 1990) (en banc). This premise underlies the "zone of danger" rule, which permits recovery for emotional distress even absent physical injury or impact, where the defendant's negligence places the plaintiff in physical peril and the plaintiff fears for her safety. *See* Mower v. Baird, 422 P.3d 837, 852 (Utah 2018). If the defendant's negligence places the plaintiff in danger of immediate bodily harm, and severe emotional harm results from the plaintiff's fear at having been placed within that "zone of danger," the defendant may be liable. This general rule is reflected in § 47(a) of the *Restatement (Third) of Torts* and has been adopted by numerous courts.

Problem 10.3. Refer back to the facts from Problem 10.1. Could Patricia recover from the Hospital on her NIED claim in a jurisdiction that employs the zone of danger test?

Note

Justifications for the rule. Recall some of the justifications listed at the beginning of the chapter and in *Mitchell* for limiting the ability of plaintiffs to recover for emotional distress absent physical injury. How, if at all, does the zone of danger rule address the concerns identified by courts concerning such claims?

4. Rules Based on Guaranties of Genuineness and Foreseeability

Even when the impact rule was common, courts recognized certain scenarios as being especially likely to result in emotional distress and in which concerns over fakery and lack of causation were reduced. These were cases in which the facts themselves provided a "guaranty of genuineness" concerning the plaintiff's claimed emotional distress. One early example was the so-called "dead body cases" mentioned previously. These were cases in which the concerns over unforeseeability of distress and fakery were, by their nature, lessened.

While the impact, physical manifestation, and zone of danger tests are all still in use, there are at least some courts that focus more heavily on the foreseeability of distress resulting from a defendant's negligence when crafting rules for NIED claims.

a. Activities, Undertakings, or Relationships in which Negligent Conduct Is Especially Likely to Cause Serious Emotional Harm

Hedgepeth v. Whitman Walker Clinic

22 A.3d 789 (D.C. 2011)

RUIZ, Associate Judge:

Appellant Terry Hedgepeth alleges that he suffered serious emotional distress after the doctor he saw at the Whitman Walker Clinic negligently informed him that he was HIV positive when, in fact, he was not. Appellant presented evidence that, as a result of the mistaken diagnosis, he was severely clinically depressed and suffered repercussions in his employment and personal life until another clinic correctly informed him that he was not afflicted with HIV, five years later. The Superior

Court granted appellees' motion for summary judgment on the grounds that appellant had failed to establish the requisite facts for the tort of negligent infliction of emotional distress, where there is no other harm. A division of this court affirmed, agreeing with the Superior Court that appellees' alleged negligence did not place appellant within a "zone of physical danger," as required for recovery of emotional distress damages by *Williams v. Baker*, 572 A.2d 1062 (D.C. 1990) (en banc).

. . .

III. Emotional Distress Damages in Established Relationships

In this appeal, appellant urges us to abandon our reliance upon the "zone of physical danger" test as the *sole* means of recovery for the tort of negligent infliction of emotional distress. Specifically, appellant and *amicus* supporting his claim argue that recovery also should be permitted in those cases where the negligent actor has a relationship or has committed to an undertaking with the plaintiff of such nature that negligent performance of a legal obligation to the plaintiff is very likely to cause serious emotional harm, and, in fact, does so. The question is not whether the "zone of physical danger" rule should be jettisoned and replaced with the proposed "relationship" or "undertaking" rule in every case. Rather, the issue presented in this appeal is whether—in addition to permitting recovery based on the "zone of physical danger" rule—the law should allow courts to conclude that a defendant has assumed a duty to avoid inflicting emotional distress in certain cases where the underlying relationship or undertaking is such that it is not only foreseeable, but especially likely, that the defendant's negligence will cause serious emotional distress to the plaintiff. For the reasons we now discuss, we agree with appellant, and adopt a supplemental rule, as defined in this opinion.

A. The Proposed Special Relationship or Undertaking Rule

Appellant's argument that the "zone of physical danger" rule should not be the sole route for recovery in all cases seeking damages for serious emotional distress finds support in Section 47[1] of the draft Restatement (Third) of Torts:

> § 47 Negligent Conduct Directly Inflicting Emotional Disturbance on Another
>
> An actor whose negligent conduct causes serious emotional disturbance to another is subject to liability to the other if the conduct:
>
> (a) places the other in immediate danger of bodily harm and the emotional disturbance results from the danger; or
>
> (b) occurs in the course of specified categories of activities, undertakings, or relationships in which negligent conduct is especially likely to cause serious emotional disturbance.

Restatement (Third) of Torts § 46 (Tentative Draft No. 5, 2007) (hereinafter, "draft Third Restatement"). Subsection (a) of Section 46, which refers to "immediate

1. Editor's note: The court originally referenced a different section number that appeared in an earlier draft. The final version of this section now appears in section 47.

danger of bodily harm," corresponds to the *Williams* "zone of physical danger" rule. Subsection (b), which refers to "specified categories of activities, undertakings, or relationships in which negligent conduct is especially likely to cause serious emotional disturbance," would encompass claims, such as appellant's, which arise from a doctor-patient relationship in which the doctor negligently misdiagnosed the patient with a grave illness, with the likely result that it would (and did) cause serious emotional distress. Thus, as articulated by the drafters of § 46 of the draft Third Restatement, a rule that finds a duty based upon "undertakings or relationships" is a supplement to—rather than a substitute for—the "zone of physical danger" rule that permits recovery in the absence of such a relationship. Under either test, only direct victims of the actor's negligence can recover.

. . .

Professor Dobbs's modern treatise on torts explains why such a rule addresses the problem of potentially infinite liability that has been of central judicial concern in emotional distress cases:

> When the defendant owes an independent duty of care to the plaintiff, there is no risk of unlimited liability to an unlimited number of people. Liability turns solely on relationships accepted by the defendant, usually under contractual arrangement. Consequently, the duty extends only to those for whom the contract was made. . . .

PROSSSER & KEETON ON TORTS, supra, § 312, at 849. We agree with the draft Third Restatement and Professor Dobbs's observation that no special rule (such as the zone of physical danger test) is necessary to guard against the risk of imposing a duty that might be unlimited or unreasonable when emotional harm is especially likely to be caused as a direct result of negligent performance of a duty to avoid such harm owed to a specific person. Such a duty can, but need not, arise from a contractual arrangement between the parties. The key point is that the requirement of a special relationship between the parties or undertaking by the defendant to the plaintiff limits the scope of the defendant's potential liability to identifiable persons, rendering the "zone of physical danger" requirement unnecessary to achieve that purpose.

. . .

Viewed against the broad spectrum of cases that permit recovery for emotional distress resulting from breach of an obligation owed to a particular person, we are hard pressed to justify a blanket prohibition on recovery where such breach has been proven simply because emotional distress is the only injury suffered. We conclude that the "zone of physical danger" rule should not preclude a plaintiff's recovery for negligently inflicted emotional distress where other factors in an existing relationship—that we now set out in this opinion—are more adequate to define, and also are adequate to limit, the defendant's responsibilities.

IV. The Duty to Avoid Inflicting Serious Emotional Distress

We hold that a plaintiff may recover for negligent infliction of emotional distress if the plaintiff can show that (1) the defendant has a relationship with the plaintiff, or has undertaken an obligation to the plaintiff, of a nature that necessarily implicates the plaintiff's emotional well-being, (2) there is an especially likely risk that the defendant's negligence would cause serious emotional distress to the plaintiff, and (3) negligent actions or omissions of the defendant in breach of that obligation have, in fact, caused serious emotional distress to the plaintiff. Whether the defendant breached her obligations is to be determined by reference to the specific terms of the undertaking agreed upon by the parties or, otherwise, by an objective standard of reasonableness applicable to the underlying relationship or undertaking, *e.g.*, in medical malpractice cases, the national standard of care. The likelihood that the plaintiff would suffer serious emotional distress is measured against an objective standard: what a "reasonable person" in the defendant's position would have foreseen under the circumstances in light of the nature of the relationship or undertaking. In addition, the plaintiff must establish that she actually suffered "serious and verifiable" emotional distress....

In the absence of such an undertaking or relationship between plaintiff and defendant, the general rule continues to be that there is no freestanding duty to avoid the negligent infliction of emotional distress to a "stranger" unless the actor's negligent conduct has put the plaintiff in danger of bodily harm, *i.e.*, the *Williams* "zone of physical danger" rule that recognizes that "a near miss may be as frightening as a direct hit." We emphasize that the issue addressed in *Williams* and that we further refine today is one of duty *vel non*, an issue of law to be determined by the court as a necessary precondition to the viability of a cause of action for negligence. It is for the court to consider the relevant evidence and make a decision on the pleadings, on summary judgment, or, where necessary, after a hearing. Once the court determines the existence of a duty to avoid inflicting emotional distress, the other elements of the cause of action—standard of care, breach, causation and damages—must be proven to the finder of fact by a preponderance of the evidence, and the defendant may present defenses, such as the plaintiff's contributory negligence. But if the court determines there is no duty as a matter of law, the litigation comes to an end, and that decision is a final order of the trial court.

...

Having set out the legal requirements, we now turn to the facts alleged by appellant....

Following the mistaken diagnosis delivered in 2000, appellant believed that he was HIV positive for five years. He became depressed and began having suicidal thoughts, which resulted in his admission to the psychiatric wards at George Washington University Hospital in January 2001, and at Sibley Hospital in 2002. He was prescribed several medications for depression. He lost his job as a restaurant manager. Appellant's relationship with his daughter also suffered as a result of his depression. Appellant used illegal drugs, suffered from an eating disorder, and began to have sexual intercourse with a woman he knew to be HIV-positive "[b]ecause [he] was diagnosed with HIV and there was no reason for [him] to live."

Appellant visited the Abundant Life Clinic in June 2005, where he was again tested for HIV. The test revealed that appellant was not HIV positive. According to Dr. Abdul Muhammad, the treating physician at Abundant Life, upon hearing the negative test result, appellant wept and appeared to him as though he were "a man being released from prison." Appellant confirmed his negative test result several weeks later at the Johns Hopkins Bayview Medical Center.

Appellees do not dispute that they owed a duty of care to appellant as their patient; appellant alleges that this duty was breached when appellees negligently misinformed him that he was HIV positive, and has presented testimonial and documentary evidence in support of his allegations. Furthermore, there is evidence in the record to support that the nature of appellees' duty to appellant necessarily implicated his emotional well-being and that it was especially likely that a doctor's breach of duty in misdiagnosing a patient with HIV-infection would result in serious emotional harm. Appellant's actions and suffering after the misdiagnosis reveal that when a patient is told that he has a life-altering or life-threatening chronic disease, this information can and does cause serious emotional distress. When the diagnosis is for HIV—a potentially fatal infection that carries a significant social stigma—the emotional impact can be catastrophic. WWC does not dispute that patients who are informed that they are HIV positive often suffer serious emotional distress. Indeed, WWC implicitly recognizes this risk; its brief recounts that WWC provides counseling to patients who test positive for HIV "to help the person understand how to live with the virus, and also to accept that, in 2010, the presence of HIV is not tantamount to a 'death sentence.'" In one commentator's view, appellant's distress is "inseparable" from breach of the appellees' "core undertakings." Nor does WWC dispute that appellant actually suffered serious emotional distress, a claim that appellant has sought to verify with evidence of his admission to two psychiatric wards, prescriptions for several anti-depressants, the deterioration of his relationships with his employer and with his daughter, and his risk-taking behavior. In sum, there is both objective and subjective evidence that serious emotional distress would result from appellees' negligent misdiagnosis of HIV.

Applying the rule we enunciate in this opinion, we conclude that on this record appellees are not entitled to summary judgment on appellant's claim of negligent infliction of emotional distress. Accordingly, we reverse and remand the case for further proceedings in the trial court consistent with this opinion.

So ordered.

Notes

Other examples. Other examples listed in the *Restatement* include where "a physician negligently diagnoses a patient with a dreaded or serious disease; a physician negligently causes the loss of a fetus; a hospital loses a newborn infant; a person injures a fetus; [and] a hospital (or another) exposes a patient to HIV infection." Restatement (Third) of Torts § 47 cmt. f. *See also* Mower v. Baird, 422 P.3d 837 (Utah 2018) (therapist working with a minor child who negligently causes child to have false memories or make false allegations of sexual abuse by parent); *Hedgepeth*, 22 A.3d at 815 (suggesting that a claim might lie against those who are appointed to act as guardians and counsel for those who are especially vulnerable: children, the elderly, and the disabled).

Recognition of similar exceptions. Even the courts in jurisdictions that retain more restrictive rules like the impact rule tend to recognize at least some exceptions like those described in this section or exceptions where the risk of emotional distress is clearly foreseeable. For example, Florida still retains *Gilliam*'s impact rule, but it has recognized a "very narrow class of cases in which the foreseeability and gravity of the emotional injury involved, and lack of countervailing policy concerns, have surmounted the policy rationale undergirding the application of the impact rule." Rowell v. Holt, 850 So. 2d 474, 478 (Fla. 2003). Examples include where a psychotherapist discloses confidential information about a patient, *see* Gracey v. Eaker, 837 So. 2d 348 (Fla. 2002), where a laboratory negligently disseminates a patient's HIV-positive test results, *see* Florida Dept. of Corrections v. Abril, 969 So. 2d 201 (Fla. 2007), or where a customer consumes contaminated food or beverages and fears for her health. *See* Hagan v. Coca-Cola Bottling Co., 804 So. 2d 1234 (Fla. 2001).

Serious or severe harm requirement. Notice in *Hegepeth* and the *Restatement* the requirement that the resulting distress be serious or severe. Recall from Chapter 2 that a plaintiff alleging intentional infliction of emotional distress must establish that the defendant's conduct resulted in severe emotional distress. Note also that under both approaches a defendant is only liable for foreseeable emotional distress; a defendant is not liable for the distress suffered by "the supersensitive plaintiff." Gammon v. Osteopathic Hosp. of Maine, Inc., 534 A.2d 1282, 1285 (Me. 1987).

Lawyers and NIED. As *Hedgepeth* notes in another part of the opinion, clients have generally had little success in their NIED claims against lawyers. The reason for this, according to *Hedgepeth*, is that "neither the purpose of the relationship nor the fiduciary's undertaking is to care for the plaintiff's emotional well-being; rather the object of the engagement is to obtain a financial, commercial or legal objective, even if its non-attainment due to the fiduciary's negligence is emotionally distressing to the client." *Hedgepeth v. Whitman Walker Clinic*, 22 A.3d 789, 815 (D.C. 2011). Is the lawyer-client relationship one that, in the words of *Hedgepeth*, "necessarily implicates the plaintiff's emotional well-being?" Or, to use the language of the *Restatement*, is the lawyer's undertaking one that, if performed negligently, "is especially likely to cause serious emotional disturbance?"

Problem 10.4. Refer back to the facts from Problem 10.1. Assume for purposes of this problem only that well before the incident with the ambulance, Patricia's son, Bob, was driving negligently. Patricia was terrified that a collision might occur as a result of Bob's negligence, although no collision would have seemed imminent to a reasonable person. Patricia claims she suffers serious emotional distress as a result of Bob "driving like a maniac." Putting aside any question of intra-family immunity, could Patricia recover from Bob on an NIED claim in a jurisdiction that employs the test from *Hedgepeth*?

b. General Negligence Principles

Camper v. Minor

915 S.W.2d 437 (Tenn. 1996)

DROWOTA, Justice.

Facts and Procedural History

On April 14, 1992, the plaintiff Camper was driving his cement truck along South Wilcox Drive, a four-lane highway in Kingsport, Tennessee. At the same time, Jennifer L. Taylor, a 16 year old driver of a car owned by Sharon Barnett, was proceeding on Reservoir Road, a two-lane road that intersects with South Wilcox Drive. As Camper approached the South Wilcox-Reservoir Road intersection, which is controlled by a stop sign, Ms. Taylor, who had been stopped at this intersection, suddenly pulled out in front of Camper. The vehicles collided, and Ms. Taylor was killed instantly. Camper exited his truck moments after the crash, walked around the front of his vehicle, and viewed Ms. Taylor's body in the wreckage from close range.

Mr. Camper subsequently brought an action against Daniel B. Minor, the administrator of Ms. Taylor's estate, and Sharon Barnett, seeking to recover for the emotional injuries he allegedly received as a result of viewing Ms. Taylor's body soon after the accident. In his complaint, Camper did not allege that he sustained any substantial physical injury in the accident; instead, he alleged that "as a result of this accident, the plaintiff suffers from personal injuries to his nerves and nervous system known as a post traumatic disorder [sic], which injury is serious and disabling to him." In his deposition, Mr. Camper testified as to the nature of his injuries as follows:

> Q: Okay. At the time of the accident, when the accident occurred, were you injured as a result of this accident?
>
> A: Not physically, but emotionally and mentally I was.
>
> Q: All right. Now—so when you say you weren't injured physically, no broken bones, no cuts, no bruises, no back problems, no nothing [sic]?
>
> A: No, sir. I had a small scrape on my knee.
>
> Q: Okay. But nothing to warrant doctors' care.
>
> A: No, sir.

In his affidavit, Mr. Camper stated "[t]hat as a result of the collision in which I was involved, I have sustained mental and emotional injuries resulting in loss of sleep, inability to function on a normal basis, outbursts of crying and depression. It has been necessary for me to be under the care and treatment of a psychiatrist and counselors and further that I am taking medication in order to help relieve me of my suffering." Camper testified in his deposition that he never feared for his own safety during the accident, and that his emotional injuries resulted solely from seeing Ms. Taylor's body in the car immediately after the accident.

About two weeks after the accident, Mr. Camper consulted a psychiatrist about his mental problems stemming from the accident. He went to the psychiatrist's office twice; but he stated that he quit going because he could not afford it and because the medication the psychiatrist prescribed left him unable to function. Camper later consulted a second psychiatrist. (This visit was three days before Camper's deposition; he stated in his deposition that his lawyer had arranged for the consultation.) This second psychiatrist referred Camper to an apparently more affordable center for counseling; at the time of the deposition, however, Camper had not yet had an appointment at this counseling center. Despite the fact that the record reflects that Camper has undergone some psychiatric treatment, it contains no expert medical evidence detailing his alleged mental and emotional injuries.

After the complaint was filed, the defendants filed a motion for summary judgment, arguing that damages for emotional injuries were not recoverable because Camper did not suffer any physical injury and because he did not, at the time of the accident, fear for his own safety. . . .

I.

The first issue for our consideration concerns the viability of Camper's claim against both defendants for his emotional damages. [The court engaged in a lengthy examination of the competing approaches in negligent infliction of emotional distress cases and concluded that the physical manifestation rule should no longer be used.]

This negative conclusion logically raises its positive counterpart: what is required to make out a prima facie case? After considering the strengths and weaknesses of the options used in other jurisdictions, we conclude that these cases should be analyzed under the general negligence approach . . . In other words, the plaintiff must present material evidence as to each of the five elements of general negligence—duty, breach of duty, injury or loss, causation in fact, and proximate, or legal, cause—in order to avoid summary judgment. Furthermore, we agree that in order to guard against trivial or fraudulent actions, the law ought to provide a recovery only for "serious" or "severe" emotional injury. A "serious" or "severe" emotional injury occurs "where a reasonable person, normally constituted, would be unable to adequately cope with the mental stress engendered by the circumstances of the case." Finally, we conclude that the claimed injury or impairment must be supported by expert medical or scientific proof.

Having so concluded, we have no alternative but to remand this case for further proceedings consistent with the approach that we adopt today. A remand is necessary because in the trial court the defendants simply argued that they were entitled to a summary judgment because (1) the plaintiff had received no physical injury—a requirement under the prior law; and (2) that the plaintiff had not been in fear for his own safety . . . Because the general negligence approach was not controlling at the time the defendants submitted their summary judgment motion, they clearly have failed to prove that no genuine issue of material fact exists as to those elements of negligent infliction of emotional distress that we adopt herein, and that they are entitled to a judgment as matter of law. Because the defendants failed to carry their initial burden pursuant to Rule 56, Tenn.R.Civ.P., we cannot approve of the summary judgment granted by the Court of Appeals.

Notes

Justifications for the rule. Recall some of the justifications listed at the beginning of the chapter and in *Mitchell* for limiting the ability of plaintiffs to recover for emotional distress absent physical injury. How, if at all, do the rules applied in *Hedgepeth* and *Camper* address the concerns identified by courts concerning such claims?

Practical lessons. If you were a lawyer in a jurisdiction that uses the *Camper* approach, what information would you want to know from a potential client before deciding to represent a client in a negligent infliction of emotional distress action?

Recognition of the *Camper* approach. Not many courts follow the *Camper* approach. But those that have adopted a more traditional negligence analysis have pointed to the "artificial devices" employed in other tests to limit liability. For example, the Supreme Judicial Council of Maine discarded all of its previous approaches to NIED in favor of "the traditional tort principle of foreseeability." Gammon v. Osteopathic Hosp. of Maine, Inc., 534 A.2d 1282, 1285 (Me. 1987). In *Gammon*, a hospital and funeral home negligently gave a son a bag containing a human leg that he believed would contain the personal effects of his father. The court acknowledged that it could have relied on the "dead body" line of cases to uphold liability, but instead chose to frame the issue simply as whether "the hospital and the mortician reasonably should have foreseen that members of Linwood Gammon's family would be vulnerable to emotional shock at finding a severed leg in what was supposed to be the decedent's personal effects." *Id.*

Problem 10.5. Refer back to the original facts from Problem 10.1. Could Patricia recover from the Hospital on her NIED claim in a jurisdiction that employs the test from *Camper*?

C. NIED: Harm to Third Persons Cases

The cases in the previous part all involved plaintiffs who were the direct victims of a defendant's negligence. In some cases, however, a plaintiff's emotional distress may stem from observing harm to another. These are sometimes referred to as "bystander" cases in that the plaintiff's distress did not stem from the plaintiff's fear for her own physical safety. Instead, the defendant's negligence injured a third party and the plaintiff suffered emotional distress as a result. In these situations, courts have historically been even more concerned about permitting liability.

For example, in *Grube v. Union Pacific Railroad Co.*, 886 P.2d 845 (Kan. 1994), the train the plaintiff was operating as an engineer collided with an automobile trapped upon a railroad crossing. One of the occupants of the car was killed. The plaintiff saw the occupant while the car was trapped and saw the look of fear on his face before the accident. The plaintiff expressed no fear for his own safety from the impending collision. After the collision, the plaintiff ran back to the scene of the accident to render aid. "He felt the pulse of the driver and touched the deceased, attempting to find a pulse." Shortly thereafter, he began to experience severe emotional distress. Applying the zone of danger test, the Kansas Supreme Court denied recovery in the plaintiff's NIED action against the railroad because his distress did not result from any fear for his own safety but instead from his fear for the deceased prior to the accident and from having been involved in the accident.

The case in this part of the chapter illustrates how the law has shifted to sometimes permit recovery in situations in which the plaintiff's distress stems from harm to third persons.

Thing v. La Chusa

771 P.2d 814 (Cal. 1989)

EAGLESON, Justice

On December 8, 1980, John Thing, a minor, was injured when struck by an automobile operated by defendant James V. La Chusa. His mother, plaintiff Maria Thing, was nearby, but neither saw nor heard the accident. She became aware of the injury to her son when told by a daughter that John had been struck by a car. She rushed to the scene where she saw her bloody and unconscious child, whom she believed was dead, lying in the roadway. Maria sued defendants, alleging that she suffered great emotional disturbance, shock, and injury to her nervous system as a result of these events, and that the injury to John and emotional distress she suffered were proximately caused by defendants' negligence.

The trial court granted defendants' motion for summary judgment, ruling that, as a matter of law, Maria could not establish a claim for negligent infliction of emotional distress because she did not contemporaneously and sensorily perceive the accident. Although prior decisions applying the guidelines suggested by this court in *Dillon v. Legg*, 441 P.2d 912, compelled the ruling of the trial court, the Court of Appeal reversed the judgment dismissing Maria's claim . . .

. . . Initially . . . in negligence cases the right to recover for emotional distress had been limited to circumstances in which the victim was himself injured and emotional distress was a "parasitic" item of damages, or if a plaintiff who had been in the "zone of danger" did not suffer injury from impact, but did suffer physical injury as a result of the emotional trauma.

Where the conduct was negligent, emotional distress caused solely by fear for a third person's safety or apprehension of injury to the third person, was first recognized as an injury for which damages could be sought in *Dillon v. Legg, supra.*

But shortly before *Dillon*, in *Amaya v. Home Ice, Fuel & Supply Co.*, 379 P.2d 513, the court had declined the opportunity to broaden the right to recover for emotional distress. *Amaya*, after confirming that the "impact rule" making a contemporaneous physical impact a prerequisite to recovery for negligently induced fright or shock was not applicable in California, held damages could not be recovered by persons outside the zone of danger created by the defendant's negligence even when that shock was reflected in physiological symptoms. The court quoted with approval the statement of the general rule of nonliability for nervous shock induced by fear for a third party applied by the Court of Appeal in *Reed v. Moore* (1957) 156 Cal. App.2d 43, 319 P.2d 80: "'As a general rule, no recovery is permitted for a mental or emotional disturbance, or for a bodily injury or illness resulting therefrom, in the absence of a contemporaneous bodily contact or independent cause of action, or an element of willfulness, wantonness, or maliciousness, in cases in which there is no injury other than one to a third person, even though recovery would have been permitted had the wrong been directed against the plaintiff. The rule is frequently applied to mental or emotional disturbances caused by another's danger, or sympathy for another's suffering. It has been regarded as applicable to a mental or emotional disturbance resulting from an injury not only to a stranger, but also to a relative of the plaintiff, such as a child, sister, father, or spouse.'"

The *Amaya* view was short lived, however. Only five years later, the decision was overruled in *Dillon v. Legg, supra.* In the ensuing 20 years, like the pebble cast into the pond, *Dillon*'s progeny have created ever widening circles of liability. Post-*Dillon* decisions have now permitted plaintiffs who suffer emotional distress, but no resultant physical injury, and who were not at the scene of and thus did not witness the event that injured another, to recover damages on grounds that a duty was owed to them solely because it was foreseeable that they would suffer that distress on learning of injury to a close relative.

In *Dillon* itself, the issue was limited. The mother and sister of a deceased infant each sought damages for "great emotional disturbance and shock and injury to her nervous system" which had caused them great mental pain and suffering. Allegedly these injuries were caused by witnessing the defendant's negligently operated vehicle collide with and roll over the infant as she lawfully crossed a street. The mother was not herself endangered by the defendant's conduct. The sister may have been. The trial court had therefore granted the defendant's motion for judgment on the pleadings as to the mother, but had denied it with respect to the sister of the decedent. Faced with the incongruous result demanded by the "zone of danger" rule which denied recovery for emotional distress and consequent physical injury unless the plaintiff himself had been threatened with injury, the court overruled *Amaya.*

Reexamining the concept of "duty" as applicable to the *Dillon* facts, the court now rejected the argument that the possibility of fraudulent claims justified denial of recovery, at least insofar as a mother who sees her child killed is concerned, as "no one can seriously question that fear or grief for one's child is as likely to cause physical injury as concern over one's own well-being." The court held instead that the right to recover should be determined by application of "the neutral principles of foreseeability, proximate cause and consequential injury that generally govern tort law."

The difficulty in defining the limits on recovery anticipated by the *Amaya* court was rejected as a basis for denying recovery, but the court did recognize that "to limit the otherwise potentially infinite liability which would follow every negligent act, the law of torts holds defendant amenable only for injuries to others which to defendant at the time were reasonably foreseeable." Thus, while the court indicated that foreseeability of the injury was to be the primary consideration in finding duty, it simultaneously recognized that policy considerations mandated that infinite liability be avoided by restrictions that would somehow narrow the class of potential plaintiffs. But the test limiting liability was itself amorphous.

In adopting foreseeability of the injury as the basis of a negligent actor's duty, the *Dillon* court identified the risks that could give rise to that duty as both physical impact and emotional disturbance brought on by the conduct. Having done so, the *Dillon* court conceded: "We cannot now predetermine defendant's obligation in every situation by a fixed category; no immutable rule can establish the extent of that obligation for every circumstance of the future." In an effort to give some initial definition to this newly approved expansion of the cause of action for NIED the court enunciated "guidelines" that suggested a limitation on the action to circumstances like those in the case before it.

"We note, first, that we deal here with a case in which plaintiff suffered a shock which resulted in physical injury and we confine our ruling to that case. In determining, in such a case, whether defendant should reasonably foresee the injury to plaintiff [mother], or in other terminology, whether defendant owes plaintiff a duty of due care, the courts will take into account such factors as the following: (1) Whether plaintiff was located near the scene of the accident as contrasted with one who was a distance away from it. (2) Whether the shock resulted from a direct emotional impact upon plaintiff from the sensory and contemporaneous observance of the accident, as contrasted with learning of the accident from others after its occurrence. (3) Whether plaintiff and the victim were closely related, as contrasted with an absence of any relationship or the presence of only a distant relationship.

. . .

Not surprisingly, this "case-to-case" or ad hoc approach to development of the law . . . has not only produced inconsistent rulings in the lower courts, but has provoked considerable critical comment by scholars who attempt to reconcile the cases.

The elements which justify and simultaneously limit an award of damages for emotional distress caused by awareness of the negligent infliction of injury to a close relative are those noted in *Ochoa*—the traumatic emotional effect on the plaintiff who contemporaneously observes both the event or conduct that causes serious injury to a close relative and the injury itself. Even if it is "foreseeable" that persons other than closely related percipient witnesses may suffer emotional distress, this fact does not justify the imposition of what threatens to become unlimited liability for emotional distress on a defendant whose conduct is simply negligent. Nor does such abstract "foreseeability" warrant continued reliance on the assumption that the limits of liability will become any clearer if lower courts are permitted to continue approaching the issue on a "case-to-case" basis some 20 years after *Dillon.*

We conclude, therefore, that a plaintiff may recover damages for emotional distress caused by observing the negligently inflicted injury of a third person if, but only if, said plaintiff: (1) is closely related to the injury victim; (2) is present at the scene of the injury producing event at the time it occurs and is then aware that it is causing injury to the victim; and (3) as a result suffers serious emotional distress—a reaction beyond that which would be anticipated in a disinterested witness and which is not an abnormal response to the circumstances.

...

The undisputed facts establish that plaintiff was not present at the scene of the accident in which her son was injured. She did not observe defendant's conduct and was not aware that her son was being injured. She could not, therefore, establish a right to recover for the emotional distress she suffered when she subsequently learned of the accident and observed its consequences. The order granting summary judgment was proper.

The judgment of the Court of Appeal is reversed.

Notes

Justifications for the rule. The concerns over fakery, foreseeability, and expansive liability are perhaps even more pronounced in NIED cases involving harm to third parties. How does the rule from *Thing* address these concerns?

Modern approaches. In these kinds of third-party cases, most courts have now adopted rules that are similar to *Dillon* or *Thing.* Some have adopted a flexible approach based on *Dillon, see, e.g., Culbert v. Sampson's Supermarkets Inc.*, 444 A.2d 433 (Me. 1982), while others have adopted a more formalized approach along the lines of *Thing. See, e.g.*, Clohessy v. Bachelor, 675 A.2d 852, 863 (Conn. 1996). The *Restatement* employs a test similar to that of *Thing.*

Suddenness of event. Section 48 of the *Restatement (Third) of the Torts* requires that the defendant's negligence cause a "sudden" serious bodily injury. Not all courts require this. *See* Henderson v. Vanderbilt University, 534 S.W.3d 426 (Tenn. Ct. App. 2017); Armstrong v. A.I. Dupont Hosp. for Children, 60 A.3d 414 (Del. Super. Ct. 2012).

Presence versus perception. Note that *Thing* requires the plaintiff to be present at the scene of the event that causes the injury. In contrast, § 48 of the *Restatement (Third) of the Torts* allows recovery where the plaintiff "perceives the event contemporaneously," which suggests that physical presence is not necessarily a requirement.

Guaranty of genuineness. Instead of the *Dillon/Thing* approach, some courts look to whether the facts provide a "guaranty of genuineness" in deciding whether to recognize a claim based on harm to a third person. In *Doe Parents No. 1 v. State, Dept. of Educ.*, 58 P.3d 545 (Haw. 2002), the Hawaii Supreme Court noted that while it normally applies a "zone of danger approach," there are cases "that present unique circumstances, which provide the requisite assurance that the plaintiff's psychological distress is trustworthy and genuine." In *Doe Parents No. 1*, the defendant allegedly reinstated a teacher accused of child molestation to a position of trust that put the teacher in close and generally unsupervised proximity with children, without first ascertaining that the teacher was actually innocent. According to the court, these circumstances provided the sort of "guaranty of genuineness" to permit the *parents* to recover for emotional distress suffered if their child was molested. *Id.* at 582.

Problem 10.6. Pam was visiting the Pleasant Hill Hospital with her fiancé, Victor. Victor left Pam in a waiting area and entered an elevator to go down to the cafeteria. Victor became trapped in the hospital's elevator between its outer door and the wall of the elevator shaft. The elevator was activated and Victor was dragged down two floors. A hospital employee saw Victor wedged within the elevator, and ran to seek help. Soon afterward, Pam and officers of the local police department arrived. The officers worked for four and one-half hours to free Victor to no avail. During their attempts, Pam watched as Victor moaned, cried out, and flailed his arms. Victor died from multiple bone fractures and massive internal hemorrhaging, while still trapped. Pam became severely depressed as a result of the incident and suffered severe emotional distress. Assume the hospital was negligent in its maintenance of the elevator.

(a) Could Pam recover on an NIED theory against the hospital in a jurisdiction that follows the *Thing v. La Chusa* approach?

(b) What legal rule do you believe is appropriate in these kinds of cases?

Problem 10.7. Victoria was a child who was undergoing radiation treatment for cancer at the Pleasant Hill Hospital. Her parents watched as she underwent the treatment. During the procedure, Victoria was lethally overexposed to radiation. The parents had no way of knowing this at the time of the procedure. The overexposure was not discovered until later when Victoria developed symptoms of radiation poisoning. The parents observed their child's appearance change dramatically on a daily basis as a result of the overexposure and became severely depressed both prior to and shortly after Victoria's death. Assume the hospital was negligent in its treatment of Victoria.

(a) Could the parents recover on an NIED theory against the hospital in a jurisdiction that follows the *Thing v. LaChusa* approach?

(b) What legal rule do you believe is appropriate in these kinds of cases?

D. Loss of Consortium

Connecticut General Statutes § 52-555b

Any claim or cause of action for loss of consortium by one spouse with respect to the death of the other spouse, which claim or cause of action may include, without limitation, claims for damages with respect to loss of the society of, affection of, moral support provided by, services provided by, sexual relations with or companionship of the other spouse, suffered because of the death of the other spouse, shall be brought with or joined with the claims and causes of action with respect to the death of the other spouse.

Loss of consortium claims are similar to, but ultimately different from, claims of negligent infliction of emotional distress. They are similar to the NIED cases involving harm to third persons in the sense that the party seeking compensation is not necessarily the party who was injured by the defendant's negligence. But they are different in the sense that the plaintiff is not seeking compensation for the emotional distress suffered by the death or injury of a loved one. Instead, as the Connecticut statute above illustrates, the plaintiff is seeking compensation for the "loss of the society of, affection of, moral support provided by, services provided by, sexual relations with or companionship of" the loved one.

Historically, only husbands had the right to bring such claims based on death or injury to the wife. In addition, early actions focused on the husband's right to recover for the loss of services resulting from the injury to the wife. In this sense, the claims were like those of an employer for the loss of services of an employee or servant. During the nineteenth century, the focus switched to the loss of support or companionship. *See* John Fabian Witt, *From Loss of Services to Loss of Support: The Wrongful Death Statutes, the Origins of Modern Tort Law, and the Making of the Nineteenth-Century Family*, 25 Law & Social Inquiry 717 (2000). In addition, both spouses now enjoy a right to recover. But as family structures and the tort have evolved, new issues have emerged.

Campos v. Coleman

123 A.3d 854 (Conn. 2015)

The named plaintiff, Gregoria Campos, in her individual capacity and in her capacity as administratrix of the estate of her late husband, Jose Mauricio Campos (decedent), and the Campos' three children, Mauricio Campos, Jose Ernesto Campos and Jose Eduardo Campos (Campos children), brought this action against the defendants, Robert E. Coleman and LQ Management, LLC (LQ Management). The plaintiffs alleged in their complaint that Coleman negligently had caused the decedent's death and included claims for the Campos children's loss of parental consortium. The defendants filed a motion to strike the loss of parental consortium claims . . . , which the trial court granted. Thereafter, a jury returned a verdict for the decedent's estate on the wrongful death claim and for Gregoria Campos on her loss of spousal consortium claim, and the trial court rendered judgment in accordance with the verdict. The Campos children then filed this appeal, contending that we should . . . allow them to pursue their claims for loss of parental consortium. . . .

In [*Mendillo v. Board of Education*, 246 Conn. 456, 461, 495–96, 717 A.2d 1177 (1998)], a majority of this court ultimately declined to recognize a minor child's claim for loss of parental consortium resulting from a tortfeasor's conduct. At the outset of our analysis of this issue in *Mendillo*, however, we candidly acknowledged that "many of [the arguments in support of recognizing such a claim] have considerable appeal. . . ." In particular, we recognized that a minor child who, by virtue of a tortfeasor's conduct, has been deprived of the love and companionship of a parent "has suffered a genuine injury, and a serious one." Underscoring this point, we explained that "we [had] recently reaffirmed that it is our state's public policy to promote the welfare of the family, and that the interest of children in not being dislocated from the emotional attachments that derive from the intimacy of daily association . . . with the parent has constitutional significance."

We also acknowledged the argument made by the plaintiffs in *Mendillo* that "permitting compensation for loss of parental consortium will enable the emotionally injured child to secure the therapy that will, in turn, help to heal the wounds caused by his or her loss. . . . [N]ot only will the minor child benefit, but society will also benefit if the child is able to function without emotional handicap. This may well offset any increase in insurance premiums."

As we further observed in *Mendillo*, another argument favoring the recognition of a derivative cause of action for parental consortium is the fact that this court already had recognized analogous causes of action for loss of spousal consortium and bystander emotional distress. With respect to the former, we acknowledged the view, as expressed by the Supreme Court of Washington, that "permitting a husband or wife but not children to recover for loss of consortium erroneously suggests that an adult is more likely to suffer emotional injury than a child" and noted the contention of the plaintiffs in *Mendillo* that, following our recognition of a derivative cause of action for spousal consortium in *Hopson*, the "logical [next step] from . . . *Hopson*['s] protect[ion of] the emotional or sentimental aspects of the husband-wife relationship [is the] protection of the similar aspects of the parent-child relationship." . . .

Finally, we observed what the plaintiffs in *Mendillo* had "characterize[d] as the emerging national trend recognizing . . . [a] cause of action [for loss of parental consortium]. . . ." We further observed that, in support of this argument, the plaintiffs in *Mendillo* had "cite[d] to a number of jurisdictions that have, since 1980, recognized a cause of action for loss of parental consortium."

Notwithstanding the conceded force of these arguments, we ultimately declined to recognize a cause of action for parental consortium, "primarily on the basis of: [1] the fact that recognition of the cause of action would require arbitrary limitations; [2] the additional economic burden that recognition would impose on the general public; [3] the uncertainty that recognition would yield significant social benefits; [4] the substantial risk of double recovery; and [5] the weight of judicial authority."

Upon reconsideration of the relevant considerations, including the five factors that this court found determinative in *Mendillo*, we now agree with the concurring and dissenting opinion in *Mendillo* that the public policy factors favoring recognition of a cause of action for loss of parental consortium outweigh those factors disfavoring recognition. More specifically, we agree that the unique emotional attachment between parents and children, the importance of ensuring the continuity of the critically important services that parents provide to their children, society's interest in the continued development of children as contributing members of society, and the public policies in favor of compensating innocent parties and deterring wrongdoing provide compelling reasons to recognize such a cause of action. With respect to the countervailing policy considerations on which we relied in *Mendillo*, we now are persuaded . . . that our concerns were overstated.

. . .

Because we no longer agree with this court's weighing of the relevant public policy factors in *Mendillo*, we now overrule our holding in that case and conclude that we should recognize a cause of action for loss of parental consortium. To decide otherwise would be inconsistent with the "the fundamental policy purposes of the tort compensation system—compensation of innocent parties, shifting the loss to responsible parties or distributing it among appropriate entities, and deterrence of wrongful conduct. . . ." *Mendillo v. Board of Education, supra*, 246 Conn. at 482, 717 A.2d 1177. Consistent with the foregoing analysis, however, we impose the following restrictions on loss of parental consortium claims. First, loss of parental consortium claims must be joined with the parent's negligence claim whenever possible, and the jury must be instructed that only the child raising the claim can recover the pecuniary value of the parent's services. Second, and relatedly, because a loss of parental consortium action "is derivative of the injured [parent's] cause of action, the consortium claim would be barred when the [action] brought by the injured [parent] has been terminated by settlement or by an adverse judgment on the merits." Third, a loss of parental consortium claim may be raised only by a person who was a minor on the date that the parent was injured, and damages may be awarded only for the period between the date of the parent's injury and the date that the child reaches the age of majority.

Notes

Death or injury. Some states permit recovery in the case of injury to the family member, not just where death occurs. *See* R.I. ST § 9-1-41.

Other claims. The further a loss of consortium claim strays from its historical link to marriage, the less likely courts are to recognize such claims. But as *Campos* illustrates, children have sometimes had success with such claims. *But see* Harrington v. Brooks Drugs, Inc., 808 A.2d 532, 534 (N.H. 2002) (rejecting such a claim). Other scenarios involving asserted loss of consortium claims have involved individuals engaged to be married and unmarried couples, *see* Private Bank v. Silver Cross Hospital and Medical Centers, 98 N.E.3d 381 (Ill. Ct. App. 2017); claims asserted by adult children for loss of parental consortium, *see North Pacific Ins. Co. v. Stucky*, 338 P.3d 56 (Mont. 2014); claims asserted by parents when a child is injured, *compare Roberts v. Williamson*, 111 S.W.3d 113 (Tex. 2003) *with* Gillispie v. Beta Const. Co., 842 P.2d 1272 (Alaska 1992); and claims by siblings and stepparents, *Ford Motor Co. v. Miles*, 967 S.W.2d 377 (Tex.1998).

Derivative nature of such claims. Courts often speak of loss of consortium claims as being derivative of the other family member's claim in the sense that the loss of consortium action must be joined with the underlying claim of the other family member and that any defenses to that underlying claim will also limit recovery on the loss of consortium claim. *See* Voris v. Molinaro, 31 A.3d 363 (Conn. 2011).

Review Question

Cindy was driving her car on a rural road when she encountered Charles and his wife, Joanne, in the middle of the road. Cindy did not know either party. However, Joanne appeared to be in distress. When Cindy stopped her vehicle to provide assistance, Charles told her that his wife was having a seizure. As Cindy used her cell phone to call 911 to request help, Charles pulled out a pistol and shot Joanne in the head. Cindy was obviously shocked. Charles then turned and faced Cindy, pointed the pistol at his head, pulled the trigger, and killed himself. Cindy suffered from post-traumatic stress disorder and major depression (both diagnosed) after witnessing the incident and was unable to return to work. She now seeks to recover from Charles' estate on a claim of negligent infliction of emotional distress.

(a) The relevant jurisdiction has adopted the *Restatement (Third) of Torts* test for negligent infliction of emotional distress in cases in which the plaintiff is the direct victim of the defendant's negligence and the *Thing v. La Chusa* test in cases in which the plaintiff suffers emotional distress that results from observing harm inflicted upon another. Can Cindy recover?

(b) Assume for purposes of this question only that the relevant jurisdiction has adopted the *Dillon v. Legg* test in cases in which the plaintiff suffers emotional distress that results from observing harm inflicted upon another. You represent Cindy. Explain why your client should prevail on her claim.

Part 3
Strict Liability

In nearly all of the cases included in this book so far, plaintiffs have sought to hold the defendants liable for the defendants' own negligence or intentional misconduct. But sometimes a defendant may be held liable even if the defendant is not at fault. This part of the book focuses on situations in which a defendant may be held strictly liable.

Chapter 11 focuses on situations in which a defendant is held vicariously liable for the torts of another person. Chapter 12 focuses on strict liability for engaging in abnormally dangerous activities. Chapter 13 examines the tort of nuisance. Chapter 14 explores products liability law, an area of tort law that has its roots in strict liability.

Chapter 11

Vicarious Liability

A. Vicarious Liability in General
- *Respondeat superior* liability in general
- The justifications for vicarious liability
- Other concepts developed in class or in readings assigned by the professor

B. Employee Status
- Distinguishing employees and independent contractors
- Control
- Relevant factors
- Gratuitous servants
- Other concepts developed in class or in readings assigned by the professor

C. Scope of Employment
- Vicarious liability stemming from negligent conduct
  - The traditional rule
  - Relevant factors
  - Going and coming rule and exceptions
  - Other concepts developed in class or in readings assigned by the professor
- Enterprise liability
  - In general
  - Justifications
  - Differences with the traditional rule
  - Other concepts developed in class or in readings assigned by the professor
- Vicarious liability stemming from intentional conduct
  - Relevant considerations
  - Other concepts developed in class or in readings assigned by the professor

D. Nondelegable Duties
- Generally defined
- Examples
- Effect of finding a duty to be nondelegable
- Other concepts developed in class or in readings assigned by the professor

Chapter Problem. Piper was a passenger in a vehicle driven by Christian. Christian worked for a company called RideAlong that (like Lyft or Uber) provides drivers to customers on demand through a cell phone application.

Christian's car collided with a car driven by Bobbi, an associate at a law firm. Piper sustained injuries as a result of the collision. She has filed a complaint seeking to hold RideAlong and Bobbi's law firm vicariously liable for the alleged torts of Christian and Bobbi.

A. Vicarious Liability in General

Vicarious liability is a form of strict liability in which a defendant is held liable for someone else's wrongdoing. One example is where one partner in a partnership is held liable vicariously liable for the wrongdoing of another partner. The most common example is the principle of *respondeat superior*, in which the principal (the employer) is held liable for the torts of the agent (the employee). These cases should be distinguished from cases in which an employer is accused of negligence in supervising an employee or in hiring an individual to begin with. Various justifications have been offered for the *respondeat superior* principle, including the idea that vicarious liability is proper since the master has control over the servant, the idea that employers have the "deep pockets" in this situation, and the idea that the rule is simply a means of allocating risks. Regardless of the justification, to establish liability on the part of an employer, a plaintiff must prove: (1) that a master-servant (or employer-employee or principal-agent) relationship existed and (2) that the tortious act of the servant occurred within the scope of that employment.

B. Employee Status

Mangual v. Berezinsky

53 A.3d 664 (N.J. Super. Ct. 2012)

ACCURSO, J.S.C. (temporarily assigned).

This interlocutory appeal arises out of a car accident in which plaintiffs suffered catastrophic injuries. On leave granted, defendant Essex Surgery Center, L.L.C. (Essex) appeals from two partial summary judgment orders in favor of plaintiffs in these consolidated cases, one determining that defendant Lazar Berezinsky (Berezinsky) was Essex's agent, and the other that Berezinsky was liable for the accident in which plaintiffs were injured. . . .

While returning home from a shopping trip on Saturday, June 7, 2008, at about 12:30 in the afternoon, plaintiffs Felix and Judith Mangual's 1971 Chevy Nova had overheated, and they had pulled onto the shoulder of Route 280 in Orange. The day was clear and dry and the traffic very light. They were standing on the shoulder outside their disabled car when a Lincoln Town Car driven by Berezinsky slammed into them. The force of the impact propelled the Manguals' car into Mrs. Mangual and trapped Mr. Mangual between it and the Town Car. Mr. Mangual suffered a broken leg and anterior meniscus tears in both legs in the accident. Mrs. Mangual's injuries required that both her legs be amputated below the knee.

The evidence adduced on the cross-motions for partial summary judgment on agency filed by plaintiffs and Essex shows that at the time of the accident, Berezinsky was driving Galina Komarov and her daughter home after Mrs. Komarov had an out-patient procedure performed by Dr. Gary Gorodokin .... Berezinsky had been hired to drive Mrs. Komarov to and from her appointment by Abram Stekolshchik (referred to by the parties, and by us hereinafter, as Arkady). Arkady was employed by Essex.

Essex is an out-patient surgical center limited to pain management procedures, which in 2008 was open only on Tuesdays and Wednesdays. Essex employed a full-time administrator and director of nursing, a handful of clerical workers and a dispatcher, Arkady, but had few other full-time employees. The physicians who performed procedures at Essex were not paid by the surgical center but by their patients or their insurance providers. Essex paid the ten or fifteen nurses who worked on Tuesdays and Wednesdays on a per diem basis.

Essex is a limited liability company formed in 2005. Richard Lipsky, M.D., serves as its non-member unpaid manager....

Dr. Lipsky testified at deposition that Essex provided transportation for all patients undergoing treatment at Essex. He explained that the high patient volume attendant to a pain management practice made patient transportation necessary in order to protect the day's schedule. In other words, the only way to insure that patients appeared on-time for their tightly scheduled appointments was for the facility to provide them transportation. Dr. Lipsky testified that the transportation was costly and was paid by Essex and not by the physicians using the facility. Arkady arranged for all patient transportation for Essex using a pool of approximately fifty drivers culled from limousine services who would drive for Essex on the side. Berezinsky was one of those drivers.

Berezinsky was a member of a limousine service cooperative in Ozone Park, New York called Inta-Boro Two-Way Radio Car (Inta-Boro). He testified at deposition that he owned the Town Car that he was driving on the day of the accident and that it was registered in his name in New York at Inta-Boro's location, which he considered his work address. Berezinsky has also owned a taxi medallion in New York City since 1988. Berezinsky's 1099-Miscellaneous Income Statements from Inta-Boro reveal that he received nonemployee compensation of $59,387.80 in 2006; $51,406.46 in 2007; and $44,772.35 in 2008. For those same periods, Berezinsky received from Essex, $14,025; $18,290; and $13,910, respectively.

Berezinsky testified that Arkady began calling him in 2006 to transport patients to and from Essex. He had no contract or set schedule; he would simply drive for Essex when Arkady needed him. Berezinsky drove for Essex on his own behalf and not for Inta-Boro. Arkady would call him a day or so ahead of time with the name and address of the patient and the time of pick-up. Berezinsky picked up the patient in his own car and drove to Essex where Arkady would assign other trips. Berezinsky maintained and repaired his own car and chose the routes of travel. Essex paid him by the hour and not by the trip. Berezinsky testified that Essex paid him $35 an hour and did not reimburse him for gas or tolls. Dr. Lipsky, however, testified that Essex paid the drivers an additional $35 for gas on the days they worked. Berezinsky testified that Arkady would give him a check from Essex for the hours he worked at the end of each shift or the next time he drove. Essex issued Berezinsky a 1099-Miscellaneous Income Statement at the end of each year.

...

Applying the factors established in *Miklos v. Liberty Coach Co.*, 48 N.J.Super. 591, 138 A.2d 762 (App.Div.1958), to these largely undisputed facts, the motion judge determined that no rational factfinder could find that Berezinsky was an independent contractor and not acting as Essex's agent while driving Mrs. Komarov at the time of the accident. We disagree.

...

New Jersey has adopted section 220 of the Restatement (Second) of Agency "as the touchstone" for determining whether one acting for another acts as a servant or agent, or as an independent contractor. Carter v. Reynolds, 175 N.J. 402, 408, 815 A.2d 460 (2003). Section 220 provides:

> (1) A servant is a person employed to perform services in the affairs of another and who with respect to the physical conduct in the performance of the services is subject to the other's control or right to control.
>
> (2) In determining whether one acting for another is a servant or an independent contractor, the following matters of facts, among others, are considered:
>
> (a) the extent of control which, by the agreement, the master may exercise over the details of the work;
>
> (b) whether or not the one employed is engaged in a distinct occupation or business;
>
> (c) the kind of occupation, with reference to whether, in the locality, the work is usually done under the direction of the employer or by a specialist without supervision;
>
> (d) the skill required in the particular occupation;
>
> (e) whether the employer or the workman supplies the instrumentalities, tools, and the place of work for the person doing the work;
>
> (f) the length of time for which the person is employed;
>
> (g) the method of payment, whether by the time or by the job;
>
> (h) whether or not the work is a part of the regular business of the employer;

(i) whether or not the parties believe they are creating the relation of master and servant; and

(j) whether the principal is or is not in business.

[Restatement (Second) of Agency § 220 (1958).]

...

We have no quarrel with the motion judge's reliance on *Miklos*. Where we part company with the motion judge is in his determination that applying *Miklos* to these facts leads inescapably to only one conclusion. The motion judge determined on the basis of facts adduced on the motions that Arkady exercised "an expansive control" over Berezinsky's actions at the time of the accident; that Berezinsky was not engaged in an occupation distinct from that of a surgical center; that Essex contributed to Berezinsky's operational costs by paying him an additional $35 for gas, despite Berezinsky's assertion to the contrary; that livery service is a part of Essex's regular surgical center business; and that Essex, although not considering Berezinsky as its agent, held him out to Mrs. Komarov as such ...

We do not determine that no rational jury could arrive at the same conclusions from these facts, but only that a rational jury could as readily conclude the opposite, that is, that Berezinsky was acting as an independent contractor. Although the facts may be largely, but not completely, undisputed, the inferences that may be drawn from these facts vary greatly. This appears to us to be ... a case in which a rational jury could go either way. Accordingly, we conclude that the entry of summary judgment was inappropriate and that the issue of whether Berezinsky was acting as Essex's agent at the time of the accident must be determined by a jury.

Notes

Control. The control test relied upon in *Mangual* is the traditional test used and focuses on whether the employer has the right to control and direct the purported employee in the performance of his work and in the manner in which the work is to be done. *See* Gale v. Greater Washington Softball Umpires Ass'n, 311 A.2d 817 (Md. 1973).

The gig economy and tort law. Historically, *respondeat superior* liability was justified on the idea that it was just to hold an employer liable for the torts of its employees since the employer retained the right to control the actions of the employees. The advent of the so-called gig economy, in which employers increasingly rely on independent contractors, "continues to present definitional challenges and reveals the pervasive practical difficulty in applying" multi-factor tests. Orly Lobel, *The Gig Economy & The Future of Employment and Labor Law*, 51 U.S.F. L. Rev. 51, 61 (2017). As one judge has observed, "These new relationships also threaten to shield businesses from liability for the harm those workers caused while laboring on their behalf." Gil v. Clara Maass Medical Center, 162 A.3d 1093, 1107 (N.J. Super. Ct. 2017) (Ostrer, J., concurring).

Gratuitous service. One who renders services for another without expectation of payment may still qualify as an agent for purposes of vicarious liability. Restatement (Second) of Agency § 225 (1958). For a principal-agent relationship to result, there must be conduct "manifesting that one of them is willing for the other to act for him subject to his control, and that the other consents so to act." Evans v. White, 682 S.W.2d 733, 734 (Ark. 1985). Thus, the uncompensated volunteer or the unpaid intern might qualify as agents for purposes of *respondeat superior* liability. *See* Whetstone v. Dixon, 616 So.2d 764, 770 (La. Ct. App. 1993) (concluding that unpaid deacon in a church was an agent where he was subject to control by the deacon board of church); Cason v. Saniford, 148 So. 3d 8 (La. Ct. App. 2014) (concluding intern was not an agent where intern paid money to be in internship program).

Problem 11.1. On the day of the accident, Piper had used an app on her phone to summon a RideAlong driver. RideAlong drivers provide their own cars, determine which hours and how many hours they want to work, and are free to decline a ride request (although drivers must sustain an acceptable ride-request-acceptance rate). RideAlong dictates the fares charged to passengers, collects the appropriate payment from each passenger, and then passes on to its drivers 75% of the fares collected while keeping the remaining portion for itself. RideAlong drivers receive payment for their work via weekly direct deposit from RideAlong, not individual passengers. Drivers are not permitted to set their own fares or accept cash payment from consumers. RideAlong requires its drivers to maintain their vehicles in clean condition and good working order; respond to ride requests within an acceptable timeframe; and display the RideAlong logo on their vehicles. In her complaint, Piper alleges that Christian drove his car in a negligent manner. She seeks to hold RideAlong vicariously liable. RideAlong responded that Christian was an independent contractor, not an employee. Thus, according to the firm, *respondeat superior* liability could not attach. Is Christian an independent contractor or an employee?

C. Scope of Employment

1. Vicarious Liability Stemming from Negligent Conduct

a. The Traditional Rule

Christensen v. Swensen

874 P.2d 125 (Utah 1994)

DURHAM, Justice

Burns provides security services for the Geneva Steel Plant ("Geneva") in Orem, Utah. Burns employed Swenson as a security guard in June 1988. On the day of the accident, July 26, 1988, Swenson was assigned to guard duty at Gate 4, the northeast entrance to the Geneva property. Security guards at Gate 4 worked eight-hour continuous shifts, with no scheduled breaks. However, employees were permitted to take ten- to fifteen-minute unscheduled lunch and restroom breaks.

When taking their lunch breaks, Gate 4 guards generally ate a bag lunch but occasionally ordered take-out food from the sole restaurant within close physical proximity to Gate 4, the Frontier Cafe. The Frontier Cafe was located directly across the street from the Geneva plant, approximately 150 to 250 yards from Gate 4. The cafe's menu was posted near the telephone at Gate 4. Aside from vending machines located within a nearby Geneva office building, the Frontier Cafe provided the sole source of food accessible to Gate 4 guards within their ten- to fifteen-minute breaks. Indeed, the Frontier Cafe was the only restaurant in the immediate area. Whether they brought their lunches or ordered from the cafe, Gate 4 guards were expected to eat at their posts.

Shortly after 11:00 a.m. on the day of the accident, Swenson noticed a lull in the traffic at Gate 4 and decided to get a cup of soup from the Frontier Cafe. She placed a telephone order for the soup from Gate 4 and then drove her automobile to the cafe. She intended to pick up the soup and return to Gate 4 to eat at her post. She expected the round trip to take approximately ten to fifteen minutes, as permitted by Burns' unscheduled break policy. On her return trip, however, she collided with plaintiffs' motorcycle at a public intersection just outside Geneva's property. Both Christensen and Fausett were injured.

Christensen and Fausett filed a negligence action against Swenson and Burns. After answering the complaint, Burns moved for summary judgment, claiming that it was not liable under the doctrine of respondeat superior because Swenson was not acting within the scope of her employment at the time of the accident. The trial court granted Burns' motion, and Christensen and Fausett appealed. The court of appeals affirmed the trial court's decision, concluding that reasonable minds could not disagree that Swenson was acting outside the scope of her employment at the time of the accident. We granted plaintiffs' petition for certiorari.

Under the doctrine of respondeat superior, employers are vicariously liable for torts committed by employees while acting within the scope of their employment. Whether an employee is acting within the scope of her employment is ordinarily a question of fact....

In *Birkner*, we stated that acts falling within the scope of employment are "'those acts which are so closely connected with what the servant is employed to do, and so fairly and reasonably incidental to it, that they may be regarded as methods, even though quite improper ones, of carrying out the objectives of employment.'" 771 P.2d at 1056 (quoting W. Page Keeton et al., Prosser and Keeton on the Law of Torts §70, at 502 (5th ed. 1984)). We articulated three criteria helpful in determining whether an employee is acting within or outside the scope of her employment. First, the employee's conduct must be of the general kind the employee is hired to perform, that is, "the employee must be about the employer's business and the duties assigned by the employer, as opposed to being wholly involved in a personal endeavor." Second, the employee's conduct must occur substantially within the hours and ordinary spatial boundaries of the employment. Finally, "the employee's conduct must be motivated, at least in part, by the purpose of serving the employer's interest."

The court of appeals held that Swenson was not substantially within the ordinary spatial boundaries of her employment because the accident did not occur on Geneva property. Christensen and Fausett argue that the court of appeals erred in its application of the second criterion identified in *Birkner.* Burns responds that the court of appeals properly construed the second *Birkner* criterion in holding that Swenson was acting outside the scope of her employment at the time of the accident.

Because the court of appeals concluded that Swenson failed to satisfy the second *Birkner* criterion, it did not address the first and third criteria. However, our review of the record indicates that reasonable minds could differ on all three criteria. Thus, to avoid a second summary judgment on remand, we address all three of the *Birkner* criteria.

The first *Birkner* criterion requires that the employee's conduct be of the general kind the employee is hired to perform, that is, "the employee must be about the employer's business and the duties assigned by the employer, as opposed to being wholly involved in a personal endeavor." Reasonable minds could differ as to whether Swenson was about Burns' business when she was involved in the traffic accident between Gate 4 and the Frontier Cafe.

We base this conclusion on two disputed issues of material fact. First, Swenson claims that Burns employed her as a security guard to "see and be seen" on and around the Geneva plant. Thus, traveling the short distance to the Frontier Cafe in uniform arguably heightened the secure atmosphere that Burns sought to project. Burns, on the other hand, claims that Swenson was not hired to perform that function. Burns' position is supported by the deposition of another security guard who stated that he considered lunch trips to the Frontier Cafe to be entirely personal in nature.

A second material issue of fact remains as to whether Burns tacitly sanctioned Gate 4 guards' practice of obtaining lunch from the Frontier Cafe. Burns expected its Gate 4 guards to work eight-hour continuous shifts and to remain at their posts as much as possible. However, because Burns also recognized that the guards must at times eat meals and use the restroom, the company permitted them to take ten- to fifteen-minute paid breaks. The record indicates that Burns was aware that its employees occasionally traveled to the Frontier Cafe during these unscheduled breaks but had never disciplined them for doing so. Indeed, Swenson asserts that a menu from the Frontier Cafe was posted in plain view at Gate 4. Thus, reasonable minds could differ as to whether Burns tacitly sanctioned, or at least contemplated, that its guards would satisfy their need for nourishment by obtaining meals from the Frontier Cafe.

The second *Birkner* criterion states that the employee's conduct must occur substantially within the hours and ordinary spatial boundaries of the employment. It is undisputed that Swenson's action occurred within the hours of her employment. She was at her post and in uniform when she decided to take advantage of a lull in plant traffic to eat lunch.

With respect to spatial boundaries, we find that reasonable minds might differ as to whether Swenson was substantially within the ordinary spatial boundaries of her employment when traveling to and from the Frontier Cafe. Again, the court of appeals concluded that Swenson did not pass this criterion because the accident did not occur on Geneva property. While it is true that Swenson was not on Geneva property when the accident occurred, she was attempting to obtain lunch from a restaurant within the geographic area accessible during her ten- to fifteen-minute break. Given the other facts of this case, reasonable minds could differ as to whether Swenson's trip to the Frontier Cafe fell substantially within the ordinary spatial boundaries of her employment.

Furthermore, Burns could not point to specific orders barring guards from leaving the facility in their own vehicles to go to the Frontier Cafe on break, although two managers opined that such behavior was prohibited. This dispute alone presents a genuine issue of material fact. If guards were expressly forbidden to drive to the Frontier Cafe to pick up lunch during their break, a jury could find that Swenson was substantially outside the ordinary spatial boundaries of her employment; if they were not so forbidden, a jury might find her to have been acting substantially within the ordinary spatial boundaries of her employment.

Under the third criterion of the *Birkner* test, "the employee's conduct must be motivated, at least in part, by the purpose of serving the employer's interest." Applying this criterion to the instant case poses the question of whether Swenson's trip to the Frontier Cafe was motivated, at least in part, by the purpose of serving Burns' interest. Reasonable minds might also differ on this question.

First, two Burns managers admitted in their depositions that employee breaks benefit both the employee and the employer. Employees must occasionally eat meals and use the restroom, and employers receive the corresponding benefit of productive, satisfied employees. Reasonable minds could differ as to whether Swenson's particular break fell into this mutual-benefit category.

Second, given the continuous-shift nature of the job and the comparatively brief breaks permitted, Burns' break policy obviously placed a premium on speed and efficiency. Swenson claimed that traveling to the Frontier Cafe enabled her to obtain lunch within the allotted period and thus maximize the time spent at her post. In this respect, reasonable minds might conclude that Swenson's conduct was motivated, at least in part, by the purpose of serving Burns' interest. Evidence indicating that Swenson tried to save time on her lunch break by phoning her order ahead, driving instead of walking, and attempting to return immediately to her post is also relevant in this regard.

In sum, we hold that reasonable minds could differ as to whether Swenson was acting within or outside the scope of her employment when she collided with plaintiffs' motorcycle. Thus, summary judgment is inappropriate. We reverse and remand for further proceedings.

Carter v. Reynolds

815 A.2d 460 (N.J. 2003)

LONG, J.

I

Defendant Alice Reynolds was the owner and operator of a vehicle that struck plaintiff, David Carter, on January 15, 1997, in Belmar, New Jersey. At the time of the accident, Reynolds, who resided in Brielle, New Jersey, was employed by the accounting firm of Stevens, Fluhr, Chismar, Alvino & Schechter, CPA, (the firm), located in Neptune, New Jersey.

At the firm, Reynolds was a non-professional, part-time employee who conducted detail work for auditors. She was responsible for the verification, checking, and preparation of bank reconciliations. Her job required her to work in the firm's Neptune office, and also to visit clients. Vincent Alvino, a partner in the firm, testified that Reynolds spent approximately sixty to seventy percent of her time at the firm's Neptune office and twenty-five to thirty percent at client locations. There was no office car available to Reynolds; thus, she was required to use her own vehicle for travel, with business mileage reimbursed by the firm under the Internal Revenue Service's (IRS) then prevailing allowance of 31 ½ cents per mile. With respect to travel reimbursement, Alvino testified that, in accordance with IRS rules, Reynolds could

> claim mileage from the office to the client assignment and from the client assignment back to the office and in the event that she was traveling from home, it would be the mileage from her home to the client or from the office to the client, whichever was closer, and that would also hold true for the return trip. If she was traveling from the client back home, she would get the shorter distance of the mileage from the client to home or the client to the office.

With respect to billing, on the days Reynolds traveled from her home to the client, she would begin billing when she arrived at the client's destination. On the days that she went directly home after meeting with a client, she would stop billing when she left the client, not when she actually arrived at home. If she had to return to the office after meeting with a client, she would bill for her travel time to the firm.

On the day in question, Reynolds spent the morning at the firm, and then traveled to Deal to a client location. Reynolds spent the remainder of the day working in Deal. She testified that she was reimbursed for the mileage from Deal to Neptune, but that she was not paid wages for her travel time. At approximately 4:29 p.m., when Reynolds was traveling from Deal to her home, the accident occurred.

On November 3, 1997, Carter filed an automobile negligence action against Reynolds. Later, Carter filed an amended complaint adding the firm as a defendant, alleging that Reynolds was an employee, servant, and/or agent of the firm when the accident occurred because she was in the scope of her employment.

The firm filed a motion for summary judgment and Carter filed a cross-motion. The trial court granted the firm's motion, leaving Reynolds as the sole defendant in the case. On Carter's motion for reconsideration based on new precedent, the trial court determined that Reynolds was, in fact, acting within the scope of her employment when she struck him and thus, granted Carter's motion for partial summary judgment with respect to *respondeat superior* liability.

The firm moved for leave to appeal the interlocutory order, which motion was granted. In a published opinion, the Appellate Division affirmed the trial court's grant of partial summary judgment to Carter, reasoning that Reynolds was acting within the scope of her employment, thus making the firm liable under the doctrine of *respondeat superior.* The firm then moved before us for leave to appeal, which motion we granted. We now affirm.

II

The heart of the firm's argument is that the Appellate Division's decision represents a fundamental change in the law regarding an employer's vicarious liability because the court jettisoned the element of control, which the firm maintains is a necessary aspect of the vicarious liability calculus. Carter counters that the Appellate Division merely recognized a well-established exception to the "going and coming" rule carved out for cases in which an employer requires an employee to use his or her own vehicle for work. Carter argues alternatively that Reynolds' activity on the day in question fell within the "special mission" exception to the going and coming rule.

III

Although as a general rule of tort law, liability must be based on personal fault, the doctrine of *respondeat superior* recognizes a vicarious liability principle pursuant to which a master will be held liable in certain cases for the wrongful acts of his servants or employees. The theoretical underpinning of the doctrine of *respondeat superior* has been described as follows: that one who expects to derive a benefit or advantage from an act performed on his behalf by another must answer for any injury that a third person may sustain from it.

Under *respondeat superior*, an employer can be found liable for the negligence of an employee causing injuries to third parties, if, at the time of the occurrence, the employee was acting within the scope of his or her employment. To establish a master's liability for the acts of his servant, a plaintiff must prove (1) that a master-servant relationship existed and (2) that the tortious act of the servant occurred within the scope of that employment. Those are two entirely distinct concepts governed by different legal principles. The former focuses on the nature of the relationship. If no master-servant relationship exists, no further inquiry need take place because the master-servant relationship is *sine qua non* to the invocation of *respondeat superior.* If such a relationship exists, its margins are the subject of the scope of employment inquiry.

. . .

B.

Once the master-servant relationship is established, it is necessary to decide the question of whether the particular tortious conduct took place within the scope of that employment relationship. Proof that the employer-employee relationship exists does not, in and of itself, create an inference that a given act done by the employee was within the scope of employment. Restatement (Second) of Agency § 228 comment b (1958).

In New Jersey, as in most other states, scope of employment is subject to analysis under Restatement sections 228 and 229, which provide in relevant part that an employee's conduct falls within the scope of employment if:

> (a) it is of the kind he is employed to perform;
>
> (b) it occurs substantially within the authorized time and space limits;
>
> (c) it is actuated, at least in part, by a purpose to serve the master,
>
> . . . .
>
> (2) Conduct of a servant is not within the scope of employment if it is different in kind from that authorized, far beyond the authorized time or space limits, or too little actuated by a purpose to serve the master.
>
> [Restatement (Second) of Agency § 228 (1958).] . . .

C.

Generally, an employee who is "going to" or "coming from" his or her place of employment is not considered to be acting within the scope of employment. That rule had its genesis in workers' compensation law and has been imported into tort law. *Courtless v. Jolliffe*, 203 W.Va. 258, 507 S.E.2d 136, 141 (1998) (per curiam) (citing 1 *Larson's Workers' Compensation Law* § 16.10 (1972)). Indeed, most jurisdictions apply the general rule that an employee who is driving his or her personal vehicle to and from the employer's workplace is not within the scope of employment for the purpose of imposing vicarious liability on the employer. The Restatement addresses the going and coming rule in section 229, comment d: "'It is essentially . . . the employee's own job of getting to or from work.'" Franklin, *supra*, 39 *S.D.L.Rev.* at 587 (quoting *Restatement (Second) of Agency* § 229 comment d (1958)).

Two rationales exist to support the "going and coming" rule. The first is that "employment is suspended from the time the employee leaves the workplace until he or she returns." That "suspension" occurs because the element of "control" is deemed lacking. The second is that the employer derives no benefit from the commute. Those rationales are essentially inversions of the Restatement standards for vicarious liability. One commentator has explained that the purpose that underlies the going and coming rule is that "it is unfair to impose unlimited liability on an employer for conduct of its employees over which it has no control and from which it derives no benefit." Franklin, *supra*, 39 *S.D.L.Rev.* at 588 (footnote omitted). In essence, when employees travel to or from work they are deemed to be acting in their own interests without constraints by the employer regarding the method or means of the commute.

There are, however, exceptions to the going and coming rule. Those exceptions are also rooted in workers' compensation law but have been engrafted onto tort law. Thus, *respondeat superior* has been held to apply to a situation involving commuting when: (1) the employee is engaged in a special errand or mission on the employer's behalf; (2) the employer requires the employee to drive his or her personal vehicle to work so that the vehicle may be used for work-related tasks; and (3) the employee is "on-call." *Mannes, supra*, 306 N.J.Super. at 354–55, 703 A.2d 944 (citations omitted).

Those so-called "dual purpose" exceptions cover cases in which, at the time of the employee's negligence, he or she can be said to be serving an interest of the employer along with a personal interest. It makes sense that those exceptions to the going and coming rule exist. Unlike ordinary commutation in which an employer really has no interest, each of the noted exceptions involves some control over the employee's actions and a palpable benefit to be reaped by the employer, thus squarely placing such conduct back into the vicarious liability construct of the Restatement.

This case involves the required-vehicle exception described above. In *Mannes*, supra, that exception was recognized but ultimately held inapplicable because at the time of the accident, the employer did not require the employee to use a particular vehicle. It was also recognized in *Pfender v. Torres*, where plaintiff was injured by the automobile negligence of Torres, an employee of Don Rosen Imports, Inc. (DRI). 336 N.J.Super. 379, 383, 385, 393–94, 765 A.2d 208 (App.Div.), certif. denied, 167 N.J. 637, 772 A.2d 938 (2001). At the time of the accident, Torres was driving to work in a car provided by DRI, which he used as a personal vehicle and which had to be available as a demonstrator at the car dealership. The car was also used during the workday for work-related errands. The trial court directed a verdict in favor of DRI at the conclusion of the evidence. The Appellate Division reversed. In so doing, the court invoked the required-vehicle exception:

> DRI's liability under that well-recognized exception is clear since Torres was driving to work when the accident happened and he was required to use the car in the performance of his employment as a demonstrator to encourage sales and to run work-related errands.
>
> [*Ibid.*]

See also O'Toole v. Carr, 175 N.J. 421, 815 A.2d 471 (2003) (recognizing required-vehicle exception). That is the backdrop for our inquiry.

IV

A master-servant relationship plainly existed between Reynolds and the firm. Further, the Appellate Division concluded that because Reynolds spent one-third of her work time on the road visiting firm clients; was required by the firm to have her own car available for such activities; and actually was returning from a client visit at the time of the accident, she came within the required-vehicle exception to the going and coming rule outlined in *Mannes* and applied in *Pfender.* We agree.

The firm's contrary view—that the required-vehicle exception is narrower than the Appellate Division realized—is based upon *Oaks v. Connors*, 339 Md. 24, 660 A.2d 423 (1995). There, the defendant was required to have a personal vehicle for traveling on his job between his employer's stores. He was involved in an accident on his way to a work assignment, and plaintiffs argued that the employer was vicariously liable because defendant was transporting a vehicle to the job site that the employer required him to have available for use in the course of his employment. The intermediate appellate court agreed. The Maryland Court of Appeals reversed. Although recognizing the required-vehicle exception and acknowledging that the employer directed the employee to have a vehicle available for work-related tasks, *Oaks* held that because the employee was neither actually performing a work-related task nor advancing his employer's business purposes at the time of the accident, the exception did not apply. The court further observed that the employer "exerted no control over the method or means by which the employee operated his vehicle."

We disagree with that rather narrow analysis. To be sure, ordinary commuting is beyond the scope of employment because of the absence of control and benefit. Driving a required vehicle, however, is a horse of another color because it satisfies the control and benefit elements of *respondeat superior.* An employee who is required to use his or her own vehicle provides an "essential instrumentality" for the performance of the employer's work. Konradi v. United States, 919 F.2d 1207, 1212 (7th Cir.1990) (finding under Indiana law, employee who drove personal truck to and from work as required "conferred a benefit on his employer because he was bringing an essential instrumentality of the employer's business"). When a vehicle must be provided by an employee, the employer benefits by not having to have available an office car and yet possessing a means by which off-site visits can be performed by its employees. It is that benefit that the *Oaks* court overlooked.

Oaks was equally wide of the mark regarding control. When an employer requires an employee to use a personal vehicle, it exercises meaningful control over the method of the commute by compelling the employee to foreswear the use of carpooling, walking, public transportation, or just being dropped off at work. *See Konradi, supra*, 919 F.2d at 1211–12 (finding that employer substantially controlled employee's commute because, among other things, employer required employee to use his personal vehicle instead of other forms of commutation (*i.e.*, bus, train, or car pooling)).

On the day in question, Reynolds actually had made an off-site visit in her car and was returning home from the off-site location when the accident occurred. She was required to use her car for the visit. Her commute therefore had a dual purpose insofar as it served interests of both Reynolds and the firm. Moreover, the firm's requirement that Reynolds use her car eliminated alternate means of transportation. Thus, the firm is liable to the Carters under the doctrine of *respondeat superior* because Reynolds' use of her personal automobile to advance her employer's business interests fell within the dual purpose, required-vehicle exception to the going and coming rule and placed her squarely both within the employment relationship and the scope of her employment at the time of the accident. Obviously this is a fact-intensive inquiry. In every case in which a plaintiff invokes the required-vehicle exception to the going and coming rule, he or she must establish that the employer, in fact, required the vehicle to be provided by the employee on the day in question.

. . .

VII

The judgment of the Appellate Division is affirmed.

Notes

Slight deviations. Sometimes an employee might not be engaging in a work-related activity when his negligence results in an injury to another. For example, the fact that an employee is engaging in horseplay when an injury occurs does not automatically take the employee's actions outside the scope of employment. But where the employee's actions amount to a substantial deviation from a work-related task, the actions are no longer within the scope of employment. Where a court will draw that line is not always clear. *Compare* Great A & P Tea Co. v. Aveilhe, 116 A.2d 162 (D.C. Ct. App. 1955) (employees not acting within scope of employment when one jokingly pushed the other over while the other was kneeling to stock cans) *with* Hughes v. Metropolitan Government of Nashville and Davidson County, 340 S.W.3d 352 (Tenn. 2011) (employee who drove front-end loader toward co-workers in a menacing fashion acting with scope of employment).

Frolics and detours. Some employees are required to travel as part of their jobs. If, as one nineteenth-century decision put it, a traveling employee goes off "on a frolic of his own, without being at all on his master's business, the master will not be liable." Joel v. Morrison, 6 C. & P. 501, 172 Eng.Rep. 1338 (1834). In such cases, "the scope of employment is suspended until the employee returns to the point of departure." Eberhardy v. Gen. Motors Corp., 404 F. Supp. 826, 830 (M.D. Fla.1975). If, instead, the employee engaged in but a minor deviation or detour along the way, the employee may still be within the scope of employment. As is typical of this area of the law, there is often much gray area between those extremes. In *McNair v. Lend Lease Trucks, Inc.*, 95 F.3d 325 (4th Cir. 1996) (en banc), a truck driver pulled his car over to the side of the road (a detour) and proceeded to a nearby bar where he became extremely intoxicated (a frolic). Three hours later, he attempted to return to his truck but was struck by a motorcycle. The individual driving the motorcycle was killed and the truck driver was allegedly negligent in cutting in front of the motorcycle as he returned to the truck. Was the employee within the scope of employment at the time of the accident?

Acting contrary to employer instructions. An employee's job involves delivering flowers in her car to customers. Her employer has instructed all of its employees to obey the speed limit at all times. On Valentine's Day, the business is overwhelmed with orders, and the employee is running behind in her deliveries. To make up time, she drives 45 m.p.h. in a 25 m.p.h. zone. Due to her speed, she is unable to slow down in time to avoid a collision. The driver of the other vehicle now seeks to hold the employer vicariously liable for the employee's negligence. Was the employee acting within the scope of employment? *See* Restatement (Third) of Agency § 7.01 cmt. c (2006).

Problem 11.2. Bobbie is an associate at the law firm of Hayes, Grevey, and Bing. For the past two years, she has taught Legal Writing as an adjunct at a nearby law school. The firm is aware of this fact. In fact, several attorneys in the firm work in similar part-time capacities. Two of the partners in the firm serve as part-time municipal court judges, for example. On the day of the accident, Bobbie was driving her car to the law school to teach. While driving, she made several firm-related calls on her cell phone, including one that ended seconds before Bobbie crashed her car into Christian's car, in which Piper was riding.

Was Bobbie acting within the scope of employment at the time of the accident for purposes of a claim against her law firm?

b. The Enterprise Liability Theory

Harris v. Trojan Fireworks Co.

120 Cal. App. 3d 157 (Cal. Ct. App. 1981)

GARST, Associate Justice

Statement of Facts

Since the appeal arose from an order dismissing the complaint, the facts stated are the facts which are alleged in the complaint.

Barajas was an employee of defendant Trojan Fireworks Company (Trojan). On Friday, December 21, 1979, at the Trojan manufacturing plant in Rialto, commencing at noon and continuing until 4 p. m., Trojan held a Christmas party for its employees at which, it is alleged, the employees were caused to attend and caused to imbibe large quantities of alcoholic beverages.

Barajas attended the party and became intoxicated to the extent that his ability to drive an automobile was substantially impaired. Nevertheless, he attempted to drive home. In this attempt he was involved in the accident which resulted in the death of James Harris and injury to Dawn and Steven Griffin.

Plaintiffs allege the death of Harris and the injuries of Dawn and Steven Griffin were the result of the accident which was proximately caused by Barajas' advanced state of intoxication.

Contentions

Plaintiffs contend that their complaint is sufficient. They contend that Barajas' intoxication, which was the proximate cause of the accident and resulting injuries and death, occurred in the course and scope of his employment so that under the doctrine of respondeat superior his employer, defendant Trojan, is liable for the resulting injuries and wrongful death.

Discussion

Respondeat Superior

As a general rule, a principal is responsible for the acts of his agent; however, an employer is often exempted from liability for injury caused to or by the employee while the employee is traveling to or from work.

This exemption of employer liability is often referred to as the "going and coming" rule. In workers' compensation cases where the rule has been applied to relieve an employer or its carrier from liability resulting from injuries to the employee, it is often stated that the injury was not incurred "in the course and scope of the employment." In third party liability cases, the negligent employee's employer is often excused from liability under the "going and coming" rule on the rationale that the employer should not be liable for acts of the employee which occur when the employee is not rendering service to his employer, or where the employer has no right of control over the employee.

...

The law now recognizes that the entire subject of torts is a reflection of social policies which fix financial responsibility for harm done. As we depart from liability for one's own act or conduct and enter into the arena of vicarious liability, the quest of liability is frequently determined by who is best able to spread the risk of loss through the prices charged for its product or liability insurance. (*Hinman v. Westinghouse Electric Company, supra*, 2 Cal.3d 956, 959–960, 88 Cal.Rptr. 188, 471 P.2d 988; *Fields v. Sanders* (1947) 29 Cal.2d 834, 180 Cal.Rptr. 684.) The underlying philosophy which holds an employer liable for an employee's negligent acts is the deeply rooted sentiment that a business enterprise should not be able to disclaim responsibility for accidents which may fairly be said to be the result of its activity.

In the case of *Rodgers v. Kemper Constr. Co., supra*, 50 Cal.App.3d 608, 124 Cal. Rptr. 143, this court stated:

> "Under the modern rationale for *respondeat superior*, the test for determining whether an employer is vicariously liable for the tortious conduct of

> his employee is closely related to the test applied in workers' compensation cases for determining whether an injury arose out of or in the course of employment. This must necessarily be so because the theoretical basis for placing a loss on the employer in both the tort and workers' compensation fields is the allocation of the economic cost of an injury resulting from a risk incident to the enterprise." (50 Cal.App.3d at p. 619, 124 Cal.Rptr. 143.)

Thus, we think it can be fairly said that liability attaches where a nexus exists between the employment or the activity which results in an injury that is foreseeable. Foreseeable is here used in the sense that the employee's conduct is not so unusual or startling that it would seem unfair to include the loss resulting from it among the other costs of the employer's business. (Rodgers v. Kemper Constr. Co., supra, 50 Cal.App.3d at p. 619, 124 Cal.Rptr. 143.)

Applying these standards of business purpose or business activity and foreseeability to the facts of the instant case it appears that there is sufficient connection between the employment or the employer's Christmas party and the employee's negligent act to justify holding the employer financially responsible for the injuries occasioned by the employee's accident. Although the accident occurred away from the employer's premises and presumably after work, we believe that the operable factors giving rise to the subsequent accident at least make a prima facie showing that the accident occurred in the course of Harris' employment with defendant.

It may be inferred that the party was for the benefit of the employer. It may be argued that the purpose of the party was to improve employer/employee relations or to increase the continuity of employment by providing employees with the fringe benefit of a party, or to improve relations between the employees by providing them with this opportunity for social contact. That Trojan intended for Barajas to attend the party is indicated by the fact that the party was held at work during work hours and Barajas was paid to attend. That Trojan intended for Barajas to consume alcohol is implied from the fact that the employer furnished the alcoholic beverages and it is further alleged that Trojan, its agents and employees caused him to imbibe large quantities of alcoholic beverages. It is further alleged that he became intoxicated at the party, to such an extent that his ability to operate a motor vehicle was substantially impaired. The complaint further alleges that while in this intoxicated condition, and at his place of employment, he entered his automobile and commenced his attempt to drive home.

...

We hold that plaintiffs have pleaded sufficient facts, which, if proved, would support a jury's determination that Barajas' intoxication occurred at the Christmas party and that his attendance at the party as well as his state of intoxication occurred within the scope of his employment. That he would attempt to drive home while still intoxicated and might have an accident was foreseeable as that term is used in *Rodgers v. Kemper Const. Co., supra*, 50 Cal.App.3d 608, 618–619, 124 Cal. Rptr. 143.

Notes

The cost of doing business. California courts have justified application of the enterprise liability partly on the basis of fairness. "The losses caused by the torts of employees, which as a practical matter are sure to occur in the conduct of the employer's enterprise, are placed upon that enterprise itself, as a required cost of doing business." Hinman v. Westinghouse Elec. Co., 2 Cal. 3d 956, 959–960 (1970). Is it fair to treat the injuries in *Harris* as a required cost of Trojan Fireworks' business?

Problem 11.3. Review the facts in Problems 11.1 and 11.2. Would Bobbie be deemed to be acting within the scope of employment at the time of the accident in a jurisdiction that employs the enterprise liability theory?

2. Vicarious Liability Stemming from Intentional Misconduct

> It is not ordinarily within the scope of a servant's authority to commit an assault on a third person.... And the cases in which liability has been imposed upon the master for assault by his servant are comparatively few. Usually assault is the expression of personal animosity and is not for the purpose of carrying out the master's business.

Texas & Pac. Ry. v. Hagenloh, 247 S.W.2d 236, 239 (Tex. 1952).

The first two cases in this part involve battery cases in which the courts apply traditional *respondeat superior* principles. The third involves a court invoking enterprise liability theory.

G.T. Management v. Gonzalez

106 S.W.3d 880 (Tex. Ct. App.—Dallas—2003)

Opinion by Justice ROSENBERG (Assigned).

About 11:00 p.m. on October 11, 1998, Gonzalez went to Club 2551, a dance club in Dallas. According to Gonzalez, about 1:00 a.m., a Club 2551 bouncer grabbed Gonzalez and asked him whether he had thrown a bottle. When Gonzalez denied it, the man called more bouncers over. The bouncers grabbed Gonzalez from behind, pinning his arms. When Gonzalez told them that they "had the wrong guy," the bouncers began hitting Gonzalez in the face with their flashlights. Gonzalez fell against a wall and was thrown down the steps at the club entrance. Ray Vasquez, the club manager, testified that the bouncers grabbed Gonzalez's arms after Gonzalez swung at Vasquez and Gonzalez and a bouncer fell against a wall and then fell down. Vasquez denied that any bouncers hit Gonzalez with flashlights or threw him down the steps. It was undisputed that Gonzalez was injured as a result of this incident. He was taken by ambulance to Parkland Hospital and received medical treatment.

[Gonzalez sued G.T. Management on a respondeat superior theory.]

The case was submitted to the court, and a verdict was rendered for Gonzalez against G.T. Management.... The court awarded Gonzalez $30,000, costs, and pre- and postjudgment interest. G.T. Management's motion for new trial was overruled by operation of law. G.T. Management appeals the judgment.

...

Because Gonzalez pleaded a respondeat superior theory, we consider whether the evidence supports the trial court's implied findings that G.T. Management was liable for Gonzalez's injuries under this theory. An employee's tortious conduct will be found to be within the scope of employment when the tortious conduct is of the same general nature as that authorized or incidental to the conduct authorized. An employer will be held liable for the act of his employee, even if the act is contrary to express orders, if it is done within the general authority of the employee. Thus, an employer may be vicariously liable for an intentional tort when the act, although not specifically authorized by the employer, is closely connected with the employee's authorized duties, that is, if the intentional tort is committed in the accomplishment of a duty entrusted to the employee, rather than because of personal animosity. When an employee commits an assault, it is for the trier of fact to determine whether the employee ceased to act as an employee and acted instead upon his own responsibility.

G.T. Management does not dispute that it employed the bouncers, but it contends that it cannot be held vicariously liable for any assault because assault was contrary to its policies and was necessarily an expression of personal animosity. In *Durand*, an employer night club was found vicariously liable for the assault of a customer by a doorman who had authority to select customers for admittance. Evidence of "overzealous enforcement" of the club's policies supported the finding of vicarious liability. However, in *Texas & Pacific Railway Co. v. Hagenloh*, 151 Tex. 191, 198, 247 S.W.2d 236, 240 (1952), relied on by G.T. Management, a railroad was held not vicariously liable for an assault of one employee by another employee whose duties did not include the use of force and who was not authorized to use force to perform those duties, even when the assault arose from a job-related investigation....

Here, fights occurred at the club, sometimes three or four per night, and the bouncers' duties were to break up the fights and walk the parties out of the club. The bouncers were expected to signal for back-up with their flashlights when fights occurred. The bouncers used choke holds to control the patrons. The bouncers were hired based primarily on their size. Thus, the evidence shows that the bouncers were authorized to use force, and their assault of Gonzalez was incidental to their use of that force. Therefore, this case is similar to *Durand*, and distinguishable from *Hagenloh*. Considering only the evidence supporting the trial court's implied finding that bouncers employed by G.T. Management committed an assault while acting as employees, we conclude that evidence is legally sufficient to support the finding. Further, considering all the evidence on this issue, we conclude the evidence is factually sufficient to support the finding.

LeBrane v. Lewis

292 So. 2d 216 (La. 1974)

TATE, Justice.

The court of appeal held that the defendant employer was not liable in tort for the act of its supervisor in stabbing a discharged employee who was still on the employment premises. We granted certiorari to review the employer's liability, if any, by reason of the doctrine of respondeat superior.

1. The Issue

The essential issue thus raised before us is whether, at the time of the intentional tort, the supervisor was acting within the scope of his employment. If so, therefore his employer is liable for the damages caused by this tort....

2. The Facts

Charles LeBrane, then 17, was employed as a kitchen helper for the Capitol House Hotel. His immediate supervisor was Lewis, the kitchen steward.

On the day of the injury, LeBrane arrived late for work. Lewis told him to take the rest of the day off and to get a haircut, since the hotel manager did not want bushy-haired employees on the food premises. LeBrane hung around an hour or so and, despite several warnings by Lewis, refused to leave. Lewis, who has authority to hire and fire, then terminated LeBrane's employment. He had LeBrane sign a termination slip and took him upstairs to the hotel manager's office for his termination pay.

The manager was out, so Lewis and LeBrane then rode down the elevator again. On the way down a heated and profane argument ensued, with, in the trial court's finding, each 'more or less inviting each other outside'.

On the way out, Lewis and LeBrane commenced fighting. Whoever the initial aggressor, the factual finding now final is that Lewis, in stabbing LeBrane as he tried to run away, used excessive force and is liable in tort.

The final stabbing took place within the loading premises at the basement level of the hotel. This was away from the kitchen, but still on the hotel premises enroute to the basement exit from the hotel.

3. The Law and its Application Here

In Louisiana, as elsewhere, an employer (master) is liable for a tort committed by his employee (servant) if, at the time, the servant is acting within the scope of his employment—acting, as our Civil Code Article 2320 phrases it, "in the exercise of the functions in which ... employed." Article 2320.

In the present case, the supervisory employee knifed and seriously injured a former co-employee on the employment premises in an employment-related dispute at or soon after the time of the co-employee's discharge by the supervisor. At least insofar as discharging the injured employee and ordering him off the premises, the supervisor was acting within the course and scope of his employment.

In holding that, nevertheless, the stabbing did not occur during the course and scope of the employment, our brethren of the intermediate court reasoned: "In our view when LeBrane and Lewis reached the basement of the hotel on the service elevator and each invited the other outside to fight, what followed had nothing to do with Lewis' employment. The altercation had at this point become a purely personal matter between LeBrane and Lewis."

In so concluding, we believe our brethren of the intermediate court were in error.

The dispute which erupted into violence was primarily employment-rooted. The fight was reasonably incidental to the performance of the supervisor's duties in connection with firing the recalcitrant employee and causing him to leave the place of employment. It occurred on the employment premises and during the hours of employment.

In short, the tortious conduct of the supervisor was so closely connected him time, place, and causation to his employment-duties as to be regarded a risk of harm fairly attributable to the employer's business, as compared with conduct motivated by purely personal considerations entirely extraneous to the employer's interests. It can thus be regarded as within the scope of the supervisor's employment, so that his employer is liable in tort to third persons injured thereby. . . .

[T[he present employee's tortious conduct occurred while the employee was at least partly actuated by his purpose of acting for his employer in the discharge of the recalcitrant co-employee (*Restatement*, Section 228), and it was reasonably consequent upon or incident to his performance of his employment function of hiring and firing sub-employees (*Restatement*, Section 229). The tortious conduct (which had also occurred within the authorized time and space limits of the employment and was thus within the scope of employment. The Supervisor Lewis's employer is therefore liable for the damages caused by his tort at work.

Lisa M. v. Henry Mayo Newhall Memorial Hospital

907 P.2d 358 (Cal. 1995)

Plaintiff Lisa M. was injured in a fall and sought treatment at defendant Henry Mayo Newhall Memorial Hospital (Hospital). Under the pretense of conducting an ultrasound imaging examination, a technician [Tripoli] sexually molested her. [Lisa M. sought to hold the hospital vicariously liable for Tripoli's actions.]

Was Tripoli's sexual battery of Lisa M. within the scope of his employment? The injurious events were causally related to Tripoli's employment as an ultrasound technician in the sense they would not have occurred had he not been so employed.

Tripoli's employment as an ultrasound technician provided the opportunity for him to meet plaintiff and to be alone with her in circumstances making the assault possible. The employment was thus one necessary cause of the ensuing tort. But, as previously discussed, in addition to such "but for" causation, respondeat superior liability requires that the risk of the tort have been engendered by, "typical of or broadly incidental to," or, viewed from a somewhat different perspective, "a generally foreseeable consequence of," Hospital's enterprise. (*Hinman v. Westinghouse Elec. Co., supra*)

. . .

As with . . . nonsexual assaults, a sexual tort will not be considered engendered by the employment unless its motivating emotions were fairly attributable to work-related events or conditions. Here the opposite was true: a technician simply took advantage of solitude with a naive patient to commit an assault for reasons unrelated to his work. Tripoli's job was to perform a diagnostic examination and record the results. The task provided no occasion for a work-related dispute or any other work-related emotional involvement with the patient. The technician's decision to engage in conscious exploitation of the patient did not arise out of the performance of the examination, although the circumstances of the examination made it possible. "If . . . the assault was not motivated or triggered off by anything in the employment activity but was the result of only propinquity and lust, there should be no liability." (*Lyon v. Carey, supra*, 533 F.2d at p. 655.)

Our conclusion does not rest on mechanical application of a motivation-to-serve test for intentional torts, which would bar vicarious liability for virtually all sexual misconduct. Tripoli's criminal actions, of course, were unauthorized by Hospital and were not motivated by any desire to serve Hospital's interests. Beyond that, however, his motivating emotions were not causally attributable to his employment. The flaw in plaintiff's case for Hospital's respondeat superior liability is not so much that Tripoli's actions were personally motivated, but that those personal motivations were not generated by or an outgrowth of workplace responsibilities, conditions or events.

Analysis in terms of foreseeability leads to the same conclusion. . . .

In arguing Tripoli's misconduct was generally foreseeable, plaintiff emphasizes the physically intimate nature of the work Tripoli was employed to perform. In our view, that a job involves physical contact is, by itself, an insufficient basis on which to impose vicarious liability for a sexual assault. To hold medical care providers strictly liable for deliberate sexual assaults by every employee whose duties include examining or touching patients' otherwise private areas would be virtually to remove scope of employment as a limitation on providers' vicarious liability. In cases like the present one, a deliberate sexual assault is fairly attributed not to any peculiar aspect of the health care enterprise, but only to "propinquity and lust" (*Lyon v. Carey* (D.C.Cir.1976) 533 F.2d 649, 655).

Here, there is no evidence of emotional involvement, either mutual or unilateral, arising from the medical relationship. Although the procedure ordered involved physical contact, it was not of a type that would be expected to, or actually did, give rise to intense emotions on either side. We deal here not with a physician or therapist who becomes sexually involved with a patient as a result of mishandling the feelings predictably created by the therapeutic relationship (*see, e.g.,* Simmons v. United States (9th Cir.1986) 805 F.2d 1363, 1369–1370; Doe v. Samaritan Counseling Center (Alaska 1990) 791 P.2d 344, 348–349), but with an ultrasound technician who simply took advantage of solitude, access and superior knowledge to commit a sexual assault.

Note

The use of force. Section 228 of the *Restatement (Second) of Agency* suggests that the use of force by an employee is within the scope of employment if it is not "unexpectable by the master." This is most likely to be the case where the nature of the job may necessarily involve the use of force. *See* Durand v. Moore, 879 S.W.2d 196 (Tex. App.—Houston 1994) (holding that evidence supported conclusion that doorman's "overzealous enforcement" of nightclub's admittance policies, which led to injury of patron, was conduct within doorman's scope of employment). Section 229 suggests that one of the factors to consider more generally in determining whether an act is within the scope of employment is whether the employee's act was "seriously criminal."

Problem 11.4. After the collision, Piper got out of the car and began to berate Christian for his careless driving. The two argued intensely for a few minutes until Christian threatened Piper with physical violence. Piper then decided to walk away from the situation. Christian followed. Piper then began running in an effort to escape Christian. Christian caught up to Piper and jerked her arm and spun her around. At this point, onlookers intervened and prevented any further violence. Piper suffered a dislocated shoulder. In addition to seeking to hold RideAlong vicariously liable for Christian's alleged negligence, she also seeks to hold RideAlong vicariously liable for Christian's battery. Was Christian acting within the scope of employment during this incident?

D. Nondelegable Duties

Pusey v. Bator

762 N.E.2d 968 (Ohio 2002)

DOUGLAS, J.

At all times relevant herein, defendant-appellee, Greif Brothers Corporation, a steel drum manufacturer, owned and operated a manufacturing plant in Youngstown, Ohio. In 1987, Greif Brothers experienced several incidents wherein trespassers stole property from its parking lot. As a result of these incidents, Lowell Wilson, the superintendent at Greif Brothers' Youngstown plant, decided to hire a security company to guard Greif Brothers' property.

In April 1987, Wilson, on behalf of Greif Brothers, entered into a contract with Youngstown Security Patrol, Inc. ("YSP") to supply a uniformed security guard to "deter theft [and] vandalism" on Greif Brothers' property during specified hours. Wilson told YSP's owner and president, Carl Testa, that he wanted the security guard to periodically check the parking lot and the inside of the building. Other than those instructions, Wilson did not instruct Testa in the manner that YSP was to protect Greif Brothers' property.

The written security contract did not specify whether the guard was to be armed or unarmed, and Wilson and Testa both later testified that they never discussed the subject. At least some of the YSP security guards that were assigned to watch Greif Brothers' property carried firearms. Wilson was aware of this because he noticed that the guards wore holsters and guns as part of their uniform. In addition, Wilson was aware of an incident in which a YSP guard discharged his weapon in the manufacturing plant while apparently using one of Greif Brothers' steel drums for target practice. Although Wilson complained to Testa about the damage, he did not indicate that the security guards should not carry firearms while protecting Greif Brothers' property.

On June 30, 1991, Testa hired Eric Bator as a YSP security guard. Notes written on the bottom of Bator's application indicate that Bator was hired as an unarmed guard but that he would take the necessary training required by the state to become certified as an armed guard. Nevertheless, because he felt uneasy performing his security duties without a weapon, Bator took his gun, in a briefcase, to work with him. Bator testified that his supervisor, Bill Kissinger, knew that Bator carried a gun while working as a YSP guard and that Bator was not licensed to work as an armed guard. Kissinger testified that he had seen Bator's gun but denied knowing that Bator carried the gun while working as a YSP guard.

YSP employed several security guards but only one guard per shift was assigned to guard Greif Brothers' property. Bator was the guard assigned to Greif Brothers' property from 11:00 p.m., August 11 to 7:00 a.m., August 12, 1991. At approximately 1:00 a.m., Bator looked out through a window in the guard office and saw two individuals, later identified as Derrell Pusey and Charles Thomas, walking through Greif Brothers' parking lot. Bator used the radio in the office to inform a YSP guard on duty at another location that two people were on Greif Brothers' property. [After words were exchanged, Bator shot Pusey.]

Derrell was transported to the hospital, where he died from his wound. Thereafter, plaintiff-appellant, Ethel Pusey, Derrell's mother, individually and as executor of Derrell's estate, filed a wrongful death and survivorship action against Bator, YSP, and Greif Brothers. YSP and Bator settled with Pusey soon after the jury trial began, leaving Greif Brothers as the only defendant.

After Pusey rested her case, Greif Brothers moved for a directed verdict pursuant to Civ.R. 50(A). The trial court granted Greif Brothers' motion. The court held that even if Derrell's death was the result of YSP's negligence, Greif Brothers was not liable because YSP was an independent contractor and, as a general rule, an employer is not liable for the negligent acts of its independent contractor. The court rejected Pusey's assertion that the nature of the work contracted for in this case qualified as an exception to the general rule.

Pusey appealed the trial court's decision to the Seventh District Court of Appeals. The court of appeals, in a split decision, affirmed the trial court's ruling and Pusey appealed to this court. The case is before this court upon our allowance of a discretionary appeal.

...

We find that, even when viewed in the light most favorable to Pusey, the evidence clearly established YSP's status as an independent contractor. Greif Brothers specified the result to be accomplished, *i.e.*, to deter vandals and thieves, but the details of how this task should be accomplished, with the exception noted above regarding periodic patrolling of the property, were left to YSP. Moreover, YSP, not Greif Brothers, hired the guards, supplied them with uniforms and equipment, paid them, and assigned them to their posts, and was responsible for training them and ensuring that they were state-certified as security guards. For the foregoing reasons, we agree with the trial court's conclusion, affirmed by the court of appeals, that YSP was an independent contractor.

As stated previously, an employer is generally not liable for the negligent acts of an independent contractor. There are, however, exceptions to this general rule, several of which stem from the nondelegable duty doctrine. Nondelegable duties arise in various situations that generally fall into two categories: (1) affirmative duties that are imposed on the employer by statute, contract, franchise, charter, or common law and (2) duties imposed on the employer that arise out of the work itself because its performance creates dangers to others, *i.e.*, inherently dangerous work. If the work to be performed fits into one of these two categories, the employer may delegate the work to an independent contractor, but he cannot delegate the duty. In other words, the employer is not insulated from liability if the independent contractor's negligence results in a breach of the duty.

Pusey claims that hiring armed guards to protect property creates a nondelegable duty because the work is inherently dangerous. Consequently, Pusey argues, even if YSP is an independent contractor, that status does not relieve Greif Brothers from liability for the damages arising from Derrell's death resulting from the alleged negligence of Bator.

Work is inherently dangerous when it creates a peculiar risk of harm to others unless special precautions are taken. Under those circumstances, the employer hiring the independent contractor has a duty to see that the work is done with reasonable care and cannot, by hiring an independent contractor, insulate himself or herself from liability for injuries resulting to others from the negligence of the independent contractor or its employees.

To fall within the inherently-dangerous-work exception, it is not necessary that the work be such that it cannot be done without a risk of harm to others, or even that it be such that it involves a high risk of such harm. It is sufficient that the work involves a risk, recognizable in advance, of physical harm to others, which is inherent in the work itself.

The exception does not apply, however, where the employer would reasonably have only a general anticipation of the possibility that the contractor may be negligent in some way and thereby cause harm to a third party. For example, one who hires a trucker to transport his goods should realize that if the truck is driven at an excessive speed, or with defective brakes, some harm to persons on the highway is likely to occur. An employer of an independent contractor may assume that a careful contractor will take routine precautions against all of the ordinary and customary dangers that may arise in the course of the contemplated work.

The inherently-dangerous-work exception does apply, however, when special risks are associated with the work such that a reasonable man would recognize the necessity of taking special precautions. The work must create a risk that is not a normal, routine matter of customary human activity, such as driving an automobile, but is rather a special danger to those in the vicinity arising out of the particular situation created, and calling for special precautions.

Greif Brothers argues that hiring armed guards to protect property does not create a peculiar risk of harm to others and, therefore, does not fit within the inherently-dangerous-work exception. The common pleas court agreed with Greif Brothers and relied on the Twelfth District Court of Appeals' holding in *Joseph v. Consol. Rail Corp.* (Oct. 30, 1987), Butler App. No. CA87-05-065, unreported, 1987 WL 19481, to support its decision.

In *Joseph*, the defendant, Conrail, hired an independent contractor to perform surveillance of an employee of Conrail to determine the validity of the employee's claim that he had injured his back. The investigators were consequently detected and confronted by the employee. In a subsequent action by the employee against Conrail for alleged damages resulting from the confrontation, the trial court granted summary judgment in favor of Conrail.

On appeal, the Butler County Court of Appeals rejected the plaintiff's contention that the inherently-dangerous-work exception was applicable. The court stated that that exception "'is limited to dangerous work, and cannot be extended to proper work dangerously done.'"

Although we agree with the holding in *Joseph*, we disagree with the trial court's determination that it is applicable to the facts of this case. One crucial difference between the work at issue in *Joseph, i.e.*, surveillance, and the work at issue herein, *i.e.*, an armed guard deterring thieves and vandals, is that an armed confrontation with a suspicious person may be required by the latter. Surveillance work, as emphasized by the *Joseph* court, is not inherently dangerous to the person being investigated because the purpose of the investigator is to remain undetected and unobtrusive. In contrast, armed YSP guards were instructed to "deter" thieves and vandals. Thus, the work contracted for contemplates a confrontation between an armed guard and persons entering the property. For the foregoing reasons, we do not agree with the trial court's determination that *Joseph* supports its conclusion that hiring armed guards to protect property is not inherently dangerous to those entering the property.

. . .

We find that work such as YSP was hired to perform does create a peculiar risk of harm to others. When armed guards are hired to deter vandals and thieves it is foreseeable that someone might be injured by the inappropriate use of the weapon if proper precautions are not taken. Thus, such an injury is one that might have been anticipated as a direct or probable consequence of the performance of the work contracted for, if reasonable care is not taken in its performance. Also, the risk created is not a normal, routine matter of customary human activity, such as driving an automobile, but is instead a special danger arising out of the particular situation created and calling for special precautions. We therefore hold that when an employer hires an independent contractor to provide armed security guards to protect property, the inherently-dangerous-work exception is triggered such that if someone is injured by the weapon as a result of a guard's negligence, the employer is vicariously liable even though the guard responsible is an employee of the independent contractor.

We do not mean to suggest by the foregoing that we have determined that Derrell's death resulted from YSP's negligence. That issue is to be determined by a finder of fact. If the fact finder so finds, however, then, pursuant to our holding herein, Greif Brothers is liable for the damages even though the negligence was that of an employee of an independent contractor.

For the foregoing reasons, we reverse the judgment of the court of appeals and remand the cause to the trial court for a fact-finder's determination whether Derrell's death was a result of YSP's negligence.

Note

Nondelegable duties. According to one author, "[t]he most often cited formulation is that a duty will be deemed nondelegable when the responsibility is so important to the community that the employer should not be permitted to transfer it to another." 5 Harper, James and Gray, Torts § 26.11, at 73 (2d ed.) (quoted in Kleeman v. Rheingold, 614 N.E.2d 712, 716 (N.Y. 1993)). An example would be the duty to provide medical care to prisoners. *See* Medley v. North Carolina Department of Corrections, 412 S.E.2d 654 (N.C. 1992) ("[T]he duty to provide adequate medical care to inmates, imposed by the state and federal Constitutions, and recognized in state statute and caselaw, is such a fundamental and paramount obligation of the state that the state cannot absolve itself of responsibility by delegating it to another."). Another would be the duty of a business owner or possessor to maintain the premises in a reasonably safe condition. Valenti v. NET Properties Management, 142 N.H. 633, 635, 710 A.2d 399 (1998).

Review Question

Kathleen is an associate in a law firm. She flew to Orlando, Florida, for a deposition on Friday and rented a car. She was scheduled to attend a work-related conference in Tampa the following Monday, so she planned to stay over for the weekend. Her firm approved of her car rental and paid for her attendance at the conference. Kathleen's mother lived in Tampa, so Kathleen decided to stay with her for the weekend instead of at a hotel. Since the firm was going to save money on hotel expenses, it had no objection to Kathleen staying with her mother. After the deposition on Friday, Kathleen stopped for dinner on the way to Tampa. She consumed four glasses of wine during dinner before getting in her car and driving toward Tampa. While driving, she negligently crossed the center line and collided with a motorcycle driven by Michael. Michael now seeks to hold Kathleen's law firm vicariously liable for Kathleen's negligence. Is he likely to succeed under the traditional *Restatement* rule?

Chapter 12

Strict Liability for Harm Caused by Abnormally Dangerous Activities

A. Strict Liability for Harm Caused by Abnormally Dangerous Activities
- Strict liability in general
- Strict liability under the *Rylands v. Fletcher* standard
- Strict liability for harm caused by engaging in abnormally dangerous activities
- Factors to consider
- Types of activities leading to strict liability
- Policy basis for imposing strict liability
- Other concepts developed in class or in readings assigned by the professor

B. Strict Liability for Harm Caused by Animals
- Livestock
- Wild animals
- Abnormally dangerous animals
- Other concepts developed in class or in readings assigned by the professor

C. Causation
- In general
- Superseding causes
- Other concepts developed in class or in readings assigned by the professor

D. Defenses
- Other concepts developed in class or in readings assigned by the professor

Chapter Problem. Henry Benjamin drove a tank truck for Texxon Oil. Tank trucks are large vehicles designed to transport up to 11,000 gallons of gasoline. Henry was transporting approximately 8,000 gallons of gas on Interstate 40 when the tank trailer, which was carrying the gas, disengaged from the tank truck. The trailer tipped over onto its right side and came crashing down in the middle of road, spilling gasoline everywhere. Henry had worked for the company for 10 years without incident. His driving record was spotless and his truck had recently undergone an inspection, which revealed no problems with the vehicle.

As the old common law developed in England, a plaintiff who wished to recover for harm caused by a defendant needed to obtain the appropriate writ, an order in the name of the king that provided a specific remedy for a particular wrong. To recover under the writ of Trespass, for example, the plaintiff needed to prove that he suffered an injury that was the result of force directly applied to the plaintiff or the plaintiff's property. So, the writ of trespass would apply where the defendant intentionally or negligently struck the plaintiff with his fist. When the plaintiff was injured in a more indirect fashion—for example, where the defendant negligently left an object in the road, which the plaintiff collided with—the plaintiff could bring an action "on the Case." At the time, it was thought that the writ of trespass imposed strict liability, whereas a plaintiff seeking to recover on the Case had to establish some form of fault on the part of the defendant. Joseph Sanders et al., *Must Torts Be Wrong? An Empirical Perspective*, 49 WAKE FOREST L. REV. 1, 3 (2014).

The Massachusetts Supreme Judicial Court's decision in *Brown v. Kendall*, 60 Mass. (6 Cush.) 292 (1850) marked a major turning point in U.S. tort law on this issue. In *Brown*, the defendant attempted to break up a dog fight by hitting the dogs with a stick. The defendant accidentally struck the plaintiff in the process. Since the injury was inflicted directly without any sort of delay, the plaintiff should theoretically not have been required to establish fault on the defendant's part in order to recover. Instead, the Massachusetts Supreme Judicial Court held that "the plaintiff must come prepared with evidence to show either that the intention was unlawful, or that the defendant was in fault; for if the injury was unavoidable, and the conduct of the defendant was free from blame, he will not be liable." In other words, liability must be based on fault.

Brown v. Kendall, then, effectively establishes the default rule for modern tort law: liability is ordinarily based on fault. But as this chapter illustrates, there are some situations in which a plaintiff may recover even without establishing fault on the defendant's part. The chapter explores how the law in this area developed as well as particular types of cases in which strict liability often applies.

A. Strict Liability for Harm Caused by Abnormally Dangerous Activities

1. Early Evolution of the Doctrine: *Rylands v. Fletcher*

Rylands v. Fletcher

Exchecquer Chamber
1 Ex. 265 (1866)

BLACKBURN, J., read the following judgment of the court

This was a Special Case stated by an arbitrator under an order of *nisi prius*, in which the question for the court is stated to be whether the plaintiff is entitled to recover any, and, if any, what, damages from the defendants by reason of the matters therein before stated.

It appears from the statement in the Case, that the plaintiff was damaged by his property being flooded by water which, without any fault on his part, broke out of a reservoir constructed on the defendants' land by the defendants' orders and maintained by the defendants. It appears from the statement in the Case, that the coal under the defendants' land had, at some remote period, been worked out, but that this was unknown at the time when the defendants gave directions to erect the reservoir, and the water in the reservoir would not have escaped from the defendants' land, and no would have been done to the plaintiff, but for this latent defect in the defendants' subsoil. It further appears from the Case that the defendants selected competent engineers and contractors and make the reservoir, and themselves personally continued in total ignorance of what we have called the latent defect in the subsoil, but that the persons employed by them, in the course of the work, became aware of the existence of ancient shafts filled up with soil, though they did not know or suspect that they were shafts communicating with old workings.

It is found that the defendants personally were free from all blame, but that in fact, proper care and skill was not used by the persons employed by them to provide for the sufficiency of the reservoir with reference to these shafts. The consequence was, that the reservoir, when filled with water, burst into the shafts, the water flowed down through them into the old workings, and thence into the plaintiff's mine, and there did the mischief.

The plaintiff, though free from all blame on his part, must bear the loss, unless he can establish that it was the consequence of some default for which the defendants are responsible. The question of law, therefore, arises: What is the liability which the law casts upon a person who like the defendants, lawfully brings on his land something which, though harmless while it remains there, will naturally do mischief if it escape out of his land? It is agreed on all hands that he must take care to keep in that which he has brought on the land, and keep it there in order that it may not escape and damage his neighbour's, but the question arises whether the duty which the law casts upon him under such circumstances is an absolute duty to keep it in at his peril, or is, as the majority of the Court of Exchequer have thought, merely a duty to take all reasonable and prudent precautions in order to keep it in, but no more. If the first be the law, the person who has brought on his land and kept there something dangerous, and failed to keep it in, is responsible for all the natural consequences of its escape. If the second be the limit of his duty, he would not be answerable except on proof of negligence, and consequently would not be answerable for escape arising from any latent defect which ordinary prudence and skill could not detect.

Supposing the second to be the correct view of the law, a further question arises subsidiary to the first, namely, whether the defendants are not so far identified with the contractors whom they employed as to be responsible for the consequences of their want of skill in making the reservoir in fact insufficient with reference to the old shafts, of the existence of which they were aware, though they had not ascertained where the shafts went to.

We think that the true rule of law is that the person who, for his own purposes, brings on his land, and collects and keeps there anything likely to do mischief if it escapes, must keep it in at his peril, and, if he does not do so, he is prima facie answerable for all the damages which is the natural consequence of its escape. He can excuse himself by showing that the escape was owing to the plaintiff's default, or, perhaps, that the escape was the consequence of *vis major*, or the act of God; but, as nothing of this sort exists here, it is unnecessary to inquire what excuse would be sufficient. The general rule, as above stated, seems on principle just. The person whose grass or corn is eaten down by the escaped cattle of his neighbour, or whose mine is flooded by the water from his neighbour's reservoir, or whose cellar is invaded by the filth of his neighbour's privy, or whose habitation is made unhealthy by the fumes and noisome vapours of his neighbour's alkali works, is damnified without any fault of his own; and it seems but reasonable and just that the neighbour who has brought something on his own property which was not naturally there, harmless to others so long as it is confined to his own property, but which he knows will be mischievous if it gets on his neighbour's, should be obliged to make good the damage which ensues if he does not succeed in confining it to his own property. But for his act in bringing it there no mischief could have accrued, and it seems but just that he should at his peril keep it there, so that no mischief may accrue, or answer for the natural and anticipated consequences. On authority this, we think, is established to be the law, whether the thing so brought be beasts or water, or filth or stenches.

...

But it was further said by MARTIN, B., that when damage is done to personal property, or even to the person by collision, neither upon land or at sea, there must be negligence in the party doing the damage to render him legally responsible. This is no doubt true, and this is not confined to cases of collision, for there are many cases in which proof of negligence is essential, as, for instance, where an unruly horse gets on the footpath of a public street and kills a passenger . . . or where a person in a dock is struck by the falling of a bale of cotton which the defendant's servants are lowering. Many other similar cases may be found. But we think these cases distinguishable from the present. Traffic on the highways, whether by land or sea, cannot be conducted without exposing those whose persons or property are near it to some inevitable risk; and, that being so, those who go on the highway, or have their property adjacent to it, may well be held to do so subject to their taking upon themselves the risk of injury from that inevitable danger, and persons who, by the license of the owners, pass near to warehouses where goods are being raised or lowered, certainly do so subject to the inevitable risk of accident. In neither case, therefore, can they recover without proof of want of care or skill occasioning the accident; and it is believed that all the cases in which inevitable accident has been held an excuse for what prima facie was a trespass can be explained on the same principle, namely, that the circumstances were such as to show that the plaintiff had taken the risk upon himself. But there is no ground for saying that the plaintiff here took upon himself any risk arising from the uses to which the defendants should choose to apply their land. He neither knew what there might be, nor could he in any way control the defendants, or hinder their building what reservoirs they liked, and storing up in them what water they pleased, so long as the defendants succeeded in preventing the water which they there brought from interfering with the plaintiff's property.

The view which we take of the first point renders it unnecessary to consider whether the defendants would or would not be responsible for the want of care and skill in the persons employed by them. We are of opinion that the plaintiff is entitled to recover, but as we have not heard any argument as to the amount, we are not able to give judgment for what damages. The parties probably will empower their counsel to agree on the amount of damages; should they differ on the principle the case may be mentioned again.

[The defendants appealed to the House of Lords.]

Rylands v. Fletcher

House of Lords
L.R. 3 H.L. 330 (1868)

THE LORD CHANCELLOR (Lord Cairns)

My Lords, the principles on which this case must be determined appear to me to be extremely simple. The Defendants, treating them as the owners or occupiers of the close on which the reservoir was constructed, might lawfully have used that close for any purpose for which it might in the ordinary course of the enjoyment of land be used; and if, in what I may term the natural user of that land, there had been any accumulation of water, either on the surface or underground, and if, by the operation of the laws of nature, that accumulation of water had passed off into the close occupied by the Plaintiff, the Plaintiff could not have complained that that result had taken place. If he had desired to guard himself against it, it would have lain upon him to have done so, by leaving, or by interposing, some barrier between his close and the close of the Defendants in order to have prevented that operation of the laws of nature.

...

On the other hand if the Defendants, not stopping at the natural use of their close, had desired to use it for any purpose which I may term a non-natural use, for the purpose of introducing into the close that which in its natural condition was not in or upon it, for the purpose of introducing water either above or below ground in quantities and in a manner not the result of any work or operation on or under the land,—and if in consequence of their doing so, or in consequence of any imperfection in the mode of their doing so, the water came to escape and to pass off into the close of the Plaintiff, then it appears to me that that which the Defendants were doing they were doing at their own peril; and, if in the course of their doing it, the evil arose to which I have referred, the evil, namely, of the escape of the water and its passing away to the close of the Plaintiff and injuring the Plaintiff, then for the consequence of that, in my opinion, the Defendants would be liable. . . .

My Lords, these simple principles, if they are well founded, as it appears to me they are, really dispose of this case.

The same result is arrived at on the principles referred to by Mr. Justice Blackburn in his judgment, in the Court of Exchequer Chamber, where he states the opinion of that Court as to the law in these words: "We think that the true rule of law is, that the person who, for his own purposes, brings on his land and collects and keeps there anything likely to do mischief if it escapes, must keep it in at his peril; and if he does not do so, is prima facie answerable for all the damage which is the natural consequence of its escape. . . ."

My Lords, in that opinion, I must say I entirely concur. Therefore, I have to move your Lordships that the judgment of the Court of Exchequer Chamber be affirmed, and that the present appeal be dismissed with costs.

LORD CRANWORTH :-

My Lords, I concur with my noble and learned friend in thinking that the rule of law was correctly stated by Mr. Justice Blackburn in delivering the opinion of the Exchequer Chamber. If a person brings, or accumulates, on his land anything which, if it should escape, may cause damage to his neighbour, he does so at his peril. If it does escape, and cause damage, he is responsible, however careful he may have been, and whatever precautions he may have taken to prevent the damage. . . .

I concur, therefore, with my noble and learned friend in thinking that the judgment below must be affirmed, and that there must be judgment for the Defendant in Error.

Note

One reading of *Rylands v. Fletcher* is that the decision is fundamentally about the use of land. Under this reading, the decision might have little relevance outside of that context. Some courts focused on the "non-natural use" portion of the opinion:

> In *Rylands v. Fletcher* the court predicated the absolute liability of the defendants on the proposition that the use of land for the artificial storage of water was not a natural use, and that, therefore, the landowner was bound at his peril to keep the waters on his own land. This basis of the English rule is to be found in the meteorological conditions which obtain there. England is a pluvial country, where constant streams and abundant rains make the storage of water unnecessary for ordinary or general purposes. When the court said in *Rylands v. Fletcher* that the use of land for storage of water was an unnatural use, it meant such use was not a general or an ordinary one; not one within the contemplation of the parties to the original grant of the land involved, nor of the grantor and grantees of

> adjacent lands, but was a special or extraordinary use, and for that reason applied the rule of absolute liability.

Turner v. Big Lake Oil Co., 96 S.W.2d 221 (Tex. 1936).

The case is more commonly cited for Justice Blackburn's idea that strict liability should apply when one engages in activity that is "likely to do mischief" if things go wrong. Therefore, if one focuses less on the fact that *Rylands v. Fletcher* involved the use of land and more on the fact that the defendant was doing something supposedly "special or extraordinary" that was "likely to do mischief" if something went wrong, the decision can be seen as a clear step in the progression toward the more modern rule discussed in Part A2 below.

Sullivan v. Dunham

55 N.E. 923 (N.Y. 1900)

VANN, J. (after stating the facts).

The main question presented by this appeal is whether one who, for a lawful purpose, and without negligence or want of skill, explodes a blast upon his own land, and thereby causes a piece of wood to fall upon a person lawfully traveling in a public highway, is liable for the injury thus inflicted. The statute authorizes the personal representative of a decedent to 'maintain an action to recover damages for a wrongful act, neglect, or default, by which the decedent's death was caused, against a natural person who, or a corporation which, would have been liable to an action in favor of the decedent, by reason thereof, if death had not ensued.' Code Civ. Proc. § 1902. It covers any action of trespass upon the person which the deceased could have maintained if she had survived the accident. Stated in another form, therefore, the question before us is whether the defendants are liable as trespassers. This is not a new question, for it has been considered, directly or indirectly, so many times by this court that a reference to the earlier authorities is unnecessary. In the leading case upon the subject the defendant, in order to dig a canal authorized by its charter, necessarily blasted out rocks from its own land with gunpowder, and thus threw fragments against the plaintiff's house, which stood upon the adjoining premises. Although there was no proof of negligence or want of skill, the defendant was held liable for the injury sustained. [Hay v. Cohoes Co., 2 N.Y. 159 (1849).]

. . .

[The principle underlying that decision], founded in public policy, that the safety of property generally is superior in right to a particular use of a single piece of property by its owner. It renders the enjoyment of all property more secure, by preventing such a use of one piece by one man as may injure all his neighbors. It makes human life safer, by tending to prevent a landowner from casting, either with or without negligence, a part of his land upon the person of one who is where he has a right to be. It so applies the maxim of 'Sic utere tuo' as to protect person and property from direct physical violence, which, although accidental, has the same effect as if it were intentional. It lessens the hardship by placing absolute liability upon the one who causes the injury. The accident in question was a misfortune to the defendants, but it was a greater misfortune to the young woman who was killed. The safety of travelers upon the public highway is more important to the state than the improvement of one piece of property by a special method is to its owner.

Notes

Justifications for strict liability. Putting aside the *Sullivan* court's focus on property, what justifies holding the defendant liable without fault? What justified holding the defendant in *Rylands v. Fletcher* strictly liable?

Evolution of the doctrine. *Rylands* and blasting cases like *Sullivan* helped form the basis for the strict liability rules regarding abnormally dangerous activities that are covered in the next section.

2. Abnormally Dangerous Activities

In 1938, the first *Restatement of Torts* recognized that "one who carries on an ultrahazardous activity" is strictly liable for the harm caused to one whom "the actor should recognize as likely to be harmed by the unpreventable miscarriage of the activity." *Id.* § 519. The only examples provided by the authors of "ultrahazardous" activities were flying airplanes (in 1938), blasting, and storing and transporting explosive substances. Almost 40 years later, the *Restatement (Second) of Torts* used the phrase "abnormally dangerous" activities to describe the same concept and provided a list of factors to consider in deciding whether a defendant's conduct qualified. Restatement (Second) of Torts § 520. The following decision examines the *Restatement* test and whether it should be applied under the facts of the case.

Indiana Harbor Belt Railroad Co. v. American Cyanamid Co.

916 F.2d 1174 (7th Cir. 1990)

POSNER, Circuit Judge.

American Cyanamid Company, the defendant in this diversity tort suit governed by Illinois law, is a major manufacturer of chemicals, including acrylonitrile, a chemical used in large quantities in making acrylic fibers, plastics, dyes, pharmaceutical chemicals, and other intermediate and final goods. On January 2, 1979, at its manufacturing plant in Louisiana, Cyanamid loaded 20,000 gallons of liquid acrylonitrile into a railroad tank car that it had leased from the North American Car Corporation. The next day, a train of the Missouri Pacific Railroad picked up the car at Cyanamid's siding. The car's ultimate destination was a Cyanamid plant in New Jersey served by Conrail rather than by Missouri Pacific. The Missouri Pacific train carried the car north to the Blue Island railroad yard of Indiana Harbor Belt Railroad, the plaintiff in this case, a small switching line that has a contract with Conrail to switch cars from other lines to Conrail, in this case for travel east.

The Blue Island yard is in the Village of Riverdale, which is just south of Chicago and part of the Chicago metropolitan area.

The car arrived in the Blue Island yard on the morning of January 9, 1979. Several hours after it arrived, employees of the switching line noticed fluid gushing from the bottom outlet of the car. The lid on the outlet was broken. After two hours, the line's supervisor of equipment was able to stop the leak by closing a shut-off valve controlled from the top of the car. No one was sure at the time just how much of the contents of the car had leaked, but it was feared that all 20,000 gallons had, and since acrylonitrile is flammable at a temperature of 30° Fahrenheit or above, highly toxic, and possibly carcinogenic (Acrylonitrile, 9 International Toxicity Update, no. 3, May–June 1989, at 2, 4), the local authorities ordered the homes near the yard evacuated. The evacuation lasted only a few hours, until the car was moved to a remote part of the yard and it was discovered that only about a quarter of the acrylonitrile had leaked. Concerned nevertheless that there had been some contamination of soil and water, the Illinois Department of Environmental Protection ordered the switching line to take decontamination measures that cost the line $981,022.75, which it sought to recover by this suit.

One count of the two-count complaint charges Cyanamid with having maintained the leased tank car negligently. The other count asserts that the transportation of acrylonitrile in bulk through the Chicago metropolitan area is an abnormally dangerous activity, for the consequences of which the shipper (Cyanamid) is strictly liable to the switching line, which bore the financial brunt of those consequences because of the decontamination measures that it was forced to take. [The district court granted summary judgment in favor of the switching line on the strict liability and dismissed the negligence claim with prejudice. The parties cross-appealed.]

The parties agree that the question whether placing acrylonitrile in a rail shipment that will pass through a metropolitan area subjects the shipper to strict liability is, as recommended in Restatement (Second) of Torts § 520, comment l (1977), a question of law, so that we owe no particular deference to the conclusion of the district court. They also agree (and for this proposition, at least, there is substantial support in the Fallon and Continental opinions) that the Supreme Court of Illinois would treat as authoritative the provisions of the Restatement governing abnormally dangerous activities. The key provision is section 520, which sets forth six factors to be considered in deciding whether an activity is abnormally dangerous and the actor therefore strictly liable.

The roots of section 520 are in nineteenth-century cases. The most famous one is *Rylands v. Fletcher*, 1 Ex. 265, *aff'd*, L.R. 3 H.L. 300 (1868), but a more illuminating one in the present context is *Guille v. Swan*, 19 Johns. (N.Y.) 381 (1822). A man took off in a hot-air balloon and landed, without intending to, in a vegetable garden in New York City. A crowd that had been anxiously watching his involuntary descent trampled the vegetables in their endeavor to rescue him when he landed. The owner of the garden sued the balloonist for the resulting damage, and won. Yet the balloonist had not been careless. In the then state of ballooning it was impossible to make a pinpoint landing.

Guille is a paradigmatic case for strict liability. (a) The risk (probability) of harm was great, and (b) the harm that would ensue if the risk materialized could be, although luckily was not, great (the balloonist could have crashed into the crowd rather than into the vegetables). The confluence of these two factors established the urgency of seeking to prevent such accidents. (c) Yet such accidents could not be prevented by the exercise of due care; the technology of care in ballooning was insufficiently developed. (d) The activity was not a matter of common usage, so there was no presumption that it was a highly valuable activity despite its unavoidable riskiness. (e) The activity was inappropriate to the place in which it took place—densely populated New York City. The risk of serious harm to others (other than the balloonist himself, that is) could have been reduced by shifting the activity to the sparsely inhabited areas that surrounded the city in those days. (f) Reinforcing (d), the value to the community of the activity of recreational ballooning did not appear to be great enough to offset its unavoidable risks.

These are, of course, the six factors in section 520. They are related to each other in that each is a different facet of a common quest for a proper legal regime to govern accidents that negligence liability cannot adequately control. The interrelations might be more perspicuous if the six factors were reordered. One might for example start with (c), inability to eliminate the risk of accident by the exercise of due care. The baseline common law regime of tort liability is negligence. When it is a workable regime, because the hazards of an activity can be avoided by being careful (which is to say, nonnegligent), there is no need to switch to strict liability. Sometimes, however, a particular type of accident cannot be prevented by taking care but can be avoided, or its consequences minimized, by shifting the activity in which the accident occurs to another locale, where the risk or harm of an accident will be less ((e)), or by reducing the scale of the activity in order to minimize the number of accidents caused by it ((f)). By making the actor strictly liable—by denying him in other words an excuse based on his inability to avoid accidents by being more careful—we give him an incentive, missing in a negligence regime, to experiment with methods of preventing accidents that involve not greater exertions of care, assumed to be futile, but instead relocating, changing, or reducing (perhaps to the vanishing point) the activity giving rise to the accident. The greater the risk of an accident ((a)) and the costs of an accident if one occurs ((b)), the more we want the actor to consider the possibility of making accident-reducing activity changes; the stronger, therefore, is the case for strict liability. Finally, if an activity is extremely common ((d)), like driving an automobile, it is unlikely either that its hazards are perceived as great or that there is no technology of care available to minimize them; so the case for strict liability is weakened.

...

Against this background we turn to the particulars of acrylonitrile. Acrylonitrile is one of a large number of chemicals that are hazardous in the sense of being flammable, toxic, or both; acrylonitrile is both, as are many others. A table in the record, drawn from Glickman & Harvey, Statistical Trends in Railroad Hazardous Material Safety, 1978 to 1984, at pp. 63–65 (Draft Final Report to the Environmental & Hazardous Material Studies Division of the Association of American Railroads, April 1986) (tab. 4.1), contains a list of the 125 hazardous materials that are shipped in highest volume on the nation's railroads. Acrylonitrile is the fifty-third most hazardous on the list. Number 1 is phosphorus (white or yellow), and among the other materials that rank higher than acrylonitrile on the hazard scale are anhydrous ammonia, liquified petroleum gas, vinyl chloride, gasoline, crude petroleum, motor fuel antiknock compound, methyl and ethyl chloride, sulphuric acid, sodium metal, and chloroform. The plaintiff's lawyer acknowledged at argument that the logic of the district court's opinion dictated strict liability for all 52 materials that rank higher than acrylonitrile on the list, and quite possibly for the 72 that rank lower as well, since all are hazardous if spilled in quantity while being shipped by rail. Every shipper of any of these materials would therefore be strictly liable for the consequences of a spill or other accident that occurred while the material was being shipped through a metropolitan area. The plaintiff's lawyer further acknowledged the irrelevance, on her view of the case, of the fact that Cyanamid had leased and filled the car that spilled the acrylonitrile; all she thought important is that Cyanamid introduced the product into the stream of commerce that happened to pass through the Chicago metropolitan area. Her concession may have been incautious. One might want to distinguish between the shipper who merely places his goods on his loading dock to be picked up by the carrier and the shipper who, as in this case, participates actively in the transportation. But the concession is illustrative of the potential scope of the district court's decision.

No cases recognize so sweeping a liability. Several reject it, though none has facts much like those of the present case....

... So we can get little help from precedent, and might as well apply section 520 to the acrylonitrile problem from the ground up. To begin with, we have been given no reason ... for believing that a negligence regime is not perfectly adequate to remedy and deter, at reasonable cost, the accidental spillage of acrylonitrile from rail cars. [A]lthough acrylonitrile is flammable even at relatively low temperatures, and toxic, it is not so corrosive or otherwise destructive that it will eat through or otherwise damage or weaken a tank car's valves although they are maintained with due (which essentially means, with average) care. No one suggests, therefore, that the leak in this case was caused by the inherent properties of acrylonitrile. It was caused by carelessness—whether that of the North American Car Corporation in failing to maintain or inspect the car properly, or that of Cyanamid in failing to maintain or inspect it, or that of the Missouri Pacific when it had custody of the car, or that of the switching line itself in failing to notice the ruptured lid, or some combination of these possible failures of care. Accidents that are due to a lack of care can be prevented by taking care; and when a lack of care can ... be shown in court, such accidents are adequately deterred by the threat of liability for negligence.

It is true that the district court purported to find as a fact that there is an inevitable risk of derailment or other calamity in transporting "large quantities of anything." 662 F.Supp. at 642. This is not a finding of fact, but a truism: anything can happen. The question is, how likely is this type of accident if the actor uses due care? For all that appears from the record of the case or any other sources of information that we have found, if a tank car is carefully maintained the danger of a spill of acrylonitrile is negligible. If this is right, there is no compelling reason to move to a regime of strict liability, especially one that might embrace all other hazardous materials shipped by rail as well. This also means, however, that the amici curiae who have filed briefs in support of Cyanamid cry wolf in predicting "devastating" effects on the chemical industry if the district court's decision is affirmed. If the vast majority of chemical spills by railroads are preventable by due care, the imposition of strict liability should cause only a slight, not as they argue a substantial, rise in liability insurance rates, because the incremental liability should be slight. The amici have momentarily lost sight of the fact that the feasibility of avoiding accidents simply by being careful is an argument against strict liability.

. . .

The district judge and the plaintiff's lawyer make much of the fact that the spill occurred in a densely inhabited metropolitan area. Only 4,000 gallons spilled; what if all 20,000 had done so? Isn't the risk that this might happen even if everybody were careful sufficient to warrant giving the shipper an incentive to explore alternative routes? Strict liability would supply that incentive. But this argument overlooks the fact that, like other transportation networks, the railroad network is a hub-and-spoke system. And the hubs are in metropolitan areas. Chicago is one of the nation's largest railroad hubs. In 1983, the latest year for which we have figures, Chicago's railroad yards handled the third highest volume of hazardous-material shipments in the nation. East St. Louis, which is also in Illinois, handled the second highest volume. Office of Technology Assessment, Transportation of Hazardous Materials 53 (1986). With most hazardous chemicals (by volume of shipments) being at least as hazardous as acrylonitrile, it is unlikely—and certainly not demonstrated by the plaintiff—that they can be rerouted around all the metropolitan areas in the country, except at prohibitive cost. Even if it were feasible to reroute them one would hardly expect shippers, as distinct from carriers, to be the firms best situated to do the rerouting. . . .

The difference between shipper and carrier points to a deep flaw in the plaintiff's case. Unlike . . . the storage cases, beginning with *Rylands* itself, here it is not the actors—that is, the transporters of acrylonitrile and other chemicals—but the manufacturers, who are sought to be held strictly liable. A shipper can in the bill of lading designate the route of his shipment if he likes, 49 U.S.C. § 11710(a)(1), but is it realistic to suppose that shippers will become students of railroading in order to lay out the safest route by which to ship their goods? Anyway, rerouting is no panacea. Often it will increase the length of the journey, or compel the use of poorer track, or both. When this happens, the probability of an accident is increased, even if the consequences of an accident if one occurs are reduced; so the expected accident cost, being the product of the probability of an accident and the harm if the accident occurs, may rise. It is easy to see how the accident in this case might have been prevented at reasonable cost by greater care on the part of those who handled the tank car of acrylonitrile. It is difficult to see how it might have been prevented at reasonable cost by a change in the activity of transporting the chemical. This is therefore not an apt case for strict liability.

. . .

In emphasizing the flammability and toxicity of acrylonitrile rather than the hazards of transporting it, . . . the plaintiff overlooks the fact that ultrahazardousness or abnormal dangerousness is, in the contemplation of the law at least, a property not of substances, but of activities: not of acrylonitrile, but of the transportation of acrylonitrile by rail through populated areas. Natural gas is both flammable and poisonous, but the operation of a natural gas well is not an ultrahazardous activity. *Cf.* Williams v. Amoco Production Co., 241 Kan. 102, 115, 734 P.2d 1113, 1123 (1987). . . . The plaintiff does not suggest that Cyanamid should switch to making some less hazardous chemical that would substitute for acrylonitrile in the textiles and other goods in which acrylonitrile is used. Were this a feasible method of accident avoidance, there would be an argument for making manufacturers strictly liable for accidents that occur during the shipment of their products (how strong an argument we need not decide). Apparently it is not a feasible method.

The relevant activity is transportation, not manufacturing and shipping. This essential distinction the plaintiff ignores. But even if the defendant is treated as a transporter and not merely a shipper, the plaintiff has not shown that the transportation of acrylonitrile in bulk by rail through populated areas is so hazardous an activity, even when due care is exercised, that the law should seek to create—perhaps quixotically—incentives to relocate the activity to nonpopulated areas, or to reduce the scale of the activity, or to switch to transporting acrylonitrile by road rather than by rail . . . . It is no more realistic to propose to reroute the shipment of all hazardous materials around Chicago than it is to propose the relocation of homes adjacent to the Blue Island switching yard to more distant suburbs. It may be less realistic. Brutal though it may seem to say it, the inappropriate use to which land is being put in the Blue Island yard and neighborhood may be, not the transportation of hazardous chemicals, but residential living. The analogy is to building your home between the runways at O'Hare.

The briefs hew closely to the Restatement, whose approach to the issue of strict liability is mainly allocative rather than distributive. By this we mean that the emphasis is on picking a liability regime (negligence or strict liability) that will control the particular class of accidents in question most effectively, rather than on finding the deepest pocket and placing liability there. At argument, however, the plaintiff's lawyer invoked distributive considerations by pointing out that Cyanamid is a huge firm and the Indiana Harbor Belt Railroad a fifty-mile-long switching line that almost went broke in the winter of 1979, when the accident occurred.

Well, so what? A corporation is not a living person but a set of contracts the terms of which determine who will bear the brunt of liability. Tracing the incidence of a cost is a complex undertaking which the plaintiff sensibly has made no effort to assume, since its legal relevance would be dubious. We add only that however small the plaintiff may be, it has mighty parents: it is a jointly owned subsidiary of Conrail and the Soo line.

The case for strict liability has not been made. Not in this suit in any event. We need not speculate on the possibility of imposing strict liability on shippers of more hazardous materials . . . We noted earlier that acrylonitrile is far from being the most hazardous among hazardous materials shipped by rail in highest volume. Or among materials shipped, period. The Department of Transportation has classified transported materials into sixteen separate classes by the degree to which transporting them is hazardous. Class number 1 is radioactive material. Class number 2 is poisons. Class 3 is flammable gas and 4 is nonflammable gas. Acrylonitrile is in Class 5. 49 C.F.R. §§ 172.101, Table; 173.2(a).

. . .

The defendant concedes that if the strict liability count is thrown out, the negligence count must be reinstated, as requested by the cross-appeal. . . .

The judgment is reversed (with no award of costs in this court) and the case remanded for further proceedings, consistent with this opinion, on the plaintiff's claim for negligence.

Notes

The *Restatement* factors. Blasting is the classic example of an abnormally dangerous activity. Applying the factors listed in the *Restatement*, be prepared to explain why blasting qualifies as an abnormally dangerous activity. Based on the reasoning in *Indiana Harbor Belt*, be prepared to explain why, from an allocative standpoint, it makes sense to employ a strict liability regime as opposed to a negligence regime in such cases.

Restatement (Third) of Torts. Section 20 of the *Restatement (Third) of Torts* condenses the six factors from the Restatement (Second) down to two: "An activity is abnormally dangerous if: (1) the activity creates a foreseeable and highly significant risk of physical harm even when reasonable care is exercised by all actors; and (2) the activity is not one of common usage."

Other examples of abnormally dangerous activities. The determination of whether an activity is abnormally dangerous is fact specific. For example, storing explosives in a suburban area has been held to be abnormally dangerous, Yukon Equip., Inc., 585 P.2d 1206 (Alaska 1978), whereas storing explosives in a rural area has been held not to be an abnormally dangerous activity. Otero v. Burgess, 505 P.2d 1251 (N.M. 1973). Other situations in which strict liability might apply depending upon the circumstances include storing and handling toxic chemicals, *see* Daigle v. Shell Oil Co., 972 F.2d 1527 (10th Cir. 1992) (denying defendant's motion to dismiss); crop dusting, *compare* Langan v. Valicopters, Inc., 567 P.2d 218 (Wash. 1977) (strict liability applies) *with* Wilson v. Greg Williams Farm, Inc., 436 S.W.3d 485 (Ark. Ct. App. 2014) (strict liability does not apply); and shooting fireworks, *compare* Beddingfield v. Linam, 127 So. 3d 1178 (Ala. 2013) (strict liability did not apply where minors were shooting bottle rockets) *with* Klein v. Pyrodyne Corp., 810 P.2d 917 (Wash. 1991) (setting off public fireworks display is an abnormally dangerous activity).

Problem 12.1. Alison House was 16 years old. She was driving home from her part-time job around 10:00 p.m. when she drove through the gasoline that had spilled onto Interstate 40. Somehow, her car ignited the gas, causing her car and Henry's tanker trailer to burst into flames. The gasoline ignited and spread several hundred yards down the road. Alison was killed. Alison's family has now brought a wrongful death action against Texxon. They seek to hold the company strictly liable for Alison's death. Should strict liability apply, or should ordinary negligence principles apply?

B. Strict Liability for Harm Caused by Animals

Another area in which strict liability may apply is in the case of harm caused by animals. *Rylands v. Fletcher* referenced the British common law principle that strict liability should apply where livestock escapes from an owner's property and causes damage to the property of another. This same principle is reflected in § 21 of the *Restatement (Third) of Torts*, although it is not followed in every jurisdiction. The owner of a wild animal is subject to strict liability for physical harm caused by the animal. An animal is "wild" if it "belongs to a category of animals that have not been domesticated and that are likely, unless restrained, to cause personal injury." *Id.* § 22. The case below discusses the rules covering domesticated animals and abnormally dangerous animals.

Rhodes v. MacHugh

361 P.3d 260 (Wash. Ct. App. 2015)

SIDDOWAY, C.J.

Comments to § 23 of the *Restatement (Third) of Torts*, which deals with strict liability imposed on the owners of abnormally dangerous animals, observe that the common law has been satisfied overall with the generalization that livestock are not excessively dangerous, but "[i]n the future, courts might wish to give consideration to particular genders . . . of a species that involve danger levels uncommon for the species itself." Restatement (Third) of Torts: Liability for Physical and Emotional Harm § 23 cmt. e (2010) (emphasis added). In this case, Jay Rhodes asks us to hold the owner of a ram (a male sheep) strictly liable for harm caused by the ram on account of the ram's gender-based dangerousness, rather than any abnormal dangerousness of which the owner was aware.

Mr. Rhodes is a particularly sympathetic plaintiff and appellant, both in the circumstances he presents and the forthrightness of his argument on appeal. But we conclude that existing Washington common law strikes the appropriate balance in imposing limited strict liability on the owners of domestic animals and otherwise imposing a duty of care commensurate with the character of their animals. We affirm the summary judgment dismissal of Mr. Rhodes's complaint.

Facts and Procedural Background

Jay Rhodes and Rodney MacHugh are longtime friends and neighbors. Both men live in Richland and have farmed for decades. Mr. Rhodes has raised cows, horses, and occasionally pigs and goats, but he described the summer of 2012 as "my first excursion with sheep. And an unfortunate one." Mr. MacHugh has bred sheep for over 30 years. Because Mr. MacHugh's land is prone to flooding, Mr. Rhodes has allowed Mr. MacHugh to keep some of his livestock on Mr. Rhodes's property.

In the summer of 2012, Mr. MacHugh and Mr. Rhodes went to a livestock yard in Lewiston, Idaho, where Mr. MacHugh purchased a ram to replace his existing ram, which he described as "in really old shape." The replacement ram was eight or nine months old[1] and weighed in the neighborhood of 150 pounds. It showed no vicious tendencies. The men took it directly to Mr. Rhodes's property where, for the following month, it caused no problems. In the weeks before Mr. MacHugh put the ram in with ewes, Mr. Rhodes described it as "real friendly. He'd come up to me several times when I was changing water, and I'd pet him."

On August 20, 2012, Mr. Rhodes went into his yard to turn on his sprinklers. By that time, Mr. MacHugh had put several ewes in the pasture with the ram. Mr. Rhodes walked past them and toward the five-foot sprinklers in the pasture. Just as he touched the valve at the top of the sprinklers, the ram butted him from behind, knocking him to the ground. According to Mr. Rhodes, the ram continued to "jump up in the air and then he'd hit me with his head," knocking him out "a couple of times," for as much as 30 minutes. Fortunately, a neighbor who stopped by to bring Mr. Rhodes some cantaloupes saw what was going on. Although Mr. Rhodes told her not to come into the pasture, she began throwing her cantaloupes at the ram, which was sufficiently distracted that Mr. Rhodes was able to crawl to the gate. She helped him out and slammed the gate on the charging ram. Mr. Rhodes, then 82 years old, suffered a concussion, five broken ribs, and a broken sternum and shoulder. He was hospitalized for 16 days.

Mr. Rhodes filed this action in an effort to recover for his injuries. He did not contend that the ram was abnormally dangerous, and he refused to accuse his friend of negligence, testifying, "I don't think Mr. MacHugh thought there was anything

1. At that age, it was a "lamb ram," but we refer to it as a ram for simplicity.

wrong" with the ram. For his part, Mr. MacHugh admitted that he had owned as many as three "mean" rams over the years, but that "on my place, if they're the least bit mean, they go real quick." He testified that he had selected this ram because it was the "friendliest" of three that the seller had raised on a bottle after their mother died.

Because Mr. Rhodes relied exclusively on a theory of strict liability that he asked the court to extend to the owners of all rams, not just those known to be abnormally dangerous, the parties presented the legal issue to the trial court on summary judgment. Mr. MacHugh's motion for summary judgment dismissing the claim was granted. Mr. Rhodes appeals.

Analysis

The sole issue on appeal is whether summary judgment in favor of Mr. MacHugh was proper because he is not strictly liable for harm caused by a ram he did not know to be abnormally dangerous. No material facts are in dispute, and we, like the trial court, are presented with a pure question of law that we review de novo.

For more than a century, the rule in Washington regarding liability for harm caused by a domestic animal[2] has been:

> "The owner or keeper of a domestic animal not naturally inclined to commit mischief, while bound to exercise ordinary care to prevent injury being done by it to another, is not liable for such injury if the animal be rightfully in the place when the mischief is done, unless it is affirmatively shown, not only that the animal was vicious, but that the owner or keeper had knowledge of the fact. When such scienter exists, the owner or keeper is accountable for all the injury such animal may do, without proof of any negligence or fault in the keeping, and regardless of his endeavors to so keep the animal as to prevent the mischief."

Lynch v. Kineth, 36 Wash. 368, 370–71, 78 P. 923 (1904) (emphasis omitted) (quoting 2 Cyc. Animals 368–69 (1901)).

Washington cases are consistent with the *Restatement (Second) of Torts* (1977). In Arnold v. Laird, 94 Wash.2d 867, 871, 621 P.2d 138 (1980), our Supreme Court noted that the *Restatement (Second)* "recognizes two separate causes of action" against the owner of a domestic animal that causes injury. Under section 509, strict liability applies where the animal "has known dangerous propensities abnormal to its class." *Arnold*, 94 Wash.2d at 871, 621 P.2d 138. Section 518, on the other hand, "provides that if there are no known abnormally dangerous propensities, the owner is liable only if he is negligent in failing to prevent the harm. The amount of care required

2. A "domestic animal," as defined by the *Restatement (Second) of Torts*, is one "that is by custom devoted to the service of mankind at the time and in the place in which it is kept." RESTATEMENT (SECOND) OF TORTS § 506(2), at 10 (1977). "[T]he test is whether the animals are as a class recognized by custom as devoted to the service of mankind." *Id.* § 506 cmt. a.

is commensurate with the character of the animal." *Id.* (emphasis omitted) (citing § 518 cmt. f).

Mr. Rhodes concedes that rams have not historically been regarded as being inherently dangerous animals. Br. of Appellant at 1–2; Restatement (Second) § 509 cmt. e ("[T]he law has not regarded bulls, stallions and rams as being abnormally dangerous animals to be kept under the strict liability stated in this Section."). Nevertheless, relying on a comment to § 23 of the most recent *Restatement*, he asks that we recognize that "[t]he dangerous propensities of rams are well-known and strict liability should attach, and this whether the animal is 'domestic' or otherwise."

The language of § 23 of the *Restatement (Third)* is similar to that of *Restatement (Second)* § 509, yet the comments to § 23 propose a possible gender-or breed-based modification of the general rule treating domestic animals as not excessively dangerous. Comment e states, in part:

> Overall, the common law has been satisfied with the generalization that livestock and dogs are not excessively dangerous and has applied this generalization to all livestock and dogs. *In the future, courts might wish to give consideration to particular genders or breeds of a species that involve danger levels uncommon for the species itself. If so, it might be appropriate to impose strict liability, without individualized scienter, on the owner of such an animal.*

Restatement (Third) § 23 cmt. e (emphasis added). Mr. Rhodes asks us to act on this acknowledgment and common knowledge that while ewes may be timid, rams are known to be dangerous.

Prior versions of the *Restatement* have not overlooked the different temperament of male domestic animals, pointing out that "[b]ulls are more dangerous than cows and steers; stallions are more dangerous than mares and geldings; rams are more dangerous than ewes and lambs." Restatement (Second) § 509 cmt. e. But historically the framework of liability for negligence has been viewed as adequate to address gender differences, and refusing to broaden strict liability has also been justified by policy reasons.

The *Restatement (Second)* recognizes the relatively dangerous propensities of male domestic animals such as bulls, stallions, and rams but characterizes them as normal to their class. As the comments to § 509 observe, "[T]hese animals have been kept for stud purposes from time immemorial so that the particular danger involved in their dangerous tendencies has become a normal incident of civilized life." Restatement (Second) § 509 cmt. e; *see also id.* § 509 cmt. d (noting that such animals "do not introduce any unusual danger, since the somewhat dangerous characteristics of these animals are a customary incident of farming"). In other words, a ram has not been considered "abnormally" dangerous for purposes of applying strict liability under § 509 because its dangerous propensities are "normal" for its species.

It is also for policy reasons that owners of male domestic animals have not been held to a standard of strict liability, because often it is the very characteristics that cause the males to be dangerous that make them useful to society. The comments to § 518 of the *Restatement (Second)* observe that "[t]he high temper normal to stud animals is so inseparable from their usefulness for breeding purposes that they are not kept at the risk of the liability stated in § 509." Restatement (Second) § 518 cmt. f. . . .

The law is not oblivious to the greater risk posed by male livestock used for breeding in the context of liability for negligence, and greater precautions are typically required in light of their characteristics. Restatement (Second) § 509 cmt. e. "The amount of care required is commensurate with the character of the animal." *Arnold*, 94 Wash.2d at 871, 621 P.2d 138. As the comments to § 518 explain, "the keeper of a bull or stallion is required to take greater precautions to confine it to the land on which it is kept and to keep it under effective control when it is taken from the land than would be required of the keeper of a cow or gelding." Restatement (Second) § 518 cmt. g.

"Rules of law . . . should not be changed for light or transient causes; but, when time and events prove the need for a change, changed they must be." State ex rel. *Wash. State Fin. Comm. v. Martin*, 62 Wash.2d 645, 666, 384 P.2d 833 (1963). Here, the utility of domestic animals remains undiminished. Those who raise them and face the greatest exposure to relatively more dangerous genders or breeds will be familiar with their characteristics. Third parties continue to have recourse for an owner's negligence, and owners are required to take greater precautions to confine and control animals in light of their characteristics. Mr. Rhodes's unfortunate excursion with Mr. MacHugh's ram does not persuade us that the limited scope of strict liability that Washington has historically imposed on the owners of domestic animals should be enlarged.[4]

Notes

The "first bite" rule. One common view is that a dog owner may reasonably believe a dog is not dangerous until the dog first bites another. After that, strict liability attaches. *See Kringle v. Elliott*, 686 S.E.2d 665 (Ga. Ct. App. 2009). ("[T]he rule does not literally require a first bite," but it is enough if the owner has knowledge that the dog has the propensity to do the particular act.)

Strict liability for dog bites. Despite the traditional rule, numerous jurisdictions have adopted a strict liability standard in the case of dog bites, usually by statute. *See Martin v. Christman*, 99 A.3d 1008, 1011 (Vt. 2014) (estimating that approximately 18 states have adopted a strict liability standard and that "the overwhelming majority" have done so by statute); Wash. Rev. Code § 16.08.040 ("The owner of any dog which shall bite any person while such person is in or on a public place or lawfully in or on a private place including the property of the owner of such dog,

4. The legislature can, of course, act. We note that by statute, and in derogation of the common law, it has imposed strict liability on the owner of a dog that bites a person, as long as the victim was in a public place or lawfully in or on a private place. RCW 16.08.040.

shall be liable for such damages as may be suffered by the person bitten, *regardless of the former viciousness of such dog or the owner's knowledge of such viciousness.*") (emphasis added).

Livestock. *Rylands v. Fletcher* mentioned the idea that "[t]he person whose grass or corn is eaten down by the escaped cattle of his neighbour" has a strict liability claim against the neighbor. This was the English common law rule. The authors of the *Restatement (Third) of Torts* summarize the current state of U.S. law as comprised of three different approaches. One approach imposes strict liability on the owner of livestock for damage caused by the trespassing livestock. The second imposes strict liability but recognizes an affirmative defense where the plaintiff has failed to erect a fence to "fence out" encroaching livestock. The third adopts a negligence standard with no "fence out" defense. *See* Restatement (Third) of Torts § 21 cmt. c.

C. Causation

Foster v. Preston Mill Co.

268 P.2d 645 (Wash. 1954)

HAMLEY, Justice.

Blasting operations conducted by Preston Mill Company frightened mother mink owned by B. W. Foster, and caused the mink to kill their kittens. Foster brought this action against the company to recover damages. His second amended complaint, upon which the case was tried, sets forth a cause of action on the theory of absolute liability . . .

After a trial to the court without a jury, judgment was rendered for plaintiff in the sum of $1,953.68. . . . Defendant appeals.

The primary question presented by appellant's assignments of error is whether, on these facts, the judgment against appellant is sustainable on the theory of absolute liability.

. . .

The modern doctrine of strict liability for dangerous substances and activities stems from Justice Blackburn's decision in *Rylands v. Fletcher*, 1 Exch. 265, decided in 1866 and affirmed two years later in *Fletcher v. Rylands*, L.R. 3 H.L. 330. As applied to blasting operations, the doctrine has quite uniformly been held to establish liability, irrespective of negligence, for property damage sustained as a result of casting rocks or other debris on adjoining or neighboring premises.

There is a division of judicial opinion as to whether the doctrine of absolute liability should apply where the damage from blasting is caused, not by the casting of rocks and debris, but by concussion, vibration, or jarring. This court has adopted the view that the doctrine applies in such cases. *Patrick v. Smith, supra*. In the *Patrick* case, it was held that contractors who set off an exceedingly large blast of powder, causing the earth for a considerable distance to shake violently, were liable to an adjoining owner whose well was damaged and water supply lost, without regard to their negligence in setting off the blast, although there was no physical invasion of the property.

However the authorities may be divided on the point just discussed, they appear to be agreed that strict liability should be confined to consequences which lie within the extraordinary risk whose existence calls for such responsibility. This limitation on the doctrine is indicated in the italicized portion of the rule as set forth in *Restatement of Torts, supra*:

> Except as stated in §§ 521-4, one who carries on an ultrahazardous activity is liable to another whose person, land or chattels the actor should recognize as likely to be harmed by the unpreventable miscarringe of the activity for harm resulting thereto *from that which makes the activity ultrahazardous*, although the utmost care is exercised to prevent the harm.' (Italics supplied.)

. . .

Applying this principle to the case before us, the question comes down to this: Is the risk that any unusual vibration or noise may cause wild animals, which are being raised for commercial purposes, to kill their young, one of the things which make the activity of blasting ultrahazardous?

We have found nothing in the decisional law which would support an affirmative answer to this question. The decided cases. as well as common experience, indicate that the thing which makes blasting ultrahazardous is the risk that property or persons may be damaged or injured by coming into direct contact with flying debris, or by being directly affected by vibrations of the earth or concussions of the air.

Where, as a result of blasting operations, a horse has become frightened and has trampled or otherwise injured a person, recovery of damages has been upheld on the theory of negligence. But we have found no case where recovery of damages caused by a frightened farm animal has been sustained on the ground of absolute liability.

If, however, the possibility that a violent vibration, concussion, or noise might frighten domestic animals and lead to property damages or personal injuries be considered one of the harms which makes the activity of blasting ultrahazardous, this would still not include the case we have here.

The relatively moderate vibration and noise which appellant's blasting produced at a distance of two and a quarter miles was no more than a usual incident of the ordinary life of the community. The trial court specifically found that the blasting did not unreasonably interfere with the enjoyment of their property by nearby landowners, except in the case of respondent's mink ranch.

It is the exceedingly nervous disposition of mink, rather than the normal risks inherent in blasting operations, which therefore must, as a matter of sound policy, bear the responsibility for the loss here sustained. We subscribe to the view expressed by Professor Harper (30 Mich.L.Rev. 1001, 1006, supra) that the policy of the law does not impose the rule of strict liability to protect against harms incident to the plaintiff's extraordinary and unusual use of land. This is perhaps but an application of the principle that the extent to which one man in the lawful conduct of his business is liable for injuries to another involves an adjustment of conflicting interests.

...

It is our conclusion that the risk of causing harm of the kind here experienced, as a result of the relatively minor vibration, concussion, and noise from distant blasting, is not the kind of risk which makes the activity of blasting ultrahazardous. The doctrine of absolute liability is therefore inapplicable under the facts of this case, and respondent is not entitled to recover damages.

The judgment is reversed.

Yukon Equipment, Inc. v. Fireman's Fund Ins. Co.

585 P.2d 1206 (Alaska 1978)

MATTHEWS, Justice.

A large explosion occurred at 2:47 a. m. on December 7, 1973, in the suburbs north of the city of Anchorage. The explosion originated at a storage magazine for explosives under lease from the federal government to petitioner E. I. du Pont de Nemours and Company, which was operated by petitioner Yukon Equipment, Inc. The storage magazine is located on a 1,870 acre tract of federal land which had been withdrawn by the Department of the Interior for the use of the Alaska Railroad for explosive storage purposes by separate orders in 1950 and 1961. The magazine which exploded was located 3,820 feet from the nearest building not used to store explosives and 4,330 feet from the nearest public highway. At the time of the explosion it contained approximately 80,000 pounds of explosives. The blast damaged dwellings and other buildings within a two mile radius of the magazine and, in some instances, beyond a two mile radius. The ground concussion it caused registered 1.8 on the Richter scale at the earthquake observation station in Palmer, some 30 miles away.

The explosion was caused by thieves. Four young men had driven onto the tract where the magazine was located, broken into the storage magazine, set a prepared charge, and fled. They apparently did so in an effort to conceal the fact that they had stolen explosives from the site a day or two earlier.

This consolidated lawsuit was brought to recover for property damage caused by the explosion. Cross-motions for partial summary judgment were filed, and summary judgment on the issue of liability was granted in favor of the respondents. Respondents presented alternative theories of liability based on negligence, nuisance, absolute liability, and trespass. The court's order granting partial summary judgment did not specify the theory on which liability was based.

Petitioners contend that none of the theories may be utilized to fix liability on them by summary judgment and further that the intentional detonation of the magazine is a superseding cause relieving them of liability under any theory. Respondents argue that the summary judgment is sustainable under the theory of absolute liability and that the intentional nature of the explosion is not a defense. We agree with respondents and affirm.

[The court concluded that storing explosives as an abnormally dangerous activity that subjected the defendants to strict liability.]

The next question is whether the intentional detonation of the storage magazine was a superseding cause relieving petitioners from liability. In *Sharp v. Fairbanks North Star Borough*, 569 P.2d 178 (Alaska 1977), a negligence case, we stated that a superseding cause exists where "after the event and looking back from the harm to the actor's negligent conduct, it appears to the court highly extraordinary that it should have brought about the harm." We further explained in *Sharp*,

> (w)here the defendant's conduct threatens a particular kind of result which will injure the plaintiff and an intervening cause which could not have been anticipated changes the situation but produces the same result as originally threatened, such a result is within the scope of the defendant's negligence.

Id. at 183 n. 9. The considerations which impel cutting off liability where there is a superseding cause in negligence cases also apply to cases of absolute liability.

Prior to the explosion in question the petitioners' magazines had been illegally broken into at least six times. Most of these entries involved the theft of explosives. Petitioners had knowledge of all of this.

Applying the standards set forth in *Sharp, supra*, to these facts we find there to have been no superseding cause. The incendiary destruction of premises by thieves to cover evidence of theft is not so uncommon an occurrence that it can be regarded as highly extraordinary. Moreover, the particular kind of result threatened by the defendant's conduct, the storage of explosives, was an explosion at the storage site. Since the threatened result occurred it would not be consistent with the principles stated in *Sharp, supra*, to hold there to have been a superseding cause. Absolute liability is imposed on those who store or use explosives because they have created an unusual risk to others. As between those who have created the risk for the benefit of their own enterprise and those whose only connection with the enterprise is to have suffered damage because of it, the law places the risk of loss on the former. When the risk created causes damage in fact, insistence that the precise details of the intervening cause be foreseeable would subvert the purpose of that rule of law.

Note

Strict liability for animals. The same causation standard that applies in the case of other abnormally dangerous activities applies in the case of wild animals and those with abnormally dangerous tendencies known by the owner. *See* Restatement (Third) of Torts § 23.

Problem 12.2. The reason why Henry's tank trailer became disengaged from his tank truck is because Mitch, another driver, clipped the trailer with his own car while attempting to pass Henry. Mitch was drunk at the time and was negligent in attempting to pass Henry. The trial judge in Alison's case concluded that strict liability should apply. Texxon now argues that Mitch's actions amount to a superseding cause that breaks the chain of causation, thus absolving Texxon from liability. Was Texxon's act of transporting the gasoline a proximate cause of Alison's death?

D. Defenses

If the defendant's fault is irrelevant to the issue of liability in a strict liability case, should the plaintiff's fault have any relevance in terms of reducing recovery? When the all-or-nothing form of contributory negligent was the norm, the *Restatement* took the position that the fact that the plaintiff was contributorily negligence was not a defense in a strict liability action. It was only where the plaintiff assumed the risk of the abnormally dangerous activity that liability was barred. Restatement (Second) of Torts § 523. With the spread of more modern comparative fault rules, § 25 of the *Restatement (Third) of Torts* takes the position that the plaintiff's fault reduces the plaintiff's recovery in accordance with the share of comparative responsibility assigned to the plaintiff.

Some strict liability dog bite statutes also have an element of assumption of risk or comparative fault about them. *See* Idaho Code § 25-2810(10) ("Any dog that physically attacks, wounds, bites or otherwise injures any person *who is not trespassing, when such dog is not physically provoked or otherwise justified*" subjects its owner to strict liability); Pocatello [Idaho] Municipal Code § 6.04.050(E) ("An adult owner/custodian of a dangerous animal shall be liable for all injuries and property damage sustained by any person or by animal caused by an *unprovoked attack* by any dangerous animal. . . ."); *see also* Boswell v. Steele, 2017 Idaho App. LEXIS 65 (Idaho Ct. App. Sep. 6, 2017) (recognizing comparative fault as a defense in dog bite cases to the extent the plaintiff "knowingly and unreasonably subject[s] himself to the risk" that an abnormally dangerous animal posed to him).

Review Question

Alice crossbred a wolf and a dog. The result is Peaches, a "wolfdog." Alice owned Peaches for five years without incident. Peaches plays fetch, likes to have her tummy rubbed, and is trustworthy around Alice's children. One day, Peaches, completely unprovoked, attacked Bob, Alice's next-door neighbor. Is Alice strictly liable for Bob's injuries?

Chapter 13

Nuisance

- The interest protected by the cause of action
- Private nuisance
  - The general test
  - Factors in assessing gravity of harm
  - Factors in assessing utility of conduct
  - Effect of moving to the nuisance
  - Remedies available
    - Availability of compensatory damages
    - Injunctive relief as a remedy
- Public nuisance
  - Difference with private nuisance
  - Impact of defendant's compliance with statute or regulation
  - Remedies available
- Other concepts developed in class or in readings assigned by the professor

Chapter Problem. Eldon operates a facility a few miles outside of the town of Pleasant Hill that supplies mice to medical researchers. The area is somewhat remote and there are only a few residences nearby. Several of his neighbors, including Luis, wish to bring a nuisance claim against the facility based on the odors emanating from the facility.

Another area in which strict liability principles may play a role is in nuisance claims. A nuisance claim exists in order to protect an individual's interest in the use and enjoyment of the individual's land. Unlike the tort of trespass, there does not have to be an actual physical intrusion onto one's property in order to sustain a nuisance claim. But, unlike trespass, the defendant's activities must result in significant harm.

While there does not have to be an actual physical intrusion, sometimes such an intrusion is present in a nuisance case. A defendant may be held strictly liable for abnormally dangerous conditions or activities that result in a nuisance. Restatement (Second) of Torts § 822 (1979). So, for example, the defendant who disposes of hazardous chemicals in a manner that results in contamination of a neighbor's property may be liable on a nuisance theory absent fault. *See* Shockley v. Hoechst

Celanese Corp., 793 F. Supp. 670 (D.S.C.1992), *rev'd in part on other grounds*, 996 F.2d 1212 (4th Cir. 1993)

More common are nuisance claims based on intentional acts, where the defendant acts with the intent to invade the plaintiff's interest in the use and enjoyment of land. In such cases, the plaintiff must establish that the invasion was intentional *and* unreasonable. *Id.*

South Camden Citizens in Action v. New Jersey Department of Environmental Protection

254 F. Supp. 2d 486 (D.N.J. 2003)

I. Introduction

Approximately two years ago, South Camden Citizens in Action [SCCIA], and the individual Plaintiffs who reside in a South Camden, New Jersey neighborhood, known as "Waterfront South," asked this Court to issue a preliminary injunction enjoining the construction and operation of a proposed cement grinding facility [by St. Lawrence Cement Co. (SLC).] [Plaintiffs brought civil rights claims, alleging that the operation of the facility would have a disparate impact on their community on the basis of race in violation of Title VI of the Civil Rights Act of 1964 and the Equal Protection Clause. In response to the defendants' motion to dismiss, the court ruled that the plaintiffs had stated a cause of action. Plaintiffs also brought private and public nuisance claims. After a long and complicated procedural history, Defendants moved to dismiss the SCCIA plaintiff' amended complaint.]

C. Nuisance

Finally, the SCCIA Plaintiffs allege that SLC, "through the operation of its [cement grinding] facility, and through the associated use of diesel trucks," has created both a public and private nuisance in the Waterfront South neighborhood. SLC moves to dismiss the nuisance claims on the basis that, because the SCCIA Plaintiffs have failed to allege that the construction of the cement grinding facility was in violation of regulations promulgated under the Clean Air Act, 42 U.S.C. § 7409(1) ("CAA"), and permits issued by the [New Jersey Department of Environmental Protection] NJDEP, they have failed to state a valid claim of either private or public nuisance.

1. Have the SCCIA Plaintiffs Stated a Claim of Private Nuisance?

According to the Supreme Court of New Jersey, "the essence of a private nuisance is an unreasonable interference with the use and enjoyment of land." Sans v. Ramsey Golf & Country Club, Inc., 29 N.J. 438, 448, 149 A.2d 599, 605 (1959).

> Litigation of this type usually deals with the conflicting interests of property owners and the question of the reasonableness of the defendant's mode of use of his land. The process of adjudication requires recognition of the reciprocal rights of each owner to reasonable use, and a balancing

> of the conflicting interests. The utility of the defendant's conduct must be weighed against the quantum of harm to the plaintiffs. The question is not simply whether a person is annoyed or disturbed, but whether the annoyance or disturbance arises from an unreasonable use of the neighbor's land or operation of his business.

The Restatement (Second) of Torts § 821D defines a private nuisance as "a nontrespassory invasion of another's interest in the private use and enjoyment of land."

... A defendant is only liable for a nuisance that "causes significant harm, of a kind that would be suffered by a normal person in the community." Restatement (Second) of Torts § 821F.

> By significant harm is meant harm of importance, involving more than slight inconvenience or petty annoyance. The law does not concern itself with trifles, and therefore there must be a real and appreciable invasion of the plaintiff's interests before he can have an action for either a public or a private nuisance. In the case of a ... private nuisance, there must be a real and appreciable interference with the plaintiff's use or enjoyment of his land before he can have a cause of action.

Id. at cmt. b.

SLC's challenge to the SCCIA Plaintiffs' claim of private nuisance is twofold. First, SLC maintains that the SCCIA Plaintiffs cannot argue that the operation of the cement grinding facility creates a private nuisance when they have failed to allege that "SLC has violated the Air Permit or has failed to comply with all of its conditions and requirements." Second, SLC contends that the SCCIA Plaintiffs "could not, as a matter of law, demonstrate that the Facility's operations caused them any significant harm." *Id.* Because the cement grinding is located in an area zoned industrial, residents in such an area "must expect a certain degree of noise, odors, and the like. Thus, in context, SLC's operation of the Facility simply cannot be considered annoying or offensive, and Plaintiffs cannot as a matter of law demonstrate that those operations cause significant harm."

A review of New Jersey case law, however, does not support SLC's first argument. A private nuisance may exist in New Jersey even when there is compliance with controlling governmental regulations. *See* Rose v. Chaikin, 187 N.J.Super. 210, 217, 453 A.2d 1378, 1381 (Ch.Div.1982) ("Whether a given use complies with controlling governmental regulations, while not dispositive on the issue of private nuisance, Monzolino v. Grossman, 111 N.J.L. 325, 328, 168 A. 673 (N.J. Err. & App.1933), does not impact on its reasonableness.").

> [A]lthough the noises may emanate from the conduct of a business duly licensed by the State ..., the character, volume, frequency, duration, time, and locality of the noises continue to be relevant factors in determining whether the alleged annoyance surpasses the requirements that the business

> operations and in fact unreasonably interferes with the ordinary comfort of human existence in the neighborhood....
>
> *Indeed, the legislature or governmental agencies cannot constitutionally confer upon individuals or private corporations acting primarily for the own profit... any right to deprive persons of the lawful enjoyment of their property.*

Hyde v. Somerset Air Serv., 1 N.J.Super. 346, 349–50, 61 A.2d 645, 646–47 (Ch. Div.1948) (emphasis added) (granting an injunction to complainants who alleged that the resulting noises of a duly licensed flight school, which conducted low altitude flight operations over their properties, constituted a private nuisance because of significant interference with the peaceful use and occupation of complainants' residences). For that reason, SLC's reliance on the Restatement (Second) of Torts § 821B cmt. f, which pertains only to claims of public nuisance, is misplaced.

As to their second argument that as a matter of law, the SCCIA Plaintiffs have failed to demonstrate that the operation of the cement grinding facility caused them substantial harm, SLC improperly asks this Court to consider the merits of the SCCIA Plaintiffs' claims in deciding SLC's Rule 12(b)(6) motion. As previously noted, it is axiomatic that a court may not consider the merits of a plaintiff's claims on a Rule 12(b)(6) motion, but rather, must accept as true the allegations in the complaint....

In the Second Amended Complaint, the SCCIA Plaintiffs allege sufficient facts that, if true, could lead a factfinder to conclude that the operation of the cement grinding facility causes substantial harm to the residents of the Waterfront South community. More specifically, the SCCIA Plaintiffs maintain that emissions from the cement grinding facility have increased the level of pollution in the air to the point that their health and safety, as well as that of their children and families, is significantly endangered. In addition, the SCCIA Plaintiffs allege that the annual ingress and egress of nearly 80,000 delivery trucks, in addition to threatening the health of those residing in the Waterfront South neighborhood, will also create noise, vibrations, and dust which will "affect the quality of life, interfere with sleep, cause property damage, and lower the self-esteem of plaintiffs...." New Jersey courts have recognized the existence of a private nuisance when similar factors have been present. *See Sans*, 29 N.J. at 448–50, 149 A.2d at 605–06 (affirming the trial court's finding that the pedestrian traffic resulting from the placement of a golf course tee near complainant's property constituted a private nuisance); *Rose*, 187 N.J.Super. at 216–20, 453 A.2d at 1381–83 (holding that because of its character, duration, and volume, the noise created by the twenty-four hour a day operations of a windmill constituted an actionable private nuisance); *Hyde*, 1 N.J.Super. at 351–53, 61 A.2d at 647–48 (finding that noise and vibrations resulting from low flying airplanes created a private nuisance).

For these reasons, I conclude that the SCCIA Plaintiffs have stated a claim of private nuisance upon which relief can be granted. Accordingly, I shall deny SLC's motion to dismiss the Fifth Count of the Second Amended Complaint which alleges a claim of private nuisance.

2. Have the SCCIA Plaintiffs Stated a Claim of Public Nuisance?

Unlike a private nuisance which contemplates the invasion of an individual's interest "in the private use and enjoyment of land, a public nuisance is 'an unreasonable interference with a right common to the general public.'" Philadelphia Elec. Co. v. Hercules, Inc., 762 F.2d 303, 315 (3d Cir.1985) (quoting Restatement (Second) of Torts § 821B(1)).

> Circumstances that may sustain a holding that an interference with a public right is unreasonable include the following:
>
> (a) Whether the conduct involves a significant interference with the public health, the public safety, the public peace, the public comfort or the public convenience, or
>
> (b) whether the conduct is proscribed by a statute, ordinance or administrative regulation, or
>
> (c) whether the conduct is of a continuing nature or has produced a permanent or long-lasting effect, and, as the actor knows or has reason to know, has a significant effect upon the public right.

Restatement (Second) of Torts § 821B(2).

In support of its motion to dismiss the claim of public nuisance, SLC advances the same argument that it made to challenge the SCCIA Plaintiffs' private nuisance claim, namely, that because it obtained permits from the NJDEP and did not violate any controlling regulations, it can not as a matter of law, be held liable for the creation of a public nuisance. Alternatively, SLC maintains that the SCCIA Plaintiffs have failed to allege that they suffered harm of a different kind than that suffered by other members of the public.

In making its first argument, SLC relies on Comment f of the Restatement (Second) of Torts § 821B, which provides:

> Although it would be a nuisance at common law, *conduct that is fully authorized by statute, ordinance or administrative regulation does not subject the actor to tort liability.* Aside from the question of the validity of the legislative enactment, there is the question of its interpretation. Legislation prohibiting some but not other conduct is not ordinarily construed as authorizing the latter. In the case of negligence as a matter of law, the standard defined by a legislative enactment is normally a minimum standard, applicable to the ordinary situations contemplated by the legislation. Thus traveling at less than the speed limit may still be negligence if traffic conditions indicate that a lesser speed is required. (See § 288C). The same general principle applies to public nuisance. Consideration may appropriately be given, however, to the fact that acts were taken in reliance upon legislation, as when expensive screening processes are installed to reduce the level of pollution to a legislative maximum.

> In addition, if there has been established a comprehensive set of legislative acts or administrative regulations governing the details of a particular kind of conduct, the courts are slow to declare an activity to be a public nuisance if it complies with the regulations. Thus, at one time courts frequently engaged in "judicial zoning," or the determination of whether a particular land use was unsuitable to a locality and therefore unreasonable. Now that most cities have complete sets of zoning regulations and agencies to plan and administer them, the courts have shown an inclination to leave the problem of the appropriate location of certain types of activities, as distinguished from the way in which they are carried on, to the administrative agencies. The variety and complexity of a problem and of the interests involved and the feeling that the particular decision should be a part of an overall plan prepared with a knowledge of matters not presented to the court and of interests not represented before it, may also promote judicial restraint and a readiness to leave the question to an administrative agency if there is one capable of handling it appropriately.

Id. (emphasis added). In response, the SCCIA Plaintiffs contend that compliance with governing regulations is only one of the factors which a court should consider in determining whether a party has established a claim of public nuisance, and that, aside from citing the Restatement (Second) of Torts and case law from other jurisdictions, SLC has provided no support for its argument.

Ironically, the SCCIA Plaintiffs cite no case law in support of their assertions, perhaps because the few New Jersey cases that have addressed the issue have concluded that a party whose actions are authorized by a governing body cannot be held liable for a public nuisance.

Very recently, however, the Appellate Division of the Superior Court of New Jersey held that handgun manufacturers may be liable for creating a public nuisance even if their conduct falls within the framework of the governing laws. *See* James v. Arms Tech., Inc., 359 N.J.Super. 291, 820 A.2d 27, 49–52 (2003). Considering the impact of the Restatement (Second) of Torts § 821B, cmt. f, the court noted that the activities in which the defendants engaged were not fully regulated.

> [W]hile it is true that some aspects of gun sales are regulated, the reality is that their [the gun industry's] marketing and distribution policies and practices exist in a regulatory vacuum, in that there is generally no regulation of the quantity, frequency, or purpose of firearm purchases or sales nor is there any national registration of purchasers or firearms. Thus the specific conduct alleged to constitute the public nuisance—fostering an illegal secondary gun market—is not closely regulated.

Id. at 52 (internal citations and quotations omitted).

There is a distinction to be drawn between *James* and this case. Not only can the argument be made that the emission of pollutants is fully regulated under both federal and state laws and the implementing regulations promulgated thereunder, see 42 U.S.C. §§ 7401 et seq. (Clean Air Act); N.J.S.A. §§ 26:2C-1 et seq., but also, in this case, the activities in which SLC engaged were affirmatively sanctioned by the NJDEP by way of air permits. Because the SCCIA Plaintiffs have not alleged that SLC's activities were not fully regulated, I conclude that the SCCIA Plaintiffs cannot state a claim of public nuisance. Accordingly, I shall grant SLC's motion to dismiss the Sixth Count of the Second Amended Complaint which alleges a claim of public nuisance.

Notes

Zoning and other forms of regulation. *South Camden Citizens in Action* involved the interplay between nuisance claims and environmental regulations. Zoning ordinances and restrictive covenants may also be implicated in nuisance cases. *See* Bagko Dev. Co. v. Jim Bagley Const. Co., 640 N.E.2d 67 (Ind. Ct. App. 1994) (involving claims of private nuisance, violation of restrictive covenant, and violation of zoning ordinances based on operation of Little League practice field).

Public nuisance actions. As *South Camden Citizens in Action* suggests, the same activity can amount to both a private and a public nuisance. *See* Armory Park Neighborhood Ass'n v. Episcopal Community Services in Arizona, 712 P.2d 914 (Ariz. 1985). The remedy sought in a public nuisance action is typically to enjoin the defendant from continuing the activity. Such suits are often brought by a state attorney general or similar official. *See* People v. Gallo, 929 P.2d 596 (Cal. 1997). But an individual whose use or enjoyment of her specific property is adversely affected by the defendant's activity may have suffered an injury different in kind from that of the general public and have standing to seek damages as well as an injunction rather than relying on the attorney general. *See* Armory Park Neighborhood Ass'n v. Episcopal Community Services in Arizona, 712 P.2d 914, 918 (Ariz. 1985).

Unreasonableness of the invasion. In determining whether an invasion is unreasonable, courts often weigh the gravity of the plaintiff's harm against the utility of the defendant's conduct. *See* Restatement (Second) of Torts § 826. In determining the gravity of the harm (or "quantum of the harm" as *South Camden Citizens in Action* refers to it), a court considers the "effect upon persons of ordinary health and sensibilities, and ordinary modes of living, and not upon those who, on the one hand, are morbid or fastidious or peculiarly susceptible to the thing complained of, or, on the other hand, are unusually insensible thereto." Jenkins v. CSX Transp., Inc., 906 S.W.2d 460 (Tenn. Ct. App.1995); *see also* Restatement (Second) of Torts § 827. In assessing the utility of the defendant's conduct, one might consider the social value of the conduct in question, the suitability of the conduct to the character of the locality, and impracticability in preventing or avoiding the invasion. Restatement (Second) of Torts § 828.

Moving to the nuisance. In *Spur Industries, Inc. v. Del E. Webb Development Co.*, 494 P.2d 700 (Ariz. 1972), the plaintiff sought to enjoin the defendant from operating its cattle feedlot. When the defendant started its operation (which consisted of 30,000 head of cattle and accompanying amount of manure), the area in question was largely agricultural in nature. The plaintiff began developing a residential area nearby with more than 1,300 lots and a golf course, but the odor and flies from the feedlot impacted the willingness of residents to live there. Should the plaintiff have the ability to enjoin the defendant's activities when the plaintiff knowingly moved to the nuisance? Should the defendant have the right to continue its activities when its activities otherwise amount to a nuisance? "The fact that the plaintiff has acquired or improved his land after a nuisance interfering with it has come into existence is not in itself sufficient to bar his action, but it is a factor to be considered in determining whether the nuisance is actionable." Restatement (Second) of Torts § 840D.

Problem 13.1. Luis and the three other homeowners in his neighborhood wish to bring a nuisance claim against Eldon based on the odors emanating from the facility. Would this be a claim of public nuisance or private nuisance?

Problem 13.2. Eldon breeds thousands of mice, which he supplies to medical testing facilities for medical research. The odor that Luis and his neighbors complain of stems from the accumulation of urine, droppings, and dead mice. Eldon's facility uses powerful fans to help regulate the temperature in the building. Unfortunately, the fans also increase the volume of the mousey odor that the plaintiffs experience. What other facts would you want to know before reaching a conclusion as to whether Eldon's invasion was unreasonable, either in terms of the gravity of the harm or the utility of Eldon's conduct? Be specific.

Problem 13.3. Eldon set up his facility 15 years ago. The facility is located several miles outside of the nearest town, and, at the time, there were no residences anywhere in the vicinity. It wasn't until the last few years that a few houses began to spring up nearby. How does this impact the unreasonableness analysis?

Note

Compensatory and punitive damages. Where the harm suffered by the plaintiff is permanent, courts may award compensatory damages in the form of the diminished market value of the plaintiff's property. *See* Crawford v. National Lead Co., 784 F. Supp. 439, 445 (S.D. Ohio 1989). Where the harm is temporary but nonetheless may take some time to abate (for example, where the plaintiff must undertake repairs or clean up), the plaintiff may recover the abatement costs or lost rental value. *See* Reeser v. Weaver Bros., Inc., 605 N.E.2d 1271 (Ohio Ct. App. 1992). Where the nuisance has already terminated and caused no ongoing harm, the plaintiff could be limited to compensatory damages (for example, emotional distress damages) for the loss of use or enjoyment of the land while the nuisance was ongoing. *See* Crawford v. National Lead Co., 784 F. Supp. 439, 445 (S.D. Ohio 1989). Nuisance cases sometimes involve mean-spirited or malicious behavior on the part of defendants, so sometimes punitive damages may be available. *See* Statler v. Catalano, 521 N.E.2d 565, 570 (Ill. Ct. App. 1988) (involving defendant who erected a barrier that prevented plaintiff from using portion of a lake on his property and who, over the course of five years, randomly subjected plaintiffs to bright lights being shone on their property at various times of night). A number of states have statutes prohibiting the construction of "spite fences"—fences that are constructed for the purpose of annoying a neighbor or otherwise injuring his use and enjoyment of land. *See* Connecticut Gen. Stat. § 52-570. The construction of such a fence might lead to injunctive relief as well as compensatory and punitive damages. *See* Austin v. Bald II, L.L.C., 658 S.E.2d 1 (N.C. Ct. App. 2008). The next case in the chapter explores in more detail the question of whether injunctive relief or compensatory damages is the appropriate remedy in a nuisance case.

Boomer v. Atlantic Cement Co.

257 N.E.2d 870 (N.Y. 1970)

BERGAN, Judge.

Defendant operates a large cement plant near Albany. These are actions for injunction and damages by neighboring land owners alleging injury to property from dirt, smoke and vibration emanating from the plant. A nuisance has been found after trial, temporary damages have been allowed; but an injunction has been denied.

The public concern with air pollution arising from many sources in industry and in transportation is currently accorded ever wider recognition accompanied by a growing sense of responsibility in State and Federal Governments to control it. Cement plants are obvious sources of air pollution in the neighborhoods where they operate.

But there is now before the court private litigation in which individual property owners have sought specific relief from a single plant operation. The threshold question raised by the division of view on this appeal is whether the court should resolve the litigation between the parties now before it as equitably as seems possible; or whether, seeking promotion of the general public welfare, it should channel private litigation into broad public objectives.

A court performs its essential function when it decides the rights of parties before it. Its decision of private controversies may sometimes greatly affect public issues. Large questions of law are often resolved by the manner in which private litigation is decided. But this is normally an incident to the court's main function to settle controversy. It is a rare exercise of judicial power to use a decision in private litigation as a purposeful mechanism to achieve direct public objectives greatly beyond the rights and interests before the court.

Effective control of air pollution is a problem presently far from solution even with the full public and financial powers of government. In large measure adequate technical procedures are yet to be developed and some that appear possible may be economically impracticable.

It seems apparent that the amelioration of air pollution will depend on technical research in great depth; on a carefully balanced consideration of the economic impact of close regulation; and of the actual effect on public health. It is likely to require massive public expenditure and to demand more than any local community can accomplish and to depend on regional and interstate controls.

A court should not try to do this on its own as a by-product of private litigation and it seems manifest that the judicial establishment is neither equipped in the limited nature of any judgment it can pronounce nor prepared to lay down and implement an effective policy for the elimination of air pollution. This is an area beyond the circumference of one private lawsuit. It is a direct responsibility for government and should not thus be undertaken as an incident to solving a dispute between property owners and a single cement plant—one of many—in the Hudson River valley.

The cement making operations of defendant have been found by the court of Special Term to have damaged the nearby properties of plaintiffs in these two actions. That court, as it has been noted, accordingly found defendant maintained a nuisance and this has been affirmed at the Appellate Division. The total damage to plaintiffs' properties is, however, relatively small in comparison with the value of defendant's operation and with the consequences of the injunction which plaintiffs seek.

The ground for the denial of injunction, notwithstanding the finding both that there is a nuisance and that plaintiffs have been damaged substantially, is the large disparity in economic consequences of the nuisance and of the injunction. This theory cannot, however, be sustained without overruling a doctrine which has been consistently reaffirmed in several leading cases in this court and which has never been disavowed here, namely that where a nuisance has been found and where there has been any substantial damage shown by the party complaining an injunction will be granted.

The rule in New York has been that such a nuisance will be enjoined although marked disparity be shown in economic consequence between the effect of the injunction and the effect of the nuisance.

The problem of disparity in economic consequence was sharply in focus in *Whalen v. Union Bag & Paper Co.*, 208 N.Y. 1, 101 N.E. 805. A pulp mill entailing an investment of more than a million dollars polluted a stream in which plaintiff, who owned a farm, was 'a lower riparian owner.' The economic loss to plaintiff from this pollution was small. This court, reversing the Appellate Division, reinstated the injunction granted by the Special Term against the argument of the mill owner that in view of 'the slight advantage to plaintiff and the great loss that will be inflicted on defendant' an injunction should not be granted. 'Such a balancing of injuries cannot be justified by the circumstances of this case', Judge Werner noted. He continued: 'Although the damage to the plaintiff may be slight as compared with the defendant's expense of abating the condition, that is not a good reason for refusing an injunction.'

Thus the unconditional injunction granted at Special Term was reinstated. The rule laid down in that case, then, is that whenever the damage resulting from a nuisance is found not 'unsubstantial', *viz.*, $100 a year, injunction would follow. This states a rule that had been followed in this court with marked consistency.

. . .

Although the court at Special Term and the Appellate Division held that injunction should be denied, it was found that plaintiffs had been damaged in various specific amounts up to the time of the trial and damages to the respective plaintiffs were awarded for those amounts. The effect of this was, injunction having been denied, plaintiffs could maintain successive actions at law for damages thereafter as further damage was incurred.

The court at Special Term also found the amount of permanent damage attributable to each plaintiff, for the guidance of the parties in the event both sides stipulated to the payment and acceptance of such permanent damage as a settlement of all the controversies among the parties. The total of permanent damages to all plaintiffs thus found was $185,000. This basis of adjustment has not resulted in any stipulation by the parties.

This result at Special Term and at the Appellate Division is a departure from a rule that has become settled; but to follow the rule literally in these cases would be to close down the plant at once. This court is fully agreed to avoid that immediately drastic remedy; the difference in view is how best to avoid it.*

One alternative is to grant the injunction but postpone its effect to a specified future date to give opportunity for technical advances to permit defendant to eliminate the nuisance; another is to grant the injunction conditioned on the payment of permanent damages to plaintiffs which would compensate them for the total economic loss to their property present and future caused by defendant's operations. For reasons which will be developed the court chooses the latter alternative.

If the injunction were to be granted unless within a short period—*e.g.*, 18 months—the nuisance be abated by improved methods, there would be no assurance that any significant technical improvement would occur.

The parties could settle this private litigation at any time if defendant paid enough money and the imminent threat of closing the plant would build up the pressure on defendant. If there were no improved techniques found, there would inevitably be applications to the court at Special Term for extensions of time to perform on showing of good faith efforts to find such techniques.

---

* Respondent's investment in the plant is in excess of $45,000,000. There are over 300 people employed there.

Moreover, techniques to eliminate dust and other annoying by-products of cement making are unlikely to be developed by any research the defendant can undertake within any short period, but will depend on the total resources of the cement industry nationwide and throughout the world. The problem is universal wherever cement is made.

For obvious reasons the rate of the research is beyond control of defendant. If at the end of 18 months the whole industry has not found a technical solution a court would be hard put to close down this one cement plant if due regard be given to equitable principles.

On the other hand, to grant the injunction unless defendant pays plaintiffs such permanent damages as may be fixed by the court seems to do justice between the contending parties. All of the attributions of economic loss to the properties on which plaintiffs' complaints are based will have been redressed.

The nuisance complained of by these plaintiffs may have other public or private consequences, but these particular parties are the only ones who have sought remedies and the judgment proposed will fully redress them. The limitation of relief granted is a limitation only within the four corners of these actions and does not foreclose public health or other public agencies from seeking proper relief in a proper court.

It seems reasonable to think that the risk of being required to pay permanent damages to injured property owners by cement plant owners would itself be a reasonable effective spur to research for improved techniques to minimize nuisance.

The power of the court to condition on equitable grounds the continuance of an injunction on the payment of permanent damages seems undoubted.

The damage base here suggested is consistent with the general rule in those nuisance cases where damages are allowed. 'Where a nuisance is of such a permanent and unabatable character that a single recovery can be had, including the whole damage past and future resulting therefrom, there can be but one recovery' (66 C.J.S. Nuisances s 140, p. 947). It has been said that permanent damages are allowed where the loss recoverable would obviously be small as compared with the cost of removal of the nuisance (Kentucky-Ohio Gas Co. v. Bowling, 264 Ky. 470, 477, 95 S.W.2d 1).

...

Thus it seems fair to both sides to grant permanent damages to plaintiffs which will terminate this private litigation. The theory of damage is the 'servitude on land' of plaintiffs imposed by defendant's nuisance. (See United States v. Causby, 328 U.S. 256, 261, 262, 267, 66 S.Ct. 1062, 90 L.Ed. 1206, where the term 'servitude' addressed to the land was used by Justice Douglas relating to the effect of airplane noise on property near an airport.)

The judgment, by allowance of permanent damages imposing a servitude on land, which is the basis of the actions, would preclude future recovery by plaintiffs or their grantees.

This should be placed beyond debate by a provision of the judgment that the payment by defendant and the acceptance by plaintiffs of permanent damages found by the court shall be in compensation for a servitude on the land.

Although the Trial Term has found permanent damages as a possible basis of settlement of the litigation, on remission the court should be entirely free to examine this subject. It may again find the permanent damage already found; or make new findings.

The orders should be reversed, without costs, and the cases remitted to Supreme Court, Albany County to grant an injunction which shall be vacated upon payment by defendant of such amounts of permanent damage to the respective plaintiffs as shall for this purpose be determined by the court.

JASEN, Judge (dissenting).

I agree with the majority that a reversal is required here, but I do not subscribe to the newly enunciated doctrine of assessment of permanent damages, in lieu of an injunction, where substantial property rights have been impaired by the creation of a nuisance.

It has long been the rule in this State, as the majority acknowledges, that a nuisance which results in substantial continuing damage to neighbors must be enjoined. To now change the rule to permit the cement company to continue polluting the air indefinitely upon the payment of permanent damages is, in my opinion, compounding the magnitude of a very serious problem in our State and Nation today.

In recognition of this problem, the Legislature of this State has enacted the Air Pollution Control Act (Public Health Law, Consol.Laws, c. 45, §§ 1264 to 1299m) declaring that it is the State policy to require the use of all available and reasonable methods to prevent and control air pollution (Public Health Law § 12651).

The harmful nature and widespread occurrence of air pollution have been extensively documented. Congressional hearings have revealed that air pollution causes substantial property damage, as well as being a contributing factor to a rising incidence of lung cancer, emphysema, bronchitis and asthma.

The specific problem faced here is known as particulate contamination because of the fine dust particles emanating from defendant's cement plant. The particular type of nuisance is not new, having appeared in many cases for at least the past 60 years. It is interesting to note that cement production has recently been identified as a significant source of particulate contamination in the Hudson Valley. This type of pollution, wherein very small particles escape and stay in the atmosphere, has been denominated as the type of air pollution which produces the greatest hazard to human health. We have thus a nuisance which not only is damaging to the plaintiffs, but also is decidedly harmful to the general public.

I see grave dangers in overruling our long-established rule of granting an injunction where a nuisance results in substantial continuing damage. In permitting the injunction to become inoperative upon the payment of permanent damages, the majority is, in effect, licensing a continuing wrong. It is the same as saying to the cement company, you may continue to do harm to your neighbors so long as you pay a fee for it. Furthermore, once such permanent damages are assessed and paid, the incentive to alleviate the wrong would be eliminated, thereby continuing air pollution of an area without abatement.

It is true that some courts have sanctioned the remedy here proposed by the majority in a number of cases, but none of the authorities relied upon by the majority are analogous to the situation before us. In those cases, the courts, in denying an injunction and awarding money damages, grounded their decision on a showing that the use to which the property was intended to be put was primarily for the public benefit. Here, on the other hand, it is clearly established that the cement company is creating a continuing air pollution nuisance primarily for its own private interest with no public benefit.

This kind of inverse condemnation may not be invoked by a private person or corporation for private gain or advantage. Inverse condemnation should only be permitted when the public is primarily served in the taking or impairment of property. The promotion of the interests of the polluting cement company has, in my opinion, no public use or benefit.

Nor is it constitutionally permissible to impose servitude on land, without consent of the owner, by payment of permanent damages where the continuing impairment of the land is for a private use. This is made clear by the State Constitution (art. I, § 7, subd. (a)) which provides that '(p)rivate property shall not be taken for *public use* without just compensation' (emphasis added). It is, of course, significant that the section makes no mention of taking for a *private* use.

In sum, then, by constitutional mandate as well as by judicial pronouncement, the permanent impairment of private property for private purposes is not authorized in the absence of clearly demonstrated public benefit and use.

I would enjoin the defendant cement company from continuing the discharge of dust particles upon its neighbors' properties unless, within 18 months, the cement company abated this nuisance.

It is not my intention to cause the removal of the cement plant from the Albany area, but to recognize the urgency of the problem stemming from this stationary source of air pollution, and to allow the company a specified period of time to develop a means to alleviate this nuisance.

. . .

In a day when there is a growing concern for clean air, highly developed industry should not expect acquiescence by the courts, but should, instead, plan its operations to eliminate contamination of our air and damage to its neighbors.

Accordingly, the orders of the Appellate Division, insofar as they denied the injunction, should be reversed, and the actions remitted to Supreme Court, Albany County to grant an injunction to take effect 18 months hence, unless the nuisance is abated by improved techniques prior to said date.

Notes

Determining the appropriate remedy. *Boomer* involves a court trying to determine the appropriate remedy. Courts sometimes say that injunctive relief may be granted where there is no other adequate legal remedy. *See* Krein v. Szewc, 403 P.3d 520 (Or. 2017). However, in some situations, compensatory damages for past loss of enjoyment and injunctive relief to prevent future harm may be appropriate. *Id.* As a form of equitable relief, courts have significant discretion when it comes to determining the appropriate injunctive relief. *See id.* (affirming award of compensatory damages for past nuisance associated with incessant barking of defendants' dog and injunctive relief ordering devocalization of dog).

Diminution of property value as harm. In some instances, a defendant's conduct might not impact a plaintiff's ability to use or enjoy the property in the ways one normally thinks of. Instead, the plaintiff's claimed harm is the possible reduction in the value of the property. But some courts say that "property depreciation alone is insufficient to constitute a nuisance." Adkins v. Thomas Solvent Co., 487 N.W.2d 715, 724 (Mich. 1992). For example, in one case, the noise from the defendant's shooting range was not sufficient to result in a nuisance, nor was there any danger to the plaintiff by the existence of the range. The Michigan Supreme Court ruled that even assuming the presence of the range resulted in reduction in property value, this was not "in itself sufficient to constitute a nuisance." Smith v. Western Wayne Co. Conservation Ass'n., 158 N.W.2d 463, 472 (Mich. 1968).

Problem 13.4. Assume for purposes of this problem that Eldon's mouse operation is determined to be a nuisance. You are the judge. What is the appropriate remedy for Luis and his neighbors?

Review Question

Paul owns a house next door to Vivienne in a small housing subdivision. Every Monday and Wednesday at 9:00 p.m. for the past two months, Paul plugs his bass guitar into his amplifier and practices for an hour. The sound is loud enough that Vivienne needs to turn up the volume of her television so that she can understand the dialogue over the sound of the bass. And the vibrations from the amplifier are intense enough that Vivienne can feel the walls vibrate a little in her living room. Vivienne is especially annoyed by the noise because her favorite television shows are on at those times, and Paul's actions interfere with her television watching. Vivienne called the police on two occasions, and on the second occasion, Paul was cited for violation of the town' noise ordinance, which prohibits sound at a level of 60 decibels across a residential real property boundary or within a noise-sensitive zone, between the hours of 7:00

a.m. and 10:00 p.m. Another portion of the ordinance describes the basis for the ordinance:

> Sec. 46-2. Findings; general policy.
>
> (a) The city council finds that:
>
> (1) Excessive sound is a serious hazard to the public health, welfare and safety and the quality of life;
>
> (2) A substantial body of science and technology exists by which excessive sound may be substantially abated; and
>
> (3) The citizens of the city have a right to and should be ensured an environment free from excessive sound that may jeopardize their health or welfare or safety or degrade the quality of life.
>
> (b) It is the policy of the city to prevent excessive sound which may jeopardize the health, welfare or safety of its citizens or degrade the quality of life.

Despite the citation, Paul continues to play his bass at night at the same volume. You are a lawyer. Vivienne is frustrated and comes to you for your advice as to how she should proceed. What advice do you have?

Chapter 14

Products Liability

A. Historical Development of Products Liability Law
- The role of privity
- The role of warranties
- The role of tort law in addressing product defects
- The § 402A test in general
- Different types of defects in general
- Special products liability rules
  - "Seller"
  - "Product"
  - Used goods
  - Potential plaintiffs
  - The economic loss rule
- Other concepts developed in class or in readings assigned by the professor

B. Manufacturing Defects
- In general
- The § 402A/consumer expectations test
- Special rules in food cases
- Prima facie case
- The malfunction doctrine
- Liability up the chain of distribution
- Other concepts developed in class or in readings assigned by the professor

C. Design Defects
- In general
- The risk-utility test in general
  - Limitations of the consumer expectation test
  - California's two-pronged test
  - Foreseeable misuse of a product
  - Unforeseeable misuse of a product
  - The crashworthiness doctrine
  - Other concepts developed in class or in readings assigned by the professor
- Application of the risk-utility test
  - Factors to consider
  - State of the art
  - Subsequent design changes.
  - Other concepts developed in class or in readings assigned by the professor

D. Information (Warning) Defects

- In general
  - The function of warnings and obvious risks
  - Addressing the appropriate audience
  - Warnings and food and drug allergies
- Special issues involving causation
  - Increased risk
  - The heeding presumption
  - Other concepts developed in class or in readings assigned by the professor
- Special issues involving duty
  - Learned intermediary doctrine
  - Sophisticated user doctrine
  - Component parts doctrine
  - Bulk supplier doctrine
  - Post-sale duty to warn
  - Other concepts developed in class or in readings assigned by the professor

E. Defenses

- Comparative fault
  - The effect of a plaintiff's own fault
  - Failure to discover a defect
- Substantial modification of product
- Compliance with regulations
- Preemption
  - Express
  - Implied
- Other concepts developed in class or in readings assigned by the professor

F. Final Thoughts on Products Liability

- Arguments in favor of tort reform applied to products liability law
- Arguments against tort reform applied to products liability law

Chapter Problem. Mary, Daniela, and Isabella all suffered injuries from what they believe are defective products. They seek to recover for their injuries.

Tenn. Code § 29-28-102. Definitions

(6) "Product liability action" for purposes of this chapter includes all actions brought for or on account of personal injury, death or property damage caused by or resulting from the manufacture, construction, design, formula, preparation, assembly, testing, service, warning, instruction, marketing, packaging or labeling of any product. "Product liability action" includes, but is not limited to, all actions based upon the following theories: strict liability in tort; negligence; breach of warranty, express or implied; breach of or

> failure to discharge a duty to warn or instruct, whether negligent, or innocent; misrepresentation, concealment, or nondisclosure, whether negligent, or innocent; or under any other substantive legal theory in tort or contract whatsoever.

The phrase "products liability" potentially conjures up a host of images: the exploding car, the circular saw with the defective blade, or the scalding hot cup of coffee. The phrase also sometimes evokes strong feelings about greedy plaintiffs, uncaring manufacturers, and the role the law should play in resolving their disputes. Perhaps the issue that thrust the concept of products liability into the public consciousness was the Ford Pinto litigation of the 1970s. As designed, the Ford Pinto was prone to fuel tank fires upon a rear-end collision. Ford was aware of the problem but continued production of the car. One of the first news stories on the problem reported that between 500 and 900 people had died in fires as a result of the Pinto's fuel line problem. *See* John R. Danley, *Polishing Up the Pinto*, BUSINESS ETHICS QUARTERLY 209 (April 2005). Not surprisingly, Ford faced substantial litigation and endured a public relations debacle. Today, products liability is often on the front line of tort reform battles.

As the above statute illustrates, the term "products liability" covers a host of potential legal theories. One reason why the phrase matters is because courts and legislatures have constructed special substantive and procedural rules that apply when a plaintiff is injured by a supposedly defective product. This chapter explores the sometimes-complicated law governing defective products. After the chapter fleshes out all of the relevant legal rules, the final section gets into some of the competing arguments concerning the relative merits of tort reform proposals as they apply to products liability

A. Historical Development

1. The Privity Requirement

Winterbottom v. Wright

10 M&W 109 (1842)

[The plaintiff entered into a contract with the Postmaster-General to drive a mail coach, which was supplied by the Postmaster-General. The Postmaster-General had contracted with the defendant to maintain the coach in good working order. The plaintiff was injured when the coach broke down due to the supposed negligence of the defendant. The plaintiff sought to recover from the defendant.]

LORD ABINGER, C.B.

I am clearly of opinion that the defendant is entitled to our judgment. We ought not to permit a doubt to rest upon this subject, for our doing so might be the means of letting in upon us an infinity of actions.... There is no privity of contract between these parties; and if the plaintiff can sue, every passenger, or even any person passing along the road, who was injured by the upsetting of the coach, might bring a similar action. Unless we confine the operation of such contracts as this to the parties who entered into them, the most absurd and outrageous consequences, to which I can see no limit, would ensue. Where a party becomes responsible to the public, by undertaking a public duty, he is liable, though the injury may have arisen from the negligence of his servant or agent. So, in cases of public nuisances, whether the act was done by the party as a servant or in any other capacity, you are liable to an action at the suit of any person who suffers. Those, however, are cases where the real ground of the liability is the public duty, or the commission of the public nuisance.... The plaintiff in this case could not have brought an action on the contract; ... By permitting this action, we should be working this injustice, that after the defendant had done everything to the satisfaction of his employer, and after all matters between them had been adjusted, and all of their accounts settled on the footing of their contract we should subject them to be ripped open by this action of tort being brought against him.

2. The Fall of Privity

MacPherson v. Buick Motor Co.

111 N.E. 1050 (N.Y. 1916)

CARDOZO, J.

The defendant is a manufacturer of automobiles. It sold an automobile to a retail dealer. The retail dealer resold to the plaintiff. While the plaintiff was in the car, it suddenly collapsed. He was thrown out and injured. One of the wheels was made of defective wood, and its spokes crumbled into fragments. The wheel was not made by the defendant; it was bought from another manufacturer. There is evidence, however, that its defects could have been discovered by reasonable inspection, and that inspection was omitted. There is no claim that the defendant knew of the defect and willfully concealed it.... The charge is one, not of fraud, but of negligence. The question to be determined is whether the defendant owed a duty of care and vigilance to any one but the immediate purchaser.

The foundations of this branch of the law, at least in this state, were laid in *Thomas v. Winchester* (6 N.Y. 397). A poison was falsely labeled. The sale was made to a druggist, who in turn sold to a customer. The customer recovered damages from the seller who affixed the label. "The defendant's negligence," it was said, "put human life in imminent danger." A poison falsely labeled is likely to injure any one who gets it. Because the danger is to be foreseen, there is a duty to avoid the injury. Cases were cited by way of illustration in which manufacturers were not subject to any duty irrespective of contract. The distinction was said to be that their conduct, though, negligent, was not likely to result in injury to any one except the purchaser. We are not required to say whether the chance of injury was always as remote as the distinction assumes. Some of the illustrations might be rejected today. The principle of the distinction is for present purposes the important thing.

Thomas v. Winchester became quickly a landmark of the law. In the application of its principle there may at times have been uncertainty or even error. There has never in this state been doubt or disavowal of the principle itself. The chief cases are well known, yet to recall some of them will be helpful. *Loop v. Litchfield* (42 N.Y. 351) is the earliest. It was the case of a defect in a small balance wheel used on a circular saw. The manufacturer pointed out the defect of the buyer, who wished a cheap article and was ready to assume the risk. The risk can hardly have been an imminent one, for the wheel lasted five years before it broke. In the meanwhile the buyer had made a lease of the machinery. It was held that the manufacturer was not answerable to the lessee. *Loop v. Litchfield* was followed in *Losee v. Clute* (51 N.Y. 494), the case of the explosion of a steam boiler. . . . It was put upon the ground that the risk of injury was too remote. The buyer in that case had not only accepted the boiler, but had tested it. The manufacturer knew that his own test was not the final one. The finality of the test has a bearing on the measure of diligence owing to persons other than the purchaser.

These early cases suggest a narrow construction of the rule. Later cases, however, evince a more liberal spirit. First in importance is *Devlin v. Smith* (89 N.Y. 470). The defendant, a contractor, built a scaffold for a painter. The painter's servants were injured. The contractor was held liable. He knew that the scaffold, if improperly constructed, was a most dangerous trap. He knew that it was to be used by the workmen. He was building it for that very purpose. Building it for their use, he owed them a duty, irrespective of his contract with their master, to build it with care.

From *Devlin v. Smith* we pass over intermediate cases and turn to the latest case in this court in which *Thomas v. Winchester* was followed. That case is *Statler v. Ray Mfg. Co.* (195 N.Y. 478, 480). The defendant manufactured a large coffee urn. It was installed in a restaurant. When heated, the urn exploded and injured the plaintiff. We held that the manufacturer was liable. We said that the urn "was of such a character inherently that, when applied to the purposes for which it was designed, it was liable to become a source of great danger to many people if not carefully and properly constructed." It may be that *Devlin v. Smith* and *Statler v. Ray Mfg. Co.* have extended the rule of *Thomas v. Winchester.* If so, this court is committed to the extension. The defendant argues that things imminently dangerous to life are poisons, explosives, deadly weapons—things whose normal function it is to injure or destroy. But whatever the rule in *Thomas v. Winchester* may once have been, it has no longer that restricted meaning. A large coffee urn (*Statler v. Ray Mfg. Co., supra*) may have within itself, if negligently made, the potency of danger, yet no one thinks of it as an implement whose normal function is destruction. What is true of the coffee urn is equally true of bottles of aerated water (*Torgesen v. Schultz*, 192 N.Y. 156). . . .

. . .

We hold, then, that the principle of *Thomas v. Winchester* is not limited to poisons, explosives, and things of like nature, to things which in their normal operation are implements of destruction. If the nature of a thing is such that it is reasonably certain to place and limb in peril when negligently made, it is then a thing of danger. Its nature gives warning of the consequences to be expected. If to the element of danger there is added knowledge that the thing will be used by persons other than the purchaser, and used without new tests then, irrespective of contract, the manufacturer of this thing of danger is under a duty to make it carefully. That is as far as we are required to go for the decision of this case. There must be knowledge of a danger, not merely possible, but probable. It is possible to use almost anything in a way that will make it dangerous if defective. That is not enough to charge the manufacturer with a duty independent of his contract. Whether a given thing is dangerous may be sometimes a question for the court and sometimes a question for the jury. There must also be knowledge that in the usual course of events the danger will be shared by others than the buyer. Such knowledge may often be inferred from the nature of the transaction. But it is possible that even knowledge of the danger and of the use will not always be enough. The proximity or remoteness of the relation is a factor to be considered. We are dealing now with the liability of the manufacturer of the finished product, who puts it on the market to be used without inspection by his customers. If he is negligent, where danger is to be foreseen, a liability will follow. We are not required at this time to say that it is legitimate to go back to the manufacturer of the finished product and hold the manufacturers of the component parts. To make their negligence a cause of imminent danger, an independent cause must often intervene; the manufacturer of the finished product must also fail in his duty of inspection. It may be that in those circumstances the negligence of the earlier members of the series as too remote to constitute, as to the ultimate user, an actionable wrong. We leave that question open to you. We shall have to deal with it when it arises. The difficulty which it suggests is not present in this case. There is here no break in the chain of cause and effect. In such circumstances, the presence of a known danger, attendant upon a known use, makes vigilance a duty. We have put aside the notion that the duty to safeguard life and limb, when the consequences of negligence may be foreseen, grows out of contract and nothing else. We have put the source of the obligation where it ought to be. We have put its source in the law.

From this survey of the decisions, there thus emerges a definition of the duty of a manufacturer which enables us to measure this defendant's liability. Beyond all question, the nature of an automobile gives warning of probable danger if its construction is defective. This automobile was designed to go fifty miles an hour. Unless its wheels were sound and strong, injury was almost certain. It was as much a thing of danger as a defective engine for a railroad. The defendant knew the danger. It knew also that the care would be used by persons other than the buyer. This was apparent from its size; there were seats for three persons. It was apparent also from the fact that the buyer was a dealer in cars, who bought to resell. The maker of this car supplied it for the use of purchasers from the dealer just as plainly as the contractor in *Devlin v. Smith* supplied the scaffold for use by the servants of the owner. The dealer was indeed the one person of whom it might be said with some approach to certainly that by him the car would not be used. Yet the defendant would have us say that he was the one person whom it was under a legal duty to protect. The law does not lead us to so inconsequent a conclusion. Precedents drawn from the days of travel by stage coach do not fit the conditions of travel today. The principle that the danger must be imminent does not change, but the things subject to the principle do change. They are whatever the needs of life in a developing civilization require them to be.

...

We think the defendant was not absolved from a duty of inspection because it bought the wheels from a reputable manufacturer. It was not merely a dealer in automobiles. It was a manufacturer of automobiles. It was responsible for the finished product. It was not at liberty to put the finished product on the market without subjecting the component parts to ordinary and simple tests. Under the charge of the trial judge nothing more was required of it. The obligation to inspect must vary with the nature of the thing to be inspected. The more probable the danger, the greater the need of caution....

The judgment should be affirmed.

Note

Fraudulent misrepresentation and privity. Another situation in which courts of this time were willing to look past the absence of privity between the injured party and the manufacturer was where the defendant was guilty of fraud or deceit in terms of representing the nature of the product. *See* Mazetti v. Armour & Co., 135 P. 633, 634 (Wash. 1913).

Problem 14.1. Mary's great-grandmother, Margaret, was injured in 1915 in New York when a negligently manufactured tea kettle exploded, resulting in personal injuries to Margaret. Margaret purchased the tea kettle from a local retailer, but the kettle was made by another company.

(a) Could Margaret recover for injuries from the manufacturer?

(b) What if the accident occurred in 1917 (one year after *MacPherson*)?

3. The Role of Warranties

As courts began to adopt *MacPherson*'s holding, the fact that a purchaser and manufacturer were not in privity no longer served as a bar to recovery based on a claim of negligence. But defendants potentially had other tools at their disposal to limit liability. The most noteworthy was the ability to disclaim warranties associated with a sale of a product.

Warranty liability is strict liability. If I sell you what I tell you is a 2020 Honda Accord, I am liable to you for breach of express warranty if the car turns out to be a 2019 Honda Accord, even if I used reasonable care in making the statement. More relevant for purposes of personal injury claims are implied warranties. There are two types of implied warranties. If I am in the business of selling cars and I sell you a car, I have impliedly warranted to you that the car is fit for the ordinary purpose for which it is manufactured and sold. If the car instead turns out to be unfit to drive on the highway, I have breached the implied warranty of merchantability even if I honestly and reasonably thought the car was roadworthy. If you make it known to me that you need a car for a particular purpose (*e.g.*, driving in dirt track races) and you rely upon my judgment in selecting a car, and the car I pick for you turns out to be inadequate for the task, I have breached the implied warranty of fitness for a particular purpose.

As the absence of privity increasingly posed less of a problem for injured consumers, consumers enjoyed some success in alleging that a manufacturer innocently or negligently misrepresented the nature of a defective product. *See* Baxter v. Ford Motor Co., 12 P.2d 409 (Wash. 1932) (permitting claim where party was injured by shattered glass from car windshield where manufacturer marketed car's windshield as being shatterproof). But if retailers and manufacturers could disclaim the existence of warranties, they could effectively limit the ability of purchasers to hold them strictly liable in the event that a product proved to be dangerous. The following case involves a court wrestling with this issue.

Henningsen v. Bloomfield Motors, Inc.

161 A.2d 69 (N.J. 1960)

[Mr. and Mrs. Henningsen purchased a 1955 Plymouth Club Sedan, manufactured by defendant Chrysler Corporation, from defendant Bloomfield Motors, Inc. When they purchased the vehicle, they signed a contract that provided "that there are no warranties, express or implied, made by either the dealer or the manufacturer on the motor vehicle, chassis, of parts furnished hereunder" with a few exceptions. Two weeks later, Mrs. Henningsen was driving when she heard a loud noise "from the bottom, by the hood." "It felt as if something cracked." The steering wheel spun in her hands; the car veered sharply to the right and crashed into a highway sign and a brick wall. The insurance inspector concluded that the accident was due to mechanical defect or failure.]

I. The Claim of Implied Warranty against the Manufacturer

There is no doubt that under early common-law concepts of contractual liability only those persons who were parties to the bargain could sue for a breach of it. In more recent times a noticeable disposition has appeared in a number of jurisdictions to break through the narrow barrier of privity when dealing with sales of goods in order to give realistic recognition to a universally accepted fact. The fact is that the dealer and the ordinary buyer do not, and are not expected to, buy goods, whether they be foodstuffs or automobiles, exclusively for their own consumption or use. Makers and manufacturers know this and advertise and market their products on that assumption; witness, the 'family' car, the baby foods, etc. The limitations of privity in contracts for the sale of goods developed their place in the law when marketing conditions were simple, when maker and buyer frequently met face to face on an equal bargaining plane and when many of the products were relatively uncomplicated and conducive to inspection by a buyer competent to evaluate their quality. With the advent of mass marketing, the manufacturer became remote from the purchaser, sales were accomplished through intermediaries, and the demand for the product was created by advertising media. In such an economy it became obvious that the consumer was the person being cultivated. Manifestly, the connotation of "consumer" was broader than that of "buyer." He signified such a person who, in the reasonable contemplation of the parties to the sale, might be expected to use the product. Thus, where the commodities sold are such that if defectively manufactured they will be dangerous to life or limb, then society's interests can only be protected by eliminating the requirement of privity between the maker and his dealers and the reasonably expected ultimate consumer. In that way the burden of losses consequent upon use of defective articles is borne by those who are in a position to either control the danger or make an equitable distribution of the losses when they do occur. As Harper & James put it, 'The interest in consumer protection calls for warranties by the maker that do run with the goods, to reach all who are likely to be hurt by the use of the unfit commodity for a purpose ordinarily to be expected.' 2 Harper & James, *supra* 1571, 1572. As far back as 1932, in the well known case of *Baxter v. Ford Motor Co.*, 168 Wash. 456, 12 P.2d 409 (Sup. Ct.1932), *affirmed* 15 P.2d 1118, 88 A.L.R. 521 (Sup.Ct.1932), the Supreme Court of Washington gave recognition to the impact of then existing commercial practices on the strait jacket of privity, saying:

> It would be unjust to recognize a rule that would permit manufacturers of goods to create a demand for their products by representing that they possess qualities which they, in fact, do not possess, and then, because there is no privity of contract existing between the consumer and the manufacturer, deny the consumer the right to recover if damages result from the absence of those qualities, when such absence is not readily noticeable.

. . .

Under modern conditions the ordinary layman, on responding to the importuning of colorful advertising, has neither the opportunity nor the capacity to inspect or to determine the fitness of an automobile for use; he must rely on the manufacturer who has control of its construction, and to some degree on the dealer who, to the limited extent called for by the manufacturer's instructions, inspects and services it before delivery. In such a marketing milieu his remedies and those of persons who properly claim through him should not depend "upon the intricacies of the law of sales. The obligation of the manufacturer should not be based alone on privity of contract. It should rest, as was once said, upon 'the demands of social justice.'" Mazetti v. Armour & Co., 75 Wash. 622, 135 P. 633, 635, 48 L.R.A.,N.S., 213 (Sup.Ct.1913)....

Accordingly, we hold that under modern marketing conditions, when a manufacturer puts a new automobile in the stream of trade and promotes its purchase by the public, an implied warranty that it is reasonably suitable for use as such accompanies it into the hands of the ultimate purchaser. Absence of agency between the manufacturer and the dealer who makes the ultimate sale is immaterial.

II. The Effect of the Disclaimer and Limitation of Liability Clauses on the Implied Warranty of Merchantability

...

The traditional contract is the result of free bargaining of parties who are brought together by the play of the market, and who meet each other on a footing of approximate economic equality. In such a society there is no danger that freedom of contract will be a threat to the social order as a whole. But in present-day commercial life the standardized mass contract has appeared. It is used primarily by enterprises with strong bargaining power and position. 'The weaker party, in need of the goods or services, is frequently not in a position to shop around for better terms, either because the author of the standard contract has a monopoly (natural or artificial) or because all competitors use the same clauses. His contractual intention is but a subjection more or less voluntary to terms dictated by the stronger party, terms whose consequences are often understood in a vague way, if at all.' Kessler,' *Contracts of Adhesion—Some Thoughts About Freedom of Contract,*' 43 Colum.L.Rev. 629, 632 (1943); Ehrenzweig, '*Adhesion Contracts in the Conflict of Laws,*' 53 Colum.L.Rev. 1072, 1075, 1089 (1953). Such standardized contracts have been described as those in which one predominant party will dictate its law to an undetermined multiple rather than to an individual. They are said to resemble a law rather than a meeting of the minds. Siegelman v. Cunard White Star, 221 F.2d 189, 206 (2 Cir.1955).

...

The warranty before us is a standardized form designed for mass use. It is imposed upon the automobile consumer. He takes it or leaves it, and he must take it to buy an automobile. No bargaining is engaged in with respect to it. In fact, the dealer through whom it comes to the buyer is without authority to alter it; his function is ministerial—simply to deliver it....

...

The task of the judiciary is to administer the spirit as well as the letter of the law. On issues such as the present one, part of that burden is to protect the ordinary man against the loss of important rights through what, in effect, is the unilateral act of the manufacturer....

...

Public policy at a given time finds expression in the Constitution, the statutory law and in judicial decisions. In the area of sale of goods, the legislative will has imposed an implied warranty of merchantability as a general incident of sale of an automobile by description. The warranty does not depend upon the affirmative intention of the parties. It is a child of the law; it annexes itself to the contract because of the very nature of the transaction. The judicial process has recognized a right to recover damages for personal injuries arising from a breach of that warranty. The disclaimer of the implied warranty and exclusion of all obligations except those specifically assumed by the express warranty signify a studied effort to frustrate that protection. True, the Sales Act authorizes agreements between buyer and seller qualifying the warranty obligations. But quite obviously the Legislature contemplated lawful stipulations (which are determined by the circumstances of a particular case) arrived at freely by parties of relatively equal bargaining strength. The lawmakers did not authorize the automobile manufacturer to use its grossly disproportionate bargaining power to relieve itself from liability and to impose on the ordinary buyer, who in effect has no real freedom of choice, the grave danger of injury to himself and others that attends the sale of such a dangerous instrumentality as a defectively made automobile. In the framework of this case, illuminated as it is by the facts and the many decisions noted, we are of the opinion that Chrysler's attempted disclaimer of an implied warranty of merchantability and of the obligations arising therefrom is so inimical to the public good as to compel an adjudication of its invalidity.

III. The Dealer's Implied Warranty

The principles that have been expounded as to the obligation of the manufacturer apply with equal force to the separate express warranty of the dealer. . . .

. . .

For the reasons set forth in Part I hereof, we conclude that the disclaimer of an implied warranty of merchantability by the dealer, as well as the attempted elimination of all obligations other than replacement of defective parts, are violative of public policy and void.

4. Toward Modern Products Liability Law

Henningsen represented an important step toward what became modern products liability law. But the decision was grounded on contract principles, with all of the attendant requirements of that area of law. The next two cases illustrate how products liability became largely the province of tort law.

Escola v. Coca Cola Bottling Co. of Fresno

150 P.2d 436 (Cal. 1944)

GIBSON, Chief Justice.

Plaintiff, a waitress in a restaurant, was injured when a bottle of Coca Cola broke in her hand. She alleged that defendant company, which had bottled and delivered the alleged defective bottle to her employer, was negligent in selling 'bottles containing said beverage which on account of excessive pressure of gas or by reason of some defect in the bottle was dangerous . . . and likely to explode.' This appeal is from a judgment upon a jury verdict in favor of plaintiff.

. . .

Although it is not clear in this case whether the explosion was caused by an excessive charge or a defect in the glass there is a sufficient showing that neither cause would ordinarily have been present if due care had been used. Further, defendant had exclusive control over both the charging and inspection of the bottles. Accordingly, all the requirements necessary to entitle plaintiff to rely on the doctrine of res ipsa loquitur to supply an inference of negligence are present.

It is true that defendant presented evidence tending to show that it exercised considerable precaution by carefully regulating and checking the pressure in the bottles and by making visual inspections for defects in the glass at several stages during the bottling process. It is well settled, however, that when a defendant produces evidence to rebut the inference of negligence which arises upon application of the doctrine of res ipsa loquitur, it is ordinarily a question of fact for the jury to determine whether the inference has been dispelled.

The judgment is affirmed.

TRAYNOR, Justice, concurring in the judgment

I concur in the judgment, but I believe the manufacturer's negligence should no longer be singled out as the basis of a plaintiff's right to recover in cases like the present one. In my opinion it should now be recognized that a manufacturer incurs an absolute liability when an article that he has placed on the market, knowing that it is to be used without inspection, proves to have a defect that causes injury to human beings. *MacPherson v. Buick Motor Co.* established the principle, recognized by this court, that irrespective of privity of contract, the manufacturer is responsible for an injury caused by such an article to any person who comes in lawful contact with it. In these cases the source of the manufacturer's liability was his negligence in the manufacturing process or in the inspection of component parts supplied by others. Even if there is no negligence, however, public policy demands that responsibility be fixed wherever it will most effectively reduce the hazards to life and health inherent in defective products that reach the market. It is evident that the manufacturer can anticipate some hazards and guard against the recurrence of others, as the public cannot. Those who suffer injury from defective products are unprepared to meet its consequences. The cost of an injury and the loss of time or health may be an overwhelming misfortune to the person injured, and a needless one, for the risk of injury can be insured by the manufacturer and distributed among the public as a cost of doing business. It is to the public interest to discourage the marketing of products having defects that are a menace to the public. If such products nevertheless find their way into the market it is to the public interest to place the responsibility for whatever injury they may cause upon the manufacturer, who, even if he is not negligent in the manufacture of the product, is responsible for its reaching the market. However intermittently such injuries may occur and however haphazardly they may strike, the risk of their occurrence is a constant risk and a general one. Against such a risk there should be general and constant protection and the manufacturer is best situated to afford such protection.

The injury from a defective product does not become a matter of indifference because the defect arises from causes other than the negligence of the manufacturer, such as negligence of a submanufacturer of a component part whose defects could not be revealed by inspection, or unknown causes that even by the device of res ipsa loquitur cannot be classified as negligence of the manufacturer. The inference of negligence may be dispelled by an affirmative showing of proper care. If the evidence against the fact inferred is "clear, positive, uncontradicted, and of such a nature that it can not rationally be disbelieved, the court must instruct the jury that the nonexistence of the fact has been established as a matter of law." Blank v. Coffin, 20 Cal.2d 457, 461, 126 P.2d 868, 870. An injured person, however, is not ordinarily in a position to refute such evidence or identify the cause of the defect, for he can hardly be familiar with the manufacturing process as the manufacturer himself is. In leaving it to the jury to decide whether the inference has been dispelled, regardless of the evidence against it, the negligence rule approaches the rule of strict liability. It is needlessly circuitous to make negligence the basis of recovery and impose what is in reality liability without negligence. If public policy demands that a manufacturer of goods be responsible for their quality regardless of negligence there is no reason not to fix that responsibility openly.

. . .

The retailer, even though not equipped to test a product, is under an absolute liability to his customer, for the implied warranties of fitness for proposed use and merchantable quality include a warranty of safety of the product. This warranty is not necessarily a contractual one, for public policy requires that the buyer be insured at the seller's expense against injury. The courts recognize, however, that the retailer cannot bear the burden of this warranty, and allow him to recoup any losses by means of the warranty of safety attending the wholesaler's or manufacturer's sale to him. Such a procedure, however, is needlessly circuitous and engenders wasteful litigation. Much would be gained if the injured person could base his action directly on the manufacturer's warranty.

. . .

As handicrafts have been replaced by mass production with its great markets and transportation facilities, the close relationship between the producer and consumer of a product has been altered. Manufacturing processes, frequently valuable secrets, are ordinarily either inaccessible to or beyond the ken of the general public. The consumer no longer has means or skill enough to investigate for himself the soundness of a product, even when it is not contained in a sealed package, and his erstwhile vigilance has been lulled by the steady efforts of manufacturers to build up confidence by advertising and marketing devices such as trade-marks. Consumers no longer approach products warily but accept them on faith, relying on the reputation of the manufacturer or the trade mark. Manufacturers have sought to justify that faith by increasingly high standards of inspection and a readiness to make good on defective products by way of replacements and refunds. The manufacturer's obligation to the consumer must keep pace with the changing relationship between them; it cannot be escaped because the marketing of a product has become so complicated as to require one or more intermediaries. Certainly there is greater reason to impose liability on the manufacturer than on the retailer who is but a conduit of a product that he is not himself able to test.

The manufacturer's liability should, of course, be defined in terms of the safety of the product in normal and proper use, and should not extend to injuries that cannot be traced to the product as it reached the market.

Greenman v. Yuba Power Products, Inc.

377 P.2d 897 (Cal. 1963)

Plaintiff brought this action for damages against the retailer and the manufacturer of a Shopsmith, a combination power tool that could be used as a saw, drill, and wood lathe. He saw a Shopsmith demonstrated by the retailer and studied a brochure prepared by the manufacturer. He decided he wanted a Shopsmith for his home workshop, and his wife bought and gave him one for Christmas in 1955. In 1957 he bought the necessary attachments to use the Shopsmith as a lathe for turning a large piece of wood he wished to make into a chalice. After he had worked on the piece of wood several times without difficulty, it suddenly flew out of the machine and struck him on the forehead, inflicting serious injuries. About ten and a half months later, he gave the retailer and the manufacturer written notice of claimed breaches of warranties and filed a complaint against them alleging such breaches and negligence.

After a trial before a jury, the court ruled that there was no evidence that the retailer was negligent or had breached any express warranty and that the manufacturer was not liable for the breach of any implied warranty. Accordingly, it submitted to the jury only the cause of action alleging breach of implied warranties against the retailer and the causes of action alleging negligence and breach of express warranties against the manufacturer. The jury returned a verdict for the retailer against plaintiff and for plaintiff against the manufacturer in the amount of $65,000. The trial court denied the manufacturer's motion for a new trial and entered judgment on the verdict. The manufacturer and plaintiff appeal. Plaintiff seeks a reversal of the part of the judgment in favor of the retailer, however, only in the event that the part of the judgment against the manufacturer is reversed.

Plaintiff introduced substantial evidence that his injuries were caused by defective design and construction of the Shopsmith. His expert witnesses testified that inadequate set screws were used to hold parts of the machine together so that normal vibration caused the tailstock of the lathe to move away from the piece of wood being turned permitting it to fly out of the lathe. They also testified that there were other more positive ways of fastening the parts of the machine together, the use of which would have prevented the accident. The jury could therefore reasonably have concluded that the manufacturer negligently constructed the Shopsmith. The jury could also reasonably have concluded that statements in the manufacturer's brochure were untrue, that they constituted express warranties, and that plaintiff's injuries were caused by their breach.

The manufacturer contends, however, that plaintiff did not give it notice of breach of warranty within a reasonable time and that therefore his cause of action for breach of warranty is barred by section 1769 of the Civil Code.

...

[T]o impose strict liability on the manufacturer under the circumstances of this case, it was not necessary for plaintiff to establish an express warranty as defined in ... the Civil Code. A manufacturer is strictly liable in tort when an article he places on the market, knowing that it is to be used without inspection for defects, proves to have a defect that causes injury to a human being. Recognized first in the case of unwholesome food products, such liability has now been extended to a variety of other products that create as great or greater hazards if defective. (Peterson v. Lamb Rubber Co., 54 Cal.2d 339, 347, 5 Cal.Rptr. 863, 353 P.2d 575 (grinding wheel); ... Gottsdanker v. Cutter Laboratories, 182 Cal.App.2d App.2d 602, 607, 6 Cal.Rptr. 320, 79 A.L.R.2d 290 (vaccine); McQuaide v. Bridgport Brass Co., D.C., 190 F.Supp. 252, 254 (insect spray); Bowles v. Zimmer Manufacturing Co., 7 Cir., 277 F.2d 868, 875, 76 A.L.R.2d 120 (surgical pin); ... Henningsen v. Bloomfield Motors, Inc., 32 N.J. 358, 161 A.2d 69, 76–84, 75 A.L.R.2d 1 (automobile); Hinton v. Republic Aviation Corporation, D.C., 180 F.Supp. 31, 33 (airplane).).

Although in these cases strict liability has usually been based on the theory of an express or implied warranty running from the manufacturer to the plaintiff, the abandonment of the requirement of a contract between them, the recognition that the liability is not assumed by agreement but imposed by law and the refusal to permit the manufacturer to define the scope of its own responsibility for defective products make clear that the liability is not one governed by the law of contract warranties but by the law of strict liability in tort. Accordingly, rules defining and governing warranties that were developed to meet the needs of commercial transactions cannot properly be invoked to govern the manufacturer's liability to those injured by their defective products unless those rules also serve the purposes for which such liability is imposed.

We need not recanvass the reasons for imposing strict liability on the manufacturer. They have been fully articulated in the cases cited above. The purpose of such liability is to insure that the costs of injuries resulting from defective products are borne by the manufacturers that put such products on the market rather than by the injured persons who are powerless to protect themselves. Sales warranties serve this purpose fitfully at best. In the present case, for example, plaintiff was able to plead and prove an express warranty only because he read and relied on the representations of the Shopsmith's ruggedness contained in the manufacturer's brochure. Implicit in the machine's presence on the market, however, was a representation that it would safely do the jobs for which it was built. Under these circumstances, it should not be controlling whether plaintiff selected the machine because of the statements in the brochure, or because of the machine's own appearance of excellence that belied the defect lurking beneath the surface, or because he merely assumed that it would safely do the jobs it was built to do. It should not be controlling whether the details of the sales from manufacturer to retailer and from retailer to plaintiff's wife were such that one or more of the implied warranties of the sales act arose. "The remedies of injured consumers ought not to be made to depend upon the intricacies of the law of sales." (Ketterer v. Armour & Co., D.C., 200 F. 322, 323; Klein v. Duchess Sandwich which Co., 14 Cal.2d 272, 282, 93 P.2d 799.) To establish the manufacturer's liability it was sufficient that plaintiff proved that he was injured while using the Shopsmith in a way it was intended to be used as a result of a defect in design and manufacture of which plaintiff was not aware that made the Shopsmith unsafe for its intended use.

Problem 14.2. Mary's grandmother, Mildred, was injured in California in when the blade of a steak knife she had just purchased from a local retailer and was using for the first time broke away from the handle, causing Mildred to slice her finger. Mildred was exercising reasonable care at the time of the accident. Her lawyer suspects that there may have been negligence in the manufacturing process, but is skeptical about the ability to prove it at trial. When Mildred purchased her set of steak knives, the store had her sign a form acknowledging that the store had disclaimed any and all warranties, express or implied.

(a) Would Mildred's inability to establish negligence on the part of the manufacturer prevent her from recovering for her injury following *Greenman*?

(b) Assuming Mildred could assert a potentially viable claim against the manufacturer, what would the effect of the retailer's warranty disclaimer be on Mildred's ability to pursue a claim against the retailer?

5. Modern Products Liability Law

The rest of the chapter will cover the various rules regarding liability for defective products. For now, it's important to note that there are significant differences among the states in terms of the controlling rules regarding products liability. But most modern products liability statutes and common law rules are based on some combination of the § 402A test from the *Restatement (Second) of Torts*, the *Restatement (Third) of Torts*, and special rules limiting the reach of products liability claims.

a. The § 402A Test

Decisions like *Henningsen* and *Greenman* influenced the development of the *Restatement (Second) of Torts'* approach to products liability law:

> (1) One who sells any product in a defective condition unreasonably dangerous to the user or consumer or to his property is subject to liability for physical harm thereby caused to the ultimate user or consumer, or to his property, if
>
> (a) the seller is engaged in the business of selling such a product, and
>
> (b) it is expected to and does reach the user or consumer without substantial change in the condition in which it is sold.

Restatement (Second) of Torts § 402A. Section 402A announces a rule of strict liability. A seller is liable even if the seller "has exercised all possible care in the preparation and sale of his product" and if privity between the buyer and the defendant is lacking. *Id.* § 402A(2).

b. The Restatement (Third) of Torts Approach

The *Restatement (Third) of Torts* expands upon the *Second Restatement.* The most noteworthy difference between the two for now is that the *Third Restatement* identifies three different types of product liability claims: manufacturing defects, design defects, and information (or warning) defects. The rest of the chapter will cover these distinctions in much greater detail.

c. Special Products Liability Rules

States have adopted a wide variety of products liability statutes and special common law rules governing defective products. Before any of the special products liability rules are implicated, however, the seller must be "engaged in the business of selling" the product. The "occasional or casual" seller of a product is not a proper defendant for purposes of the rule described above (although some other tort theory, like misrepresentation, might be appropriate). *See* Restatement (Third) of Torts: Products Liability § 1, cmt. c (1998). In addition, special products liability rules only apply to defective *products.* A "product" is "tangible personal property distributed commercially for use or consumption." *Id.* § 19(a). Where the essence of a transaction involves the provision of a service rather than the purchase of a product, the plaintiff's theory of recovery is something other than a products liability claim. *See* Cafazzo v. Central Medical Health Services, Inc., 668 A.2d 521 (Pa. 1995) (concluding physician was not a "seller" for purposes of strict products liability claim where physician implanted an allegedly defective prosthesis).

Generally speaking, the seller of a used product is not subject to the same rules as the seller of a new product. One who sells a used defective product may be held liable where the seller fails to exercise reasonable care (such as by failing to conduct a reasonable inspection that would have detected the defect). The seller of used goods may also be subject to liability where a manufacturing defect exists "and the seller's marketing of the product would cause a reasonable person in the position of the buyer to expect the used product to present no greater risk of defect than if the product were new." Restatement (Third) of Torts: Products Liability § 8. But generally, the special products liability rules only apply to the distribution of new products.

Another issue that sometimes emerges is who qualifies as a potential plaintiff. Some jurisdictions limit coverage to foreseeable users or consumers of defective products who are injured. *See* Bourne v. Marty Gilman, Inc., 452 F.3d 632, 635 (7th Cir. 2006) (referencing Ind. Code § 34-20-2-1). In some cases, the injured party is technically neither a user nor a consumer of the product in the traditional sense. For example, an employee who comes home with asbestos on his clothing may cause injury to a family member who inhales the asbestos. The family member is an innocent bystander, not a user or consumer of the product. Nonetheless, courts often apply duty or scope of risk analysis in such cases and analyze whether harm to the injured party was foreseeable. *See* Martin v. Cincinnati Gas and Elec. Co., 561 F.3d 439 (6th Cir. 2009).

Special damages rules may also apply to products liability claims. Some states impose caps on recovery for noneconomic or punitive damages. The most noteworthy issue regarding damages in products liability cases is the economic loss rule. If a car engine explodes due to a defect and the owner is injured, the owner may have a tort claim based on a products liability theory. If the exploding car damages some other property of the owner, the owner may also have a products liability claim for that damage. If, however, the car explodes and only the car itself is damaged, the owner's claim sounds in contract under the majority approach, not tort. *See* Giddings & Lewis, Inc. v. Industrial Risk Insurers, 348 S.W.3d 729 (Ky. 2011). Pure economic loss or standalone harm to a product itself is the domain of contract law.

Problem 14.3. Mary's mother, Millie, was grilling steaks on her back porch recently when the grill caught on fire due to a defect. A nearby table and chairs also caught on fire and were destroyed. Millie suffered injuries as well. Millie purchased the grill from a local hardware store that regularly stocks grills produced by the manufacturer, but only sells a few grills a month; most of the store's sales come from other items. Could Millie recover on a products liability theory from the hardware store for damage caused by the defective grill? If so, for what harm could she recover?

B. Manufacturing Defects

Manufacturing defects are the easiest type of defect case to conceptualize. A manufacturing defect occurs "when the product departs from its intended design." Restatement (Third) of Torts: Products Liability § 2(a). "The exploding bottle in

Escola v. Coca Cola Bottling Co. is the prototypical example of a manufacturing defect." Webb v. Special Elec. Co., Inc., 370 P.3d 1022, 1029–30 (Cal. 2016). The power tool from *Greenman* is another example. The first case below deals with the requirements of the prima facie case. The second deals with a specific issue of proof of a defect.

Estate of Pinkham v. Cargill, Inc.

55 A.3d 1 (Maine 2012)

JABAR, J.

I. Background

Viewing the evidence in the light most favorable to the non-prevailing party, the summary judgment record supports the following facts. On or about August 23, 2004, at about 9:00 p.m., Stanley Pinkham consumed a hot turkey sandwich during his break as a line cook at Dysart's Truck Stop and Restaurant. Cargill manufactured the boneless turkey product in Pinkham's sandwich, and the kitchen staff at Dysart's occasionally found pieces of bone in that turkey product. In the middle of or immediately after eating the sandwich, Pinkham experienced severe and sudden pain in his upper abdominal area and thought that he might be suffering from a heart attack. Shortly thereafter, he was taken by ambulance to Eastern Maine Medical Center. At the hospital, Donald M. Clough, M.D., initially evaluated Pinkham and determined that he most likely had an "esophageal tear or perforation."

Unable to locate the injury in a laparotomy procedure, Clough called in Scott D. Stern, D.O., a specialist in gastroenterology, to perform an upper endoscopy. Stern discovered a small perforation in Pinkham's esophagus as well as a small food bolus containing fragments of bony or cartilaginous material. Although Stern removed the food substance from the area of the esophageal perforation, he did not remove any food product or other substance from Pinkham's body. After Stern located the site of the injury, Clough called in Felix Hernandez, M.D., to perform thoracic surgery to repair the esophageal perforation.

During his deposition as well as in a letter addressed to Pinkham's Nurse Case Manager, Stern noted that there were small, white cartilaginous fragments that appeared to be bone fragments in the food bolus, measuring no more than one or two millimeters in size. When questioned at his deposition about what caused Pinkham's esophageal injury, Stern agreed that it was a "perforation secondary to a foreign body." Stern noted that even if Pinkham had a pre-existing condition that made his esophagus more susceptible to injury, an additional factor would most likely have to be present for this type of injury to occur. He explained that the additional factor could be aggressive retching or vomiting, or a foreign body. Finally, Stern said that, aside from a foreign body or aggressive retching or vomiting, he could not think of any other cause of an esophageal perforation.

On May 13, 2009, the Estate filed a complaint naming Cargill and Poultry Products of Maine, Inc., as defendants. The complaint requested relief for Pinkham's esophageal injury, citing Maine's law establishing liability for "[d]efective or unreasonably dangerous goods" as the basis for Cargill's liability. 14 M.R.S. § 221 (2011). On October 13, 2010, Cargill filed a motion for summary judgment and a statement of material facts. The Estate opposed the motion for summary judgment and filed an opposing statement of material facts, to which Cargill filed a response. [The court granted Cargill's motion.]

II. Discussion

A. "Reasonable Expectation" Test

We have not yet had the opportunity to decide what test should apply to strict liability claims involving food products. Our only decision addressing liability for an injury caused by a food product was decided in 1967, *Kobeckis*, 225 A.2d 418, six years before Maine's strict liability statute addressing "[d]effective or unreasonably dangerous goods," 14 M.R.S. § 221, was enacted. P.L.1973, ch. 466, § 1 (effective Oct. 3, 1973). In that case, we held that live trichinae in raw pork was a "natural . . . attribute" of pork and therefore the merchant was not liable for injuries cause by the trichinae.

Currently, there are two tests that courts apply when faced with a defective food product claim. The traditional test, and the one most similar to what we used in *Kobeckis*, is called the "foreign-natural" doctrine. The United States District Court for the District of Nebraska best defined this test: "The 'foreign-natural' doctrine provides there is no liability if the food product is natural to the ingredients; whereas, liability exists if the substance is foreign to the ingredients, and the manufacturer can be held liable for injuries." Newton v. Standard Candy Co., No. 8:06CV242, 2008 WL 752599, at *2, 2008 U.S. Dist. LEXIS 21886, at *6 (D.Neb. Mar. 19, 2008). Likewise, the Supreme Court of Illinois best defined the "reasonable expectation" test: "The reasonable expectation test provides that, regardless whether a substance in a food product is natural to an ingredient thereof, liability will lie for injuries caused by the substance where the consumer of the product would not reasonably have expected to find the substance in the product." Jackson v. Nestle-Beich, Inc., 147 Ill.2d 408, 168 Ill.Dec. 147, 589 N.E.2d 547, 548 (1992).

We have previously noted that Maine's strict liability statute[7] was fashioned after the *Restatement (Second) of Torts* § 402A (1965). The Restatement comments define

7. Maine's strict liability statute states:

> One who sells any goods or products in a defective condition unreasonably dangerous to the user or consumer or to his property is subject to liability for physical harm thereby caused to a person whom the manufacturer, seller or supplier might reasonably have expected to use, consume or be affected by the goods, or to his property, if the seller is engaged in the business of selling such a product and it is expected to and does reach the user or consumer without significant change in the condition in which it is sold. This section applies although the seller has exercised all possible care in the preparation and

"[d]efective condition" as a product that is "in a condition not contemplated by the ultimate consumer." Restatement (Second) of Torts §402A cmt. g. The comments also define "[u]nreasonably dangerous": "The article sold must be dangerous to an extent beyond that which would be contemplated by the ordinary consumer who purchases it, with the ordinary knowledge common to the community as to its characteristics." *Id.* cmt. i.

These comments to the Restatement are consistent with the "reasonable expectation" test. Both the Restatement and the test consider the condition of the product as it compares to the ordinary consumer's reasonable expectation for that product.

With this framework in mind, we adopt the "reasonable expectation" test in Maine, to be used in strict liability cases alleging a defective food product pursuant to section 221. We conclude that, in enacting section 221, the Legislature intended to align itself with the Restatement's objectives, and therefore the Legislature intended the "reasonable expectation" test to be used in applying the language of section 221.

B. Genuine Dispute as to Material Facts

With the proper test for evaluating the Estate's strict liability claim established, we can now turn our attention to whether the Estate presented enough evidence to create a genuine issue of material fact, and therefore survive summary judgment and proceed to trial. We conclude that the Estate did present sufficient evidence to create a genuine issue of material fact and to establish a prima facie case for products liability.

The Estate presented evidence that creates a genuine issue of material fact as to whether the turkey product caused Pinkham's injury. Stern testified that he believed that the injury was a "perforation secondary to a foreign body." He opined that even if Pinkham had a pre-existing condition making him more susceptible to an esophageal injury, a second factor—such as a foreign body, retching, or vomiting—would still most likely need to be present to cause Pinkham's injury. The record demonstrates that the "foreign body" was either a small piece of bone or cartilage, or a larger piece of bone. There is direct evidence of the presence of the smaller pieces of bone or cartilage: Stern actually saw them. There is no direct evidence of a larger piece of bone, but the summary judgment record does contain indirect evidence that a larger piece of bone could have been present in the turkey product Pinkham consumed, but may have passed, undetected, from Pinkham's throat. The indirect evidence is found in the deposition of a Dysart's employee, who testified that larger pieces of bone had regularly been discovered in Cargill's "boneless" turkey product in the past, and in the expert deposition testimony of John F. Erkkinen, M.D., who acknowledged that a larger bone piece could have passed through Pinkham's esophagus and into his stomach.

> sale of his product and the user or consumer has not bought the product from or entered into any contractual relation with the seller.

14 M.R.S. §221 (2011).

Whether a consumer would reasonably expect to find a particular item in a food product is normally a question of fact that is left to a jury. The Superior Court noted this, but nonetheless decided that a food bolus containing one-to-two-millimeter bone fragments is not defective as a matter of law. In making this determination, the court erred. The question of whether a consumer would reasonably expect to find a turkey bone or a bone fragment large and/or sharp enough to cause an esophageal perforation in a "boneless" turkey product is one best left to the fact-finder. At trial, the jury will have an opportunity to determine whether a foreign body in the turkey product caused Pinkham's injury, what the foreign body was, and whether Cargill is liable as a result.

C. Inference of Defect

The Restatement (Third) of Torts: Products Liability § 3[11] provides for the possibility of an inference that the product was defective in the absence of a known specific defect. Once again, we are faced with a Restatement provision that we have not explicitly adopted. The United States District Court for the District of Maine has twice inferred that we would adopt this provision when given the opportunity. We acknowledge the accuracy of the District Court's prediction and hold that, on remand, the Estate may seek recovery pursuant to this provision.

Whether there is proof that an injury was not "solely the result of causes other than [a] product defect existing at the time of sale or distribution," Restatement (Third) of Torts: Prods. Liab. § 3(b) is a question of fact for a jury to decide. Even without proof of a specific defect, there is evidence that could lead to the inference that the turkey product was defective. Stern opined that dysphagia or bad reflux alone would not cause an esophageal perforation; he stated that something else most likely would have to occur such as aggressive retching or vomiting, or the presence of a foreign body. Because Cargill offered no evidence that aggressive retching or vomiting occurred, the only other likely cause of Pinkham's esophageal perforation was a foreign body in the food that Pinkham digested. Cargill does have evidence that Pinkham had been complaining of difficulty swallowing in the weeks before he ate the turkey sandwich, and it may be successful in preventing the Estate from establishing that the injury occurred as a result of a defect in its turkey product. Given the record presented at summary judgment, however, Pinkham's estate is entitled to the opportunity to have a fact-finder decide whether it should receive the benefit of the inference.

---

11. Section 3 of the Restatement provides:

> It may be inferred that the harm sustained by the plaintiff was caused by a product defect existing at the time of sale or distribution, without proof of a specific defect, when the incident that harmed the plaintiff:
>
> (a) was of a kind that ordinarily occurs as a result of product defect; and
>
> (b) was not, in the particular case, solely the result of causes other than product defect existing at the time of sale or distribution.

Restatement (Third) of Torts: Prods. Liab. § 3 (1998).

Under these facts, section 3(b) of the Restatement permits the inference that the harm sustained by Pinkham was caused by a product defect and that the injury sustained was of a kind that ordinarily occurs as a result of a product defect and was not solely the result of causes other than the defect.

Notes

The ordinary consumer expectation test/reasonable expectation. The test embodied in comment i to Restatement (Second) of Torts §402A as referenced in *Estate of Pinkham* remains the standard test in manufacturing defect cases.

The foreign-natural doctrine. As *Estate of Pinkham* explains, a good number of jurisdictions rely upon the foreign-natural distinction in deciding manufacturing defects involving objects in food. *See* Mexicali Rose v. Superior Court, 822 P.2d 1292 (Cal. 1992) (sustaining defendant's motion to dismiss where the plaintiff swallowed a chicken bone in an enchilada). The rationale is that "[i]f the injury-producing substance is natural to the preparation of the food served, it can be said that it was reasonably expected by its very nature." *Id.* at 1301. Which of the two competing rules is most in line with the justifications for strict liability?

Malfunction doctrine. The rule discussed in *Estate of Pinkham* regarding an inference of defect is sometimes referred to as the "malfunction doctrine." Farmer v. International Harvester Co., 553 P.2d 1306, 1311 (Idaho 1976) ("proof of malfunction is circumstantial evidence of a defect in a product since a product will not ordinarily malfunction within the reasonable contemplation of a consumer in the absence of defect"). The determination of whether a product malfunctioned due to a defect ordinarily involves a consideration of circumstantial evidence, including "the age of a product and the length of its use, the severity of its use, the state of its repair, its expected useful life and the fact that the source of the malfunction is an enclosed system relatively immune from tampering or alteration once the product leaves the manufacturer's control." *Id.* at 1312.

Liability up the chain of distribution. Note that under Maine's test (which is the same as the *Restatement* test), the product must be in a defective condition at the time it leaves the defendant's control before liability may attach. There may be multiple parties involved in a distribution chain, so there may potentially be multiple defendants in a products liability action. For example, in *Estate of Pinkham*, the plaintiff sued the manufacturer of the sandwich *and* Poultry Products of Maine, the wholesale supplier of the turkey. Some states place limits on the ability of a plaintiff to recover from a retailer in limited situations, such as through adoption of the "sealed container doctrine." *See* N.C. Gen. Stat. §99B-2(a) ("No product liability action, except an action for breach of express warranty, shall be commenced or maintained against any seller when the product was acquired and sold by the seller in a sealed container or when the product was acquired and sold by the seller under circumstances in which the seller was afforded no reasonable opportunity to inspect the product in such a manner that would have or should have, in the exercise of reasonable care, revealed the existence of the condition complained of.").

Piltch v. Ford Motor Co.

778 F.3d 628 (7th Cir. 2015)

BAUER, Circuit Judge.

Howard Piltch and Barbara Nelson-Piltch (the "Piltches") were traveling in their 2003 Mercury Mountaineer in February 2007 when they hit a patch of black ice, causing the car to slide off the road and into a wall. Upon impact, none of the car's air bags deployed and both Piltches were injured. [The Piltches were involved in a previous car accident in 2006 in which the air bags did not deploy. Following the accident, the Piltches had the vehicle repaired. They did not confirm whether the restraint control module, which monitors a crash and decides whether to deploy air bags, was reset during or after repairs after the 2006 collision. But Mr. Piltch explained that it was his understanding that it had been reset. In 2009, following the second accident in 2007, the Piltches sold the Mountaineer. The buyer happened to be a mechanic who reprogrammed the vehicle's blackbox, wiping any data that might remain from the crash.] The Piltches filed the present action in Indiana state court against Ford Motor Company ("Ford") in 2010, alleging the vehicle was defective under Indiana law. Ford removed the action to federal court, and shortly thereafter moved for summary judgment. On March 28, 2014, the district court granted Ford's summary judgment motion holding that, without expert testimony, the Piltches could not create an issue of fact as to proximate cause.

. . . .

. . . To demonstrate a manufacturing defect, the plaintiff must show that "the product . . . deviates from its intended design." [Hathaway v. Cintas Corp. Serv., Inc., 903 F.Supp.2d 669, 673 (N.D. Ind. 2012)] (applying Indiana law and citing *Restatement (Third) of Torts: Products Liability* § 2(a) (1988)). The Piltches contend that the Mountaineer's owner's manual establishes the intended design of the air bags, and that the state of the air bags during and after the 2007 collision indicates a departure from that intended design.

[T]he Piltches argue that this evidence, taken together, raises a genuine issue of material fact as to defect even in the absence of expert testimony. In *Cansler*, the court found that the plaintiff designated sufficient circumstantial evidence on the issue of whether the air bags in question were defective, rendering expert testimony unnecessary to create a triable issue of fact. The circumstantial evidence included the plaintiff's testimony about the speed of the car just before the collision and a mechanic's testimony about the damage to the vehicle after the collision. Though not an expert, the mechanic was deemed a "skilled witness" who could testify to opinions or inferences based on facts within his personal knowledge, in addition to his observations. The mechanic testified that he had almost two decades of experience examining automobile wrecks with deployed air bags. After examining the plaintiff's car three to four days after the accident, he opined that "based on his observations of other vehicles that had been in accidents severe enough to cause front frame damage [like the plaintiff's], the air bag in [the plaintiff's] Corvette should have deployed." The plaintiff also presented the car's owner's manual, which detailed the conditions that would warrant air bag deployment, including the threshold velocity of impact that would trigger deployment.

[T]he Piltches do not provide testimony about the accident other than their own. We also do not have testimony on the state of the car following the collision. This is especially problematic considering the Piltches preserved neither the Mountaineer nor, critically, the Mountaineer's blackbox, which could have contained details about the crash. Without this information, and without an accident reconstruction expert or otherwise "skilled witness" to fill in some of these blanks, a layperson would be unable to discern whether the circumstances of the crash should have triggered air bag deployment or not. Furthermore, the presentation of the Mountaineer's owner's manual does nothing to elevate this evidence out of the realm of speculation. [T]he conditions for air bag deployment in the Mountaineer's manual are written in broad generalities. The manual merely states that the air bags are designed to activate when the vehicle sustains sufficient longitudinal deceleration. However, it neither defines "sufficient," nor specifies the precise impact speeds at which the air bags are expected to deploy.

Problem 14.4. Mary purchased a glass "oven proof" baking dish from Best Homes, a retailer of baking products. The dish was manufactured by Good Gourmet, Inc. The dish is advertised as "oven proof" because it is designed to minimize the stresses put into the glass by the rapid changes in temperature that the glass undergoes in its normal usage. Mary alleges that she had used the dish for seven months when the dish exploded when she removed it from a heated oven. A piece of glass struck and cut her arm.

(a) Who would be proper defendants if Mary chose to bring a products liability action?

(b) What would be the elements of a prima facie case in Mary's manufacturing defect case?

(c) Could Mary establish that a product defect caused her injuries based solely on the facts presented?

(d) If you represented the defendant, what evidence or information would you seek to obtain in order disprove the existence of a manufacturing defect?

C. Design Defects

Problem 14.5. Daniela is a licensed cosmetologist with 15 years of experience. She recent purchased a pair of Q-36 scissors, manufactured by TrimLine, Inc. The Q-36 design replaced Trimline's Q-35 design, which had been produced for years. While cutting a customer's hair, the tip of the blade accidentally pierced and became embedded in Daniela's wrist/forearm area. She continues to suffer reduced mobility in her wrist and incurred $50,000 in medical expenses. Consider her situation as you read the material below.

As products liability law developed, the focus was originally on manufacturing defects. As one author has pointed out, the authors of the *Restatement (Second) of Torts* cited only manufacturing defect cases in support of the rule that appears in § 402A. Victor Schwartz, *The Restatement, Third, Torts: Products Liability: A Model of Fairness and Balance*, 10 Kan. J.L. & Pub. Policy 41, 42 (2000). But not all products liability cases involve products that depart from their intended design. In some cases, a product functions exactly in keeping with its design, but a user is still injured. In such cases, the plaintiff might be able to recover on the theory that the product was defective in terms of its basic design.

1. The Risk-Utility Test in General

It is virtually impossible to describe a majority rule with respect to design defect cases. There are too many variations and conflicting standards. However, the majority are based on or at least closely resemble the test articulated in section 2 of the *Restatement (Third) of Torts: Products Liability.* The series of cases below all originated in California and are included, in part, to present a snapshot of one jurisdiction's approach to the issue of design defects. They are also included as an example of the sort of risk-utility analysis ultimately adopted by the *Restatement (Third).*

Soule v. General Motors Corp.

882 P.2d 298 (Cal. 1994)

BAXTER, Justice.

Plaintiff's ankles were badly injured when her General Motors (GM) car collided with another vehicle. She sued GM, asserting that defects in her automobile allowed its left front wheel to break free, collapse rearward, and smash the floorboard into her feet. GM denied any defect and claimed that the force of the collision itself was the sole cause of the injuries. Expert witnesses debated the issues at length. Plaintiff prevailed at trial, and the Court of Appeal affirmed the judgment.

Facts

On the early afternoon of January 16, 1984, plaintiff was driving her 1982 Camaro in the southbound center lane of Bolsa Chica Road, an arterial street in Westminster. There was a slight drizzle, the roadway was damp, and apparently plaintiff was not wearing her seat belt. A 1972 Datsun, approaching northbound, suddenly skidded into the path of plaintiff's car. The Datsun's left rear quarter struck plaintiff's Camaro in an area near the left front wheel. Estimates of the vehicles' combined closing speeds on impact vary from 30 to 70 miles per hour.

The collision bent the Camaro's frame adjacent to the wheel and tore loose the bracket that attached the wheel assembly (specifically, the lower control arm) to the frame. As a result, the wheel collapsed rearward and inward. The wheel hit the underside of the "toe pan"—the slanted floorboard area beneath the pedals—causing the toe pan to crumple, or "deform," upward into the passenger compartment.

Plaintiff received a fractured rib and relatively minor scalp and knee injuries. Her most severe injuries were fractures of both ankles, and the more serious of these was the compound compression fracture of her left ankle. This injury never healed properly. In order to relieve plaintiff's pain, an orthopedic surgeon fused the joint. As a permanent result, plaintiff cannot flex her left ankle. She walks with considerable difficulty, and her condition is expected to deteriorate.

. . .

Plaintiff sued GM for her ankle injuries, asserting a theory of strict tort liability for a defective product. She claimed the severe trauma to her ankles was not a natural consequence of the accident, but occurred when the collapse of the Camaro's wheel caused the toe pan to crush violently upward against her feet. Plaintiff attributed the wheel collapse to a manufacturing defect, the substandard quality of the weld attaching the lower control arm bracket to the frame. She also claimed that the placement of the bracket, and the configuration of the frame, were defective designs because they did not limit the wheel's rearward travel in the event the bracket should fail.

[Plaintiff's experts opined that the failed bracket was a result of a manufacturing defect. GM's experts disputed this. The rest of the decision focuses on the design defect issue.]

. . . Plaintiff's experts also emphasized the alternative frame and bracket design used by the Ford Mustang of comparable model years. They asserted that the Mustang's design, unlike the Camaro's, provided protection against unlimited rearward travel of the wheel should a bracket assembly give way.

. . . Expert witnesses for GM . . . countered the assertions of defective design. GM asserted that the Camaro's bracket was overdesigned to withstand forces in excess of all expected uses. According to expert testimony adduced by GM, the Mustang's alternative frame and bracket configuration did not fit the Camaro's overall design goals and was not distinctly safer for all collision stresses to which the vehicle might be subjected. Indeed, one witness noted, at least one more recent Ford product had adopted the Camaro's design.

A second major thrust of GM's defense was that the force of the collision, rather than any product defect, was the sole cause of plaintiff's ankle injuries. Using the results of accident reconstruction, computer simulations, and actual crash tests, GM sought to prove that the probable collision force concentrated on the left front wheel of plaintiff's Camaro exceeded the "yield strength" of any feasible weld or design.

...

The court instructed the jury that a manufacturer is liable for "enhanced" injuries caused by a manufacturing or design defect in its product while the product is being used in a foreseeable way. Over GM's objection, the court gave the standard design defect instruction without modification. This instruction advised that a product is defective in design "if it fails to perform as safely as an ordinary consumer would expect when used in an intended or reasonably foreseeable manner *or* if there is a risk of danger inherent in the design which outweighs the benefit of the design." (Italics added.)

The jury was also told that in order to establish liability for a design defect under the "ordinary consumer expectations" standard, plaintiff must show (1) the manufacturer's product failed to perform as safely as an ordinary consumer would expect, (2) the defect existed when the product left the manufacturer's possession, (3) the defect was a "legal cause" of plaintiff's "enhanced injury," and (4) the product was used in a reasonably foreseeable manner.

...

In a series of special findings, the jury determined that the Camaro contained a defect (of unspecified nature) which was a "legal cause" of plaintiff's "enhanced injury." The jury further concluded that although plaintiff was guilty of comparative fault, her conduct was not a legal cause of her enhanced injuries. Plaintiff received an award of $1.65 million.

GM appealed. Among other things, it argued that the trial court erred by instructing on ordinary consumer expectations in a complex design-defect case, and by failing to give GM's special instruction on causation.

...

Discussion

1. Test for design defect.

A manufacturer, distributor, or retailer is liable in tort if a defect in the manufacture or design of its product causes injury while the product is being used in a reasonably foreseeable way. (*Cronin v. J.B.E. Olson Corp.* (1972) 8 Cal.3d 121, 126–130, 104 Cal.Rptr. 433, 501 P.2d 1153 [*Cronin*]; *Greenman v. Yuba Power Products, Inc.* (1963) 59 Cal.2d 57, 62, 27 Cal.Rptr. 697, 377 P.2d 897 [*Greenman*].) Because traffic accidents are foreseeable, vehicle manufacturers must consider collision safety when they design and build their products. Thus, whatever the cause of an accident, a vehicle's producer is liable for specific collision injuries that would not have occurred but for a manufacturing or design defect in the vehicle.

...

In *Barker v. Lull Engineering Co., supra*, 20 Cal.3d 413, 143 Cal.Rptr. 225, 573 P.2d 443 (*Barker*), the operator of a high-lift loader sued its manufacturer for injuries he received when the loader toppled during a lift on sloping ground. The operator alleged various design defects which made the loader unsafe to use on a slope.

... At a minimum, said *Barker*, a product is defective in design if it does fail to perform as safely as an ordinary consumer would expect. This principle, *Barker* asserted, acknowledges the relationship between strict tort liability for a defective product and the common law doctrine of warranty, which holds that a product's presence on the market includes an implied representation "'that it [will] safely do the jobs for which it was built.'"

However, *Barker* asserted, the *Restatement* had erred in proposing that a violation of ordinary consumer expectations was necessary for recovery on this ground. "As Professor Wade has pointed out, ... the expectations of the ordinary consumer cannot be viewed as the exclusive yardstick for evaluating design defectiveness because '[i]n many situations ... *the consumer would not know what to expect*, because he would have *no idea* how safe the product could be made.'" (20 Cal.3d at p. 430, 143 Cal.Rptr. 225, 573 P.2d 443, quoting Wade, *On the Nature of Strict Tort Liability for Products* (1973) 44 Miss.L.J. 825, 829, italics added.)

Thus, *Barker* concluded, "a product may be found defective in design, even if it satisfies ordinary consumer expectations, if through hindsight the jury determines that the product's design embodies 'excessive preventable danger,' or, in other words, if the jury finds that the risk of danger inherent in the challenged design outweighs the benefits of such design. *Barker* held that under this latter standard, "a jury may consider, among other relevant factors, the gravity of the danger posed by the challenged design, the likelihood that such danger would occur, the mechanical feasibility of a safer alternative design, the financial cost of an improved design, and the adverse consequences to the product and to the consumer that would result from an alternative design."

...

In *Barker*, we offered two alternative ways to prove a design defect, each appropriate to its own circumstances. The purposes, behaviors, and dangers of certain products are commonly understood by those who ordinarily use them. By the same token, the ordinary users or consumers of a product may have reasonable, widely accepted minimum expectations about the circumstances under which it should perform safely. Consumers govern their own conduct by these expectations, and products on the market should conform to them.

In some cases, therefore, "ordinary knowledge ... as to ... [the product's] characteristics" (Rest.2d Torts, supra, § 402A, com. i., p. 352) may permit an inference that the product did not perform as safely as it should. If the facts permit such a conclusion, and if the failure resulted from the product's design, a finding of defect is warranted without any further proof. The manufacturer may not defend a claim that a product's design failed to perform as safely as its ordinary consumers would expect by presenting expert evidence of the design's relative risks and benefits.

However, as we noted in *Barker*, a complex product, even when it is being used as intended, may often cause injury in a way that does not engage its ordinary consumers' reasonable minimum assumptions about safe performance. For example, the ordinary consumer of an automobile simply has "no idea" how it should perform in all foreseeable situations, or how safe it should be made against all foreseeable hazards.

An injured person is not foreclosed from proving a defect in the product's design simply because he cannot show that the reasonable minimum safety expectations of its ordinary consumers were violated. Under *Barker*'s alternative test, a product is still defective if its design embodies "excessive preventable danger," that is, unless "the benefits of the . . . design outweigh the risk of danger inherent in such design." But this determination involves technical issues of feasibility, cost, practicality, risk, and benefit which are "impossible" to avoid. In such cases, the jury must consider the manufacturer's evidence of competing design considerations, and the issue of design defect cannot fairly be resolved by standardless reference to the "expectations" of an "ordinary consumer."

As we have seen, the consumer expectations test is reserved for cases in which the everyday experience of the product's users permits a conclusion that the product's design violated minimum safety assumptions, and is thus defective regardless of expert opinion about the merits of the design. It follows that where the minimum safety of a product is within the common knowledge of lay jurors, expert witnesses may not be used to demonstrate what an ordinary consumer would or should expect. Use of expert testimony for that purpose would invade the jury's function and would invite circumvention of the rule that the risks and benefits of a challenged design must be carefully balanced whenever the issue of design defect goes beyond the common experience of the product's users.

By the same token, the jury may not be left free to find a violation of ordinary consumer expectations whenever it chooses. Unless the facts actually permit an inference that the product's performance did not meet the minimum safety expectations of its ordinary users, the jury must engage in the balancing of risks and benefits required by the second prong of *Barker.*

Accordingly, as *Barker* indicated, instructions are misleading and incorrect if they allow a jury to avoid this risk-benefit analysis in a case where it is required. Instructions based on the ordinary consumer expectations prong of *Barker* are not appropriate where, as a matter of law, the evidence would not support a jury verdict on that theory. Whenever that is so, the jury must be instructed solely on the alternative risk-benefit theory of design defect announced in *Barker.*

GM suggests that the consumer expectations test is improper whenever "crashworthiness," a complex product, or technical questions of causation are at issue. Because the variety of potential product injuries is infinite, the line cannot be drawn as clearly as GM proposes. But the fundamental distinction is not impossible to define. The crucial question in each individual case is whether the circumstances of the product's failure permit an inference that the product's design performed below the legitimate, commonly accepted minimum safety assumptions of its ordinary consumers.

GM argues at length that the consumer expectations test is an "unworkable, amorphic, fleeting standard" which should be entirely abolished as a basis for design defect. In GM's view, the test is deficient and unfair in several respects. First, it defies definition. Second, it focuses not on the objective condition of products, but on the subjective, unstable, and often unreasonable opinions of consumers. Third, it ignores the reality that ordinary consumers know little about how safe the complex products they use can or should be made. Fourth, it invites the jury to isolate the particular consumer, component, accident, and injury before it instead of considering whether the whole product fairly accommodates the competing expectations of all consumers in all situations. Fifth, it eliminates the careful balancing of risks and benefits which is essential to any design issue.

In its amicus curiae brief, the Product Liability Advisory Council, Inc. (Council) makes similar arguments. The Council proposes that all design defect claims be resolved under a single risk-benefit analysis geared to "reasonable safety."

We fully understand the dangers of improper use of the consumer expectations test. However, we cannot accept GM's insinuation that ordinary consumers lack any legitimate expectations about the minimum safety of the products they use. In particular circumstances, a product's design may perform so unsafely that the defect is apparent to the common reason, experience, and understanding of its ordinary consumers. In such cases, a lay jury is competent to make that determination.

Nor are we persuaded by the Council's proposal. In essence, it would reinvest product liability claims with the requirement of "unreasonable danger" that we rejected in *Cronin* and *Barker*.

When use of the consumer expectations test is limited as *Barker* intended, the principal concerns raised by GM and the Council are met. Within these limits, the test remains a workable means of determining the existence of design defect. We therefore find no compelling reason to overrule the consumer expectations prong of *Barker* at this late date, and we decline to do so.

Applying our conclusions to the facts of this case, however, we agree that the instant jury should not have been instructed on ordinary consumer expectations. Plaintiff's theory of design defect was one of technical and mechanical detail. It sought to examine the precise behavior of several obscure components of her car under the complex circumstances of a particular accident. The collision's exact speed, angle, and point of impact were disputed. It seems settled, however, that plaintiff's Camaro received a substantial oblique blow near the left front wheel, and that the adjacent frame members and bracket assembly absorbed considerable inertial force.

An ordinary consumer of automobiles cannot reasonably expect that a car's frame, suspension, or interior will be designed to remain intact in any and all accidents. Nor would ordinary experience and understanding inform such a consumer how safely an automobile's design should perform under the esoteric circumstances of the collision at issue here. Indeed, both parties assumed that quite complicated design considerations were at issue, and that expert testimony was necessary to illuminate these matters. Therefore, injection of ordinary consumer expectations into the design defect equation was improper.

We are equally persuaded, however, that the error was harmless, because it is not reasonably probable defendant would have obtained a more favorable result in its absence....

Here there were no instructions which specifically remedied the erroneous placement of the consumer expectations alternative before the jury. Moreover, plaintiff's counsel briefly reminded the jury that the instructions allowed it to find a design defect under either the consumer expectations or risk-benefit tests. However, the consumer expectations theory was never emphasized at any point. As previously noted, the case was tried on the assumption that the alleged design defect was a matter of technical debate. Virtually all the evidence and argument on design defect focused on expert evaluation of the strengths, shortcomings, risks, and benefits of the challenged design, as compared with a competitor's approach.

Neither plaintiff's counsel nor any expert witness on her behalf told the jury that the Camaro's design violated the safety expectations of the ordinary consumer. Nor did they suggest the jury should find such a violation regardless of its assessment of such competing design considerations as risk, benefit, feasibility, and cost. The jury never made any requests which hinted it was inclined to apply the consumer expectations test without regard to a weighing of risks and benefits.

Under these circumstances, we find it highly unlikely that a reasonable jury took that path. We see no reasonable probability that the jury disregarded the voluminous evidence on the risks and benefits of the Camaro's design, and instead rested its verdict on its independent assessment of what an ordinary consumer would expect. Accordingly, we conclude, the error in presenting that theory to the jury provides no basis for disturbing the trial judgment.[8]

---

8. In a separate argument, raised for the first time in GM's brief on the merits, both GM and the Council urge us to reconsider *Barker*'s holding—embodied in the standard instruction received by this jury—that under the risk-benefit test, the manufacturer has the burden of proving that the utility of the challenged design outweighs its dangers. We explained in *Barker* that placement of the risk-benefit burden on the manufacturer is appropriate because the considerations which influenced the design of its product are "peculiarly within ... [its] knowledge." Furthermore, we observed, the "fundamental policies" of *Greenman* dictate that a manufacturer who seeks to escape design defect liability on risk-benefit grounds "should bear the burden of persuading the trier of fact that its product should not be judged defective...." GM argues that *Barker* unfairly requires the manufacturer to "prove a negative"—*i.e.*, the absence of a safer alternative design. The Council suggests our "peculiar knowledge" rationale is unrealistic under liberal modern discovery rules. We are not persuaded. *Barker* allows the evaluation of competing designs, but it does not require proof that the challenged design is the safest possible alternative. The manufacturer need only show that given the inherent complexities of design, the benefits of its chosen design outweigh the dangers. Moreover, modern discovery practice neither redresses the inherent technical imbalance

Notes

The Restatement (Third) of Torts: Products Liability. The authors of the *Restatement (Third)* viewed *Soule's* risk-utility test as being consistent with the rule described in section 2 of the *Restatement*, which explains that a product is defective in design:

> when the foreseeable risks of harm posed by the product could have been reduced or avoided by the adoption of a reasonable alternative design by the seller or other distributor, or a predecessor in the commercial chain of distribution, and the omission of the alternative design renders the product not reasonably safe.

Consumer expectations. Some states continue to employ the strict liability consumer expectations test in design defect cases. *See* Delaney v. Deere and Co., 999 P.2d 930, 944 (Kan. 2000). Others have followed California's lead and created a two-pronged test. *See* Ray v. BIC Corp., 925 S.W.2d 527 (Tenn. 1996). The majority do not include consumer expectations as part of the formal test and instead rely upon some type of risk-utility test. Do consumer expectations have any relevance under such an approach? Imagine you bought the most comfortable sweater you have ever owned. Unfortunately, due to the fabric used, the sweater causes 90% of buyers to break out in a horrible rash. Should a consumer have to go through the trouble of identifying a reasonable alternative design and demonstrating why that design is superior?

Burden of proof. California's approach to the burden of proof issue is definitely in the minority.

Foreseeable misuse of the product. *Soule* speaks repeatedly about "foreseeable" use of a product. To what extent must a manufacturer design a product with foreseeable *misuse* in mind? For example, it may be a misuse of a car to drive at excessive speeds, but it is certainly a foreseeable misuse. Because it is foreseeable, a car manufacturer has a duty to design its car in a manner so that it is reasonably safe even when it is driven above the speed limit. The impact that foreseeable misuse of a product may have on a consumer's ability to recover full damages is discussed later in this chapter in the section on defenses. But note that "[t]he absence of misuse is part of the plaintiff's case. Misuse is not an affirmative defense. Thus, the plaintiff has the burden of showing that there was no misuse or that the misuse was objectively foreseeable." Jurado v. Western Gear Works, 619 A.2d 1312, 1317 (N.J. 1993).

Unforeseeable misuse of the product. When a plaintiff is injured as a result of using the product for a purpose or in a manner that is not objectively foreseeable, the product is not defectively designed. Jurado v. Western Gear Works, 619 A.2d 1312, 1317 (N.J. 1993). "If, for instance, a plaintiff undertakes to use his power saw

---

between manufacturer and consumer nor dictates that the injured consumer should bear the primary burden of evaluating a design developed and chosen by the manufacturer. GM and the Council fail to convince us that *Barker* was incorrectly decided in this respect.

as a nail clipper and thereby snips his digits, he will not be heard to complain." *Id.* (citations omitted). Again, unforeseeable misuse of a product is not technically an affirmative defense but is instead evidence relevant to the question of whether the product was defective to begin with. What should qualify as "foreseeable" misuse? *See* Iliades v. Dieffenbacher North America Inc., 915 N.W.2d 338 (Mich. 2018) (stating the answer depends on whether manufacturer was aware, or should have been aware, of the misuse when the product was manufactured).

Pruitt v. General Motors Corp.

72 Cal. App. 4th 1480 (Cal. Ct. App. 1999)

GILBERT, Acting P. J.

On March 22, 1995, Pruitt was driving her 1991 Chevrolet Beretta manufactured by GMC. The seat belt and shoulder harness were buckled. She turned left at an intersection and collided with an oncoming car. The driver's side air bag deployed within an instant of impact.

Pruitt suffered three fractures of her lower mandible which required surgery. She sustained medical expenses of $66,224.

In her product liability cause of action against GMC, Pruitt alleged that the air bag deployed in a low-speed collision causing her injuries.

At trial, the court granted Pruitt's motion to exclude expert testimony offered by GMC regarding the expectations of an ordinary consumer and granted GMC's motion to preclude Pruitt's testimony about her expectations concerning the safety of the air bag. Nevertheless, at trial Pruitt testified that she did not expect the air bag to injure her.

. . .

Pruitt contends the jury should have been instructed on the consumer expectations test.

Pruitt requested and the trial court refused to instruct the jury that, "A product is defective in design: if it fails to perform as safely as an ordinary consumer would expect when used in an intended or reasonably foreseeable manner."

Our Supreme Court discussed the application of the consumer expectation test in *Soule v. General Motors Corp.* (1994) 8 Cal.4th 548, 567 [34 Cal.Rptr.2d 607, 882 P.2d 298]: "[T]he consumer expectations test is reserved for cases in which the everyday experience of the product's users permits a conclusion that the product's design violated minimum safety assumptions, and is thus defective regardless of expert opinion about the merits of the design. . . ."

. . .

The deployment of an air bag is, quite fortunately, not part of the "everyday experience" of the consuming public. Minimum safety standards for air bags are not within the common knowledge of lay jurors. Jurors are in need of expert testimony to evaluate the risks and benefits of the challenged design. Even Pruitt's own expert testified that in designing air bags there are tradeoffs involving complex technical issues. The trial court correctly refused to give the consumer expectations instruction.

Notes

Crashworthiness. In the typical products liability case, the product causes the accident. In a car crash case, for example, the brakes fail or the brakes were poorly designed, leading to a crash. In cases like *Pruitt*, however, the complaint is that the design of the vehicle actually increased the extent of the injury following a crash. Under the crashworthiness doctrine, a car manufacturer may be held liable for injuries sustained in an accident where a defect caused or enhanced the injuries. *See* Camacho v. Honda Motor Co., Ltd., 741 P.2d 1240 (Colo. 1987). *Soule* and *Pruitt* are examples.

Problem 14.6. Refer back to the facts in Problem 14.5. Daniela's injury occurred when she attempted to put the Q-36 scissors down for a moment. As she put the scissors down, the comb she was holding caught on the thumb hole of the shears, causing the shears to roll open. Daniela used her left hand to close the shears when the back side of the blade gently tapped, pierced, and sliced into her wrist. Daniela had to physically pull the shears from her wrist. Daniela has now brought a design defect claim against TrimLine. Which part of the California test for design defects should apply to Daniela's situation?

2. Application of the Risk-Utility Test

Soule lists several nonexclusive factors involved in the risk-utility analysis. Decisions from other courts list similar, but slightly different, factors. The *Restatement (Third)* also lists a number of factors to consider, including the magnitude and probability of the foreseeable risks of harm; the instructions and warnings accompanying the product; the nature and strength of consumer expectations regarding the product; the likely effects of the alternative design on production costs; the effects of the alternative design on product longevity, maintenance, repair, and esthetics; and the range of consumer choice among products. Restatement (Third) of Torts: Products Liability § 2 cmt. e.; *see also* Ray by Holman v. Bic Corp., 925 S.W.2d 527, 532 (Tenn. 1996) (listing "usefulness, costs, seriousness and likelihood of potential harm, and the myriad of other factors often lumped into . . . a risk-utility test"). The point is simply that the risk-utility test—however it is defined—ordinarily requires a common-sense comparison between an alternative design and the design that caused the injury. *Id.* § 2 cmt. d. But first, the plaintiff must establish that there was, in fact, a reasonable alternative design. This section explores special issues of proof involved in the design defect determination.

General Motors Corp. v. Sanchez

997 S.W.2d 584 (Tex. 1999)

Justice GONZALES delivered the opinion for a unanimous Court.

Because there were no witnesses, relatively little is known first hand about the circumstances of the accident that is the basis of this litigation. Lee Sanchez, Jr. left his home to feed a pen of heifers in March 1993. The ranch foreman found his lifeless body the next morning and immediately called Sanchez's father. Apparently, Sanchez's 1990 Chevy pickup had rolled backward with the driver's side door open pinning Sanchez to the open corral gate in the angle between the open door and the cab of the truck. Sanchez suffered a broken right arm and damaged right knee where the gate crushed him against the door pillar, the vertical metal column to which the door is hinged. He bled to death from a deep laceration in his right upper arm.

The Sanchez family, his estate, and his wife sued General Motors Corporation and the dealership that sold the pickup for negligence, products liability, and gross negligence based on a defect in the truck's transmission and transmission-control linkage. The plaintiffs presented circumstantial evidence to support the following theory of how the accident happened. Sanchez drove his truck into the corral and stopped to close the gate. He mis-shifted into what he thought was Park, but what was actually an intermediate, "perched" position between Park and Reverse where the transmission was in "hydraulic neutral." Expert witnesses explained that hydraulic neutral exists at the intermediate positions between the denominated gears, Park, Reverse, Neutral, Drive, and Low, where no gear is actually engaged. Under this scenario, as Sanchez walked toward the gate, the gear shift slipped from the perched position of hydraulic neutral into Reverse and the truck started to roll backwards. It caught Sanchez at or near the gate and slammed him up against it, trapping his right arm and knee. He was pinned between the gate and the door pillar by the pressure the truck exerted while idling in Reverse. Struggling to free himself, Sanchez severed an artery in his right arm and bled to death after 45 to 75 minutes.

...

The trial court rendered judgment for actual and punitive damages of $8.5 million for the plaintiffs.

II.

A design defect renders a product unreasonably dangerous as designed, taking into consideration the utility of the product and the risk involved in its use. A plaintiff must prove that there is a safer alternative design in order to recover under a design defect theory. An alternative design must substantially reduce the risk of injury and be both economically and technologically feasible. We first examine the evidence concerning the operation of the transmission in Sanchez's truck and then determine whether the plaintiffs have proven a safer alternative design.

A

Most of the plaintiff's design evidence came in through the testimony of the plaintiffs' expert, Simon Tamny, who testified about the operation of the 700R4 transmission in Sanchez's truck. He opined that the G.M. transmission and transmission-control linkage presented a particular risk. All transmissions have an intermediate position between Reverse and Park. It is impossible, under federal standardization guidelines, to design a gear shift without an intermediate position between Reverse and Park. However, Tamny testified that G.M.'s transmission has the added danger that internal forces tend to move the gear selector toward Reverse rather than Park when the driver inadvertently leaves the lever in this intermediate position. Tamny explained how G.M. could alter the design to make the operation of the 700R4 safer.

. . .

It is possible for the gear shift to be moved to a position between Reverse and Park, called hydraulic neutral by the parties. In hydraulic neutral, the roller is perched at the peak between the two gears. . . . Tamny performed an experiment in which he moved the gear selector of Sanchez's truck to this position six times. He disturbed the friction of the linkage four times by slapping the steering wheel; once by revving the engine, and once he took no action. In each case, the gear shift slipped into Reverse.

B

Tamny offered a few alterations to G.M.'s design that he contended would reduce the risk of injury.

. . .

Tamny admitted that his design change would not totally eliminate the possibility of leaving the gearshift in the intermediate position of hydraulic neutral. However, according to Tamny, his design change would totally eliminate the possibility of slipping into Reverse from hydraulic neutral. Tamny described his design change as a "99% solution" to the mis-shift problem. While his design change would not eliminate the risk that the car might roll in hydraulic neutral, it would eliminate the most dangerous risk of migration to Reverse and powered movement without a driver.

C

G.M. does not challenge that Tamny's design was technically and economically feasible. Instead, G.M. argues that, as a matter of law, Tamny's design is inadequate to prove a substantial reduction in the risk of injury because: (1) the design was not proved safer by testing; (2) the design was not published and therefore not subjected to peer review; and (3) G.M.'s statistical evidence proved that other manufacturers, whose designs incorporated some of Tamny's suggestions, had the same accident rate as G.M. These arguments however, go to the reliability and therefore the admissibility of expert evidence rather than the legal sufficiency of the evidence of a product defect.

. . .

[T]he plaintiffs did not have to build and test an automobile transmission to prove a safer alternative design. A design need only prove "capable of being developed." The *Restatement (Third) of Torts: Products Liability* takes the position that "qualified expert testimony on the issue suffices, even though the expert has produced no prototype, if it reasonably supports the conclusion that a reasonable alternative design could have been practically adopted at the time of sale." Furthermore, assuming we could consider evidence contrary to the verdict, no manufacturer has incorporated Tammy's design into an existing transmission. For that reason alone, G.M.'s statistical evidence comparing the safety of different existing designs could not conclusively establish the safety of Tamny's design.

The evidence supporting Tamny's conclusion that his design is safer raises a fact question that the jury resolved in favor of the plaintiffs. We conclude that the plaintiffs have presented more than a scintilla of evidence that Tamny's alternative design substantially reduced the risk of injury.

Camacho v. Honda Motor Co.

741 P.2d 1240 (Colo. 1987)

KIRSHBAUM, Justice.

I

In March 1978, Jaime Camacho (Camacho) purchased a new 1978 Honda Hawk motorcycle, model CV400T2, from a Honda dealer. In May 1978, while driving the motorcycle through an intersection, Camacho collided with an automobile and sustained serious leg injuries. Camacho and his wife filed an action against Honda seeking damages for personal injuries, property losses, loss of consortium and exemplary damages. The action was based on several theories, including strict liability. The Camachos alleged that the motorcycle was a defectively designed, unreasonably dangerous product under the Restatement (Second) of Torts section 402A because it was not equipped with "crash bars"—tubular steel bars attached to the motorcycle frame to protect the rider's legs in the event of a collision. They asserted that if such crash bars had been installed on the motorcycle, Camacho's leg injuries would have been mitigated.

Two mechanical engineers employed by the Camachos testified in depositions that, in light of their extensive research work on motorcycle crash bars, including testing conducted for the United States Department of Transportation, the state of the art in mechanical engineering and motorcycle design was such that effective injury-reducing, leg protection devices were feasible in March 1978 and that several manufacturers other than Honda had made such devices available as optional equipment; that, although room for further improvement of crash bars existed in March 1978, crash bars then available from manufacturers other than Honda provided some protection in low-speed collisions and, in particular, would have reduced or completely avoided the serious leg injuries suffered by Camacho; and that Honda itself had conducted some of the seminal research on crash bars in 1969, as the result of which Honda's engineers had concluded that injury-reducing crash bars could be manufactured by strengthening the steel bars which had been tested and providing strong bolts to attach the bars to the motorcycle frame.

Honda moved for summary judgment, arguing that as a matter of law a motorcycle lacking crash bars cannot be deemed unreasonably dangerous. The trial court granted the motion, concluding that (1) because the danger of leg injury was obvious and foreseeable, Honda had no duty to totally alter the nature of its product by installing crash bars; and (2) Honda had no duty under the crashworthiness doctrine to add a safety feature to its product to reduce the severity of injuries resulting from accidents.

In agreeing with the trial court's conclusions, the Court of Appeals held that the determination of whether a product is unreasonably dangerous because of a design defect is to be made on the basis of whether the extent of the danger "would have been fully anticipated by or within the contemplation of" the ordinary user or consumer. Because the criteria applied by the trial court and the Court of Appeals are inconsistent with our decisions in *Ortho Pharmaceutical Corp. v. Heath*, 722 P.2d 410 (Colo.1986), and *Union Supply Co. v. Pust*, 196 Colo. 162, 583 P.2d 276 (1978), we reverse and remand for further proceedings.

II

. . .

The crashworthiness doctrine has been applied to accidents involving motorcycles. Honda argues, however, that motorcycles are inherently dangerous motor vehicles that cannot be made perfectly crashworthy and, therefore, that motorcycle manufacturers should be free of liability for injuries not actually caused by a defect in the design or manufacture of the motorcycle. We find no principled basis to conclude that liability for failure to provide reasonable, cost-acceptable safety features to reduce the severity of injuries suffered in inevitable accidents should be imposed upon automobile manufacturers but not upon motorcycle manufacturers. The use of motorcycles for transportation over roadways is just as foreseeable as the use of automobiles for such purpose. The crashworthiness doctrine does not require a manufacturer to provide absolute safety, but merely to provide some measure of reasonable, cost-effective safety in the foreseeable use of the product. Honda acknowledges that motorcycle accidents are just as foreseeable as automobile accidents and that motorcycle riders face a much greater risk of injury in the event of an accident than do occupants of automobiles. In view of the important goal of encouraging maximum development of reasonable, cost-efficient safety features in the manufacture of all products, the argument that motorcycle manufacturers should be exempt from liability under the crashworthiness doctrine because serious injury to users of that product is foreseeable must be rejected.

III

In determining the extent of liability of a product manufacturer for a defective product, this court has adopted the doctrine of strict products liability as set forth in the Restatement (Second) of Torts section 402A (1965).

... [T]he consumer contemplation concept embodied in comment i, while illustrative of a particular problem, does not provide a satisfactory test for determining whether particular products are in a defective condition unreasonably dangerous to the user or consumer. In the final analysis, the principle of products liability contemplated by section 402A is premised upon the concept of enterprise liability for casting defective products into the stream of commerce. The primary focus must remain upon the nature of the product under all relevant circumstances rather than upon the conduct of either the consumer or the manufacturer. Total reliance upon the hypothetical ordinary consumer's contemplation of an obvious danger diverts the appropriate focus and may thereby result in a finding that a product is not defective even though the product may easily have been designed to be much safer at little added expense and no impairment of utility. W.P. Keeton, D. Dobbs, R. Keeton & D. Owen, *Prosser and Keeton on The Law of Torts* § 99 at 66 (5th ed. 1984). Uncritical rejection of design defect claims in all cases wherein the danger may be open and obvious thus contravenes sound public policy by encouraging design strategies which perpetuate the manufacture of dangerous products.

In *Ortho Pharmaceutical Corp. v. Heath*, 722 P.2d 410 (Colo. 1986), we recently recognized that exclusive reliance upon consumer expectations is a particularly inappropriate means of determining whether a product is unreasonably dangerous under section 402A where both the unreasonableness of the danger in the design defect and the efficacy of alternative designs in achieving a reasonable degree of safety must be defined primarily by technical, scientific information. Moreover, manufacturers of such complex products as motor vehicles invariably have greater access than do ordinary consumers to the information necessary to reach informed decisions concerning the efficacy of potential safety measures. The principles that have evolved in the law of products liability have in part been developed to encourage manufacturers to use information gleaned from testing, inspection and data analysis to help avoid the "massive problem of product accidents."

... In *Ortho* we noted that the following factors are of value in balancing the attendant risks and benefits of a product to determine whether a product design is unreasonably dangerous:

> (1) The usefulness and desirability of the product—its utility to the user and to the public as a whole.
>
> (2) The safety aspects of the product—the likelihood that it will cause injury and the probable seriousness of the injury.
>
> (3) The availability of a substitute product which would meet the same need and not be as unsafe.

(4) The manufacturer's ability to eliminate the unsafe character of the product without impairing its usefulness or making it too expensive to maintain its utility.

(5) The user's ability to avoid danger by the exercise of care in the use of the product.

(6) The user's anticipated awareness of the dangers inherent in the product and their avoidability because of general public knowledge of the obvious condition of the product, or of the existence of suitable warnings or instructions.

(7) The feasibility, on the part of the manufacturer, of spreading the loss by setting the price of the product or carrying liability insurance.

Ortho Pharmaceutical Corp. v. Heath, 722 P.2d 410, 414 (relying on Wade, *On the Nature of Strict Tort Liability for Products*, 44 Miss. L.J. 825, 837–38 (1973)). The factors enumerated in *Ortho* are applicable to the determination of what constitutes a product that is in a defective unreasonably dangerous condition. By examining and weighing the various interests represented by these factors, a trial court is much more likely to be fair to the interests of both manufacturers and consumers in determining the status of particular products.

The question of the status of the motorcycle purchased by Camacho involves in part the interpretation of mechanical engineering data derived from research and testing—interpretation which necessarily includes the application of scientific and technical principles. In addition, the question posed under the crashworthiness doctrine is not whether the vehicle was obviously unsafe but rather whether the degree of inherent dangerousness could or should have been significantly reduced. The record contains some evidence to support the conclusion that Honda could have provided crash bars at an acceptable cost without impairing the motorcycle's utility or substantially altering its nature and Honda's failure to do so rendered the vehicle unreasonably dangerous under the applicable danger-utility test. It is far from certain, however, that the ultimate answer to this question can be determined on the basis of the limited facts thus far presented to the trial court.

. . .

The Camachos proffered evidence that the Honda Hawk motorcycle could have been equipped with crash bars which would mitigate injuries in low-speed, angled-impact collisions such as the one in which Camacho was involved. The Camachos' expert witnesses' interpretation of research and testing data indicated that the maneuverability of the motorcycle could be retained by making the crash bars no wider than the handlebars, that the stability of the motorcycle could be retained by mounting the crash bars relatively close to the center of gravity and that the addition of crash bars would not impair the utility of the motorcycle as a fuel efficient, open-air vehicle nor impair the safety of the motorcycle in accidents which varied in kind from the accident involving Camacho. These conclusions are all strenuously disputed by Honda. However, precisely because the factual conclusions reached by expert witnesses are in dispute, summary judgment as to whether the design strategies of Honda were reasonable is improper.

Notes

Application of the risk-utility test. What other facts would the *Camacho* court need in order to make a decision as to whether Honda's product was unreasonably dangerous (or not reasonably safe)?

State of the art. Both *Camacho* and *Sanchez* reference the feasibility of an alternative design. Closely related to the question of whether a design is feasible is whether the defendant's existing design was "state of the art." The phrase "state of the art" generally refers "to what feasibly could have been done," Falada v. Trinity Industries, Inc., 642 N.W.2d 247, 250 (Iowa 2002), or in terms of the most advanced scientific and technological knowledge existing at the time. *See* Wiska v. St. Stanislaus Social Club, Inc., 390 N.E.2d 1133 (Mass. 1979). Some define the term in terms of whether the defendant's product was the safest actually on the market. *See* North Dakota Cent. Code § 28-01.4-03. Some jurisdictions refer to the "state of the art defense." *Falada*, 642 N.W.2d at 248. What should be the effect of the fact that the defendant's product was manufactured in accordance with industry customs? *See* McLaughlin v. Sikorsky Aircraft, 148 Cal. App. 3d 203 (Cal. Ct. App. 1983); Howard v. Omni Hotels Management Corp., 203 Cal. App. 4th 403 (Cal. Ct. App. 2012).

Subsequent design changes. The question of whether a product is defective is assessed at the time the product left the defendant's hands. Ordinarily, evidence that a defendant changed its approach following an accident is inadmissible in a negligence case. *See* Fed. R. Evid. 703. What relevance, if any, should there be in a products liability action to the fact that a manufacturer subsequently changed the design of its product following an accident?

Inherently unsafe products. Are there some products that have so little value and are so inherently dangerous under the risk-utility analysis that a plaintiff should be relieved of the need to identify a reasonable alternative design and can argue that the product simply should not be produced? Armor-piercing bullets, for example? *See* McCarthy v. Olin Corporation, 119 F.3d 148 (2d Cir. 1997). Grain alcohol? Cigarettes? *See* Cal. Civ Code § 1714.45(a)(2).

Problem 14.7. Daniela introduced evidence that the tips of the Q-36 scissors were significantly more pointed than the tips of every other model on the market and that more rounded tips are the norm in the industry. In addition, the tips of the Q-36 were unusually narrow, turning them into what Daniela's lawyer called "virtually a stabbing instrument." Assume that the risk-utility test applies to Daniella's design defect claim. What would be the likely result? What other information might you want in order to effectively analyze the issue?

D. Information (Warning) Defects

Problem 14.8. Isabella and her family went camping one night. In an effort to keep warm in the tent overnight, they used an Outdoorsman Heatmaster 5000 radiant heater. During the night, the heater released deadly amounts of carbon monoxide. Isabella died as a result. Her estate now seeks to bring a wrongful death claim against Outdoorsman based on the failure to include an adequate warning concerning the dangers of the heater.

1. In General

One step a manufacturer might take to reduce consumers' safety expectations would be to warn consumers about the potential dangers associated with the product. *See* Jackson v. Nestle-Beich, Inc., 589 N.E.2d 547 (Ill. 1992). This might, in turn, reduce the potential for harm, thereby rendering the design safer. Sometimes the failure to provide a consumer with necessary information might itself be the source of a products liability claim. Under the standard approach, inadequate information may render a product defective "when the foreseeable risks of harm posed by the product could have been reduced or avoided by the provision of reasonable instructions or warnings by the seller or other distributor, or a predecessor in the commercial chain of distribution, and the omission of the instructions or warnings renders the product not reasonably safe." Restatement (Third) of Torts: Products Liability § 2(c).

Hood v. Ryobi America Corp.

181 F.3d 608 (4th Cir. 1999)

WILKINSON, Chief Judge:

Hood purchased a Ryobi TS-254 miter saw in Westminster, Maryland on February 25, 1995, for the purpose of performing home repairs. The saw was fully assembled at the time of purchase. It had a ten-inch diameter blade mounted on a rotating spindle controlled by a finger trigger on a handle near the top of the blade. To operate the saw, the consumer would use that handle to lower the blade through the material being cut.

Two blade guards shielded nearly the entire saw blade. A large metal guard, fixed to the frame of the saw, surrounded the upper half of the blade. A transparent plastic lower guard covered the rest of the blade and retracted into the upper guard as the saw came into contact with the work piece.

A number of warnings in the operator's manual and affixed to the saw itself stated that the user should operate the saw only with the blade guards in place. For example, the owner's manual declared that the user should "KEEP GUARDS IN PLACE" and warned: "ALWAYS USE THE SAW BLADE GUARD. Never operate the machine with the guard removed"; "NEVER operate this saw without all guards in place and in good operating condition"; and "WARNING: TO PREVENT POSSIBLE SERIOUS PERSONAL INJURY, NEVER PERFORM ANY CUTTING OPERATION WITH THE UPPER OR LOWER BLADE GUARD REMOVED." The saw itself carried several decals stating "DANGER: DO NOT REMOVE ANY GUARD. USE OF SAW WITHOUT THIS GUARD WILL RESULT IN SERIOUS INJURY"; "OPERATE ONLY WITH GUARDS IN PLACE"; and "WARNING . . . DO NOT operate saw without the upper and lower guards in place."

The day after his purchase, Hood began working with the saw in his driveway. While attempting to cut a piece of wood approximately four inches in height Hood found that the blade guards prevented the saw blade from passing completely through the piece. Disregarding the manufacturer's warnings, Hood decided to remove the blade guards from the saw. Hood first detached the saw blade from its spindle. He then unscrewed the four screws that held the blade guard assembly to the frame of the saw. Finally, he replaced the blade onto the bare spindle and completed his cut.

Rather than replacing the blade guards, Hood continued to work with the saw blade exposed. He worked in this fashion for about twenty minutes longer when, in the middle of another cut, the spinning saw blade flew off the saw and back toward Hood. The blade partially amputated his left thumb and lacerated his right leg.

Hood admits that he read the owner's manual and most of the warning labels on the saw before he began his work. He claims, however, that he believed the blade guards were intended solely to prevent a user's clothing or fingers from coming into contact with the saw blade. He contends that he was unaware that removing the blade guards would permit the spinning blade to detach from the saw. But Ryobi, he claims, was aware of that possibility. In fact, another customer had sued Ryobi after suffering a similar accident in the mid-1980s.

On December 5, 1997, Hood sued several divisions of Ryobi in the United States District Court for the District of Maryland. Hood raised claims of failure to warn and defective design under several theories of liability. On cross-motions for summary judgment the district court entered judgment for the defendants on all claims, finding that in the face of adequate warnings Hood had altered the saw and caused his own injury. Hood appeals.

II.

A manufacturer may be liable for placing a product on the market that bears inadequate instructions and warnings or that is defective in design. Hood asserts that Ryobi failed adequately to warn of the dangers of using the saw without the blade guards in place. Hood also contends that the design of the saw was defective. We disagree on both counts.

A.

Hood first complains that the warnings he received were insufficiently specific. Hood admits that Ryobi provided several clear and conspicuous warnings not to operate the saw without the blade guards. He contends, however, that the warnings affixed to the product and displayed in the operator's manual were inadequate to alert him to the dangers of doing so. In addition to Ryobi's directive "never" to operate a guardless saw, Hood would require the company to inform of the actual consequences of such conduct. Specifically, Hood contends that an adequate warning would have explained that removing the guards would lead to blade detachment.

We disagree. Maryland does not require an encyclopedic warning. Instead, "a warning need only be one that is reasonable under the circumstances." Levin v. Walter Kidde & Co., 251 Md. 560, 248 A.2d 151, 153 (1968). A clear and specific warning will normally be sufficient—"the manufacturer need not warn of every mishap or source of injury that the mind can imagine flowing from the product." Liesener v. Weslo, Inc., 775 F.Supp. 857, 861 (D. Md.1991); *see* Levin, 248 A.2d at 154 (declining to require warning of the danger that a cracked syphon bottle might explode and holding "never use cracked bottle" to be adequate as a matter of law). In deciding whether a warning is adequate, Maryland law asks whether the benefits of a more detailed warning outweigh the costs of requiring the change.

Hood assumes that the cost of a more detailed warning label is minimal in this case, and he claims that such a warning would have prevented his injury. But the price of more detailed warnings is greater than their additional printing fees alone. Some commentators have observed that the proliferation of label detail threatens to undermine the effectiveness of warnings altogether. *See* James A. Henderson, Jr. & Aaron D. Twerski, *Doctrinal Collapse in Products Liability: The Empty Shell of Failure to Warn*, 65 N.Y.U. L.Rev. 265, 296–97 (1990). As manufacturers append line after line onto product labels in the quest for the best possible warning, it is easy to lose sight of the label's communicative value as a whole. Well-meaning attempts to warn of every possible accident lead over time to voluminous yet impenetrable labels—too prolix to read and too technical to understand.

By contrast, Ryobi's warnings are clear and unequivocal. Three labels on the saw itself and at least four warnings in the owner's manual direct the user not to operate the saw with the blade guards removed. Two declare that "serious injury" could result from doing so. This is not a case where the manufacturer has failed to include any warnings at all with its product. Ryobi provided warnings sufficient to apprise the ordinary consumer that it is unsafe to operate a guardless saw—warnings which, if followed, would have prevented the injury in this case.

It is apparent, moreover, that the vast majority of consumers do not detach this critical safety feature before using this type of saw. Indeed, although Ryobi claims to have sold thousands of these saws, Hood has identified only one fifteen-year-old incident similar to his. Hood has thus not shown that these clear, unmistakable, and prominent warnings are insufficient to accomplish their purpose. Nor can he prove that increased label clutter would bring any net societal benefit. We hold that the warnings Ryobi provided are adequate as a matter of law.

Liriano v. Hobart Corp.

170 F.3d 264 (2d Cir. 1999)

CALABRESI, Circuit Judge

Luis Liriano was severely injured on the job in 1993 when his hand was caught in a meat grinder manufactured by Hobart Corporation ("Hobart") and owned by his employer, Super Associated ("Super"). The meat grinder had been sold to Super with a safety guard, but the safety guard was removed while the machine was in Super's possession and was not affixed to the meat grinder at the time of the accident. The machine bore no warning indicating that the grinder should be operated only with a safety guard attached.

Liriano sued Hobart under several theories, including failure to warn. Hobart brought a third-party claim against Super. The United States District Court for the Southern District of New York (Shira A. Scheindlin, J.) dismissed all of Liriano's claims except the one based on failure to warn, and the jury returned a verdict for Liriano on that claim. It attributed five percent of the liability to Hobart and ninety-five percent to Super. . . .

Hobart and Super appealed, arguing (1) that as a matter of law, there was no duty to warn, and (2) that even if there had been a duty to warn, the evidence presented was not sufficient to allow the failure-to-warn claim to reach the jury . . . .

. . .

If the question before us were . . . simply whether meat grinders are sufficiently known to be dangerous so that manufacturers would be justified in believing that further warnings were not needed, we might be in doubt. . . . [M]ost New Yorkers would probably appreciate the danger of meat grinders . . . . Any additional warning might seem superfluous. On the other hand, Liriano was only seventeen years old at the time of his injury and had only recently immigrated to the United States. He had been on the job at Super for only one week. He had never been given instructions about how to use the meat grinder, and he had used the meat grinder only two or three times. And, as Judge Scheindlin noted, the mechanism that injured Liriano would not have been visible to someone who was operating the grinder. It could be argued that such a combination of facts was not so unlikely that a court should say, as a matter of law, that the defendant could not have foreseen them or, if aware of them, need not have guarded against them by issuing a warning. That argument would draw strength from the Court of Appeals' direction that the question of whether a warning was needed must be asked in terms of the information available to the injured party rather than the injured party's employer and its added comment that "in cases where reasonable minds might disagree as to the extent of the plaintiff's knowledge of the hazard, the question is one for the jury."

Nevertheless, it remains the fact that meat grinders are widely known to be dangerous. Given that the position of the New York courts on the specific question before us is anything but obvious, we might well be of two minds as to whether a failure to warn that meat grinders are dangerous would be enough to raise a jury issue.

But to state the issue that way would be to misunderstand the complex functions of warnings. As two distinguished torts scholars have pointed out, a warning can do more than exhort its audience to be careful. It can also affect what activities the people warned choose to engage in. See James A. Henderson, Jr., and Aaron D. Twerski, *Doctrinal Collapse in Products Liability: The Empty Shell of Failure to Warn*, 65 N.Y.U. L. Rev. 265, 285 (1990). And where the function of a warning is to assist the reader in making choices, the value of the warning can lie as much in making known the existence of alternatives as in communicating the fact that a particular choice is dangerous. It follows that the duty to warn is not necessarily obviated merely because a danger is clear.

To be more concrete, a warning can convey at least two types of messages. One states that a particular place, object, or activity is dangerous. Another explains that people need not risk the danger posed by such a place, object, or activity in order to achieve the purpose for which they might have taken that risk. Thus, a highway sign that says "Danger—Steep Grade" says less than a sign that says "Steep Grade Ahead—Follow Suggested Detour to Avoid Dangerous Areas."

If the hills or mountains responsible for the steep grade are plainly visible, the first sign merely states what a reasonable person would know without having to be warned. The second sign tells drivers what they might not have otherwise known: that there is another road that is flatter and less hazardous. A driver who believes the road through the mountainous area to be the only way to reach her destination might well choose to drive on that road despite the steep grades, but a driver who knows herself to have an alternative might not, even though her understanding of the risks posed by the steep grade is exactly the same as those of the first driver. Accordingly, a certain level of obviousness as to the grade of a road might, in principle, eliminate the reason for posting a sign of the first variety. But no matter how patently steep the road, the second kind of sign might still have a beneficial effect. As a result, the duty to post a sign of the second variety may persist even when the danger of the road is obvious and a sign of the first type would not be warranted.

One who grinds meat, like one who drives on a steep road, can benefit not only from being told that his activity is dangerous but from being told of a safer way. As we have said, one can argue about whether the risk involved in grinding meat is sufficiently obvious that a responsible person would fail to warn of that risk, believing reasonably that it would convey no helpful information. But if it is also the case—as it is—that the risk posed by meat grinders can feasibly be reduced by attaching a safety guard, we have a different question. Given that attaching guards is feasible, does reasonable care require that meat workers be informed that they need not accept the risks of using unguarded grinders? Even if most ordinary users may—as a matter of law—know of the risk of using a guardless meat grinder, it does not follow that a sufficient number of them will—as a matter of law—also know that protective guards are available, that using them is a realistic possibility, and that they may ask that such guards be used. It is precisely these last pieces of information that a reasonable manufacturer may have a duty to convey even if the danger of using a grinder were itself deemed obvious.

Consequently, the instant case does not require us to decide the difficult question of whether New York would consider the risk posed by meat grinders to be obvious as a matter of law. A jury could reasonably find that there exist people who are employed as meat grinders and who do not know (a) that it is feasible to reduce the risk with safety guards, (b) that such guards are made available with the grinders, and (c) that the grinders should be used only with the guards. Moreover, a jury can also reasonably find that there are enough such people, and that warning them is sufficiently inexpensive, that a reasonable manufacturer would inform them that safety guards exist and that the grinder is meant to be used only with such guards. Thus, even if New York would consider the danger of meat grinders to be obvious as a matter of law, that obviousness does not substitute for the warning that a jury could, and indeed did, find that Hobart had a duty to provide. It follows that we cannot say, as a matter of law, that Hobart had no duty to warn Liriano in the present case. We therefore decline to adopt appellants' argument that the issue of negligence was for the court only and that the jury was not entitled, on the evidence, to return a verdict for Liriano.

Notes

The function of warnings and obvious risks. Obviously, there is no breach of duty for the failure to warn of an obvious risk. *See* Evans v. Lorillard Tobacco Co., 990 N.E.2d 997 (Mass. 2013). Why did that rule not apply in *Liriano*?

Addressing the appropriate audience. A warning must be sufficient to put a reasonable person on notice as to the dangers of a product, but the defendant must also consider who the reasonable people using the product are likely to be. The warning must "convey to the typical user of average intelligence the information necessary to permit the user to avoid the risk and to use the product safely." Stanley Industries, Inc. v. W.M. Barr & Co., Inc., 784 F. Supp. 1570, 1575 (S.D. Fla. 1992). For example, if it is foreseeable that a dangerous product is likely to be used non-English speakers, a warning might need to be made in Spanish. *Id.* at 1576 (recognizing such a duty where the defendant marketed pesticide using Hispanic media in Miami).

Warnings and food and drug allergies. A peanut butter manufacturer probably doesn't need to include a warning that its product contains peanuts. But at what point does the manufacturer of a particular food or drug that contains a known allergen owe a duty to warn about the presence of an allergen? The consequence of consuming the allergen? *See* Restatement Third of Torts: Products Liability § 2 cmt. k ("When the presence of the allergenic ingredient would not be anticipated by a reasonable user or consumer, warnings concerning its presence are required.").

Problem 14.9. The Heatmaster 5000 radiant heater contained the following warning on the product itself: "For outdoor or well ventilated construction use only. Never use inside house, camper, tent, vehicle or other unventilated or enclosed areas." Isabella's son says he believes Isabella read the warning prior to using the heater. Outdoorsman has moved for summary judgment on the estate's information defect claim. What should the result be?

2. Special Issues Involving Causation

Liriano v. Hobart Corp.

170 F.3d 264 (2d Cir. 1999)

[See the facts and procedural history above regarding Liriano's accident involving the meat grinder.]

On rebriefing following the Court of Appeals decision, Hobart has made another argument as to why the jury should not have been allowed to find for the plaintiff. In this argument, Hobart raises the issue of causation. It maintains that Liriano "failed to present any evidence that Hobart's failure to place a warning [on the machine] was causally related to his injury." Whether or not there had been a warning, Hobart says, Liriano might well have operated the machine as he did and suffered the injuries that he suffered. Liriano introduced no evidence, Hobart notes, suggesting either that he would have refused to grind meat had the machine borne a warning or that a warning would have persuaded Super not to direct its employees to use the grinder without the safety attachment.

Hobart's argument about causation follows logically from the notion that its duty to warn in this case merely required Hobart to inform Liriano that a guard was available and that he should not use an unguarded grinder. The contention is tightly reasoned, but it rests on a false premise. It assumes that the burden was on Liriano to introduce additional evidence showing that the failure to warn was a but-for cause of his injury, even after he had shown that Hobart's wrong greatly increased the likelihood of the harm that occurred. But Liriano does not bear that burden. When a defendant's negligent act is deemed wrongful precisely because it has a strong propensity to cause the type of injury that ensued, that very causal tendency is evidence enough to establish a prima facie case of cause-in-fact. The burden then shifts to the defendant to come forward with evidence that its negligence was not such a but-for cause.

We know, as a general matter, that the kind of negligence that the jury attributed to the defendant tends to cause exactly the kind of injury that the plaintiff suffered. Indeed, that is what the jury must have found when it ruled that Hobart's failure to warn constituted negligence. In such situations, rather than requiring the plaintiff to bring in more evidence to demonstrate that his case is of the ordinary kind, the law presumes normality and requires the defendant to adduce evidence that the case is an exception. Accordingly, in a case like this, it is up to the defendant to bring in evidence tending to rebut the strong inference, arising from the accident, that the defendant's negligence was in fact a but-for cause of the plaintiff's injury. *See* Zuchowicz v. United States, 140 F.3d 381, 388 nn. 6–7, 390–91 (2d Cir.1998).

Note

Heeding presumptions. *Liriano* illustrates one way that courts deal with the causation issue. Another is through the recognition of a rebuttable presumption that the plaintiff would have heeded a warning had one been given. The presumption can be overcome through evidence that the plaintiff would not have heeded an adequate warning had one been given. *See* In re Prempro Products Liab. Litigation, 586 F.3d 547 (8th Cir. 2009) (ruling in defendant's favor where plaintiff responded, "Why would you read a manual?" when asked whether he had read the manual for a front-end loader).

3. Special Issues Involving Duty

Recall from earlier that liability may attach to any number of defendants along the distribution chain, ranging from the manufacturer to the ultimate seller of the product. This same rule applies in the case of information or warning defects. Thus, the general rule is that the duty to warn applies to all entities in a product's chain of distribution. The following case examines the learned intermediary doctrine, one of the most common exceptions to the general rule.

Watts v. Medicis Pharmaceutical Corp.

365 P.3d 944 (Ariz. 2016)

Vice Chief Justice PELANDER, opinion of the Court.

Medicis Pharmaceutical Corporation manufactures and distributes Solodyn, which contains minocycline. In its full prescribing informational materials for Solodyn, Medicis warns: "The long-term use of minocycline in the treatment of acne has been associated with drug-induced lupus-like syndrome, autoimmune hepatitis and vasculitis." Those materials also state: "Autoimmune syndromes, including drug-induced lupus-like syndrome, autoimmune hepatitis, vasculitis and serum sickness have been observed with tetracycline-class drugs, including minocycline. Symptoms may be manifested by arthralgia, fever, rash and malaise. Patients who experience such symptoms should be cautioned to stop the drug immediately and seek medical help."

In April 2008, Amanda Watts, then a minor, sought medical treatment for acne and received a prescription for Solodyn from her medical provider. Watts apparently did not receive the full prescribing information noted above, but did receive two other publications about the drug. The first was a "MediSAVE" card, which her medical provider gave to her, that outlined a discount-purchasing program for Solodyn. The MediSAVE card and its accompanying information stated that "[t]he safety of using [Solodyn] longer than 12 weeks has not been studied and is not known." Second, Watts received an informational insert about Solodyn from her pharmacist. The insert warned that patients should consult a doctor if symptoms did not improve within twelve weeks. Watts used Solodyn as prescribed for twenty weeks.

About two years later, Watts received another prescription for Solodyn and took it as directed for another twenty weeks. In October 2010, Watts was hospitalized and diagnosed with drug-induced lupus and hepatitis, both allegedly side effects from using Solodyn. Although she has recovered from the hepatitis, doctors expect her to have lupus for the rest of her life.

Watts sued Medicis alleging consumer fraud and product liability, seeking both compensatory and punitive damages. In her statutory [Consumer Fraud Act] claim, Watts alleged that in connection with the sale or advertisement of Solodyn, Medicis knowingly misrepresented and omitted material facts on the MediSAVE card she received and on which she relied. She also alleged that the drug was defective and unreasonably dangerous because Medicis failed to adequately warn her of the consequences of its long-term use. The superior court granted Medicis's motion to dismiss.

The court of appeals vacated the judgment of dismissal and remanded the case for further proceedings. . . .

We granted review because the legal issues are of statewide importance and likely to recur.

A.

Generally, a claim of strict products liability may be based on "informational defects encompassing instructions and warnings" that render a product defective and unreasonably dangerous. Gosewisch v. Am. Honda Motor Co., 153 Ariz. 400, 403, 737 P.2d 376, 379 (1987). To establish such a claim, the plaintiff must prove, among other things, that the manufacturer had a duty to warn of the product's dangerous propensities and that the lack of an adequate warning made the product defective and unreasonably dangerous. "In certain contexts, however, the manufacturer's or supplier's duty to warn end users of the dangerous propensities of its product is limited to providing an adequate warning to an intermediary, who then assumes the duty to pass the necessary warnings on to the end users." Centocor, Inc. v. Hamilton, 372 S.W.3d 140, 154 (Tex. 2012). This legal doctrine is known as the LID.

In 1978, our court of appeals adopted the LID in a product liability case against pharmaceutical companies that manufactured a drug that allegedly was unsafe due to informational defects. Dyer v. Best Pharmacal, 118 Ariz. 465, 577 P.2d 1084 (App.1978). . . .

As subsequent Arizona cases have recognized, the LID is based on principles of duty, not causation. *See, e.g.*, Dole Food Co. v. N.C. Foam Indus., Inc., 188 Ariz. 298, 302–03, 935 P.2d 876, 880–81 (App.1996) (assessing factors to determine when, under the LID, the "manufacturer's duty to warn is ordinarily satisfied"); *see also* Restatement (Third) of Torts: Prod. Liab. § 6 cmt. b (Am. Law Inst. 1998) ("Third Restatement") ("The rationale supporting this 'learned intermediary' rule is that only health-care professionals are in a position to understand the significance of the risks involved and to assess the relative advantages and disadvantages of a given form of prescription-based therapy. The duty then devolves on the health-care provider to supply to the patient such information as is deemed appropriate under the circumstances so that the patient can make an informed choice as to therapy."). Thus, the court of appeals here correctly remarked that, "[i]n its application, the [LID] appears to be less a rule of causation and more a standard for determining when a drug manufacturer has satisfied its duty to warn."

Manufacturers generally have a duty to warn consumers of foreseeable risks of harm from using their products. *See* Third Restatement at § 2. But under the LID, if the manufacturer provides complete, accurate, and appropriate warnings about the product to the learned intermediary, it fulfills its duty to warn the consumer. *See id.* at § 6. The premise for the LID is that certain types of goods (such as prescription drugs) are complex and vary in effect, depending on the end user's unique circumstances, and therefore can be obtained only through a qualified intermediary like a prescribing physician, who can evaluate the patient's condition and weigh the risks and benefits. As applied to prescription drug manufacturers, the Third Restatement states the doctrine as follows:

> A prescription drug or medical device is not reasonably safe due to inadequate instructions or warnings if reasonable instructions or warnings regarding foreseeable risks of harm are not provided to:
>
> (1) prescribing and other health-care providers who are in a position to reduce the risks of harm in accordance with the instructions or warnings; or
>
> (2) the patient when the manufacturer knows or has reason to know that health-care providers will not be in a position to reduce the risks of harm in accordance with the instructions or warnings.

Third Restatement § 6(d).

Although the court of appeals has embraced the LID, this Court has not yet addressed the doctrine. In our view, the Third Restatement properly states the LID, and therefore we adopt § 6(d) as our expression of it. Adopting the doctrine places us with the majority of jurisdictions that have considered the matter. *See generally Centocor*, 372 S.W.3d at 158 n. 17 (noting that "the highest courts of at least thirty-five states have adopted some form of the [LID] within the prescription drug products-liability context or cited favorably to its application within this context").

Contrary to Watts's assertion, the LID does not create a blanket immunity for pharmaceutical manufacturers. The doctrine does not apply, for instance, if the manufacturer fails to provide adequate warnings to the learned intermediary. In that event, as Medicis acknowledged at oral argument in this Court, a patient could sue and directly recover from a drug manufacturer based on its failure to properly warn the prescribing physician.

Watts also asserts, and the court of appeals agreed, that the underlying rationale for the LID is no longer viable. But we find persuasive the reasoning of the Texas Supreme Court in rejecting this argument.

> Prescription drugs are likely to be complex medicines, esoteric in formula and varied in effect. As a medical expert, the prescribing physician can take into account the propensities of the drug, as well as the susceptibilities of his patient. His is the task of weighing the benefits of any medication against its potential dangers. The choice he makes is an informed one, an individualized medical judgment bottomed on a knowledge of both patient and palliative. Pharmaceutical companies then, who must warn ultimate purchasers of dangers inherent in patent drugs sold over the counter, in selling prescription drugs are required to warn only the prescribing physician, who acts as a "learned intermediary" between manufacturer and consumer.... Because patients can obtain prescription drugs only through their prescribing physician or another authorized intermediary and because the "learned intermediary" is best suited to weigh the patient's individual needs in conjunction with the risks and benefits of the prescription drug, we are in agreement with the overwhelming majority of other courts that have considered the learned intermediary doctrine and hold that, within the physician-patient relationship, the learned intermediary doctrine applies and generally limits the drug manufacturer's duty to warn to the prescribing physician.

Centocor, 372 S.W.3d at 159 (citations omitted); see also Larkin, 153 S.W.3d at 763–64 (stating that policy reasons support the LID because (1) the "prescribing physician is in a superior position to impart the warning and can provide an independent medical decision as to whether use of the drug is appropriate for treatment of a particular patient," (2) the "manufacturers lack effective means to communicate directly with each patient," and (3) any duty to directly warn the end user would unduly interfere with the physician-patient relationship).

In finding the policy rationale for the LID unpersuasive, the court of appeals relied on *State ex rel. Johnson & Johnson Corp. v. Karl*, 220 W.Va. 463, 647 S.E.2d 899 (2007). In *Karl*, the West Virginia Supreme Court found the LID outdated and that "existing law of comparative contribution among joint tortfeasors is adequate to address issues of liability among physicians and drug companies...." No other court has followed *Karl*, and several courts have criticized it.... Like these other courts, we do not find *Karl* persuasive.

Watts alternatively urges this Court to adopt a direct-to-consumer ("DTC") advertising exception to the LID. *See* Perez v. Wyeth Labs. Inc., 161 N.J. 1, 734 A.2d 1245, 1247, 1256 (1999) (concluding that "when mass marketing of prescription drugs seeks to influence a patient's choice of a drug, a pharmaceutical manufacturer that makes direct claims to consumers for the efficacy of its product should not be unqualifiedly relieved of a duty to provide proper warnings of the dangers or side effects of the product," and "[c]onsumer-direct advertising of pharmaceuticals thus belies each of the premises on which the [LID] rests"). The Third Restatement, however, provides a different exception to the LID that sufficiently protects consumers. *See* Third Restatement § 6(d)(2) ("A prescription drug or medical device is not reasonably safe due to inadequate instructions or warnings if reasonable instructions or warnings regarding foreseeable risks of harm are not provided to: . . . the patient when the manufacturer knows or has reason to know that health-care providers will not be in a position to reduce the risks of harm in accordance with the instructions or warnings.").

In light of this broad exception, we decline to recognize a DTC advertising exception, which has been adopted only in New Jersey.

. . .

Watts did not allege in her complaint that she received the full prescribing informational materials, but she did allege that "Medicis provided" those warnings, without specifying to whom, and attached them as an exhibit to her complaint. Watts also did not specifically allege that Medicis breached its duty by giving inadequate or otherwise defective warnings to her prescribing physician and other health-care providers who were in a position to reduce the risks of harm. She did allege more generally, however, that "Medicis failed to provide an adequate warning of the danger" of using Solodyn for more than twelve weeks.

Viewed in a light most favorable to Watts, her complaint implies that Medicis failed to give appropriate warnings to her or the pertinent health-care provider. Accordingly, we vacate the superior court's dismissal of Watts's product liability claim and remand the case for further proceedings. If Medicis establishes that there is no genuine factual dispute that it provided complete, adequate warnings for Solodyn to Watts's prescribing physician and other health-care providers who were in a position to reduce the risks of harm, the LID applies and, as a matter of law, Medicis satisfied its duty to warn and would be entitled to summary judgment on the product liability claim.

Notes

Watts addressed one exception to the general rule that the duty to warn applies to all entities in a product's chain of distribution. There are several other related exceptions to this rule, as well as special issues regarding the duty to warn more generally:

Sophisticated user doctrine. Closely related to the rule that there is no duty to warn of obvious risks of a product is the sophisticated user doctrine. Under this rule, if the end user of a product has special knowledge or expertise concerning a product, a supplier is not liable for the failure to warn of the dangers associated with the product. For example, in *Johnson v. American Standard, Inc.*, 179 P.3d 905, 916 (Cal. 2008), the defendant manufactured and supplied air conditioning equipment that contained R-22, refrigerant that can decompose into phosgene gas and cause health issues. Air conditioning (HVAC) technicians had "generally known of the dangers this exposure could cause since as early as 1931." Plaintiff was a certified HVAC technician who had completed several training courses in the field. The California Supreme Court held that the sophisticated user doctrine shielded American Standard for liability for its failure to warn of the dangers associated with its product because here was undisputed evidence that HVAC technicians could reasonably be expected to know of the dangers, even if this particular technician claimed not to know.

Component parts doctrine. "[W]hile component part sellers should be responsible for defects in their own product, and must warn purchasers about risks associated with the use of their product, they cannot reasonably be expected to monitor the development of all potential products into which their components are integrated." Webb v. Special Elec. Co., 370 P.3d 1022, 1032 (Cal. 2016). In such cases, the seller has no duty to warn the immediate buyer or end user unless the component was defective or the seller was involved in integrating the component into the product. *Id.*

Bulk supplier doctrine. This doctrine parallels the component parts doctrine, but involves raw materials like "sand, gravel, or kerosene [that] cannot be defectively designed." Restatement (Third) of Torts: Products Liability § 5, com. c. If the raw materials are supplied to a sophisticated buyer in bulk, the supplier has no duty to warn subsequent buyers of the end product.

Post-sale duty to warn. To be actionable, a product must be defective at the time of sale or distribution. Under what circumstances should a defendant have an obligation to warn consumers about the dangers of a product that the seller was unaware of at the time of sale? The *Restatement (Third) of Torts* takes the position that such a duty is owed when "a reasonable person in the seller's position would provide such a warning." *Id.* § 10(a). The *Restatement (Third)* provides several factors to consider in making this determination, including whether those to whom a warning might be provided can be identified, whether a warning can be effectively communicated, and the seriousness of the risk of harm if no warning is provided. *See* Patton v. Hutchinson Wil-Rich Mfg. Co., 861 P.2d 1299 (Kan. 1993) (discussing other considerations in deciding whether manufacturer is required to provide a post-sale warning). However, the majority of courts have rejected the argument that there is also a post-sale duty to retrofit a product that was not defective when originally sold on the theory that product recalls "are properly the province of administrative agencies, as the federal statutes that expressly delegate recall authority to various agencies suggest." Ostendorf v. Clark Equipment Co., 122 S.W.3d 530, 534 (Ky. 2003).

E. Defenses

1. Comparative Fault

At the time that products liability law began to develop, the all-or-nothing defense of assumption of risk was still quite common. Gradually, comparative fault largely replaced assumption of risk. Originally, liability for defective products was viewed as being strict in nature. With the advent of the risk-utility tests employed in information and some design defect cases, the defendant's fault began to play a greater role. These developments led to a reexamination of what role a plaintiff's fault should play in apportioning liability.

General Motors Corp. v. Sanchez

997 S.W.2d 584 (Tex. 1999)

[Some of the facts of the case appear in Part C2 above. The plaintiffs presented circumstantial evidence that Sanchez shifted the gear of his truck into what he thought was Park but which was actually in a position known as "hydraulic neutral." The gear then shifted into Reverse after Sanchez left his truck. The truck rolled backwards, pinning Sanchez against a gate. The jury found against GM.]

The principal question in this case is when does the doctrine of comparative responsibility apply in a products-liability case....

I

[Contrary to the plaintiffs' theory,] G.M. suggested that Sanchez simply left the truck in Neutral and it rolled down the five degree slope toward the gate. Finally, G.M. argued that even if the accident was caused by a mis-shift as alleged by the plaintiffs, the mis-shift was a result of operator error, and not a defect in design.

The jury rejected G.M.'s theories and found that G.M. was negligent, the transmission was defectively designed, and G.M.'s warning was so inadequate as to constitute a marketing defect. The jury also found that Sanchez was fifty percent responsible for the accident, but the trial court disregarded this finding. The trial court rendered judgment for actual and punitive damages of $8.5 million for the plaintiffs.

...

III

The jury found that Sanchez was fifty percent responsible for his accident. G.M. argues that this finding should be applied to reduce its liability for damages whether in negligence or strict liability. However, the plaintiffs argue that Sanchez's actions amounted to no more than a failure to discover or guard against a product defect and ... such negligence does not constitute a defense to strict liability....

Before 1987, . . . [i]f strict liability was asserted against any defendant, comparative negligence did not apply. . . .

In 1987, the Legislature changed Chapter 33 of the Texas Civil Practice and Remedies Code to a system of] comparative responsibility. Under comparative responsibility, a court reduces a claimant's damages recovery by the "percentage of responsibility" attributed to him by the trier of fact. The new statute expressly included suits based on strict tort liability. It defined "Percentage of responsibility" as the percentage that a party "cause[d] or contribute[d] to cause in any way, whether by *negligent act or omission*, . . . [or] by *other conduct or activity violative of the applicable legal standard*" the harm for which damages are sought. Thus, as the emphasized language indicates, the new statute applies to a claimant's conduct that violated the duty to use ordinary care or some other applicable legal standard.

. . . The position of *Restatement (Third)*, section 17(a), is that a plaintiff's conduct should be considered to reduce a damages recovery if it fails to conform to applicable standards of care, similar to the Texas 1987 statutory scheme. However, comment "d" to *Restatement (Third)* states:

> [W]hen the defendant claims that the plaintiff failed to discover a defect, there must be evidence that the plaintiff's conduct in failing to discover a defect did, in fact, fail to meet a standard of reasonable care. In general, a plaintiff has no reason to expect that a new product contains a defect and would have little reason to be on guard to discover it.

We believe that a duty to discover defects, and to take precautions in constant anticipation that a product might have a defect, would defeat the purposes of strict liability. Thus, we hold that a consumer has no duty to discover or guard against a product defect, but a consumer's conduct other than the mere failure to discover or guard against a product defect is subject to comparative responsibility. Public policy favors reasonable conduct by consumers regardless of whether a product is defective. A consumer is not relieved of the responsibility to act reasonably nor may a consumer fail to take reasonable precautions regardless of a known or unknown product defect. . . . Because we conclude that a consumer has no duty to discover or guard against a product defect, we next determine whether the decedent's conduct in this case was merely the failure to discover or guard against a product defect or some other negligence unrelated to a product defect.

The truck's owner's manual describes safety measures designed to ensure that the truck would not move when parked: (1) set the parking brake; (2) place the truck completely in Park; (3) turn off the engine; (4) remove the key from the ignition; and (5) check that Park is fully engaged by pulling down on the gear shift. Sanchez's father testified that his son probably read the entire owner's manual. The plaintiff's own experts agreed at trial that Sanchez failed to perform any of the safety measures described in the owner's manual and that performing any one of them would have prevented the accident. This evidence is sufficient to support the jury's negligence finding.

Regardless of any danger of a mis-shift, a driver has a duty to take reasonable precautions to secure his vehicle before getting out of it. The danger that it could roll, or move if the engine is running, exists independently of the possibility of a mis-shift. For instance, the driver could inadvertently leave a vehicle in gear or a mechanical problem unrelated to a product defect could prevent Park from fully engaging. A moving vehicle without a driver is a hazard to public safety. The state licenses drivers who have demonstrated the minimum knowledge and skill necessary to safely operate a motor vehicle. Many, perhaps most, consumer products may be operated without a license, including lawn and garden equipment, household appliances, and powered hand tools. It follows then that, because of this licensing requirement, as well as other special duties imposed on drivers, more is expected of an operator of a motor vehicle than of users of most other consumer products. Thus, although we do not expect the average driver to have the engineering background to discover defects in their car's transmission, we do expect the reasonably prudent driver to take safety precautions to prevent a runaway car. Sanchez had a responsibility to operate his truck in a safe manner. The fact that the precautions demanded of a driver generally would have prevented this accident does not make Sanchez's negligence a mere failure to discover or guard against a mis-shift.

. . .

Sanchez's actions amounted to conduct other than a mere failure to discover or guard against a product defect. We hold as a matter of law that such conduct must be scrutinized under the duty to use ordinary care or other applicable duty. We conclude that there was legally sufficient evidence to support the jury's verdict that Sanchez breached the duty to use ordinary care and was fifty percent responsible for the accident.

. . . Accordingly, we reverse the court of appeals judgment and render judgment that the plaintiffs recover their actual damages reduced by the jury's finding of fifty percent comparative responsibility.

Notes

Apples and oranges? Where liability for a defective product is truly strict, there is some tension in saying that "the user's negligence is material when the seller's is not," *Smith v. Smith*, 278 N.W.2d 155 (S.D. 1979), and that a jury is being asked to compare "apples and oranges." Daly v. General Motors Corp., 20 Cal. 3d 725 (1978). Is this still a concern when a court is using the risk-utility analysis of the *Restatement (Third)*? Most courts follow *Sanchez*'s approach.

Foreseeable misuse of a product. Recall from earlier that a product may still be deemed defective even if it was misused by the ultimate consumer, provided it was misused in a foreseeable way.

2. Substantial Modification of the Product

Recall that the defectiveness of a product is judged at the time the product left the control of the defendant. What should be the effect if a user or third party modifies or alters the product after it has left the defendant's control, but such modification was foreseeable or even predictable? Below are two different approaches to this issue.

Michigan Compiled Law

§ 600.2947 Product liability action; liability of manufacturer or seller.

(1) A manufacturer or seller is not liable in a product liability action for harm caused by an alteration of the product unless the alteration was reasonably foreseeable. Whether there was an alteration of a product and whether an alteration was reasonably foreseeable are legal issues to be resolved by the court.

§ 600.2945 Definitions.

(a) "Alteration" means a material change in a product after the product leaves the control of the manufacturer or seller. Alteration includes a change in the product's design, packaging, or labeling; a change to or removal of a safety feature, warning, or instruction; deterioration or damage caused by failure to observe routine care and maintenance or failure to observe an installation, preparation, or storage procedure; or a change resulting from repair, renovation, reconditioning, recycling, or reclamation of the product.

Jones v. Ryobi, Ltd.

37 F.3d 423 (8th Cir. 1994)

FAGG, Circuit Judge.

Jennifer Jones was employed at Business Cards Tomorrow (BCT) as the operator of a small printing press known as an offset duplicator. Jones seriously injured her left hand when she caught it in the moving parts of the press. . . .

The press involved in Jones's injury operates by passing blank paper through several moving parts, imprinting an image on the paper, and dispensing the printed paper through upper and lower "eject wheels." To avoid streaking the freshly printed image, on each job the operator must adjust the eject wheels to ensure the wheels do not touch the freshly printed area. The press was manufactured and sold to BCT equipped with both a plastic guard that prevented the operator from reaching into the moving parts to adjust the eject wheels, and an electric interlock switch that automatically shut off the press if the guard was opened. Sometime after the press was manufactured and delivered to BCT, the guard was removed and the interlock switch was disabled to allow the press to run without the guard. Because this modification increased production by saving the few seconds required to stop and to restart the press when the operator adjusted the eject wheels, the modification was a common practice in the printing industry.

Jones learned to operate the press by watching other BCT employees. Jones testified she knew the guard was missing and knew it was dangerous to have her hands near the unguarded moving parts, but her supervisor pressured her to save time by adjusting the eject wheels while the press was running. Jones feared she would be fired if she took the time to stop the press. While Jones was adjusting the eject wheels on the running press, a noise startled her. Jones jumped and her left hand was caught in the press's moving parts and crushed.

. . .

To recover on a theory of . . . defective design under Missouri law, Jones must prove she was injured as a direct result of a defect that existed when the press was sold. Jasinski v. Ford Motor Co., 824 S.W.2d 454, 455 (Mo. Ct. App.1992) (explaining elements of defective design claim). Jones had the burden to show the press had not been modified to create a defect that could have proximately caused her injury. Jones failed to meet this burden because her evidence showed the press had been substantially modified by removing the safety guard and disabling the interlock switch, and showed the modification caused her injury. When a third party's modification makes a safe product unsafe, the seller is relieved of liability even if the modification is foreseeable. Jones did not show who modified the press, but her evidence clearly showed that a third party, not the manufacturer or the distributor, was responsible for the modification.

Although the manufacturer provided tools for general maintenance of the press that could also be used to remove the guard, we do not believe this made the manufacturer responsible for the guard's removal. Jones produced no evidence that any representative of the manufacturer or the distributor removed the guard or instructed BCT to remove the guard from the press involved in Jones's injury. Indeed, the distributor's service representative testified he told BCT's owner several times the guard should be replaced, but BCT's owner shrugged off the suggestion. Because BCT knew the guard was missing and the interlock switch was disabled, but did not follow the distributor's advice to repair the disabled safety features, the distributor's service work on the press did not extend the distributor's liability to defects that were not present when the press was sold.

Jones argues the modification rule does not apply because the press was not safe even before the modification. We disagree. The press was safe before the modification because the press would not run without the safety guard covering the moving parts. . . . Although several witnesses testified the press operated more efficiently without the safety guard and interlock switch, other witnesses testified similar presses operated satisfactorily with the designed safety features intact. The press could be operated safely without removing the guard because the eject wheels did not have to be adjusted while the press was running. Jones's expert witness opined the press was unsafe as designed, but the expert based his view on the printing industry's tendency to disable the press's safety features to achieve greater production. Thus, the expert's testimony does not show the press was unreasonably dangerous when used in the same condition as when it was sold.

Because Jones's evidence showed a third party's modification, not a defect existing when the press was sold, was the sole cause of her injury, her . . . product liability claim for defective design fails as a matter of law. The district court thus properly granted the manufacturer's and the distributor's JAML motions.

. . .

HEANEY, Senior Circuit Judge, dissenting.

Viewing the evidence in the light most favorable to Jones, as we must, I cannot subscribe to the majority's opinion that the offset duplicator was safe as originally manufactured.

. . .

The testimony of Dr. Creighton, Jones's expert witness, is alone sufficient to support the inference that the offset duplicator was not safe as originally designed. . . . He testified that the duplicator's guard, in addition to not being fail-safe, was made of material "that will break . . . readily," did not allow for proper ventilation of the internal components of the machine, and invited removal. . . .

Further, although not direct proof that the duplicator was defectively designed, the fact that an overwhelming majority of machines had their guards removed after their delivery is evidence that the duplicator was incapable of operating efficiently according to industry standards. According to ITEK representative Brad Gruenewald, nearly ninety-eight percent of all machines he came into contact with had their safety covers removed. Indeed, Gruenewald testified that he told duplicator operators in effect to remove the guard in order to alleviate problems with ink emulsification that occurred as a result of humidity which frequently became trapped inside the plastic shield.

. . .

In my judgment there was sufficient evidence to support the inference that the offset duplicator was unreasonably dangerous and thus was defectively designed. This case should have met its fate in the hands of the jury members, not the district court's and not now ours.

Notes

Foreseeability of the modification. *Jones* states the minority approach on the issue of the foreseeability of a modification or alteration of a product. *See, e.g.*, Ind. Code § 34-20-6-5 (recognizing a defense where the modification or alteration is not reasonably expected by the seller); Conn. Gen. Stat. Ann. § 52-572p (providing that a defendant is not liable unless "the alteration or modification was the result of conduct that reasonably should have been anticipated by the product seller'). If it is foreseeable to a manufacturer that an end user will remove a safety device or otherwise substantially alter a product, what might the manufacturer do to limit potential liability on a design defect theory?

The substantial modification "defense." *Jones* treats the modification issue as part of the plaintiff's prima facie case. Other courts and statutes often refer to the substantial modification or substantial alteration *defense. See* Ind. Code § 34-20-6-5; Elliot v. Sears, Roebuck & Co., 642 A.2d 709 (1994). The same issue of nomenclature also arises regarding whether it is part of a plaintiff's prima facie case to show that the product was not misused in an unforeseeable way or whether misuse is better viewed as an affirmative defense. *See* Perez v. VAS S.p.A., 188 Cal. App. 4th 658, 678 n.6 (Cal. Ct. App. 2010) (discussing this issue in the context of jury instructions).

3. Compliance with Regulations

The Consumer Products Safety Commission (CPSC) is an independent federal regulatory agency that, among other things, promulgates and enforces safety regulations for potentially dangerous products. The CPSC also works with industry groups and consumer groups to develop voluntary safety standards for consumer products. State statutes and regulations may also set safety standards for consumer products.

To what extent should the fact that a product complies with these types of standards shield a manufacturer or seller from liability? In a traditional negligence action, the fact that a defendant's actions comply with an applicable regulation may be evidence that the defendant was not negligent, but it does not establish that the defendant was exercising reasonable care. Some state products liability statutes articulate the same position and simply provide that the fact that a manufacturer's product complied with an applicable state or federal regulation may be introduced as evidence that the product was not defective. Others go further:

Colo. Rev. Stat. Ann. § 13-21-403. Presumptions

(1) In any product liability action, it shall be rebuttably presumed that the product which caused the injury, death, or property damage was not defective and that the manufacturer or seller thereof was not negligent if the product:

. . .

(b) Complied with, at the time of sale by the manufacturer, any applicable code, standard, or regulation adopted or promulgated by the United States or by this state, or by any agency of the United States or of this state.

(2) In like manner, noncompliance with a government code, standard, or regulation existing and in effect at the time of sale of the product by the manufacturer which contributed to the claim or injury shall create a rebuttable presumption that the product was defective or negligently manufactured.

4. Preemption

In some instances, a manufacturer's compliance with federal law pertaining to a consumer product may serve as a complete bar to recovery in a products liability action. Federal statutes may expressly or impliedly preempt state law, including statutory or common law products liability actions. In *Riegel v. Medtronic*, 552 U.S. 312 (2008), the Supreme Court held that the express preemption clause of the Medical Device Amendments of 1976 preempts state suits that challenge the safety of certain medical devices that have been approved by the FDA as part of its premarket approval process. The Act prohibited states from establishing requirements that are "different from, or in addition to, any requirement applicable under" the Medical Device Act. 21 U.S.C. § 360k(a). The *Riegel* court held that state tort duties impose requirements on the medical devices in question that are "different from or in addition to the federal requirements."

In contrast, implied preemption occurs in one of two ways. Where "compliance with both federal and state regulations is a physical impossibility," *Florida Lime & Avocado Growers, Inc. v. Paul*, 373 U.S. 132, 142–143, (1963), or where state law "stands as an obstacle to the accomplishment and execution of the full purposes and objectives of Congress," *Felder v. Casey*, 487 U.S. 131, 138, (1988), "conflict preemption" exists. Where federal law is "so pervasive as to make reasonable the inference that Congress left no room for the States to supplement it," *Fidelity Federal Savings & Loan Assn. v. De la Cuesta*, 458 U.S. 141, 153 (1982), "field preemption" exists. In *Wyeth v. Levine*, 555 U.S. 555 (2009), the Supreme Court considered whether a state products liability claim based on an inadequate warning regarding medication was preempted by federal law. The warning had already been approved by the federal Food and Drug Administration (FDA). Citing the presumption that the "powers of the States were not to be superseded by the Federal Act unless that was the clear and manifest purpose of Congress"—particularly in a field that the states have traditionally occupied—the Court held that the plaintiff's claims were not impliedly preempted by the approval authority given to the FDA.

F. Final Thoughts on Products Liability

Products liability is one of the major battlegrounds of the tort reform wars. Perhaps the most common argument in favor of imposing stricter limits on the ability of plaintiffs to recover for injuries caused by allegedly defective products is that the threat of liability deters innovation. "Innovation depends on the ability to experiment and make mistakes," argues Deborah J. La Fetra, an attorney with the Pacific Legal Foundation, a libertarian-minded public interest law firm. "A fair legal system must provide for the evolution of technology and manufacturing or risk the loss of inventions that benefit all members of society." Deborah J. La Fetra, *Freedom, Responsibility, and Risk: Fundamental Principles Supporting Tort Reform*, 36 IND. L. REV. 645, 647 (2003). As an example, La Fetra cites the medical field:

> In 1983, Merrill Dow Pharmaceuticals voluntarily removed Bendectin from the American market in response to multi-million dollar claims that it caused birth defects in children carried by women who took the drug during pregnancy to combat nausea and vomiting (*i.e.*, morning sickness). Despite Bendectin's use in over thirty million pregnancies, experts were sharply divided on whether the drug caused birth defects; the majority opinion, however, was that Bendectin "was not a significant teratogen." The FDA and most courts held there was no increased risk of birth defects associated with Bendectin. Despite the legal vindication of Bendectin, the American market continues to lack any drugs approved for the treatment of morning sickness, and American pharmaceutical companies have not chosen to invest in research for a new morning sickness drug. Even members of the plaintiffs' bar concede that Bendectin was driven from the market by unjustified litigation.

Id. at 653.

Those on the other side of the debate argue that "[p]roperly understood, American tort law contains a number of features that are accommodative of, rather than pointedly antagonistic toward, disruptive technological innovation." James A. Henderson Jr., *Tort vs. Technology: Accommodating Disruptive Innovation*, 47 ARIZ. ST. L.J. 1145, 1146 (2015). Professor Ben Barton used the examples of playground design to counter the innovation arguments of tort reform proponents. As evidence of the harms brought about by expanded products liability, tort reformers have sometimes pointed to the fact that traditional playgrounds have increasingly been stripped of their traditional features (like seesaws and monkey bars) for fear of potential liability. Barton argues that "the traditional playground was done in by a combination of liability concerns and regulatory measures from the Consumer Product Safety Commission (CPSC)," but that this was not necessarily a bad thing. For one, "Beginning in the 1970s there was a dawning realization that playgrounds were the cause of many serious childhood injuries and deaths." Benjamin J. Barton, *Tort Reform, Innovation, and Playground Design*, 58 FLA. L. REV. 265, 292 (2006).

In addition, Barton argues, "this new focus on liability and playground safety" has spawned meaningful innovation when it comes to playground design:

> Colorful, modular play areas are replacing the "traditional" playground all over America. Interestingly, the "new" playground design is not only more concerned with safety, but also much more reflective of child development and child play concerns. Additionally, new playgrounds are much easier to maintain than the old playgrounds (because rubber-covered steel and plastic is much more durable than wood or other materials), and require less parental or governmental oversight of play. Admittedly, relative judgments about playground design are subjective, but I find it hard to believe that there are many who would choose the old prison yard-style playgrounds over the new style. New playgrounds have more activities,

> encourage group and imaginative play, and still have swings, slides, and climbing elements.

Id. at 294.

The arguments over the proper scope of products liability law are unlikely to stop anytime soon. New innovations, like autonomous or driverless cars, have spurred substantial debate in terms of the potential liability for manufacturers and sellers. *See* Mark A. Geistfeld, *A Roadmap for Autonomous Vehicles: State Tort Liability, Automobile Insurance, and Federal Safety Regulation*, 105 Cal. L. Rev. 1611 (2017) (discussing the host of potential liability issues involved). And old debates, like whether gun manufacturers should be required to implement new design features in order to reduce the number of gun-related injuries, continue to the present. *See* Adames v. Sheahan, 909 N.E.2d 742 (Ill. 2009) (concluding federal Protection of Lawful Commerce in Arms Act barred a design defect claim based on the manufacturer's failure to incorporate safety devices such as a child-resistant manual safety, a grip safety, and personalized gun technology "that would have prevented unauthorized users, such as children, from firing the gun"); Andrew J. McClurg, *The Second Amendment Right to Be Negligent*, 68 Fla. L. Rev. 1, 7–8 (2016) ("Because no federal gun safety design regulations exist, the absence of a threat of tort liability leaves gun manufacturers with little incentive to implement safer gun designs, such as personalized gun technology that would prevent unauthorized users from operating a firearm."); Richard C. Ausness, *Gun Control Through Tort Law*, 68 Fla. L. Rev. F. 101, 108 (2017) (responding to McClurg's article and suggesting that "perhaps we should consider whether some of these benefits can be achieved more cheaply by imposing certain theft prevention measures by regulation instead of relying on tort liability").

Review Question

Jack purchased a package of PecanTastic bars, a delicious candy featuring pecans and caramel covered in dark chocolate. The wrapper advertised the fact that these were the ingredients of the candy. When Jack bit into his first PecanTastic bar, he broke a tooth on a pecan shell embedded in the candy. While it is impossible to completely remove all traces of shells from pecans in the candy-making process, Choco-Buddies, a competitor to PecanTastic, employs a different removal process that effectively removes 99.8% of all shells.

Briefly identify all of the various products liability claims Jack might assert, the parties against whom he might assert them, and any issues that are likely to arise during the litigation process concerning those claims. (You can assume that the relevant jurisdiction employs California's test for design defect claims.)

Part 4
Dignitary Torts

Dignitary torts are so named because they are wrongs that subject another to indignity. The torts of battery, assault, false imprisonment, and intentional infliction of emotional distress, which were all covered in Part 1, actually fall into this category. But this part of the book focuses primarily on two other tort theories designed to protect one's dignity—defamation and invasion of privacy.

Chapter 15

Defamation

A. Defamation: The Prima Facie Case

- Publication
  - Slander versus libel
  - Publication defined
  - Liability for repeating or republishing
  - Other concepts developed in class or in readings assigned by the professor
- Of defamatory statements
  - "Defamatory" defined
  - Rules of interpretation
  - Defamation by implication
  - Other concepts developed in class or in readings assigned by the professor
- Of and concerning the plaintiff
  - "Of and concerning the plaintiff" defined
  - Small group defamation
  - Other concepts developed in class or in readings assigned by the professor
- Damages
  - Types of damages recoverable
  - Common law rules: libel and slander per se
  - Other concepts developed in class or in readings assigned by the professor
- The role of truth
  - Burden of proof
  - Substantial truth
  - Other concepts developed in class or in readings assigned by the professor
- Actionable and non-actionable statements
  - Kinds of statements that are actionable
  - Kinds of statements that are not actionable
  - Other concepts developed in class or in readings assigned by the professor

B. Constitutional Constraints on Defamation

- Public officials and public figures
  - The constitutional fault standard required
  - Justifications for the fault standard
  - Who qualifies as a public official

    - Who qualifies as a public figure
    - The meaning of "actual malice"
    - Other concepts developed in class or in readings assigned by the professor
  - Private figures and matters of public concern or controversy
    - The constitutional fault standard required
    - The effect of *Gertz* on presumed damages
    - The fault standard in practice following *Gertz*
    - Actual malice and falsity
    - Other concepts developed in class or in readings assigned by the professor
  - Private figures and matters of private concern
    - The constitutional fault standard required
    - Public controversies, matters of public concern, and matters of private concern
    - Other concepts developed in class or in readings assigned by the professor
  - The actual malice standard
    - Ways of establishing reckless disregard
    - Clear and convincing proof
    - Other concepts developed in class or in readings assigned by the professor
  - Classifying plaintiffs as public figures or private figures
    - All-purpose public figure
      - "All-purpose public figure" defined
      - The burden of proof for all-purpose public figures
      - Justifications for imposing this burden
    - Limited-purpose public figure
      - "Limited-purpose public figure" defined
      - The burden of proof for limited-purpose public figures
      - Justifications for imposing this burden
    - Involuntary limited-purpose public figure
      - "Involuntary limited-purpose public figure" defined
      - The burden of proof for involuntary public figures
      - Justifications for imposing this burden
    - Other concepts developed in class or in readings assigned by the professor

C. Privileges and Defenses
  - Absolute privileges
    - Truth
    - Consent
    - Judicial proceedings privilege
    - Other concepts developed in class or in readings assigned by the professor
  - Qualified privileges
    - Common interest privilege
    - Public interest privilege
    - Privilege to protect one's own interest or that of others
    - Fair comment
    - How such privileges are lost

- Other concepts developed in class or in readings assigned by the professor
- Media privileges
  - Fair reporting privilege
  - Neutral reporting privilege
  - Other concepts developed in class or in readings assigned by the professor

Chapter Problem. Fred Winchell owns a small automotive repair shop. His wife, Rachel Winchell, stays at home to raise the couple's four children. The Winchells regularly attend the public meetings of the Pleasant Hill School Board. Both of the Winchells regularly speak out at these meetings and offer their opinions regarding various matters. Donna Edwards is a parent with a child in the same school as one of the Winchells' children. Donna recently posted a photo of the Winchells' car and an accompanying derogatory comment on her Facebook page. Fred and Rachel are now suing Donna on a defamation theory.

The tort of defamation exists primarily to protect one's reputational interest. The history of the tort goes back centuries, but modern technology has greatly enhanced the ability of one person to damage the reputation of another. Thus, the tort is perhaps more relevant now than ever.

As it exists today, defamation is one of the more complicated torts. States have long employed a host of distinctions and categories in establishing the rules for defamation. In the 1960s, the Supreme Court added a new layer of complexity by establishing constitutional rules that impacted the common law rules of defamation. As a result, "[t]here is simply no way succinctly to state the elements of a modern cause of action for defamation." Rodney A. Smolla, 2 Law of Defamation § 1:34 (2d ed.). Despite this, this chapter tries to present the rules regarding defamation as clearly as possible. Part A of this chapter covers the basic issues that are likely to be present in most defamation actions before turning in Part B to the special constitutional rules that apply. Part C addresses some of the more common defenses and privileges.

A. Defamation: The Prima Facie Case

Defamation may consist of slander—typically thought of as the spoken form of defamation—or libel—typically thought of as written or more permanent forms of defamation. Historically, the distinction often mattered for purposes of defining the plaintiff's prima facie case. Given the greater permanence of a libelous statement, a defamation plaintiff did not have to establish that a defamatory statement was false in order to establish a prima facie case at common law. Instead, the defendant bore the burden of establishing that the statement was true in order to avoid liability. Likewise, in the case of libel, a plaintiff often did not have to establish that the defendant knew or had reason to know that the statement was false. Today, the exact elements of a prima facie case may vary from jurisdiction to jurisdiction. But in every case, a plaintiff will need to establish that there was a publication of a defamatory statement of and concerning the plaintiff. The rules may vary as to what sort of damages a plaintiff must establish and which party bears the burden of proof with respect to the question of whether the defamatory statement was true or false. Finally, there will sometimes be a question as to whether the statement in question is actionable to begin with, such as in the case of a statement of opinion.

1. Publication

Regardless of whether the defamatory communication takes the form of libel or slander, liability for defamation requires publication of a defamatory statement. The defamatory statement need not be "publicized" in the sense of being communicated to a large number of people; it is enough that it was communicated to at least one person other than the person defamed. Doe v. Am. Online, Inc., 783 So. 2d 1010, 1016 (Fla. 2001). Of course, the communication must also be understood by at least that person. *See* Economopoulos v. A.G. Pollard Co., 105 N.E. 896 (Mass. 1914) (concluding that no publication occurred where statement was made in Greek and no one who heard statement spoke Greek). The publication element is satisfied by either an intentional publication (where the defendant acts for the purpose of communicating with the third person or knows that such communication is substantially certain to occur) or a negligent publication (for example, where the defendant leaves a defamatory letter lying around in plain sight and the letter is read by another). Restatement (Second) of Torts § 577 cmt. k.

Despite the seeming simplicity of the publication requirement, there are some subtleties. For example, where one manager says something negative about an employee to another manager in the company, has there been a communication about the employee to a third person, or is this just the company speaking to itself through its agents? *See* Bals v. Verduzco, 600 N.E.2d 1353 (Ind. 1992) (stating the majority rule that there has been no publication). The Internet has increased the potential for defamation liability exponentially. Under the traditional common law rule, the property owner who intentionally and unreasonably fails to remove defamatory graffiti from the bathroom wall is treated as having made a publication of the graffiti himself. Restatement (Second) of Torts § 577(2). The individual who merely *delivers or transmits* material containing defamatory material (like a newspaper delivery person) is not treated as having made a publication of the defamatory statement. However, a person who repeats a defamatory statement originally made by another (like the gossipy neighbor or the newspaper editor) is treated as having published the statement under the theory that a talebearer may cause as much damage to the reputation of another as the original talemaker. Harris v. Minvielle, 19 So. 925 (La. 1896).

How should these rules apply in the case of electronic communications? Section 230(c) of the Communications Decency Act (CDA) reverses the common law rules in the case of Internet service providers whose sites are used by others to communicate defamatory information. Under the CDA, providers are not treated as the publisher or speaker of the defamatory content. This provision has been held to shield online service providers from liability for defamation and related torts where the law historically has provided for such liability. *See, e.g.*, Hassell v. Bird, 420 P.3d 776 (Cal. 2018); Zeran v. America Online, Inc., 129 F.3d 327 (4th Cir. 1997). Why would Congress want to shield online service providers from liability in these kinds of cases, even when they are aware that they are providing a forum for people who are making false and defamatory statements about others?

Problem 15.1. When Donna posted the photo and derogatory statement on Facebook, she only had a few Facebook friends. Two of her friends "liked" the post. One of those told several other people all about the post, while the other shared Donna's post on her own page. After that, the original post went viral in the local community.

(a) Which of these individuals published the information about the Winchells?

(b) Which of the publications qualify as libel and which qualify as slander?

2. Defamatory Statements

Marcone v. Penthouse International Magazine for Men

754 F.2d 1072 (3d Cir. 1985)

ADAMS, Circuit Judge.I.

Marcone is an attorney residing in Delaware County, a suburb of Philadelphia. During the mid-1970's he gained notoriety in part through his representation of the Pagans, a motorcycle gang headquartered in Marcus Hook, Pennsylvania, and a rival gang, the Warlocks. Marcone was also linked to these motorcycle gangs on a non-professional basis. In this regard, law enforcement agents stated that Marcone frequented "the Castle," a 40-room mansion in Delaware County which served as the Pagans' headquarters. Among other things, the Castle was connected with the disappearance and death of five young women in 1976. An article in the Philadelphia Inquirer dated March 18, 1976, reported that Marcone once stated that he "occasionally went on weekend trips" with one of the motorcycle gangs.

In February of 1976, a grand jury in Detroit, Michigan, handed down an indictment charging Marcone and 24 other co-defendants with conspiring "to knowingly, intentionally and unlawfully possess with intent to distribute, and to distribute marijuana" in violation of 21 U.S.C. §§841(a)(1), 846 (1982). In particular, the indictment charged that "[d]uring May, 1974, FRANK MARCONE gave $25,000 in United States currency to FREDERICK R. FREY in Philadelphia, Pennsylvania for the purpose of purchasing multi-hundred pound quantities of marijuana in California." Law enforcement agents stated that Marcone and the three other co-defendants from the Philadelphia area had frequent meetings at the Castle.

On May 19, 1976, the government withdrew the charges against Marcone without prejudice to his being reindicted in Philadelphia. An assistant United States Attorney in Detroit explained that the charges were dropped because of "legal technicalities" in tying Marcone to the larger conspiracy which involved defendants from San Diego to Montreal. For reasons not explained in the record, Marcone was not subsequently reindicted in Philadelphia.

Penthouse published an article in its November 1978 issue entitled "The Stoning of America." Written by Edward Rasen, the article concerned the emergence of marijuana trade as a multibillion dollar industry. The subtitle stated that "marijuana is now big agribusiness—a $12 billion a year corporate growth crop." The article proceeded to report, in part, about "criminal attorneys and attorney criminals" involved in drug transactions . . .

Example[]: . . . "Frank Marcone, an attorney from the Philadelphia area, contributed down payments of up to $25,000 on grass transactions. Charges against him were dismissed because he cooperated with further investigations."

Marcone brought suit against *Penthouse* charging that the article libeled him since it declared that he was guilty of an offense for which he was only indicted, and since it stated that charges were dropped against him because he cooperated with the authorities. Plaintiff alleges that these two statements are untrue and that they have caused him harm and subjected him to ridicule.

A.

First, defendant contends that plaintiff has not met the burden of proving the article's defamatory character. This is so, *Penthouse* maintains, because the questioned remarks are incapable of defamatory meaning. Whether a statement is capable of defamatory meaning is a question the judge, as distinguished from the jury, must determine, and the district court ruled that the article was capable of a defamatory meaning.

According to Pennsylvania law, a statement is defamatory if it "tends so to harm the reputation of another as to lower him in the estimation of the community or to deter third persons from associating or dealing with him." The threshold determination of whether a statement is capable of defamatory meaning depends "on the general tendency of the words to have such an effect"; no demonstration of any actual harm to reputation is necessary.

Penthouse attempts to demonstrate that each individual phrase in the article, in isolation, cannot be understood as libelous. Thus, for example, it asserts that "cooperated with further investigations" cannot be defamatory. The proper test, however, requires that the allegedly libelous communication be read as a whole, in context.

As the district court observed, "The Stoning of America" refers to "attorney criminals" and lists as one of the examples:

> Frank Marcone, an attorney from the Philadelphia area, contributed down payments of up to $25,000 on grass transactions. Charges against him were dismissed because he cooperated with further investigations.

This statement suggests that Marcone has committed a crime. Statements imputing the commission of an indictable offense are capable of defamatory meaning as a matter of law. Thus *Penthouse*'s argument that the article could not possibly have defamed Marcone is not valid.

May v. Greater Kansas City Dental Society

863 S.W.2d 941 (Mo. Ct. App. 1993)

HANNA, Judge.

In the summer of 1989, the Internal Revenue Service (IRS) mailed an inquiry to several hundred dentists in the Kansas City area seeking information about Dr. May. Specifically, the inquiry requested names of and information about patients whom the various dentists had referred to Dr. May. Dr. Nelson was one of the dentists who received a letter and IRS summons concerning patients he may have referred to Dr. May. That IRS summons was the incentive for his article.

On or about April 1, 1990, Dr. Nelson published an article in The Professional Journal of the Greater Kansas City Dental Society, the Midwestern Dentist, entitled "For Whom the Bell Tolls, or Beware: The G-Man Cometh!" The Midwestern Dentist is a monthly newsletter published by the Dental Society and at the time of the article, Dr. Nelson was the president of the Dental Society. At the time, Dr. May specialized in endodontics.

Although the article does not mention May by name, he claims to be the subject of the article because it contains a reference to an IRS investigation of "one of our profession." He argues that the article contains offensive references to him. The objectionable terms are: "yo-yo," "wacko," "at odds with the federal government," and "axe murderer." Plaintiff May argues that as a result of defendant Nelson's article, he lost patient referrals and eventually, in 1992, closed his dental practice due to a lack of referrals.

[The plaintiff alleged defamation among other claims, including intentional infliction of emotional distress. The court sustained the defendant's motion to dismiss for failure to state a claim. The plaintiff appealed.]

... The word ["yo-yo] is referenced in the article as follows:

> I called my attorney, the Greater Kansas City Society office, the American Dental Association attorney, Roger Weis with the Missouri Dental Association and the Missouri State Dental Board to see what my options were, and what was the legal implication of distributing patient names, addresses and phone numbers without their consent. My attorney said to give them the names and don't mess around. "You could petition the court to determine cause, etc., but why mess with them for some yo-yo?" he said. The American Dental Association returned my call later that day, and the attorney told me she could not provide legal advice, only my attorney licensed to practice in Missouri could do that, but that precedent probably allowed the IRS to obtain that information.

...

The plaintiff suggests that "yo-yo" denotes an individual who is not stable. While "yo-yo" cannot be categorized as an accolade, it is difficult to define precisely. It is probably susceptible to various interpretations, most of which would not be flattering. It is voguish slang casting one in an unfavorable light and possibly has some relationship to the movement and uses of the more familiar meaning of the word: a double-disc cylinder-shaped object that falls and raises by manipulation of a string.

In the first instance, whether the words are defamatory is a question of law for the court's determination, and the offending words must be considered in the context of the entire publication. The title of the article—"For Whom the Bell Tolls, or Beware: The G-Man Cometh!"—is a factor to be considered if the title accurately reflects the contents of the article. In this respect, the text of the article and its title convey a legitimate concern regarding the invasion of the patients' privacy by the federal government and the effect of a mistaken IRS probe on the reputation of any dentist investigated. Later in the article, the author observes the sobering impact of a visit from the IRS to one's office about a patient referred to "this dentist based on the knowledge he was a competent specialist, licensed by the state and probably convenient to your patient[.]" The theme of the article and title is one that expresses concern with the IRS's attempts to obtain information from the files of a professional. The reference to "some yo-yo" is in this context.

The court in *Coots v. Payton*, 365 Mo. 180, 280 S.W.2d 47 (banc 1955), defined defamation as "to speak evil of one maliciously, to dishonor, to render infamous." *Id.* at 53. The court went on to observe that the offending language is not libelous simply because it is unpleasant and annoys or irks plaintiff and subjects him to jests or banter, so as to affect his feelings. The attorney's response to Nelson's inquiry could reasonably be understood as an expression of frustration that a serious problem had arisen because a dentist had gotten himself crosswise with the government. Such a construction of the comment would not be construed to harm and injure the reputation and character of plaintiff so "as to provoke him to public wrath and expose him to public hatred, contempt, and ridicule. . . .".

The offending word takes its meaning from the context of the article. "Yo-yo" is used in the context of the attorney's comment about plaintiff's involvement with the IRS. The word does not attach to, nor is it descriptive of May in his professional capacity. It does not make reference to a professional quality, the absence or presence of which is essential to the practice of dentistry. The word may have a different meaning to different people, but considering the word in the context of the whole article, we conclude that it does not carry a defamatory meaning within the definition of the law. The word is not used to describe him as one having a lack of knowledge, skill, or capacity to perform his duties. The plaintiff fails to sustain the meaning he ascribes to the word, an unstable person in his professional capacity, as a meaning reasonably understood by the publication's readership.

Notes

Defamatory statements. *Marcone* and *May* employ different standards in terms of what qualifies as a "defamatory" statement. Both, however, are commonly used by courts.

Rules of interpretation. Note that *Marcone* and *May* both reference the well-accepted rule of interpretation that the allegedly defamatory statement must be read in the context of the whole article. Similarly, in considering whether a statement is defamatory, nearly every jurisdiction follows the rule of reasonable construction: "The meaning of a communication is that which the recipient correctly, or mistakenly but reasonably, understands that it was intended to express." Restatement (Second) Torts § 563 (1977). If the communication is capable of either a defamatory or innocent meaning, "the plaintiff has the burden of proving that it was reasonably understood in the sense that would make it defamatory." Restatement (Second) Torts § 613 cmt. c (1977).

Defamation by implication. Closely related to the above rules of interpretation is the concept of defamation by implication. "An implied statement, just as a statement made in direct language, can be defamatory." Woods v. Evansville Press Co., 791 F.2d 480, 486 (7th Cir. 1986). For example, in *Schultz v. Reader's Digest Ass'n.*, 468 F. Supp. 551 (E.D. Mich. 1979), an article took the position that famed union leader Jimmy Hoffa had been murdered. According to the article, Hoffa was supposed to meet with three individuals at a restaurant (one of whom was the plaintiff), but Hoffa feared that the meeting might be a setup. According to the court, when read in context, this passage in the article could be read as implying that the plaintiff had been involved in setting up Hoffa to be murdered, although the article never explicitly said as much. As such, it was potentially actionable. *See also* Memphis Pub. Co. v. Nichols, 569 S.W.2d 412 (Tenn. 1978) (holding that although a news article was literally true, "[w]hen read and construed in the sense in which the reader would ordinarily understand it, the clear implication of the article is that [the parties] had an adulterous relationship").

Problem 15.2. The photo that Donna posted online was of the back of the Winchells' minivan, which contained several stickers depicting the Confederate Battle Flag. Donna posted the photo and the following text: "Look! It turns out that Winchell is racist!" Was the post was defamatory?

3. Of and Concerning the Plaintiff

Elias v. Rolling Stone LLC

872 F.3d 97 (2d Cir. 2017)

Forrest, District Judge:

George Elias, IV, Stephen Hadford, and Ross Fowler (collectively, "Plaintiffs") appeal from a June 28, 2016 decision of the United States District Court for the Southern District of New York (Castel, J.) dismissing their defamation claims against *Rolling Stone*, LLC ("Rolling Stone"), Sabrina Rubin Erdely, and Wenner Media LLC ("Wenner Media") (collectively, "Defendants"). Plaintiffs' defamation action arises from a now-retracted *Rolling Stone* magazine article written by Erdely titled, "A Rape on Campus: A Brutal Assault and Struggle for Justice at UVA" (the "Article") as well as a subsequent online podcast appearance by Erdely discussing the Article (the "Podcast"). The Article, first published in the November 19, 2014 online edition of the magazine, presented a detailed account of an alleged violent gang rape of a woman named "Jackie" by seven male participants and two male onlookers (including a man named "Drew") in a bedroom of the Phi Kappa Psi fraternity house at the University of Virginia ("UVA").

Following widespread national attention to the Article's allegations, it was discovered that "Jackie," the Article's main subject as well as Erdely's principal source, had fabricated the story. In the wake of this discovery, *Rolling Stone* retracted the Article and issued an apology on April 5, 2015.

On July 29, 2015, Plaintiffs sued *Rolling Stone*, Erdely, and Wenner Media for defamation. Plaintiffs, who were undergraduate students and members of the Phi Kappa Psi fraternity at UVA when Jackie's rape purportedly occurred, alleged that the Article and Podcast defamed them by identifying them individually as participants in Jackie's alleged rape and by identifying them collectively as members of a group of Phi Kappa Psi fraternity brothers at the time the rape allegedly occurred.

Defendants moved to dismiss Plaintiffs' complaint for failure to state a claim under Federal Rule of Civil Procedure 12(b)(6). By Memorandum and Order dated June 28, 2016, the District Court granted Defendants' motion in its entirety. The District Court held that Plaintiffs had not sufficiently pled that Defendants' statements were "of and concerning" them, as is necessary to sustain a claim for defamation. The District Court found that, as a matter of law, the statements were insufficient to be "of and concerning" each Plaintiff individually and were also insufficient to support small group defamation.

[The Article stated that Jackie attended a party at the Phi Kappa Psi Phi Kappa Psi with her date, a Phi Kappa Psi brother pseudonymously named "Drew," a junior whom she "met while [they were] working lifeguard shifts together at the university pool." "According to the Article, Drew then invited Jackie to an upstairs bedroom," where she was forcibly raped by multiple men. The Article described the gang rape as a sort of initiation ritual.]

Discussion

...

B. Applicable Legal Principles

[C]entral to this appeal, a defamation plaintiff must allege that the purportedly defamatory statement was "of and concerning" him or her, *i.e.*, that "[t]he reading public acquainted with the parties and the subject" would recognize the plaintiff as a person to whom the statement refers. Carlucci v. Poughkeepsie Newspapers, Inc., 57 N.Y.2d 883, 885, 456 N.Y.S.2d 44, 442 N.E.2d 442 (1982); *see also* New York Times Co. v. Sullivan, 376 U.S. 254, 288–91, 84 S.Ct. 710, 11 L.Ed.2d 686 (1964). Whether a plaintiff has satisfied this requirement is typically resolved by the court at the pleading stage. "'It is not necessary that the world should understand the libel; it is sufficient if those who know the plaintiff can make out that she is the person meant.'" Geisler v. Petrocelli, 616 F.2d 636, 639 (2d Cir. 1980) (quoting Fetler v. Houghton Mifflin Co., 364 F.2d 650, 651 (2d Cir. 1966)) (alteration omitted). "[W]here extrinsic facts are relied upon to prove such reference the party alleging defamation must show that it is reasonable to conclude that the publication refers to him or her and the extrinsic facts upon which that conclusion is based were known to those who read or heard the publication." Chicherchia v. Cleary, 207 A.D.2d 855, 616 N.Y.S.2d 647, 648 (2d Dep't 1994).

C. The Article

On appeal, Plaintiffs argue that they have sufficiently pled that the allegedly defamatory statements in the Article were "of and concerning" them. Specifically, Plaintiffs argue, first, that they have plausibly alleged that the defamatory statements in the Article were "of and concerning" them individually . . .

1. Elias

Elias alleged that the Article was "of and concerning him" individually because during the time of the purported rape, he was both a Phi Kappa Psi brother in the class of 2013 and was known to live in the bedroom at the top of the first flight of stairs in the fraternity house. . . . [T]he alleged rape took place on the second floor of the fraternity house; the complaint alleged that Elias's bedroom was one of only three in the Phi Kappa Psi house on the second floor that could fit ten people (the number involved in the alleged gang rape) and was the only bedroom on the second floor accessible by way of the staircase without having to pass through an electronic keypad lock. The complaint also alleged that upon release of the Article, family, friends, acquaintances, coworkers, and reporters easily identified Plaintiff Elias as one of the alleged attackers and, among other things, interrogated him, humiliated him, and scolded him.

The decision below found these facts insufficient to plausibly allege that the Article was "of and concerning" Elias. Drawing all inferences in Plaintiffs' favor, we disagree.

The District Court based its determination on two observations: first, that there were several bedrooms on the second floor and the Article contained no details distinguishing Elias's bedroom from the others; and second, that the Article did not mention the presence or absence of a keypad lock. Drawing all reasonable inferences in Plaintiffs' favor, however, the absence of any mention of a keypad lock is properly construed to support the inference that Drew and Jackie did not encounter such a lock between the stairs and the bedroom. Considering that Elias was a member of Phi Kappa Psi; he graduated in 2013 (the year that the alleged perpetrators graduated); he lived in the fraternity house in the only bedroom on the second floor that was both large enough to fit the description of the alleged location of the rape and easily accessible by non-residents; and he was in fact identified by others as one of the alleged attackers, Elias has sufficiently pled that the Article was "of and concerning" him. At this stage of the proceedings, Elias has shown that it is plausible that a reader who knew Elias could identify him based on the allegedly defamatory statements in the Article.

2. Fowler

Fowler alleged that the Article was "of and concerning him" individually because during the time of the purported rape, he was a Phi Kappa Psi brother in the class of 2013, he had a prominent role in initiating new fraternity members, and he regularly swam at the UVA aquatic center.... Fowler was the rush chair for Phi Kappa Psi in the 2010–2011 academic year and was active in the rush process during the 2011–2012 academic year. And as Erdely's Podcast gloss corroborates, the Article described a kind of fraternity initiation ritual, with the alleged attackers egging on one unaroused participant by stating: "Don't you want to be a brother?" and "We all had to do it, so you do, too." The Article also stated that "Drew" worked as a lifeguard and Jackie ran into Drew at the UVA pool.

We conclude that based on these facts, Fowler like Elias has plausibly alleged that the Article was "of and concerning" him. Fowler was a member of Phi Kappa Psi who graduated in 2013. And although Fowler was not a lifeguard, he visited the UVA pool regularly, where Jackie was reported to have met Drew and encountered Drew on multiple occasions. In addition, as Fowler argues, the alleged statements by the attackers, "Don't you want to be a brother?" and "We all had to do it," can plausibly be interpreted to suggest that Jackie's gang rape was related to the fraternity's initiation process, in which Fowler had a prominent role. The District Court rejected this interpretation, explaining that the statements "are plausibly read as a boast—a type of perverse puffery." Again, however, such statements are to be read in the light most favorable to Plaintiffs and the relevant determination is whether Fowler's proffered interpretation is plausible, not whether other plausible interpretations exist. Like Elias, Fowler was also actually identified after the Article was published as one of the participants in the alleged gang rape and received harassing texts, emails, and comments from peers, co-workers, and reporters.

In short, Fowler has plausibly pled that the Article was "of and concerning" him.

3. Hadford

The District Court determined that Hadford failed to plausibly allege that the Article was "of and concerning" him. Hadford's defamation claim rests primarily on the fact that, in addition to being a Phi Kappa Psi member who graduated in 2013, he rode his bike through campus regularly for fifteen months after graduating. Like the District Court, we conclude that Hadford's allegations are too speculative to withstand Defendants' motion to dismiss.

According to the Article, Dean Eramo told Jackie in late-2014 that "all the boys involved [in the rape] have graduated," indicating that the attackers graduated in either 2013 or 2014. The Article further states that Jackie was "mystified" by this because she had "just seen one of the boys riding his bike on the grounds." Hadford argues that because he "lived on campus after graduating and rode his bike around campus," "[r]eaders aware of those facts would reasonably conclude that Hadford must have been the person who Jackie saw riding his bike on campus."

While Hadford's interpretation is possible, we conclude that he has not pled sufficient facts to render it plausible that the Article was "of and concerning" him individually. For example, there is no allegation that it is unusual for UVA alumni to bike through campus such that a reasonable reader familiar with Hadford's biking habits would conclude that the Article plausibly referred to him. The facts alleged with regard to Hadford are "'merely consistent with' . . . defendant's liability," and are thus insufficient to survive Defendants' motion to dismiss. Iqbal, 556 U.S. at 678, 129 S.Ct. 1937 (quoting Twombly, 550 U.S. at 557, 127 S.Ct. 1955).

Notes

Small group defamation. If a defendant defames an entire group, does each member of that group have a defamation claim? Ordinarily, "a statement made about an organization is not understood to refer to any of its individual members unless that person is distinguished from other members of the group." Three Amigos SJL Rest., Inc. v. CBS News Inc., 132 A.D.3d 82, 15 N.Y.S.3d 36, 41 (1st Dep't 2015). But where a defamatory statement refers to all members of a small group, the statement can be reasonably read to refer to each individual in the group. Thus, "an individual belonging to a small group may maintain an action for individual injury resulting from a defamatory comment about the group, by showing that he is a member of the group." Brady v. Ottaway Newspapers, Inc., 84 A.D.2d 226, 445 N.Y.S.2d 786, 790 (2d Dep't 1981). In *Elias*, there were 53 members of Phi Kappa Psi, and the article implied that the other members of the fraternity knew about the rape (even if not all of them participated in it). Would this be sufficient to establish that the article was "of and concerning" each member of the fraternity?

Fictional characters. According to the *Restatement*, a statement is of and concerning the plaintiff if the "recipient correctly, or mistakenly but reasonably, understands that it was intended to refer" to the plaintiff. Restatement (Second) of Torts § 564. In *Smith v. Stewart*, 660 S.E.2d 822 (Ga. 2008), the defendant authored *The Red Hat Club*, a New York Times bestseller. One of the characters in the book, SuSu, was portrayed as "an unrehabilitated alcoholic . . . foul-mouthed, insensitive and ill-mannered, a 'right-wing reactionary' and atheist, and a 'loose cannon' with a bad temper." In support of her claim, the plaintiff pointed out that the character of SuSu bore so many similarities to the plaintiff, whom the author had known for 50 years, that Stewart's friends "did not discuss the book around Stewart because they did not want to embarrass her." The Georgia Supreme Court ruled that a genuine issue of material fact existed as to whether the book stated actual facts about the plaintiff herself.

Problem 15.3. Rachel Winchell was running for the Pleasant Hill School Board at the time Donna posted on Facebook. The minivan in the picture was registered to her husband Fred. Some of Donna's post read, "Look! It turns out that Winchell is racist! . . . We'll have to remind people of that before election day." Was the statement of and concerning Rachel? Was it of and concerning Fred? If you represented the Winchells, what other information would you want to gather?

4. Damages

Damages recoverable for defamation include damage to one's reputation, as well as emotional distress and any resulting economic or physical harm. One potentially important distinction between libel and slander is that, historically, unless the defamatory statement constituted libel or slander per se, a plaintiff had to establish special harm (*i.e.*, pecuniary damage). In the case of libel, a plaintiff did not have to establish special harm at common law. Economic damage could be presumed because of the "greater permanency, dissemination, and credence attached to printed as opposed to spoken words." Marcone v. Penthouse International Magazine for Men, 754 F.2d 1072, 1080 (3d Cir. 1985) (quotations omitted). This rule was quite beneficial for many plaintiffs given the difficulty of establishing that a defamatory statement resulted in economic loss somehow. This rule still exists in some jurisdictions. At common law, slander typically required proof of special damage before a plaintiff could recover. If a statement qualifies as "slander per se," the plaintiff is relieved of the burden of proving special harm caused by the slander. There are four recognized categories of statements that amount to slander per se. These are statements that impute to another:

(a) a criminal offense,

(b) a loathsome disease,

(c) a matter incompatible with his business, trade, profession, or office, or

(d) serious sexual misconduct.

Restatement (Second) of Torts § 570.

Where a plaintiff established that the defamation consisted of libel or slander per se, some courts permitted a jury to award presumed damages, *i.e.*, recovery without any evidence of any kind of injury. The ability of plaintiffs to recover presumed damages has been limited by the Supreme Court decisions in Part B. Indeed, some jurisdictions have abolished the doctrine altogether.

Marcone v. Penthouse International Magazine for Men

754 F.2d 1072 (3d Cir. 1985)

ADAMS, Circuit Judge.I.

[The facts in this case appear in Part A2 *supra*. The Third Circuit concluded that the statements concerning Marcone could be construed as being defamatory.]

Defendants next contend that even if its article was capable of being defamatory, Marcone's reputation in the community was so tarnished before the publication that no further harm could have occurred. Penthouse's assertion is that Marcone was, in effect, libel proof before the publication of the allegedly libelous statement. *See* Cardillo v. Doubleday & Co., 518 F.2d 638, 639–40 (2d Cir.1975); Sharon v. Time, Inc., 575 F.Supp. 1162, 1168–72 (S.D.N.Y.1983); Wynberg v. National Enquirer, Inc., 564 F.Supp. 924, 927–28 (C.D.Cal.1982).

In *Wynberg*, for example, the court held that a plaintiff, who had a brief but highly publicized romance with Elizabeth Taylor was libel proof. Wynberg had been convicted of criminal conduct on five separate occasions, including a conviction for contributing to the delinquency of minors. The court concluded that

> When, for example, an individual engages in conspicuously anti-social or even criminal behavior, which is widely reported to the public, his reputation diminishes proportionately. Depending upon the nature of the conduct, the number of offenses, and the degree and range of publicity received, there comes a time when the individual's reputation for specific conduct, or his general reputation for honesty and fair dealing is sufficiently low in the public's estimation that he can recover only nominal damages for subsequent defamatory statements.

To bolster its claim that Marcone is entitled only to nominal damages, *Penthouse* cites a string of items of negative publicity regarding Marcone, from 1976 onward.

For example, his indictment in connection with drug trafficking in 1976 was widely publicized in the Philadelphia-area media. Moreover, a number of newspaper articles linked Marcone to the Castle, a gathering place for motorcycle gangs and a haven for a variety of illegal activities. In addition, in 1978 Marcone was tried for failing to file Federal Income tax returns for 1971 and 1972. Marcone was tried for criminal income tax evasion in 1978, and although the case ended in a hung jury, it was widely reported by the local media. Marcone was also fined at least twice for contempt of court for his failure to appear at scheduled hearings. The second of these contempt convictions occurred in 1979, however, after the Penthouse article was published. Finally, in 1978 Marcone was fined for punching a police officer who had stopped Marcone's car for a traffic violation.

While such evidence suggests that Marcone's reputation was sullied before the article was published, we cannot say as a matter of law that Marcone was libel proof. *See* Buckley v. Littell, 539 F.2d 882, 889 (2d Cir.1976) (libel proof doctrine is narrow), *cert. denied*, 429 U.S. 1062, 97 S.Ct. 785, 50 L.Ed.2d 777 (1977). Evidence of a tarnished reputation is admissible and should be considered as a factor to mitigate the level of compensatory damages. In the present case, the jury was informed of the evidence regarding Marcone's reputation, and its verdict for compensatory damages may well reflect the diminished status of Marcone in November of 1978.

Problem 15.4. The Winchells allege that when one of their former customers, Bruce MacGowan, learned about Donna's Facebook post, he was outraged and decided to take his business elsewhere. The original estimate for the repairs on MacGowan's car that Fred's auto shop was going to perform was $5,000. The Winchells have been unable to locate MacGowan for purposes of their defamation suit. Would they need to introduce evidence regarding MacGowan's supposed reasons for going to another mechanic in order to prevail on their defamation claim?

5. The Role of Truth

At common law, the fact that a defamatory statement was true served as an absolute defense for the defendant. A plaintiff was not necessarily required to establish the falsity of the statement in order to establish a prima facie case. Part B later in the chapter addresses the role that truth plays in modern cases and who bears the burden in terms of establishing the truth or falsity of a statement.

Regardless of who bears the burden with respect to the truth or falsity of a statement, if it is established that the statement was true, there can be no liability. What it means to say that a statement is "true" (or at least "not false"), however, is a complicated question. Some statements may be mostly true but a little bit false.

Sometimes the headline or teaser of a story may be misleading but the gist of the article as a whole is true. This section explores the concept of truth in the context of defamation claims.

Collins v. Detroit Free Press, Inc.

627 N.W.2d 5 (Mich. Ct. App. 2001)

PER CURIAM.

Defendants appeal by leave granted the trial court's order denying their motion for summary disposition of plaintiff's defamation action. We reverse and remand for further proceedings.

Plaintiff was the United States Representative for Michigan's 15th Congressional District, located in Detroit. In 1996, plaintiff was seeking reelection to a fourth term, and she faced opposition in the August primary election. In May 1996, plaintiff was interviewed by defendant Ann Hazard-Hargrove, an employee of defendant States News Service in Washington, D.C. The interview was tape-recorded and transcribed. The Washington defendants provided the tape and the transcript of the interview to defendant Detroit Free Press, Inc. On July 17, 1996, the Detroit Free Press published a story, based on the interview, concerning plaintiff's views on racism. The article attributed the following quotation to plaintiff:

> All white people, I don't believe, are intolerant. That's why I say I love the individuals, but I *hate* the race....

On July 30, 1996, plaintiff issued a news release in response to the story. Plaintiff explained that she had "summarized [her] thoughts on racism by stating that [she] loved the individual but that '[she] hated the (sins committed by) the white race against people of color throughout history.'" On July 31, 1996, a story circulated on the Associated Press wire service repeating the original quotation and indicating that defendants had verified the quotation and found it to be accurate.

On August 9, 1996, after plaintiff had lost the primary election for her congressional seat, the Detroit Free Press published a retraction. The Free Press admitted that plaintiff had been quoted "incorrectly," said that it "clearly made a mistake," and indicated that the Free Press would consider disciplinary action against the reporter and editors involved. After the tape and transcript of the interview had been reviewed, the Free Press admitted that plaintiff had actually said:

> All white people, I don't believe, are intolerant. That's why I say, I love the individuals, but I *don't like* the race. [Emphasis added.]

Plaintiff filed the instant action asserting claims of defamation, intentional infliction of emotional distress, intentional publication of injurious falsehoods, false light invasion of privacy, violation of the consumer protection act, and conspiracy. Defendants moved for summary disposition, arguing that the "gist" or "sting" of the original article was substantially true. The trial court rejected this argument and determined that "hate" and "dislike" had substantially different meanings, especially in this context. The court was satisfied that "the word 'hate' can have a major effect on the minds of the readers, particularly in the minds of the readers in a jurisdiction such as Detroit."

...

To avoid liability, it is not necessary for "defendants to prove that a publication is literally and absolutely accurate in every minute detail." *Rouch*, 487 N.W.2d 205 [Mich. 1982]. Rather, substantial truth is an absolute defense to a defamation claim. Michigan courts have held that "'[s]light inaccuracies of expression are immaterial provided that the defamatory charge is true in substance.'" *Id.* (quoting 3 Restatement Torts, 2d, § 581A, comment f, p. 237. "'It is sufficient for the defendant to justify so much of the defamatory matter as constitutes the sting of the charge, and it is unnecessary to repeat and justify every word ... so long as the substance of the libelous charge be justified,'" and "'the inaccuracy in no way alters the complexion of the affair, and would have no different effect on the reader than that which the literal truth would produce....'" *Rouch, supra* at 259, 487 N.W.2d 205, quoting McAllister v. Detroit Free Press Co., 85 Mich. 453, 460–461, 48 N.W. 612 (1891). "Thus, the test look[s] to the sting of the article to determine its effect on the reader; if the literal truth [would have] produced the same effect, minor differences [a]re deemed immaterial." *Rouch, supra* at 259, 487 N.W.2d 205.

"The substantial truth doctrine is frequently invoked to solve two recurring problems: minor inaccuracies and technically incorrect or flawed use of legal terminology" ... However, the doctrine has not been limited to such situations. *See id.* at 258–271, 487 N.W.2d 205. Indeed, such a limitation would make little sense, given that, in addition to being a defense, the substantial truth doctrine provides the common law "definition of falsity" that a plaintiff must meet in order to prevail on a defamation claim. In other words, for purposes of establishing a prima facie case of defamation, a "statement is not considered false unless it 'would have a different effect on the mind of the reader from that which the pleaded truth would have produced.'" *Masson, supra* at 517, 111 S.Ct. 2419 (citation omitted)....

Where the allegedly defamatory statement is a purported quotation, the question is whether, viewing the evidence in the light most favorable to the plaintiff, "the published passages differ materially in meaning from the [plaintiff's] statements so as to create an issue of fact for a jury as to falsity." *Id.* at 521, 111 S.Ct. 2419....

In this case, the original article quoted plaintiff as having said, "I hate the race." In fact, plaintiff had said, "I don't like the race." According to plaintiff's news release, the comments were made in the context of discussing how racism had personally affected her. The printed quotation, although admittedly inaccurate, does not paint a "very different picture" from the actual quotation. *See id.* at 523–524, 111 S.Ct. 2419. Plaintiff does not contest portions of the article in which she was quoted as saying that "God is going to have to burn [racism] out of white people" or that "the only reason Dr. Martin Luther King was successful was because he said if blood had to flow, let it be my black blood, and not the blood of my white brother, and white people like to hear that kind of stuff." Plaintiff was also quoted as saying that white people "don't even realize how they benefit from racism." Also, immediately following the subject misquotation, the article contains the following quotation which provides some context to plaintiff's statement: "I've got a lot of friends who are white. At one time, all my friends were white, so it's like I don't like the race, I like the individuals." Further, a review of the interview as a whole reveals that plaintiff used the terms "love" and "like," and "hate" and "don't like" loosely and interchangeably during the uncontested printed portions of the interview.

When the article is viewed in its entirety, the difference between the two quotations is not material. The gist of the actual statement was the same as the subject misquotation. Because we find no material difference between the printed statement and plaintiff's actual words, we conclude that there is no genuine issue of material fact regarding material falsity or substantial truth. Accordingly, the trial court erred in denying defendants' motion for summary disposition.

Note

Substantial truth. Which of the following statements are false (or substantially untrue) under the *Collins* approach?

(a) A newspaper article stating, in the context of a story about public employees' use of taxpayer-funded vehicles, that the plaintiff had used a state car to drive 72 miles to work when, in fact, the distance was only 55 miles. Stevens v. Independent Newspapers, Inc., 15 Media L. Rep. 1097, 1988 Del. Super. LEXIS 89 (Del. Super. Ct., 1988).

(b) A television news report in which the reporter stated that the plaintiff was "facing criminal charges" over her treatment of customers when, in fact, the plaintiff had never been charged with a crime although her conduct may have constituted potential violations of consumer protection laws. Terry v. Journal Broadcast Corp., 840 N.W.2d 255 (Wis. Ct. App. 2013).

(c) A newspaper article stating that plaintiff, a candidate for office, had spent 24 hours in jail for firing a gun after a motorist accidentally leaned on her horn, when, in fact, plaintiff had spent 24 hours in jail for displaying a weapon after a motorist accidentally leaned on her horn. Read v. Phoenix Newspapers, Inc., 819 P.2d 939 (Ariz. 1991).

6. Actionable and Non-Actionable Statements

False and defamatory statements are actionable as defamation. But there may be statements that fall into a gray area in which it is difficult to classify the statements as actually being "false" or "defamatory." The following section explores how the law of defamation treats such statements.

Milkovich v. Lorain Journal Co.

497 U.S. 1 (1990)

Chief Justice REHNQUIST delivered the opinion of the Court.

Respondent J. Theodore Diadiun authored an article in an Ohio newspaper implying that petitioner Michael Milkovich, a local high school wrestling coach, lied under oath in a judicial proceeding about an incident involving petitioner and his team which occurred at a wrestling match. Petitioner sued Diadiun and the newspaper for libel, and the Ohio Court of Appeals affirmed a lower court entry of summary judgment against petitioner. This judgment was based in part on the grounds that the article constituted an "opinion" protected from the reach of state defamation law by the First Amendment to the United States Constitution....

This lawsuit is before us for the third time in an odyssey of litigation spanning nearly 15 years. Petitioner Milkovich, now retired, was the wrestling coach at Maple Heights High School in Maple Heights, Ohio. In 1974, his team was involved in an altercation at a home wrestling match with a team from Mentor High School. Several people were injured. In response to the incident, the Ohio High School Athletic Association (OHSAA) held a hearing at which Milkovich and H. Don Scott, the Superintendent of Maple Heights Public Schools, testified. Following the hearing, OHSAA placed the Maple Heights team on probation for a year and declared the team ineligible for the 1975 state tournament. OHSAA also censured Milkovich for his actions during the altercation. Thereafter, several parents and wrestlers sued OHSAA in the Court of Common Pleas of Franklin County, Ohio, seeking a restraining order against OHSAA's ruling on the grounds that they had been denied due process in the OHSAA proceeding. Both Milkovich and Scott testified in that proceeding. The court overturned OHSAA's probation and ineligibility orders on due process grounds.

The day after the court rendered its decision, respondent Diadiun's column appeared in the News-Herald, a newspaper which circulates in Lake County, Ohio, and is owned by respondent Lorain Journal Co. The column bore the heading "Maple Beat the Law with the 'Big Lie,'" beneath which appeared Diadiun's photograph and the words "TD Says." The carryover page headline announced "... Diadiun says Maple told a lie." The column contained the following passages:

> "'... [A] lesson was learned (or relearned) yesterday by the student body of Maple Heights High School, and by anyone who attended the Maple-Mentor wrestling meet of last Feb. 8.
>
> "'A lesson which, sadly, in view of the events of the past year, is well they learned early.
>
> "'It is simply this: If you get in a jam, lie your way out.
>
> "'If you're successful enough, and powerful enough, and can sound sincere enough, you stand an excellent chance of making the lie stand up, regardless of what really happened.

"'The teachers responsible were mainly head Maple wrestling coach, Mike Milkovich, and former superintendent of schools H. Donald Scott.

.....

"'Anyone who attended the meet, whether he be from Maple Heights, Mentor, or impartial observer, knows in his heart that Milkovich and Scott lied at the hearing after each having given his solemn oath to tell the truth.

"'But they got away with it.

"'Is that the kind of lesson we want our young people learning from their high school administrators and coaches?

"'I think not.'"

Milkovich v. News-Herald, 46 Ohio App. 3d 20, 21, 545 N.E.2d 1320, 1321—1322 (1989).

The common law generally did not place any ... restrictions on the type of statement that could be actionable. Indeed, defamatory communications were deemed actionable regardless of whether they were deemed to be statements of fact or opinion.

... Respondents would have us recognize ... First-Amendment-based protection for defamatory statements which are categorized as "opinion" as opposed to "fact."

If a speaker says, "In my opinion John Jones is a liar," he implies a knowledge of facts which lead to the conclusion that Jones told an untruth. Even if the speaker states the facts upon which he bases his opinion, if those facts are either incorrect or incomplete, or if his assessment of them is erroneous, the statement may still imply a false assertion of fact. Simply couching such statements in terms of opinion does not dispel these implications; and the statement, "In my opinion Jones is a liar," can cause as much damage to reputation as the statement, "Jones is a liar." As Judge Friendly aptly stated: "[It] would be destructive of the law of libel if a writer could escape liability for accusations of [defamatory conduct] simply by using, explicitly or implicitly, the words 'I think.'" ...

[R]espondents do not really contend that a statement such as, "In my opinion John Jones is a liar," should be protected by a separate privilege for "opinion" under the First Amendment. But they do contend that in every defamation case the First Amendment mandates an inquiry into whether a statement is "opinion" or "fact," and that only the latter statements may be actionable. ... But we think the "'breathing space'" which "'[f]reedoms of expression require in order to survive,'" *Hepps*, 475 U.S., at 772, 106 S.Ct., at 1561, is adequately secured by existing constitutional doctrine without the creation of an artificial dichotomy between "opinion" and fact.

Foremost, we think *Hepps* stands for the proposition that a statement on matters of public concern must be provable as false before there can be liability under state defamation law, at least in situations, like the present, where a media defendant is involved. Thus, unlike the statement, "In my opinion Mayor Jones is a liar," the statement, "In my opinion Mayor Jones shows his abysmal ignorance by accepting the teachings of Marx and Lenin," would not be actionable. *Hepps* ensures that a statement of opinion relating to matters of public concern which does not contain a provably false factual connotation will receive full constitutional protection.

Next, [another] line of cases provides protection for statements that cannot "reasonably [be] interpreted as stating actual facts" about an individual. *Falwell*, 485 U.S., at 50, 108 S.Ct., at 879. This provides assurance that public debate will not suffer for lack of "imaginative expression" or the "rhetorical hyperbole" which has traditionally added much to the discourse of our Nation. *See id.*, at 53–55, 108 S.Ct., at 880–882.

We are not persuaded that, in addition to these protections, an additional separate constitutional privilege for "opinion" is required to ensure the freedom of expression guaranteed by the First Amendment. The dispositive question in the present case then becomes whether a reasonable factfinder could conclude that the statements in the Diadiun column imply an assertion that petitioner Milkovich perjured himself in a judicial proceeding. We think this question must be answered in the affirmative. As the Ohio Supreme Court itself observed: "[T]he clear impact in some nine sentences and a caption is that [Milkovich] 'lied at the hearing after . . . having given his solemn oath to tell the truth.'" *Scott*, 25 Ohio St.3d, at 251, 496 N.E.2d, at 707. This is not the sort of loose, figurative, or hyperbolic language which would negate the impression that the writer was seriously maintaining that petitioner committed the crime of perjury. Nor does the general tenor of the article negate this impression.

We also think the connotation that petitioner committed perjury is sufficiently factual to be susceptible of being proved true or false. A determination whether petitioner lied in this instance can be made on a core of objective evidence by comparing, *inter alia*, petitioner's testimony before the OHSAA board with his subsequent testimony before the trial court. As the Scott court noted regarding the plaintiff in that case: "[W]hether or not H. Don Scott did indeed perjure himself is certainly verifiable by a perjury action with evidence adduced from the transcripts and witnesses present at the hearing. Unlike a subjective assertion the averred defamatory language is an articulation of an objectively verifiable event." *Id.* at 252, 496 N.E.2d, at 707. So too with petitioner Milkovich.

The numerous decisions discussed above establishing First Amendment protection for defendants in defamation actions surely demonstrate the Court's recognition of the Amendment's vital guarantee of free and uninhibited discussion of public issues. But there is also another side to the equation; we have regularly acknowledged the "important social values which underlie the law of defamation," and recognized that "[s]ociety has a pervasive and strong interest in preventing and redressing attacks upon reputation." . . .

We believe our decision in the present case holds the balance true. The judgment of the Ohio Court of Appeals is reversed, and the case is remanded for further proceedings not inconsistent with this opinion.

Reversed.

Cashion v. Smith

749 S.E.2d 526 (Va. 2013)

Opinion by Justice WILLIAM C. MIMS.

I. Background and Material Proceedings Below

In November 2009, Dr. Robert Smith, a trauma surgeon, and Dr. Bradley Cashion, an anesthesiologist, provided emergency care to a critically injured patient. Dr. Smith is employed full-time by Carilion Medical Center ("Carilion"). Dr. Cashion was employed by Anesthesiology Consultants of Virginia, Inc., which provides services to Carilion. Despite the efforts of Dr. Smith and Dr. Cashion, the patient died during surgery.

Following the patient's death, Dr. Smith criticized Dr. Cashion in the operating room. Dr. Smith, in front of several other members of the operating team, made the following remarks to Dr. Cashion:

> "He could have made it with better resuscitation."
>
> "This was a very poor effort."
>
> "You didn't really try."
>
> "You gave up on him."
>
> "You determined from the beginning that he wasn't going to make it and purposefully didn't resuscitate him."

Immediately thereafter, Dr. Smith addressed Dr. Cashion in the hallway outside the operating room, stating: "You just euthanized my patient." Nurse Sherri Zwart, who also had been in the operating room, and Dr. James Crawford, Chief of Anesthesia at Carilion, were present in the hallway at the time. In a subsequent meeting that evening between Drs. Smith, Cashion, and Crawford, Dr. Smith repeatedly stated that Dr. Cashion "euthanized" the patient.

Dr. Cashion filed an amended complaint alleging defamation . . . against Dr. Smith and Carilion, which Dr. Cashion alleged to be liable under a theory of *respondeat superior.* Dr. Smith and Carilion filed demurrers and pleas in bar asserting, among other things, that Dr. Smith's statements were non-actionable expressions of opinion or rhetorical hyperbole. . . .

[The circuit court entered an order sustaining the demurrers and granting the pleas in bar as to the non-euthanasia statements on the ground that they were non-actionable expressions of opinion, but overruled the demurrers as to the euthanasia statements. The defendants later moved for summary judgment as to the euthanasia statements. The circuit court ruled that the statement was not rhetorical hyperbole but that a qualified privilege applied. Dr. Cashion appealed.]

II. Analysis

A. Opinion or Statements of Fact

The question of whether the non-euthanasia statements were expressions of opinion is a question of law. We therefore review the circuit court's ruling de novo.

"When a statement is relative in nature and depends largely on a speaker's viewpoint, that statement is an expression of opinion." *Hyland*, 277 Va. at 47, 670 S.E.2d at 750. However, statements may be actionable if they have a "'provably false factual connotation'" and thus "are capable of being proven true or false." Fuste v. Riverside Healthcare Ass'n, 265 Va. 127, 575 S.E.2d 858, 861–62 (2003) (quoting WJLA-TV v. Levin, 264 Va. 140, 156, 564 S.E.2d 383, 392 (2002)).

The statements "[t]his was a very poor effort," "[y]ou didn't really try," and "[y]ou gave up on him," fall into the former class because they are subjective and wholly depend on Dr. Smith's viewpoint. However, the statements that the patient "could have made it with better resuscitation" and "[y]ou determined from the beginning that he wasn't going to make it and purposefully didn't resuscitate him" do not.

The statement that the patient "could have made it with better resuscitation" directly attributes the patient's death to Dr. Cashion, insinuating that he either failed to perform some action necessary to the patient's recovery or acted affirmatively to prevent it. Insinuations may constitute defamatory statements. The statement asserts that the patient was capable of surviving, but for the quality of Dr. Cashion's treatment. Whether the quality of Dr. Cashion's treatment caused or even contributed to the patient's death is an allegation of fact capable of being proven true or false, such as through expert opinion testimony. The second statement goes further, not only attributing the patient's death to Dr. Cashion's action or inaction but accusing him of purposefully causing the death by withholding treatment. Such a statement is indistinguishable from the alleged accusations of euthanasia.

Accordingly, the circuit court erred by ruling that these two statements were non-actionable expressions of opinion. We therefore will reverse this portion of its judgment and remand for further proceedings.

[The court reversed the circuit's ruling with respect to the existence of a qualified privilege, concluding that a jury issue existed.]

C. Rhetorical Hyperbole

Dr. Smith and Carilion assert in assignments of cross-error that Dr. Smith's statements accusing Dr. Cashion of committing euthanasia constitute nothing more than rhetorical hyperbole and therefore are not actionable. We disagree.

Under Virginia law, rhetorical hyperbole is not defamatory. Statements characterized as rhetorical hyperbole are those from which "no reasonable inference could be drawn that the individual identified in the statements, as a matter of fact, engaged in the conduct described." Whether a statement constitutes rhetorical hyperbole is a question of law for the court to determine.

In this case, as noted above, some of Dr. Smith's statements can reasonably be interpreted as allegations of fact capable of being proven true or false. Considering the context in which the statements were made, a listener could believe that Dr. Cashion engaged in the conduct Dr. Smith attributed to him, *i.e.*, euthanizing the patient or causing or contributing to the patient's death by providing deficient care. Dr. Smith's position as a surgeon, having just left the operating room where the patient died, and his relationship to Dr. Cashion, an anesthesiologist whose participation in the surgery afforded him the opportunity to cause or contribute to the patient's death, support the inference that Dr. Smith was conveying what he believed to be factual information about Dr. Cashion. Thus, we agree with the circuit court's determination that the statements were not rhetorical hyperbole. We therefore will affirm this portion of the circuit court's judgment.

Notes

Undisclosed facts. As *Milkovich* suggests, a statement of opinion is actionable "if it implies the allegation of undisclosed defamatory facts as the basis for the opinion." Restatement (Second) of Torts § 566 (1965). Where, however, the facts that form the basis for an opinion are disclosed or are otherwise known (and are themselves accurate), the statement of opinion is not actionable. *Id.*

Name calling. "[N]ame calling and verbal abuse are to be taken as statements of opinion, not fact, and therefore will not give rise to an action for libel." Johnson v. Delta-Democrat Pub. Co., 531 So. 2d 811, 814 (Miss. 1988). At what point does a statement cease to be mere name calling and become actionable defamation?

Problem 15.5. The photo of the Winchells' minivan that appeared on Donna's Facebook page contained several stickers, including a Confederate Battle Flag next to the word "SECEDE," the phrase "Southern by the Grace of God," and the phrase "the League of the Confederacy" (which happens to be the name of an organization labeled by some as a white supremacist organization and that expressly advocates for secession from the United States by the states that formerly comprised the Confederacy). Beneath this photo, Donna wrote, "Look! It turns out that Winchell is racist! *That explains some of her behavior!* We'll have to remind people of that before election day." (emphasis added) Is this statement actionable?

Review Question

Alison worked for Quick Stop, a convenience store chain. Beth worked for Convenience Plus, another chain. The two were friends. Beth was thinking about hiring Priscilla, a Quick Stop employee, for a management position. She called Alison to ask for Alison's opinion regarding Priscilla. Alison hesitated before responding, "In my opinion, she is a bit of a troublemaker. She was denied a promotion last year, so that probably tells you everything you need to know about her." Beth ended up not hiring Priscilla as a result. Priscilla has now sued Alison on a defamation theory.

Could Priscilla establish a prima facie case of defamation as it existed at common law?

B. Defamation: Constitutional Constraints

Constitutional law began to play a significant role in defamation law in the 1960s. Prior to that time, liability for defamation was often strict in nature. The fact that the defendant did not know or had no reason to know that the defamatory publication was false did not necessarily prevent the plaintiff from establishing a prima facie case. But defamation is a speech-based tort, and in 1964 the Supreme Court considered how the First Amendment impacted state defamation law. The result was a new focus on the status of the plaintiff, the degree of fault on the part of the defendant necessary to establish liability, and the role of truth in defamation actions.

1. Public Officials and Public Figures

New York Times Co. v. Sullivan

376 U.S. 254 (1964)

Mr. Justice BRENNAN delivered the opinion of the Court.

We are required in this case to determine for the first time the extent to which the constitutional protections for speech and press limit a State's power to award damages in a libel action brought by a public official against critics of his official conduct.

Respondent L. B. Sullivan is one of the three elected Commissioners of the City of Montgomery, Alabama. He testified that he was 'Commissioner of Public Affairs and the duties are supervision of the Police Department, Fire Department, Department of Cemetery and Department of Scales.' He brought this civil libel action against the four individual petitioners, who are Negroes and Alabama clergymen, and against petitioner the New York Times Company, a New York corporation which publishes the New York Times, a daily newspaper. A jury in the Circuit Court of Montgomery County awarded him damages of $500,000, the full amount claimed, against all the petitioners, and the Supreme Court of Alabama affirmed.

Respondent's complaint alleged that he had been libeled by statements in a full-page advertisement that was carried in the New York Times on March 29, 1960. Entitled 'Heed Their Rising Voices,' the advertisement began by stating that 'As the whole world knows by now, thousands of Southern Negro students are engaged in widespread non-violent demonstrations in positive affirmation of the right to live in human dignity as guaranteed by the U.S. Constitution and the Bill of Rights.' It went on to charge that 'in their efforts to uphold these guarantees, they are being met by an unprecedented wave of terror by those who would deny and negate that document which the whole world looks upon as setting the pattern for modern freedom.... Succeeding paragraphs purported to illustrate the 'wave of terror' by describing certain alleged events. The text concluded with an appeal for funds for three purposes: support of the student movement, 'the struggle for the right-to-vote,' and the legal defense of Dr. Martin Luther King, Jr., leader of the movement, against a perjury indictment then pending in Montgomery.

. . . The advertisement was signed at the bottom of the page by the 'Committee to Defend Martin Luther King and the Struggle for Freedom in the South,' and the officers of the Committee were listed.

Of the 10 paragraphs of text in the advertisement, the third and a portion of the sixth were the basis of respondent's claim of libel. They read as follows:

Third paragraph:

> In Montgomery, Alabama, after students sang 'My Country, 'Tis of Thee' on the State Capitol steps, their leaders were expelled from school, and truckloads of police armed with shotguns and tear-gas ringed the Alabama State College Campus. When the entire student body protested to state authorities by refusing to re-register, their dining hall was padlocked in an attempt to starve them into submission.

Sixth paragraph:

> Again and again the Southern violators have answered Dr. King's peaceful protests with intimidation and violence. They have bombed his home almost killing his wife and child. They have assaulted his person. They have arrested him seven times—for 'speeding,' 'loitering' and similar 'offenses.' And now they have charged him with 'perjury'—a felony under which they could imprison him for ten years. . . .

Although neither of these statements mentions respondent by name, he contended that the word 'police' in the third paragraph referred to him as the Montgomery Commissioner who supervised the Police Department, so that he was being accused of 'ringing' the campus with police. He further claimed that the paragraph would be read as imputing to the police, and hence to him, the padlocking of the dining hall in order to starve the students into submission. As to the sixth paragraph, he contended that since arrests are ordinarily made by the police, the statement 'They have arrested (Dr. King) seven times' would be read as referring to him; he further contended that the 'They' who did the arresting would be equated with the 'They' who committed the other described acts and with the 'Southern violators.' Thus, he argued, the paragraph would be read as accusing the Montgomery police, and hence him, of answering Dr. King's protests with 'intimidation and violence,' bombing his home, assaulting his person, and charging him with perjury. Respondent and six other Montgomery residents testified that they read some or all of the statements as referring to him in his capacity as Commissioner.

It is uncontroverted that some of the statements contained in the two paragraphs were not accurate descriptions of events which occurred in Montgomery. [For example, "[t]he campus dining hall was not padlocked on any occasion, and the only students who may have been barred from eating there were the few who had neither signed a preregistration application nor requested temporary meal tickets.

Although the police were deployed near the campus in large numbers on three occasions, they did not at any time 'ring' the campus, and they were not called to the campus in connection with the demonstration on the State Capitol steps, as the third paragraph implied."]

Respondent made no effort to prove that he suffered actual pecuniary loss as a result of the alleged libel.[3] One of his witnesses, a former employer, testified that if he had believed the statements, he doubted whether he 'would want to be associated with anybody who would be a party to such things that are stated in that ad,' and that he would not re-employ respondent if he believed 'that he allowed the Police Department to do the things that the paper say he did.' But neither this witness nor any of the others testified that he had actually believed the statements in their supposed reference to respondent.

The cost of the advertisement was approximately $4800, and it was published by *the Times* upon an order from a New York advertising agency acting for the signatory Committee.... The manager of the Advertising Acceptability Department testified that he had approved the advertisement for publication because he knew nothing to cause him to believe that anything in it was false, and because it bore the endorsement of 'a number of people who are well known and whose reputation' he 'had no reason to question.' Neither he nor anyone else at *the Times* made an effort to confirm the accuracy of the advertisement, either by checking it against recent Times news stories relating to some of the described events or by any other means.

In affirming the judgment, the Supreme Court of Alabama sustained the trial judge's rulings and instructions in all respects. It held that '(w)here the words published tend to injure a person libeled by them in his reputation, profession, trade or business, or charge him with an indictable offense, or tends to bring the individual into public contempt,' they are 'libelous per se'; that 'the matter complained of is, under the above doctrine, libelous per se, if it was published of and concerning the plaintiff'; and that it was actionable without 'proof of pecuniary injury..., such injury being implied.' It approved the trial court's ruling that the jury could find the statements to have been made 'of and concerning' respondent, stating: 'We think it common knowledge that the average person knows that municipal agents, such as police and firemen, and others, are under the control and direction of the city governing body, and more particularly under the direction and control of a single commissioner. In measuring the performance or deficiencies of such groups, praise or criticism is usually attached to the official in complete control of the body.' In sustaining the trial court's determination that the verdict was not excessive, the court said that malice could be inferred from *the Times*' 'irresponsibility' in printing the advertisement while '*the Times* in its own files had articles already published which would have demonstrated the falsity of the allegations in the advertisement';

3. Approximately 394 copies of the edition of the Times containing the advertisement were circulated in Alabama. Of these, about 35 copies were distributed in Montgomery County. The total circulation of the Times for that day was approximately 650,000 copies.

from the Times' failure to retract for respondent while retracting for the Governor, whereas the falsity of some of the allegations was then known to *the Times* and 'the matter contained in the advertisement was equally false as to both parties'; and from the testimony of *the Times*' Secretary that, apart from the statement that the dining hall was padlocked, he thought the two paragraphs were 'substantially correct.' The court reaffirmed a statement in an earlier opinion that 'There is no legal measure of damages in cases of this character.' It rejected petitioners' constitutional contentions with the brief statements that 'The First Amendment of the U.S. Constitution does not protect libelous publications' and 'The Fourteenth Amendment is directed against State action and not private action.'

I.

We may dispose at the outset of two grounds asserted to insulate the judgment of the Alabama courts from constitutional scrutiny. The first is the proposition relied on by the State Supreme Court—that 'The Fourteenth Amendment is directed against State action and not private action.' That proposition has no application to this case. Although this is a civil lawsuit between private parties, the Alabama courts have applied a state rule of law which petitioners claim to impose invalid restrictions on their constitutional freedoms of speech and press. It matters not that that law has been applied in a civil action and that it is common law only, though supplemented by statute. The test is not the form in which state power has been applied but, whatever the form, whether such power has in fact been exercised. *See* Ex parte Virginia, 100 U.S. 339, 346–347, 25 L. Ed. 676; American Federation of Labor v. Swing, 312 U.S. 321, 61 S. Ct. 568, 85 L. Ed. 855.

The second contention is that the constitutional guarantees of freedom of speech and of the press are inapplicable here, at least so far as *the Times* is concerned, because the allegedly libelous statements were published as part of a paid, 'commercial' advertisement. . . .

[The Court held that the advertisement was not a commercial advertisement in the traditional sense in that it "communicated information, expressed opinion, recited grievances, protested claimed abuses, and sought financial support on behalf of a movement whose existence and objectives are matters of the highest public interest and concern." Accordingly, the Court held "that if the allegedly libelous statements would otherwise be constitutionally protected from the present judgment, they do not forfeit that protection because they were published in the form of a paid advertisement."]

II.

Under Alabama law as applied in this case, a publication is 'libelous per se' if the words 'tend to injure a person . . . in his reputation' or to 'bring (him) into public contempt'; the trial court stated that the standard was met if the words are such as to 'injure him in his public office, or impute misconduct to him in his office, or want of official integrity, or want of fidelity to a public trust. . . . Once 'libel per se' has been established, the defendant has no defense as to stated facts unless he can persuade the jury that they were true in all their particulars. His privilege of 'fair comment' for expressions of opinion depends on the truth of the facts upon which the comment is based. Unless he can discharge the burden of proving truth, general damages are presumed, and may be awarded without proof of pecuniary injury. A showing of actual malice is apparently a prerequisite to recovery of punitive damages, and the defendant may in any event forestall a punitive award by a retraction meeting the statutory requirements. Good motives and belief in truth do not negate an inference of malice, but are relevant only in mitigation of punitive damages if the jury chooses to accord them weight.

The question before us is whether this rule of liability, as applied to an action brought by a public official against critics of his official conduct, abridges the freedom of speech and of the press that is guaranteed by the First and Fourteenth Amendments.

Respondent relies heavily, as did the Alabama courts, on statements of this Court to the effect that the Constitution does not protect libelous publications. Those statements do not foreclose our inquiry here. None of the cases sustained the use of libel laws to impose sanctions upon expression critical of the official conduct of public officials.... Like insurrection, contempt, advocacy of unlawful acts, breach of the peace obscenity, solicitation of legal business, and the various other formulae for the repression of expression that have been challenged in this Court, libel can claim no talismanic immunity from constitutional limitations. It must be measured by standards that satisfy the First Amendment.

The general proposition that freedom of expression upon public questions is secured by the First Amendment has long been settled by our decisions. The constitutional safeguard, we have said, 'was fashioned to assure unfettered interchange of ideas for the bringing about of political and social changes desired by the people.' Roth v. United States, 354 U.S. 476, 484, 77 S. Ct. 1304, 1308, 1 L. Ed.2d 1498. 'The maintenance of the opportunity for free political discussion to the end that government may be responsive to the will of the people and that changes may be obtained by lawful means, an opportunity essential to the security of the Republic, is a fundamental principle of our constitutional system.' Stromberg v. California, 283 U.S. 359, 369, 51 S. Ct. 532, 536, 75 L. Ed. 1117. '(I)t is a prized American privilege to speak one's mind, although not always with perfect good taste, on all public institutions,' Bridges v. California, 314 U.S. 252, 270, 62 S. Ct. 190, 197, 86 L. Ed. 192, and this opportunity is to be afforded for 'vigorous advocacy' no less than 'abstract discussion.' N.A.A.C.P. v. Button, 371 U.S. 415, 429, 83 S. Ct. 328, 9 L. Ed.2d 405. The First Amendment, said Judge Learned Hand, 'presupposes that right conclusions are more likely to be gathered out of a multitude of tongues, than through any kind of authoritative selection. To many this is, and always will be, folly; but we have staked upon it our all.' United States v. Associated Press, 52 F. Supp. 362, 372 (D.C. S.D.N.Y.1943). Mr. Justice Brandeis, in his concurring opinion in Whitney v. California, 274 U.S. 357, 375–376, 47 S. Ct. 641, 648, 71 L. Ed. 1095, gave the principle its classic formulation:

> Those who won our independence believed . . . that public discussion is a political duty; and that this should be a fundamental principle of the American government. They recognized the risks to which all human institutions are subject. But they knew that order cannot be secured merely through fear of punishment for its infraction; that it is hazardous to discourage thought, hope and imagination; that fear breeds repression; that repression breeds hate; that hate menaces stable government; that the path of safety lies in the opportunity to discuss freely supposed grievances and proposed remedies; and that the fitting remedy for evil counsels is good ones. Believing in the power of reason as applied through public discussion, they eschewed silence coerced by law—the argument of force in its worst form. Recognizing the occasional tyrannies of governing majorities, they amended the Constitution so that free speech and assembly should be guaranteed.

Thus we consider this case against the background of a profound national commitment to the principle that debate on public issues should be uninhibited, robust, and wide-open, and that it may well include vehement, caustic, and sometimes unpleasantly sharp attacks on government and public officials. The present advertisement, as an expression of grievance and protest on one of the major public issues of our time, would seem clearly to qualify for the constitutional protection. The question is whether it forfeits that protection by the falsity of some of its factual statements and by its alleged defamation of respondent.

Authoritative interpretations of the First Amendment guarantees have consistently refused to recognize an exception for any test of truth—whether administered by judges, juries, or administrative officials—and especially one that puts the burden of proving truth on the speaker. The constitutional protection does not turn upon 'the truth, popularity, or social utility of the ideas and beliefs which are offered.' N.A.A.C.P. v. Button, 371 U.S. 415, 445, 83 S. Ct. 328, 344, 9 L. Ed.2d 405. As Madison said, 'Some degree of abuse is inseparable from the proper use of every thing; and in no instance is this more true than in that of the press.' 4 Elliot's Debates on the Federal Constitution (1876), p. 571. In Cantwell v. Connecticut, 310 U.S. 296, 310, 60 S. Ct. 900, 906, 84 L. Ed. 1213, the Court declared:

> In the realm of religious faith, and in that of political belief, sharp differences arise. In both fields the tenets of one man may seem the rankest error to his neighbor. To persuade others to his own point of view, the pleader, as we know, at times, resorts to exaggeration, to vilification of men who have been, or are, prominent in church or state, and even to false statement. But the people of this nation have ordained in the light of history, that, in spite of the probability of excesses and abuses, these liberties are, in the long view, essential to enlightened opinion and right conduct on the part of the citizens of a democracy.

That erroneous statement is inevitable in free debate, and that it must be protected if the freedoms of expression are to have the 'breathing space' that they 'need . . . to survive,' *N.A.A.C.P. v. Button*, 371 U.S. 415, 433, 83 S. Ct. 328, 338, 9 L.

Ed.2d 405, was also recognized by the Court of Appeals for the District of Columbia Circuit in *Sweeney v. Patterson*, 76 U.S. App. D.C. 23, 24, 128 F.2d 457, 458 (1942), cert. denied, 317 U.S. 678, 63 S. Ct. 160, 87 L. Ed. 544. Judge Edgerton spoke for a unanimous court which affirmed the dismissal of a Congressman's libel suit based upon a newspaper article charging him with anti-Semitism in opposing a judicial appointment. He said:

> Cases which impose liability for erroneous reports of the political conduct of officials reflect the obsolete doctrine that the governed must not criticize their governors.... The interest of the public here outweighs the interest of appellant or any other individual. The protection of the public requires not merely discussion, but information. Political conduct and views which some respectable people approve, and others condemn, are constantly imputed to Congressmen. Errors of fact, particularly in regard to a man's mental states and processes, are inevitable.... Whatever is added to the field of libel is taken from the field of free debate.

What a State may not constitutionally bring about by means of a criminal statute is likewise beyond the reach of its civil law of libel. The fear of damage awards under a rule such as that invoked by the Alabama courts here may be markedly more inhibiting than the fear of prosecution under a criminal statute. Alabama, for example, has a criminal libel law which subjects to prosecution 'any person who speaks, writes, or prints of and concerning another any accusation falsely and maliciously importing the commission by such person of a felony, or any other indictable offense involving moral turpitude,' and which allows as punishment upon conviction a fine not exceeding $500 and a prison sentence of six months. Alabama Code, Tit. 14, s 350.... The judgment awarded in this case—without the need for any proof of actual pecuniary loss—was one thousand times greater than the maximum fine provided by the Alabama criminal statute, and one hundred times greater than that provided by the Sedition Act. And since there is no double-jeopardy limitation applicable to civil lawsuits, this is not the only judgment that may be awarded against petitioners for the same publication. Whether or not a newspaper can survive a succession of such judgments, the pall of fear and timidity imposed upon those who would give voice to public criticism is an atmosphere in which the First Amendment freedoms cannot survive.

The state rule of law is not saved by its allowance of the defense of truth....

A rule compelling the critic of official conduct to guarantee the truth of all his factual assertions—and to do so on pain of libel judgments virtually unlimited in amount—leads to a comparable 'self-censorship.' Allowance of the defense of truth, with the burden of proving it on the defendant, does not mean that only false speech will be deterred. Even courts accepting this defense as an adequate safeguard have recognized the difficulties of adducing legal proofs that the alleged libel was true in all its factual particulars. Under such a rule, would-be critics of official conduct may be deterred from voicing their criticism, even though it is believed to be true and even though it is in fact true, because of doubt whether it can be proved in court or fear of the expense of having to do so. They tend to make only statements which 'steer far wider of the unlawful zone.' Speiser v. Randall, *supra*, 357 U.S., at 526, 78 S. Ct. at 1342, 2 L. Ed.2d 1460. The rule thus dampens the vigor and limits the variety of public debate. It is inconsistent with the First and Fourteenth Amendments.

The constitutional guarantees require, we think, a federal rule that prohibits a public official from recovering damages for a defamatory falsehood relating to his official conduct unless he proves that the statement was made with 'actual malice'—that is, with knowledge that it was false or with reckless disregard of whether it was false or not.

. . .

III.

We hold today that the Constitution delimits a State's power to award damages for libel in actions brought by public officials against critics of their official conduct. Since this is such an action, the rule requiring proof of actual malice is applicable. While Alabama law apparently requires proof of actual malice for an award of punitive damages, here general damages are concerned malice is 'presumed.' Such a presumption is inconsistent with the federal rule. . . . Since the trial judge did not instruct the jury to differentiate between general and punitive damages, it may be that the verdict was wholly an award of one or the other. But it is impossible to know, in view of the general verdict returned. Because of this uncertainty, the judgment must be reversed and the case remanded.

Since respondent may seek a new trial, we deem that considerations of effective judicial administration require us to review the evidence in the present record to determine whether it could constitutionally support a judgment for respondent. This Court's duty is not limited to the elaboration of constitutional principles; we must also in proper cases review the evidence to make certain that those principles have been constitutionally applied. This is such a case, particularly since the question is one of alleged trespass across 'the line between speech unconditionally guaranteed and speech which may legitimately be regulated.' Speiser v. Randall, 357 U.S. 513, 525, 78 S. Ct. 1332, 1342, 2 L. Ed.2d 1460. . . .

Applying these standards, we consider that the proof presented to show actual malice lacks the convincing clarity which the constitutional standard demands, and hence that it would not constitutionally sustain the judgment for respondent under the proper rule of law. The case of the individual petitioners requires little discussion. Even assuming that they could constitutionally be found to have authorized the use of their names on the advertisement, there was no evidence whatever that they were aware of any erroneous statements or were in any way reckless in that regard. The judgment against them is thus without constitutional support.

As to *the Times*, we similarly conclude that the facts do not support a finding of actual malice. The statement by *the Times*' Secretary that, apart from the padlocking allegation, he thought the advertisement was 'substantially correct,' affords no constitutional warrant for the Alabama Supreme Court's conclusion that it was a 'cavalier ignoring of the falsity of the advertisement (from which), the jury could not have but been impressed with the bad faith of *The Times*, and its maliciousness inferable therefrom.' The statement does not indicate malice at the time of the publication; even if the advertisement was not 'substantially correct'—although respondent's own proofs tend to show that it was—that opinion was at least a reasonable one, and there was no evidence to impeach the witness' good faith in holding it....

Finally, there is evidence that *the Times* published the advertisement without checking its accuracy against the news stories in *the Times*' own files. The mere presence of the stories in the files does not, of course, establish that *the Times* 'knew' the advertisement was false, since the state of mind required for actual malice would have to be brought home to the persons in *the Times*' organization having responsibility for the publication of the advertisement. With respect to the failure of those persons to make the check, the record shows that they relied upon their knowledge of the good reputation of many of those whose names were listed as sponsors of the advertisement, and upon the letter from A. Philip Randolph, known to them as a responsible individual, certifying that the use of the names was authorized. There was testimony that the persons handling the advertisement saw nothing in it that would render it unacceptable under *the Times*' policy of rejecting advertisements containing 'attacks of a personal character'; their failure to reject it on this ground was not unreasonable. We think the evidence against *the Times* supports at most a finding of negligence in failing to discover the misstatements, and is constitutionally insufficient to show the recklessness that is required for a finding of actual malice.

We also think the evidence was constitutionally defective in another respect: it was incapable of supporting the jury's finding that the allegedly libelous statements were made 'of and concerning' respondent.

[The proposition that criticism of a government body is attached to the official in control of the body] has disquieting implications for criticism of governmental conduct. For good reason, 'no court of last resort in this country has ever held, or even suggested, that prosecutions for libel on government have any place in the American system of jurisprudence.' The present proposition would sidestep this obstacle by transmuting criticism of government, however impersonal it may seem on its face, into personal criticism, and hence potential libel, of the officials of whom the government is composed.... We hold that such a proposition may not constitutionally be utilized to establish that an otherwise impersonal attack on governmental operations was a libel of an official responsible for those operations. Since it was relied on exclusively here, and there was no other evidence to connect the statements with respondent, the evidence was constitutionally insufficient to support a finding that the statements referred to respondent.

The judgment of the Supreme Court of Alabama is reversed and the case is remanded to that court for further proceedings not inconsistent with this opinion.

Reversed and remanded.

Notes

Clarifying who qualifies as a "public official." In *New York Times, Inc. v. Sullivan*, the Supreme Court classified an elected Commissioner of Public Affairs, whose duties involved supervision of the Police Department, Fire Department, Department of Cemetery and Department of Scales, as a public official. The Court did little to further flesh out the contours of this classification, however. Two years later in *Rosenblatt v. Baer*, 383 U.S. 75 (1966), the Court provided slightly more guidance. To qualify as a public official for purposes of the actual malice analysis, the employee's position must have "such apparent importance that the public has an independent interest in the qualifications and performance of the person who holds it, beyond the general public interest in the qualifications and performance of all government employees." The Court noted that the thrust of the *New York Times* decision is that public criticism and debate of public issues should be robust and open. Therefore, there is a strong interest in debate "about those persons who are in a position significantly to influence the resolution of those issues." This means, then, "that the 'public official' designation applies at the very least to those among the hierarchy of government employees who have, or appear to the public to have, substantial responsibility for or control over the conduct of governmental affairs."

Judges, district attorneys, and police chiefs have all been held to be public officials for purposes of *New York Times* analysis. Courts have sometimes split as to whether firefighters and public school teachers qualify. Some courts have concluded that police officers—not just police chiefs or other high-ranking officers—should be treated as public officers. These courts have reasoned that "law enforcement is a uniquely governmental affair" and that police officers "vested with substantial responsibility for the safety and welfare of the citizenry in areas impinging most directly and intimately on daily living." Roche v. Egan, 433 A.2d 757, 762 (Me. 1981). Does the *Rosenblatt* standard provide courts with sufficient guidance on this important issue?

Extension to public figures. The *New York Times* case involved a public official as the plaintiff. In *Curtis Publishing Co. v. Butts*, 388 U.S. 130 (1967), the Court extended the *New York Times* standard to cases involving *public figures* as plaintiffs. That case involved an article alleging that Butts, the athletic director for the University of Georgia, conspired to fix a football game with the University of Alabama. Although Butts was the athletic director for a public university, "he was employed by the Georgia Athletic Association, a private corporation, rather than by the State itself." *Id.* at 135. Therefore, he could not be a public official. However, "Butts had previously served as head football coach of the University and was a well-known and respected figure in coaching ranks." *Id.* at 136. He continued to command "a substantial amount of independent public interest" at the time of the publication of the article. *Id.* at 154. Thus, the Court concluded he was a public figure. For reasons similar to those articulated in *New York Times Co. v. Sullivan*, the Court concluded that the actual malice standard applied to Butts' libel action. A later section in this chapter will explore the contours of public figure status in the defamation context in greater detail.

The meaning of "actual malice." The actual malice standard the Court adopted in *New York Times* is a difficult standard for plaintiffs to satisfy. The Supreme Court's use of the term "actual malice" was rather unfortunate since malice in the traditional sense of the word is not actually required. Nor is the Court's "reckless disregard" language particularly illuminating. It took subsequent cases to develop the meaning of the term:

> In *St. Amant* [*v. Thompson*, 390 U.S. 727 (1968)] Deputy Sheriff Thompson sued St. Amant, a candidate for public office, for defamation. Based on a source whose reputation he did not know and without any independent investigation, St. Amant incorrectly asserted that Thompson had taken bribes. The Supreme Court held that on those facts actual malice was lacking because "[t]here must be sufficient evidence to permit the conclusion that the defendant in fact entertained serious doubts as to the truth of his publication." *St. Amant*, 390 U.S. at 731.

Marcone v. Penthouse International Magazine for Men, 754 F.2d 1072, 1089 (3d Cir. 1985). Section 4 below will explore the actual malice concept in greater detail.

2. Private Figures and Matters of Public Concern or Controversy

Gertz v. Robert Welch, Inc.

418 U.S. 323 (1974)

Mr. Justice POWELL delivered the opinion of the Court.

This Court has struggled for nearly a decade to define the proper accommodation between the law of defamation and the freedoms of speech and press protected by the First Amendment. With this decision we return to that effort. We granted certiorari to reconsider the extent of a publisher's constitutional privilege against liability for defamation of a private citizen.

I

In 1968 a Chicago policeman named Nuccio shot and killed a youth named Nelson. The state authorities prosecuted Nuccio for the homicide and ultimately obtained a conviction for murder in the second degree. The Nelson family retained petitioner Elmer Gertz, a reputable attorney, to represent them in civil litigation against Nuccio.

Respondent publishes *American Opinion*, a monthly outlet for the views of the John Birch Society. Early in the 1960's the magazine began to warn of a nationwide conspiracy to discredit local law enforcement agencies and create in their stead a national police force capable of supporting a Communist dictatorship. As part of the continuing effort to alert the public to this assumed danger, the managing editor of American Opinion commissioned an article on the murder trial of Officer Nuccio. For this purpose he engaged a regular contributor to the magazine. In March 1969 respondent published the resulting article under the title 'FRAME-UP: Richard Nuccio And The War On Police.' The article purports to demonstrate that the testimony against Nuccio at his criminal trial was false and that his prosecution was part of the Communist campaign against the police.

In his capacity as counsel for the Nelson family in the civil litigation, petitioner attended the coroner's inquest into the boy's death and initiated actions for damages, but he neither discussed Officer Nuccio with the press nor played any part in the criminal proceeding. Notwithstanding petitioner's remote connection with the prosecution of Nuccio, respondent's magazine portrayed him as an architect of the 'frame-up.' According to the article, the police file on petitioner took 'a big, Irish cop to lift.' The article stated that petitioner had been an official of the 'Marxist League for Industrial Democracy, originally known as the Intercollegiate Socialist Society, which has advocated the violent seizure of our government.' It labeled Gertz a 'Leninist' and a 'Communist-fronter.' It also stated that Gertz had been an officer of the National Lawyers Guild, described as a Communist organization that 'probably did more than any other outfit to plan the Communist attack on the Chicago police during the 1968 Democratic Convention.'

These statements contained serious inaccuracies. The implication that petitioner had a criminal record was false. Petitioner had been a member and officer of the National Lawyers Guild some 15 years earlier, but there was no evidence that he or that organization had taken any part in planning the 1968 demonstrations in Chicago. There was also no basis for the charge that petitioner was a 'Leninist' or a 'Communist-fronter.' And he had never been a member of the 'Marxist League for Industrial Democracy' or the 'Intercollegiate Socialist Society.'

The managing editor of American Opinion made no effort to verify or substantiate the charges against petitioner. Instead, he appended an editorial introduction stating that the author had 'conducted extensive research into the Richard Nuccio Case.' And he included in the article a photograph of petitioner and wrote the caption that appeared under it: 'Elmer Gertz of Red Guild harasses Nuccio.' Respondent placed the issue of American Opinion containing the article on sale at newsstands throughout the country and distributed reprints of the article on the streets of Chicago.

Petitioner filed a diversity action for libel in the United States District Court for the Northern District of Illinois. He claimed that the falsehoods published by respondent injured his reputation as a lawyer and a citizen.

II

The principal issue in this case is whether a newspaper or broadcaster that publishes defamatory falsehoods about an individual who is neither a public official nor a public figure may claim a constitutional privilege against liability for the injury inflicted by those statements.

III

We begin with the common ground. Under the First Amendment there is no such thing as a false idea. However pernicious an opinion may seem, we depend for its correction not on the conscience of judges and juries but on the competition of other ideas. But there is no constitutional value in false statements of fact. Neither the intentional lie nor the careless error materially advances society's interest in 'uninhibited, robust, and wide-open' debate on public issues. New York Times Co. v. Sullivan, 376 U.S., at 270, 84 S. Ct., at 721. They belong to that category of utterances which 'are no essential part of any exposition of ideas, and are of such slight social value as a step to truth that any benefit that may be derived from them is clearly outweighed by the social interest in order and morality.' Chaplinsky v. New Hampshire, 315 U.S. 568, 572, 62 S. Ct. 766, 769, 86 L. Ed. 1031 (1942).

The legitimate state interest underlying the law of libel is the compensation of individuals for the harm inflicted on them by defamatory falsehood. We would not lightly require the State to abandon this purpose ....

Some tension necessarily exists between the need for a vigorous and uninhibited press and the legitimate interest in redressing wrongful injury.... In our continuing effort to define the proper accommodation between these competing concerns, we have been especially anxious to assure to the freedoms of speech and press that 'breathing space' essential to their fruitful exercise. To that end this Court has extended a measure of strategic protection to defamatory falsehood.

The *New York Times* standard defines the level of constitutional protection appropriate to the context of defamation of a public person. Those who, by reason of the notoriety of their achievements or the vigor and success with which they seek the public's attention, are properly classed as public figures and those who hold governmental office may recover for injury to reputation only on clear and convincing proof that the defamatory falsehood was made with knowledge of its falsity or with reckless disregard for the truth. This standard administers an extremely powerful antidote to the inducement to media self-censorship of the common-law rule of strict liability for libel and slander. And it exacts a correspondingly high price from the victims of defamatory falsehood. Plainly many deserving plaintiffs, including some intentionally subjected to injury, will be unable to surmount the barrier of the *New York Times* test. Despite this substantial abridgment of the state law right to compensation for wrongful hurt to one's reputation, the Court has concluded that the protection of the *New York Times* privilege should be available to publishers and broadcasters of defamatory falsehood concerning public officials and public figures. We think that these decisions are correct, but we do not find their holdings justified solely by reference to the interest of the press and broadcast media in immunity from liability. Rather, we believe that the *New York Times* rule states an accommodation between this concern and the limited state interest present in the context of libel actions brought by public persons. For the reasons stated below, we conclude that the state interest in compensating injury to the reputation of private individuals requires that a different rule should obtain with respect to them.

... [W]e have no difficulty in distinguishing among defamation plaintiffs. The first remedy of any victim of defamation is self-help—using available opportunities to contradict the lie or correct the error and thereby to minimize its adverse impact on reputation. Public officials and public figures usually enjoy significantly greater access to the channels of effective communication and hence have a more realistic opportunity to counteract false statements then private individuals normally enjoy. Private individuals are therefore more vulnerable to injury, and the state interest in protecting them is correspondingly greater.

More important than the likelihood that private individuals will lack effective opportunities for rebuttal, there is a compelling normative consideration underlying the distinction between public and private defamation plaintiffs. An individual who decides to seek governmental office must accept certain necessary consequences of that involvement in public affairs. He runs the risk of closer public scrutiny than might otherwise be the case. And society's interest in the officers of government is not strictly limited to the formal discharge of official duties. As the Court pointed out in *Garrison v. Louisiana*, 379 U.S., at 77, 85 S. Ct., at 217, the public's interest extends to 'anything which might touch on an official's fitness for office.... Few personal attributes are more germane to fitness for office than dishonesty, malfeasance, or improper motivation, even though these characteristics may also affect the official's private character.'

Those classed as public figures stand in a similar position. Hypothetically, it may be possible for someone to become a public figure through no purposeful action of his own, but the instances of truly involuntary public figures must be exceedingly rare. For the most part those who attain this status have assumed roles of especial prominence in the affairs of society. Some occupy positions of such persuasive power and influence that they are deemed public figures for all purposes. More commonly, those classed as public figures have thrust themselves to the forefront of particular public controversies in order to influence the resolution of the issues involved. In either event, they invite attention and comment.

Even if the foregoing generalities do not obtain in every instance, the communications media are entitled to act on the assumption that public officials and public figures have voluntarily exposed themselves to increased risk of injury from defamatory falsehood concerning them. No such assumption is justified with respect to a private individual. He has not accepted public office or assumed an 'influential role in ordering society.' He has relinquished no part of his interest in the protection of his own good name, and consequently he has a more compelling call on the courts for redress of injury inflicted by defamatory falsehood. Thus, private individuals are not only more vulnerable to injury than public officials and public figures; they are also more deserving of recovery.

For these reasons we conclude that the States should retain substantial latitude in their efforts to enforce a legal remedy for defamatory falsehood injurious to the reputation of a private individual.

We hold that, so long as they do not impose liability without fault, the States may define for themselves the appropriate standard of liability for a publisher or broadcaster of defamatory falsehood injurious to a private individual. This approach provides a more equitable boundary between the competing concerns involved here. It recognizes the strength of the legitimate state interest in compensating private individuals for wrongful injury to reputation, yet shields the press and broadcast media from the rigors of strict liability for defamation....

IV

Our accommodation of the competing values at stake in defamation suits by private individuals allows the States to impose liability on the publisher or broadcaster of defamatory falsehood on a less demanding showing than that required by *New York Times*. This conclusion is not based on a belief that the considerations which prompted the adoption of the *New York Times* privilege for defamation of public officials and its extension to public figures are wholly inapplicable to the context of private individuals. Rather, we endorse this approach in recognition of the strong and legitimate state interest in compensating private individuals for injury to reputation. But this countervailing state interest extends no further than compensation for actual injury. For the reasons stated below, we hold that the States may not permit recovery of presumed or punitive damages, at least when liability is not based on a showing of knowledge of falsity or reckless disregard for the truth.

The common law of defamation is an oddity of tort law, for it allows recovery of purportedly compensatory damages without evidence of actual loss. Under the traditional rules pertaining to actions for libel, the existence of injury is presumed from the fact of publication. Juries may award substantial sums as compensation for supposed damage to reputation without any proof that such harm actually occurred. The largely uncontrolled discretion of juries to award damages where there is no loss unnecessarily compounds the potential of any system of liability for defamatory falsehood to inhibit the vigorous exercise of First Amendment freedoms. Additionally, the doctrine of presumed damages invites juries to punish unpopular opinion rather than to compensate individuals for injury sustained by the publication of a false fact. More to the point, the States have no substantial interest in securing for plaintiffs such as this petitioner gratuitous awards of money damages far in excess of any actual injury.

We would not, of course, invalidate state law simply because we doubt its wisdom, but here we are attempting to reconcile state law with a competing interest grounded in the constitutional command of the First Amendment. It is therefore appropriate to require that state remedies for defamatory falsehood reach no farther than is necessary to protect the legitimate interest involved. It is necessary to restrict defamation plaintiffs who do not prove knowledge of falsity or reckless disregard for the truth to compensation for actual injury. We need not define 'actual injury,' as trial courts have wide experience in framing appropriate jury instructions in tort actions. Suffice it to say that actual injury is not limited to out-of-pocket loss. Indeed, the more customary types of actual harm inflicted by defamatory falsehood include impairment of reputation and standing in the community, personal humiliation, and mental anguish and suffering. Of course, juries must be limited by appropriate instructions, and all awards must be supported by competent evidence concerning the injury, although there need be no evidence which assigns an actual dollar value to the injury.

We also find no justification for allowing awards of punitive damages against publishers and broadcasters held liable under state-defined standards of liability for defamation. In most jurisdictions jury discretion over the amounts awarded is limited only by the gentle rule that they not be excessive. Consequently, juries assess punitive damages in wholly unpredictable amounts bearing no necessary relation to the actual harm caused. And they remain free to use their discretion selectively to punish expressions of unpopular views. Like the doctrine of presumed damages, jury discretion to award punitive damages unnecessarily exacerbates the danger of media self-censorship, but, unlike the former rule, punitive damages are wholly irrelevant to the state interest that justifies a negligence standard for private defamation actions. They are not compensation for injury. Instead, they are private fines levied by civil juries to punish reprehensible conduct and to deter its future occurrence. In short, the private defamation plaintiff who establishes liability under a less demanding standard than that stated by *New York Times* may recover only such damages as are sufficient to compensate him for actual injury.

V

Because the jury was allowed to impose liability without fault and was permitted to presume damages without proof of injury, a new trial is necessary. We reverse and remand for further proceedings in accord with this opinion.

Notes

Uncertainty following *Gertz*. *Gertz* involved defamatory statements that obviously involved matters of public concern. But there was some question as to whether the *Gertz* approach was limited to cases involving private-figure plaintiffs who had been defamed with reference to a matter of public concern, or whether it applied regardless of whether the statement implicated matters of public concern. *See Dun & Bradstreet, Inc. v. Greenmoss Builders, Inc.*, 472 U.S. 749, 785 (1985) (Brennan, J., dissenting). There was also some question—given the Court's repeated references in *Gertz* to publishers and broadcasters—whether *Gertz* was limited to cases involving media defendants. Both of these issues were resolved to some extent in *Dun & Bradstreet, Inc. v. Greenmoss Builders, Inc.*, which is covered in the next section.

The fault standard in practice following *Gertz*. Following *Gertz*, state courts have struck the balance identified in *Gertz* in different ways. Some states have chosen to require a showing of actual malice in *Gertz*-type cases. *See* Bandido's, Inc. v. Journal Gazette Co., 575 N.E.2d 324, 326 (Ind. 1991). However, most states simply require the lesser standard of negligence. Rodney A. Smolla, 1 Law of Defamation § 3:30 (2d ed.)

Actual malice and falsity. When the defamatory speech is on a matter of public concern, as a matter of constitutional law, the plaintiff bears the burden of proving the speech was false, regardless of whether the plaintiff is a public or private figure. Philadelphia Newspapers, Inc. v. Hepps, 475 U.S. 767, 776 (1986).

3. Private Figures and Matters of Private Concern

Dun & Bradstreet, Inc. v. Greenmoss Builders, Inc.

472 U.S. 749 (1985)

Justice POWELL announced the judgment of the Court and delivered an opinion, in which Justice REHNQUIST and Justice O'CONNOR joined.

In *Gertz v. Robert Welch, Inc.*, 418 U.S. 323 (1974), we held that the First Amendment restricted the damages that a private individual could obtain from a publisher for a libel that involved a matter of public concern. More specifically, we held that in these circumstances the First Amendment prohibited awards of presumed and punitive damages for false and defamatory statements unless the plaintiff shows "actual malice," that is, knowledge of falsity or reckless disregard for the truth. The question presented in this case is whether this rule of *Gertz* applies when the false and defamatory statements do not involve matters of public concern.

I

Petitioner Dun & Bradstreet, a credit reporting agency, provides subscribers with financial and related information about businesses. All the information is confidential; under the terms of the subscription agreement the subscribers may not reveal it to anyone else. On July 26, 1976, petitioner sent a report to five subscribers indicating that respondent, a construction contractor, had filed a voluntary petition for bankruptcy. This report was false and grossly misrepresented respondent's assets and liabilities. That same day, while discussing the possibility of future financing with its bank, respondent's president was told that the bank had received the defamatory report. He immediately called petitioner's regional office, explained the error, and asked for a correction. In addition, he requested the names of the firms that had received the false report in order to assure them that the company was solvent. Petitioner promised to look into the matter but refused to divulge the names of those who had received the report.

...

Respondent then brought this defamation action in Vermont state court. It alleged that the false report had injured its reputation and sought both compensatory and punitive damages. The trial established that the error in petitioner's report had been caused when one of its employees, a 17-year-old high school student paid to review Vermont bankruptcy pleadings, had inadvertently attributed to respondent a bankruptcy petition filed by one of respondent's former employees. Although petitioner's representative testified that it was routine practice to check the accuracy of such reports with the businesses themselves, it did not try to verify the information about respondent before reporting it.

After trial, the jury returned a verdict in favor of respondent and awarded $50,000 in compensatory or presumed damages and $300,000 in punitive damages. Petitioner moved for a new trial. It argued that in *Gertz v. Robert Welch, Inc., supra,* this Court had ruled broadly that "the States may not permit recovery of presumed or punitive damages, at least when liability is not based on a showing of knowledge of falsity or reckless disregard for the truth," and it argued that the judge's instructions in this case permitted the jury to award such damages on a lesser showing. The trial court indicated some doubt as to whether *Gertz* applied to "non-media cases," but granted a new trial "[b]ecause of . . . dissatisfaction with its charge and . . . conviction that the interests of justice require[d]" it. App. 26.

The Vermont Supreme Court reversed. . . . It held that the balance between a private plaintiff's right to recover presumed and punitive damages without a showing of special fault and the First Amendment rights of "nonmedia" speakers "must be struck in favor of the private plaintiff defamed by a nonmedia defendant." Accordingly, the court held "that as a matter of federal constitutional law, the media protections outlined in *Gertz* are inapplicable to nonmedia defamation actions."

Recognizing disagreement among the lower courts about when the protections of *Gertz* apply, we granted certiorari. We now affirm, although for reasons different from those relied upon by the Vermont Supreme Court.

IV

We have never considered whether the *Gertz* balance obtains when the defamatory statements involve no issue of public concern. To make this determination, we must employ the approach approved in *Gertz* and balance the State's interest in compensating private individuals for injury to their reputation against the First Amendment interest in protecting this type of expression. This state interest is identical to the one weighed in *Gertz.* There we found that it was "strong and legitimate." A State should not lightly be required to abandon it . . .

The First Amendment interest, on the other hand, is less important than the one weighed in *Gertz.* We have long recognized that not all speech is of equal First Amendment importance. It is speech on "'matters of public concern'" that is "at the heart of the First Amendment's protection." First National Bank of Boston v. Bellotti, 435 U.S. 765, 776, 98 S. Ct. 1407, 1415, 55 L.Ed.2d 707 (1978), citing Thornhill v. Alabama, 310 U.S. 88, 101, 60 S. Ct. 736, 743, 84 L.Ed. 1093 (1940). . . .

In contrast, speech on matters of purely private concern is of less First Amendment concern. As a number of state courts, including the court below, have recognized, the role of the Constitution in regulating state libel law is far more limited when the concerns that activated *New York Times* and *Gertz* are absent. In such a case,

> [t]here is no threat to the free and robust debate of public issues; there is no potential interference with a meaningful dialogue of ideas concerning self-government; and there is no threat of liability causing a reaction of self-censorship by the press. The facts of the present case are wholly without the First Amendment concerns with which the Supreme Court of the United States has been struggling. Harley-Davidson Motorsports, Inc. v. Markley, 279 Or. 361, 366, 568 P.2d 1359, 1363 (1977).

While such speech is not totally unprotected by the First Amendment, its protections are less stringent.... In light of the reduced constitutional value of speech involving no matters of public concern, we hold that the state interest adequately supports awards of presumed and punitive damages—even absent a showing of "actual malice."

V

The only remaining issue is whether petitioner's credit report involved a matter of public concern. In a related context, we have held that "[w]hether ... speech addresses a matter of public concern must be determined by [the expression's] content, form, and context ... as revealed by the whole record." Connick v. Myers, *supra*, 461 U.S., at 147–148. These factors indicate that petitioner's credit report concerns no public issue. It was speech solely in the individual interest of the speaker and its specific business audience. *Cf.* Central Hudson Gas & Elec. Corp. v. Public Service Comm'n of New York, 447 U.S. 557, 561 (1980). This particular interest warrants no special protection when—as in this case—the speech is wholly false and clearly damaging to the victim's business reputation. Moreover, since the credit report was made available to only five subscribers, who, under the terms of the subscription agreement, could not disseminate it further, it cannot be said that the report involves any "strong interest in the free flow of commercial information." *Id.* at 764. There is simply no credible argument that this type of credit reporting requires special protection to ensure that "debate on public issues [will] be uninhibited, robust, and wide-open." New York Times Co. v. Sullivan, 376 U.S., at 270.

In addition, the speech here, like advertising, is hardy and unlikely to be deterred by incidental state regulation. It is solely motivated by the desire for profit, which, we have noted, is a force less likely to be deterred than others. Arguably, the reporting here was also more objectively verifiable than speech deserving of greater protection. In any case, the market provides a powerful incentive to a credit reporting agency to be accurate, since false credit reporting is of no use to creditors. Thus, any incremental "chilling" effect of libel suits would be of decreased significance.

VI

We conclude that permitting recovery of presumed and punitive damages in defamation cases absent a showing of "actual malice" does not violate the First Amendment when the defamatory statements do not involve matters of public concern. Accordingly, we affirm the judgment of the Vermont Supreme Court.

Notes

Public controversies, matters of public concern, and matters of private concern. The Court's use of language has not always been terribly precise in this area. In *New York Times v. Sullivan*, the Court first spoke of the need to establish actual malice in the context of discussion of "public issues." However, subsequent cases made clear that one did not become a public figure simply by being associated with a "public" or "newsworthy" issue. Time, Inc. v. Firestone, 424 U.S. 448 (1976). Gradually, the Court began to speak more often of whether a "public controversy" existed with respect to an issue at the time of the defamatory statement. Wolston v. Reader's Digest Ass'n, Inc., 443 U.S. 157, 164–66 (1979). The *Dun & Bradstreet* decision uses the terms "matter of public concern" and "matter of private concern."

Defining the concept further. Courts have used a variety of phrases in attempting to define what qualifies as a public controversy or matter of public concern. *See* Avins v. White, 627 F.2d 637, 647 (3d Cir. 1980) (stating to qualify as a controversy, there "must be a real dispute, the outcome of which affects the general public or some segment of it"); Street v. National Broadcasting Co., 645 F.2d 1227, 1234 (6th Cir. 1981) (concluding that infamous rape trials qualified as a public controversy because they "were the focus of major public debate over the ability of our courts to render even-handed justice"); Lerman v. Flynt Distributing Co., Inc., 745 F.2d 123, 138 (2d Cir.1984) ("A public 'controversy' is any topic upon which sizeable segments of society have different, strongly held views.").

4. The Actual Malice Standard

All of the cases in Sections 1–3 involved the appropriate classification of a defamation plaintiff. The ultimate classification of the defamation plaintiff, in turn, dictates the level of fault the plaintiff must establish on the part of the defendant. Where a defamation plaintiff must establish actual malice on the part of a defendant, the plaintiff faces a considerable burden.

Palin v. New York Times Co.

264 F. Supp. 3d 527 (S.D.N.Y. 2017)

JED S. RAKOFF, U.S.D.J.

Background

In her one-count complaint filed on June 27, 2017, plaintiff Sarah Palin, an acknowledged public figure, alleged that defendant The New York Times Company (the "Times") defamed her in an editorial published on June 14, 2017, the defamatory statements in which were not corrected until the next day. On July 14, 2017, the Times moved to dismiss the complaint for failure to state a claim as a matter of law, and the matter was promptly briefed by both sides.

. . .

Although, therefore, if the Court were to solely limit its evaluation to the face of the complaint, it would readily grant the motion to dismiss, the Court has instead evaluated the plausibility of the complaint in light of such background facts developed during the evidentiary hearing that, as shown by the parties' post-hearing briefs, were either undisputed (at least for purposes of the instant motion) or, where disputed, are taken most favorably to plaintiff. In brief, the pertinent factual allegations are as follows:

On the morning of June 14, 2017, James Hodgkinson opened fire on members of Congress and current and former congressional aides playing baseball at a field in Virginia. That same day, Elizabeth Williamson, an editorial writer at the Times, proposed that the Times editorial board write a piece about the shooting. Before she began writing, James Bennet—the Times' editorial page editor—asked Ms. Williamson to look at editorials the Times had previously published in the aftermath of a January 7, 2011 attack carried out by Jared Lee Loughner at a political event in Tucson, Arizona. In this shooting spree, Loughner shot nineteen people, severely wounding United States Congresswoman Gabrielle Giffords and killing six others, including Chief U.S. District Court Judge John Roll and a nine-year-old girl. Mr. Bennet asked a researcher to send Ms. Williamson these editorials, which the researcher did, copying Mr. Bennet.

Shortly following Loughner's attack, speculation arose about a connection between the crime and plaintiff Palin. This speculation focused on a map (the "SarahPAC Map") circulated by plaintiff's political action committee, SarahPAC, prior to the shooting. The map depicted stylized crosshairs placed over the geographic locations of congressional districts that Republicans were targeting in an upcoming election, including Representative Gabrielle Giffords' district, as well as photos (below the map) of the incumbent Democrats. In the end, however, articles published in the Times and elsewhere stated that no such connection had been established between the circulation of the SarahPAC Map and the Loughner shooting.

Ms. Williamson sent a first draft of the editorial to Mr. Bennet around 5:00 pm on June 14. The original draft stated, in relevant part, that " [n]ot all the details [of the Hodgkinson shooting] are known yet, but a sickeningly familiar pattern is emerging: a deranged individual with a gun—perhaps multiple guns—and scores of rounds of ammunition uses politics as a pretense for a murderous shooting spree.... Just as in 2011, when Jared Lee Loughner opened fire in a supermarket parking lot, grievously wounding Representative Gabby Giffords and killing six people, including a nine year-old girl, Mr. Hodgkinson's rage was nurtured in a vile political climate. Then, it was the pro-gun right being criticized: in the weeks before the shooting Sarah Palin's political action committee circulated a map of targeted electoral districts that put Ms. Giffords and 19 other Democrats under stylized crosshairs." ...

After receiving Ms. Williamson's draft, Mr. Bennet "effectively rewr[o]te the piece." Mr. Bennet's revised version of the editorial was published online on the evening of June 14, 2017 and in print on June 15, 2017 under the title "America's Lethal Politics." The two paragraphs here relevant read as follows:

> Was this attack [by Hodgkinson] evidence of how vicious American politics has become? Probably. In 2011, when Jared Lee Loughner opened fire in a supermarket parking lot, grievously wounding Representative Gabby Giffords and killing six people, including a 9-year-old girl, the link to political incitement was clear. Before the shooting, Sarah Palin's political action committee circulated a map of targeted electoral districts that put Ms. Giffords and 19 other Democrats under stylized cross hairs.
>
> Conservatives and right-wing media were quick on Wednesday to demand forceful condemnation of hate speech and crimes by anti-Trump liberals. They're right. Though there's no sign of incitement as direct as in the Giffords attack, liberals should of course hold themselves to the same standard of decency that they ask of the right.

However, within a day or so of publication, the Times twice revised (and corrected) the text of the editorial, and separately also issued two corrections online beginning on or about 11:15 am on June 15. The corrections were also in the print editions of the Times on June 16. [The corrections explained that the editorial incorrectly stated that a link existed between political rhetoric and the 2011 shooting of Representative Gabby Giffords. In fact, no such link was established.]

Despite these corrections, plaintiff, less than three weeks later, filed the instant complaint alleging that the Times defamed her by including within the original version of the editorial the subsequently-corrected errors.

Discussion

On a motion to dismiss, the Court accepts all well-pleaded factual allegations as true and draws all reasonable inferences in favor of the non-moving party. However, conclusory allegations are not entitled to be assumed true. *Ashcroft v. Iqbal*, 556 U.S. 662, 680–681, 129 S.Ct. 1937, 173 L.Ed.2d 868 (2009). Moreover, to survive a motion to dismiss, a complaint must contain "enough facts to state a claim for relief that is plausible on its face." *Bell Atl. Corp. v. Twombly*, 550 U.S. 544, 570, 127 S.Ct. 1955, 167 L.Ed.2d 929 (2007).

Additionally, in a defamation case, these standards must be applied consistently with the First Amendment protections famously put forward in *New York Times v. Sullivan*, 376 U.S. 254, 84 S.Ct. 710, 11 L.Ed.2d 686 (1964) and its progeny. Thus, in "defamation cases, Rule 12(b)(6) not only protects against the costs of meritless litigation, but provides assurance to those exercising their First Amendment rights that doing so will not needlessly become prohibitively expensive." [After discussing the other elements of a defamation claim, the court turned to the actual malice issue.]

3. Actual Malice

Public figures who seek damages for defamatory statements must . . . do more than prove that the statements about them were false. They must also prove by "clear and convincing evidence" that the statements were made with "actual malice"—that is, with knowledge that the statements were false or with reckless disregard as to their falsity. Reckless disregard can be established by "evidence of an intent to avoid the truth," *Harte-Hanks Comms., Inc. v. Connaughton*, 491 U.S. 657, 693, 109 S. Ct. 2678, 105 L.Ed.2d 562 (1989), evidence that the defendant "entertained serious doubts as to the truth of his publication," *St. Amant v. Thompson*, 390 U.S. 727, 731, 88 S.Ct. 1323, 20 L.Ed.2d 262 (1968), or evidence that the defendant acted with a "high degree of awareness of [a statement's] probable falsity," *Garrison v. State of Louisiana*, 379 U.S. 64, 74, 85 S.Ct. 209, 13 L.Ed.2d 125 (1964). But even then, a defamation complaint by a public figure must allege sufficient particularized facts to support a claim of actual malice by clear and convincing evidence, or the complaint must be dismissed.

Here, ... the complaint fails on its face to adequately allege actual malice, because it fails to identify any individual who possessed the requisite knowledge and intent and, instead, attributes it to the Times in general. This will not suffice. "When there are multiple actors involved in an organizational defendant's publication of a defamatory statement, the plaintiff must identify the individual responsible for publication of a statement, and it is that individual the plaintiff must prove acted with actual malice." *Dongguk Univ.*, 734 F.3d at 123; *see Sullivan*, 376 U.S. at 287, 84 S.Ct. 710 ("[T]he state of mind required for actual malice would have to be brought home to the persons in the [defendant's] organization having responsibility for the publication of the [statement].").

But even assuming, in light of the evidentiary hearing, that the complaint should now be construed as asserting actual malice on the part of Mr. Bennet—the primary, if not sole author of the sentences in question and the Times' editorial page editor—plaintiff still fails to meet the actual malice standard. That standard is grounded in "a profound national commitment to the principle that debate on public issues be uninhibited, robust, and wide-open, and that it may well include vehement, caustic, and sometimes unpleasantly sharp attacks on government and public officials." *Sullivan*, 376 U.S. at 270, 84 S.Ct. 710. *Sullivan* and succeeding cases "have emphasized that the stake of the people in public business and the conduct of public officials is so great that neither the defense of truth nor the standard of ordinary care would protect against self-censorship and thus adequately implement First Amendment policies." *St. Amant*, 390 U.S. at 731–732, 88 S.Ct. 1323.

Coupling this protective overlay with the more technical requirement that a public figure, in order to survive a motion to dismiss a claim of defamation, must allege specific facts that plausibly evidence actual malice in a clear and convincing manner, it is plain that plaintiff has not and cannot meet this standard, even with the benefit of the facts brought forth by the evidentiary hearing.

To put the matter simply, Bennet as the undisputed testimony shows—wrote the putatively offending passages of the editorial over a period of a few hours and published it very soon thereafter. Shortly after that, his mistakes in linking the

SarahPAC Map to the Loughner shooting were called to his attention, and he immediately corrected the errors, not only in the editorial itself but also by publishing corrections both electronically and in print. Such behavior is much more plausibly consistent with making an unintended mistake and then correcting it than with acting with actual malice.

Plaintiff's response is, first, to posit that the Times in general, and Mr. Bennet in particular, had a motive to defame Mrs. Palin. As to the Times in general, the complaint alleges that "there is existing hostility toward Mrs. Palin" and "her name and attacks upon her inflame passions and thereby drive viewership and Web clicks to media companies." As to the alleged "hostility," it goes without saying that the Times editorial board is not a fan of Mrs. Palin. But neither the fact of that opposition, nor the supposition that a sharp attack on a disfavored political figure will increase a publication's readership, has ever been enough to prove actual malice. For "it is hardly unusual for publications to print matter that will please their subscribers; many publications set out to portray a particular viewpoint or even to advance a partisan cause. Defamation judgments do not exist to police their objectivity." *Reuber v. Food Chem. News, Inc.*, 925 F.2d 703, 716 (4th Cir. 1991).

Here, moreover, as previously noted, it is not the Times' collective knowledge and intent that is relevant but rather Mr. Bennet's. As to hostility, the best that plaintiff can muster is that Mr. Bennet has a long association with liberal publications and that his brother is the Democratic senator from Colorado who was endorsed by Congresswoman Giffords' political action committee in his 2016 election and whose opponent was endorsed by Mrs. Palin in that same election. If such political opposition counted as evidence of actual malice, the protections imposed by *Sullivan* and its progeny would swiftly become a nullity.

As for the alleged economic motive, there is not a shred of factual support, either in the complaint or in the evidentiary hearing, for the supposition that considerations of attracting readership ever entered Mr. Bennet's mind when he was drafting this particular editorial. Indeed, if that were his goal, one would have expected him to mention Mrs. Palin's name more than once in the editorial or use her name in the social media promoting the editorial, neither of which was done.

In her complaint, plaintiff also relies on her allegations that the Times cited "no source" for the challenged statements and failed to conduct an adequate investigation into their veracity, allegations that plaintiff now suggests apply to Mr. Bennet as well. As to the Times in general, this allegation is undercut by the fact that the original draft of the editorial that Ms. Williamson sent Mr. Bennet, as well as the version published, included a hyperlink to an article that described in some detail the SarahPAC Map and its circulation and concluded that there was no proven link between that circulation and the Loughner shooting. "The hyperlink is the twenty-first century equivalent of the footnote for purposes of attribution in defamation law." *See Adelson v. Harris*, 973 F.Supp.2d 467, 484 (S.D.N.Y. 2013). The inclusion of this article through the hyperlink shows, first, that the Times did do some research before publishing the editorial (despite the very limited time available) and, second, that the allegation of actual malice is even more improbable because the Times included as a hyperlink an article undercutting its own conclusions.

Once again, however, it is Mr. Bennet's knowledge and intent that are ultimately at issue so far as actual malice is concerned, and Bennet testified that he himself did not read the hyperlinked article when rewriting the editorial nor do any further investigation of his own (though he was copied on a communication sent by the researcher that he had directed to find and examine prior Times editorials regarding Mrs. Palin and the Loughner shooting). But it is well-established that supposed research failures do not constitute clear and convincing evidence of actual malice, even of the "reckless" kind. Indeed, in *Sullivan* itself, the Supreme Court recognized that the editorial advertisement there at issue contained facts contradicted by earlier news stories printed in the New York Times. The Court held that the existence of these prior stories did not establish actual malice in part because failure to investigate "supports at most a finding of negligence in failing to discover the misstatements."

Similarly, failure to comply with journalistic policies—which the complaint here also alleges, although in wholly conclusory fashion,—cannot establish actual malice absent allegations supporting an inference of reckless disregard. *See, e.g., Harte-Hanks*, 491 U.S. at 665, 109 S.Ct. 2678 ("[A] public figure plaintiff must prove more than an extreme departure from professional standards" to demonstrate actual malice).

. . .

The Court has considered plaintiff's other alleged evidence of actual malice and finds it too inconsequential to be worth further discussion. The Court has also considered whether the various items of supposed evidence of actual malice discussed above, even if individually insufficient to support an inference of actual malice, are collectively sufficient to support an inference of actual malice. But, as the foregoing discussion demonstrates, each and every item of alleged support for plaintiff's claim of actual malice consists either of gross supposition or of evidence so weak that, even together, these items cannot support the high degree of particularized proof that must be provided before plaintiff can be said to have adequately alleged clear and convincing evidence of actual malice.

We come back to the basics. What we have here is an editorial, written and rewritten rapidly in order to voice an opinion on an immediate event of importance, in which are included a few factual inaccuracies somewhat pertaining to Mrs. Palin that are very rapidly corrected. Negligence this may be; but defamation of a public figure it plainly is not.

For the foregoing reasons, the Court grants defendant's motion to dismiss. Because, moreover, this Court has canvassed in the discussion above all the various additions that plaintiff has even remotely suggested it would include in an amended complaint, the dismissal is "with prejudice," that is, final. Clerk to enter judgment.

SO ORDERED.

Notes

***Palin* on appeal.** On appeal, the Second Circuit Court of Appeals held that the lower court had improperly relied on matters outside the pleading in considering the motion to dismiss without converting the motion to one for summary judgment. According to Palin's amended complaint, Bennett had a predetermined argument he wanted to make in the editorial, which led him to publish an editorial with reckless disregard as to its falsity or knowing that the facts contained were false. According to the Second Circuit, Palin had plausibly alleged a claim of defamation for purposes of the motion to dismiss. *Palin v. New York Times Co.*, 940 F.3d 804 (2d Cir. 2019).

The impact of *Twombly* and *Iqbal* on defamation claims. *Palin* was decided on a Rule 12(b)(6) motion. As you may have already read in your Civil Procedure class, *Bell Atlantic Corp. v. Twombly*, 550 U.S. 544 (2007), and *Ashcroft v. Iqbal*, 556 U.S. 662 (2009) (together, sometimes referred to as "*Twiqbal*"), dramatically heightened the pleading standard for plaintiffs. According to one author, "The *Twiqbal* pleading standard requires a court to evaluate a motion to dismiss for failure to state a claim by, first, discarding conclusory allegations, and second, determining whether the remaining factual allegations state a claim that is 'plausible on its face.' While Federal Rule of Civil Procedure 9(b) permits malice to be pleaded 'generally,' all Circuit Courts of Appeals that have addressed the issue have applied the plausibility standard to allegations of malice under Rule 9(b)." Judy M. Cornett, *Pleading Actual Malice in Defamation Actions after Twiqbal: A Circuit Survey*, 17 Nev. L.J. 709, 710 (2017). The result, according to the author, is that defendants have "virtual immunity" where the actual malice standard applies. *Id.*

Striking the appropriate balance. Does the actual malice standard as applied in cases involving public figures or public officials strike the appropriate balance between free speech and one's interest in his or her reputation? What would it take for a plaintiff to establish that a defendant acted with actual malice?

5. Classifying Plaintiffs as Public Figures or Private Figures

Again, Sections 1–3 above all dealt with how plaintiffs should be classified for purposes of their defamation claims. As Section 4 illustrated, how a court classifies a plaintiff may, as a practical matter, make it exceedingly difficult for a plaintiff to recover if it is determined that the plaintiff needs to establish that the defendant acted with actual malice. *Gertz* held that the *New York Times* actual malice standard did not apply to the plaintiff in that case, a lawyer, because he was not a public official or a public figure. Subsequent decisions have attempted to flesh out the contours of the "public figure" concept in more detail. Distinguishing between public and private figures is not always easy. Over time, several different categories of "public figures" have emerged, further complicating the analysis. The following section explores these distinctions.

In *Gertz*, the Court concluded that designation as a public figure may rest on two possible bases and explained why Gertz did not fit either:

> In some instances an individual may achieve such pervasive fame or notoriety that he becomes a public figure for all purposes and in all contexts. More commonly, an individual voluntarily injects himself or is drawn into a particular public controversy and thereby becomes a public figure for a limited range of issues. In either case such persons assume special prominence in the resolution of public questions.
>
> Petitioner has long been active in community and professional affairs. He has served as an officer of local civic groups and of various professional organizations, and he has published several books and articles on legal subjects. Although petitioner was consequently well known in some circles, he had achieved no general fame or notoriety in the community. None of the prospective jurors called at the trial had ever heard of petitioner prior to this litigation, and respondent offered no proof that this response was atypical of the local population. We would not lightly assume that a citizen's participation in community and professional affairs rendered him a public figure for all purposes. Absent clear evidence of general fame or notoriety in the community, and pervasive involvement in the affairs of society, an individual should not be deemed a public personality for all aspects of his life. It is preferable to reduce the public-figure question to a more meaningful context by looking to the nature and extent of an individual's participation in the particular controversy giving rise to the defamation.
>
> In this context it is plain that petitioner was not a public figure. He played a minimal role at the coroner's inquest, and his participation related solely to his representation of a private client. He took no part in the criminal prosecution of Officer Nuccio. Moreover, he never discussed either the criminal or civil litigation with the press and was never quoted as having done so. He plainly did not thrust himself into the vortex of this public issue, nor did he engage the public's attention in an attempt to influence its outcome. We are persuaded that the trial court did not err in refusing to characterize petitioner as a public figure for the purpose of this litigation.

Gertz v. Robert Welch, Inc., 418 U.S. 323, 351–52 (1974).

The first case in this section examines the distinctions among the all-purpose (or general-purpose) public figures, limited-purpose public figures, and private figures identified in *Gertz*.

Wolston v. Reader's Digest Ass'n, Inc.

443 U.S. 157 (1979)

Mr. Justice REHNQUIST delivered the opinion of the Court.

In 1974, respondent Reader's Digest Association, Inc., published a book entitled KGB, the Secret Work of Soviet Agents (KGB), written by respondent John Barron.

The book describes the Soviet Union's espionage organization and chronicles its activities since World War II. [A passage identified petitioner Ilya Wolston as a Soviet agent.]

Petitioner sued the author and publishers of KGB in the United States District Court for the District of Columbia, claiming that the passages in KGB stating that he had been indicted for espionage and had been a Soviet agent were false and defamatory. The District Court granted respondents' motion for summary judgment. The court held that petitioner was a "public figure" and that the First Amendment therefore precluded recovery unless petitioner proved that respondents had published a defamatory falsehood with "'actual malice'—that is, with knowledge that it was false or with reckless disregard of whether it was false or not," New York Times Co. v. Sullivan, 376 U.S. 254, 280, 84 S. Ct. 710, 726, 11 L.Ed.2d 686 (1964). 429 F. Supp., at 172, 176. While the District Court agreed that the above-quoted portions of KGB appeared to state falsely that petitioner had been indicted for espionage, it ruled, on the basis of affidavits and deposition testimony, that the evidence raised no genuine issue with respect to the existence of "actual malice" on the part of respondents.

During 1957 and 1958, a special federal grand jury sitting in New York City conducted a major investigation into the activities of Soviet intelligence agents in the United States. As a result of this investigation, petitioner's aunt and uncle, Myra and Jack Soble, were arrested in January 1957 on charges of spying. The Sobles later pleaded guilty to espionage charges, and in the ensuing months, the grand jury's investigation focused on other participants in a suspected Soviet espionage ring, resulting in further arrests, convictions, and guilty pleas. On the same day the Sobles were arrested, petitioner was interviewed by agents of the Federal Bureau of Investigation at his home in the District of Columbia. Petitioner was interviewed several more times during the following months in both Washington and in New York City and traveled to New York on various occasions pursuant to grand jury subpoenas.

On July 1, 1958, however, petitioner failed to respond to a grand jury subpoena directing him to appear on that date. Petitioner previously had attempted to persuade law enforcement authorities not to require him to travel to New York for interrogation because of his state of mental depression. On July 14, a Federal District Judge issued an order to show cause why petitioner should not be held in criminal contempt of court. These events immediately attracted the interest of the news media, and on July 15 and 16, at least seven news stories focusing on petitioner's failure to respond to the grand jury subpoena appeared in New York and Washington newspapers.

Petitioner appeared in court on the return date of the show-cause order and offered to testify before the grand jury, but the offer was refused. A hearing then commenced on the contempt charges. Petitioner's wife, who then was pregnant, was called to testify as to petitioner's mental condition at the time of the return date of the subpoena, but after she became hysterical on the witness stand, petitioner agreed to plead guilty to the contempt charge. He received a 1-year suspended sentence and was placed on probation for three years, conditioned on his cooperation with the grand jury in any further inquiries regarding Soviet espionage. Newspapers also reported the details of the contempt proceedings and petitioner's guilty plea and sentencing. In all, during the 6-week period between petitioner's failure to appear before the grand jury and his sentencing, 15 stories in newspapers in Washington and New York mentioned or discussed these events. This flurry of publicity subsided following petitioner's sentencing, however, and, thereafter, he succeeded for the most part in returning to the private life he had led prior to issuance of the grand jury subpoena. At no time was petitioner indicted for espionage.

... We explained in *Gertz* that the rationale for extending the *New York Times* [actual malice] rule to public figures was two-fold. First, we recognized that public figures are less vulnerable to injury from defamatory statements because of their ability to resort to effective "self-help." They usually enjoy significantly greater access than private individuals to channels of effective communication, which enable them through discussion to counter criticism and expose the falsehood and fallacies of defamatory statements. Second, and more importantly, was a normative consideration that public figures are less deserving of protection than private persons because public figures, like public officials, have "voluntarily exposed themselves to increased risk of injury from defamatory falsehood concerning them." We identified two ways in which a person may become a public figure for purposes of the First Amendment:

> For the most part those who attain this status have assumed roles of especial prominence in the affairs of society. Some occupy positions of such persuasive power and influence that they are deemed public figures for all purposes. More commonly, those classed as public figures have thrust themselves to the forefront of particular public controversies in order to influence the resolution of the issues involved. 418 U.S., at 345, 94 S. Ct., at 3009.

Neither respondents nor the lower courts relied on any claim that petitioner occupied a position of such "persuasive power and influence" that he could be deemed one of that small group of individuals who are public figures for all purposes. Petitioner led a thoroughly private existence prior to the grand jury inquiry and returned to a position of relative obscurity after his sentencing. He achieved no general fame or notoriety and assumed no role of special prominence in the affairs of society as a result of his contempt citation or because of his involvement in the investigation of Soviet espionage in 1958.

Instead, respondents argue, and the lower courts held, that petitioner falls within the second category of public figures—those who have "thrust themselves to the forefront of particular public controversies in order to influence the resolution of the issues involved"—and that, therefore, petitioner is a public figure for the limited purpose of comment on his connection with, or involvement in, Soviet espionage in the 1940's and 1950's. Both lower courts found petitioner's failure to appear before the grand jury and citation for contempt determinative of the public-figure issue. The District Court concluded that by failing to appear before the grand jury and subjecting himself to a citation for contempt, petitioner "became involved in a controversy of a decidedly public nature in a way that invited attention and comment, and thereby created in the public an interest in knowing about his connection with espionage. . . ." Similarly, the Court of Appeals stated that by refusing to comply with the subpoena, petitioner "stepped center front into the spotlight focused on the investigation of Soviet espionage. In short, by his voluntary action he invited attention and comment in connection with the public questions involved in the investigation of espionage."

We do not agree with respondents and the lower courts that petitioner can be classed as such a limited-purpose public figure. First, the undisputed facts do not justify the conclusion of the District Court and Court of Appeals that petitioner "voluntarily thrust" or "injected" himself into the forefront of the public controversy surrounding the investigation of Soviet espionage in the United States. It would be more accurate to say that petitioner was dragged unwillingly into the controversy. The Government pursued him in its investigation. Petitioner did fail to respond to a grand jury subpoena, and this failure, as well as his subsequent citation for contempt, did attract media attention. But the mere fact that petitioner voluntarily chose not to appear before the grand jury, knowing that his action might be attended by publicity, is not decisive on the question of public-figure status. In *Gertz*, we held that an attorney was not a public figure even though he voluntarily associated himself with a case that was certain to receive extensive media exposure. We emphasized that a court must focus on the "nature and extent of an individual's participation in the particular controversy giving rise to the defamation." In *Gertz*, the attorney took no part in the criminal prosecution, never discussed the litigation with the press, and limited his participation in the civil litigation solely to his representation of a private client. Similarly, petitioner never discussed this matter with the press and limited his involvement to that necessary to defend himself against the contempt charge. It is clear that petitioner played only a minor role in whatever public controversy there may have been concerning the investigation of Soviet espionage. We decline to hold that his mere citation for contempt rendered him a public figure for purposes of comment on the investigation of Soviet espionage.

Petitioner's failure to appear before the grand jury and citation for contempt no doubt were "newsworthy," but the simple fact that these events attracted media attention also is not conclusive of the public-figure issue. A private individual is not automatically transformed into a public figure just by becoming involved in or associated with a matter that attracts public attention. . . . A libel defendant must show more than mere newsworthiness to justify application of the demanding burden of *New York Times*.

Nor do we think that petitioner engaged the attention of the public in an attempt to influence the resolution of the issues involved. Petitioner assumed no "special prominence in the resolution of public questions." *See* Gertz v. Robert Welch, Inc.,

418 U.S., at 351, 94 S. Ct., at 3012. His failure to respond to the grand jury's subpoena was in no way calculated to draw attention to himself in order to invite public comment or influence the public with respect to any issue. He did not in any way seek to arouse public sentiment in his favor and against the investigation. Thus, this is not a case where a defendant invites a citation for contempt in order to use the contempt citation as a fulcrum to create public discussion about the methods being used in connection with an investigation or prosecution. To the contrary, petitioner's failure to appear before the grand jury appears simply to have been the result of his poor health. He then promptly communicated his desire to testify and, when the offer was rejected, passively accepted his punishment. There is no evidence that petitioner's failure to appear was intended to have, or did in fact have, any effect on any issue of public concern. In short, we find no basis whatsoever for concluding that petitioner relinquished, to any degree, his interest in the protection of his own name.

This reasoning leads us to reject the further contention of respondents that any person who engages in criminal conduct automatically becomes a public figure for purposes of comment on a limited range of issues relating to his conviction.

. . .

Accordingly, the judgment of the Court of Appeals is

Reversed.

Note

Public figures within a community. A person may be an all-purpose public figure within a particular community or geographic area despite not having attained pervasive fame or notoriety on a national level. *See* Steere v. Cupp. 602 P.2d 1267 (Kan. 1979).

Gertz suggested that "[h]ypothetically, it may be possible for someone to become a public figure through no purposeful action of his own, but the instances of truly involuntary public figures must be exceedingly rare." Some courts have been willing to recognize the involuntary public figure as a category of public figures. The following case explores whether the plaintiff was a voluntary limited-purpose figure, an involuntary limited-purpose public figure, or a private figure.

Atlanta Journal-Constitution v. Jewell

555 S.E.2d 175 (Ga. Ct. App. 2002)

JOHNSON, Presiding Judge.

[This case arises] from coverage by the Atlanta Journal-Constitution of the 1996 bombing in Centennial Olympic Park and Richard Jewell's involvement in that incident. The initial media coverage of the Olympic Park bombing portrayed Jewell as a hero for his role in discovering the bomb, alerting authorities, and evacuating bystanders from the immediate vicinity, no doubt saving lives. Subsequently, however, the Federal Bureau of Investigation (FBI) focused its investigation on Jewell. The resulting media coverage of the criminal investigation caused Jewell and his family considerable anguish, while converting Jewell's status from hero to suspect. The investigation ultimately cleared Jewell of any involvement in the bombing. And through subsequent media coverage of the investigation, his role in these events has once again been depicted as the positive role it was originally believed to be.

. . .

Jewell moved for partial summary judgment, asserting the trial court should find that he is a private, versus a public, figure. Specifically, the trial court was asked to determine whether, by his public appearances, Jewell became a limited-purpose public figure prior to the Atlanta Journal-Constitution's public disclosure that he was under investigation in connection with the bombing of the Olympic Park. The trial court determined that Jewell is a "voluntary limited purpose public figure" and thereby required him to meet the actual malice standard of proof set forth in *New York Times Co. v. Sullivan* in this defamation action. Jewell appeals this ruling.

In considering this issue, we repeat the basic facts of the case. At the time of the park bombing, Jewell was working as a security guard in the park. Shortly before the explosion, he spotted a suspicious and unattended package and reported its existence to the Georgia Bureau of Investigation. Around the same time, an anonymous 911 call informed police that a bomb had been placed in the park. After he reported the existence of the package, and at a time when police believed the package contained a bomb but did not know when it would explode, Jewell assisted police in moving park patrons away from the package. He also assisted in the evacuation of the five-story tower where the package was located.

Following the explosion of the bomb, but before he became a suspect, Jewell granted one photo shoot and ten interviews. [Several of the interviews were with national media sources.] . . . .

Four days after the bombing, the Atlanta Journal-Constitution published a front-page article headlined "FBI suspects 'hero' guard may have planted bomb." Subsequently, Jewell alleges, approximately 19 articles portrayed him as an individual who was guilty or likely guilty of criminal involvement in the bombing, who had a motive for the bombing, and who had an aberrant personality and a bizarre employment history.

The central issue presented by this appeal is whether Jewell, as the plaintiff in this defamation action, is a public or private figure, as those terms are used in defamation cases. This is a critically important issue, because in order for a "public figure" to recover in a suit for defamation, there must be proof by clear and convincing evidence of actual malice on the part of the defendant. Plaintiffs who are "private persons" must only prove that the defendant acted with ordinary negligence. Jewell contends the trial court erred in finding that he is a "public figure" for purposes of this defamation action. We disagree.

. . .

The trial court held that Jewell is a voluntary limited-purpose public figure. Jewell argues that he is not because he did not assume a role of special prominence in the controversy over the safety of Olympic Park, he did not voluntarily thrust himself to the forefront of the controversy of the safety of Olympic Park, and he did not intentionally seek to influence the resolution or outcome of any public controversy surrounding the safety of Olympic Park. Jewell further claims that the alleged defamation in this case is not germane to his participation in the controversy over safety at Olympic Park.

In *Silvester v. American Broadcasting Cos.*, the Eleventh Circuit adopted a three-prong test to determine whether a person is a limited-purpose public figure. Under this test, the court must isolate the public controversy, examine the plaintiff's involvement in the controversy, and determine whether the alleged defamation was germane to the plaintiff's participation in the controversy. Whether a person is a public figure, general or limited, is a question of law for the court to resolve.

(a) In isolating the public controversy, the court must look to those controversies that are already the subject of debate in the public arena. The trial court dismissed Jewell's argument that the public controversy was "who bombed the Olympic Park," finding this too narrowly defined the controversy. According to the trial court, the public controversy following the bombing and prior to the alleged defamatory statements included the broader question of the safety of the general public in returning to the Olympic Park area. Safety of the park and other Olympic venues after the bombing involved a real dispute. The outcome of that dispute would affect the general public or some segment of it in an appreciable way, and the ramifications of the dispute would be felt by persons who were not direct participants in the public discussion. Neither party argues on appeal that the trial court erred in reaching this conclusion.

(b) The trial court next examined Jewell's involvement in the controversy. A plaintiff in a libel case must be deemed a public figure if he purposefully tries to influence the outcome of a public controversy or, because of his position in the controversy, could realistically be expected to have an impact on its resolution. A tangential involvement is insufficient. In examining the nature and extent of Jewell's participation in the issue of Olympic Park safety, the court can look to Jewell's past conduct, the extent of press coverage, and the public reaction to his conduct and statements. The court must examine these factors as they existed before the alleged defamation was published. An analysis of these factors shows that Jewell assumed a role of special prominence in the Olympic Park safety debate.

While Jewell asserts that his media role was limited to that of an eyewitness and that he did not attempt to shape the resolution of any controversy, Jewell's participation in interviews and the information he related about the controversy was not so circumscribed. In fact, the extensive media coverage Jewell received as the individual who discovered the bomb and helped evacuate the public led one federal judge to describe him as a "media hero." The Detroit News headlined its article about the bombing: "Hero: Keen eyesight, level head thrust guard into spotlight."

While we can envision situations in which news coverage alone would be insufficient to convert Jewell from private citizen to public figure, we agree with the trial court that Jewell's actions show that he voluntarily assumed a position of influence in the controversy. Jewell granted ten interviews and one photo shoot in the three days between the bombing and the reopening of the park, mostly to prominent members of the national press. While no magical number of media appearances is required to render a citizen a public figure, Jewell's participation in the public discussion of the bombing exceeds what has been deemed sufficient to render other citizens public figures. Even Jewell commented that the number of interviews he gave—up to two or three within a fifteen-minute period—was so great that he still cannot remember them all. The fact is that Jewell was prominent enough to require the assistance of a media handler to field press inquiries and coordinate his media appearances.

... Jewell stated that he had spotted the bag after a group of rowdy, college-aged men had left the park. And he announced on CNN that he had matched one of the men to a composite sketch. These statements gave the impression that police had solid leads and the park was safe. Jewell also repeatedly offered assurances that his training had been sufficient to handle the situation, that other law enforcement personnel had received adequate training to handle the situation, and that law enforcement personnel did all they could in response to the situation. In addition, Jewell spoke with a television crew conducting interviews on whether the Olympic Games should continue and whether the park should reopen. He offered encouragement to members of the public who had continued coming to the Olympic Games.

Jewell should have known, and likely did know, that his comments would be broadcast and published to millions of American citizens searching for answers in the aftermath of the bombing. Clearly, his repeated comments regarding the adequacy of the law enforcement preparation, the appropriateness of the response to the bombing, and the safety of those returning to the park could realistically be expected to have an impact on the controversy's resolution.

Jewell claims he gave the interviews only to accommodate the desires of his employer and that he never intended to have any influence on the matters. Whether a person has voluntarily injected himself into a public controversy in order to have an impact on its outcome cannot be determined solely by reference to the actor's subjective motives. The court must ask whether a reasonable person would have concluded that Jewell would play or was seeking to play a major role in determining the outcome of the controversy. Viewed objectively, Jewell's numerous media appearances in the days following the bombing reveal that he attempted to improve the public's perception of security at the park. The media spokesman who facilitated many of the interviews told Jewell he was under no obligation to do any interviews, but Jewell nevertheless voluntarily made media appearances. This evidence was sufficient to support the trial court's determination that Jewell was a voluntary limited-purpose public figure.

c) The third prong of the *Silvester* test requires the court to ascertain whether the allegedly defamatory statements were germane to Jewell's participation in the controversy. Anything which might touch on the controversy is relevant. Misstatements wholly unrelated to the controversy do not require a showing of actual malice to be actionable.

As recognized in *Waldbaum*, a publication is germane to a plaintiff's participation in a controversy if it might help the public decide how much credence should be given to the plaintiff. Here, Jewell was on the scene in his role as a security guard, he found the bomb and reported its existence to authorities, and he helped evacuate people from the scene. During interviews, he discussed his participation in the events, his previous training, the training and reactions of other law enforcement personnel on the scene, and urged the public to show the bomber that this type of activity would not be tolerated.

Certainly, the information reported regarding Jewell's character was germane to Jewell's participation in the controversy over the Olympic Park's safety. A public figure's talents, education, experience, and motives are relevant to the public's decision to listen to him. The articles and the challenged statements within them dealt with Jewell's status as a suspect in the bombing and his law enforcement background.

Even if the trial court erred in finding that Jewell was a voluntary limited-purpose public figure, the record contains clear and convincing evidence that, at the very least, Jewell was an involuntary limited-purpose public figure. While, in general, a public figure voluntarily puts himself into a position to influence the outcome of the controversy, "[o]ccasionally, someone is caught up in the controversy involuntarily and, against his will, assumes a prominent position in its outcome. Unless he rejects any role in the debate, he too has 'invited comment' relating to the issue at hand." The decision in *Dameron v. Washington Magazine* [779 F.2d 736, 741–742 (D.C.Cir.1985)] provides an excellent example of the types of circumstances in which an individual can become an involuntary public figure.

In *Dameron*, the plaintiff claimed defamation in connection with a magazine article that mentioned his role as the sole air traffic controller on duty at the time of a notorious airliner crash. Although the plaintiff had not availed himself of the media to speak on the public issues relating to the crash, he was nonetheless held to be an involuntary public figure. The plaintiff's sole role in the controversy over the cause of the crash was that he was the air traffic controller on duty at the time of the crash and he subsequently testified at a National Transportation Safety Board hearing on the crash.

The same considerations that led the *Dameron* court to find the plaintiff in that case was an involuntary public figure require the same conclusion in this case. Even if we found that Jewell did not "inject" himself into the controversy, "[i]njection is not the only means by which public-figure status is achieved. Persons can become involved in public controversies and affairs without their consent or will." Jewell, who had the misfortune to have a tragedy occur on his watch, is such a person.

Like the plaintiff in *Dameron*, Jewell was an ordinary citizen who was unknown to the public before the Olympic Park bombing, never sought to capitalize on the fame he achieved through his actions in events surrounding the bombing, and never acquired any notoriety apart from the bombing and the investigation which followed. However, there is no question that Jewell played a central, albeit possibly involuntary, role in the controversy over Olympic Park safety. Jewell happened to be the security guard on duty at the time of the bombing, happened to be the security guard who found the bomb, and happened to be involved in the evacuation of the public from the area where the bomb was located. He became embroiled in the ensuing discussion and controversy over park safety and became well known to the public in this one very limited connection. Whether he liked it or not, Jewell became a central figure in the specific public controversy with respect to which he was allegedly defamed: the controversy over park safety.

Notes

Justifications for requiring a showing of actual malice. *Gertz* and *Wolston* both justify imposing the heightened actual malice standard on voluntary public figures on the grounds that such individuals have a greater ability to resort to self-help in responding to defamatory statements and because they have assumed the risk of negative publicity. Do these justifications apply to Jewell's situation?

Voluntary limited-purpose public figures. *Gertz* talked about an individual engaging the public's attention in an attempt to influence the outcome of a public issue. Is that what Jewell did? Some courts focus less on the existence of some type of public controversy and the plaintiff's attempts to influence the outcome of debate on the issue and more on the fact that the plaintiff has voluntarily sought public attention on a matter that impacts the public. For example, restaurants and other places of public accommodations are often classified as public figures for purposes of statements concerning the services they provide because restaurants actively seek public patrons and offer services to the public at large. *See, e.g.*, Steaks Unlimited, Inc. v. Deaner, 623 F.2d 264, 272–73 (3d Cir. 1980) (concluding restaurant was a public figure based, in part, on its extensive advertising).

Involuntary limited-purpose public figures. Should there be such a category? Some courts have refused or at least been reluctant to recognize the existence of an involuntary public figure category. *See* Wells v. Liddy, 186 F.3d 505, 538 (4th Cir. 1999), cert. denied, 528 U.S. 1118 (2000) (commenting that "[s]o rarely have courts determined that an individual was an involuntary public figure that commentators have questioned the continuing existence of that category"). Was Richard Jewell the sort of person the *Gertz* court had in mind when it alluded to the possibility of someone becoming a public figure after being involuntarily drawn into a controversy? According to the Fourth Circuit Court of Appeals, to be an involuntary public figure, one must: (1) be a central figure in a significant public controversy and

(2) have assumed the risk of publicity, even if one did not seek to publicize her views or influence discussion on an issue of public controversy. Wells v. Liddy, 186 F.3d 505, 540 (4th Cir. 1999).

Problem 15.6. Recall that Rachel Winchell was running for the Pleasant Hill School Board at the time Donna posted on Facebook. Based on the material above, should Rachel be classified as a public official, a public figure, or a private figure? If a public figure, what kind of public figure?

Problem 15.7. Assuming your conclusion to the previous question is correct, what would be the effect in terms of Rachel's burden of proof?

Problem 15.8. Recall that Fred Winchell owns a small automotive repair shop. Assuming he could satisfy the other requirements of a defamation claim, should he be classified as a public official, a public figure, or a private figure? If a public figure, what kind of public figure?

Problem 15.9. Assuming your conclusion to the previous question is correct, what would be the effect in terms of Fred's burden of proof?

C. Defamation: Privileges and Defenses

1. Absolute Privileges

As the name implies, absolute privileges are absolute in nature. In other words, if the requirements of the privilege are satisfied, the actor is shielded from liability "irrespective of his purpose in publishing the defamatory matter, his belief in its truth, or even his knowledge of its falsity." Finkelstein, Thompson, & Loughran v. Hemispherx Biopharma, Inc., 774 A.2d 332, 338 (D.C. 2001). Given the broad reach of an absolute privilege, courts recognize only a few situations in which defamatory publications are so privileged.

Depending upon whether the plaintiff is a public figure or public official, truth may be an absolute defense to a defamation claim. *See* Collins v. Detroit Free Press, Inc., 627 N.W.2d 5 (2001). Consent is an absolute defense to a claim of defamation just as it is an absolute defense to any type of intentional tort claim. *See* Restatement (Second) of Torts § 583 (1977). Executive, legislative, and judicial officers may also be entitled to invoke an absolute privilege with respect to statements made in the performance of their official functions. *See id.* §§ 585, 590, 591.

Participants in a judicial proceeding may also enjoy an absolute privilege with respect to publications occurring in the course of the proceeding. Also known as the litigation privilege, this privilege applies to statements made by parties, witnesses, and lawyers who have a sufficient relation to a legal proceeding.

Messina v. Krakower

439 F.3d 755 (D.C. Cir. 2006)

Karyne Messina and Susan Fontana were equal owners and co-presidents of a corporation called Totally Italian.com, Inc. By December 2002, the two had become embroiled in disputes regarding the management of the business. To assist her in resolving those conflicts, Fontana retained the services of Krakower and his law firm. Krakower drafted a letter to Messina, outlining Fontana's grievances and proposing a process that would allow one owner to buy out the other. The letter is the source of Messina's defamation claim against Krakower and the law firm.

... "[D]espite its name, the judicial proceedings privilege does not protect only statements that are made in the institution of a lawsuit or in the course of litigation." *Finkelstein*, 774 A.2d at 341. Rather, the "privilege extends to some statements that are made prior to the commencement of litigation, for instance, 'in ... communications preliminary to the proceeding.'" *Id.* (quoting Restatement § 586 cmt. a). "An actual outbreak of hostilities is not required, so long as litigation is truly under serious consideration." *Finkelstein*, 774 A.2d at 343. In particular, the privilege applies to "written correspondence between parties' counsel concerning threatened lawsuit[s]," *id.* at 341 (*citing McBride*, 658 A.2d at 207–08); "statements relating to threat[s] of litigation," including statements "'analogous to [those] that are often contained in demand letters,'" *id.* (quoting Conservative Club of Washington v. Finkelstein, 738 F.Supp. 6, 14 (D.D.C.1990)); and statements made during "'settlement discussions,'" *id.* (quoting *Brown*, 402 F.2d at 213).

Krakower's letter plainly falls within these contours. The letter explained that it was "for settlement purposes," proposed a "win/win scenario," and warned of a "lose/lose scenario" if settlement failed and Fontana were "forced to commence legal proceedings and/or dissolution of the Corporation." ... As the district court determined, it is plain on the face of the letter that it was "'preliminary to a judicial proceeding' in that it was sent for the very purpose of attempting settlement prior to litigation." *Messina v. Fontana*, 260 F.Supp.2d 173, 178 (D.D.C.2003) (quoting *Restatement* § 586).

Green Acres Trust v. London

688 P.2d 617 (Ariz. 1984)

Appellants Green Acres Trust and Green Acres Memorial Gardens, Inc. ("Green Acres") brought a defamation action against all of the appellees based on oral and written statements published by the appellees during a "press conference" preliminary to the initiation of a class action against Green Acres. [The appellees were lawyers who represented plaintiffs in a class action against Green Acres. The lawyers invited a local reporter to a meeting in which they shared a copy of the complaint the lawyers were about to file. The reporter then wrote a story containing negative information about Green Acres described in the complaint and from conversations with the lawyers. The lawyers argued that the defamatory communications to the reporter were protected by the litigation privilege.]

. . . In *Asay v. Hallmark Cards*, [594 F.2d 692 (8th Cir.1979)], the . . . court concluded that the application of the absolute privilege defense was dependent upon an analysis of the occasion for the communication and the substance of the communication. Focusing on the occasion of the statements, the *Asay* court concluded that since "[p]ublication to the news media is not ordinarily sufficiently related to a judicial proceeding to constitute a privileged occasion," the absolute privilege should not immunize such publication to the media. The court found that this conclusion harmonized with the public policy underlying the privilege:

> The salutary policy of allowing freedom of communication in judicial proceedings does not warrant or countenance the dissemination and distribution of defamatory accusations outside of the judicial proceeding. No public purpose is served by allowing a person to unqualifiedly make libelous or defamatory statements about another, but rather such person should be called upon to prove the correctness of his allegations or respond in damages.

Id. at 698. We conclude that the *Asay* ruling represents the better position considering the competing interests to be protected. We believe that both content and manner of extra-judicial communications must bear "some relation to the proceeding." The requirements of *Asay* that the recipient of the extra-judicial communication have some relationship to the proposed or pending judicial proceeding for the occasion to be privileged is sound. Ordinarily the media will lack such a connection to a judicial proceeding.

Notes

The duty of diligent representation. Lawyers owe a duty to their client to diligently represent the interests of their clients within the bounds of the law. *See* ABA Model Rules of Professional Conduct R. 1.3 (2017). In the case of lawyers, the judicial proceedings privilege is said to be necessary to preserve lawyers' willingness to be zealous advocates for their clients without fear of liability. Is an absolute privilege necessary to accomplish this goal? *See* Paul T. Hayden, *Reconsidering the Litigator's Absolute Privilege to Defame*, 54 Ohio St. L.J. 985 (1993).

Witness perjury. Given the obviously crucial role that witness testimony plays in a judicial proceeding, the privilege usually covers witness testimony. In the case of witnesses, the privilege is said to be essential so that witnesses do not fear the threat of a defamation action when they testify. *See* Paul T. Hayden, *Reconsidering the Litigator's Absolute Privilege to Defame*, 54 Ohio St. L.J. 985, 1054 (1993). One of the consequences of this rule is that there can be no recovery under a defamation theory by an individual who has been defamed in a proceeding by a witness.

2. Qualified Privileges

Qualified or conditional privileges may provide a defense for a defendant. But as the name suggests, the privilege is not absolute in nature. Courts recognize the existence of a qualified or conditional privilege when the societal interest implicated is of "an intermediate degree of importance, so that the immunity conferred is not absolute, but is conditioned upon publication in a reasonable manner and for a proper purpose." Green Acres Trust v. London, 688 P.2d 617, 624 (Ariz.1984). The following case addresses two common qualified privileges.

a. Common Interest Privilege

Kelley v. Tanoos

865 N.E.2d 593 (Ind. 2007)

SULLIVAN, Justice.

On January 17, 2001, a bullet grazed the head of Daniel T. Tanoos, Superintendent of the Vigo County School Corporation ("School Corporation"), when someone fired a shotgun at him from outside his house. The police identified Paul "Jay" Kelley as a suspect because of his known animosity toward Tanoos. At the time of the incident, Kelley was Supervisor of Safety and Security at the Gibault School, a juvenile residential treatment facility also in Vigo County. James Sinclair was the Executive Director and Chief Executive Officer of Gibault, Inc.

The day after the shooting, there were rumors on the Gibault campus that Kelley was a suspect. The police came to Gibault School and interviewed some of Kelley's fellow employees. When police contacted Gibault a second time and indicated that they would like to speak to some Gibault employees again, they were told they should interview the employees on their own time rather than while the employees were working. This led to a rumor that Gibault was not cooperating with the police investigation and strained relations between the School Corporation and Gibault School. Concerned, Sinclair sent Tanoos a letter suggesting they meet.

Tanoos called the police, who expressed interest in the meeting because Kelley would be a topic of discussion. The police gave Tanoos questions to ask and a wire to wear so that the conversation could be recorded. At the meeting, which occurred on December 21, 2001, Tanoos attempted to coax information from Sinclair. In particular, Tanoos made the following statements about Kelley:

> "I'm as convinced as the police are that Jay Kelley did it."

Kelley was never charged with any crime arising from the shooting incident. On December 10, 2002, Kelley filed a lawsuit for defamation against Tanoos. He subsequently learned of the taped conversation during the trial of one Marty Ketner, who was identified as a suspect in February 2002, tried, and acquitted. The parties filed cross-motions for summary judgment. The trial court, without findings of fact or conclusions of law, granted Tanoos's motion and denied Kelley's.

. . .

Our courts have recognized two distinct rationales for holding certain communications qualifiedly privileged. The first is the well-established common interest privilege that protects communication made in connection with membership qualifications, employment references, intracompany communications, and the extension of credit. This privilege is intended to facilitate "full and unrestricted communication on matters in which the parties have a common interest or duty." *Chambers*, 577 N.E.2d at 615.

Tanoos contends that his statements to Sinclair are protected by the common interest privilege. To support this contention, Tanoos argues that both he and Sinclair were executives in partnered education institutions, that Sinclair employed Kelley as a school guard, and that tension between the School Corporation and Gibault had arisen as a result of Gibault's refusal to cooperate with the police investigation. Chiefly, Tanoos argues that both he and Sinclair share a common interest "in discerning the potentially violent propensities of an individual guarding school-age Vigo County community children. . . ."

As stated by the court in *Elliott v. Roach*:

> In viewing such arguments, this court is cognizant not only of the broad legal categories represented by such terms as "interest" and "duty," but also of an underlying consideration whenever privilege is alleged—namely, whether the evidence shows the defamer in fact acted for a privileged purpose and in good faith. It has properly been held
>
> > "The privilege attaches only if the communication was made in good faith to serve the interests of the publisher and the person to whom it is addressed, and it does not exist if the privileged occasion was abused. There is no privilege if the publication was made primarily for the purpose of furthering an interest that is not entitled to protection, or if the defendant acted principally through motives of ill will, or, so it is held, if he acted recklessly. Whether a defendant acted in good faith in making a statement usually is a question of fact for the jury."

409 N.E.2d at 673 (quoting 50 Am.Jur.2d Libel and Slander § 197 at 702–03 (1970)).

There is a limit to the scope of protection available under the qualified privilege doctrine. A communication otherwise protected by a qualified privilege may lose its protection if it is shown that: "(1) the communicator was primarily motivated by ill will in making the statement; (2) there was excessive publication of the defamatory statements; or (3) the statement was made without belief or grounds for belief in its truth." *Bals*, 600 N.E.2d at 1356. "And although the term 'malice' is frequently applied in viewing such acts, it appears 'the essence of the concept is not the speaker's spite but his abuse of the privileged occasion by going beyond the scope of the purposes for which privilege exists.'" *Elliott*, 409 N.E.2d at 673.

It is evident that the legal question of a shared interest or duty must be answered before the associated factual question of whether the defamer acted for a protected purpose. In this case, we are unable to conclude that Tanoos's statements to Sinclair are protected by the common interest privilege because there is evidence that the interests of Tanoos and Sinclair are not sufficiently concurrent to make Tanoos's statements qualifiedly privileged.

Here, there is substantial evidence that Tanoos's principal interest in making the statements was in having his attempted murderer apprehended, while Sinclair's principal interest was in repairing strained relations between the School Corporation and Gibault. Even assuming Tanoos acted from less subjective motives, absent a more particular shared interest, protecting himself or school-age Vigo County community children does not give rise to the protection of a privilege.

To illustrate, compare *Gatto v. St. Richard School, Inc.*, 774 N.E.2d 914 (Ind. Ct.App.2002), a case Tanoos cites for support to this one. In *Gatto*, the common interest privilege was held to have applied to a school's communication to students' parents about the termination of a school employee. There, the court reasoned, "Parents and schools have a 'corresponding interest' in the free flow of information about administrators and faculty members." The school's communication to parents was privileged because both the parents' and the school's interest was particular to a discrete group of children and the alleged defamatory statements were relevant to that particularized interest.

The relationship between the concurrent interest and the defamatory remarks found in *Gatto* and in comparable cases is not readily apparent in the case before us. In *Gatto* the parents and the school officials shared a joint interest in the welfare of particularized children. Here, Tanoos shares no special relationship with Gibault students. The only interest, if any, Tanoos has for Gibault students is a generalized interest in their wellbeing. Even assuming, arguendo, that Tanoos and Sinclair shared a joint interest in repairing strained relations between the School Corporation and Gibault, Tanoos's remarks to Sinclair regarding Kelley were not, as a matter of law, relevant to that interest. In sum, "The information [Tanoos] profess[ed] to [provide] was volunteered, and the purpose for which it was conveyed to [Kelley's] employer was solely for the benefit of [Tanoos], and was not intended to benefit the employer by giving him, in good faith and for a just purpose, information necessary for his protection against a knavish servant." Over v. Schiffling, 102 Ind. 191, 26 N.E. 91, 92 (1885).

Accordingly, we conclude that Tanoos's statements to Sinclair are not protected by a common interest privilege as a matter of law. We believe that to hold otherwise would bring within the common interest privilege in future cases communications not entitled to protection given the purpose of the privilege.

Note

Common interests. Other examples where the common interest privilege might apply include communications between members of the same church with respect to possible misconduct by the church's pastor, *Ex parte Bole*, 103 So. 3d 40 (Ala.

2012); tenants regarding possible crimes by their landlord, *Liberman v. Gelstein*, 605 N.E.2d 344 (N.Y. 1992); and managers within a company regarding conduct of an employee, *Bals v. Verduzco*, 600 N.E.2d 1353 (Ind. 1992).

Problem 15.10. When Donna posted the photo and derogatory statement on Facebook, she only had a few Facebook friends. All of them were parents of children at the school attended by Donna's children and the Winchell children. Should the common interest privilege protect Donna from liability?

b. The Public Interest Privilege

Kelley v. Tanoos

865 N.E.2d 593 (Ind. 2007)

[The facts appear above.]

In addition to the common interest privilege, Indiana courts have also recognized what section 598 of the Restatement (Second) of Torts (1977) calls a "public interest privilege." ... [I]t is well established that in Indiana, communications made to law enforcement to report criminal activity are qualifiedly privileged. This so-called public interest privilege is intended to encourage private individuals to assist law enforcement with investigating and apprehending criminals.

The *Restatement*, under the purview of the public interest privilege, articulates a broader scope of protection than adopted in Indiana:

> The privilege stated in ... Section [598] affords protection to a private citizen who publishes defamatory matter to a third person even though he is not a law enforcement officer, under circumstances which, if true, would give to the recipient a privilege to act for purposes of preventing a crime or of apprehending a criminal or fugitive from justice.

Restatement (Second) of Torts § 598 cmt. f (1977).

... Indiana courts have not adopted this reading of the public interest privilege and therefore do not protect such communications to private citizens. Tanoos, through his *amici*, asks us to extend the public interest privilege to cover communications to private citizens, and to extend its protection to him.

We agree with the *amici* and the *Restatement* and think the public interest privilege, under a limited number of circumstances, protects communications to private citizens. Statements reporting criminal activity to law enforcement, as stated *supra*, are privileged to enhance public safety by facilitating the investigation of suspected criminal activity. We think certain statements to private citizens may further the same end.

In *Pate v. Service Merchandise Co., Inc.*, the Tennessee Court of Appeals adopted this view of the public interest privilege and held that a store clerk who reported suspicious criminal activity to a private security guard and theft victim was protected by the public interest privilege. That court reasoned:

> [E]ven though the investigation was not conducted by the local police, the investigation by the security department could have led to the apprehension of the criminal. It is reasonable for anyone in the position of the clerks to believe that the identification would affect the public interest of preventing crime. The public interest privilege is grounded in public policy, and we should encourage cooperation with an investigation of a criminal matter.

Pate v. Service Merchandise Co., Inc., 959 S.W.2d 569, 576–77 (Tenn. Ct. App.1996).

Just as statements to law enforcement further a public interest, similar statements made to a private citizen may further the same interest. That interest is grounded in a public policy intended to encourage private citizens and victims not only to report crime, but also to assist law enforcement with investigating and apprehending individuals who engage in criminal activity.

The rationale for privileging communications to law enforcement and to certain private citizens is applicable here. Tanoos's statements, made at least in part at the behest of law enforcement, to Sinclair were designed to elicit information about Kelley to further an ongoing criminal investigation. It is reasonable to conclude that when law enforcement and the victim of a crime work in concert, the likelihood of apprehending the perpetrator of the crime increases. As noted by the court in *Pate*, "The victim of a crime has the unfortunate privilege of acting to apprehend a criminal. Most times it would be impossible for the police to successfully investigate and apprehend criminals without the actions of the victim." *Id.* at 577. Accordingly, we hold that Tanoos's statements to Sinclair are qualifiedly privileged by the public interest privilege as a matter of law.

...

If a communication is found to be qualifiedly privileged, the burden is on the plaintiff to show that the privilege has been abused. Unless only one conclusion can be drawn from the evidence, the question of whether the privilege has been abused is for the jury.

Kelley argues that if Tanoos's statements are qualifiedly privileged, Tanoos lost the privilege because he used the privileged occasion for an improper purpose. [Kelley also contended that the privileges was lost because Tanoos did not believe or have reason to believe certain statements he made to Sinclair. The court rejected these arguments.]

... Because Kelley has failed to designate evidence that demonstrates Tanoos abused the privileged occasion, summary judgment is appropriate.

c. The Privilege to Protect One's Own Interest or that of Another

Qualified privilege to protect one's own interest. An individual may also enjoy a qualified privilege where the defendant reasonably believes that the publication of defamatory information will help protect an important interest of the defendant herself. Restatement (Second) of Torts § 594. Importantly, the defendant must be seeking to protect a sufficiently important interest before the privilege will apply. For example, in *Anderson v. Beach*, 897 N.E.2d 361 (Ill. Ct. App. 2008), the defendant disclosed the contents of a letter she had written to her superior to several other co-workers. In her letter, the defendant, a police officer, claimed that the plaintiff, another officer, had assaulted and tried to strike her and had failed to provide backup when responding to a disturbance. The defendant disclosed the contents of the letter to some of her co-workers, in part, because "she had concerns about her reputation among her fellow officers" and because she had concerns over her own safety. The court concluded that "it would not have been unreasonable for Beach to conclude that by informing her fellow officers of her problems with Anderson, she could enlist their assistance for herself." *Id.* at 368.

Qualified privilege to protect the interest of others. An individual may also be conditionally privileged to disclose information to a third person if the individual reasonably believes that the information: (a) "affects a sufficiently important interest of the recipient or a third person and (b) the recipient is one to whom the publisher is under a legal duty to publish the defamatory matter or is a person to whom its publication is otherwise within the generally accepted standards of decent conduct." Restatement (Second) of Torts § 595. An example would be the lawyer or the doctor who is under an ethical obligation to report the serious misconduct of another lawyer or doctor to the appropriate professional authorities. *See* ABA Model Rules of Professional Conduct R. 8.3(a) (involving duty on the part of a lawyer to report the misconduct of another lawyer); Agee v. Grunert, 349 F. Supp. 2d 838 (D. Vt. 2004) (involving physician who was under an ethical obligation to report the impairment of another doctor).

Employment references. Another clear example of the conditional privilege to protect others would be the situation where an employer provided a negative reference to a prospective employer about an employee's performance. *See* Miron v. University of New Haven Police Dept., 931 A.2d 847, 853–54 (Conn. 2007). In many states, the legislature has enacted specific employment reference statutes that codify existing common law privileges. *See* J. Hoult Verkerke, *Legal Regulation of Employment Reference Practices*, 65 U. Chi. L. Rev. 115, 132 (1998).

d. Fair Comment Privilege

At common law, the fair comment privilege protected a statement of opinion regarding a matter of public concern, provided the defendant stated the facts upon which the opinion was based. The privilege no longer has much relevance in most jurisdictions as the various constitutional rules discussed in this chapter developed. *See* Dan B. Dobbs et al., The Law of Torts § 567 (2d ed.). For example, as discussed in *Milkovich, supra*, there should be no liability where the defendant states an opinion on any matter (not just one of public concern) and discloses the facts upon which that opinion is based (provided the underlying facts are, themselves, accurate). That said, the privilege does still appear in some jurisdictions. *See* Lindenmuth v. McCreer, 165 A.3d 544 (Md. Ct. App. 2017) (recognizing the existence of the privilege).

3. Media Privileges

There are also several privileges that apply specifically to the media. These privileges are arguably less important than they were before the Supreme Court's *New York Times v. Sullivan* line of cases. Nonetheless, they still exist as a matter of statutory or common law in many jurisdictions and may sometimes have a role to play.

a. Fair Reporting Privilege

Vernon's Texas Statutes and Codes Annotated

§ 73.002. Privileged Matters

(a) The publication by a newspaper or other periodical of a matter covered by this section is privileged and is not a ground for a libel action. This privilege does not extend to the republication of a matter if it is proved that the matter was republished with actual malice after it had ceased to be of public concern.

(b) This section applies to:

(1) a fair, true, and impartial account of:

(A) a judicial proceeding, unless the court has prohibited publication of a matter because in its judgment the interests of justice demand that the matter not be published;

(B) an official proceeding, other than a judicial proceeding, to administer the law;

(C) an executive or legislative proceeding (including a proceeding of a legislative committee), a proceeding in or before a managing board of an educational or eleemosynary institution supported from the public revenue, of the governing body of a city or town, of a county commissioners court, and of a public school board or a report of or debate and statements made in any of those proceedings; or

(D) the proceedings of a public meeting dealing with a public purpose, including statements and discussion at the meeting or other matters of public concern occurring at the meeting. . . .

Notes

The nature of the privilege. What additional protection, if any, does this statute provide for newspapers and other periodicals that such entities don't already enjoy as a matter of constitutional law?

The effect of malice. In some jurisdictions, the fair reporting privilege exists as a matter of common law. Courts are split on the question of whether the existence of common law malice (in the sense of spite or ill will) or perhaps actual malice defeats the existence of the fair reporting privilege. RODNEY A. SMOLLA, 2 LAW OF DEFAMATION § 8:70.50 (2d ed.).

Problem 15.11. After the Winchells sued Donna Edwards for defamation, the local newspaper, the *Pleasant Hill Gazette*, published a story about the first day of the trial. The story reported that the Winchells were suing Donna after Donna "used social media to allege that the Winchells supported a white supremacist group." The reporter based this statement on statements by Donna's lawyer during his opening statement to the jury. The lawyer repeatedly emphasized the fact that the Winchells' vehicle had a sticker from "the League of the Confederacy" (which happens to be the name of an organization labeled by some as a white supremacist organization and that expressly advocates for secession from the United States by the states that formerly comprised the Confederacy). During the opening statement, the lawyer barely mentioned Donna's actual statement on Facebook that "Winchell is racist!" Donna was outraged when she saw the article in the paper and stated "I never said Winchell supported a white supremacist group!" She is thinking about suing the paper for defamation. Assume that the state in which Pleasant Hill is located has a statute in place that is identical to Texas' statute above. Would the statute shield the *Pleasant Hill Gazette* from liability in a subsequent defamation claim brought by Donna?

b. The Neutral Reporting Privilege

As you read the next case regarding the neutral reporting privilege, consider why a media outlet would need such a privilege (a) in general and (b) when the actual malice standard would already apply.

Edwards v. National Audubon Society, Inc.

556 F.2d 113 (2d Cir. 1977)

[Throughout the 1960s and 70s, there was national debate as to the impact the pesticide DDT was having on bird populations. In the foreword to a publication by the National Audubon Society, the editor of the publication wrote that "[a]nytime you hear a 'scientist' say" that bird populations are increasing, "you are in the presence of someone who is being paid to lie" by the pesticide industry. The *New York Times* accurately reported these statements in an article. The Audubon Society publication did not list names of the scientists in question, but the editor provided the

New York Times reporter with a list of name, which the *New York Times* article ran. Those individuals sued the *New York Times* among others. At trial, the jury was instructed that the *Times* could be found guilty of actual malice if the reporter had serious doubts about the truth of the statement that the plaintiffs were paid liars, even if he did not have any doubt that he was reporting the Audubon Society's allegations faithfully. The jury returned a verdict in favor of the plaintiffs.]

Implicit in the jury's verdict against Clement is the finding, which we must accept, that the Times accurately reported the five scientists whose names were furnished by [the editor] were the "paid liars" referred to in the *American Birds* Foreword. We believe that a libel judgment against the *Times*, in the face of this finding of fact, is constitutionally impermissible.

At stake in this case is a fundamental principle. Succinctly stated, when a responsible, prominent organization like the National Audubon Society makes serious charges against a public figure, the First Amendment protects the accurate and disinterested reporting of those charges, regardless of the reporter's private views regarding their validity. What is newsworthy about such accusations is that they were made. We do not believe that the press may be required under the First Amendment to suppress newsworthy statements merely because it has serious doubts regarding their truth. Nor must the press take up cudgels against dubious charges in order to publish them without fear of liability for defamation. The public interest in being fully informed about controversies that often rage around sensitive issues demands that the press be afforded the freedom to report such charges without assuming responsibility for them.

Note

Recognition of the privilege. Some courts have been unwilling to recognize this type of neutral reporting privilege, reasoning that it is not found in the text of a state constitution or is otherwise contrary to the *New York Times* line of cases. *See* Dickey v. CBS Inc., 583 F.2d 1221 (3d Cir. 1978); Norton v. Glenn, 860 A.2d 48, 50 (Pa. 2004); Englezos v. Newspress and Gazette Co., 980 S.W.2d 25 (Mo. Ct. App. 1998).

Problem 15.12. Before the Winchells sued Donna but after Donna's post had gone viral, a reporter for the local Pleasant Hill television station did a story about the situation. The reporter knew Rachel and Fred Winchell and did not believe them to be racists. Nonetheless, since she knew that Rachel was running for a seat on the local school board, she decided to run the story.

If a court were to recognize the neutral reporting privilege described in *Edwards*, would it shield the reporter from liability in a defamation suit brought by Fred?

Review Question

Vic Hernandez is a high school baseball coach. A few of his players had a tendency to step outside of the batter's box when a pitch was coming toward the plate for fear of being hit. To address the problem, Coach Hernandez instructed players on the proper technique to use if they were actually about to be hit by a pitch. To do this, he stood 15 feet away and threw tennis balls at the players at half speed while they were in the batter's box and instructed them on how to limit the impact from a pitch. Becky Johnson, the mother of one of the players, was livid when she learned from her son about this practice. She approached Hernandez after practice one day to complain about the fact that her son was hit. The two soon began arguing, with the argument quickly turning personal. Later that night, Becky sent an email to the other parents on the team, the parents on the junior varsity team (who were not yet coached by Hernandez), and the school principal "alerting" them to the fact that "Coach Hernandez is now forcing players to stand in the batter's box while he throws baseballs at them as hard as he can in an attempt to 'toughen them up.'" A local reporter learned of the email and ran a short story describing the situation and accurately quoting Becky's email. Coach Hernandez eventually sues Becky and the reporter for defamation.

Assume that Hernandez is able to make out a prima facie case of defamation (including establishing the falsity of Becky's statements). Are Becky's statements nonetheless covered under the common interest privilege?

Chapter 16

Invasion of Privacy

A. Intrusion Upon the Seclusion of Another
- The difference with other privacy torts
- Intentional intrusion upon the solitude or seclusion of another
- The concept of seclusion
- Forms of intrusion
- Highly offensive to a reasonable person
- Interplay between the elements
- Other concepts developed in class or in readings assigned by the professor

B. Publicity Given to Private Facts
- The difference with other privacy torts
- Private facts
- Publicity
- Disclosure that would be highly offensive to a reasonable person
- Facts not of legitimate concern to the public
- Reckless disregard of the private nature of the fact or facts disclosed
- Other concepts developed in class or in readings assigned by the professor

C. False Light
- The difference with other privacy torts
- The difference with defamation
- Overlap with defamation and the judicial reluctance to recognize the tort.
- The fault standard
- Other concepts developed in class or in readings assigned by the professor

D. Misappropriation of the Right of Publicity
- The difference with other privacy torts
- Advertising or for purposes of trade
- Noncommercial uses
- Other concepts developed in class or in readings assigned by the professor

Chapter Problem. For six weeks, Pamela was a patient at the Pleasant Hill Hospital, a private psychiatric facility. Susan, a famous television personality, was at the facility during the same time. Susan had been the subject of intense media coverage just prior to checking in to the facility following widespread reports of erratic behavior and a possible eating disorder. A photographer for the *Pleasant Hill Times* was able to obtain photographs of Susan that were included in news story about Susan's stay at the hospital. The photographs also featured Pamela.

The genesis of the recognition of a right to privacy in tort law is usually credited to an 1890 law review article written by Samuel D. Warren and Louis D. Brandeis. *The Right to Privacy*, 4 HARV. L. REV. 193 (1890). Warren and Brandeis argued that the common law recognized "the right to be let alone," *id.* at 193, the violation of which should lead to a tort remedy. While it is debatable whether such a right existed at the time of the article, one certainly crystalized after its publication. Today, there are four widely recognized privacy theories, all of which are grouped under the general heading of "invasion of privacy." Each privacy tort seeks to protect a particular component of one's right to privacy, although as the cases make clear, there is often some overlap among the four torts.

A. Intrusion Upon the Seclusion of Another

The first and most widely recognized of the privacy torts protects one's "interest in solitude or seclusion, either as to his person or as to his private affairs or concerns." Restatement (Second) of Torts § 652B cmt. a. According to the *Restatement*, "One who intentionally intrudes, physically or otherwise, upon the solitude or seclusion of another or his private affairs or concerns, is subject to liability to the other for invasion of privacy, if the intrusion would be highly offensive to a reasonable person." *Id.* § 652B.

1. Intentional Intrusion upon the Solitude or Seclusion of Another

In re Marriage of Tigges

758 N.W.2d 824 (Iowa 2008)

HECHT, Justice.

A husband surreptitiously recorded on videotape his wife's activities in the marital home. The district court entered a judgment for money damages in favor of the wife who claimed the videotaping constituted a tortious invasion of her privacy. The court of appeals affirmed the judgment, rejecting the husband's contention the wife had no reasonable expectation of privacy in the marital home she shared with him. On further review of the decision of the court of appeals, we conclude a claim for invasion of privacy is legally viable under the circumstances of this case, and therefore affirm the judgment.

I. Factual and Procedural Background.

Upon our de novo review we make the following findings of fact. The long relationship between Jeffrey and Cathy Tigges was plagued by trust issues. Even before their marriage, Jeffrey and Cathy had recorded each other's telephone conversations without the other's knowledge and consent. Apparently undeterred by their history of discord, they were married on December 31, 1999.

Jeffrey surreptitiously installed recording equipment and recorded Cathy's activities during the marriage in the marital home.[1] The equipment included a video cassette recorder positioned above a ceiling, a camera concealed in an alarm clock located in the bedroom regularly used by Cathy, and a motion sensing "optical eye" installed in the headboard of the bed in that room. Cathy discovered her activities in the bedroom had been recorded when she observed Jeffrey retrieving a cassette from the recorder in August 2006.

During the ensuing confrontation, Jeffrey damaged the cassette. Cathy took possession of it and restored it with the assistance of others. When she viewed the tape, Cathy discovered it revealed nothing of a graphic or demeaning nature. Although the tape was not offered in evidence, we credit Cathy's testimony that it recorded the "comings and goings" from the bedroom she regularly used. Notwithstanding the unremarkable activities recorded on the tape, Cathy suffered damage as a consequence of Jeffrey's actions. She felt violated, fearing Jeffrey had placed, or would place, other hidden cameras in the house.

Jeffrey filed a petition for dissolution of marriage. In her answer, Cathy alleged she was entitled to compensation for Jeffrey's "tortious . . . violation of her privacy rights" as a consequence of his surreptitious placement of the video equipment and recording of her activities. Cathy alleged she should be awarded tort damages in this dissolution action or, in the alternative, the claim should be "reserved upon entry of [the] Decree." The district court found Jeffrey had invaded Cathy's privacy and entered judgment in the amount of $22,500.

Jeffrey contends on appeal the judgment against him for money damages must, as a matter of law, be reversed. He urges this court to conclude his actions were not tortious because Cathy had no reasonable expectation of privacy precluding his recording of her activities in the marital home. Jeffrey further asserts on appeal Cathy cannot recover damages for the alleged invasion because the only publication of the tape was undertaken by Cathy when she permitted her sister to watch it.

---

1. The district court found the videotaping occurred when "the parties were separated and residing in separate residences." The court of appeals concluded "the incidents testified to by Cathy clearly occurred while the parties were still residing in the same house together as husband and wife." We find the record lacks sufficient clarity to determine by a preponderance of the evidence whether Jeffrey was residing in the marital home or in a separate residence when he installed the cameras and when the recording was accomplished. A resolution of this factual issue is not essential to our decision, however, as we conclude Jeffrey's activities intruded on Cathy's right to privacy whether or not he was residing in the marital home when the surreptitious videotaping occurred.

[The Iowa Supreme Court had previously adopted the *Restatement* approach to this tort: Thus, under the court's articulation of the relevant test, a plaintiff must prove (1) "the defendant intentionally intruded upon the seclusion that the plaintiff 'has thrown about [his or her] person or affairs,'" and (2) the intrusion "would be 'highly offensive to a reasonable person.'"]

III. Discussion.

A. The Expectation of Privacy within the Marital Relationship. Although this court has never been called upon to decide whether a claim may be brought by one spouse against the other for an invasion of privacy resulting from surreptitious videotaping, the question has been confronted by courts in other jurisdictions....

As we have already noted, in the case before this court the record is unclear whether Jeffrey installed the equipment and accomplished the recording of Cathy's activities before or after the parties separated. We conclude, however, the question of whether Jeffrey and Cathy were residing in the same dwelling at the time of Jeffrey's actions is not dispositive on this issue. Whether or not Jeffrey and Cathy were residing together in the dwelling at the time, we conclude Cathy had a reasonable expectation that her activities in the bedroom of the home were private when she was alone in that room. Cathy's expectation of privacy at such times is not rendered unreasonable by the fact Jeffrey was her spouse at the time in question, or by the fact that Jeffrey may have been living in the dwelling at that time.

Our conclusion is consistent with the decision reached by the Texas Court of Appeals in *Clayton v. Richards*, 47 S.W.3d 149 (Tex. App. 2001). In that case, Mrs. Clayton hired Richards to install video equipment in the bedroom shared by Mrs. Clayton and her husband. After discovering the scheme, Mr. Clayton sued his wife and Richards, alleging invasion of his privacy. The trial court denied Mrs. Clayton's motion for summary judgment, but granted the one filed by Richards. On appeal, the Texas Court of Appeals concluded Richards' liability turned on whether Mrs. Clayton's acts were tortious under Texas law. In its analysis of whether Mr. Clayton had a reasonable expectation of privacy in the bedroom he shared with his spouse, the court observed:

> A spouse shares equal rights in the privacy of the bedroom, and the other spouse relinquishes some of his or her rights to seclusion, solitude, and privacy by entering into marriage, by sharing a bedroom with a spouse, and by entering into ownership of the home with a spouse. *However, nothing in the . . . common law suggests that the right to privacy is limited to unmarried individuals.*
>
> *When a person goes into the privacy of the bedroom, he or she has a right to the expectation of privacy in his or her seclusion. A video recording surreptitiously made in that place of privacy at a time when the individual believes that he or she is in a state of complete privacy could be highly offensive to the ordinary reasonable person.* The video recording of a person without

> consent in the privacy of his or her bedroom *even when done by the other spouse could be found to violate his or her rights of privacy.*
>
> As a spouse with equal rights to the use and access of the bedroom, it would not be illegal or tortious as an invasion of privacy for a spouse to open the door of the bedroom and view a spouse in bed. It could be argued that a spouse did no more than that by setting up a video camera, but that the viewing was done by means of technology rather than by being physically present. It is not generally the role of the courts to supervise privacy between spouses in a mutually shared bedroom. *However, the videotaping of a person without consent or awareness when there is an expectation of privacy goes beyond the rights of a spouse because it may record private matters, which could later be exposed to the public eye. The fact that no later exposure occurs does not negate that potential and permit willful intrusion by such technological means into one's personal life in one's bedroom.*

Id. at 155–56 (citations omitted) (emphasis added).

Prior to catching Jeffrey in the act of removing the cassette from the concealed recorder, Cathy was unaware of his video surveillance scheme. Citing our decision in *Stessman v. American Black Hawk Broadcasting Co.*, 416 N.W.2d 685 (Iowa 1987), Jeffrey nonetheless contends his conduct is not actionable because Cathy was in "public view" in the home he owned jointly with her. In *Stessman*, the plaintiff sued a broadcasting company for invasion of privacy for videotaping her, despite her objection, while she was eating in a public restaurant, and publishing the tape. The district court dismissed Stessman's petition for failure to state a claim, concluding she was, as a matter of law, in "public view" at the time the recording was made. On appeal, this court rejected the notion that Stessman was in "public view" as a matter of law. *Id.* at 687 (noting it was not inconceivable the plaintiff was seated in a private dining room within the restaurant at the time the recording was made). "[T]he mere fact a person can be seen by others does not mean that person cannot legally be 'secluded.'" *Id.* (quoting *Huskey* v. NBC, Inc., 632 F.Supp. 1282, 1287–88 (N.D.Ill.1986)). Furthermore, "visibility to some people does not strip [the plaintiff] of the right to remain secluded from others." *Id.* (quoting *Huskey*, 632 F.Supp. at 1287–88).

Even if we assume for purposes of our analysis that Cathy was observed by other family members including Jeffrey, who, from time to time, entered the bedroom with her knowledge and consent, she was not in "public view" and did not forfeit her right to seclusion at other times when she was alone in that room. As we observed in *Stessman*, "[p]ersons are exposed to family members and invited guests in their own homes, but that does not mean they have opened the door to television cameras." *Id.* (quoting *Huskey*, 632 F.Supp. at 1287–88). Any right of access to the bedroom held by Jeffrey did not include the right to videotape Cathy's activities without her knowledge and consent.

We find persuasive the courts' characterizations of a spouse's right of privacy in Miller and Clayton. Cathy did not forfeit through marriage her expectation of privacy as to her activities when she was alone in the bedroom. Accordingly, we conclude Cathy had a reasonable expectation of privacy under the circumstances presented in this case.

B. The Elements of an Invasion of Privacy Claim.

1. Intentional intrusion. [Based on the previous discussion, the court concluded that Jeffrey's conduct "clearly constituted an intentional intrusion upon Cathy's privacy."]

2. Highly offensive to a reasonable person. Jeffrey contends the judgment in favor of Cathy must be reversed because the videotaping captured nothing that would be viewed as highly offensive to a reasonable person. He emphasizes the videotape captured nothing of a "private" or "sexual" nature in the bedroom. This contention is without merit, however, because the content of the videotape is not determinative of the question of whether Jeffrey tortiously invaded Cathy's privacy. The intentional, intrusive, and wrongful nature of Jeffrey's conduct is not excused by the fact that the surreptitious taping recorded no scurrilous or compromising behavior. The wrongfulness of the conduct springs not from the specific nature of the recorded activities, but instead from the fact that Cathy's activities were recorded without her knowledge and consent at a time and place and under circumstances in which she had a reasonable expectation of privacy.

. . . We conclude Cathy met her burden to prove Jeffrey's intrusive videotaping would be highly offensive to a reasonable person.

IV. Conclusion.

Cathy had a reasonable expectation of privacy when she was alone in her bedroom. Jeffrey's covert video surveillance intentionally intruded upon Cathy's expectation of privacy. The intrusion was highly offensive to a reasonable person. We therefore affirm the decision of the court of appeals.

Notes

The concept of seclusion. *Tigges* focuses primarily on the seclusion issue, specifically whether Cathy had a reasonable expectation of privacy at the time of the recording. This part of the standard test has both a subjective and objective quality to it. *See* Danai v. Canal Square Associates, 862 A.2d 395 (D.C. Ct. App. 2004) (concluding that while tenant may have had a subjective expectation of privacy in her trash, that expectation was not objectively reasonable when she knew the items she voluntarily placed in the trash were readily accessible to a third party).

The analogy to the Fourth Amendment. The Fourth Amendment to the U.S. Constitution provides a right to be free from unreasonable searches on the part of the government. But first, one must have a reasonable expectation of privacy in the thing that is searched. Not surprisingly, Fourth Amendment jurisprudence has shaped the common law involving invasion of privacy. *See* Tagouma v. Investigative Consultant Services, Inc., 4 A.3d 170 (Pa. Super. 2010) (relying upon Fourth

Amendment police search-and-seizure cases for the conclusion that plaintiff had no reasonable expectation of privacy when his activities were in plain view).

Other forms of intrusion. The tort requires an intentional intrusion upon one's seclusion. In *Tigges*, the intrusion occurred through the use of a mechanical device, but it may also occur by something as similar as opening an another's mail. *See, e.g., Chaconas v. JP Morgan Chase Bank*, 713 F. Supp. 2d 1180, 1185 (S.D. Cal. 2010) (involving debt collector who hounded plaintiff by phone to collect a debt); Doe v. High-Tech Institute, Inc., 972 P.2d 1060 (Colo. Ct. App. 1998) (concluding plaintiff stated a claim where school obtained plaintiff's consent to test his blood for rubella but also tested blood for HIV); Pingatore v. Union Pacific Railroad Company, 530 S.W.3d 372 (Ark. Ct. App. 2017) (affirming summary judgment in favor of employer in claim based upon drug testing of employee).

2. Highly Offensive to a Reasonable Person

McLain v. Boise Cascade Corp.

533 P.2d 343 (Or. 1975)

McALLISTER, Justice.

Plaintiff was employed by Boise Cascade Corporation as a glue mixer. On May 19, 1972 he strained his back when he fell while carrying a 100 pound sack of flour to a glue machine. Plaintiff was taken to the office of Dr. D. H. Searing in Salem. Dr. Searing sent plaintiff to the hospital where he was placed in traction. On June 6, 1972, Dr. Searing wrote to Richard Cyphert, then in charge of the Boise Cascade Workmen's Compensation program, advising that plaintiff might be disabled for as much as 12 months. Dr. John D. White was called in as a consultant. He performed a myelogram on plaintiff and reported to Mr. Cyphert that he found no evidence of nerve root or lumbar disc disease and that it was possible that plaintiff was 'consciously malingering.' Cyphert received this letter on June 22, 1972.

On the basis of Dr. White's report Mr. Cyphert notified plaintiff his compensation payments would be terminated. At about that time Mr. Cyphert also was informed that plaintiff was performing part-time work for a mortuary while he was ostensibly disabled. On June 27, 1972 plaintiff received a written release from Dr. White permitting him to return to work with the restriction that he was not to lift more than 50 pounds. Plaintiff returned to work and was assigned an easier job, but was unable to work due to continued pain in his hip.

Plaintiff then consulted an attorney, who filed a request for a hearing with the Workmen's Compensation Board asking that plaintiff's temporary disability payments be reinstated. Mr. Cyphert received a copy of this request on July 5, 1972. On July 12, 1972 Mr. Cyphert hired the defendant United Diversified Services, Inc., to conduct a surveillance of the plaintiff to check the validity of plaintiff's claim of injury. United assigned two of its employees, Rick Oulette and Steve Collette, to conduct a surveillance. The two investigators took 18 rolls of movie film of plaintiff while he was engaged in various activities on his property outside his home. Some of the film showed plaintiff mowing his lawn, rototilling his garden and fishing from a bridge near his home.

Plaintiff lived at Independence on a large square lot containing slightly more than two acres. The property is bounded on the north by the Hopville Road, on the east by a pond, on the west by property owned by Lindsey Ward, a neighbor. To the south is a field which apparently also belongs to Mr. Ward.

Some of the film of plaintiff was taken from a barn behind plaintiff's house, which apparently belonged to Ward, although the record is not clear on that point. Other film was taken by Collette while plaintiff was fishing from a bridge on the Hopville Road near the northeast corner of plaintiff's property. The record is not clear as to where Mr. Collette was standing while taking that film. The remaining rolls of film were taken by Mr. Collette from a point near some walnut trees at the southeast corner of plaintiff's property.

There was a barbed wire fence a short distance west of the east boundary of plaintiff's tract and west of the row of walnut trees from which some of the film was taken. Collette testified that he stayed east of the fence and did not know that he was on plaintiff's land. He testified, however, that he crossed over a fence under the bridge near the northeast corner of plaintiff's property in order to get to his vantage point near the walnut trees. He probably trespassed on plaintiff's property when he crossed the fence, but that does not appear clearly from the record.

On one occasion while Collette was near the walnut trees he was seen by plaintiff. When Collette realized he had been seen, he left the area. He had parked his pickup truck on Ward's property near the southwest corner of plaintiff's tract, but abandoned the pickup when he was spotted by McLain and retrieved his truck later.

McLain did not learn about the film and picture taking until the film was shown at the Workmen's Compensation Hearing.

United's investigators did not question any of plaintiff's neighbors or friends and limited their activities to taking pictures while plaintiff was engaged in various activities outside his home. Plaintiff testified that these activities could have been viewed either by neighbors or passersby on the highway. Plaintiff further testified that he was not embarrassed or upset by anything that appeared in the films. He said:

> Q You did all of the things that were shown in the film? There was no deception in the film?
>
> A No.
>
> Q You agree that what you saw there was what you did?
>
> A Right.
>
> Q And you weren't embarrassed by it or mad or upset?
>
> A No, the only thing I was mad about was the fact they snuck around behind my back.

> Q The thing that really bothered you was that somebody filmed you without telling you, isn't that right?
>
> A Right.
>
> Q Other than that, it just made you mad that somebody did that without telling you? Other than that, that is all there was to it?
>
> A Right. And I didn't think anybody had any right on my property without permission.

It is now well established in Oregon that damages may be recovered for violation of privacy.

The general rule permitting recovery for such intrusion is stated in *Restatement of the Law of Torts 2d*, . . . as follows:

> One who intentionally intrudes, physically or otherwise, upon the solitude or seclusion of another or his private affairs or concerns, is subject to liability to the other for invasion of his privacy, if the intrusion would be highly offensive to a reasonable person.

Restatement (Second) of Torts §652B (1977).* *See, also*, PROSSER, TORTS (4th ed. 1971), 807; *Prosser, Privacy*, 48 CAL.L.REV. 383, 389 (1960).

. . . We quote from the Annotation, *Right of Privacy-Surveillance*, 13 A.L.R.3d 1025, 1027:

> Where the surveillance, shadowing, and trailing is conducted in a reasonable manner, it has been held that owing to the social utility of exposing fraudulent claims and because of the fact that some sort of investigation is necessary to uncover fictitious injuries, an unobtrusive investigation, even though inadvertently made apparent to the person being investigated, does not constitute an actionable invasion of his privacy.

In *Forster v. Manchester, supra*, 189 A.2d at 150, the court stated:

> It is not uncommon for defendants in accident cases to employ investigators to check on the validity of claims against them. Thus, by making a claim for personal injuries appellant must expect reasonable inquiry and investigation to be made of her claim and to this extent her interest in privacy is circumscribed. . . .

If the surveillance is conducted in a reasonable and unobtrusive manner the defendant will incur no liability for invasion of privacy. On the other hand, if the surveillance is conducted in an unreasonable and obtrusive manner the defendant will be liable for invasion of privacy.

---

* Editor's note: The original version of the opinion included the language from a draft of the *Restatement*. This version includes the language from the final version of the *Restatement*, which is nearly identical to the draft version.

In this case we think the court below properly granted a nonsuit for the cause of action for invasion of privacy. In the first place, the surveillance and picture taking were done in such an unobtrusive manner that plaintiff was not aware that he was being watched and filmed. In the second place, plaintiff conceded that his activities which were filmed could have been observed by his neighbors or passersby on the road running in front of his property. Undoubtedly the investigators trespassed on plaintiff's land while watching and taking pictures of him, but it is also clear that the trespass was on the periphery of plaintiff's property and did not constitute an unreasonable surveillance 'highly offensive to a reasonable [person].'

Plaintiff does not contend that the surveillance in this case was per se actionable. Plaintiff contends only that the surveillance became actionable when the investigators trespassed on plaintiff's property. Plaintiff's brief states the issue as follows:

> The issue before this Court is whether trespass upon another's homestead for the purpose of conducting an unauthorized surveillance gives rise to an action for violation of the right of privacy, ...

We think trespass is only one factor to be considered in determining whether the surveillance was unreasonable. Trespass to peer in windows and to annoy or harass the occupant may be unreasonable. Trespass alone cannot automatically change an otherwise reasonable surveillance into an unreasonable one. The one trespass which was observed by plaintiff did not alert him to the fact that he was being watched or that his activities were being filmed. The record is clear that the trespass was confined to a narrow strip along the east boundary of plaintiff's property. All the surveillance in this case was done during daylight hours and when plaintiff was exposed to public view by his neighbors and passersby.

By the same reasoning we think the court did not err in striking the claim for punitive damages in the cause of action for trespass. Assuming that the trespass in this case was intentional there was no evidence of intent to harm, harass or annoy the plaintiff. The surveillance took place near the boundaries of plaintiff's property. The trespass was unlawful, but did not injure plaintiff, nor was it intended to injure him. We think the court properly withdrew from consideration by the jury the claim for punitive damages on account of the trespass.

Note

Intrusion highly offensive to a reasonable person. What factors should go into the determination of whether an intrusion would be highly offensive to a reasonable person? For each of the following cases, you can assume that there was an intentional intrusion upon the plaintiff's seclusion. Could a jury find that the intrusions were highly offensive to a reasonable person? Why or why not?

> (a) Plaintiff was involved in a child custody dispute. Defendant, who was a party on the other side of the dispute, persuaded another individual to pretend to be friends with Plaintiff's family so that the individual could enter Plaintiff's house and learn information that would be useful to Defendant

in the custody matter. The individual "befriended" the family and then reported back to Defendant that she had observed Plaintiff's underage son consuming alcohol within Plaintiff's house.

(b) Over a three-month period, a telemarketing company placed 33 telemarketing calls to the plaintiff's home for the purpose of selling him property. The first call was a prerecorded voice message, and the next two calls were placed by a live agent. After the third call, the plaintiff requested that his name be placed on a "do not call" list as provided for under federal law. The remaining 30 calls were prerecorded messages. All of the calls occurred during the day.

3. Interplay between the Elements

McClain focuses more heavily on whether the intrusion was highly offensive to a reasonable person, and more specifically the manner in which the surveillance was conducted. But there is also some issue as to whether there had been an intrusion upon McClain's *seclusion* to begin with. There may not always be a clear distinction between the two concepts. As the California Supreme Court has explained, "privacy, for purposes of the intrusion tort, is not a binary, all-or-nothing characteristic. There are degrees and nuances to societal recognition of our expectations of privacy." Sanders v. American Broadcasting Companies, 978 P.2d 67, 72 (Cal. 1999). The cases that follow help illustrate that principle and how courts view the concept of "privacy."

Ruzicka Elec. and Sons, Inc. v. International Broth. of Elec. Workers, Local 1, AFL-CIO

427 F.3d 511 (8th Cir. 2005)

Ruzicka Electric, a Missouri corporation founded and headed by Ruzicka, provides commercial electrical services. Local 1 is a labor union representing electricians in eastern Missouri. Ruzicka Electric and Local 1 do not have a history of friendly relations. . . .

In April 1998, Local 1 hired a private investigator to investigate Ruzicka Electric and Ruzicka. The private investigator, in turn, hired four additional investigators to conduct surveillance. The investigators surveilled Ruzicka's private residence with the purpose "to establish a daily routine . . . [and] to see what time [Ruzicka] got home." . . .

. . . Ruzicka . . . explained his property is lined with about 100 feet of trees, including evergreen trees, stating, "You simply cannot see through there. It is not possible." Based on his knowledge of his property, Ruzicka testified a person would have to be on his property to see the things the surveillance notes depict.

Ruzicka maintains he was appalled, amazed, shocked, and angered when he discovered "somebody had been lurking around on my property . . . taking videotapes of me and my family [and] had been on my property until 11:00 at night on a Saturday."

[Ruzicka alleged several violations of federal labor law related to other activities on the part of Local 1 as well as a claim of unreasonable intrusion upon his seclusion. The Eighth Circuit Court of Appeals applied Missouri law, which essentially follows the *Restatement* rule.]

We conclude Ruzicka easily established the first two elements of his invasion of privacy claim. Ruzicka testified he built his home for privacy and seclusion, and his property was set off from the public and was lined with 100 feet of trees. Ruzicka even posted no trespassing signs. Indeed, Missouri protects Ruzicka's personal residence from criminal trespass. *See* Mo.Rev.Stat. § 569.140. There can be no doubt Ruzicka's home is "a secret and private subject matter" that Ruzicka has a right to keep private.

Thus, the critical issue is whether Ruzicka produced sufficient evidence for a reasonable jury to find Local 1's investigators obtained information about Ruzicka's home "through some method objectionable to the reasonable" person. We conclude he has. Ruzicka testified his property's layout precluded anyone from viewing the home from public places. He specifically explained it is impossible to see from public property whether the lights in his home were on or off, noting a person would have to be on his property to make those determinations. If Ruzicka's testimony and evidence is believed, a reasonable jury could conclude Local 1's investigators trespassed on Ruzicka's private property to conduct surveillance of him and his family. We believe a reasonable person may object to strangers entering his posted private property to record when he sleeps and awakes inside his home, and may consider such as highly offensive. [W]e believe the third element presents a jury question. Because Ruzicka presented sufficient evidence on his invasion of privacy claim to present the claim to a jury, we reverse the district court's grant of judgment as a matter of law to Local 1, and remand the claim for a new trial.

Fletcher v. Price Chopper Foods of Trumann, Inc.

220 F.3d 871 (8th Cir. 2000)

In early October 1997, Fletcher learned that her right foot had developed a staph infection. Fletcher immediately informed two coworkers of her condition; coworkers eventually conveyed the information to the local store manager. PCF's corporate manager, Marlene Sawyer, testified that she decided to terminate Fletcher's employment that evening because Arkansas health regulations forbid persons infected with a communicable disease (such as staph) from working in the food preparation industry. Sawyer also admitted, however, that she viewed Fletcher as an "insurance risk" due to Fletcher's prosthetic limb and decreased mobility.

Following her termination, Fletcher applied for state unemployment benefits in Arkansas. In her application, Fletcher claimed that she did not have a staph infection at the time PCF terminated her employment. When Sawyer learned of Fletcher's claim that she had not been infected with staph, Sawyer decided to resolve the inconsistency in Fletcher's story.

Sawyer contacted Fletcher's doctor to ascertain whether Fletcher in fact had a staph infection. Sawyer spoke to Nurse Flemon, who informed Sawyer that such information could not be conveyed without a medical authorization form. According to Flemon, Sawyer responded that PCF employees sign medical information waivers when they begin work at PCF. Sawyer agreed to fax to the doctor's office a copy of Fletcher's authorization. Sawyer proceeded to fax a copy of Fletcher's *workers' compensation form* that contained a medical authorization. Sawyer also informed Nurse Flemon that, on one occasion, Fletcher had removed the bandage from her foot during work. Flemon interpreted Sawyer's remarks to mean that Fletcher had exposed her infection to the air, an act proscribed by Fletcher's doctor. Based on this information, Fletcher's doctor wrote to Sawyer informing her that Fletcher was indeed infected with the staph virus. The doctor reiterated that Fletcher should not remove her bandages.

[Fletcher brought a discrimination claim under the Americans with Disabilities Act as well as invasion of privacy claim. Fletcher prevailed at trial on the privacy claim. On appeal, the Eighth Circuit applied Arkansas law, which essentially follows the *Restatement* approach.]

Fletcher introduced evidence that Sawyer obtained information about her staph infection by subterfuge. Fletcher equates subterfuge with "highly offensive" conduct. . . .

. . . Sawyer could have employed proper means to discover whether Fletcher actually had a staph infection at the time of her discharge. During her rebuttal argument, Fletcher's counsel conceded that PCF could have obtained a subpoena for the doctor's testimony during Fletcher's unemployment benefits application process. That concession comports with our understanding of Arkansas unemployment benefits law: PCF would have had an opportunity (perhaps even a duty) to subpoena Fletcher's doctor.

Because Sawyer might have availed herself of proper discovery means—even though she did not—we conclude as a matter of law that Sawyer's conduct was not highly offensive. Fletcher urges a contrary conclusion and refers us to an illustration in § 652B. Illustration 4 prescribes liability for one who procures evidence to use in a civil suit by forging a court document to obtain confidential bank records of his adversary. *See* Restatement (Second) of Torts § 652B, cmt. b, illus. 4 (1977). Illustration 4 does not foreclose our decision, however, because the felonious conduct of the actor in the hypothetical is qualitatively different from Sawyer's conduct. While we readily acknowledge that Sawyer's conduct was morally reproachable, her conduct does not rise to the level of forgery, a felony. Hence Sawyer's decision to bypass proper channels in obtaining information from Fletcher's doctor does not bring her conduct within the ambit of Illustration 4.

Fletcher therefore failed to adduce sufficient evidence at trial to permit a jury to conclude that Sawyer intruded in a highly offensive manner.

We also find that Fletcher failed to establish the third element of her intrusion claim—privacy. At trial, Fletcher asserted a privacy interest in the medical fact that she was infected with the staph virus at the time of her termination. PCF acknowledges that, as a general matter, an individual's medical records are private. But PCF contends that Fletcher's behavior, coupled with the circumstances surrounding her termination, failed to demonstrate an intent to maintain privacy in the information.

A legitimate expectation of privacy is the touchstone of the tort of intrusion upon seclusion. "[T]he plaintiff in an invasion of privacy case must have conducted himself or herself in a manner consistent with an actual expectation of privacy."

Fletcher's behavior did not indicate that she intended to keep knowledge of her staph infection private. When Fletcher learned that she had a staph infection, she informed two coworkers of her condition. Fletcher's revelation of private information to coworkers eliminated Fletcher's expectation of privacy by making what was formerly private a topic of office conversation. *See* Moffett v. Gene B. Glick Co., Inc., 621 F.Supp. 244, 283 (N.D. Ind. 1985) (applying § 652B of the Restatement per Indiana law).

In *Moffett*, a white female suffered repeated sexual and racial taunts from several coworkers because she dated a black man. Moffett's supervisor also removed items from her desk and attempted to eavesdrop on her conversations with her boyfriend. The court acknowledged that Moffett's coworkers and supervisor intentionally interfered with her personal affairs. Yet the court dismissed Moffett's intrusion claim because she failed to demonstrate adequate "seclusion." Moffett admitted that she had discussed her interracial relationship with her coworkers. The court found that "[b]y discussing that relationship in the office environment, [Moffett] cannot now claim some kind of solitude or seclusion for the relationship in that environment." *Id.* at 283.

Moffett suggests that even extraordinarily offensive conduct may not be redressed via the tort of intrusion upon seclusion unless a plaintiff demonstrates a legitimate expectation of privacy. Much like the plaintiff in *Moffett*, Fletcher lost her expectation of privacy when she shared knowledge of her staph infection with coworkers.

The timing of Fletcher's disclosure to her fellow coworkers also suggests she did not intend to keep the knowledge of her staph infection to herself. Fletcher testified that the first thing she did upon learning that she was infected was to inform her coworkers. One who seeks to maintain privacy in a newly-discovered piece of information does not immediately reveal that information to others. Fletcher's actions do not indicate a subjective expectation of privacy.

. . .

More fundamentally, Fletcher's staph infection significantly impacted her fitness to work at PCF. Employees infected with communicable diseases may not, as a general matter, work in the food service industry. It is beyond dispute that the staph virus has the potential to infect others. Hence Fletcher's medical condition was a matter of legitimate concern to PCF, since her staph infection jeopardized her future employment at PCF. When such concern for the public health exists, an employer's need to know trumps an employee's right to privacy.

For all of these reasons, we conclude that Fletcher lacked a reasonable expectation of privacy with respect to knowledge of her staph infection. As a matter of law, the jury could not reasonably conclude that Fletcher established "seclusion."

Note

Privacy statutes. While the intrusion upon the seclusion tort is widely recognized, there are also a plethora of privacy statutes that provide a civil remedy in the event of a violation. *See* Americans with Disabilities Act, 42 U.S.C. § 12112(d)(4)(A) (prohibiting disability-related questions of employees and applicants); Cal. Civ. Code §§ 1708–1728 (paparazzi statute providing for punitive damages where an invasion of privacy involving the use of visual images, sound recordings, or other physical impression was for commercial purposes); Health Insurance Portability and Accountability Act (HIPAA) Privacy Rule, 45 C.F.R. Part 160 (requiring appropriate safeguards to protect the privacy of personal health information and setting limits and conditions on the uses and disclosures that may be made of such information without patient authorization).

Problem 16.1. The *Pleasant Hill Times*' story about Susan did not mention Pamela by name, but it did include her image in the photograph that ran along with the article. The photographer trespassed onto the hospital's secluded grounds and, with a telephoto lens, took pictures from 300 yards away of Pamela and Susan outdoors. That night, the hospital's medical director telephoned an editor at the paper and requested that the paper not publish any patient photographs. The paper nonetheless ran the story and the accompanying photograph. Would Pamela and Susan be successful if they brought claims of intrusion upon the seclusion?

B. Publicity Given to Private Life

With intrusion upon the seclusion, the tort is complete upon the intrusion. Thus, the tort truly does protect "the right to be let alone" as envisioned by Warren and Brandeis. The second form of invasion of privacy torts—publicity given to private life—protects "the right to be free of unwarranted publicity." Bremmer v. Journal-Tribune Pub. Co., 76 N.W.2d 762, 764 (Iowa 1956).

Ozer v. Borquez

940 P.2d 371 (Colo. 1997)

[Borquez was an associate attorney for Ozer & Mullen, P.C. (the Ozer law firm). On February 19, 1992, Borquez learned that his partner was diagnosed with Acquired Immune Deficiency Syndrome (AIDS). Borquez' physician advised him that he should be tested for the human immunodeficiency virus (HIV) immediately. Borquez advised the president and shareholder of the law firm, Robert Ozer (Ozer) about the situation and asked him to keep the information confidential. After speaking with Borquez, Ozer telephoned his wife, Renee Ozer, and told her of Borquez' disclosure. Renee was a shareholder of the Ozer law firm and the supervisor of the Colorado Springs and Pueblo offices of the law firm. Renee in turn disclosed Borquez' situation to a staff attorney at the Colorado Springs office. Additionally, Ozer informed the law firm's office manager about Borquez' disclosure and discussed Borquez' disclosure with two of the law firm's secretaries. On February 21, 1992, Borquez returned to the office and became upset when he learned that everyone in the law firm knew about his situation. On February 26, 1992, one week after Borquez made his disclosure to Ozer, Borquez was fired. Borquez filed suit against the Ozer law firm and against Ozer as an individual, claiming wrongful discharge and invasion of privacy. The jury found in favor of Borquez and awarded him damages totaling $90,841. The jury set compensatory damages at $30,841 for the wrongful discharge claim and $20,000 for the invasion of privacy claim, and awarded exemplary damages in the sum of $40,000. The Ozer firm appealed.]

[A] majority of jurisdictions have recognized that the right of privacy encompasses a tort claim based on unreasonable publicity given to one's private life.

In accordance with these jurisdictions, we now recognize in Colorado a tort claim for invasion of privacy in the nature of unreasonable publicity given to one's private life. In order to prevail on such a claim, we hold that the following requirements must be met: (1) the fact or facts disclosed must be private in nature; (2) the disclosure must be made to the public; (3) the disclosure must be one which would be highly offensive to a reasonable person; (4) the fact or facts disclosed cannot be of legitimate concern to the public; and (5) the defendant acted with reckless disregard of the private nature of the fact or facts disclosed.

The first requirement of a tort claim for invasion of privacy in the nature of unreasonable publicity given to one's private life is that the facts disclosed be private in nature. The disclosure of facts that are already public will not support a claim for invasion of privacy. In contrast, facts related to an individual's sexual relations, or "unpleasant or disgraceful" illnesses, are considered private in nature and the disclosure of such facts constitutes an invasion of the individual's right of privacy. Restatement (Second) of Torts § 652D cmt. b (1976).

The second requirement of a tort claim for invasion of privacy based on unreasonable publicity given to one's private life is that the disclosure be made to the public. The requirement of public disclosure connotes publicity, which requires communication to the public in general or to a large number of persons, as distinguished from one individual or a few.[7]

Although the disclosure must be made to the general public or to a large number of persons, there is no threshold number which constitutes "a large number" of persons. Rather, the facts and circumstances of a particular case must be taken into consideration in determining whether the disclosure was sufficiently public so as to support a claim for invasion of privacy. *See, e.g.*, Kinsey v. Macur, 107 Cal.App.3d 265, 165 Cal.Rptr. 608, 611 (1980) (holding that defendant's dissemination of copies of a letter to only twenty people constituted public disclosure).

The third requirement of a tort claim for invasion of privacy in the nature of unreasonable publicity given to one's private life is that the disclosure be one which would be highly offensive to a reasonable person. The term "highly offensive" has been construed to mean that the disclosure would cause emotional distress or embarrassment to a reasonable person. The determination of whether a disclosure is highly offensive to the reasonable person is a question of fact and depends on the circumstances of a particular case.

The fourth requirement of a tort claim for invasion of privacy in the nature of unreasonable publicity given to one's private life is that the facts disclosed are not of legitimate concern to the public. The right of privacy may potentially clash with the rights of free speech and free press guaranteed by the United States and Colorado Constitutions. The rights of free speech and free press protect the public's access to information on matters of legitimate public concern. As such, the right of the individual to keep information private must be balanced against the right to disseminate newsworthy information to the public. *See* Gilbert v. Medical Econs. Co., 665 F.2d 305, 307 (10th Cir.1981). As the Tenth Circuit Court of Appeals stated in *Gilbert*, "to properly balance freedom of the press against the right of privacy, every private fact disclosed in an otherwise truthful, newsworthy publication must have some substantial relevance to a matter of legitimate public interest." *Id.* at 308; *see also* Virgil v. Time, Inc., 527 F.2d 1122, 1129 (9th Cir.1975) (holding that liability may be imposed for invasion of privacy only if matter publicized is of a kind which is not of legitimate concern to public).

The term newsworthy is defined as "[a]ny information disseminated 'for purposes of education, amusement or enlightenment, when the public may reasonably be expected to have a legitimate interest in what is published.'" *Gilbert*, 665 F.2d at 308 (quoting Restatement (Second) of Torts § 652D cmt. j (1976)). In determining whether a subject is of legitimate public interest, "[t]he line is to be drawn when the publicity ceases to be the giving of information to which the public is entitled, and becomes a morbid and sensational prying into private lives for its own sake."

---

7. We note that public disclosure may occur where the defendant merely initiates the process whereby the information is eventually disclosed to a large number of persons. *See* Beaumont v. Brown, 401 Mich. 80, 257 N.W.2d 522, 530 (1977).

Restatement (Second) of Torts §652D cmt. h (1976). The newsworthiness test "properly restricts liability for public disclosure of private facts to the extreme case, thereby providing the breathing space needed by the press." *Gilbert*, 665 F.2d at 308. As such, the requirement that the facts disclosed must not be of legitimate concern to the public protects the rights of free speech and free press guaranteed by the United States and Colorado Constitutions.

The final requirement of a tort claim for invasion of privacy in the nature of unreasonable publicity given to one's private life is that the defendant acted with reckless disregard of the private nature of the fact or facts disclosed. A person acts with reckless disregard if, at the time of the publicity, the person knew or should have known that the fact or facts disclosed were private in nature.

Accordingly, we recognize in Colorado a tort claim for invasion of privacy in the nature of unreasonable publicity given to one's private life. We therefore affirm the court of appeals' recognition of this tort claim.

IV.

The final issue before us is whether the court of appeals correctly held that the jury was properly instructed on Borquez' invasion of privacy tort claim based on unreasonable publicity given to one's private life. . . .

. . . Because the trial court instructed the jury regarding the term "publication" rather than "publicity," and because the terms "publication" and "publicity" are not interchangeable, we hold that the trial court's instruction was erroneous. We therefore reverse the court of appeals' holding on this issue.

Notes

Matters of legitimate public concern. What should qualify as a matter of legitimate public concern in today's society, when intimate details surrounding the lives of celebrities and quasi-celebrities are routinely publicized? *See* Veilleux v. National Broadcasting Co., 206 F.3d 92 (1st Cir. 2001) (holding that truck driver's positive drug test was a matter of public concern when included as part of television news report); Virgil v. Time, Inc., 527 F.2d 1122 (9th Cir. 1975) ("The fact that [one] engage[s] in an activity in which the public can be said to have a general interest does not render every aspect of their lives subject to public disclosure."). Assume in *Fletcher*, *supra*, that Fletcher had kept the fact of her staph infection confidential but that her employer disclosed the fact to Fletcher's co-workers. Was the fact of her infection a matter of legitimate concern to her co-workers? Should that be sufficient to defeat Fletcher's claim, or must the matter be of legitimate concern to the broader public?

Statutory causes of action. There are various federal and state statutes that create a private right of action in the case of a disclosure of private information. *See* HIPAA, 42 U.S.C. §1320d-2(b)(ii); ADA, 42 U.S.C. §12112(d)(3)(B). In New Jersey, health care providers who maintain a medical record that "contains identifying information about a person who has or is suspected of having AIDS or HIV infection" must keep the record confidential. N.J.S.A. 26:5C-7. "A person who has or is suspected of having AIDS or HIV infection who is aggrieved as a result of the violation of this act may commence a civil action against the individual or institution who committed the violation to obtain appropriate relief, including actual damages, equitable relief and reasonable attorney's fees and court costs." N.J.S.A. 26:5C-14(a).

Problem 16.2. The article in the *Pleasant Hill Times* included a quote from one of Susan's friends that Susan was suffering from depression and an eating disorder when she was admitted to the Pleasant Hill Hospital. According to her friend, Susan's outlook had significantly improved during her stay at the hospital. The article did not mention Pamela by name, but instead simply referred to her as a friend of Susan's in the caption underneath the picture of the two walking outside. Would Susan have a claim for public disclosure of private facts? Would Pamela?

C. False Light

The third type of invasion of privacy claim is false light. As described by one court, "one who gives publicity to a matter concerning another that places the other before the public in a false light" is liable if: "(a) the false light in which the other was placed would be highly offensive to a reasonable person, and (b) the actor had knowledge of or acted in reckless disregard as to the falsity of the publicized matter and the false light in which the other would be placed." Welling v. Weinfeld, 866 N.E.2d 1051, 1054 (Ohio 2007). With its focus on falsity, the false light tort obviously resembles the defamation tort. One suggested distinction is that with false light, there need not be an actual false statement; it is enough that the defendant's actions create a misleading impression. However, it is now widely recognized that defamation can be accomplished by implication or innuendo and through the use of misleading photographs. So, how does the tort differ from defamation? The case below explores this issue.

Crump v. Beckley Newspapers, Inc.

320 S.E.2d 70 (W. Va. 1984)

The appellant in this case, Sue S. Crump, appeals from an order of the Circuit Court of Raleigh County granting summary judgment for the defendant/appellee, Beckley Newspapers, Inc. She asserts that the trial court erred in granting summary judgment because issues of material fact existed which should have been submitted for jury consideration. We agree and reverse the decision of the trial court.

On December 5, 1977, the defendant published an article in one of its newspapers concerning women coal miners. Photographs of the plaintiff, a miner with the

Westmoreland Coal Company, taken with her knowledge and consent, were used by the defendant in conjunction with the article. Her name was specifically mentioned, and her picture appeared with Jacqueline Clements, another miner. After publication of this article in 1977, Crump had no contact with the defendant, and the defendant did not request permission to use her picture or name in any other newspaper article.

On September 23, 1979, an article entitled "Women Enter 'Man's' World" appeared in one of the defendant's newspapers. The article generally addressed some of the problems faced by women miners, and by women who desire employment in the mining industry. The article related incidents in which two Kentucky women were "'stripped, greased and sent out of the mine' as part of an initiation rite"; in which a woman miner in southwestern Virginia was physically attacked twice while underground; and in which one Wyoming woman "was dangled off a 200-foot water tower accompanied by the suggestion that she quit her job. She did." The article also discussed other types of harassment and discrimination faced by women miners. Although Crump's name was not mentioned in the article, her 1977 photograph was used, accompanied by a caption which read, "Women are entering mines as a regular course of action."

As a result of the unauthorized publication of Crump's photograph in conjunction with the article, she states in an affidavit submitted below that she was questioned by friends and acquaintances concerning the incidents contained in the article and concerning whether she had been the subject of any harassment by her employer or by fellow employees. She had, in fact, experienced no such harassment. Crump also states that the article caused one reader to ask her whether she had ever been "stripped, greased and sent out of the mine." She alleges that the unfavorable attention precipitated by the publication of her photograph in conjunction with the article has damaged her reputation and caused her a great deal of embarrassment and humiliation. Therefore, she seeks recovery from the defendant for damages resulting from their unauthorized publication of her photograph.

...

Although closely related, defamation and invasion of privacy remain distinct theories of recovery entitled to separate consideration. Possessing different historical antecedents, each requires different elements of proof. Despite the lack of clarity in the plaintiff's complaint, it is clear that it sufficiently stated a cause of action for invasion of privacy meriting its consideration by the trial court. Therefore, it is necessary to develop the theory and to analyze the facts presented in order to determine whether genuine issues of material fact remain.

[P]ublicity which unreasonably places another in a false light before the public is an actionable invasion of privacy. One form in which false light invasions of privacy often appears is the use of another's photograph to illustrate an article or book with which the person has no reasonable connection, and which places the person in a false light. For example, in *Leverton v. Curtis Pub. Co.*, 192 F.2d 974 (3d Cir. 1951), a photograph of a child being helped to her feet after nearly being struck by an automobile through no fault of her own was initially published in a local newspaper. Approximately twenty months later, however, in an article published in the Saturday Evening Post on the role of pedestrian carelessness in traffic accidents, the plaintiff's photograph was used as an illustration of such carelessness. The Third Circuit affirmed the jury verdict for the plaintiff, holding that her privacy had been invaded because she had been presented in a false light.

. . .

Despite the similarities between defamation and false light causes of action, there are also a number of important differences. First, "each action protects different interests: privacy actions involve injuries to emotions and mental suffering, while defamation actions involve injury to reputation." Second, "[t]he false light need not be defamatory, although it often is, but it must be such as to be offensive to a reasonable person." Finally, although widespread publicity is not necessarily required for recovery under a defamation cause of action, it is an essential ingredient to any false light invasion of privacy claim. Therefore, false light invasion of privacy is a distinct theory of recovery entitled to separate consideration and analysis.

. . .

Turning to the facts surrounding the present case, it is clear that genuine issues of material fact remain which preclude the granting of summary judgment for the defendant on the false light invasion of privacy cause of action. First, as in the appellant's defamation cause of action, whether the statements in the article involved referred to the appellant with regards to her privacy cause of action is a question of fact for the jury. Second, when the communication involved in a false light case does not clearly favor one construction over another, the determination of what light it places the plaintiff is for the jury. This consideration is related to the first in that the key factual issue upon remand is whether the article implied that Crump had suffered harassment in the course of her employment, thereby either defaming her or placing her in a false light before the public. . . .

Accordingly, the trial court's order granting summary judgment for the defendant is reversed, and the plaintiff's defamation and false light causes of action are remanded for a trial on the merits.

Reversed and remanded.

Notes

Remand. Based on the facts as presented, does it sound like Crump could establish a prima facie case on her false light theory? Does it sound like she could establish a prima facie case on a defamation claim?

Other examples. Reese v. Pook & Pook, LLC, 158 F. Supp. 3d 271 (E.D. Pa. 2016) (magazine article characterizing antique toy collector's collection as "middle market" was not offensive enough to support a false light claim); Uhl v. CBS, Inc., 476 F. Supp. 1134 (W.D. Pa. 1979) (television broadcast that used editing to make it appear as if plaintiff had engaged in the "unsportsmanlike and unethical act of shooting a goose on the ground" instead of in the air stated a false light claim); Gill v. Curtis Pub. Co., 239 P.2d 630 (Cal. 1952) (photograph of a husband and wife in an affectionate pose taken without their permission or knowledge was used to illustrate an article that stated that "love at first sight" was founded upon 100% sex attraction and would be followed by divorce could form the basis of a false light claim).

The fault standard. Another area in which defamation and false light may overlap is with the applicable fault standard. Some courts define false light in terms of whether the defendant acts with actual malice. *See* Welling v. Weinfeld, 866 N.E.2d 1051, 1054 (Ohio 2007). Others hold that where the plaintiff is a private individual, the *New York Times*/constitutional requirement of actual malice does not apply. Uhl v. CBS, Inc., 476 F. Supp. 1134 (W.D. Pa. 1979).

Overlap with defamation and the judicial reluctance to recognize the tort. Given the potential impact on free speech and the overlap with other privacy theories and defamation, some courts have refused to recognize the false light tort. *See* Jews for Jesus, Inc. v. Rapp, 997 So. 2d 1098, 1113 (Fla. 2008) (refusing to recognize tort and stating "there are relatively few scenarios where defamation is inadequate and false light provides a potential for relief").

Problem 16.3. The article in the *Pleasant Hill Times* referenced the fact that several patients at the facility had attempted suicide. The article also mentioned Susan's alleged depression and eating disorder and quoted one of the doctors at the facility as saying, "Patients at the facility are experiencing a variety of mental health issues. The fact that they have so much in common allows the patients to bond and provide support for one another during their struggles." The caption beneath the photo of Pamela and Susan repeated this quote from the doctor. Susan has never attempted suicide. Could she prevail on a false light claim in a jurisdiction that recognizes such claims?

D. Misappropriation of the Right of Publicity

The final privacy theory resembles a property claim as much as it does a privacy claim. The material below illustrates the evolution of the theory in one jurisdiction. Other states have adopted a similar approach.

Roberson v. Rochester Folding Box Co.

64 N.E. 442 (N.Y. 1902)

PARKER, C. J.

The appellate division has certified that the following questions of law have arisen in this case, and ought to be reviewed by this court: (1) Does the complaint herein state a cause of action at law against the defendants, or either of them? (2) Does the complaint herein state a cause of action in equity against the defendants, or either of them? These questions are presented by a demurrer to the complaint, which is put upon the ground that the complaint does not state facts sufficient to constitute a cause of action.

... The complaint alleges that the Franklin Mills Company, one of the defendants, was engaged in a milling business and in the manufacture and sale of flour; that before the commencement of the action, without the knowledge or consent of plaintiff, defendants, knowing that they had no right or authority so to do, had obtained, made, printed, sold, and circulated about 25,000 lithographic prints, photographs, and likenesses of plaintiff, made in a manner particularly set up in the complaint; that upon the paper upon which the likenesses were printed and above the portrait there were printed, in large, plain letters, the words, 'Flour of the Family,' and below the portrait, in large capital letters, 'Franklin Mills Flour,' and in the lower right-hand corner, in smaller capital letters, 'Rochester Folding Box Co., Rochester, N. Y.'; that upon the same sheet were other advertisements of the flour of the Franklin Mills Company; that those 25,000 likenesses of the plaintiff thus ornamented have been conspicuously posted and displayed in stores, warehouses, saloons, and other public places; that they have been recognized by friends of the plaintiff and other people, with the result that plaintiff has been greatly humiliated by the scoffs and jeers of persons who have recognized her face and picture on this advertisement, and her good name has been attacked, causing her great distress and suffering, both in body and mind; that she was made sick, and suffered a severe nervous shock, was confined to her bed, and compelled to employ a physician, because of these facts; that defendants had continued to print, make, use, sell, and circulate the said lithographs, and that by reason of the foregoing facts plaintiff had suffered damages in the sum of $15,000. The complaint prays that defendants be enjoined from making, printing, publishing, circulating, or using in any manner any likenesses of plaintiff in any form whatever; for further relief (which it is not necessary to consider here); and for damages.

It will be observed that there is no complaint made that plaintiff was libeled by this publication of her portrait. The likeness is said to be a very good one, and one that her friends and acquaintances were able to recognize. Indeed, her grievance is that a good portrait of her, and therefore one easily recognized, has been used to attract attention toward the paper upon which defendant mill company's advertisements appear. Such publicity, which some find agreeable, is to plaintiff very distasteful, and thus, because of defendants' impertinence in using her picture, without her consent, for their own business purposes, she has been caused to suffer mental distress where others would have appreciated the compliment to their beauty implied in the selection of the picture for such purposes; ... There is no precedent for such an action to be found in the decisions of this court. Indeed, the learned judge who wrote the very able and interesting opinion in the appellate division said, while upon the threshold of the discussion of the question: 'It may be said, in the first place, that the theory upon which this action is predicated is new, at least in instance, if not in principle, and that few precedents can be found to sustain the claim made by the plaintiff, if, indeed, it can be said that there are any authoritative cases establishing her right to recover in this action.' Nevertheless that court reached the conclusion that plaintiff had a good cause of action against defendants, in that defendants had invaded what is called a "right of privacy"; in other words, the right to be let alone. Mention of such a right is not to be found in Blackstone, Kent, or any other of the great commentators upon the law; nor, so far as the learning of counsel or the courts in this case have been able to discover, does its existence seem to have been asserted prior to about the year 1890, when it was presented with attractiveness, and no inconsiderable ability, in the Harvard Law Review (volume 4, p. 193) in an article entitled "Rights of a Citizen to His Reputation." ... If such a principle be incorporated into the body of the law through the instrumentality of a court of equity, the attempts to logically apply the principle will necessarily result not only in a vast amount of litigation, but in litigation bordering upon the absurd, for the right of privacy, once established as a legal doctrine, cannot be confined to the restraint of the publication of a likeness, but must necessarily embrace as well the publication of a word picture, a comment upon one's looks, conduct, domestic relations or habits.

The legislative body could very well interfere and arbitrarily provide that no one should be permitted for his own selfish purpose to use the picture or the name of another for advertising purposes without his consent. In such event no embarrassment would result to the general body of the law, for the rule would be applicable only to cases provided for by the statute. The courts, however, being without authority to legislate, are required to decide cases upon principle, and so are necessarily embarrassed by precedents created by an extreme, and therefore unjustifiable, application of an old principle.

...

An examination of the authorities leads us to the conclusion that the so-called "right of privacy" has not as yet found an abiding place in our jurisprudence, and, as we view it, the doctrine cannot now be incorporated without doing violence to settled principles of law by which the profession and the public have long been guided.

The judgment of the appellate division and of the special term should be reversed, and questions certified answered in the negative, without costs, and with leave to the plaintiff to serve an amended complaint within 20 days, also without costs.

Note

The New York legislature responded to *Roberson* "by enacting the Nation's first statutory right to privacy (L. 1903, ch. 132), now codified as sections 50 and 51 of the Civil Rights Law. Section 50 prohibits the use of a living person's name, portrait or picture for 'advertising' or 'trade' purposes without prior written consent (Civil

Rights Law § 50). Section 50 provides criminal penalties and section 51 a private right of action for damages and injunctive relief." Howell v. New York Post Co., Inc., 612 N.E.2d 699, 703 (N.Y. 1993). Other states adopted similar statutes or common law rules prohibiting the misappropriation of another's name or likeness. *See* Restatement (Second) of Torts § 652C.

Lohan v. Perez

924 F. Supp. 2d 447 (E.D.N.Y. 2013)

HURLEY, Senior District Judge:

Plaintiff Lindsay Lohan ("plaintiff") commenced this action against defendants Armando Christian Perez (a/k/a Pitbull) ("Perez") [and others] (collectively, "defendants"), asserting that defendants violated Sections 50 and 51 of the New York Civil Rights Law by using plaintiff's "name, characterization, and personality for advertising purposes, and for purposes of trade and commercial benefits" without her consent. Plaintiff has also asserted claims for unjust enrichment and intentional infliction of emotional distress, and seeks monetary and injunctive relief.

[Lohan alleged that the defendants used her name without her consent as part of the song "Give me Everything." ("The Song.")] Specifically, approximately one-third of the way through the song, plaintiff's name is used as follows: "So, I'm tip-toein', to keep flowin'/ I got it locked up like Lindsay Lohan." . . .

Discussion

I. Defendants' Motion to Dismiss

B. Plaintiff's Claim Under the New York Civil Rights Law is Dismissed

1. Legal Standard

"New York does not recognize a common-law right of privacy." By enacting Sections 50 and 51 of the New York Civil Rights Law, however, the New York legislature sought to "provide a limited statutory right of privacy." *Id.* Section 50 of the Civil Rights Law makes it a misdemeanor for a person to "use[ ] for advertising purposes, or for the purposes of trade, the name, portrait or picture of any living person without having first obtained the written consent of such person. . . ." N.Y. Civ. Rights Law § 50 (McKinney 2012). Section 51 provides:

> Any person whose name, portrait, picture or voice is used within this state for advertising purposes or for the purposes of trade without the written consent first obtained as above provided [in Section 50] may maintain an equitable action in the supreme court of this state against the person, firm or corporation so using his name, portrait, picture or voice, to prevent and restrain the use thereof; and may also sue and recover damages for any injuries sustained by reason of such use and if the defendant shall have knowingly used such person's name, portrait, picture or voice in such manner as is forbidden or declared to be unlawful by section fifty of this article, the jury, in its discretion, may award exemplary damages. . . .

N.Y. Civ. Rights Law § 51 (McKinney 2012). The New York Court of Appeals has made clear that the prohibitions set forth in Sections 50 and 51 of the Civil Rights Law "are to be strictly limited to nonconsensual commercial appropriations of the name, portrait or picture of a living person," and "prohibit the use of pictures, names or portraits 'for advertising purposes or for the purposes of trade' only, and nothing more."

To prevail on a statutory right to privacy claim pursuant to the New York Civil Rights Law, a plaintiff must prove: "(1) use of plaintiff's name, portrait, picture or voice (2) 'for advertising purposes or for the purposes of trade' (3) without consent and (4) within the state of New York." Only the second element appears to be in dispute here.

2. The Song is a Protected Work of Art

Defendants assert initially that "the First Amendment presents a complete defense" to plaintiff's claims under the New York Civil Rights Law because that statute "does not apply to works of art."

Courts interpreting the New York Civil Rights Law have concluded that "pure First Amendment speech in the form of artistic expression . . . deserves full protection, even against [another individual's] statutorily-protected privacy interests." *Hoepker*, 200 F.Supp.2d at 350. Thus, the use of an individual's name—even without his consent—is not prohibited by the New York Civil Rights Law if that use is part of a work of art.

The Supreme Court has made clear that "[m]usic, as a form of expression and communication, is protected under the First Amendment." Ward v. Rock Against Racism, 491 U.S. 781, 790, 109 S.Ct. 2746, 105 L.Ed.2d 661 (1989). Thus, because the Song is a protected work of art, the use of plaintiff's name therein does not violate the New York Civil Rights Law.

3. Plaintiff's Name was not Used in the Song for Advertising or Purposes of Trade

Somewhat relatedly, defendants argue that plaintiff's name was not used in the Song "for advertising or trade purposes within the meaning of the statute." Specifically, defendants assert that plaintiff's name "does not promote a product or service" or "seek 'solicitation for patronage,'" and because plaintiff's name is not used in the Song's title or refrain, her name is not being used to promote the Song itself. Thus, defendants contend, the second element articulated in *Hoepker* has not been satisfied.

The fact that the Song was presumably created and distributed for the purpose of making a profit does not mean that plaintiff's name was used for "advertising" or "purposes of trade" within the meaning of the New York Civil Rights Law. *See, e.g.*, Time, Inc. v. Hill, 385 U.S. 374, 397, 87 S.Ct. 534, 17 L.Ed.2d 456 (1967) (interpreting New York Civil Rights Law and concluding: "'That books, newspapers, and magazines are published and sold for profit does not prevent them from being a form of expression whose liberty is safeguarded by the First Amendment.'") (quoting Joseph

Burstyn, Inc. v. Wilson, 343 U.S. 495, 501–02, 72 S.Ct. 777, 96 L.Ed. 1098 (1952)); Ann-Margret v. High Society Magazine, Inc., 498 F.Supp. 401, 406 (S.D.N.Y.1980) ("[S]imple use in a magazine that is published and sold for profit does not constitute a use for advertising or trade sufficient to make out an actionable claim, even if its manner of use and placement was designed to sell the article so that it might be paid for and read.") (internal quotation marks omitted). Indeed, plaintiff has not offered any argument to the contrary.

Even if the Court were to conclude that plaintiff had sufficiently alleged that her name was used in the Song for purposes of advertising or trade, the isolated nature of the use of her name would, in and of itself, prove fatal to her New York Civil Rights Law claim. "Courts in New York are reluctant to impose liability under §§ 50–51 for incidental use of a person's name or image because of the danger of imposing an uncalled-for burden and hazard on publishers." Netzer v. Continuity Graphic Assocs., Inc., 963 F.Supp. 1308, 1326 (S.D.N.Y.1997) (internal alteration and quotation marks omitted). "Whether a use falls within [the incidental use] exception to liability is determined by the role that the use of the plaintiff's name or likeness plays in the main purpose and subject of the work at issue." Preston v. Martin Bregman Prods., Inc., 765 F.Supp. 116, 119 (S.D.N.Y.1991). Here, plaintiff's name is mentioned one time in only one of 104 lines of the Song. It is not used in the Song's title or the refrain, and appears entirely incidental to the theme of the Song. Overall, the use of plaintiff's name is an "isolated reference [ ] of [a] fleeting and incidental nature which the Civil Rights law does not find offensive."

Accordingly, the Court concludes that plaintiff has failed to adequately allege a cause of action under the New York Civil Rights Law and, as such, her first claim for relief is dismissed.

Notes

Noncommercial uses. The use of a person's name, likeness, etc. is typically not actionable where the person's identity is used "in news reporting, commentary, entertainment, works of fiction or nonfiction, or in advertising that is incidental to such uses." *Restatement of Unfair Competition* § 47. For the defendant's use of another's identify to be protected, however, the use must actually fit into one of these categories. For example, in 2007, professional wrestler Chris Benoit murdered his wife, Nancy, and son before taking his own life. Several months later, *Hustler* magazine published nude photographs of Nancy alongside a short biographical piece about her. The Eleventh Circuit Court of Appeals held that the use of Nancy's photographs was not protected under Georgia's newsworthiness exception to the right of publicity statute because the short biography was "merely incidental to its publication of her nude photographs." Toffoloni v. LFP Publishing Group, 572 F.3d 1201 (11th Cir. 2009).

Right of publicity. Some courts draw a distinction between the torts of misappropriation of name and violations of the right of publicity. According to the Missouri Supreme Court, the misappropriation of name tort "protects against intrusion upon an individual's private self-esteem and dignity, while the right of publicity protects against commercial loss caused by appropriation of an individual's [identity] for commercial exploitation." *Doe v. TCI Cablevision*, 110 S.W.3d 363, 368 (Mo. 2003) (quotations omitted). The elements of the two torts, however, "are essentially the same." *Id.*

Other indicia of identity. Some statutes and common law rules provide greater protection than New York's statute by prohibiting a defendant from using "a person's name, likeness, *or other indicia of identity*." *See* Restatement (Third) of Unfair Competition §46; Carson v. Here's Johnny Portable Toilets, Inc., 698 F.2d 831 (6th Cir. 1983) (concluding phrase "Here's Johnny" was closely associated with Johnny Carson); Midler v. Ford Motor Co., 849 F.2d 460 (9th Cir. 1988) (concluding defendant's use of a "sound alike" in a commercial can amount to a misappropriation of plaintiff's identity).

Problem 16.4. Assume that Pamela and Susan file suit against the *Pleasant Hill Times* in a jurisdiction with a statute like New York's Civil Rights Law §§50 and 51. Could either recover?

Review Question

Johnny and Joan are a celebrity couple. They recently fired their housekeeper, Lita. Lita still had a key to the couple's house, so the day after being fired, she entered the couple's house, went to their bedroom, opened a drawer in Joan's nightstand, and removed a nude picture of Joan. Then, purely out of spite and to embarrass the couple, Lita posted the picture on Lita's social media accounts.

Which invasion of privacy theories, if any, could the couple (together or individually) successfully bring against Lita?

Part 5

Economic Torts

The next two chapters focus on situations in which the harm suffered is primarily economic in nature. Chapter 17 covers situations in which the defendant's misrepresentation of fact—made knowingly or negligently—causes economic damage to the plaintiff. In the case of the tort of interference with contractual relations, the defendant intentionally interferes with the plaintiff's contractual relationship with another, thereby causing pecuniary harm. This tort and its various permutations are addressed in Chapter 18.

Chapter 17

Misrepresentation

A. Fraudulent Misrepresentation
- The basic elements of the prima facie case
- The following concepts:
  - False representation
    - When nondisclosure of fact may amount to a representation
    - When omission and concealment of fact may amount to a representation
    - When representation of opinion, intention, or law may amount to a representation of fact
  - Materiality
  - Knowledge of falsity
  - Intent to deceive
  - Justifiable reliance
  - Proximate cause
  - Damages
  - Other concepts developed in class or in readings assigned by the professor

B. Negligent misrepresentation
- The requirements of the privity test
- The Restatement § 552 test
  - The basic elements of the test
  - In the course of his business, profession, or employment, or in any other transaction in which he has a pecuniary interest
  - Justifiable reliance upon the information
  - Potential plaintiffs
- Other possible approaches
- Other concepts developed in class or in readings assigned by the professor

Chapter Problem. Luis and Ruth entered into two separate agreements for Luis to purchase two small office buildings owned by Ruth. Before they entered into the agreements, Ruth sent Luis a "Seller's Real Property Disclosure Statement" for each property. The Disclosure Statement expressly stated that it was "intended to assist [Ruth] in organizing and presenting all material facts concerning the Property" and that Ruth is "obligated to fully and accurately disclose in writing to a buyer all 'material facts' concerning the property." Luis has now asserted claims of fraudulent and negligent misrepresentation against Ruth in connection with the sale of both properties.

One who relies upon an innocently made misrepresentation of fact may have a right to rescind any resulting contract. But one who wishes to recover damages based upon another's misrepresentation must establish fault on the part of the other party. Thus, the tort plaintiff must proceed on a claim of fraudulent misrepresentation (also known as "deceit") or negligent misrepresentation. This chapter explores both theories.

A. Fraudulent Misrepresentation

1. The Prima Facie Case

Dier v. Peters

815 N.W.2d 1 (Iowa 2012)

MANSFIELD, Justice.

This case presents the question whether an individual who made voluntary expenditures based on a mother's fraudulent representation that he had fathered her child has a cause of action against the mother for recovery of those payments. . . .

I. Factual Background and Procedural History.

Because this case was decided on a motion to dismiss for failure to state a claim, we assume the factual allegations of the petition are true. O.D. was born to Cassandra Jo Peters on February 10, 2009. Peters knew that Joseph O. Dier was not the child's biological father, but nonetheless told Dier that he was. Based on the mother's representations, Dier provided financial support for the mother and the child.

Dier filed an application in the district court to establish custody of the minor child. After Peters received the report of the child custody evaluator, she was afraid she would not get custody of the child and requested a paternity test. That test excluded Dier as the biological father. Dier then requested a second paternity test which again excluded him as the biological father.

On August 2, 2011, Dier filed a separate petition at law seeking reimbursement from Peters of monies "expended to the Defendant, monies for the minor child, and monies expended in custody litigation." On August 25, Peters moved to dismiss the petition. She asserted that Dier's petition "fail[ed] to state a claim upon which relief can be granted for the reason that the State of Iowa does not recognize an action for 'paternity fraud' nor has the Iowa Legislature created any such action by statute."

Dier resisted the motion, arguing that Peters "engaged in fraudulent activity in enticing me to believe that I was the child's father and securing financial assistance from me from the beginning of the child's birth until recently." He asked that the district court "overrule the Motion to Dismiss as this matter is fraudulent and the Defendant has acted with utmost malice and hatred."

On September 20, 2011, the district court granted Peters' motion to dismiss. In its order dismissing Dier's action, the trial court concluded that the "current status of the law demands that this case be dismissed." Dier now appeals.

III. Analysis

. . .

A. Traditional Law of Fraud. . . . Dier is not seeking relief under Iowa Code section 600B.41A(4)(b), which permits a putative father who has overcome the establishment of paternity to avoid all unpaid and future support obligations. Rather, Dier has brought a common law action for fraud seeking as damages monies voluntarily paid based on an allegedly fraudulent representation. From our vantage point, Dier's cause of action appears to fit comfortably within the traditional boundaries of fraud law.

In order to prevail on a common law fraud claim the plaintiff must prove the following:

> (1) [the] defendant made a representation to the plaintiff, (2) the representation was false, (3) the representation was material, (4) the defendant knew the representation was false, (5) the defendant intended to deceive the plaintiff, (6) the plaintiff acted in [justifiable] reliance on the truth of the representation . . . , (7) the representation was a proximate cause of [the] plaintiff's damages, and (8) the amount of damages.

Spreitzer v. Hawkeye State Bank, 779 N.W.2d 726, 735 (Iowa 2009) (quoting Gibson v. ITT Hartford Ins. Co., 621 N.W.2d 388, 400 (Iowa 2001)). . . .

1 & 2. *False representation.* Dier alleges that Peters told him he was the child's biological father. The two subsequent paternity tests demonstrate that this representation was false.

3. *Materiality.* In order to recover in an action for fraud the alleged false misrepresentation must be material. We have said that a fact is material if it substantially affects the interest of the party alleged to have been defrauded. We have also said that a fraudulent misrepresentation is material if it is likely to induce a reasonable person to act. According to the Restatement (Second) of Torts, a matter is material if:

> (a) a reasonable man would attach importance to its existence or nonexistence in determining his choice of action in the transaction in question; or
>
> (b) the maker of the representation knows or has reason to know that its recipient regards or is likely to regard the matter as important in

> determining his choice of action, although a reasonable man would not so regard it.

Restatement (Second) of Torts § 538, at 80 (1977).

Dier has alleged a material misrepresentation. Being the father of a child is an important matter, bringing with it legal, financial, and moral responsibilities. Dier alleges that his decision to voluntarily incur the expenses associated with supporting the child and her mother were "based upon the representations made by the Defendant" and that Peters "used this assertion to secure monies from [him]." These allegations support his claim that the false representation induced him to act and that the defendant knew that he was likely to regard the assertion "as important in determining his choice of action." See Restatement (Second) of Torts § 538, at 80. We cannot say that a reasonable person would not have attached significant importance to the specific fraudulent misrepresentation in this case.

4. *Knowledge of falsity.* The knowledge of falsity element of a fraud claim is also commonly known as the scienter element. "The element of scienter requires a showing that alleged false representations were made with knowledge they were false [but t]his requirement is met when the evidence shows such representations were made in reckless disregard of their truth or falsity." B & B Asphalt Co. v. T.S. McShane Co., 242 N.W.2d 279, 284 (Iowa 1976).

We have held that a plaintiff can prevail on the scienter element by demonstrating:

> the defendant had actual knowledge of the falsity, possessed reckless disregard for the truth, falsely stated or implied that the representations were based on personal knowledge or investigation, or had a special relationship with the plaintiff and therefore had a duty to disclose.

McGough v. Gabus, 526 N.W.2d 328, 331 (Iowa 1995).

Here Dier specifically alleges that "the Defendant knew that the Plaintiff was not the biological father of the child." Thus, he has alleged scienter.

5. *Intent to deceive.* We have held that the intent to deceive element, like the scienter element, may be proved in one of two ways: "by proof that the speaker (1) has actual knowledge of the falsity of the representation or (2) speaks in reckless disregard of whether those representations are true or false." *Rosen*, 539 N.W.2d at 350.

Dier alleges that Peters not only knew he was not the biological father, but "used this assertion to secure monies from [him]." These allegations are sufficient to survive a motion to dismiss on the intent to deceive element. Dier has also bolstered his petition with the further allegation that Peters only announced later that Dier was not the child's biological father out of fear Dier would get custody of the child following a child custody evaluator's report.

6. *Justifiable reliance.* To bring a fraud claim, the plaintiff must have justifiably relied on the false representation. "[T]he justified standard followed in Iowa means the reliance does not necessarily need to conform to the standard of a reasonably prudent person, but depends on the qualities and characteristics of the particular

plaintiff and the specific surrounding circumstances." *Id.* Still, the individual to whom the fraudulent misrepresentation is made is "'required to use his senses, and cannot recover if he blindly relies on a misrepresentation the falsity of which would be patent to him if he had utilized his opportunity to make a cursory examination or investigation.'" *Lockard*, 287 N.W.2d at 878 (quoting Restatement (Second) of Torts § 541 cmt. a, at 89).

Dier alleges that Peters told him he was the child's biological father, and that "based upon th[is] representation," he "provided for the child, provided for the Defendant and engaged in litigation . . . as to the custody of the child." At the pleading stage, these allegations are sufficient. It is true that a paternity test could have established at the outset whether Dier was the child's father, notwithstanding any representation by Peters. But we are unwilling to hold as a matter of law that a putative father can never rely on a mother's representation that he is the father and must immediately insist upon paternity testing. Dier's allegations are adequate on the justifiable reliance element.

7. *Proximate cause.* Proximate cause "address[es] the question whether the losses that in fact resulted from the reliance were connected to the misrepresentation in a way to which the law attaches legal significance." *Spreitzer*, 779 N.W.2d at 740.

Dier alleges that he provided financial support and incurred the expense of custody litigation "based upon the representations made by the Defendant." These allegations are sufficient to plead proximate cause. Not only does Dier allege he spent money based on the misrepresentation, but common sense tells us that the misrepresentation increased the likelihood he would spend this money.

8. *Damages.* "A showing of resulting injury or damages is an element in a fraudulent misrepresentation case." Sanford v. Meadow Gold Dairies, Inc., 534 N.W.2d 410, 413 (Iowa 1995). Fraud that does not result in an ascertainable injury is not actionable.

As damages, Dier seeks reimbursement of financial support provided to Peters and the minor child and expenses incurred during the custody litigation. These items are out-of-pocket expenses that are generally considered recoverable damages in a fraud case, the theory here being that Dier would not have incurred these expenses but for the misrepresentation.

However, we have consistently held that "[a] successful party ordinarily cannot recover attorney fees unless they are authorized by statute or agreement." Audus v. Sabre Commc'ns Corp., 554 N.W.2d 868, 874 (Iowa 1996). Yet we have long recognized an exception to this rule when a person, due to the tort of another, is required to protect his interests by bringing or defending an action against a third person. In such cases, we have allowed the plaintiff to recover his or her attorney fees in the third-party action from the tortfeasor. This view is in accord with the Restatement (Second) of Torts section 914(2) . . .

Dier has alleged that he was forced to engage in custody litigation as a result of Peters' fraudulent misrepresentation. But the exception to the general rule noted above does not apply because the custody action was against Peters, not a third party. Therefore, to the extent Dier is seeking the recovery of his costs and attorneys' fees in the earlier litigation with Peters, this request seems to fall outside the scope of historically recoverable fraud damages.

With the foregoing exception, Dier has not alleged, or asked this court to adopt, a new cause of action or theory of recovery. Rather, he has stated a claim for traditional common law fraud.... Although the facts in this case are somewhat novel, Dier has alleged a well-recognized civil wrong without contorting any of the elements to conform to his facts. We have said that "tribunals [should have] the liberty to deal with [fraud] in whatever form it may present itself." *Rosen*, 539 N.W.2d at 349.

...

B. Public Policy. Despite the apparent fit between this case and common law fraud, defendant contends that judicial recognition of a cause of action for paternity fraud would be contrary to Iowa public policy. She relies on the Nebraska Supreme Court's decision in *Day*, a case where a father sought recovery of court-ordered child support he had been required to pay from 1991 to 1999 for a child who had been born in 1987 while he was married to the child's mother. 653 N.W.2d at 477. There the Nebraska Supreme Court reasoned:

> Robert's fraud and assumpsit claims are for Robin's misrepresentation that led Robert to make investments of time, emotion, and money in Adam that he would not have made had he known that Adam was not his biological son. In effect, Robert is saying, "He is not my son; I want my money back." Robert's fraud and assumpsit causes of action focus on the burdens of the parent-child relationship, while ignoring the benefits of the relationship. We do not believe that having a close and loving relationship "imposed" on one because of a misrepresentation of biological fatherhood is the type of "harm" that the law should attempt to remedy.
>
> ...

Id. at 479 (internal citations omitted).

While these concerns are legitimate, we are not ultimately persuaded by them. For one thing, O.D. is not fifteen years old, like the child in *Day*, but three. We are not persuaded that allowing the present cause of action to go forward would impose additional stress on the child, who is not a party to the case, and likely need not participate in it or even be aware of it. It is true that Dier's success in the litigation could diminish the resources that Peters has available in the future to support O.D., but this would be true of any lawsuit against Peters. We have never afforded parents a general defense from tort liability on the ground they need all their money to raise their children.

Also, we need to consider the public policy implications of an opposite ruling. We recognize fraud as a cause of action partly to deter lying. One good reason to allow fraud claims to go forward in the area of paternity fraud is to avoid the situation that has allegedly arisen here.

. . .

This state has a recognized public policy interest in providing a remedy for fraud. As an Illinois court reasoned in allowing a paternity fraud claim to go forward, "public policy does not serve to protect people engaging in behavior such as that with which plaintiff's complaint charges" nor does it "allow defendant[s] to use [their children] to avoid responsibility for the consequences of [their] alleged deception." Koelle v. Zwiren, 284 Ill.App.3d 778, 220 Ill.Dec. 51, 672 N.E.2d 868, 875 (1996). For the foregoing reasons, we conclude that allowing Dier's claim to go forward would not be contrary to public policy.

Notes

Rule 9(b). Rule 9(b) of the Federal Rules of Civil Procedure requires that when a party alleges fraud or mistake, "the party must state with particularity the circumstances constituting fraud or mistake. Malice, intent, knowledge, and other conditions of a person's mind may be alleged generally."

Representation of opinion. To what extent can an opinion amount to a false misrepresentation? Much like in the case of defamation, an opinion may be actionable as a misrepresentation if there are undisclosed facts known to the defendant that are incompatible with that opinion. So, the statement that "Alice is a safe driver" may be actionable as a false representation if the speaker knows that Alice has multiple recent citations for reckless driving but does not disclose that fact. *See* Restatement (Second) of Torts § 539. This is likely to be the case where the speaker "is understood to have special knowledge of facts unknown to the recipient." *Id.* cmt. b.

To what extent is one justified in relying upon a statement of opinion? For example, is one justified in relying upon a statement by a salesperson that "this car is a great deal"? That "this car is in good shape"? *See* Restatement (Second) of Torts §§ 539, 542.

Representation of intention. A statement about one's intention to do an act in the future is not actionable unless one does not actually have that intention. *Id.* § 530.

Damages. In the case of a fraudulent misrepresentation, a plaintiff is entitled to receive

> (a) the difference between the value of what he has received in the transaction and its purchase price or other value given for it; and
>
> (b) pecuniary loss suffered otherwise as a consequence of the recipient's reliance upon the misrepresentation.

Id. § 549(1). Punitive damages may also be available. *See* Echols v. Beauty Built Homes, Inc., 647 P.2d 629, 632 (Ariz. 1982).

Problem 17.1. Luis purchased the properties so that they could serve as wellness centers, which provide counseling, family mediation services, and yoga instruction. When Luis looked at the first property, he told Ruth about his plans and asked her about the neighborhood. Ruth replied, "It's a nice, quiet neighborhood." The neighborhood actually is generally quiet, but for the trains that pass nearby every hour for roughly five minutes at a time. Is Ruth's statement actionable as a misrepresentation?

Problem 17.2. Luis told Ruth that, given the nature of Luis' wellness center, it was important to him that clients, counselors, and instructors could interact in near-total peace and quiet. Assuming Ruth's statement was actionable as a misrepresentation, was it material?

Problem 17.3. While Luis was first looking at the first property, Ruth described some of the renovations she had undertaken and mentioned that she had recently installed a new hot water heater. This was not true, and the hot water heater had to be replaced several weeks after Luis purchased the property. A quick look into the property's utility closet on Luis' part would have revealed that the hot water was old and showings signs of rust. Assuming Luis relied on Ruth's misrepresentation regarding the water heater, was his reliance justified?

2. Nondisclosure, Omission, and Concealment as Misrepresentation of Fact

Matthews v. Kincaid

746 P.2d 470 (Alaska 1987)

MATTHEWS, Justice.

Appellant Matt Matthews listed his four-plex for sale with Century 21 Heritage Homes & Investments, where he was a real estate broker. The property had no off-street parking. Matthews filled out a listing agreement, in which he left the space next to "parking units" blank. He submitted an "as-built" survey of the lot, which showed no available parking. He also submitted a subdivision plat, which clearly distinguished his lot from adjacent lots with off-street parking.

Appellee, Suzanne Kincaid, purchased the property for $155,000. Kincaid never spoke to Matthews, but dealt with another Century 21 agent, Diane Albert. When Albert first showed Kincaid the four-plex, she assured Kincaid that parking was available in the parking lot of the six-plex next door. Kincaid thought that this was an odd arrangement, as the lot seemed too small for ten cars, and was separated from the four-plex by a chain link fence. However, Albert repeated her representation as to parking when she and Kincaid visited the four-plex a second time.

Albert subsequently contacted Matthews to determine whether parking was available for the four-plex. Matthews gave her the "pat answer" that he furnished to all prospective tenants, buyers, and agents: that parking was available on the street for 22 out of 24 hours a day. There was conflicting testimony at trial as to whether Albert later communicated this information to Kincaid. Albert claimed that she did correct her earlier misrepresentations as to off-street parking. Kincaid disagreed and testified that she believed that the lot next door was available for parking when she closed the sale.

After she purchased the property, one of Kincaid's tenants told her that they were being told not to park in the lot next door. About a year after the purchase, the city closed the street on which the property was located to parking and towed away several of the tenants' cars. The property was subsequently foreclosed by the holder of the first deed of trust which Kincaid had assumed.

Kincaid subsequently brought suit against Matthews, Albert, and Century 21, seeking damages for the fraudulent or negligent misrepresentation that the property contained off-street parking. She settled with Albert and Century 21 prior to trial. The case proceeded to trial against Matthews alone on three theories: first, that he committed fraud; second, that he negligently misrepresented the availability of parking; and third, that he was legally responsible for the misrepresentations made by his agent, Diane Albert. A jury found that Matthews committed both fraudulent and negligent misrepresentation, and awarded Kincaid a total of $98,258.20 in damages. The superior court denied Matthews' motions for judgment notwithstanding the verdict and for a new trial.

Matthews appeals, arguing that there was insufficient evidence of misrepresentation or fraud to sustain the jury verdict, or to justify instructions on those subjects.

To prevail in an action for fraudulent or negligent misrepresentation the plaintiff must prove the existence of either an affirmative misrepresentation or an omission where there is a duty to disclose. The parties agree that Matthews made no affirmative misrepresentations. Kincaid therefore had to prove that Matthews had a duty to disclose certain information which he failed to disclose.

The Restatement (Second) of Torts suggests that a duty to disclose will arise in five situations.[3] Each involves facts that are concealed or unlikely to be discovered because of the special relationship between the parties, the course of their dealings,

---

3. Section 551(2) provides:

(2) One party to a business transaction is under a duty to exercise reasonable care to disclose to the other before the transaction is consummated,

(a) matters known to him that the other is entitled to know because of a fiduciary or other similar relation of trust and confidence between them; and

(b) matters known to him that he knows to be necessary to prevent his partial or ambiguous statement of the facts from being misleading; and

or the nature of the fact itself. A duty to disclose is rarely imposed where the parties deal at arm's length and where the information is the type which the buyer would be expected to discover by ordinary inspection and inquiry.

In this case the lack of off-street parking is an obvious fact which the ordinary purchaser would be expected to discover, by ordinary inspection and inquiry, before she bought the property advertised for sale. Any person who viewed the property could see that there was no parking area on Matthews' lot. Although there was a parking area in front of the multi-unit dwelling next door, it was too small to accommodate the tenants of both buildings. Further, the area was separated from Matthews' lot by a chain link fence, and therefore was not easily mistaken for Matthews' property.

Furthermore, the parties did not enjoy a relationship of trust and confidence which might require Matthews to discuss patently obvious facts such as the lack of off-street parking. Matthews and Kincaid never spoke to each other until after the sale. As seller and buyer of commercial real estate, they were bargaining adversaries who dealt entirely through the real estate agent, Diane Albert.

Finally, Matthews took no action likely to mislead Kincaid. The listing agreement that he left with the real estate agent did have a space for parking information, which Matthews left blank. His silence on this matter, however, would not lead a reasonable person to believe that she could park in the neighbor's fenced-off parking lot. Matthews furnished the real estate agent with a lot survey and a subdivision plat which clearly show the dimensions of Matthews' lot. These do not encompass the parking area next door. Thus, Kincaid acted unreasonably if she purchased the property with the belief that she was also purchasing the parking lot next door.

We see no facts which might impose on Matthews an affirmative duty to disclose the lack of off-street parking to Kincaid. The jury thus should not have been instructed on the subjects of fraud and misrepresentation. The verdict holding Matthews liable for nondisclosure is therefore set aside and the case REMANDED for further action consistent with this opinion.[5]

(c) subsequently acquired information that he knows will make untrue or misleading a previous representation that when made was true or believed to be so; and

(d) the falsity of a representation not made with the expectation that it would be acted upon, if he subsequently learns that the other is about to act in reliance upon it in a transaction with him; and

(e) facts basic to the transaction, if he knows that the other is about to enter into it under a mistake as to them, and that the other, because of the relationship between them, the customs of the trade or other objective circumstances, would reasonably expect a disclosure of those facts.

5. The jury returned a special verdict. One provision of the special verdict was an instruction that the issue of Matthews' vicarious liability should not be decided if Matthews was found to be liable for fraud or negligent misrepresentation. Thus, this issue must be considered on remand.

Notes

Objective circumstances imposing a duty to disclose. *Matthews* suggests that a duty to disclose may exist where the objective circumstances make it unlikely that a buyer would discover the fact in question. Under what circumstances would that be the case? One relevant circumstance might be the relative sophistication of the parties. For example, the Wisconsin Supreme Court has explained, "[w]here the vendor is in the real estate business and is skilled and knowledgeable and the purchaser is not, the purchaser is in a poor position to discover a condition which is not readily discernible, and the purchaser may justifiably rely on the knowledge and skill of the vendor." Ollerman v. O'Rourke Co., 288 N.W.2d 95, 107 (Wis. 1980).

Facts basic to the transaction. "A basic fact is a fact that is assumed by the parties as a basis for the transaction itself. It is a fact that goes to the basis, or essence, of the transaction." Restatement (Second) of Torts, § 551 cmt. j.

Omissions. The omission of a fact that essentially renders a statement a half-truth may also amount to a misrepresentation. *See* Jacobson v. Hofgard, 168 F. Supp. 3d 187 (D.D.C. 2016).

Concealment. One who intentionally prevents another from acquiring material information is likewise treated as having made a misrepresentation of fact. Restatement (Second) of Torts, § 550.

Problem 17.4. Assume for purposes of this question only that Ruth was also a lawyer who happened to be representing Luis in an unrelated matter at the time of the transaction. Would Ruth's failure to tell Luis about the presence of the trains at the first property amount to a misrepresentation?

Problem 17.5. Before Luis purchased the second property, he reviewed the Disclosure Statement prepared by Ruth. One question asked, "What type of waste water/sewage system do you have?" Ruth checked boxes to indicate that the property was "connected" to a "Private Sewer." Another part of the Disclosure Statement asked the seller to provide additional information to any answer as necessary, so Ruth attached the wastewater agreement that she originally entered into with the party providing the private sewer services. The agreement was dated more than 10 years prior to the day Ruth completed the Disclosure Statement. The agreement provided that Ruth agreed to pay the party $150 per month for monthly maintenance charges and a $75 a month cleanout charge. Also indicated in the agreement was the supplier's reservation of "the right to adjust the amount annually in a sum not exceeding twenty percent (20%) of the amount paid in the year immediately preceding." When Luis received his first wastewater bill, he was surprised to see that his bill was for almost $1,700. After inquiring further, he learned that the service provider had increased the amount by 20% as provided for in the wastewater agreement every year since the original agreement. The service provider told Luis that he is unwilling to negotiate a new rate.

(a) Could Luis establish that Ruth made a misrepresentation of fact?

(b) If so, was the misrepresentation material?

Problem 17.6. Assume for purposes of this question only that Ruth knew when the train passed by the property and that quiet was very important to Luis. So, she scheduled Luis' visit at a time when she knew there would be no train and hustled Luis out of the property just before the train was due. Could Louis establish that Ruth made a misrepresentation of fact?

B. Negligent Misrepresentation

As its name suggests, the tort of negligent misrepresentation does not require proof of an intent to deceive. The tort most often arises when one party, as part of its business, is negligent in providing information to another and the other party relies to its detriment on the misrepresentation. The first case in this section is one of the earliest and most famous cases involving this general fact pattern. The second illustrates the majority approach with respect to the tort.

1. The Privity Test

Ultramares Corp. v. Touche

174 N.E. 441 (N.Y. 1931)

CARDOZO, C. J.

The action is in tort for damages suffered through the misrepresentations of accountants, the first cause of action being for misrepresentations that were merely negligent, and the second for misrepresentations charged to have been fraudulent.

In January, 1924, the defendants, a firm of public accountants, were employed by Fred Stern & Co., Inc., to prepare and certify a balance sheet exhibiting the condition of its business as of December 31, 1923. They had been employed at the end of each of the three years preceding to render a like service. Fred Stern & Co., Inc., which was in substance Stern himself, was engaged in the importation and sale of rubber. To finance its operations, it required extensive credit and borrowed large sums of money from banks and other lenders. All this was known to the defendants. The defendants knew also that in the usual course of business the balance sheet when certified would be exhibited by the Stern Company to banks, creditors, stockholders, purchasers, or sellers, according to the needs of the occasion, as the basis of financial dealings. Accordingly, when the balance sheet was made up, the defendants supplied the Stern Company with thirty-two copies certified with serial numbers as counterpart originals. Nothing was said as to the persons to whom these counterparts would be shown or the extent or number of the transactions in which they would be used. In particular there was no mention of the plaintiff, a corporation doing business chiefly as a factor, which till then had never made advances to the Stern Company, though it had sold merchandise in small amounts. The range of the transactions in which a certificate of audit might be expected to play a part was as indefinite and wide as the possibilities of the business that was mirrored in the summary.

By February 26, 1924, the audit was finished and the balance sheet made up. It stated assets in the sum of $2,550,671.88 and liabilities other than capital and surplus in the sum of $1,479,956.62, thus showing a net worth of $1,070,715.26. [In reality, "The books had been falsified by those in charge of the business," and the corporation was insolvent. The plaintiff made several loans to Stern on the basis of the audit showing Stern to be in sound financial condition. Eventually, Stern went bankrupt. The plaintiff brought suit against Touche to recover the loss of the value of the loans. The jury returned a verdict in favor of the plaintiff for $187,576.32 on its negligence claim. The trial judge dismissed the plaintiff's fraudulent misrepresentation claim.]

We think the evidence supports a finding that the audit was negligently made, though in so saying we put aside for the moment the question whether negligence, even if it existed, was a wrong to the plaintiff. [The court then explained how the audit was conducted.]

If the defendants owed a duty to the plaintiff to act with the same care that would have been due under a contract of employment, a jury was at liberty to find a verdict of negligence upon a showing of a scrutiny so imperfect and perfunctory. No doubt the extent to which inquiry must be pressed beyond appearances is a question of judgment, as to which opinions will often differ. No doubt the wisdom that is born after the event will engender suspicion and distrust when old acquaintance and good repute may have silenced doubt at the beginning. All this is to be weighed by a jury in applying its standard of behavior, the state of mind, and conduct of the reasonable man. Even so, the adverse verdict, when rendered, imports an alignment of the weights in their proper places in the balance and a reckoning thereafter. The reckoning was not wrong upon the evidence before us, if duty be assumed.

We are brought to the question of duty, its origin and measure.

The defendants owed to their employer a duty imposed by law to make their certificate without fraud, and a duty growing out of contract to make it with the care and caution proper to their calling. Fraud includes the pretense of knowledge when knowledge there is none. To creditors and investors to whom the employer exhibited the certificate, the defendants owed a like duty to make it without fraud, since there was notice in the circumstances of its making that the employer did not intend to keep it to himself. A different question develops when we ask whether they owed a duty to these to make it without negligence. If liability for negligence exists, a thoughtless slip or blunder, the failure to detect a theft or forgery beneath the cover of deceptive entries, may expose accountants to a liability in an indeterminate amount for an indeterminate time to an indeterminate class. The hazards of a business conducted on these terms are so extreme as to enkindle doubt whether a flaw may not exist in the implication of a duty that exposes to these consequences....

The assault upon the citadel of privity is proceeding in these days apace. How far the inroads shall extend is now a favorite subject of juridical discussion. In the field of the law of contract there has been a gradual widening of the doctrine of Lawrence v. Fox, 20 N. Y. 268, until today the beneficiary of a promise, clearly designated as such, is seldom left without a remedy. Seaver v. Ransom, 224 N. Y. 233, 238, 120 N. E. 639, 2 A. L. R. 1187. Even in that field, however, the remedy is narrower where the beneficiaries of the promise are indeterminate or general. Something more must then appear than an intention that the promise shall redound to the benefit of the public or to that of a class of indefinite extension. The promise must be such as to 'bespeak the assumption of a duty to make reparation directly to the individual members of the public if the benefit is lost.' Moch Co. v. Rensselaer Water Co., 247 N. Y. 160, 164, 159 N. E. 896, 897, 62 A. L. R. 1199; American Law Institute, Restatement of the Law of Contracts, § 145. In the field of the law of torts a manufacturer who is negligent in the manufacture of a chattel in circumstances pointing to an unreasonable risk of serious bodily harm to those using it thereafter may be liable for negligence though privity is lacking between manufacturer and user. MacPherson v. Buick Motor Co., 217 N. Y. 382, 111 N.E. 1050; American Law Institute, Restatement of the Law of Torts, § 262. A force or instrument of harm having been launched with potentialities of danger manifest to the eye of prudence, the one who launches it is under a duty to keep it within bounds. Moch Co. v. Rensselaer Water Co., supra, at page 168 of 247 N. Y., 159 N. E. 896, 898. Even so, the question is still open whether the potentialities of danger that will charge with liability are confined to harm to the person, or include injury to property. In either view, however, what is released or set in motion is a physical force. We are now asked to say that a like liability attaches to the circulation of a thought or a release of the explosive power resident in words.

[N]othing in our previous decisions commits us to a holding of liability for negligence in the circumstances of the case at hand, and that such liability, if recognized, will be an extension of the principle of those decisions to different conditions, even if more or less analogous. The question then is whether such an extension shall be made.

The extension, if made, will so expand the field of liability for negligent speech as to make it nearly, if not quite, coterminous with that of liability for fraud....

We have said that the duty to refrain from negligent representation would become coincident or nearly so with the duty to refrain from fraud if this action could be maintained. A representation, even though knowingly false, does not constitute ground for an action of deceit unless made with the intent to be communicated to the persons or class of persons who act upon it to their prejudice. Affirmance of this judgment would require us to hold that all or nearly all the persons so situated would suffer an impairment of an interest legally protected if the representation had been negligent. We speak of all 'or nearly all,' for cases can be imagined where a casual response, made in circumstances insufficient to indicate that care should be expected, would permit recovery for fraud if willfully deceitful. Cases of fraud between persons so circumstanced are, however, too infrequent and exceptional to make the radii greatly different if the fields of liability for negligence and deceit be figured as concentric circles. The like may be said of the possibility that the negligence of the injured party, contributing to the result, may avail to overcome the one remedy, though unavailing to defeat the other.

Liability for negligence if adjudged in this case will extend to many callings other than an auditor's. Lawyers who certify their opinion as to the validity of municipal or corporate bonds, with knowledge that the opinion will be brought to the notice of the public, will become liable to the investors, if they have overlooked a statute or a decision, to the same extent as if the controversy were one between client and adviser. Title companies insuring titles to a tract of land, with knowledge that at an approaching auction the fact that they have insured will be stated to the bidders, will become liable to purchasers who may wish the benefit of a policy without payment of a premium. These illustrations may seem to be extreme, but they go little, if any, farther than we are invited to go now. Negligence, moreover, will have one standard when viewed in relation to the employer, and another and at times a stricter standard when viewed in relation to the public. Explanations that might seem plausible, omissions that might be reasonable, if the duty is confined to the employer, conducting a business that presumably at least is not a fraud upon his creditors, might wear another aspect if an independent duty to be suspicious even of one's principal is owing to investors. 'Every one making a promise having the quality of a contract will be under a duty to the promisee by virtue of the promise, but under another duty, apart from contract, to an indefinite number of potential beneficiaries when performance has begun. The assumption of one relation will mean the involuntary assumption of a series of new relations, inescapably hooked together' Moch Co. v. Rensselaer Water Co., supra, at page 168 of 247 N. Y., 159 N. E. 896, 899. 'The law does not spread its protection so far' Robins Dry Dock & Repair Co. v. Flint, supra, at page 309 of 275 U. S., 48 S. Ct. 134, 135.

Our holding does not emancipate accountants from the consequences of fraud. It does not relieve them if their audit has been so negligent as to justify a finding that they had no genuine belief in its adequacy, for this again is fraud. It does no more than say that, if less than this is proved, if there has been neither reckless misstatement nor insincere profession of an opinion, but only honest blunder, the ensuing liability for negligence is one that is bounded by the contract, and is to be enforced between the parties by whom the contract has been made. We doubt whether the average business man receiving a certificate without paying for it, and receiving it merely as one among a multitude of possible investors, would look for anything more.

[The court concluded there was sufficient evidence to permit a jury to find in favor of the plaintiffs on the fraudulent misrepresentation claim.]

Note

Subsequent developments in New York. The *Ultramares* privity test has subsequently been expanded in New York to include relationships that "sufficiently approach[] privity." Credit Alliance Corp. v. Arthur Andersen & Co., 483 N.E.2d 110 (N.Y. 1985). In the context of an accounting firm that provided inaccurate financial information, the New York Court of Appeals in *Credit Alliance Corp.* held that:

> [b]efore accountants may be held liable in negligence to noncontractual parties who rely to their detriment on inaccurate financial reports, certain prerequisites must be satisfied: (1) the accountants must have been aware that the financial reports were to be used for a particular purpose or purposes; (2) in the furtherance of which a known party or parties was intended to rely; and (3) there must have been some conduct on the part of the accountants linking them to that party or parties, which evinces the accountants' understanding of that party or parties' reliance.

Id. at 118. A few other jurisdictions have adopted this newer "near privity" rule from New York. *See, e.g.*, Colonial Bank v. Ridley & Schweigert, 551 So. 2d 390 (Ala. 1989).

2. The Section 552 Test

Blue Bell, Inc. v. Peat, Marwick, Mitchell & Co.

715 S.W.2d 408 (Tex. Ct. App.—Dallas 1986)

AKIN, Justice.

. . . Blue Bell, Inc., appeals from a summary judgment granted in favor of Peat, Marwick, Mitchell, & Co. ("PMM"). Blue Bell had sued PMM, alleging four causes of action: negligent misrepresentation; fraud; breach of warranty; and breach of fiduciary duty. PMM moved for summary judgment, and its motion was granted by the trial court. On appeal, Blue Bell contends that the trial court erred in granting summary judgment as to each of its causes of action. We agree that the trial court erred in granting summary judgment as to Blue Bell's negligent misrepresentation cause of action and, accordingly, reverse and remand this cause for trial on the merits. We affirm the trial court's judgment as to Blue Bell's other causes of action.

In 1972 Blue Bell, a clothing manufacturer located in North Carolina, established an account for and began extending credit to Myers Department Stores, Inc., a Texas corporation based in Arlington, Texas ("Myers (Texas)"). Blue Bell and Myers (Texas) apparently enjoyed a satisfactory business relationship. In 1980 Myers (Texas) and an affiliated company, Myers Department Stores of Fort Worth,

Inc. ("Myers (Fort Worth)"), were acquired by a newly-formed Delaware corporation, Myers Department Stores, Inc. ("Myers (Delaware)"). The Myers entities will be collectively referred to as "Myers."

Shortly after the acquisition, PMM was engaged by Myers (Delaware) to audit the financial records of Myers (Delaware) and its subsidiary corporations, Myers (Texas) and Myers (Fort Worth), as of and for the fiscal year ended February 1, 1981. PMM audited two sets of financial statements. On April 24, 1981, PMM completed the field work on its audit examination of the combined financial statements1 of Myers (Texas) and Myers (Fort Worth). On May 29, 1981, PMM completed the field work on its audit examination of the consolidated balance sheet of Myers (Delaware) and its subsidiaries, Myers (Texas) and Myers (Fort Worth). On June 3, 1981, PMM forwarded to Myers the consolidated balance sheet, the combined financial statements, and accountants' reports on both statements. Several days later PMM made a minor revision in the combined financial statements and, at Myers' request, provided seventy copies of the revised statements to replace the twenty-five copies of the original statements.

Myers furnished the original and revised combined financial statements, and the accompanying accountants' report, to Blue Bell. Blue Bell allegedly relied upon these documents in extending substantial amounts of credit to Myers (Texas). These extensions of credit continued until July 23, 1982. On November 4, 1982, Myers filed for bankruptcy. Blue Bell recovered through bankruptcy proceedings only a portion of the balance due on its account with Myers (Texas). Consequently, Blue Bell filed suit against PMM.

1. Negligent Misrepresentation

We consider first Blue Bell's contention that PMM failed to conclusively establish that it owed no legal duty to Blue Bell. In response, PMM argues that as a matter of law it owed no legal duty to Blue Bell because there was no privity of contract between them. We disagree with PMM. This contention was decided against PMM's position in *Shatterproof Glass Corp. v. James*, 466 S.W.2d 873 (Tex.Civ.App.—Fort Worth 1971, writ ref'd n.r.e.). There the court expressly held that, within the scope defined by section 552 of the Restatement (Second) of Torts,

> an accountant may be held liable to third parties who rely upon financial statements, audits, etc., prepared by the accountant in cases where the latter fails to exercise ordinary care in the preparation of such statements, audits, etc., and the third party because of such reliance suffers financial loss or damages.

Id. at 880. Section 552 of the *Restatement* provides, in pertinent part:

> (1) One who, in the course of his business, profession or employment, or in any other transaction in which he has a pecuniary interest, supplies false information for the guidance of others in their business transactions, is subject to liability for pecuniary loss caused to them by their justifiable reliance upon the information, if he fails to exercise reasonable care or competence in obtaining or communicating the information.

(2) Except as stated in Subsection (3), the liability stated in Subsection (1) is limited to loss suffered:

(a) by the person or one of a limited group of persons for whose benefit and guidance he intends to supply the information or knows that the recipient intends to supply it; and

(b) through reliance upon it in a transaction that he intends the information to influence or knows that the recipient so intends or in a substantially similar transaction.

RESTATEMENT (SECOND) OF TORTS § 552 (1977) (emphasis added).

Initially, we note that, although the court in *Shatterproof Glass* relied upon adoption of the quoted section of the *Restatement*, it also quoted extensively from one commentator who advocates even broader liability than that set forth in Section 552. *See Comment: "Auditors' Responsibility for Misrepresentation: Inadequate Protection for Users of Financial Statements,"* 44 Washington Law Rev. 139 (1968). In this comment, the author supports liability of an auditor to all those whom he should reasonably expect to rely on his certification of financial statements. *Id.* at 191–92. Many other law-review writers have also advocated that the test for the scope of an accountant's liability should extend beyond that propounded by the Restatement to include all relying third parties who were reasonably foreseeable to the accountant at the time he made his report. Furthermore, three jurisdictions have recently adopted foreseeability as the test for liability of accountants for negligence to third parties. International Mortgage Co. v. John P. Butler Accountancy Corp., 177 Cal.App.3d 806, 223 Cal.Rptr. 218 (4th Dist.1986); Citizens State Bank v. Timm, Schmidt & Co., 13 Wis.2d 376, 335 N.W.2d 361 (1983); H. Rosenblum, Inc. v. Adler, 93 N.J. 324, 461 A.2d 138 (1983). Although we find the reasoning of the cases and commentators urging adoption of the foreseeability test persuasive, we need not decide whether that test should be adopted in this case.

Instead, we look to section 552 of the Restatement (Second) and decide that, as we construe this section, a fact issue exists as to whether Blue Bell falls within the "limited class" as used in that section. Although we need not go so far today as to adopt the broad standard of foreseeability advocated by some of the commentators, we conclude that the apparent attempt in comment h. under this section to limit the class of third parties who may recover to those actually and specifically known by the defendant is too artificial a distinction. Consequently, we adopt a less restrictive interpretation of section 552 than would be indicated by the comments thereunder, particularly Comment h., illustration 10.* To allow liability to turn on the fortuitous

* Editor's note: This illustration provides as follows:

10. A, an independent public accountant, is retained by B Company to conduct an annual audit of the customary scope for the corporation and to furnish his opinion on the corporation's financial statements. A is not informed of any intended use of the financial statements; but A knows that the financial statements, accompanied by an

occurrence that the accountant's client specifically mentions a person or class of persons who are to receive the reports, when the accountant may have that same knowledge as a matter of business practice, is too tenuous a distinction for us to adopt as a rule of law. Instead, we hold that if, under current business practices and the circumstances of that case, an accountant preparing audited financial statements knows or should know that such statements will be relied upon by a limited class of persons, the accountant may be liable for injuries to members of that class relying on his certification of the audited reports.

Among the factors relevant to this issue is the fact that Blue Bell was a trade creditor of Myers at the time PMM prepared the financial statements in question and that PMM was, therefore, aware of Blue Bell as one of a limited number of existing trade creditors who would, in all probability, be receiving copies of the financial statements. Furthermore, PMM supplied Myers with seventy copies of the financial statements, indicating knowledge by PMM that third parties would be given the reports. We hold that a current trade creditor is one of a limited class of people contemplated by the language in the *Restatement*. Consequently, in deciding whether PMM "had a duty to Blue Bell," a fact finder must determine whether PMM knew or should have known that members of such a limited class would receive copies of the audited financial statements it prepared.

...

Next, Blue Bell contends that PMM failed to establish as a matter of law that it did not provide false information. PMM takes the contrary position, arguing that the summary judgment evidence conclusively showed that the data on the combined financial statements was accurate and that neither the combined financial statements nor the accompanying accountants' report contained any misrepresentations. We agree with Blue Bell.

The accountants' report contained the following statement:

> In our opinion, the aforementioned 1981 combined financial statements present fairly the combined financial position of Myers Department Stores, Inc. (a Texas corporation) and affiliated company as of February 1, 1981 and the combined results of their operations and the changes in their financial position for the year then ended, in conformity with generally accepted accounting principles applied on a basis consistent with that of the preceding year.

---

auditor's opinion, are customarily used in a wide variety of financial transactions by the corporation and that they may be relied upon by lenders, investors, shareholders, creditors, purchasers and the like, in numerous possible kinds of transactions. In fact B Company uses the financial statements and accompanying auditor's opinion to obtain a loan from X Bank. Because of A's negligence, he issues an unqualifiedly favorable opinion upon a balance sheet that materially misstates the financial position of B Company, and through reliance upon it X Bank suffers pecuniary loss. A is not liable to X Bank.

Blue Bell argues that the combined financial statements alone did not "present fairly" an accurate picture of the financial situation of Myers (Texas) and Myers (Fort Worth) and that, in order to obtain the true picture, reference to the consolidated balance sheet was necessary. . . . We note that there is summary judgment evidence in the record from Bernard Augen, Blue Bell's expert, that the combined statements were misleading and that the "consolidated financial statement was necessary for a fair presentation" of the true financial situation of Myers (Texas) and Myers (Fort Worth). Furthermore, with respect to the note concerning the pledge of the subsidiaries' assets to secure the parent's indebtedness, Augen testified that despite this note the combined statements are misleading because they give a reader no way of knowing:

> (a) that the parent company had no assets other than its investment in subsidiaries, (b) that the parent company had a debt of $2,900,000, of which $1,385,417 was due within one year and could only be paid from funds generated from the subsidiaries or from additional borrowings, and (c) that interest payments on the above debt would have to be paid from funds generated from the subsidiaries, (d) that the equity of the consolidated group was approximately $2,500,000 less than that shown in the subsidiaries' balance sheet even though there were assets other than the subsidiaries, and (e) that rather than operating at a profit of approximately $545,000 as shown on the statement, the stores were probably operating at a loss after interest, amortization of leasehold costs and other expenses that were booked on the parent. Without disclosure of this information, a reader had a right to assume that the combined financial statement fairly presented the financial position and results of operation for the Myers Department Stores.

Accordingly, we hold that PMM failed to negate a fact issue concerning whether PMM provided false or misleading information.

Next, Blue Bell contends that PMM did not conclusively establish that PMM exercised reasonable care in the preparation of the combined financial statements. We agree with this contention. Bernard Augen stated in his affidavit that the combined financial statements "did not appear to have been prepared in accordance with generally accepted accounting principles" and provided an example supporting his conclusion. Because we must take evidence favorable to the non-movant, Blue Bell, as true, we conclude that a fact issue was raised as to whether PMM exercised reasonable care in preparing the combined financial statements.

Lastly, with respect to its negligent misrepresentation cause of action, Blue Bell contends that PMM failed to establish as a matter of law that Blue Bell's reliance on the combined financial statements and the accompanying accountants' report was not justified . . . in so relying and that such alleged negligence was the sole proximate cause of Blue Bell's damages. We agree that a fact issue has been raised regarding these questions by the deposition testimony of Joe Abston, the PMM partner in charge of the Myers' audit [who testified that a party might make a decision as to whether to extend credit based on either the combined financial statement or the consolidated financial statement.] In view of this testimony, we hold that PMM failed to negate a fact issue as to whether Blue Bell's reliance on the combined financial statements was justified and, consequently, whether Blue Bell was contributorily negligent in so relying.

Since PMM has failed to negate fact issues with respect to each element of Blue Bell's negligent misrepresentation cause of action, we hold that the trial court erred in granting summary judgment as to this cause of action.

2. Fraud

Blue Bell contends that the trial court erred in granting summary judgment for PMM on Blue Bell's cause of action for fraud. We disagree. The elements of actionable fraud are: (1) that a material representation was made; (2) that it was false; (3) that, when the speaker made it, he knew it was false or made it recklessly without any knowledge of its truth and as a positive assertion; (4) that the speaker made it with the intention that it should be acted upon by the party; (5) that the party acted in reliance upon it; and (6) that the party thereby suffered injury. We hold that the summary judgment evidence conclusively established that PMM did not make the representation at issue with the intention that it should be acted upon by Blue Bell. Accordingly, we hold that the trial court did not err in granting summary judgment as to Blue Bell's cause of action for fraud.

. . .

The mere fact that it should be known that another will rely upon a misrepresentation does not, of itself, establish that the misrepresentation was made with the intent to induce reliance. The "intent" element of a fraud action imports a significantly greater degree of purposeful conduct than does the "foreseeability" element of a negligence action. Apart from its argument that "foreseeability" of reliance establishes the requisite intent, Blue Bell adduced no summary judgment evidence tending to show that PMM intended to induce Blue Bell's reliance on PMM's representations. Accordingly, there was no genuine issue of fact raised as to this element of Blue Bell's cause of action for fraud.

Notes

Majority approach. Section 552 represents the majority approach in negligent misrepresentation cases. In a subsequent case, the Texas Supreme Court adopted section 552 as written, thus impliedly overruling *Blue Bell*'s modification. *See McCamish, Martin, Brown & Loeffler v. F.E. Appling Interests*, 991 S.W.2d 787 (Tex. 1999). Note also that *Blue Bell* identified another possible approach to determining the potential class of plaintiffs, one based on foreseeability. Which of these approaches do you prefer?

Defendants in other contexts. Section 552 has been applied in a variety of contexts beyond the audit scenario presented in *Blue Bell, Inc. See* Greycas, Inc. v. Proud, 826 F.2d 1560 (7th Cir. 1987) (lawyer negligently failed to conduct title search and reported misinformation to client); Hagans v. Woodruff, 830 S.W.2d 732, 736 (Tex.

App.—Houston 1992) (real estate broker who made misrepresentations regarding the quality of a house); Cook Consultants, Inc. v. Larson, 700 S.W.2d 231, 234 (Tex. App.—Dallas 1985) (surveyor incorrectly reported that house was within property line).

Justifiable reliance and comparative fault. A plaintiff whose reliance was unreasonable may be prohibited from recovering in a negligent misrepresentation action. Unlike in the case of fraudulent misrepresentation, justifiable reliance in the negligent misrepresentation context involves an objective standard of reasonableness. *See* Straub v. Vaisman & Co., 540 F.2d 591, 598 (3d Cir. 1976).

Problem 17.7. Esther, one of Luis' employees, tagged along with Luis when Luis went to look at one of the properties for a second time. Ruth's real estate agent, Mary, showed Esther and Luis around the property. Esther explained that she might end up living close to whichever building Luis purchased since she would manage one of the properties. She explained that her child had special needs at school, so she wanted to know whether the area was zoned for a particular school, which was known to have the resources necessary to care for children like Esther's. Mary replied that the area was zoned for that particular school. Relying upon the agent's representation, Esther bought a home nearby. However, the agent was mistaken about the school, and the school that Esther's child attended lack the necessary resources. Esther was forced to seek a transfer to the school she originally wanted her child to attend and had to pay someone to transport her child to and from the school and care for the child after school. Esther wishes to sue Mary for negligent misrepresentation. What possible obstacles do you foresee in a jurisdiction that has adopted § 552?

Problem 17.8. Sammy, one of Luis' friends, worked in the local county assessor's office. Luis was interested in the property values of nearby lots, so he asked Sammy if he could provide information about those property values. Sammy's job involved doing this sort of thing for members of the public who paid a fee, but Sammy agreed to do it for free as a favor to Luis. Unfortunately, Sammy made a mistake when reviewing the information and provided Luis with information about different properties with much higher values. Assume that Luis sues Sammy for negligent misrepresentation in a jurisdiction that has adopted § 552. Does § 552 allow for a claim against Sammy?

Review Question

QuickCar Co. entered into negotiations with Edna to serve as QuickCar's new Vice President of Technology. Edna was not satisfied with QuickCar's initial compensation package, so she proposed that she also be given stock options in the company. The two sides negotiated for another two weeks before finally agreeing on a compensation package that included significant stock options. Unbeknownst to Edna, at the time she first started negotiating about the stock options, QuickCar was in secret discussions with Apex Car Rental about a possible merger agreement by which Apex would buy out QuickCar. QuickCar was not optimistic about this possibility initially, but by the time Edna signed her agreement with QuickCar, QuickCar viewed the odds of a merger as high. QuickCar reached a merger agreement with Apex Car Rental two days after Edna signed her agreement. The merger effectively rendered Edna's stock options worthless. Apex was willing to retain Edna as Vice President of Technology, but the two sides were unable to negotiate a new stock option agreement to replace the old one. Edna quit her job and sued QuickCar on a fraudulent misrepresentation theory. Is she likely to prevail?

Chapter 18

Interference with Contractual Relations

A. The Prima Facie Tort Approach
- Elements of the prima facie case
    - Specific information regarding individual elements
    - Criticisms of the prima facie tort approach
- The role of privilege or justification
    - Specific privileges or justifications
        - Competition
        - Financial interest in the business of another
        - Responsibility for the welfare of another
        - Providing truthful information or honest advice
        - Defendant asserting a bona fide claim.
- Other concepts developed in class or in readings assigned by the professor

B. The Improper Purpose or Improper Means Test
- In general
- Other concepts developed in class or in readings assigned by the professor

C. Decoupling the Interference Torts
- Interference with contract versus interference with prospective contractual relations
    - The prima facie case for interference with contract
    - The prima facie case for interference with prospective contractual relations
        - "Independently wrongful acts"
    - Justifications for the distinction
- Other concepts developed in class or in readings assigned by the professor
- Interference with contract versus interference with contract terminable at will
    - Possible approaches regarding the prima facie case for interference with contracts terminable at will
    - Justifications for the distinction
- Other concepts developed in class or in readings assigned by the professor

Chapter Problem. Kovacs Transportation is in the business of facilitating the transportation of primates and other animals from other countries to the United States. Kovacs' chief competitor is Zaius Transportation.

Interference claims seem easy enough to understand on their face. The paradigmatic case is the 1853 British case of *Lumley v. Gye*, 2 El. & Bl. 216 (1853), in which the defendant persuaded a singer to breach her service contract with the owner of an opera house. The Court of the Queen's Bench held that the defendant was liable for enticing Wagner away. Thus, in the simplest case, when two parties have an existing contractual relationship and a third party interferes with that relationship, causing pecuniary damage, there is a right of recovery.

In practice, however, interference claims have proven to be particularly frustrating to courts and litigants alike. One area of disagreement has been whether to recognize liability where the defendant intended to interfere with a relationship, but did not employ any sort of wrongful means or act from any sort of improper motive. In short, what is it that makes an interference "tortious"? A related question is whether the rule that applies in the case of intentional interference with a contractual relationship should apply in the case of an intentional interference with a *prospective* contractual relationship. The result has been that the law in the field has developed in "an illogical and piecemeal fashion," Lyn L. Stevens, *Interference with Economic Relations—Some Aspects of the Turmoil in the Intentional Torts*, 12 OSGOODE HALL L.J. 595, 595 (1974), and is said to lack "clear principles or doctrinal foundations." Gary Myers, *The Differing Treatment of Efficiency and Competition in Antitrust and Tortious Interference Law*, 77 MINN. L. REV. 1097, 1110 (1993). As such, it is almost impossible to discuss interference claims in terms of majority rules.

Nonetheless, this chapter examines how the law in this area has evolved and where it seems to be heading.

A. The Prima Facie Tort Approach

1. The Prima Facie Case

Imperial Ice Co. v. Rossier

112 P.2d 631 (Cal. 1941)

TRAYNOR, Justice.

The California Consumers Company purchased from S. L. Coker an ice distributing business, inclusive of good will, located in territory comprising the city of Santa Monica and the former city of Sawtelle. In the purchase agreement Coker contracted as follows: 'I do further agree in consideration of said purchase and in connection therewith, that I will not engage in the business of selling and or distributing ice, either directly or indirectly, in the above described territory so long as the purchasers, or anyone deriving title to the good will of said business from said purchasers, shall be engaged in a like business therein.' Plaintiff, the Imperial Ice Company, acquired from the successor in interest of the California Consumers Company full title to this ice distributing business, including the right to enforce the covenant not to compete. Coker subsequently began selling in the same territory in violation of the contract ice supplied to him by a company owned by W. Rossier, J. A. Matheson, and Fred Matheson. Plaintiff thereupon brought this action in the superior court for an injunction to restrain Coker from violating the contract and to restrain Rossier and the Mathesons from inducing Coker to violate the contract. The complaint alleges that Rossier and the Mathesons induced Coker to violate his contract so that they might sell ice to him at a profit. The trial court sustained without leave to amend a demurrer to the complaint of the defendants Rossier and Matheson and gave judgment for those defendants. Plaintiff has appealed from the judgment on the sole ground that the complaint stated a cause of action against the defendants Rossier and the Mathesons for inducing the breach of contract.

The question thus presented to this court is under what circumstances may an action be maintained against a defendant who has induced a third party to violate a contract with the plaintiff.

It is universally recognized that an action will lie for inducing breach of contract by resort to means in themselves unlawful such as libel, slander, fraud, physical violence, or threats of such action. Most jurisdictions also hold that an action will lie for inducing a breach of contract by the use of moral, social, or economic pressures, in themselves lawful, unless there is sufficient justification for such inducement.

Such justification exists when a person induces a breach of contract to protect an interest which has greater social value than insuring the stability of the contract. Thus, a person is justified in inducing the breach of a contract the enforcement of which would be injurious to health, safety, or good morals. The interest of labor in improving working conditions is of sufficient social importance to justify peaceful labor tactics otherwise lawful, though they have the effect of inducing breaches of contracts between employer and employee or employer and customer. In numerous other situations, justification exists depending upon the importance of the interest protected. The presence or absence of ill-will, sometimes referred to as 'malice', is immaterial, except as it indicates whether or not an interest is actually being protected.

It is well established, however, that a person is not justified in inducing a breach of contract simply because he is in competition with one of the parties to the contract and seeks to further his own economic advantage at the expense of the other. Whatever interest society has in encouraging free and open competition by means not in themselves unlawful, contractual stability is generally accepted as of greater importance than competitive freedom. Competitive freedom, however, is of sufficient importance to justify one competitor in inducing a third party to forsake another competitor if no contractual relationship exists between the latter two. A person is likewise free to carry on his business, including reduction of prices, advertising, and solicitation in the usual lawful manner although some third party may be induced thereby to breach his contract with a competitor in favor of dealing with the advertiser. Again, if two parties have separate contracts with a third, each may resort to any legitimate means at his disposal to secure performance of his contract even though the necessary result will be to cause a breach of the other contract. A party may not, however, under the guise of competition actively and affirmatively induce the breach of a competitor's contract in order to secure an economic advantage over that competitor. The act of inducing the breach must be an intentional one. If the actor had no knowledge of the existence of the contract or his actions were not intended to induce a breach, he cannot be held liable though an actual breach results from his lawful and proper acts. . . .

The contract gave to plaintiff the right to sell ice in the stated territory free from the competition of Coker. The defendants, by virtue of their interest in the sale of ice in that territory, were in effect competing with plaintiff. By inducing Coker to violate his contract, as alleged in the complaint, they sought to further their own economic advantage at plaintiff's expense. Such conduct is not justified. Had defendants merely sold ice to Coker without actively inducing him to violate his contract, his distribution of the ice in the forbidden territory in violation of his contract would not then have rendered defendants liable. They may carry on their business of selling ice as usual without incurring liability for breaches of contract by their customers. It is necessary to prove that they intentionally and actively induced the breach. Since the complaint alleges that they did so and asks for in injunction on the grounds that damages would be inadequate, it states a cause of action, and the demurrer should therefore have been overruled.

The judgment is reversed.

Torbett v. Wheeling Dollar Sav. & Trust Co.

314 S.E.2d 166 (W. Va. 1983)

Ms. Torbett was hired by [Wheeling Dollar Savings & Trust] in February, 1969, and in October, 1974, was promoted to trust officer with no salary increase. She was offered a job at another bank in November of that year, informed her employer that she would leave unless she received an immediate raise and an assistant, and Wheeling Dollar agreed to her terms and granted her a twenty-three percent (23%) raise effective November 20. On November 27, she was asked to sign a contract that included [a covenant not to compete by accepting nearby employment for a period of two years].

In December, 1978, Torbett voluntarily quit her job and she alleged she was offered employment with another bank provided that she was safe from Wheeling Dollar's covenant. . . . [T]he Plaintiff knew that the Defendant would attempt to hold her to the contract and take necessary action to prevent her from working, because they had previously taken such steps as to another former employee, therefore, she filed this Complaint and action for declaratory judgment [to prevent defendant from enforcing the covenant. Torbett claimed a loss of her employment opportunity as a result of the covenant.]

The trial court decided that the . . . covenant violated public policy and Torbett was entitled to damages of $35,000 for lost income since she left her job.

The Covenant

[The West Virginia Supreme Court of Appeals held that Wheeling Dollar was not seeking to protect a legitimate interest, and therefore "the absence of such protectible interest makes the covenant unenforceable because it violates public policy."]

Tortious Interference

Wheeling Dollar challenges Torbett's right to get damages: her complaint did not charge that the bank breached her contract, nor did she name any tort committed by it. We can find only one cause of action for damages that could possibly support any recovery by her, and that is for tortious interference with prospective employment or business relations. She did not plead this, and we remand so that she may amend her complaint to allege this tort, Wheeling Dollar may answer, and both parties can make their proofs. In doing this, we make absolutely no judgment about the merits of her cause or of affirmative defenses that Wheeling Dollar may have.

We have recognized tortious interference with business interests, with contractual relations, and with a testamentary bequest, all akin to that which Ms. Torbett may have suffered.

Our research reveals that the tort of interference bears many names. The encyclopedic compilation, American Jurisprudence Second, covers it in a category called only Interference, for lack of better rubric. 45 Am.Jur.2d, *Interference.* This genre of tort may include interference with existing or prospective contractual, business or employment relationships . . . .

Most often plaintiffs in tort actions for interference with prospective contractual relations are businesses. It appears that in employer-employee contexts employees generally seek this remedy when an employer as interfered by conveying false or pejorative information to a potential new employer. . . . A plaintiff must prove:

(1) existence of a contractual or business relationship or expectancy [with Security National Bank or Half Dollar Bank];

(2) an intentional act of interference by a party outside that relationship or expectancy [Wheeling Dollar's restrictive covenant on her];

(3) proof that the interference caused the harm sustained; and

(4) damages.

If this plaintiff makes a prima facie case for interference, Wheeling Dollar may prove lawful justification or privilege for its behavior as an affirmative defense. Lowell v. Mother's Cake and Cookie Co., 79 Cal.App.3d 13, 144 Cal.Rptr. 664, 6 A.L.R.4th 184 (1978).

We understand that this opinion may severely curb use of restrictive covenants in future employment contracts. A scrivener must decide whether his covenant is sufficiently narrow to protect only legitimate business interests in a reasonable fashion, or risk his employer-client to damages if its mere existence interferes with an employment opportunity. Frivolous noncompetition clauses in employment contracts will probably be avoided.

We remand to the trial court for further proceedings consistent herewith.

Affirmed in part; reversed and remanded in part.

NEELY, Justice dissenting:

I dissent because today's decision opens the door for vexatious litigation that will frustrate legitimate business interests and make it impossible for both employers and employees to bargain about their commercial relationship.

The majority's opinion holds that a mutual, voluntary commercial agreement becomes a tortious act when a court finds the contract unenforceable. Neither precedent nor logic supports such a holding.

... There is ... an understandable dearth of cases in which the breacher attempts to sue the victim of the breach for allowing him to make a bargain that the breaching party no longer finds satisfying.

Tiernan v. Charleston Area Med. Ctr., Inc.

506 S.E.2d 578 (W. Va. 1998)

[Betty Tiernan's employment at Charleston Area Medical Center was terminated.] After termination, Ms. Tiernan secured per diem employment as a nursing supervisor with Arthur B. Hodges Center, Inc., (hereinafter "ABHC") a geriatric patient nursing home affiliated with CAMC. [Tiernan was hired as an at-will employee, meaning she could be fired for good reason, bad reason, or no reason at all.] When CAMC learned of Ms. Tiernan's employment with ABHC, CAMC contacted ABHC and informed ABHC that Ms. Tiernan was also working as a union organizer. ABHC provided no further work for Ms. Tiernan upon learning of her union activities.

Tiernan filed suit against CAMC, [alleging among other theories,] that CAMC tortiously interfered with her business relationship with ABHC.

... In syllabus point 2 of *Torbett v. Wheeling Dollar Sav. & Trust Co.*, 173 W.Va. 210, 314 S.E.2d 166 (1983), we discussed the necessary requirements to prove a prima facie case of tortious interference in an employment relationship ... :

> To establish prima facie proof of tortious interference, a plaintiff must show:
>
> (1) existence of a contractual or business relationship or expectancy;
>
> (2) an intentional act of interference by a party outside that relationship or expectancy;

> (3) proof that the interference caused the harm sustained; and
>
> (4) damages.
>
> If a plaintiff makes a prima facie case, a defendant may prove justification or privilege, affirmative defenses....

This Court has never addressed the issue of whether truth, in and of itself, bars a claim for tortious interference with a business relationship.... [T]he Restatement (Second) of Torts §772 (1979) states the following regarding the giving of advice:

> Advice as Proper or Improper Interference
>
> One who intentionally causes a third person not to perform a contract or not to enter into a prospective contractual relation with another does not interfere improperly with the other's contractual relation, by giving the third person
>
> (a) *truthful information*, or
>
> (b) honest advice within the scope of a request for the advice.

(Emphasis added.) A majority of the courts which have interpreted and adopted §772 of the Restatement have held that truth is an absolute bar to a claim for tortious interference with a business relationship....

In the instant proceeding there is no evidence showing that the communication by CAMC with ABHC was for the purpose of giving "advice" about Ms. Tiernan. The communication was "truthful information" regarding what CAMC knew about Ms. Tiernan. Therefore, the applicable provision of the *Restatement* in the instant case is §772(a), not §772(b). The comment to §772(a) states that truthful information is an absolute bar to a claim of tortious interference "whether or not the information is requested." Ms. Tiernan does not dispute that the information given was truthful.... [W]e now adopt §722 of the *Restatement* in its entirety. Therefore, the circuit court's alternative grounds for granting summary judgment on the tortious interference claim was correct.

Notes

The prima facie tort approach. The courts in *Imperial Ice*, *Torbett*, and *Tiernan* all apply essentially the same rule with respect to the delineation between the plaintiff's prima facie case and the defendant's need to establish a privilege or justification for the interference. But the relationships that were interfered with in each case were different. *Imperial Ice* alludes to the idea that defendants may be privileged to interfere in some cases with respect to noncontractual relationships but not contractual ones. The rest of the chapter will focus on how courts have started to draw distinctions in terms of the fact patterns and how rules apply in interference cases.

Criticisms and uncertainty. Some of the primary criticisms of the interference torts typically involve the argument that they inject uncertainty into the business world and that they are inefficient and potentially anti-competitive in nature. The dissenting opinion in *Torbett*, for example, argued that the decision "opens the door for vexatious litigation that will frustrate legitimate business interests and make it impossible for both employers and employees to bargain about their commercial relationship." *Torbett*, 314 S.E.2d at 317 (Neely, J., dissenting). In *Chaves v. Johnson*, 335 S.E.2d 97 (Va. 1985), the plaintiff, an architect, entered into a contract with a city to provide services. Another architect wrote a letter to town officials arguing that he had greater experience and could do the job more cheaply. The town cancelled the contract with the plaintiff and awarded it to the defendant. Applying the same test used by *Imperial Ice*, *Torbett*, and *Tiernan*, the Virginia Supreme Court reinstated a jury verdict in favor of the plaintiff on his interference claim. Is that problematic, or should the law prohibit such action?

Damages. Think back to *Lumley v. Gye* at the beginning of the chapter. The plaintiff obviously could not recover breach of contract damages from the breaching party and then the same breach of contract damages from the interfering defendant. What advantages do interference claims present for plaintiffs, then?

Problem 18.1. Kovacs Transportation had a contract with Nairobi Air, the company that shipped many of the primates that Kovacs dealt with to the United States. Kovacs terminated its contract with Nairobi Air. The financial impact ultimately forced Nairobi Air into bankruptcy. Kovacs then was able to purchase some of Nairobi Air's fleet at a reduced price for its own use. Nairobi Air has now sued Kovacs for breach of contract. It has also sued Foley Consulting, an outside consulting company hired by Kovacs, for interference with contract. According to Nairobi Air's complaint, Foley Consulting advised Kovacs to cancel its contract with Nairobi in order to force Nairobi Air into bankruptcy and allow Kovacs to purchase the fleet at a reduced rate.

(a) Based on these facts, can Nairobi Air establish a prima facie case of interference against Foley under the prima facie tort approach used in *Imperial Ice*, *Torbett*, and *Tiernan*?

(b) Would it matter if Kovacs' termination of the contract was not actually a breach of the contract?

(c) Could Nairobi Air sue Kovacs on an interference theory?

2. Privileges and Justifications

Under the test used in *Imperial Ice*, *Torbett*, and *Tiernan*, once a plaintiff establishes the elements of a prima facie case, the defendant can avoid liability only if the defendant establishes that the intentional interference was privileged or justified. For example, *Tiernan* explored the defenses of truth and honest advice, both of which appear in the *Restatement*. There are several other widely recognized privileges:

Defendant engaged in competition with the plaintiff. Perhaps the most common interference scenario involves one competitor engaging in competition with another. Section 768 of the *Restatement (Second) of Torts* describes the rule in such cases:

> One who intentionally causes a third person not to enter into a prospective contractual relation with another who is his competitor or not to continue an existing contract terminable at will does not interfere improperly with the other's relation if
>
> (a) the relation concerns a matter involved in the competition between the actor and the other and
>
> (b) the actor does not employ wrongful means and
>
> (c) his action does not create or continue an unlawful restraint of trade and
>
> (d) his purpose is at least in part to advance his interest in competing with the other.

Defendant with a financial interest in the business of another. One who has a financial interest in the business of another and who intentionally causes that party not to enter into a contractual relationship with the plaintiff does not interfere improperly with that relationship if she does not employ wrongful means and acts to protect her interest from being prejudiced by the relationship. Restatement (Second) of Torts § 769. Thus, the creditor who, in order to protect his financial interest, persuades the debtor not to do business with the plaintiff should not be held liable, provided he does not employ improper means. Although the *Restatement* limits the rule to interferences with prospective contractual relations, some courts have extended the rule to interferences with contracts terminable at will. *See* Geib v. Alan Wood Steel Co., 419 F. Supp. 1205 (E.D. Pa. 1976).

Defendant responsible for the welfare of another. One who is charged with responsibility for the welfare of another and who intentionally causes that person not to perform a contract or not to enter into a prospective contractual relationship with the plaintiff does not interfere improperly if he does not employ wrongful means and acts to protect the welfare of the person. Restatement (Second) of Torts § 770. The rule would apply to a parent-child relationship, as well as relationships like those of attorney and client. Brown Mackie College v. Graham, 981 F.2d 1149, 1153 (10th Cir. 1992).

Defendant providing truthful information or honest advice within the scope of a request for the advice. Section 772 of the Restatement (Second) of Torts lists two types of action that do not amount to improper interference. First, as discussed in *Tiernan*, a defendant who provides truthful information to another that causes the other not to perform a contract or not to enter into a prospective contractual relationship does not interfere improperly. Restatement (Second) of Torts § 772(a). This is true even if the defendant is motivated solely by spite or ill will. At the same time, the so-called "advisor's privilege" shields from liability the defendant who provides honest advice within the scope of a request for the advice. *Id.* § 772(b).

Defendant asserting a bona fide claim. Employer believes that Former Employee is about to violate the noncompete agreement the parties signed by entering into a new employment relationship with Prospective Employer. Employer honestly and in good faith believes the noncompete agreement to be valid. Therefore, Employer notifies Prospective Employer that it plans to take whatever legal action is necessary to enforce the noncompete agreement if Prospective Employer hires Former Employee. As a result, Prospective Employer decides not to hire Former Employee. Employer has not interfered improperly under the rule described in Restatement (Second) of Torts § 773. Emery v. Merrimack Valley Wood Products, Inc., 701 F.2d 985 (1st Cir. 1983).

For each of the problems below, assume that the relevant jurisdiction uses the prima facie tort approach used in *Imperial Ice*, *Torbett*, and *Tiernan*.

Problem 18.2. Refer back to Problem 18.1. Assuming Nairobi Air could establish a prima facie case of tortious interference against Foley, were Foley's actions privileged?

Problem 18.3. Taiping Air entered into a contract with Kovacs for Taiping Air to transport several primates to Kovacs' facilities. The contract could only be terminated for cause. Chengdu Air is one of Taiping Air's competitors. Chengdu reached out to Kovacs and offered to provide the same services as Taiping at a cheaper rate. Kovacs then breached its contract with Taiping Air and entered into a contract with Chengdu. The breach resulted in Taiping being unable to fulfill another service contract with another company and losing considerable money. Taiping sues Chengdu on an interference theory. Were Chengdu's actions privileged?

Problem 18.4. Zaius Transportation is Kovacs' primary competitor. Kovacs knew that Zaius and a prospective buyer were in the process of negotiating the sale of one of Zaius' properties. Kovacs induced the prospective buyer not to purchase the property by threatening not to do business with the prospective buyer in the future. Zaius sues Kovacs on an interference theory. Were Kovacs' actions privileged?

Problem 18.5. Furious at Kovacs for its actions, Zaius wrote a letter to one of the zoos that Kovacs deals with and truthfully informed the zoo that Kovacs' license to import animals had been suspended for several weeks a few months ago for 45 violations of the Animal Welfare Act based on unsanitary and inadequate cages. There is a paper trail clearly establishing that Zaius wrote the letter out of ill will toward Kovacs and for the purpose of causing the zoo to terminate its contract with Kovacs. Its actions were successful, and Kovacs sued Zaius on an interference theory. Were Zaius' actions privileged?

Problem 18.6. Great American Bank is one of Kovacs' creditors. The Bank was concerned about the behavior of one Kovacs' vice presidents and the negative attention he had been bringing to the company. The vice president had an employment contract under which he could only been fired "for good cause." It was debatable whether Kovacs had such cause to fire the vice president. Nonetheless, Great American Bank pressured Kovacs into firing the vice president. The vice president sued Great American Bank on an interference theory. Were its actions privileged?

B. The Improper Purpose or Improper Means Test

With the publication of the Restatement (Second) of Torts, the authors of the *Restatement* took a half-step away from the prima facie tort approach. Rather than use the terms "privilege" or "justification," the authors chose to define the tort in terms of intentional and *improper* interference. For liability to attach, the defendant must have "intentionally and improperly" interfered with a contract or prospective contractual relation. Restatement (Second) of Torts §§ 766A and 766B. To determine whether a defendant "improperly" interfered, the finder of fact was instructed to consider seven separate factors. Restatement (Second) of Torts § 767. Given the difficulty in applying this malleable, seven-factor test in practice, virtually no courts have adopted it.

The most noteworthy feature of the *Restatement* test for purposes of this chapter, however, was its inclusion of the defendant's mental state as a proper consideration in determining whether an interference is improper. The defendant's motive is relevant to this determination, as is the interest the defendant is seeking to advance through the interference. Thus, the fact that the defendant acted solely out of ill will might render an interference improper. *Id.* cmt. d. The nature of the actor's conduct is another consideration under the *Restatement.* The fact that the defendant employed violent or other improper means to accomplish the interference might also render the interference improper. *Id.* cmt. c. While few courts fully adopted the *Restatement* approach, some, at least, started moving in a similar direction.

Top Service Body Shop, Inc. v. Allstate Ins. Co.

582 P.2d 1365 (Or. 1978)

LINDE, Justice.

Plaintiff, the operator of an automobile body repair shop in Coos Bay, Oregon, sued defendant insurance company for general and punitive damages for injuries alleged to result from defendant's wrongful practices in directing insurance claimants to have repairs made at body shops other than plaintiff's. The complaint pleaded causes of action grounded in two theories: First, tortious interference with plaintiff's business, and second, inducement of other body shops to accord defendant discriminatory price advantages prohibited by statute.... Defendant answered by general denials and an affirmative defense to the tort claim asserting a privilege of acting in its own legitimate financial interests. Plaintiff replied that defendant's methods and intent took its actions beyond any such privilege.

The trial resulted in jury verdicts for plaintiff in amounts of $20,000 compensatory and $250,000 punitive damages on the tort claim and $45,000 in treble damages on the price discrimination claim.

I. The claim of tortious interference.

Although other jurisdictions have decided numerous claims of tortious interference with business relations, this court has had few occasions to consider the elements of this tort.

Either the pursuit of an improper objective of harming plaintiff or the use of wrongful means that in fact cause injury to plaintiff's contractual or business relationships may give rise to a tort claim for those injuries. PROSSER, HANDBOOK OF THE LAW OF TORTS § 130 at 952 (4th ed. 1971). However, efforts to consolidate both recognized and unsettled lines of development into a general theory of "tortious interference" have brought to the surface the difficulties of defining the elements of so general a tort without sweeping within its terms a wide variety of socially very different conduct.[3] These difficulties are shown by the changing treatment of the subject in the American Law Institute's *Restatement of the Law of Torts*. The main problem is what weight to give to the defendant's objective in interfering with plaintiff's contract or with plaintiff's prospective business relations. If the focus in defining the tort is on defendant's wrongful motive or use of wrongful means, this element will likely be a necessary part of plaintiff's case. If the tort is defined

---

3. During one period of history, the tort of interference with contracts was a main legal weapon against labor organization. *See, e.g.*, Hitchman Coal & Coke Co. v. Mitchell, 245 U.S. 229, 38 S. Ct. 65, 62 L.Ed. 260 (1917) (injunction); Vegelahn v. Guntner, 167 Mass. 92, 44 N.E. 1077 (1896); PROSSER, HANDBOOK OF THE LAW OF TORTS s 129 at 946–947 (4th ed. 1971).

primarily as an invasion of plaintiff's protected interests, defendant's reasons are likely to be treated as questions of justification or privilege....

[T]he decision in *Nees v. Hocks*, 272 Or. 210, 536 P.2d 512 (1975), rejected the concept that every intentional infliction of harm is prima facie a tort unless justified. Finding that this concept was no longer needed to escape the rigidity of the common-law forms of pleading, the court concluded that it created as many difficulties as it solved. However, the court found that the plaintiff had effectively pleaded and proved that her discharge by defendant was tortious by reason of an improper motive.

We conclude that the approach of *Nees v. Hocks* is equally appropriate to claims of tort liability for intentional interference with contractual or other economic relations. In summary, such a claim is made out when interference resulting in injury to another is wrongful by some measure beyond the fact of the interference itself. Defendant's liability may arise from improper motives or from the use of improper means. They may be wrongful by reason of a statute or other regulation, or a recognized rule of common law, or perhaps an established standard of a trade or profession....

In the present case, Top Service pleaded both improper motives and improper means of interference. It alleged that Allstate sought to and did induce Top Service's patrons not to have Top Service repair their automobiles, making false statements about the quality of plaintiff's workmanship and threats about withdrawing insurance coverage or subjecting the settlement of claims to possible arbitration. It also alleged that this was done "with the sole design of injuring Plaintiff and destroying his business," and in an endeavor to "compel Plaintiff to abandon the same." If proved, along with damages and causation, these allegations satisfy the elements of the tort we have reviewed above.

Taken most favorably to plaintiff, as is proper after a verdict for plaintiff, the evidence showed that Allstate has a practice of designating certain repair shops in the locality as "competitive shops" to which it prefers to send insurance claimants for whose repairs Allstate is obligated; that Top Service at one time was a "drive-in" shop for Allstate, where claimants would be directed for an estimate by an Allstate insurance adjuster; that after a dispute Top Service's owner decided that it would not continue as a drive-in shop for Allstate; and that thereafter Allstate adjusters would actively discourage claimants under its insurance policies from taking work to be paid for by Allstate to Top Service, sending them instead to other shops on its preferred list. As specific bases for an inference of destructive purpose, Top Service lists two occasions when Allstate adjusters disparaged the quality of Top Service's work (apart from its relative cost), although Allstate personnel had generally considered Top Service a high quality shop; Allstate's willingness to disappoint its own insured who preferred Top Service; one occasion when Allstate took its option to "total" a car, *i.e.* to pay off its value, when the insured wanted it repaired at Top Service; and finally Allstate's resort to "improper and unlawful means" to direct business away from Top Service to other shops. Without setting forth here the excerpts of the record cited by plaintiff, we agree with the trial court that these acts were wholly consistent with Allstate's pursuit of its own business purposes as it saw them and did not suffice to support an inference of the alleged improper purpose to injure Top Service. The court's ruling on this point was not error.

[The court found there was insufficient evidence that the defendant had acted with an improper purpose.]

Plaintiff contends that its case did not depend solely on proof of Allstate's wrongful motive. It argues that, contrary to the trial court's conclusion, Allstate would not be privileged to interfere with plaintiff's business relations by unlawful or otherwise improper means even in pursuit of its own business objectives. As unlawful or improper practices, plaintiff points to defendant's disparagement of its services, the price discriminations [mentioned earlier in the opinion], and violation of other statutory policies, [including a statute prohibiting the disparagement of goods or services by making false representations]. Plaintiff's contention may well be a correct view of the law, as we have reviewed it above, but it does not help plaintiff on this appeal. The difficulty is that the case was submitted to the jury solely on the theory of liability for purposely seeking to harm plaintiff's business. Even if defendant might also have been liable on an alternative theory of tortious interference by improper means, we cannot reinstate the verdict on that theory, which was not presented to the jury. Since the trial court did not err in its ruling under the theory on which the case was submitted, the judgment on the first cause of action must be affirmed.

Notes

Other courts. Again, while it is difficult to speak in terms of majority rules in this area, a number of courts have adopted the *Top Service Body Shop* approach. *See, e.g.*, Leingang v. Pierce County Med. Bureau, Inc., 930 P.2d 288 (Wash. 1997); United Truck Leasing Corp. v. Geltman, 551 N.E.2d 20 (Mass. 1990).

The role of malice. Some have criticized the decision of some courts to take a defendant's motivation into account when determining the wrongfulness of the defendant's conduct: "[P]ure malice is not a perfect predictor of anticompetitive effect, because an actor motivated by pure malice may choose competitive means to accomplish his purpose: if TP hates B for personal reasons and spitefully searches for a more advantageous opportunity for A so as to interfere with B's contract with A, he nonetheless may produce a social benefit." Harvey S. Perlman, *Interference with Contract and Other Economic Expectancies*, 49 U. Chi. L. Rev. 61, 95 (1982). What role, if any, should malice play in the analysis of whether a defendant's interference was improper?

Interference with contract versus interference with prospective contracts. Note that the plaintiff's prima face case under the *Top Service Body Shop* test is the same regardless of whether the interference is with an existing contract or a mere prospective contractual relationship.

C. Decoupling the Interference Torts

There remains a considerable amount of disagreement regarding the proper treatment of interference claims. However, a few trends have started to develop within the past two decades. The following section examines two of those trends as interference law perhaps continues to stumble toward a more unified approach.

1. Interference with Contract versus Interference with Prospective Contractual Relations

Neither the prima facie tort approach from the beginning of the chapter nor the *Top Service* approach from the previous section draw a distinction between interferences with existing contracts and interferences with prospective contractual relations. Should the law treat these situations differently?

Della Penna v. Toyota Motor Sales, U.S.A., Inc.

902 P.2d 740 (Cal. 1995)

ARABIAN, Justice.

We granted review to reexamine, in light of divergent rulings from the Court of Appeal and a doctrinal evolution among other state high courts, the elements of the tort variously known as interference with "prospective economic advantage," "prospective contractual relations," or "prospective economic relations," and the allocation of the burdens of proof between the parties to such an action.

I

John Della Penna, an automobile wholesaler doing business as Pacific Motors, brought this action for damages against Toyota Motor Sales, U.S.A., Inc., and its Lexus division, alleging that certain business conduct of defendants both violated provisions of the Cartwright Act, California's state antitrust statute (Bus. & Prof .Code, § 16700 et seq.), and constituted an intentional interference with his economic relations. The impetus for Della Penna's suit arose out of the 1989 introduction into the American luxury car market of Toyota's Lexus automobile. Prior to introducing the Lexus, the evidence at trial showed, both the manufacturer, Toyota Motor Corporation, and defendant, the American distributor, had been concerned at the possibility that a resale market might develop for the Lexus in Japan. Even though the car was manufactured in Japan, Toyota's marketing strategy was to bar the vehicle's sale on the Japanese domestic market until after the American roll-out; even then, sales in Japan would only be under a different brand name, the "Celsior." Fearing that auto wholesalers in the United States might re-export Lexus models back to Japan for resale, and concerned that, with production and the availability of Lexus models in the American market limited, re-exports would jeopardize its fledgling network of American Lexus dealers, Toyota inserted in its dealership agreements a "no export" clause, providing that the dealer was "authorized to sell [Lexus automobiles] only to customers located in the United States. [Dealer] agrees that it will not sell [Lexus automobiles] for resale or use outside the United States. [Dealer] agrees to abide by any export policy established by [distributor]."

Following the introduction into the American market, it soon became apparent that some domestic Lexus units were being diverted for foreign sales, principally to Japan. To counter this effect, Toyota managers wrote to their retail dealers, reminding them of the "no-export" policy and explaining that exports for foreign resale could jeopardize the supply of Lexus automobiles available for the United States market. In addition, Toyota compiled a list of "offenders"—dealers and others believed by Toyota to be involved heavily in the developing Lexus foreign resale market—which it distributed to Lexus dealers in the United States. American Lexus dealers were also warned that doing business with those whose names appeared on the "offenders" list might lead to a series of graduated sanctions, from reducing a dealer's allocation to possible reevaluation of the dealer's franchise agreement.

During the years 1989 and 1990, plaintiff Della Penna did a profitable business as an auto wholesaler purchasing Lexus automobiles, chiefly from the Lexus of Stevens Creek retail outlet, at near retail price and exporting them to Japan for resale. By late 1990, however, plaintiff's sources began to dry up, primarily as a result of the "offenders list." Stevens Creek ceased selling models to plaintiff; gradually other sources declined to sell to him as well.

In February 1991, plaintiff filed this lawsuit against Toyota Motors, U.S.A., Inc., alleging both state antitrust claims under the Cartwright Act and interference with his economic relationship with Lexus retail dealers. At the close of plaintiff's case-in-chief, the trial court granted Toyota's motion for nonsuit with respect to the remaining Cartwright Act claim (plaintiff had previously abandoned a related claim—unfair competition—prior to trial). The tort cause of action went to the jury, however, under the standard BAJI instructions applicable to such claims with one significant exception. At the request of defendant and over plaintiff's objection, the trial judge modified BAJI No. 7.82—the basic instruction identifying the elements of the tort and indicating the burden of proof—to require plaintiff to prove that defendant's alleged interfering conduct was "wrongful."[1]

---

1. The standard instruction governing "intentional interference with prospective economic advantage," BAJI No. 7.82, describes the essential elements of the claim as (1) an economic relationship between the plaintiff and another, "containing a probable future economic benefit or advantage to plaintiff," (2) defendant's knowledge of the existence of the relationship, (3) that defendant "intentionally engaged in acts or conduct designed to interfere with or disrupt" the relationship, (4) actual disruption, and (5) damage to the plaintiff as a result of defendant's acts. The modification sought by defendant and adopted by the trial court consisted in adding the word "wrongful" in element (3) between the words "in" and "acts." The trial court also read to the jury plaintiff's special jury instruction defining the "wrongful acts" required to support liability as conduct "outside the realm of legitimate business transactions. . . . Wrongfulness may lie in the method used or by virtue of an improper motive."

The jury returned a divided verdict, nine to three, in favor of Toyota. After Della Penna's motion for a new trial was denied, he appealed. In an unpublished disposition, the Court of Appeal unanimously reversed the trial court's judgment, ruling that a plaintiff alleging intentional interference with economic relations is not required to establish "wrongfulness" as an element of its prima facie case, and that it was prejudicial error for the trial court to have read the jury an amended instruction to that effect. The Court of Appeal remanded the case to the trial court for a new trial; we then granted Toyota's petition for review and now reverse.

II

B

[By the time of the *Restatement (Second) of Torts* reformulation in §766B] an increasing number of state high courts had traveled well beyond the *Second Restatement*'s reforms by redefining and otherwise recasting the elements of the economic relations tort and the burdens surrounding its proof and defenses. In *Top Service Body Shop, Inc. v. Allstate Ins. Co.*, (1978) 283 Or. 201, 582 P.2d 1365 (*Top Service*), the Oregon Supreme Court, assessing this "most fluid and rapidly growing tort," noted that "efforts to consolidate both recognized and unsettled lines of development into a general theory of 'tortious interference' have brought to the surface the difficulties of defining the elements of so general a tort without sweeping within its terms a wide variety of socially very different conduct."

Recognizing the force of these criticisms, the court went on to hold in *Top Service, supra*, that a claim of interference with economic relations "is made out when interference resulting in injury to another is wrongful by some measure beyond the fact of the interference itself. Defendant's liability may arise from improper motives or from the use of improper means. They may be wrongful by reason of a statute or other regulation, or a recognized rule of common law, or perhaps an established standard of a trade or profession. No question of privilege arises unless the interference would be wrongful but for the privilege; it becomes an issue only if the acts charged would be tortious on the part of an unprivileged defendant."

Over the past decade or so, close to a majority of the high courts of American jurisdictions have imported into the economic relations tort variations on the *Top Service* line of reasoning, explicitly approving a rule that requires the plaintiff in such a suit to plead and prove the alleged interference was either "wrongful," "improper," "illegal," "independently tortious" or some variant on these formulations.

III

In California, the development of the economic relations tort has paralleled its evolution in other jurisdictions.... In *Imperial Ice Co. v. Rossier* (1941) 18 Cal.2d 33, 112 P.2d 631, ... California ... joined the majority of jurisdictions in adopting the view of the first *Restatement of Torts* by stating that "an action will lie for unjustifiably inducing a breach of contract."

In the aftermath of *Imperial Ice Co. v. Rossier*, our early economic relations cases were principally of two types, either the classic master and servant pattern of the pre-*Lumley v. Gye* cases (*see, e.g.*, Buxbom v. Smith (1944) 23 Cal.2d 535, 548, 145 P.2d 305 [hiring away of plaintiff's employees by defendant, after plaintiff had built up his business to distribute defendant's publication and defendant had breached distribution contract, held actionable as "an unfair method of interference with advantageous relations"]) or those involving circumscribed kinds of business relations in which the plaintiff, typically a real estate broker or attorney working on a contingency, sued to recover fees after defendant had refused to share property sales proceeds or a personal injury.

[W]e are thus presented with the opportunity to consider whether to expressly reconstruct the formal elements of the interference with economic relations tort to achieve a closer alignment with the practice of the trial courts, emerging views within the Court of Appeal, the rulings of many other state high courts, and the critiques of leading commentators. We believe that we should.

IV

In searching for a means to recast the elements of the economic relations tort and allocate the associated burdens of proof, we are guided by an overmastering concern articulated by high courts of other jurisdictions and legal commentators: The need to draw and enforce a sharpened distinction between claims for the tortious disruption of an existing contract and claims that a prospective contractual or economic relationship has been interfered with by the defendant. Many of the cases do in fact acknowledge a greater array of justificatory defenses against claims of interference with prospective relations. Still, in our view and that of several other courts and commentators, the notion that the two torts are analytically unitary and derive from a common principle sacrifices practical wisdom to theoretical insight, promoting the idea that the interests invaded are of nearly equal dignity. They are not.

The courts provide a damage remedy against third party conduct intended to disrupt an existing contract precisely because the exchange of promises resulting in such a formally cemented economic relationship is deemed worthy of protection from interference by a stranger to the agreement. Economic relationships short of contractual, however, should stand on a different legal footing as far as the potential for tort liability is reckoned. Because ours is a culture firmly wedded to the social rewards of commercial contests, the law usually takes care to draw lines of legal liability in a way that maximizes areas of competition free of legal penalties.

A doctrine that blurs the analytical line between interference with an existing business contract and interference with commercial relations less than contractual is one that invites both uncertainty in conduct and unpredictability of its legal effect. The notion that inducing the breach of an existing contract is simply a subevent of the "more inclusive" class of acts that interfere with economic relations, while perhaps theoretically unobjectionable, has been mischievous as a practical matter. Our courts should, in short, firmly distinguish the two kinds of business contexts, bringing a greater solicitude to those relationships that have ripened into agreements, while recognizing that relationships short of that subsist in a zone where the rewards and risks of competition are dominant.

Beyond that, we need not tread today. It is sufficient to dispose of the issue before us in this case by holding that a plaintiff seeking to recover for alleged interference with prospective economic relations has the burden of pleading and proving that the defendant's interference was wrongful "by some measure beyond the fact of the interference itself." (*Top Service, supra*, 582 P.2d at p. 1371.) It follows that the trial court did not commit error when it modified BAJI No. 7.82 to require the jury to find that defendant's interference was "wrongful." And because the instruction defining "wrongful conduct" given the jury by the trial court was offered by plaintiff himself, we have no occasion to review its sufficiency in this case. The question of whether additional refinements to the plaintiff's pleading and proof burdens merit adoption by California courts—questions embracing the precise scope of "wrongfulness," or whether a "disinterested malevolence," in Justice Holmes's words (American Bank & Trust Co. v. Federal Reserve Bank (1921) 256 U.S. 350, 358, 41 S.Ct. 499, 500, 65 L. Ed. 983) is an actionable interference in itself, or whether the underlying policy justification for the tort, the efficient allocation of social resources, justifies including as actionable conduct that is recognized as anticompetitive under established state and federal positive law (*see, e.g.*, Perlman, *Interference with Contract and Other Economic Expectancies; A Clash of Tort and Contract Doctrine, supra*, 49 U.Chi.L.Rev. 61)—are matters that can await another day and a more appropriate case.

Conclusion

We hold that a plaintiff seeking to recover for an alleged interference with prospective contractual or economic relations must plead and prove as part of its case-in-chief that the defendant not only knowingly interfered with the plaintiff's expectancy, but engaged in conduct that was wrongful by some legal measure other than the fact of interference itself. The judgment of the Court of Appeal is reversed and the cause is remanded with directions to affirm the judgment of the trial court.

MOSK, Justice, concurring.

The prima facie tort doctrine exhibits a specific deficiency with regard to the tort of intentional interference with prospective economic advantage. "Since not all interference [is] actionable, or even morally wrong, it cannot be said that there [is] some principle against interference. Since there is no hint in such abstract statements of liability as to what might constitute a defense it is difficult to believe that there is actually any principle involved at all. It has rather the faded ambience of a 'universal truth' once thought to be discoverable in law. In any event, this [leaves] the defendant in an interference case knowing he [is] entitled to some defense, but not knowing what defenses would be accounted sufficient." (Dobbs, *Tortious Interference With Contractual Relationships, supra*, 34 Ark.L.Rev. at p. 345.)

Further, liability under the tort may threaten values of greater breadth and higher dignity than those of the tort itself.

One is the common law's policy of freedom of competition. "'The policy of the common law has always been in favor of free competition, which proverbially is the life of trade. So long as the plaintiff's contractual relations are merely contemplated or potential, it is considered to be in the interest of the public that any competitor should be free to divert them to himself by all fair and reasonable means. . . . In short, it is no tort to beat a business rival to prospective customers. Thus, in the absence of prohibition by statute, illegitimate means, or some other unlawful element, a defendant seeking to increase his own business may cut rates or prices, allow discounts or rebates, enter into secret negotiations behind the plaintiff's back, refuse to deal with him or threaten to discharge employees who do, or even refuse to deal with third parties unless they cease dealing with the plaintiff, all without incurring liability.'" (A-Mark Coin Co. v. General Mills, Inc. (1983) 148 Cal.App.3d 312, 323–324, 195 Cal.Rptr. 859).

. . .

To this end, we should clearly define the tort, basing it on stable and circumscribed ground, and eschewing the prima facie tort doctrine, the "protectionist" premise, and the interfering party's motive. Our focus should be on objective conduct and consequences. Further, our concern should be with such conduct and consequences as are unlawful.

It follows that the tort may be satisfied by intentional interference with prospective economic advantage by independently tortious means.

Quelimane Co. v. Stewart Title Guaranty Co.

960 P.2d 513 (Cal. 1998)

Plaintiffs contend that the allegations of the first cause of action . . . state a cause of action for interference with existing and prospective contractual relations. Defendant's only rebuttal is that since there was nothing wrong in its refusal to issue the policy of title insurance to Constant, there can be no interference with existing and prospective contractual relations. Wrongfulness independent of the inducement to breach the contract is not an element of the tort of intentional interference with existing contractual relations, however.

"The elements which a plaintiff must plead to state the cause of action for intentional interference with contractual relations are (1) a valid contract between plaintiff and a third party; (2) defendant's knowledge of this contract; (3) defendant's intentional acts designed to induce a breach or disruption of the contractual relationship; (4) actual breach or disruption of the contractual relationship; and (5) resulting damage." The Court of Appeal held that plaintiffs could not state a cause of action for interference with contractual relations because the allegations did not establish that defendants' conduct was wrongful for any reason other than its impact on the contracts for the purchase of tax-defaulted property. This holding fails to properly distinguish the torts of interference with prospective economic advantage and intentional interference with an existing contract.

Because interference with an existing contract receives greater solicitude than does interference with prospective economic advantage, it is not necessary that the defendant's conduct be wrongful apart from the interference with the contract itself.

As we explained in *Della Penna v. Toyota Motor Sales, U.S.A., Inc.*, it is necessary to distinguish the tort of interference with an existing contract because the exchange of promises which cements an economic relationship as a contract is worthy of protection from a stranger to the contract. Intentionally inducing or causing a breach of an existing contract is therefore a wrong in and of itself. Because this formal economic relationship does not exist and damages are speculative when remedies are sought for interference in what is only prospective economic advantage, *Della Penna* concluded that some wrongfulness apart from the impact of the defendant's conduct on that prospect should be required. Implicit in the *Della Penna* holding is a conclusion that this additional aspect of wrongfulness is not an element of the tort of intentional interference with an existing contract.

...

The complaint here alleged a contract between plaintiff Western Land Bank and Robert Constant. Knowledge of the contract is alleged impliedly in the allegation that defendant First American refused to issue a policy of title insurance unless Constant initiated a quiet title action. Disruption is alleged in the allegation that Constant then failed to complete payment. Damages are alleged in the lost benefits of the transactions and related legal costs....

We conclude that the complaint sufficiently alleges a cause of action for intentional interference with existing contractual relations.

Notes

Decoupling the interference torts. A number of other courts have similarly decoupled the torts of interference with contract and interference with prospective contractual relations. *See* Berry & Gould, P.A. v. Berry, 757 A.2d 108, 113 (Md. 2000) ("[W]rongful or malicious interference with economic relations is interference by conduct that is independently wrongful or unlawful, quite apart from its effect on the plaintiff's business relationships."); Maximus, Inc. v. Lockheed Information Management Systems Co., Inc., 493 S.E.2d 375, 378 (Va. 1997) (holding that in the case of interference with prospective contractual relations, a plaintiff must also establish that the defendant "used improper means or methods to interfere with the expectancy").

Subsequent developments in California. In a subsequent decision, the California Supreme Court explained that an act is independently wrongful "if it is proscribed by some constitutional, statutory, regulatory, common law, or other determinable legal standard." *Korea Supply Co. v. Lockheed Martin Corp.*, 63 P.3d 937, 954 (Cal. 2003).

Independently wrongful acts. *Korea Supply Co.* attempted to clarify *Della Penna*'s holding. But what exactly does it mean to say that a defendant's conduct must be "proscribed by some constitutional, statutory, regulatory, common law, or other determinable legal standard"? Does this mean the defendant's actions have to amount to a separate, freestanding tort? If so, what purpose does the tort of interference with prospective contractual relations serve?

In *Wal-Mart Stores, Inc. v. Sturges*, 52 S.W.3d 711 (Tex. 2001), the Texas Supreme Court decoupled the interference torts in much the same manner that *Della Penna* and *Quelimane* did. The Court held that "to recover for tortious interference with a prospective business relation a plaintiff must prove that the defendant's conduct was independently tortious or wrongful." Importantly, the court clarified that by the phrase "independently tortious,"

> we do not mean that the plaintiff must be able to prove an independent tort. Rather, we mean only that the plaintiff must prove that the defendant's conduct would be actionable under a recognized tort. Thus, for example, a plaintiff may recover for tortious interference from a defendant who makes fraudulent statements about the plaintiff to a third person without proving that the third person was actually defrauded. If, on the other hand, the defendant's statements are not intended to deceive, . . . then they are not actionable.

Id. at 726. Elsewhere, the court explained that "independently tortious" conduct is conduct "that would violate some other recognized tort *duty*." *Id.* at 713 (emphasis added). Thus, "a defendant who threatened a customer with bodily harm if he did business with the plaintiff would be liable for interference because his conduct toward the customer—assault—was independently tortious," even if the plaintiff could not recover from the defendant for assault. *Id.* "Conduct that is merely 'sharp' or unfair is not actionable and cannot be the basis for an action for tortious interference with prospective relations, and we disapprove of cases that suggest the contrary." *Id.* at 726.

Violation of professional standards as improper interference. According to the *Restatement (Second) of Torts*, violation of a professional code of conduct or established custom or practice within a field may be evidence of improper interference. Restatement (Second) of Torts § 767 cmt. c. Would such a violation qualify as an independently wrongful act under the *Della Penna* approach?

Problem 18.7. Lucy was a former Kovacs employee. Shortly after quitting her job, she was offered a job with Zaius. Kovacs learned of the offer and before Lucy was able to accept, Kovacs contacted Zaius and informed Zaius that Lucy had signed a noncompete agreement with Zaius. Kovacs informed Zaius that it planned to file an action to enforce that agreement if necessary. Lucy had no specialized skill or training and did not deal directly with customers while she was at Kovacs, but the noncompete agreement prohibited her from accepting employment with any company engaged in the animal importation business for a period of 20 years. After learning of the existence and details of the noncompete agreement, Zaius thought the agreement was almost certainly unenforceable. However, it did not want to risk the trouble of hiring Lucy and possibly provoking Kovacs into filing an interference suit against Zaius for hiring Lucy. So, Zaius rescinded its offer to Lucy. Lucy has now sued Kovacs on an interference theory. What is the most likely result in a jurisdiction that follows the approach used in California?

2. Interference with Contract versus Interference with Contract Terminable at Will

If the law recognizes a distinction between an interference with a contract and an interference with a prospective contractual relation, should there also be a distinction between a contract that can only lawfully be terminated for cause and one that can lawfully be terminated at will? The following case deals with that issue.

Duggin v. Adams

360 S.E.2d 832 (Va. 1987)

STEPHENSON, Justice.

The question presented in this appeal is whether a motion for judgment contains allegations sufficient to state a cause of action for tortious interference with a terminable-at-will sales contract.

Kenneth D. Duggin, Trustee, sued C. Douglas Adams, claiming that Adams tortiously interfered with Duggin's contract rights with Betty B. Williams for the purchase of a tract of land in Fairfax County. Adams demurred to the allegations contained in Duggin's motion for judgment. The trial court sustained the demurrer. After denying Duggin's "Motion for Reconsideration and/or Leave to Amend," the court entered final judgment for Adams. Duggin appeals.

Duggin's motion for judgment contains the following allegations: In July 1978, Duggin entered into a contract to purchase approximately four and one-half acres of land from Williams for $950,000. Adams, an attorney-at-law licensed to practice in the Commonwealth, represented Williams throughout the transaction with Duggin.

[According to the complaint, as Williams' attorney, learned that a third party, Centennial, was willing to pay an additional fee in order to purchase the land from Duggin, thereby making the property more valuable.] Adams used this knowledge to "willfully, wantonly, intentionally, maliciously and wrongfully [lay] plans to deprive [Duggin] of this valuable property right and to thereby enrich himself." The essential elements of Adams' plan were to (1) secure cancellation of the Williams-Duggin contract, (2) induce Williams to contract to sell the land to Adams, and (3) sell the Williams-Adams contract to Centennial.

In carrying out his plan, Adams wrote a letter to Duggin, dated June 30, 1981, wrongfully accusing Duggin of breaching the contract and stating that Duggin had forfeited his deposit. Because Adams knew that the contract had not been breached, his letter "was a malicious, knowing, intentional and wrongful act . . . to fraudulently mislead and intimidate [Duggin] into giving up his contract rights."

On the same day that Centennial notified Adams that it was ready to settle with Williams, "Adams willfully, wantonly, wrongfully and maliciously induced... Williams to sign a contract, which Adams had prepared, giving Adams the right to purchase the subject property and requiring Williams to cancel her contract with Duggin." Williams then sent Duggin a letter, prepared by Adams, "purporting to cancel" the contract....

...Throughout the entire Williams-Duggin transaction, Adams represented that he was acting only as Williams' attorney. In doing so, Adams "willfully, wantonly, and maliciously concealed his true role and the fact that he had begun to act in his own behalf." While Duggin had the right to expect Adams to adhere to the canons and ethics of the Virginia State Bar, Adams, to the contrary, engaged in "deceptive, willful, wanton, malicious and secret self dealing" for his own personal gain. "Adams' willful, wanton, wrongful, knowing, intentional and malicious conduct... was aggravated, unjustified and in utter disregard of [Duggin's] contract rights and property interests."

Duggin provided Williams with confidential information concerning the development of the property and his assignment agreement with Centennial. "Adams had access to this confidential information which [Duggin] would not have disclosed to Adams had he known [that] Adams would attempt to use [the] information for his own personal gain and to [Duggin's] pecuniary loss.... Adams used his position as... Williams' attorney and his resulting access to confidential information, without disclosing his true interest in the matter, to enhance his own competitive position regarding the subject real estate transaction."

We now consider whether these allegations were sufficient to survive a demurrer. A party to a contract has property rights in the performance of and anticipated profits from the contract, and these rights are entitled to protection in the courts. Thus, one who intentionally interferes with another's contractual rights is subject to tort liability.

The requisite elements for a prima facie showing of a tortious interference with a contract that is not terminable at will are: "(1) the existence of a valid contractual relationship or business expectancy; (2) knowledge of the relationship or expectancy on the part of the interferor; (3) intentional interference inducing or causing a breach or termination of the relationship or expectancy; and (4) resultant damage to the party whose relationship or expectancy has been disrupted." Once a plaintiff shows that an intentional interference with a contract not terminable at will caused him damage, the burden to show that the interference was justified, privileged, or not improper shifts to the defendant.

Unlike a party to a contract for a definite term, however, an individual's interest in a contract terminable at will is essentially only an expectancy of future economic gain, and he has no legal assurance that he will realize the expected gain. Thus, the cause of action for interference with contractual rights provides no protection from the mere intentional interference with a contract terminable at will. In short, the

trial court in Cory's matter to disqualify Pauline from representing Cory on the basis of a conflict of interest. These actions resulted in a delay in Cory's litigation. The trial court ruled that there was no conflict of interest and that Daniella's motion was borderline frivolous. But the ethics investigation continued to delay the proceedings. As a result of the delay, Cory terminated his lawyer-client representation agreement with Pauline and hired a new lawyer. Eventually, the state agency that regulates the conduct of lawyers concluded that Pauline did not have a conflict of interest. Pauline then filed an interference claim against Daniella. She alleges that Daniella's ethics complaint and motion were frivolous and were filed in an attempt to force Pauline's withdrawal in Cory's case in order to gain a tactical advantage. Could Pauline's complaint survive a motion to dismiss in a jurisdiction that follows the approach of the courts in California (*Della Penna*, *Quelimane*, and *Reeves*) and Virginia (*Duggin*)?

Part 6

Damages

As discussed in the Introduction, there are many policy values that may underlie tort law. But compensation and deterrence are unquestionably at the top of most lists. The role that damages may play in a tort action has appeared throughout the cases in the book. But this chapter focuses exclusively on the issue of damages, whether they take the form of monetary damages, designed to compensate the victim for harm, or monetary damages, designed primarily to deter future misconduct.

Chapter 19

Damages

A. Compensatory Damages
- Purpose of compensatory damages
- Standard for awarding compensatory damages
- Pecuniary damages
  - Past medical expenses
    - The collateral source rule
  - Reducing awards for future losses to present value
  - Future lost wages and lost earning capacity
  - Future medical and related expenses
- Nonpecuniary damages
  - Pain and suffering damages in general
  - Loss of enjoyment of life

B. Punitive damages
- In general
  - Purposes
  - Standards for awarding punitive damages
  - Punitive damages awards against employers
- Constitutional limitations
  - Due process
  - Guideposts

C. Damage Caps and Tort Reform
- In general
- Pro-tort reform arguments
- Anti-tort reform arguments

D. Wrongful Death Statutes

E. Other Approaches to Recovery
- Workers' compensation
- Victim compensation funds

Chapter Problem. Jeffrey was 12 years old when he was injured through the negligence of the defendant, a power company. Jeffrey was riding his bike when he struck a downed power line that had been negligently maintained by the defendant. Jeffrey suffered severe and extensive burns and "blowout holes" on legs, left arm, and right hand. More than 80% of his head and face was burned, 70% to the third degree or worse. He remained in the hospital for four months following the accident. Surgeons performed numerous skin grafts and attempted to fashion a functioning right eyelid, which Jeffrey still cannot close. The operations have left Jeffrey's face and scalp severely scarred. Because his facial nerves and muscles have been burned away, even additional surgery will never restore his ability to smile. More operations to his face and the rest of his body will be needed. While still in the hospital, Jeffrey was treated by hypnosis to relieve pain, prevent regurgitation of food, and restore a will to live. Since emerging from the hospital Jeffrey has faced teasing and ridicule from his peers and startled reactions and revulsion from strangers.

There is no dispute as to the defendant's liability. Jeffrey's family has hired you to represent Jeffrey in a negligence action against the defendant.

A. Compensatory Damages

As the name suggests, compensatory damages are provided to compensate a victim for actual harm suffered. Compensatory damages provide a remedy for two main types of harm: pecuniary harm (often referred to as "special damages") and nonpecuniary harm (often referred to as "general damages").

1. Pecuniary Damages

Calva-Cerqueira v. United States

281 F. Supp. 2d 279 (D.D.C. 2003)

URBINA, District Judge.

I. Introduction

This case involves a 1998 collision ("the accident") between a bus owned and operated by defendant United States and an automobile operated by plaintiff Enrique Calva-Cerqueira. As a result of the accident, the plaintiff suffers from paralysis, decreased sensation in the left side of his body and is wheelchair bound. The plaintiff, who was 18-years-old at the time of the accident, brings this case pursuant to the Federal Tort Claims Act ("FTCA"), 28 U.S.C. § 2671 et seq. . . .

II. Findings of Fact

On August 3, 2000 the court granted the defendant's motion to bifurcate the liability and damages portions of this action. On May 3, 2001, after a three-day bench trial on the issue of liability, the court determined that the defendant was liable for the accident and resultant injuries to the plaintiff. Beginning on December 9, 2002, the court presided over an eight-day bench trial on the issue of the plaintiff's damages. On February 25, 2003, the parties filed proposed findings of fact and conclusions of law.

. . .

On Sunday, June 14, 1998, the plaintiff was involved in a tragic motor vehicle accident. On that morning, the plaintiff, then 18 years old, was driving his car eastbound on Eye Street, S.W. at its intersection with South Capitol Street in Washington, D.C. The other vehicle involved in the accident was a Smithsonian Institution bus, which was proceeding southbound on South Capitol Street when it collided with the plaintiff's car. The plaintiff's car weighed an estimated 3,380 pounds (including occupants), while the Smithsonian bus weighed an estimated 25,950 pounds (including occupants). The bus driver was driving in excess of the applicable 25 mph speed limit when she drove through a red light and into the intersection where she hit the plaintiff's car.

III. Conclusions of Law

A. Legal Standard for Compensatory Damages

In cases arising under the FTCA, the law of the state where the misconduct occurred governs substantive tort liability, including the nature and measure of damages to be awarded. "In the District of Columbia, the primary purpose of compensatory damages in personal injury cases 'is to make the plaintiff whole.'" District of Columbia v. Barriteau, 399 A.2d 563, 566 (D.C.1979) (quoting Kassman v. Am. Univ., 546 F.2d 1029, 1033 (D.C.Cir.1976)).

Courts must base compensatory damages awards on substantial evidence and not on mere speculation. . . . While the plaintiff need not prove damages to a mathematical certainty, the court must have a reasonable basis upon which to estimate the damages.

Regarding damages for the future consequences of a tort, an item is recoverable if the plaintiff proves by a reasonable certainty that the future consequence would have occurred or will occur. Courts have defined the "reasonable certainty" standard as identical to the preponderance of the evidence standard. In addition, courts should only award damages for future medical expenses when the expenses are reasonable and necessary.

. . .

C. Past Medical Care Expenses

The plaintiff requests an award of $899,325 for the medical care expenses that he incurred because of the accident. The defendant does not contest this amount, but asks the court to subtract from this award the amounts that his health care providers forgave or "wrote-off." The defendant explains that the amount that the plaintiff actually paid—as opposed to the amount paid plus the written-off amounts—represents the reasonable value of the care. The plaintiff objects to this request, arguing that pursuant to the collateral source rule, any written-off amounts are irrelevant and the award for past medical expenses should be $899,325, the amount billed.

Plaintiffs are entitled to recover for past medical care expenses as well as the cost of reasonable diagnostic examinations. In the District of Columbia, compensatory damages are subject to the collateral source rule, which states that "payments to the injured party from a collateral source are not allowed to diminish damages recoverable from the tortfeasor." Hardi v. Mezzanotte, 818 A.2d 974, 984 (D.C. 2003). This collateral source rule applies when either (1) the source of the benefit is independent of the tortfeasor or (2) the plaintiff contracted for the possibility of a double recovery.

The collateral source rule explicitly permits compensatory damages to include written-off amounts. In *Hardi*, the health care provider reduced the required payment pursuant to a contractual agreement with the injured plaintiff's insurance company. Just as the defendant argues here, Dr. Hardi argued that the plaintiff should not be able to recover written-off amounts. The court ruled that the collateral source rule applied and the injured plaintiff should receive the benefit of the agreement "including any reduction in payments that the insurance carrier was able to negotiate [for the plaintiff]." The court relied in part on a case where the hospital did not charge for medical services, explaining that "the interests of society are likely to be better served if the injured person is benefitted than if the wrongdoer is benefitted."

The collateral source rule applies in this case because the source of the benefit, the plaintiff's medical care providers' alleged writing-off of costs, is independent of the tortfeasor. The collateral source rule permits the plaintiff to recover all of his medical costs, regardless of any written-off amounts. Accordingly, the court awards the plaintiff $899,325 as damages for his past medical expenses.

D. Discounting to Present Value Awards for Future Damages

Before addressing the substance of the damages awards for future lost wages and medical and related expenses, the court discusses the methodology of calculating the present value of an award for future losses. . . .

Courts must discount to present value lump-sum damages awards intended to compensate for future medical costs or future lost wages. The leading case regarding calculating the present value of future damages is *Pfeifer*, which involves calculating future lost wages in an action brought pursuant to the Longshoremen's and Harbor Workers' Compensation Act, 33 U.S.C. §§ 904–05. In discounting a lump-sum award for future damages to present value, the discounting methodology must take into account two factors. First, the methodology must take into account the time-value of money, that is, the fact that money awarded today can be invested to earn a return. Second, the methodology must consider the effects of inflation. The discount rate should be based on the interest that can be earned with the safest available investments.

. . .

[T]o calculate the present value of the damages in a manner that accounts for medical costs that [may] rise faster than the rate of inflation, the court uses one net discount rate to calculate the present value of the future medical costs and a second net discount rate to calculate the present value of the future lost wages.

E. The Plaintiff's Award for Future Lost Wages

The court now turns to the plaintiff's claims for future lost wages. The plaintiff seeks an award of $2,562,906, and the defendant asserts that the award should be $546,663.

Considering the plaintiff's request for future lost wages, the court must evaluate whether he has proven the future consequences of the accident by a reasonable certainty. In order for the estimate of future lost wages to be reliable, the court must base it on facts specific to the plaintiff. Because the plaintiff has not yet chosen a livelihood, the court must determine future lost earnings on the basis of potential rather than demonstrated earning capacity. The court must extrapolate that potential from the plaintiff's individual characteristics such as age, sex, socio-economic status, family characteristics, criminal behavior, academic record, intelligence and dexterity. Further, "the plaintiff's occupational abilities, industriousness, work habits and experience are relevant" in estimating the future earnings he would accrue over the course of his lifetime. *McDavitt*, 804 A.2d at 290.

Accordingly, the court considers that before the accident the plaintiff had several problems, including (1) the past abuse of alcohol, marijuana, cocaine, inhalants, and intravenous drugs, (2) the present abuse of marijuana and (3) a diagnosis of depression. The plaintiff's prospects improved, however, in January 1997 when he returned to the United States to live with his mother, largely due to her close supervision of him. At the time of the accident, the plaintiff was in school, was excelling in his position at Kentucky Fried Chicken, was a devoted and reliable member of a soccer team, and was planning to attend [a community college]. The plaintiff's brother's path had provided him with a road map to graduate school. Indeed, his entire family is very well-educated: his mother has a doctorate degree, his father is a pediatrician, his brother is in medical school, and an uncle and a cousin are veterinarians. *Athridge*, 950 F.Supp. at 1193 (finding it reasonably likely that an injured adolescent would have earned a professional degree given his family's academic history and his own academic record). Significantly, the plaintiff was a bright young man with good cognitive functions, fluency in English and Spanish, and a decent academic record. The court also found credible the testimony of the plaintiff's vocational rehabilitation expert, Dr. Davis, that but for the accident the plaintiff would have completed college and two years of graduate study. In sum, the evidence demonstrates to a reasonable certainty that but for the accident the plaintiff would have completed college and two years of graduate study.

After determining the amount of future earnings that the plaintiff would have earned but for the tort, the court must discount the amount to its present value. Dr. Lurito, the plaintiff's expert economist, relied on Dr. Davis' conclusion that, absent the 1998 injury, the plaintiff would probably have graduated from college and completed two years of graduate study. Dr. Lurito testified that the plaintiff's estimated after-tax future lost wages, reduced to present value with a zero percent net discount rate (obtained by subtracting a 4.5 percent growth rate from a 4.5 percent after-tax discount rate), amount to $2,562,906. Because the court concludes that

Dr. Lurito's calculations are reasonable and based on substantial evidence, the court awards the plaintiff $2,562,906 for future lost wages.

F. The Plaintiff's Award for Future Medical and Related Expenses

Considering the issue of future medical and related expenses, the court notes that the plaintiff asks for $15,435,836 for these future costs. The defendant argues that this award should be $3,805,000. In estimating the cost of the plaintiff's future medical and related expenses, the court recognizes the significant discrepancy between the parties' estimates.

The plaintiff is entitled to an award for future medical and related expenses that are reasonable and necessary. Yearly evaluations and diagnostic examinations are proper items of damages when recommended to ensure that the plaintiff's treatment is proceeding properly and that any physical, emotional or developmental difficulties are diagnosed early. Equipment purchases are also a proper item of damages where the evidence shows that the plaintiff's development will improve with the assistance of such equipment. When the plaintiff's future need for full-time attendant care is more likely than not, an award including such care is proper. The argument that the plaintiff does not need attendant care because a family member is providing it is unpersuasive. In addition, a plaintiff has no duty to mitigate her damages award by accepting a less costly form of medical care. Rather, the plaintiff "may select from among a number of reasonable alternatives."

After listening to and reviewing the extensive testimony regarding the plaintiff's life care plan, the court concludes that the plaintiff's experts recommend all of the items in the plaintiff's life care plan as reasonable and necessary for the future treatment of his injuries as caused by the accident. Furthermore, while the provisions for the plaintiff's attendant care is highly contested and costly—especially because the plaintiff's plan does not include group care—the court concludes that the plaintiff has no duty to accept a less costly form of care. Thus, the award of damages to pay for eight hours per day of skilled attendant care and 16 hours per day of non-skilled attendant care is proper. The court concludes that the plaintiff has proven to a reasonable certainty that the items listed in his proposed life care plan are reasonable and medically necessary.

Notes

The collateral source rule. The collateral source rule mentioned in *Calva-Cerqueira* remains one of the more controversial areas in tort law. There are various justifications for the rule, including the idea that in the case of insurance benefits for which the plaintiff has already paid, allowing a jury to take those benefits into account when assessing damages would deny the plaintiff the benefit of the bargain and provide the defendant with a windfall. Critics counter that if the goal of providing tort damages is to make the plaintiff whole, the collateral source rule allows for double recovery and provides a windfall for the plaintiff. A number of states have abolished or modified the rule. *See* Ala. Code. §6-5-522 (providing that in product liability suits, proof that plaintiff's medical expenses were paid by medical, hospital, or workers' compensation insurance is admissible); Idaho Code § 6-1606 ("Evidence of payment by collateral sources is admissible to the court *after* the finder of fact has rendered an award," at which point the award is "reduced by the court to the extent the award includes compensation for damages which have been compensated independently from collateral sources"); Nebraska Rev. Stat. § 44-2819 (providing that evidence of "any nonrefundable medical reimbursement insurance shall not be admissible in evidence or brought to the attention of the jury, but such nonrefundable medical reimbursement insurance benefits, less all premiums paid by or for the claimant, may be taken as a credit against any judgment rendered").

Future lost wages and lost earning capacity. *Calva-Cerqueira* involved a plaintiff who was unable to earn *any* wages in the future due to the defendant's negligence. Some plaintiffs might instead suffer lost earning capacity as a result of a defendant's negligence, *i.e.*, the loss of the ability to earn higher-paying jobs in the future. Assume that a particular plaintiff is a psychologist. She claims that as a result of the defendant's actions, she was unable to open her own practice as she had planned and was instead forced to accept a lower-paying job. What evidence would she need to present in order to establish her lost earning capacity to the point of reasonable certainty and not mere speculation? *See* Samuelson v. Dept. of State Hospitals, 2016 Cal. App. Unpub. LEXIS 8012 (Oct. 28, 2016).

Problem 19.1. Refer back to the facts from the Chapter Problem. List at least five pieces of factual information you would need to develop, as Jeffrey's attorney, in order to help your client obtain compensation for the pecuniary damages to which he is entitled. Identify at least three types of witnesses you would need to line up to testify as to the propriety of the pecuniary damages you would seek on Jeffrey's behalf.

2. Nonpecuniary Damages

a. Pain and Suffering

Calva-Cerqueira v. United States

281 F. Supp. 2d 279 (D.D.C. 2003)

[The facts appear in the excerpt above. In this portion of the opinion, the court considered the plaintiff's claim for pain and suffering.]

B. Pain and Suffering

The plaintiff requests an award of $8,000,000 for his past and future pain and suffering as caused by the accident. The defendant argues that an award of $750,000 would be reasonable.

The plaintiff in the instant action has presented substantial evidence to prove that he suffers from severe and permanent injuries, physical and mental disabilities, pain, emotional distress, disfigurement, deformity and inconvenience as a result of the defendant's negligence. *Wood*, 859 F.2d at 1492; *see also Doe*, 492 A.2d at 861 (explaining that pain and suffering damages are appropriate for "conscious" pain and suffering). The plaintiff has proven that he appreciates many of his deficits. For example, he suffers mental anguish when he hears that he will never walk again, he is self conscious about his surgical scars, he is frustrated and anxious over questions of sexuality, and he feels hurt and frustrated when he upsets others by his inability to learn and understand. Beyond these items, the record also attests to many other losses and a great deal of pain, suffering, and mental anguish. For example, the plaintiff has paralysis and decreased sensation in the left side of his body. He is wheelchair bound and has to wear painful braces at all times. His stretching and other exercises are very painful. Prior to the accident, the plaintiff was healthy, intelligent, looking forward to attending college and a skilled soccer player.

In *Athridge v. Iglesias*, the court considered brain injuries similar to those of the instant plaintiff. Like the plaintiff in this case, the plaintiff in *Athridge* suffered brain damage resulting in loss of memory; damage to the frontal lobe resulting in lost ability to socialize, concentrate and modify behavior; physical impairment; loss of ability to integrate information and execute plans; and emotional trauma. While the plaintiff in *Athridge* functioned well enough to hold part-time minimum wage employment, the plaintiff in this case will most likely not be able to secure paid employment, though he might be able obtain volunteer employment. In *Athridge*, the court awarded the plaintiff $4,000,000 for the pain and suffering he had endured and would continue to endure, noting that the defendant must compensate the plaintiff for his severe mental and physical injuries.

Considering the pain and suffering that the plaintiff has already suffered and will continue to suffer throughout his life because of his injuries, and considering the $4,000,000 damage award in *Athridge* for a plaintiff with similar but slightly less severe injuries, the court awards the plaintiff $5,000,000 in pain and suffering damages. Especially when compared to the plaintiff in *Athridge*, the plaintiff's injuries provide a reasonable basis for this award.

Notes

Jury instructions. A typical example of jury instructions regarding pain and suffering damages is something along the lines of the following: "In making an award for such damages, you must use your best judgment and establish an amount of damages that is fair and reasonable in light of the evidence before you." Willis v. Settle, 162 S.W.3d 169 (Tenn. Ct. App. 2004). Is the lack of guidance to juries a weakness or a virtue of the system?

Statements to the jury. The "anchoring effect" theory postulates that the greater the amount of requested compensation (the *ad damnum* demand), the greater the jury verdict. One study found that jurors "reacted more negatively to, and were less influenced by, plaintiff *ad damnums* for pain and suffering than to damage requests in categories grounded in more objective evidence." Shari Seidman Diamond et al.,

Damage Anchors on Real Juries, 8 J. Empirical Legal Stud. 148, 148–49 (2011). Some courts prohibit lawyers from referencing specific dollar amounts in closing arguments, while others place limits on a lawyer's ability to provide an explanation or some type of mathematical formula as the basis for the *ad damnum* request (for example, putting a dollar value on pain and suffering for one day and then multiplying that figure by every day for the rest of the plaintiff's life). *See* Crum v. Ward, 122 S.E.2d 18 (W. Va. 1961); Certified T.V. & Appliance Co., Inc. v. Harrington, 109 S.E.2d 126 (Va. 1959).

Comparators. The *Calva-Cerqueira* court looked to pain and suffering awards in other cases to judge the reasonableness of the parties' respective positions on the issue in that case. In *Jutzi-Johnson v. U.S.*, 263 F.3d 753 (7th Cir. 2001), the defendant was negligent in supervising a prisoner who hung himself. The prisoner experienced several minutes of pain before dying. In the ensuing wrongful death action, the trial judge awarded $1.6 million in pain and suffering damages. On appeal, the defendant argued that this amount was unreasonable and pointed to lower awards in other prisoner suicide cases. The plaintiff pointed to other cases with higher pain and suffering awards involving plaintiffs who suffered over a period of hours. Is it appropriate to look to other cases in an effort to determine what an appropriate range of damages would be? If so, what would be the appropriate comparison in *Jutzi-Johnson*?

Multipliers. Personal injury lawyers often speak in terms of "multipliers" when estimating a reasonable award for pain and suffering (or general) damages. Where a plaintiff's medical costs are relatively small, a plaintiff's lawyer might estimate the pain and suffering damages to be 1.5 to 3 times that amount. Where the incurred medical costs are greater, it stands to reason that the pain and suffering is greater, so a multiplier of 4 or 5 might be more appropriate.

Problem 19.2. Refer back to the facts of the Chapter Problem. You represent Jeffrey. How much will you suggest to the jury that it should award Jeffrey in order to compensate him for his past and future pain and suffering?

b. Loss of Enjoyment of Life

McDougald v. Garber

536 N.E.2d 372 (N.Y. 1989)

WACHTLER, Chief Judge.

The specific questions raised here deal with assessment of nonpecuniary damages and are (1) whether some degree of cognitive awareness is a prerequisite to recovery for loss of enjoyment of life and (2) whether a jury should be instructed to consider and award damages for loss of enjoyment of life separately from damages for pain and suffering. We answer the first question in the affirmative and the second question in the negative.

On September 7, 1978, plaintiff Emma McDougald, then 31 years old, underwent a Caesarean section and tubal ligation at New York Infirmary. Defendant Garber performed the surgery; defendants Armengol and Kulkarni provided anesthesia. During the surgery, Mrs. McDougald suffered oxygen deprivation which resulted in severe brain damage and left her in a permanent comatose condition. This action was brought by Mrs. McDougald and her husband, suing derivatively, alleging that the injuries were caused by the defendants' acts of malpractice.

[The trial judge instructed the jury, "If you conclude that Emma McDougald is so neurologically impaired that she is totally incapable of experiencing any unpleasant or painful sensation, then, obviously, she cannot be awarded damages for conscious pain . . ." The judge also instructed, "Damages for the loss of the pleasures and pursuits of life, however, require no awareness of the loss on the part of the injured person. . . . It is possible, however, for an injured person to lose the enjoyment of life without experiencing any conscious pain and suffering. Damages for this item of injury relate not to what Emma McDougald is aware of, but rather to what she has lost."]

A jury found all defendants liable and awarded Emma McDougald a total of $9,650,102 in damages, including $1,000,000 for conscious pain and suffering and a separate award of $3,500,000 for loss of the pleasures and pursuits of life. The balance of the damages awarded to her were for pecuniary damages—lost earnings and the cost of custodial and nursing care. Her husband was awarded $1,500,000 on his derivative claim for the loss of his wife's services. On defendants' posttrial motions, the Trial Judge reduced the total award to Emma McDougald to $4,796,728 by striking the entire award for future nursing care ($2,353,374) and by reducing the separate awards for conscious pain and suffering and loss of the pleasures and pursuits of life to a single award of $2,000,000. Her husband's award was left intact. On cross appeals, the Appellate Division affirmed and later granted defendants leave to appeal to this court. [Only the issue of nonpecuniary damages was in dispute on appeal.]

We begin with the familiar proposition that an award of damages to a person injured by the negligence of another is to compensate the victim, not to punish the wrongdoer. The goal is to restore the injured party, to the extent possible, to the position that would have been occupied had the wrong not occurred. To be sure, placing the burden of compensation on the negligent party also serves as a deterrent, but purely punitive damages—that is, those which have no compensatory purpose—are prohibited unless the harmful conduct is intentional, malicious, outrageous, or otherwise aggravated beyond mere negligence.

Damages for nonpecuniary losses are, of course, among those that can be awarded as compensation to the victim. This aspect of damages, however, stands on less certain ground than does an award for pecuniary damages. An economic loss can be compensated in kind by an economic gain; but recovery for noneconomic losses such as pain and suffering and loss of enjoyment of life rests on "the legal fiction that money damages can compensate for a victim's injury." We accept this fiction, knowing that although money will neither ease the pain nor restore the victim's abilities, this device is as close as the law can come in its effort to right the wrong. We have no hope of evaluating what has been lost, but a monetary award may provide a measure of solace for the condition created.

Our willingness to indulge this fiction comes to an end, however, when it ceases to serve the compensatory goals of tort recovery. When that limit is met, further indulgence can only result in assessing damages that are punitive. The question posed by this case, then, is whether an award of damages for loss of enjoyment of life to a person whose injuries preclude any awareness of the loss serves a compensatory purpose. We conclude that it does not.

Simply put, an award of money damages in such circumstances has no meaning or utility to the injured person. An award for the loss of enjoyment of life "cannot provide [such a victim] with any consolation or ease any burden resting on him . . . He cannot spend it upon necessities or pleasures. He cannot experience the pleasure of giving it away" (Flannery v. United States, 4th Cir., 718 F.2d 108, 111, *cert. denied* 467 U.S. 1226, 104 S.Ct. 2679, 81 L.Ed.2d 874).

We recognize that, as the trial court noted, requiring some cognitive awareness as a prerequisite to recovery for loss of enjoyment of life will result in some cases "in the paradoxical situation that the greater the degree of brain injury inflicted by a negligent defendant, the smaller the award the plaintiff can recover in general damages." The force of this argument, however—the temptation to achieve a balance between injury and damages—has nothing to do with meaningful compensation for the victim. Instead, the temptation is rooted in a desire to punish the defendant in proportion to the harm inflicted. However relevant such retributive symmetry may be in the criminal law, it has no place in the law of civil damages, at least in the absence of culpability beyond mere negligence.

Accordingly, we conclude that cognitive awareness is a prerequisite to recovery for loss of enjoyment of life. We do not go so far, however, as to require the fact finder to sort out varying degrees of cognition and determine at what level a particular deprivation can be fully appreciated. With respect to pain and suffering, the trial court charged simply that there must be "some level of awareness" in order for plaintiff to recover. We think that this is an appropriate standard for all aspects of nonpecuniary loss. No doubt the standard ignores analytically relevant levels of cognition, but we resist the desire for analytical purity in favor of simplicity. A more complex instruction might give the appearance of greater precision but, given the limits of our understanding of the human mind, it would in reality lead only to greater speculation.

We turn next to the question whether loss of enjoyment of life should be considered a category of damages separate from pain and suffering.

. . .

There is no dispute here that the fact finder may, in assessing nonpecuniary damages, consider the effect of the injuries on the plaintiff's capacity to lead a normal life. Traditionally, in this State and elsewhere, this aspect of suffering has not been treated as a separate category of damages; instead, the plaintiff's inability to enjoy life to its fullest has been considered one type of suffering to be factored into a general award for nonpecuniary damages, commonly known as pain and suffering.

Recently, however, there has been an attempt to segregate the suffering associated with physical pain from the mental anguish that stems from the inability to engage in certain activities, and to have juries provide a separate award for each.

Some courts have resisted the effort, primarily on the ground that duplicative and therefore excessive awards would result. Other courts have allowed separate awards, noting that the types of suffering involved are analytically distinguishable. Still other courts have questioned the propriety of the practice but held that, in the particular case, separate awards did not constitute reversible error.

. . .

We do not dispute that distinctions can be found or created between the concepts of pain and suffering and loss of enjoyment of life. If the term "suffering" is limited to the emotional response to the sensation of pain, then the emotional response caused by the limitation of life's activities may be considered qualitatively different. But suffering need not be so limited—it can easily encompass the frustration and anguish caused by the inability to participate in activities that once brought pleasure. Traditionally, by treating loss of enjoyment of life as a permissible factor in assessing pain and suffering, courts have given the term this broad meaning.

If we are to depart from this traditional approach and approve a separate award for loss of enjoyment of life, it must be on the basis that such an approach will yield a more accurate evaluation of the compensation due to the plaintiff. We have no doubt that, in general, the total award for nonpecuniary damages would increase if we adopted the rule. That separate awards are advocated by plaintiffs and resisted by defendants is sufficient evidence that larger awards are at stake here. But a larger award does not by itself indicate that the goal of compensation has been better served.

The advocates of separate awards contend that because pain and suffering and loss of enjoyment of life can be distinguished, they must be treated separately if the plaintiff is to be compensated fully for each distinct injury suffered. We disagree. Such an analytical approach may have its place when the subject is pecuniary damages, which can be calculated with some precision. But the estimation of nonpecuniary damages is not amenable to such analytical precision and may, in fact, suffer from its application. Translating human suffering into dollars and cents involves no mathematical formula; it rests, as we have said, on a legal fiction. The figure that emerges is unavoidably distorted by the translation. Application of this murky process to the component parts of nonpecuniary injuries however analytically distinguishable they may be) cannot make it more accurate. If anything, the distortion will be amplified by repetition.

Thus, we are not persuaded that any salutary purpose would be served by having the jury make separate awards for pain and suffering and loss of enjoyment of life. We are confident, furthermore, that the trial advocate's art is a sufficient guarantee that none of the plaintiff's losses will be ignored by the jury.

The errors in the instructions given to the jury require a new trial on the issue of nonpecuniary damages to be awarded to plaintiff Emma McDougald.

Accordingly, the order of the Appellate Division, insofar as appealed from, should be modified, with costs to defendants, by granting a new trial on the issue of nonpecuniary damages of plaintiff Emma McDougald, and as so modified, affirmed.

Note

Hedonic damages. Damages for the loss of enjoyment of life are sometimes referred to as hedonic damages. Most courts do not allow separate recovery for such damages. *See, e.g.*, Dockery v. U.S., 663 F. Supp. 2d 111 (N.D.N.Y. 2009) (applying New York law); Golnick v. Callender, 860 N.W.2d 180, 195 (Neb. 2015). Courts have reached different conclusions on the specific questions presented in *McDougald*. *See* Eyoma v. Falco, 589 A.2d 653, 662 (N.J. Super. Ct. App. Div. 1991) (permitting recovery); Flannery v. United States, 297 S.E.2d 433, 438 (W. Va. 1982) (same).

Problem 19.3. You plan to file your personal injury lawsuit on behalf of Jeffrey in a jurisdiction that has never considered the question of whether damages for loss of enjoyment of life should be awarded separately from ordinary pain and suffering damages. You know that if you request such damages, the defendant will likely cite the arguments from the *McDougald* opinion. Would it be to your client's advantage to argue in favor of such a separate damages determination? If so, what arguments would you make in order to persuade the court to recognize such damages?

B. Punitive Damages

Punitive damages serve a different function from compensatory damages. As the name suggests, punitive damages are designed to punish and deter extreme misconduct. *See* Exxon Shipping Co. v. Baker, 554 U.S. 471, 492 (2008) (stating "the consensus today is that punitives are aimed not at compensation but principally at retribution and deterring harmful conduct"). Courts will instruct juries as to the standard to apply in deciding whether punitive damages are warranted. But the amount that a jury awards is often the subject of controversy.

1. In General

Bolsta v. Johnson

848 A.2d 306 (Vt. 2004)

Appellant Sarah Bolsta appeals the trial court's denial of a punitive damages award in her personal injury action based upon a motor vehicle collision caused by a drunk driver, Michael Johnson. We agree that the actions of the driver do not constitute the kind of malicious, intentional acts that punitive damages are designed to address, and therefore, we affirm.

The accident occurred in September 1999. Johnson failed to stop at an intersection controlled by a stop sign, causing a collision with appellant's oncoming vehicle. Appellant's car was totaled, and she suffered several injuries, including a broken kneecap and permanent damage to her knee mechanism. According to witness testimony, immediately after the accident Johnson took beer bottles from his vehicle, and broke them on the road. The officer who conducted the investigation of the accident concluded that Johnson was at fault. Johnson was uninsured.

Johnson was processed for driving under the influence of alcohol, and was found to have a BAC of 0.156 approximately two hours after the accident. Johnson stated that he had consumed two beers and three shots in the hour prior to the accident, and admitted being "slightly" under the influence of alcohol. Johnson had a suspended license—resulting from a prior DUI conviction—and three prior convictions for driving with a suspended license in Vermont. He was charged in district court with DUI, second offense, and with driving with a suspended license, fourth offense. Johnson entered no contest pleas to both charges.

Appellant commenced a personal injury action against Johnson and against appellant's uninsured motorist insurance carrier, Concord General Mutual Insurance Co. In her complaint, she sought both compensatory and punitive damages for Johnson's negligence. Because Johnson failed to answer or make an appearance, appellant was granted a default judgment. Appellant and Concord Mutual reached a settlement, and the insurance carrier was dismissed from the case. The court then determined that Johnson owed appellant compensatory damages in the amount of $131,921.35. The court rejected appellant's motion for punitive damages, finding that the standard articulated in *Brueckner v. Norwich University*, 169 Vt. 118, 730 A.2d 1086 (1999), had not been met, as there was no evidence of the requisite element of malice. This appeal followed.

Punitive damages are permitted upon evidence of malice, "[w]here the defendant's wrongdoing has been intentional and deliberate, and has the character of outrage frequently associated with crime." *Id.* at 129, 730 A.2d at 1095 (quoting W. Keeton et al., Prosser and Keeton on the Law of Torts § 2 (5th ed. 1984)). Actual malice may be shown by conduct manifesting personal ill will or carried out under circumstances evincing insult or oppression, or conduct showing a reckless disregard to the rights of others. In any case, however, there must be some evidence of bad motive, as mere negligence or even recklessness are not sufficient to show malice and therefore do not justify the imposition of punitive damages. Accordingly, in *Brueckner* we found that it was inappropriate to impose punitive damages against Norwich University for its conscious inaction and inattention to the issue of hazing despite numerous—often serious—incidents, because there was no evidence of bad motive.

Appellant claims that Johnson's conduct and history of conduct is either sufficient to prove malice as required for punitive damages under the *Brueckner* standard or, alternatively, that the standard should be amended. Appellant argues that punitive damages are warranted when a repeat drink driver or a person who repeatedly drives with a suspended license injures another driver through negligent driving. Appellant asserts that to purposefully and repeatedly commit these crimes requires a bad spirit or wrong intention, because the driver consciously chooses to pursue a course of conduct knowing that it creates a substantial risk of significant harm to others. According to appellant, the reasoning used to deny punitive damages to the plaintiff in *Brueckner* is inapposite in this case, as the conduct at issue is distinguishable. Appellant argues that unlike defendant Norwich University in *Brueckner*, defendant Johnson willfully committed criminal acts. In essence, defendant would have us adopt a rule that drunk driving is per se evidence of malice sufficient to impose punitive damages in every case in which the negligent act of a drunk driver causes injury. We are unwilling to do so because such a rule would be inconsistent with our standard for imposing punitive damages.

We have previously rejected the contention that violation of the law is sufficient evidence of malice. Willful violation of the law is insufficient evidence of malice, if not accompanied by "a showing of bad faith." *See* Bruntaeger v. Zeller, 147 Vt. 247, 254, 515 A.2d 123, 127 (1986) (punitive damages properly denied despite violation of consumer fraud statute because defendant's conduct was wrongful but not malicious); Meadowbrook Condo. Ass'n v. S. Burlington Realty Corp., 152 Vt. 16, 28, 565 A.2d 238, 245 (1989) (willful violation of consumer protection statute is wrongful conduct, but not evidence of degree of malice required for punitive damages). However wrongful, Johnson's conduct does not evince more than a reckless disregard of the right of others. As we pointed out in *Brueckner*, allowing punitive damages solely on that basis presents "the danger of . . . a test which may be so flexible that it can become virtually unlimited in its application."

We are aware that some jurisdictions have adopted a "per se" approach. Many other states, however, determine whether punitive damages are warranted in DUI cases by conducting an individualized inquiry into the driver's conduct and any other aggravating circumstances. We find this latter approach preferable and consistent with our jurisprudence.

The trial court's findings regarding punitive damages will be disturbed only if the court abused its discretion. Given the evidence in this case, there was no abuse. Defendant was found to have a BAC of 0.156 at the time of processing, and a suspended license resulting from a prior DUI conviction in 1997. While Johnson's conduct can be characterized as negligent or even reckless, there are no special circumstances, such as personal ill will or bad motive, to support a finding of actual malice. It was well within the court's discretion to conclude that "[t]he actions of defendant in this case do not constitute the kind of malicious, intentional acts that punitive damages are designed to address."

Taylor v. Superior Court

598 P.2d 854 (Cal. 1979)

RICHARDSON, Justice.

We consider whether punitive damages (Civ.Code, s 3294) are recoverable in a personal injury action brought against an intoxicated driver....

Petitioner Taylor is the plaintiff in a civil action against defendant and real party Stille (and others) for damages arising from an automobile accident. Because the matter is presented to us following the sustaining of defendant's demurrer as to the prayer for punitive damages, the issues are framed by the allegations of the complaint which we now examine. In pertinent part, the complaint alleged that the car driven by Stille collided with plaintiff's car, causing plaintiff serious injuries; that Stille is, and for a substantial period of time had been, an alcoholic "well aware of the serious nature of his alcoholism" and of his "tendency, habit, history, practice, proclivity, or inclination to drive a motor vehicle while under the influence of alcohol"; and that Stille was also aware of the dangerousness of his driving while intoxicated.

The complaint further alleged that Stille had previously caused a serious automobile accident while driving under the influence of alcohol; that he had been arrested and convicted for drunken driving on numerous prior occasions; that at the time of the accident herein, Stille had recently completed a period of probation which followed a drunk driving conviction; that one of his probation conditions was that he refrain from driving for at least six hours after consuming any alcoholic beverage; and that at the time of the accident in question he was presently facing an additional pending criminal drunk driving charge.

In addition, the complaint averred that notwithstanding his alcoholism, Stille accepted employment which required him both to call on various commercial establishments where alcoholic beverages were sold, and to deliver or transport such beverages in his car. Finally, it is alleged that at the time the accident occurred, Stille was transporting alcoholic beverages, "was simultaneously driving ... while consuming an alcoholic beverage," and was "under the influence of intoxicants."

...

Section 3294 of the Civil Code authorizes the recovery of punitive damages in noncontract cases "where the defendant has been guilty of oppression, fraud, or malice, express or implied...." As we recently explained, "This has long been interpreted to mean that malice in fact, as opposed to malice implied by law, is required. The malice in fact, referred to . . . as *animus malus*, may be proved under section 3294 either expressly (by direct evidence probative on the existence of hatred or ill will) or by implication (by indirect evidence from which the jury may draw inferences).

Other authorities have amplified the foregoing principle. Thus it has been held that the "malice" required by section 3294 "implies an act conceived in a spirit of mischief or with criminal indifference towards the obligations owed to others." In Dean Prosser's words: "Where the defendant's wrongdoing has been intentional and deliberate, and has the character of outrage frequently associated with crime, all but a few courts have permitted the jury to award in the tort action 'punitive' or 'exemplary' damages . . . . Something more than the mere commission of a tort is always required for punitive damages. There must be circumstances of aggravation or outrage, such as spite or 'malice,' or a fraudulent or evil motive on the part of the defendant, *or such a conscious and deliberate disregard of the interests of others that his conduct may be called wilful or wanton.*" (italics added.)

Defendant's successful demurrer to the complaint herein was based upon plaintiff's failure to allege any actual intent of defendant to harm plaintiff or others. Is this an essential element of a claim for punitive damages? As indicated by Dean Prosser, courts have not limited the availability of punitive damages to cases in which such an intent has been shown. As we ourselves have recently observed, in order to justify the imposition of punitive damages the defendant "'. . . must act with the intent to vex, injure, or annoy, *or with a conscious disregard of the plaintiff's rights.*'"

. . .

[A] conscious disregard of the safety of others may constitute malice within the meaning of section 3294 of the Civil Code. In order to justify an award of punitive damages on this basis, the plaintiff must establish that the defendant was aware of the probable dangerous consequences of his conduct, and that he willfully and deliberately failed to avoid those consequences.

elements P must prove for P.D.

[The court held that the defendant's actions, as alleged, which involved the defendant being under the influence of intoxicants at the time of the collision and the defendant having had multiple arrests and accidents stemming from alcohol consumption, could support an award of punitive damages.]

Defendant's final contention is that many instances of simple negligent conduct not involving consumption of alcoholic beverages could also be alleged to involve a conscious disregard of the safety of others. For example, one who willfully disobeys traffic signals or speed limit laws arguably possesses such a state of mind and culpability. That case is not before us and we express no opinion on it, holding only that one who voluntarily commences, and thereafter continues, to consume alcoholic beverages to the point of intoxication, knowing from the outset that he must thereafter operate a motor vehicle demonstrates, in the words of Dean Prosser, "such a conscious and deliberate disregard of the interests of others that his conduct may be called willful or wanton." (Prosser, *supra*, § 2, at pp. 9–10.) Although the circumstances in a particular case may disclose similar willful or wanton behavior in other forms, ordinarily, routine negligent or even reckless disobedience of traffic laws would not justify an award of punitive damages.

Notes

Standards for awarding punitive damages. The indicators for whether an award of punitive damages is warranted are often similar to those in intentional infliction of emotional distress cases. *See* Restatement (Second) of Torts § 908(2) (1979) ("Punitive damages may be awarded for conduct that is outrageous."); In re Sansone, 99 B.R. 981, 987 (C.D. Cal. Bkrtcy. Ct. 1989) (recognizing award of punitive damages is appropriate where there has been misuse or abuse of authority or power); Henley v. Phillip Morris, Inc., 114 Cal. App. 4th 1429 (2004) (stating the fact that the defendant took advantage of the known vulnerability of the victim may justify a punitive damages award).

Wealth of the defendant. "In assessing punitive damages, the trier of fact can properly consider . . . the wealth of the defendant." Restatement (Second) of Torts § 908(2) (1979). Why is this permitted? Evidence of a defendant's wealth might prejudice a jury on the issues of liability and compensatory damages. As a result, some courts bifurcate the proceedings so that *if* the jury determines that punitive damages are warranted, the plaintiff may *then* introduce evidence of the defendant's wealth. *See* Campen v. Stone, 635 P.2d 1121 (Wyo. 1981).

Punitive damages awards against employers. Most courts take the position that while an employer may be held vicariously liable for the torts of an employee and be required to pay compensatory damages, an employer "is not liable for punitive damages for the same act, unless it is proved, over and above the fact that the agent was acting within the scope of his authority, that the principal participated in, authorized, or ratified the actual tortious conduct of the agent." Sanchez v. Securities Acceptance Corporation, 260 P.2d 703, 706–07 (N.M. 1953).

Problem 19.4. The power company's negligence in Jeffrey's case stemmed from its failure to trim trees located within the company's easement to avoid the damaging of the power lines. The company's own inspections had revealed months earlier that the trees in the area needed to be trimmed and that several branches were in imminent danger of falling. Despite this, the company did not trim the trees. Eventually, a branch fell, causing the downed power line that injured Jeffrey. Is Jeffrey entitled to punitive damages from the power company?

2. Constitutional Limitations

State Farm Mutual Automobile Insurance Co. v. Campbell

538 U.S. 408 (2003)

Justice KENNEDY delivered the opinion of the Court.

We address once again the measure of punishment, by means of punitive damages, a State may impose upon a defendant in a civil case. The question is whether, in the circumstances we shall recount, an award of $145 million in punitive damages, where full compensatory damages are $1 million, is excessive and in violation of the Due Process Clause of the Fourteenth Amendment to the Constitution of the United States.

I

In 1981, Curtis Campbell (Campbell) was driving with his wife, Inez Preece Campbell, in Cache County, Utah. He decided to pass six vans traveling ahead of them on a two-lane highway. Todd Ospital was driving a small car approaching from the opposite direction. To avoid a head-on collision with Campbell, who by then was driving on the wrong side of the highway and toward oncoming traffic, Ospital swerved onto the shoulder, lost control of his automobile, and collided with a vehicle driven by Robert G. Slusher. Ospital was killed, and Slusher was rendered permanently disabled. The Campbells escaped unscathed.

In the ensuing wrongful death and tort action, Campbell insisted he was not at fault. Early investigations did support differing conclusions as to who caused the accident, but "a consensus was reached early on by the investigators and witnesses that Mr. Campbell's unsafe pass had indeed caused the crash." 65 P.3d 1134, 1141 (Utah 2001). Campbell's insurance company, petitioner State Farm Mutual Automobile Insurance Company (State Farm), nonetheless decided to contest liability and declined offers by Slusher and Ospital's estate (Ospital) to settle the claims for the policy limit of $50,000 ($25,000 per claimant). State Farm also ignored the advice of one of its own investigators and took the case to trial, assuring the Campbells that "their assets were safe, that they had no liability for the accident, that [State Farm] would represent their interests, and that they did not need to procure separate counsel." To the contrary, a jury determined that Campbell was 100 percent at fault, and a judgment was returned for $185,849, far more than the amount offered in settlement.

At first State Farm refused to cover the $135,849 in excess liability. Its counsel made this clear to the Campbells: "'You may want to put for sale signs on your property to get things moving.'" Nor was State Farm willing to post a supersedeas bond to allow Campbell to appeal the judgment against him. Campbell obtained his own counsel to appeal the verdict. During the pendency of the appeal, in late 1984, Slusher, Ospital, and the Campbells reached an agreement whereby Slusher and Ospital agreed not to seek satisfaction of their claims against the Campbells. In exchange the Campbells agreed to pursue a bad faith action against State Farm and to be represented by Slusher's and Ospital's attorneys. The Campbells also agreed that Slusher and Ospital would have a right to play a part in all major decisions concerning the bad-faith action. No settlement could be concluded without Slusher's and Ospital's approval, and Slusher and Ospital would receive 90 percent of any verdict against State Farm.

In 1989, the Utah Supreme Court denied Campbell's appeal in the wrongful-death and tort actions. State Farm then paid the entire judgment, including the amounts in excess of the policy limits. The Campbells nonetheless filed a complaint against State Farm alleging bad faith, fraud, and intentional infliction of emotional distress. The trial court initially granted State Farm's motion for summary judgment because State Farm had paid the excess verdict, but that ruling was reversed on appeal. On remand State Farm moved *in limine* to exclude evidence of alleged conduct that occurred in unrelated cases outside of Utah, but the trial court denied the motion. At State Farm's request the trial court bifurcated the trial into two phases conducted before different juries. In the first phase the jury determined that State Farm's decision not to settle was unreasonable because there was a substantial likelihood of an excess verdict.

Before the second phase of the action against State Farm we decided *BMW of North America, Inc. v. Gore*, 517 U.S. 559, 116 S.Ct. 1589, 134 L.Ed.2d 809 (1996), and refused to sustain a $2 million punitive damages award which accompanied a verdict of only $4,000 in compensatory damages. Based on that decision, State Farm again moved for the exclusion of evidence of dissimilar out-of-state conduct. The trial court denied State Farm's motion.

The second phase addressed State Farm's liability for fraud and intentional infliction of emotional distress, as well as compensatory and punitive damages. The Utah Supreme Court aptly characterized this phase of the trial:

> "State Farm argued during phase II that its decision to take the case to trial was an 'honest mistake' that did not warrant punitive damages. In contrast, the Campbells introduced evidence that State Farm's decision to take the case to trial was a result of a national scheme to meet corporate fiscal goals by capping payouts on claims company wide. This scheme was referred to as State Farm's 'Performance, Planning and Review,' or PP & R, policy. To prove the existence of this scheme, the trial court allowed the Campbells to introduce extensive expert testimony regarding fraudulent practices by State Farm in its nation-wide operations. Although State Farm moved prior to phase II of the trial for the exclusion of such evidence and continued to object to it at trial, the trial court ruled that such evidence was admissible to determine whether State Farm's conduct in the Campbell case was indeed intentional and sufficiently egregious to warrant punitive damages." 65 P.3d, at 1143.

Evidence pertaining to the PP & R policy concerned State Farm's business practices for over 20 years in numerous States. Most of these practices bore no relation to third-party automobile insurance claims, the type of claim underlying the Campbells' complaint against the company. The jury awarded the Campbells $2.6 million in compensatory damages and $145 million in punitive damages, which the trial court reduced to $1 million and $25 million respectively. Both parties appealed.

The Utah Supreme Court sought to apply the three guideposts we identified in *Gore, supra*, and it reinstated the $145 million punitive damages award. Relying in large part on the extensive evidence concerning the PP & R policy, the court concluded State Farm's conduct was reprehensible. The court also relied upon State Farm's "massive wealth" and on testimony indicating that "State Farm's actions, because of their clandestine nature, will be punished at most in one out of every 50,000 cases as a matter of statistical probability," and concluded that the ratio between punitive and compensatory damages was not unwarranted. Finally, the court noted that the punitive damages award was not excessive when compared to various civil and criminal penalties State Farm could have faced, including $10,000 for each act of fraud, the suspension of its license to conduct business in Utah, the disgorgement of profits, and imprisonment. We granted certiorari.

II

We recognized in *Cooper Industries, Inc. v. Leatherman Tool Group, Inc.*, 532 U.S. 424, 121 S.Ct. 1678, 149 L.Ed.2d 674 (2001), that in our judicial system compensatory and punitive damages, although usually awarded at the same time by the same decisionmaker, serve different purposes. Compensatory damages "are intended to redress the concrete loss that the plaintiff has suffered by reason of the defendant's wrongful conduct." By contrast, punitive damages serve a broader function; they are aimed at deterrence and retribution.

While States possess discretion over the imposition of punitive damages, it is well established that there are procedural and substantive constitutional limitations on these awards. The Due Process Clause of the Fourteenth Amendment prohibits the imposition of grossly excessive or arbitrary punishments on a tortfeasor. The reason is that "[e]lementary notions of fairness enshrined in our constitutional jurisprudence dictate that a person receive fair notice not only of the conduct that will subject him to punishment, but also of the severity of the penalty that a State may impose." To the extent an award is grossly excessive, it furthers no legitimate purpose and constitutes an arbitrary deprivation of property.

Although these awards serve the same purposes as criminal penalties, defendants subjected to punitive damages in civil cases have not been accorded the protections applicable in a criminal proceeding. This increases our concerns over the imprecise manner in which punitive damages systems are administered. We have admonished that "[p]unitive damages pose an acute danger of arbitrary deprivation of property. Jury instructions typically leave the jury with wide discretion in choosing amounts, and the presentation of evidence of a defendant's net worth creates the potential that juries will use their verdicts to express biases against big businesses, particularly those without strong local presences." *Honda Motor, supra*, at 432, 114 S.Ct. 2331;

see also Haslip, supra, at 59, 111 S.Ct. 1032 (O'CONNOR, J., dissenting) ("[T]he Due Process Clause does not permit a State to classify arbitrariness as a virtue. Indeed, the point of due process—of the law in general—is to allow citizens to order their behavior. A State can have no legitimate interest in deliberately making the law so arbitrary that citizens will be unable to avoid punishment based solely upon bias or whim"). Our concerns are heightened when the decisionmaker is presented, as we shall discuss, with evidence that has little bearing as to the amount of punitive damages that should be awarded. Vague instructions, or those that merely inform the jury to avoid "passion or prejudice" do little to aid the decisionmaker in its task of assigning appropriate weight to evidence that is relevant and evidence that is tangential or only inflammatory.

In light of these concerns, in *Gore, supra*, we instructed courts reviewing punitive damages to consider three guideposts: (1) the degree of reprehensibility of the defendant's misconduct; (2) the disparity between the actual or potential harm suffered by the plaintiff and the punitive damages award; and (3) the difference between the punitive damages awarded by the jury and the civil penalties authorized or imposed in comparable cases. We reiterated the importance of these three guideposts in *Cooper Industries* and mandated appellate courts to conduct de novo review of a trial court's application of them to the jury's award. Exacting appellate review ensures that an award of punitive damages is based upon an "'application of law, rather than a decisionmaker's caprice.'"

III

Under the principles outlined in *BMW of North America, Inc. v. Gore*, this case is neither close nor difficult. It was error to reinstate the jury's $145 million punitive damages award. We address each guidepost of *Gore* in some detail.

A

"[T]he most important indicium of the reasonableness of a punitive damages award is the degree of reprehensibility of the defendant's conduct." *Gore*, 517 U.S., at 575, 116 S.Ct. 1589. We have instructed courts to determine the reprehensibility of a defendant by considering whether: the harm caused was physical as opposed to economic; the tortious conduct evinced an indifference to or a reckless disregard of the health or safety of others; the target of the conduct had financial vulnerability; the conduct involved repeated actions or was an isolated incident; and the harm was the result of intentional malice, trickery, or deceit, or mere accident. The existence of any one of these factors weighing in favor of a plaintiff may not be sufficient to sustain a punitive damages award; and the absence of all of them renders any award suspect. It should be presumed a plaintiff has been made whole for his injuries by compensatory damages, so punitive damages should only be awarded if the defendant's culpability, after having paid compensatory damages, is so reprehensible as to warrant the imposition of further sanctions to achieve punishment or deterrence.

Applying these factors in the instant case, we must acknowledge that State Farm's handling of the claims against the Campbells merits no praise. The trial court found that State Farm's employees altered the company's records to make Campbell appear less culpable. State Farm disregarded the overwhelming likelihood of liability and the near-certain probability that, by taking the case to trial, a judgment in excess of the policy limits would be awarded. State Farm amplified the harm by at first assuring the Campbells their assets would be safe from any verdict and by later telling them, postjudgment, to put a for-sale sign on their house. While we do not suggest there was error in awarding punitive damages based upon State Farm's conduct toward the Campbells, a more modest punishment for this reprehensible conduct could have satisfied the State's legitimate objectives, and the Utah courts should have gone no further.

This case, instead, was used as a platform to expose, and punish, the perceived deficiencies of State Farm's operations throughout the country. The Utah Supreme Court's opinion makes explicit that State Farm was being condemned for its nationwide policies rather than for the conduct directed toward the Campbells. This was, as well, an explicit rationale of the trial court's decision in approving the award, though reduced from $145 million to $25 million.

A State cannot punish a defendant for conduct that may have been lawful where it occurred. Nor, as a general rule, does a State have a legitimate concern in imposing punitive damages to punish a defendant for unlawful acts committed outside of the State's jurisdiction. Any proper adjudication of conduct that occurred outside Utah to other persons would require their inclusion, and, to those parties, the Utah courts, in the usual case, would need to apply the laws of their relevant jurisdiction.

Here, the Campbells do not dispute that much of the out-of-state conduct was lawful where it occurred. They argue, however, that such evidence was not the primary basis for the punitive damages award and was relevant to the extent it demonstrated, in a general sense, State Farm's motive against its insured. This argument misses the mark. Lawful out-of-state conduct may be probative when it demonstrates the deliberateness and culpability of the defendant's action in the State where it is tortious, but that conduct must have a nexus to the specific harm suffered by the plaintiff. A jury must be instructed, furthermore, that it may not use evidence of out-of-state conduct to punish a defendant for action that was lawful in the jurisdiction where it occurred. *Gore*, 517 U.S., at 572–573, 116 S.Ct. 1589 (noting that a State "does not have the power . . . to punish [a defendant] for conduct that was lawful where it occurred and that had no impact on [the State] or its residents"). A basic principle of federalism is that each State may make its own reasoned judgment about what conduct is permitted or proscribed within its borders, and each State alone can determine what measure of punishment, if any, to impose on a defendant who acts within its jurisdiction.

For a more fundamental reason, however, the Utah courts erred in relying upon this and other evidence: The courts awarded punitive damages to punish and deter conduct that bore no relation to the Campbells' harm. A defendant's dissimilar acts, independent from the acts upon which liability was premised, may not serve as the basis for punitive damages. A defendant should be punished for the conduct that harmed the plaintiff, not for being an unsavory individual or business. Due process does not permit courts, in the calculation of punitive damages, to adjudicate the merits of other parties' hypothetical claims against a defendant under the guise of the reprehensibility analysis, but we have no doubt the Utah Supreme Court did that here. 65 P.3d, at 1149 ("Even if the harm to the Campbells can be appropriately characterized as minimal, the trial court's assessment of the situation is on target: 'The harm is minor to the individual but massive in the aggregate'"). Punishment on these bases creates the possibility of multiple punitive damages awards for the same conduct; for in the usual case nonparties are not bound by the judgment some other plaintiff obtains.

The same reasons lead us to conclude the Utah Supreme Court's decision cannot be justified on the grounds that State Farm was a recidivist. Although "[o]ur holdings that a recidivist may be punished more severely than a first offender recognize that repeated misconduct is more reprehensible than an individual instance of malfeasance," in the context of civil actions courts must ensure the conduct in question replicates the prior transgressions.

The Campbells have identified scant evidence of repeated misconduct of the sort that injured them. Nor does our review of the Utah courts' decisions convince us that State Farm was only punished for its actions toward the Campbells. Although evidence of other acts need not be identical to have relevance in the calculation of punitive damages, the Utah court erred here because evidence pertaining to claims that had nothing to do with a third-party lawsuit was introduced at length. Other evidence concerning reprehensibility was even more tangential. For example, the Utah Supreme Court criticized State Farm's investigation into the personal life of one of its employees and, in a broader approach, the manner in which State Farm's policies corrupted its employees. The Campbells attempt to justify the courts' reliance upon this unrelated testimony on the theory that each dollar of profit made by underpaying a third-party claimant is the same as a dollar made by underpaying a first-party one. For the reasons already stated, this argument is unconvincing. The reprehensibility guidepost does not permit courts to expand the scope of the case so that a defendant may be punished for any malfeasance, which in this case extended for a 20-year period. In this case, because the Campbells have shown no conduct by State Farm similar to that which harmed them, the conduct that harmed them is the only conduct relevant to the reprehensibility analysis.

B

Turning to the second *Gore* guidepost, we have been reluctant to identify concrete constitutional limits on the ratio between harm, or potential harm, to the plaintiff and the punitive damages award. 517 U.S., at 582, 116 S.Ct. 1589 ("[W]e have consistently rejected the notion that the constitutional line is marked by a simple mathematical formula, even one that compares actual and potential damages to the punitive award"); *TXO, supra*, at 458, 113 S.Ct. 2711. We decline again to impose a bright-line ratio which a punitive damages award cannot exceed. Our jurisprudence and the principles it has now established demonstrate, however, that, in practice, few awards exceeding a single-digit ratio between punitive and compensatory damages, to a significant degree, will satisfy due process. In *Haslip*, in upholding a punitive damages award, we concluded that an award of more than four times the amount of compensatory damages might be close to the line of constitutional impropriety. 499 U.S., at 23–24, 111 S.Ct. 1032. We cited that 4-to-1 ratio again in *Gore*. 517 U.S., at 581, 116 S.Ct. 1589. The Court further referenced a long legislative history, dating back over 700 years and going forward to today, providing for sanctions of double, treble, or quadruple damages to deter and punish. While these ratios are not binding, they are instructive. They demonstrate what should be obvious: Single-digit multipliers are more likely to comport with due process, while still achieving the State's goals of deterrence and retribution, than awards with ratios in range of 500 to 1, or, in this case, of 145 to 1.

Nonetheless, because there are no rigid benchmarks that a punitive damages award may not surpass, ratios greater than those we have previously upheld may comport with due process where "a particularly egregious act has resulted in only a small amount of economic damages." The converse is also true, however. When compensatory damages are substantial, then a lesser ratio, perhaps only equal to compensatory damages, can reach the outermost limit of the due process guarantee. The precise award in any case, of course, must be based upon the facts and circumstances of the defendant's conduct and the harm to the plaintiff.

In sum, courts must ensure that the measure of punishment is both reasonable and proportionate to the amount of harm to the plaintiff and to the general damages recovered....

C

The third guidepost in *Gore* is the disparity between the punitive damages award and the "civil penalties authorized or imposed in comparable cases." We note that, in the past, we have also looked to criminal penalties that could be imposed. The existence of a criminal penalty does have bearing on the seriousness with which a State views the wrongful action. When used to determine the dollar amount of the award, however, the criminal penalty has less utility. Great care must be taken to avoid use of the civil process to assess criminal penalties that can be imposed only after the heightened protections of a criminal trial have been observed, including, of course, its higher standards of proof. Punitive damages are not a substitute for the criminal process, and the remote possibility of a criminal sanction does not automatically sustain a punitive damages award.

Here, we need not dwell long on this guidepost. The most relevant civil sanction under Utah state law for the wrong done to the Campbells appears to be a $10,000 fine for an act of fraud, an amount dwarfed by the $145 million punitive damages award. The Supreme Court of Utah speculated about the loss of State Farm's business license, the disgorgement of profits, and possible imprisonment, but here again its references were to the broad fraudulent scheme drawn from evidence of out-of-state and dissimilar conduct. This analysis was insufficient to justify the award.

IV

An application of the *Gore* guideposts to the facts of this case, especially in light of the substantial compensatory damages awarded (a portion of which contained a punitive element), likely would justify a punitive damages award at or near the amount of compensatory damages. The punitive award of $145 million, therefore, was neither reasonable nor proportionate to the wrong committed, and it was an irrational and arbitrary deprivation of the property of the defendant. The proper calculation of punitive damages under the principles we have discussed should be resolved, in the first instance, by the Utah courts.

The judgment of the Utah Supreme Court is reversed, and the case is remanded for further proceedings not inconsistent with this opinion.

Justice SCALIA, dissenting.

I adhere to the view expressed in my dissenting opinion in *BMW of North America, Inc. v. Gore* that the Due Process Clause provides no substantive protections against "excessive" or "'unreasonable'" awards of punitive damages. I am also of the view that the punitive damages jurisprudence which has sprung forth from *BMW v. Gore* is insusceptible of principled application; accordingly, I do not feel justified in giving the case *stare decisis* effect. I would affirm the judgment of the Utah Supreme Court.

Justice GINSBURG, dissenting.

The large size of the award upheld by the Utah Supreme Court in this case indicates why damages-capping legislation may be altogether fitting and proper. Neither the amount of the award nor the trial record, however, justifies this Court's substitution of its judgment for that of Utah's competent decisionmakers. In this regard, I count it significant that, on the key criterion "reprehensibility," there is a good deal more to the story than the Court's abbreviated account tells.

Ample evidence allowed the jury to find that State Farm's treatment of the Campbells typified its "Performance, Planning and Review" (PP & R) program; implemented by top management in 1979, the program had "the explicit objective of using the claims-adjustment process as a profit center.". "[T]he Campbells presented considerable evidence," the trial court noted, documenting "that the PP & R program . . . has functioned, and continues to function, as an unlawful scheme . . . to deny benefits owed consumers by paying out less than fair value in order to meet preset, arbitrary payout targets designed to enhance corporate profits." That policy, the trial court observed, was encompassing in scope; it "applied equally to the handling of both third-party and first-party claims."

Evidence the jury could credit demonstrated that the PP & R program regularly and adversely affected Utah residents. Ray Summers, "the adjuster who handled the Campbell case and who was a State Farm employee in Utah for almost twenty years," described several methods used by State Farm to deny claimants fair benefits, for example, "falsifying or withholding of evidence in claim files." A common tactic, Summers recounted, was to "unjustly attac[k] the character, reputation and credibility of a claimant and mak[e] notations to that effect in the claim file to create prejudice in the event the claim ever came before a jury." State Farm manager Bob Noxon, Summers testified, resorted to a tactic of this order in the Campbell case when he "instruct[ed] Summers to write in the file that Todd Ospital (who was killed in the accident) was speeding because he was on his way to see a pregnant girlfriend." In truth, "[t]here was no pregnant girlfriend." Expert testimony noted by the trial court described these tactics as "completely improper."

The trial court further determined that the jury could find State Farm's policy "deliberately crafted" to prey on consumers who would be unlikely to defend themselves. In this regard, the trial court noted the testimony of several former State Farm employees affirming that they were trained to target "the weakest of the herd"—"the elderly, the poor, and other consumers who are least knowledgeable about their rights and thus most vulnerable to trickery or deceit, or who have little money and hence have no real alternative but to accept an inadequate offer to settle a claim at much less than fair value."

The Campbells themselves could be placed within the "weakest of the herd" category. The couple appeared economically vulnerable and emotionally fragile. At the time of State Farm's wrongful conduct, "Mr. Campbell had residuary effects from a stroke and Parkinson's disease."

To further insulate itself from liability, trial evidence indicated, State Farm made "systematic" efforts to destroy internal company documents that might reveal its scheme, efforts that directly affected the Campbells. For example, State Farm had "a special historical department that contained a copy of all past manuals on claim-handling practices and the dates on which each section of each manual was changed." Yet in discovery proceedings, State Farm failed to produce any claim-handling practice manuals for the years relevant to the Campbells' bad-faith case.

State Farm's inability to produce the manuals, it appeared from the evidence, was not accidental. Documents retained by former State Farm employee Samantha Bird, as well as Bird's testimony, showed that while the Campbells' case was pending, Janet Cammack, "an in-house attorney sent by top State Farm management, conducted a meeting ... in Utah during which she instructed Utah claims management to search their offices and destroy a wide range of material of the sort that had proved damaging in bad-faith litigation in the past—in particular, old claim-handling manuals, memos, claim school notes, procedure guides and other similar documents." "These orders were followed even though at least one meeting participant, Paul Short, was personally aware that these kinds of materials had been requested by the Campbells in this very case."

...

The Court dismisses the evidence describing and documenting State Farm's PP & R policy and practices as essentially irrelevant, bearing "no relation to the Campbells' harm." It is hardly apparent why that should be so. What is infirm about the

Campbells' theory that their experience with State Farm exemplifies and reflects an overarching underpayment scheme, one that caused "repeated misconduct of the sort that injured them?" The Court's silence on that score is revealing: Once one recognizes that the Campbells did show "conduct by State Farm similar to that which harmed them," it becomes impossible to shrink the reprehensibility analysis to this sole case, or to maintain, at odds with the determination of the trial court, that "the adverse effect on the State's general population was in fact minor."

Evidence of out-of-state conduct, the Court acknowledges, may be "probative [even if the conduct is lawful in the State where it occurred] when it demonstrates the deliberateness and culpability of the defendant's action in the State where it is tortious. . . ." "Other acts" evidence concerning practices both in and out of State was introduced in this case to show just such "deliberateness" and "culpability." The evidence was admissible, the trial court ruled: (1) to document State Farm's "reprehensible" PP & R program; and (2) to "rebut [State Farm's] assertion that [its] actions toward the Campbells were inadvertent errors or mistakes in judgment." Viewed in this light, there surely was "a nexus" between much of the "other acts" evidence and "the specific harm suffered by [the Campbells]."

I remain of the view that this Court has no warrant to reform state law governing awards of punitive damages. Even if I were prepared to accept the flexible guides prescribed in *Gore*, I would not join the Court's swift conversion of those guides into instructions that begin to resemble marching orders. For the reasons stated, I would leave the judgment of the Utah Supreme Court undisturbed.

Notes

Other Supreme Court decisions. The Court has visited the issue of excessive punitive damages awards on numerous occasions in the past few decades. In *Pacific Mut. Life Ins. Co. v. Haslip*, 499 U.S. 1, 18 (1991), the Court noted that it could not "draw a mathematical bright line between the constitutionally acceptable and the constitutionally unacceptable that would fit every case." Two years later in *TXO Production Corp. v. Alliance Resources Corp.*, 509 U.S. 443 (1993), the Court concluded that a punitive damages award of $10 million in a case with $19,000 in actual damages was grossly excessive in violation of due process. In *BMW of North America, Inc. v. Gore*, 517 U.S. 559 (1996), the Court concluded that a 500:1 ratio between punitives and compensatory damages in a fraud case offended due process. In 2007, the Court held that that a jury cannot directly punish a defendant for harm caused to others who are not part of the case, but a jury may take into account harm to others when assessing the reprehensibility of the defendant's conduct under the first *Gore* guidepost. *See* Phillip Morris USA v. Williams, 549 U.S. 346 (2007).

Other limitations on punitive damages awards. There may be other limitations on a jury's punitive damages award. In *Exxon Shipping Co. v. Baker*, 554 U.S. 471 (2008), the Supreme Court considered the propriety of a jury award of $5 billion, later reduced by the appellate court to $2.5 billion. The total compensatory damages awarded were $507.5 million. The case stemmed from the grounding of the oil tanker *Exxon Valdez* on an Alaskan reef, which caused tremendous environmental and economic harm. In a fractured opinion, the Court held that the punitive damages award was excessive as a matter of maritime common law. Part C below explores statutory limitations on punitive damages awards.

Problem 19.5. The power company's installation of the line in Jeffrey's case amounted to a trespass above a neighbor's property. The power company knew its actions would amount to a trespass before it was installed but refused to accede to the neighbor's demand to cease construction. The neighbor sued for trespass, and the jury awarded $750 in compensatory damages. The jury also awarded $10,000 in punitive damages. The power company has appealed this award on due process grounds. Is the award constitutionally permissible?

C. Damage Caps and Tort Reform

Problem 19.6. Assume that Jeffrey has $2 million in special damages. Under your contingent fee agreement, you are entitled to 40% of Jeffrey's recovery. Your expenses (expert witness fees, etc.) amounted to $200,000, all of which will be deducted from Jeffrey's recovery. The relevant jurisdiction has enacted a statute containing a damages cap in tort actions. Under the cap, punitive damages are capped at a 1:1 ratio in terms of compensatory damages to punitives. Recovery for noneconomic damages is also capped at $250,000. Assume the jury awards the full $2 million amount for pecuniary damages and the statutory cap of $250,000 for pain and suffering damages. How much would the jury need to award in punitive damages in order for Jeffrey to be made whole?

1. Damage Caps and Tort Reform in General

Tort reform has been the subject of considerable debate and controversy in recent decades. The term "tort reform" potentially covers a variety of statutory measures addressing the civil litigation system. For example, the elimination of joint and several liability is a feature of tort reform in some jurisdictions.

One of the most common features of tort reform statutes is the damage cap. The statutes typically place limits either on the amount of noneconomic damages or punitive damages a plaintiff may recover in a tort action, although some place overall limits on recovery. *See* Ind. Code Ann. § 34-18-14-3(a)(3) (placing a cap on total damages in medical malpractice cases of $1.65 million). Most statutes do not place caps on noneconomic damages in tort cases in general. But a majority do place caps on noneconomic damages in certain categories of cases, such as medical malpractice or products liability cases. The amounts vary. *See* Cal. Civ. Code § 3333.2(b) ($250,000 in tort actions); Wis. Stat. Ann. § 893.55(d)(1) ($750,000 in medical malpractice actions). Some states waive or increase the cap on pain and suffering damages where the plaintiff suffers permanent disfigurement or similar consequences. *See* W. Va. Code Ann. § 55-7B-8(b) (expanding the cap on noneconomic damages in medical malpractice cases to $500,000 where the malpractice results in permanent and serious disfigurement, or an injury that permanently prevents the plaintiff from caring for herself).

Some states place a dollar cap on punitive damages. *See* Ga. Code Ann. § 51-12-5.1(g). ($250,000). But the most common approach is to use a multiplier of a victim's compensatory damages. Three times a plaintiff's compensatory damages is common. *See* Ala. Code § 6-11-21(a) (three times the compensatory damages of the party claiming punitive damages or five hundred thousand dollars ($500,000), whichever is greater). Mississippi takes the interesting approach of linking the size of a punitive damages award to the wealth of the defendant. At one extreme, a plaintiff can recover up to $20 million in punitive damages from a defendant with a net worth of more than $1 billion. At the other extreme, a plaintiff can recover up to 2% of the net worth of a defendant with a net worth of $50 million or less. *See* Miss. Code Ann. § 11-1-65(3)(a). A few states expand or eliminate a cap on punitive damages where the defendant's conduct is especially egregious. *See* Alaska Stat. Ann. § 9.17.020(g) (creating a higher cap where the defendant acted for financial gain and knew of the potential consequences of its actions); Miss. Code Ann. § 11-1-65(3)(d) (eliminating punitives cap if the defendant was convicted of a felony that caused the injury or was under the influence of alcohol or drugs).

Several states have enacted constitutional provisions prohibiting statutory caps on damages. The courts in some others have held that statutes that place limits on damages are unconstitutional. Courts have struck down such statutes on equal protection grounds, *North Broward Hosp. Dist. v. Kalitan*, 219 So. 3d 49 (Fla. 2017), separation of powers grounds, *Lebron v. Gottlieb Mem. Hosp*, 930 N.E.2d 895 (Ill. 2010), or as being in violation of the constitutional right to a jury trial. Atlanta Oculoplastic Surgery, P.C. v. Nestlehutt, 691 S.E.2d 218 (Ga. 2010).

2. The Pro-Tort Reform Arguments

Perhaps the most common argument advanced by tort reform proponents is that there has been an increase in frivolous litigation as well as an overall increase in litigation. Tort reform is necessary in order to deter potential litigants and their lawyers from seeking to "win the litigation lottery" by filing baseless claims in the hopes of recovering substantial damages. *See generally* LAWRENCE J. MCQUILLAN ET AL., JACKPOT JUSTICE (2007). Closely related to these kinds of arguments is the concern that such litigation adversely impacts business and, in the case of medical malpractice claims, health-care providers. *See id.* at vii ("[T]he economic drag of the American tort system costs billions, lowering the standard of living for ordinary citizens nationwide."). The result in the case of medical malpractice claims is decreased quality of care and increased health care costs. *See id.* at 20 (linking rising health care costs to "liability-driven medical expenditures").

Unchecked tort liability may also deter the development of innovative new products and medical advancements. *See* Deborah J. La Fetra, *Freedom, Responsibility, and Risk: Fundamental Principles Supporting Tort Reform*, 36 Ind. L. Rev. 645, 648–49 (2003). While one of the goals of tort law in general and punitive damages in particular is deterrence, supporters of tort reform and damage caps argue that unchecked punitive damages may result in overdeterrence. For example, Professor Victor E. Schwartz has pointed to a survey of corporate executives reporting that "that fear of liability suits had prompted thirty-six percent of the firms to discontinue a product and thirty percent to decide against introducing a new product." Victor E. Schwartz et al., *Reining in Punitive Damages "Run Wild": Proposals for Reform by Courts and Legislatures*, 65 Brook. L. Rev. 1003, 1011 (1999). For these reasons, among others, Professor Schwartz and his co-authors have argued in favor of caps on noneconomic and punitive damages:

> We support permitting punitive damages awards against larger businesses up to two times the amount awarded to the claimant for economic and noneconomic losses, or $250,000, whichever is greater. This flexible approach accomplishes punishment and deterrence in the unusual situation where there is serious misconduct and relatively minor actual damages. We also support limiting the maximum single punishment against an individual or small business to two times the amount awarded to the claimant for economic and noneconomic losses, or $250,000, whichever is less (*i.e.*, $250,000 would be the maximum). This recommendation reflects the practical reality that a punitive damages award exceeding $250,000 would bankrupt most individuals and small businesses.

Id. at 1015–16.

3. The Anti-Tort Reform Arguments

Opponents respond that concerns over increased litigation are dramatically overstated. *See* David A. Hyman & Charles Silver, *Medical Malpractice Litigation and Tort Reform: It's the Incentives, Stupid*, 59 Vand. L. Rev. 1085, 1089 (2006) ("Popular perceptions notwithstanding, the evidence is quite clear that while many patients are injured, few ever sue."). They also assert that tort law permits juries to tailor damage awards to the needs of individual plaintiffs; damage caps take away the flexibility juries need to adequately compensate victims. *See* Thomas C. Galligan Jr., *The Tragedy in Torts*, 5 Cornell J.L. & Pub. Pol'y 139, 173 (1996). An additional argument against the damage caps found in some tort reform statutes is that noneconomic and punitive damages serve to offset a plaintiff's litigation costs. Since plaintiffs' lawyers work on a contingent fee basis under which their fee is contingent upon the plaintiff recovering money, a plaintiff who only recovers his pecuniary damages may be undercompensated once his attorney takes the agreed-upon fee. Therefore, noneconomic and punitive damages may be the means by which both lawyer and client are fully compensated.

In terms of deterrence, opponents of damage caps argue that damage awards beyond compensation for economic losses may be necessary to deter "either especially egregious behavior or behaviors where the probability of detecting negligence is low." Joanna M. Shepherd, *Tort Reforms' Winners and Losers: The Competing Effects of Care and Activity Levels,* 55 UCLA L. Rev. 905, 913 (2008).

> Suppose that in only a fraction of cases the victim discovers that her injuries were caused by tortious conduct and sues. For example, studies have shown that in only a small proportion of cases do victims of medical malpractice even discover that their doctors have erred, much less file a lawsuit. To achieve adequate deterrence, damages in the few suits that are filed must exceed the compensatory level. Otherwise, the potential tortfeasor may recognize that most of the time he pays nothing, and only rarely pays the compensatory amount; the average that he faces is much less than the compensatory amount. Because he is not internalizing the full costs of his actions on others, he will either engage in dangerous activities too frequently or take insufficient precautions when he does engage in them. By raising liability costs in the few suits that succeed, punitive damages can increase deterrence to the appropriate level.

Id. Noneconomic damages are also necessary in order to deter misconduct. "The only way to make a potential tortfeasor internalize the nonpecuniary harms he imposes on others is to make him pay for them with noneconomic damages. If he is not compelled to pay the damages, he will be underdeterred, because he will not consider all of the costs that his conduct imposes." *Id.* at 914.

D. Wrongful Death Statutes

Throughout the book, there have been numerous cases involving claims brought by surviving family members against defendants whose wrongful acts caused the death of a loved one. At common law, one's right to bring an action against a tortfeasor expired upon one's own death. Eventually, states enacted wrongful death statutes to permit survivors to seek compensation from a tortfeasor in the event of a family member's death. Survivors may be able to recover damages sustained by the deceased as well as their own incidental damages caused by the death. *See* Jordan v. Baptist Three Rivers Hosp., 984 S.W.2d 593, 598 (Tenn. 1999).

One form of incidental damages a surviving family member may be able to collect is loss of consortium damages, a topic covered in Chapter 10. Loss of consortium damages measure the intangible benefits a family member receives from the continued existence of other family members. This includes such things as attention, guidance, care, protection, training, companionship, cooperation, affection, love, and in the case of a spouse, sexual relations. *See* Jordan v. Baptist Three Rivers Hosp., 984 S.W.2d 593 (Tenn. 1999). A spouse may seek to recover such damages. The origins of this claim trace at least back to the idea that a tortfeasor who injured a man's wife had a right to recover for the loss of services provided by his wife. "However, the wife had no reciprocal action for negligent injury to her husband's consortium since she had no independent legal status: 'husband and wife were one; and he was the one.'" Frank v. Superior Court of Arizona, 722 P.2d 955, 958 n.6 (quoting 3 W. Blackstone, Commentaries on the Law of England 433–36 (3rd ed. 1884)). Eventually, the theory was expanded to permit recovery by wives and, potentially, other family members.

E. Other Approaches to Recovery

1. Workers' Compensation

Modern workers' compensation law developed, in part, as a response to the strictures of tort law as it existed in the early twentieth century. An employee who was injured on the job obviously had to establish negligence on the part of an employer or fellow employee in order to recover. But if the injured employee was himself negligent or had assumed the risk of another's negligence, there could be no recovery. Moreover, under the old fellow servant rule, an employee who was injured on the job by another employee could not recover from the employer. The result was that, at a time when the dangers of workplace injuries were increasing due to increased mechanization in the workplace, employees faced numerous obstacles when they sought recovery for those injuries.

Workers' compensation is a matter of state law. Today, an employee who is injured by an accident arising out of and in the course of employment is entitled to compensation, regardless of the fault of the employer. Likewise, the employee is entitled to compensation regardless of any comparative fault on the part of the employee. The workers' compensation system represents a tradeoff. Employees are entitled to compensation without having to establish fault, but the workers' compensation system is the employee's exclusive basis of recovery. An employee who is injured by an accident arising out of and in the course of employment is generally prohibited from bringing a tort claim against the employer. This may mean that compensation is significantly less than it otherwise might be. But, again, an employee may potentially benefit by not having to establish fault on the part of the employer.

Most states recognize an intentional tort exception to the exclusivity provisions contained in workers' compensation statutes. The exceptions vary from state to state, but typically permit an employee to bring a tort claim where the employer acts with the specific or deliberate intent to injure the employee. *See, e.g.*, Baker v. Westinghouse Elec. Corp., 637 N.E.2d 1271, 1273 (Ind. 1994). Gross negligence or conduct that the employer knows is substantially certain to result in harm is not sufficient. *See* Houdek v. ThyssenKrupp Materials N.A., Inc., 983 N.E.2d 1253, 1258 (Ohio 2012); Fenner v. Municipality of Anchorage, 53 P.3d 573, 577 (Alaska 2002).

2. Victim Compensation Funds

Following the September 11 attacks, Congress created a victim compensation fund that would provide compensation for those were injured by the attacks or whose family members were killed in the attacks. Those who sought compensation did not have to establish fault on the part of airlines or other potential defendants. Instead, they had to establish that they were present at the affected locations during the relevant period and had a physical injury or illness that was on a list of covered conditions. A special master was appointed by the U.S. Attorney General. He reviewed each claim and made an award that took into account the different types of damages covered in this chapter. The fund paid out more than 5,500 claims with an average of $1.2 million each ($2 million for people who lost family members and $300,000 for those who were injured). *See* Gillian K. Hadfield, *Framing the Choice between Cash and the Courthouse: Experiences with the 9/11 Victim Compensation Fund*, 42 Law & Soc'y Review 645, 646 (2008). In addition to the desire to compensate victims, Congress was motivated by a desire to prevent potentially massive litigation costs to airlines.

The tradeoff for victims was that to be eligible to receive compensation from the fund, they had to waive their right to bring a lawsuit. Victims had to evaluate whether the greater certainty and speed of recovery offered by the fund outweighed the potential for a higher jury award in a court proceeding. The vast majority of victims chose the victim compensation fund route. Despite this, more than half of those who chose this route found the decision difficult, due often to concerns about the inability of the fund to punish or hold responsible those who were at fault or to deter similar events in the future. *Id.* at 663.

Similar victim compensation funds have been set up in other high-profile tragic situations, including the BP oil spill, the Boston Marathon bombing, and the Aurora, Colorado, movie theater shooting. The existence of these types of funds raises interesting questions concerning the role of tort law beyond merely providing compensation and the extent to which such funds could (or should) be used as substitute to traditional civil litigation.

Review Question

Padma was visiting a casino with friends. While walking through the casino, she noticed a five-cent token sitting in the tray of a slot machine. Seeing no chairs at the machine and no one around, Padma picked up the token. Before she could insert the token in the slot machine, a security guard for the hotel roughly grabbed Padma by the arm and told her that she needed to come along with him. As the guard walked Padma back to an office with no windows, he informed her that the casino had a policy against "slot-walking," the practice of walking by slot machines and picking up stray tokens. Once inside the office, the security guard berated Padma. He asked who else she was working with, accused her of stealing casino property, and used a racial slur. When Padma tried to leave, the security guard told her that she could not leave and that if she tried, he would handcuff her to the desk. Eventually, the security guard let Padma go, but only after telling her she had to leave the casino and was banned from ever returning.

Padma sued the casino for false imprisonment. The jury returned a verdict for compensatory damages in the amount of $800 for Padma's emotional distress. The jury also awarded punitive damages in the amount of $50,000. The casino has now appealed, challenging both the jury's decision to award punitive damages in the first place as well as the amount of those damages. Discuss all issues.

Index

NUISANCE

PRODUCTS LIABILITY

PROXIMATE CAUSE